Nation of Nations

A CONCISE NARRATIVE
OF THE AMERICAN REPUBLIC

James West Davidson

William E. Gienapp
Harvard University

Christine Leigh Heyrman
University of Delaware

Mark H. Lytle
Bard College

Michael B. Stoff
University of Texas, Austin

OVERTURE
BOOKS
McGraw-Hill
College

Boston   Burr Ridge, IL   Dubuque, IA   Madison, WI   New York   San Francisco   St. Louis
Bangkok   Bogotá   Caracas   Lisbon   London   Madrid
Mexico City   Milan   New Delhi   Seoul   Singapore   Sydney   Taipei   Toronto

McGraw-Hill College

A Division of The McGraw·Hill Companies

NATION OF NATIONS: A CONCISE NARRATIVE OF THE AMERICAN REPUBLIC, SECOND EDITION

This book is printed on acid-free paper.

2 3 4 5 6 7 8 9 0 DOC/DOC 9 3 2 1 0 9

ISBN 0–07–303375–8

Editorial director: *Jane E. Vaicunas*
Senior sponsoring editor: *Lyn Uhl*
Developmental editor: *Monica Freedman*
Senior marketing manager: *Suzanne Daghlian*
Senior project manager: *Marilyn Rothenberger*
Production supervisor: *Deborah Donner*
Designer: *Laurie Jean Entringer*
Photo research coordinator: *John C. Leland*
Supplement coordinator: *Rita Hingtgen*
Compositor: *York Graphic Services, Inc.*
Typeface: *10/12 Janson*
Printer: *R. R. Donnelley & Sons Company/Crawfordsville, IN*

The credits section for this book begins on page C.1 and is considered an extension of the copyright page.

Library of Congress Cataloging-in-Publication Data

Nation of nations : a concise narrative of the American republic /
    James West Davidson . . . [et al.]. —2nd ed.
        p.   cm.
    Adapted from Nation of nations : a narrative history of the
American republic, 2nd ed. © 1994.
    Includes bibliographical references and index.
    ISBN 0–07–303375–8 (acid-free paper)
    1. United States—History.   I. Davidson, James West.
E178.4.N345   1999
973—dc21   98–21631
                                                                                              CIP

www.mhhe.com

Contents

List of Maps and Charts   xxv

Preface to the Second Concise Edition   xxviii

Introduction   xxxi

PART ONE
GLOBAL ESSAY: THE CREATION OF A NEW AMERICA   1

CHAPTER ONE
Old World, New Worlds   5

THE MEETING OF EUROPE AND AMERICA   6
The Portuguese Wave 8 ~ The Spanish and Columbus 10

EARLY NORTH AMERICAN CULTURES   11
*The First Inhabitants 11 ~ Societies of Increasing Complexity 12
Mesoamerican Empires 13*

THE EUROPEAN BACKGROUND OF AMERICAN COLONIZATION   16
*Life and Death in Early Modern Europe 16 ~ The Conditions of
Colonization 17*

SPAIN'S EMPIRE IN THE NEW WORLD   18
*Spanish Conquest 18 ~ Role of the Conquistadors 20 ~ Spanish
Colonization 21 ~ The Effects of Colonial Growth 22*

THE REFORMATION IN EUROPE   23
*Backdrop to Reform 23 ~ The Teachings of Martin Luther 23
The Contribution of John Calvin 24 ~ The English Reformation 25*

ENGLAND'S ENTRY INTO AMERICA   26
*The English Colonization of Ireland 26 ~ Renewed Interest in the
Americas 27 ~ The Failures of Frobisher and Gilbert 28
Raleigh's Roanoke Venture 30 ~ A Second Attempt 31*

EYEWITNESS TO HISTORY: A Spanish Conquistador Visits the Aztec
Marketplace in Tenochtitlán 14

COUNTERPOINT: The Role of Human Sacrifice 15

CHAPTER TWO

The First Century of Settlement in the Colonial South

33

ENGLISH SOCIETY ON THE CHESAPEAKE 35
*The Mercantilist Impulse 36 ~ The Virginia Company 36
Reform and a Boom in Tobacco 37 ~ Settling Down in the
Chesapeake 40 ~ The Founding of Maryland and the Renewal of
Indian Wars 40 ~ Changes in English Policy in the Chesapeake 42*

CHESAPEAKE SOCIETY IN CRISIS 43
*The Conditions of Unrest 43 ~ Bacon's Rebellion and Coode's
Rebellion 43 ~ From Servitude to Slavery 45 ~ A Changing
Chesapeake Society 46 ~ The Chesapeake Gentry 47*

FROM THE CARIBBEAN TO THE CAROLINAS 48
*Paradise Lost 49 ~ The Founding of the Carolinas 50 ~ Early
Instability 51 ~ White, Red, and Black: The Search for Order 53
The Founding of Georgia 54*

THE SPANISH BORDERLANDS 55

EYEWITNESS TO HISTORY: A Virginia Settler Describes the Indian War of
1622 to Officials in England 39

COUNTERPOINT: Beyond the Black Legend 58

CHAPTER THREE

The First Century of Settlement in the Colonial North

61

THE FOUNDING OF NEW ENGLAND 64
*The Puritan Movement 64 ~ The Pilgrim Settlement at Plymouth
Colony 65 ~ The Puritan Settlement at Massachusetts Bay 66*

NEW ENGLAND COMMUNITIES 67
*Stability and Order in Early New England 68 ~ Congregational
Church Order 69 ~ Colonial Governments 71 ~ Communities in
Conflict 71 ~ Heretics 72 ~ Goodwives and Witches 74
Whites and Indians in Early New England 75*

THE MIDDLE COLONIES 77
*The Founding of New Netherlands 77 ~ English Rule in New York 77
The League of the Iroquois 78 ~ The Founding of New Jersey 80
Quaker Odysseys 81 ~ Patterns of Settlement 82
Quakers and Politics 83*

ADJUSTMENT TO EMPIRE 83
*The Dominion of New England 84 ~ The Aftershocks of the Glorious
Revolution 84 ~ Leisler's Rebellion 85 ~ Royal Authority in
America in 1700 85*

EYEWITNESS TO HISTORY: A Puritan New Englander Wrestles with
Her Faith   70

COUNTERPOINT: Bewitched by Salem Village   75

CHAPTER FOUR
The Mosaic of Eighteenth-Century America   88

FORCES OF DIVISION   90
Immigration and Natural Increase   90   ~   The Settlement of the
Backcountry   92   ~   Social Conflict on the Frontier   93   ~   Boundary
Disputes and Tenant Wars   94   ~   Eighteenth-Century Seaports   95
Social Conflict in Seaports   97

SLAVE SOCIETIES IN THE EIGHTEENTH-CENTURY SOUTH   96
The Slave Family and Community   98   ~   Slave Resistance in the
Eighteenth Century   99

ENLIGHTENMENT AND AWAKENING IN AMERICA   101
The Enlightenment in America   102   ~   The First Great
Awakening   103   ~   The Aftermath of the Great Awakening   103

ANGLO-AMERICAN WORLDS OF THE EIGHTEENTH CENTURY   106
English Economic and Social Development   106   ~   Inequality in
England and America   107   ~   Politics in England and America   108
The Imperial System before 1760   110

TOWARD THE SEVEN YEARS' WAR   112

EYEWITNESS TO HISTORY: Benjamin Franklin Attends the Preaching of
George Whitefield   104

COUNTERPOINT: The African American Response to Enslavement   101

PART TWO
GLOBAL ESSAY: THE CREATION OF
A NEW REPUBLIC   114

CHAPTER FIVE
Toward the War for American Independence   116

THE SEVEN YEARS' WAR   117
The Years of Defeat   117   ~   The Years of Victory   118   ~   Postwar
Expectations   119

THE IMPERIAL CRISIS   121
New Troubles on the Frontier   121   ~   George Grenville's New
Measures   121   ~   The Beginning of Colonial Resistance   124
Riots and Resolves   126   ~   Repeal of the Stamp Act   128   ~   The

Townshend Acts 129 ~ The Resistance Organizes 130 ~ The Boston Massacre 131 ~ Resistance Revived 132 ~ The Empire Strikes Back 133

TOWARD THE REVOLUTION   135
The First Continental Congress 135 ~ The Last Days of the British Empire in America 137 ~ The Fighting Begins 138 ~ Common Sense 138

EYEWITNESS TO HISTORY: Thomas Hutchinson Recounts the Destruction of His Boston Home during the Stamp Act Riots 127

COUNTERPOINT: A Revolution Within a Revolution? 134

CHAPTER SIX

The American People and the American Revolution   141

THE DECISION FOR INDEPENDENCE   143
The Second Continental Congress 143 ~ The Declaration 144 American Loyalists 145

THE FIGHTING IN THE NORTH   146
The Two Armies at Bay 147 ~ Laying Strategies 149 The Campaigns in New York and New Jersey 150 ~ Capturing Philadelphia 151 ~ Disaster at Saratoga 152

THE TURNING POINT   153
An Alliance Formed 153 ~ Winding Down the War in the North 154 ~ War in the West 156 ~ The Home Front in the North 156

THE STRUGGLE IN THE SOUTH   157
The Siege of Charleston 157 ~ The Partisan Struggle in the South 158 ~ Greene Takes Command 159 ~ African Americans in the Age of Revolution 161

THE WORLD TURNED UPSIDE DOWN   162
Surrender at Yorktown 163 ~ The Significance of a Revolution 164

EYEWITNESS TO HISTORY: A North Carolina Soldier Witnesses the Partisan War in the Southern Backcountry 159

COUNTERPOINT: Fear of Civil War 146

CHAPTER SEVEN

Crisis and Constitution   166

REPUBLICAN EXPERIMENTS   167
The State Constitutions 167 ~ From Congress to Confederation 169

THE TEMPTATIONS OF PEACE   170
    The Temptations of the West 170 ~ Foreign Intrigues 171
    Disputes among the States 172 ~ The More Democratic West 174
    The Northwest Territory 174 ~ Slavery and Sectionalism 177
    Wartime Economic Disruption 179

REPUBLICAN SOCIETY   180
    The New Men of the Revolution 181 ~ The New Women of the
    Revolution 181 ~ "Republican Motherhood" and Education 183
    The Attack on Aristocracy 183

FROM CONFEDERATION TO CONSTITUTION   185
    The Jay–Gardoqui Treaty 185 ~ Shays' Rebellion 185
    Framing a Federal Constitution 187 ~ The Virginia and New Jersey
    Plans 188 ~ The Deadlock Broken 189 ~ Ratification 190
    Changing Revolutionary Ideals 191

EYEWITNESS TO HISTORY: A Traveler from Virginia Considers the Ruins
of an Ancient Indian Civilization in the Ohio Valley 175

COUNTERPOINT: Radicalism and the American Revolution 184

CHAPTER EIGHT

The Republic Launched   193

1789: A SOCIAL PORTRAIT   195
    The Semisubsistence Economy of Crèvecoeur's America 196 ~ The
    Commercial Economy of Franklin's America 197 ~ The Constitution
    and Commerce 198

THE NEW GOVERNMENT   199
    Organizing the Government 199 ~ The Bill of Rights 200
    Hamilton's Financial Program 201 ~ Opposition to Hamilton's
    Program 202 ~ The Specter of Aristocracy 204

EXPANSION AND TURMOIL IN THE WEST   204
    The Resistance of the Miamis 204 ~ The Whiskey Rebellion 205

THE EMERGENCE OF POLITICAL PARTIES   206
    The French Revolution 206 ~ Washington's Neutral Course 207
    The Federalists and Republicans Organize 207 ~ The 1796
    Election 208 ~ Federalist and Republican Ideologies 209

THE PRESIDENCY OF JOHN ADAMS   210
    The Quasi-War with France 211 ~ Suppression at Home 211
    The Election of 1800 212 ~ Political Violence in the
    Early Republic 213 ~ The Federalists' Legacy 215

EYEWITNESS TO HISTORY: A Farmer Becomes Involved
in the World of Commerce   214

COUNTERPOINT: Key Differences between Republicans and Federalists   210

CHAPTER NINE

The Jeffersonian Republic   217

JEFFERSON IN POWER   218
    Jefferson's Character and Philosophy   218   ~   Republican Principles   220
    Jefferson's Economic Policies   220   ~   John Marshall and Judicial
    Review   221

JEFFERSON AND WESTERN EXPANSION   222
    The Louisiana Purchase   222   ~   Lewis and Clark   223

WHITES AND INDIANS ON THE FRONTIER   224
    The Course of White Settlement   225   ~   A Changing
    Environment   226   ~   The Second Great Awakening   226
    Pressure on Indian Lands and Culture   228   ~   The Prophet, Tecumseh,
    and the Pan-Indian Movement   229

THE SECOND WAR FOR AMERICAN INDEPENDENCE   232
    Neutral Rights   232   ~   The Embargo   232   ~   Madison and the
    Young Republicans   234   ~   The Decision for War   234   ~   National
    Unpreparedness   235   ~   "A Chance Such as Will Never Occur
    Again"   236   ~   The British Invasion   236   ~   The Hartford
    Convention   238

AMERICA TURNS INWARD   238
    Monroe's Presidency   239   ~   The Monroe Doctrine   239   ~   The
    End of an Era   240

EYEWITNESS TO HISTORY: Isaac Clark Is Impressed by the British Navy   233

COUNTERPOINT: Tecumseh versus the Prophet   231

PART THREE
GLOBAL ESSAY: THE REPUBLIC TRANSFORMED
AND TESTED   242

CHAPTER TEN

The Opening of America   244

THE MARKET REVOLUTION   245
    The New Nationalism   246   ~   The Cotton Trade   246   ~   The
    Transportation Revolution   247   ~   Agriculture in the Market
    Economy   248   ~   John Marshall and the Promotion of Enterprise   250
    General Incorporation Laws   251

A RESTLESS TEMPER 251
  Population Growth 252 ~ The Restless Movement West 253
  Urbanization 254

THE RISE OF FACTORIES 256
  Technological Advances 256 ~ Textile Factories 257
  Lowell and the Environment 259 ~ Industrial Work 260
  The Shoe Industry 261 ~ The Labor Movement 262

SOCIAL STRUCTURES OF THE MARKET SOCIETY 263
  Economic Specialization 264 ~ Materialism 264 ~ The Emerging
  Middle Class 265 ~ The Distribution of Wealth 266 ~ Social
  Mobility 266 ~ A New Sensitivity to Time 266

PROSPERITY AND ANXIETY 267
  The Panic of 1819 268 ~ The Missouri Crisis 266

EYEWITNESS TO HISTORY: The Mere Love of Moving 255

COUNTERPOINT: Workers and Industrialization 262

CHAPTER ELEVEN
The Rise of Democracy

271

EQUALITY AND OPPORTUNITY 273
  The Tension between Equality and Opportunity 273

THE NEW POLITICAL CULTURE OF DEMOCRACY 274
  The Election of 1824 274 ~ Social Sources of the New Politics 275
  The Acceptance of Political Parties 276

JACKSON'S RISE TO POWER 278
  President of the People 278 ~ The Political Agenda in the Market
  Economy 281

DEMOCRACY AND RACE 281
  Accommodate or Resist? 281 ~ Trail of Tears 282 ~ Free Blacks
  in the North 284 ~ The African American Community 285
  The Minstrel Show 286

THE NULLIFICATION CRISIS 287
  The Growing Crisis in South Carolina 287 ~ Calhoun's Theory of
  Nullification 288 ~ The Nullifiers Nullified 289

THE BANK WAR 289
  The National Bank and the Panic of 1819 290 ~ Biddle's Bank 290
  The Bank Destroyed 291 ~ Jackson's Impact on the Presidency 291

VAN BUREN AND DEPRESSION 292
  "Van Ruin's" Depression 292 ~ The Whigs' Triumph 293

THE JACKSONIAN PARTY SYSTEM 294
    Democrats, Whigs, and the Market *294* ~ *The Social Bases of the Two Parties* *295* ~ *The Triumph of the Market* *296*

EYEWITNESS TO HISTORY: Andrew Jackson's Tumultuous Inauguration 279

COUNTERPOINT: How Democratic Was Jacksonian Democracy? 277

CHAPTER TWELVE
The Fires of Perfection

298

REVIVALISM AND THE SOCIAL ORDER 300
    Finney's New Measures and New Theology *300* ~ *Religion and the Market Economy* *301* ~ *The Rise of African American Churches* *303* ~ *The Significance of the Second Great Awakening* *304*

WOMEN'S SPHERE 304
    The Ideal of Domesticity *304* ~ *The Middle-Class Family in Transition* *306*

AMERICAN ROMANTICISM 307
    The Transcendentalists *307* ~ *The Clash between Nature and Civilization* *308* ~ *Songs of the Self-Reliant and Darker Loomings* *308*

THE AGE OF REFORM 309
    Utopian Communities *309* ~ *The Mormon Experiment* *311*
    Socialist Communities *312* ~ *The Temperance Movement* *312*
    Educational Reform *313* ~ *The Asylum Movement* *314*

ABOLITIONISM 315
    The Beginnings of the Abolitionist Movement *315* ~ *The Spread of Abolitionism* *317* ~ *Opponents and Divisions* *318* ~ *The Women's Rights Movement* *319* ~ *The Schism of 1840* *320*

REFORM SHAKES THE PARTY SYSTEM 321
    Women and the Right to Vote *321* ~ *The Maine Law* *321*
    Abolitionism and the Party System *322*

EYEWITNESS TO HISTORY: The Slave Mortimer Describes His Conversion Experience 302

COUNTERPOINT: Reformers and Social Control 314

CHAPTER THIRTEEN
The Old South

325

THE SOCIAL STRUCTURE OF THE COTTON KINGDOM 327
    Deep South, Upper South *327* ~ *The Rural South* *328*
    Distribution of Slavery *330* ~ *Slavery as a Labor System* *330*

CLASS STRUCTURE OF THE WHITE SOUTH 332
    The Slaveowners 332 ~ *Tidewater and Frontier* 333
    The Master at Home 334 ~ *The Plantation Mistress* 334
    Yeoman Farmers 336 ~ *Poor Whites* 337

THE PECULIAR INSTITUTION 338
    Work and Discipline 339 ~ *Slave Maintenance* 340
    Resistance 340

SLAVE CULTURE 341
    The Slave Family 342 ~ *Songs and Stories of Protest and
    Celebration* 344 ~ *The Lord Calls Us Home* 345 ~ *The Slave
    Community* 347 ~ *Free Black Southerners* 347

SOUTHERN SOCIETY AND THE DEFENSE OF SLAVERY 348
    The Virginia Debate of 1832 348 ~ *The Proslavery
    Argument* 349 ~ *Closing Ranks* 349 ~ *Sections and the
    Nation* 350

EYEWITNESS TO HISTORY: An Enslaved Woman Picks a Husband 343

COUNTERPOINT: The Role of Religion in the Lives of Slaves 346

CHAPTER FOURTEEN
Western Expansion and the Rise
of the Slavery Issue

  353

DESTINIES: MANIFEST AND OTHERWISE 355
    The Roots of Manifest Destiny 356 ~ *The Mexican Borderlands* 356
    The Texas Revolution 358 ~ *The Republic of Texas* 358

THE TREK WEST 359
    The Overland Trail 359 ~ *Indians and the Trail Experience* 362

THE POLITICAL ORIGINS OF EXPANSION 362
    Tyler's Texas Ploy 363 ~ *Van Overboard* 363 ~ *To the
    Pacific* 364 ~ *The Mexican War* 364 ~ *The Price of Victory* 366
    The Rise of the Slavery Issue 366

NEW SOCIETIES IN THE WEST 367
    Farming in the West 367 ~ *The Gold Rush* 367 ~ *Instant City:
    San Francisco* 370 ~ *The Mormons in Utah* 371 ~ *Temple City:
    Salt Lake City* 372 ~ *Shadows on the Moving Frontier* 373

ESCAPE FROM CRISIS 373
    A Two-Faced Campaign 374 ~ *The Compromise of 1850* 375
    Away from the Brink 377

EYEWITNESS TO HISTORY: Disappointment in the Gold Diggings 368

COUNTERPOINT: Women in the West 361

CHAPTER FIFTEEN
The Union Broken   380

SECTIONAL CHANGES IN AMERICAN SOCIETY   382
*The Growth of a Railroad Economy 382 ~ Railroads and the Prairie
Environment 384 ~ Railroads and the Urban Environment 385
Rising Industrialization 385 ~ Immigration 386 ~ Southern
Complaints 387*

THE POLITICAL REALIGNMENT OF THE 1850S   388
*The Kansas–Nebraska Act 388 ~ The Collapse of the Second American
Party System 390 ~ The Know-Nothings 390 ~ The Republicans
and Bleeding Kansas 391 ~ The Caning of Charles Sumner 391
The Election of 1856 393*

THE WORSENING CRISIS   395
The Dred Scott *Decision 395 ~ The Panic of 1857 396 ~ The
Lecompton Constitution 397 ~ The Lincoln–Douglas Debates 397
The Beleaguered South 399*

THE ROAD TO WAR   400
*A Sectional Election 401 ~ Secession 401 ~ The Outbreak of
War 402 ~ The Roots of a Divided Nation 404*

EYEWITNESS TO HISTORY: A Northerner Views *Uncle Tom's Cabin*
on the Stage 394

COUNTERPOINT: Lincoln's Motives in the Fort Sumter Crisis 404

CHAPTER SIXTEEN
Total War and the Republic   408

THE DEMANDS OF TOTAL WAR   409
Political Leadership 410 ~ The Border States 412

OPENING MOVES   413
*Blockade and Isolate 413 ~ Grant in the West 414 ~ Eastern
Stalemate 416*

EMANCIPATION   418
*The Logic of Events 418 ~ The Emancipation Proclamation 419
African Americans' Civil War 420 ~ Black Soldiers 421*

THE CONFEDERATE HOME FRONT   422
*The New Economy 422 ~ New Opportunities for Southern Women 423
Confederate Finance and Government 423 ~ Hardship and
Suffering 424*

THE UNION HOME FRONT 425
   Government Finances and the Economy 425 ~ *A Rich Man's War* 426 ~ *Women and the Workforce* 426 ~ *Civil Liberties and Dissent* 427

GONE TO BE A SOLDIER 428
   Camp Life 428 ~ *Southern Individualism* 429 ~ *The Changing Face of Battle* 430

THE UNION'S TRIUMPH 431
   Lincoln Finds His General 431 ~ *War in the Balance* 433
   The Twilight of the Confederacy 435

THE IMPACT OF WAR 438

EYEWITNESS TO HISTORY: A Georgia Plantation Mistress in Sherman's Path 437

COUNTERPOINT: Who Freed the Slaves? 419

CHAPTER SEVENTEEN

Reconstructing the Union 441

PRESIDENTIAL RECONSTRUCTION 442
   Lincoln's 10 Percent Plan 442 ~ *The Mood of the South* 443
   Johnson's Program of Reconstruction 444 ~ *The Failure of Johnson's Program* 444 ~ *Johnson's Break with Congress* 445 ~ *The Fourteenth Amendment* 446 ~ *The Elections of 1866* 447

CONGRESSIONAL RECONSTRUCTION 448
   The Land Issue 448 ~ *Impeachment* 449

RECONSTRUCTION IN THE SOUTH 450
   Black Officeholding 451 ~ *White Republicans in the South* 451
   Reforms under the New State Governments 452 ~ *Economic Issues and Corruption* 452

BLACK ASPIRATIONS 453
   Experiencing Freedom 453 ~ *The Black Family* 454 ~ *The Schoolhouse and the Church* 454 ~ *New Working Conditions* 455
   The Freedmen's Bureau 456 ~ *Planters and a New Way of Life* 457

THE ABANDONMENT OF RECONSTRUCTION 458
   The Election of Grant 458 ~ *The Grant Administration* 459
   Growing Northern Disillusionment 460 ~ *The Triumph of White Supremacy* 460 ~ *The Disputed Election of 1876* 462 ~ *Racism and the Failure of Reconstruction* 463

EYEWITNESS TO HISTORY: The Mississippi Plan in Action 462

COUNTERPOINT: Should Johnson Have Been Removed from Office? 450

PART FOUR
GLOBAL ESSAY: THE UNITED STATES IN AN INDUSTRIAL AGE

466

CHAPTER EIGHTEEN
The New Industrial Order

468

THE DEVELOPMENT OF INDUSTRIAL SYSTEMS 469
Natural Resources and Industrial Technology 471 ~ Systematic Invention 472 ~ Transportation and Communication 473 ~ Finance Capital 474 ~ The Corporation 474 ~ A Pool of Labor 475

RAILROADS: AMERICA'S FIRST BIG BUSINESS 477
A Managerial Revolution 477 ~ Competition and Consolidation 478 The Challenge of Finance 478

THE GROWTH OF BIG BUSINESS 480
Growth in Consumer Goods 480 ~ Carnegie Integrates Steel 481 ~ Rockefeller and the Great Standard Oil Trust 482 ~ The Mergers of J. Pierpont Morgan 483 Corporate Defenders 484 ~ Corporate Critics 484 The Costs of Doing Business 486

THE WORKERS' WORLD 487
Industrial Work 487 ~ Children, Women, and African Americans 490 ~ The American Dream of Success 491

THE SYSTEMS OF LABOR 492
Early Unions 492 ~ The Knights of Labor 493 The American Federation of Labor 493 ~ The Limits of Industrial Systems 494 ~ Management Strikes Again 496

EYEWITNESS TO HISTORY: An Englishman Visits Pittsburgh in 1898 470

COUNTERPOINT: American Business Leaders: Robber Barons or Captains of Industry? 487

CHAPTER NINETEEN
The Rise of an Urban Order

498

A NEW URBAN AGE 499
The Urban Explosion 500 ~ The Great Global Migration 501 The Shape of the City 503 ~ Urban Transport 503 ~ Bridges and Skyscrapers 504 ~ Slum and Tenement 505

RUNNING AND REFORMING THE CITY 506
Boss Rule 507 ~ Rewards, Accomplishments, and Costs 508 Nativism, Revivals, and the Social Gospel 508 ~ The Social Settlement Movement 510

CITY LIFE   510
  The Immigrant in the City 510 ~ Urban Middle-Class Life 514
  Victorianism and the Pursuit of Virtue 515 ~ Challenges to
  Convention 516

CITY CULTURE   517
  Public Education in an Urban Industrial World 518 ~ Higher Learning
  and the Rise of the Professional 519 ~ Higher Education for
  Women 520 ~ A Culture of Consumption 520 ~ Leisure 521
  Arts and Entertainment 522

EYEWITNESS TO HISTORY: A Chinese Immigrant Names
His Children 513

COUNTERPOINT: The "New" Immigrants: Who Came and Why? 514

CHAPTER TWENTY
Agrarian Domains: The South and the West   525

THE SOUTHERN BURDEN   526
  Agriculture in the New South 527 ~ Tenancy and
  Sharecropping 527 ~ Southern Industry 529 ~ Timber and
  Steel 529 ~ The Sources of Southern Poverty 530

LIFE IN THE NEW SOUTH   531
  Rural Life 531 ~ The Church 532 ~ Segregation 534

WESTERN FRONTIERS   535
  The Western Landscape 536 ~ Indian Peoples and the Western
  Environment 536 ~ Whites and the Western Environment: Competing
  Visions 537

THE WAR FOR THE WEST   539
  Contact and Conflict 539 ~ Custer's Last Stand–And the
  Indians 541 ~ Killing with Kindness 542 ~ Borderlands 544

BOOM AND BUST IN THE WEST   545
  Mining Sets a Pattern 545 ~ The Transcontinental Railroad 546
  Cattle Kingdom 547

THE FINAL FRONTIER   549
  Farming on the Plains 550 ~ A Plains Existence 550
  The Urban Frontier 551

EYEWITNESS TO HISTORY: An Indian Girl Is Shorn at
Boarding School 543

COUNTERPOINT: How to Define the Frontier? 535

CHAPTER TWENTY-ONE
The Political System under Strain

554

THE POLITICS OF PARALYSIS 555
Political Stalemate 556 ~ *The Parties* 557 ~ *The Issues* 558
The White House from Hayes to Harrison 560 ~ *Ferment in the States and Cities* 561

THE REVOLT OF THE FARMERS 562
The Harvest of Discontent 562 ~ *The Origins of the Farmers'
Alliance* 565 ~ *The Alliance Peaks* 566 ~ *The Election of
1892* 567

THE NEW REALIGNMENT 568
The Depression of 1893 568 ~ *The Rumblings of Unrest* 569
The Battle of the Standards 570 ~ *Campaign and Election* 571
The Rise of Jim Crow Politics 573 ~ *The African American
Response* 574 ~ *McKinley in the White House* 575

VISIONS OF EMPIRE 576
Imperialism, European-Style and American 576 ~ *The Shaping of
Foreign Policy* 578 ~ *William Henry Seward* 579 ~ *The United
States and Latin America* 580 ~ *Prelude in the Pacific* 581
Crisis in Venezuela 583

THE IMPERIAL MOMENT 584
Mounting Tensions 584 ~ *The Imperial War* 586 ~ *War in
Cuba* 587 ~ *Peace and the Debate over Empire* 588 ~ *America's
First Asian War* 590 ~ *An Open Door in China* 591

EYEWITNESS TO HISTORY: A Nebraska Farmer Laments His Plight 564

COUNTERPOINT: Origins of the Welfare State 558

CHAPTER TWENTY-TWO
The Progressive Era

594

THE ROOTS OF PROGRESSIVE REFORM 596
Progressive Beliefs 597 ~ *The Pragmatic Approach* 598 ~ *The
Progressive Method* 598

THE SEARCH FOR THE GOOD SOCIETY 600
Poverty in a New Light 600 ~ *Expanding the "Woman's
Sphere"* 601 ~ *Social Welfare* 604 ~ *Woman Suffrage* 605

CONTROLLING THE MASSES 606
Stemming the Immigrant Tide 607 ~ *The Curse of Demon
Rum* 608 ~ *Prostitution* 608

THE POLITICS OF MUNICIPAL AND STATE REFORM 609
The Reformation of the Cities 609 ~ Progressivism in
the States 610

PROGRESSIVISM GOES TO WASHINGTON 612
TR 612 ~ A Square Deal 614 ~ Bad Food and Pristine
Wilds 616 ~ The Troubled Taft 618 ~ Roosevelt Returns 619
The Election of 1912 619

WOODROW WILSON AND THE POLITICS OF MORALITY 621
Early Career 621 ~ The Reforms of the New Freedom 621
Labor and Social Reform 623 ~ The Limits of Progressive
Reform 623

EYEWITNESS TO HISTORY: Jane Addams Fights Child Labor 603

COUNTERPOINT: What Was Progressivism? 597

CHAPTER TWENTY-THREE
The United States and the Old World Order 626

PROGRESSIVE DIPLOMACY 627
Big Stick in the Caribbean 628 ~ A "Diplomatist of the Highest
Rank" 628 ~ Dollar Diplomacy 629

WOODROW WILSON AND MORAL DIPLOMACY 630
Missionary Diplomacy 630 ~ Intervention in Mexico 631

THE ROAD TO WAR 633
The Guns of August 633 ~ Neutral but Not Impartial 634
The Diplomacy of Neutrality 635 ~ Peace, Preparedness,
and the Election of 1916 636 ~ Wilson's Final Peace
Offensive 637

WAR AND SOCIETY 639
The Slaughter of Stalemate 639 ~ "You're in the Army Now" 640
Mobilizing the Economy 642 ~ War Work 643
Great Migrations 644 ~ Propaganda and Civil Liberties 645
Over There 647

THE LOST PEACE 649
The Treaty of Versailles 649 ~ The Battle for the Treaty 650
Red Scare 652

EYEWITNESS TO HISTORY: An African American Woman's View of the
1919 Race Riots 646

COUNTERPOINT: Why Did the United States Go to War? 638

PART FIVE
GLOBAL ESSAY: THE PERILS OF DEMOCRACY 656

CHAPTER TWENTY-FOUR
The New Era 658

THE ROARING ECONOMY 661
Technology and Consumer Spending 661 ~ *The Booming Construction Industry* 661 ~ *The Automobile* 662 ~ *The Business of America* 663 ~ *Welfare Capitalism* 664 ~ *The Consumer Culture* 665

A MASS SOCIETY 667
The New Woman 668 ~ *Mass Media* 670 ~ *A Youth Culture* 671 ~ *"Ain't We Got Fun?"* 672 ~ *The Art of Alienation* 673 ~ *A "New Negro"* 673

DEFENDERS OF THE FAITH 675
Nativism and Immigration Restriction 675 ~ *The "Noble Experiment"* 676 ~ *KKK* 677 ~ *Fundamentalism versus Darwinism* 679

REPUBLICANS ASCENDANT 680
The Politics of Normalcy 680 ~ *The Policies of Mellon and Hoover* 681 *Distress Signals* 683 ~ *The Election of 1928* 684

EYEWITNESS TO HISTORY: A Mexican Laborer Sings of the Sorrows of the New Era 666

COUNTERPOINT: Were the 1920s a Sharp Break with the Past? 682

CHAPTER TWENTY-FIVE
Crash and Depression 687

THE GREAT BULL MARKET 688
The Rampaging Bull 689 ~ *The Great Crash* 690 *The Causes of the Great Depression* 690 ~ *The Sickening Slide* 692

THE AMERICAN PEOPLE IN THE GREAT DEPRESSION 693
Hard Times 693 ~ *The Depression Family* 695 *Working Women, Anxious Children* 696 ~ *Play* 698 *The Golden Age of Radio and Film* 699 ~ *"Dirty Thirties": An Ecological Disaster* 700 ~ *Mexican Americans and African Americans* 702

THE TRAGEDY OF HERBERT HOOVER 704
The Failure of Relief 704 ~ *Herbert Hoover* 705 ~ *The Hoover*

Depression Program 706 ~ Stirrings of Discontent 707 ~ The
Bonus Army 709 ~ The Election of 1932 710

EYEWITNESS TO HISTORY: A Salesman Loses Everything 697

COUNTERPOINT: What Caused the Great Depression? 692

CHAPTER TWENTY-SIX
The New Deal 712

THE EARLY NEW DEAL (1933–1935) 714
  The Democratic Roosevelts 714 ~ Saving the Banks 715
  Relief for the Unemployed 717 ~ The Riddle of Recovery 719
  The NRA in Trouble 720 ~ Planning for Agriculture 720

A SECOND NEW DEAL (1935–1936) 721
  Voices of Protest 722 ~ The Second Hundred Days 724 ~ The
  Election of 1936 725

THE NEW DEAL AND THE AMERICAN PEOPLE 726
  The New Deal and Western Water 727 ~ The Limited Reach
  of the New Deal 727 ~ Tribal Rights 729 ~ A New Deal for
  Women 730 ~ The Rise of Organized Labor 731 ~ Campaigns
  of the CIO 732 ~ "Art for the Millions" 733

THE END OF THE NEW DEAL (1937–1940) 734
  "Packing" the Courts 735 ~ The New Deal at Bay 736
  The Legacy of the New Deal 737

EYEWITNESS TO HISTORY: "My Day": The First Lady Tours Tennessee 716

COUNTERPOINT: Assessing the New Deal 739

CHAPTER TWENTY-SEVEN
America's Rise to Globalism 741

THE UNITED STATES IN A TROUBLED WORLD 742
  Pacific Interests 742 ~ Becoming a Good Neighbor 743
  The Diplomacy of Isolationism 744 ~ Neutrality Legislation 745
  Inching toward War 746 ~ Hitler's Invasion 747
  Retreat from Isolationism 749 ~ Disaster in the Pacific 750

A GLOBAL WAR 751
  Strategies for War 752 ~ Gloomy Prospects 752 ~ A Grand
  Alliance 753 The Naval War in the Pacific 754 ~ Turning Points in
  Europe 755 ~ Those Who Fought 755 ~ Uneasy Recruits 756
  Women at War 757

WAR PRODUCTION   757
> Mobilizing for War   758   ~   Science Goes to War   759
> War Work and Prosperity   760   ~   Organized Labor   760
> Women Workers   761

A QUESTION OF RIGHTS   762
> Italians and Asian Americans   762   ~   Minorities on the Job   765
> Urban Unrest   767   ~   The New Deal in Retreat   768

WINNING THE WAR AND THE PEACE   768
> The Fall of the Third Reich   769   ~   Two Roads to Tokyo   770
> Big Three Diplomacy   771   ~   The Road to Yalta   771
> The Fallen Leader   773   ~   The Holocaust   774   ~   A Lasting
> Peace   775   ~   Atom Diplomacy   776

EYEWITNESS TO HISTORY: A Woman Learns Shipyard Welding   762

COUNTERPOINT: Did Roosevelt Deliberately Invite War?   751

PART SIX
GLOBAL ESSAY: THE UNITED STATES
IN A NUCLEAR AGE   780

CHAPTER TWENTY-EIGHT
Cold War America   782

THE RISE OF THE COLD WAR   783
> American Suspicions   784   ~   Communist Expansion   785   ~   A Policy
> of Containment   786   ~   The Truman Doctrine   787   ~   The Marshall
> Plan   787   ~   NATO   788   ~   The Atomic Shield versus the Iron
> Curtain   789   ~   Atomic Deterrence   790

POSTWAR PROSPERITY   791
> Postwar Adjustments   792   ~   The New Deal at Bay   793   ~   The
> Election of 1948   794   ~   The Fair Deal   795

THE COLD WAR AT HOME   796
> The Shocks of 1949   796   ~   The Loyalty Crusade   798   ~   HUAC
> and Hollywood   798   ~   The Ambitions of Senator McCarthy   799

FROM COLD WAR TO HOT WAR AND BACK   801
> Police Action   801   ~   The Chinese Intervene   802   ~   Truman versus
> MacArthur   802   ~   K1C2: The Election of 1952   804   ~   The Fall
> of McCarthy   805

EYEWITNESS TO HISTORY: Harry Truman Disciplines His
"Big General"   806

COUNTERPOINT: What Were Stalin's Intentions?   785

CHAPTER TWENTY-NINE
The Suburban Era 809

THE RISE OF THE SUBURBS 810
A Boom in Babies and in Housing 811 ~ Suburbs and Cities Transformed 812

THE CULTURE OF SUBURBIA 814
American Civil Religion 815 ~ "Homemaking" Women in the Workaday World 816 ~ The Flickering Gray Screen 817

THE POLITICS OF CALM 818
The Eisenhower Presidency 818 ~ The Conglomerate World 820

NATIONALISM IN AN AGE OF SUPERPOWERS 821
To the Brink? 821 ~ Brinksmanship in Asia 822 ~ The Superpowers 823 ~ Nationalism Unleashed 823 ~ The Response to Sputnik 825 ~ Thaws and Freezes 826

CIVIL RIGHTS AND THE NEW SOUTH 828
The Changing South and African Americans 828 ~ The NAACP and Civil Rights 829 ~ The Brown Decision 830 ~ A New Civil Rights Strategy 830 ~ Little Rock and the White Backlash 832

CRACKS IN THE CONSENSUS 833
Critics of Mass Culture 833 ~ Juvenile Delinquency, Rock and Roll, and Rebellion 834

EYEWITNESS TO HISTORY: Growing Up with the Threat of Atomic War 827

COUNTERPOINT: Assessing Eisenhower 819

CHAPTER THIRTY
Liberalism and Beyond 837

A LIBERAL AGENDA FOR REFORM 838
The Social Structures of Change 838 ~ The Election of 1960 839 ~ The Hard-Nosed Idealists of Camelot 840

NEW FRONTIERS 841
Cold War Frustrations 842 ~ Confronting Khrushchev 843 ~ The Missiles of October 843 ~ The (Somewhat) New Frontier at Home 846 ~ The Reforms of the Warren Court 846

THE CIVIL RIGHTS CRUSADE 848
Riding to Freedom 848 ~ Civil Rights at High Tide 849 ~ The Fire Next Time 853 ~ Black Power 854 ~ Violence in the Streets 855

LYNDON JOHNSON AND THE GREAT SOCIETY 856
The Origins of the Great Society 856 ~ The Election of 1964 858
The Great Society 858

THE COUNTERCULTURE 860
Activists on the New Left 860 ~ The Rise of the Counterculture 862
The Rock Revolution 863 ~ The West Coast Scene 864

EYEWITNESS TO HISTORY: A Mississippi College Student Attends the
NAACP Convention 850

COUNTERPOINT: What Triggered the Upheavals of the 1960s? 861

CHAPTER THIRTY-ONE
The Vietnam Era 867

THE ROAD TO VIETNAM 869
Lyndon Johnson's War 871 ~ Rolling Thunder 872

SOCIAL CONSEQUENCES OF THE WAR 873
The Soldiers' War 873 ~ The War at Home 875

THE UNRAVELING 878
Tet Offensive 878 ~ The Shocks of 1968 880 ~ Whose Silent
Majority? 881

THE NIXON ERA 883
Vietnamization—and Cambodia 884 ~ Fighting a No-Win War 885
The Move toward Détente 885 ~ Nixon's New Federalism 887
Stagflation 888

"SILENT" MAJORITIES AND VOCAL MINORITIES 888
Hispanic Activism 889 ~ The Choices of American Indians 891
Gay Rights 892 ~ Social Policies and the Court 892 ~ Us versus
Them 893 ~ Triumph 894

THE END OF AN ERA 894

EYEWITNESS TO HISTORY: A Disabled Vietnam Veteran Joins a Los Angeles
Antiwar Demonstration 882

COUNTERPOINT: Whose War? 877

CHAPTER THIRTY-TWO
The Age of Limits 897

THE LIMITS OF REFORM 898
Consumerism 898 ~ Environmentalism 900 ~ Feminism 902
Equal Rights and Abortion 904

POLITICAL LIMITS: WATERGATE 905
  *The President's Enemies 906 ~ Break-In 906 ~ To the Oval
  Office 907 ~ Resignation 908*

A FORD, NOT A LINCOLN 909
  *Kissinger and Foreign Policy 909 ~ Economic Limits and American
  Diplomacy 910 ~ Détente 912 ~ The Limits of a Post-Watergate
  President 912 ~ Fighting Inflation 914 ~ The Election of
  1976 914*

JIMMY CARTER: RESTORING THE FAITH 915
  *The Search for Direction 915 ~ A Sick Economy 917 ~ Leadership,
  Not Hegemony 917 ~ Saving Détente 918 ~ The Middle East:
  Hope and Hostages 919 ~ A President Held Hostage 920*

EYEWITNESS TO HISTORY: Recounting the Early Days of the
Feminist Movement 903

COUNTERPOINT: Interpreting the Environmental Movement 901

CHAPTER THIRTY-THREE
A Nation Still Divisible

923

THE CONSERVATIVE REBELLION 925
  *Born Again 925 ~ The Catholic Conscience 926 ~ The Media as
  Battleground 928 ~ The Election of 1980 928*

PRIME TIME WITH RONALD REAGAN 929
  *The Great Communicator 929 ~ The Reagan Agenda 930 ~ The
  Reagan Revolution in Practice 931 ~ The Impact of Reaganomics 933
  The Military Buildup 934*

STANDING TALL IN A CHAOTIC WORLD 935
  *Terrorism in the Middle East 935 ~ Mounting Frustrations in Central
  America 936 ~ The Iran-Contra Connection 936 ~ Cover
  Blown 937 ~ From Cold War to Glasnost 939 ~ The Election of
  1988 939*

AN END TO THE COLD WAR 939
  *A Post–Cold War Foreign Policy 940 ~ The Persian Gulf War 941
  Domestic Doldrums 942 ~ The Conservative Court 942
  Disillusionment and Anger 944 ~ The Election of 1992 945*

THE CLINTON PRESIDENCY 945
  *The New World Disorder 946 ~ Recovery—but Reform? 947
  Revolution Reborn 948 ~ Morality and Politics 949*

A NATION OF NATIONS IN THE TWENTY-FIRST CENTURY 950
  The New Immigration 951 ~ Equality Still Denied 953

EYEWITNESS TO HISTORY: The President's Budget Director Discusses the "Reagan Revolution"   932

COUNTERPOINT: Defining the New Conservatism   926

APPENDIX   A.1

THE DECLARATION OF INDEPENDENCE   A.1

THE CONSTITUTION OF THE UNITED STATES OF AMERICA   A.4

PRESIDENTIAL ELECTIONS   A.19

JUSTICES OF THE SUPREME COURT   A.23

A SOCIAL PROFILE OF THE AMERICAN REPUBLIC   A.25
   *Population   A.25   ~   Vital Statistics   A.25   ~   Life Expectancy   A.26
   Regional Origin of Immigrants   A.26   ~   Recent Trends in
   Immigration   A.27   ~   American Workers and Farmers   A.28
   The Economy and Federal Spending   A.28   ~   American Wars   A.29*

Bibliography   B.1

Photo Credits   C.1

Index   I.1

List of Maps and Charts

Principal Routes of European Exploration   10
Indians of North America, circa 1500   12
Spanish America, circa 1600   20
Colonies of the Chesapeake   41
The Carolinas and the Caribbean   52
Spanish Missions in North America, ca. 1675   57
Early New England   68
Patterns of Settlement in the Eighteenth Century   91
The Distribution of the American Population, 1775   100
Overseas Trade Networks   111
The Seven Years' War in America   118
European Claims in North America, 1750 and 1763   120
The Appalachian Frontier, 1750–1775   122
The Fighting in the North, 1775–1777   150
The Fighting in the South, 1780–1781   160
Western Land Claims, 1782–1802   173
The Ordinance of 1785   176
Exploration and Expansion: The Louisiana Purchase   224
The Indian Response to White Encroachment   230
The War of 1812   237
The Transportation Network of a Market Economy, 1840   249
Development of the Lowell Mills   260
The Missouri Compromise and the Union's Boundaries in 1820   269
Indian Removal   283
Cotton and Other Crops of the South   329
The Spread of Slavery, 1820–1860   331
Sioux Expansion and the Horse and Gun Frontier   354
The Overland Trail   360
The Mexican War   365
Territorial Growth and the Compromise of 1850   375
Growth of the Railroad Network, 1850–1860   383
The Kansas–Nebraska Act   389
The Pattern of Secession   403
Resources of the Union and the Confederacy, 1861   410
The War in the West, 1861–1862   415
The War in the East, 1861–1862   417
The War in the East, 1863–1865   432
The War in the West, 1863–1865   434
A Georgia Plantation after the War   456

Steel Production, 1880 and 1914   471
Occupational Distribution, 1880 and 1920   476
Railroads, 1870–1890   479
Boom and Bust Business Cycle, 1865–1900   486
Immigration, 1860–1920   502
Tenant Farmers, 1900   528
Natural Environment of the West   538
The Indian Frontier   540
The Mining and Cattle Frontiers   548
The Voting Public, 1860–1912   556
The Election of 1896   572
Imperialist Expansion, 1900   577
The United States in the Pacific   589
Woman Suffrage   606
The Election of 1912   620
American Interventions in the Caribbean, 1898–1930   631
The War in Europe, 1914–1917   634
The Final German Offensive and Allied Counterattack, 1918   648
Areas of Population Growth   660
The Election of 1928   685
Unemployment, 1925–1945   694
Federal Budget and Surplus/Deficit, 1920–1940   707
Unemployment Relief, 1934   718
What the New Deal Did . . .   738
World War II in Europe and North Africa   748
World War II in the Pacific and Asia   770
Cold War Europe   788
The Korean War   803
The United States Birthrate, 1900–1989   811
The World of the Superpowers   844
The War in Vietnam   870
Oil and Conflict in the Middle East, 1948–1995   911
Poverty in America, 1970–1990   934
Hispanic and Asian Populations   952

About the Authors

James West Davidson received his Ph.D. from Yale University. A historian who has pursued a full-time writing career, he is the author of numerous books, among them *After the Fact: The Art of Historical Detection* (with Mark H. Lytle), *The Logic of Millennial Thought: Eighteenth-Century New England*, and *Great Heart: The History of a Labrador Adventure* (with John Rugge).

William E. Gienapp has a Ph.D. from the University of California, Berkeley. He taught at the University of Wyoming before going to Harvard University, where he is Professor of History. In 1988 he received the Avery O. Craven Award for his book *The Origins of the Republican Party, 1852–1856*. His essay "The Antebellum Era" appeared in the *Encyclopedia of Social History* (1992), and he is a coauthor of *Why the Civil War Came* (1996).

Christine Leigh Heyrman is Associate Professor of History at the University of Delaware. She received a Ph.D. in American Studies from Yale University and is the author of *Commerce and Culture: The Maritime Communities of Colonial Massachusetts, 1690–1750*. Most recently she received the Bancroft Prize for *Southern Cross: The Beginnings of the Bible Belt* (1997), a book about popular religious culture in the Old Southwest.

Mark H. Lytle, who was awarded a Ph.D. from Yale University, is Professor of History and Environmental Studies and Chair of the American Studies Program at Bard College. He is also Director of the Master of Arts in Teaching Program at Bard. His publications include *The Origins of the Iranian-American Alliance, 1941–1953* and *After the Fact: The Art of Historical Detection* (with James West Davidson), and most recently, "An Environmental Approach to American Diplomatic History," in *Diplomatic History*. He is at work on *The Uncivil War: America in the Vietnam Era*.

Michael B. Stoff is Associate Professor of History at the University of Texas at Austin, where he is director of graduate studies in history. The recipient of a Ph.D. from Yale University, he wrote *Oil, War, and American Security: The Search for a National Policy on Foreign Oil, 1941–1947* and *Manhattan Project: A Documentary Introduction to the Atomic Age*. He has been honored many times for his teaching, most recently with the Friar's Centennial Teaching Excellence Award.

Preface to the
Second Concise Edition

Nation of Nations was written in the belief that students would be drawn more readily to the study of history if their text emphasized a narrative approach. Clearly, many of our readers agree, and to them we owe thanks for the warm reception the text has been given.

This edition provides a briefer alternative to the full-length text. In the belief that the original authors could best preserve both the themes and the narrative approach of the longer work, we have done the abridgment ourselves. Indeed, the task forced us to think again about the core elements of narrative history, for the task of condensing a full-length survey presents devilish temptations. Most teachers rightly resist sacrificing breadth of coverage; yet if an edition is to be concise, the words, the sentences, the paragraphs must go. The temptation is to excise the apparently superfluous "details" of a full-dress narrative: trimming character portraits, cutting back on narrative color, lopping off concrete examples. Yet too draconian a campaign risks producing either a barebones compendium of facts or a bloodless thematic outline, dispossessed of the tales that engaged the reader in the first place.

The intent, then, is to provide a text that remains a *narrative*—a history with enough contextual detail for readers to grasp the story. The fuller introductions to each chapter, a distinctive feature of the original text, have been preserved, though streamlined where possible. Within each chapter, we have attempted to maintain a balance between narrative and thematic analysis. Paradoxically, this has occasionally meant *adding* material to the concise edition: replacing longer stories with shorter emblematic sketches or recasting sections to ensure that students are not overwhelmed by the compression of too many details into too few paragraphs.

Each chapter of the concise edition also includes two additional features. The first, "Eyewitness to History," is designed to reinforce the centrality of narrative. Each Eyewitness is a primary source excerpt; some are written by eminent Americans, others by little-known folk who were intimately involved in the changes affecting their times. In either case, the vivid first-person accounts serve to draw readers further into the story. But we also hope that they will encourage students to recognize the hidden complexities of narrative. The diversity of materials and perspectives should make it clear that one of the historian's primary tasks is to step back and place the welter of overlapping, often conflicting narratives in a larger context.

A second feature, entitled "Counterpoint," is new to this concise edition. In it, we explore contrasting ways historians have interpreted a central topic covered by the chapter. We were led to do this, paradoxically, by the very success of the narrative approach, for some professors have written suggesting that precisely because the tale flows so smoothly, students may be seduced into thinking that the writing of history is without controversy—that the past must have occurred precisely as we have sketched it and that any questions of interpretations must be minor matters. To combat this misimpression, our Counterpoint discussions in each chapter are *not* separated out as boxed features; instead, they are integrated into the narrative so that students come to understand such debates as an inevitable (and productive) part of writing history.

In other ways, the approach of this concise edition remains the same as in the first edition. We continue to use marginal headings to help readers focus on key terms and concepts. Each chapter also concludes with a timeline of significant events. And each of the book's six parts begins with an essay setting American events in a global perspective. We believe it important to show that the United States did not develop in a geographic or cultural vacuum and that the broad forces shaping it also influenced other nations.

Over the past decade during which we have worked on this book we have been immensely grateful to the many reviewers generous enough to offer constructive comments and suggestions. To name them all would require more space than this preface itself occupies. But we cannot omit specific mention of those readers who have provided advice on the shaping of the concise edition of *Nation of Nations*. They include Janet Allured, McNeese State University; Virginia Paganelli Caruso, Henry Ford Community College; Kathryn Dabelow, Pasadena City College; Alan C. Downs, Georgia Southern University; Linda Killen, Radford University; Kenneth L. Kitchen, Trident Technical College; Michael J. Gillis, California State University–Chico; Shane Maddock, U.S. Coast Guard Academy; Jay Mullen, Southern Oregon University; Sydney Nathans, Duke University; Gary L. Shumway, California State University–Fullerton; Albert J. Smith, Modesto Junior College. The first concise edition also benefited from the advice of Michael Bellesiles, Emory University; James Crisp, North Carolina State University; Ann Ellis, Kennesaw State College; Norman Enhorning, Adirondack Community College; Jerry Felt, University of Vermont; Mary Ferrari, Radford University; Renee Shively Leonard; Steven White, Lexington Community College; James Woods, Georgia Southern; and William Woodward, Seattle Pacific University.

The division of labor for this book was determined by our respective fields of scholarship: Christine Heyrman, the colonial era, in which Europeans, Africans, and Indians participated in the making of both a new America and a new republic; William Gienapp, the 90 years in which the young nation first flourished, then foundered on the issues of section and slavery; Michael Stoff, the post–Civil War era, in which industrialization and urbanization brought the nation more centrally into an international system frequently disrupted by depression and war; and Mark Lytle, the modern era, in which Americans finally faced the reality that even the boldest dreams of national greatness are bounded by the finite nature of power and resources both natural and human. Finally, because the need to specialize inevitably imposes limits on any project as broad as this one, our fifth author, James Davidson, served as a general editor and writer, with the intent of fitting individual parts to the whole, as well as providing a measure of continuity, style, and overarching purpose. In producing this collaborative effort, all of us have shared the conviction that the best history speaks to a larger audience.

James West Davidson
William E. Gienapp
Christine Leigh Heyrman
Mark H. Lytle
Michael B. Stoff

Introduction

History is both a discipline of rigor, bound by rules and scholarly methods, and something more: the unique, compelling, even strange way in which we humans define ourselves. We are all the sum of the tales of thousands of people, great and small, whose actions have etched their lines upon us. History supplies our very identity—a sense of the social groups to which we belong, whether family, ethnic group, race, class, or gender. It reveals to us the foundations of our deepest religious beliefs and traces the roots of our economic and political systems. It explores how we celebrate and grieve, sing the songs we sing, weather the illnesses to which time and chance subject us. It commands our attention for all these good reasons and for no good reason at all, other than a fascination with the way the myriad tales play out. Strange that we should come to care about a host of men and women so many centuries gone, some with names eminent and familiar, others unknown but for a chance scrap of information left behind in an obscure letter.

Yet we do care. We care about Sir Humphrey Gilbert, "devoured and swallowed up of the Sea" one black Atlantic night in 1583; about George Washington at Kips Bay, red with fury as he takes a riding crop to his retreating soldiers. We care about Octave Johnson, a slave fleeing through Louisiana swamps trying to decide whether to stand and fight the approaching hounds or take his chances with the bayou alligators; about Clara Barton, her nurse's skirts so heavy with blood from the wounded that she must wring them out before tending to the next soldier. We are drawn to the fate of Chinese laborers, chipping away at the Sierras' looming granite; a Georgian named Tom Watson seeking to forge a colorblind political alliance; and desperate immigrant mothers, kerosene in hand, storming Brooklyn butcher shops that have again raised prices. We follow, with a mix of awe and amusement, the fortunes of the quirky Henry Ford ("Everybody wants to be somewhere he ain't"), turning out identical automobiles, insisting his factory workers wear identical expressions ("Fordization of the Face"). We trace the career of young Thurgood Marshall, crisscrossing the South in his own "little old beat-up '29 Ford," typing legal briefs in the back seat, trying to get black teachers to sue for equal pay, hoping to get his people somewhere they weren't. The list could go on and on, spilling out as it did in Walt Whitman's *Leaves of Grass:* "A southerner soon as a northerner, a planter nonchalant and hospitable, A Yankee bound my own way . . . a Hoosier, a Badger, a Buckeye, a Louisianian or Georgian . . . ." Whitman embraced and celebrated them all, inseparable strands of what made him an American and what made him human:

> In all people I see myself, none more and not one a barleycorn less,
> And the good or bad I say of myself I say of them.

To encompass so expansive an America Whitman turned to poetry; historians have traditionally chosen narrative as their means of giving life to the past. That mode of explanation permits them to interweave the strands of economic, political, and social history in a coherent chronological framework. By choosing narrative, they affirm the multicausal nature of historical explanation—the insistence that events be portrayed in context. By choosing narrative, they are also acknowledging that, while long-term economic and social trends shape societies in significant ways, events often take on a logic (or an illogic) of their own, jostling one another, being deflected by unpredictable personal decisions, sudden deaths, natural catastrophes, and chance. There are literary reasons, too, for preferring a narrative approach, since it supplies a dramatic force usually missing from more structural analyses of the past.

In some ways, surveys like this one are the natural antithesis of narrative history. They strive, by definition, to be comprehensive: to furnish a broad, orderly exposition of their chosen field. Yet to cover so much ground in so limited a space necessarily deprives readers of the context of more detailed accounts. Then, too, the resurgence of social history—with its concern for class and race, patterns of rural and urban life, the spread of market and industrial economies— lends itself to more analytic, less chronological treatments. The challenge facing historians is to incorporate these areas of research without losing the story's narrative drive or the chronological flow that orients readers to the more familiar events of our past.

In the end, it is counterproductive to treat political and social history as distinct spheres. There is no simple way to separate the world of ordinary Americans or the marketplace of boom and bust from the corridors of political maneuvering or the ceremonial pomp of an inauguration. The primary question of this narrative—how the fledgling, often tumultuous confederation of "these United States" managed to transform itself into an enduring republic—is not only political but necessarily social. In order to survive, a republic must resolve conflicts among citizens of different geographic regions and economic classes, of diverse racial and ethnic origins, of competing religions and ideologies. The resolution of these conflicts has produced tragic consequences, perhaps, as often as noble ones. But tragic or noble, the destiny of these states cannot be understood without comprehending both the social and the political dimensions of the story.

The Creation of a New America

It is now half a millennium—a full 500 years—since the civilizations of Europe and Africa first made sustained contact with those of North America. The transformations arising out of that event have been astonishing. To gain a rough sense of the scale involved, both in time and space, it is worth standing for a moment not at the beginning of our story but somewhere nearer its midpoint: with Meriwether Lewis and William Clark in August 1805, as they stand atop the continental divide on their traverse of North America. The two men, on orders from President Thomas Jefferson, had been sent on the first American exploratory mission to report on the lands west of the Mississippi. From Lewis and Clark's vantage point, high in the Rocky Mountains, what can we see?

At first glance we see pretty much what we expect to see: a vast, seemingly endless land stretching from sea to sea. But living as we do in the late twentieth century, we tend to take for granted that the domain spread before us is united as a continental republic under a single national government. Only hindsight makes this proposition seem natural. In 1800 the sheer size of the land made the notion of political unity difficult to grasp, for the United States themselves remained a group of colonies only recently unified. Even Jefferson, who possessed the vision to send Lewis and Clark on their mission, had long been in the habit of referring to Virginia as "my country." And the lands west of the Mississippi were still controlled primarily by scores of independent Indian nations.

Just how diverse the landscape was can be seen by the methods Lewis and Clark used to communicate. With no common language spanning the territory, speech making became a series of translations that reflected the route over which the party had traveled. In present-day Idaho, Clark addressed the Tushepaw tribe in English. His speech was translated into French by a trapper in the party; then a second trapper translated into Minataree, a language that his Indian wife, Sacajawea, understood. Sacajawea, the only female member of the party, had grown up farther west with the Shoshone, so she in turn translated the Minataree into Shoshone, which a boy from the Tushepaw nation understood. He translated the Shoshone into his own people's tongue.

If the Louisiana Territory seemed a patchwork of governments and cultures, the young "United States" appeared nearly as heterogeneous. Dutch-speaking patroons could be found along New York's Hudson River, Welsh and German farmers along Pennsylvania's Lancaster Pike, Swedes in Delaware, Gaelic-speaking Scots scattered up and down the Appalachian backcountry, African Americans speaking the Gullah dialect along the Carolina coast. In 1800 many of these settlers knew more about their homelands in Europe or Africa than they did about other regions of North America.

Thus our first task in studying the American past becomes one of translation. We must view events not with the jaded eyes of the late twentieth century but with the fresh eyes of an earlier era. Then the foregone conclusions vanish. How does the American nation manage to unite millions of square miles of territory into one governable republic? How do New York and San Francisco (a city not even in existence in Lewis and Clark's day) come to be linked in a complex economy as well as in a single political system? Such questions take on even more significance when we recall that Europe—roughly the same size as the United States—is today still divided into over four dozen independent nations speaking some 33 languages, not to mention another 100 or so spoken within the former Soviet Union. A united Europe has not emerged, and indeed seems even farther away after the momentous breakup of the Soviet empire.

How, then, did this American republic—this "teeming nation of nations," to use Walt Whitman's phrase—come to be? In barest outline, that is the question that drives our narrative across half a millennium.

The question becomes even more challenging if we move toward the beginning of our story. In 1450, about the time Christopher Columbus was born, only the first stirrings of European expansion to the west had begun. To be sure, Scandinavian seafarers led by Leif Ericsson had reached the northern reaches of the Americas, planting a settlement in Newfoundland in 1001 A.D. But news of Vinland, as Leif called his colony, never reached Europe, and the site was soon abandoned and forgotten. In Columbus' day localism still held sway. Italy was divided into five major states and an equal number of smaller territories. The Germanic peoples were united loosely in the Holy Roman Empire, which (as historians have long delighted in pointing out) was neither holy, Roman, nor an empire. French kings ruled over only about half of what is now France. Spain was divided into several kingdoms, with some areas held by Christians and others by Islamic Moors, whose forebears came from Africa. England, a contentious little nation, was beginning a series of bitter civil conflicts among the nobility, known eventually as the Wars of the Roses. The only country pushing beyond the boundaries of the known European world was Portugal, whose sailors were advancing down the coast of Africa in search of gold and slaves.

Localism was also evident in the patterns of European transportation and trade. For the most part, goods moving overland were carried by wheeled carts or pack animals over rutted paths. Rivers and canals provided another option, but lords repeatedly taxed boats that crossed their territories. On the Seine River, greedy tollkeepers lay in wait every six or seven miles. Travel across the Mediterranean Sea and along Europe's northern coastlines was possible, but storms and pirates made the going dangerous and slow. Under good conditions a ship might reach London from Venice in only 9 days; under bad it might take 50.

European peoples at this time had some dealings—though not extensive ones—with Africa. What contact there was arose primarily from sharing the Mediterranean Sea. North African culture had been shaped since the seventh century by the religion of Islam, whose influence spread even up through Spain. Farther south in Africa, the kingdom of Songhai prospered along the Niger River. But Africans from the interior regions were linked with Europeans primarily through trading caravans, which made their way across the Sahara Desert with African gold—essential to Europe's economy. The west African coast, which faced the Atlantic, was only beginning to receive the attention of the Portuguese.

If Europe in 1450 was less unified and dynamic than we might have imagined, the civilizations of North and South America were more complex and populous than historians once thought. Earlier estimates suggested that when Europeans first arrived, about 10 million people were living in Central and South America, with another million living north of Mexico. More recently these figures have been raised tenfold, to perhaps as many as 100 million people in Central and South America and 5 to 10 million north of Mexico. In 1492, when Columbus landed on Hispaniola, that island alone may have held some 7 to 8 million people—a number roughly equal to the entire population of Spain. Tenochtitlán, capital of the Aztec empire, held an estimated 250,000 inhabitants, perhaps double the size of the largest European cities of the day. Such dense urban populations were supported by sophisticated agricultural techniques, including canals, irrigation, and drainage systems.

North America was far from being as heavily populated, but neither was it sparsely settled. From one end of the continent to the other, native cultures actively shaped their environments, burning the forests and plains to promote the growth of vegetation as well as animal populations, which they harvested. As we shall see, Amerindian agricultural achievements were so remarkable that they eventually revolutionized eating habits across the rest of the globe.

Here then are three worlds—Europe, Africa, the Americas—poised on the brink of contact. What social and economic forces led so many Europeans—desperate and opportunistic, high-minded and idealistic—to turn westward in pursuit of their dreams? How did the civilizations of North and South America react to the European invaders? And not least, how did the mix of cultures from Africa, Europe, and North America come together to create what was truly a new America, in which some of the most independent-minded individuals prospered in provinces that exhibited some of the harshest examples of human slavery? These are among the questions we seek to answer as our narrative unfolds.

CHAPTER ONE

Old World, New Worlds

All the world lay before them. Or so it seemed to mariners from England's seafaring coasts, pushing westward toward unknown lands in the far Atlantic. Since the time of King Arthur, the English living along the rugged southwestern coasts of Devon and Cornwall had followed the sea. From the wharves of England's West Country seaports like Bristol, ships headed west and north to Ireland, bringing back animal hides as well as timber for houses and barrels. Or they turned south, fetching wines from France and olive oil or figs and raisins from the Spanish and Portuguese coasts. In return, West Country ports offered woven woolen cloth and codfish, caught wherever the best prospects beckoned.

The search for cod had long drawn West Country sailors north and west, toward Iceland. In the 1480s and 1490s, however, a few English pushed even

Cabot discovers Newfoundland

farther west. Old maps, after all, claimed that the bountiful *Hy-Brasil*—Gaelic for "Isle of the Blessed"—lay somewhere west of Ireland. These western ventures returned with little to show for their daring until the coming of an Italian named Giovanni Caboto, called John Cabot by the English. Cabot, who hailed from Venice, obtained the blessing of King Henry VII to hunt for unknown lands. From the port of Bristol his lone ship set out in the spring of 1497.

This time the return voyage brought news of a "new-found" island where the trees were tall enough to make fine masts and the codfish were plentiful. After returning to Bristol, Cabot marched off to London to inform His Majesty, received 10 pounds as his reward, and with the proceeds dressed himself in dashing silks. The multitudes of London flocked after him, wondering over "the Admiral"; then Cabot returned triumphantly to Bristol to undertake a more ambitious search for a northwest passage to Asia. He set sail with five ships in 1498 and was never heard from again.

By the 1550s Cabot's island, now known as Newfoundland, attracted 400 vessels annually, fishermen not only from England but also from France, Portugal,

The fishing season

and Spain. The trip was not easy. Individual merchants or a few partners outfitted small ships with provisions, fishing boats, and guns to ward off sea-roving pirates. As early in the season as they dared, crews of 10 or 20 would catch the spring easterlies, watching as familiar roofs and primitive lighthouses burning smoky coal sank beneath the horizon.

Weeks after setting sail the sailors sighted Newfoundland's fog-shrouded beaches. Seals and walruses played along the rocks offshore, and the encircling sea teemed with cod and flounder, salmon and herring. Throughout the summer men launched little boats from each harbor and fished offshore all day and into the night. With lines and nets, and baskets weighted with stones, they scooped fish from the sea and then dried and salted the catch on the beach. In odd hours, sailors traded with the native Indians, who shared their summer fishing grounds and the skins of fox and deer.

St. John's, Newfoundland, served as the hub of the North Atlantic fishery. Portuguese, English, and French vessels all dropped anchor there, either to take on supplies in the spring or to prepare for the homeward voyage in autumn. Besides trading, there was much talking, for these seafarers knew as much as anyone about the world of wonders opening to Europeans. They were acquainted with names like Cristoforo Colombo, the Italian from Genoa whom Cabot might have known as a boy. They listened to Portuguese tales of sailing around Africa in pursuit of Asian spices and to stories of Indian empires to the south, rich in gold and silver.

Indeed, Newfoundland was one of the few places in the world where so many ordinary folk of different nations could gather and talk, crammed aboard dank ships moored in St. John's harbor, huddled before blazing fires on its beaches, or crowded into smoky makeshift taverns. When the ships sailed home in autumn, the tales went with them, repeated in the tiniest coastal villages by those pleased to have cheated death and the sea one more time. Eager to fish, talk, trade, and take profits, West Country mariners were almost giddy at the prospect of Europe's expanding horizons.

THE MEETING OF EUROPE AND AMERICA

Most seafarers who fished the waters of Newfoundland's Grand Banks remain unknown today. Yet it is well to begin with these ordinary fisherfolk, for the European discovery of the Americas cannot be looked upon simply as the voyages of a few bold explorers. Adventurers like Christopher Columbus or John Cabot were only the most visible representatives of a much larger expansion of European peoples and culture that began in the 1450s. That expansion arose out of a series of gradual but telling changes in the fabric of European society—changes that were reflected in the lives of ordinary seafarers as much as in the careers of explorers decked out in flaming silks.

Some of these changes were technological, arising out of advances in the arts of navigating and shipbuilding and the use of gunpowder. Some were economic, involving the development of trade networks like those linking Bristol with ports in Iceland and Spain. Some were demographic, bringing about a rise in Europe's population after a devastating century of plague. Other changes were religious, adding a dimension of devout belief to the political rivalries that fueled discoveries in the Americas. Yet others were political, making it possible for kingdoms to centralize and extend their influence across the ocean. Portugal, Spain, France, and England—all possessing coasts along the Atlantic—led the way in exploration, spurred on by Italian "admirals" like Caboto and Colombo, Spanish *conquistadores* like Cortés and Pizarro, and English sea dogs like Humphrey Gilbert and Walter Raleigh. Ordinary folk rode these currents too. The great and the small alike were propelled by forces that were remolding the face of Europe.

Changes in European society

The Portuguese Wave

In 1450 all of the world known to western Europeans was Asia and Africa. Most sailors traveled only along the coast of western Europe, following the shores between Norway and the southern tip of Spain, seldom daring to lose sight of land. Beginning in the fifteenth century, bolder seafarers groped down the coast of western Africa, half-expecting to be boiled alive in the Atlantic as they approached the equator. Europeans had traded with Asia through the Muslims of the eastern Mediterranean and across an overland route called the "Silk Road." But they had only vague notions about "the Indies"—China and Japan, the Spice Islands, and the lands lying between Thailand and India. What little they knew, they had learned mainly from Marco Polo, whose account of his travels in the East was not published until 1477, more than 150 years after his death.

But a revolution in European geography began in the middle decades of the fifteenth century, as widening networks of travel and trade connected Europeans to civilizations beyond western Europe. The Portuguese took the lead, encouraged by Prince Henry, known as the Navigator. The devout Henry, a member of Portugal's royal family, had heard tales of Prester John, a Catholic priest rumored to rule a Christian kingdom somewhere beyond the Muslim kingdoms of Africa and Asia. Henry dreamed of joining forces with Prester John and trapping the Muslims in a vise. To that end, he helped finance a series of expeditions down the coast of west Africa. He founded an informal school of navigation on the Portuguese coast, supplying shipmasters with information about wind and currents, as well as navigational charts.

Revolution in geography

This stately ivory mask made by a west African artist in the early sixteenth century is adorned with 10 bearded heads of white men, representing Portuguese explorers and traders.

Portuguese merchants, who may or may not have believed in Prester John, never doubted there was money to be made in Africa. They invested in Prince Henry's voyages in return for trading monopolies of ivory and slaves, grain and gold. A few may have hoped that the voyages down the coast of west Africa would lead to a direct sea route to the Orient. By discovering such a route, Portugal would be able to cut out the Muslim merchants who funneled all the Asian trade in silks, dyes, drugs, and perfumes through Mediterranean ports.

While Portugal's merchants were establishing trading posts along the west coast of Africa, its mariners were discovering islands in the Atlantic: the Canaries, Madeira, and the Azores. Settlers planted sugarcane and imported slaves from Africa to work their fields. The Portuguese might have pressed even farther west, but for the daring of Bartholomeu Dias. In 1488 Dias rounded the Cape of Good Hope on the southern tip of Africa, sailing far enough up that continent's eastern coast to claim discovery of a sea route to India. Ten years later Vasco da Gama reached India itself, and Portuguese interests ultimately extended to Indochina and China. With the trade of Africa and Asia to occupy them, they showed less interest in exploring the Atlantic.

The Portuguese focus on Africa and Asia

By 1500, all of seafaring Europe sought the services of Portuguese pilots, prizing their superior maps and skills with the quadrant. That instrument made it possible to determine latitude fairly accurately, allowing ships to plot their position after months out of the sight of land. The Portuguese had also pioneered the caravel, a lighter, more maneuverable ship that could sail better against contrary winds and in rough seas.

The Spanish and Columbus

From among the international community of seafarers and pilots, it was a sailor from Genoa, Cristoforo Colombo, who led the Spanish to the Americas. Columbus (the Latinized version of his name survives) had knocked about in a number of harbors, picking up valuable navigation skills by sailing Portugal's merchant ships to Madeira, west Africa, and the North Atlantic.

That experience instilled in Columbus the belief that the quickest route to the Indies lay west, across the Atlantic—and that his destiny was to prove it. Perhaps a mere 4500 miles, he reckoned, separated Europe from Japan. His wishful estimate raised eyebrows whenever Columbus asked European monarchs for the money to meet his destiny. Most educated Europeans agreed that the world was round, but they also believed that the Atlantic barrier between themselves and Asia was far wider than Columbus allowed. The kings of England, France, and Portugal dismissed him as a crackpot.

Almost a decade of rejection had grayed Columbus' red hair when Spain's monarchs, Ferdinand and Isabella, finally agreed to subsidize his expedition in 1492. For the past 20 years they had worked to drive the Muslims out of their last stronghold on the Iberian peninsula, the Moorish kingdom of Granada. In 1492 they completed this *reconquista*, or battle of reconquest, expelling many Jews as well. Yet the Portuguese, by breaking the Muslim stranglehold on trade with Asia, had taken the lead in the competition to smite the Islamic powers. Ferdinand and Isabella were so desperate to even the score with Portugal that jealousy overcame common sense: they agreed to take a risk on Columbus.

The reconquista

Columbus' first voyage across the Atlantic could only have confirmed his conviction that he was destiny's darling. His three ships, no bigger than fishing vessels that sailed to Newfoundland, plied their course over placid seas, south from Seville to the Canary Islands and then due west. On October 11, branches, leaves, and flowers floated by their hulls, signals that land lay near. Just after midnight, a sailor spied cliffs shining white in the moonlight. On the morning of October 12, the *Niña*, the *Pinta*, and the *Santa Maria* set anchor in a shallow sapphire bay, and their crews knelt on the white coral beach. Columbus christened the place San Salvador (Holy Savior).

Like many men of destiny, Columbus did not recognize his true destination. At first he confused his actual location, the Bahamas, with an island off the coast of Japan. He coasted along Cuba and Hispaniola (Haiti), expecting at any moment to catch sight of gold-roofed Japanese temples or to happen upon a fleet of Chinese junks. He encountered instead a gentle, generous people who knew nothing of the Great Khan, but who showed him their islands. He dubbed the Arawak people "Indians"—inhabitants of the Indies.

Columbus crossed the Atlantic three more times between 1493 and 1504. On his second voyage he established a permanent colony at Hispaniola and explored other Caribbean islands. On his third voyage he reached Venezuela on

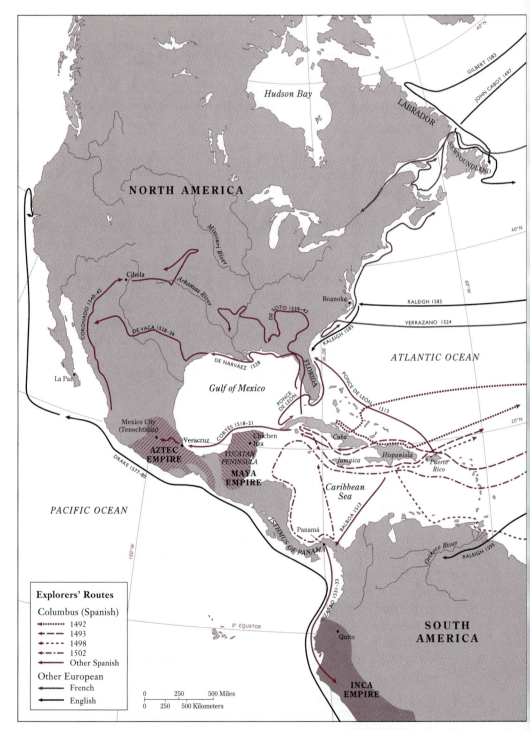

PRINCIPAL ROUTES OF EUROPEAN EXPLORATION

The four voyages of Columbus the continent of South America; and on his last sailing he made landfalls throughout Central America. Everywhere he looked for proof that these lands formed part of Asia.

Columbus died in 1506, rich in titles, treasure, and tales—everything but recognition. During the last decade of his life, most Spaniards no longer believed that Columbus had discovered the Indies or anyplace else of significance. Instead, another Italian stamped his own name on the New World. Amerigo Vespucci, a Florentine banker with a flair for self-promotion, cruised the coast of Brazil in 1501 and again in 1503. His sensational report misled a German mapmaker into crediting Vespucci with discovering the barrier between Europe and Asia, and so naming it "America."

EARLY NORTH AMERICAN CULTURES

The Americas were a new world only to European latecomers. To the Asian peoples and their native American descendants who had settled the continents tens of thousands of years earlier, Columbus' new world was their own old world. But the first nomadic hunters who crossed from Siberia over the Bering Strait to Alaska probably did not consider themselves discoverers or recognize what they had found—a truly new world wholly uninhabited by humans.

The First Inhabitants

The first passage of people from Asia to America probably took place during a prehistoric glacial period—either before 35,000 B.C. or about 10,000 years later—when huge amounts of the world's water froze into sheets of ice. Sea levels dropped so drastically that the Bering Strait became a broad, grassy plain. Across that land bridge between the two continents both humans and animals escaped icebound Siberia for ice-free Alaska. Whenever the first migration took place, the movement of Asians to America continued, even after 8000 B.C. when world temperatures rose again and the water from melting glaciers flooded back into the ocean, submerging the Bering Strait. Over a span of 25,000 years settlement spread down the Alaskan coast, then deeper into the North American mainland, and finally throughout Central and South America.

Native Americans remained nomadic hunters and gatherers for thousands of years, as did many Europeans, Africans, and Asians of those millennia. But American cultures gradually diversified, especially after about 5500 B.C., when the peoples of central Mexico discovered how to cultivate food crops. As this "agricultural revolution" spread slowly northward, native American societies were able to grow larger and develop distinctive forms of economic, social, and political organization. By the end of the fifteenth century, the inhabitants of

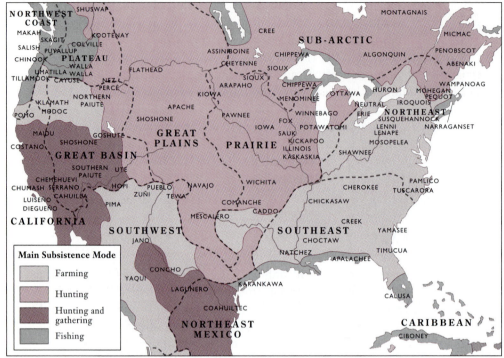

INDIANS OF NORTH AMERICA, CIRCA 1500

North America, perhaps 5 to 10 million people, spoke as many as 1000 languages. Although later Europeans, like Columbus, lumped these societies together by calling them Indian, any cultural unity had vanished long before 1492.

The simplest Indian societies were those that still relied on hunting and gathering, like the Eskimos of the Arctic and the Serrano, Cahuilla, Luiseño, and Diegueño of southern California, Arizona, and the Baja peninsula of Mexico. Stark deserts and frozen tundra defied cultivation and yielded food supplies that could sustain nomadic bands numbering no more than about 50 people. Families occasionally joined together for a collective hunt or wintered in common quarters, but for most of the year they scattered across the landscape, the women gathering plants and seeds, making baskets, and cooking meals while the men hunted for meat and hides. Political authority lay with either the male family head or the "headman" of a small band. "Shamans"—any tribesmen claiming spiritual powers—enlisted the supernatural to assist individuals.

Societies of Increasing Complexity

In the densely forested belt that stretched from Newfoundland to the Bering Strait, resources more generous than those of the tundra to the north made for larger populations and more closely knit societies. Northeastern bands like the

Hunters and gatherers   Montagnais, the Micmac, and the Penobscot and northwestern tribes like the Yellowknife and the Beaver traveled forests in moccasins and snowshoes, stalking deer, elk, moose, bear, and caribou; they speared fish in icy lakes and streams from birch-bark canoes. Their environment encouraged cooperative economic pursuits. Leading men assigned several families to specific territories that they hunted together, dividing the returns among the whole band. Religious beliefs strengthened the ties of kinship: each family had a "totem," a particular animal from which they claimed descent.

While men dominated Indian bands based on hunting, women assumed more influence in societies that relied for part of their food on settled agriculture. Among the Pueblo peoples of Arizona and New Mexico, the Hopi and *Women in agricultural societies*   Zuñi tribes, men hunted bison and cultivated corn and beans, but women owned the fields, the crops, and even the tools. They also owned the sun-baked dwellings of adobe and stone, some of which rose to several stories, that housed the families of their daughters. By 1540 some 70 Pueblo villages flourished, as more reliable food supplies swelled the size and number of clans (families sharing a common ancestry). A council of religious elders drawn from the different clans governed each village. Pueblo religious ceremonies, in contrast to those of simpler Indian societies, involved elaborate rituals celebrating tribal unity and seeking the gods' blessing for hunts and harvests. Thousands of miles to the northeast, in a natural setting far different from the semiarid Southwest, the Iroquois created a remarkably similar culture.

More complex Indian civilizations arose in the bountiful environments of the Pacific Northwest and the coastal region reaching from Virginia to Texas. The seas and rivers from eastern Alaska to northern California teemed with fish, humpback whales, seals, and otters. In the Southeast fertile soil and temperate climate encouraged the cultivation of maize, rice, and a variety of fruits. By harvesting these resources and developing techniques to preserve food supplies, settlements could become larger and more complex. Far less egalitarian than nomadic hunting bands or even the Pueblo and Iroquois, these tribes developed elaborate systems of status. Among southeastern tribes like the Natchez, below the chief, or "Great Sun," stood a hereditary nobility of lesser "Suns," who demanded elaborate displays of respect from the lowly "Stinkards," the common people.

Mesoamerican Empires

Even more advanced were the vast agricultural empires of Mesoamerica—south and central Mexico and Guatemala. As the Roman empire was declining in Europe, the civilization of the Mayas was flourishing in the lowland jungles of Central America. They built cities filled with palaces, bridges, aqueducts, baths, astronomical observatories, and temples topped by pyramids. Their priests de-

E Y E W I T N E S S   T O   H I S T O R Y

A Spanish Conquistador Visits the Aztec Marketplace in Tenochtitlán

n reaching the market-place . . . we were astounded at the great number of people and the quantities of merchandise, and at the orderliness and good arrangements that prevailed, for we had never seen such a thing before. . . . Every kind of merchandise was kept separate and had its fixed place marked for it.

Let us begin with the dealers in gold, silver, and precious stones, feathers, cloaks, and embroidered goods, and male and female slaves who are also sold there. They bring as many slaves to be sold in that market as the Portuguese bring Negroes from Guinea. Some are brought there attached to long poles by means of collars round their necks to prevent them from escaping, but others are left loose. Next there were those who sold coarser cloth, and cotton goods and fabrics made of twisted thread, and there were chocolate merchants. . . . In this way you could see every kind of merchandise to be found anywhere in New Spain, laid out in the same way as goods are laid out in my own district [in Spain] of Medina del Campo, a center for fairs, where each line of stalls has its own particular sort. So it was in this great market. There were those who sold sisal cloth and ropes and the sandals they wear on their feet . . . and in another part were skins of tigers and lions, otters, jackals, and deer, badgers, mountain cats, and other wild animals.

. . . I must also mention, with all apologies, that they sold many canoe-loads of human excrement, which they kept in the creeks near the market. This was for the manufacture of salt and the curing of skins, which they say cannot be done without it. I know that many gentlemen will laugh at this, but I assure them it is true. I may add that on all the roads they have shelters made of reeds or straw or grass so that they can retire when they wish to do so, and purge their bowels unseen by passers-by, and also in order that their excrement shall not be lost.

Bernal Diaz, *The Conquest of New Spain*, translated by J M Cohen (New York: Penguin Classics, 1963), pp. 232–233. Copyright © J M Cohen, 1963.

veloped a written language, their mathematicians discovered the zero, and their astronomers devised a calendar more accurate than any then existing.

The Aztecs, who invaded central Mexico from the north in the fourteenth century, built on the Mayas' achievements. Within a century Aztec conquest had created an empire of several million people. The capital, Tenochtitlán, was a glittering island metropolis with a population in 1400 of perhaps a quarter of a million—several times the size of London. The Great Temple of the Sun dominated the center of the city, and through the canals leading to Tenochtitlán flowed gold, silver, exotic feathers, cocoa, and millions of pounds of maize—all trade goods and tribute from other Mexican city-states conquered by the Aztecs.

Rise of the Aztecs

In many ways, the world of the Aztecs paralleled the societies of early modern Europe. Both worlds were predominantly rural, most of their inhabitants living in small villages and engaging in agriculture. In both worlds, merchants and specialized craftworkers clustered in cities, organized themselves into guilds, and clamored for protection from the government. And, as in Europe, Aztec noble and priestly classes took the lead in politics and religion, demanding tribute from the common people.

The question of human sacrifice aside, there was at least one crucial difference between Aztec and European civilizations. Aztec expansion did not take the form of colonial settlements that spanned the oceans—indeed, the globe. That difference reflected a host of distinctive changes in European social, economic, and political development during the fourteenth and fifteenth centuries. It was these transformations that made it possible for bold sailors like Columbus and Cabot or anonymous fisherfolk and traders to dream of profit, glory, and empire.

COUNTERPOINT   *The Role of Human Sacrifice*

Some students of history, however, emphasize that the Aztecs differed from Europeans in one particularly striking way: they practiced ritual human sacrifice. Every year, Aztec priests wielding razor-sharp knives sliced open the chests of thousands of captives and offered up to the sun hearts still beating, the essence of life. Indeed, the primary purpose of Aztec warfare was less to extend their empire than to maintain a steady supply of captives for such rites. Aztecs believed that they were the chosen people—chosen to nourish the earth by sustaining the life of the sun with offerings of human blood. Put simply, the Aztecs slaughtered other human beings in the name of religion. As one recent historian noted, "In numbers, the elevated sense of ceremony which accompanied the theatrical shows involved, as in its significance in the official religion, human sacrifice in Mexico was unique."

But were the Aztecs really so different in this regard from invading Europeans? The sense of being a "chosen people" that underlay Aztec rituals also inspired Christians in their own crusades. They campaigned ruthlessly against "Muslim infidels," massacred Jews, and executed thousands of witches during the Middle Ages and even into the seventeenth century. Put just as simply, European Christians, too, slaughtered other human beings in the name of religion. But it was a similarity that Europeans found convenient to overlook. They preferred to portray themselves as "civilizers" of a people whose "savagery" was proved by the practice of human sacrifice.

THE EUROPEAN BACKGROUND OF AMERICAN COLONIZATION

Europe in the age of discovery was a world graced by the courage of explorers like Columbus and the genius of artists like Michelangelo. It was also a world riddled with war, disease, and uncertainty. In 1450 the continent was still recovering from the ravages of the Black Death. Under such vibrant, often chaotic conditions, a sense of crisis mixed with a sense of possibility. Indeed, it was this blend of desperation and ambition that made the newly discovered Americas so attractive to Europeans. Here were strange and distant lands like the island paradises spoken of in legends, like that of the fabled kingdom of Atlantis. Here were opportunities and riches for the daring to grasp. Here were salvation and security for those escaping a world full of violence and sin or oppressed by disease and poverty.

Life and Death in Early Modern Europe

During the fourteenth and the fifteenth centuries 90 percent of Europe's people, widely dispersed in small villages, made their living from the land. But warfare, poor transportation, and low grain yields all created food shortages, and undernourishment produced a population prone to disease. Under these circumstances life was nasty, brutish, and usually short. One-quarter of all children died in the first year of life. People who reached the ripe age of 40 counted themselves fortunate.

It was also a world of sharp inequalities, where nobles and aristocrats enjoyed several hundred times the income of peasants or craftworkers. It was a world with no strong, centralized political authority, where kings were weak and warrior lords held sway over small towns and tiny fiefdoms. It was a world of hierarchy and dependence, where the upper classes provided land and protection for the lower orders. It was a world of violence and sudden death, where homicide, robbery, and rape occurred with brutal frequency. It was a world where security and order of any kind seemed so fragile that most people clung to tradition and feared change.

Into that world in 1347 came the Black Death. In only four years that plague swept away one-third of Europe's population, disrupting both agriculture and commerce. Yet the sudden drop in population restored the balance be-

Plague and recovery

tween people and resources. Survivors of the Black Death found that the relative scarcity of workers and consumers made for better wages, lower prices, and more land.

But by the time Columbus reached America, nearly 150 years after the outbreak of the Black Death, Europe again confronted its old problem. Too many people were again competing for a limited supply of food and land. Throughout the sixteenth century diets became poorer, land and work less available, crime and beggary more common. Inflation compounded these problems when prices doubled at the end of the fifteenth century and then quadrupled between 1520 and 1590. To keep pace with the "Price Revolution," landlords raised rents, adding to the burden of Europe's peasantry.

To Europe's hopeful and desperate alike, this climate of disorder and uncertainty led to dreams that the New World would provide an opportunity to renew the Old. As Columbus wrote eagerly of Hispaniola: "This island and all others are very fertile to a limitless degree. . . . There are very large tracts of cultivated land. . . . In the interior there are mines and metals." Columbus and many other Europeans expected that the Americas would provide land for the landless, work for the unemployed, and wealth beyond the wildest dreams of the daring.

The Conditions of Colonization

Sixteenth-century Europeans sought to colonize the Americas, not merely to escape from scarcity and disruption at home. They were also propelled across the Atlantic by dynamic changes in their society. Revolutions in technology, economics, and politics made overseas settlement practical and attractive to seekers of profit and power.

The improvements in navigation and sailing also fostered an expansion of trade. By the late fifteenth century Europe's merchants and bankers had devised

Expansion of trade and capital

more efficient ways of transferring money and establishing credit in order to support commerce across the longer distances. And although rising prices and rents pinched Europe's peasantry, that same inflation enriched those who had goods to sell, money to lend, and land to rent. Wealth flowed into the coffers of sixteenth-century traders, financiers, and landlords, creating a pool of capital that those investors could plow into colonial development. Both the commercial networks and the private fortunes needed to sustain overseas trade and settlement were in place by the time of Columbus' discovery.

The direction of Europe's political development also paved the path for American colonization. After 1450 strong monarchs in Europe steadily enlarged

Political centralization

the sphere of royal power at the expense of warrior lords. Henry VII, the founder of England's Tudor dynasty, Francis I of France, and Ferdinand and Isabella of Spain began the trend, forging modern nation-states by extending their political control over more territory, people, and resources. Those larger, more centrally organized states were able to marshal the resources necessary to support colonial outposts and to sustain the professional armies and navies capable of protecting empires abroad.

It was the growing power of monarchs as well as commercial and techno-logical development that allowed Europeans to establish permanent settle-

Limits to Aztec expansion

ments—even empires—in a world lying an ocean away. That ac-complishment had eluded the Aztecs, who lacked knowledge of ocean navigation. Equally important, Aztec rulers had not estab-lished their sovereign authority over powerful nobles. Without strong central-ized power, rulers were hard-pressed to launch a more ambitious expansion. While their armies put down disturbances in conquered territories and pro-tected trade routes, the Aztecs never exported their people or their way of life to other places. Instead, conquered city-states retained their distinctive lan-guages and customs—and bitterly resented Aztec rule. The result was an em-pire vulnerable to division from within and to attack from abroad.

SPAIN'S EMPIRE IN THE NEW WORLD

By the reckoning of the Aztecs it was the year 12-House, a time, they believed, when the fate of the whole world hung by a thread. According to their calen-dar, a 52-year cycle had come to an end. Now the gods might extinguish the sun with a flood or a great wind. The end of this particular cycle had been marked with a chilling omen. In one of the canals, fishermen caught a bird "the color of ashes" with a strange mirror in the crown of its head. They brought the creature to their ruler, Moctezuma II, who looked in the mirror and saw ranks of men mounted on animals resembling deer and moving across a plain.

Two years later, the Aztecs' worst fears were fulfilled. Dust rose in whirl-winds on the roads from the hooves of horses and the boots of men in battle array. "It was as if the earth trembled beneath them, or as if the world were spinning . . . as it spins during a fit of vertigo," one Aztec scribe recorded. This was no image in a magic mirror: Hernando Cortés and his army of Spaniards were marching on Tenochtitlán. By Cortés' calculations, it was A.D. 1519.

Spanish Conquest

To Cortés and the other Spanish explorers who had followed Columbus across the Atlantic over the previous quarter century, a new and remarkable world was

Balboa and Magellan

opening. By 1513 the Spanish had explored and mastered the Caribbean basin. In that year too, Vasco Nuñez de Balboa crossed the Isthmus of Panama and glimpsed the Pacific Ocean. North and South America were revealed as continents of vast size, separated from Asia by another ocean. And Ferdinand Magellan finally did reach the Orient by sailing west across the vast Pacific. After his death in the Philippines in 1521, his shipmates completed the first circumnavigation of the globe.

From their bases in the islands of the Caribbean, the Spanish pressed outward. To the north they met mostly with disappointment. Juan Ponce de León vainly scoured the shores of the Florida peninsula for the fabled "Fountain of Youth," while Hernando de Soto trekked through Florida and into the southeastern interior as far west as the Mississippi River. Between 1540 and 1542 Francisco Vásquez de Coronado moved through Arizona, New Mexico, Texas, Oklahoma, and Kansas. But reports of fantastic cities of gold proved to be merely the stuff of dreams.

During these same decades, however, the Spanish found golden opportunities elsewhere. Those who had first rushed to Hispaniola immediately started scouring the island for gold—and enslaving Indians to work the mines. As for

Cortés conquers the Aztecs

Cortés, when Moctezuma's ambassadors met him on the road to Tenochtitlán in 1519 and attempted to appease him with gold ornaments and other gifts, an Indian witness recorded that "the Spaniards . . . picked up the gold and fingered it like monkeys. . . . Their bodies swelled with greed." For nearly half a year Cortés dominated the indecisive Moctezuma by imprisoning him in his own capital. The Aztecs drove the Spanish out after Moctezuma's death, but Cortés returned with reinforcements, set siege to Tenochtitlán, and in 1521 conquered it. The Aztec empire lay in ruins.

The dignity and grace of this Mexican woman, drawn in the 1550s, possibly by a Spanish priest, may reflect the sympathetic influence of Bartolomé de Las Casas—sentiments most Spaniards did not share.

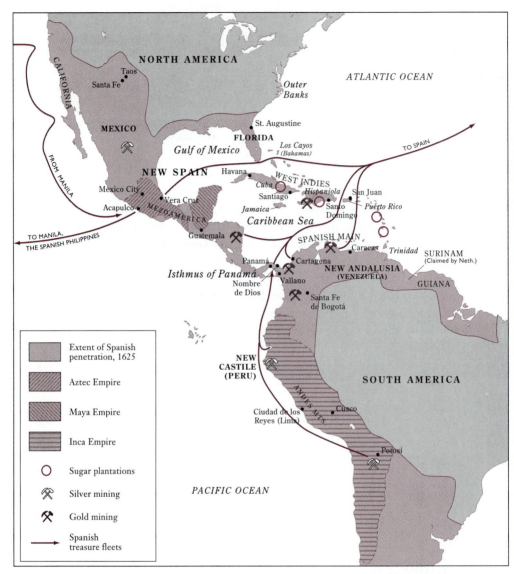

SPANISH AMERICA, CIRCA 1600   By 1600, Spain was extracting large amounts
of gold and silver from Central and South America, as well as
profits from sugar plantations in the Caribbean.

Role of the Conquistadors

To the conquistadors—a motley lot of minor nobles, landless gentlemen, and
professional soldiers—the Americas seemed more than a golden opportunity.
They resented the Spanish monarchy's growing strength at home and aimed to
re-create in the New World a much older world of their own dreaming. Like
medieval knights, Cortés and other conquistadors hoped to establish themselves

as a powerful nobility that would enjoy virtual independence from the Spanish Crown an ocean away.

For a time the conquistadors succeeded. By the 1540s Cortés and just 1500 men had taken all of Mexico and the southwestern portion of North America. During the 1550s the ruthless Pizarro brothers and an even smaller band of conquistadors sailed along South America's Pacific coast and overthrew the Incas in Peru, an Andean civilization as impressive as that of the Aztecs. They also laid claim to Ecuador, Chile, Argentina, and Bolivia.

How did a handful of gentlemen heading a rabble of soldiers, seamen, and criminals bring down sophisticated Indian empires in the span of a generation?

Reasons for Spain's success
Certainly, the Spanish enjoyed the edge of surprise and technological superiority. The sight of ships and the explosion of guns at first terrified the Indians, as did men on horseback whom they took at first to be single creatures. The only domesticated animals known to the Aztecs were small dogs; the Spanish provided them with their first glimpse of horses and, later, cattle, sheep, oxen, pigs, goats, donkeys, mules, and chickens.

What delivered a more lasting shock to Indian civilizations was exposure to European infections. Smallpox, influenza, typhus, and measles, disease strains against which they had developed no biological resistance, ravaged entire villages and tribes. Tenochtitlán surrendered to Cortés after a siege of 85 days, during which many died from starvation but many more died of smallpox contracted from the Spanish.

An equally important factor in the swift conquest was the political disunity within Indian empires. The Aztecs and Incas had subdued the native Indian populations of Mexico and Peru only 100 years before the Spanish invasion. Resentment at Aztec and Inca rule brought the conquistadors eager allies among the subject Indian tribes. But by aiding the Spanish overthrow of the Aztecs and the Incas, the native Indians only substituted one set of overlords for another.

Spanish Colonization

The conquistadors did not long enjoy their mastery in the Americas. The Spanish monarchs who had just tamed an aristocracy at home were not about

Royal control replaces the conquistadors
to allow a colonial nobility to arise across the Atlantic. The Crown bribed the conquistadors into retirement—or was saved the expense when men like the Pizarro brothers were assassinated by their own followers. The task of governing Spain's new colonies passed from the conquistadors to a small army of officials, soldiers, lawyers, and Catholic bishops, all appointed by the Crown, reporting to the Crown, and loyal to the Crown. Headquartered in urban centers like Mexico City (formerly Tenochtitlán), an elaborate, centralized bureaucracy administered the Spanish empire, regulating nearly every aspect of economic and social life.

Few Spaniards besides imperial officials settled in the Americas. By 1600 only about 5 percent of the colonial population was of Spanish descent, the other 95 percent being either Indian or African. Even by 1800 only 300,000 Spanish immigrants had come to Central and South America. Indians remained on the lands that they had farmed under the Aztecs and the Incas, now paying Spanish overlords their taxes and producing livestock for export. The Indians were not enslaved outright, but the Spanish compelled them to work for specified periods of time, a system of forced labor known as *encomienda*. The Spanish also established sugar plantations in the West Indies; these were worked by black slaves who were being imported from Africa in large numbers by 1520.

Spain's colonies returned even more spectacular profits after 1540, when silver deposits were discovered in both Mexico and Peru. European investors and *Discovery of silver* Spanish immigrants who had profited from cattle raising and sugar planting poured their capital into silver mining. The Spanish government pressed whole villages of Indians to serve in the mines, joining black slaves and free white workers employed there. Local farmers who supplied mining centers with food and Spanish merchants in Seville who exported European goods to Potosí profited handsomely. So did the Spanish Crown, which claimed one-fifth of the silver extracted.

The Effects of Colonial Growth

Its American riches made Spain the dominant power in Europe. But that dominance was purchased at a fearful human cost. Devastated by warfare, disease, and exploitation, the Indians of the Caribbean were virtually wiped out within a century. In Mesoamerica, a native population of 20 million was reduced to 2 million.

Only a few of the Spanish spoke out against the exploitation of the natives. Among them was Bartolomé de Las Casas, a Spanish priest who became a *Las Casas* bishop in southern Mexico. His writings, reprinted in many translations and illustrated with gruesome drawings, circulated throughout Europe, becoming the basis of the "Black Legend" of Spanish oppression in the Americas.

Most did not share Las Casas' scruples. They justified their conquest by claiming that they had "delivered" the Indians from Aztec and Inca tyranny and replaced native "barbarism" and "paganism" with European civilization and Christianity. The extent of the Spanish conquest itself fostered a heady sense of superiority. By the beginning of the seventeenth century Spain's dominions in the Americas spanned 8000 miles, stretching from Baja California to the Straits of Magellan at South America's southern tip. The prevailing mood was captured by the portrait of a Spanish soldier that adorns the frontispiece of his book about the West Indies. He stands with one hand on his sword and the other holding a pair of compasses on top of a globe. Beneath is inscribed the motto "By compasses and the sword/More and more and more and more."

THE REFORMATION IN EUROPE

Spain met with little interference in the Americas from rival European nations for most of the sixteenth century. One reason was religious upheaval in Europe. During the second decade of the sixteenth century—the same decade in which Cortés laid siege to Tenochtitlán—enormous religious changes swept Europe. That revolution in Christianity, known as the Protestant Reformation, also played a crucial role in shaping the later history of the Americas.

Backdrop to Reform

During the Middle Ages, the Roman Catholic church defined what it meant to be a Christian in western Europe. Like other institutions of medieval society, the Catholic church was a hierarchy. At the top was the pope in Rome, and under him were the descending ranks of other church officials—cardinals, archbishops, bishops. At the bottom of the Catholic hierarchy were parish priests, each serving his own village, as well as monks and nuns living in monasteries and convents. But medieval popes were weak, their power felt little in the lives of most Europeans. Like political units of the era, religious institutions of the Middle Ages were local and decentralized.

As the monarchs of Europe grew more powerful, so too did the popes. By 1500 a large bureaucracy of church officials supported the papacy. The Catholic

Rise of the papacy

church acquired land throughout Europe and added to its income by tithing (collecting taxes from church members) and by collecting fees from those appointed to church offices. In the thirteenth century, church officials also began to sell "indulgences." For ordinary believers, who expected to spend time after death purging their sins in purgatory, the purchase of an indulgence promised to shorten that punishment by supposedly drawing on a "treasury of merit" amassed by the good works of Christ and the saints.

By the fifteenth century the Catholic church and the papacy had become enormously powerful but increasingly indifferent to popular religious concerns. Church officials meddled in secular politics. Popes and bishops flaunted their wealth, while poorly educated parish priests neglected their pastoral duties. At the same time, popular demands for religious assurance grew increasingly intense. The concern for salvation swelled in response to the disorienting changes sweeping the continent during the fifteenth and sixteenth centuries—the widening gulf between rich and poor, the rise in prices, and the discovery of America.

The Teachings of Martin Luther

Into this climate of heightened spirituality stepped Martin Luther, who abandoned studying the law to enter a monastery. Like many contemporaries, Luther was consumed by fears over his eternal fate. He was convinced that he was damned, and he could not find any consolation in the Catholic church. Catholic doctrine taught that a person could be saved by faith in God and by his or her own good works—by leading a virtuous life, observing the sacraments (such as baptism, the Mass, and penance), making pilgrimages to holy places, and praying to Christ and the saints. Since Luther believed that human nature was innately evil, he despaired of being able to lead a life that "merited" salvation. If men and women were so bad, he reasoned, how could they ever win their way to heaven with good works?

Luther finally broke through his despair by reading the Bible. It convinced him that God did not require fallen mankind to earn salvation. Salvation, he *Justification by faith alone* concluded, came by faith alone, the "free gift" of God to undeserving sinners. The ability to live a good life could not be the *cause* of salvation but its *consequence*: once men and women believed that they had saving faith, moral behavior was possible. That idea, known as "justification by faith alone," Luther elaborated between 1513 and 1517.

Luther was ordained a priest and then assigned to teach at a university in Wittenberg, Germany. Still, he became increasingly critical of the Catholic church as an institution. In 1517 he posted on the door of a local church 95 theses attacking the Catholic hierarchy for selling salvation in the form of indulgences.

The novelty of this attack was not Luther's open break with Catholic teaching. Challenges to the church had cropped up throughout the Middle Ages. What was new was the passion behind Luther's attacks. Using the earthy Germanic tongue he expressed the anxieties of so many devout laypeople and their outrage at the church hierarchy's neglect. The "gross, ignorant asses and knaves at Rome," he warned, should keep their distance from Germany, or else "jump into the Rhine or the nearest river, and take . . . a cold bath."

The pope and his representatives in Germany at first tried to silence Martin Luther, then excommunicated him. But opposition only pushed Luther toward *Attacks on church authority* more radical positions. He asserted that the church and its officials were not infallible; only the Scriptures were without error. Every person, he said, should read and interpret the Bible for himself or herself. In an even more direct assault on church authority, he advanced an idea known as "the priesthood of all believers." Catholic doctrine held that salvation came only through the church and its clergy, a privileged group that possessed special access to God. Luther asserted that every person had the power claimed by priests.

Although Luther had not intended to start a schism within Catholicism, independent Lutheran churches were forming in Germany by the 1520s. And during the 1530s, Luther's ideas spread throughout Europe, where they were eagerly taken up by other reformers.

The Contribution of John Calvin

The most influential of Luther's successors was John Calvin, a French lawyer turned theologian. Calvin agreed with Luther that men and women could not merit their salvation. But while Luther's God was a loving deity who extended his mercy to sinful humankind, Calvin conceived of God as an awesome sovereign, all-knowing and all-powerful, the controlling force in human history who

The elect

would ultimately triumph over Satan. To bring about that final victory, Calvin believed, God had selected certain people as his agents for ushering in his heavenly kingdom. These people—"the saints," or "the elect"—had been "predestined" by God for eternal salvation in heaven.

Calvin's emphasis on predestination led him to another distinctively Protestant notion—the doctrine of calling. How could a person learn whether he or she belonged to the elect who were saved? Calvin answered: strive to behave like a saint. God expected his elect to serve the good of society by unrelenting work in a "calling," or occupation, in the world. In place of the Catholic belief in the importance of good works, Calvin emphasized the goodness of work itself. Success in attaining self-control, in bringing order into one's own life and the entire society, revealed that a person might be among the elect.

Calvin fashioned a religion to change the world. Where Luther believed that Christians should accept the existing social order, Calvin called on Christians

An activist theology

to become activists, reshaping society and government to conform with God's laws laid down in the Bible. He wanted all of Europe to become like Geneva, the Swiss city that he had converted into a holy commonwealth where the elect regulated the behavior and morals of everyone else. And unlike Luther, who wrote primarily for a German audience, Calvin addressed his most important book, *The Institutes of the Christian Religion* (1536), to Christians throughout Europe. Reformers from every country flocked to Geneva to learn more about Calvin's ideas.

The English Reformation

While the Reformation went forward in Europe, King Henry VIII of England was striving for a goal more modest than those of Luther and Calvin. He wanted only to produce a male heir to carry on the Tudor dynasty. When his wife, Catherine of Aragon, gave birth to a daughter, Mary, Henry decided to do something less modest. He set out to get his marriage to Catherine annulled by the pope. This angered Catherine's father, the king of Spain, who convinced the pope to refuse. Defiantly Henry went ahead with the divorce and married his mistress, Anne Boleyn.

Henry then widened this breach with Rome by making himself, and not the pope, the head of the Church of England. In 1534 Parliament formalized the

Henry VIII breaks with Rome

relationship with the Act of Supremacy. But Henry, who fancied himself a theologian, had no fondness for Protestant doctrine. Under his leadership the Church of England remained essentially Catholic in its teachings and rituals.

England's Protestants gained ground during the six-year reign of Edward VI, but then found themselves persecuted when his Catholic half-sister, Mary, became queen in 1553. Five years later the situation turned again, when Elizabeth (Anne Boleyn's daughter) took the throne, proclaiming herself the defender of Protestantism.

Still, Elizabeth was no radical Calvinist. A vocal minority of her subjects were reformers of that stripe, calling for the English church to purge itself of

English Puritans bishops, elaborate ceremonies, and other Catholic "impurities." Because of the austerity and zeal of such Calvinist radicals, their opponents proclaimed them "Puritans."

The Protestant Reformation shattered the unity of Christendom in western Europe. Spain, Ireland, and Italy remained firmly Catholic. England, France, Scotland, the Netherlands, and Switzerland developed either dominant or substantial Calvinist constituencies. Much of Germany and Scandinavia opted for Lutheranism. As these religious groups competed for political power and the loyalties of believers, brutal wars racked sixteenth-century Europe. Protestants and Catholics slaughtered each other in the name of Christianity.

ENGLAND'S ENTRY INTO AMERICA

In 1562 Queen Elizabeth gave her blessing to an English army that set sail for France, to aid Calvinists there being suppressed by the government. Perhaps the most dashing of the army's captains was a red-faced and robust West Country gentleman, Sir Humphrey Gilbert.

Like so many West Country boys in search of honor and fortune, Gilbert was eager to seize the main chance. In the early 1560s, that seemed to be fighting for the Protestant cause in France. Gilbert's stepfather, the seafarer Walter Raleigh, had done a good deal of his own seizing, mostly from Spanish silver ships along the South American coast. Like the conquistadors, Raleigh wanted more. He merely decided he could get more a bit more easily if he let Spain dig and refine the silver first.

If France had not beckoned, Humphrey Gilbert would surely have been happy to harass the Spanish too, along with his stepbrother, the young Walter

Ambitious West Country gentlemen Raleigh (named after his plundering father). But as Gilbert and young Raleigh came of age, they began to consider more ambitious schemes than the mere plundering of treasure. They looked to conquer Spain's empire—or, at least, to carve out for England a rival empire of its own. During the late 1570s and 1580s, when Queen Elizabeth felt confident enough to challenge Spain in the Americas, Gilbert and Raleigh were ready to lead the way.

The English Colonization of Ireland

During the 1560s, however, England was too deeply distracted by religious and political turmoil to pursue empire across the Atlantic. For Elizabeth, privateers like the senior Walter Raleigh stirred up more trouble than they were worth.

Reasons for England to soothe Spain

Spain, after all, was England's ally against a common rival, France. And the Netherlands, which was then controlled by Spain, imported English cloth. Elizabeth had good reason to pursue a policy that would soothe Spain, not offend it.

The queen also worried about Catholic Ireland to the west. She feared that the French or the Spanish might use the island as a base for invading England. Beginning in 1565 Elizabeth encouraged a number of her subjects, mainly gentlemen and aristocrats from the West Country, to sponsor private ventures for subduing the native Irish and settling English families on Irish land. Among the gentlemen eager to win fame and fortune were Humphrey Gilbert and Walter Raleigh.

The English invaders of Ireland, almost all ardent Protestants, regarded the native Catholic inhabitants as superstitious, pagan savages. Thus did the English justify their conquest: by proclaiming it their duty to teach the Irish the discipline of hard work, the rule of law, and the truth of Christianity. And while the Irish were learning civilized ways, they would not be allowed to buy land or hold office or serve on juries or give testimony in courts or learn a trade or bear arms.

When the Irish rebelled at that program of "liberation," the English ruthlessly repressed native resistance, slaughtering combatants and civilians. Most

English repression of the Irish

English in Ireland, like most Spaniards in America, believed that native peoples who resisted civilization and Christianity should be subdued at any cost. No scruples stopped Humphrey Gilbert, in an insurgent county, from planting the path to his camp with the severed heads of Irish rebels.

England's efforts to settle and subdue Ireland would serve as a rough model for later efforts at colonization. The approach was essentially military, like that of the conquistadors. More ominously, it sanctioned the savage repression of any "inferior race." Not only Gilbert but also Raleigh and many other West Country gentry soon turned their attention toward North America. "Neither reputation, or profytt is to be wonne" in Ireland, concluded Gilbert. They wanted more.

Renewed Interest in the Americas

After hard service in France and Ireland, Gilbert and Raleigh returned to England. Her cautious bureaucrats who had been enlarging royal power considered the two swaggering gentlemen insufferable if not downright dangerous, much as the Spanish officials distrusted their conquistadors. Still, England was becoming more receptive to the schemes of such hotheaded warrior lords for challenging Spain overseas. English Protestantism, English nationalism, and English economic interests all came together to increase support for English exploration and colonization.

The turning point for the English came during the 1570s when Calvinist Dutch in the Netherlands rebelled against their rule by Catholic Spain. The

Spanish retaliated savagely by sacking the city of Antwerp, which was England's major European market for cloth. Forced to look elsewhere for markets and in-

Joint stock companies

vestment opportunities, merchants combined in joint stock companies to develop a trade with Africa, Russia, the East Indies, and the Mediterranean. These private corporations, in which many shareholders pooled small amounts of capital, also began to plow money into Atlantic privateering voyages.

Joining English merchants in the new interest in overseas exploration were gentry families. The high birthrate among England's upper classes throughout the sixteenth century had produced a surplus of younger sons, who stood to inherit no share of family estates. The shortage of land for their sons at home stirred up support among the gentry for England to claim territory across the Atlantic.

With the support of England's leading merchants and gentlemen, Elizabeth now needed little encouragement to adopt a more belligerent stance toward Spain. But she got more encouragement from Spain itself, which made no secret of wanting to restore England to Catholicism, by armed invasion if necessary. Elizabeth was not yet prepared to provoke open warfare with Spain, but she watched with interest the exploits of a new generation of English explorers in North America.

The Failures of Frobisher and Gilbert

The adventurer who first caught the queen's eye was Martin Frobisher, the veteran of slaving voyages to west Africa, privateering raids in the Atlantic, the fighting in Ireland, and other unsavory enterprises. In 1576 he sailed on another search for a Northwest Passage to Asia.

After sailing north of Labrador, Frobisher returned to England with an Eskimo (plucked, kayak and all, from the Atlantic) and a shiny black stone that seemed to be gold ore. With royal backing, Frobisher made two more voyages to his "New Peru" in 1577 and 1578, hauling back nearly 2000 tons of black rock. When upon closer inspection all of the rock turned out to be "fool's gold," his reputation fell under a cloud.

Because Humphrey Gilbert had refused to invest in this fiasco, Frobisher's disgrace became Gilbert's opportunity. In 1578 Elizabeth granted Gilbert a vague patent—the first English colonial charter—to explore, occupy, and govern any territory in America "not actually possessed of any Christian prince or people." That charter, ignoring the Indian possession of North America, made Gilbert lord and proprietor of all the land lying between Florida and Labrador.

Gilbert pictured himself and his heirs as manorial lords of a colony filled with loyal tenant farmers paying rents in return for protection. In a sense his dreams resembled those of Spain's conquistadors: to recreate an older, nearly

Gilbert's colonial plans

feudal world that would remain largely free of royal control. Yet Gilbert's vision also looked forward to a utopian society. He planned to encourage England's poor to emigrate by providing them free land and a government "to be chosen by consent of the people."

In the end, the dreams foundered in a stormy present. Gilbert set sail in June 1583, but a late start forced him to turn back before he could scout the North American coast. Then his two ships met with foul weather. Gilbert, with characteristic bravado, sat on the deck of the smaller *Squirrel*, reading a book. "We are as neere to Heaven by sea as by land," he shouted across the heaving swells. The men aboard the *Golden Hind* recognized the words of Thomas More, whose *Utopia*—a dialogue about an ideal society in the New World— Gilbert held in his hand. Gilbert was nearer to heaven than he hoped: around midnight, the crew of the *Golden Hind* saw the lights of the *Squirrel* extinguished and the ship "devoured and swallowed up by the sea."

Martin Frobisher, his face frozen in a glare, a horse-pistol fixed in his fist, exemplified the ruthless ambition of England's West Country adventurers.

Raleigh's Roanoke Venture

Raleigh had been eager to accompany his stepbrother's ill-fated expedition, but Elizabeth's many favors made it hard for him to leave. He was dining on food from palace kitchens, sleeping in a bed adorned with green velvet and spangled plumes of white feathers. Still, Raleigh was restless—and envious when another West Country adventurer, Sir Francis Drake, returned from circumnavigating the globe in 1580, his ships heavy with Spanish plunder.

Raleigh's ambitions led him to Richard Hakluyt, a clergyman with a passion for spreading knowledge of overseas discoveries. At Raleigh's request,

Hakluyt publicizes America

Hakluyt wrote an eloquent plea to Elizabeth for the English settlement of America, titled *A Discourse Concerning Westerne Planting*. The temperate and fertile lands of North America, Hakluyt argued, would provide a perfect base from which to harry the Spanish, search for a Northwest Passage, and extend the influence of Protestantism. He also stressed the advantages of colonies as sources of new commodities, as markets for English goods, and as havens for the poor and unemployed.

Raleigh's chance to settle American lands finally came in 1584, when Elizabeth granted him a patent nearly identical with that of Gilbert. By the summer Raleigh had sent Philip Amadas and Arthur Barlowe across the Atlantic, their two small ships coasting the Outer Banks of present-day North Carolina. Amadas and Barlowe established cordial relations with the Roanoke tribe, ruled by a "werowance," or chief, named Wingina. The following summer a full-scale expedition returned to Roanoke Island.

Raleigh apparently aimed to establish on Roanoke a mining camp and a military garrison modeled on Frobisher's venture of the 1570s. In a stroke of ge-

The first colony at Roanoke

nius, he included in the company of 108 men a scientist, Thomas Hariot, to study the country's natural resources and an artist, John White, to make drawings of the Virginia Indians. *A Briefe and True Reporte of the New Found Land of Virginia* (1588), written by Hariot and illustrated by White, served as one of the principal sources about North America and its Indian inhabitants for more than a century. Far less inspired was Raleigh's choice to lead the expedition—two veterans of the Irish campaigns, Sir Richard Grenville and Ralph Lane. Even his fellow conquistadors in Ireland considered Lane proud and greedy, and Grenville was given to breaking wineglasses between his teeth and then swallowing the shards to show that he could stand the sight of blood, even his own.

The bullying ways of both men quickly alienated the natives of Roanoke. After a year, in response to rumors of an imminent Indian attack, Lane and his men attacked Wingina's main village and killed him. All that averted an Indian counterattack was the arrival of Drake and Frobisher, fresh from freebooting up and down the Caribbean. The settlement's 102 survivors piled onto the pirate fleet and put an ocean between themselves and the avenging Roanokes.

A Second Attempt

Undaunted, Raleigh organized a second expedition to plant a colony farther north, in the Chesapeake Bay. He now projected an agricultural community modeled on Humphrey Gilbert's manorial dreams. He recruited 119 men, women, and children, members of the English middle class, granting each person an estate of 500 acres. He also appointed as governor the artist John White, who brought along a suit of armor for ceremonial occasions.

From the moment of first landfall in July 1587, everything went wrong. The expedition's pilot, Simon Ferdinando, insisted on putting off the colonists at Roanoke Island rather than the Chesapeake. Even before Ferdinando weighed anchor, the settlers were skirmishing with the local Indians. Sensing that the situation on Roanoke could quickly become desperate, White sailed back with Ferdinando, hoping to bring reinforcements.

But White returned home in 1588 when the massive Spanish navy, the Armada, was marshaling for an assault on England. Blocked by the war with Spain, Raleigh left the Roanoke colonists to shift for themselves. When White finally returned to Roanoke Island in 1590, he found only an empty fort and a few cottages in a clearing. The sole clue to the colony's fate was carved on a post: CROATOAN. It was the name of a nearby island off Cape Hatteras.

Had the Roanoke colonists fled to Croatoan for safety? Had they moved to the mainland and joined Indian tribes in the interior? Had they been killed by Wingina's people? The fate of the "lost colony" remains a mystery. White sailed back to England, leaving behind the little cluster of cottages that would soon be overgrown with vines and his suit of armor that was already "almost eaten through with rust."

All the world lay before them. Or so it had seemed to the young men from England's West Country who dreamed of gold and glory, conquest and colonization. Portugal had sent slave and gold traders to Africa, as well as merchants to trade with the rich civilizations of the Indies. Spanish conquerors like Cortés had toppled Indian empires and brought home silver. But England's would-be conquistadors had met only with frustration. In 1600, over a century after Columbus' first crossing, not a single English settlement existed anywhere in the Americas. The Atlantic had swallowed up Gilbert and his hopes for a manorial utopia; Roanoke lay in ruins.

What was left of the freebooting world of West Country adventurers? Raleigh, his ambition unquenchable, sailed to South America in quest of a rich city named El Dorado. In 1603, however, Elizabeth's death brought to the English throne her cousin James I, the founder of the Stuart dynasty. The new king arrested the old queen's favorite for treason and left him to languish 15 years in the Tower of London. Set free in 1618 at the age of 64, Raleigh returned to South America, his lust for El Dorado undiminished. Along the way he plundered some Spanish silver ships, defying James' orders. It was a fatal mistake, for England had made peace with Spain. Raleigh lost his head.

James I did not want to harry the king of Spain; he wanted to imitate him. The Stuarts were even more determined than the Tudors to enlarge the sphere of royal power. There would be no room in America for a warrior nobility of conquistadors, no room for a feudal fiefdom ruled by the likes of Raleigh or Gilbert. Instead, there would be English colonies in America like the new outpost of Jamestown, planted on the Chesapeake Bay in Virginia in 1607. There would be profitable plantations and other bold enterprises, enriching English royalty and managed by loyal, efficient bureaucrats. Settling America would strengthen English monarchs, paving their path to greater power, just as the dominions of Mexico and Peru had enlarged the authority of the Spanish crown. America would be the making of kings and queens.

Or would it? For some in Europe, weary of freebooting conquistadors and sea rovers, the order and security that Crown rule and centralized states promoted in western Europe would be enough. But others, the desperate and idealistic men and women who sailed to the world that lay before them, would want more.

SIGNIFICANT EVENTS

ca. 50,000–25,000 B.P. (before the present)	First Asian penetration of the Americas
ca. 1300 A.D.	Rise of the Aztec empire
1271–1295	Marco Polo travels to China from Italy
1347	First outbreak of the Black Death
1420s	Portuguese settlements in the Atlantic islands
1488	Dias rounds the tip of Africa
1492	Columbus discovers America
1497	John Cabot discovers Newfoundland
1498	Da Gama reaches India
1517	Luther posts his 95 theses
1519–1522	Magellan circumnavigates the globe
1521	Tenochtitlán surrenders to Cortés
1540	Discovery of silver in Mexico and Peru
1558	Elizabeth I becomes queen of England
1565	England begins its conquest of Ireland
1576–1578	Frobisher searches for Northwest Passage
1583	Gilbert's quest for a North American colony
1584–1590	Roanoke voyages

CHAPTER TWO

The First Century of Settlement in the Colonial South

In the year 1617, as Europeans counted time, on a bay they called the Chesapeake, in a land they named Virginia, an old Indian chief surveyed his domain. It had all worked according to plan, and Powhatan, leader of the Pamunkeys, had laid his plans carefully. While in his prime, the tall, robust man had drawn some 30 smaller tribes along the Virginia coast into a powerful confederacy.

By 1607 Powhatan's confederacy numbered nearly 9000, a political alliance that had overcome formidable obstacles. The natives of Virginia, like the other

Powhatan's confederacy

peoples who inhabited the length of eastern North America, were seminomadic. They lived for most of the year in small villages and ranged over tribal hunting and fishing grounds, following the game from one season to the next. Rivalries over trade, territorial boundaries, and leadership had often erupted into armed conflict. Some coastal tribes had fiercely resisted Powhatan's efforts to incorporate them; other tribes to the west still threatened the security of his confederacy. After 1607 Powhatan was forced to take into account yet another tribe. The English, as this new people called themselves, came by sea, followed a river deep into his territory, and built a fort on a swampy, mosquito-infested site that they called Jamestown.

Powhatan was not frightened. The English did have larger boats and louder, more deadly weapons. But the Indians quickly learned how to use guns, and they vastly outnumbered the English, an inferior race who seemed unlikely to live long and prosper in Powhatan's land. They could not even manage to feed themselves from the rich resources of the Chesapeake. With bows and arrows, spears and nets, Indian men brought in an abundance of meat and fish. The fields tended by Indian women yielded crops of corn, beans, squash, and melon, and edible nuts and fruits grew wild. Still the English starved, and not just during the first months of their settlement but for several years after.

Powhatan could understand why the English refused to grow food. Cultivating crops, like building houses, or making clothing, pottery, and baskets, or caring for children, was women's work, and the English settlement included no women until two arrived in the fall of 1608. Yet even after more women came, the English still starved, and they expected—no, they demanded—that the Indians supply them with food.

Most incredible to Powhatan was that the inferior English considered themselves a superior people. They boasted constantly about the power of their god—they had only one—and denounced the Indians' "devil-worship" of "false gods." The English also boasted without end about the power of their king, James I, who expected Powhatan to become his vassal. The English had even planned a "coronation" to crown Powhatan as a "subject king."

It was inconceivable to Powhatan that he should bow before this King James, the ruler of so savage a race. When the Indians made war, they killed the male warriors of rival tribes but adopted their women and children. But when Powhatan's people withheld food or defended their land from these invaders, the English retaliated by murdering Indian women and children. Worse, the English could not even keep order within their own tribe. Too many of them wanted to be chiefs, and they squabbled constantly.

Only one man, a brash fellow called Captain John Smith, had briefly been able to bring order to the English settlement. Powhatan granted him a grudging respect, though Smith would have enslaved the Indians if it had been in his power. But Smith returned to England in 1609 after being injured when some of the white people's gunpowder blew up by mistake. Thereafter the English returned to squabbling and starving. Small wonder that some English had deserted their settlement to live among Powhatan's people. Anyone could see the superiority of Indian culture to English ways.

The temptation to wipe out the helpless, troublesome, arrogant tribe of English—or simply to let them starve—had been almost overwhelming. But

Powhatan's strategy

Powhatan allowed the English to survive because he had decided that even these barbaric people had their uses. English labor, English trading goods, and, most important, English guns would help him quell resistance within his confederacy and subdue his Indian rivals in the west. In 1614 Powhatan cemented his claim on the English and their weapons with the marriage between his favorite child, Pocahontas, and a white settler, John Rolfe.

By 1617 events had vindicated Powhatan's strategy of tolerating the English. His empire flourished, ready to be passed on to his brother, Opechancanough. Powhatan's people still outnumbered the English, who seldom starved outright now but continued to fight among themselves and sicken and die. Only one thing had changed in the Chesapeake by 1617: the English were clearing woodland along the rivers and planting tobacco.

That was the doing of Powhatan's son-in-law, Rolfe, a man as strange as any of his tribe, all of them eager to store up wealth and worldly goods. Rolfe had been obsessed with finding a crop that could be grown in Virginia and then sold for gain across the sea. When he succeeded by growing tobacco, other English followed his lead. Odder still, not women but men tended the tobacco fields. Here was more evidence of English inferiority. Men wasted long hours laboring when they might supply their needs with far less effort.

In 1617 Powhatan, ruler of the Pamunkeys, surveyed his empire, and sometime in that year, he looked no longer. He had lived long enough to see the tobacco fields lining the riverbanks, straddling the charred stumps of felled trees. But he died believing that he had bent the English to his purposes—died before those stinking tobacco weeds spread over the length of his land and sent his hard-won empire up in smoke.

ENGLISH SOCIETY ON THE CHESAPEAKE

While the chief of the Chesapeake was expanding his dominions and consolidating his power, the king of England was doing the same. Just as Spain had begun to profit from the riches of silver mines and sugar plantations, James I of England hoped that the wealth and power of his kingdom would grow as English colonists settled the American coasts north of Spain's empire. The first newcomers clustered along the many bays of the Chesapeake, as well as in a few island outposts of the Caribbean. A generation later, during the 1670s and 1680s, colonists from the Caribbean hopscotched to the mainland to found colonies along the Carolina coast. As the English struggled to put down roots, the ambitions of merchants and planters and kings clashed with the conflicting goals of Indian leaders like Powhatan.

The result was a chaotic and deadly landscape. During much of the seventeenth century, ambitious colonists scrambled to control the land and the labor
Instability of the southern colonies needed to secure profits from tobacco, sugar, and rice. Only after decades of uncertainty, violence, and high mortality did the colonies along the southern Atlantic crescent begin to prosper. Even then, stability was bought at a high price. In order to supply the workers so desperately sought by plantation owners, English colonists introduced the institution of slavery.

The Mercantilist Impulse

When European powers established permanent colonies in America, they were putting into practice a theory about how best to attain national wealth and in-
Mercantilism fluence. That idea, which guided Europe's commercial expansion for 200 years, was named "mercantilism" by the eighteenth-century economist Adam Smith. Mercantilists called for the state to regulate and protect industry and commerce. Their objective was to enrich the nation by fostering a favorable balance of trade. Once the value of exports ex-

ceeded the cost of imports, they theorized, gold and silver would flow into home ports.

If a nation could dispense entirely with imports from other countries, so much the better, and it was here that the idea of colonies entered the mercantilist scheme. Colonial producers would supply raw materials that the mother country could not produce, while colonial consumers swelled demand for the finished goods and financial services that the mother country could provide.

Mercantilist notions appealed to Europe's monarchs. A thriving trade meant that more taxes and customs duties would fill royal coffers, increasing royal power. That logic led James I to lend his approval to the private venture that brought the first white settlers to the Chesapeake.

The Virginia Company

In 1606 the king granted a charter to a number of English merchants, gentlemen, and aristocrats, incorporating them as the Virginia Company of London. The members of the new joint stock company sold stock in their venture to

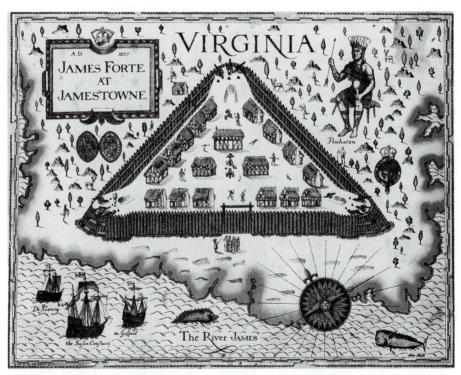

The Jamestown fort's heavy palisades and its strategic location upriver and some distance inland underscore the colonists' concern for defense—as does the imposing figure of Powhatan seated at the right.

English investors, as well as awarding a share to those willing to settle in Virginia at their own expense. With the proceeds from the sale of stock, the company planned to send to Virginia hundreds of poor and unemployed people as well as scores of skilled craftworkers. These laborers were to serve the company for seven years in return for their passage, pooling their efforts to produce any commodities that would return a profit to stockholders. In the spring of 1607 the first expedition dispatched by the Virginia Company, 104 men and boys, founded Jamestown.

Making the first of many mistakes, Jamestown's settlers pitched their fort on an inland peninsula in order to prevent a surprise attack from the Spanish.

Jamestown's problems

Unfortunately, the marshy, thickly wooded site served as an ideal breeding ground for malaria. The Virginia Company settlers, weakened by bouts of malaria and then beset by dysentery, typhoid, and yellow fever, died by the scores.

Even before sickness took its toll, many of Jamestown's first settlers had little taste for labor. The gentlemen of the expedition expected to lead rather than to work, while most other members of the early colonizing parties were gentlemen's servants and craftworkers who knew nothing about growing crops. The settlers resorted to bullying Powhatan's people for food. Many colonists suffered from malnutrition, which heightened their susceptibility to disease. Only 60 of Jamestown's 500 inhabitants lived through the winter of 1609–1610, known as the "starving time." Some desperate colonists unearthed and ate corpses; one settler even butchered his wife.

Reports of starvation and staggering death rates stiffened the Virginia Company's resolve: in 1611 it imposed on the colonists what amounted to martial law. Company officials in Virginia organized the settlers into work gangs and severely punished the lazy and the disorderly. Still the company failed to turn a profit. And after 1617, skirmishes with the Indians became more brutal and frequent, as rows of tobacco plants steadily invaded tribal lands.

Reform and a Boom in Tobacco

Desperate to salvage their investment, Virginia Company managers in 1618 set in place sweeping reforms. To attract more capital and colonists, the com-

Key reforms

pany established a "headright" system for granting land to individuals. Those already settled in the colony received 100 acres apiece. New settlers each received 50 acres, and anyone who paid the passage of other immigrants to Virginia—either family members or servants—received 50 acres per "head." The company also abolished martial law, allowing the planters to elect a representative assembly. Along with a governor and an advisory council appointed by the company, the House of Burgesses had the authority to make laws for the colony. It met for the first time in 1619, beginning what would become a strong tradition of representative government in the English colonies.

The new measures met with immediate success. The free and unfree laborers who poured into Virginia during the 1620s made up the first wave of an English migration to the Chesapeake that numbered between 130,000 and 150,000 over the seventeenth century. Drawn from the ranks of ordinary English working people, the immigrants were largely men, outnumbering women by six to one. Most were young, ranging in age from 15 to 24. Because of their youth, most lacked skills or wealth. Some of those who came to the Chesapeake as free immigrants prospered, because during the 1620s the demand for tobacco soared and prices spiked in Europe. But for the vast majority of settlers—and, specifically, the three-quarters of all immigrants who arrived in the Chesapeake as indentured servants—the future was far grimmer.

For most new servants, the crossing to Virginia was simply the last of many moves made in the hope of finding work. Although England's population had been rising since the middle of the fifteenth century, the demand *Indentured* for farm laborers was falling because many landowners were con- *servants* verting croplands into pastures for sheep. The search for work pushed young men and women out of their villages, sending them through the countryside and then into the cities. Down and out in London, Bristol, or Liverpool, some chanced a move to America, by signing indentures. Pamphlets promoting immigration promised abundant land and quick riches once servants had finished their terms of four to seven years.

Even the most skeptical immigrants were shocked at what they found. The death rate in Virginia during the 1620s was higher than that of England during times of epidemic disease. The life expectancy for Chesapeake men who reached the age of 20 was a mere 48 years; for women it was lower still. Servants fared worst of all, since malnutrition, overwork, and abuse made them vulnerable to disease. As masters scrambled to make quick profits, they extracted the maximum amount of work before death carried off their laborers. An estimated 40 percent of servants did not survive to the end of their indentured terms.

The expanding cultivation of tobacco also claimed many lives by putting unbearable pressure on Indian land. After Powhatan's death in 1617, leadership of the confederacy passed to Opechancanough, who watched, *War with the* year after year, as the tobacco mania grew. In March 1622 he co- *confederacy* ordinated a sweeping attack on white settlements that killed about one-fifth of Virginia's white population. Swift English retaliation wiped out whole tribes and cut down an entire generation of young Indian men.

News of the Indian war jolted English investors into determining the true state of their Virginia venture. It came to light that, despite the tobacco boom, the Virginia Company was plunging toward bankruptcy. Nor was that the worst news. Stockholders discovered that over 3000 immigrants had not survived the brutal conditions of Chesapeake life. An investigation by James I brought out the grisly truth, causing the king to dissolve the Virginia Company and take

EYEWITNESS TO HISTORY

A Virginia Settler Describes the Indian War of 1622 to Officials in England

Such was the treacherous dissumulation of that people who then had contrived our destruction, that even two dayes before the Massacre, some of our men were guided thorow [through] the woods by them in safety. . . as well on the Friday morning (the fatal day) of the 22 of March . . . they came unarmed into our houses, without Bowes or arrowes, or other weapons, with Deere, Turkies, Fish, Furres, and other provisions, to sell and trucke with us, for glasse, beades, and other trifles: yea in some places sate downe at Breakfast with our people at their tables, whom immediately with their owne tooles and weapons, eyther laid downe, or standing in their houses, they basely and barbarously murthered [murdered], not sparing eyther age or sexe, man, woman, or childe. . . . In which manner they also slew many of our people then at their severall workes and husbandries in the fields . . . some in planting Corne and Tobacco, some in gardening, some in making Bricke, building, sawing, and other kindes of husbandry, they well knowing in what places and quarters each of our men were, in regard of their daily familiarity, and resort to us for trading and other negotiations, which the more willingly was by us continued and cherished for the desire we had of effecting that great masterpeece of workes, their conversion. And by this meanes that fatall Friday morning, there fell under the bloudy and barbarous hands of that perfidious and inhumane people, contrary to all lawes of God and men, of Nature and Nations, three hundred forty seven men, women and children, most by their owne weapons; and not being content with taking away life alone, they fell after again upon the dead, making as well as they could, a fresh murder, defacing, dragging and mangling the dead carkasses into many pieces, and carrying some parts away in derision, with base and brutish triumph.

Edward Waterhouse, *A Declaration of the State of the Colonie and Affaires in Virginia* (1622). Susan Myra Kingsbury, ed., *The Records of the Virginia Company of London*, (Washington, D.C., 1906-1935) III, pp. 459–556.

control of the colony himself in 1624. Henceforth Virginia would be governed as a royal colony.

Settling Down in the Chesapeake

During the 1630s and 1640s the fever of the tobacco boom broke, and a more settled social and political life emerged in Virginia. The settlers who had become wealthy by exploiting servant labor now began to acquire political power. They established local bases of influence in Virginia's counties, serving as justices of the peace and sheriffs, maintaining roads and bridges, collecting taxes, and supervising local elections. They organized all able-bodied adult males into militias for local defense and sat on vestries, the governing bodies of local Anglican parishes, hiring the handful of clergy who came to Virginia and providing for the neighborhood poor.

The biggest tobacco planters of each county also dominated colony politics. Even though King James had replaced the Virginia Company's government with his own royal administration, the colony's elected assembly continued making laws for the colony. Along with the council (the upper house of the legislature), the assembly resisted interference in Virginia's affairs from the royal governor, the king's representative.

The colony's growing stability was reflected in improved conditions for less powerful Virginians. Although servants still streamed into the colony, the price of tobacco leveled off. That meant planters were less likely to drive their servants to death in search of overnight fortunes. As tobacco became less profitable, planters raised more corn and cattle, and mortality rates declined as food supplies rose. Freed servants who survived their indentures usually worked a few more years as hired hands or tenant farmers. In doing so, most managed to save enough money to buy their own land and become independent planters. For women who survived servitude, prospects were even better. With wives at a premium, single women stood a good chance of improving their status by marriage. By 1650 Virginia could boast about 15,000 inhabitants, with more servants and free immigrants coming to the colony every year.

Decline in mortality rates

The Founding of Maryland and the Renewal of Indian Wars

Unlike Virginia, which was first settled by a private corporation and later converted into a royal colony, Maryland was founded by a single aristocratic family, the Calverts. Indeed, it was the first of several such "proprietary" colonies given by English monarchs to loyal followers. Thus in 1632, Maryland became the private preserve of the Calverts. They held absolute authority to dispose of 10 million acres of land, administer justice, and establish a civil government. All of these powers they exercised, granting estates, or "manors," to their friends and dividing other holdings into smaller farms for ordinary immigrants. From all of these "tenants"—that is, every settler in the

Proprietary colonies

colony—the Calverts collected "quitrents" every year, fees for use of the land. The Calverts appointed a governor and a council to oversee their own interests, while allowing the largest landowners to dispense local justice in manorial courts and make laws for the entire colony in a representative assembly.

Virginians liked nothing at all about their neighbors in the northerly bays of the Chesapeake. To begin with, the Calvert family was Catholic and had ex-

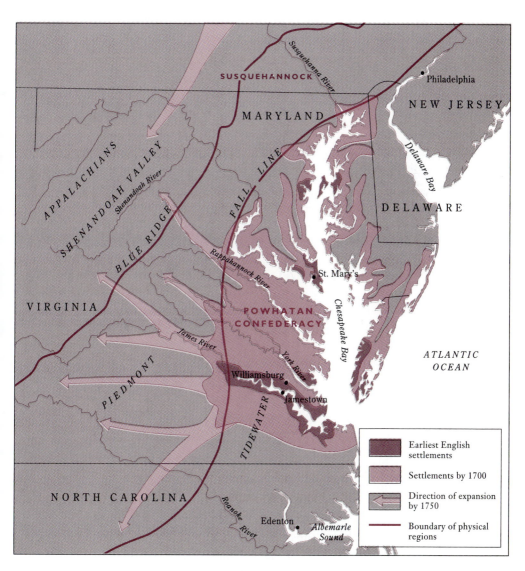

COLONIES OF THE CHESAPEAKE   Settlements in Virginia and Maryland spread out along the many bays of the Chesapeake, where tobacco could easily be loaded from plantation wharves. The fall line on rivers, dividing the Tidewater and Piedmont regions, determined the extent of commercial agriculture, since ships could not pick up exports beyond that point.

tended complete religious freedom to all Christians, making Maryland a haven for Catholics. Worse, the Marylanders were a source of economic competition. Two thousand inhabitants had settled on Calvert holdings by 1640, virtually all of them planting tobacco on land coveted by the Virginians.

Another obstacle to Virginia's expansion was the remnant of the Powhatan confederacy, still determined to repel white invaders. Opechancanough led a new generation of Indians into battle in 1644 against the encroaching Virginia planters. The hostilities inflicted as many casualties on both sides as the fighting in 1622.

Changes in English Policy in the Chesapeake

Throughout the 1630s and 1640s colonial affairs drew little concern from royal officials. England itself had become engulfed by first a political crisis and then a civil war.

The conflict grew out of efforts by both James I and Charles I (who succeeded his father in 1625) to expand their royal power and rule the nation without the nuisance of having to consult Parliament. When Parliament condemned Charles for usurping its power to raise money, he simply dissolved that body in 1629. But when the Scots invaded England in 1639, Charles found he could raise funds to pay for an army only by calling Parliament back into session. By then, many of the merchants and landed gentlemen who were members had de-

The English Civil War

cided that the Stuart kings themselves might be dispensable. In 1642 Parliament and its Puritan allies squared off against Charles I and his royalist supporters, defeated them in battle, and, in 1649, beheaded the king. England became a republic ruled by Oliver Cromwell, the man who had led Parliament's army.

In truth, Cromwell's "republic" more accurately resembled a military dictatorship. After his death, most English were happy to see their throne restored in 1660 to Charles II, the son of the beheaded king. And the new king was determined to ensure that not only his subjects at home but his American colonies abroad contributed to England's prosperity. His colonial policy was reflected in a series of regulations known as the Navigation Acts.

The first, passed by Parliament in 1660, gave England and English colonial merchants a monopoly on the shipping and marketing of all colonial goods.

The Navigation Acts

It also ordered that the colonies could export certain "enumerated commodities" only to England or other British ports. These goods included sugar, tobacco, cotton, ginger, and indigo (a blue dye). In 1663 Parliament added another regulation, giving British merchants a virtual monopoly on the sale of European manufactured goods to Americans by requiring that most imports going to the colonies had to pass through England. In 1673 a third Navigation Act placed duties on the coastal trade of the American colonies and provided for customs officials to collect tariffs and enforce commercial regulations.

CHESAPEAKE SOCIETY IN CRISIS

The regulations of trade put in place by Restoration kings Charles II and James II and their Parliaments had a decisive impact on colonials. Accustomed to conducting their affairs as they pleased—and they were often pleased to trade with the Dutch—Chesapeake planters chafed under the Navigation Acts. What was worse, the new restrictions came at the same time as a downturn in tobacco prices. In the effort to consolidate its empire, England unintentionally worsened the economic and social difficulties of Chesapeake society.

The Conditions of Unrest

The Chesapeake colonies were heading for trouble partly because of their success. As inhabitants had started to live longer, more servants survived their terms of service and set up as independent tobacco planters.

Diminishing opportunities

More planters meant more production, and overproduction sent the price of tobacco plummeting, especially between 1660 and 1680. To maintain their advantage, the biggest planters bought up all of the prime property along the coast, forcing newly freed servants to become tenants or to settle on unclaimed land in the interior. Either way, poorer men lost. Depending on bigger planters for land and credit made the small farmers vulnerable to debt. Moving to the frontier made them vulnerable to Indian attack.

The slim resources of small planters were stretched even thinner, not only from county taxes but also from export duties on tobacco paid under the Navigation Acts. During the hard times after 1660, many small planters fell deeply into debt, and some were forced back into servitude. By 1676 one-quarter of Virginia's free white men were landless. Many former servants were unable to gain a foothold even as tenants.

Diminishing opportunity in the 1660s and 1670s provided the tinder for unrest in Virginia. As the discontent of poor men mounted, so did the worries of big planters. The assembly of the colony lengthened terms of servitude, hoping to limit the number of servants entering the free population. It curbed the political rights of landless men, hoping to stifle opposition by depriving them of the vote. But these measures only set off a spate of mutinies among servants and protests over rising taxes among small planters.

Bacon's Rebellion and Coode's Rebellion

Those tensions came to a head in 1676 when civil war erupted. The immediate catalyst of the rebellion was renewed skirmishing between whites expanding westward and Indians. Virginia's royal governor, William Berkeley, favored building forts to contain the Indian threat, but frontier farmers opposed his plan as an expensive and ineffective way to defend their scattered plantations. As they clamored for an expedition to punish the Indians, Nathaniel Bacon stepped forward to lead it.

Wealthy and well connected, Bacon had arrived recently from England, expecting to receive every favor from the governor—including permission to trade

Nathaniel Bacon

with the Indians from his frontier plantation. But Berkeley and a few select friends already held a monopoly on the Indian trade. When they declined to include Bacon, he took up the cause of his poorer frontier neighbors against their common enemy, the governor. Other recent, well-to-do immigrants who resented being excluded from Berkeley's circle of power and patronage also joined Bacon.

In the summer of 1676 Bacon marched into Jamestown with a body of armed men and bullied the assembly into approving his expedition to kill Indians. While Bacon carried out that grisly business, slaughtering friendly as well as hostile tribes, Berkeley rallied his supporters and declared Bacon a rebel. Bacon retaliated by turning his forces against those led by the governor. Both sides sought allies by offering freedom to servants and slaves willing to join their ranks. Many were willing: for months the followers of Bacon and Berkeley plundered one another's plantations. In September 1676 Bacon reduced Jamestown itself to a mound of ashes. It was only his death from dysentery a month later that snuffed out the rebellion.

Political upheaval also shook Maryland, where colonists had long resented the Calvert's rule. As proprietors, the Calverts and their favorites monopolized political offices, just as Berkeley's circle had in Virginia. Well-to-do planters wanted a share of the power. Smaller farmers, like those in Virginia, wanted a less expensive and more representative government. Compounding the tensions were religious differences: the Calverts and their friends were Catholic, but other colonists, including its most successful planters, were Protestant.

The unrest among Maryland's discontented planters peaked in July 1689. A former member of the assembly, John Coode, gathered an army, captured the

Coode's Rebellion

proprietary governor, and then took his grievances to authorities in England. There Coode received a sympathetic hearing. The Calverts' charter was revoked and not restored until 1715, by which time the family had become Protestant.

After 1690 rich planters in both Chesapeake colonies fought among themselves less and cooperated more. In Virginia older leaders and newer arrivals divided the spoils of political office. In Maryland Protestants and

Growing stability

Catholics shared power and privilege. Those arrangements ensured that no future Bacon or Coode would mobilize restless gentlemen against the government. By acting together in legislative assemblies, they managed to curb the power of royal and proprietary governors for decades.

But the greater unity among the Chesapeake's leading families did little to ease that region's most fundamental problem. That was the sharp inequality of white society. The gulf between rich and poor planters, which had been etched ever more deeply by the troubled tobacco economy, persisted long after the rebellions of Bacon and Coode. All that saved white society in the Chesapeake from renewed crisis and conflict was the growth of black slavery.

From Servitude to Slavery

Like the tobacco plants that spread across Powhatan's land, a labor system based on slavery had not figured in the first plans for the Chesapeake. Both early promoters and planters preferred buying English servants to importing alien African slaves. Black slaves, because they served for life, were more expensive than white workers, who served only for several years. Since neither white nor black emigrants lived long, cheaper servant labor was the logical choice. The black population of the Chesapeake remained small for most of the seventeenth century, comprising just 5 percent of all inhabitants in 1675.

The first Africans landed in Virginia in 1619, brought by the Dutch, who dominated the slave trade until the middle of the eighteenth century. The lives

The lives of servants and slaves

of those newcomers resembled the lot of white servants, with whom they shared harsh work routines and living conditions. White and black bound laborers socialized with each other and formed sexual liaisons. They conspired to steal from their masters and ran away together, and if caught, they endured similar punishments. There was more common ground: many of the first black settlers did not arrive directly from Africa but came from the Caribbean, where some had learned English and adopted Christian beliefs. And not all were slaves: some were indentured servants, and a handful were free.

A number of changes after 1680 caused planters to invest more heavily in slaves than in servants. First, declining mortality rates in the Chesapeake made slaves the more profitable investment. Although slaves were more expensive than servants, planters could now expect to get many years of work from their bondspeople. Equally important, masters would have title to the children that slaves would now live long enough to have. At the same time, the influx of white servants was falling off just as the pool of available black labor was expanding. When the Royal African Company lost its monopoly on the English slave trade in 1698, other merchants entered the market. The number of Africans sold by British dealers swelled to 20,000 annually.

During the decades after 1680, more than 80 percent of black people imported as slaves came directly from Africa. Much of the trade centered on the coast of Africa that Portuguese explorers had first probed, between the Senegal and Niger rivers. Seized by other Africans, captives were yoked together at the neck and marched hundreds of miles through the interior to the Atlantic shores of Senegambia, the Windward Coast, and the Gold Coast. Farther south, slaves were also taken from the agrarian societies of Angola.

After the trauma of capture and the long trek to the ocean, there followed the horror of the Middle Passage, a journey of 5000 miles across the Atlantic

Middle Passage to America. As many as 200 black men, women, and children were crowded onto each slave ship, but perhaps one out of every six did not live through the crossing. Shipmasters crammed their human cargo onto platforms built between the decks of their vessels, tiers spaced so low that sitting upright was impossible. Among white sailors and slaves alike, the death toll from disease was staggering.

When the numb, exhausted survivors of the Middle Passage reached American ports, they faced more challenges to staying alive. The first year in the colonies was the most deadly for new, unseasoned slaves. The sickle cell genetic trait gave black Africans a greater immunity than white Europeans had to malaria, but slaves were highly susceptible to respiratory infections. One-quarter of all Africans died during their first year in the Chesapeake, and among Carolina and Caribbean slaves, mortality rates were even higher. In addition to the new disease environment, Africans were forced to adapt to lives without freedom in a wholly unfamiliar country and culture.

A Changing Chesapeake Society

Exchanging a labor system based on servitude for one based on slavery transformed the character of Chesapeake society. Most obviously, the number of black Virginians rose sharply. By 1740, 40 percent of all Virginians were black, and most were African-born. Unlike black men and women who had arrived earlier, they had little familiarity with English language and culture. This larger, more distinctively African community was also locked into a slave system that was becoming ever more rigid and demeaning. By the late decades of the seventeenth century, laws were in place making it more difficult for masters to free slaves. Other legislation systematically separated the races by prohibiting free black settlers from owning white servants and outlawing interracial marriages and sexual relationships. The legal code encouraged white contempt for black Virginians in a variety of other ways. While masters were prohibited from whipping their white servants on the bare back, slaves had no such protection. And "any Negro that shall presume to strike any white" was to receive 30 lashes for that rash act.

The new laws both reflected and encouraged racism among white colonists of all classes. Deepening racial hatred, in turn, made it unlikely that poor white planters, tenants, and servants would ever join with poor black slaves to chal-

Racism lenge the privilege of great planters. Instead of identifying with the plight of the slaves, the Chesapeake's poorer white residents considered black Virginians their natural inferiors. They could pride themselves on sharing with wealthy white gentlemen the same skin color and on being their equals in the eyes of the law.

The leaders of the Chesapeake colonies cultivated unity among white in-

Opportunities for white settlers habitants by improving economic prospects for freed servants and lesser planters. The Virginia assembly lowered taxes, allowing small planters to keep more of their earnings. New laws also gave most white male Virginians a vote in elections, allowing them an outlet to express their grievances. Economic trends toward the end of the seventeenth century contributed to the greater prosperity of small planters, as tobacco prices rose slightly and then stabilized. As a result of Bacon's savage campaign against the Virginia Indians, new land on the frontier became available. Even the domestic lives of ordinary men improved as the numbers of men and women in the white population evened out around the turn of the century.

After 1700 the Chesapeake evolved into a more stable society. Virginia and Maryland became colonies of farming families, most of them headed by small planters who owned between 50 and 200 acres. These families held no slaves, or at most two or three. And they accepted, usually without question, the social and political leadership of their acknowledged "superiors," great planters who styled themselves the "gentry."

The Chesapeake Gentry

The new Chesapeake gentry were the sons of well-to-do London merchant families, many of whom had intermarried with England's landed gentry. For both classes Virginia offered new prospects for land and commercial wealth. Enterprising fathers sent their sons to the Chesapeake between 1640 and 1670 to establish family interests in America by creating vast plantations.

The gentry's fortunes rested in part on the cultivation of tobacco on thousands of acres by hundreds of slaves. But the leading planters made even more

George Booth, the son of a wealthy planter family in Gloucester County Virginia was being raised for mastery. The young man's self-assured stance, the bow and arrows, the dog at his feet clutching the kill, the classical busts of women flanking his figure, and his family estate in the distance all suggest the gentry's concern for controlling the natural and social worlds.

*The basis of
gentry power*

money by marketing the tobacco of their humbler neighbors, selling them manufactured goods, supplying them with medical and legal services, lending money, and hiring out slaves. Unlike the rough-hewn barons of the early tobacco boom, the gentry's profit did not depend on wringing work from poor whites. It hinged instead on wringing work from black slaves while converting their white "inferiors" into modestly prosperous small planters and paying clients.

But the gentry wanted more than money: they wanted the respect of lesser whites. On election days, when voters in the county assembled, each approached in his turn the gentleman candidate he preferred, publicly announced his vote, and sometimes made a brief, flattering speech about his choice. At militia musters, when every able-bodied man in the county gathered, gentlemen officers led the military drills. On court days, defendants and plaintiffs testified before gentlemen justices of the peace, bedecked in wigs and robes and seated on raised benches. And every Sunday, when many in the county came to worship at the Anglican chapel, families filed into the church in order of their social rank, with the gentlemen vestry heading the procession. The courthouse and church, the tavern and training field—all served as theaters in which the new Chesapeake gentry dramatized their superiority and lesser men deferred.

If anything, the evolving plantation societies of Virginia and Maryland were becoming even more unequal, because the rise of slavery sharpened economic

*Stability in the
Chesapeake*

distinctions within the white population. Those who owned slaves enjoyed a decided economic edge over those who did not. But while extreme economic inequality persisted, social tension between richer and poorer white settlers lessened. As racism unified all classes within white society and economic and political gains eased discontent among small planters, the changing character of the Chesapeake's leaders also reduced social friction. The unscrupulous scoundrels who once dominated society had been replaced by gentlemen planters who fancied themselves the "fathers" of their plantations and neighborhoods.

FROM THE CARIBBEAN TO THE CAROLINAS

During the same decade that the English invaded Powhatan's land, they began to colonize the Caribbean. A century earlier, Columbus had charted the route: ships picked up the trade winds off Madeira and the Canary Islands and headed west across the Atlantic to paradise. At journey's end the surf broke over shores rimmed with white sand beaches that rose sharply to coral terraces, then to broad plateaus or mountain peaks shrouded in rain forests.

Paradise was lost to the Indians of the Caribbean, or at least to those few remaining alive. European diseases, combined with Spanish exploitation, had

*Transformation
of the Caribbean*

eliminated virtually all the natives of Hispaniola by the 1520s. Over the next century those living in Cuba, Puerto Rico, the Bahamas, the Lesser Antilles, and Jamaica would follow. And the "paradise" that remained was filled with plants and animals that would have been strange to natives only a century earlier. Hogs and cattle, now wild, had been imported by Europeans, as had figs, oranges, pomegranates, and African yams. That ecological migration of flora and fauna would continue to transform the Americas in the century to come.

Paradise was lost to the English as well. At first they came to the Caribbean intending not to colonize but to steal from the Spanish. Even after 1604 when some English settled on the islands, few intended to stay. Yet not only did the English establish permanent plantation colonies in the West Indies, their Caribbean settlements became the jumping-off points for a new colony on the North American mainland, South Carolina. Because of the strong West Indian influence, South Carolina developed a social order in some ways distinct from that of the Chesapeake. Yet in other ways, the development of the Carolinas paralleled Virginia and Maryland's path from violence, high mortality, and uncertainty toward relative stability.

Paradise Lost

The English had traded and battled with the Spanish in the Caribbean since the 1560s. From those island bases English buccaneers conducted an illegal trade with Spanish settlements, sacked the coastal towns, and plundered silver ships bound for Seville. Weakened by decades of warfare, Spain could not hold the West Indies. The Dutch drove a wedge into Caribbean trade routes, and the French and the English began to colonize the islands.

In the 40 years after 1604, some 30,000 immigrants from the British Isles planted crude frontier outposts on St. Kitts, Barbados, Nevis, Montserrat, and Antigua. The settlers—some free, many others indentured servants, and almost all young men—devoted themselves to working as little as possible, drinking as much as possible, and returning to England as soon as possible. They cultivated for export a poor quality of tobacco, which returned just enough to maintain straggling settlements of small farms.

Then, nearly overnight, sugar cultivation transformed the Caribbean. In the 1640s Barbados planters learned from the Dutch how to process sugarcane. The _Caribbean sugar_ Dutch also supplied African slaves to work the cane fields and marketed the sugar for high prices in the Netherlands. Sugar plantations and slave labor rapidly spread to other English and French islands as Europeans developed an insatiable sweet tooth for the once scarce commodity. Caribbean sugar made more money for England than the total volume of commodities exported by all of the mainland American colonies.

Even though its great planters became the richest people in English America, they could not have confused the West Indies with paradise. Throughout the seventeenth century, disease took a fearful toll, and island populations grew only because of immigration. In the scramble for land, small farmers were pushed onto tiny plots that barely allowed them to survive.

The desperation of bound laborers posed another threat. After the conversion to sugar, black slaves gradually replaced white indentured servants in the cane fields. By the beginning of the eighteenth century, black inhabitants outnumbered white residents by four to one. Fear of servant mutinies and slave rebellions frayed the nerves of island masters. They tried to contain the danger by imposing harsh slave codes and inflicting brutal punishments on white and black laborers alike. But planters lived under a constant state of siege. One visitor to Barbados observed that whites fortified their homes with parapets from which they could pour scalding water on attacking servants and slaves. During the first century of settlement, seven major slave uprisings shook the English islands.

Slavery in the Caribbean

As more people, both white and black, squeezed onto the islands, some settlers looked for a way out. With all of the land in use, the Caribbean no longer offered opportunity to freed servants or even planters' sons. It was then that the West Indies started to shape the history of the American South.

The Founding of the Carolinas

The colonization of the Carolinas began with the schemes of Virginia's royal governor, William Berkeley, and Sir John Colleton, a supporter of Charles I who had been exiled to the Caribbean at the end of England's civil war. Colleton saw that the Caribbean had a surplus of white settlers, and Berkeley knew that Virginians needed room to expand as well. Together the two men set their sights on the area south of Virginia. Along with a number of other aristocrats, they convinced Charles II to make them joint proprietors in 1663 of a place they called the Carolinas, in honor of the king.

A few hardy souls from Virginia had already squatted around Albemarle Sound in the northern part of the Carolina grant. The proprietors provided them with a governor and a representative assembly. About 40 years later, in 1701, they set off North Carolina as a separate colony. The desolate region quickly proved a disappointment. Lacking good harbors and navigable rivers, the colony had no convenient way of marketing its produce. North Carolina remained a poor colony, its sparse population engaged in general farming and the production of masts, pitch, tar, and turpentine.

North Carolina

The southern portion of the Carolina grant held far more promise, especially in the eyes of one of its proprietors, Sir Anthony Ashley Cooper, earl of Shaftesbury. In 1669 he sponsored an expedition of a few hundred English and Barbadian immigrants, who planted the first permanent settlement in South Carolina. By 1680 the colonists established the center of economic, social, and political life at the confluence of the Ashley and the Cooper rivers, naming the site Charles Town (later Charleston) after the king.

South Carolina

Most of the Carolina proprietors regarded their venture simply as land speculation. But Cooper, like others before him, hoped to create an ideal soci-

The Fundamental Constitutions

ety in America. Cooper's utopia was one in which a few landed aristocrats and gentlemen would rule with the consent of many smaller propertyholders. With his personal secretary, John Locke, Cooper drew up an intricate scheme of government, the Fundamental Constitutions. The design provided Carolina with a proprietary governor and a hereditary nobility who, as a Council of Lords, would recommend all laws to a Parliament elected by lesser landowners.

The Fundamental Constitutions met the same fate as other lordly dreams for America. Instead of peacefully observing its provisions, Carolinians plunged into the political wrangling that had plagued Maryland's proprietary rule. Assemblies resisted the sweeping powers granted to the proprietary governors. Ordinary settlers protested against paying quitrents claimed by the proprietors. Political unrest in North Carolina triggered three rebellions between 1677 and 1711. In South Carolina opposition to the proprietors gathered strength more slowly, but finally exploded with equal force.

Early Instability

Immigrants from Barbados, the most numerous among the early settlers, came quickly to dominate South Carolina politics. Just as quickly, they objected to proprietary power. To offset the influence of the Barbadians, most of whom were Anglican, the proprietors encouraged the migration of French Huguenots and English Presbyterians and Baptists. The stream of newcomers only heightened tensions, splitting South Carolinians into two camps with competing political and religious loyalties.

Meanwhile, settlers spread out along the coastal plain. Searching for a profitable export, the first colonists raised grains and cattle, foodstuffs that they exported to the West Indies. South Carolinians also developed a large trade in deerskins with coastal tribes like the Yamasee and the Creeks and

Indian slavery

Catawbas of the interior. More numerous than the Indians of the Chesapeake and even more deeply divided, the Carolina tribes competed to become the favored clients of white traders. Southeastern Indian economies quickly became dependent on English guns, rum, and clothing. To repay their debts to white traders, Indians enslaved and sold to white buyers large numbers of men, women, and children taken in wars waged against rival tribes.

Provisions, deerskins, and Indian slaves proved less profitable for South Carolinians than rice, which became the colony's cash crop by the opening of the eighteenth century. Constant demand for rice in Europe made South Carolina the richest colony and South Carolina planters the richest people on the mainland of North America.

Unfortunately, South Carolina's swampy coast, so perfectly suited to growing rice, was less suited for human habitation. Weakened by chronic malaria, settlers died in epic numbers from yellow fever, smallpox, and respiratory in-

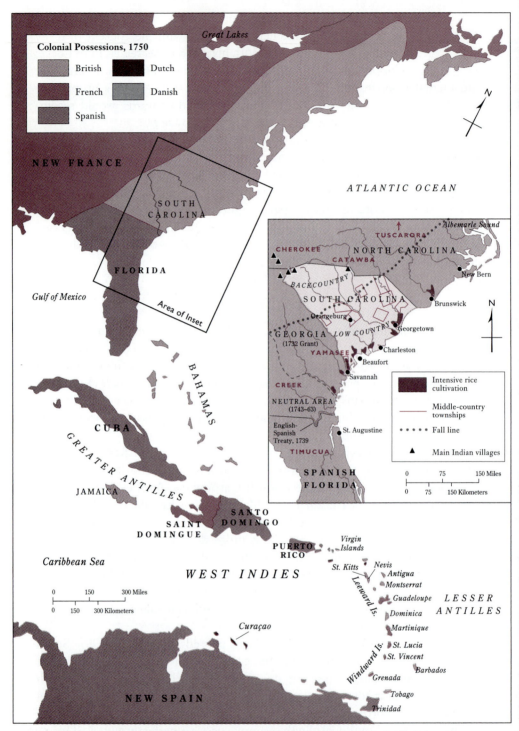

Colonial Possessions, 1750

British
French
Spanish
Dutch
Danish

Great Lakes

NEW FRANCE

ATLANTIC OCEAN

SOUTH CAROLINA

FLORIDA

Gulf of Mexico

Area of Inset

Albemarle Sound

TUSCARORA

CHEROKEE   NORTH CAROLINA
CATAWBA

New Bern

BACKCOUNTRY

SOUTH CAROLINA

Brunswick

Orangeburg

Georgetown

GEORGIA *LOW COUNTRY*
(1732 Grant)

YAMASEE   Charleston

Beaufort

Savannah

CREEK

NEUTRAL AREA
(1743–63)

English-
Spanish
Treaty, 1739   St. Augustine

TIMUCUA

SPANISH
FLORIDA

Intensive rice
cultivation

Middle-country
townships

Fall line

Main Indian villages

0   75   150 Miles

0   75   150 Kilometers

BAHAMAS

CUBA

GREATER ANTILLES

JAMAICA

SANTO
DOMINGO

SAINT
DOMINGUE

PUERTO
RICO

*Virgin
Islands*

Caribbean Sea

St. Kitts   Nevis
              Antigua
              Montserrat
WEST INDIES   Guadeloupe   LESSER
              Dominica   ANTILLES
Leeward Is.   Martinique

0   150   300 Miles

0   150   300 Kilometers

Curaçao

Windward Is.   St. Lucia
                St. Vincent

Grenada   Barbados

Tobago

NEW SPAIN   Trinidad

THE CAROLINAS AND THE CARIBBEAN   The map underscores the link between
West Indian and Carolina settlements. Emigrants from Barbados dominated
politics in early South Carolina, while Carolinians provided foodstuffs, grain,
and cattle to the West Indies.

fections. The white population grew slowly, through immigration rather than natural increase, and numbered a mere 10,000 by 1730.

Early South Carolinians had little in common but the harsh conditions of frontier existence. Most colonists lived on isolated plantations; early deaths fragmented families and neighborhoods. Immigration after 1700 only intensified the colony's ethnic and religious diversity, adding Swiss and German Lutherans, Scots-Irish Presbyterians, Welsh Baptists, and Spanish Jews. The colony's only courts were in Charleston; churches and clergy of any denomination were scarce. On those rare occasions when early Carolinians came together, they gathered at Charleston to escape the pestilent air of their plantations, to sue each other for debt and to haggle over prices, or to fight over religious differences and proprietary politics.

White, Red, and Black: The Search for Order

By the opening decades of the eighteenth century, South Carolina seemed as strife-torn and unstable as the early Chesapeake colonies. In addition to internal tensions, external dangers threatened the very life of the Carolina settlements. The Spanish were rattling their sabers in Florida, the French filtering into the Gulf region, and pirates lurking along the North Carolina coast.

Most menacing were the Indians, and in 1715 they struck. The Yamasee of the coast allied themselves with the Creeks farther inland, launching a series of

Yamasee War

assaults that nearly pushed white Carolinians into the sea. All that saved the colony was an alliance with the Cherokee, another interior tribe who, in return for trading privileges, mounted a counterattack against their Indian rivals.

As colonists reeled from the Yamasee War, opposition mounted against the proprietors, who had done nothing to protect their vulnerable colony. Military expenses had also forced Carolinians to fall into greater debt, to pay higher taxes, and to struggle with an inflated currency that month by month became

The end of proprietary rule

worth less. Even Presbyterians, Baptists, and Huguenots, who had once defended the proprietors, shifted their sympathies because they disapproved of more recent attempts to establish the Church of England as South Carolina's official religion. During the 1720s, mass meetings and riots so disrupted government that it all but ground to a halt. Finally, in 1729, the Crown formally established royal government; by 1730 economic recovery had done much to ease the strife. Even more important in bringing greater political stability, the white colonists of South Carolina came to realize that they must unite if they were to counter the Spanish in Florida and the French and their Indian allies to the southwest.

The growing black population gave white Carolinians another reason to maintain a united front. During the first decades of settlement, frontier condi-

Slavery in South Carolina

tions and the scarcity of labor had forced masters to allow enslaved Africans greater freedom within bondage. White and black laborers shared chores on small farms. On stockraising plantations, called "cowpens," black cowboys ranged freely over the countryside. Black contributions to the defense of the colony also reinforced racial interdependence and muted white domination. Whenever the Spanish, the French, or the Indians threatened, black Carolinians were enlisted in the militia.

White Carolinians depended on black labor even more after turning to rice as their cash crop. Indeed, the skills of west Africans in cultivating rice led to a greater demand for them. But whites harbored deepening fears of the workers whose labor built planter fortunes. As early as 1708 black men and women had become a majority in the colony, and by 1730 they outnumbered white settlers by two to one. Like Caribbean planters, white Carolinians put into effect strict slave codes that converted their colony into an armed camp and snuffed out the freedoms that black settlers had enjoyed earlier.

The ever-present threat of revolt on the part of the black majority gave all white South Carolinians an incentive to cooperate, whatever their religion, politics, or ethnic background. To be sure, the colony's high death rates and cultural differences persisted, while local government and churches remained weak. Yet against all these odds, white South Carolinians prospered and political peace prevailed after 1730. Any course except harmony would have exacted too high a price.

The Founding of Georgia

After 1730 South Carolinians could also take comfort from the founding of a new colony on their southern border. South Carolinians liked Georgia a great deal more than the Virginians had liked Maryland, for the colony formed a defensive buffer between British North America and Spanish Florida.

Enhancing the military security of South Carolina was only one reason for the founding of Georgia. More important to General James Oglethorpe and

James Oglethorpe

other idealistic English gentlemen was the aim of aiding the "worthy poor" by providing them with land, employment, and a new start. They envisioned a colony of hardworking small farmers who would produce silk and wine, sparing England the need to import those commodities. That dream seemed within reach when George II made Oglethorpe and his friends the trustees of the new colony in 1732, granting them a charter for 21 years. At the end of that time Georgia would revert to royal control.

The trustees did not, as legend has it, empty England's debtors' prisons to populate Georgia. They freed few debtors but recruited from every country in Europe paupers who seemed willing to work hard—and who professed Protestantism. They paid their passage and provided each with 50 acres of land, tools, and a year's worth of supplies. The trustees encouraged settlers who could pay their own way to come by granting them larger tracts of land. Much to the trustees' dismay, that generous offer was taken up not only by many hoped-for Protestants but also by several hundred Ashkenazim (German Jews) and

Sephardim (Spanish and Portuguese Jews), who established a thriving community in early Savannah.

The trustees were determined to ensure that Georgia became a small farmers' utopia. Rather than selling land the trustees gave it away, but none of the

Utopian designs

colony's settlers could own more than 500 acres. The trustees also outlawed slavery and hard liquor, in order to cultivate habits of industry and sustain equality among whites. This design for a virtuous and egalitarian utopia was greeted with little enthusiasm by Georgians. They pressed for a free market in land and argued that the colony could never prosper until the trustees revoked their ban on slavery. Since the trustees had provided for no elective assembly, settlers could express their discontent only by moving to South Carolina—which many did during the early decades.

In the end, the trustees caved in to the opposition. They revoked their restrictions on land, slavery, and liquor a few years before the king assumed control of the colony in 1752. Under royal control, Georgia continued to develop an ethnically and religiously diverse society like that of South Carolina. In addition, its economy was similarly based on rice cultivation and the Indian trade.

Although South Carolina and the English West Indies were both more opulent and more embattled societies than Virginia and Maryland, the plantation

Similarities among the plantation colonies

colonies stretching from the Chesapeake to the Caribbean had much in common. Everywhere planters depended on a single staple crop, which brought both wealth and political power to those commanding the most land and the most labor. Everywhere the biggest planters relied for their success on the very people whom they deeply feared: enslaved African Americans. Everywhere that fear was reflected in the development of repressive slave codes and the spread of racism throughout all classes of white society.

THE SPANISH BORDERLANDS

When the English founded Jamestown, Spanish settlement in the present-day United States consisted of one feeble fort in southeastern Florida and a single outpost in New Mexico. Hoping both to intimidate privateers who preyed on

St. Augustine and Santa Fe

silver ships and to assert their sovereign claim to the Americas, Spain had established St. Augustine on the Florida coast in 1565. But for decades the place remained a squalid garrison town of a few hundred soldiers and settlers beleaguered by hurricanes, pirates, and Indians. Meanwhile, the Spanish planted a straggling settlement under azure skies and spectacular mesas near present-day Santa Fe in 1598. Their desire was to create colonies in the Southwest that would prove more richly profitable than even those in Central and South America.

Defending both outposts proved so great a drain on royal resources that the Spanish government considered abandoning its footholds in North America.

This Native American drawing on a canyon wall in present-day Arizona represents the progress of the Spanish into the Southwest. The prominence of horses underscores their novelty to the Indians, an initial advantage enjoyed by the invaders. "The most essential thing in new lands is horses," one of Coronado's men emphasized. "They instill greatest fear in the enemy and make the Indians respect the leaders of the army." Many Indian peoples soon put the horse to their own uses, however, and even outshone the Spanish in their riding skills.

Only the pleas of Catholic missionaries, who hoped to convert the native peoples, persuaded the Crown to sustain its support. But even by 1700, St. Augustine could boast only about 1500 souls, a motley assortment of Spaniards, black slaves, and Hispanicized Indians. New Mexico's colonial population amounted to fewer than 3000 Spanish ranchers, soldiers, and clergy, scattered among the "haciendas" (cattle and sheep ranches), "presidios" (military garrisons), and Catholic mission along the Rio Grande river. There, the native Pueblo Indians numbered some 30,000.

Still, during these years the Catholic clergy remained active, creating mission communities designed to incorporate native tribes into colonial society. In

Mission communities New Mexico, Franciscan friars supervised Pueblo women (who traditionally built their people's adobe homes) in the construction of over 30 missions. By 1675 in Florida, perhaps 10,000 Indians were living in 35 Indian villages where the friars came to stay.

Unlike the English, the Spanish projected a place in their colonies for the Indians. Homes, workshops, granaries, and stables clustered around the church. The missionaries taught Indians European agricultural techniques and crafts. At mission schools, adults as well as children learned to say prayers, sing Christian hymns, and speak Spanish. In 1675, when the Bishop of Cuba toured Florida's missions, he spoke enthusiastically of converts who embraced "with devotion the mysteries of our holy faith."

The Indians were selective, however, in the European "mysteries" they chose to adopt. Some natives regarded the friars' presence simply as a means of protecting themselves against the harsher treatment of Spanish soldiers and ranchers. Other Indians used the Spanish presence to give them the upper hand in dealing with rival tribes, just as Powhatan had used white Virginians to further his own designs. And in their religious ceremonies, many natives simply placed Jesus, Mary, and Christian saints beside the other deities they honored.

Indian and Spanish cultures bumped up against each other in material ways as well. When the Spanish at St. Augustine found the climate unsuitable for growing wheat, olives, and grapes, they turned to Indian maize, beans, and squash. Indians adopted domesticated animals from Europe—horses, cattle, sheep, mules, and donkeys. Watermelons and peach trees, brought to the

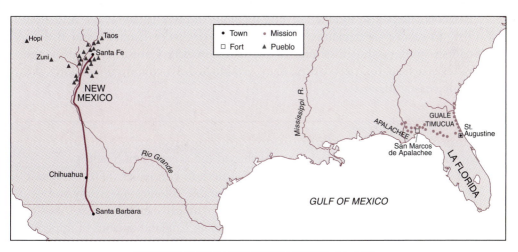

SPANISH MISSIONS IN NORTH AMERICA CA. 1675
From St. Augustine, Spanish missionaries spread north into Guale Indian villages in present-day Georgia and westward among the Indians of Timacua, Apalachee, and Apalachicola. In New Mexico, missions radiated outward from the Rio Grande, as distant as Hopi Pueblo in the west.

Atlantic coast by the Spanish, spread quickly along Indian trade routes, often ahead of Europeans themselves.

To their dismay, Indians discovered that in the long run, becoming "civilized" usually meant learning to work for Spanish masters as docile servants. The labor was harsh enough to send many to an early death. European diseases, too, took a gruesome toll among mission Indians. As the population dropped sharply, the demand by Spanish colonists rose for increasingly scarce Indian labor.

As the abuses increased, so did the resentment. Indians regularly fled the mission settlements; others made life miserable for their "benefactors." One

Indian resistance

padre at Taos Pubelo was served corn tortillas laced with urine and mouse meat. On occasion discontent and anger ignited major insurrections. The most successful was the Pueblo Revolt of 1680, which would drive the Spanish out of New Mexico for more than a decade. Popé, an Indian spiritual leader in Taos, coordinated an uprising of several Pueblo tribes that vented the full force of their hatred of Spanish rule. They killed 400 people in outlying haciendas, burned their Spanish-style houses and churches to the ground, and even exterminated the livestock introduced by the Spanish. The attack wiped out one-fifth of the Spanish population of 2500 and sent survivors scurrying for refuge down Dead Man's Road to El Paso, Texas.

Despite native opposition, the Spanish persisted, especially as they saw their European rivals making headway in North America. As a counterweight to English settlements in South Carolina and French forts near the mouth of the Mississippi River, the Spanish added a second military outpost in Florida, at Pensacola. They also founded several missions in present-day Texas. And after 1769, to secure their claims to the Pacific coast from England and Russia, Spanish soldiers and missionaries began colonizing California. Led by the Franciscan friar Junípero Serra, they established 20 communities along the Pacific coastal plain.

COUNTERPOINT   *Beyond the Black Legend*

For many centuries, the Black Legend shaped the accounts of Spanish colonization written by most English and American chroniclers. This was the conviction that Spaniards were uniquely deplorable colonizers—greedy and corrupt, cruel and treacherous, fanatical and tyrannical—an opinion that had first taken hold during the sixteenth century in an England envious of imperial Spain's new power and wealth. But late in the nineteenth century, American historians rejected this interpretation. Indeed, they embraced its opposite: a strongly pro-Spanish view of the New World's Hispanic past that celebrated the valor of explorers, the dedication of missionaries, the achievements of government officials. That challenge to the Black Legend performed the invaluable service of reminding people in the United States that besides the familiar cast of colonizers among the English, French, and Dutch, the Spanish had also made crucial contributions to their heritage. But it was also a perspective that romanticized Spanish colonialism, all to readily overlooking the toll taken on Native Americans by colonization.

This emphasis on Spain's "frontiering genius" dominated histories of the American Southwest until the 1960s. But thereafter, a new generation of scholars, many of them Chicanos, drew attention to the fact that most inhabitants of the Spanish Southwest were "mestizos" or Mexican. In their view, it is important to recover the story of colonization as it was experienced by native peoples as well as Spaniards, and to recognize that whatever "triumphs" Spain achieved often came at a terrible cost to the Indians. Telling that more complicated story of how cultures cooperated and contended with one another on the borderlands of Spain's empire does not mean reviving the Black Legend. But it is a call for recounting the history of the early Southwest fully, from both sides, an effort that will yield a richer understanding of what was gained and what was lost on this historic American frontier.

Empire . . . utopia . . . independence. . . . For more than a century after the founding of Jamestown in 1607, those dreams inspired the inhabitants of the Chesapeake, the Carolinas and Georgia, the Caribbean, and the American Southwest. The regions served as staging grounds where kings and common-ers, free and unfree, men and women, red, white, and black played out their hopes. Most met only disappointment and many, disaster in the painful decades before the new colonies achieved a measure of stability.

The dream of an expanding empire faltered for the Spanish, who found no new El Dorado in the Southwest. The dream of empire failed, too, when James I and Charles I, England's early Stuart kings, found their power checked by Parliament. And the dream foundered fatally for Powhatan's successors, who were unable to resist both white diseases and land-hungry tobacco planters.

English lords had dreamed of establishing feudal utopias in America. But proprietors like the Calvert family in Maryland and Cooper in the Carolinas found themselves hounded by frontier planters and farmers who sought eco-nomic and political power. Georgia's trustees struggled in vain to nurture their dream of a utopia for the poor. The dream of a Spanish Catholic utopia brought by missionaries to the American Southwest dimmed with Indian resistance.

The dream of independence proved the most deceptive of all, especially for the inhabitants of England's colonies. Just a bare majority of the white ser-vant immigrants to the Chesapeake survived to enjoy freedom. The rest were struck down by disease or worn down at the hands of tobacco barons eager for profit. Not only in the Chesapeake but also in the Caribbean and the Carolinas, real independence eluded the English planters. Poorer people were dependent on richer people for land and leadership; they deferred to them at church and on election days and depended on them to buy crops or to extend credit. Even the richest planters depended on the English and Scottish merchants who supplied them with credit and marketed their crops, as well as the English officials who made colonial policy.

And everywhere in the American South and Southwest, white people's lingering dreams were realized only through the labor of the least free members of colonial America. In the Southwest the Spanish made servants of the Indians. Along the southern Atlantic coast and in the Caribbean, English plantation owners (like the Spanish before them) turned for labor to the African slave trade. Only after slavery became firmly established as a social and legal institution did England's southern colonies begin to settle down and grow: during the late seventeenth century for the Chesapeake region and the early eighteenth for the Carolinas. That stubborn reality would haunt Americans of all colors who continued to dream of freedom and independence.

SIGNIFICANT EVENTS

late 1500s	Formation of Powhatan's confederacy
1603	James I becomes king of England; beginning of Stuart dynasty
1604	First English settlements in the Caribbean
1607	English settle Jamestown
1610	Founding of Santa Fe
1619	First Africans arrive in Virginia
1620s	Tobacco boom in Virginia
1622	White–Indian warfare in Virginia
1624	Virginia becomes a royal colony
1625	Charles I becomes king of England
1632	Calvert founds Maryland
1640s	Sugar boom begins in the Caribbean
1660	Parliament passes the first of the Navigation Acts
1669	First permanent settlement in South Carolina
1676	Bacon's Rebellion in Virginia
1680	Pueblo Revolt in New Mexico
1689	Coode's Rebellion in Maryland
ca. 1700	Rice boom begins in South Carolina
1715	Yamasee uprising in South Carolina
1732	Chartering of Georgia

CHAPTER THREE

The First Century of Settlement in the Colonial North

They came to her one night while she slept. Into her dreams drifted a small island, and on the island were tall trees and living creatures, one of them wearing the fur of a white rabbit. When she told of her vision, no one took her seriously, not even the wise men among her people, shamans and conjurers whose business it was to interpret dreams. No one, that is, until two days later, when the island appeared to all, floating toward shore. On the island, as she had seen, were tall trees, and on their branches—bears. Or creatures that looked so much like bears that the men grabbed their weapons and raced to the beach, eager for the good hunt sent by the gods. They were disappointed. The island was not an island at all, but a strange wooden ship planted with the trunks of trees. And the bears were not bears at all but a strange sort of men whose bodies were covered with hair. Strangest among them, as she had somehow known, was a man dressed all in white. He commanded great respect among the bearlike men as their shaman, or "priest."

In that way, foretold by the dreams of a young woman, the Micmac Indians in 1869 recounted their tribe's first meeting with whites more than two centuries earlier. Uncannily, the traditions of other northern tribes record similar dreams predicting the European arrival: "large canoes with great white wings like those of a giant bird," filled with pale bearded men bearing "long black tubes." Perhaps the dreamers gave shape in their sleep to stories heard from other tribes who had actually seen white strangers and ships. Or perhaps, long before they ever encountered Europeans, these Indians imagined them, just as Europeans fantasized about a new world. The first whites seen by those tribes might have been English or Dutch. But probably, like the party met by the Micmacs, they were French, the most avid early adventurers in the northern reaches of the Americas.

For the time being, few French had dreams of their own about settling in the Americas. Jacques Cartier looked for a Northwest Passage to Asia in 1535,

61

Cartier and Champlain

and instead discovered the St. Lawrence River. But not until 1605 did the French plant a permanent colony, at Port Royal in Acadia (Nova Scotia). Three years later, Samuel de Champlain shifted French interests to the St. Lawrence valley, where he founded Quebec. His plan was to follow the network of rivers and lakes leading from Quebec into the interior, exploring the continent for furs and a passage to the Pacific.

Over the next several decades the handful of soldiers, traders, and missionaries who came to New France established friendly relations with tribes of expert fishers and hunters. There were the Algonquin and Montagnais of the St. Lawrence valley; and in the fertile meadows and rich forests around Georgian Bay there was Huronia, a nation 25,000 strong. In return for French goods, these peoples traded beaver, otter, and raccoon they had trapped. The furs went to make fashionable European hats, while mink and marten were sent to adorn the robes of high-ranking European officials and churchmen. The French had a name for what New France had become by 1630—a *comptoir*, a storehouse for the skins of dead animals, not a proper colony.

That began to change when other French with their own dreams took responsibility for Canada. Louis XIII and his chief minister, Cardinal Richelieu, hoped that American wealth might be the making of France and its monarchs. In the 1630s they granted large tracts of land and a trading monopoly to a group of private investors, the Company of the Hundred Associates. The Associates brought a few thousand French farmers across the Atlantic and scattered them over 200 miles of company lands along the St. Lawrence.

Religious zeal, as much as the hope of profit, spurred France's renewed interest in colonization. Throughout Europe the Catholic church was enjoying a revival of religious piety as a result of the Counterreformation, an effort to correct those abuses that had prompted the Protestant Reformation. To reclaim members lost to Protestantism, the Counterreformation also launched an aggressive campaign of repression in Europe and missionary work abroad.

The shock troops of these missions, not only in the Americas but also in India and Japan, were the Jesuits, members of the Society of Jesus. With

The Jesuits

Richelieu's encouragement Jesuit missionaries streamed into Canada to assist other French settlers in bringing the Indians the "right" kind of Christianity. At first, it seemed unlikely that the Jesuits would shake the Indians' strong belief in the superiority of their own cultures. In Indian eyes these spiritual soldiers were a joke—men with effeminate robes and "very ugly" beards, who were forbidden physical pleasure by their vow of celibacy. The Jesuits were also a nuisance. Not content to preach at French settlements and Indian villages, they undertook "flying" missions to the nomadic tribes, tagging along with Indian trappers. Once in the wilderness the Jesuits were a disaster—tangling in their snowshoes as they marched through wintry drifts, trying for a first and last time to stand in canoes, refusing to carry any weapons, and sponging off the Indians for food and shelter.

Some Indians gradually formed a better opinion of the French and their priests. French traders, known as *coureurs du bois,* and their soldiers often adopted the native way of life and married Indian women. More to the point, the French were still relatively few. Interested primarily in trade, they had no designs on Indian land. The Jesuits, too, won acceptance among some tribes. Their lack of interest in Indian land, furs, and women made them a novelty among white men, while their greater immunity to the diseases that killed many Indians confirmed their claims to superior power. And once the Jesuits got the hang of native tongues, they showed a talent for smooth talk that the Indians, who prized oratory, greatly admired.

Throughout the seventeenth century, the French in North America remained relatively few. Instead, it was English Protestants who established the most populous settlements along the north Atlantic coast, challenging Indian dreams with religious visions of their own. Just as Jesuit crusaders of the Counterreformation shaped the culture of New France, so the zealous followers of John Calvin left their unmistakable imprint on New England.

Converts of the French Jesuits, these women of the Caughnawaga tribe (right) are kneeling before a statue of the Virgin Mary, taking vows of celibacy. One cuts her hair, a symbol of banishing pride, in imitation of the practice of Catholic nuns like Marguerite Bourgeoys (left), who founded a religious community dedicated to the education of young girls.

THE FOUNDING OF NEW ENGLAND

The English regarded the northern part of North America as a place in which only the mad French could see possibility. English fisherfolk who strayed from Newfoundland to the coast of Acadia and New England carried home descriptions of the long, lonely coast, rockbound and rugged. Long winters of numbing cold melted into short summers of steamy heat. There were no minerals to mine, no crops suitable for export, no large native population available for enslaving. The Chesapeake, with its temperate climate and long growing season, seemed a much likelier spot.

But by 1620, worsening conditions at home instilled in some English men and women the mixture of desperation and idealism needed to settle an uninviting, unknown world. Religious differences among English Protestants became a matter of sharper controversy during the seventeenth century. Along with the religious crisis came mounting political tensions and continuing problems of unemployment and recession. The anticipation of even worse times to come swept men and women to the shores of New England.

The Puritan Movement

The settlement of New England started with a king who chose his enemies unwisely. James I, shortly after succeeding Elizabeth I in 1603, vowed to purge England of all radical Protestant reformers. The radicals James had in mind were the Puritans, most of whom were either Presbyterians or Congregationalists. Although both groups of Puritan reformers embraced Calvin's ideas, they differed on the best form of church organization. Individual Presbyterian churches (or congregations) were guided by higher governing bodies of ministers and laypersons. Congregationalists, on the other hand, believed that each congregation should conduct its own affairs independently, answering to no other authority.

King James angered not only the Puritans but also members of Parliament, who objected to his attempts to levy taxes without their consent. The enmity of both Parliament and the Puritans did not bode well for James' reign. In Parliament he faced influential landowners and merchants, who were convinced that law was on their side. And in the Puritans he faced determined zealots who were convinced that God was on their side.

Like all Christians, Protestant and Catholic, the Puritans believed that God was all-knowing and all-powerful. And like all Calvinists, the Puritans emphasized that idea of divine sovereignty known as predestination. At

Predestination the center of their thinking was the belief that God had ordained the outcome of history, including the eternal fate of every human being. The Puritans found comfort in their belief in predestination because it provided their lives with meaning and purpose. They felt assured that a sovereign God was directing the fate of individuals, nations, and all of creation. The Puritans strove to play their parts in that divine drama of history and to discover in their performances some signs of personal salvation.

The divine plan, as the Puritans understood it, called for reforming both church and society along the lines laid down by John Calvin. It seemed to the Puritans that England's government hampered rather than promoted religious purity and social order. It tolerated drunkenness, theatergoing, gambling, extravagance, public swearing, and Sabbath breaking.

What was worse, the state had not done enough to purify the English church of the "corruptions" of Roman Catholicism. The Church of England counted as its members everyone in the nation, saint and sinner alike. To the Puritans, belonging to a church was no birthright. They wished to limit membership and the privileges of baptism and communion to godly men and women. The Puritans also deplored the hierarchy of bishops and archbishops in the Church of England, as well as its elaborate ceremonies in which priests wore ornate vestments. Too many Anglican clergy were "dumb dogges" in Puritan eyes, too poorly educated to instruct churchgoers in the truths of Scripture or to deliver a decent sermon.

Puritan calls for reform

Because English monarchs had refused to take stronger measures to reform church and society, the Puritans became their outspoken critics. Elizabeth I had tolerated this opposition, but James I would not endure it and intended to rid England of these radicals. With some of the Puritans, known as the Separatists, he seemed to succeed.

The Pilgrim Settlement at Plymouth Colony

The Separatists were Congregationalists who concluded that the Church of England was too corrupt to be reformed. They abandoned Anglican worship and met secretly in small congregations. From their first appearance in England during the 1570s, the Separatists suffered persecution from the government—fines, imprisonment, and in a few cases, execution. Always a tiny minority within the Puritan movement, the Separatists were people from humble backgrounds, craftworkers and farmers without the influence to challenge the state. By 1608 some had become so discouraged that they migrated to Holland, where the Dutch government permitted complete freedom of religion. But when their children began to adopt Dutch customs and other religions, some Separatists decided to move again, this time to Virginia.

It can only be imagined what fate would have befallen the unworldly Separatists if they had actually settled in the Chesapeake during the tobacco boom. But a series of mistakes—including an error in charting the course of their ship, the *Mayflower*—landed the little band in New England instead. In November 1620, some 88 Separatist "Pilgrims" set anchor at a place they called Plymouth on the coast of present-day southeastern Massachusetts. They were sick with scurvy, weak from malnutrition, and

Early difficulties

shaken by a shipboard mutiny; and neither the site nor the season invited settlement. As one of their leaders, William Bradford, later remembered:

> For summer being done, all things stand upon them with a weatherbeaten face, and the whole country, full of woods and thickets represented a savage hue. If they looked behind them, there was the mighty ocean which they had passed and was now as a main bar and gulf to separate them from all the civil parts of the world.

Few Pilgrims could have foreseen founding the first permanent white settlement in New England, and many did not live long enough to enjoy the distinction. They had arrived too late to plant crops, and the colonists had failed to bring an adequate supply of food. By the spring of 1621, half of the immigrants had died. English merchants who had financed the *Mayflower* voyage failed to send supplies to the struggling colony.

Plymouth might have become another doomed colony if the Pilgrims had not received better treatment from native inhabitants than they did from their English backers. Samoset and Squanto, two Indians who had learned to speak English from visiting fishermen, introduced the settlers to native strains of corn. They also arranged a treaty between the Pilgrims and the region's main tribe, the Wampanoags.

The Pilgrims also set up a government for their colony, the framework of which was the Mayflower Compact. That agreement provided for a governor and several assistants to advise him, all to be elected annually by Plymouth's adult males. The Plymouth settlers had no clear legal basis for their land claims or their government, for they had neither a royal charter nor approval from the Crown. But English authorities, distracted by problems closer to home, left the tiny colony of farmers alone.

The Mayflower Compact

The Puritan Settlement at Massachusetts Bay

Among the Crown's distractions were two groups of Puritans more numerous and influential than the gentle Pilgrims. They included both the Presbyterians and the majority of Congregationalists who, unlike the Pilgrim Separatists, still considered the Church of England capable of being reformed. But the 1620s brought these Puritans only fresh discouragements. In 1625 Charles I inherited his father's throne and all his enemies. When Parliament attempted to limit the king's power, Charles simply dissolved it in 1629 and proceeded to rule without it. When Puritans pressed for reform, he supported a host of measures proposed by his archbishop, William Laud, for purging England's parishes of ministers with Puritan leanings.

This persecution swelled a second wave of Puritan migration that also drew from the ranks of Congregationalists. Unlike the humble Separatists, these emigrants included merchants, landed gentlemen, and lawyers who organized the

Massachusetts Bay Company in 1629. Those able Puritan leaders aimed to build a better society in America, an example to the rest of the world. Unlike the Separatists, they had a strong sense of mission and destiny. They were not abandoning the English church, they insisted, but merely regrouping for another assault on corruption from across the Atlantic.

Despite the company's Puritan leanings, it somehow obtained a royal charter confirming its title to most of present-day Massachusetts and New Hampshire. Advance parties in 1629 established the town of Salem on the coast well north of Plymouth. In 1630 the company's first governor, John Winthrop, sailed from England with a dozen other company stockholders and a fleet of men and women committed to the Puritan cause. Winthrop, a landed gentleman, was both a tough-minded lawyer and a visionary determined to set an example for the world. "We shall be as a city on a hill," he told his fellow passengers during the crossing on the ship *Arabella*.

Once established in the Bay Colony, Winthrop and the other stockholders transformed the charter for their trading company into the framework of government for a colony. The company's governor became the colony's chief executive; the company's other officers, the governor's assistants. The charter provided for annual elections of the governor and his assistants by company stockholders, known as the freemen. But to create a broad base of support for the new government, Winthrop and his assistants expanded the freemanship in 1631 to include every adult male church member.

Establishing the colony's government

The governor, his assistants, and the freemen together made up the General Court of the colony, which passed all laws, levied taxes, established courts, and made war and peace. In 1634 the whole body of the freemen stopped meeting and instead each town elected representatives or deputies to the General Court. Ten years later, the deputies formed themselves into the lower house of the Bay Colony legislature, and the assistants formed the upper house. By refashioning a company charter into a civil constitution, Massachusetts Bay Puritans gained full control of their future, fulfilling their dream of shaping society, church, and state to their liking.

NEW ENGLAND COMMUNITIES

Contrary to expectations, New England proved more hospitable to the English than the Chesapeake. The character of the migration itself gave New England settlers an advantage, for most arrived in family groups—not as young, single, indentured servants of the sort whose discontents unsettled Virginia society. The heads of New England's first households were typically free men—farmers, artisans, and merchants. Most were skilled and literate. Since husbands usually migrated with their wives and children, the ratio of men to women within the population was fairly evenly balanced.

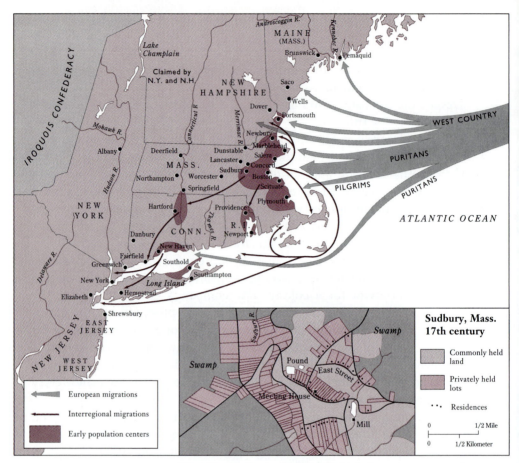

EARLY NEW ENGLAND   New England remained a relatively homogeneous and stable region, with everyday life centered in small towns like Sudbury (located to the west of Boston). Most families lived close to one another in houses clustered around the meetinghouse.

Most immigrants, some 21,000, came in a cluster between 1630 and 1642. Thereafter new arrivals tapered off because of the outbreak of the English Civil War. This relatively rapid settlement fostered solidarity because immigrants shared a common past of persecution and a strong desire to create an ordered society modeled on Scripture.

The "Great Migration"

Stability and Order in Early New England

Puritan emigrants and their descendants thrived in New England. The first generation of colonists lived to an average age of 70, nearly twice as long as Virginians and 10 years longer than English men and women. With 90 percent of all children reaching adulthood, the typical family consisted of seven or eight children who came to maturity. Because of low death

Long-lived New Englanders

rates and high birthrates, the number of New Englanders doubled about every 27 years—while the populations of Europe and the Chesapeake barely reproduced themselves. By 1700, New England and the Chesapeake each had populations of approximately 100,000. But whereas the southern population grew because of continuing immigration, New England's expanded through natural increase.

As immigrants arrived in the Bay Colony after 1630, they carved out an arc of small villages around Massachusetts Bay. Within a decade settlers pressed into Connecticut, Rhode Island, and New Hampshire. Connecticut and Rhode Island received separate charters from Charles II in the 1660s, guaranteeing their residents the rights to land and government. New Hampshire, to which Massachusetts laid claim in the 1640s, did not become a separate colony until 1679. The handful of hardy souls settled along the coast of present-day Maine had also accepted the Massachusetts Bay Colony's authority.

Early New Englanders planted most of their settlements with an eye to stability and order. Unlike the Virginians, who scattered across the Chesapeake to isolated plantations, most New Englanders established tightly knit communities like those they had left behind in England. In fact, migrating families from the *Patterns of settlement* same village or congregation back in England often petitioned the colony government for a tract of land to found their own new town. All prospective adult townsmen initially owned in common this free grant of land, along with the right to set up a local government. Townsmen gradually parceled out among themselves the land granted by the colony. Each family received a lot for a house along with about 150 acres of land in nearby fields. Farmers left many of their acres uncultivated, as a legacy for future generations, for most had only the labor of their own families to work their land. While the Chesapeake abounded with servants and tenant farmers, almost every adult male in rural New England owned property.

The economy that supported most of New England's families and towns offered few chances for anyone to get rich. Farmers could coax a yield of food crops sufficient to feed their families, but the stony soil and long winters could not support cash crops like tobacco, rice, or sugar. With no resources for commercial agriculture, New England farmers also had no incentive to import large numbers of servants and slaves or to create large plantations.

Strong family institutions contributed to New England's order and stability. While the early deaths of parents regularly splintered Chesapeake families, two adult generations were often on hand to encourage order within New England households. Husbands and fathers exacted submission from wives and strict obedience from children, even after young people had come of age.

Congregational Church Order

Equally important in preserving local order was the church. Most settlers formed churches as quickly as they founded towns, and each congregation ran its own affairs, hiring and dismissing ministers, admitting and disciplining members.

A Puritan New Englander Wrestles with Her Faith

Many times hath Satan troubled me concerning the verity of the scriptures, many times by Atheisme how I could know whether there was a God; I never saw any miracles to confirm me, and those which I read of how did I know but they were feigned. That there is a God my Reason would soon tell me by the wondrous workes that I see, the vast frame of the Heaven and the Earth, the order of all things, night and day, Summer and Winter, Spring and Autumne, the dayly providing for this great houshold upon the Earth, the preserving and directing of All to its proper end. The consideration of these things would with amazement certainly resolve me that there is an Eternall Being.

But how should I know he is such a God as I worship in Trinity, and such a Saviour as I rely upon? though: this hath thousands of Times been suggested to mee, yet God hath helped me over. I have argued thus with myself. That there is a God I see. If ever this God hath revealed himself, it must bee in his word, and this must bee it or none. Have I not found that operation by it no humane Invention can work upon the Soul? hath not Judgments befallen Diverse who have scorned and contemd it? hath it not been preserved through: All Ages maugre all the heathen Tyrants and all of the enemyes who have opposed it? Is there any story but that which showes the beginnings of Times, and how the world came to bee as wee see? Doe wee not know the prophecyes in it fulfilled which could not have been so long foretold by any but God himself?

John Harvard Ellis, Ed., *The Works of Anne Bradstreet in Prose and Verse*. Charlestown, MA A.E. Cutter, 1867, pp. 3–10.

Membership in New England's Congregational churches was voluntary, but it was not available for the asking. Those wishing to join had to satisfy the church that they had experienced "conversion." Puritans understood conversion to mean a turning of the heart and soul toward God, a spiritual rebirth that was reflected by a pious and disci-

Church membership

plined life. In New England, believers who could credibly relate their conversions to the minister and other church members gained admission to membership. Most early New Englanders sought and received church membership, a status that entitled them to receive communion and to have their children baptized. Widespread membership also enabled the churches to oversee public morality and to expel wayward members for misbehavior.

Everywhere in New England except Rhode Island, civil laws obliged everyone to attend worship services on the Sabbath and to pay taxes to support

Separation of church and state

Congregationalist ministers. Although the separation between church and state was incomplete, it had progressed further in New England than in most nations of Europe. New England ministers did not serve as officers in the civil government, and the Congregational churches owned no property. By contrast, Catholic and Anglican church officials wielded real temporal power in European states, and the churches held extensive tracts of land.

Colonial Governments

The final institution fostering order in daily life was the town meeting, the basis of local self-government. In every New England village, all white adult male inhabitants met regularly at the meetinghouse to decide matters of local importance. Nearly all of them could vote for town officials. The town fathers generally set the meeting's agenda and offered advice, but the unanimous consent of townsmen determined all decisions. Reaching consensus was a practical necessity because the town fathers had no means of enforcing unpopular decisions.

Colony governments in early New England also evolved into representative and responsive institutions. Typically the central government of each colony, like the General Court of Massachusetts Bay, consisted of a governor and a bicameral legislature, including an upper house, or council, and a lower house, or assembly. All officials were elected annually by the freemen—white adult men entitled to vote in colony elections. Voting qualifications varied, but the number of men enfranchised made up a much broader segment of society than in seventeenth-century England.

Communities in Conflict

Not every community in early New England was a small, self-sufficient farming village in which strong families, town fathers, and watchful churches pursued the ideals of Puritanism. Along the edges of settlement, several towns departed dramatically from the usual patterns.

One such outpost was Marblehead, a fishing port on the Massachusetts coast settled by immigrant fisherfolk from every port in the British Isles. Most

Commerce and "company towns"

eked out a bare existence as suppliers and employees of Boston merchants, who managed Marblehead's fishery. Single men dominated the population, and their brawls and drunken cavorting often spilled out of the town's many taverns into the streets. Local government remained weak for most of the seventeenth century, and inhabitants managed to avoid founding a local church for 50 years.

The rest of Massachusetts tolerated chaotic "company towns" like Marblehead because their inhabitants produced what few commodities New England could trade to the rest of the world. Marblehead's fish found a ready market in Catholic Spain and Portugal. In exchange, New Englanders acquired wine, sugar, molasses, textiles, and iron goods—commodities that they needed but could not produce.

More commonly, conflicts in New England towns were likely to arise over religious differences. Although most New Englanders called themselves Puritans and Congregationalists, the very fervency of their convictions often led them to disagree about how best to carry out the teachings of the Bible and the ideas of John Calvin. The Puritans of Plymouth Colony, for example, believed that religious purity required renouncing the Church of England, while those of the Bay Colony clung to the hope of reforming the Anglican church from within.

Conflict over religious differences

Even within Massachusetts Bay, Puritans differed among themselves about how to organize their churches. During the first decades of settlement, those differences led to the founding of new colonies in New England. In 1636 Thomas Hooker, the minister of Cambridge, Massachusetts, led part of his congregation to Connecticut, where they established the first English settlement. Somewhat more liberal than other Bay Puritans, Hooker favored more lenient standards for church membership. He also opposed the Bay's policy of limiting voting in colony elections to church members. By contrast, New Haven (a separate colony until it became part of Connecticut in 1662) was begun in 1638 by strict Congregationalists who found Massachusetts too liberal. Massachusetts recognized its southern neighbors, including Separatist Plymouth, as colonies within the Puritan fold, respectable suburbs of Winthrop's city on a hill.

Heretics

The same could not be said of Rhode Island, for that little colony on Narragansett Bay began as a ghetto for heretics. While voluntary migration formed Connecticut and New Haven, enforced exile filled Rhode Island with men and women whose radical ideas unsettled the rest of Massachusetts.

Roger Williams, Rhode Island's founder, had come to New England in 1631, serving as a respected minister of Salem. But soon Williams announced

Roger Williams that he was a Separatist, like the Pilgrims of Plymouth. He encouraged the Bay Colony to break all ties to the corrupt Church of England. He also urged a more complete separation of church and state than most New Englanders were prepared to accept, and later in his career he endorsed full religious toleration. Finally, Williams denounced the Bay's charter—the legal document that justified Massachusetts' existence—on the grounds that the king had no right to grant land that he had not purchased from the Indians. When Williams boldly suggested that Massachusetts actually inform the king of his mistake, angry authorities prepared to deport him. Instead Williams fled the colony in the dead of winter to live with the Indians. In 1636, he became the founder of Providence, later to be part of Rhode Island.

Another charismatic heretic from Massachusetts arrived soon after. Anne Hutchinson, a skilled midwife and the spouse of a wealthy merchant, came to *Anne Hutchinson* Boston in 1634. Enthusiasm for her minister, John Cotton, started her on a course of explaining his sermons to gatherings of her neighbors—and then to elaborating ideas of her own in which many of the Bay's leaders detected the dangerous heresy of "Antinomianism."

The Bay Puritans, like all Calvinists, denied that men and women could "earn" salvation simply by obeying God's laws. They held that salvation came through divine grace, not human actions. But many Puritans believed that the ability to lead an upright life was a natural consequence of being saved. A minority in the Puritan movement, including Anne Hutchinson, rejected that notion. Hutchinson contended that outward obedience to God's laws indicated nothing whatsoever about the soul's inward state. Those predestined for salvation knew it intuitively, she said, and could recognize the same grace in others.

When most of the Bay Colony's ministers rejected her views, Anne Hutchinson denounced them. Her attack on the clergy, along with the popularity of her preaching among many important merchant families, prompted the Bay Colony government to expel Hutchinson and her followers for sedition in 1638. She settled briefly in Rhode Island before moving on to Long Island, where she died in an Indian attack.

Colony leaders were especially critical of Hutchinson because she was a woman, who by their lights should have remained less assertive of her beliefs. *Quakers* In later religious controversies, the devil of dissent assumed the shape of a woman as well. The Quakers, one of the most radical religious groups produced by the Protestant Reformation in England, sent Ann Austin and Mary Fisher as their first missionaries to the Bay. Women were among the most active early converts, and one of them, Mary Dyer, was hanged for her persistence, along with three Quaker men, in 1656. Like the Antinomians, the Quakers attached great significance to an inward state of grace, called the "Light Within." Through that inner light, the Quakers claimed, God revealed his will directly to believers, enabling men and women to attain spiritual perfection. Because they held that everyone had immediate access to God, the Quakers also dispensed with a clergy and the sacraments.

Goodwives and Witches

If Anne Hutchinson and Mary Dyer had been men, their ideas would still have been deemed heretical. On the other hand, if these women had been men, they might have found other ways to express their intelligence and magnetism. But life in colonial New England offered women, especially married women, little scope for their talents.

Most adult women were hardworking farmwives who cared for large households of children. Between marriage and middle age, most New England wives were pregnant except when breast-feeding. When they were not nursing or minding children, mothers were producing and preparing much of what was consumed and worn by their families. They planted vegetable gardens and pruned fruit trees, salted beef and pork and pressed cider, milked cows and churned butter, kept bees and tended poultry, cooked and baked, washed and ironed, spun, wove, and sewed. While husbands and sons engaged in farmwork that changed with the seasons, took trips to taverns and mills, and went off to hunt or fish, housebound wives and daughters were locked into a humdrum routine with little time for themselves.

By placing a woman at the center of his composition, the artist who sketched this Quaker meeting called attention to one of that sect's most controversial practices. Women were allowed to speak in Quaker worship services and to preach at public gatherings of non-Quakers.

Women suffered legal disadvantages as well. English common law and colonial legal codes accorded married women no control over property. Wives could

Legal barriers for women

not sue or be sued, they could not make contracts, and they surrendered to their husbands any property that they possessed before marriage. Divorce was almost impossible to obtain until the late eighteenth century. Only widows and a few single women had the same property rights as men, but they could not vote in colony elections.

The one arena in which women could attain something approaching equal standing with men was the churches. Women wielded the greatest influence among the Quakers. They could speak in Quaker meetings, preach as missionaries, and oversee the behavior of other female members in "women's meetings." Puritan women could not become ministers, but after the 1660s they made up the majority of church members. In some churches membership enabled them to vote for ministerial candidates and to voice opinions about admitting and disciplining members. Puritan doctrine itself rejected the medieval Catholic suspicion of women as "a necessary evil," seeing them instead as "a necessary good." Even so, the Puritan ideal of the virtuous woman was a chaste, submissive "helpmeet," a wife and mother who served God by serving men.

Communities sometimes responded to assertive women with accusations of witchcraft. Like most early modern Europeans, New Englanders believed

Witchcraft

in wizards and witches, men and women who were said to acquire supernatural powers by signing a compact with Satan. A total of 344 New Englanders were charged with witchcraft during the first century of settlement, with the notorious Salem Village episode of 1692 producing the largest outpouring of accusations and 20 executions. More than three-quarters of all accused witches were women, usually middle-aged and older, and most of those accused were regarded as unduly independent. Before they were charged with witchcraft, many had been suspected of heretical religious beliefs, others of sexual impropriety. Still others had inherited or stood to inherit property.

COUNTERPOINT   *Bewitched by Salem Village*

Few events in American history have compelled the imagination of historians more than the witchcraft hysteria that wracked one small New England village early in the 1690s. It is true that colonial America witnessed nothing like the recurring mass panics over witchcraft that swept through early modern Europe for centuries and resulted in the executions of thousands of men and women. The outbreak of accusations that led to the deaths of 20 accused Salem Village "witches" was, as one eminent American historian observed, "a small episode in the history of a great superstition." Even so, many scholars have been lured into closely investigating the Salem tragedy in the hope that it may shed light on that lost world of the past in which it took place and lead to a richer understanding of early New England society and culture.

In recent years, many historians studying the Salem Village tragedy—and, indeed, witchcraft in general—have focused on the preponderance of women accused of that crime. For those scholars, what witchcraft panics illustrate is the deep and widespread hostility to women in all early modern cultures. But other scholars think that women were targeted as witches only because they were the most vulnerable members of these societies and thus fell prey to being scapegoated during periods of uncertainty and instability. In the case of Salem Village, some historians argue that witchcraft hysteria arose in response to communal divisions over commercial development—that subsistence farmers who both resented and coveted the new wealth of their more profit-minded neighbors vented their frustrations in charges of witchcraft. Other historians believe that political upheavals in New England during the early 1690s so disrupted the local judicial system that Salem Villagers seeking redress for their grievances fell back on charging their adversaries with witchcraft, charges that were handled by specially appointed courts. Still other historians see the late seventeenth century as a period when New England Puritans felt deeply threatened by the growth of rival groups like the Quakers and Anglicans, noting that a high percentage of those accused of witchcraft came from families related by blood or marriage to those religious "outsiders." All of these interpretations of what happened in Salem Village enrich our understanding of the role of witchcraft beliefs in early New England and the changing character of that society.

Whites and Indians in Early New England

Most white settlers in New England, like those in the Chesapeake, condemned the "savagery" and "superstition" of the Indians around them. Unlike the French, however, the Puritans made only a few efforts to spread their faith to the Indians.

In truth, the "godly" New Englanders had more in common with the natives in the region than they might have cared to admit. Perhaps 100,000 Algonkian-speaking men and women lived in the area reaching from the Kennebec River in Maine to Cape Cod. Like the Puritans, they relied for food on fishing in spring and summer, hunting in winter, cultivating and harvesting food crops in spring and fall. And, to an even greater degree than among white settlers, Indian political authority was local. Within each village, a single leader known as the "sachem" or "sagamore" directed economic life, administered justice, and negotiated with other tribes and English settlers. Like New England's town fathers, a sachem's power depended on keeping the trust and consent of his people.

Puritans and Indians

The Indians of New England shared one other characteristic with all Europeans: they quarreled frequently with neighboring nations. The antagonism among the English, Spanish, Dutch, and French was matched by the hostilities among the Abenaki, Pawtucket, Massachusett, Narragansett, and

Wampanoag tribes of the north Atlantic coast. Rivalries kept different tribes from forging an effective defense against white colonials. New England settlers, like those in the Chesapeake, exploited Indian disunity.

The first New England natives to put up a strong resistance to Europeans were the Pequots, whom white settlers encountered when they began to push *War* into Connecticut. Had the Pequots allied with their neighbors, the Narragansetts, they could have retarded English expansion. But the Narragansetts, bitter enemies of the Pequots, allied with the English instead. Together they virtually destroyed the Pequots in 1637. This playing of one tribe off against another finally left the Wampanoags of Plymouth as the only coastal tribe capable of resisting Puritan expansion. In 1675, their sachem Metacomet, whom the English called King Philip, organized an uprising that devastated white frontier settlements.

Faced with shortages of food and ammunition, Metacomet called for assistance from the Abenaki, a powerful Maine tribe, and from the Iroquois of New York. But those tribes withheld their support, not wishing to jeopardize their trade with the English. In the summer of 1676 Metacomet met his death in battle, and the Indian offensive collapsed. In seventeenth-century New England, as in the Chesapeake, the clash between Indians and white settlers threatened the very survival of both groups. Perhaps 20,000 whites and Indians lost their lives in Metacomet's War.

THE MIDDLE COLONIES

The inhabitants of the Middle Colonies—New York and New Jersey, Pennsylvania and Delaware—enjoyed more secure lives than most southern colonials. But they lacked the common bonds that lent stability to early New England. Instead, in each of the Middle Colonies a variety of ethnic and religious groups vied for wealth from farming and the fur trade and contended bitterly against governments that commanded little popular support.

The Founding of New Netherlands

New York was settled in 1624 as New Netherlands, an outpost of the Dutch West India Company. Far more impressed with the commercial potential of Africa and South America, the company limited its investment in North America to a few fur trading posts along the Hudson, Connecticut, and Delaware rivers.

Intent only on trade, the Dutch had little desire to plant permanent colonies abroad because they enjoyed prosperity and religious freedom at home. Most of New Netherlands' few settlers clustered in the village of New Amsterdam on Manhattan Island at the mouth of the Hudson. One hundred and fifty miles upriver lay a fur trading outpost, Fort Orange (Albany), and by the 1660s a few other farming villages dotted the west end of Long Island, upper Manhattan

Ethnic and religious diversity

Island, Staten Island, and the lower Hudson valley. In all, there were fewer than 9000 New Netherlanders—a mixture of Dutch, Belgians, French, English, Portuguese, Swedes, Finns, and Africans. The first blacks had arrived in 1626, imported as slaves; some later became free, intermarried with whites, and even owned white indentured servants.

This ethnic diversity ensured a variety of religions. Although the Dutch Reformed Church predominated, other early New Netherlanders included Lutherans, Quakers, and Catholics. There were Jews as well, refugees from Portuguese Brazil, who were required by law to live in a ghetto in New Amsterdam. Yet another religious group kept to themselves by choice: New England Congregationalists. Drawn by promises of cheap land and self-government, they planted farming communities on eastern Long Island during the 1640s.

New Netherlanders knew that their cultural differences hampered the prospects for a stable social and political life. The Dutch West India Company made matters worse by appointing corrupt, dictatorial governors who ruled without an elective assembly. The company also provided little protection for its outlying settlers; when it did attack neighboring Indian nations, it did so savagely, triggering terrible retaliations. By the time the company went bankrupt in 1654, it had virtually abandoned its American colony.

New Englanders on Long Island, who had insisted on a free hand in governing their own villages, now began to demand a voice in running the colony as well. By the 1660s they were openly challenging Dutch rule and calling for English conquest of the colony.

English Rule in New York

Taking advantage of the disarray in New Netherlands, Charles II ignored Dutch claims in North America and granted his brother James, the duke of York, a proprietary charter there. It granted James all of New Netherlands to Delaware Bay, as well as Maine, Martha's Vineyard, and Nantucket Island. In 1664 James sent an invading fleet, whose mere arrival caused the Dutch to surrender.

English management of the new colony, renamed New York, did little to ease ethnic tensions or promote political harmony. The Dutch resented English rule, and only after a generation of intermarriage and acculturation did that resentment fade. James also failed to win friends among Long Island's New Englanders. He grudgingly gave in to their demand for an elective assembly in 1683, but rejected its first act, the Charter of Liberties, which would have guaranteed basic political rights. The chronic political strife discouraged prospective settlers. By 1698 the colony numbered only 18,000 inhabitants, and New York City, the former New Amsterdam, was an overgrown village of a few thousand.

Many French colonials showed an abiding interest in and respect for native American culture. Among them was George Heriot, who produced a series of watercolor sketches of Iroquois ceremonies, including this portrayal of a calumet (or peace-pipe) dance.

The League of the Iroquois

While New York's colonists wrangled, many of its native Indians succumbed to the same pressures that shattered the natives of New England and the Chesapeake. Only one tribe of Indians in New York's interior, the Iroquois nation, actually gained greater strength from contacts with whites.

Like the tribes of South Carolina, the Indians of northern New York became important suppliers of furs to white traders. As in the Carolinas, powerful tribes dominated the interior, far outnumbering white settlers. The handful of Dutch and, later, English traders had every reason to keep peace with the Indians. But the fur trade heightened tensions among interior tribes. At first the Mahicans had supplied furs to the Dutch, but by 1625 the game in their territory had been exhausted and the Dutch had taken their business to the Iroquois. When the Iroquois faced the same extinction of fur-bearing animals in the 1640s, they found a solution. With Dutch encouragement and Dutch guns, the Iroquois virtually wiped out the neighboring Huron nation and seized their hunting grounds.

The Indian trade

The destruction of the Huron made the Iroquois the undisputed power on the northern frontier. More successfully than Powhatan's confederacy in the Chesapeake, the League of the Iroquois welded different tribes into a coherent political unit. This union of the Five Nations (to become six after the Tuscaroras joined them in 1712) included the Mohawk, Oneida, Onondaga, Cayuga, and Seneca tribes and stretched from the lands around the upper Hudson in the east to the Genesee River in the west. Political strength enabled the Iroquois to deal effectively with their Algonkian rivals in New England as well as European newcomers. As the favored clients of the Dutch and, later, the English, they became opponents of the French.

The League's strength rested on an even more remarkable form of political and social organization, one in which men and women shared authority. The

Iroquois women

most powerful women anywhere in colonial North America were the matriarchs of the Iroquois. Matrilineal kinship formed the basis of Iroquois society, as it did among the Pueblos of the Southwest. When men married, they joined their wives' families, households over which the eldest female member presided. But unlike Pueblo women, Iroquois matriarchs also wielded political influence. The most senior Iroquois women selected the confederation's council of chiefs, advised them, and "dehorned"—removed from office—those deemed unfit. Throughout the eighteenth century, the League of the Iroquois continued to figure as a major force in North America.

The Founding of New Jersey

New Jersey took shape in the shadow of its stronger neighbors to the north. Its inhabitants were less united and powerful than the Iroquois, less wealthy and influential than New Yorkers, and less like-minded and self-governing than New Englanders.

Confusion attended New Jersey's beginnings. The lands lying west of the Hudson and east of the Delaware River had been part of the Duke of York's proprietary grant. But in 1664 he gave about 5 million of these acres to Lord Berkeley and Sir George Carteret, two of his favorites who were already involved in the proprietary colonies of the Carolinas. New Jersey's new owners guaranteed settlers land, religious freedom, and a representative assembly in exchange for a small quitrent, an annual fee for the use of the land. The proprietors' terms promptly drew Puritan settlers from New Haven, Connecticut. At the same time, unaware that James had already given New Jersey to Berkeley and Carteret, New York's Governor Richard Nicolls granted Long Island Puritans land there.

More complications ensued when Berkeley and Carteret decided to divide New Jersey into east and west and sell both halves to Quaker investors—a prospect that outraged New Jersey's Puritans. Although some English Friends migrated to West Jersey, the Quakers quickly decided that two Jerseys were less desirable than one Pennsylvania and resold both East and West Jersey to speculators. In the end the Jerseys became a patchwork of religious and ethnic groups. Settlers who shared a common religion or national origin formed communities and established small family farms. When the Crown finally reunited east and west as a single royal colony in 1702, New Jersey was overshadowed by settlements not only to the north but now, also, to the south.

Quaker Odysseys

Religious and political idealism similar to that of the Puritans inspired the settlement of Pennsylvania, making it an oddity among the Middle Colonies. The oddity began with an improbable founder, William Penn. Young Penn devoted his early years to disappointing his distinguished father, Sir William Penn, an admiral in the royal navy. Several years after being expelled from college, he finally chose a career that may have made the admiral yearn for mere disappointment: young Penn undertook a lifelong commitment to put into practice Quaker teachings. By the 1670s he had emerged as one of the Society of Friends' acknowledged leaders.

    The Quakers behaved in ways and believed in ideas that most people regarded as odd. They dressed in a deliberately plain and severe manner. They

Quaker beliefs withheld from their social superiors the customary marks of respect, such as bowing, kneeling, and removing their hats. They refused to swear oaths or to make war. They allowed women public roles of religious leadership. That pattern of behavior reflected their egalitarian ideals, the belief that all men and women shared equally in the "Light Within." Some 40,000 English merchants, artisans, and farmers embraced Quakerism by 1660, and many suffered fines, imprisonment, and corporal punishment.

    Since the English upper class has always prized eccentricity among its members, it is not surprising that Penn, despite his Quakerism, remained a favorite

Young William Penn (1666) at about the time he became a Quaker.

Pennsylvania established

of Charles II. More surprising is that the king's favor took the extravagant form of presenting Penn in 1681 with all the land between New Jersey and Maryland. Perhaps the king was repaying Penn for the large sum that his father had lent the Stuarts. Or perhaps the king was hoping to export England's Quakers to an American colony governed by his trusted personal friend.

Penn envisioned that his proprietary colony would provide a refuge for Quakers while producing quitrents for himself. To publicize his settlement, he distributed pamphlets praising its attractions throughout the British Isles and Europe. The response was overwhelming: by 1700 its population stood at 21,000. The only early migration of equal magnitude was the Puritan colonization of New England.

Patterns of Settlement

Perhaps half of Pennsylvania's settlers arrived as indentured servants, while the families of free farmers and artisans made up the rest. The majority were Quakers from Britain, Holland, and Germany, but the colonists also included Catholics, Lutherans, Baptists, Anglicans, and Presbyterians. In 1682 when Penn purchased and annexed the Three Lower Counties (later the colony of Delaware), his settlement included the Dutch, Swedes, and Finns living there, about 1000 people.

Quakers from other colonies—West Jersey, Maryland, and New England—also flocked to the new homeland. Those experienced settlers brought skills and connections that contributed to Pennsylvania's rapid economic growth. Farmers sowed their rich lands into a sea of wheat, which merchants exported to the Caribbean. The center of the colony's trade was Philadelphia, a superb natural harbor situated at the confluence of the Delaware and Schuylkill rivers.

In contrast to New England's landscape of villages, the Pennsylvania countryside beyond Philadelphia was dotted with dispersed farmsteads. Commercial agriculture required larger farms, which kept settlers at greater distances from one another. As a result, the county rather than the town became the basic unit of local government in Pennsylvania.

Another reason that farmers did not need to cluster their homes within a central village was that the coastal Indians, the Lenni Lenapes (also called

Quakers and Indians

Delawares by the English), posed no threat. Thanks to two of the odder Quaker beliefs—their commitment to pacifism and their conviction that the Indians rightfully owned their land—peace prevailed between native inhabitants and newcomers. Before Penn sold any land to white settlers, he purchased it from the Indians.

"Our Wildernesse flourishes as a Garden," Penn declared late in 1683, and in fact, his colony lived up to its promises. New arrivals readily acquired good land on liberal terms, while Penn's Frame of Government instituted a representative assembly and guaranteed all inhabitants the basic English civil liberties and complete freedom of worship.

Quakers and Politics

Even so, Penn's colony suffered constant political strife. Rich investors whom he had rewarded with large tracts of land and trade monopolies dominated the council, which held the sole power to initiate legislation. That power and Penn's own claims as proprietor set the stage for controversy. Members of the representative assembly battled for the right to initiate legislation. Farmers opposed Penn's efforts to collect quitrents. The Three Lower Counties agitated for separation, their inhabitants feeling no loyalty to Penn or Quakerism.

Penn finally bought peace at the price of approving a complete revision of his original Frame of Government. In 1701 the Charter of Privileges, Penn-

Penn's compromises

sylvania's new constitution, stripped the council of its legislative power, leaving it only the role of advising the governor. The charter also limited Penn's privileges as proprietor to the ownership of ungranted land and the power to veto legislation. Thereafter an elective unicameral assembly, the only single-house legislature in the colonies, dominated Pennsylvania's government.

As Pennsylvania prospered, Philadelphia became the commercial and cultural center of England's North American empire. Gradually the interior of Pennsylvania filled with immigrants who harbored no "odd" ideas about Indian rights—mainly Germans and Scots-Irish—and the Lenni Lenapes and other tribes were bullied into moving farther west. As for William Penn, he returned to England and spent time in a debtors' prison after being defrauded by his unscrupulous colonial agents. He died in 1718, an ocean away from his American utopia.

ADJUSTMENT TO EMPIRE

In the year 1685, from the city of London, a new English king surveyed his American domains. The former duke of York, now James II, had hoped that America might contribute to the making of kings and queens. Like earlier Stuart monarchs, James hoped to ride to absolute power on a wave of colonial wealth, just as Spain's monarchs had during the previous century. To encourage colonial settlement, Stuart kings had chartered the private trading companies of Virginia, Plymouth, and Massachusetts Bay. They had rewarded their aristocratic favorites with huge tracts of land: Maryland, the Carolinas, New York, New Jersey, and Pennsylvania.

Yet to what end? Although North America now abounded in places named in honor of English monarchs, the colonies themselves lacked any strong ties to the English state. In only three colonies—New Hampshire, New York, and Virginia—

did England exercise direct control through royally appointed governors and councils. Until Parliament passed the first Navigation Acts in 1660, England had not even set in place a coherent policy for regulating colonial trade. What was more disheartening, ungrateful colonists were resisting their duty to enrich the English state and the Stuarts. New Englanders seemed the worst of the lot: they ignored the Navigation Acts altogether and traded openly with the Dutch.

What was needed, in James's view, was an assertion of royal authority over America, starting with Massachusetts. His brother, Charles II, had laid the

Control over the colonies tightened

groundwork in 1673 by persuading Parliament to authorize the placement of customs agents in colonial ports to suppress illegal trade. When reports of defiance continued to surface, the king delivered the decisive blow: an English court in 1684 revoked Massachusetts' original charter, leaving the Bay Colony without a legal basis for its claim to self-government.

The Dominion of New England

Charles died the following year, leaving James II to finish the job of reorganization. In 1686, at the king's urging, the Lords of Trade consolidated the colonies of Connecticut, Plymouth, Massachusetts Bay, Rhode Island, and New Hampshire into a single entity to be ruled by a royal governor and a royally appointed council. By 1688 he had added New York and New Jersey to that domain, now called the Dominion of New England. Showing the typical Stuart distaste for representative government, James also abolished all northern colonial assemblies. The king's aim to centralize authority over such a large territory made the Dominion not only a royal dream but a radical experiment in English colonial administration.

Sir Edmund Andros, a tough professional soldier sent to Boston as the Dominion's royal governor, quickly came to rival his king for the title of most

Edmund Andros

unpopular man north of Pennsylvania. Andros set in force policies that outraged every segment of New England society. He strictly enforced the Navigation Acts, which slowed down commerce and infuriated merchants and workers in the maritime trades. He commandeered a Boston meetinghouse for Anglican worship and immediately angered devout Congregationalists. He abolished all titles to land granted under the old charter, alarming farmers and speculators. He imposed arbitrary taxes, censored the press, and forbade all town meetings, thereby alienating almost everyone.

The Aftershocks of the Glorious Revolution

About the same time northern colonials were reaching the end of their patience with Andros, the English decided they had taken enough from his royal master. James II had revealed himself to be the wrong sort of Stuart—one who tried to dispense with Parliament and embraced Catholicism besides. As they had before with Charles I, Parliament dispensed with the king. In a quick, bloodless coup d'état known as the Glorious Revolution, Parliament forced James into exile in 1688 and placed on the throne of England his daughter, Mary, and her Dutch husband, William of Orange. Mary was the right sort of Stuart. A staunch Protestant, she agreed to rule with Parliament.

The deposing of James II proved so popular among New Englanders that even before Parliament had officially proclaimed William and Mary king and

The Dominion overthrown

queen, Boston's militia seized Governor Andros and sent him home in April 1689. William and Mary officially dismembered the Dominion and reinstated representative assemblies everywhere in the northern colonies. Connecticut and Rhode Island were restored their old charters, but Massachusetts received a new charter in 1691. Under its terms Massachusetts, Plymouth, and present-day Maine were combined into a single royal colony headed by a governor appointed by the Crown rather than elected by the people. The charter also made property ownership rather than church membership the basis of voting rights and imposed religious toleration.

Leisler's Rebellion

The new charter did not satisfy all New Englanders, but they soon adjusted to the political realities of royal rule. By contrast, the violent political infighting that plagued New York mirrored that colony's instability.

Word of revolution in England and rebellion in Massachusetts roused New Yorkers into armed opposition in May 1689. Declaring their loyalty to William and Mary, the New York City militia forced from office Andros' second-in-command, the Dominion's lieutenant governor. In his place they installed one of their own leaders, Jacob Leisler, a German merchant.

Since James II had won few friends in New York, the rebellion met no opposition. But Leisler could not win commanding support for his authority. While Protestant Dutch farmers, artisans, and small shopkeepers stood by him, the leaders of the colony—an intermarried elite of English and Dutch merchants—considered Leisler an upstart who threatened their own influence. After royal rule was restored to New York in 1691, a jury comprised of Englishmen convicted Leisler and his son-in-law, Jacob Milburne, of treason. Their executions guaranteed a long life to the bitter political rivalries that Leisler's rebellion had fueled in New York.

Royal Authority in America in 1700

In the wake of upheaval at home and in North America, England focused its imperial policy on reaping maximum profit from the colonial trade. In 1696

Closer regulation of trade

Parliament enlarged the number of customs officials stationed in each colony to enforce the Navigation Acts. To help prosecute smugglers, Parliament established colonial vice-admiralty courts, tribunals without juries presided over by royally appointed justices. To keep current on all colonial matters, the king appointed a new Board of Trade to replace the old Lords of Trade. The new enforcement procedures generally succeeded in discouraging smuggling and in channeling colonial trade through England.

That was enough for England and its monarchs for half a century thereafter. English kings and queens gave up any dreams of imposing the kind of centralized administration of colonial life that James II had attempted in his Dominion of New England. To be sure, royal control had increased over the previous half century. By 1700 royal governments had been established in Virginia, New York, Massachusetts, and New Hampshire. New Jersey, the Carolinas, and Georgia would shortly be added to the list. Royal rule meant that the monarch appointed governors and (everywhere except Massachusetts) also appointed their councils. Royally appointed councils could veto any law passed by a colony's representative assembly, royally appointed governors could veto any law passed by both houses, and the Crown could veto any law passed by both houses and approved by the governor.

Despite the ability to veto, the sway of royal power remained more apparent than real after 1700. The Glorious Revolution asserted once and for all that

The limits of royal power

Parliament's authority—rule by the legislative branch of government—would be supreme in the governing of England. In the colonies members of representative assemblies grew more adept at dealing with royal governors and more protective of their rights. They guarded most jealously their strongest lever of power—the right of the lower houses to levy taxes.

The political reality of the assemblies' power reflected a social reality as well. No longer mere outposts along the Atlantic, the colonies of 1700 were becoming more firmly rooted societies. Their laws and traditions were based not only on what they had brought from England but on the conditions of life in America. That social reality had already ensured that Stuart ambitions to shape the future of North America would prove no more practical than the designs of lordly proprietors or the dreams of religious reformers.

Still, the dream of empire would revive among England's rulers in the middle of the eighteenth century—in part because the same dream had never died among the rulers of France. By 1663, Louis XIV had decided that kings could succeed where the enterprise of private French traders had failed: he placed New France under royal rule. Thereafter France's fortunes in America steadily improved. Soldiers strengthened Canada's defenses, colonists and traders expanded the scope of French influence, and the Jesuits made more converts among the interior tribes. Under the Sun King, as Louis was known to admiring courtiers, royal rule became absolute, and the hopes for empire grew absolutely. Louis and his heirs would continue their plans for the making of France by contending for empire with the English, both in the Old World and in the New.

SIGNIFICANT EVENTS

late 1500s	Formation of the League of the Iroquois
1535	Cartier discovers the St. Lawrence
1608	Champlain founds Quebec on the St. Lawrence; Separatists flee to Holland
1620	Pilgrims land at Plymouth
1624	Dutch found New Netherlands
1630	Winthrop fleet arrives at Massachusetts Bay
1637	Pequot War
1642–1648	English Civil War
1649	Charles I executed
1660	English monarchy restored: Charles II becomes king
1664	New Netherlands becomes English New York; founding of New Jersey
1675–1676	Metacomet's War
1681	Founding of Pennsylvania
1685	James II becomes king of England
1686	Dominion of New England established
1688	Glorious Revolution; William and Mary become monarchs of England
1689	Massachusetts Bay overthrows Andros; Leisler's rebellion in New York
1692	Witchcraft trials in Salem
1696	Creation of the Board of Trade and Plantations

CHAPTER FOUR

The Mosaic of Eighteenth-Century America

n the morning of June 29, 1754, about 150 Iroquois sat facing the colonial commissioners in Albany, New York. In front of the governor's house, servants had set up rows of long wooden planks, upon which the delegates from the Six Nations of the Iroquois now sat. The commissioners themselves, 25 in all, were not about to make do with planks; each had his own chair. They represented seven colonies, from Massachusetts Bay on the north to Maryland on the south.

Governor James DeLancey of New York stood and read a proclamation of welcome, pledging to "brighten the Chain of Friendship" between the Iroquois and the English. As each paragraph of the governor's speech was translated, the Iroquois were presented with a decorative belt, to which they responded with a ceremonial "*Yo-heigh-eigh*," shouted in unison. The noise unsettled those colonials attuned to the subtleties of Iroquois diplomacy. Normally, each nation voiced its agreement individually: six *Yo-heigh-eighs* coming one after another. By mixing them together, noted one observer, the delegates "had a mind to disguise that all the Nations did not universally give their hearty assent" to uniting with the English.

Unity—and not merely the unity of the Iroquois—was much on the mind of one commissioner from Philadelphia. Several chairs to the left of Governor DeLancey sat the most influential member of the Pennsylvania delegation, Benjamin Franklin. He knew that the question of whether the Iroquois would unite in an alliance with British America was only half the issue for this gathering at Albany. Equally important was whether the British colonies themselves could unite, to deal effectively with France's threat throughout North America. Franklin had a plan for bringing the colonies together, but whether they would pay any notice remained an open question.

In a sense that plan grew out of a lifetime of experience, for the imperial rivalry between England and France had begun well before Franklin's birth and

Rivalry between France and England

had flared, on and off, throughout his adult years. In 1689 England had joined the Netherlands and the League of Augsburg (several German-speaking states) in a war against France. While the main struggle raged on the continent of Europe, French and English colonials, joined by their Indian allies, skirmished in what was known as King William's War. Peace returned in 1697, but only until 1702, when the Anglo-French struggle resumed again, four years before Franklin was born. It continued throughout his boyhood, until 1713.

For a quarter of a century thereafter, the two nations waged a kind of cold war, competing for position and influence. At stake was not so much control over people or even territory but control over trade. In North America, France and England vied for access to the sugar islands of the Caribbean, a monopoly on supplying manufactured goods to New Spain, and title to the fur trade. The British had the advantage of numbers: nearly 400,000 subjects in the colonies in 1720, compared with only about 25,000 French spread along a thin line of fishing stations and fur trading posts. Yet the French steadily strengthened their chain of forts, stretching from the mouth of the Mississippi north through the Illinois country and into Canada. The forts helped channel the flow of furs from the Great Lakes and the Mississippi River valley into Canada, thus keeping them out of the clutches of English traders. And the forts neatly encircled England's colonies, confining their settlement to the eastern seaboard.

Fighting again engulfed Europe and the colonies in 1744. King George's War, as the colonials dubbed it, ended four years later, but peace did nothing to diminish the old rivalry. As English traders and settlers filtered steadily into the Ohio River valley, the French built a new line of forts in 1752, from south of Lake Erie to the Ohio River. Two years later they erected Fort Duquesne at the strategic forks of the Ohio, flush against the border of Franklin's Pennsylvania. That startled Pennsylvania and other colonies into sending commissioners to Albany in 1754 to coordinate efforts to deal with the worsening crisis. Franklin put the message plainly in his newspaper, the *Pennsylvania Gazette*, in a cartoon of a snake cut into segments. It was inscribed "Join, or Die."

As France and England maneuvered for the empire, the Iroquois League maintained a cool neutrality. They were uneasy at the prospect of a North America without the French. Without French competition for Indian furs, what would spur British colonials to offer fair prices and trade goods of high quality? Without the arc of French forts encircling the British colonies, what would halt the westward spread of white settlement? Increasingly, too, the Iroquois were impressed by the show of French military might.

For the time being, the commissioners at Albany could do little to satisfy Iroquois doubts, except lavish as much hospitality as their budgets would allow. In the end the Iroquois made vague promises of loyalty, and then hauled away 30 wagons full of presents.

But would the colonies themselves unite? On the way to the Albany Congress Franklin had sketched out a framework for colonial cooperation. He proposed

The Albany Plan of Union

establishing "one general government" for British North America: a federal council composed of representatives from each colony, presided over by a president-general appointed by the Crown. The council would assume all responsibility for colonial defense and Indian policy, building forts and patrolling harbors with taxes levied on all Americans. The commissioners were bold enough to accept the plan, alarmed by the wavering Iroquois and the looming French threat.

But the union born at Albany was smothered by the jealous colonies, who were unwilling to sing *yo-heigh-eigh* either in unison or separately. Not a single assembly approved the Albany Plan of Union. And no American legislature was ready to surrender its cherished right to tax inhabitants of its own colony—not to a federal council or to any other body. "Everyone cries, a union is necessary," Franklin wrote Governor Shirley of Massachusetts in disgust; "but when they come to the manner and form of the union, their weak noodles are perfectly distracted." If the Albany Congress proved one thing, it was that American colonials were hopelessly divided.

FORCES OF DIVISION

Franklin, of course, should have known better than to hope for an intercolonial union. A practical man not given to idle dreams, he recognized the many forces of division at work in America. He knew that the colonies were divided by ethnic and regional differences, as well as racial and religious prejudices. Year after year small wooden ships brought to American seaports a bewildering variety of immigrants—especially in Philadelphia, where Franklin had lived since 1723. From his efforts to reorganize the post office Franklin knew, too, that Americans were separated by vast distances, poor transportation, and slow communications. He knew how suspicious frontier districts remained of seaboard communities and how the eastern seaboard disdained the backcountry. Taken all in all, the British settlements in America were, in the eighteenth century, a diverse and divided lot.

Immigration and Natural Increase

One of the largest immigrant groups—250,000 black men, women, and children—had come to the colonies from Africa not by choice but in chains. White arrivals included many English immigrants but also a quarter of a million Scots-Irish, the descendants of seventeenth-century Scots who had regretted settling in northern Ireland; perhaps 135,000 Germans; and a sprinkling of Swiss, Swedes, Highland Scots, and Spanish Jews. Most non-English white immigrants were fleeing lives torn by famine, warfare, and religious persecution. Many had paid for passage by signing indentures to work as servants in America.

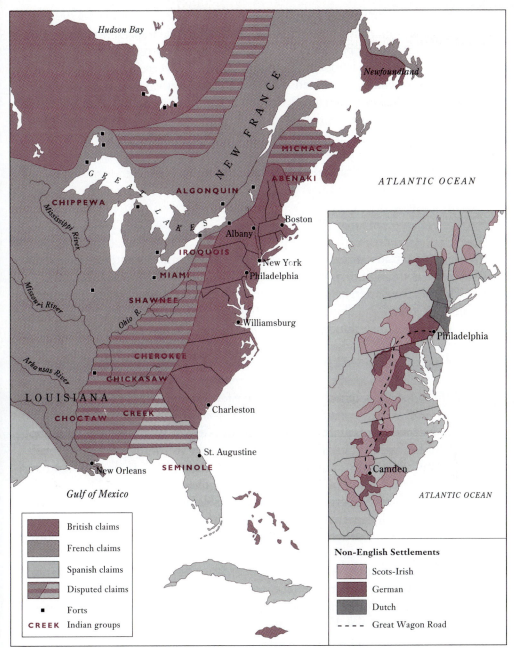

PATTERNS OF SETTLEMENT IN THE EIGHTEENTH CENTURY   The French, English, and Indian nations all jockeyed for power and position across North America. The French expanded their fur trade through the interior, while English settlement at midcentury began to press the barrier of the Appalachians. Many non-English settlers spilled into the backcountry: the Scots-Irish and Germans followed the Great Wagon Road through the western parts of the middle and southern colonies, while the Dutch and Germans moved up the Hudson River valley.

The immigrants and slaves who arrived in the colonies between 1700 and 1775 swelled population that was already growing dramatically from natural increase. The birthrate in eighteenth-century America was triple

High birthrate

what it is today. Most women bore between five and eight children, and most children survived to maturity. Indeed, the consequences of this population explosion so intrigued Franklin that he wrote an essay on the subject in 1751. He recognized that ethnic and religious diversity, coupled with the hectic pace of westward expansion, made it hard for colonials to share any common identity. Far from fostering political union, almost every aspect of social development set Americans at odds with one another.

The Settlement of the Backcountry

To white immigrants from Europe, weary of war or worn by want, the seaboard's established communities must have seemed havens of order and stability. But by the beginning of the eighteenth century, even the children of long-time settlers could not acquire land along the coast. In older New England towns, three and four generations were putting pressure on a limited supply of land, while wasteful farming practices had depleted the soil of its fertility. Farther south, earlier settlers had already snatched up the farmland of Philadelphia's outlying counties, the prime Chesapeake tobacco property, and lowcountry rice swamps.

With older rural communities offering few opportunities to either native-born or newly arrived white families, both groups were forced to create new communities on the frontier. The peopling of New England's frontier—Maine, New Hampshire, and Vermont—was left mainly to the descendants of old Yankee families. Better opportunities for new immigrants to acquire land at cheaper prices lay south of New York. By the 1720s German and Scots-Irish immigrants as well as native-born settlers were pouring into western Pennsylvania. Some settled permanently, but others streamed southward into the backcountry of Virginia and the Carolinas, where they encountered native-born southerners pressing westward.

Backcountry settlers endured greater isolation than other colonials. From many farms it was a day's ride to the nearest courthouse; taverns and churches

Isolation of the backcountry

were often as distant. Isolation hindered the formation of strong social bonds, as did the mobility of backcountry settlers. Many families pulled up stakes three or four times before settling permanently. Houses reflected that transience: most families crowded into one-room shacks wal d with mud, turf, or crude logs.

The backc try meant economic isolation as well. Large portions of the interior were cut off from water transport because they were located above the fall line, where rivers flowing to the Atlantic became unnavigable. By 1755 several crude wagon roads linked western Pennsylvania and Virginia to towns farther east, including Philadelphia, but transporting crops and driving livestock overland proved prohibitively expensive. Cut off from outside markets, farmers grew only enough to feed their households. Most backcountry inhabitants could not afford to invest in a slave or even a servant. Those conditions made the frontier, more than anywhere else in America, a society of equals.

Hard work dominated the lives of backcountry settlers. Besides doing the usual chores of farm women, western wives and daughters joined male family *Frontier women* members in the fields. Men found some release from their harsh lives in coarse, aggressive behavior—epic bouts of drinking, fighting, and slaughtering game. But frontier women had few consolations and longed to live closer to neighbors and churches. The reactions of women to being resettled on the frontier can be imagined from the promise that one Scottish husband offered his wife: "We would get all these trees cut down . . . [so] that we would see from house to house."

Social Conflict on the Frontier

Despite the discomforts of frontier life, cheap land lured many families to the West. Benjamin Franklin had observed the hordes of Scots-Irish and German immigrants lingering in Philadelphia just long enough to scrape together the purchase price of a frontier farm. From Franklin's point of view, the backcountry performed a valuable service by siphoning off surplus people from congested eastern settlements. But he knew, too, that the frontier was an American Pandora's box. Once opened, the West unleashed discord, especially between the eastern seaboard and the backcountry.

In Pennsylvania, Franklin himself mediated one such contest between east and west. In 1763 a band of Scots-Irish farmers known as "the Paxton Boys" *The Paxton Boys* protested the government's inadequate protection of frontier settlers by killing a number of Indians. Then the Paxton Boys took their protests and their guns to Philadelphia, marching as far as Lancaster before Franklin intervened and promised redress of their grievances.

Strife between east and west was even deadlier and more enduring in North and South Carolina. In both colonies legislatures dominated by coastal planters refused to grant inland settlers equitable political representation or *Regulation movements* even basic legal institutions. In response to those injustices, two protest movements emerged in the Carolina interior, each known as the Regulation.

Farmers in the South Carolina backcountry organized their Regulation in the 1760s, after that colony's assembly refused to set up courts in the backcountry. Westerners were desperate for protection from outlaws who stole livestock, kidnapped and raped women, and tortured and murdered men. In the absence of courts the Regulators acted as vigilantes, meting out their own brand of grisly frontier justice against these criminals. Regulator threats to march on Charleston itself finally panicked eastern political leaders into extending the court system, but bitter memories lingered among westerners.

Western North Carolinians organized their Regulation to protest not the absence of a legal system but the corruption of local government. Lawyers and merchants, backed by wealthy eastern planters, moved into the western parts of that colony and seized control of politics. Then they used local office to exploit frontier settlers, charging exorbitant fees for legal services, imposing high taxes, and manipulating debt laws. Western farmers responded to these abuses with the Regulation: they seized county courts and finally squared off against an eastern militia led by the governor. Easterners crushed the Regulators at the Battle of Alamance in 1771 but left frontier North Carolinians with an enduring hostility to the seaboard.

Ethnic differences heightened sectional tensions between east and west. While people of English descent predominated along the Atlantic coast, *Ethnic conflicts* Germans, Scots-Irish, and other white minorities were concentrated in the interior. Many English colonials regarded these new immigrants as culturally inferior. Charles Woodmason, an Anglican missionary in the Carolina backcountry, lamented the arrival of "5 or 6000 Ignorant, mean, worthless, beggarly Irish Presbyterians, the Scum of the Earth, the Refuse of Mankind," who "delighted in a low, lazy, sluttish, heathenish, hellish life."

German immigrants were generally credited with having steadier work habits, as well as higher standards of sexual morality and personal hygiene. But like the clannish Scots-Irish, the Germans preferred to live, trade, and worship among themselves. By 1751 Franklin was warning that the Germans would retain their separate language and customs: the Pennsylvania English would be overrun by "the Palatine Boors."

Boundary Disputes and Tenant Wars

The settlement of the frontier also triggered disputes between colonies over their boundaries. The most serious of these border wars pitted New York *Green Mountain Boys* against farmers from New England who had settled in present-day Vermont: Ethan Allen and the Green Mountain Boys. In the 1760s New York, backed by the Crown, claimed land that Allen and his friends had already purchased from New Hampshire. When New York tried to extend its rule over Vermont, Allen led a successful guerrilla resistance, harassing Yorker settlers and officials, occupying Yorker courthouses, and setting up a competing judicial system in the Green Mountains.

The spread of settlement also set the stage for mass revolts by tenants in those areas where proprietors controlled vast amounts of land. In eastern New Jersey, proprietors insisted that squatters pay quitrents on land that had become increasingly valuable. When the squatters, many of them migrants from New England, refused to pay rents, buy the land, or move, the proprietors began evictions, touching off riots in the 1740s. Tenant unrest also raged in New York's Hudson River valley. In the 1680s the royal governor had granted several prominent merchant families large estates in that region. By the middle of the eighteenth century, there were about 30 manors around New York City and Albany, totaling some 2 million acres and worked by several thousand tenants. Newcomers from New England, however, demanded to own land and preached their ideas to Dutch and German tenants. Armed insurrection exploded in 1757 and again, more violently, in 1766. Tenants refused to pay rents, formed mobs, and stormed the homes of landlords.

Eighteenth-Century Seaports

While most Americans on the move settled on the frontier, others swelled the populations of colonial cities. By present-day standards such cities were small, harboring from 8000 to 22,000 citizens by 1750. The scale of seaports remained intimate, too: all of New York City was clustered at the southern tip of Manhattan Island, and the length of Boston or Charleston could be walked in less than half an hour.

All major colonial cities were seaports, their waterfronts fringed with wharves and shipyards. A jumble of shops, taverns, and homes crowded their streets; the spires of churches studded their skylines. By the 1750s, the grandest and most populous was Philadelphia, which boasted straight, neatly paved streets, flagstone sidewalks, and three-story brick buildings. Older cities like Boston and New York had a more medieval aspect: most of their dwellings and shops were wooden structures with tiny windows and low ceilings, rising no higher than two stories to steeply pitched roofs. The narrow cobblestone streets of Boston and New York also challenged pedestrians, who competed for space with livestock being driven to the butcher, roaming herds of swine and packs of dogs, clattering carts, carriages, and horses.

Commerce, the lifeblood of seaport economies, was managed by merchants who tapped the wealth of surrounding regions. Traders in New York and

The commercial classes

Philadelphia shipped the Hudson and Delaware valleys' surplus of grain and livestock to the West Indies. Boston's merchants sent fish to the Caribbean and Catholic Europe, masts to England, and rum to west Africa. Charlestonians exported indigo to English dyemakers and rice to southern Europe. Other merchants specialized in the import trade, selling luxuries and manufactured goods produced in England—fine fabrics, ceramics, tea, and farming implements. Wealth brought many merchants political power: they dominated city governments and shared power in colonial assemblies with lawyers and the largest farmers and planters.

Skilled craftworkers or artisans made up the middling classes of colonial cities. The households of master craftworkers usually included a few younger and less skilled journeymen working in other artisans' shops. Unskilled boy apprentices not only worked but also lived under the watchful eye of their masters. Some artisans specialized in the maritime trades as shipbuilders, blacksmiths, and sailmakers. Others, like butchers, millers, and distillers, processed and packed raw materials for export. Still others served the basic needs of city dwellers—the men and, occasionally, women who baked bread, mended shoes, combed and powdered wigs, and tended shops and taverns.

On the lowest rung of a seaport's social hierarchy were free and bound workers. Free laborers were mainly young white men and women—journeymen

Free and bound workers

artisans, sailors, fishermen, domestic workers, seamstresses, and prostitutes. The ranks of unfree workers included apprentices and indentured servants doing menial labor in shops and on the docks. Black men and women also made up a substantial part of the bound labor force of colonial seaports. While the vast majority of African slaves were sold to southern plantations, a smaller number were bought by urban merchants and craftworkers. Laboring as porters at the docks, as assistants in craft shops, or as servants in wealthy households, black residents made up almost 20 percent of the population in New York City and 10 percent in Boston and Philadelphia.

The character of slavery in northern seaports changed decisively during the mid-eighteenth century. When wars raging in Europe reduced the supply of white indentured servants, colonial cities imported a larger number of Africans. Those newcomers brought to urban black culture a new awareness of a common west African past. The influence of African traditions appeared most vividly in an annual event known as "Negro election day," celebrated in northern seaports. During the festival, similar to ones held in west Africa, some black men and women paraded in their masters' clothes or mounted on their horses. An election followed, to choose black "kings," "governors," and "judges," who then "held court" and settled minor disputes among white and black members of the community. "Negro election day" did not challenge the established racial order with its temporary reversal of roles, but it did allow the black community of seaports to honor their own leaders.

The availability of domestic workers, both black and white, made for leisured lives among women from wealthy white families. Even those city women who

Women in cities

could not afford household help spent less time on domestic work than farming wives and daughters. Although some housewives grew vegetables in backyard gardens or kept a few chickens, large markets stocked by outlying farmers supplied most of the food for urban families.

For women who had to support themselves, seaports offered a number of employments. Young single women from poorer families worked in wealthier households as maids, cooks, laundresses, seamstresses, or nurses. The highest-paying occupations for women, midwifery and dressmaking, both required long apprenticeships and expert skills. The wives of artisans and traders sometimes assisted their husbands and, as widows, often continued to manage groceries, taverns, and printshops. But most women were confined to caring for households, husbands, and children; fewer than 1 out of every 10 women in seaports worked outside their own homes.

All seaport dwellers—perhaps 1 out of every 20 Americans—enjoyed a more stimulating environment than other colonials. The wealthiest could attend an

Urban diversions and hazards

occasional ball or concert; those living in New York or Charleston might even see a play performed by touring English actors. The middling classes could converse with other tradespeople at private social clubs and fraternal societies. Men of every class found diversion in drink and cockfighting. Crowds of men, women, and children swarmed to tavern exhibitions of trained dogs and horses or the spectacular waxworks of one John Dyer, featuring "a lively Representation of Margaret, Countess of Herrinburg, who had 365 Children at one Birth."

But city dwellers, then as now, paid a price for their pleasures. Commerce was riddled with risk: ships sank and wars disrupted trade. When such disasters struck, the lower classes suffered most. The ups and downs of seaport economies, combined with the influx of immigrants, swelled the ranks of the poor in all cities by the mid-eighteenth century. Furthermore, epidemics and catastrophic fires occurred with greater frequency and produced higher mortality rates in congested seaports than in the countryside.

Social Conflict in Seaports

The swelling of seaport populations, like the movement of whites to the West, often churned up trouble. English, Scots-Irish, Germans, Swiss, Dutch, French, and Spanish jostled uneasily against one another in the close quarters of Philadelphia and New York. To make matters worse, religious differences heightened ethnic divisions. Jewish funerals in New York, for example, drew crowds of hostile and curious Protestants, who heckled the mourners.

Class resentment also stirred unrest. Some merchant families flaunted their wealth, building imposing town mansions and dressing in the finest imported fashions. During hard times, expensive coaches and full warehouses became targets of mob vandalism. Crowds also gathered to intimidate and punish other groups who provoked popular hostility—unresponsive politicians, prostitutes, and "press gangs." Impressment, attempts to force colonials to serve in the British navy, triggered some of the most violent urban riots.

SLAVE SOCIETIES IN THE EIGHTEENTH-CENTURY SOUTH

Far starker than the inequalities and divisions among seaport dwellers were those between white and black in the South. By 1775 one out of every five Americans was of African ancestry, and over 90 percent of all black Americans lived in the South, most along the seaboard. Here, on tobacco and rice plantations, slaves fashioned a distinctive African American society and culture. But they were able to build stable families and communities only late in the eighteenth century, and against enormous odds.

Whether a slave was auctioned off to the Chesapeake or to the Lower South shaped his or her future in important ways. Slaves in the lowcountry of South

The Chesapeake versus the Lower South

Carolina and Georgia lived on large plantations with as many as 50 other black workers, about half of whom were African-born. They had infrequent contact with either their masters or the rest of the sparse white population. "They are as 'twere, a Nation within a Nation," observed Francis LeJau, an Anglican priest in the lowcountry. And their work was arduous, for rice required constant cultivation. Black laborers tended young plants and hoed fields in the sweltering summer heat of the mosquito-infested lowlands. During the winter and early spring, they built dams and canals to regulate the flow of water into the rice fields. But the use of the "task system" rather than gang labor widened the window of freedom within slavery. When a slave had completed his assigned task for the day, one planter explained, "his master feels no right to call upon him."

Many Chesapeake slaves, like those in the Lower South, were African-born, but most lived on smaller plantations with fewer than 20 fellow slaves. Less densely concentrated than in the lowcountry, Chesapeake slaves also had more contact with whites. Unlike Carolina's absentee owners who left white overseers and black drivers to run their plantations, Chesapeake masters actively managed their estates and subjected their slaves to closer scrutiny.

The Slave Family and Community

After the middle of the eighteenth century, a number of changes fostered the growth of black families and the vitality of slave communities. As slave importations began to taper off, the rate of natural reproduction among blacks started to climb. As the proportion of new Africans dropped and the number of native-born black Americans grew, the ratio of men to women in the slave community became more equal. Those changes and the appearance of more large plantations, even in the Chesapeake, created more opportunities for black men and women to find partners and form families. Elaborate kinship networks gradually developed, often extending over several plantations in a single neighborhood.

Even so, black families remained vulnerable. If a planter fell on hard times, members of black families might be sold off to different buyers to meet his debts. When a master died, black families might be divided among surviving heirs. Even under the best circumstances, fathers might be hired out to other planters for long periods or sent to work in distant quarters.

Black families struggling with terrible uncertainties were sustained by the distinctive African American culture evolving in the slave community. The high

Influence of African culture

percentage of native Africans among the eighteenth-century American black population made it easier for slaves to retain the ways of their lost homeland. Christianity won few converts, in part because white masters feared that baptizing slaves might make them more

The Old Plantation affords a rare glimpse of life in the
slave quarters. At this festive gathering, both men and
women dance to the music of a molo (a stringed
instrument similar to a banjo) and drums.

rebellious, but also because African Americans preferred their traditional religions. African influence appeared as well in the slaves' agricultural skills and practices, folktales, music, and dances.

Slave Resistance in the Eighteenth Century

Inevitably, slavery forced upon the enslaved a need to cope with the institution's barbarities, and enslaved African Americans both resisted captivity and developed strategies for survival. Among newly arrived Africans, collective attempts at escape were most common. Groups of slaves, often made up of newcomers from the same tribe, fled inland and formed "Maroon" communities of runaways. These efforts were usually unsuccessful because the Maroon settlements were large enough to be easily detected.

More acculturated blacks adopted subtler ways of subverting slavery. Domestics and field hands alike faked illness, feigned stupidity and laziness, broke tools, pilfered from storehouses, hid in the woods for weeks at a time, or simply took off to visit other plantations. Other slaves, usually escaping bondage as solitary individuals, found a new life as craftworkers, dock laborers, or sailors in the relative anonymity of colonial seaports.

Less frequently, black rebellion took direct and violent form. Whites in communities with large numbers of blacks lived in dread of arson, poisoning, and insurrection. Four slave conspiracies were reported in Virginia before 1750.

The Stono Rebellion   In South Carolina, more than two decades of abortive uprisings and insurrection scares culminated in the Stono Rebellion of 1739, the largest slave revolt of the colonial period. Nearly 100 African Americans, led by a slave named Jemmy, seized arms from a store in the coastal district of Stono and killed several white neighbors before they were caught and killed by the white militia.

Despite the growing rebelliousness of black slaves, southern planters continued to import Africans throughout the eighteenth century. The practice mystified Franklin, revealing at least one gap in his knowledge: the crucial importance of slavery in the southern economy. But unlike some of his Quaker neighbors in Pennsylvania, who were beginning to object to slavery on moral

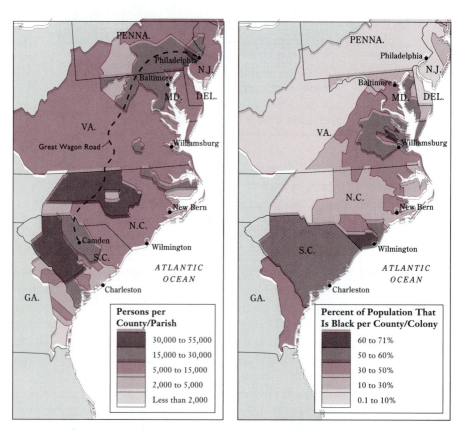

THE DISTRIBUTION OF THE AMERICAN POPULATION, 1775   The African American population expanded dramatically during the eighteenth century, especially in the southern colonies. While the high volume of slave imports accounts for most of the growth in the first half of the century, natural increase was responsible for the rising black population during later decades.

and humanitarian grounds, Franklin's reservations—like his opposition to German immigration—were overtly racist. "Why increase the sons of Africa by planting them in America," he asked, "where we have so fair an opportunity, by excluding all blacks and tawnys, of increasing the lovely white and red?"

COUNTERPOINT *The African American response to enslavement*

It is only in the last twenty years that historians have come to appreciate how various and enduring were the ways in which black men and women resisted bondage. In the 1960s, when scholars began to explore the impact of slavery on African Americans, many portrayed blacks as passive victims of a brutal system. They concluded that the experience of captivity left African Americans so disoriented and demoralized that they lost the will to fight back. Indeed, one influential historian compared the regimen of southern plantations to that in Nazi concentration camps during World War II, arguing that both were "total institutions" that utterly tranformed the personalities of those subject to such repressive conditions. To survive the horrors of slavery, blacks became docile, submissive, dependent, even childlike.

That interpretation has been sharply challenged since the mid-1970s by other historians who argue for the resourcefulness and resilience of the African American in bondage. Without denying the harness of the slave system, these scholars have shown that most southern plantations were not so tightly and efficiently controlled as to cripple the personalities of slaves. On the contrary, they believe that blacks created space within those settings to fashion a sustaining family and communal life, institutions that endowed them with a strong sense of personal and collective identity. They contend, too, that relationships between masters and slaves were often complex interactions in which blacks could negotiate terms for better treatment. There is much evidence to confirm that some slaves became expert at showing masters that their productivity depended on having some measure of freedom—being permitted to set their work schedules, to meet at night for religious services, to choose their mates.

ENLIGHTENMENT AND AWAKENING IN AMERICA

The differences among eighteenth-century colonials resulted in more than clashes between regions, races, classes, and ethnic groups. Those differences also made for diversity in the ways that Americans thought and believed. City dwellers were more attuned to European culture than were people living in small villages or on the frontier. White males from well-to-do families of English ancestry were far more likely to receive college educations than those from poorer or immigrant households. White women of every class and background were excluded from higher education, and slaves received no formal education at all. Where they lived, how well they lived, whether they were male or female, native-born or immigrant, slave or free—all these variables fostered among colonials distinctive worldviews, differing attitudes and assumptions about the individual's relationship to nature, society, and God.

The Enlightenment in America

The diversity of colonials' inner lives became even more pronounced during the eighteenth century because of the Enlightenment, an intellectual movement that started in Europe during the seventeenth century. The leading figures of the Enlightenment, the "philosophes," stressed the power of human reason to promote progress by revealing the laws that governed both nature and society. In the American colonies the Enlightenment influenced some curious artisans in major seaports, as well as wealthy merchants, lawyers, and landowners with the leisure and education to read the latest books from Europe.

Like many devotees of the Enlightenment, Franklin was most impressed by its emphasis on useful knowledge and experimentation. He pondered air currents and then invented a stove that heated houses more efficiently. He toyed with electricity and then invented lightning rods to protect buildings in thunderstorms. Other amateur colonial scientists constructed simple telescopes, classified animal species native to North America, or sought to explain epidemics in terms of natural causes.

Some clergy educated at American colleges (six had been established by 1763) were touched by the Enlightenment, adopting a more liberal theology that stressed

Rational versus traditional Christianity

the reasonableness of Christian beliefs. By the middle of the eighteenth century this "rational Christianity" commanded a small following among colonials, usually Anglicans or liberal Congregationalists. Their God was not the Calvinists' awesome deity, but a benevolent creator who offered salvation to all, not just to a small, predestined elite. They believed that God's greatest gift to mankind was reason, which enabled all human beings to follow the moral teachings of Jesus. They muted the Calvinist emphasis on human sinfulness and the need for a soul-shattering conversion.

Enlightenment philosophy and rational Christianity did not affect the outlook of most colonials. By the middle of the eighteenth century, over half of all white men (and a smaller percentage of white women) were literate. But most colonial readers were not equipped to tackle the learned writings of Enlightenment philosophes. As a result, the outlook of most colonials contrasted sharply with that of the cosmopolitan few. The great majority of Americans still looked for ultimate truth in biblical revelation rather than human reason and explained the workings of the world in terms of divine providence rather than natural law.

Widespread attachment to traditional Christian beliefs was strengthened by the hundreds of new churches built during the first half of the eighteenth century. Church attendance ran highest in the northern colonies, where some 80 percent of the population turned out for public worship on the Sabbath. In the South, because of the greater distances involved and the shortage of clergy, about half of all colonials regularly attended Sunday services.

Despite the prevalence of traditional religious beliefs, many ministers expressed concern about the dangerous influence of rational Christianity. They also worried that the lack of churches might tempt many frontier families to abandon Christianity altogether. Exaggerated as these fears may have been, the consequence was a major religious revival that swept the colonies during the middle decades of the eighteenth century.

The First Great Awakening

The Great Awakening, as the revival came to be called, deepened the influence of older forms of Protestant Christianity and, specifically, Calvinism throughout British America. Participation in the revival was the only experience that a large number of people everywhere in the colonies had in common. But the Great Awakening also heightened religious divisions among Americans.

The first stirrings of revival appeared in the 1730s among Presbyterians and Congregationalists in the Middle Colonies and New England. Many ministers in these churches preached an "evangelical" message, emphasizing the need for individuals to experience "a new birth" through religious conversion. Among them was the Reverend Jonathan Edwards of Northampton, Massachusetts. Edwards' preaching combined moving descriptions of God's grace with terrifying portrayals of eternal damnation. "The God that holds you over the pit of hell, much as one holds a spider or some loathsome insect over the fire, abhors you and is dreadfully provoked," he declaimed to one congregation; ". . . there is no other reason to be given, why you have not dropped into hell since you arise in the morning, but that God's hand has held you up."

These local revivals of the 1730s were mere tremors compared to the earthquake of religious enthusiasm that shook the colonies with the arrival in the fall

The appeal of George Whitefield

of 1739 of George Whitefield. This handsome, cross-eyed "boy preacher" from England electrified crowds from Georgia to New Hampshire during his two-year tour of the colonies. He and his many imitators among colonial ministers turned the church into a theater, enlivening sermons with dramatic gestures, flowing tears, and gruesome depictions of hell's torments. The drama of such performances appealed to people of all classes, ethnic groups, and races. By the time Whitefield sailed back to England in 1741, thousands of awakened souls were joining older churches or forming new ones.

The Aftermath of the Great Awakening

Whitefield also left behind a raging storm of controversy. Many "awakened" church members now openly criticized their ministers as cold, unconverted, and uninspiring. To supply the missing fire, some laymen—"and even Women and

E Y E W I T N E S S   T O   H I S T O R Y

Benjamin Franklin Attends the Preaching
of George Whitefield

I happened . . . to attend one of his Sermons, in the Course of which I perceived he intended to finish with a Collection, and I silently resolved he should get nothing from me. I had in my Pocket a Handful of Copper Money, three or four silver Dollars, and five Pistoles in Gold. As he proceeded I began to soften, and concluded to give the Coppers. Another Stroke of his Oratory made me asham'd of that, and determin'd me to give the Silver; and he finish'd so admirably, that I emptied my Pocket wholly into the Collectors' Dish, Gold and all. . . .

Some of Mr. Whitefield's Enemies affected to suppose that he would apply these Collections to his own private Emolument; but I, who was intimately acquainted with him, (being employ'd in printing his Sermons and Journals, etc.) never had the least Suspicion of his Integrity, but am to this day decidedly of Opinion that he was in all his Conduct a perfectly *honest Man*. And methinks my Testimony in his Favor ought to have the more Weight, as we had no religious Connection. He us'd indeed sometimes to pray for my Conversion, but never had the Satisfaction of believing that his Prayers were heard. Ours was a mere civil Friendship, sincere on both Sides, and lasted to his Death.

He had a loud and clear Voice, and articulated his Words and Sentences so perfectly that he might be heard and understood at a great distance, especially as his Auditors, however numerous, observ'd the most exact Silence. He preach'd one Evening from the Top of the Court House Steps, which are in the Middle of Market Street. . . . I had the Curiosity to learn how far he could be heard by retiring backwards down the Street towards the River. . . . I computed that he might well be heard by more than Thirty Thousand.

Benjamin Franklin, *The Autobiography of Benjamin Franklin* (New York: Washington Square Press, 1960), pp. 131–133. Copyright © 1965 by Washington Square Press. Copyright renewed © 1993 by Ralph Ketcham. Reprinted by permission of Pocket Books, a division of Simon & Schuster, Inc.

Religious controversies

Common Negroes"—took to "exhorting" any audience willing to listen. The most popular ministers became "itinerants," traveling like Whitefield from one town to another. Throughout the colonies conservative and moderate clergy questioned the unrestrained emotionalism and the disorder that attended the gatherings of lay exhorters and itinerants.

George Whitefield drew critics as well as admirers in both England and America. In this satirical English cartoon, he is depicted as a money-grubbing evangelist, while his audience, which consists mainly of women, is taken in by his pose of sanctity and youthful good looks.

Although Americans had been fighting over religion well before the Great Awakening, the new revivals left colonials even more divided along religious lines. The largest single group of churchgoers in the northern colonies remained within the Congregational and Presbyterian denominations. But both these groups split into factions that either supported or condemned the revivals. Some conservative Presbyterians and Congregationalists, disgusted with the disorder, defected to the Quakers and the Anglicans, who had shunned the revival. On the other hand the most radical converts joined forces with the warmest champions of the Awakening, the Baptists.

While northern churches splintered and bickered, the fires of revivalism spread to the South and its backcountry. From the mid-1740s until the 1770s, *Evangelicalism on the frontier* scores of new Presbyterian and Baptist churches were formed, but conflict often accompanied religious zeal. Ardent Presbyterians in the Carolina backcountry disrupted Anglican worship by loosing packs of dogs in local chapels. In northern Virginia, Anglicans took the offensive against the Baptists, whose strict moral code sounded a silent reproach to the hard-drinking, high-stepping, horse-racing, slaveholding gentry. County officials, prodded by resentful Anglican parsons, harassed, fined, and imprisoned Baptist ministers.

And so a diverse lot of Americans found themselves continually at odds with one another. Because of differences in religion and education, colonials quarreled over whether rational Christianity enlightened the world or emotional revivalists destroyed its order. Because of ethnic and racial tensions, Spanish Jews found themselves persecuted, and African Americans searched for ways to resist their white masters. Because of westward expansion, Carolina Regulators waged war against coastal planters, while colonial legislatures from Massachusetts to Virginia quarreled over western boundaries.

Benjamin Franklin surely understood the depth of those divisions as he made his way toward the Albany Congress in the spring of 1754. He himself had brooded over the boatloads of non-English newcomers. He had lived in two booming seaports and felt the explosive force of the frontier. He personified the Enlightenment—and he had heard George Whitefield himself preach from the steps of the Philadelphia courthouse.

How, then, could Franklin, who knew how little held the colonials together, sustain his hopes for political unity? The answer may be that even in 1754, the majority of colonials were of English descent. And these free, white Americans liked being English. That much they had in common.

ANGLO-AMERICAN WORLDS OF THE EIGHTEENTH CENTURY

Most Americans prided themselves in being English. When colonials named their towns and counties, they named them after places in their parent country. When colonials established governments, they turned to England for their political models. They frequently claimed "the liberties of freeborn Englishmen" as their birthright. Even in diet, dress, furniture, architecture, and literature, colonists adopted English standards of taste.

Yet American society had developed in ways significantly different from that of Great Britain.* Some differences made colonials feel inferior, ashamed of their simplicity when compared with London's sophistication. But they also came to appreciate the greater equality of colonial society and the more representative character of colonial governments. If it was good to be English, it was better still to be English in America.

English Economic and Social Development

The differences between England and America began with their economies. Large financial institutions like the Bank of England and influential corporations like the East India Company were driving England's commercial development. New textile factories and mines were deepening its industrial

---

*When England and Scotland were unified in 1707, the nation as a whole became known officially as Great Britain; its citizens, as British.

development. Although most English men and women worked at agriculture, it, too, had become a business. Members of the gentry rented their estates to tenants, members of the rural middle class. In turn, these tenants hired workers from the swollen ranks of England's landless to perform the actual farm labor. By contrast, most colonial farmers owned their land, and most family farms were a few hundred acres. The scale of commerce and manufacturing was equally modest.

England's more developed economy fostered the growth of London and other cities. Americans abroad quickly recognized that even major colonial seaports could not match London, a teeming colossus of 675,000 in 1750. Touring colonials gloried in the British Museum and gawked at cathedrals. They strolled through fashionable shops, fingering fine textiles and inspecting handsome carriages. But there was an underside to the splendor. London seethed with filth, crime, and desperate poverty. The poor and the unemployed as well as pickpockets and prostitutes crowded into its gin-soaked slums, taverns, and brothels. The contrast between the luxuries enjoyed by a wealthy few Londoners and the misery of the many, disquieted colonial observers.

Inequality in England and America

The opportunities for great wealth provided by England's more developed economy created deep class distinctions, as did the inherited privileges of its

Class distinctions aristocracy. The members of the upper class, the landed aristocracy and gentry, made up less than 2 percent of England's population but owned 70 percent of its land. By right of birth, English aristocrats claimed membership in the House of Lords; by custom, certain powerful gentry families dominated the other branch of Parliament, the House of Commons. England's titled gentlemen shared power and wealth and often family ties with the rich men of the city—major merchants, successful lawyers, and lucky financiers. They too exerted political influence through the House of Commons. The colonies had their own prominent families, but no titled ruling class holding political privilege by hereditary right. And even the wealthiest colonial families lived in far less magnificence than their English counterparts.

If England's upper classes lived more splendidly, its lower classes were larger and worse off than those in the colonies. Less than a third of England's inhabitants belonged to the "middling sort" of traders, professionals, artisans, and tenant farmers. More than two-thirds struggled for survival at the bottom of society. By contrast, the colonial middle class counted for nearly three-quarters of the white population. With land cheap, labor scarce, and wages for both urban and rural workers 100 percent higher in America than in England, it was much easier for colonials to accumulate savings and then buy farms of their own.

Colonials were both fascinated and repelled by English society. They gushed over the grandeur of aristocratic estates and imported suits of livery for their ser-

Coffeehouses like this establishment in London were favorite gathering places for Americans visiting Britain. Here merchants and mariners, ministers and students, lobbyists and tourists warmed themselves, read newspapers, and exchanged gossip.

Ambivalent Americans

vants and tea services for their wives. They exported their sons to Britain for college educations at Oxford and Cambridge, medical school at Edinburgh, and legal training at London's Inns of Court.

But colonials recognized that England's ruling classes purchased their luxury and leisure at the cost of the rest of the nation. In his *Autobiography*, Benjamin Franklin painted a devastating portrait of the degraded lives of his fellow workers in a London printshop, who drowned their disappointments by drinking throughout the workday, even more excessively on the Sabbath, and then faithfully observing the holiday of "St. Monday's" to nurse their hangovers. Like Franklin, many colonials believed that gross inequalities of wealth would endanger liberty. They regarded the idle among England's rich and poor alike as ominous signs of a degenerate nation.

Politics in England and America

Colonials were also of two minds about England's government. While they praised the English constitution as the basis of all liberties, they were alarmed by the actual workings of English politics. In theory, England's "balanced constitution" was designed to give every order of English society some voice in the workings of government. While the Crown represented the monarchy and the House of Lords the aristocracy, the House of Commons represented the democracy, the

England's balanced constitution

people of England. In fact, the monarch's executive ministers had become dominant by creating support for their policies in Parliament through patronage—or, put more bluntly, bribery.

Over the course of the eighteenth century, a large executive bureaucracy had evolved in order to enforce laws, collect taxes, and wage the nearly constant wars in Europe and America. The power to appoint all military and treasury officials, customs and tax collectors, judges and justices of the peace lay with the monarch and his or her ministers. By the middle of the eighteenth century, almost half of all members of Parliament held such Crown offices or government contracts. Royal patronage was also used to manipulate parliamentary elections. The executive branch used money or liquor to bribe local voters into selecting their candidates. The small size of England's electorate fostered executive influence. Perhaps one-fourth of all adult males could vote, and many electoral districts were not adjusted to keep pace with population growth and resettlement. The notorious "rotten boroughs" each elected a member of Parliament to represent fewer than 500 easily bribable voters, while some large cities like Manchester and Leeds, newly populous because of industrial growth, had no representation in Parliament at all.

Tools for "managing" Parliament

Americans liked to think that their colonial governments mirrored the ideal English constitution. In terms of formal structure, there were similarities. Most colonies had a royal governor who represented the monarch in America and a bicameral (two-house) legislature made up of a lower house (the assembly) and an upper house (or council). The democratically elected assembly, like the House of Commons, stood for popular interests, while the council, some of which were elected and others appointed, more roughly approximated the House of Lords.

Colonial governments

But these formal similarities masked real differences between English and colonial governments. On the face of it, royal governors had much more power than the English Crown. Unlike kings and queens, royal governors could veto laws passed by assemblies; they could dissolve those bodies at will; they could create courts and dismiss judges. However, governors who asserted such powers found that their assemblies protested that popular liberty was being endangered. In any showdown most royal governors had to give way, for they lacked the government offices and contracts that bought loyalty. The colonial legislatures possessed additional leverage, since all of them retained the sole authority to levy taxes.

Even if the governors had enjoyed greater patronage powers, their efforts to influence colonial legislatures would have been frustrated by the sheer size of the American electorate. There were too many voters in America to bribe. Over half and possibly as many as 70 percent of all white adult colonial men were enfranchised. Property requirements were the same in America as in England, but widespread ownership of land in the colonies allowed most men to meet the qualifications easily.

The colonial electorate was also more watchful. Representatives were required to reside in the districts that they served, and a few even received binding instructions from their constituents about how to vote. Representation was also apportioned according to population far more equitably than in England. Since they were so closely tied to their constituents' wishes, colonial legislators were far less likely than members of Parliament to be swayed by executive pressure.

Most Americans were as pleased with their inexpensive and representative colonial governments as they were horrified by the conduct of politics in England. John Dickinson, a young Pennsylvanian training as a lawyer in London, was scandalized by a Parliamentary election he witnessed in 1754. The king and his ministers had spent over 100,000 pounds sterling to buy support for their candidates, he wrote his father, and "if a man cannot be brought to vote as he is desired, he is made dead drunk and kept in that state, never heard of by his family and friends, till all is over and he can do no harm."

The Imperial System before 1760

Colonials like Dickinson thought long and hard about the condition of England's society and politics. Meanwhile, the English thought about their colonies little, understood them less, and wished neither to think about them more nor to understand them better.

That indifference contributed to England's haphazard administration of its colonies. The Board of Trade and Plantations, created in 1696, gathered information about Atlantic trading and fishing, reviewed laws and petitions drawn up by colonial assemblies, and exchanged letters and instructions with royal governors. But the Board of Trade was only an advisory body.

Real authority over the colonies was divided among an array of other agencies. The Treasury oversaw customs and gathered other royal revenues; the Admiralty Board enforced regulations of trade; the War Office orchestrated colonial defense. But these departments spent most of their hours handling more pressing responsibilities. Colonial affairs stood at the bottom of their agendas. Most British officials in America seemed equally indifferent. Often enough, they had been awarded their jobs in return for political support, not in recognition of administrative ability.

But the branch of England's government most indifferent to America was Parliament. Aside from passing an occasional law to regulate trade, restrict manufacturing, or direct monetary policy, Parliament made no effort to assert its authority in America. Its members assumed that Parliament's sovereignty extended over the entire empire, and nothing had occurred to make them think otherwise.

For the colonies, this chaotic and inefficient system of colonial administration worked well enough. The very weakness of imperial oversight left Americans with a great deal of freedom. Even England's regulation of trade rested lightly on the shoulders of most Americans. Southern planters were obliged to send their rice, indigo, and tobacco to

The benefits of benign neglect

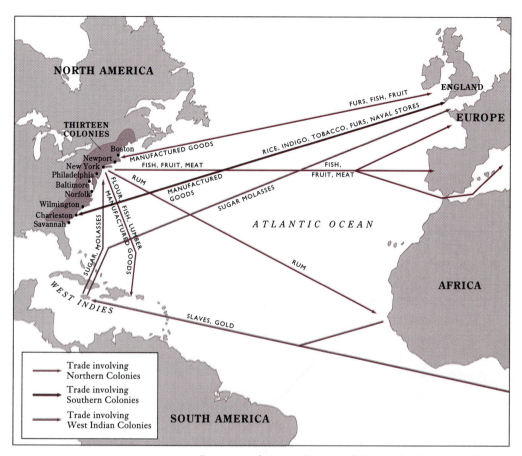

OVERSEAS TRADE NETWORKS   Commercial ties to Spain and Portugal, Africa, and the Caribbean sustained the growth of both seaports and commercial farming regions on the British North American mainland and enabled colonials to purchase an increasing volume of finished goods from England.

Britain only, but they enjoyed favorable credit terms and knowledgeable marketing from English merchants. Colonials were prohibited from finishing iron products and exporting hats and textiles, but they had scant interest in developing domestic industries. Americans were required to import all manufactured goods through England, but by doing so, they acquired high-quality goods at low prices. At little sacrifice, most Americans obeyed imperial regulations. Only sugar, molasses, and tea were routinely smuggled.

Following this policy of benign neglect the British empire muddled on to the satisfaction of most people on both sides of the Atlantic. Economic growth and political autonomy allowed most Americans to like being English, despite their misgivings about their parent nation. The beauty of it was that Americans could be English in America, enjoying greater economic opportunity and political equality. If imperial arrangements had remained as they were in 1754, the empire might have muddled on indefinitely. But because of the French and the Indians on the American frontier, the British empire began to change. And those changes made it increasingly hard for Americans to be English in America.

TOWARD THE SEVEN YEARS' WAR

In the late spring of 1754, while Benjamin Franklin dreamed of unifying Americans, a young Virginian dreamed of military glory. As Franklin rode toward Albany, the young man, an inexperienced officer, led his company of Virginia militia toward Fort Duquesne, the French stronghold on the forks of the Ohio.

Less than a year earlier, the king's ministers had advised royal governors in America to halt the French advance into the Ohio country. The Virginia government organized an expedition against Fort Duquesne, placing at its head the young man who combined an imposing physique with the self-possession of an English gentleman. He wanted, more than anything, to become an officer in the regular British army.

But events in the Ohio country during that spring and summer did not go George Washington's way. French soldiers easily captured Fort Necessity, his

Washington at Fort Necessity

crude outpost near Fort Duquesne. In early July, as the Albany Congress was debating, Washington was surrendering to a French force in the Pennsylvania backcountry and beating a retreat back to Virginia. By the end of 1754, he had resigned his militia command and retired to his plantation at Mount Vernon. The disaster at Fort Necessity had dashed his dreams of martial glory and a regular army commission. He had no future as a soldier.

With the rout of Washington and his troops, the French grew bolder and the Indians more restless. The renewal of war between England and France was certain by the beginning of 1755. This time the contest between the two powers would decide the question of sovereignty over North America. That, at least, was the dream of William Pitt, who was about to become the most powerful man in England.

Even by the standards of English politicians, William Pitt was an odd character. Subject to bouts of illness and depression and loathed for his opportunism

The ambitions of William Pitt

and egotism, Pitt surmounted every challenge, buoyed by a strong sense of destiny—his own and that of England. He believed that England must seize the world's trade, for trade meant wealth and wealth meant power. As early as the 1730s, Pitt recognized that the only obstacle between England and its destiny was France—and that the contest between the two for world supremacy would be decided in America. During King George's War, Pitt had mesmerized the House of Commons and the nation with his spellbinding oratory about England's imperial destiny. But the mounting cost of fighting prompted the government to accept peace with France in 1748. In frustration Pitt retired from public life.

But while Pitt sulked in his library, the rivalry for the American frontier moved toward a showdown. The French pressed their front lines eastward; the English pushed for land westward; the Indians maneuvered for position. Heartened by the news from America, Pitt clung to his dream of English commercial dominion and French defeat. By the late spring of 1754, as Benjamin Franklin and George Washington rode toward their defeats, William Pitt knew that he would have his war with France and his way with the world.

Other dreams would wait longer for fulfillment. The Albany Congress had demonstrated that a few Americans like Franklin had seen beyond the diversity of a divided colonial world to the possibility of union, however unaccustomed and untried. But it would take another war, one that restructured an empire, before some Americans saw in themselves a likeness that was not English.

SIGNIFICANT EVENTS

1689–1697	King William's War (War of the League of Augsburg)
1702	Anne becomes queen of England
1702–1713	Queen Anne's War (War of the Spanish Succession)
1714	George I becomes king of England, beginning Hanover dynasty
1727	George II becomes king of England
1730s–1740s	Rise in importation of black slaves in northern colonies
1739	George Whitefield's first preaching tour in America; Stono Rebellion in South Carolina
1744–1748	King George's War (War of the Austrian Succession)
1751	Franklin's essay on population
1754	The Albany Congress; Washington surrenders at Fort Necessity
1760–1769	South Carolina Regulation
1763	Paxton Boys march in Pennsylvania
1766	Tenant rebellion in New York
1766–1771	North Carolina Regulation (Battle of Alamance, 1771)

The Creation of a New Republic

s Benjamin Franklin had observed in 1751, the population of British North America was doubling approximately every 25 years. This astonishing rate was quite possibly the fastest in the world at the time. Even so, the surge was merely one part of a more general global rise in population during the second half of the eighteenth century. In sheer numbers China led the way. Its population of 150 million in 1700 had doubled to more than 313 million by the end of the century. Europe's total rose from about 118 million in 1700 to about 187 million a century later, the greatest growth coming on its eastern and western flanks, in Great Britain and Russia. African and Indian populations seem to have increased as well.

Climate may have been one reason for the worldwide rise. In Europe, warmer and drier seasons produced generally better harvests. Furthermore, health and nutrition improved globally with the spread of native American crops. Irish farmers discovered that a single acre planted with the lowly American potato could support an entire family. The tomato added crucial vitamins to the Mediterranean diet, while maize provided more calories per acre than any European or African grain. In China the American sweet potato thrived in hilly regions where rice would not grow.

Not only plants but diseases were carried back and forth by European ships. As we have seen, contact between previously isolated peoples produced extreme mortality from epidemics. But after more than two centuries of sustained contact, Indians developed increased biological resistance to European and African illnesses. The frequent circulation of diseases worldwide led to a more stable environment in which populations began to swell.

During the years in which Europeans explored the Atlantic frontiers of North and South America, Slavic and Romanian pioneers were moving eastward into the Eurasian steppes. There they turned sparsely settled pastoral lands into feudal manors and farms. In northern forests unsuitable for farming, Russian fur traders advanced eastward across Siberia until they reached the Pacific in the 1630s. By the 1780s Russian pioneers had pushed into Alaska and down the Pacific American coast, bumping up against western Europeans who were harvesting furs from Canada's forests and streams.

Both flanks of this European thrust often depended on forced labor, especially in agricultural settings. As we have seen, the institution of slavery in North America became increasingly restrictive over the course of the seventeenth century. Similarly, the plight of serfs worsened from 1500 to 1650, as the demand for labor increased in eastern Europe. In 1574 Polish nobles received the right to punish their serfs entirely as they pleased—including execution, if they chose. By 1603, Russian peasants were routinely sold along with the land they worked.

The eighteenth-century Enlightenment penetrated eastern Europe too, as it had the urban centers of North America. Russia's Peter the Great absorbed many ideas when he traveled to England and western Europe. As czar (1689–1725), he attempted to put them to use in westernizing Russia. During the years Catherine the Great ruled (1762–1796), she imported Western architects, sculptors, and musicians to grace her court. But Catherine's limits to toleration were made brutally clear in 1773. The same year that a group of rowdy Americans were dumping tea into Boston harbor, a Cossack soldier named Emelian Pugachev launched a peasant rebellion, seeking to abolish serfdom and taxes. Catherine ruthlessly imprisoned and executed Pugachev. In 1775 she granted Russian nobles even more absolute control over their serfs.

The Americans who rebelled more successfully in 1775 did so not out of a serf's desperation—quite the opposite. With the significant exception of enslaved African Americans, the distance between the poorest and richest colonials was smaller than anywhere in Europe. And the British tradition of representative government ensured a broader involvement of citizens in governing themselves. Thus an American Revolution was hardly inevitable in 1776.

As we shall see, the timing of the colonists' break with Great Britain was the result of specific decisions made on both sides of the Atlantic. Given the failure of the Albany Plan of Union in 1754, it is perhaps surprising that the war for independence ended in the creation of a new and remarkably stable American republic. But that is exactly what happened. American colonials, who in 1763 liked being English and gloried in the British empire, gradually came to think of themselves as independent Americans, subject neither to a British monarch nor to Parliament.

CHAPTER FIVE

Toward the War for American Independence

Americans liked being English. They had liked being English from the beginning of colonial settlement, but they liked it more than ever for a few years after 1759. One wonderful day during those years—September 16, 1762—Bostonians turned out to celebrate belonging to the British empire. Soldiers mustered on the Common; bells pealed from the steeples of local churches; the charge of guns fired from the battery resounded through towns; strains of orchestra music from an outdoor concert floated through the city's crowded streets and narrow alleys. When darkness fell and bonfires illuminated the city, Bostonians consumed "a vast quantity of liquor," drinking "loyal healths" to their young king, George III, and in celebration of Britain's victory in the Seven Years' War.

When the great news of that triumph reached the North American mainland in the fall of 1762, similar celebrations broke out all over the colonies. But the party in America had begun long before, with a string of British victories in French Canada in the glorious year of 1759. It continued through 1760 when all of Canada fell to Anglo-American forces and George III became England's new king. In February of 1763, when the Treaty of Paris formally ended the war, Britain had become the largest and most powerful empire in the Western world. Americans were among His Majesty's proudest subjects.

Thirteen years after the celebration of 1762, Boston was a different place. Pride in belonging to the empire had shriveled to shrill charges that England conspired to enslave its colonies. Massachusetts led the way, drawing other colonies deep into resistance. Bostonians initiated many of the petitions and resolves against British authority. When words did not work, they ignited riots, harassed British officials, baited British troops, and destroyed British property. In 1775, they were laying plans for rebellion against the British empire.

An ironic fate overtook that generation of Americans who loved being English, boasted of their rights as Britons, and celebrated their membership in

116

the all-conquering empire. That very pride drove colonials into rebellion, for the men who ran the British empire after 1763 would not allow Americans to be English. Even before the Seven Years' War, some colonials saw that diverging paths of social and political development made them different from the

A process of disillusionment

English. After the Seven Years' War, events demonstrated to even more colonials that they were not considered the political equals of the English who lived in England. As their disillusionment with the empire deepened, British North Americans from Massachusetts to Georgia slowly discovered a new identity as Americans and declared their independence from being English.

THE SEVEN YEARS' WAR

The Seven Years' War, which actually lasted nine years, pitted Britain and its ally, Prussia, against France, in league with Austria and Spain. The battle raged from 1754 until 1763, ranging over the continent of Europe, the coast of west Africa, India, the Philippines, the Caribbean, and North America.

The Years of Defeat

The war started when the contest over the Ohio River valley among the English, the French, and the Indians led to George Washington's surrender at Fort Necessity in 1754 (page 112). That episode stiffened Britain's resolve to assert its own claims to the Ohio country. In the summer of 1755, as two British reg-

Braddock's defeat

iments led by Major General Edward Braddock approached the French outpost at Fort Duquesne on the forks of the Ohio, they were ambushed and cut to pieces by a party of French and Indians. Washington led the mortally wounded Braddock and the remnants of his army in a retreat. During the summer of Braddock's defeat, New Englanders fared somewhat better against French forces in Nova Scotia and deported 6000 farmers from that region. The Acadians, as they were known, had their land confiscated, and they were dispersed throughout the colonies.

There followed two disastrous years for Britain and its allies. When England and France formally declared war in May 1756, John Campbell, the earl of Loudoun, took command of the North American theater. American soldiers and colonial assemblies alike hated Lord Loudoun. They balked at his efforts to take command over colonial troops and dragged their heels at his demands for men and supplies. Meanwhile, the French strengthened their position in Canada by appointing a new commanding general, Louis Joseph, the marquis de Montcalm. Montcalm drove southward, capturing key British forts and threatening the security of both New York and New England. While he prospered in America, the British were also taking a beating from the French in Europe and in India.

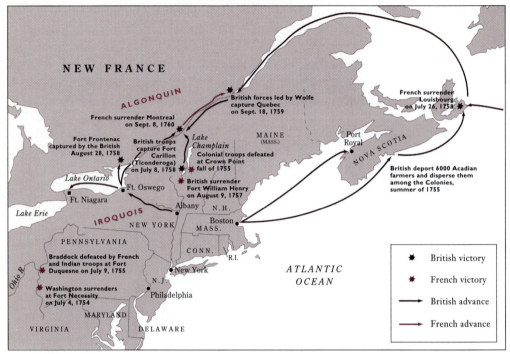

NEW FRANCE

ALGONQUIN

British forces led by Wolfe
capture Quebec
on Sept. 18, 1759

French surrender Montreal
on Sept. 8, 1760

French surrender
Louisbourg
on July 26, 1758

Fort Frontenac
captured by the British
August 28, 1758

British troops
capture Fort
Carillon
(Ticonderoga)
on July 8, 1758

Lake
Champlain

MAINE
(MASS.)

Port
Royal

NOVA SCOTIA

Colonial troops defeated
at Crown Point
fall of 1755

Ft. Oswego

Lake Ontario

British surrender
Fort William Henry
on August 9, 1757

British deport 6000 Acadian
farmers and disperse them
among the Colonies,
summer of 1755

Ft. Niagara

Albany   N.H.

Lake Erie

IROQUOIS

NEW YORK

Boston
MASS.

PENNSYLVANIA

CONN.

R.I.

ATLANTIC
OCEAN

Braddock defeated by French
and Indian troops at Fort
Duquesne on July 9, 1755

New York

N.J.

Ohio R.

Washington surrenders
at Fort Necessity
on July 4, 1754

Philadelphia

MARYLAND

VIRGINIA

DELAWARE

✳	British victory
✳	French victory
→	British advance
→	French advance

THE SEVEN YEARS' WAR IN AMERICA

During the years when the French seemed unstoppable, the British looked for help from the strongest tribes of the interior—the Iroquois in the North, the Creek, Choctaw, and Cherokee in the South. Instead, Benjamin Franklin's worst fears were realized: most tribes adopted neutrality or joined the French. As France seemed certain to carry the continent, Indian attacks on English frontier settlements increased.

The Years of Victory

As British fortunes worsened throughout 1756 and 1757, William Pitt resumed his political career and took personal control over the war. "I know that I can

William Pitt turns the tide

save this country and that no one else can," he announced. Leaving the fighting in Europe to the Prussians, Pitt focused the full strength of the British military on beating the French in America. Pitt also renewed colonial support for the war effort by replacing Lord Loudoun and giving his successor far more limited authority over colonial troops. And Pitt sent requests for men and money directly to each colonial assembly—accompanied by promises of reimbursement in gold and silver.

With Pitt now in control, the tide of battle turned. In July of 1758, the British gained control of the St. Lawrence River when the French fortress at Louisbourg fell before the combined force of the Royal Navy and British and colonial troops. In August, a force of New Englanders strangled France's frontier defenses by capturing Fort Frontenac, thereby isolating French forts lining the Great Lakes and the Ohio valley. The Indians, seeing the French routed from the interior, switched their allegiance to the English.

The British succeeded even more brilliantly in 1759. In Canada, Brigadier General James Wolfe gambled on a daring stratagem and won Quebec from

Wolfe and Montcalm battle for Quebec

Montcalm. Under the cover of darkness, naval squadrons landed Wolfe's men beneath the city's steep bluffs, where they scaled the heights to a plateau known as the Plains of Abraham. Montcalm matched Wolfe's recklessness and offered battle. Five days later both Wolfe and Montcalm lay dead, along with 1400 French soldiers and 600 British and American troops. Quebec had fallen to the British. A year later the French surrender of Montreal ended the fighting in North America.

The Treaty of Paris, signed in February 1763, ended the French presence on the continent of North America. The terms confirmed British title to all French territory east of the Mississippi as well as to Spanish Florida. (Spain had made the mistake of entering the war, against Britain, in 1762.) France ceded to its ally Spain all of its land lying west of the Mississippi and the port of New Orleans.

Postwar Expectations

Britain's victory gave rise to great expectations among Americans. The end of the war, they were sure, meant the end of high taxes. The terms of the peace,

Colonial pride and optimism

they were confident, meant the opening of the Ohio valley's fertile land. The prosperity of the war years alone made for a mood of optimism. British military spending and William Pitt's subsidies had made money for farmers, merchants, artisans, and anyone else who had anything to do with supplying the army or navy. Colonials also took pride in their contributions of troops and money to the winning of the war. In view of that support, Americans expected to be accorded more consideration within the British empire. Now, as one anonymous pamphleteer put it, Americans would "not be thought presumptuous, if they consider[ed] themselves upon an equal footing" with English in the parent country.

But if Americans took pride in being English, most imperial officials in America thought that they had done a poor job of showing it. British statesmen

English resentments

complained that colony assemblies had been tightfisted when it came to supplying the army. British commanders charged that colonial troops had been lily-livered when it came to fighting the French. Such charges were unjust, but they stuck in the minds of many Britons, who concluded that the Americans were selfish and self-interested, unconcerned with the welfare of the empire as a whole. Britain had accumulated a huge national debt that would saddle the nation with high taxes for years to come. To make matters worse, some Britons suspected that, with the French removed from North America, the colonies would move toward independence.

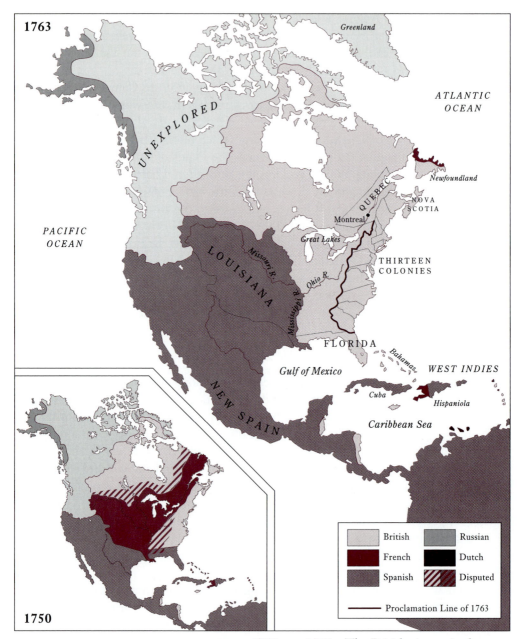

EUROPEAN CLAIMS IN NORTH AMERICA, 1750 AND 1763   The British victory in the
Seven Years' War secured their title to a large portion of the present-day
United States and Canada.

Americans in 1763 were not, in truth, revolutionaries in the making. They
were loyal British subjects in the flush of postwar patriotism. Americans in
1763, deeply divided among themselves, were not even "Americans." But most
postwar English colonials did expect to enjoy a more equal status in the empire.
And most Britons had no inclination to accord them that equality. The differ-

ing expectations of the colonies' place in the empire poised the postwar generation for crisis.

THE IMPERIAL CRISIS

It was common sense. Great Britain had waged a costly war to secure its empire in America; now it needed to consolidate those gains. The empire's North American territory needed to be protected, its administration tightened, and its colonies made as profitable as possible to the parent nation. In other words, the empire needed to be centralized. That conclusion dictated Britain's decision to leave several thousand troops in America after the Seven Years' War. The British army would prevent France from trying to regain its lost territory.

New Troubles on the Frontier

Keeping troops in North America made sense because of the Indians, too. With the French gone, English traders, speculators, and settlers would swarm into the West. Without the French as trading partners, Indian tribes were in a weaker position to deal with the British. No longer could they count on a steady supply of arms and ammunition from European rivals competing for their furs. The Indians were edgy, expecting the worst, and the British were worried.

Events bore out British fears. In the early 1760s a Lenni Lenape prophet, Neolin, began advising the tribes to return to their native ways and resist the

Pontiac's Rebellion

spread of white settlement. Pontiac, an Ottawa chief, embraced Neolin's message of renaissance and rebellion. Other interior tribes joined Pontiac's offensive, and during the summer of 1763 they captured all the British outposts west of Pittsburgh. British troops and American militia finally smothered Pontiac's Rebellion.

Thereafter British administrators discovered another use for troops in America—to enforce the newly issued Proclamation of 1763. That order, issued

Proclamation of 1763

by England's Board of Trade, prohibited white settlement past the crest of the Appalachian Mountains. Restricting westward movement might ease Indian fears, the British hoped, and so stave off future conflicts. It might also keep the colonials confined to the seaboard, where they were more easily subject to the control of the empire.

George Grenville's New Measures

A final reason for keeping troops in the colonies occurred to the British by 1764: an armed presence could enforce American acceptance of other new and sensible measures for tightening the empire. Those measures were the solutions of George Grenville, the First Lord of the Treasury, to the financial problems facing England after the Seven Years' War.

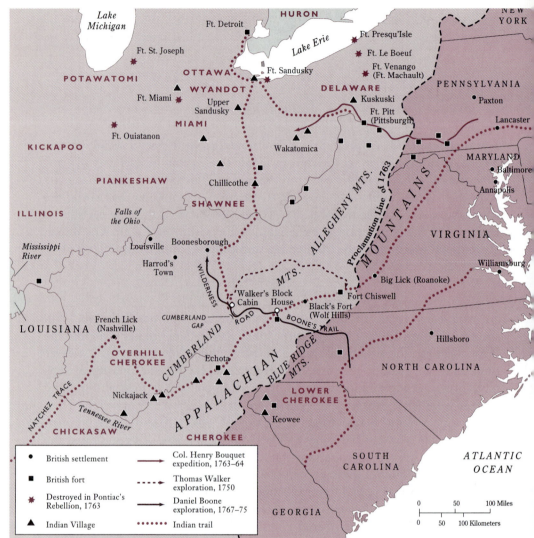

THE APPALACHIAN FRONTIER, 1750–1775 Increasingly, land-hungry colonials spilled into the west through the Cumberland Gap, a notch in the chain of mountains stretching the length of the North American interior. A route through the gap was scouted in 1750 by Dr. Thomas Walker and a party of Virginians on behalf of a company of land speculators. In 1763, Indians led by Pontiac seized eight British forts before troops under Colonel Henry Bouquet stopped the offensive. In 1775 Daniel Boone led the first large party of pioneers through the gap to Boonesborough, in present-day Kentucky.

Britain's national debt had doubled in the decade after 1754. Adding to that burden was the drain of supporting troops in the colonies. Grenville recognized that English taxpayers alone could not shoulder the costs of winning and maintaining an empire. As matters stood, heavy taxes were already triggering protests among hard-pressed Britons. Americans, by contrast, paid comparatively low taxes to their colonial governments and little in trade duties to the empire. Indeed, Grenville discovered that the colonial customs service paid out four times more in salaries to its collectors than it gathered in duties, operating at a net loss.

The income from customs duties was slim because colonial merchants evaded the Molasses Act of 1733. That tariff imposed a hefty duty of six pence

Molasses Act of 1733

on every gallon of molasses imported from the French and Dutch sugar islands. Parliament had designed the duty to encourage colonists to consume more British molasses, which carried a higher price but came duty-free. New England merchants, who distilled molasses into rum and then traded it to the southern colonies and to west Africa, claimed that the British sugar islands could not satisfy the demands of their distilleries. Regrettably, the merchants were forced to import more molasses from the French and Dutch. More regrettably, to keep their costs low and the price of their rum competitive, they had to bribe British customs officials. With the going rate for bribes ranging from a halfpenny to a penny and a half per gallon, the whole regrettable arrangement made handsome profits for both merchants and customs inspectors.

George Grenville reasoned that if Americans could pay out a little under the table to protect an illegal trade, they would willingly pay a little more to go

Sugar Act

legitimate. Parliament agreed. In April 1764 it passed the Revenue Act, commonly called the Sugar Act, which actually lowered the duty on foreign molasses from six to three pence a gallon. But Grenville intended to enforce the new duty and to crack down on smugglers. Those caught on the wrong side of the law were to be tried in admiralty courts, where verdicts were handed down by royally appointed judges rather than colonial juries more likely to sympathize with their fellow citizens.

By tightening customs enforcement, Grenville hoped to raise more revenue from the American trade. Unlike the earlier Navigation Acts, which imposed duties mainly to regulate trade, the Sugar Act's duties were intended mainly to yield revenue. Even so, Grenville regarded his demands as modest: he did not expect colonials to help reduce England's national debt or even to cover the entire cost of their defense.

Grenville made other modest proposals, all approved by Parliament. There was the Currency Act of 1764, which prohibited the colonies from making their

Currency and Quartering Acts

paper money legal tender. That prevented Americans from paying their debts to British traders in currency that had fallen to less than its face value. There was the Quartering Act of 1765, which obliged any colony in which troops were stationed to provide them with suitable accommodations. That contributed to the cost of keeping British forces in America. Finally, in March of 1765, Parliament passed the Stamp Act.

The Stamp Act placed taxes on legal documents, customs papers, newspapers, almanacs, college diplomas, playing cards, and dice. After November 1, 1765, all these items had to bear a stamp signifying that their possessor had paid

Stamp Act   the tax. Violators of the Stamp Act, like those disobeying the Sugar Act, were to be tried without juries in admiralty courts. The English had been paying a similar tax for nearly a century, so it seemed to Grenville and Parliament that colonials could have no objections.

Every packet boat from London that brought news of Parliament passing another one of Grenville's measures dampened postwar optimism. For all of the differences between the colonies and England, Americans still held much in common with the English. Those shared ideas included firm beliefs about why the British constitution, British customs, and British history all served to protect liberty and the rights of the empire's free-born citizens. For that reason the new measures, which seemed like common sense to Grenville and Parliament, did not make sense at all to Americans.

The Beginning of Colonial Resistance

Like other Britons, colonials in America accepted a maxim laid down by the English philosopher John Locke: property guaranteed liberty. Property, in this

Locke on property and liberty   view, was not merely real estate, or wealth, or material possessions. It was the source of strength for every individual, providing the freedom to think and act independently. Protecting the individual's right or property was the main responsibility of government, for if personal property was not sacred, then neither was personal liberty.

It followed from this close connection between property, power, and liberty that no people should be taxed without their consent or that of their elected representatives. The power to tax was the power to destroy by depriving a person of property. Yet both the Sugar Act and the Stamp Act were taxes passed by members of Parliament, none of whom had been elected by colonials.

Like the English, colonials also prized the right of trial by jury as one of their basic constitutional liberties. Yet both the Sugar Act and the Stamp Act would prosecute offenders in the admiralty courts, not through local courts, thus depriving colonials of the freedom claimed by all other English men and women.

The concern for protecting individual liberties was only one of the convictions shaping the colonies' response to Britain's new policies. Equally important

Influence of the English Opposition   was their deep suspicion of power itself, a preoccupation that colonials shared with a minority of radical English thinkers. These radicals were known by a variety of names—the "Country Party," the "Commonwealthmen," and "the Opposition." They drew their inspiration from the ancient tradition of classical republicanism, which held that representative government safeguarded liberty more reliably than either monarchy or oligarchy. Underlying that judgment was the belief that human beings were driven by passion and insatiable ambition. One person, or even a few people, could not be entrusted with governing, because they would inevitably become corrupted by power and turn into tyrants. Even in representative governments, the people were obliged to watch those in power at all times: the price of liberty was eternal vigilance.

The Opposition believed that the people of England were not watching their rulers closely enough. During the first half of the eighteenth century, they argued, the entire executive branch of England's government—monarchs and their ministers—had been corrupted by their appetite for power. Proof of their ambition was the executive bureaucracy of military and civil officials that steadily grew larger, interfered more with citizens' lives, and drained increasing amounts of money from taxpayers. Even more alarming, in the Opposition's view, the executive branch's bribery of members of Parliament was corrupting the representative branch of England's government. They warned that a sinister conspiracy originating in the executive branch of government threatened English liberty.

Opposition thinkers commanded little attention in England, where they were dismissed as a discontented radical fringe. But they were revered by political leaders in the American colonies. The Opposition's view of politics confirmed colonial anxieties about England, doubts that ran deeper after 1763. Parliament's attempt to tax the colonies and the quartering of a standing army on the frontier confirmed all too well the Opposition's portrayal of how powerful rulers turned themselves into tyrants and reduced the people whom they ruled to slaves.

In sum, Grenville's new measures led some colonials to suspect that ambitious men ruling England might be conspiring against American liberties. At the very least, the new measures implied that colonials were not the political equals of the English living in England. They were not entitled to taxation by consent or to trial by jury. To be treated like second-class citizens wounded colonials' pride and mocked their postwar expectations. The heady dreams of the role that the colonies would play in the British empire evaporated, leaving behind the bitter dregs of disappointment. And after the passage of the Stamp Act, dismay mushroomed into militant protest.

Britain's determination to centralize its empire after 1763 was a disaster of timing, not just psychologically but also economically. By then, the colonies were in the throes of a recession. The boom produced in America by government spending during the war had collapsed once subsidies were withdrawn. Colonial merchants were left with full stocks of imported goods gathering dust on their shelves. Farmers lost the brisk and profitable market of the army.

Impact of postwar recession

Colonial response to the Sugar Act reflected the painful postwar readjustments. New England merchants led the opposition, objecting to the Sugar Act principally on economic grounds. But with the passage of the Stamp Act, the terms of the imperial debate widened, and resistance intensified within all of the colonies. The Stamp Act hit all colonials, not just New England merchants. It took money from the pockets of anyone who made a will, filed a deed, traded out of a colonial port, bought a newspaper, consulted an almanac, graduated from college, took a chance at dice, or played cards. More important, the Stamp Act served notice that Parliament possessed the rightful authority to tax the colonies directly and for the sole purpose of raising revenue.

Riots and Resolves

That unprecedented assertion provoked an unprecedented development: the first display of colonial unity. A nearly unanimous chorus of outrage greeted Parliament's claim that it could tax the colonies. During the spring and summer of 1765, American assemblies passed resolves denying Parliament that authority. The right to tax Americans belonged to colonial assemblies alone, they argued, by the law of nature and by the liberties guaranteed in colonial charters and in the British constitution.

Virginia's assembly, the House of Burgesses, took the lead in protesting the Stamp Act, prodded by Patrick Henry, a young lawyer from western Virginia.

Patrick Henry's resolves

The Burgesses passed Henry's resolutions upholding their exclusive right to tax Virginians. They stopped short of adopting those resolves that called for outright resistance to the Stamp Act. When news of Virginia's stand spread to the rest of the colonies, other assemblies followed suit, affirming that the sole right to tax Americans resided in their elected representatives. But some colonial newspapers deliberately printed a different story—that the Burgesses had approved all of Henry's resolves, including one that sanctioned disobedience to any Parliamentary tax. That prompted a few assemblies to endorse resistance. In October 1765 delegates from nine colonies convened in New York, where they prepared a joint statement of the American position and petitioned the king and Parliament to repeal both the Sugar Act and the Stamp Act.

Meanwhile, colonial leaders turned to the press to arouse popular opposition to the Stamp Act. Disposed by the writings of the English Opposition to think of politics in conspiratorial terms, they warned that Grenville and the king's other ministers schemed to deprive the colonies of their liberties by unlawfully taxing their property. The Stamp Act was only the first step in a sinister plan to enslave Americans. Whether or not dark fears of a ministerial conspiracy haunted most colonials in 1765, many resisted the Stamp Act. The merchants of Boston, New York, and Philadelphia agreed to stop importing English goods in order to pressure British traders to lobby for repeal. In every colony, organizations emerged to ensure that the Stamp Act, if not repealed, would never be enforced.

The new resistance groups, which styled themselves the "Sons of Liberty," consisted of traders, lawyers, and prosperous artisans. With great success, they

Sons of Liberty

organized the lower classes of seaports in opposition to the Stamp Act. The sailors, dockworkers, poor artisans, apprentices, and servants who poured into the streets resembled mobs that had been organized

E Y E W I T N E S S   T O   H I S T O R Y

Thomas Hutchinson Recounts the Destruction of His Boston Home during the Stamp Act Riots

n the evening whilst I was at supper and my children round me some-body ran in and said the mob were coming. I directed my children to fly to a secure Place and shut up my house as I had done before intending not to quit it but my eldest daughter repented her leaving me and hastened back and protested she would not quit the house unless I did. I could not stand against this and withdrew with her to a neighbouring house where I had been but a few minutes before the hellish crew fell upon my house with the Rage of devils and in a moment with axes split down the doors and entered my son be-ing in the great entry heard them cry damn him he is upstairs we'll have him. Some ran immediately as high as the top of the house others filled the rooms below and cellars. . . . Messages soon came one after another to the house where I was to inform me the mob were coming in Pursuit of me and I was obliged to retire thro yards and gardens to a house more remote where I remained un-til 4 o'clock by which time one of the best finished houses in the Province had nothing remaining but bare walls and floors. Not contented with tearing off all the wainscot and hangings and splitting the doors to pieces . . . they began to take the slate and boards from the roof and were prevented only by the ap-proaching daylight from a total demolition of the building. The garden fence was laid flat and all my trees, etc. broke down to the ground. Such ruins were never seen in America. Besides my Plate and family Pictures houshold furniture of every kind my own children and servants apparel they carried off about 900 pounds sterling in money and emptied the house of every thing . . . not leaving a single book or paper in it and have scattered or destroyed all the manuscripts and other papers I had been collecting for 30 years.

Thomas Hutchinson to Richard Jackson, August 30, 1765, Massachusetts Archives, IIVI, pp. 146–147.

from time to time earlier in the century. Previous riots against houses of pros-titution, merchants who hoarded goods, or supporters of smallpox inoculation had not been spontaneous, uncontrolled outbursts. Crowds chose their targets and their tactics carefully and then carried out the communal will with little violence.

In every colonial city, the mobs of 1765 burnt the stamp distributors in effigy, insulted them on the streets, demolished their offices, and attacked their homes. By the first of November, the day that the Stamp Act took effect, most of the stamp distributors had resigned.

Repeal of the Stamp Act

Meanwhile, the repeal of the Stamp Act was already in the works back in England. The man who came—unintentionally—to America's relief was George III. The young king was a good man, industrious, and devoted to the empire, but he was also immature and not overendowed with intellect. Insecurity made the young king an irksome master, and he ran through ministers rapidly. By the end of 1765, George had dismissed Grenville for reasons unrelated to the uproar in America and appointed a new first minister, the marquis of Rockingham. Rockingham had opposed the Stamp Act from the outset, and he had no desire to enforce it. He received support from London merchants, who were beginning to feel the pinch of the American nonimportation campaign, and secured repeal of the Stamp Act in March 1766.

The Stamp Act controversy demonstrated to colonials how similar in political outlook they were to one another and how different they were from the

Virtual versus actual representation

British. Americans had found that they shared the same assumptions about the meaning of representation. To counter colonial objections to the Stamp Act, Grenville and his supporters had claimed that Americans *were* represented in Parliament, even though they had elected none of its members. Americans were virtually represented, Grenville insisted, for each member of Parliament stood for the interests of the whole empire, not just those of the particular constituency that had elected him.

Colonials could see no virtue in the theory of virtual representation. After all, the circumstances and interests of colonials, living an ocean apart, were so different from those of Britons. The newly recognized consensus among Americans was that colonials could be truly represented only by those whom they had elected. Their view, known as actual representation, emphasized that elected officials were directly accountable to their constituents.

Americans also had discovered that they agreed about the extent of Parliament's authority over the colonies: it stopped at the right to tax. Colonials conceded Parliament's right to legislate and to regulate trade for the good of the whole empire. But taxation, in their view, was the free gift of the people through their representatives—who were not sitting in Parliament.

Members of Parliament had brushed aside colonial petitions and resolves, all but ignoring their constitutional argument. To make its authority perfectly

Declaratory Act

clear, Parliament accompanied the repeal of the Stamp Act with a Declaratory Act, asserting that it had the power to make laws for the colonies "in all cases whatsoever." In fact, the Declaratory Act clarified nothing: did Parliament understand the power of legislation to include the power of taxation?

The Townshend Acts

In the summer of 1766 George III—again inadvertently—gave the colonies what should have been an advantage by changing ministers again. The king replaced Rockingham with William Pitt, who enjoyed great favor among colonials for his leadership during the Seven Years' War and for his opposition to the Stamp Act. Almost alone among British politicians, Pitt had grasped and approved the colonists' constitutional objections to taxation.

If the man who believed that Americans were "the sons not the bastards of England" had been well enough to govern, matters between Great Britain and the colonies might have turned out differently. But almost immediately after Pitt took office, his health collapsed, and power passed into the hands of Charles Townshend, the chancellor of the exchequer. Townshend's two main concerns were to strengthen the authority of Parliament and royal officials in the colonies at the expense of American assemblies and to raise more revenue at the expense of American taxpayers. In 1767 he persuaded Parliament to tax the lead, paint, paper, glass, and tea that Americans imported from Britain.

Townshend used several strategies to limit the power of colonial assemblies. First, he instructed the royal governors to take a firmer hand. To set the example, he singled out for punishment the New York legislature, which was refusing to comply with provisions of the Quartering Act of 1765. The New York

This 1766 porcelain of *Lord Chatham and America* attests to the popularity of William Pitt, Earl of Chatham, among Americans who resisted the Stamp Act. The artist's representation of "America" as a black woman kneeling in gratitude echoes the colonists' association of taxation with slavery.

assembly held that the cost of quartering the troops constituted a form of indirect taxation. But Parliament backed Townshend, suspending the New York assembly in 1767 until it agreed to obey the Quartering Act.

Townshend also dipped into the revenue from his new tariffs in order to support royal officials. That freed them from the influence of colonial assemblies, which had previously funded the salaries of governors, customs collectors, and judges. Townshend's policies enlarged the number of those bureaucrats. To ensure more effective enforcement of all the duties on imports, he created an American Board of Customs Commissioners, who appointed a small army of new customs collectors. He also established three new vice-admiralty courts in Boston, New York, and Charleston to bring smugglers to justice.

The Resistance Organizes

In Townshend's efforts to centralize the administration of the British empire, Americans saw new evidence that they were not being treated like the English. In newspapers and pamphlets colonial leaders repeated their earlier arguments against taxation. The most widely read publication, "A Letter from a Farmer in Pennsylvania," was the work of John Dickinson, who urged Americans to protest the Townshend duties with a show of superior virtue—hard work, thrift, simplicity, and home manufacturing. By consuming fewer imported English luxuries, Dickinson argued, Americans would advance the cause of repeal. The Townshend Acts also shaped the destiny of Samuel Adams, a leader in the Massachusetts assembly and a consummate political organizer and agitator. First his enemies and later his friends claimed that Adams had decided on independence for America as early as 1768. In that year he persuaded the assembly to send to other colonial legislatures a circular letter condemning the acts and calling for a united American resistance.

John Dickinson and Samuel Adams

As John Dickinson and Samuel Adams whipped up public outrage against the Townshend Acts, the Sons of Liberty again organized the opposition in the streets. Customs officials, like the stamp distributors before them, became targets of popular hatred. But the customs collectors gave as good as they got, using the flimsiest excuses to seize American vessels for violating royal regulations and shaking down American merchants for what amounted to protection money. The racketeering in the customs service brought tensions in Boston to a flashpoint in June 1768 after officials seized and condemned the *Liberty*, a sloop belonging to one of the city's biggest merchants, John Hancock. Several thousand Bostonians vented their anger in a night of rioting, searching out and roughing up customs officials.

The Liberty *seized*

The new secretary of state for the colonies, Lord Hillsborough, responded by sending two regiments of troops to Boston. In the fall of 1768 the redcoats, like a conquering army, paraded into town under the cover of warships lying off the harbor. In the months that followed, citizens bristled when challenged on the streets by armed soldiers.

The *Liberty* riot and the arrival of British troops in Boston pushed colonial assemblies to coordinate their resistance more closely. Most legislatures endorsed the Massachusetts circular letter and adopted agreements not to import or to consume British goods. The reluctance among some merchants to revive nonimportation in 1767 gave way to greater enthusiasm by 1768, and by early 1769, such agreements were in effect throughout the colonies.

Protests against the Townshend Acts raised the stakes by creating new institutions to carry forward the resistance. Subscribers to the nonimportation

Committees of inspection

agreements established "committees of inspection" to enforce the ban on trade with Britain. The committees publicly denounced merchants who continued to import, vandalized their warehouses, forced them to stand under the gallows, and sometimes resorted to tar and feathers.

After 1768 the resistance also brought a broader range of colonials into the politics of protest. Artisans, who recognized that nonimportation would spur domestic manufacturing, began to organize as independent political groups. In many towns, women took an active part in opposing the Townshend duties. The "Daughters of Liberty" took to heart John Dickinson's advice: they wore homespun clothing instead of English finery, served coffee instead of tea, and boycotted shops selling British goods.

The Boston Massacre

The situation in Boston deteriorated steadily. British troops found themselves regularly cursed by citizens and occasionally pelted with stones, dirt, and human excrement. The British regulars were particularly unpopular among Boston's laboring classes because they competed with them for jobs. Off-duty soldiers moonlighted as maritime laborers, and they sold their services at cheaper rates than the wages paid to locals. By 1769, brawls between British regulars and waterfront workers broke out with unsettling frequency.

With some 4000 redcoats enduring daily contact with some 15,000 Bostonians under the sway of Samuel Adams, what happened on the night of March 5, 1770, was nearly inevitable. A crowd gathered around the customshouse for the sport of heckling its guard of 10 soldiers. The redcoats panicked and fended off insults and snowballs with live fire, hitting 11 rioters and killing 5. Labeling the bloodshed "the Boston Massacre," Adams and other propagandists publicized that "atrocity" throughout the colonies.

While Townshend's policies spurred the resistance in America, Parliament recognized that Townshend's duties only discouraged sales to colonials and encouraged them to manufacture at home. The way to repeal had been cleared by the unexpected death of Townshend shortly after Parliament adopted his proposals. In 1770 his successor, Lord North, convinced Parliament to repeal all the Townshend duties except the one on tea, allowing that tax to stand as a source of revenue and as a symbol of their authority.

Resistance Revived

Repeal of the Townshend duties took the wind from the sails of American resistance for more than two years. But the controversy between England and the colonies had not been resolved. Beneath the banked fires of protest smoldered the live embers of Americans' political inequality. Any shift in the wind could fan those embers into flames.

The wind did shift, quite literally, on Narragansett Bay in 1772, running aground the *Gaspee*, a British naval schooner in hot pursuit of Rhode Island smugglers. Providence residents celebrated its misfortune with a bonfire built on the ship's deck. Outraged British officials sent a special commission to look into the matter, intending once again to bypass the established colonial court system. The arrival of the Gaspee Commission reignited the imperial crisis, and American resistance flared again.

It did so through an ingenious mechanism, the committees of correspondence. Established in all the colonies by their assemblies, the committees drew

Committees of correspondence

up statements of American rights and grievances, distributed those documents within and among the colonies, and solicited responses from towns and counties. The brainchild of Samuel Adams, the committee structure formed a new communications network, one that fostered an intercolonial agreement on resistance to British measures. The committees also spread the scope of the resistance from colonial seaports into rural areas, engaging farmers and other country folk in the opposition to Britain.

The committees had much to talk about when Parliament passed the Tea Act in 1773. The law was an effort to bail out the bankrupt East India Company by granting that corporation a monopoly on the tea trade to Americans. Since the company could use agents to sell its product directly, cutting out the middlemen, it could offer a lower price than that charged by colonial merchants. Still, many colonials saw the act as Parliament's attempt to trick them into accepting its authority to tax the colonies.

In early winter of 1773 the tempest over the Tea Act peaked in Boston, with popular leaders calling for the cargoes to be returned immediately to England.

Boston Tea Party

On the evening of December 16, thousands of Bostonians, as well as farmers from the surrounding countryside, packed into the Old South Meetinghouse. Some members of the audience knew what Samuel Adams had on the evening's agenda, and they awaited their cue. It came when Adams told the meeting that they could do nothing more to save their country. War whoops rang through the meetinghouse, the crowd spilled onto the streets and out to the waterfront, and the Boston Tea Party commenced. From the throng emerged 50 men dressed as Indians to disguise their identities. The party boarded three vessels docked off Griffin's Wharf, broke open casks containing 90,000 pounds of tea, and brewed a beverage worth 10,000 pounds sterling in Boston harbor.

The Empire Strikes Back

The Boston Tea Party proved to British satisfaction that the colonies aimed at independence. To reassert its authority, Parliament passed the Coercive Acts,

Coercive Acts

dubbed in the colonies the "Intolerable Acts." In March 1774, two months after hearing of the Tea Party, Parliament passed the Boston Port Bill, closing that harbor to all oceangoing traffic until such time as the king saw fit to reopen it. He would not see fit until colonials paid the East India Company for their losses. During the next three months, Parliament approved three other "intolerable" laws designed to punish Massachusetts. The Massachusetts Government Act handed over the colony government to royal

While the new political activism of some American women often amused male leaders of the resistance, it inspired the scorn of some partisans of British authority. When the women of Edenton, North Carolina, renounced imported tea, this British cartoon mocked them.

officials. Even convening town meetings would require royal permission. The Impartial Administration of Justice Act permitted any royal official accused of a crime in Massachusetts to be tried in England or in another colony. The Quartering Act allowed the housing of British troops in private homes—not only in Massachusetts but in all the colonies.

Many colonials saw the Coercive Acts as proof of a plot to enslave the colonies. In truth, the taxes and duties, laws and regulations of the last decade *were* part of a deliberate design—a commonsensical plan to centralize the administration of the British empire. But those efforts by the king's ministers and Parliament to run the colonies more efficiently and profitably were viewed by more and more Americans as a sinister conspiracy against their liberties.

Week after week in the spring of 1774, reports of legislative outrages came across the waters. Shortly after approving the Coercive Acts, Parliament passed
Quebec Act
the Quebec Act, which established a permanent government in what had been French Canada. Ominously, it included no representative assembly; it also officially recognized the Roman Catholic church and extended the bounds of the province to include all land between the Mississippi and Ohio rivers. Suddenly New York, Pennsylvania, and Virginia found themselves bordering a British colony whose subjects had no voice in their own government.

As alarm deepened in the wake of the Coercive Acts, one colony after another called for an intercolonial congress—like the one that had met during the
First Continental Congress called
Stamp Act crisis—to determine the best way to defend their freedom. But many also remained unsettled about where the logic of their actions seemed to be taking them: toward a denial that they were any longer English.

COUNTERPOINT *A revolution within a revolution?*

Throughout the twentieth century, some historians have contended that the American Revolution was more than a fight for home rule—it was also a fight over who should rule at home, one that pitted ordinary people against the colonial elite. The most recent advocates of that view have found that American society became more unequal during the eighteenth century, as wealth and political power grew more concentrated in the hands of leading families of planters, merchants, and lawyers. The result, they contended, was a rising disaffection among humbler folk, whose participation in protests and riots expressed not only their grievances against the British empire but also their hostility to wealthy colonials. In the course of defying Parliament and the king, ordinary farmers and artisans, and even people beneath them in the social structure, developed their own "popular ideology," a political outlook more egalitarian and democratic than the republican views held by gentlemen who led the resistance to Britain.

But other historians are more skeptical. While agreeing that mounting inequalities heightened tensions during the decades before the Revolution, they argue that all classes of white colonials embraced a common political outlook: republicanism. What promoted that unity of belief and feeling was that most white men owned land and had the right to vote. As members of a propertied, politically empowered middle class, a majority of white colonials wanted only to throw off their connection with Britain; they had no incentive to seek more drastic changes in their society. Indeed, their moderate political aspirations were ably expressed by republicanism, which spoke directly to the concerns of most white Americans both by upholding property rights as the basis of personal freedom and by warning that any group of people who became too wealthy or powerful posed a threat to the liberty of the people.

TOWARD THE REVOLUTION

By the beginning of September 1774, when 55 delegates to the First Continental Congress gathered in Philadelphia, the news from Massachusetts was bad. The colony verged on anarchy, it was reported, as its inhabitants resisted the enforcement of the Massachusetts Government Act.

In the midst of this atmosphere of crisis, the members of Congress also had to take one another's measure. Many of the delegates had not traveled outside their own colonies. (All but Georgia sent representatives.) Although the delegates encountered a great deal of diversity, they quickly discovered that they esteemed the same traits of character, attributes that they called "civic virtue." These traits included simplicity and self-reliance, industry and thrift, and, above all, an unselfish commitment to the public good. Most members of the Congress also shared a common mistrust of England, associating the mother country with vice, extravagance, and corruption.

Still, the delegates had some misgivings about those from other colonies. Massachusetts in particular brought with it a reputation—well deserved, considering that Samuel Adams was along—for radical action and a willingness to use force to accomplish its ends.

The First Continental Congress

As the delegates settled down to business, their aim was to reach agreement on the basis of American rights, the limits of Parliament's power, and the proper tactics for resisting the Coercive Acts. Congress quickly agreed on the first point. The delegates affirmed that the law of nature, the colonial charters, and the British constitution provided the foundations of American liberties. This position was what most colonials had argued since 1765. On the two other issues, Congress charted a middle course between the demands of radicals and the reservations of conservatives.

Since the time of the Stamp Act, most colonials had insisted that Parliament had no authority to tax the colonies. But later events had demonstrated that

Parliament could undermine colonial liberties by legislation as well as by taxation. The suspension of the New York legislature, the Gaspee Commission, and the Coercive Acts all fell into this category. Given those experiences, the delegates adopted a Declaration of Rights and Grievances on October 14, 1774, asserting the right of the colonies to tax and legislate for themselves. The Declaration of Rights thus limited Parliament's power over Americans more strictly than colonials had a decade earlier.

By denying Parliament's power to make laws for the colonies, the Continental Congress blocked efforts of the most conservative delegates to

Joseph Galloway's plan

reach an accommodation with England. Their leading advocate, Joseph Galloway of Pennsylvania, proposed a plan of union with Britain similar to the one set forth by the Albany Congress in 1754. Under it, a grand council of the colonies would handle all common concerns, with any laws it passed subject to review and veto by Parliament. For its part, Parliament would have to submit for the grand council's approval any acts it passed affecting America. A majority of delegates judged that Galloway's proposal left Parliament too much leeway in legislating for colonials, and they rejected his plan.

Although the Congress denied Parliament the right to impose taxes or to make laws, delegates stopped short of declaring that it had no authority at all in the colonies. They approved Parliament's regulation of trade, but only because of the interdependent economy of the empire. And although some radical pamphleteers were attacking the king for plotting against American liberties, Congress acknowledged the continuing allegiance of the colonies to George III. In other words, the delegates called for a return to the situation that had existed in the empire before 1763, with Parliament regulating trade and the colonies exercising all powers of taxation and legislation.

On the question of resistance, Congress satisfied the desires of its most radical delegates by drawing up the Continental Association, an agreement to cease

The Association

all trade with Britain until the Coercive Acts were repealed. They agreed that their fellow citizens would immediately stop drinking East India Company tea, and that by December 1, 1774, merchants would no longer import goods of any sort from Britain. A ban on the export of American produce to Britain and the West Indies would go into effect a year later, during September 1775—the lag being a concession to southern rice and tobacco planters, who wanted to market their crops.

Although the Association provided for the total cessation of trade, Congress did not approve another part of the radicals' agenda: making preparations for war. Congress approved a defensive strategy of civil disobedience but drew the line at authorizing proposals to strengthen and arm colonial militias.

Thus the First Continental Congress steered a middle course. Although determined to bring about repeal of the Coercive Acts, it held firm in resisting any revolutionary course of action. If British officials had responded to its recommendations and restored the status quo of 1763, the war for independence might have been postponed—perhaps indefinitely. On the other hand, even though the Congress did not go to the extremes urged by the radicals, its decisions drew colonials further down the road to independence.

The Last Days of the British Empire in America

Most colonials applauded the achievements of the First Continental Congress. They expected that the Association would bring about a speedy repeal of the Coercive Acts. But fear that the colonies were moving toward a break with Britain led others to denounce the doings of the Congress. Conservatives were convinced that if independence was declared, chaos would ensue. Colonials, they argued, would quarrel over land claims and sectional tensions and religious differences, as they had so often in the recent past. But without Britain to referee such disputes, the result would be civil war, followed by anarchy.

The man in America with the least liking for the Continental Congress sat in the hottest seat in the colonies, that of the governor of Massachusetts.

Thomas Gage in Boston

General Thomas Gage now watched as royal authority crumbled in Massachusetts and the rebellion spread to other colonies. In October 1774 a desperate Gage dissolved the Massachusetts legislature, which then formed itself into a Provincial Congress, assumed the government of the colony, and began arming the militia. Gage then started to fortify Boston and pleaded for more troops—only to find his fortifications damaged by saboteurs and his requests for reinforcements ignored by Britain.

Outside Boston, royal authority fared no better. Farmers in western Massachusetts forcibly closed the county courts, turning out royally appointed justices and establishing their own tribunals. Popularly elected committees of in-

Collapse of royal authority

spection charged with enforcing the Association took over towns everywhere in Massachusetts, not only restricting trade but also regulating every aspect of local life. The committees called upon townspeople to display civic virtue by renouncing "effeminate" English luxuries like tea and fine clothing and "corrupt" leisure activities like dancing, gambling, and racing. The committees also assigned spies to report on any citizen unfriendly to the resistance. "Enemies of American liberty" risked being roundly condemned in public or beaten and pelted with mud and dung by hooting, raucous mobs.

Throughout the colonies a similar process was under way. During the winter and early spring of 1775, provincial congresses, county conventions, and local committees of inspection were emerging as revolutionary governments, replacing royal authority at every level. As the spectacle unfolded before General Gage, he concluded that only force could subdue the colonies. It would take more than he had at his command, but reinforcements might be on the way. In February of 1775, Parliament had approved an address to the king declaring that the colonies were in rebellion.

The Fighting Begins

As spring came to Boston, the city waited. A band of artisans, organized as spies and express riders by Paul Revere, watched General Gage and waited for him to act. Gage waited for reinforcements from Lord North and watched the hostile town. On April 14 word from North finally arrived: Gage was to seize the leaders of the Provincial Congress. That would behead the rebellion, North said. Gage knew better than to believe North—but he also knew that he had to do something.

On the night of April 18 the sexton of Boston's Christ Church hung two lamps from its steeple. It was a signal that British troops had moved out of Boston and were now marching toward the arms and ammunition stored by the Provincial Congress in Concord. As the lamps flashed the signal, Revere and a comrade, William Dawes, rode out to arouse the countryside.

When the news of a British march reached Lexington, its militia of about 70 farmers, chilled and sleepy, mustered on the Green at the center of the small rural town. Lexington Green lay directly on the road to Concord.

Lexington and Concord

At about four in the morning 700 British troops massed on the Green, and their commander, Major John Pitcairn, ordered the Lexington militia to disperse. The townsmen, outnumbered and overawed, began to obey. Then a shot rang out—whether the British or the Americans fired first is unknown—and then two volleys burst from the ranks of the redcoats. With a cheer the British set off for Concord, five miles distant, leaving eight Americans dead on Lexington Green.

By dawn, hundreds of militiamen from nearby towns were surging into Concord. The British entered Concord at about seven in the morning and moved, unopposed, toward their target, a house lying across the bridge that spanned the Concord River. While three companies of British soldiers searched for American guns and ammunition, three others, posted on the bridge itself, had the misfortune to find those American arms—borne by the rebels and being fired with deadly accuracy. By noon, the British were retreating to Boston.

The narrow road from Concord to Boston's outskirts became a corridor of carnage. Pursuing Americans fired on the column of fleeing redcoats from the cover of fences and forests. By the end of April 19, the British had sustained 273 casualties; the Americans, 95. It was only the beginning. By evening of the next day, some 20,000 New England militia had converged on Boston for a long siege.

Common Sense

The bloodshed at Lexington Green and Concord's North Bridge committed colonials to a course of rebellion—and independence. That was the conclusion drawn by Thomas Paine, who urged other Americans to do the same.

Paine himself was hardly an American at all. He was born in England, apprenticed first as a corsetmaker, appointed later a tax collector, and fated finally

Thomas Paine, author of *Common Sense*

to become midwife to the age of republican revolutions. Paine came to Philadelphia late in 1774, set up as a journalist, and made the American cause his own. "Where liberty is, there is my country," he declared. In January 1776 he wrote a pamphlet to inform colonials of their identity as a distinct people and their destiny as a nation. *Common Sense* enjoyed tremendous popularity and wide circulation, selling 120,000 copies within three months of its publication.

After Lexington and Concord, Paine wrote, as the imperial crisis passed "from argument to arms, a new era for politics is struck—a new method of thinking has arisen." That new era of politics for Paine was the *Thomas Paine argues for independence* age of republicanism. He denounced monarchy as a foolish and dangerous form of government, one that violated the dictates of reason as well as the word of the Bible. By ridicule and remorseless argument, he severed the ties of colonial allegiance to the king. *Common Sense* scorned George III as "the Royal Brute of Britain," who had enslaved the chosen people of the new age—the Americans.

Nor did Paine stop there. He rejected the idea that colonials were or should want to be English. Britain, he told his readers, far from being a tender parent, had bled colonials of their wealth and preyed on their liberties. Why suffer such enslavement? The colonies occupied a huge continent an ocean away from the tiny British Isles—clear proof that nature itself had fashioned America for independence. England lay locked in Europe, doomed to the corruption of an Old World. America had been discovered anew to become an "asylum of liberty."

Many Americans had liked being English, but being English hadn't worked. Perhaps that is another way of saying that over the course of nearly two centuries colonial society and politics had evolved in such a way that the identity between the Americans and the English no longer fit. By the end of the Seven Years' War, the colonies had established political institutions that made the rights of "freeborn Britons" more available to ordinary citizens in America than in the nation that had created those liberties. Perhaps, then, most Americans had succeeded *too* well at becoming English, regarding themselves as political equals entitled to basic constitutional freedoms. In the space of less than a generation, the logic of events made clear that despite all the English and Americans shared, in the distribution of political power they were fundamentally at odds. And the call to arms at Lexington and Concord made retreat impossible.

On that point Paine was clear. It was the destiny of Americans to be republicans, not monarchists. It was the destiny of Americans to be independent, not subject to British dominion. It was the destiny of Americans to be American, not English. That, according to Thomas Paine, was common sense.

SIGNIFICANT EVENTS

1755	Braddock defeated by French and Indians
1756	England and France declare war
1759	Decisive English victory at Quebec
1760	George III becomes king of England
1763	Treaty of Paris ends the Seven Years' War; Pontiac's Rebellion; royal proclamation prohibits settlement west of the Appalachians
1764	Sugar Act; Currency Act
1765	Stamp Act; Quartering Act
1766	Repeal of the Stamp Act; Declaratory Act
1767	Townshend duties; Parliament suspends New York assembly
1770	Boston Massacre; repeal of most Townshend duties
1772	Gaspee Commission
1773	Boston Tea Party
1774	Coercive Acts; First Continental Congress meets at Philadelphia
1775	Battles of Lexington and Concord
1776	Thomas Paine's *Common Sense* published

CHAPTER SIX

The American People and the American Revolution

F rom a high place somewhere in the city—Beacon Hill, perhaps, or Copse Hill—General Thomas Gage looked down on Boston. Through a spyglass his gaze traveled over the church belfries and steeples, the roofs of brick and white frame houses. Finally he fixed his sights on a figure far in the distance across the Charles River. The man was perched atop a crude fortification on Breed's Hill, an elevation lying just below Bunker Hill on the Charlestown peninsula. Gage took the measure of his enemy: an older man, past middle age, a sword swinging beneath his homespun coat, a broad-brimmed hat shading his eyes. As he passed the spyglass to his ally, an American loyalist, Gage asked Abijah Willard if he knew the man on the fort. Willard peered across the Charles and identified his own brother-in-law, Colonel William Prescott. A veteran of the Seven Years' War, Prescott was now a leader in the rebel army laying siege to Boston.

"Will he fight?" Gage wondered aloud.

"I cannot answer for his men," Willard replied, "but Prescott will fight you to the gates of hell."

Fight they did on June 17, 1775, both William Prescott and his men. The evening before, three regiments had followed the colonel from Cambridge to

Battle of Bunker Hill

Breed's Hill—soldiers drawn from the thousands of militia who had surrounded British-occupied Boston after the bloodshed at Lexington and Concord. Through the night, they dug trenches and built up high earthen walls atop the hill. At the first light of day, a British warship spotted the new rebel outpost and opened fire. By noon barges were ferrying British troops under Major General William Howe across the half-mile of river that separated Boston from Charlestown. The 1600 raw rebel troops tensed at the sight of scarlet-coated soldiers streaming ashore, glittering bayo-

141

nets grasped at the ready. The rebels were farmers and artisans, not professional soldiers, and they were frightened out of their wits.

But Prescott and his men held their ground. The British charged Breed's Hill twice, and Howe watched in horror as streams of fire felled his troops. Finally, during the third British frontal assault, the rebels ran out of ammunition and were forced to withdraw. Redcoats poured into the rebel fort, bayoneting its handful of remaining defenders. By nightfall the British had taken Breed's Hill and the rest of the Charlestown peninsula. They had bought a dark triumph at the cost of 228 dead and 800 wounded.

The cost came high in loyalties as well. The fighting on Breed's Hill fed the hatred of Britain that had been building since April. Throughout America, preparations for war intensified: militia in every colony mustered; communities stockpiled arms and ammunition. Around Charlestown civilians fled the countryside, abandoning homes and shops set afire by the British shelling of Breed's Hill. "The roads filled with frightened women and children, some in carts with their tattered furniture, others on foot fleeing into the woods," recalled Hannah Winthrop, one of their number.

The bloody, indecisive fight on the Charlestown peninsula known as the Battle of Bunker Hill actually took place on Breed's Hill. And the exchange between Thomas Gage and Abijah Willard that is said to have preceded the battle may not have taken place at all. But the story has persisted in the folklore of the American Revolution. Whether it really happened or not, the conversation between Gage and Willard raised the question that both sides wanted answered: were Americans willing to fight for independence from British rule? It was one thing, after all, to oppose the British ministry's policy of taxation. It was another to support a rebellion for which the ultimate price of failure was hanging for treason. And it was another matter entirely for men to wait nervously atop a hill as the seasoned troops of one's own "mother country" marched toward them with the intent to kill.

Indeed, the question "will they fight?" was revolutionary shorthand for a host of other questions concerning how ordinary Americans would react to

Americans react to the Revolution

the tug of loyalties between long-established colonial governments and a long-revered parent nation and monarch. For slaves, the question revolved around their allegiance to masters who spoke of liberty or to their masters' enemies who promised liberation. For those who led the rebels, it was a question of strengthening the resolve of the undecided, coordinating resistance, instilling discipline—translating the *will* to fight into the ability to do so. And for those who believed the rebellion was a madness whipped up by artful politicians, it was a question of whether to remain silent or risk speaking out, whether to take up arms for the king or flee. All these questions were raised, of necessity, by the act of revolution. But the barrel of a rifle shortened them to a single, pointed question: will you fight?

THE DECISION FOR INDEPENDENCE

The delegates to the Second Continental Congress gathered at Philadelphia on May 10, 1775, just one month after the battles at Lexington and Concord. They had to determine whether independence or reconciliation offered the best way to protect the liberties of their colonies.

For a brash, ambitious lawyer from Braintree, Massachusetts, British abuses dictated only one course. "The Cancer [of official corruption] is too deeply rooted," wrote John Adams, "and too far spread to be cured by anything short of cutting it out entire." Yet during the spring and summer of 1775, even strong advocates of independence did not openly seek a separation from Britain. If independence was to be achieved, radicals needed to forge greater agreement among Americans. Moderates and conservatives harbored deep misgivings about independence: they had to be brought along slowly.

The Second Continental Congress

To bring them along, Congress adopted the "Olive Branch Petition" in July 1775. Drawn up by Pennsylvania's John Dickinson, the document affirmed American loyalty to George III and asked the king to disavow the policies of his principal ministers. At the same time Congress issued a declaration denying that the colonies aimed at independence. Yet, less than a month earlier, Congress had authorized the creation of a rebel military force, the Continental Army, and had issued paper money to pay for the troops.

A Congress that sued for peace while preparing for war was a puzzle that British politicians did not even try to understand, least of all Lord George

Aggressive British response

Germain. A tough-minded statesman now charged with overseeing colonial affairs, Germain was determined to subdue the rebellion by force. George III proved just as stubborn: he refused to receive the Olive Branch Petition. By the end of that year Parliament had shut down all trade with the colonies and had ordered the Royal Navy to seize colonial merchant ships on the high seas. In November 1775 Virginia's royal governor, Lord Dunmore, offered freedom to any slaves who would join the British. During January of the next year, he ordered the shelling of Norfolk, Virginia, reducing that town to smoldering rubble.

British belligerence withered the cause of reconciliation within Congress and the colonies. Support for independence gained more momentum from the overwhelming reception of *Common Sense* in January 1776. Radicals in Congress realized that the future was theirs and were ready to act. In April 1776 the delegates opened American trade to every nation in the world except Great Britain; a month later Congress advised the colonies to establish new state governments. And on June 7 Virginia's Richard Henry Lee offered the motion "that these United Colonies are, and of right ought to be, free and independent States . . .

and that all political connection between them and the State of Great Britain is, and ought to be, totally dissolved."

The Declaration

Congress postponed a final vote on Lee's motion until July. Some opposition still lingered among delegates from the Middle Colonies, and a committee appointed to write a declaration of independence needed time to complete its work. That committee included some of the leading delegates in Congress: John Adams, Benjamin Franklin, Connecticut's Roger Sherman, and New York's Robert Livingston. But the man who did most of the drafting was a young planter and lawyer from western Virginia.

Thomas Jefferson was just 33 years old in the summer of 1776 when he withdrew to his lodgings on the outskirts of Philadelphia, pulled a portable writing desk onto his lap, and wrote the statement that would explain American independence to a "candid world." In the document's brief opening section, Jefferson set forth a general justification of revolution that invoked the "self-evident truths" of human equality and "unalienable rights" to "life, liberty, and the pursuit of happiness." These natural rights had been "endowed" to all persons "by their Creator," the Declaration

Thomas Jefferson

In John Trumbull's painting, the Committee of Five—including Adams (left), Jefferson (second from the right), and Franklin (right)—submit the Declaration of Independence to the Continental Congress.

pointed out; thus there was no need to appeal to the narrower claim of the "rights of Englishmen."

While the first part of the Declaration served notice that Americans no longer considered themselves English, its second and longer section denied England any authority in the colonies. In its detailed history of American grievances against the British empire, the Declaration referred only once to Parliament. Instead, it blamed George III for a "long train of abuses and usurpations" designed to achieve "absolute despotism." Unlike *Common Sense*, the Declaration denounced only the reigning king of England; it did not attack the institution of monarchy itself. But like *Common Sense*, the Declaration affirmed that government originated in the consent of the governed and it upheld the right of the people to overthrow oppressive rule. Congress adopted the Declaration of Independence on July 4, 1776.

Blaming George III

American Loyalists

Colonial political leaders embraced independence because they believed that a majority of Americans would support a revolution. But the sentiment for independence was not universal. Those who would not back the rebellion, supporters of the king and Parliament, numbered perhaps one-fifth of the population in 1775. While they proclaimed themselves "loyalists," their rebel opponents dubbed them "tories." That division made the Revolution a conflict pitting Americans against one another as well as the British. In truth, the war for independence was the first American civil war.

Predictably, the king and Parliament commanded the strongest support in colonies that had been wracked by internal strife earlier in the eighteenth century. In New York, New Jersey, Pennsylvania, and the Carolinas, not only did memories of old struggles sharpen worries of future upheaval, but old enemies often took different sides in the Revolution. The Carolina backcountry emerged as a stronghold of loyalist sentiment because of influential local men who cast their lot with Britain. To win support against Carolina's rebels, whose ranks included most wealthy coastal planters, western loyalist leaders played on ordinary settlers' resentments of privileged easterners. Grievances dating back to the 1760s also influenced the revolutionary allegiances of former land rioters of New York and New Jersey. If their old landlord opponents opted for the rebel cause, the tenants took up loyalism.

Other influences also fostered allegiance to Britain. Government officials who owed their jobs to the empire, major city merchants who depended on British trade, and Anglicans living outside the South retained strong ties to the parent country. Loyalists were also disproportionately represented among recent emigrants from the British Isles. The inhabitants of Georgia, the newest colony, inclined toward the king, as did the Highland Scots, many of whom had arrived in the colonies as soldiers during the Seven Years' War or had worked for a short time in the southern backcountry as tobacco merchants and Indian traders.

COUNTERPOINT   *Contrasting veiws of loyalists*

Historians of the American revolution written by rebel partisans as well as many later chronicles have not treated the loyalists kindly. Often such accounts portray those who opposed independence as traitors at worst or, at best, timid, misguided souls. But within the last generation, many historians have taken a more dispassionate view, finding that many who took up the king's cause had not lacked sympathy for the resistance. Loyalist leaders like Joseph Galloway and Daniel Leonard had opposed the Stamp Act in 1765 and disapproved of imperial policy thereafter. It was not until the crisis reached a fever pitch in 1774 that more colonials cast their lot with the king. Worse than British taxation, in their view, was the radicalism of American resistance—the dumping of tea into Boston harbor, the forming of the Association, and the defying of royal authority.

Such acts of defiance touched what was for loyalists the rawest nerve: a deep seated fear of the divisions and instability of colonial society. Without the British around to maintain order, they warned, differences among Americans would result in civil war. On the eve of the Revolution, Jonathan Boucher, a New York loyalist, warned with uncanny foresight that "we should as soon expect to see . . . the wolf and the lamb feed together, as Virginians form a cordial union with the saints of New England." It would take the passage of less than a century for such fears to be borne out by events—the Union divided and the North and South locked in a fratricidal war. In prizing liberty over order, the rebels acted on principle. But as the loyalists predicted, that choice came at a terrible cost both to them and to their descendants.

Although a substantial minority, loyalists never became numerous enough anywhere to pose a serious threat to the Revolution. A more formidable threat was posed by the British army. And the greatest threat of all was posed by those very Americans who claimed that they wanted independence. For the question remained: would they fight?

THE FIGHTING IN THE NORTH

In the summer of 1775 Americans who wished to remain neutral probably outnumbered either loyalists or rebels. From the standpoint of mere survival, staying neutral made more sense than fighting for independence. Even the most ardent advocates of American rights had reason to harbor doubts, given the odds against the rebel colonists defeating the armed forces of the British empire.

Perhaps no friend of American liberty saw more clearly how slim the chances of a rebel victory were than George Washington. But Washington's principles,

George Washington, general

and his sense of honor, prevailed. June of 1775 found him, then 43 years old, attending the deliberations of the Second Continental Congress and dressed—a bit conspicuously—in his officer's uniform. The other delegates listened closely to his opinions on military matters, for Washington was the most celebrated American veteran of the Seven Years' War who remained young enough to lead a campaign. Better still, as a southerner he could bring his region into what thus far had remained mostly New England's fight. Congress readily appointed him commander-in-chief of a newly created Continental Army.

The Two Armies at Bay

Thus did Washington find himself, only a month later, looking to bring order to the rebel forces around Boston. He knew he faced a formidable foe.

Highly trained, ably led, and efficiently equipped, the king's troops were seasoned professionals. Rigorous drills and often savage discipline by an aristocratic officer corps welded rank-and-file soldiers, men drawn mainly from the bottom of British society, into a sleek fighting machine. At the height of the campaign in America, reinforcements brought the number of British troops to

Hunting shirts, like the one worn by this rifleman (second from the right), captured the imagination of the French army officer in America who made these watercolor sketches of the uniforms of revolutionary soldiers. The enlistment of blacks (infantryman at the far left) drew the artist's attention as well.

50,000, strengthened by some 30,000 Hessian mercenaries from Germany and the support of half the ships in the British navy, the largest in the world.

Washington was more modest about the army under his command, and he had much to be modest about. At first Congress recruited his fighting force of 16,600 rebel "regulars," the Continental Army, from the ranks of local New England militia bands. Although enlistments swelled briefly during the patriotic enthusiasm of 1775, for the rest of the war Washington's Continentals suffered chronic shortages of men and supplies. Even strong supporters of the Revolution hesitated to join the regular army, with its low pay, strict discipline, and constant threat of disease and danger. Most men preferred to fight instead as members of local militia units, the "irregular" troops who turned out to support the regular army whenever British forces came close to their neighborhoods.

"Regulars" versus the militia

The general reluctance to join the Continental Army created a host of difficulties for its commander and for Congress. Washington wanted and needed an army whose size and military capability could be counted on in long campaigns. He could not create an effective fighting force out of civilians who mustered out occasionally with the militia or enlisted for short stints in the Continental Army. Washington's desire for a professional military establishment clashed with the preferences of most republican leaders. They feared standing armies and idealized "citizen-soldiers"—men of selfless civic virtue who volunteered whenever needed—as the backbone of the common defense. "Oh, that I was a soldier," chubby John Adams fantasized in 1775. "Everyone must and will and shall be a soldier."

But everyone did not become a soldier, and the dwindling number of volunteers gradually overcame republican fears of standing armies. In September 1776 Congress set terms in the Continental Army at a minimum of three years or for the duration of the war and assigned each state to raise a certain number of troops. They offered every man who enlisted in the army a cash bounty and a yearly clothing issue; enlistees for the duration were offered 100 acres of land as well. Still the problem of recruitment persisted. Less than a year later, Congress recommended that the states adopt a draft, but Congress had no authority to compel the states to meet their troop quotas.

Even in the summer of 1775, before enlistments fell off, Washington was worried. As his Continentals laid siege to British-occupied Boston, he measured them against the adversary and found them wanting. Inexperienced officers provided no real leadership, and the men under their command shirked the most basic responsibilities of soldiers. They slipped away from camp at night; they left sentry duty before being relieved; they took potshots at the British; they tolerated filthy conditions in their camps.

While Washington strove to impose discipline on his Continentals, he also attempted, without success, to rid himself of "the Women of the Army." When American men went off to fight, their wives usually stayed at home. To women then fell the sole responsibility for running farms and businesses, raising children, and keeping households

Women of the army

together. They helped to supply the troops by sewing clothing, making blankets, and saving rags and lead weights for bandages and bullets. Other women on the home front organized relief for the widows and orphans of soldiers and protests against merchants who hoarded scarce commodities.

But the wives of poor men who joined the army were often left with no means to support their families. Thousands of such women—1 for every 15 soldiers—drifted after the troops. In return for half-rations, they cooked and washed for the soldiers; and after battles, they nursed the wounded, buried the dead, and scavenged the field for clothing and equipment. An even larger number of women accompanied the redcoats: their presence was the only thing that Washington did not admire about the British army and could barely tolerate in his own. But the services that they performed were indispensable, and women followed the troops throughout the war.

Laying Strategies

At the same time that he tried to discipline the Continentals, Washington designed a defensive strategy to compensate for their weakness. To avoid exposing raw rebel troops on "open ground against their Superiors in number and Discipline," he planned to fight the British from strong fortifications. With that aim in mind, in March 1776, Washington barricaded his army on Dorchester Heights, an elevation commanding Boston harbor from the south. That maneuver, which allowed American artillery to fire on enemy warships, confirmed a decision already made by the British to evacuate their entire army from Boston and sail for Halifax, Nova Scotia.

Britain had hoped to reclaim its colonies with a strategy of strangling the resistance in Massachusetts. But by the spring of 1776 they saw clearly that more was required than a show of force against New England. *British assumptions* Instead the situation called for Britain to wage a conventional war in America, capturing major cities and crushing the Continental forces in a decisive battle. Military victory, the British believed, would enable them to restore political control and reestablish imperial authority.

The first target was New York City. General William Howe and Lord George Germain, the British officials now charged with overseeing the war, chose that seaport for its central location and—they hoped—its large loyalist population. They planned for Howe's army to move from New York City up the Hudson River, meeting ultimately with British troops under General Sir Guy Carleton coming south from Canada. Either the British drive would lure Washington into a major engagement, crushing the Continentals, or, if unopposed, the British offensive would cut America in two, smothering resistance to the south by isolating New England.

Unfortunately for the British, the strategy was sounder than the men placed in charge of executing it. General Howe took to extremes the conventional wis-

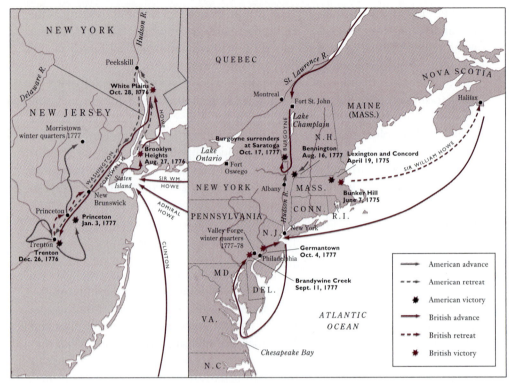

THE FIGHTING IN THE NORTH, 1775–1777

Howe brothers

dom of eighteenth-century European warfare, which aimed as much at avoiding heavy casualties as at winning victories against the enemy. Concern for preserving manpower addicted Howe to caution, when daring more would have carried the day. Howe's brother, Admiral Lord Richard Howe, the head of naval operations in America, also stopped short of pressing the British advantage, owing to his personal desire for reconciliation. The reluctance of the Howe brothers to fight became the formula for British frustration in the two years that followed.

The Campaigns in New York and New Jersey

However cautiously, British forces landed on Staten Island in New York harbor during July 1776. The Continentals marched from Boston and fortified Brooklyn Heights on Long Island, the key to the defenses of New York City on Manhattan Island. By mid-August, 32,000 British troops, including 8000 Hessians, the largest expeditionary force of the eighteenth century, faced Washington's army of 23,000.

At dawn on August 22 the Howe brothers moved on Long Island and easily pushed the rebel army back across the East River to Manhattan. After lin-

British capture New York City gering on Long Island for a month, the Howes again lurched into action, ferrying their forces to Kip's Bay, just a few miles south of Harlem. When the British landed, the handful of rebel defenders at Kip's Bay fled—straight into the towering wrath of Washington, who happened on the scene during the rout. For once the general lost his habitual self-restraint, flogged both officers and men with his riding crop, and came close to being captured himself. But the Howes remained reluctant to hit hard, letting Washington's army escape from Manhattan to Westchester County.

Throughout the fall of 1776 General Howe's forces followed as Washington's fled southward into New Jersey. By mid-November, as the British advance picked up speed, the rebels stepped up their retreat and crossed the Delaware River into Pennsylvania on December 7. There Howe stopped, pulling back most of his army to winter in New York City and leaving the Hessians to hold the British line of advance along the New Jersey side of the Delaware River.

Although the retreat through New York and New Jersey had shriveled rebel strength to only 3000 men, Washington decided that the campaign of 1776 was not over. On a snowy Christmas night, the Continentals floated back across the *Rebel victories at Trenton and Princeton* Delaware, picked their way across roads sleeted with ice, and finally slid into Hessian-held Trenton at eight in the morning. One thousand German soldiers, still recovering from their spirited Christmas celebration and caught completely by surprise, quickly surrendered. Washington's luck held on January 3, 1777, when the Continentals defeated British troops on the outskirts of Princeton, New Jersey.

During the winter of 1776–1777 the British lost more than battles: they alienated the very civilians whose loyalties they had hoped to ensure. In New York City the presence of the main body of the British army brought shortages of food and housing and caused constant friction between soldiers and city dwellers. In the New Jersey countryside still held by the Hessians, the situation was more desperate. Forced to live off the land, the Germans aroused resentment among local farmers by seizing "hay, oats, Indian corn, cattle, and horses, which were never or but very seldom paid for," as one loyalist admitted. The Hessians ransacked and destroyed homes and churches; they kidnapped and raped young women.

Many neutrals and loyalists who had had enough of the king's soldiers now took their allegiance elsewhere. Bands of militia on Long Island, along the Hudson River, and all over New Jersey rallied to support the Continentals.

Capturing Philadelphia

In the summer of 1777 General Howe still hoped to entice the Continentals into a decisive engagement or to seize a major seaport and its surrounding countryside. But he had now decided to goad the Americans into battle by capturing Philadelphia. Rather than risk his army on a march through hostile New Jersey, he approached the rebel capital by sea. In early August the redcoats disembarked on the Maryland shore and headed for Philadelphia, 50 miles away. Washington's army hurried south from New Jersey to protect the new nation's

Brandywine and Germantown

capital. Washington engaged Howe twice: in September at Brandywine Creek and in October in an early dawn attack at Germantown, but both times the rebels were beaten back. He had been unable to prevent the British occupation of Philadelphia.

Still, the rebels could take satisfaction from the troubles that beset the British even in victory. In Philadelphia, as in New York, British occupation jacked up demand and prices for food, fuel, and housing. Philadelphians complained of redcoats looting their shops, trampling their gardens, and harassing them on the streets. Elizabeth Drinker, the wife of a Quaker merchant, confided in her diary that "I often feel afraid to go to bed."

Even worse, the British march through Maryland and Pennsylvania had outraged civilians, who fled before the army and then returned to find their homes and barns bare, their crops and livestock gone. Everywhere Howe's men went in the middle states, they left in their wake Americans with compelling reasons to support the rebels. Worst of all, just days after Howe marched his occupying army into Philadelphia in the fall of 1777, another British commander in North America was surrendering his entire army to rebel forces at Saratoga, New York.

Disaster at Saratoga

The calamity that befell the British at Saratoga was the doing of a glory-mongering general, John "Gentleman Johnny" Burgoyne. After his superior officer, Sir Guy Carleton, bungled a drive into New York during the summer of 1776, Burgoyne won approval to command another attack from Canada. At the end of June 1777 he set out from Quebec with a force of 9500 redcoats, 2000 women and children, and an elaborate baggage train that included the commander's silver dining service, his dress uniforms, and numerous cases of champagne. As Burgoyne's huge entourage lumbered southward, a handful of Continentals and a horde of New England militia assembled several miles below Saratoga at Bemis Heights under the command of General Horatio Gates.

On September 19 Gates's rebel scouts, nested high in the trees on Bemis Heights, spied the glittering bayonets of Burgoyne's approaching force. Benedict

Burgoyne surrenders at Saratoga

Arnold, a brave young officer, led several thousand rebels into the surrounding woods, meeting Burgoyne's men in a clearing at Freeman's Farm. At the end of the day British reinforcements finally pushed the rebels back from a battlefield piled high with the bodies of soldiers from both sides. Burgoyne tried to flee back to Canada, but got no farther than Saratoga, where he surrendered his army to Gates on October 17.

Saratoga changed everything. With Burgoyne's surrender, the rebels succeeded in convincing France that, with a little help, the Americans might well reap the fruits of victory.

THE TURNING POINT

France had been waiting for revenge against Britain ever since its humiliating defeat in the Seven Years' War. Since the mid-1760s, as France's agents in America sent home reports of a rebellion brewing, a scheme for evening the score had been taking shape in the mind of the French foreign minister, Charles Gravier de Vergennes. He reckoned that France might turn discontented colonials into willing allies against Britain.

An Alliance Formed

Vergennes approached the Americans cautiously. He wanted to make certain that the rift between Britain and its colonies would not be reconciled and that the rebels in America stood a fighting chance. Although France had been secretly supplying the Continental Army with guns and ammunition since the spring of 1776, Vergennes would go no further than covert assistance.

Congress approached their former French enemies with equal caution. Would France, the leading Catholic monarchy in Europe, make common cause with the republican rebels? A few years earlier American colonials had fought against the French in Canada; only recently they had renounced a king, and for centuries they had overwhelmingly adhered to Protestantism.

The string of defeats dealt the Continental Army during 1776 convinced Congress that they needed the French enough to accept both the contradictions and the costs of such an alliance. In November Congress appointed a three-member commission to negotiate not only aid from France but also a formal alliance. Its senior member was Benjamin Franklin, who enchanted all of Paris when he arrived in town sporting a simple fur cap and a pair of spectacles (something no fashionable Frenchman wore in public). Hailed as a homespun sage, Franklin played the role of American innocent to the hilt and watched as admiring Parisians stamped his face on everything from the top of commemorative snuffboxes to the bottom of porcelain chamber pots.

*Franklin
in Paris*

Still, Franklin understood that mere popularity could not produce the alliance sought by Congress. It was only news that Britain had surrendered an entire army at Saratoga that finally convinced Vergennes that the rebels could actually win. In February 1778 France signed a treaty of commerce and friendship and a treaty of alliance, which Congress approved in May. Under the terms of the treaties, both parties agreed to accept nothing short of independence for America. France pledged to renounce all future claims in continental North America and to relinquish any territory captured in the war. The alliance left the British no choice other than to declare war on France. Less than a year later Spain joined France, hoping to recover territory lost to England in earlier wars.

Winding Down the War in the North

The Revolution widened into a global war after 1778. Preparing to fight France and Spain dictated a new British strategy in America. No longer could the British concentrate on crushing the Continental Army; instead they would disperse their forces to fend off challenges all over the world. In May Sir Henry Clinton replaced William Howe as commander-in-chief and received orders to withdraw from Philadelphia to New York City. There, and in Newport, Rhode Island, Clinton was to maintain defensive bases for harrying northern coastal towns.

Valley Forge

Only 18 miles outside of Philadelphia, at Valley Forge, Washington and his Continentals were assessing their own situation. Some 11,000 rebel soldiers had passed a harrowing winter in that isolated spot, starving for want of food, freezing for lack of clothing, huddling in miserable huts, and hating the British who lay 18 miles away in Philadelphia. The army also cursed their fellow citizens, for the misery of the soldiers resulted from congressional weakness and disorganization and civilian corruption and indifference. Congress lacked both money to pay and maintain the army and an efficient system for dispensing provisions to the troops. Most farmers and merchants preferred to supply the British, who could pay handsomely, than to do business with financially strapped Congress and the Continentals. What little did reach the army often was food too rancid to eat or clothing too rotten to wear. Perhaps 2500 perished at Valley Forge, the victims of cold, hunger, and disease.

Social composition of the Continental Army

Why did civilians who supported the rebel cause allow the army to suffer? Probably because by the winter of 1777, the Continentals came mainly from social classes that received little consideration at any time. The respectable, propertied farmers and artisans who had laid siege to Boston in 1775 had stopped enlisting. Serving in their stead were single men in their teens and early twenties, some who joined the army out of desperation, others who were drafted, still others who were hired as substitutes for the more affluent. The landless sons of farmers, unemployed laborers, drifters, petty criminals, vagrants, indentured servants, slaves, even captured British and Hessian soldiers—all men with no other means and no other choice—were swept into the Continental Army. The social composition of the rebel rank and file had come to resemble that of the British army. It is the great irony of the Revolution: a war to protect liberty and property was waged by those Americans who were poorest and least free.

The beginning of spring in 1778 brought a reprieve. Supplies arrived at Valley Forge, and so did a fellow calling himself Baron von Steuben, a penniless Prussian soldier of fortune. Although Washington's men had shown spirit and resilience ever since Trenton, they still lacked discipline and training. Those defects and more von Steuben began to remedy. Barking orders and spewing curses in German and French, the baron (and his translators) drilled the rebel regiments to march in formation and to handle their bayonets like proper Prussian soldiers. By the summer of 1778, morale had rebounded as

The soldiers depicted in this 1777 illustration
("pinched with cold") condemn civilian neglect and
the profiteering of private contractors ("damned
Extortioners") who supplied the Continental Army.
Such grievances provoked mutinies within the army.

professional pride fused solidarity among Continental ranks in the crucible of Valley Forge.

Spoiling for action after their long winter, Washington's army, now numbering nearly 13,500, set out to harass Clinton's army as it marched overland from Philadelphia to New York. The Continentals caught up with the British force on June 28 at Monmouth Courthouse, where a long, confused battle ended in a draw. After both armies retired for the night, Clinton's forces slipped away to safety in New York City. Washington pursued, longing to launch an all-out assault on New York City, but he lacked the necessary numbers.

While Washington waited outside New York City, his army started to come apart. During the two hard winters that followed, resentments mounted among *Army uprisings* the rank and file over spoiled food, inadequate clothing, and arrears in pay. The army retaliated with mutinies. Between 1779 and 1780 officers managed to quell uprisings in three New England regiments. But in January 1781 both the Pennsylvania and the New Jersey lines mutinied outright and marched on Philadelphia, where Congress had reconvened. Order returned only after Congress promised back pay and provisions and Washington put two ringleaders in front of a firing squad.

War in the West

Trouble also loomed on the western frontier. There both the British and the rebels sought support from the Indians because the most powerful tribes determined the balance of power. Most of the tribes remained neutral, but those who took sides usually joined the British, who had tried to stem the tide of colonials taking Indian lands.

While George Rogers Clark and his few hundred rebel troops helped to contain British and Indian raids in the Old Northwest, General John Sullivan led an expedition against the Iroquois in upstate New York. Loyalists under Major John Butler and Iroquois fighters under a Mohawk chief, Thayendanegea (called Joseph Brant by the English), had conducted a series of raids along the New York and Pennsylvania frontiers. Sullivan and his expedition routed the marauders and burned over 40 Indian villages.

The Home Front in the North

While fighting flared on the frontier and British troops attacked a few Connecticut coastal towns in 1779, most northern civilians enjoyed a respite from the war. Since the outbreak of the fighting at Lexington and Concord, every rumor of approaching enemy troops had pitched any imperiled neighborhoods into a panic. Refugees on foot and in hastily packed carts filled the roads, fleeing the advancing armies. Those who remained to protect their homes and property might be caught in the crossfire of contending forces or cut off from supplies of food and firewood. Loyalists who remained in areas occupied by rebel troops faced harassment, imprisonment, or the confiscation of their property. Rebel sympathizers met similar fates in regions held by the British. Disease, however, disregarded political allegiances: military camps and occupied towns spawned epidemics of dysentery and smallpox that devastated civilians as well as soldiers, rebels and loyalists alike.

While plundering armies destroyed civilian property wherever they marched, military demands disrupted family economies throughout the north-

Women and the war

ern countryside. The seasons of intense fighting drew men off into military service just when their labor was most needed on family farms. Wives and daughters were left to assume the work of husbands and sons while coping with loneliness, anxiety, and grief. Often enough, the disruptions, flight, and loss of family members left lasting scars. Two years after she fled before Burgoyne's advance into upstate New York, Ann Eliza Bleecker confessed to a friend, "Alas! the wilderness is within: I muse so long on the dead until I am unfit for the company of the living."

Despite these hardships, many women vigorously supported the revolutionary cause in a variety of ways. The Daughters of Liberty joined in harassing those who opposed the rebel cause. One outspoken loyalist found himself surrounded by angry women who stripped off his shirt, covered him with molasses, and plastered him with flower petals. In more genteel fashion, groups of well-to-do women collected not only money but medicines, food, and pewter to melt for bullets.

THE STRUGGLE IN THE SOUTH

Between the autumn of 1778 and the summer of 1781, while Washington and his restless army waited outside New York City, the British opened another theater in the American war. Despite their armed presence in the North, the British had come to believe that their most vital aim was to regain their colonies

Britain's southern strategy

in the mainland South. The Chesapeake and the Carolinas were more profitable to the empire and more strategically important, being so much closer to rich British sugar islands in the West Indies. That new "southern strategy" prompted Clinton to dispatch forces to the Caribbean and Florida. In addition, the British laid plans for a new offensive drive into the Carolinas and Virginia.

English politicians and generals believed that the war could be won in the South. Loyalists were numerous, they believed, especially in the backcountry. Resentment of the seaboard, a rebel stronghold, would breed readiness among frontier folk to take up arms for the king at the first show of British force. And southern rebels—especially the vulnerable planters along the coast—could not afford to turn their guns away from their slaves. So, at least, the British theorized. All that was needed, they concluded, was for the British army to establish a beachhead in the South and then, in league with loyalists, drive northward, pacifying the population while pressing up the coast.

The Siege of Charleston

The southern strategy worked well for a short time in a small place. In November 1778 Clinton sent 3500 troops to Savannah, Georgia. The resistance in the tiny colony quickly collapsed, and a large number of loyalists turned out to help the British. Encouraged by that success, the British moved on to South Carolina.

During the last days of 1779, an expedition under Clinton himself set sail from New York City. Landing off the Georgia coast, his troops mucked through malarial swamps to the peninsula lying between the Ashley and the Cooper rivers. At the tip of that neck of land stood Charleston, and the British began to lay siege. By then, an unseasonably warm spring had set in, making the area a heaven for mosquitoes and a hell for human beings. Sweltering and swatting, redcoats weighted down in their woolen uniforms inched their siegeworks toward the city. By early May Clinton's army closed in, and British shelling was setting fire to houses within the city. On May 12 Charleston surrendered.

Clinton sailed back to New York at the end of June 1780, leaving behind 8300 redcoats to carry the British offensive northward to Virginia. The man charged with leading that campaign was his ambitious and able subordinate, Charles, Lord Cornwallis.

The Partisan Struggle in the South

Cornwallis's task in the Carolinas was complicated by the bitter animosity between rebels and loyalists there. Many Carolinians had taken sides years before Clinton's conquest of Charleston. In the summer and fall of 1775 the supporters of Congress and the new South Carolina revolutionary government mobbed, tortured, and imprisoned supporters of the king in the backcountry. These attacks only hardened loyalist resolve: roving bands seized ammunition, broke their leaders out of jail, and besieged rebel outposts. But within a matter of months, a combined force of rebel militias from the coast and the frontier managed to defeat loyalist forces in the backcountry.

With the fall of Charleston in 1780, the loyalist movement on the frontier returned to life. Out of loyalist vengefulness and rebel desperation issued the

Rebels and loyalists battle for the backcountry

brutal civil war that seared the southern backcountry after 1780. Neighbors and even families fought and killed each other as members of roaming rebel and tory militias. The intensity of partisan warfare in the backcountry produced unprecedented destruction. All of society, observed one minister, "seems to be at an end. Every person keeps close on his own plantation. Robberies and murders are often committed on the public roads. . . . Poverty, want, and hardship appear in almost every countenance."

Cornwallis, when confronted with the chaos, erred fatally. He did nothing to stop his loyalist allies or his own troops from mistreating civilians. A Carolina loyalist admitted that "the lower sort of People, who were in many parts originally attached to the British Government, have suffered so severely . . . that Great Britain has now a hundred enemies, where it had one before." Although rebels and loyalists alike plundered and terrorized the backcountry, Cornwallis's forces bore more of the blame and suffered the consequences.

A growing number of civilians outraged by the king's men cast their lot with the rebels. That upsurge of popular support enabled Francis Marion, the "Swamp Fox," and his band of white and black raiders to cut British lines of communication between Charleston and the interior. It swelled another rebel militia led by the "Gamecock," Thomas Sumter, who bloodied loyalist forces throughout the central part of South Carolina. It mobilized the "over-the-mountain men," a rebel militia in western Carolina, who claimed victory at the Battle of King's Mountain in October 1780. By the end of 1780, these successes had persuaded most civilians that only the rebels could restore order.

If rebel fortunes prospered in the partisan struggle, they faltered in the conventional warfare being waged at the same time in the South. In August of 1780

British victory at Camden

the Continentals commanded by Horatio Gates lost a major engagement to the British force at Camden, South Carolina. In the fall of 1780 Congress replaced Gates with Washington's candidate for the southern command, Nathanael Greene, an energetic, 38-year-old Rhode Islander and a veteran of the northern campaigns.

EYEWITNESS TO HISTORY

A North Carolina Soldier Witnesses the Partisan War in the Southern Backcountry

The evening after our battle with the Tories, we having a considerable number of prisoners, I recollect a scene which made a lasting impression on my mind. I was invited by some of my comrades to go and see some of the prisoners. We went to where six were standing together. Some discussion taking place, I heard some of our men cry out, "Remember Buford," [a rebel soldier killed by loyalists] and the prisoners were immediately hewed to pieces with broadswords. At first I bore the scene without any emotion, but upon a moment's reflection, I felt such horror as I never did before nor have since, and, returning to my quarters and throwing myself upon my blanket, I contemplated the cruelties of war until overcome and unmanned by a distressing gloom from which I was not relieved until commencing our march next morning before day by moonlight. I came to Tarleton's camp [a British officer], which he had just abandoned leaving lively rail fires. Being on the left of the road as we marched along, I discovered lying upon the ground something with the appearance of a man. Upon approaching him, he proved to be a youth about sixteen who, having come to view the British through curiosity, for fear he might give information to our troops, they had run him through with a bayonet and left him for dead. Though able to speak, he was mortally wounded. The sight of this unoffending boy, butchered . . . relieved me of my distressful feelings for the slaughter of the Tories, and I desired nothing so much as the opportunity of participating in their destruction.

Moses Hall in John C. Dann, ed., *The Revolution Remembered: Eyewitness Accounts of the War for Independence* (Chicago: University of Chicago Press, 1980), pp. 202–203.

Greene Takes Command

Greene bore out Washington's confidence by grasping the military situation in the South. He understood the needs of his 1400 hungry, ragged, and demoralized troops and instructed von Steuben to lobby Virginia for food and clothing. He understood the importance of the rebel militias and sent Lieutenant Colonel

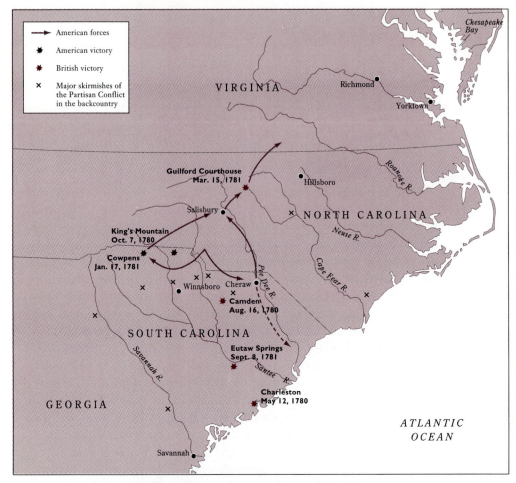

THE FIGHTING IN THE SOUTH, 1780–1781

In December 1780 Nathanael Greene made the crucial decision to split his army, sending Daniel Morgan west, where he defeated the pursuing Banastre Tarleton at Cowpens. Meanwhile Greene regrouped and replenished at Cheraw, keeping Cornwallis off balance with a raid (dotted line) toward Charleston and the coast. Then, with Cornwallis in hot pursuit, Greene and Morgan rejoined at Salisbury, retreating into Virginia. Cornwallis was worn down in this vain pursuit and lost three-quarters of the troops he began with before finally abandoning the Carolina campaign.

Henry "Lighthorse Harry" Lee to assist Marion's raids. He understood the weariness of southern civilians and prevented his men from plundering the countryside.

Above all, Greene understood that his forces could never hold the field against the whole British army. That led him to break the first rule of conventional warfare: he divided his army. In December 1780 he dispatched to western South Carolina a detachment of 600 men under the command of Brigadier General Daniel Morgan of Virginia.

Back at the British camp, Cornwallis worried that Morgan and his rebels, if left unchecked, might rally the entire backcountry against the British. On the other hand, Cornwallis reckoned that he could not commit his entire army to the pursuit of Morgan's men, for then Greene and his troops might retake Charleston. The only solution, unconventional to be sure, was for Cornwallis to divide *his* army. That he did, sending Lieutenant Colonel Banastre Tarleton and 1100 men west after Morgan. Cornwallis had played

Cowpens

right into Greene's hands: the rebel troops might be able to defeat a British army split into two pieces. For two weeks Morgan led Tarleton's troops on a breakneck chase across the Carolina countryside. In January 1781 at an open meadow called Cowpens, Morgan routed Tarleton's force.

Now Cornwallis took up the chase. Morgan and Greene joined forces and agreed to keep going north until the British army wore out. Cornwallis finally stopped at Hillsboro, North Carolina, but few local loyalists responded to his call for reinforcements. To ensure that loyalist ranks remained thin, Greene decided to make a show of force near the tiny village of Guilford Courthouse. On a brisk March day the two sides joined battle, each sustaining severe casualties before Greene was forced to retreat. But the high cost of victory convinced Cornwallis that he could not put down the rebellion in the Carolinas.

Although Nathanael Greene's command provided the Continentals with effective leadership in the South, it was the resilience of rebel militias that

*Value of
the militia*

thwarted the British offensive in the Carolinas. Many Continental Army officers complained about the militia's lack of discipline, its habit of melting away when homesickness set in or harvest approached, and its record of cowardice under fire in conventional engagements. But when set the task of ambushing supply trains and dispatch riders, harrying bands of local loyalists, or making forays against isolated British outposts, the militia came through. Many southern civilians refused to join the British or to provide the redcoats with food and information because they knew that once the British army left their neighborhoods, the rebel militia would always be back. The Continental Army in the South lost many conventional battles, but the militia kept the British from restoring political control over the backcountry.

African Americans in the Age of Revolution

The British also lost in the Carolinas because they did not seek greater support from those southerners who would have fought for liberty *with* the British: African American slaves.

Black Americans, virtually all in bondage, made up one-third of the population between Delaware and Georgia. Since the beginning of the resistance to Britain, white southerners had worried that the watchwords of liberty and equality would spread to the slave quarters. Gripped by the fear of slave rebellion, southern revolutionaries began to take precautions. Marylanders disarmed black inhabitants and issued extra guns to the white militia. Charlestonians hanged and then burned the body of Thomas Jeremiah, a free black who was convicted of spreading the word to others that the British "were come to help the poor Negroes."

Southern whites fully expected the British to turn slave rebelliousness to their strategic advantage. As early as 1775, Virginia's royal governor, Lord

White fears of rebellion

Dunmore, confirmed white fears by offering to free any slave who joined the British. When Clinton invaded the South in 1779, he renewed that offer. Janet Schaw, an English woman visiting her brother's North Carolina plantation, reported that his neighbors had heard that loyalists were "promising every Negro that would murder his master and family he should have his Master's plantation. . . . The Negroes have got it amongst them and believe it to be true."

But in Britain there was overwhelming opposition to organizing support among African Americans. British leaders dismissed Dunmore's ambitious scheme to raise a black army of 10,000 and another plan to create a sanctuary for black loyalists on the southeastern coast. Turning slaves against masters, they recognized, was not the way to conciliate southern whites.

Even so, southern fears of insurrection made the rebels reluctant to enlist black Americans as soldiers. At first, Congress barred African Americans from the Continental Army. But as the rebels became more desperate for manpower, policy changed. Northern states actively encouraged black enlistments, and in the Upper South, some states allowed free men of color to join the army or permitted slaves to substitute for their masters.

Slaves themselves sought freedom from whichever side seemed most likely to grant it. In 1775 more than 800 took up Dunmore's offer and deserted their

African American quests for liberty

masters, and thousands more flocked to Clinton's forces after the fall of Charleston. For many runaways the hope of liberation proved an illusion. Although some served the British army as laborers, spies, and soldiers, many died of disease in army camps or were sold back into slavery in the West Indies. An estimated 5000 black soldiers served in the revolutionary army in the hope of gaining freedom. In addition, the number of runaways to the North soared during the Revolution. All told, some 55,000 slaves fled to freedom, some escaping behind British lines, others into the North.

The slave revolts so dreaded by southern whites never materialized. Possibly the boldest slaves were drawn off into the armies; possibly greater white precautions discouraged schemes for black rebellions. In South Carolina, where the potential for revolt was greatest, most slaves chose to remain on plantations rather than risking a collective resistance and escape in the midst of the fierce partisan warfare.

THE WORLD TURNED UPSIDE DOWN

Despite his losses in the Carolinas, Cornwallis still believed that he could score a decisive victory against the Continental Army. The theater he chose for that showdown was the Chesapeake. During the spring of 1781, he and his army joined forces along the Virginia coast with the hero of Saratoga and newly turned loyalist, Benedict Arnold. Embarrassed by debt and disgusted by Congress's shabby treatment of the Continental Army, Arnold had started exchanging rebel secrets for British money in 1779 before defecting outright in 1780. By June of 1781 Arnold and Cornwallis were fortifying a site on the tip of the peninsula formed by the York and the James rivers, a place called Yorktown.

Meanwhile, Washington and his French ally, the Comte de Rochambeau, met in Connecticut to plan a major attack. Rochambeau urged a coordinated land–sea assault on the Virginia coast. Washington insisted instead on a full-scale offensive against New York City. Just when the rebel commander was about to have his way, word arrived that a French fleet under the Comte de Grasse was sailing for the Chesapeake to blockade Cornwallis by sea. Washington's Continentals headed south.

Surrender at Yorktown

By the end of September, 7800 Frenchmen, 5700 Continentals, and 3200 militia had sandwiched Yorktown between the devil of an allied army and the deep blue sea of French warships. "If you cannot relieve me very soon," Cornwallis wrote to Clinton, "you must expect to hear the worst." The British navy did arrive— but seven days after Cornwallis surrendered to the rebels on October 19, 1781.

It need not have ended at Yorktown, but timing made all the difference. At the end of 1781 and early in 1782, the British army received setbacks in the other theaters of the war: India, the West Indies, and Florida. The French and the Spanish were everywhere in Europe as well, gathering in the English Channel, planning a major offensive against Gibraltar. The cost of the fighting was already enormous. British leaders recognized that the rest of the empire was at stake and set about cutting their losses in America.

The Treaty of Paris, signed on September 3, 1783, was a diplomatic triumph for the American negotiators: Benjamin Franklin, John Adams, and John *Treaty of Paris* Jay. They dangled before Britain the possibility that a generous settlement might weaken American ties to France. The British jumped at the bait. They recognized the independence of the United States and agreed to ample boundaries for the new nation: the Mississippi River on the west, the 31st parallel on the south, and the present border of Canada on the north. American negotiators then persuaded a skeptical France to approve the treaty by arguing that, as allies, they were bound to present a united front to the British. When the French finally persuaded Spain, the third member of the alliance, to reduce its demands on Britain for territorial concessions, the treaty became an accomplished fact. The Spanish settled for Florida and Minorca, an island in the Mediterranean.

The Significance of a Revolution

If the Treaty of Paris marked both the end of a war and the recognition of a new nation, the surrender at Yorktown captured the significance of a revolution. Those present at Yorktown on that clear autumn afternoon in 1781 watched as the British second-in-command to Cornwallis (who had sent word that he was "indisposed") surrendered his superior's sword. He offered the sword first, in a face-saving gesture, to the French commander Rochambeau, who politely refused and pointed to Washington. But the American commander-in-chief, out of a mixture of military protocol, nationalistic pride, and perhaps even wit, pointed to *his* second-in-command, Benjamin Lincoln.

Some witnesses recalled that British musicians arrayed on the Yorktown green played "The World Turned Upside Down." Their recollections may have been faulty, but the story has persisted as part of the folklore of the American Revolution—and for good reasons. The world had, it seemed, turned upside down with the coming of American independence. The colonial rebels shocked the British with their answer to the question: would they fight?

The answer had been yes—but on their own terms. By 1777 most propertied Americans avoided fighting in the Continental Army. Yet whenever the war reached their homes, farms, and businesses, many Americans gave their allegiance to the new nation by turning out with rifles or supplying homespun clothing, food, or ammunition. They rallied around Washington in New Jersey, Gates in upstate New York, Greene in the Carolinas. Middle-class American men fought, some from idealism, others out of self-interest, but always on their own terms, as members of the militia. These citizen-soldiers turned the world upside down by defeating professional armies.

Of course, the militia did not bear the brunt of the fighting. That responsibility fell to the Continental Army, which by 1777 drew its strength from the poorest ranks of American society. Yet even the Continentals, for all their desperation, managed to fight on their own terms. Some asserted their rights by raising mutinies, until Congress redressed their grievances. All of them, as the Baron von Steuben observed, behaved differently from European soldiers. Americans followed orders only if the logic of commands was explained to them. The Continentals, held in contempt by most Americans, turned the world upside down by sensing their power and asserting their measure of personal independence.

Thus did a revolutionary generation turn the world upside down. Descended from desperate, idealistic, and self-interested men and women who settled colonies named for kings and queens—ruled by kings and queens who aimed to increase the wealth and power of their dynasties and their nations—these Americans rebelled against a king. They wanted more than a monarch. But what more did they want? What awaited in a world turned upside down by republican revolutionaries?

SIGNIFICANT EVENTS

1775 — Second Continental Congress convenes at Philadelphia; Congress creates the Continental Army; Battle of Bunker Hill

1776 — Publication of *Common Sense*; British troops evacuate Boston; Declaration of Independence; British occupy New York City, forcing Washington to retreat through New Jersey into Pennsylvania; Washington counterattacks at Battle of Trenton

1777 — British summer drive to occupy Philadelphia: battles of Brandywine Creek, Germantown; Burgoyne surrenders at Saratoga; Continental Army encamps for winter at Valley Forge

1778 — France allies with rebel Americans; France and Britain declare war; British shift focus to the South; Savannah falls

1780 — British occupy Charleston; partisan warfare of Marion, Sumter; rebel victory at King's Mountain, South Carolina; Nathanael Greene takes southern command

1781 — Engagements at Cowpens, Guilford Courthouse; Cornwallis surrenders at Yorktown

1783 — Treaty of Paris

CHAPTER SEVEN

Crisis and Constitution

"I am not a Virginian, but an American," Patrick Henry declared in the Virginia House of Burgesses. Most likely he was lying. Certainly no one listening took him seriously, for the newly independent colonists did not identify themselves as members of a nation. They would have said, as did Thomas Jefferson, "Virginia, Sir, is my country." Or as John Adams wrote to another native son, "Massachusetts is our country." Jefferson and Adams were men of wide political vision and experience: both were leaders in the Continental Congress and more inclined than most to think nationally. But like other members of the revolutionary generation, they identified deeply with their home states and even more deeply with their home counties and towns.

It followed that allegiance to the states, not the Union, determined the shape of the first republican political experiments. For a decade after independence, the revolutionaries were less committed to creating an American nation than to organizing 13 separate state republics. The Declaration of Independence referred explicitly not to *the* United States but to *these* United States. It envisioned not one republic so much as a federation of 13.

Only when peace was restored during the decade of the 1780s were Americans forced to face some unanswered questions raised by their revolution.

How close a union? The Declaration proclaimed that these "free and independent states" had "full power to levy war, conclude peace, contract alliances, establish commerce." Did that mean that New Jersey, as a free and independent state, could sign a trade agreement with France, excluding the other states? If the United States was to be more than a loose federation, how could it assert power on a national scale? Similarly, American borderlands to the west presented problems. If these territories were settled by Americans, would they eventually join the United States? Go their own ways as independent nations? Become new colonies of Spain or England?

Such problems were more than political; they were rooted in social realities. For a political union to succeed, the inhabitants of 13 separate states had to start thinking of themselves as Americans. When it came right down to it, what united a Vermont farmer working his rocky fields and a South Carolina gentleman presiding over a vast rice plantation? What bonds existed between a Kentuckian rafting the Ohio River and a Salem merchant sailing to China for porcelain?

And in a society where all citizens were said to be "created equal," the inevitable social inequalities had to be confronted. How could women participate in the Revolution's bid for freedom if they were not free to vote or to hold property? How could black Americans feel a bond with white Americans when so often the only existing bonds had been forged with chains? To these questions there were no final answers in 1781. And as the decade progressed, the sense of crisis deepened. Americans worried that factions and selfish interest groups would pull "these" United States apart. The new republican union, which spread out over so many miles, constituted a truly unprecedented venture. A good deal of experimenting would be needed if it was to succeed.

REPUBLICAN EXPERIMENTS

After independence was declared in July 1776, many of America's best political minds turned to draw up constitutions for their individual states. In truth, the state constitutions were crucial republican experiments, the first efforts at establishing a government of and by the people. All the revolutionaries agreed that the people—not a king or a few privileged aristocrats—should rule. Yet they were equally certain that republican governments were best suited to small

Belief in the need for small republics

territories. They believed that the new United States was too sprawling and its people too diverse to be safely consolidated into a single national republic. They feared, too, that the government of a large republic would inevitably grow indifferent to popular concerns, being distant from many of its citizens. Without being under the watchful eye of the people, representatives would become less accountable to the electorate and turn tyrannical. A federation of small state republics, they reasoned, would stand a far better chance of enduring.

The State Constitutions

The new state constitutions retained the basic form of their old colonial governments, most providing for a governor and a bicameral legislature. But while most states did not alter the basic structure of their governments, they changed dramatically the balance of power among the different branches of government.

From the republican perspective in 1776, the greatest problem of any government lay in curbing executive power. What had driven Americans into re-

Curbing executive power

bellion was the abuse of authority by the king and his appointed officials. To ensure that the executive could never again threaten popular liberty, the new states either accorded almost no power to their governors or abolished that office entirely. The governors had no authority to convene or dissolve the legislature. They could not veto the legislatures' laws, grant land, or erect courts. Most important from the republican point of view, governors had few powers to appoint other state officials. All these limits were designed to deprive the executive of any patronage or other form of influence over the legislature.

What the state governors lost, the legislatures gained. To ensure that those powerful legislatures truly represented the will of the people, the new state constitutions called for annual elections and required candidates for

Strengthening legislative powers

the legislature to live in the district they represented. Many states even asserted the right of voters to instruct the men elected to office how to vote on specific issues. Although no state granted universal manhood suffrage, most reduced the amount of property required of qualified voters. Finally, state supreme courts were also either elected by the legislatures or appointed by an elected governor.

By investing all power in popular assemblies, Americans abandoned the British system of mixed government. In one sense, that change was fairly democratic. A majority of voters within a state could do whatever they wanted, unchecked by governors or courts. On the other hand, the arrangement opened the door for legislatures to turn as tyrannical as governors. The revolutionaries

Americans responded to independence with rituals of "killing the king," like this New York crowd in 1776, which is pulling down a statue of George III. Americans also expressed their mistrust of monarchs by establishing state governments with weak executive branches.

brushed that prospect aside: republican theory assured them that the people possessed a generous share of civic virtue, the capacity for selfless pursuit of the general welfare.

In an equally momentous change, the revolutionaries insisted on written state constitutions. Whenever government appeared to exceed the limits of its

Written constitutions

authority, Americans wanted to have at hand the written contract between rulers and ruled. When eighteenth-century Englishmen used the word "constitution," they meant the existing arrangement of government—not an actual document but a collection of parliamentary laws, customs, and precedents. But Americans believed that a constitution should be a written code that stood apart from and above government, a yardstick against which the people measured the performance of their rulers. After all, they reasoned, if Britain's constitution had been written down, available for all to consult, would American rights have been violated?

From Congress to Confederation

While Americans lavished attention on their state constitutions, the national government nearly languished during the decade after 1776. With the coming of independence, the Second Continental Congress conducted the common business of the federated states. It created and maintained the Continental Army, issued currency, and negotiated with foreign powers.

But while Congress acted as a central government by common consent, it lacked any legal basis for its authority. To redress that need, in July 1776 Congress appointed a committee to draft a constitution for a national government. The more urgent business of waging and paying for the war made for delay, as did the consuming interest in framing state constitutions. Congress finally approved the first national constitution in November 1777, but it took four more years for all of the states to ratify these Articles of Confederation.

The Articles of Confederation provided for a government by a national legislature—essentially a continuation of the Second Continental Congress.

Articles of Confederation

That body had the authority to declare war and make peace, conduct diplomacy, regulate Indian affairs, appoint military and naval officers, and requisition men from the states. In affairs of finance it could coin money and issue paper currency. Extensive as these responsibilities were, Congress could not levy taxes or even regulate trade. The crucial power of the purse rested entirely with the states, as did the final power to make and execute laws. Even worse, the national government had no distinct executive branch. Congressional committees, constantly changing in their membership, not only had to make laws but had to administer and enforce them as well.

Those weaknesses of the federal government appear more evident in hindsight. Most American leaders of the 1770s had given little thought to federalism, the organization of a United States. Political leaders had not yet recognized the need for dividing power between the states and the national government. With the new nation in the midst of a military crisis, Congress assumed—correctly in most cases—that the states did not have to be forced to contribute men and money to the common defense. Creating a strong national government would have antagonized many Americans, who after all had just rebelled against the distant, centralized authority of Britain's king and Parliament.

Guided by republican political theory and by their colonial experience, American revolutionaries created a loose confederation of 13 independent state republics under a nearly powerless national government. They succeeded so well, the United States almost failed to survive its first decade of independence. The problem was that lessons from the colonial past were not always useful guides to postwar realities. Only when events forced Americans to think nationally did they begin to consider the possibility of reinventing "these United States"—this time under the yoke of a truly federal republic.

THE TEMPTATIONS OF PEACE

The surrender of Cornwallis at Yorktown in 1781 marked the end of military crisis in America. But as the threat from Britain receded, so did the source of American unity. The many differences among Americans, most of which lay submerged during the struggle for independence, surfaced in full force. Those domestic divisions, combined with challenges to the new nation from Britain and Spain, created conflicts that neither the states nor the national government proved equal to handling.

The Temptations of the West

The greatest opportunities and the greatest problems for postwar Americans awaited in the rapidly expanding West. With the boundary of the new United States now set at the Mississippi River, more settlers spilled across the Appalachians, planting farmsteads and towns throughout Ohio, Kentucky, and Tennessee. By 1790 places that had been almost uninhabited by whites in 1760 held more than 2.25 million people, one-third of the nation's population.

After the Revolution, as before, western settlement fostered intense conflict. American claims that its territory stretched all the way to the Mississippi were by no means taken for granted by European and Indian powers. The West also confronted Americans with questions about their own national identity. Would the newly settled territories enter the nation as states on an equal footing with the original 13 states? Would they be ruled as dependent colonies? The fate of the West, in other words, constituted a crucial test of whether "these" United States could grow and still remain united.

As the stumps dotting the landscape indicate, western farmers first sought
to "improve" their acreage by felling trees. But their dwellings were far
less substantial than those depicted in this idealized sketch of an "American New
Cleared Farm." And while some Indians guided parties of whites into the West,
as shown in the foreground, more often they resisted white encroachment. For
that reason, dogs, here perched placidly in canoes, were trained to alert their white
masters to the approach of Indians.

Foreign Intrigues

Both the British from their base in Canada and the Spanish in Florida and
Louisiana hoped to chisel away at American borders. Their considerable success in the 1780s exposed the weakness of Confederation diplomacy.

Before the ink was dry on the Treaty of Paris, Britain's ministers were secretly
instructing Canadians to maintain their forts and trading posts inside the United
States's northwestern frontier. They reckoned—correctly—that with the Continental Army disbanded, the Confederation could not force the British to withdraw.

The British also made mischief along the Confederation's northern borders,
mainly with Vermont. For decades, Ethan Allen and his Green Mountain Boys
had waged a war of nerves with neighboring New York, which claimed Vermont
as part of its territory. After the Revolution the Vermonters petitioned Congress
for statehood, demanding independence of both New York and New Hampshire.
When Congress dragged its feet, the British tried to woo Vermont into their
empire as a province of Canada. That flirtation with the British pressured
Congress into granting Vermont statehood in 1791.

The loyalty of the southwestern frontier was even less certain. By 1790
more than 100,000 settlers had poured through the Cumberland Gap to reach

Spanish designs on the Southwest Kentucky and Tennessee. But the commercial possibilities of the region depended entirely on access to the Mississippi and the port of New Orleans, since it was far too costly to ship southwestern produce over the rough trails east across the Appalachians. And the Mississippi route was still dominated by the Spanish, who controlled Louisiana as well as forts along western Mississippi shores as far north as St. Louis. The Spanish, seeing their opportunity, closed the Mississippi to American navigation in 1784. That action prompted serious talk among southwesterners about seceding from the United States and joining Spain's empire.

The Spanish also tried to strenghten their hold on North America by making common cause with the Indians. Of particular concern to both groups was protecting Florida, which had reverted to Spain's possession, from the encroachment of American settlers filtering south from Georgia. Florida's governor alerted his superiors back in Spain to the threat posed by those backwoodsmen who were "nomadic like Arabs and . . . distinguished from savages only in their color, language, and the superiority of their depraved cunning and untrustworthiness." So Spanish colonial officals responded eagerly to the overtures of Alexander McGillivray, a young Indian leader whose mother was of French-Creek descent and whose father was a Scots trader. His efforts brought about a treaty of alliance between the Creeks and the Spanish in 1784, quickly followed by similar alliances with the Choctaws and the Chickasaws. What cemented such treaties were the trade goods that the Spanish agreed to supply to the tribes. Securing European gunpower and guns had become essentail to southeastern Indians, because their entire economies now revolved around hunting and selling deerskins to white traders.

Disputes among the States

As if foreign intrigues were not divisive enough, the states continued to argue among themselves over western land claims. The old royal charters for some colonies had extended their boundaries all the way to the Mississippi and beyond. (See the map, page 173.) But the charters were often vague, granting both Massachusetts and Virginia, for example, undisputed possession of present-day Wisconsin. In contrast, other charters limited state boundaries to within a few hundred miles of the Atlantic coast. "Landed" states like Virginia wanted to secure control over the large territory granted by their charters. "Landless" states (which included Maryland, Delaware, Pennsylvania, Rhode Island, and New Jersey) called on Congress to restrict the boundaries of landed states and to convert western lands into a domain administered by the Confederation.

Landed versus landless states

The landless states lost the opening round of the contest over ownership of the West. The Articles of Confederation acknowledged the old charter claims of the landed states. Then Maryland, one of the smallest landless states, retaliated by refusing to ratify the Articles. Since every state had to approve the

Articles before they were formally accepted, the fate of the United States hung in the balance. One by one the landed states relented. The last holdout, Virginia, in January 1781 ceded its charter rights to land north of the Ohio River. Once Virginia ceded, Maryland ratified the Articles in February 1781, four long years after Congress had first approved them.

WESTERN LAND CLAIMS, 1782–1802   The Confederation's settlement of conflicting western land claims was an achievement essential to the consolidation of political union. Some states asserted that their original charters extended their western borders to the Mississippi River. A few states, like Virginia, claimed western borders on the Pacific Ocean.

The More Democratic West

More bitterly disputed than land claims in the West was the issue concerning the sort of men westerners elected to political office. The state legislatures of the 1780s were both larger and more democratic in their membership than the old colonial assemblies. Before the Revolution no more than a fifth of the men serving in the assemblies were middle-class farmers or artisans; government was almost exclusively the domain of the wealthiest merchants, lawyers, and planters. After the Revolution twice as many state legislators were men of moderate wealth. The shift was more marked in the North, where middle-class men predominated among representatives. But in every state, some men of modest means, humble background, and little formal education attained political power.

State legislatures became more democratic in membership mainly because as backcountry districts grew, so did the number of their representatives. Since western districts tended to be less developed economically and culturally, their leading men were less rich and cultivated than the seaboard elite. Wealthy, well-educated gentlemen thus became a much smaller and less powerful group within the legislatures because of greater western representation and influence.

Changing composition of state legislatures

But many republican gentlemen, while endorsing government by popular consent, doubted whether ordinary people were fit to rule. The problem, they contended, was that the new western legislators concerned themselves only with the narrow interests of their constituents, not with the good of the whole state. As Ezra Stiles, the president of Yale College, observed, the new breed of politicians were those with "the all-prevailing popular talent of coaxing and flattering," who "whenever a bill is read in the legislature . . . instantly thinks how it will affect his constituents." And if state legislatures could not rise above petty bickering and narrow self-interest, how long would it be before civic virtue and a concern for the general welfare simply withered away?

The Northwest Territory

Such fears of "democratic excess" also influenced policy when Congress debated what to do with the Northwest Territory. Carved out of the land ceded by the states to the national government, the Northwest Territory comprised the present-day states of Ohio, Indiana, Illinois, Michigan, and Wisconsin. With so many white settlers moving into these lands, Congress was faced with a crucial test of its federal system. If the Confederation could not expand in an orderly way beyond the original 13 colonies, the new territories might well become independent countries or even colonies of Spain or Britain. Congress dealt with the issue of expansion by adopting three ordinances.

The first, drafted by Thomas Jefferson in 1784, divided the Northwest Territory into 10 states, each to be admitted to the Union on equal terms as soon as its population equaled that in any of the existing states. In the mean-

E Y E W I T N E S S   T O   H I S T O R Y

A Traveler from Virginia Considers the Ruins of an Ancient Indian Civilization in the Ohio Valley

have often observed while travelling thro' this country, a number of round hillocks, raised from 15 feet high and under and from 50 to 100 yards around them. It seems evident that those places are not natural, but are the work of man. The only question seems to be, "What were they made for?" Some have supposed they were once places of defence. But the most probable opinion is, that they are burying places of the former inhabitants of this country. On digging into these, I am informed, great quantities of bones are found, lying in a confus'd promiscuous manner. Some authors inform us that once in ten years the Indians collect the bones of their dead, and bring them all to one place and bury them. Thus they proceed, putting one layer over another till they get them to the height above mentioned.

An object, however, of a different kind now presents itself to our view . . . a neck of land about 4 or 500 yards wide. Across this neck of land lies an old wall, joining the river at each end and enclosing, I suppose, about 100 acres of land. This wall is composed of earth dug from the outside, where a ditch of some depth is still discernible. The wall at present is so mouldered down that a man could easily ride over it. It is however about 10 feet, as near as I can judge, in perpendicular height, and gives growth to a number of large trees. In one place I observe a breach in the wall about 60 feet wide, where I suppose the gate formerly stood through which the people passed in and out of this stronghold. Compared with this, what feeble and insignificant works are those of Fort Hamilton or Fort Washington! They are no more in comparison to it than a rail fence is to a brick wall.

18 November 1795, Journal of the Reverend James Smith. Richard H. Collins Papers, Durrett Collection, University of Chicago.

Jefferson's plan for the Northwest — time, Jefferson provided for democratic self-government of the territory by all free adult males. A second ordinance of 1785 set up an efficient mechanism for dividing and selling public lands. The Northwest Territory was surveyed into townships of six miles square. Each township then was divided into 36 lots of one square mile, or 640 acres.

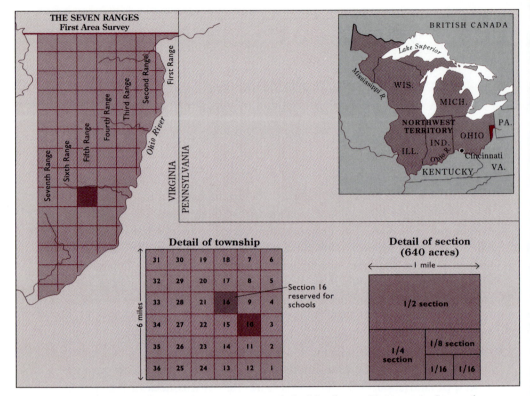

THE ORDINANCE OF 1785 Surveyors entered the Northwest Territory in September of 1785, imposing on the land regular grids of six square miles to define new townships, as shown on this range map of a portion of Ohio. Farmers purchased blocks of land within townships, each one mile square, from the federal government or from land speculators.

Congress waited in vain for buyers to flock to the land offices it established. The cost of even a single lot—$640—was too steep for most farmers. Disappointed by the shortage of buyers and desperate for money, Congress finally accepted a proposition submitted by a private company of land speculators that offered to buy some 6 million acres in present-day southeastern Ohio. That several members of Congress numbered among the company's stockholders no doubt added to enthusiasm for the deal.

The transaction concluded, Congress calmed the speculators' worries that incoming settlers might enjoy too much self-government by scrapping Jefferson's

Northwest Ordinance

democratic design and substituting the Northwest Ordinance of 1787. That ordinance provided for a period in which Congress held sway in the territory through its appointees—a governor, a secretary, and three judges. When the population reached 5000 free adult males, a legislature was to be established, although its laws required the governor's approval. A representative could sit in Congress but had no vote. When the population reached 60,000, the inhabitants might apply for statehood, and the whole Northwest Territory was to be divided into not less than three or more than five states. The ordinance also guaranteed basic rights—freedom of religion and trial by jury—and provided for the support of public education.

Congress's plan completely ignored the rights of the Shawnee, Chippewa, and other Indian peoples who lived in the region. To them, it made no difference that the British had ceded their lands to the Americans. And in terms of Jefferson's democratic ideals for white inhabitants, the ordinance of 1787 also fell short. Still, Congress had succeeded in extending republican government to the West and incorporating the frontier into the new nation. Congress also outlawed slavery throughout the territory.

That decision had an unexpected, almost ironic consequence. The Northwest Ordinance went a long way toward establishing a federal system that would minimize tensions between the East and the West, a major source of postwar conflict. The Republic now had a peaceful, orderly way to expand its federation of states. Yet by limiting the spread of slavery in the northern states, Congress deepened the critical social and economic differences between North and South, evident already in the 1780s.

Slavery and Sectionalism

When white Americans declared their independence, they owned nearly half a million black Americans. African Americans of the revolutionary generation, most of them enslaved, constituted 20 percent of the total population of the colonies in 1775, and nearly 90 percent of them lived in the South. Yet few political leaders directly confronted the issue of whether slavery should be permitted to exist in a truly republican society.

When political discussion did stray toward the subject of slavery, southerners—especially ardent republicans—bristled defensively. Theirs was a

Republicanism and slavery

difficult position, riddled with contradictions. On the one hand, they had condemned parliamentary taxation as tantamount to political "slavery" and had rebelled, declaring that all men were "created equal." On the other hand, enslaved African Americans formed the basis of the South's plantation economy. To surrender slavery, southerners believed, would be to usher in economic ruin.

Some planters in the Upper South resolved the dilemma by freeing their slaves. Such decisions were made easier by changing economic conditions in the Chesapeake. As planters shifted from tobacco toward wheat, a crop demanding a good deal less labor, Virginia and Maryland liberalized their manumission statutes, laws providing for freeing slaves. Between 1776 and 1789, most southern states also joined the North in prohibiting the importation of slaves, and a few antislavery societies appeared in the Upper South. But no southern state legally abolished slavery. Masters defended their right to hold human property in the name of republicanism.

Negro Methodists Holding a Meeting in a Philadelphia Alley evokes the vibrancy of black religious life in the city that became a haven for free African Americans. (The Metropolitan Museum of Art, New York)

Eighteenth-century republicans regarded property as crucial, for it provided a man and his family with security, status, and wealth. More important, it provided a measure of independence: to be able to act freely, without fear or favor of others. People without property were dangerous, republicans believed, because the poor could never be politically independent. Southern defenders of slavery thus argued that free, propertyless black people would pose a political threat to the liberty of propertied white citizens. Subordinating the human rights of blacks to the property rights of whites, southern republicans reached the paradoxical conclusion that their freedom depended on keeping African Americans in bondage.

The North followed a different course. Because its economy depended far less on slave labor, black emancipation did not run counter to powerful economic interests. Antislavery societies, the first founded by the Quakers in 1775, spread throughout the northern states during the next quarter century. Over the same period the legislatures of most northern states provided for the immediate or gradual abolition of slavery. Freedom for most northern African Americans came slowly, but by 1830 there were fewer than 3000 slaves out of a total northern black population of 125,000.

The Revolution, which had been fought for liberty and equality, did little to change the status of most black Americans. By 1800 more enslaved African Americans lived in the United States than had lived there in 1776. Slavery continued to grow in the Lower South as the rice culture of the Carolinas and Georgia expanded and as the new cotton culture spread westward.

Still, a larger number of slaves than ever before became free during the war and in the decades following, whether through military service, successful escape, manumission, or gradual emancipation. All these developments fostered the growth of free black communities, especially in the Upper South and in northern cities. By 1810 free African Americans made up 10 percent of the total population of Maryland and Virginia. The composition of the postwar free community changed as well. Before independence most free blacks had been either mulattoes—the offspring of interracial unions—or former slaves too sick or aged to have value as laborers. By contrast, the free population of the 1780s became darker skinned, younger, and healthier. This group injected new vitality into black communal life, organizing independent schools, churches, and mutual benefit societies for the growing number of "free people of color."

Growth of the free black community

After the Revolution slavery ceased to be a national institution. It became the "peculiar institution" of a single region, the American South. The isolation of slavery in one section set North and South on radically different courses of social development, sharpening economic and political divisions.

Wartime Economic Disruption

With the outbreak of the Revolution, Americans had suffered an immediate loss of the manufactured goods, markets, and credit that Britain had formerly supplied. Matters did not improve with the coming of peace. France and Britain flooded the new states with their manufactures, and postwar Americans, eager for luxuries, indulged in a most unrepublican spending spree. The flurry of buying left some American merchants and consumers as deeply in debt as their governments. When loans from private citizens and foreign creditors like France had proved insufficient to finance the fighting, both Congress and the states printed paper money—a whopping total of $400 million. The paper currency was backed only by the government's promise to redeem the bills with money from future taxes, since legislatures balked at the unpopular alternative of levying taxes during the war. For the bills to be redeemed, the United States had to survive, so by the end of 1776, when Continental forces sustained a series of defeats, paper money started to depreciate dramatically. By 1781 it was virtually without value, and Americans coined the expression "not worth a Continental."

Public and private debt

The printing of paper money, combined with a wartime shortage of goods, triggered an inflationary spiral of scarcer and scarcer goods costing more and

Postwar inflation

more worthless dollars. In this spiral, creditors were gouged by debtors, who paid them back with depreciated currency. At the same time soaring prices for food and manufactured goods eroded the buying power of wage earners and small farmers. And the end of the war brought on demands for prompt repayment from the new nation's foreign creditors as well as from soldiers seeking back pay and pensions.

Congress could do nothing. With no power to regulate trade, it could neither dam the stream of imported goods rushing into the states nor stanch the flow of gold and silver to Europe to pay for these items. With no power to prohibit the states from issuing paper money, it could not halt depreciation. With no power to regulate wages or prices, it could not curb inflation. With no power to tax, it could not reduce the public debt. Efforts to grant Congress greater powers met with determined resistance from the states.

Within states, too, economic problems aroused discord. Some major merchants, creditors, and large commercial farmers had profited handsomely during the war by selling supplies to the American, British, and French army at high prices or by preying on enemy vessels as privateers. Eager to protect their windfall, they lobbied state legislatures for an end to inflationary monetary policies. That meant passing high taxes to pay wartime debts, a paper currency that was backed up with gold and silver, and an active policy to encourage foreign trade.

Political divisions over economic policy

Less affluent men fought back, pressing legislatures for programs that met their needs. Western farmers, often in debt, urged the states to print more paper money and to pass laws lowering taxes and postponing the foreclosure of mortgages. Artisans opposed merchants by calling for protection from low-priced foreign imports that competed with the goods they produced. They set themselves against farmers as well by demanding price regulation of the farm products they consumed. In the continuing struggle, the state legislatures became the battleground of competing economic factions.

As the 1780s wore on, conflicts mounted. So long as the individual states remained sovereign, the Confederation was crippled—unable to conduct foreign affairs effectively, unable to set coherent economic policy, unable to deal with discontent in the West. Equally dismaying was the discovery that many Americans, instead of being selflessly concerned for the public good, selfishly pursued their private interests.

REPUBLICAN SOCIETY

The war for independence transformed not only America's government and economy but also its society and culture. Inspired by the Declaration's ideal of equality, some Americans rejected the subordinate position assigned to them under the old colonial order. Westerners, newly wealthy entrepreneurs, urban artisans, and women all claimed greater freedom, power, and recognition. The authority of the traditional leaders of government, society, and the family came under a new scrutiny; the impulse to defer to social superiors became less automatic. The new assertiveness demonstrated how deeply egalitarian assumptions were taking root in American culture.

The New Men of the Revolution

The Revolution gave rise to a new sense of social identity and a new set of ambitions among several groups of men who had once accepted a humbler status. The war also offered opportunities to aspiring entrepreneurs everywhere, and often they were not the same men who had prospered before the war. At a stroke, independence swept away the prominence of loyalists, whose ranks included an especially high number of government officials, large landowners, and major merchants. And while loyalists found their properties confiscated by revolutionary governments, other Americans grew rich. Many northern merchants gained newfound wealth from privateering or military contracts. Commercial farmers in the mid-Atlantic states prospered from the high food prices caused by wartime scarcity and army demand.

Winners and losers

The Revolution effected no dramatic redistribution of wealth. Indeed, the gap between rich and poor increased during the 1780s. But those families newly enriched by the Revolution came to demand and receive greater social recognition and political influence. The republican ideal of "an aristocracy of merit" justified their ambitions.

City craftworkers pushed for recognition too. Their experience in organizing boycotts against British goods during the imperial crisis gave artisans a greater taste of politics. With the Revolution accomplished, they clamored for men of their own kind to represent them in government. Their assertiveness came as a rude shock to gentlemen like South Carolina's William Henry Drayton, who balked at sharing power with men "who never were in a way to study" anything except "how to cut up a beast in the market to the best advantage, to cobble an old shoe in the neatest manner, or to build a necessary house."

Urban artisans

While master craftworkers competed for political office, the laborers who worked for them also exhibited a new sense of independence. Recognizing that their interests were often distinct from those of masters, journeymen formed new organizations to secure higher wages. Between 1786 and 1816 skilled urban laborers organized the first major strikes in American history.

The New Women of the Revolution

Not long after the fighting with Britain had broken out, Margaret Livingston of New York wrote to her sister Catherine, "You know that our Sex are doomed to be obedient in every stage of life so that we shant be great gainers by this contest." By war's end, however, Eliza Wilkinson from rural South Carolina was complaining boldly to a woman friend: "The men say we have no business with political matters . . . it's not our sphere. . . . [But] I won't have it thought that because we are the weaker Sex (as to bodily strength my dear) we are Capable of nothing more, than minding the Dairy . . . surely we may have enough sense to give our Opinions."

What separated Margaret Livingston's resignation from Eliza Wilkinson's assertion of personal worth and independence was the Revolution. Eliza Wilkinson had managed her parents' plantation during the war and defended it from British marauders. Other women discovered similar reserves of skill and resourcefulness. When soldiers returned home, some were surprised to find their wives and daughters, who had been running family farms and businesses, less submissive and more self-confident.

But American men had not fought a revolution for the equality of American women. In fact, male revolutionaries gave no thought to the role of women in

Exclusion of women from politics

the new nation, assuming that those of the "weaker sex" were incapable of making informed and independent political decisions. Most women of the revolutionary generation agreed that the proper female domain was the home, not the public arena of politics. Still, the currents of the Revolution occasionally left gaps that allowed women to display their political interests. When a loosely worded provision in the New Jersey state constitution gave the vote to "all free inhabitants" owning a specified amount of property, white widows and single women went to the polls. Only in 1807 did the state legislature close the loophole.

Artists in the new republic often personified freedom as a young female, shown here as "Miss Liberty," bearing an American flag, even as male revolutionaries excluded women from the political life of the new nation.

"Republican Motherhood" and Education

Even though women's primary sphere remained the home, the Revolution brought about changes. Reformers like Benjamin Rush and Judith Sargent Murray argued that only educated and independent-minded women could raise the informed and self-reliant citizens that a republican government required. The notion of "republican motherhood" contributed to the most dramatic change in the lives of women after the war: the spread of female literacy.

Between 1780 and 1830 the number of American colleges and secondary academies rose dramatically, and some of these new institutions were devoted

Improved schooling and literacy rates

to educating women. Not only did the number of schools for women increase, but these schools also offered a solid academic curriculum. By 1850—for the first time in American history— there were as many literate women as there were men. To counter popular prejudices, the defenders of female education contended that schooling for women would produce the ideal republican mother. An educated woman, as one graduate of a female academy claimed, would "inspire her brothers, her husband, or her sons with such a love of virtue, such just ideas of the true value of civil liberty . . . that future heroes and statesmen shall exaltingly declare, it is to my mother that I owe this elevation."

The Revolution also prompted some states to reform their marriage laws, making divorce somewhat easier, although it remained extremely rare. But

Women's legal status

while women won greater freedom to divorce, courts became less concerned to enforce a widow's traditional legal claim to one- third of her spouse's real estate. And married women still could not sue or be sued, make wills or contracts, or buy and sell property. Any wages that they earned went to their husbands; so did all personal property that wives brought into a marriage; so did the rents and profits of any real estate they owned. Despite the high ideals of "republican motherhood," most women re- mained confined to the "domestic sphere" of the home and deprived of the most basic legal and political rights.

The Attack on Aristocracy

Why wasn't the American Revolution more revolutionary? Independence se- cured the full political equality of white men who owned property, but women were still deprived of political rights, African Americans of human rights. Why did the revolutionaries stop short of extending equality to the most unequal groups in American society—and with so little sense that they were being inconsistent?

In part, the lack of concern was rooted in republican ideas themselves. Republican ideology viewed property as the key to independence and power.

Republican view of equality   Lacking property, women and black Americans were easily consigned to the custody of husbands and masters. Then, too, prejudice played its part: the perception of women and blacks as naturally inferior beings.

But revolutionary leaders also failed to press for greater equality because they conceived their crusade in terms of eliminating the evils of a European past dominated by kings and aristocrats. They believed that the great obstacle to equality was monarchy—kings and queens who bestowed hereditary honors and political office on favored individuals and granted legal privileges and monopolies to favored churches and businesses. These artificial inequalities posed the real threat to liberty, most republicans concluded. In other words, the men of the Revolution were intent on attaining equality by leveling off the top of society. It did not occur to most republicans that the cause of equality could also be served by raising up the bottom—by attacking the laws and prejudices that kept African Americans enslaved and women dependent.

The most significant reform of the republican campaign against artificial privilege was the dismantling of state-supported churches. Most states had a re-

Disestablishment   ligious establishment. In New York and the South, it was the Anglican church; in New England, the Congregational church. Since the 1740s, dissenters who did not worship at state churches had protested laws that taxed all citizens to support the clergy of established denominations. After the Revolution, as more dissenters became voters, state legislators gradually abolished state support for Anglican and Congregational churches.

Not only in religious life but in all aspects of their culture, Americans rejected inequalities associated with a monarchical past. In that spirit reformers attacked the

Society of Cincinnati   Society of Cincinnati, a group organized by former officers of the Continental Army in 1783. The society, which was merely a social club for veterans, was forced to disband for its policy of passing on its membership rights to eldest sons. In this way, critics charged, the Cincinnati was creating artificial distinctions and perpetuating a hereditary warrior nobility.

Today many of the republican efforts at reform seem misdirected. While only a handful of revolutionaries worked for the education of women and the emancipation of slaves, enormous zeal went into fighting threats from a monarchical past that had never existed in America. Yet the threat from kings and aristocrats was real to the revolutionaries—and indeed remained real in many parts of Europe. Their determination to sweep away every shred of formal privilege ensured that these forms of inequality never took root in America.

COUNTERPOINT   *Radicalism and the American Revolution*

Not all historians agree that the American Revolution was an essentially conservative movement, one that effected little fundamental social change. On the contrary, some argue that the Revolution had radical consequences, dramatically transforming not only government but society. True, unlike later revolutions in France and Russia, the American Revolution did not involve the violent overthrow of a ruling class by a nonruling class. Even so, these scholars believe that the birth of republican goverment not only created a more egalitarian culture in the new United States than existed anywhere else in the world but also spurred the rise of a liberal, democratic, and capitalist society.

The real radicalism of the American Revolution, in this view, lay in its challenging the age-old belief that gentlemen and common men were two separate kinds of human beings. For centuries, most people of every social rank in both the Old World and the New had accepted the notion that gentlefolk were innately superior because of their high birth, classical learning, polite refinements, and leisured existences. Ordinary people were held to be naturally ignorant, driven by the basest desires and needs, and so dulled by lives of toil that they were incapable of elevated thought or noble behavior. But American revolutionaries shattered that hierarchical way of thinking by celebrating the common sense of the common man and asserting that all human beings are naturally equal in their moral capacity to judge right from wrong. Indeed, revolutionaries went even further, endowing ordinary people and their labor with dignity by elevating the importance of productive work and by depicting industrious farmers and artisans as more virtuous than the idle rich.

In short, historians contending for the radicalism of the American Revolution believe that to emphasize the inequalites of race and gender that persisted in the new United States is to overlook the very real change that republicanism achieved. It accorded common white men unprecedented respect and power at the same time that it created a government dedicated to promoting their liberty, security, and prosperity.

FROM CONFEDERATION TO CONSTITUTION

While Americans in many walks of life sought to realize the republican commitment to equality, leaders in Congress wrestled with the problem of preserving the nation itself. With the new republic slowly rending itself to pieces, some political leaders concluded that neither the Confederation nor the state legislatures were able to remedy the basic difficulties facing the nation. But how could the states be convinced to surrender their sovereign powers? The answer came in the wake of two events—one foreign, one domestic—that lent momentum to the cause of strengthening the central government.

The Jay–Gardoqui Treaty

The international episode that threatened to leave the Confederation in shambles was a debate over a proposed treaty with Spain. In 1785 southwesterners still could not legally navigate the Mississippi and were still threatening to secede from the union and annex their territory to Spain's American empire. To shore up southwestern loyalties, Congress instructed its secretary of foreign affairs, John Jay, to negotiate an agreement with Spain preserving American rights to navigate on the Mississippi River. But the Spanish emissary, Don Diego de Gardoqui, sweet-talked Jay into accepting a treaty by which the United States would give up all rights to the Mississippi for 25 years. In return, Spain agreed to grant trading privileges to American merchants.

Jay, a New Yorker, knew more than a few northern merchants who were eager to open new markets. But when the proposed treaty became public knowledge, southwesterners denounced it as nothing short of betrayal. The treaty was never ratified, but the hostility stirred up during the debate revealed the strength of sectional feelings.

Shays' Rebellion

On the heels of this humiliation by Spain came an internal conflict that challenged the notion that individual states could maintain order in their own territories. The trouble erupted in western Massachusetts, where many small farmers were close to ruin. Yet they still had to pay mortgages on their farms, still had other debts, and were perpetually short of money. In 1786 the lower house of the Massachusetts legislature obliged the farmers with a package of relief measures. But creditors in eastern Massachusetts, determined to safeguard their own investments, persuaded the upper house to defeat the measures.

In the summer of 1786 western farmers responded, demanding that the upper house of the legislature be abolished and that the relief measures go into effect. That autumn 2000 farmers rose in armed rebellion, led by Captain Daniel Shays, a veteran of the Revolution. They closed the county courts to halt creditors from foreclosing on their farms and marched on the federal arsenal at Springfield. The state militia quelled the uprising by February 1787, but the insurrection left many in Massachusetts and the rest of the country thoroughly shaken.

Alarmed conservatives saw Shays' Rebellion as the consequence of radical democracy. "The natural effects of pure democracy are already produced among us," lamented one republican gentleman; "it is a war against virtue, talents, and property carried on by the dregs and scum of mankind." He was wrong. Daniel Shays' rebels were no impoverished rabble. They were reputable members of western communities who wanted their property protected and believed that government existed to provide that protection. The Massachusetts state legislature had been unable to safeguard the property of farmers from the inroads of recession or to protect the property of creditors from the armed debtors who closed the courts. It had failed, in other words, to fulfill the most basic aim of republican government.

Response to agrarian unrest

Other states with discontented debtors feared what the example of western Massachusetts might mean for the future of the Confederation itself. But by 1786 Shays' Rebellion supplied only the sharpest jolt to a movement for reform

James Madison, the scholar and statesman whose ideas and political skill shaped the Constitution

that was already under way. Even before the rebellion, a group of Virginians had proposed a meeting of the states to adopt a uniform system of commercial regulations. Once assembled at Annapolis in September 1786, the delegates from five states agreed to a more ambitious undertaking. They called for a second, broader meeting in Philadelphia, which Congress approved, for the "express purpose of revising the Articles of Confederation."

Framing a Federal Constitution

It was the wettest spring anyone could remember. The 55 men who traveled over muddy roads to Philadelphia in May 1787 arrived drenched and bespattered. Fortunately, most of the travelers were men in their thirties and forties, young enough to survive a good soaking. Since most were gentlemen of some means—planters, merchants, and lawyers with powdered wigs and prosperous paunches—they could recover from the rigors of their journey in the best accommodations offered by America's largest city.

The delegates came from all the states except Rhode Island. The rest of New England supplied shrewd backroom politicians—Roger Sherman and Oliver Ellsworth from Connecticut and Rufus King and Elbridge Gerry, Massachusetts men who had learned a trick or two from Sam Adams. The middle states marshaled much of the intellectual might: two Philadelphia lawyers, John Dickinson and James Wilson; one Philadelphia financier, Robert Morris; and the aristocratic Gouverneur Morris. From New York there was Alexander Hamilton, the mercurial and ambitious young protégé of Washington. South Carolina provided fiery orators, Charles Pinckney and John Rutledge.

It was "an assembly of the demi-gods," gushed Thomas Jefferson, who, along with John Adams, was serving as a diplomat in Europe when the convention met. In fact, the only delegate who looked even remotely divine was the convention's presiding deity. Towering a full half foot taller than most of his colleagues, George Washington displayed his usual self-possession from a chair elevated on the speaker's platform where the delegates met, in the Pennsylvania State House. At first glance, the delegate of least commanding presence was

James Madison

Washington's fellow Virginian, James Madison. Short and slightly built, the 36-year-old Madison had no profession except hypochondria. But he was an astute politician and a brilliant political thinker who, more than anyone else, shaped the framing of the federal Constitution.

The delegates from 12 different states had two things in common. They were all men of considerable political experience, and they all recognized the need for a stronger national union. So when the Virginia delegation introduced Madison's outline for a new central government, the convention was ready to listen.

The Virginia and New Jersey Plans

What Madison had in mind was a truly national republic, not a confederation of independent states. His "Virginia Plan" proposed a central government with

Madison's Virginia Plan

three branches: legislative, executive, and judicial. Furthermore, the legislative branch, Congress, would possess the power to veto all state legislation. In place of the Confederation's single assembly, Madison substituted a bicameral legislature, with a lower house elected directly by the people and an upper house chosen by the lower from nominations made by state legislatures. Representatives to both houses would be apportioned according to population—a change from practice under the Articles, in which each state had a single vote in Congress. Madison also revised the structure of government that had existed under the Articles by adding an executive, who would be elected by Congress, and an independent federal judiciary.

After two weeks of debate over the Virginia Plan, William Paterson, a lawyer from New Jersey, presented a less radical counterproposal. While his "New

Paterson's New Jersey Plan

Jersey Plan" increased Congress's power to tax and to regulate trade, it kept the national government as a unicameral assembly, with each state receiving one vote in Congress under the policy of equal representation. The delegates took just four days to reject Paterson's plan. Most endorsed Madison's design for a stronger central government.

Even so, the issue of apportioning representation continued to divide the delegates. While smaller states pressed for each state having an equal vote in Congress, larger states backed Madison's provision for basing representation on population. Underlying the dispute over representation was an even deeper rivalry between southern and northern states. While northern and southern populations were nearly equal in the 1780s, and the South's population was growing more rapidly, the northern states were more numerous. Giving the states equal votes would put the South at a disadvantage. Southerners feared being outvoted in Congress by the northern states and felt that only proportional representation would protect the interests of their section.

That division turned into a deadlock as the wet spring burned off into a blazing summer. Delegates suffered the daily torture of staring at a large sun painted on the speaker's chair occupied by Washington. The stifling heat was made even worse because the windows remained shut, to keep any news of the proceedings from drifting out onto the Philadelphia streets.

The Deadlock Broken

Finally, as the heat wave broke, so did the political stalemate. On July 2 a committee headed by Benjamin Franklin suggested a compromise. States would be equally represented in the upper house of Congress, each state legislature ap-

Compromise over representation

pointing two senators to six-year terms. That satisfied the smaller states. In the lower house of Congress, which alone could initiate money bills, representation was to be apportioned according to population. Every 30,000 inhabitants would elect one representative for a two-year term. A slave was to count as three-fifths of a free person in the calculation of population, and the slave trade was to continue until 1808. That satisfied the larger states and the South.

By the end of August the convention was prepared to approve the final draft of the Constitution. The delegates agreed that the executive, now called the president, would be chosen every four years. Direct election seemed out of the question—after all, how could citizens in South Carolina know any-

Electoral College

thing about a presidential candidate who happened to live in distant Massachusetts, or vice versa? But if voters instead chose presidential electors, those eminent men would likely have been involved in national politics, have known the candidates personally, and be prepared to vote wisely. Thus the Electoral College was established, with each state's total number of senators and representatives determining its share of electoral votes.

An array of other powers ensured that the executive would remain independent and strong: he would have command over the armed forces, authority to conduct diplomatic relations, responsibility to nominate judges and officials

Separation of powers

in the executive branch, and the power to veto congressional legislation. Just as the executive branch was made independent, so too the federal judiciary was separated from the other two branches of government. Madison believed that this clear separation of powers was essential to a balanced republican government.

Madison's only real defeat came when the convention refused to give Congress veto power over state legislation. Still, the new bicameral national legislature enjoyed much broader authority than Congress had under the Confederation, including the power to tax and to regulate commerce. The Constitution also limited the powers of state legislatures, prohibiting them from levying duties on trade, coining money or issuing paper currency, and conducting foreign relations. The Constitution and the acts passed by Congress were declared the supreme law of

Amending the Constitution

the land, taking precedence over any legislation passed by the states. And changing the Constitution would not be easy. Amendments could be proposed only by a two-thirds vote of both houses of Congress or in a convention requested by two-thirds of the state legislatures. Ratification of amendments required approval by three-quarters of the states.

On September 17, 1787, thirty-nine of the forty-two delegates remaining in Philadelphia signed the Constitution. Charged only to revise the Articles, the delegates had instead written a completely new frame of government. And to speed up ratification, the convention decided that the Constitution would go into effect after only nine states had approved it. They further declared that the people themselves—not the state legislatures—would pass judgment on the Constitution in special ratifying conventions. To serve final notice that the new central government was a republic of the people and not merely another confederation of states, Gouverneur Morris of Pennsylvania hit on a happy turn of phrase to introduce the Constitution. "We the People," the document begins, "in order to form a more perfect union. . . ."

Ratification

With grave misgivings on the part of many, the states called for conventions to decide whether to ratify the new Constitution. Those with the gravest misgivings—the Anti-Federalists as they came to be called—voiced familiar re-

The Anti-Federalists

publican fears. Older and less cosmopolitan than their Federalist opponents, the Anti-Federalists drew upon their memories of the struggle with England to frame their criticisms of the Constitution. Expanding the power of the central government at the expense of the states, they warned, would lead to corrupt and arbitrary rule by new aristocrats. Extending a republic over a large territory, they cautioned, would separate national legislators from the interests and close oversight of their constituents.

Madison responded to these objections in *The Federalist Papers*, a series of 85 essays written with Alexander Hamilton and John Jay during the winter of 1787–1788. He countered Anti-Federalist concerns over the centralization of

The Federalist Papers

power by pointing out that each separate branch of the national government would keep the others within the limits of their legal authority. That mechanism of checks and balances would prevent the executive from oppressing the people while preventing the people from oppressing themselves.

To answer Anti-Federalist objections to a national republic, Madison drew on the ideas of an English philosopher, David Hume. In his famous tenth essay in *The Federalist Papers*, Madison argued that in a great republic, "the Society becomes broken into a greater variety of interests, of pursuits, of passions, which check each other." The larger the territory, the more likely it was to contain multiple political interests and parties, so that no single faction could dominate. Instead, each would cancel out the others.

The one Anti-Federalist criticism Madison could not get around was the absence of a national bill of rights. Opponents insisted on an explicit statement

Bill of Rights

of rights to secure the freedoms of individuals and minorities from being violated by the federal government. Madison finally promised to place a bill of rights before Congress immediately after the Constitution was ratified.

Throughout the early months of 1788, Anti-Federalists continued their opposition. But they lacked the articulate and influential leadership that rallied behind the Constitution and commanded greater access to the public press. In the end, too, Anti-Federalist fears of centralized power proved less compelling than Federalist prophecies of the chaos that would follow if the Constitution were not adopted.

By June 1788 all but three states had voted in favor of ratification. The last holdout—to no one's surprise Rhode Island—finally came aboard in May 1790, after Madison had carried through on his pledge to submit a bill of rights to the new Congress. Indeed, these 10 amendments proved to be the Anti-Federalists' most impressive legacy.

Changing Revolutionary Ideals

Within the life span of a single generation, Americans had declared their independence twice. In many ways the political freedom claimed from Britain in 1776 was less remarkable than the intellectual freedom that Americans achieved by agreeing to the Constitution. The Constitution represented both a triumph of imagination and common sense and a rejection of some older, long-cherished republican beliefs.

Americans thought long and hard before changing their minds, but many did. Committed at first to limiting executive power by making legislatures supreme, they at last ratified a constitution that provided for an independent executive and a balanced government. Committed at first to preserving the sovereignty of the states, they at last established a national government with authority independent of the states. Committed at first to the proposition that a national republic was impossible, they at last created an impossibility that still endures.

What, then, became of the last tenet of the old republican creed—the belief that civic virtue would sustain popular liberty? The hard lessons of the war

Interest rather than virtue

and the crises of the 1780s withered confidence in the capacity of Americans to sacrifice their private interests for the public welfare. Many came to share Washington's sober view that "the few . . . who act upon Principles of disinterestedness are, comparatively speaking, no more than a drop in the Ocean." The Constitution reflected the new recognition that interest rather than virtue shaped the behavior of most people most of the time and that the clash of diverse interest groups would remain a constant of public life.

Yet Madison and many other Federalists did not believe that the competition between private interests would somehow result in policies fostering public welfare. That goal would be met instead by the new national government acting as "a disinterested and dispassionate umpire in disputes between different passions and interests in the State." The Federalists looked to the national government to fulfill that role because they trusted that a large republic, with its millions of citizens, would yield more of that scarce resource—disinterested gentlemen dedicated to serving the public good. Such gentlemen, in Madison's words, "whose enlightened views and virtuous sentiments render them superior to local prejudices," would fill the small number of national offices.

Not all the old revolutionaries agreed. Anti-Federalists drawn from the ranks of ordinary Americans still believed that common people were more virtuous and gentlemen more interested than the Federalists allowed. "These lawyers and men of learning, and moneyed men, that talk so finely," complained one Anti-Federalist, would "get all the power and all of the money into their own hands, and then they will swallow up all us little folks." Instead of being dominated by enlightened gentlemen, the national government should be composed of representatives from every social class and occupational group.

The narrow majorities by which the Constitution was ratified reflected the continuing influence of such sentiments, as well as fear that the states were surrendering too much power. That fear made Patrick Henry so ardent an Anti-Federalist that he refused to attend the Constitutional Convention in 1787, saying that he "smelt a rat." "I am not a Virginian, but an American," Henry had once declared. Most likely he was lying. Or perhaps Patrick Henry, a southerner and a slaveholder, could see his way clear to being an "American" only so long as sovereignty remained firmly in the hands of the individual states. Henry's convictions, 70 years hence, would rise again to haunt the Union.

SIGNIFICANT EVENTS

1777	Continental Congress approves the Articles of Confederation
1781	Articles of Confederation ratified
1784	Spain closes the Mississippi River to American navigation
1785	Jay–Gardoqui Treaty negotiated but not ratified
1786	Shays' Rebellion; Annapolis convention calls for revising the Articles
1787	Congress adopts the Northwest Ordinance; Constitutional Convention
1787–1788	Publication of *The Federalist Papers*
1788	New Hampshire becomes ninth state to ratify Constitution
1791	Bill of Rights adopted

CHAPTER EIGHT

The Republic Launched

ne spring evening in 1794 General John Neville was riding home from Pittsburgh with his wife and granddaughter. Coming up a hill his wife's saddle started to slip, so Neville dismounted to tighten the girth. As he adjusted the strap, he heard the clip-clop of horses' hooves, followed by a gruff voice. "Are you Neville the excise officer?"

Still busy with his wife's saddle, Neville replied "yes," without turning around.

"Then I must give you a whipping!" announced the rider, leaping from his horse. He grabbed the startled Neville by the hair and lunged at his throat, and the two began tussling. Breaking free, Neville finally managed to knock the man down and subdue him. He recognized his assailant as Jacob Long, a local farmer. After Long fled, the badly shaken Neville resumed his journey.

John Neville was not accustomed to such treatment. As one of the wealthiest men in the area, he expected respect from those of lower social rank. And he had received it—at least he had until becoming embroiled in a controversy over the new "whiskey tax" on distilled spirits. In a frontier district like western Pennsylvania, farmers regularly distilled their grain into whiskey for barter and sale. Not surprisingly, the excise tax, passed by Congress in 1791, was notoriously unpopular. Even so, Neville had accepted an appointment as one of the tax's regional inspectors. For three years he had endured threats as he tried to enforce the law, but this roadside assault clearly indicated that popular hostility was rising.

As spring turned to summer, the grain ripened, and so did the people's anger. In mid-July, a federal marshall arrived to serve summonses to a number of farmer-distillers who had not paid taxes. One, William Miller, squinted at the paper and was amazed to find the government ordering him to set aside "all manner of business and excuses" and appear in court—hundreds of miles away in Philadelphia—in little more than a month. Even worse, the papers claimed he owed $250.

Frontier farmers in Pennsylvania tar and feather a federal tax collector
during the Whiskey Rebellion. The political violence of the 1790s
led Americans to wonder whether the new government would succeed
in uniting a socially diverse nation.

And there, next to this unknown federal marshall, stood the stiff-backed,
unyielding John Neville.

"I felt myself mad with passion," recalled Miller. "I thought $250 would
ruin me; and . . . I felt my blood boil at seeing General Neville along to pilot
the sheriff to my very door." Meanwhile word of the marshall's presence brought
30 or 40 laborers swarming from a nearby field. Armed with muskets and pitch-
forks, they appeared both angry and well-liquored. When a shot rang out,
Neville and the marshall beat a hasty retreat.

Within hours, news of Neville's doings spread to a nearby militia company.
Enraged by what they considered this latest trampling on individual liberty, the
militia marched to Neville's fortified house the next morning. A battle ensued,
and the general, aided by his slaves, beat back the attackers. A larger group,

numbering 500 to 700, returned the following day to find Neville fled and his home garrisoned by a group of soldiers from nearby Fort Pitt. The mob burned down most of the outbuildings and, after the soldiers surrendered, torched Neville's home.

Throughout the region that summer, anonymous broadsides threatened those who "opposed the virtuous principles of republican liberty," liberty poles appeared with flags proclaiming "liberty and no excise," and marauding bands in disguise roamed the countryside, burning homes, banishing individuals, and attacking tax collectors and other enemies. To many citizens who learned of the disturbances, such echoes of the revolutionary 1760s and 1770s were deeply distressing. In the space of only 15 years, Americans had already overturned two governments: England's colonial administration and the Articles of Confederation. As the aged Benjamin Franklin remarked in 1788, although Americans were quite proficient at overthrowing governments, it remained to be seen whether they were any good at sustaining them. Six years later, Franklin's warning seemed prophetic.

Yet Federalists—supporters of the Constitution—had recognized from the beginning how risky it was to unite a territory as large as the United States's 890,000 square miles. Yankee merchants living along Boston wharves had economic interests and cultural traditions quite different from those of backcountry farmers who raised hogs, tended a few acres of corn, and distilled whiskey. Even among farmers, there was a world of difference between a South Carolina planter who shipped tons of rice to European markets and a Vermont family whose stony fields yielded barely enough to survive. Could the new government established by the Constitution provide a framework strong enough to unite such a socially diverse nation?

1789: A SOCIAL PORTRAIT

When the Constitution went into effect, the United States stretched from the Atlantic Ocean to the Mississippi River. The first federal census, compiled in 1790, put the population at approximately 4 million people, divided about evenly between the northern and southern states. The Republic's population was overwhelmingly concentrated along the eastern seaboard. Only about 100,000 settlers lived beyond the Appalachians in the Tennessee and Kentucky territories, which were soon to become states. The area north of the Ohio River was virtually unsettled by whites.

Within the Republic's boundaries were two major racial groups that lacked effective political influence: African Americans and Indians. In 1790 black Americans numbered 750,000, almost one-fifth of the total population. Over 90 percent lived in the southern states from Maryland to Georgia; most were slaves who worked on tobacco and rice plantations. The census did not count the number of Indians living east of the Mississippi. North of the Ohio, the powerful Miami Confederacy discouraged settlement, while to the south, five strong, well-organized tribes—the Creeks, Cherokees, Chickasaws, Choctaws, and Seminoles—dominated the region from the Appalachians to the Mississippi River.

That situation would change, however, as the white population continued to double approximately every 22 years. The primary cause was natural increase,

Population growth

for in 1790 the average American white woman gave birth to nearly eight children.* The age at first marriage was about 25 for men, 24 for women; but it was significantly lower in newly settled areas (on average perhaps 21 for males and younger for females), which contributed to the high birthrate.

This youthful, growing population remained overwhelmingly rural. Only 24 towns or cities boasted a population of 2500 or more, and 19 out of 20 Americans lived outside them. In fact, in 1800 over 80 percent of American families were engaged in agriculture. In such a rural environment the move-

Poor transportation

ment of people, goods, and information was slow. Few individuals used the expensive postal system, and most roads were still little more than dirt paths. In 1790 the country had 92 newspapers, published weekly or semiweekly, mostly in towns and cities along major avenues of transportation. Americans off the beaten path only occasionally heard news of the outside world.

What would divide Americans most broadly over the coming decades was whether they were primarily semisubsistence farmers, living largely on the produce of their own land and labor, or were tied more closely to the larger commercial markets. As the United States began its life under the new federal union, the distinction between a semisubsistence economy and a commercial economy was a crucial one.

The Semisubsistence Economy of Crèvecoeur's America

Most rural white Americans lived off the produce of their own land in a barter economy. It was this world that a French writer, Hector St. John de Crèvecoeur, described so well.

Arriving in 1759, Crèvecoeur traveled widely in the British colonies before settling for a number of years as a farmer in the Hudson River valley. He published in 1783 his *Letters from an American Farmer*, asking in them the question that had so often recurred to him: "What then is the American, this new man?"

For Crèvecoeur what distinguished American society was the widespread equality of its people, especially the rural farmers. Americans were hostile to

---

*Because the 1790 census did not include significant data on the black population, many of the statistical figures quoted for this era apply only to white Americans.

Equality
anything that smacked of aristocratic privilege. Furthermore, the conditions of the country promoted equality. Land was abundant and widely distributed, citizens lived decently, and the population was not divided into the wealthy few and the desperate many. (Like most of his contemporaries, Crèvecoeur glided rather quickly over the plight of black slaves.) "We are the most perfect society now existing in the world," he boasted.

Although Crèvecoeur waxed romantic about the conditions of American life, he painted a reasonably accurate portrait of most of the interior of the northern states and the backcountry of the South. Wealth in those areas, while not distributed equally, was spread fairly broadly. And subsistence remained the goal of most white families. "The great effort was for every farmer to produce anything he required within his own family," one European visitor noted. In such an economy women played a key role. Wives and daughters had to be skilled in making articles such as candles, soap, clothing, and hats, since the cost of buying such items was steep.

With labor scarce and expensive, farmers also depended on their neighbors to help clear fields, build homes, and harvest crops. If a farm family produced
Barter economy
a small surplus, they usually exchanged it locally rather than selling it for cash in a distant market. In this barter economy money was seldom seen. Instead, residents in the countryside "supply their needs . . . by direct reciprocal exchanges," a French traveler recorded. "They write down what they give and receive on both sides and at the end of the year they settle a large variety of exchanges with a very small quantity of coin."

Indian economies were also based primarily on subsistence. In the division of labor women raised crops, while men fished or hunted—not only for meat but also for skins to make clothing. Because Indians followed game more seasonally than white settlers, their villages were moved to several different locations over the course of a year. But both whites and Indians in a semisubsistence economy moved periodically to new fields after the old ones were exhausted.

Despite the popular image of both the independent "noble savage" and the self-reliant yeoman farmer, virtually no one in the backcountry operated within a truly subsistence economy. While farmers tried to grow most of the food their families ate, they normally bought salt, sugar, and coffee. In addition, necessities such as iron, glass, lead, and powder had to be purchased, usually at a country store, and many farmers hired artisans to make items such as shoes and to weave cloth. Similarly, Indians quickly became enmeshed in the wider world of European commerce, exchanging furs for iron tools or clothing and ornamental materials.

The Commercial Economy of Franklin's America

Outside the backcountry, Americans were tied much more closely to a commercial economy. Here, merchants, artisans, and even farmers did not subsist on what they produced but instead sold goods or services in a wider market and lived on their earnings. Cities and towns, of course, played a key part in the commercial economy. But so did the agricultural regions near the seaboard and along navigable rivers.

For commerce to flourish, goods had to move from producers to market cheaply enough to reap profits. Water offered the only cost-effective transportation over any distance; indeed, it cost as much to ship goods a mere 30 miles over primitive roads as to ship by boat 3000 miles across the Atlantic to London. Where transportation was prohibitively expensive, farmers had no incentive to increase production, and an economy of barter and semisubsistence persisted.

Commercial society differed from Crèvecoeur's world in another important way: its wealth was less equally distributed. By 1790, the richest 10 percent of those living in cities and in the plantation districts of the Tidewater South owned about 50 percent of the wealth. In the backcountry the top 10 percent was likely to own 25 to 35 percent.

Inequality of wealth

Crèvecoeur argued that the American belief in equality sustained this society of small, relatively equal farm families. But he failed to see how much that equality rested on isolation. In areas with access to markets, Americans were more acquisitive and materialistic. Although semisubsistence farm families were eager to rise in life and acquire material goods, only those in the commercial economy could realistically pursue these dreams.

The man who gained international renown as a self-made citizen of commercial America was Benjamin Franklin. In his writings and in the example of his own life, Franklin offered a vision of the new nation that contrasted with Crèvecoeur's ideal of a subsistence America. He had arrived in Philadelphia as a runaway apprentice but by hard work and talent rose to be one of the leading citizens of his adopted city. The preface to Franklin's popular *Poor Richard's Almanack*, as well as his countless essays, spelled out simple maxims for Americans seeking the upward path. "The way to wealth is as plain as the way to market," he noted. "It depends chiefly on two words, industry and frugality." Those anxious to succeed should "remember that time is money." The kind of success he preached depended on taking advantage of commerce and a wider market. As a printer, Franklin was able to lead a life of acquisition and social mobility because he could distribute his almanacs and newspapers to ever-greater audiences.

Benjamin Franklin and commercial values

The ethics of Franklin's marketplace threatened to destroy Crèvecoeur's egalitarian America. At the time of Franklin's death in 1790, the ideal that Crèvecoeur had so eloquently described still held sway across much of America. But the political debate of the 1790s showed clearly that Franklin's world of commerce and markets was slowly transforming the nation.

The Constitution and Commerce

In many ways the fight over ratification of the Constitution represented a struggle between the commercial and the subsistence-oriented elements of American society. Urban merchants and workers as well as commercial farmers and planters generally rallied behind the Constitution. They took a broader, more cosmopolitan view of the nation's future, and they had a more favorable view of government power.

Americans who remained a part of the semisubsistence barter economy tended to oppose the Constitution. More provincial in outlook, they feared concentrated power, were suspicious of cities and commercial institutions, opposed aristocracy and special privilege, and in general just wanted to be left alone. In defeat they remained suspicious that a powerful government would tax them to benefit the commercial sectors of the economy.

And so in 1789 the United States embarked on its new national course, with two rival visions of the direction that the fledgling Republic should take. Which vision would prevail—a question that was as much social as it was political—increasingly divided the generation of revolutionary leaders during the 1790s.

THE NEW GOVERNMENT

Whatever the Republic was to become, Americans agreed that George Washington personified it. When the first Electoral College cast its votes, Washington was unanimously elected, the only president in history so honored. John Adams became vice president. Loyalty to the new Republic rested to a great degree on the trust and respect Americans gave Washington.

Time has transformed Washington from a man into a monument: remote and unknowable, stiff, unbowing, impenetrable. Even during his own lifetime,

Washington's character

he had no close friends in public life and discouraged familiarity. Cautious and deliberate, the president usually asked for written advice and made his decision only after weighing the options carefully. Critics complained about his formal public receptions, the large number of servants, and the coach emblazoned with his coat of arms—all aristocratic habits. Still, as much as Washington craved honor and military fame, he did not hunger for power and accepted the office of the presidency only reluctantly.

Organizing the Government

Washington realized that as the first occupant of the executive office, everything he did was fraught with significance. "I walk on untrodden ground," he commented. "There is scarcely any part of my conduct which may not hereafter be drawn into precedent."

Congress authorized the creation of four departments—War, Treasury, State, and Attorney General—whose heads were to be appointed with the con-

The cabinet

sent of the Senate. Washington's most important choices were Alexander Hamilton as secretary of the treasury and Thomas Jefferson to head the State Department. At first the president did not meet regularly with his advisers as a group, but gradually the idea of a cabinet that met to discuss policy matters evolved.

Washington's trip from Virginia to New York City to assume the presidency was a triumphant procession as Americans greeted him with unbridled enthusiasm bordering on adulation. Here women strew flowers before him as he passes through Trenton.

The Constitution created a federal Supreme Court but beyond that was silent about the court system. The Judiciary Act of 1789 set the size of the

Federal judiciary Supreme Court at 6 members; it also established 13 federal district courts and 3 circuit courts of appeal. The Judiciary Act made it clear that federal courts had the right to review decisions of the state courts and specified cases over which the Supreme Court would have original jurisdiction. Washington appointed John Jay of New York, a staunch Federalist, as the first chief justice.

The Bill of Rights

Congress also confronted the demand for a bill of rights, which had become an issue during the debate over ratification. At that time, nearly 200 amendments had been put forward in one form or another. Supporters of the Constitution were particularly alarmed over proposals to restrict the federal power to tax. As leader of the Federalist forces in the House of Representatives, James Madison moved to head off any large-scale changes that would weaken federal power by submitting a bill of rights that focused on civil liberties.

Ultimately Congress sent 12 amendments to the states. By December 1791, 10 had been ratified and incorporated into the Constitution. The advocates of strong federal power, like Hamilton, were relieved that "the structure of the government, and the mass and distribution of its powers," remained unchanged.

These first 10 amendments, known as the Bill of Rights, were destined to be of crucial importance in defining personal liberty in the United States. Among the rights guaranteed were freedom of religion, the press, and speech, as well as the right to assemble and petition and the right to bear arms. The amendments also established clear procedural safeguards, including the right to a trial by jury and protection against illegal searches and seizures. They prohibited excessive bail, cruel and unusual punishment, and the quartering of troops in private homes. At the same time, an attempt in Congress to apply these same guarantees to state governments failed.

Protected rights

Hamilton's Financial Program

Before adjourning, Congress called on Alexander Hamilton, as secretary of the treasury, to report on the nation's finances. Hamilton undertook the assignment eagerly, for he did not intend to be a minor figure in the new administration.

Hamilton grew up on the islands of the West Indies, scarred by the stigmas of poverty and illegitimacy. To compensate, he was driven constantly to seek respectability and money. He served as a military aide to Washington during the Revolution, and marriage to the daughter of a wealthy New York politician gave him influential connections he could draw on in his political career. Hamilton's haughty manner, jealousy, and penchant for intrigue made him many enemies. He was a brilliant thinker, yet he felt out of place in the increasingly democratic society emerging around him. "All communities divide themselves into the few and the many," he declared. ". . . The people are turbulent and changing; they seldom judge or determine right."

Hamilton's character

Convinced that human nature was at bottom selfish, Hamilton believed that the government needed to appeal to the self-interest of the rich and wellborn in order to succeed. "Men," he observed succinctly, "will naturally go to those who pay them best." He took as his model Great Britain, whose greatness he attributed to its system of public finance and its preeminence in commerce and manufacturing. Thus Hamilton set out to achieve two goals. He intended to use federal power to encourage manufacturing and commerce, in order to make the United States economically strong and independent of Europe. And he was determined to link the interests of the wealthy with those of the new government.

Neither goal could be achieved until the federal government solved its two most pressing financial problems: revenue and credit. Without revenue it could not be effective, and without credit—the faith that the government would repay its debts—it would lack the ability to borrow. Hamilton proposed that all $52 million of the federal debt be paid in full (or funded). He also recommended that the federal government assume responsibility for the remaining $25 million in debts that individual states owed. He intended with these policies to enhance the new federal government's

Funding and assumption

Hamilton, though short of stature, cut a dashing figure with his erect bearing, strutting manner, meticulous dress, and carefully powdered hair. Declared the wife of the British ambassador: "I have scarcely ever been more charmed with the vivacity and conversation of any man."

power and strengthen its creditworthiness. Hamilton also proposed a series of excise taxes, including a controversial 25 percent levy on whiskey, to help meet government expenses.

After heated debate, Congress deadlocked over funding and assumption. Finally, over dinner with Hamilton, Jefferson and Madison of Virginia agreed to

Location of the capital

support his proposal if, after 10 years in Philadelphia, the permanent seat of government was located in the South, on the Potomac River between Virginia and Maryland. Aided by this understanding, funding and assumption passed Congress. In 1791 Congress also approved a 20-year charter for the first Bank of the United States. The bank would hold government deposits and issue bank notes that would be received in payment of all debts owed the federal government. Congress proved less receptive to the rest of Hamilton's program, although a limited tariff to encourage manufacturing and several excise taxes, including the one on whiskey, won approval.

Opposition to Hamilton's Program

The passage of Hamilton's program caused a permanent rupture among supporters of the Constitution. Eventually the two warring factions organized themselves into political parties: the Republicans, led by Jefferson and Madison, and the Federalists, led by Hamilton and Adams.[*] But the division emerged slowly over several years.

---

[*]The Republican party of the 1790s, sometimes referred to as the Jeffersonian Republicans, is not to be confused with the modern-day Republican party, which originated in the 1850s.

Hamilton's program promoted the commercial sector at the expense of semisubsistence-agrarian groups. Thus it rekindled many of the concerns that

Fears over Hamilton's program

had surfaced during the struggle over ratification of the Constitution. The ideology of the Revolution had stressed that republics inevitably contained groups who sought power in order to destroy popular liberties and overthrow the republic. To some Americans, Hamilton's program seemed a clear threat to establish a privileged and powerful financial aristocracy—perhaps even a monarchy.

Who, after all, would benefit from the funding proposal? During and after the Revolution, the value of notes issued by the Continental Congress dropped sharply. Speculators had bought up most of these notes for a fraction of their face value from small farmers and workers. Equally disturbing, members of Congress had been purchasing the notes before the adoption of Hamilton's program. Madison urged that only the original holders of the debt be reimbursed in full, but Hamilton rejected this idea, since commercial speculators were precisely the class of people he hoped to bind to the new government.

Similarly, when stock in the Bank of the United States went on sale, speculators snapped up all the shares in an hour. The price of a share skyrocketed from $25 to $300 in two months. Jefferson was appalled by the mania Hamilton's program encouraged. "The spirit of gambling, once it has seized a subject, is incurable," he asserted. "The taylor who has made thousands in one day, tho he has lost them the next, can never again be content with the slow and moderate earnings of his needle."

The national bank struck its critics as a dangerous mimicking of English corruption. Indeed, in Great Britain the Bank of England played a powerful role

Opposition to a national bank

not only in fueling the economy but in controlling Parliament by making loans to members, and Jefferson warned that the same thing would happen in the United States. These fears were heightened because Americans had little experience with banks: only three existed in the country when the Bank of the United States was chartered. Then, too, banks and commerce were a part of the urban environment that rural Americans so distrusted. Moreover, the tariff favored one group in society—manufacturers—at the expense of other groups.

After Congress approved the bank bill, Washington hesitated to sign it. When he consulted his cabinet, Jefferson stressed that the Constitution did not

Strict construction versus implied powers

specifically authorize Congress to charter a bank. Both he and Madison upheld the idea of strict construction—that the Constitution should be interpreted narrowly and the federal government restricted to powers expressly delegated to it. Otherwise, the federal government would be the judge of its own powers, and there would be no safeguard against the abuse of power.

Hamilton countered that the Constitution contained implied as well as enumerated powers. He particularly emphasized the clause that permitted Congress to make all laws "necessary and proper" to carry out its duties. A bank would be useful in carrying out the enumerated powers of regulating commerce and maintaining the public credit; therefore Congress had a right to decide whether to establish one. In the end Washington accepted Hamilton's forceful arguments and signed the bill.

The Specter of Aristocracy

Hamilton's opponents feared the development of an aristocracy in the United States. Because Hamilton's program deliberately aided the rich and created a class of citizens whose wealth derived from the federal government, it strengthened these traditional fears. "Money will be put under the direction of government," charged Philip Freneau, a leading Republican editor, "and the government will be put under the direction of money."

Many who opposed Hamilton's financial program had also been against the Constitution, but leadership of the opposition fell to Jefferson and Madison, who had staunchly worked for ratification. Although Jefferson and Madison were planters, well accustomed to the workings of the marketplace, they still distrusted cities and commerce and Hamilton's aristocratic ways.

Economically Hamilton's program was a success. The government's credit was restored, and the national bank ended the inflation of the previous two

Hamilton's success

decades and created a sound currency. And Hamilton's theory of implied powers and broad construction gave the nation the flexibility necessary to respond to unanticipated crises.

EXPANSION AND TURMOIL IN THE WEST

In the peace treaty of 1783, Britain ceded to the United States the territory between the Appalachian Mountains and the Mississippi River. Even so, British troops continued to hold the forts in the Northwest, and Indian tribes controlled most of this region. To demonstrate the government's effectiveness, Washington moved to extend control over the West.

The Resistance of the Miamis

In principle, the United States recognized the rights of Indians to their lands. Furthermore, it had promised that any purchase of Indian land would be made only by treaty and not through private agreements. Nevertheless, the government was determined to buy out Indian titles in order to promote white settlement.

By 1790 the United States had acquired the Indian lands in most of Kentucky and about one-quarter of Tennessee. North of the Ohio, however, the Miami Confederacy (composed of eight western tribes headed by the Miami) stoutly refused to sell territory. Eventually Washington dispatched an army of 2000, commanded by "Mad Anthony" Wayne, to compel a resolution. At the Battle

Indian defeat at Fallen Timbers

of Fallen Timbers in August 1794 Wayne won a decisive victory. In the Treaty of Greenville (1795), he forced the tribes to cede the southern two-thirds of the area between Lake Erie and the Ohio River, thus opening up the Northwest to white settlement.

The Whiskey Rebellion

Westerners approved of the administration's military policy against the Indians. They were far less pleased that in 1791 Congress had passed a new excise tax on distilled liquors. Most property owners along the frontier found it hard to make ends meet, and for many settlers the sale of whiskey provided essential income.

When news of the law reached them, farmers in the western districts of several states defied federal officials and refused to pay, launching a "whiskey rebellion." The greatest unrest flared in western Pennsylvania, where General Neville was burned out of his home (page 195). That summer an even larger gathering of angry, impoverished farmers threatened to march on Pittsburgh. For rural residents, the city had become a symbol of the corrupt cosmopolitan influences that threatened their liberty. Many in the crowd relished the idea of looting the property of wealthy residents. "I have a bad hat now, but I expect to have a better one soon," shouted one of the mob.

To distant easterners, the Whiskey Rebellion at first appeared serious. Hamilton, who had pushed the whiskey tax in order to demonstrate the power

Collapse of resistance

of the new government, saw the matter as a question of authority. "Shall there be government, or no government?" he asked. An alarmed Washington led an army of 13,000 men into the Pennsylvania countryside to overawe the populace and subdue the rebels. Hamilton soon took charge, but to his disappointment the troops met no organized resistance. "An insurrection was announced and proclaimed and armed against," Jefferson scoffed, "but could never be found." Even some of Hamilton's allies conceded that he had overreacted.

Western unhappiness was also eased somewhat when Washington sent Thomas Pinckney to negotiate a treaty with Spain, which controlled Florida

Pinckney's Treaty

and the mouth of the Mississippi. Pinckney's Treaty, which the Senate unanimously ratified in 1796, set the 31st parallel as the southern boundary of the United States and granted Americans free navigation of the Mississippi, with the right to deposit goods at New Orleans for reshipment to ports in the East and abroad. No longer could Spain try to detach the western settlements from American control by promising to open the Mississippi to their trade.

THE EMERGENCE OF POLITICAL PARTIES

Members of the revolutionary generation fervently hoped that political parties would not take root in the United States. "If I could not go to heaven but with a party, I would not go at all," remarked Jefferson. Critics condemned parties because they divided society, were dominated by narrow special interests, and placed selfishness and party loyalty above a concern for the public good. Yet the United States was the first nation to establish truly popular parties.

Social conditions encouraged the rise of parties. Because property owner-ship was widespread, the nation had a broad suffrage. When parties acted as

Social conditions and parties   representatives of economic and social interest groups, they be-came one means by which a large electorate could make its feel-ings known. In addition, the United States had the highest liter-acy rate in the world and the largest number of newspapers, further encouraging political interest and participation. Finally, the fact that well-known patriots of the Revolution headed both the Federalists and the Republicans helped defuse the charge that either party was hostile to the Revolution or the Constitution.

The French Revolution

While domestic issues at first split the supporters of the Constitution, it was a crisis in Europe that initially pushed Americans toward political parties. When the French Revolution began in 1789, Americans hailed it as the first stirring of liberty on the European continent. By 1793, however, enthusiasm for the French Revolution began to cool as radical elements began a reign of terror, ex-ecuting the king and queen and many of the nobility. When France went to war in 1793 with England, Americans were deeply divided over whether the United States should continue its old alliance with France.

Hamilton and his allies viewed the French Revolution as sheer anarchy. Its leaders seemed to be destroying the very institutions that held civilization to-

Differing views of the Revolution   gether: the church, social classes, property, law and order. The United States, Hamilton argued, should renounce the 1778 treaty of alliance with France and side with Britain. For Jefferson and his followers, the issue was republicanism versus monarchy. France was a sister republic, and despite deplorable excesses, its revolution was spreading the doc-trine of liberty. Jefferson argued that the United States should maintain its treaty of alliance with France and insist that as neutrals, Americans had every right to trade with France as much as with England.

As tempers flared, each faction suspected the worst of the other. To the Jeffersonians, Hamilton and his friends seemed part of a monarchist conspiracy. "The ultimate object of all this," Jefferson said of Hamilton's policies, "is to prepare the way for a change, from the present republican forms of Government, to that of a monarchy." As for the Hamiltonians, they viewed Jefferson and his faction as disciples of French radicals, conspiring to establish mob rule in the United States.

Washington's Neutral Course

Washington was convinced that in order to prosper, the United States must remain independent of Europe and its unending quarrels and wars. Thus he issued a proclamation of American neutrality.

Under international law, neutrals could trade with belligerents—nations at war—so long as the trade had existed before the outbreak of hostilities and

Neutral rights did not involve war supplies. But both France and Great Britain began intercepting American ships and confiscating cargoes. At the same time, Britain impressed into service American sailors it suspected of being British subjects. Despite these abuses, Hamilton continued to support a friendly policy toward Britain. He realistically recognized, as did Washington, that the United States was not strong enough to challenge Britain militarily. Moreover, Hamilton's domestic program depended on trade with Britain, which purchased 75 percent of America's exports and provided 90 percent of its imports.

In addition to violating neutral rights and practicing impressment, Great Britain continued to occupy the western forts it had promised to evacuate in

Jay's Treaty 1783, and it closed the West Indies, a traditional source of trade, to American ships. Washington sent John Jay to Britain as a special minister to resolve these differences, but Jay persuaded the British only to withdraw their troops from the Northwest. The West Indies remained closed to American shipping. In essence, Jay's Treaty reinforced the United States's position as an economic satellite of Britain.

To Republicans, Jay had been all too willing to bend to British demands. Their opposition in the Senate meant that the treaty was ratified in June 1795 by the narrowest possible margin.

The Federalists and Republicans Organize

Thus events in Europe contributed directly to the rise of parties in America. The war, Jefferson commented, "kindled and brought forward the two parties with an ardour which our own interests merely, could never excite." By the mid-1790s both sides were organizing on a national basis. Hamilton took the lead in coordinating the Federalist party, which grew out of the voting bloc in Congress that enacted his economic program. Increasingly, Washington drew closer to Federalist advisers and policies and became the symbol of the party.

The guiding genius of the opposition was Hamilton's one-time colleague James Madison. Jefferson, who resigned as secretary of state at the end of 1793,

Organization of an opposition party became the symbolic head of the party. The disputes over Jay's Treaty and the whiskey tax gave the Republicans popular issues, and they began organizing on the state and local levels. Unlike the Federalists, who cloaked themselves in Washington's mantle and claimed to uphold the government and the Constitution, the Republicans had to overcome the ingrained idea that an opposition party was seditious and therefore illegitimate.

As more and more members of Congress allied themselves with one faction or the other, voting became increasingly partisan. By 1796 even minor matters were decided by party votes. Gradually, party organization filtered downward to local communities.

The 1796 Election

Weary of the abuse heaped on him by the opposition press, Washington announced in 1796 that he would not accept a third term. In his Farewell Address he warned against the dangers of parties and urged a return to the earlier nonpartisan system. But when the Republicans chose Thomas Jefferson to oppose John Adams, the possibility of a nonparty constitutional system ended.

The framers of the Constitution did not anticipate that political parties would run competing candidates for both the presidency and the vice presidency. They provided that the candidate with the most electoral votes would be president and the second highest would become vice president. Ever the intriguer, Hamilton tried to manipulate the electoral vote to defeat Adams, whom he disliked. But in the ensuing confusion, Adams won with 71 electoral votes, while his rival, Jefferson, gained the vice presidency with 68 votes.

The fault line between the two parties reflected basic divisions in American life. Geographically, the Federalists were strongest in New England, with its

Typifying the rising party spirit of the 1790s, this anti-Republican cartoon portrays Washington with American troops repulsing an invasion of bloodthirsty French radicals while Jefferson attempts to hold his chariot back. This cartoon appealed to American nationalism by linking the opposition with foreign influence and disloyalty.

Support for the two parties strong commercial ties to Great Britain and its powerful tradition of hierarchy and order. Of the southernmost states, the Federalists enjoyed significant strength only in aristocratic South Carolina. The Republicans won solid support in semisubsistence areas like the West, where Crèvecoeur's farmers were only weakly linked to the market. The middle states were closely contested, although the most cosmopolitan and commercially oriented elements remained the core of Federalist strength.

The Republicans won the backing of most of the old Anti-Federalist opponents of the Constitution, as well as a number of Americans who had firmly backed the new union. These supporters included some commercial farmers in the North and planters in the South and, increasingly, urban workers and small shopkeepers who were repelled by the aristocratic tone of the Federalists. The Republicans were often led by ambitious men of new wealth who felt excluded by the entrenched Federalist elite. Jefferson also attracted the support of immigrants and members of dissenting religious sects who lacked cultural acceptance.

Federalist and Republican Ideologies

In different ways, each party looked both forward and backward: toward certain traditions of the past as well as toward newer social currents that would shape America in the nineteenth century.

Most Federalists viewed themselves as a kind of natural aristocracy making a last desperate stand against the excesses of democracy. They clung to the notion that the upper class should rule over their social and economic inferiors. Pessimistic in their view of human nature, Federalists opposed unbridled individualism and were obsessed by fear of the "mob." In a republic, they argued, government had to restrain popular power. *Federalist ideas*

Although the Federalists resolutely opposed the rising tide of democracy and individualism, they were remarkably forward-looking in their economic ideas. They believed that the government ought to use its power to actively encourage growth of commerce and manufacturing.

The Republicans, in contrast, looked backward to the traditional Revolutionary fear that government power threatened liberty. The Treasury, they cried, was corrupting Congress, the army would enslave the people, and broad construction would make the federal government all-powerful. To them, Federalist attitudes and policies illustrated the corruption eating away at American morals, just as England had become corrupt before 1776. *Republican ideas*

Nor did their economic ideals anticipate future American development. For Republicans, agriculture and not commerce stood as the centerpiece of American liberty and virtue. To be sure, some commercial activity was necessary, especially to sell America's agricultural surplus abroad. But Jefferson and his followers believed that republican values would be preserved only by limiting commerce and promoting household manufacturing instead of industry. They also failed to appreciate the role of financial institutions in promoting economic development.

On the other hand, the Jeffersonians were more farsighted in matters of equality and personal liberty. Their faith in the people put them in tune with the emerging egalitarian temper of society. Eagerly they embraced the virtues of individualism, hoping to limit government in order to free individuals to develop to their full potential without interference.

COUNTERPOINT *Key Differences between Federalists and Republicans*

Some historians have painted the conflict between the Federalist and Republican parties as a clash between aristocracy and democracy. The Federalists, in their view, looked to create and sustain an American aristocracy that combined social, economic, and political prestige, and thus were hostile to the mass of Americans. The Jeffersonians, in contrast, represented the democratic impulses in the country and thus enjoyed far wider popular support.

Despite its appeal, this interpretation overlooks the fact that the leaders of both parties were hardly ordinary citizens but instead men of wealth and privilege. Moreover, Jefferson's party was especially strong in the more aristocratic South. Indeed, his victory in 1800 depended on the three-fifths clause, which increased the South's electoral votes by counting slaves in apportioning representation in the House of Representatives. Without the additional representation slavery gave the southern states, John Adams, the supposed aristocratic candidate, would have won.

Other historians trace party divisions back to the republican ideology of the Revolution. In their view, both parties favored republican government, but disagreed about the relationship between economic growth and republicanism. The Jeffersonians upheld the traditional attitude that republicanism rested on public virtue, and that wealth, luxury, idleness, and speculation would undermine the moral fiber of the people. To the Federalists commerce was not a threat to the Republic but the means to strengthen it, by stimulating popular interest in public life and causing Americans to think nationally rather than locally. Thus the two parties differed not over republican institutions but over the role commerce should play in a republic.

THE PRESIDENCY OF JOHN ADAMS

As president, John Adams became the nominal head of the Federalists, but in many ways he was out of step with his party. He felt no pressing need to aid the wealthy, nor was he fully committed to Hamilton's commercial–industrial vision. He also opposed any alliance with Britain.

Increasingly Adams and Hamilton clashed over policies and party leadership. Although Hamilton had resigned from the Treasury Department in 1795, key members of Adams's cabinet regularly turned to him for advice. Indeed, they opposed Adams so often that the frustrated president sometimes dealt with them, according to Jefferson, "by dashing and trampling his wig on the floor." The feud between the two rivals did not bode well for the Federalist party.

The Quasi-War with France

Adams began his term trying to stave off war with France, whose navy and privateers continued to raid American ships. In 1797 he dispatched three envoys

XYZ Affair to France, but the French foreign minister demanded a bribe even to open negotiations. The American representatives refused, and when news of these discussions became public, it was known as the XYZ Affair (because in the official documents the letters X, Y, and Z were substituted for the names of the French officials involved). A tremendous outcry ensued.

Federalist leaders saw a chance to retain power by exploiting the crisis and going to war with France. With war fever running high, Congress in 1798 en-

The Quasi-War larged the army and navy. An unofficial naval war—the so-called Quasi-War—broke out with France as ships in each navy openly and freely raided the fleets of the other.

Eager for war, Hamilton dreamed of using the army to seize Louisiana and Florida from Spain, France's ally. He even toyed with provoking resistance in Virginia in order to justify suppression of the Republican party. Hamilton's hotheaded behavior, however, helped cool Adams's willingness to go to war.

Suppression at Home

Meanwhile, Federalist leaders attempted to suppress disloyalty at home. In the summer of 1798 Congress passed several measures known together as the Alien and Sedition Acts. The Alien Act, which was never used, authorized the presi-

Alien and Sedition Acts dent to arrest and deport aliens suspected of "treasonable" leanings. To limit the number of immigrant voters—most of them Republicans—the Naturalization Act increased the period of residence from 5 to 14 years to become a naturalized citizen. But most controversial was the Sedition Act, which established heavy fines and even imprisonment for writing, speaking, or publishing anything of "a false, scandalous and malicious" nature against the government or any officer of the government. To cries that such censorship violated the First Amendment's guarantees of freedom of speech and the press, Federalists replied that sedition and libel were not protected by the Constitution.

Because of the partisan way it was enforced, the Sedition Act quickly became a symbol of tyranny. Federalists convicted and imprisoned a number of prominent Republican editors. At the same time, the crisis over the Sedition Act forced Republicans to develop a broader conception of freedom of the press.

Freedom of the press

Previously, most Americans had agreed that newspapers should not be restrained before publication, but that they could be punished afterward for sedition. Jefferson and others now argued that only overtly seditious acts, not opinions, should be subject to prosecution, a view the courts eventually endorsed.

The Republican-controlled legislatures of Virginia and Kentucky responded to the crisis of 1798 by each passing a set of resolutions. Madison secretly wrote

Virginia and Kentucky resolutions

those for Virginia and Jefferson, those for Kentucky. These resolutions proclaimed that the Constitution was a compact between sovereign states, that the federal government had been delegated strictly limited powers, and that states had the right to interpose their authority when the government exceeded those powers and threatened the liberties of citizens.

But Jefferson and Madison were not ready to rend a union that had so recently been forged. Jefferson and Madison intended for the Virginia and Kentucky resolutions to rally public opinion to the Republican cause and opposed any effort to resist federal authority by force. During the last year of the Adams administration, the Alien and Sedition Acts quietly expired. Once in power, the Republicans repealed the Naturalization Act.

The Election of 1800

With a naval war raging on the high seas and the Alien and Sedition Acts sparking debate at home, Adams suddenly shocked his party by negotiating a peace

Federalist split

treaty with France. It was a courageous act, for Adams not only split his party in two but also ruined his own chances for reelection by forcing Hamilton's pro-British wing of the party into open opposition.

With the Federalist party split, Republican prospects for 1800 brightened. Again the party chose Jefferson to run against Adams, along with Aaron Burr for vice president. Their efficient party organization mobilized supporters, whereas the Federalists' highhanded policies and disdain for the "mob" alienated countless ordinary citizens. Noah Webster put his finger on his fellow Federalists' problem: "They have attempted to resist the force of public opinion, instead of falling into the current with a view to direct it."

Sweeping to victory, the Republicans won control of both houses of Congress for the first time. Adams ran ahead of his party, but Jefferson outdis-

Jefferson's election

tanced him, 73 electoral votes to 65. Once again, the election demonstrated the fragility of the fledgling political system. Jefferson and Burr received an equal number of votes, but the Constitution, with no provision for political parties, did not distinguish between the votes for president and vice president. With the election tied, the decision lay with the House of Representatives, which deadlocked for almost a week.

Generating strong popular emotions, elections in the early Republic involved many more voters than ever before. In this detail of an early nineteenth-century painting by John Lewis Krimmel, party workers bring electors to the Philadelphia polls in carriages, while voters heatedly argue about candidates and celebrate.

Jefferson was finally elected on the thirty-sixth ballot. In 1804 the Twelfth Amendment corrected the problem, specifying that electors were to vote separately for president and vice president.

Political Violence in the Early Republic

The deadlocked election provided a tense end to the decade, with some Federalists even swearing they would "go without a constitution and take the risk of civil war." Indeed, it is easy for Americans today to forget how violent and unpredictable the politics of the 1790s had been.

Some of the violence was physical. The leading Republican newspaper editor in Philadelphia plunged into a street brawl with his Federalist rival; Representatives Matthew Lyon and Roger Griswold slugged it out on the floor of Congress. The political rhetoric of the era was equally extreme. Republicans accused patriots like Washington and Hamilton of being British agents and monarchists; Federalists portrayed Jefferson as an irreligious radical and the Republicans as "blood-drinking cannibals." Washington complained that he was abused "in such exaggerated and indecent terms as could scarcely be applied . . . to a common pickpocket."

E Y E W I T N E S S   T O   H I S T O R Y

A Farmer Becomes Involved
in the World of Commerce

A short story of myself, will show you how it came hard times—and no money—with me, at the age of 65, who have lived well these forty years. My parents were poor, and they put me at 12 years of age to a farmer, with whom I lived till I was 21. . . . At 22 I married me a wife, and a very working young woman she was; we took a farm of 40 acres on rent, by industry we gained a-head fast. . . . In 10 years I was able to buy me a farm of 60 acres. . . . I then in a manner grew rich, and soon added another 60 acres, with which I was content. . . .

About this time I married my oldest daughter to a clever lad. . . . I fitted her out well, and to her mind, for I told her to take of the best of my wool and flax, and to spin herself gowns, coats, stockings and shifts; nay, I suffered her to buy some cotton, and make into sheets. . . . At this time my farm gave me and my whole family a good living on the produce of it, and left me one year with another 150 silver dollars, for I never laid out (besides my taxes) more than 10 dollars a year, which was for salt, nails, and the like; nothing to wear, eat or drink was purchased, as my farm provided all: with this saving I put money to interest, bought cattle, fatted and sold them, and made great profit.

In two years after, my second daughter was courted. My wife says, . . . Sarah must be fitted out a little, she ought to fare as well as neighbour N——'s Betty; I must have some money to go to town. Well, wife, it shall be as you think best; I never was stingy, but it seems to me that what we spin at home will do. However, wife goes down in a few days, and returns with a calico gown, a cal-

---

What accounts for this torrent of violence—both real and rhetorical—in the first decade of the Republic? For one, Federalists and Republicans alike rec-

Ideology of republicanism

ognized how fragile a form of government republicanism had proved over the long course of history. Its repeated failure left political leaders uneasy and uncertain about the American experiment. Then, too, the ideology of the American Revolution stressed the need to guard constantly against conspiracies to subvert liberty. All too quickly, turbulent foreign events heightened domestic suspicions.

In such overheated circumstances, both Republicans and Federalists readily assumed the worst of one another. Neither side grasped that political parties were essential in a democracy to express and resolve peacefully differences imanco petticoat, a set of stone teacups, half a dozen pewter tea spoons, and a tea kettle, things that we never seen in my house before. They cost but little, I did not feel it, and I confess I was pleased to see them. Sarah was as well fitted out as any girl in the township.

In 3 years more my third daughter had a spark, and wedding being concluded upon, wife comes again for the purse. But when she returned, what did I see! a silken gown, silk for a cloak, looking glass, china tea gear, and a hundred other things, with the empty purse.

But this was not the worst of it, Mr. Printer. Some time before the marriage of this last daughter, and ever since, this charge increased in my family. Besides all sorts of household furniture unknown to us before, cloathing of every sort is bought, and the wheel goes only for the purpose of exchanging our substantial cloath of flax and wool, for gauze, ribbons, silk, tea, etc. My butter, which used to go to market, and brought money, is now expended on the tea-table; . . . my lambs, which used also to bring cash, are now eaten at home, or if sent to market, are brought back in things of no use. So that, instead of laying up 150 dollars a year, I find now all my loose money is gone, my best debts called in and expended; and being straitened, I can't carry on my farm to so good advantage; . . . that what it costs to live (though a less family, and all able to work) is fifty or sixty dollars a year more than what all my farm brings me. Now this has gone on a good many years, and has brought hard times into my family; and if I can't reform it, ruin must follow. . . .

I am determined to alter my way of living to what it was 20 years ago. . . . Not one thing to eat, drink or wear shall come into my house, which is not raised on my farm, or in my township, or in the country, except iron work . . . no tea, sugar, coffee or rum. The tea kettle shall be sold. I shall then, Mr. Printer, live and die with a good conscience.

"A Farmer," Pittsburgh *Gazette*, November 18, 1786.

among competing social, geographic, and economic interests. Instead, each party considered the other a faction, and therefore illegitimate. Each longed to reestablish a one-party system.

The Federalists' Legacy

As John Adams prepared to leave office, he looked back on the 12 years that the Federalist party had held power with mixed feelings. Under Washington's firm

Federalists' achievements

leadership and his own, the Federalists had made the Constitution a workable instrument of government. They had proved that republicanism was compatible with stability and order, and they had established economic policies and principles of foreign affairs that even their opponents would continue.

But most Federalists took no solace in such reflections, for the tide of history seemed to be running against them. As the champions of government by the well-born, they had waged one last desperate battle to save their disintegrating world—and had lost. Power had fallen into the hands of the ignorant and unwashed rabble, led by that demagogue Thomas Jefferson. Federalists shared fully the view of the British minister, who concluded in 1800 that the entire American political system was "tottering to its foundations."

The great American experiment in republicanism had failed. Of this most Federalists were certain. And surely, if history was any judge, the destruction of liberty and order would soon follow.

SIGNIFICANT EVENTS

1789	First session of Congress; Washington inaugurated president; French Revolution begins; Judiciary Act passed
1790	Funding and assumption approved
1791	Bank of the United States chartered; first 10 amendments (Bill of Rights) ratified
1792	Washington reelected
1793	Execution of French king and queen; war breaks out between France and England; Washington's Neutrality Proclamation
1794	Battle of Fallen Timbers; Whiskey Rebellion
1795	Jay's Treaty ratified; Treaty of Greenville signed
1796	Pinckney's Treaty ratified; first contested presidential election—Adams defeats Jefferson
1798	XYZ Affair; Alien and Sedition Acts passed; Virginia and Kentucky resolutions
1798–1799	Quasi-War with France
1800	Adams sends new mission to France; Jefferson defeats Adams
1801	The House elects Jefferson president

CHAPTER NINE

The Jeffersonian Republic

n September 29, 1800, following a rather rocky courtship, Margaret Bayard married Samuel H. Smith. Even though Samuel was well educated and from a socially prominent family, Margaret's father consented to the marriage reluctantly, for the Bayards were staunch Federalists and Smith was an ardent Republican. Indeed, Thomas Jefferson had asked Smith, a Philadelphia editor, to follow the government to Washington, D.C., and establish a party newspaper in the new capital. After the wedding ceremony, the couple traveled to the new seat of government along the Potomac River.

When the Smiths arrived in Washington, they found a raw village of 3200 people. Samuel began publishing the *National Intelligencer*, the first national newspaper in the United States, while Margaret's social charm and keen intelligence made their home a center of Washington society. When she met Jefferson about a month after her arrival, she found herself captivated by his gracious manners, sparkling conversation, and gentlemanly bearing. Whatever remained of her Federalist sympathies vanished, and she became (perhaps as her father feared) a devoted supporter of the Republican leader.

In eager anticipation she went to the Senate chamber on March 4, 1801, to witness Jefferson's inauguration. To emphasize the change in attitude of the new

Jefferson's inauguration

administration, the president-elect walked to the capitol with only a small escort. Absent were the elaborate ceremonies of the years of Federalist rule. When the swearing-in was completed, the new president returned to his lodgings at Conrad and McMunn's boardinghouse, where he declined a place of honor and instead took his accustomed seat at the foot of the table. Only several weeks later did he finally move to his official residence.

As Margaret Smith proudly watched the proceedings, she could not help thinking of the most striking feature of this transfer of power: it was peaceful. "The changes of administration," she commented, "which in every government and in every age have most generally been epochs of confusion, villainy and blood-shed, in our happy country take place without any species of distraction, or disor-der." After the fierce controversies of the previous decade and the harsh rhetoric of the election of 1800, to see the opposition party take power peacefully—the first such occurrence in the nation's history—was indeed remarkable.

Once in power, Jefferson set out to reshape the government and society into closer harmony with Republican principles. He later referred to his election as "the Revolution of 1800," asserting that it "was as real a revolution in the prin-ciples of our government as that of 1776 was in its form." That statement is an exaggeration, perhaps. But the rule of the Republican party during the follow-ing two decades set the nation on a distinctly more democratic tack. And in working out its relationship with Britain and France, as well as with the Indian nations of the West, America achieved a sense of its own nationhood that came only with time and the passing of the Revolutionary generation.

JEFFERSON IN POWER

Thomas Jefferson was the first president to be inaugurated in the new capital of Washington, D.C. Because the Federalists believed that government was the paramount power in a nation, they had intended that the city would be a new Rome—a cultural, intellectual, and commercial center of the Republic.

The new city, however, fell far short of this grandiose dream. Its streets were filled with tree stumps and became impenetrable seas of mud after a rain.

The new capital city

Much of the District was wooded, and virtually all of it re-mained unoccupied. A British diplomat grumbled over leaving Philadelphia, the previous capital, with its bustling commerce, regular communication with the outside world, and lively society, to conduct business in "a mere swamp."

Yet the isolated and unimpressive capital reflected the new president's atti-tude toward government. Distrustful of centralized power of any kind, Jefferson deliberately set out to remake the national government into one of limited scope that touched few people's daily lives.

Jefferson's Character and Philosophy

Jefferson himself reflected that vision of modesty. Even standing nearly 6 feet, 3 inches, the 57-year-old president lacked an impressive presence. Despite his wealth and genteel birth into Virginia society, Jefferson disliked pomp and with his informal manners and careless dress projected an image of republican simplicity.

Jefferson was a product of the Enlightenment, with its faith in the power of human reason to improve society and decipher the universe. "I steer my bark with Hope in the head," he once declared, "leaving fear astern."

Jefferson considered "the will of the majority" to be "the only sure guardian of the rights of man," which he defined as "life, liberty, and the pursuit of happiness." Although he conceded that the masses might err, he was confident they would soon return to correct principles. Yet in good republican fashion, he feared those in power, even if they had been elected by the people. Government seemed at best a necessary evil.

To Jefferson, agriculture was a morally superior way of life. "Those who labour in the earth are the chosen people of God, if ever he had a chosen peo-

Agrarianism

ple," he wrote in *Notes on the State of Virginia* (1787). Like Crèvecoeur, Jefferson praised rural life for nourishing the honesty, independence, and virtue so essential in a republic. Government would "remain virtuous . . . as long as [the American people] are chiefly agricultural," he assured his associate James Madison. Rather than encouraging large-scale factories, Jefferson wanted to preserve small household manufacturing, which was an essential part of the rural economy. Commerce should exist primarily to sell America's agricultural surplus.

Although Jefferson asserted that "the tree of liberty must be refreshed from time to time by the blood of patriots and tyrants," his reputation as a radical

Jefferson's radicalism exaggerated

was undeserved. While he wanted to extend the suffrage to a greater number of Americans, he clung to the traditional republican idea that voters should own property and thus be economically independent. One of the largest slaveholders in the country, he increasingly muffled his once-bold condemnation of slavery, and despite his belief in free speech he did not have any qualms about state governments punishing political criticism.

Despite his aristocratic upbringing, Jefferson was awkward, reserved, and ill-at-ease in public. But in private conversation he sparkled.

Jefferson was an exceedingly complex, at times contradictory personality. But like most politicians, he was flexible in his approach to problems and tried to balance means and ends. And like most leaders, he quickly discovered that he confronted very different problems in power than he had in opposition.

Republican Principles

Once Jefferson settled into the executive mansion, he took steps to return the government to the republican ideals of simplicity and frugality. The states
Limited government rather than the federal government, he asserted, were "the most competent administrators for our domestic concerns and the surest bulwarks against antirepublican tendencies." Ever the individualist, he recommended a government that left people "free to regulate their own pursuits of industry and improvement."

In his inaugural address, Jefferson also went out of his way to soothe the feelings of defeated Federalists. He promised to uphold the government's credit and protect commerce as the "handmaiden" of agriculture—both Federalist concerns. Agreeing with Washington, he proposed friendship with all nations and "entangling alliances" with none. Finally, he called on Americans to unite for the common good: "We have called by different names brethren of the same principles. We are all republicans—we are all federalists."

The election of 1800 had made clear that opposition parties could be a legitimate part of American politics, and Jefferson, in this statement, seemed to endorse the validity of a party system. In reality, however, he hoped to restore one-party rule to the country by winning over moderate and honest Federalists and isolating the party's extremists, whom he still attacked as monarchists.

Jefferson's Economic Policies

But what would Jefferson do about Hamilton's economic program? As he promised in his inaugural address, the new president proceeded to cut spending, reduce the size of the government, and begin paying off the national debt. He abolished the internal taxes enacted by the Federalists, including the controversial levy on whiskey, and thus was able to get rid of all tax collectors and inspectors. "What farmer, what mechanic, what laborer, ever sees a tax gatherer in the United States?" boasted Jefferson in 1805. Land sales and the tariff duties would supply the funds needed to run the government.

The most serious spending cuts were made in the military branches. Jefferson slashed the army budget in half, reducing the army to 3000 men. In a national emergency, he reasoned, the militia could defend the country. Jefferson reduced the navy even more, halting work on powerful frigates authorized during the Quasi-war with France and replacing them with inexpensive gunboats.

By such steps, Jefferson made significant progress toward paying off Hamilton's hated national debt. He lowered it from $83 million to only $57 million by the end of his two terms in office, despite the added financial burden of the Louisiana Purchase (page 223). Still, Jefferson did not entirely dismantle the Federalists' economic program. Funding and assumption could not be reversed—the nation's honor was pledged to paying these debts, and Jefferson fully understood the importance of maintaining the nation's credit. The tariff had to be retained as a source of revenue to meet government expenses. More surprising, Jefferson expanded the operations of the national bank and, in words reminiscent of Hamilton, advocated tying banks and members of the business class to the government by rewarding those who supported the Republican party.

Failure to abolish Hamilton's program

Throughout his presidency, Jefferson often put pragmatic considerations above unyielding principles. As he himself expressed it, "What is practicable must often control what is pure theory."

John Marshall and Judicial Review

Having lost both the presidency and control of Congress in 1800, the Federalists took steps to shore up their power before Jefferson assumed office. They did so by expanding the size of the federal court system. The Judiciary Act of 1801 created 6 circuit courts and 16 new judgeships, along with a number of marshals, attorneys, and clerks. Adams quickly filled these with Federalists, but in 1802, by a strict party vote, Congress repealed the 1801 law and eliminated the new courts.

Among Adams's last-minute appointments was that of William Marbury as justice of the peace for the District of Columbia. When James Madison assumed the office of secretary of state in the new administration, he found a batch of undelivered commissions, including Marbury's. Wishing to appoint loyal Republicans to these posts, Jefferson instructed Madison not to hand over the commissions, whereupon Marbury sued under the Judiciary Act of 1789. Since that act gave the Supreme Court original jurisdiction in cases against federal officials, the case of *Marbury v. Madison* went directly to the Court in 1803.

Marbury v. Madison

Chief Justice John Marshall, a Federalist and one of Adams's outgoing appointments, seized on this case to affirm the Court's greatest power, the right to review statutes and interpret the meaning of the Constitution. "It is emphatically the province of and duty of the judicial department to say what the law is," he wrote in upholding the doctrine of judicial review. This idea meant that the Court "must of necessity expound and interpret" the Constitution and the laws when one statute conflicted with another or when a law violated the framework of the Constitution. Marshall found that the section of the Judiciary Act of 1789 that granted the Supreme Court original jurisdiction in the case was unconstitutional. Since the Constitution specified those cases in which the Court had such jurisdiction, they could not be enlarged by statute. *Marbury v. Madison* was so critical to the development of the American constitutional system that it has been called the keystone of the constitutional arch.

Judicial review

Marshall and his colleagues later asserted the power of the Court to review the constitutionality of state laws in *Fletcher v. Peck* (1810) when it struck down a Georgia law. In subsequent decisions, it also brought state courts under the final authority of the Supreme Court. In fact, during his tenure on the bench, Marshall extended judicial review to all acts of government. Since Marshall's time the Supreme Court has successfully defended its position as the final judge of the meaning of the Constitution.

JEFFERSON AND WESTERN EXPANSION

The Federalists feared the West as a threat to social order and stability. Frontiersmen, sneered New Englander Timothy Dwight, were "too idle; too talkative; too passionate; . . . and too shiftless to acquire either property or character." Farther south, another observer referred to squatters on western lands as "ragged, dirty, brawling, browbeating monsters, six feet high, whose vocation is robbing, drinking, fighting, and terrifying every peaceable man in the community."

Jefferson, on the other hand, viewed the West as the means to preserve the values of an agrarian republic. He anticipated that as settled regions of the

Empire of liberty

country became crowded, many rural residents would migrate to the cities in search of work unless cheap land beckoned farther west. America's vast spaces provided land that would last for a thousand generations, he predicted in his inaugural address, enough to transform the United States into "an empire of liberty."

To encourage rapid settlement of the West, the Republican Congress in 1801 reduced the minimum purchase of federal lands from 640 to 320 acres. (Even so, speculators accounted for most sales under the new law.) Nevertheless, the West was overwhelmingly Republican. Thus the admission of new western states would strengthen Jefferson's party and hasten the demise of the Federalists. From the Jeffersonian perspective, western expansion was a blessing economically, socially, and politically.

The Louisiana Purchase

Because Spain's colonial empire was disintegrating, Americans were confident that before long they would gain control of Florida and of the rest of the Mississippi, either through purchase or military occupation. This comforting prospect was shattered, however, when Spain secretly ceded Louisiana—the territory lying between the Mississippi River and the Rocky Mountains—to France. Under the leadership of Napoleon Bonaparte, France had become the most powerful nation on the European continent, with the military might to protect its new colony and block American expansion. American anxiety intensified when Spain, while still in control of Louisiana, abruptly revoked Americans' right to navigate the lower Mississippi guaranteed by Pinckney's Treaty (page 205). Western farmers, who were suddenly denied access to the sea, angrily protested Spain's highhanded action.

Jefferson dispatched James Monroe to Paris to join Robert Livingston, the American minister, to negotiate the purchase of New Orleans and West Florida

Sale of Louisiana

from the French and thus secure control of the Mississippi. With war looming again in Europe, Napoleon needed money and thus, in April 1803, offered to sell not just New Orleans but all of Louisiana to the United States. This proposal flabbergasted Livingston and Monroe. Their instructions said nothing about acquiring all of Louisiana, and they had not been authorized to spend what the French demanded. With no time to consult Jefferson, Livingston and Monroe agreed to buy Louisiana for approximately $15 million. In one fell swoop, the American negotiators had doubled the country's size by adding some 830,000 square miles.

Jefferson, naturally, was immensely pleased at the prospect of acquiring so much territory, which seemed to guarantee the survival of his agrarian repub-

Jefferson's pragmatism

lic. At the same time, as someone who favored the doctrine of strict construction, he found the legality of the act deeply troubling. The Constitution, after all, did not specifically authorize the acquisition of territory by treaty. Livingston and Monroe urged haste, however, and in the end, Jefferson sent the treaty to the Senate for ratification, noting privately, "The less we say about constitutional difficulties the better." Once again pragmatism had triumphed over theory.

West Florida, which bordered part of the lower Mississippi, remained in Spanish hands, and Jefferson's efforts to acquire this region were unsuccessful. Nevertheless, western commerce could flow down the Mississippi unhindered to the sea. The Louisiana Purchase would rank as the greatest achievement of Jefferson's presidency.

Lewis and Clark

Early in 1803, even before the Louisiana Purchase was completed, Congress secretly appropriated $2500 to send an exploring party up the Missouri River to the Pacific. This expedition was led by Meriwether Lewis, Jefferson's secretary, and William Clark.

Jefferson instructed Lewis and Clark to map the region and make detailed observations of the soil, climate, rivers, minerals, and plant and animal life. They were also to look for a practical overland route to the Pacific and engage in diplomacy with the Indians along the way. Equally important, by pushing onward to the Pacific, Lewis and Clark would strengthen the American title to Oregon, which several nations claimed but none effectively controlled.

In the spring of 1804 Lewis and Clark, accompanied by 48 men, set off up the Missouri. After wintering in present-day North Dakota, they crossed the

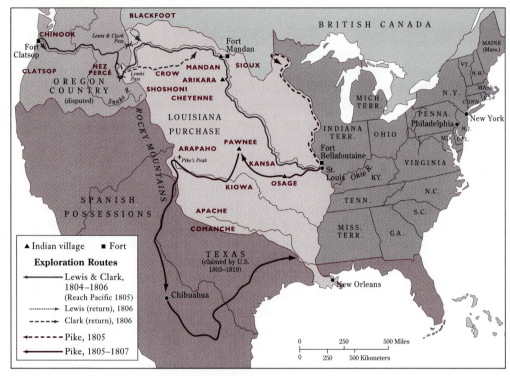

EXPLORATION AND EXPANSION: THE LOUISIANA PURCHASE   The vast, largely uncharted Louisiana Purchase lay well beyond the most densely populated areas of the United States. The Lewis and Clark expedition along with Lieutenant Zebulon Pike's exploration of the upper Mississippi River and the Southwest opened the way for westward expansion.

Exploration of the West — Rockies and made it to the Oregon coast, where they spent the winter before returning overland the following year. Having traveled across half the continent in both directions, navigated countless rapids, and conducted negotiations with numerous tribes, the party arrived in St. Louis in September 1806, two and a half years after they had departed. Lewis and Clark had collected thousands of useful plant and animal specimens, discovered several passes through the Rockies, and produced a remarkably accurate map, their most valuable contribution to western exploration.

WHITES AND INDIANS ON THE FRONTIER

In February 1803, as American diplomats prepared to leave for France in hopes of gaining title to western lands, another delegation was visiting Washington with a similar purpose. Black Hoof, a Shawnee chief from the Ohio River valley, asked Secretary of War Henry Dearborn to issue a deed to the tribe's lands in western Ohio. The deed, said Black Hoof, would ensure that his people could "raise good Grain and cut Hay for our Cattle" and guarantee "that nobody would take advantage" of them. The astonished Dearborn was not about to give the Shawnee any document that would strengthen their title to land in Ohio. But he did promise to provide some plows and cattle.

Unlike many Shawnees, Black Hoof had decided that the best way to get along with white Americans was to adopt their ways. For a number of years he

Black Hoof chooses assimilation

and his tribe settled along the Auglaize River, built log cabins, cleared land to raise corn, potatoes, cabbage, and turnips, and even planted an apple orchard. But in 1808, after the government refused to pay a Quaker missionary who was providing technical support, Black Hoof's followers became increasingly dependent on government payments. Even Black Hoof admitted, "The white people . . . have been our ruin."

The Shawnee along the Auglaize were only one of many Indian tribes forced to make hard choices as white Americans streamed into the fertile lands of the Ohio River valley. In 1790 only about 100,000 whites lived in the West. By 1800 that number had jumped to almost 400,000 and, a decade later, to more than a million. By 1820 more than 2 million whites lived in a region they had first entered only 50 years earlier.

In this backcountry, where white and Indian cultures mixed and often clashed, both peoples experienced the breakdown of traditional cultural systems. White immigrants pushing into Indian territory often lacked the structures of community such as churches, schools, and legal institutions. But Indian cultures were also severely stressed by the availability of white trade goods and by the more settled agricultural ways of white farmers, with their domesticated animals and fenced-in fields. Above all, Indians had to deal with the unceasing hunger of whites for Indian lands.

The Course of White Settlement

Following the Treaty of Greenville (page 205), white settlers poured into the Ohio Territory by wagon and flatboat. Time after time the pattern of settlement remained the same: in the first wave came backwoods families who laboriously cleared a few acres of forest by girdling the trees, removing the brush, and planting corn between the dead trunks. Their isolated one-room log cabins were crude, dark, and windowless, with mud stuffed between the chinks; the furniture and utensils were sparse and homemade. Such settlers were mostly squatters without legal title to their land. As a region began to fill up, these restless pioneers usually sold their improvements and headed west again.

The waves of settlement that followed were more permanent. Many of the newcomers were young unmarried men who left crowded regions in the East

Maturing society

seeking new opportunities. Once established, they quickly married and started families. Like the pioneers before them, most engaged in semisubsistence agriculture. As their numbers increased and a local market developed, they switched to surplus agriculture, growing and making much of what the family needed while selling or exchanging the surplus to obtain essential items. "The woman told me that they spun and wove all the cotton and woolen garments of the family, and knit all the stockings," a visitor to an Ohio farm wrote. "Her husband, though not a shoemaker by trade, made all the shoes. She manufactured all the soap and candles they used." The wife sold butter and chickens in order to buy coffee, tea, and whiskey.

A Changing Environment

The inrush of new settlers significantly reduced the amount of original forest west of the Appalachian Mountains. Because Americans equated clearing the forest with progress, they had "an unconquerable aversion to trees," one observer noted, and "whenever a settlement is made they cut away all before them without mercy; not one is spared. . . ." By 1850 they had cleared at least 100 million acres. The resulting landscape was often bleak looking, with stumps left to slowly rot and the ground, "rugged and ill-dressed" . . . "as if nothing could ever be made to spring from it."

The rapid cutting of the forest led to the sharp decline of large animals, such as deer and bears, while the bison soon disappeared east of the Mississippi River. The loss of forest cover, combined with the new plowing of the land, increased runoff after rains, which lowered the water table and made destructive floods more frequent. The climate changed as well: it was hotter in the summer and the winds blew more fiercely, causing erosion in the summer and chilling gusts in the winter. Finally, deforestation also made the Ohio valley more unhealthy by creating wasteland with pools of stagnant water, which became breeding places for mosquitoes that spread diseases like malaria.

Effects of deforestation

The Second Great Awakening

It was the sparsely settled regions that became most famous for a series of revivals, known collectively as the Second Great Awakening. Like the first national outpouring of religious enthusiasm 50 years earlier, these revivals were fanned by ministers who traveled the countryside preaching to groups anywhere they could. Beginning in the late 1790s Congregationalists, Presbyterians, and Baptists all participated in these revivals, but the Methodists were the most enthusiastic and most organized in their support.

News of several revivals in Kentucky in the summer of 1800 quickly spread, and people came from 50 and 100 miles around, camping in makeshift tents and holding services out of doors. This new form of worship, the camp meeting, reached its climax at Cane Ridge, Kentucky, in August 1801. At a time when the largest city in the state had only 2000 people,

Cane Ridge

Although the clergy at camp meetings were male, women played prominent roles, often pressing husbands to convert. Worshipers, especially those on the "anxious bench" below the preacher, were often overcome with emotion.

over 10,000 gathered for a week to hear dozens of ministers. "The vast sea of human beings seemed to be agitated as if by storm," recalled one skeptic, who himself was converted at Cane Ridge. "Some of the people were singing, others praying, some crying for mercy in the most piteous accents" while "shrieks and shouts . . . rent the very heavens." In the overwhelming emotion of the moment, converts might dance, laugh hysterically, fall down, or jerk uncontrollably as they sought assurance of their salvation.

In the South, African Americans, including slaves, attended camp meetings and enthusiastically participated in the tumultuous services. Indeed, revivals

African Americans and revivals

were a major force in spreading Christianity to African Americans and producing slave conversions. Revivalists' clear and vivid speech, their acceptance of the moral worth of every individual regardless of race, and their emphasis on the conversion experience rather than abstract theology had the same appeal to black listeners, who had little formal schooling, that they had to poorly educated white churchgoers. Blacks worshiped separately from and sometimes together with whites. As was the case with white worshipers, the Baptist and Methodist churches received the bulk of African American converts.

The revivals quickly found critics, who decried the emotionalism and hysteria they produced. For a time Presbyterians and Baptists withdrew from camp meetings, leaving the field to the Methodists. Eventually even the Methodists sought to dampen excessive emotion by restricting admittance and patrolling the meeting grounds.

Revivals like Cane Ridge provided an emotional release from the hard, isolated life on the frontier. For families with few neighbors, camp meetings of-

Attraction of revivals

fered a chance to participate in a wider social gathering. And for those at the bottom of the social hierarchy, the revivalists' message emphasized an individual's ability to gain personal triumph and salvation, regardless of his or her station in life. In the swiftly changing borderlands north and south of the Ohio River, where society seemed constantly in flux, revivals brought a sense of uplift and comfort.

Pressure on Indian Lands and Culture

As white settlers continued to pour into the backcountry, the pressure to acquire Indian lands increased. Jefferson endorsed the policy that tribes either would have to assimilate into American culture by becoming farmers and abandoning their seminomadic hunting or would have to move west of the Mississippi River. Jefferson argued that otherwise the Indians faced extermination, but he also recognized that by becoming farmers they would need less land.

The hard truth about white policies toward Indians was that however enlightened individuals might be, the demographic pressure of high birthrates and aggressive expansion ensured conflict between the two cultures. Anglo-Americans never doubted the superiority of their ways. Even a student of the Enlightenment like Jefferson could become cynical. He encouraged the policy of selling goods on credit in order to lure Indians into debt, observing, "When these debts get beyond what the individuals can pay, they become willing to lop them off by a cession of lands." Between 1800 and 1810 whites pressed Indians into ceding more than 100 million acres in the Ohio River valley.

The loss of so much land to white settlement devastated traditional Indian cultures by reducing hunting grounds and making game and food scarce. "Stop

Destruction of Indian cultures

your people from killing our game," the Shawnees complained in 1802 to federal Indian agents. "They would be angry if we were to kill a cow or hog of theirs, the little game that remains is very dear to us." Tribes also became dependent on white trade to obtain blankets, guns, metal utensils, alcohol, and decorative beads. To pay for these goods with furs, Indians often overtrapped, which caused them to invade the lands of neighboring tribes, provoking wars. The debilitating effects of alcohol, which Indians turned to as a means of coping with cultural stress, were especially marked during these years.

Among the Shawnees in the Ohio River valley, the strain produced by white expansion led to alcoholism, growing violence among tribal members, family disintegration, and the collapse of the clan system designed to regulate relations among different villages. These problems might have been lessened by separation from white culture, but the Shawnees had become dependent on trade for articles they could not produce themselves. The question of how to deal with white culture became a matter of anguished debate. Black Hoof, as we have seen, attempted to accommodate to white ways. But for most Indians, the course of assimilation was unappealing and fraught with risk.

The Prophet, Tecumseh, and the Pan-Indian Movement

Other Shawnees looked to revitalize their culture by severing all ties with the white world. Among the Shawnees, Lalawethika, also known as the Prophet, sparked a religious revival that began in 1805. Inspired by a series of visions, he took a new name, Tenskwatawa (the Open Door), to express his mission to "reclaim the Indians from bad habits and to cause them to live in peace with all mankind."

Tenskwatawa urged the Shawnee to renounce whiskey and white goods and return to their old ways of hunting with bows and arrows, eating customary

Prophet's message

foods like corn and beans, and wearing traditional garb. Seeking to revitalize Shawnee culture, the Prophet condemned intertribal violence and denounced the idea of private instead of communal property. Except for guns, which could be used in self-defense, his followers were to cease all contact with whites and discard all white trading goods.

Setting up headquarters at a newly built village of Prophetstown in Indiana in 1808, Tenskwatawa led a religious revival among the tribes of the Northwest, who were increasingly concerned about the loss of their lands. Just as thousands of white settlers traveled to Methodist or Baptist camp meetings where preachers denounced the evils of liquor and called for a return to a purer life, so thousands from northern tribes traveled to the Prophet's village for inspiration.

While Tenskwatawa's strategy of revitalization was primarily religious, his older brother Tecumseh turned to political and military solutions. William

Tecumseh advocated political unity to preserve Indian lands and cultures. He was the dominant figure among the western tribes until he died fighting alongside the British in the War of 1812.

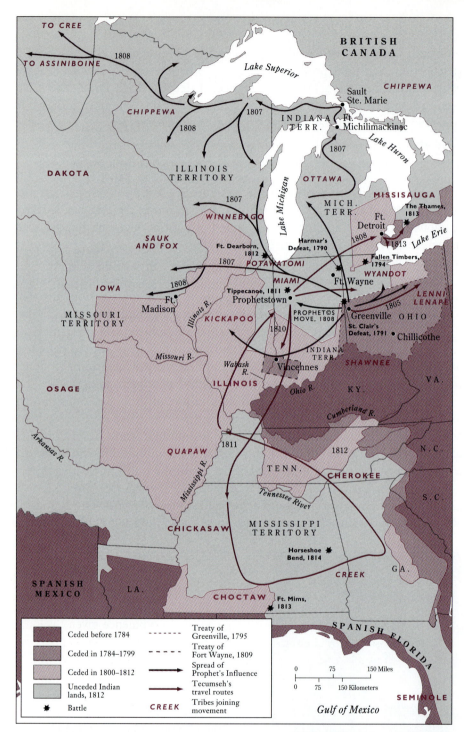

THE INDIAN RESPONSE TO WHITE ENCROACHMENT   With land cessions and white western migration placing increased pressure on Indian cultures after 1790, the Prophet's revivals quickly spread throughout the Great Lakes region. Tecumseh eventually eclipsed the Prophet as the major leader of Indian resistance, but his trips South to forge political alliances met with less success.

Tecumseh's movement

Henry Harrison described Tecumseh as "one of those uncommon geniuses which spring up occasionally to produce revolutions and overturn the established order of things." In 1809 when the Lenni Lenape and Miami tribes ceded yet another 3 million acres in Indiana and Illinois under the Treaty of Fort Wayne, Tecumseh repudiated the treaty. Traveling throughout the Northwest, he urged tribes to forget their old rivalries and unite under his leadership to protect their lands from the flood of white settlers. As Tecumseh began to overshadow the Prophet, Harrison aptly termed him "really the efficient man—the Moses of the family."

Tecumseh's failure in the South

After recruiting a number of northwestern tribes for his confederacy, Tecumseh in 1811 traveled through the South, where he encountered greater resistance. In general, the southern tribes were more prosperous, were more used to white ways, and felt less immediate pressure on their land than did northern tribes. So Tecumseh's southern mission ended largely in failure.

To compound his problems, while he was away a force of Americans under Governor Harrison defeated the Prophet's forces at the Battle of Tippecanoe in November and then destroyed Prophetstown. Tecumseh became convinced that the best way to contain white expansion was to play off the Americans against the British in the Great Lakes region. Indeed, by 1811 the two nations were on the brink of war.

COUNTERPOINT   *Tecumseh versus the Prophet*

Inevitably, the contrast between the tactics of the Prophet and those of Tecumseh have invited comparisons. For many years, historians saw Tecumseh as a towering figure who advocated the most effective response to white pressure on tribal lands. Perhaps because white historians lived in a nation whose story centered on the union of one nation from out of many, they tended to sympathize with Tecumseh's ideas of a Pan-Indian confederacy and military resistance under a centralized authority. From this perspective, the Prophet was a minor figure whose ideas were irrelevant and doomed to failure.

More recently, historians have challenged the prominence given Tecumseh over his brother. The Prophet's religious message, these revisionists point out, was much more in harmony with Indian cultures. As a result, the Prophet attracted a much larger following. Tecumseh's idea of a Pan-Indian confederacy, in constrast, ran counter to Indian cultures, bypassed traditional sources of authority within individual tribes, and ignored long-standing intertribal rivalries. Ironically, his ideas were closer to those of white society. Indeed, it was for precisely this reason that American officials had a high opinion of Tecumseh and so many historians since have been sympathetic: he responded much the way whites would have. But within the context of tribal cultures, the Prophet's movement had the greater impact.

THE SECOND WAR FOR
AMERICAN INDEPENDENCE

As Tecumseh pushed for a Pan-Indian alliance, Jefferson was looking to restore American political unity by wooing all but the most extreme Federalists into the Republican camp. The president easily won reelection in 1804 over Federalist Charles Cotesworth Pinckney, carrying 15 of 17 states. Jefferson's goal of one-party rule seemed at hand.

That unity was threatened, however, by renewed fighting in Europe. Only two weeks after Napoleon agreed to sell Louisiana to the United States, war broke out between France and Great Britain. As in the 1790s, the United States found itself caught between the world's two greatest powers. In his struggle to maintain American neutrality, Jefferson's controversial policies momentarily revived the two-party system.

Neutral Rights

At first the war benefited American trade because of the disruption in European agriculture. That stimulated demand for American foodstuffs and other raw materials. As the fighting drove most nonneutral ships from the seas, American shipping dominated the carrying trade, and the nation's foreign trade doubled between 1803 and 1805.

Even so, Americans were angered when the British navy resumed its impressment of sailors and even passengers from American ships. Anywhere from

Impressment

4000 to 10,000 sailors were impressed by British naval officers, who did not always bother to distinguish naturalized from native-born Americans. Voicing American indignation, John Quincy Adams characterized impressment as an "authorized system of kidnapping upon the ocean."

By 1805, the war had demonstrated the British navy's clear superiority at sea, while Napoleon's army enjoyed a decisive edge on land. Adopting a strategy of

Seizure of American ships

attrition, each country began to raid America's ocean commerce with the other side. Between 1803 and 1807, Britain seized over 500 American ships; France, over 300. When Britain issued new regulations in 1807, known as the Orders in Council, tightly controlling neutral trade with France, Napoleon authorized the seizure of any neutral ship that obeyed these regulations. An irate Jefferson complained of France and England, "The one is a den of robbers, the other of pirates." Then in June 1807 a British frigate fired on the U.S. warship *Chesapeake* in American waters and seized four deserters from the Royal Navy. Public opinion clamored for military retaliation.

The Embargo

Yet Jefferson shrank from declaring war. He announced instead a program of "peaceable coercion," designed to protect neutral rights without war. The plan not only prohibited American ships from trading with foreign ports, it stopped

EYEWITNESS TO HISTORY

Isaac Clark Is Impressed by the British Navy

, Isaac Clark, of Salem . . . Massachusetts, on solemn oath declare, that I was born in the Town of Randolph; . . . that on the 14th day of June, 1809, I was impressed and forcibly taken from the ship *Jane* of Norfolk, by the sailing master . . . of his majesty's ship *Porcupine*, Robert Elliot, commander. I had a protection [i.e., passport] from the Customhouse in Salem, which I showed to captain Elliot: he swore that I was an Englishman, tore my protection to pieces before my eyes, and threw it overboard, and ordered me to go to work—I told him I did not belong to his flag, and I would do no work under it. He then ordered my legs to be put in irons, and the next morning ordered the master at arms to . . . give me two dozen lashes; after receiving them, he ordered him to keep me in irons, and give me one biscuit and one pint of water for 24 hours. After keeping me in this situation for one week, I was . . . asked by captain Elliot if I would go to my duty—on my refusing, he . . . gave me two dozen more [lashes] and kept me on the same allowance another week— then . . . asked if I would go to work; I still persisted . . . [and he] gave me the third two dozen lashes, ordered a very heavy chain put round my neck . . . and that no person . . . give me any thing to eat or drink, but my one biscuit and pint of water for 24 hours, until I would go to work. I was kept in this situation for nine weeks, when being exhausted by hunger and thirst, I was obliged to yield. After being on board the ship more than two years and a half, and being wounded in an action with a French frigate, I was sent to the hospital—when partially recovered I was sent on board the *Impregnable*, a 98 gun ship. . . . The American consul received a copy of my protection from Salem, and procured my discharge on the 29th of April [1812].

Clement Cleveland Sawtell, "Impressment of American Seamen by the British," *Essex Institute Historical Collections*, v. 76 (October 1940), pp. 318–319. Reprinted by permission.

the export of all American goods. Jefferson was confident that American exports were so essential to the two belligerents, they would quickly agree to respect American neutral rights. In December 1807 Congress passed the Embargo Act.

The president had seriously miscalculated. Under the embargo, American exports plunged from $108 million in 1807 to a mere $22 million a year later.

Economic impact At the same time, imports fell from almost $145 million to about $58 million. As the center of American shipping, New England port cities were hurt the most and protested the loudest. In the face of widespread smuggling, Jefferson simply gave up trying to enforce the act during his last months in office.

Madison and the Young Republicans

Following Washington's example, Jefferson did not seek a third term. A caucus of Republican members of Congress selected James Madison to run against Federalist Charles Cotesworth Pinckney. Madison won an easy triumph.

Few men have assumed the presidency with more experience than James Madison. A leading nationalist in the 1780s, the father of the Constitution, a key floor leader in Congress, the founder of the Republican party, Jefferson's secretary of state and closest adviser, Madison had spent over a quarter of a century in public life. Yet as president he lacked the force of leadership and the inner strength to impose his will on less capable individuals.

With a president reluctant to fight for what he wanted, leadership passed from the executive branch to Congress. There, the elections of 1810 swept in *War Hawks* a new generation of Republicans who were much more nationalistic. They sought an ambitious program of economic development and were aggressive expansionists, especially those from frontier districts. Their feisty willingness to go to war earned them the name of War Hawks. Though they numbered fewer than 30 in Congress, they quickly became the driving force in the Republican party.

The Decision for War

During Jefferson's final week in office in early 1809, Congress repealed the Embargo Act and reopened trade except with Britain and France. The following year it authorized trade with France and England but decreed that if one of the two belligerents agreed to stop interfering with American shipping, trade with the other would be prohibited.

In this situation, Napoleon outmaneuvered the British by announcing that he would set aside the French trade regulations. Madison eagerly took the *Growing conflict with Great Britain* French emperor at his word and reimposed a ban on trade with England. It soon became clear that Napoleon had no intention of lifting restrictions, but Madison refused to rescind his order unless the British revoked the Orders in Council. In the ensuring disputes, American anger focused on the British, who seized many more ships than the French and continued to impress American sailors. Westerners also accused the British of stirring up hostility among the Indian tribes.

The embargo produced hard times in Britain, and finally on June 16, 1812, the British ministry suspended the Orders in Council. But it was too late. Two days earlier, unaware of the change in policy, the United States had declared war on Britain.

Angered by the continued violations of American neutrality and pressed by the War Hawks to defend American honor, Madison on June 1 asked for a de-

Debate over going to war

claration of war. The vote of 79 to 49 in the House and 19 to 13 in the Senate mostly followed party lines, with every Federalist voting against war. As the representatives of commercial inter-

ests, particularly in New England, Federalists were convinced that war would ruin American commerce. They also still identified with Britain as the champion of order and conservatism. The handful of Republicans who joined the Federalists represented coastal districts, which were most vulnerable to the Royal Navy.

Clearly, the vote for war could not be explained as a matter of outraged Americans protecting neutral rights. The coastal areas, which were most affected, preferred trade over high principle. On the other hand, members of Congress from the South and the West, regions that had a less direct interest in the issue, clamored most strongly for war. Their constituents were eager to seize territory in Canada or in Florida (owned by Britain's ally Spain) and were outraged by British intrigues with Indians along the frontier.

Perhaps most important, the War Hawks were convinced that Britain had never truly accepted the verdict of the American Revolution. To them, American independence—and with it republicanism—hung in the balance. For Americans hungering for acceptance in the community of nations, nothing rankled more than being treated by the British as colonials. John Quincy Adams expressed this point of view when he declared: "In this question something besides dollars and cents is concerned and no alternative [is] left but war or the abandonment of our rights as an independent nation."

National Unpreparedness

With Britain preoccupied with Napoleon, the War Hawks expected that the United States would win an easy victory. In truth, the United States was totally unprepared for war. Crippled by Jefferson's cutbacks, the navy was unable to remove the British blockade of the American coast. But the Great Lakes, which were inaccessible to the Royal Navy, held the key to the naval war, and when hostilities began, neither side had an advantage there. The army was small and poorly led, and volunteering lagged, even in states where sentiment for war was highest. Congress was also reluctant to levy taxes to finance the war.

A three-pronged American invasion of Canada failed dismally in 1812. The Americans fared better in 1813, when Commander Oliver Hazard Perry won a

Battle of Lake Erie

decisive victory on Lake Erie. Perry's triumph gave the United States control of Lake Erie and greatly strengthened the American position in the Northwest.

"A Chance Such as Will Never Occur Again"

As the United States struggled to organize its forces, Tecumseh discerned his long-awaited opportunity to drive Americans out of the western territories. "Here is a chance . . . such as will never occur again," he told a war council, "for us Indians of North America to form ourselves into one great combination." Joining up with the British, Tecumseh traveled south in the fall to coordinate a concerted offensive with his Creek allies for the following summer. He left a bundle of red sticks with eager Creek soldiers, who were to remove one stick each day from the bundle and attack when the sticks had run out.

A number of the older Creeks were more acculturated and preferred an American alliance. But about 2000 younger "Red Stick" Creeks launched a se-

Defeat of the Creeks

ries of attacks. Once again, the Indians' lack of unity was a serious handicap, as warriors from the Cherokee, Choctaw, and Chickasaw tribes, traditional Creek enemies, allied with the Americans. At the Battle of Horseshoe Bend in March 1814, General Andrew Jackson and his Tennessee militia soundly defeated the Red Stick Creeks. Jackson promptly dictated a peace treaty under which the Creeks ceded 22 million acres of land in the Mississippi Territory. They and the other southern tribes still retained significant landholdings, but Indian military power had been broken in the Old Southwest.

Farther north, in October 1813 American forces under General William Henry Harrison defeated the British and their Indian allies at the Battle of the

Tecumseh's death

Thames. In the midst of heavy fighting Tecumseh was slain—and with him died any hope of a Pan-Indian movement.

The British Invasion

As long as the war against Napoleon continued, the British were unwilling to divert army units to North America. But in 1814 Napoleon was at last defeated. Free to concentrate on America, the British devised a coordinated strategy to invade the United States in the northern, central, and southern parts of the country. The main army headed south from Montreal but was checked when Captain Thomas Macdonough destroyed the British fleet on Lake Champlain.

Meanwhile, a smaller British force captured Washington and burned several public buildings, including the capitol and the president's home. The British withdrew, however, after they failed to capture Baltimore, their principal objective. Witnessing the unsuccessful British attack on Fort McHenry in the city's harbor, Francis Scott Key penned the verses of "The Star Spangled Banner," which was eventually adopted as the national anthem.

The third British target was New Orleans, where a formidable army of 7500 British troops was opposed by a hastily assembled American force commanded

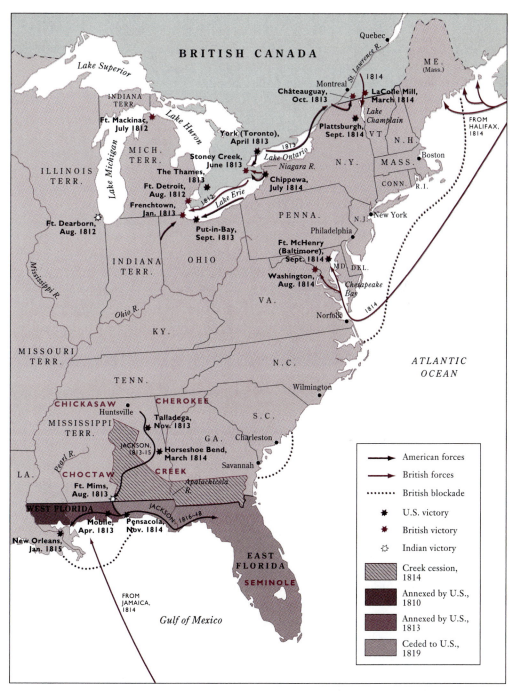

THE WAR OF 1812   After the American victory on Lake Erie and the defeat of the western Indians at the Battle of the Thames, the British adopted a three-pronged strategy to invade the United States, culminating with an attack on New Orleans. But they met their match in Andrew Jackson, whose troops marched to New Orleans after fighting a series of battles against the Creeks and forcing them to cede a massive tract of land.

Jackson's victory at New Orleans

by Major General Andrew Jackson. Jackson's outnumbered and ill-equipped forces won a stunning victory, which made him an overnight hero. The Battle of New Orleans enabled Americans to forget the war's many failures and to boast that once again the United States had humbled the world's greatest military power.

The Hartford Convention

In December 1814, while Jackson was organizing the defense of New Orleans, New England Federalists met in Hartford to voice their grievances. Rejecting calls for secession, the delegates proposed a series of amendments to the Constitution that demonstrated their displeasure with the government's economic policies and their resentment of the South's national political power. The burst of national pride following Jackson's victory, however, badly undercut the Hartford Convention's position, as did news that American negotiators in Ghent, Belgium, had signed a treaty ending the war.

Like the war itself, the Treaty of Ghent accomplished little. All the major issues between the two countries were either ignored or referred to future com-

Treaty of Ghent

missions for settlement. As John Quincy Adams commented, "Nothing was adjusted, nothing was settled—nothing in substance but an indefinite suspension of hostilities was agreed to." Both sides were simply relieved to end the conflict.

AMERICA TURNS INWARD

Adams was right in concluding that in international relations the war had settled nothing. Psychologically, however, the nation's mood had perceptibly changed. "Let any man look at the degraded condition of this country before the war," declaimed young Henry Clay, a leading War Hawk. "The scorn of the universe, the contempt of ourselves. . . . What is our present situation? Respectability and character abroad—security and confidence at home." Indeed, the return of peace brought with it an outburst of American nationalism. Jackson's drubbing of the British at New Orleans strengthened Americans' confidence in their country's destiny. "We have stood the contest, single-handed, against the conqueror of Europe," wrote Supreme Court Justice Joseph Story to a friend, "and we are at peace, with all our blushing victories thick crowding on us."

The upsurge in nationalism sounded the death knell of the Federalist party, whose members had opposed the embargo and flirted with secession at the

Death of the Federalist party

Hartford Convention. Although the party had made its best showing in years in 1812, when Madison narrowly won reelection, its support collapsed in the 1816 election. Madison's secretary of state, James Monroe, resoundingly defeated Federalist Rufus King of New York. Four years later Monroe ran for reelection unopposed.

Monroe's Presidency

The spirit of postwar harmony produced the so-called Era of Good Feelings, presided over by James Monroe, the last president of the Revolutionary generation. Monroe, like Jefferson before him, hoped to eliminate political parties, which he considered unnecessary in a free government. Like Washington, he thought of himself as the head of the nation rather than of a party.

Monroe's greatest achievements were diplomatic, accomplished largely by his talented secretary of state, John Quincy Adams, the son of President John Adams. An experienced diplomat, Adams thought of the Republic in continental terms and sought to promote expansion to the Pacific. Such a vision required dealing with Spain, which had never recognized the legality of the Louisiana Purchase. In addition, between 1810 and 1813 the United States had occupied and unilaterally annexed Spanish West Florida.

Spain was distracted by the rebellion of its Latin American colonies and feared that the United States might invade Texas or other Spanish territory. As a

Transcontinental Treaty

result, Spain agreed to the Transcontinental or Adams–Onís Treaty in February 1819. Its terms set the boundary between American and Spanish territory all the way to the Pacific. Spain not only gave up its claims to the Pacific Northwest, it ceded Florida in exchange for the U.S. government's assuming $5 million in claims against Spain by American citizens. Understanding the strategic commitment to expanding across the continent, Adams wrote in his diary, "The acknowledgement of a definite line of boundary to the South Sea [the Pacific] forms a great epoch in our history."

The Monroe Doctrine

The United States came to terms not only with Spain but, even more important, with Great Britain as well. Following the War of 1812, the British aban-

Improved relations with Britain

doned their connections with the western Indian tribes and no longer attempted to block American expansion to the Rocky Mountains. In addition, the two countries signed a commercial treaty, fixed the 49th parallel as the northern boundary of the Louisiana Purchase, and agreed to joint control of the Oregon Territory for 10 years, subject to renewal.

In this atmosphere of goodwill, George Canning, the British foreign secretary, proposed in August 1823 that the United States and Britain issue a joint statement disavowing any expansionist aims in Latin America and opposing the transfer of Spain's colonies to any foreign power. John Quincy Adams, however, forcefully argued that the United States should not make any pledge against acquiring territory in the future, particularly in Texas, Mexico, and the Caribbean, and Monroe finally decided to make an independent statement.

He included it in his annual message to Congress on December 2, 1823. Monroe reaffirmed that the United States would not intervene in European affairs, a principle of American foreign policy since Washington's Farewell Address. He also announced that the United States would not interfere with already established European colonies in the Western Hemisphere. But any intervention, he warned, in the new republics of Latin America would be considered a hostile act: "The American continents . . . are henceforth not to be considered as subjects for future colonization by any European powers." The essence of this policy was the concept of two worlds, one old and one new, each refraining from interfering in the other's affairs.

American public opinion hailed Monroe's statement and then promptly forgot it. Only years later would it be referred to as the Monroe Doctrine. Still, it

American independence reaffirmed

represented the culmination of the American quest since 1776 for independence and sovereignty. Monroe's declaration underlined the United States's determination not to act in world affairs as a satellite of Britain. Ever since the adoption of the Constitution, the issue of independence had been at the center of American politics. It had surfaced during the 1790s, in Hamilton's quarrel with Jefferson over whether to favor Britain or France and in the differing responses of Americans to the French Revolution. It colored the debates over the embargo and finally once again came to a head in 1812 with the second war for American independence.

The End of an Era

The growing reconciliation with Great Britain ended the external threat to the Republic. Isolated from Europe and protected by the British fleet, the United

Contrasting visions of independence

States was free to turn its attention inward, to concentrate on expanding across the vast continent and on developing its resources. Yet how would the nation be developed? Jefferson had dreamed of an "empire of liberty," delighting in western expansion as the means to preserve a nation of small farmers, like those Crèvecoeur had celebrated.

Younger, more nationalistic Republicans had a different vision. They spoke of protective tariffs to help foster American industries, and better roads and canals to link farmers with towns, cities, and wider markets. The tone of these new Republicans was not aristocratic, like that of the Federalists of old. Still, their dream of a national, commercial republic resembled Franklin's and Hamilton's more than Jefferson's. They looked to profit from speculation in land, from the increasing market for cotton, from the new methods of industrial manufacturing. If these people represented the rising generation, what would be the fate of Crèvecoeur's semisubsistence farm communities? The answer was not yet clear.

In one of those remarkable coincidences that Americans hailed as a sign of Providence's favor, Thomas Jefferson and John Adams died within hours of each other on July 4, 1826, the fiftieth anniversary of the adoption of the Declaration of Independence. Partners in the struggle to secure American independence, these revolutionary giants had become bitter foes in the heated party battles of the 1790s and resumed a warm friendship only after they had retired from public life. Their reconciliation was in tune with the surge of American nationalism, but their time was past. Leadership belonged now to a new generation of Americans who confronted different problems and challenges. Revolutionary America had passed from the scene. The dawn of a new nation was at hand.

SIGNIFICANT EVENTS

1790s	Second Great Awakening begins
1801	Adams's last-minute appointments; Marshall becomes chief justice; Jefferson inaugurated in Washington; Cane Ridge revival
1803	*Marbury v. Madison;* Louisiana Purchase; war resumes between Great Britain and France
1804–1806	Lewis and Clark expedition
1805	Prophet's revivals begin
1807	*Chesapeake* affair; Embargo Act passed
1808	Madison elected president
1809	Embargo repealed; Tecumseh's confederacy organized
1810	*Fletcher v. Peck*
1811	Battle of Tippecanoe
1812	War declared against Great Britain
1813–1814	Creek War
1813	Tecumseh killed
1814	Washington burned; Hartford Convention; Treaty of Ghent
1815	Battle of New Orleans
1816	Monroe elected president
1818	United States–Canada boundary fixed to the Rockies; joint occupation of Oregon established
1819	Transcontinental Treaty; United States acquires Florida
1823	Monroe Doctrine proclaimed

The Republic Transformed and Tested

Two remarkable transformations began sweeping the world in the late eighteenth century. Both of them were so wrenching and far-reaching that they have been called revolutions. The first was a cascade of political revolts that led to increased democratic participation in the governing of many nation-states. The second was the application of machine labor and technological innovation to agricultural and commercial economies—known as the industrial revolution.

Proclaiming the values of liberty and equality, Americans in 1776 led the way with their own democratic revolution. In 1789, however, the center of revolutionary attention shifted to France. There, as in America, the ideals of the Enlightenment helped justify the rejection of rule by monarchy. Increasingly, however, the crowds marching through the streets of Paris adopted a more radical and violent stance, reflecting the burdens of the harsh feudal system as well as other social pressures. The worldwide rise in population of the previous half-century had left the French capital overcrowded, underfed, and thoroughly unruly. Paradoxically, the population pressure that had pushed matters to a crisis was relieved as the Revolution gave way to the emperor Napoleon, in whose wars of conquest the number of French soldiers killed almost offset the natural increase of the nation's population.

In Latin America, democratic and nationalist movements also spread. Just as Great Britain had attempted to pay for its colonial defenses with new revenue from its colonies, so the Spanish Crown raised taxes in the Americas, with similar results. From 1808 to 1821 Spain's American provinces declared their independence one by one. During the uprisings the writings of Jefferson and Thomas Paine circulated, as did translations of the French *Declaration of the Rights of Man*. Democracy did not always root itself in the aftermath of these revolutions, but democratic ideology remained a powerful social catalyst.

The industrial revolution was less violent but no less dramatic in its effects. It began in Great Britain, where canals built toward the end of the eighteenth century improved the transportation network, just as they would in the United States during the 1820s and 1830s. In Britain, too, James Watt in 1769 invented an engine that harnessed the power of steam, used eventually to drive mechanical textile looms. As steam power was applied to ships and rail locomotives, the reach of commercial markets widened. More dependable shipping made it possible to bring cotton from the Egyptian port of Alexandria to factories in British Manchester and American cotton from the Arkansas Red River country to New England.

In many ways the narrative of the young American republic is the story of how one nation worked out the implications of these twin revolutions, industrial and democratic. After the War of 1812 a market economy began rapidly to transform the agricultural practices of Crèvecoeur's semisubsistence America. Urban areas of the North became more diversified and industrial, as young women took jobs in textile mills and young men labored at flour mills processing grain to be shipped east. In a different way, the industrial revolution also transformed the rural South. Cotton would never have become king there without the demand for it created by textile factories.

The industrial revolution thus transformed both the North and the South— but in conflicting ways. Although the economies of the two regions depended on each other, slavery came increasingly to be the focus of disputes between them. The industrial revolution's demand for cotton increased both southern profits and a demand for slave labor. Yet the spread of democratic ideology worldwide created increased pressure to abolish slavery. In France the revolutionary government struck it down in 1794. The British empire outlawed it in 1833, about the time that American abolitionists, influenced by their British friends, became more active in opposing it. In eastern Europe the near-slavery of feudal serfdom was being eliminated as well: in 1848 within the Hapsburg empire, in 1861 in Russia, in 1864 in Romania.

If the purpose of a democratic republic is to resolve conflicts among its members in a nonviolent manner, then in 1861 the American republic failed. It took four years of bitter fighting to reconcile the twin paths of democracy and industrial development. Given the massive size of the territory involved and the depth of sectional divisions, it is perhaps not surprising that a union so diverse did not hold without the force of arms. That the separation was not final—that in the end, reunion emerged out of conflict—is perhaps one reason why the tale is so gripping.

CHAPTER TEN

The Opening of America

I n the years before the Civil War, the name of Chauncey Jerome could be found traced in neat, sharp letters in a thousand different places across the globe: everywhere from the fireplace mantels of southern planters to the log huts of Illinois prairie farmers, and even in Chinese trading houses in Canton. For Chauncey Jerome was a New England clockmaker, whose clever, inexpensive, and addictive machines had conquered the markets of the world.

Jerome, a Connecticut Yankee, had apprenticed himself to a carpenter during his boyhood, but after the War of 1812 he decided to try his luck as a clockmaker. For years he eked out a living peddling his products from farmhouse to farmhouse, until 1824, when his career took off thanks to a "very showy" bronze looking-glass clock. The new model he had designed sold as fast as the clocks could be manufactured. Between 1827 and 1837 Jerome's factory produced more clocks than any other in the country. But when the Panic of 1837 struck, Jerome had to scramble to avoid financial ruin.

Looking for a new opportunity, he set out to produce an inexpensive brass "one-day" clock—so called because its winding mechanism kept it running that long. Traditionally, the works of these clocks were made of wood, and the wheels and teeth had to be painstakingly cut by hand. Jerome's brass version proved more accurate than earlier types and cheaper to boot. Costs came down further when he began to use interchangeable parts and combined his operations for making cases and movements within a single factory in New Haven, Connecticut. By systematically organizing the production process, Jerome brought the price of a good clock within the reach of ordinary people. So popular were the new models that desperate competitors began attaching Jerome labels to their own inferior imitations.

Disaster struck again in 1855, when Jerome took on several unreliable partners. Within a few years his business faltered, then failed. At the age of 62, the once-prominent business leader found himself working again in a clock factory as an ordinary mechanic. He lived his last years in poverty.

Chauncey Jerome's life spanned the transition from the master–apprentice system of production to the beginnings of mechanization and the rise of the factory system. By 1850 the notion of independent American farmers living mainly on what they themselves produced (Crèvecoeur's vision of the 1780s) had become a dream of the past. In its place stood a commercial republic in which a full-blown national market encompassed most settled areas of the country.

The concept of the market is crucial here. Americans tied themselves to one another eagerly, even aggressively, through the mechanism of the free *Market economy* market. They sold cotton or wheat and bought manufactured cloth or brass one-day clocks. They borrowed money not merely to buy a house or farm but also to speculate and profit. They relied, even in many rural villages, on cash and paper money instead of bartering for goods and services. American life moved from less to more specialized forms of labor. It moved from subsistence-oriented to more commercially oriented outlooks and from face-to-face local dealings to impersonal, distant transactions. It shifted from the mechanically simple to the technologically complex and from less dense patterns of settlement on farms to more complex arrangements in cities and towns. Such were the changes Chauncey Jerome witnessed—indeed, changes he helped to bring about himself, with his clocks that divided the working days of Americans into more disciplined, orderly segments.

As these changes took place, Jerome sensed that society had taken on a different tone—that the marketplace and its ethos had become dominant. "It is all money and business, business and money which make the man now-a-days," he complained. "Success is every thing, and it makes very little difference how, or what means he uses to obtain it." The United States, according to one foreign traveler, had become "one gigantic workshop, over the entrance of which there is the blazing inscription '*No admission here except on business.*'"

THE MARKET REVOLUTION

This national system of markets began to develop following the War of 1812. As the United States entered a period of unprecedented economic expansion, the economy became varied enough to sustain and even accelerate its growth. Before the war it had been tied largely to international trade. If European nations suddenly stopped purchasing American commodities like tobacco and timber, the domestic economy faltered, as happened during the European wars of the 1790s and again after 1803. Since so many Americans remained rural and primarily self-sufficient, they could not absorb any increase in goods produced by American manufacturers.

But the War of 1812 marked the turning point in the creation and expansion of a domestic market. First the embargo and then the war itself stimulated

Growth of a domestic market

the growth of manufacturing, particularly in textiles. In addition, war had also bottled up capital in Europe. When peace was restored, this capital flowed into the United States seeking investments. Finally, the war experience led the federal government to adopt policies designed to spur economic expansion.

The New Nationalism

After the war with Britain, leadership passed to a new generation of the Republic—younger men like Henry Clay, John C. Calhoun, and John Quincy Adams. Each was an ardent nationalist eager to use federal power to promote rapid development of the nation. Increasingly dominant within the Republican party, they advocated the "New Nationalism," a set of economic policies designed to foster the prosperity of all regions of the country and bind the nation more tightly together.

Even James Madison saw the need for increased federal activity, given the problems the government experienced during the war. The national bank had closed its doors in 1811 when its charter expired, and the result had been financial chaos. With Madison's approval, Congress in 1816 chartered the Second

A new national bank and a protective tariff

Bank of the United States for a period of 20 years. Madison also agreed to a mildly protective tariff to aid fledgling American industries by raising the price of competing foreign goods. Passed in 1816, it set an average duty of 20 percent on selected imports. The measure enjoyed wide support in the North and West, while a number of southern representatives voted against it.

Madison also recommended that the government provide aid for internal improvements such as roads, canals, and bridges. The war had demonstrated

Bonus Bill veto

how cumbersome it was to move troops or supplies overland. Madison, however, believed that federal funds could not be used for merely local projects, so he vetoed the Bonus Bill, by which money was to be distributed to the states for internal improvements. This represented only a temporary setback for the nationalists, however, for even Madison was willing to support projects broader in scope, and his successor, James Monroe, approved additional ones.

The Cotton Trade

The most important spur to American economic development after 1815 was the growing cotton trade. Cotton production was limited, however, until in

Cotton gin

1793 Eli Whitney invented the cotton gin, a mechanical device that removed sticky seeds from the lint. With a slave now able to clean 50 pounds of cotton a day (compared with only one by hand), and with prices high on the world market, cotton production in the Lower South soared. By 1840 the South produced more than 60 percent of the world supply, which accounted for almost two-thirds of all American exports.

The cotton trade was the major expansive force in the economy until 1839. Northern factories increasingly made money by turning raw cotton into cloth, while northern merchants reaped profits from shipping the cotton and then re-shipping the textiles. Planters used the income they earned to purchase food-stuffs from the West and goods and services from the Northeast.

The Transportation Revolution

For a market economy to become truly national, a transportation network link-ing various parts of the nation was essential. The economy had not become self-sustaining earlier partly because the only means of transporting goods cheaply was by water. Thus trade was limited largely to coastal and international markets, for even on rivers, bulky goods moved easily in only one direction: downstream.

All that changed, however, after 1815. From 1825 to 1855—the span of a single generation—the cost of transportation on land fell 95 percent, while its speed increased fivefold. As a result, new regions were drawn quickly into the market.

Canals attracted considerable investment capital, especially after the success of the wondrous Erie Canal. Built between 1818 and 1825, the canal stretched *The canal age* 364 miles from Albany on the Hudson River to Buffalo on Lake Erie. Its construction by the state was an act of faith, for in 1816 the United States had only 100 miles of canals, none longer than 28 miles. Then, too, the proposed route ran through forests, disease-ridden swamps, and unsettled wilderness.

The project paid for itself within a few years. The Erie Canal reduced the cost of shipping a ton of goods from Buffalo to New York City from more than 19 cents a mile to less than 3 cents; by 1860 the cost had fallen to less than a penny. Where the canal's busy traffic passed, settlers flocked, and towns like Rochester and Lockport sprang up and thrived by moving goods and serving markets. The steady flow of goods eastward gave New York City the dominant position in the scramble for control of western trade.

New York's commercial rivals, like Philadelphia and Baltimore, were soon frantically trying to build their own canals to the West. Western states like Ohio and Indiana, convinced that prosperity depended on cheap transportation, con-structed canals to link interior regions with the Great Lakes. By 1840 the na-tion had completed more than 3300 miles of canals—a length greater than the distance from New York City to Seattle—at a cost of about $125 million. Almost half of that amount came from state governments.

Because of its vast expanse, the United States was particularly dependent on river transportation. But shipping goods downstream from Pittsburgh to New

Steamboats Orleans took 6 weeks, and the return journey required 17 weeks or more. Steamboats reduced the time of a trip from New Orleans to Louisville from 90 to 8 days, while cutting upstream costs by 90 percent.

Robert Fulton in 1807 demonstrated the commercial possibilities of propelling a boat with steam when his ship, the *Clermont*, traveled from New York City to Albany on the Hudson River. But steamboats had the greatest effect on transportation on western rivers, where the flat-bottomed boats could haul heavy loads even in low water. The number of steamboats operating in those waters jumped from 17 in 1817 to 727 in 1855. Since steamboats could make many more voyages annually, the carrying capacity on the western rivers increased 100-fold between 1820 and 1860.

Governments did not invest heavily in steamboats as they had in canals, except for removing obstacles to navigation. Although railroads would end the steamboat's dominance by 1860, it was the major form of western transportation during the establishment of a national market economy and was the most important factor in the rise of manufacturing in the Ohio and upper Mississippi valleys.

The first significant railroads appeared in the 1830s, largely as feeder lines to canals. Soon enough, cities and towns saw that their future depended on having *Railroads* good rail links. The country had only 13 miles of track in 1830, but 10 years later railroad and canal mileage were almost exactly equal (3325 miles). By 1850, the nation had a total of 8879 miles. Railroad rates were usually higher, but railroads were twice as fast as steamboats, offered more direct routes, and could operate year-round. Although railroads increasingly dominated the transportation system after 1850, canals and steamboats were initially the key to creating a national market.

Agriculture in the Market Economy

The new forms of transportation had a remarkable effect on Crèvecoeur's yeoman farm families: they became linked ever more tightly to a national market system. Before the canal era, wheat could be shipped at a profit no farther than 50 miles. But given cheap transportation, farmers eagerly increased their output in order to sell the surplus at distant markets. In this shift to-*Commercial agriculture* ward commercial agriculture, farmers began cultivating more acres, working longer hours, and adopting scientific farming methods, including crop rotation and the use of manures as fertilizer. Instead of bartering goods with friends and neighbors, they more often paid cash or depended on banks to extend them credit. Instead of marketing crops themselves, they began to rely on regional merchants. Like southern planters, western wheat farmers increasingly sold in a world market.

As transportation and market networks connected more areas of the nation, they encouraged regional specialization. The South increasingly concentrated on staple crops for export, and the West grew foodstuffs, particularly grain. By

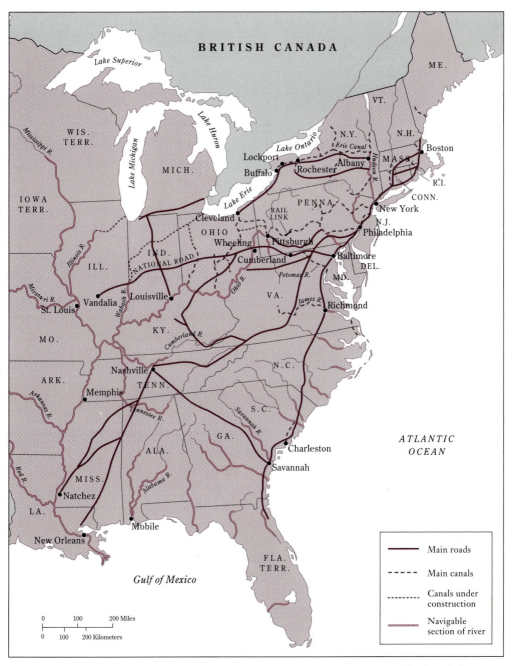

THE TRANSPORTATION NETWORK OF A MARKET ECONOMY, 1840   Canals played their
most important role in the Northeast, where they linked eastern cities to western
rivers and the Great Lakes. Steamboats were most crucial in the extensive river
systems of the South and the West.

1850, Wisconsin and Illinois were major wheat-producing states. Eastern farmers, unable to compete with wheat yields of western farms, shifted to producing fruits, vegetables, and dairy products for rapidly growing urban areas.

Although foreign commerce expanded too, it was overshadowed by the dramatic growth in domestic markets, which absorbed more and more of the goods and services being produced. The cities of the East no longer looked primarily to the sea for their trade; they looked to southern and western markets. That, indeed, was a revolution in markets.

John Marshall and the Promotion of Enterprise

For a national market system to flourish, a climate favorable to investment had to exist. Under the leadership of Chief Justice John Marshall, the Supreme Court became the branch of the federal government most aggressive in protecting the new forms of business central to the growing market economy.

Marshall, who presided over the Court from 1801 to 1835, at first glance seemed an unlikely leader. Informal in manners and almost sloppy in dress, he was nonetheless a commanding figure: tall and slender, with twinkling eyes and a contagious laugh. His forceful intellect was reinforced by his ability to persuade. Time after time he convinced his colleagues to uphold the sanctity of private property and the power of the federal government to promote economic growth.

In the case of *McCulloch v. Maryland* (1819) the Court upheld the constitutionality of the Second Bank of the United States. Just as Alexander Hamilton

Constitutionality of the national bank

had argued in the debate over the first national bank, Marshall emphasized that the Constitution gave Congress the power to make all "necessary and proper" laws to carry out its delegated powers. If Congress believed that a bank would help it meet its responsibilities, such as maintaining the public credit and regulating the currency, then it was constitutional. "Let the end be legitimate," Marshall wrote, "let it be within the scope of the Constitution, and all means which are appropriate, which are plainly adapted to that end, which are not prohibited . . . are constitutional." By upholding Hamilton's doctrine of implied powers, Marshall enlarged federal power to an extraordinary degree.

He also encouraged a more freewheeling commerce in *Gibbons v. Ogden* (1824), which gave Marshall a chance to define the greatest power of the fed-

Interstate commerce

eral government in peacetime, the right to regulate interstate commerce. In striking down a steamboat monopoly granted by the state of New York, the chief justice gave the term "commerce" the broadest possible definition, declaring that it covered all commercial dealings, and that Congress's power over interstate commerce could be "exercised to its utmost extent." The result was increased business competition throughout society.

At the heart of most commercial agreements were private contracts, made between individuals or companies. Marshall took an active role in defining con-

Contracts

tract law, which was then in its infancy. The case of *Fletcher v. Peck* (1810) showed how far he was willing to go to protect private property. The justices unanimously struck down a Georgia law rescinding a land grant to a group of speculators that had been obtained by bribing the legislature. A grant was a contract, Marshall declared, and since the Constitution forbade states from impairing "the obligation of contracts," the legislature could not interfere with the grant once it had been made. Although the framers of the Constitution probably meant contracts to refer only to agreements between private parties, Marshall made no distinction between public and private agreements, thereby greatly expanding the meaning of the contract clause.

The most celebrated decision Marshall wrote on the contract clause was in *Dartmouth College v. Woodward*, decided in 1819. This case arose out of the attempt by New Hampshire to alter the college's charter of 1769. The Court overturned the state law on the grounds that state charters were also contracts and could not be altered by later legislatures. By this ruling Marshall intended to protect corporations, which conducted business under charters granted by individual states.

Thus the Marshall Court sought to encourage economic risk-taking by protecting property and contracts, by limiting state interference, and by creating a climate of business confidence.

General Incorporation Laws

Corporations were not new in American business, but as the economy expanded, they grew in number. By pooling investors' resources, they also provided a way to raise capital for large-scale undertakings. Then, too, corporations offered the advantage of limited liability: that is, an investor was liable only for the amount he or she had invested, which limited a person's financial risk. Ventures such as banks, insurance companies, railroads, and manufacturing firms—which all required a large amount of capital—increasingly were incorporated.

Advantages of corporations

Originally, state legislatures were required to approve a special charter for each new corporation. Beginning in the 1830s, states adopted general incorporation laws that automatically granted a corporation charter to any applicant who met certain minimum qualifications. This reform made it much easier and faster to secure a charter and stimulated organization of the national market.

A RESTLESS TEMPER

"An American . . . wants to perform within a year what others do within a much longer period," observed one German emigrant. Indeed, between 1815 and 1850, the nation reverberated with almost explosive energy. The French commentator Alexis de Tocqueville was astonished, like most Europeans, at the restless mobility of the average American. "Born often under another sky, placed in the middle of an always moving scene, . . . the American . . . grows accustomed only to change, and ends by regarding it as the natural state of man."

This emphasis on speed affected nearly every aspect of American life. Steamboat captains risked boiler explosions for the honor of having the fastest boat on the river, prompting the visiting English novelist Charles Dickens to comment that traveling under these conditions seemed like taking up "lodgings on the first floor of a powder mill." American technology emphasized speed over longevity. Unlike European railroads, American railroads were lightweight, were hastily constructed, and paid little heed to the safety or comfort of passengers. Americans ate so quickly that one disgruntled European insisted food was "pitch-forked down."

High-speed society

Horatio Greenough, a sculptor who returned to the United States in 1836 after an extended stay abroad, was amazed and a bit frightened by the pace he witnessed. "Go ahead! is the order of the day," he observed. "The whole continent presents a scene of scrambling and roars with greedy hurry." If the economic hallmark of this new order was the growth of a national market, there were social factors that also contributed to American restlessness.

Population Growth

The American population continued to double about every 22 years—more than twice the birthrate of Great Britain. The census, which stood at fewer than 4 million in 1790, surpassed 23 million in 1850. Although the birthrate

Europeans were shocked that Americans bolted their food or gorged themselves on anything within reach, as this English drawing indicates.

peaked in 1800, it declined only slowly before 1840. In the 1840s, it dropped about 10 percent, the first significant decrease in American history.

At the same time, many basic population characteristics changed little throughout the first half of the nineteenth century. Life expectancy did not improve significantly, the population remained quite young, and early marriage remained the norm, especially in rural areas.

From 1790 to 1820 natural increase accounted for virtually all of the country's population growth. But immigration, which had been disrupted by the Napoleonic Wars in Europe, revived after 1815. In the 1830s some 600,000 immigrants arrived, more than double the number in the quarter century after 1790.

The Restless Movement West

The vast areas of land available for settlement absorbed much of the burgeoning population. As settlers streamed west, speculation in western lands reached frenzied proportions. Whereas only 68,000 acres of the public domain had been sold during the year 1800, sales peaked in 1818, at a staggering 3.5 million acres.

The Panic of 1819 sent sales and prices crashing, and in the depression that followed many farmers lost their farms. Congress reacted by abolishing credit sales and demanding payment in cash, but it tempered this policy by lowering the price of the cheapest lands to $1.25 an acre and reducing the minimum tract to 80 acres.

Even so, speculators purchased most of the public lands sold, since there was no limit on the amount of acreage an individual or a land company could

Land speculation buy. These land speculators played a leading role in settlement of the West. To hasten sales, they usually sold land partially on credit—a vital aid to poorer farmers. They also provided loans to purchase needed tools and supplies. Many farmers became speculators themselves, buying up property in the neighborhood and selling it to latecomers at a tidy profit. "Speculation in real estate has been the ruling idea and occupation of the Western mind," one Englishman reported in the 1840s. "Clerks, labourers, farmers, storekeepers merely followed their callings for a living while they were speculating for their fortunes."

Given such rapid settlement, geographic mobility became one of the most striking characteristics of the American people. The 1850 census revealed that

Geographic mobility nearly half of all native-born free Americans lived outside the state where they had been born. In Boston from 1830 to 1860 perhaps one-third of the inhabitants changed their place of residence each year. The typical American "has no root in the soil," visiting Frenchman Michel Chevalier observed, but "is always in the mood to move on, always ready to start in the first steamer that comes along from the place where he had just now landed."

It was the search for opportunity, more than anything else, that accounted for such restlessness. An American moved, noted one British observer, "if by so doing he can make $10 where before he made $8." Often, the influence of the market uprooted Americans too. In 1851, a new railroad line bypassed the village of Auburn, Illinois. Despite its pretty location, residents quickly abandoned it and moved to the new town that sprang up around the depot. A neighboring farmer purchased the old village, plowed up the streets, and Auburn reverted to a cornfield.

Urbanization

Even with the growth of a national market, the United States remained a rural nation. Nevertheless, the four decades after 1820 witnessed the fastest rate of urbanization in American history. As a result, the ratio of farmers to city dwellers steadily dropped from 15 to 1 in 1800 to 5.5 to 1 in 1850.

Reasons for urban growth

Improved transportation, the declining productivity of many eastern farms, the beginnings of industrialization, and the influx of immigrants all stimulated the growth of cities.

The most heavily urbanized area of the country was the Northeast, where in 1860 more than a third of the population lived in cities.* Important urban centers such as St. Louis and Cincinnati arose in the West. The South, with only 10 percent of its population living in cities, was the least urbanized region.

---

*The Northeast included New England and the mid-Atlantic states (New York, Pennsylvania, and New Jersey). The South comprised the slave states plus the District of Columbia.

St. Louis, a major urban center that developed in the West, depended
on the steamboat to sustain its commerce,
as this 1859 illustration makes clear.

The Mere Love of Moving

In the course of the next morning, while we were sitting in the public parlour, at the hotel, a party came in which we soon recognized as . . . one of the groups of wanderers we had overtaken the day before [on the road]. . . . A gentleman came forward who claimed the chief of the party for his brother . . . [and] broke out thus—"Well! this is the strangest resolution for a man of your years to take into his head! Why, where are you going?"

"I am going to Florida, to be sure. . . . It is the finest country in the world—a delightful climate—rich soil—plenty of room."

"Have you been there?" asked his brother.

"No, not yet," said the wanderer; "but I know all about it. . . ."

"Pray tell me, what have you done with your estate in Maryland, on which you were fixed when I last got tidings of you? . . ."

"I've sold that property."

"What, all?"

"Yes, all, every inch of it, and I have brought away every movable thing with me. Here we are, . . . my wife, my son there, and my daughter—all my slaves, too, my furniture, horses, and so forth."

"And now, pray, answer me this question—were you not well off where you were located before—had you not plenty of good land?"

"Oh yes, plenty. . . ."

"What, then, possesses you to go seeking for a fresh place in such a country as Florida, where you must be content to take up your quarters amongst tadpoles and mosquitoes?"

While the hardy rover was puzzling himself in search of a reasonable answer, his wife took up the discourse, and . . . said, "It is all for the mere love of moving. We have been doing so all our lives—just moving from place to place—never resting—as soon as ever we get comfortably settled, then it is time to be off to something new."

Basil Hall, *Travels in the United States* (Edinburgh: 3 vols., Cadell and Co., 1829), v. 3, pp. 129–132.

All of these changes—the amazing growth of the population, the quickening movement westward, and the rising migration to the cities—pointed to a fundamental reorientation of American development. Expansion was the keynote of the new America, and the prospects it offered both excited and unsettled Americans.

THE RISE OF FACTORIES

It was an isolated life, growing up in a rural, hilly Vermont. But stories of the textile factories that had sprung up in Lowell and other towns in Massachusetts reached even small villages like Barnard. Mary Paul was working there as a domestic servant when she asked her father for permission to move to Lowell. "I am in need of clothes which I cannot get about here," she explained. In 1845 two other friends from Barnard helped her find her first job at the Lowell mills, from which she earned $128 in 11 months. After four years she returned home, but now found "countryfied" life too confining. This time she left her rural hometown for good.

Mary Paul was one of thousands of rural Americans whose lives were fundamentally altered by the economic transformations of the young republic. The changes in her lifestyle and her working habits demonstrated that the new factories and industries needed more than technological innovation to run smoothly. Equally crucial, labor needed to be reorganized.

Technological Advances

Before 1815 manufacturing had been done in homes or shops by skilled artisans. As master craftworkers, they imparted the knowledge of their trades to apprentices and journeymen. In addition, women often worked in their homes part-time under the putting-out system, making finished articles from raw material supplied by merchant capitalists. After 1815 this older form of manufacturing began to give way to factories with machinery tended by unskilled or semiskilled laborers.

From England came many of the earliest technological innovations. But Americans often improved on the British machines or adapted them to more extensive uses. In contrast to the more traditional societies of Europe, "everything new is quickly introduced here," one visitor commented in 1820. "There is no clinging to old ways; the moment an American hears the word 'invention' he pricks up his ears." From 1790 to 1860 the United States Patent Office granted more patents than England and France combined.

To protect their economic advantage, the British forbade the export of any textile machinery or emigration of any craftworker trained in its construction. But in 1790 a mill worker named Samuel Slater eluded English authorities and built the first textile mill in America. Two decades later, the Boston merchant Francis Cabot Lowell imitated British designs for a power loom and then improved on them.

The first machines required highly skilled workers both to build and to repair them. Eli Whitney had a better idea. Having won a contract to produce

Interchangeable parts

10,000 rifles for the government, he developed machinery that would mass-produce parts that were interchangeable from rifle to rifle. Such parts had to be manufactured to rigid specifica-

tions, but once the process was perfected, these parts allowed a worker to assemble a rifle quickly with only a few tools. Simeon North applied the same
principle to the production of clocks, and Chauncey Jerome followed North's
example and soon surpassed him.

What rail and steam engines did for transportation, Samuel F. B. Morse's
telegraph did for communications. Morse patented a device that sent electrical

Revolution in communications
pulses over a wire in 1837, and before long telegraph lines fanned
out in all directions, linking various parts of the country in instantaneous communication. By 1852 there were 23,000 miles of
lines, and by 1860, more than 50,000. The new form of communication sped
business information, helped link the transportation network, and enabled
newspapers to provide readers with up-to-date news.

Indeed, the invention of the telegraph and the perfection of a power press
(1847) by Robert Hoe and his son Richard revolutionized journalism. The mechanical press sharply increased the speed with which sheets could be printed
over the old hand method and brought newspapers within economic reach of
ordinary families. Hoe's press had a similar impact on book publishing, as thousands of copies could be printed at affordable prices.

Textile Factories

The factory system originated in the Northeast, where capital, water power, and
transportation facilities were available. As in England, the production of cloth
was the first manufacturing process to use the new technology on a large scale.
Eventually all the processes of manufacturing fabrics were brought together in
a single location, and machines did virtually all the work.

In 1820 a group of wealthy Boston merchants, known as the Boston
Associates, set up operations at Lowell, Massachusetts, which soon became the

Textile city of Lowell
nation's most famous center of textile manufacturing. Its founders
intended to avoid the misery that surrounded English factories
by combining paternalism with high profits. Instead of relying
mostly on child labor or a permanent working class, the Lowell mills employed
daughters of New England farm families. Female workers lived in company
boardinghouses under the watchful eye of a matron. To its many visitors, Lowell
presented an impressive sight, with huge factories and well-kept houses. Female
workers were encouraged to attend lectures and use the library; they even published their own magazine, the *Lowell Offering*.

In reality, factory life involved strict work rules and long hours of tedious,
repetitive work. At Lowell, for example, workers could be fined for lateness or
misconduct, such as talking on the job, and the women's morals in the boardinghouses were strictly guarded. Work typically began at 7 A.M. (earlier in the
summer) and continued until 7 at night, six days a week. With only 30 minutes
for the noon meal, many workers had to run to the boardinghouse and back to
avoid being late. Winter was the "lighting up" season, when work began before

daylight and ended after dark. The only light after sunset came from whale oil lamps that filled the long rooms with smoke.

Although the labor was hard, the female operators earned from $2.40 to $3.20 a week, wages that were considered good by the standards of the time.

Female workers

(Domestic servants and seamstresses were paid less than a dollar a week.) The average "mill girl" was between 16 and 30 years old. Most were not working to support their families back home on the farm; instead they wanted to accumulate some money for perhaps the first time in their lives and sample some of life's pleasures. "I must . . . have something of my own before many more years have passed," Sally Rice wrote when her parents asked her to return home to Somerset, Vermont. "And where is that something coming from if I go home and earn nothing?"

Like Rice, few women in the mills intended to work permanently. Most stayed no more than five years before getting married. The sense of sisterhood that united women in the boardinghouses made it easier for farm daughters to adjust to the stress and regimen the factory imposed on them. So did their view of the situation as temporary rather than permanent.

As competition in the textile industry intensified, factory managers undertook to raise productivity. In the mid-1830s the mills began to increase the

Lowell mills become less paternal

workloads and speed up the machinery. Even these changes failed to maintain previous profits, and on several occasions factories cut wages. The ever-quickening pace of work finally provoked resistance among the women in the mills. Several times in the 1830s wage cuts sparked strikes in which a minority of workers walked out. In the 1840s workers' protests focused on the demand for a 10-hour day.

"There are very many young ladies at work in the factories that have given up milinary dressmaking and school-keeping for to work in the mill," wrote Malenda Edwards in 1839. This young woman was one of them.

As the mills expanded, a smaller proportion of the workers lived in company boardinghouses and moral regulations were relaxed. But the greatest change was a shift in the workforce from native-born females to Irish immigrants, including men and children. The Irish, who made up only 8 percent of the Lowell workforce in 1845, amounted to almost half by 1860. Desperately poor and eager for any work, they did not view their situation as temporary. Wages continued to decline, and a permanent working class took shape.

Lowell and the Environment

Lowell was a city built on water power. Early settlers had used the power of the Merrimack River to run mills, but never on the scale of the textile factories. As the market spread, Americans came to link progress with the fullest use of the environment's natural resources.

By 1836, Lowell had seven canals, with a supporting network of locks and dams, to govern the Merrimack's flow and distribute water to the city's 26

Reshaping the area's waterscape

mills. As more and more mills were built, both at Lowell and other sites, the Associates erected dams at several points along the river to store water and divert it into power canals for factories. At Lawrence, they constructed the largest dam in the world at the time, a 32-foot-high granite structure that spanned 1600 feet across the river. But even dammed, the Merrimack's waters proved insufficient. So the Associates gained control of over 100 square miles of New Hampshire lakes that fed the river system. Damming these lakes provided a regular flow of water, especially in the drier summer months. In the course of establishing this elaborate water control system, they came to see water as a form of property, divorced from the owership of land along the river. Water became a commodity that was measured in terms of its power to operate a certain number of spindles and looms.

By regulating the river's waters, the Boston Associates made the Merrimack Valley the nation's greatest industrial center in the first half of the nineteenth

Damaging effects

century. But not all who lived in the valley benefited. By raising water levels, the dams flooded farmlands, blocked the transportation of logs downstream, and damaged mills upstream by reducing the current and creating backwater that impeded waterwheels. The dams also devastated the fish population by preventing upstream spawning, while factories routinely dumped their wastes into the river to be carried downstream, thereby eventually contaminating water supplies. Epidemics of typhoid, cholera, and dysentery occurred with increasing frequency, so that by midcentury Lowell had a reputation as a particularly unhealthy city.

In the end, the factory system fundamentally transformed the environment. Far from existing in harmony with its rural surroundings, Lowell, with its clattering machines and dammed rivers, presented a glaring constrast to rural life. The founding vision of Lowell had disappeared.

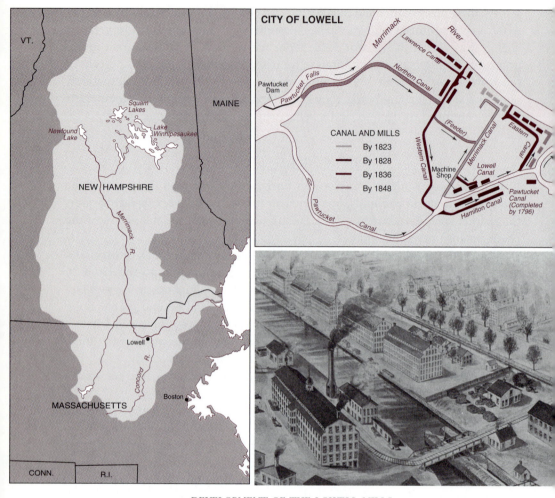

DEVELOPMENT OF THE LOWELL MILLS

As more mills were built at Lowell, the demand increased for water to power them. By 1859 the mills drew water from lakes 80 to 100 miles upstream, including Winnipesaukee, Squam, and Newfound. The map at left shows the watersheds affected. In the city of Lowell (right), a system of canals was enlarged over several decades. In the painting (done in 1845), the machine shop can be seen at left, with a row of mills alongside a canal. Rail links tied Lowell and Boston together.

Industrial Work

The creation of an industrial labor force that was accustomed to working in factories did not occur easily. Before the rise of the factory, artisans had worked

Artisan system

within the home. Apprentices were considered part of the family, and masters were responsible not only for teaching their apprentices a trade but also for providing them some education and for supervising their moral behavior. Journeymen knew that if they perfected their skill, they could become respected master artisans with their own shops. Nor did skilled artisans work by the clock, at a steady pace, but rather in bursts of intense labor alternating with greater leisure.

The factory changed that. Factory goods were not so finished or elegant as those done by hand, and pride in craftsmanship gave way to rates of productiv-

Transformation of work

ity. At the same time, workers were required to discard old habits, for industrialism demanded a worker who was sober, dependable, and self-disciplined. Absenteeism, lateness, and drunkenness hurt productivity and disrupted the regular factory routine. Thus industrialization not only produced a fundamental change in the way work was organized. It transformed the very nature of work.

The first generation to experience these changes did not adopt the new attitudes easily. The factory clock became the symbol of the new work rules. One mill worker who finally quit complained revealingly about "obedience to the ding-dong of the bell—just as though we are so many living machines." With the loss of personal freedom also came the loss of standing in the community. The master–apprentice relationship gave way to factories' sharp separation of workers from management. Few workers rose through the ranks to supervisory positions, and even fewer could achieve the artisan's dream of setting up their own businesses. Even well-paid workers sensed their decline in status.

The Shoe Industry

Shoemaking illustrates one way the artisan tradition was undermined. Traditionally, a skilled cobbler possessed a good knowledge of leather, had the ability to cut out the various parts of a shoe, and could stitch and glue those parts together. He then sold the shoes in the same shop where he and his apprentices made them. Unlike the textile industry, shoemaking was not rapidly transformed in this period by a shift to heavy machinery. Even so, expanding transportation networks and national markets fundamentally altered this business.

Micajah Pratt, a cobbler from Lynn, Massachusetts, discovered that if he could make shoes cheaply enough, there were ready markets in the South and

Lynn, center of shoe manufacturing

West. So he hired workers to produce shoes in larger and larger central shops. Pratt cut costs further by using new production techniques, such as standardized patterns and sole-cutting machines. Pratt eventually employed as many as 500 men and women.

Unable to keep up with demand, he and other manufacturers hired farmers, fishermen, and their families in surrounding towns to do part-time work at home. Women and girls sewed the upper parts of a shoe, men and boys attached the bottoms. While slow, this mode of production allowed wages to be reduced still further. A few highly paid workers performed critical tasks like cutting the leather, but most work was done either in large central shops or in homes. With workers no longer able to make an entire shoe, in little more than a generation shoemaking ceased to be a craft. Though not organized in a factory setting, it had become essentially an assembly-line process.

The Labor Movement

In this newly emerging economic order, workers sometimes organized to protect their rights and traditional ways of life. Craftworkers such as carpenters, printers, and tailors formed unions, and in 1834 individual unions came together in the National Trades' Union.

Union leaders argued that labor was degraded in America: workers endured long hours, low pay, and low status. Unlike most American social thinkers of the day, they accepted the idea of conflict between different classes. They did not believe that the interests of workers and employers could be reconciled, and they blamed the plight of labor on monopolies, especially banking and paper money, and on machines and the factory system.

If the unions' rhetoric sounded radical, the solutions they proposed were moderate. Reformers agitated for public education, abolition of imprisonment for debt, political action by workers, and effective unions as the means to guarantee social equality and restore labor to its former honored position. Proclaiming the republican virtues of freedom and equality, they attacked special privilege, denounced the lack of equal opportunity, and decried workers' loss of independence.

The labor movement gathered some momentum in the decade before the Panic of 1837, but in the depression that followed, labor's strength collapsed. During hard times, few workers were willing to strike or engage in collective action. Nor did skilled craftworkers, who spearheaded the union movement, feel a particularly strong bond with semiskilled factory workers and unskilled laborers. More than a decade of agitation did finally win the 10-hour day for some workers by the 1850s, and the courts also recognized workers' right to strike, but these gains had little immediate impact.

Difficulties of the union movement

Workers were united in resenting the industrial system and their loss of status, but they were divided by ethnic and racial antagonisms, gender, conflicting religious perspectives, occupational differences, party loyalties, and disagreements over tactics. For them, the factory and industrialism were not agents of opportunity but reminders of their loss of independence and a measure of control over their lives.

COUNTERPOINT *Workers and Industrialization*

The process of industrialization was both sweeping and complex, so it is not surprising that historians have disagreed over its impact on workers. Economic historians generally emphasize industrialization's benefits. Focusing on wages and the standard of living, they estimate that between 1820 and 1860 real wages rose anywhere from 60 to 100 percent. Even the incomes of unskilled workers grew, thanks partly to higher wages but mostly due to the lower cost of consumer items, which were now mass-produced. In 1800 only prosperous families could enjoy items like matched chairs, finished furniture, carpets, clocks, silverware, and ceramic dishes. By midcentury, however, such items were well within reach of working families. Inexpensive textiles enlarged personal wardrobes, allowed for more frequent changes of clothing, and thus promoted cleanliness. Workers' diets also benefited from the variety of foods newly available in stores. These gains spread throughout all ranks of free white society.

Labor historians, who emphasize instead workers' attitudes, have painted a bleaker picture. As workers ceased to be skilled craftspeople, they sensed that manual labor no longer commanded respect in the community. Moreover, even though their standard of living might be increasing, workers were receiving a smaller *proportion* of the wealth their labor produced. Given this increasingly unequal distribution of wealth, they fell further behind employers and professionals, who no longer did manual labor. In addition, they faced a lifetime of hard, tedious work with only a limited chance of rising into the middle class. From this perspective, industrialization took a heavy psychological toll by weakening factory laborers' pride and independence and hardening class lines. Their despair was voiced by a group of cotton mill workers who protested that workers were becoming "mere machine[s] producing wealth by perpetual exertion, yet living a life of unceasing anxiety and want. . . ."

SOCIAL STRUCTURES OF
THE MARKET SOCIETY

Thousands of miles beyond Lowell's factory gates a different sort of American roamed, who at first appeared unconnected to the bustle of urban markets. These were the legendary mountain men, who flourished from the mid-1820s through the mid-1840s. Traveling across the Great Plains, along upland streams, and over the passes of the Rockies, outdoorsmen like Jim Bridger, Jedediah Smith, and James Walker wore buckskin hunting shirts, let their hair grow to their shoulders, and stuck pistols and tomahawks in their belts. Wild and exotic, the mountain men became romantic symbols of the American quest for individual freedom.

Yet these wanderers, too, were tied to the emerging market society. The mountain men hunted beaver pelts and shipped them east, to be turned into fancy hats for gentlemen. The fur trade was not a sporting event but a business, dominated by organizations like John Jacob Astor's American Fur Company, and the trapper was the agent of an economic structure that stretched from the mountains to eastern

The mountain men tied to market society

cities and even to Europe. Most of these men went into the wilderness not to flee civilization but to make money—to accumulate capital in order to set themselves up in society. Of those who survived the fur trade, almost none remained permanently outside civilization but returned and took up new careers as shop-keepers, traders, ranchers, politicians, and even bankers. Far from rejecting society's values, the mountain men sought respectability. They, like farmers, were expectant capitalists for whom the West was a land of opportunity.

The revolution in markets, in other words, affected Americans from all walks of life: mountain men as well as merchants, laborers as well as farmers. Equally critical, it restructured American society as a whole.

Economic Specialization

To begin with, the spread of the market produced greater specialization. As we have seen, transportation networks made it possible for farmers to concentrate on producing certain crops, while factories could focus on making a single item such as cloth or shoes. Within factories, the division of labor meant that the process of manufacturing an item became more specialized. No longer did cobblers produce a pair of shoes from start to finish; the operation was broken down into more specialized (and less skilled) tasks.

This process evolved at different rates. Textiles and milling were completely mechanized, while other sectors of the economy, such as shoes and men's clothing, depended little on machinery. Moreover, large factories were the exception rather than the rule. A great deal of manufacturing was still done in smaller shops with few employees. Still, the tendency was toward more technology, greater efficiency, and increasing specialization.

Specialization had consequences at home as well as in the workplace. The average eighteenth-century American woman produced items like thread, cloth,

Decline of women's traditional work

clothing, and candles in the home for family use. As factories spread, however, household manufacturing all but disappeared, and women lost many of the economic functions they had previously performed in the family unit. Again, textiles are a striking example. Between 1815 and 1860, the price of cotton cloth fell from 18 to 2 cents a yard, and because it was also smoother and more brightly colored than homespun, most women purchased cloth rather than made it themselves. Similarly, the development of ready-made men's clothing reduced the amount of sewing women did, especially in urban centers. As Chapter 12 will make clearer, the growth of industry led to an economic reorganization of the family and a new definition of women's role in society.

Materialism

European visitors were struck during these years by how much Americans were preoccupied with material goods. The new generation did not invent materialism, but the spread of the market after 1815 made it much more evident. "I know of no country, indeed," Tocqueville commented, "where the love of money has taken stronger hold on the affections of men."

In a nation that had no legally recognized aristocracy, no established church, and class lines that were only informally drawn, wealth became the most obvi-

Wealth and status

ous symbol of status. Dismissing birth as "a mere idea," one magazine explained, "Wealth is something substantial. Everybody knows that and feels it." Materialism reflected more than a desire for goods and physical comfort. It represented a quest for respect and recognition. "Americans boast of their skill in money making," one contemporary observed, "and as it is the only standard of dignity and nobility and worth, they endeavor to obtain it by every possible means."

The emphasis on money and material goods left its mark on the American character. Often enough, it encouraged sharp business practices and promoted a greater tolerance of wealth acquired by questionable means. Americans also emphasized practicality over theory. The esteem of the founding generation for intellectual achievement was mostly lost in the scramble for wealth that seemed to consume the new generation.

The Emerging Middle Class

In the years after 1815, a new middle class took shape in American society. A small class of shopkeepers, professionals, and master artisans had existed earlier,

Separation of middle class from manual laborers

but the creation of a national market economy greatly expanded its size and influence. As specialization increased, office work and selling were more often physically separated from the production and handling of merchandise. Businessmen, professionals, storekeepers, clerks, office workers, and supervisors began to think of themselves as a distinct social group. Members of the growing middle class had access to more education and enjoyed greater social mobility. They were paid not only more but differently. A manual worker might earn $300 a year, paid as wages computed on an hourly basis. Professionals received a yearly salary and might make $1000 a year or more.

Middle-class neighborhoods, segregated along income and occupational lines, also began to develop in towns and cities. In larger cities improved transportation enabled middle-class residents to move to surrounding suburbs and commute to work. Leisure also became segregated, as separate working-class and middle-class social organizations and institutions emerged.

As middle-class Americans accumulated greater wealth, they were able to consume more. Thus material goods became emblems of success and status—

Material goods as emblems of success

as clockmaker Chauncey Jerome sadly discovered when his business failed and his wealth vanished. Indeed, this materialistic ethos was most apparent in the middle class, as they strove to set themselves apart from other groups in society.

The middle class also came to embrace a new concept of marriage, the family, and the home, as we will see in Chapter 12. Along with occupation and income, moral outlook also marked class boundaries during this period.

The Distribution of Wealth

As American society became more specialized, greater extremes of wealth appeared. Chauncey Jerome demonstrated that if one's market were the nation— or even the world—greater riches could be amassed than by selling locally. And as the new markets created fortunes for the few, the factory system lowered the wages of workers by dividing labor into smaller, less skilled tasks.

Indeed, local tax records reveal a growing concentration of wealth at the top of the social pyramid after 1815. Wealth was most highly concentrated in large

Growing inequality of wealth

eastern cities and in the cotton kingdom of the South, but everywhere the tendency was for the rich to get richer and own a larger share of the community's total wealth. By 1860, 5 percent of American families owned more than 50 percent of the nation's wealth. In villages where the market revolution had not penetrated, wealth tended to be less concentrated.

In a market society, the rich were able to build up their assets because those with capital were in a position to increase it dramatically by taking advantage of new investment opportunities. Although a few men, such as Cornelius Vanderbilt and John Jacob Astor, vaulted from the bottom ranks of society to the top, most of the nation's richest individuals came from wealthy families.

Social Mobility

The existence of great fortunes is not necessarily inconsistent with the idea of social mobility or property accumulation. Although the gap between the rich and the poor widened after 1820, even the incomes of most poor Americans rose, because the total amount of wealth produced in America had become much larger. From about 1825 to 1860 the average per capita income almost doubled to $300. Voicing the popular belief, a New York judge proclaimed, "In this favored land of liberty, the road to advancement is open to all."

Social mobility existed in these years, but not as much as contemporaries boasted. Most laborers—or more often their sons—did manage to move up the

Limits to social mobility

social ladder, but only a rung or two. Few unskilled workers rose higher than to a semiskilled occupation. Even the children of skilled workers normally did not escape the laboring classes to enter the middle-class ranks of clerks, managers, or lawyers. For most workers improved status came in the form of a savings account or home ownership, which gave them some security during economic downswings and in old age.

A New Sensitivity to Time

It was no accident that Chauncey Jerome's clocks spread throughout the nation along with the market economy. The new methods of doing business involved a new and stricter sense of time. Factory life necessitated a more regimented schedule, where work began at the sound of a bell, workers kept machines going at a constant pace, and the day was divided into hours and even minutes.

Clocks began to invade private as well as public space. With mass production ordinary families could now afford clocks, and even farmers became more sensitive to time as they were integrated into the market. As one frontier traveler reported in 1844, "In Kentucky, in Indiana, in Illinois, in Missouri, and here in every dale in Arkansas, and in cabins where there was not a chair to sit on, there was sure to be a Connecticut clock."

PROSPERITY AND ANXIETY

As Americans watched their nation's frontiers expand and its economy grow, many began to view history in terms of an inevitable and continuous improvement. The path of commerce, however, was not steadily upward. Rather it advanced in a series of wrenching boom–bust cycles: accelerating growth, followed by a crash and then depression.

The country remained extraordinarily prosperous from 1815 until 1819, only to sink into a depression that lasted from 1819 to 1823. During the next

Boom–bust cycle cycle, the economy expanded slowly during the 1820s, followed by almost frenzied speculation in the 1830s. Then came the inevitable contraction in 1837, and the country suffered an even more severe depression from 1839 to 1843. The third cycle followed the familiar pattern: gradual economic growth during the 1840s, frantic expansion in the 1850s, and a third depression that began in 1857 and lasted until the Civil War. In each of these depressions, thousands of workers were thrown out of work, overextended farmers lost their farms, and many businesses closed their doors.

The impact of the boom–bust cycle can be seen in the contrasting fates of two Americans who moved west in search of opportunity. In 1820, 17-year-old Benjamin Remington left Hancock, Massachusetts, for western New York, which was just being opened to white settlement. After working at several jobs, he managed to purchase on credit a 150-acre farm near the growing city of Rochester. Remington's timing was ideal. In 1823, two years after his arrival, the new Erie Canal was completed as far as Rochester. Wheat prices rose, flour shipments from the region shot up, and Remington prospered supplying food for eastern markets. Over the years, he added to his acreage, built a comfortable house for his family, and was elected town supervisor. For Remington, the West was indeed a land of opportunity.

Somewhat younger, Addison Ward moved west when he came of age in 1831, leaving Virginia for Indiana. Unfortunately, by the time Ward arrived in Greene County, the best land had already been claimed. All he could afford was 80 acres of rough government land, which he bought in 1837 largely on credit. The region lacked adequate transportation to outside markets, but the economy was booming, and the state had begun an ambitious internal improvements program. Ward's timing, however, could not have been worse. Almost immediately the country entered a depression, driving farm prices and land values downward. Overwhelmed by debts, Ward sold his farm and fell into the ranks of tenant farmers. He continued to struggle until his death around 1850. Catching the wrong end of the boom–bust cycle, Ward never achieved economic success and social respectability.

In such an environment, prosperity, like personal success, seemed all too fleeting. Because Americans believed the good times would not last—that the

Popular anxiety

bubble would burst and another "panic" set in—their optimism was often tinged by insecurity and anxiety. They knew too many individuals like Chauncey Jerome, who had been rich and then lost all their wealth in a downturn.

The Panic of 1819

The initial shock of this boom-and-bust psychology came with the Panic of 1819, the first major depression in the nation's history. From 1815 to 1818 cotton had commanded truly fabulous prices on the Liverpool market, reaching 32.5 cents a pound in 1818. In this heady prosperity, the federal government extended liberal credit for land purchases, and the new national bank encouraged merchants and farmers to borrow in order to catch the rising tide.

But in 1819 the price of cotton collapsed and took the rest of the economy with it. As the inflationary bubble burst, land values, which had been driven to

National depression

new heights by the speculative fever, plummeted 50 to 75 percent almost overnight. As the economy went slack, so did the demand for western foodstuffs and eastern manufactured goods and services, sending the nation reeling into a severe depression.

Because the market economy had spread to new areas, this downturn affected not only urban Americans but those living in the countryside as well. Many farmers, especially in newly settled regions, had bought their land on credit, and others in established areas had expanded their operations in anticipation of future returns. When prices fell, both groups were hard-pressed to pay their debts. New cotton planters in the Southwest, who were especially vulnerable to fluctuations in the world market, were particularly hard hit.

The Missouri Crisis

The Panic of 1819 brought an end to the optimism that had followed the War of 1812, as the New Nationalism's spirit of cooperation gave way to jealousy and conflict between competing interests and social groups. Scrambling to weather the economic storm, southern planters, Yankee merchants, and western farmers looked first to their own welfare. So it was probably not surprising that smoldering sectional animosities flared up in 1819, when the Missouri Territory applied for admission as a slave state.

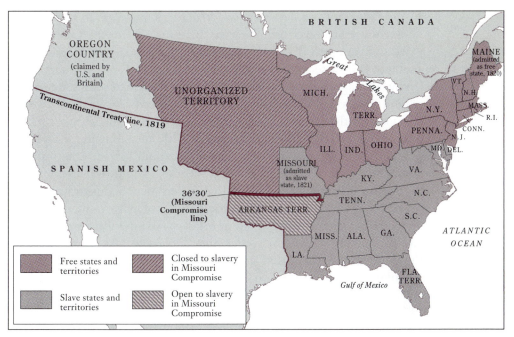

THE MISSOURI COMPROMISE AND THE UNION'S BOUNDARIES IN 1820

Congress had prohibited the African slave trade in 1808, the earliest year this could be done under the Constitution, but prior to the controversy over Missouri, slavery had not been a major issue in American politics. In the absence of any specific federal legislation, slavery had crossed the Mississippi River into the Louisiana Purchase. Louisiana entered the Union in 1812 as a slave state, and in 1818 Missouri, which had about 10,000 slaves in its population, asked permission to come in, too.

At this time, there were 11 free and 11 slave states. As the federal government became stronger and more active, both the North and the South became increasingly anxious about maintaining their political power. The North's greater population gave it a majority in the House of Representatives, 105 to 81. The Senate was evenly balanced, since each state had two senators regardless of population. But Maine, which previously had been part of Massachusetts, requested admission as a free state. That would upset the balance unless Missouri came in as a slave state.

Representative James Tallmadge of New York disturbed this delicate state of affairs when in 1819 he suddenly introduced an amendment designed to establish a program of gradual emancipation in Missouri. The debate that followed was bitter, as for the first time Congress directly debated the morality of slavery. The House approved the Tallmadge amendment, but the Senate refused to accept it, and the two houses deadlocked.

When Congress reconvened in 1820, Henry Clay of Kentucky promoted what came to be known as the Missouri Compromise. Under its terms Missouri

Missouri Compromise

was admitted as a slave state and Maine as a free state. In addition, slavery was forever prohibited in the remainder of the Louisiana Purchase north of 36°30′ (the southern boundary of Missouri). Clay's proposal, the first of several sectional compromises he would engineer in his long career, won congressional approval, ending the crisis. But southern fears for the security of slavery and northern fears about its spread remained.

Sectional tensions, though ominous, tended to ebb and flow with events. Meanwhile, the Panic of 1819 affected the political life of the nation in even more direct ways. As the depression deepened and hardship spread, Americans viewed government policies as at least partly to blame. The postwar nationalism, after all, had been based on the belief that government should stimulate economic development through a national bank and protective tariff, by improving transportation, and by opening up new lands. As Americans struggled to make sense of their new economic order, they looked to take more direct control of the government that was so actively shaping their lives. During the 1820s, the popular response to the market and the Panic of 1819 produced a strikingly new kind of politics in the Republic.

SIGNIFICANT EVENTS

1790	Slater's textile mill opens
1793	Eli Whitney invents the cotton gin
1798	Whitney develops system of interchangeable parts
1810	*Fletcher v. Peck*
1810–1820	Cotton boom begins in the South
1811	First steamboat trip from Pittsburgh to New Orleans
1816	Second Bank of the United States chartered; protective tariff enacted
1817	Bonus Bill veto
1818–1825	Erie Canal constructed
1819	*Dartmouth College v. Woodward; McCulloch v. Maryland*
1819–1823	Panic and depression
1820	Missouri Compromise enacted; Lowell mills established
1824	*Gibbons v. Ogden*
1825–1850	Canal era
1834	National Trades' Union founded
1837	Panic
1839–1843	Depression
1844	Samuel F. B. Morse sends first intercity telegraphic message
1847	Rotary printing press invented

CHAPTER ELEVEN

The Rise of Democracy

The notice, printed in a local newspaper, made the rounds in the rural Pearl River district of Mississippi. A traveler, the advertisement announced, had lost a suitcase while fording the Tallahala River. The contents included "6 ruffled shirts, 6 cambric handkerchiefs, 1 hair-brush, 1 tooth-brush, 1 nail-brush. . . ."

As the list went on, the popular reaction would inevitably shift from amusement to disdain: "1 pair curling tongs, 2 sticks pomatum . . . 1 box pearl-powder, 1 bottle Cologne, 1 [bottle] rose-water, 4 pairs silk stockings, and 2 pairs kid gloves." The howls of derision that filled the air could only have increased upon learning that anyone finding said trunk was requested to contact the owner—Mr. Powhatan Ellis of Natchez.

Powhatan Ellis was no ordinary backcountry traveler. Born into a genteel Virginia family, Ellis had moved in 1816 to the raw Southwest to seek his fortune. With his cultivated tastes, careful dress, and stately dignity, he upheld the tradition of the gentleman politician. In Virginia he would have commanded respect: indeed, in Mississippi he had been appointed district judge and U.S. senator. But for the voters along the Pearl River, the advertisement for his trunk of ruffled shirts, hair oils, and fancy "skunkwater" proved to be the political kiss of death. His opponents branded him an aristocrat and a dandy, and his support among the piney woods farmers evaporated faster than a morning mist along Old Muddy on a sweltering summer's day.

No one was more satisfied with this outcome than the resourceful Franklin E. Plummer, one of Ellis's political enemies. In truth, while the unfortunate Powhatan Ellis had lost a trunk fording a stream, he had not placed the advertisement trying to locate it. That was the handiwork of Plummer, who well understood the new playing field of American politics in the 1820s. Born in New England, Plummer had made his way as a young man to the new state of Mississippi, where he set himself up as an attorney, complete with a law library of three books. Plummer's shrewdness and oratorical talent made up for his lack of legal training, however, and he was quickly elected to the legislature.

Plummer's ambition soon flowed beyond the state capital, and in 1830 he announced his candidacy for Congress. At first few observers took his candidacy seriously. In his campaign, however, he boldly portrayed himself as the champion of the people battling the aristocrats of Natchez. Contrasting his humble background with that of his wealthy opponent, Plummer proclaimed: "We are taught that the highway to office, distinction and honor, is as free to the *meritorious poor* man, as to the *rich;* to the man who has risen from obscurity by his own individual exertions, as to him who has inherited a high and elevated standing in society, founded on the patrimony of his ancestors." Taking as his slogan "Plummer for the People, and the People for Plummer," he was easily elected.

Champion of the people

Plummer was a campaigner who knew how to effect the common touch. Once, as he canvassed the district with his opponent, the pair stopped at a farmhouse. When his opponent, seeking the farmer's vote, kissed the daughter, Plummer picked up a toddling boy and began picking red bugs off him, telling the enchanted mother, "They are powerful bad, and mighty hard on babies." On another occasion, while his opponent slept, Plummer rose at dawn to help milk the family's cow—and won another vote.

As long as Plummer maintained his image as one of the people, he remained invincible. But in 1835 when he ran for the U.S. Senate, his touch deserted him. Borrowing money from a Natchez bank, he purchased a stylish coach, put his servant in a uniform, and campaigned across the state. Aghast at such aristocratic pretensions, his followers promptly abandoned him, and he was soundly defeated. He died in 1852 in obscurity and poverty.

Franklin Plummer was being pulled two ways by the forces transforming American society. As the previous chapter explained, the growth of commerce and new markets opened up opportunities for more and more Americans during these years. "Opportunity" was one of the bywords of the age. Through his connections with bankers and the well-to-do, Plummer saw the opportunity to accumulate wealth and to gain status and respect.

Yet at the same time that new markets were producing a more stratified, unequal society, the nation's politics were becoming more democratic. The new political system that developed after 1820 differed strikingly from that of the early Republic. Just as national markets linked the regions of America economically, the new system of national politics with its mass electioneering techniques involved more voters than ever before. Plummer's world reflected that new political culture. And its central feature—another byword on everyone's lips—was "equality." In truth, the relation between the new equalities of politics and the new opportunities of the market was an uneasy one.

EQUALITY AND OPPORTUNITY

Middle- and upper-class Europeans who visited the United States during these decades were especially sensitive to the egalitarian quality of American life. Coming from the more stratified society of Europe, they were immediately struck—often unfavorably—by the "democratic spirit" that had become "infused into all the national habits and all the customs of society."

To begin with, they discovered that only one class of seats was available on stagecoaches and railcars. These were filled according to the rough-and-ready rule of first come, first served. In steamboat dining rooms or at country taverns, everyone ate at a common table, sharing food from the same serving plates. As one upper-class gentleman complained, "The rich and the poor, the educated and the ignorant, the polite and the vulgar, all herd on the cabin floor, feed at the same table, sit in each others laps, as it were."

Indeed, the democratic "manners" of Americans seemed not just shocking but downright rude. Europeans were used to social inferiors speaking only if spoken to. But Americans felt free to strike up a conversation with anyone, including total strangers. Frances Trollope was offended by the "coarse familiarity of address" between classes, while another visitor complained that in a nation where every citizen felt free to shake the hand of another, it was impossible to know anyone's social station.

Americans were self-consciously proud of such democratic behavior, which they viewed as a valued heritage of the Revolution. The keelboaters who carried the future King Louis-Philippe of France on a trip down the Mississippi made their republican feelings plain when the keelboat ran aground. "You kings down there!" bellowed the captain. "Show yourselves and do a man's work, and help us three-spots pull off this bar!" The ideology of the Revolution made it clear that, in the American deck of cards at least, "three-spots" counted as much as jacks, kings, and queens. Kings were not allowed to forget that—and neither was Franklin Plummer.

The Tension between Equality and Opportunity

While Americans praised opportunity and equality, a fundamental tension existed between these values. Inevitably, widespread opportunity would produce inequality of wealth. In Crèvecoeur's America, a rough equality of wealth and status had prevailed because of the lack of access to a market. But by the 1820s and 1830s, as the opportunities of the market expanded, wealth became much more unevenly distributed. Thus the new generation had to confront contradictions in the American creed that their parents had been able to conveniently ignore.

By equality, Americans did not mean equality of wealth or property. "I know of no country where profounder contempt is expressed for the theory of per-

Meaning of equality

manent equality of property," Alexis de Tocqueville wrote. Nor did equality mean that all citizens had equal talent or capacity. "Distinctions in society will always exist under every just government," Andrew Jackson declared. "Equality of talents, or education, or of wealth cannot be produced by human institutions."

In the end, what Americans upheld was equality of opportunity, not equality of condition. "True republicanism requires that every man shall have an equal chance—that every man shall be free to become as unequal as he can," one American commented. In an economy that could go bust as well as boom, Americans agreed that one primary objective of government was to safeguard opportunity. Thus the new politics of democracy walked hand in hand with the new opportunities of the market.

THE NEW POLITICAL CULTURE OF DEMOCRACY

The stately James Monroe, with his powdered hair and buckled shoes and breeches, was not part of the new politics. But in 1824 as he neared the end of his second term, a host of new leaders in the Republican party looked to succeed him. The Republican congressional caucus finally settled on William H.

Death of the caucus system

Crawford of Georgia as the party's presidential nominee. Condemning "King Caucus" as undemocratic, three other Republicans, all ardent nationalists, refused to withdraw from the race: Secretary of State John Quincy Adams, John C. Calhoun, Monroe's secretary of war, and Henry Clay, the Speaker of the House.

None of these men bargained on the sudden emergence of another Republican candidate, Andrew Jackson, the hero of the Battle of New Orleans. Because of his limited experience, no one took Jackson's candidacy seriously at first, including Jackson himself. But soon the general's supporters and rivals began receiving reports of his popularity. A typical account from Cincinnati read, "Strange! Wild! Infatuated! All for Jackson!" Savvy politicians soon flocked to his standard, but it was the people who first made Jackson a serious candidate.

The Election of 1824

Calhoun eventually dropped out of the race, but none of the four remaining candidates received a majority of the popular vote. Still, Jackson led the field and also finished first in the Electoral College. Under the terms of the Twelfth Amendment, the House was to select a president from the top three candidates. Henry Clay, who finished fourth and therefore was eliminated, met privately with Adams and then rallied the votes in the House needed to put Adams over the top.

Two days later, Adams announced that Clay would be his secretary of state, the usual steppingstone to the presidency. Jackson and his supporters promptly charged that there had been a "corrupt bargain" between Adams and Clay. Before Adams had even assumed office, the 1828 race was under way.

More significant, the election of 1824 shattered the old party system. Henry Clay and John Quincy Adams began to organize a new party, known as the

Second party system

National Republicans to distinguish it from Jefferson's old party. Jackson's disappointed supporters eventually called themselves Democrats. By the mid-1830s, when the National Republicans gave way to the Whigs, the second American party system was in place. Once established, it dominated the nation's politics until the 1850s.

Social Sources of the New Politics

Why was it that a new style and new system of politics emerged in the 1820s? We have already seen that a revolution in markets, stimulated by new transportation networks, was under way. We have seen, too, that the scramble to

New attitudes toward government

bring western lands into the market generated a speculative land boom that collapsed in the Panic of 1819. The rise of the new political culture was rooted in these social conditions. During the sharp depression that followed, many Americans became convinced that government policy had aggravated, if not actually produced, hard times. Consequently, they decided that the government had a responsibility to relieve distress and promote prosperity.

The connection made between government policy and economic well-being stimulated rising popular interest in politics during the 1820s. Agitation mounted, especially at the state level, for government to enact debtor relief and provide other assistance. Elections became the means through which the majority expressed its policy preferences, by voting for candidates pledged to specific programs. The older idea that representatives should be independent, voting their best judgment, gave way to the notion that representatives were to carry out the will of the people, as expressed in the results of elections.

With more citizens championing the "will of the people," pressure mounted to open up the political process. Most states eliminated property qualifications

Democratic reforms

for voting in favor of white manhood suffrage, under which all adult white males were allowed to vote. Similarly, property requirements for officeholders were reduced or dropped.

Presidential elections became more democratic as well. By 1832 South Carolina was the only state where the legislature rather than the voters still chose presidential electors. Parties began to hold conventions as a more democratic method of nominating candidates and approving a platform. And because a presidential candidate had to carry a number of states in different sections of the country, the backing of a national party, with effective state and local organizations, became essential.

As the new reforms went into effect, voter turnout soared. Whereas in the 1824 presidential election, only 27 percent of eligible voters had bothered to go to the polls, in 1840, 78 percent of eligible voters cast ballots, probably the highest turnout in American history.

The Acceptance of Political Parties

All these developments favored the emergence of a new type of politician: one whose life was devoted to party service and who often depended for his living on public office. As the number of state internal improvement projects increased during the 1820s, so did the number of government jobs that could sup-

Professional politicians

port party workers. No longer was politics primarily the province of the wealthy, who spent only part of their time on public affairs. Instead, political leaders were more likely to come from the middle ranks of society, especially outside the South. Indeed, as Franklin Plummer demonstrated, a successful politician now had to mingle with the masses and voice their feelings—requirements that put the wealthy elite at a disadvantage.

In many ways, Martin Van Buren, whose career took him to the Senate and eventually the White House, epitomized the new breed of politician. The son of a New York tavernkeeper, Van Buren lacked a magnetic personality, but he was a master organizer and tactician, highly adept at using the new party system. Unlike the older Revolutionary generation, who regarded political parties as dangerous and destructive, Van Buren argued that they were not only "inseparable from free governments" but "in many and material respects . . . highly useful to the country." While conceding they were subject to abuse, he stressed that competing parties would scrutinize each other and check abuses at the same time that they kept the masses informed.

Andrew Jackson was one of the first political leaders to grasp the new politics, in which the ordinary citizen reigned supreme. "Never for a moment be-

The new style of politics

lieve that the great body of the citizens . . . can deliberately intend to do wrong," he asserted, endorsing an often-expressed refrain of American politics. Party leaders everywhere avoided aristocratic airs when on the stump and often dressed in plain clothing and used informal language. Politics became mass entertainment, with campaign hoopla frequently overshadowing issues. Parades, massive rallies, and barbecues were used to rouse voters, and treating to drinks became an almost universal campaign tactic. ("The way to men's hearts is down their throats," quipped one Kentucky vote-getter.) Although politicians talked often about principles, political parties were pragmatic organizations, intent on gaining and holding power.

The Jacksonian era has been called the Age of the Common Man, but such democratic tendencies had distinct limits. Women and slaves were not allowed to vote, nor could free African Americans (except in a few states) or Indians.

"The Will of the People the Supreme Law" reads the banner at this county election. Election day remained an all-male event, as well as a time of excitement, heated debate, and boisterous celebration. As citizens give their oath to an election judge, diligent party workers dispense free drinks, solicit support, offer party tickets, and keep a careful tally of who has voted.

Limitations of the democratic political system Nor did the parties always deal effectively with (or even address) basic problems in society. Still, the importance of Van Buren's insight was fundamental. Popular political parties provided an essential mechanism for peacefully resolving differences among competing interest groups, regions, and social classes.

COUNTERPOINT *How Democratic Was Jacksonian Democracy?*

How democratic was the new political system? Some historians have painted these reforms as truly dramatic. With the caucus system replaced by political conventions, ordinary citizens like Franklin Plummer found it easier to run for office. With more Americans able to vote, party leaders could not easily ignore their constituents. These historians conclude that whatever the new political system's limitations, the party system addressed many of the problems confronting the country. Public policy reflected public opinion rather than the wishes of the elites.

Other historians have been more skeptical. Despite the tide of democratic reforms, both race and gender still defined citizenship. Whatever their power, "the people" referred only to adult white males. Women and minorities lacked public power. Other critics have insisted that democratic reform can be seen as meaningful only if it actually changes the distribution of power in society. Even with more Americans voting, the leaders of both parties generally remained wealthier and better edcuated than their constituents. Neither party was led by ordinary farmers and workers, the two largest groups in society. Privileged men like Andrew Jackson and Henry Clay simply adopted new campaign techniques to win popular support. The result, according to these historians, was that under the leadership of such men the political system evaded or ignored the real problems of privilege and the growing concentration of wealth in society.

JACKSON'S RISE TO POWER

When he assumed the presidency in 1825, John Quincy Adams might have worked to create a mass-based party. On the state level, the new democratic
John Quincy Adams' presidency style of politics was already making headway. But Adams, a talented diplomat and a great secretary of state, possessed hardly a political bone in his body. Cold and tactless, he could build no popular support for the ambitious and often farsighted programs he proposed. His desire to promote not only manufacturing and agriculture but also the arts, literature, and science left his opponents aghast.

Nor would Adams take any steps to gain reelection. Henry Clay finally undertook to organize the National Republicans, but he labored under serious handicaps. The new style of politics came into its own nationally only when Andrew Jackson swept to power at the head of a new party, the Democrats.

President of the People

Building a new coalition was a tricky business. Because Jackson's new party was made up of conflicting interests, "Old Hickory" remained vague about his own position on many issues. Thus the campaign of 1828 soon degenerated into a series of personal attacks, splattering mud on all involved. When the votes were counted, Jackson won handily.

The election marked the beginning of politics as Americans have practiced it ever since, with two disciplined national parties actively competing for votes,
Significance of the 1828 election emphasizing personalities over issues, and resorting to mass electioneering techniques. Yet in terms of public policy, the meaning of the election was anything but clear. The people had voted for Jackson as a national hero without any real sense of what he would do with his newly won power.

Andrew Jackson's Tumultuous Inauguration

When the speech was over, and the President made his parting bow, the barrier that had separated the people from him was broken down and they rushed up the steps all eager to shake hands with him. It was with difficulty he made his way through the Capitol and down the hill to . . . his horse. . . . Such a cortege as followed him! Country men, farmers, gentlemen, mounted and dismounted, boys, women and children, black and white. Carriages, wagons and carts all pursuing him to the President's house. . . . What a scene did we witness [at the White House]! The *Majesty of the People* had disappeared, and a rabble, a mob, of boys, negros, women, children, scrambling fighting, romping . . . the whole house had been inundated by the rabble mob. . . . The President, after having been *literally* nearly pressed to death and almost suffocated and torn to pieces by the people in their eagerness to shake hands with Old Hickory, had retreated through the back way . . . and had escaped to his lodgings at Gadsby's. Cut glass and china to the amount of several thousand dollars had been broken in the struggle to get the refreshments; punch and other articles had been carried out in tubs and buckets, but had it been in hogsheads it would have been insufficient, ice-creams, and cake and lemonade, for 20,000 people, for it is said that number were there, tho' I think the estimate exaggerated. Ladies fainted, men were seen with bloody noses, and such a scene of confusion took place as it is impossible to describe,—those who got in could not get out by the door again, but had to scramble out of windows. . . .

This concourse had not been anticipated and therefore not provided against. Ladies and gentlemen, only had been expected at this Levee, not the people en masse. But it was the People's day, and the People's President and the People would rule.

Margaret Bayard Smith, *The First Forty Years of Washington Society* (New York: Charles Scribner's Sons, 1906), pp. 294–296.

Certainly the people looked for change. Ordinary citizens came from miles around to see Jackson sworn in. At the White House reception pandemonium reigned. The crowd trampled on the furniture, smashed mirrors, and ruined carpets and draperies. "It was a proud day for the people," boasted Amos

Kendall, one of the new president's advisers. Supreme Court Justice Joseph Story was less enraptured: "I never saw such a mixture. The reign of King Mob seemed triumphant."

Whether loved as a man of the people or hated as a demagogue leading the mob, Jackson was the representative of the new democracy. The first president from west of the Appalachians, he was a man of action, and though he had a quick mind, he had little use for learning. His troops had nicknamed him Old Hickory out of respect for his toughness, but that strength sometimes became arrogance, and he could be vindictive and a bully. He was not a man to provoke, as his reputation for dueling indicated.

Jackson's character

For all these flaws, Jackson was a shrewd politician. He knew how to manipulate men and could be affable or abusive as the occasion demanded. He also displayed a keen sense of public opinion, reading the shifting national mood better than any of his contemporaries.

As the nation's chief executive, he defended the spoils system, under which public offices were awarded to political supporters, as a democratic reform. Rotation in office, he declared, would guard against insensitive bureaucrats who presumed that they held their positions by right. The cabinet, he believed, existed more to carry out his will than to offer counsel, and throughout his term he insisted on his way—and usually got it.

Spoils system

Jackson's stubborn determination shines through in this portrait by Asher Durand, painted in 1835. "His passions are terrible," Jefferson noted. "When I was President of the Senate, he was Senator, and he could never speak on account of the rashness of his feelings. I have seen him attempt it repeatedly, and as often choke with rage. His passions are, no doubt, cooler now; he has been much tried since I knew him, but he is a dangerous man." (Collection of the New York Historical Society.)

The Political Agenda in the Market Economy

Jackson took office at a time when the market economy was expanding throughout America and the nation's population was spreading geographically. The three major problems his administration faced were directly caused by the resulting growing pains.

First, the demand for new lands put continuing pressure on Indians, whose valuable cornfields and hunting grounds could produce marketable commodities like cotton and wheat. Second, as the economies of the North, South, and West became more specialized, their rival interests forced a confrontation over the tariff. And finally, the booming economy focused attention on the role of credit and banking in society and on the new commercial attitudes that were a central part of the developing market economy. The president attacked all three issues in his characteristically combative style.

DEMOCRACY AND RACE

As a planter, Jackson benefited from the international demand for cotton that was drawing new lands into the market. He had gone off to the Tennessee frontier in 1788, a rowdy, ambitious young man who could afford to purchase only one slave. Caught up in the speculative mania of the frontier, he became a prominent land speculator, established himself as a planter, and by the time he became president owned nearly 100 slaves. His popularity derived not only from defeating the British but also from opening extensive tracts of valuable Indian lands to white settlement.

Even so, in 1820 an estimated 125,000 Indians remained east of the Mississippi River. In the Southwest the Choctaws, Creeks, Cherokees, Chickasaws, and Seminoles retained millions of acres of prime land in the heart of the cotton kingdom. Led by Georgia, southern states demanded that the federal government clear these titles.

As white pressure for removal intensified, a shift in the attitude toward Indians and race increasingly occurred. Previously whites had generally attrib-

New attitudes toward race

uted cultural differences among whites, blacks, and Indians to the environment. After 1815 the dominant white culture stressed "innate" racial differences that could never be erased. A growing number of Americans began to argue that the Indian was a permanently inferior savage who blocked progress.

Accommodate or Resist?

The clamor among southern whites for removal placed the southwestern tribes in a difficult situation. Understandably, they strongly rejected the idea of abandoning their lands. They diverged, however, over how to respond. Among the

Cherokees, mixed-bloods led by John Ross advocated a program of accommodation by adopting white ways to prevent removal. After a bitter struggle Ross prevailed, and in 1827 the Cherokees adopted a written constitution modeled after that of the United States. They also enacted the death penalty for any member who sold tribal lands to whites without consent of the governing general council. Developing their own alphabet, they published a bilingual newspaper, *The Cherokee Phoenix*.

The division between traditionalists and those favoring accommodation reflected the fact that Indians too had been drawn into a web of market relationships. As more Cherokee families began to sell their surplus crops, they ceased to share property communally as in the past. Cherokee society became more stratified and unequal, just as white society had, and economic elites dominated the tribal government. Nor were the Cherokees untouched by the cotton boom. Some tribal leaders, particularly half-bloods who could deal easily with white culture, became wealthy planters who owned many slaves and thousands of acres of cotton land. Largely of mixed ancestry, slaveholders were the driving force behind acculturation.

Changing nature of Cherokee society

As cotton cultivation expanded among the Cherokees, slavery became harsher and a primary means of determining status, just as in southern white society. The general council passed several laws forbidding intermarriage with blacks and excluding blacks and mulattoes from voting or holding office. Ironically, at the same time that white racial attitudes toward Indians were deteriorating, the Cherokees' view of African Americans drew closer to that of white society.

Trail of Tears

As western land fever increased and racial attitudes hardened, Jackson prodded Congress to provide funds for Indian removal. At the same time, the Georgia legislature declared Cherokee laws null and void and decreed that tribal members would be tried in state courts. In 1830 Congress finally passed a removal bill.

But the Cherokees brought suit in federal court against Georgia's actions. In 1832 in the case of *Worcester v. Georgia*, the Supreme Court, in an opinion written by Chief Justice John Marshall, ruled that Georgia had no right to extend its laws over Cherokee territory. Pronouncing Marshall's decision "stillborn," Jackson ignored the Court's edict and went ahead with plans for removal.

Cherokees fight removal

Although Jackson assured Indians that they could be removed only voluntarily, he paid no heed when state governments harassed tribes into surrendering lands. Under the threat of coercion, the Choctaws, Chickasaws, and Creeks reluctantly agreed to move to tracts in present-day Oklahoma. In the process, land-hungry schemers cheated tribal members out of as much as 90 percent of their land allotments.

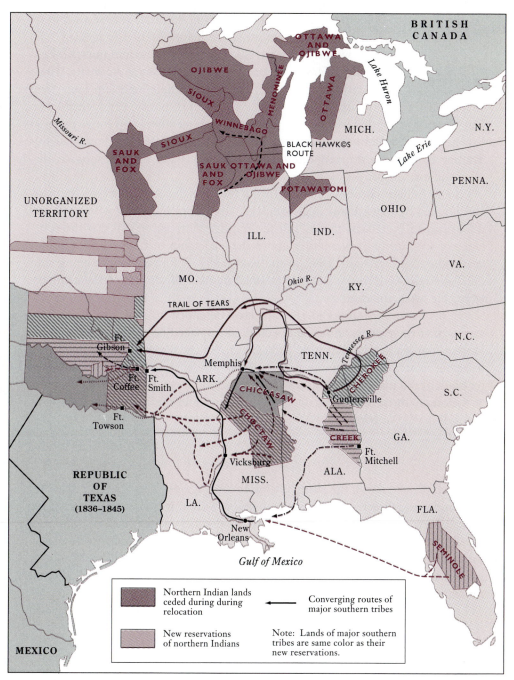

INDIAN REMOVAL   During Jackson's presidency, the federal government concluded
nearly 70 treaties with Indian tribes in the Old Northwest as well as in the South.
Under their terms, the United States acquired approximately 100 million
acres of Indian land.

The Cherokees held out longest, but to no avail. In order to deal with more pliant leaders of the tribe, Georgia authorities kidnapped Chief John Ross, who

Removal of the Cherokees

had led the resistance to relocation, and threw him into jail. Ross was finally released but not allowed to negotiate the treaty, which stipulated that the Cherokees leave their lands no later than 1838. When that time came, most refused to go. In response, President Martin Van Buren had the U.S. Army round up resistant members and force them, at bayonet point, to join the westward march. Of the 15,000 who traveled this Trail of Tears, approximately one-quarter died along the way of exposure, disease, and exhaustion.

Some Indians chose resistance. In the Old Northwest a group of the Sauk and Fox led by Black Hawk recrossed the Mississippi into Illinois in 1832 and were crushed by federal troops and the militia. More successful was the resistance of a minority of Seminoles under the leadership of Osceola. Despite his death, they held out until 1842 in the Everglades of Florida before being subdued and removed. In the end, only a small number of southern tribe members were able to escape removal.

In his Farewell Address in 1837, Jackson defended his policy by piously asserting that the eastern tribes had been finally "placed beyond the reach of injury or oppression, and that [the] paternal care of the General Government will hereafter watch over them and protect them." Indians, however, knew the bitter truth of the matter. Without effective political power, they found themselves at the mercy of the pressures of the marketplace and the hardening racial attitudes of white Americans.

Free Blacks in the North

Unlike Indian removal, the rising discrimination against free African Americans did not depend directly on presidential action. Still, it was Jackson's Democratic party, which so loudly trumpeted its belief in democracy, that was also the most strongly proslavery and the most hostile to black rights. The intensifying racism that accompanied the emergence of democracy in American life bore down with particular force on free African Americans. "The policy and power of the national and state governments are against them," commented one northerner. "The popular feeling is against them—the interests of our citizens are against them. Their prospects . . . are dreary, and comfortless."

In the years before the Civil War, the free states never had a large free black population. Only about 171,000 lived in the North in 1840, about a quarter of whom were mulattoes. Although free African Americans made up less than 2 percent of the North's population, most states enacted laws to keep them in an inferior position. (For a discussion of free African Americans in the South, see page 347.)

Most black northerners lacked any meaningful political rights. Black men could vote on equal terms with whites in only five New England states. New

Discrimination against free blacks

York imposed a property requirement only on black voters, which disfranchised all but a handful of African American males. Moreover, in New Jersey, Pennsylvania, and Connecticut, African American men lost the right to vote after having previously enjoyed that privilege.

Black northerners were also denied basic civil rights that white northerners enjoyed. Five states forbade them to testify against whites, and either law or custom kept African Americans from juries everywhere except in Massachusetts. In addition, several western states passed black exclusion laws prohibiting free African Americans from immigrating into the state. These laws were seldom enforced, but they were available to harass the free black population.

Segregation, or the physical separation of the races, was widely practiced in the free states. African Americans were excluded from public transportation or assigned to special, separate sections. Throughout the North they could not go into most hotels and restaurants, and if permitted to enter theaters and lecture halls, they sat in the corners and balconies. In white churches, they sat in separate pews and took communion after white members. In virtually every community, black children were excluded from the public schools or forced to attend overcrowded and poorly funded separate schools. Commented one English visitor: "We see, in effect, two nations—one white and another black—growing up together . . . but never mingling on a principle of equality."

Discrimination pushed African American males into the lowest paying and most unskilled jobs: servants, sailors, waiters, and common laborers. African

Black poverty

American women normally continued working after marriage, mostly as servants, cooks, laundresses, and seamstresses, since their wages were critical to the family's survival. Blacks were willing strikebreakers, because white workers, fearing economic competition and loss of status, were overtly hostile and excluded them from trade unions. A number of antiblack riots erupted in northern cities during these years. Forced into abject poverty, free blacks in the North suffered from inadequate diet, were more susceptible to disease, and in 1850 had a life expectancy 8 to 10 years less than that of whites.

"None but those who experience it can know what it is—this constant, galling sense of cruel injustice and wrong," grieved Charlotte Forten, a free African American from Philadelphia.

The African American Community

African Americans responded to this oppression by founding self-help societies, and the black community centered on institutions such as black churches, schools, and mutual aid societies. They also agitated against slavery in the South and for equal rights in the North. After 1840 black frustration generated a nationalist movement that emphasized racial unity, self-help, and, for some, renewal of ties with Africa.

Because of limited economic opportunity, the African American community was not as diversified as white society in terms of occupation and wealth. There were distinctions, nevertheless, that rested on wealth and skin color. In general, mulattoes (lighter-skinned blacks) had greater opportunity to become more literate and skilled, were better off economically, and were more likely to be community leaders. Mulattoes' feelings of superiority were reflected in marriage choices, as they usually shunned darker-skinned blacks.

The Minstrel Show

Originating in the 1830s and 1840s and playing to packed houses in cities and towns throughout the nation, the minstrel show became the most popular form of entertainment in Jacksonian America. Featuring white actors performing in blackface, these shows revealed the deep racism embedded in American society. They dealt in the broadest of racial stereotypes, ridiculing blacks as physically different and portraying them as buffoons.

Although popular across the country, minstrelsy found its primary audience

Appeal of minstrelsy

in northern cities. Its basic message was that African Americans could not cope with freedom and therefore did not belong in the North. Slaves were portrayed as happy and contented, whereas free blacks were caricatured either as strutting dandies or as helpless ignoramuses. Drawing its patrons from workers, Irish immigrants, and the poorer elements in society, minstrelsy assured these white champions of democracy that they remained superior.

The unsettling economic, social, and political changes of the Jacksonian era heightened white Americans' fear of failure, which stimulated racism. The pop-

This sawyer working in New York City evidences the dignity free blacks maintained in the face of unrelenting hostility and discrimination.

*Deepening
racism*

ular yet unrealistic expectation was that any white man might become rich. Yet in fact, 20 percent or more of white adult males of this era never accumulated any property. Their lack of success prompted them to relieve personal tensions through increased hostility to their black neighbors. The power of racism in Jacksonian America stemmed in part, at least, from the fact that equality remained part of the nation's creed, while it steadily receded as a social reality.

THE NULLIFICATION CRISIS

Indian removal and antiblack discrimination provided one answer to the question of who would be given equality of opportunity in America's new democratic society: Indians and African Americans would not. The issue of nullification raised a different, equally pressing question. As the North, South, and West increasingly specialized economically in response to the market revolution, how would various regions or interest groups accommodate their differences?

The Growing Crisis in South Carolina

South Carolina had been particularly hard hit by the depression of 1819. When prosperity returned to the rest of the nation, many of the state's cotton planters remained economically depressed. With lands exhausted from years of cultivation, they could not compete with the fabulous yields of frontier planters in Alabama and Mississippi.

Under these difficult conditions, South Carolinians increasingly blamed federal tariffs for their miseries. When Congress raised the duty rates in 1824, they assailed the tariff as an unfair tax that raised the prices of goods they imported, while benefiting other regions of the nation. Other southern states opposed the 1824 tariff as well, though none so vehemently as South Carolina.

The one southern state in which black inhabitants outnumbered whites, South Carolina had also been growing more sensitive about the institution of slavery. In

*Denmark Vesey's
conspiracy*

1822 Denmark Vesey, a daring and resourceful free black carpenter in Charleston, secretly organized a plan to seize control of the city and raise the standard of black liberty. At the last moment, white officials thwarted the conspiracy and executed Vesey and his chief lieutenants; nevertheless, white South Carolinians were convinced that other conspirators still lurked in their midst. As an additional measure of security, they began to push for stronger constitutional protection of slavery. After all, the constitutional doctrine of broad construction and implied powers had already been employed to justify higher protective tariffs. What was to prevent it from being used to end slavery? "In contending against the tariff, I have always felt that we were combatting against the symptom instead of the disease," argued Chancellor William Harper of South Carolina. "Tomorrow may witness [an attempt] to relieve . . . your slaves."

When Congress, over the protests of the state's representatives, raised the duty rates still higher in 1828 with the so-called Tariff of Abominations, South Carolina's legislature published the *South Carolina Exposition and Protest*, which outlined for the first time the theory of nullification. Only later was it revealed that its author was Jackson's own vice president, John C. Calhoun.

Calhoun's Theory of Nullification

Educated at Yale and a distinguished law school, Calhoun was the most impressive intellect of his political generation. During the 1820s the South Carolina leader made a slow but steady journey away from nationalism toward an extreme states' rights position. When he was elected Jackson's vice president, South Carolinians assumed that tariff reform would be quickly forthcoming. But Jackson and Calhoun soon quarreled, and Calhoun lost all influence in the administration.

In his theory of nullification, Calhoun argued that the Union was a compact between sovereign states. Thus the people of each state, acting in special conventions, had the right to nullify any federal law that exceeded the powers granted to Congress under the Constitution. The law would then become null and void in that state. In response, Congress could either repeal the law or propose a constitutional amendment expressly giving it the power in question. If the amendment was ratified, the nullifying state could either accept the decision or exercise its ultimate right as a sovereign state and secede from the Union.

The Union as a compact between sovereign states

Daniel Webster outlines his nationalist theory of the Constitution and the Union in a speech replying to Senator Robert Hayne of South Carolina, who is sitting (front, center) with his hands together. Leaning forward on his desk at the extreme left, Vice President Calhoun listens intently.

In debating Calhoun's theory, Senator Daniel Webster of Massachusetts replied sharply that the Union was not a compact of sovereign states. The people, and not the states, he argued, had created the Constitution. Webster also insisted that the federal government did not merely act as the agent of the states but had sovereign powers in those areas where it had been delegated responsibility. Finally, Webster endorsed the doctrine of judicial review, which gave the Supreme Court authority to determine the meaning of the Constitution.

The Nullifiers Nullified

When Congress passed another tariff in 1832 that failed to give the state any relief, South Carolina's legislature called for the election of delegates to a popular convention, which overwhelmingly adopted an ordinance in November that declared the tariffs of 1828 and 1832 "null, void, and no law, nor binding upon this state, its officers or citizens" after February 1, 1833.

Jackson, who had spent much of his life defending the nation, was not about to tolerate any defiance of his authority or the federal government's.

Idea of a perpetual Union

In his Proclamation on Nullification, issued in December 1832, he insisted that the Union was perpetual and that under the Constitution, no state had the right to secede. To reinforce his announced determination to enforce the tariff laws, Congress passed the Force Bill, reaffirming the president's military powers.

Yet Jackson was also a skillful politician. At the same time that he threatened South Carolina, he urged Congress to reduce the tariff rates. With no other state willing to follow South Carolina's lead, Calhoun reluctantly joined

Compromise of 1833

forces with Henry Clay to work out a compromise tariff in 1833. South Carolina's convention repealed the nullifying ordinance, and the crisis came to an end.

Whatever its virtues as a theory, Calhoun's doctrine had proved too radical for the rest of the South. Even so, the controversy convinced many southerners that they were becoming a permanent minority. "We are divided into slaveholding and non-slaveholding states," concluded nullifier William Harper, "and this is the broad and marked distinction that must separate us at last." As that feeling of isolation grew, it was not nullification but the threat of secession that ultimately became the South's primary weapon.

THE BANK WAR

Jackson understood well the political ties that bound the nation. He grasped much less firmly the economic and financial connections that linked regions of the country through banks and national markets. His clash with the Second Bank of the United States led to the greatest crisis of his presidency.

The National Bank and the Panic of 1819

Chartered by Congress in 1816 for a 20-year period, the Second Bank of the United States initially suffered from woeful mismanagement. At first it helped fuel the speculative pressures in the economy. Then it turned about-face and sharply contracted credit by calling in loans when the depression hit in 1819.

Monster bank

Critics viewed the Bank's policies not as a consequence but as the cause of the financial downswing. To many Americans, the Bank had already become a monster.

The psychological effects of the Panic of 1819 were almost as momentous as the economic. The shock of the depression made the 1820s a time of soul-searching, during which many uneasy farmers and workers came to view the hard times as punishment for having lost sight of the old virtues of simplicity, frugality, and hard work. For these Americans, banks were a symbol of the commercialization of American society and the rapid passing of a simpler way of life.

Biddle's Bank

In 1823 Nicholas Biddle, a rich 37-year-old Philadelphia businessman, became president of the national bank. Biddle was intelligent and thoroughly familiar with the banking system, but he was also impossibly arrogant. He set out to use the bank to regulate the amount of credit available in the economy, and thereby provide the nation with a sound currency.

The government regularly deposited its revenues in the national bank. These revenues were paid largely in bank notes (paper money) issued by state-chartered

Central bank's regulation of the economy

banks. If Biddle believed that a state bank had issued more notes than was safe, he presented them to that bank and demanded they be redeemed in specie (gold or silver). Because banks did not have enough specie reserves to back all the paper money they issued, the only way a state bank could continue to redeem its notes was to call in its loans and reduce the amount of its notes in circulation. This action had the effect of lessening the amount of credit in the economy. On the other hand, if Biddle felt that a bank's credit policies were reasonable, he simply returned the state bank notes to circulation without presenting them for redemption.

Under Biddle's direction the Bank became a financial colossus with enormous power over state banks and over the economy. Yet Biddle used this power responsibly to provide the United States a sound paper currency, which the expanding economy needed.

Although the Bank had strong support in the business community, workers complained that they were often paid in depreciated state bank notes that could

Hostility to the Second Bank

be redeemed only for a portion of their face value, a practice that cheated them of their full wages. They called for a "hard money" currency of only gold and silver. Hard money advocates viewed bankers and financiers as profiteers who manipulated the paper money system to enrich themselves at the expense of honest farmers and laborers.

The Bank Destroyed

Jackson's own experiences left him with a deep distrust of banks and paper money. In 1804 his Tennessee land speculations had brought him to the brink of bankruptcy, from which it took years of painful struggle to free himself. Reflecting on his personal situation, he became convinced that banks and paper money threatened to corrupt the Republic.

As president, Jackson periodically called for reform of the banking system, but Biddle refused even to consider curbing the Bank's powers. Already distracted by the nullification controversy, Jackson warned Biddle not to inject the bank issue into the 1832 campaign. When Biddle went ahead and applied for a renewal of the Bank's charter in 1832, four years early, Jackson was furious. "The Bank is trying to kill me," he stormed to Van Buren, *"but I will kill it."*

Despite the president's opposition, Congress passed a recharter bill in the summer of 1832. Immediately Jackson vetoed it as unconstitutional (rejecting

Jackson's veto

Marshall's earlier ruling in *McCulloch v. Maryland*). Condemning the Bank as an agent of special privilege, the president pledged to protect "the humble members of society—the farmer, mechanics, and laborers" against "the advancement of the few at the expense of the many."

When Congress failed to override Jackson's veto, the Bank became a central issue of the 1832 campaign. Jackson's opponent was Henry Clay, a National Republican who eagerly accepted the financial support of Biddle and his bank. Clay went down to defeat, and once reelected, Jackson was determined to destroy the Bank. He believed that as a private corporation the Bank wielded a dangerous influence over government policy and the economy, and he was justly incensed over its interference in the election.

To cripple the Bank, the president simply ordered all the government's federal deposits withdrawn. Since such an act clearly violated federal law, Jackson was forced

Removal of the deposits

to transfer one secretary of the treasury and fire another before he finally found an ally, Roger Taney, willing to take the job and carry out the edict. Taney (pronounced "Taw-ney") gradually withdrew the government's funds while depositing new revenues in selected state banks.

Biddle fought back by deliberately precipitating a brief financial panic in 1833, but Jackson refused to budge. Eventually Biddle had to relent, and Jackson's victory was complete. When the Bank's charter expired in 1836, no national banking system replaced it.

Jackson's Impact on the Presidency

Jackson approached the end of his administration in triumph. Indian removal was well on its way to completion, the nullifiers had been confounded, and the

Presidential power strengthened

"Monster Bank" had been destroyed. In the process, Jackson immeasurably enlarged the power of the presidency. "The President is the direct representative of the American people," he lectured the Senate when it opposed him. "He was elected by the people, and is responsible to them." With this declaration, Jackson redefined the character of the presidential office and its relationship to the people.

Jackson also converted the veto into an effective presidential power. During his two terms in office, he vetoed 12 bills, compared with only 9 for all previous presidents combined. Moreover, where his predecessors had vetoed bills only on strict constitutional grounds, Jackson felt free to block laws simply because he thought them bad policy. The threat of such action became an effective way to shape pending legislation to his liking, which fundamentally strengthened the power of the president over Congress. The development of the modern presidency began with Andrew Jackson.

VAN BUREN AND DEPRESSION

With the controls of the national bank removed, state banks rapidly expanded their activities, including the printing of more money. As the currency expanded, so did the number of banks: from 329 in 1829 to 788 in 1837. A spiraling inflation set in, as prices rose 50 percent after 1830 and interest rates by half as much.

As prices soared, so did speculative fever. By 1836 land sales, which had been only $2.6 million four years earlier, approached $25 million. Almost all of
Specie Circular these lands were bought entirely on credit with bank notes. In July 1836 Jackson issued the Specie Circular, which decreed that the government would accept only specie for the purchase of public land. Land sales drastically declined, but the speculative pressures in the economy were by now too great to be reversed.

"Van Ruin's" Depression

During Jackson's second term, his opponents had gradually come together in a new party, the Whigs. Led by Henry Clay, they charged that "King Andrew I" had dangerously concentrated power in the presidency. The Whigs also embraced Clay's "American System," designed to spur national economic development through a protective tariff, a national bank, and federal aid for internal improvements. In 1836 the Democrats nominated Martin Van Buren, who triumphed over three Whig sectional candidates.

Van Buren had less than two months in office to savor his triumph before the speculative mania collapsed, and with it the economy. After a brief recovery, the bottom fell out of the international cotton market in
Panic of 1837 1839 and the country entered a serious depression. It was not until 1843 that the economy revived.

Public opinion identified hard times with the policies of the Democratic party. Since he continued to oppose a new national bank, Van Buren instead
Independent Treasury persuaded Congress in 1840 to create an Independent Treasury to keep the government's funds. Its offices were forbidden to accept paper currency, issue any bank notes, or make any loans.

This Whig cartoon blames the Democratic party for the depression that began during Van Buren's administration. Barefoot workers go unemployed, and women and children beg and sleep in the streets. Depositors clamor for their money from a bank that has suspended specie payments, while the pawnbroker and liquor store do a thriving business and the sheriff rounds up debtors.

The government's money would be safe, as Van Buren intended, but it would also remain unavailable to banks to make loans and stimulate the economy. Whigs, on the other hand, hoped to encourage manufacturing and revive the economy by passing a protective tariff, continuing state internal improvement projects, protecting corporations, and expanding the banking and credit system.

As the depression deepened, thousands of workers were unemployed and countless businesses failed. Nationally, wages fell 30 to 50 percent. "Business of all kinds is completely at a stand," wrote New York business and civic leader Philip Hone in 1840, "and the whole body politic sick and infirm, and calling aloud for a remedy."

The Whigs' Triumph

For the 1840 presidential campaign the Whigs turned to William Henry Harrison, who had defeated the Shawnee Indians at Tippecanoe, to oppose Van Buren. In the midst of the worst depression of the century, Whigs

First modern presidential campaign

employed the democratic electioneering techniques that Jackson's supporters had perfected. They hailed Harrison as a man of the people while painting Van Buren as a dandy and an aristocrat who wore a corset, ate off gold plates with silver spoons, and used cologne. Whig rallies featured hard cider and log cabins to reinforce Harrison's image as a man of the people. Ironically, Harrison had been born into one of Virginia's most aristocratic families and was living in a 16-room mansion in Ohio. But the Whig campaign, by casting the election as a contest between aristocracy and democracy, was perfectly attuned to the prevailing national spirit.

In the campaign of 1840, Whigs for the first time also prominently involved women, urging them to become politically informed in order to morally instruct

Women take a new political role their husbands. Women attended Whig rallies, conducted meetings, made speeches, and wrote campaign pamphlets, activities previously performed solely by men. "I never took so much interest in politics in my life," Mary Steger of Richmond confessed to a friend. Democrats were uneasy about this innovation, yet had no choice but to follow suit. Within a few years the presence of women at party rallies was commonplace.

The election produced a record turnout, with nearly four-fifths of the eligible voters going to the polls. Although the popular vote was fairly close (Harrison led by about 150,000 votes out of 2.4 million cast), in the Electoral College he won an easy victory, 234 to 60.

The "log cabin" campaign marked the final transition from the deferential politics of the Federalist era to the egalitarian politics that had emerged in the wake of the Panic of 1819. As the *Democratic Review* conceded after the Whigs' victory in 1840, "We have taught them how to conquer us."

THE JACKSONIAN PARTY SYSTEM

It is easy, given the hoopla of democratic campaigning, to be distracted from the central fact that the new political system was directly shaped by the social and economic strains of an expanding nation. Whigs and Democrats held different attitudes toward the changes brought about by the market, banks, and commerce.

Democrats, Whigs, and the Market

The Democrats tended to view society as a continuing conflict between "the people"—farmers, planters, and workers—and a set of greedy aristocrats. This

Democratic ideology "paper money aristocracy" of bankers, stock jobbers, and investors manipulated the banking system for their own profit, Democrats claimed, and sapped the nation's virtue by encouraging speculation and the desire for sudden, unearned wealth. For Democrats, the Bank War became a battle to restore the old Jeffersonian Republic with its values of simplicity, frugality, hard work, and independence. This is what Jackson meant when he said that removal of the deposits from Biddle's Bank would "preserve the morals of the people."

Jackson understood the dangers private banks posed to a democratic society. Yet Democrats, in effect, wanted the rewards and goods that the market offered without sacrificing the features of a simple agrarian republic. They wanted the wealth that the market produced without the competitive society, the complex dealings, the dominance of urban centers, and the loss of independence that came with it.

Whigs, on the other hand, were more comfortable with the market. For them, commerce and economic development were agents of civilization. Nor

Whig ideology

did they envision any conflict in society between farmers and mechanics on the one hand and businesspeople and bankers on the other. The government's responsibility was to provide a well-regulated economy that guaranteed opportunity for citizens of ability. In such an economy, banks and corporations were not only useful but necessary. A North Carolina Whig well expressed the party's vision of society: "All should be mutual friends and helpers to each other, and who ever aids and assists his fellow men from good motives, by lending money, by affording employment by precept or example, is a benefactor to his fellow men."

Whigs and Democrats differed not only in their attitudes toward the market but also about how active government should be. Despite Andrew Jackson's

Democrats' belief in limited government

inclination to be a strong president, Democrats as a rule believed in limited government. Government's role in the economy was to promote competition by destroying monopolies and special privileges. As one New Jersey Democratic newspaper declared, "All Bank charters, all laws conferring special privileges, with all acts of incorporation, for purposes of private gain, are monopolies, in as much as they are calculated to enhance the power of wealth, produce inequalities among the people and to subvert liberty."

In keeping with this philosophy of limited government, Democrats also rejected the idea that moral beliefs were the proper sphere of government action. Religion and politics, they believed, should be kept clearly separate, and they generally opposed humanitarian legislation.

The Whigs, in contrast, viewed government power positively. They believed that it should be used to protect individual rights and public liberty, and

Whigs' belief in active government

that it had a special role where individual effort was ineffective. By regulating the economy and competition, the government could ensure equal opportunity. Indeed, for Whigs the concept of government promoting the general welfare went beyond the economy. Northern Whigs in particular also believed that government power should be used to foster the moral welfare of the country. They were much more likely to favor temperance or antislavery legislation and aid to education. Whigs portrayed themselves not only as the party of prosperity, but also as the party of respectability and proper behavior.

The Social Bases of the Two Parties

In some ways the social makeup of the two parties was similar. To be competitive, Whigs and Democrats both had to have significant support among farmers, the largest group in society, and workers. Neither party could carry an election by appealing exclusively to the rich or the poor.

The Whigs, however, found more support among the business and commercial classes, especially after the Bank War. Whigs appealed to planters who needed credit to finance their cotton and rice trade in the world market, to farmers eager to sell their surpluses, and to workers who wished to rise in society. Democrats attracted farmers isolated from the market or uncomfortable with it, workers alienated from the emerging industrial system, and rising entrepreneurs who wanted to break monopolies and open the economy to newcomers like themselves. The Whigs were strongest in the towns, cities, and rural areas that were fully integrated into the market economy, whereas Democrats dominated areas of semisubsistence farming that were more isolated and languishing economically. Attitude toward the market, rather than economic position, was more important in determining party affiliation.

The Triumph of the Market

Jacksonian politics evolved out of the social and economic dislocation produced by rapidly expanding economic opportunity. Yet efforts to avoid the costs of the market while preserving its benefits were doomed to fail. In states where the Democrats eliminated all banks, so much hardship and financial chaos ensued that some system of banking was soon restored. The expansion of the economy after 1815 had caught farmers as well as urban residents in an international network of trade and finance, tying them to the price of cotton in Liverpool or the interest rates of the Bank of England. There was no rolling back the market in a return to the ideals of Crèvecoeur.

The new national parties—like the new markets spreading across the nation—had become essential structures uniting the American nation. They advanced an ideology of equality and opportunity, which stood as a goal for the nation even though women, African Americans, and Indians were excluded. The new politics developed a system of truly national parties, competing with one another, involving large numbers of ordinary Americans, resolving differences through compromise and negotiation. Along with the market, democracy had become an integral part of American life.

SIGNIFICANT EVENTS

1819–1823	Panic and depression
1822	Denmark Vesey conspiracy
1823	Biddle becomes president of the Bank of the United States
1824	Tariff duties raised; Jackson finishes first in presidential race
1825	House elects John Quincy Adams president
1827	Cherokees adopt written constitution
1828	Tariff of Abominations; *South Carolina Exposition and Protest*; Jackson elected president
1830	Webster–Hayne debate; Indian Removal Act
1830–1838	Indian removal
1832	*Worcester v. Georgia*; Jackson vetoes recharter of the national bank; Black Hawk war; Jackson reelected; South Carolina nullifies tariff; Jackson's Proclamation on Nullification
1833	Force Bill; tariff duties reduced; Jackson removes deposits from the Bank of the United States
1833–1834	Biddle's panic
1834	Whig party organized
1835–1842	Second Seminole war
1836	Specie Circular; Van Buren elected president
1837	Panic of 1837
1838	Trail of Tears
1839–1843	Depression
1840	Independent Treasury Act; Harrison elected president
1842	First professional minstrel troupe

CHAPTER TWELVE

The Fires of Perfection

In 1826 the Reverend Lyman Beecher was probably the most celebrated minister of the Republic, and the pulpit of Hanover Street Church was his to command. Beecher looked and spoke like a pious farmer, but every Sunday he was transformed when he mounted the pulpit of Boston's most imposing church. From there, he would blaze forth denunciations of dancing, drinking, dueling, or "infidelity," all the while punctuating his sermon with pump-handle strokes of the right hand.

Nor were Beecher's ambitions small. His goal was nothing less than to bring the kingdom of Christ to the nation and the world. Like many ministers, Beecher had studied the intriguing final book of the New Testament, the

Prophecies of the millennium

Revelation to John. The Revelation foretold in the latter days of the Earth a glorious millennium—a thousand years of peace and triumph—when the saints would rule and evil would be banished from the world. Beecher was convinced that the long-awaited millennium might well begin in the United States.

Personal experience reinforced this optimism. Born to a sturdy line of New England blacksmiths in 1775, Beecher entered Yale College during the high tide of postwar nationalism—and, some said, the lowest ebb of religion among young people. In the revivals of the Second Great Awakening that came to many colleges in 1802, Beecher had been one of those converted.

But he was hardly a stodgy Puritan. Much of Beecher's boundless energy went into raising a family of 11 children, every one of whom he prayed would take leading roles in bringing the kingdom of God to America. He loved to wrestle on the floor with his sons or go "berrying" with his daughters. Still, the religious dimension of their lives was constant. The family attended two services on Sunday, a weekly prayer meeting, and a monthly "concert of prayer," where the devout met to pray for the conversion of the world. Beecher's son

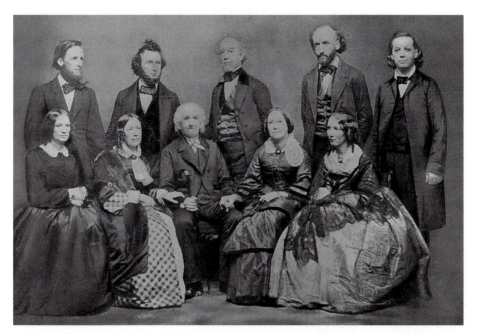

Lyman Beecher (center) with his family in 1855. Five of his six sons, all of whom were ministers, stand in back. In front, daughters Catharine (holding his arm to steady it for the long exposure) and Isabella are on the left; Harriet, the author of *Uncle Tom's Cabin*, is at the far right.

Thomas remembered his father commanding: "Overturn and overturn till He whose right it is shall come and reign, King of nations and King of saints."

To usher in the kingdom of God entire communities and even nations would have to be swept with a divine fire. Toward that end Beecher joined other

Benevolent associations

Protestant ministers in supporting a host of religious reforms and missionary organizations. Such benevolent associations distributed Bibles, promoted Sunday Schools, and ministered to the poor. Beecher also directed his righteous artillery on a host of evils that seemed to be obstructing God's kingdom. With scorn he attacked elite Unitarians, whose liberal, rational creed rejected the divinity of Jesus. But he also condemned what he viewed as sinful pastimes of the lower class: playing cards, gambling, and drinking. And he denounced Roman Catholic priests and nuns as superstitious, devious agents of "Antichrist."

Beecher's efforts at "moral reform" antagonized many immigrants and other working people who enjoyed liquor or lotteries. Thus when a blaze broke out in the basement of his church in 1830, unsympathetic local firefighters stood by while the splendid structure burned to the ground. The fires of spiritual reform had been halted, temporarily, by a blaze of a literal sort.

Any fire, real or spiritual, is unpredictable as it spreads from one scrap of tinder to the next. That proved to be the case with reform movements of the

Differing goals of reformers

1820s and 1830s, as they moved in diverging, sometimes contradictory ways. What did it mean, after all, to bring in Christ's kingdom? The goals of the early reform societies were moral rather than social. Leaders like Beecher sought to convert individuals and to church the unchurched, with the help of religious revivals and benevolent associations. Their conservative aim, as he expressed it, was to restore America to "the moral government of God."

Other Christians, however, began to focus on social issues like slavery, the inequality of women, and the operation of prisons. To these problems they demanded more radical solutions. Ironically, many of Beecher's children went well beyond his more conservative strategies for hastening the millennium. They spoke out for abolition, women's rights, and education in ways that left their father distinctly uncomfortable. In their activities the Beechers reflected the diversity of the reform impulse itself.

REVIVALISM AND THE SOCIAL ORDER

Society during the Jacksonian era was undergoing deep and rapid changes. The revolution in markets brought both economic expansion and periodic depressions, and in the ensuing uncertainty some reformers sought stability and moral order in the religious community. The bonds of unity created by a revival brought a sense of peace in the midst of a society in change. Revivals could reinforce strength and discipline, too, in an emerging industrial culture that demanded sobriety and regular working habits.

Other reformers, however, sought to check the excesses of Jacksonian America by radically remaking institutions or devising utopian, experimental ways of living and working together. The drive for renewal, in other words, led reformers sometimes to preserve social institutions, other times to overturn them. It led them sometimes to liberate, other times to control. And the conflicting ways in which these dynamics operated could be seen in the electric career of Charles Grandison Finney.

Finney's New Measures and New Theology

As a young man, Finney experienced a soul-shattering conversion in 1821 that led him to give up his law practice to become an itinerant minister. Between the mid-1820s and the early 1830s he conducted a series of spectacular revivals in the booming port cities along the new Erie Canal.

Like George Whitefield before him, Finney had an entrancing voice that carried great distances. His success, however, resulted as much from his use of

Protracted meetings and the anxious bench

special techniques—"the new measures." Finney held "protracted meetings" night after night to build excitement. Speaking bluntly, he prayed for sinners by name, encouraged women to testify in public gatherings, and placed those struggling with conversion on the "anxious bench" at the front of the church. Such techniques all heightened the emotions of the conversion process. The cries of agonized prayers, groans, and uncontrolled crying often resounded through the hall.

Finney's new measures had actually been used during the frontier revivals of the Second Great Awakening (page 226). His contribution was to popularize the techniques and use them systematically. "A revival is not a miracle," he coolly declared, "it is a purely scientific result of the right use of constituted means."

Finney also rejected many religious doctrines of Calvinism, including predestination, which maintained that God had already determined which individuals were destined to be saved or damned, and no human effort could change this decision. But by the 1820s such a proposition seemed unreasonable to citizens of a democratic republic. Leaving the Lord little role in the drama of human deliverance, Finney embraced the doctrine of free will. All men and women who wanted to could be saved. To those anxious about their salvation, he thundered, "Do it!"

Free will and perfectionism

With salvation within reach of every individual, what might be in store for society at large? "If the church would do her duty," Finney confidently predicted, "the millennium may come in this country in three years." By the 1830s Finney had taken to preaching not merely faith in human progress but something more—human perfectibility. Embracing this new theology of "perfectionism," he boldly asserted that all Christians should "aim at being holy and not rest satisfied until they are as perfect as God." And a true Christian would not rest until society was made perfect as well.

By preaching an optimistic message of free will and salvation to all, Finney and his eager imitators transformed Protestantism. But not all clergy applauded. For Lyman Beecher, as well as many supporters of the Second Great Awakening, Finney's new measures went too far, while his theology of perfectionism verged on heresy. Undaunted by such criticism, Finney continued his revivals. As for Lyman Beecher, in 1832 he accepted the presidency of Lane Seminary in Cincinnati. By moving to the West, he planned to train the right sort of revivalists to bring about the kingdom of God in America.

Religion and the Market Economy

Revival audiences responded to the call for reform partly because they were unsettled by the era's rapid social changes. In the North, evangelical religion proved strongest not in isolated backwaters but in frontier areas just entering the market economy. Rochester, New York, a booming flour-milling center on the Erie Canal, epitomized that social environment.

E Y E W I T N E S S   T O   H I S T O R Y

The Slave Mortimer Describes His Conversion Experience

One day while in the field plowing I heard a voice. . . . Again the voice called, "Morte! Morte!" With this I stopped, dropped the plow, and started running, but the voice kept on speaking to me saying, "Fear not, my little one, for behold! I come to bring you a message of truth."

Everything got dark, and I was unable to stand any longer. I began to feel sick, and there was a great roaring. I tried to cry and move but I was unable to do either. I looked up and saw that I was in a new world. There were plants and animals, and all, even the water where I stooped down to drink, began to cry out, "I am blessed but you are damned! I am blessed but you are damned!" With this I began to pray, and a voice on the inside began to cry, "Mercy! Mercy! Mercy!"

. . . I again prayed, and there came a soft voice saying, "My little one, I have loved you with an everlasting love. You are this day made alive and freed from hell. You are a chosen vessel unto the Lord. Be upright before me, and I will guide you unto all truth. My grace is sufficient for you. Go, and I am with you. Preach the gospel, and I will preach with you. . . ."

About this time my master came down [to] the field. . . . I told him I had been talking with God Almighty . . . and suddenly I fell for shouting, and I shouted and began to preach. . . . When I had finished . . . my master looked at me and seemed to tremble. He told me to catch the horse and come on with him to the barn. . . .

I went on to the barn and found my master there waiting for me. Again I began to tell him of my experience. . . . My master sat . . . listening to me, and then began to cry. He turned from me and said in a broken voice, "Morte, I believe you are a preacher. From now on you can preach to the people here on my place in the old shed by the creek. But tomorrow morning, Sunday, I want you to preach to my family and neighbors. So put on your best clothes and be in front of the big house early in the morning about nine o'clock."

. . . The next morning at the time appointed I stood up on two planks in front of the porch of the big house and, without a Bible or anything, I began to preach to my master and the people. . . . My soul caught on fire, and soon I had them all in tears.

Clifton H. Johnson, ed., *God Struck Me Dead* (Philadelphia: Pilgrim Press, 1962), pp. 15–18.

When Charles Finney came to town in the winter of 1830–1831, Rochester was a community in crisis. It had grown in a decade and a half from a village of 300 souls to a commercial city of more than 20,000. That wrenching expansion produced sharp divisions among the town's leaders, a large working class that increasingly lived apart from employers and beyond their moral control, and a rowdy saloon culture catering to canal boatmen and other transients. Finney preached almost daily in Rochester for six months, and assisted by local ministers, his revivals doubled church membership. Religion helped bring order to what had been a chaotic and fragmented city.

Although revivals like Finney's Rochester triumph drew converts from all segments of American society, they appealed especially to the middle class.

Revivalism's appeal to the middle class

Lawyers, merchants, retailers, and manufacturers all played central roles in the larger market economy and invested in factories and railroads. The market put intense pressure on these upwardly mobile citizens: they viewed success as a reflection of moral character, yet also feared that they would lose their wealth in the next economic downturn.

Workers, too, were among the converted. Among other things, joining a church reflected a desire to get ahead in the new economy by accepting moral self-discipline. To a striking degree, social mobility and church membership were linked. In Rochester two-thirds of the male workers who were church members improved their occupational status in a decade. By contrast, workers who did not join a church rarely stayed in town more than a few years, and those who stayed were likely to decline in status.

Revivalists like Finney were interested in saving souls, not money, and their converts were most concerned with their spiritual state. Even so, evangelical Protestantism reinforced values needed to succeed in the new competitive economy. Churchgoers accepted the values of hard work and punctuality, self-control and sobriety. In that sense, religion was one means of social control in a disordered society.

The Rise of African American Churches

Independent black churches grew in size and importance as well, as African Americans in urban areas increasingly resented being treated as second-class worshipers. In 1787, Richard Allen, a popular black preacher, was roughly ousted when he tried to pray in the area of a Philadelphia church reserved for whites. In 1794 he organized the Bethel Church, where African Americans would be free to worship without discrimination.

In the early nineteenth century, similar tensions led to the formation of black Methodist and Baptist churches in a number of northern and southern cities. The most important was the African Methodist Episcopal (AME) church. Growing fears for the security of slavery caused southern white communities, especially in the Deep South, to suppress independent black churches after

1820. But these churches, which were strongly evangelical, continued to grow in the North. By 1860 the AME Church had about 20,000 members.

The Significance of the Second Great Awakening

As a result of the Second Great Awakening, the dominant form of Christianity in America became evangelical Protestantism. Membership in the major Protestant churches—Congregational, Presbyterian, Baptist, and Methodist—soared. By 1840 an estimated half of the adult population was nominally connected to some church, with the Methodists emerging as the largest Protestant denomination in both the North and the South.

Evangelicalism was in harmony with the basic values of early nineteenth-century Americans. Its emphasis on the ability of everyone to bring about his

Evangelicalism and American values

or her salvation upheld the American belief in individualism. By catering to a mass audience without social distinctions, the revivals reinforced the American belief in democracy and equality. And Finney's invincibly optimistic doctrine of perfectionism was exactly attuned to the spirit of the age.

WOMEN'S SPHERE

Throughout the tumult of revivals, in the midst of benevolent association meetings, at "concerts of prayer," women played crucial roles. Indeed, during the Second Great Awakening, female converts outnumbered males by about three to two. Usually the first convert in a family was a woman, and many men who converted were related to women who had come forward earlier.

Women played such an important role in the Awakening partly because of changes in their own social universe. Instead of parents arranging the marriages

Revivalism and women's changing lives

of their children, couples were beginning to wed more often on the basis of affection. Under such conditions, a woman's prospects for marriage became less certain, and in older areas like New England, the migration of so many young men compounded this uncertainty. At the same time, marriage remained essential for a woman's economic security. The unpredictability of these social circumstances drew young women toward religion. Women between the ages of 12 and 25 were especially susceptible to conversion. Joining a church heightened a young woman's sense of purpose. By establishing respectability and widening her social circle of friends, it also enhanced her chances of marriage.

The Ideal of Domesticity

The era's changing economic order brought other pressures to bear on wives and mothers. Most men now worked outside the home, while the rise of factories led to a decline in part-time work such as spinning, which women had once performed to supplement family income. Moreover, except on the frontier, home manufacturing was no longer essential, for the family purchased articles that women previously had made, such as cloth, soap, and candles.

This growing separation of the household from the workplace meant that the home took on a new social identity. It was idealized as a place of "domesticity," a haven away from the competitive, workaday world, with the mother firmly at its center. If men's sphere was the world of factories, offices, and fields, women's sphere was the home, where they were to dispense love and comfort and teach moral values to husbands and children. "Love is our life our reality, business yours," Mollie Clark told one suitor.

Separate spheres of influence

Women, who were considered morally stronger, were also held to a higher standard of sexual purity. A man's sexual infidelity, while hardly condoned, brought no lasting shame. But a woman who engaged in sexual relations before marriage or was unfaithful afterward was threatened with everlasting disgrace. Under this double standard, women were to be passive and submerge their identities in those of their husbands.

Most women of the era did not see this ideology as a rationale for male dominance. On the contrary, women played an important role in creating the ideal of domesticity, none more than Lyman Beecher's daughter Catharine. Like earlier advocates of "republican motherhood," Catharine Beecher argued that women exercised power as moral guardians of the nation. The proper care of a middle-class household was also a crucial responsibility, and Beecher wrote several books on efficient home management. "There is no one thing more necessary to a housekeeper in performing her varied duties, than a *habit of system and order*," she told readers. "For all the time afforded us, we must give account to God."

Catharine Beecher and women as moral guardians

Catharine Beecher also advocated giving women greater educational opportunities in order to become schoolteachers. Conceiving of the school as an extension of the home, she maintained that teachers, like mothers, should instill sound moral values in children. Women also exerted their moral authority through benevolent organizations, which fostered close friendships among women.

Most women hardly had time to make the ideal of domesticity the center of their lives. Farmers' wives had to work constantly, while lower-class families could not get by without the wages of female members. Still, most middle-class women tried to live up to the ideal, and many found the effort confining. "The great trial is that I have nothing to do," one complained. "Here I am with abundant leisure and capable, I believe, of accomplishing some good, and yet with no object on which to expend my energies."

Women's socially defined role as guardians of morality helps explain their prevalence among converts. Religious activity was one way that women could exert influence over society and one area where wives need not be subordinate to their husbands. For some males, women's prominence in revivals threatened a dangerous equality between the sexes. One unhappy man in Rochester complained about the effect of Finney's visit to his home: "He *stuffed* my wife with

As business affairs grew increasingly separate from the family in the nineteenth century, the middle-class home became a female domain. As a wife and mother, a woman was to dispense love and moral guidance to her husband and her children.

tracts, and alarmed her fears, and nothing short of meetings, night and day, could atone for the many fold sins my poor, simple spouse had committed." Then, getting to the heart of the matter, he added, "She made the miraculous discovery, that she had been 'unevenly yoked.' From this unhappy period, peace, quiet, and happiness have fled from my dwelling, never, I fear, to return."

The Middle-Class Family in Transition

As the middle-class family adapted to the pressures of competitive society by becoming a haven of moral virtue, it developed a new structure and new set of attitudes closer in spirit to the modern family. One basic change was the rise of privacy. The family was increasingly seen as a sheltered retreat from the outside world. In addition, the pressures to achieve success led middle-class young adults to delay marriage, since a husband was expected to support his wife.

Smaller family size was a result of delaying marriage as well, since wives began bearing children later. Especially among the urban middle class, women be-

Smaller, more private families

gan to use birth control to space children further apart and minimize the risks of pregnancy. These practices contributed to a decline in the birthrate, from slightly more than 7 children per family in 1800 to 5.4 in 1850—a 25 percent drop. Family size was directly related to the success ethic, since in the newer, market-oriented society children needed extended education and special training in order to succeed, and thus were a greater financial burden.

Indeed, more parents showed greater concern about providing their children with advantages in the race for success. Middle-class families were increasingly willing to bear the additional expense of educating their sons longer, and they also frequently equalized inheritances rather than giving priority to the eldest son or favoring sons over daughters.

AMERICAN ROMANTICISM

The Unitarians in Boston had become accustomed to being attacked by evangelical ministers like Lyman Beecher. They were less prepared to be criticized by one of their own—and on their own home ground, no less. Yet that was what happened when a Unitarian minister named Ralph Waldo Emerson addressed the students of Harvard Divinity School one summer evening in July 1838.

Emerson warned his listeners that the true church seemed "to totter to its fall, almost all life extinct." Outside, nature's world was alive and vibrant: "The grass grows, the buds burst, the meadow is spotted with fire and gold in the tint of flowers." But from the pulpits of too many congregations came lifeless preaching. "In how many churches, by how many prophets, tell me," Emerson demanded, "is man made sensible that he is an infinite Soul?" Leaving the shocked audience to ponder his message, Emerson and his wife drove home beneath a night sky illuminated by the northern lights.

Emerson's Divinity School Address glowed much like that July aurora. The address lacked the searing fire of Finney's revivals. Yet it was bold in its own way, because it reflected a second major current of thought that shaped the reform movements of the era. That was the intellectual movement known as Romanticism.

Romanticism began in Europe as a reaction against the Enlightenment. The Enlightenment had placed reason at the center of human achievement; Romanticism instead emphasized the importance of emotion and intuition as sources of truth. It gloried in the unlimited potential of the individual, who might soar if freed from the restraints of institutions. In elevating inner feelings and heartfelt convictions, Romanticism reinforced the emotionalism of religious revivals. Philosophically, its influence was strongest among intellectuals who took part in the Transcendental movement and in the dramatic flowering of American literature. And like revivalism, Romanticism offered its own paths toward perfectionism.

European origins

The Transcendentalists

Above all, Romanticism produced individualists. Thus Transcendentalism is difficult to define, for its members resisted being lumped together. It blossomed in the mid-1830s, when a number of Unitarian clergy like George Ripley and Ralph Waldo Emerson resigned their pulpits, loudly protesting the church's smug, lifeless teachings. The new "Transcendentalist Club" attracted a small following among other discontented Boston intellectuals, including Margaret Fuller, Bronson Alcott, and Orestes Brownson.

Like European Romantics, American Transcendentalists emphasized feeling over reason, seeking a spiritual communion with nature. By transcend they meant to go beyond or to rise above—specifically above reason and beyond the material world. As part of creation, every human being contained a spark of divinity, Emerson avowed. Transcendentalists also shared in Romanticism's glorification of the individual. "Trust thyself. Every heart vibrates to that iron string," Emerson advised. Like the devout at Finney's revivals, who sought to perfect themselves and society, listeners who flocked to Emerson's lectures were infused with the spirit of optimistic reform.

As the currents of Romanticism percolated through American society, the country's literature came of age. In 1820 educated Americans still tended to ape the fashions of England and Europe. But as the population grew, education increased, and the country's literary market expanded, American writers looked with greater interest at the customs and character of their own society. Emerson's address "The American Scholar" (1837) constituted a declaration of literary independence. "Our long dependence, our long apprenticeship to the learning of other lands draws to a close," he proclaimed. "Events, actions arise, that must be sung, that will sing themselves."

The Clash between Nature and Civilization

In extolling nature, many of America's new Romantic writers betrayed a concern that the advance of civilization, with its market economy and crowded urban centers, might destroy the natural simplicity of the land.

Cooper and wilderness

James Fenimore Cooper focused on the clash between nature and civilization in his Leatherstocking Tales, a series of five novels written between 1823 and 1841. Cooper clearly admired his hero, Natty Bumppo, a self-reliant frontiersman who represented the nobility and innocence of the wilderness. At the same time, Cooper viewed the culture of the frontier as a threat to the civilization he prized so highly.

Henry David Thoreau, too, used nature as a backdrop to explore the conflict between the unfettered individual and the constraints of society. In 1845

Thoreau and individualism

Thoreau built a cabin on the edge of Walden Pond in Concord, living by himself for 16 months to demonstrate the advantages of self-reliance. His experiences became the basis for *Walden* (1854), which eloquently denounced Americans' frantic competition for material goods and wealth. Only in nature, Thoreau argued, could one find true independence, liberty, equality, and happiness. Voicing the anti-institutional impulse of Romanticism, he took individualism to its antisocial extreme.

Songs of the Self-Reliant and Darker Loomings

In contrast to Thoreau's exclusiveness, Walt Whitman was all-inclusive, embracing American society in its infinite variety. A journalist and laborer in the New York City area, Whitman was inspired by the common people, whose

Whitman and democracy

"manners, speech, dress, friendships . . . are unrhymed poetry." In taking their measure in *Leaves of Grass* (1855), he pioneered a new, modern form of poetry, unconcerned with meter and rhyme, filled with frank imagery and sexual references. Emerson and other critics were put off by such roughhewn methods, but Whitman, like the Transcendentalists, exalted emotions, nature, and the individual.

More brooding in spirit were Nathaniel Hawthorne and Herman Melville, two intellectuals who did not share the Transcendentalists' sunny optimism.

The skeptics: Hawthorne and Melville

Hawthorne wrote of the power of the past to shape future generations and the consequences of pride, selfishness, envy, and secret guilt. In *The Scarlet Letter* (1850), set in New England's Puritan era, Hawthorne searingly portrayed the sufferings of a woman who bore an illegitimate child, as well as the Puritan neighbors who harshly condemned her.

Herman Melville's dark masterpiece, *Moby-Dick* (1851), drew on his youthful experiences aboard a whaling ship. The novel's Captain Ahab relentlessly drives his crew in pursuit of the great white whale Moby-Dick. In Melville's telling, Ahab becomes a powerful symbol of American character: the prototype of the ruthless businessman despoiling nature's resources in his ferocious pursuit of success.

But awash in the many opportunities opening before them, most Americans ignored such searching criticism. They preferred to celebrate, with Emerson, the glories of democracy and the individual's quest for perfection.

THE AGE OF REFORM

In the glowing fires of a fervent camp meeting, the quest for perfection often proved hard to control. At the Cane Ridge revival of 1800, the Methodist Peter Cartwright had his hands full trying to stop less orthodox preachers from gathering converts. Quite a few worshipers had joined a group known as the Shakers. Cartwright had to ride around the neighborhood "from cabin to cabin" trying to cure people of the Shaker "delusion."

The Shakers were only one group that demonstrated more radical possibilities for democratic change. While the mainline benevolent societies aimed at a more conservative reformation of individual sinners, the more radical offshoots of Romanticism and perfectionism sought to remake society at large.

Utopian Communities

One radical way of reforming the world was by withdrawing from it, to form a utopian community that would demonstrate the possibilities of perfection. Such communities looked to replace the competitive individualism of American society with a purer spiritual unity and group cooperation. During the early 1840s,

Dancing was an integral part of the Shakers' religion, as this picture of a service at Lebanon, New York, indicates. In worshiping, men and women formed separate lines with their hands held out and moved back and forth in rhythm while singing religious songs. Note the presence of African Americans in the community.

Brook Farm for example, Emerson's friend George Ripley organized Brook Farm, a Transcendentalist community near Boston where members could live "a more wholesome and simple life than can be led amidst the pressure of our competitive institutions." Other utopian communities were more directly linked to religious movements and figures, but religious or secular, such communities shared the optimism of perfectionism and millennialism.

The Shakers proved to be one of the most long-lived utopian experiments. Ann Lee, the daughter of an English blacksmith, led a small band of followers *Mother Ann Lee and the Shakers* to America in 1774. Through a series of religious visions Lee became convinced that her own life would reveal the female side of the divinity, just as Christ had come to earth exemplifying the male side. The Shaker movement's greatest growth, however, came after Lee's death, when her followers recruited converts at revivals like Cane Ridge. The new disciples founded about 20 communal settlements based on the teachings of Mother Ann, as she was known. Convinced that the end of the world was at hand and that there was no need to perpetuate the human race, Shakers practiced celibacy, separating the sexes as far as practical. Men and women normally worked apart, ate at separate tables, and had separate living quarters.

Shaker communities accorded women unusual authority and equality. Community tasks were generally assigned along gender lines, with women performing household chores and men laboring in the fields. Leadership of the church, however, was split equally between men and women. The sect's members worked hard, lived simply, and impressed outsiders with their cleanliness and order. Lacking any natural increase, membership began to decline after 1850, from a peak of about 6000 members.

The Oneida Community, founded by John Humphrey Noyes, also set out to alter the relationship between the sexes, though in a rather different way.

The Oneida Community and complex marriage

Noyes, a convert of Charles Finney, took Finney's doctrine of perfection to extremes. While Finney argued that men and women should strive to achieve perfection, Noyes announced that he had actually reached this blessed state. Settling in Putney, Vermont, and after 1848 in Oneida, New York, Noyes set out to create a community organized on his religious ideals.

In pursuit of greater freedom, Noyes preached the doctrine of "complex marriage," by which commune members were permitted to have sexual relations with one another, but only with the approval of the community and after a searching examination of the couple's motives. Noyes eventually undertook experiments in planned reproduction by selecting "scientific" combinations of parents to produce morally perfect children.

Noyes attracted over 200 members to the Oneida Community. But in 1879 an internal dispute drove him from power and the community splintered. In 1881 its members reorganized as a business enterprise.

The Mormon Experience

The Church of Jesus Christ of Latter-Day Saints, whose members were generally known as Mormons, was founded by a young man named Joseph Smith in western New York, where the fires of revivalism flared regularly. In 1827, at the age of only 22, Smith announced that he had discovered a set of golden tablets on which was written the *Book of Mormon*. Proclaiming that he had a commission from God to reestablish the true church, Smith gathered a group of devoted followers.

Like Charles Finney's more liberal theology, Mormonism declared that salvation was available to all. Moreover, Mormon culture upheld the middle-class values of hard work, thrift, self-control, and material success. And by teaching that Christ would return to rule the earth, it shared in the hope of a coming millennial kingdom.

Mormonism was an outgrowth less of evangelicalism, however, than of the primitive gospel movement, which sought to reestablish the ancient church. In

Movement to restore the ancient church

restoring what Smith called "the ancient order of things," Mormons created a theocracy uniting church and state, reestablished biblical priesthoods and titles, and adopted temple rituals. Smith undertook to gather the saints in a "city of Zion," first in Ohio and then in Missouri, in preparation for Christ's return. But his unorthodox teachings provoked bitter persecution wherever he went, and mob violence finally hounded him out of Missouri in 1839. In reponse, Smith established a new holy city, Nauvoo, along the Mississippi River in Illinois.

At Nauvoo, Smith introduced the most distinctive features of Mormon theology, including baptism for the dead, eternal marriage, and polygamy, or plural

City of Zion: Nauvoo

marriage. As a result, Mormonism increasingly diverged from traditional Christianity and became a distinct new religion. Neighboring residents, alarmed by the Mormons' growing political power and reports that Smith had adopted polygamy, demanded that Nauvoo's charter be revoked and the Church suppressed. In 1844 Smith was murdered by an anti-Mormon mob. The Mormons abandoned Nauvoo in 1846, and the following year Brigham Young, Smith's successor, led them westward to Utah (page 371). Nauvoo ceased to be a holy city.

Socialist Communities

The hardship and poverty that accompanied the growth of industrial factories inspired utopian communities based on science and reason rather than religion.

Owen's New Harmony

Robert Owen, a Scottish industrialist, came to the United States in 1824 and founded the community of New Harmony in Indiana. Owen believed that the character of individuals was shaped by their surroundings, and that by changing those surroundings, one could change human character. Unfortunately, most of the 900 or so volunteers who flocked to New Harmony lacked the skills and commitment needed to make the community a success, and bitter factions soon split the settlement.

The experience of New Harmony and other communities demonstrated that the United States was poor soil for socialistic experiments. Wages were too high and land too cheap to interest most Americans in collectivist ventures. And individualism was too strong to create a commitment to cooperative action.

The Temperance Movement

The most significant reform movements of the period sought not to withdraw from society but to change it directly. One of the most determined of these was the temperance movement.

The origins of the campaign lay in the heavy drinking of the early nineteenth century. Alcohol consumption soared after the Revolution, so that by 1830 the average American consumed four gallons of absolute alcohol a year, the highest level in American history and nearly triple present-day levels. Anne Royale, whose travels took her cross country by stage, reported, "When I was in Virginia, it was too much whiskey—in Ohio, too much whiskey—in Tennessee, it is too, too much whiskey!" The social costs for such habits were high: broken families, abused and neglected wives and children, sickness and disability, poverty, and crime. The temperance movement undertook to eliminate these problems by curbing drinking.

Led largely by clergy, the movement at first focused on drunkenness and did not oppose moderate drinking. But in 1826 the American Temperance Society was founded, taking voluntary abstinence as its goal. During the next decade approximately 5000 local temperance societies were founded. As the movement gained momentum, annual per capita consumption of alcohol dropped sharply, so that by 1845 it had fallen below two gallons a year.

The move toward abstinence

The temperance movement was more sustained and more popular than other reforms. It appealed to young and old, to urban and rural residents, to workers and businesspeople. And it was the only reform movement with significant support in the South. Its success came partly for social reasons. Democracy necessitated sober voters; factories required sober workers. Temperance attracted the upwardly mobile—professionals and skilled artisans anxious to improve their social standing. Finally, temperance advocates stressed the suffering that men inflicted on women and children, and thus the movement appealed to women as a means to defend the home and carry out their domestic mission.

Educational Reform

In 1800 Massachusetts was the only state requiring free public schools supported by community funds. The call for tax-supported education arose first among workers, as a means to restore their deteriorating position in society. But middle-class reformers quickly took control of the movement, looking to uplift common citizens and make them responsible. Reformers appealed to business leaders by arguing that the new economic order needed educated workers.

Under Horace Mann's leadership, Massachusetts adopted a minimum-length school year, provided for training of teachers, and expanded the curriculum to include subjects such as history, geography, and various applied skills. Still, outside of Massachusetts there were only a few high schools. Moreover, compulsory attendance was rarely required, and many poor parents sent their children to work instead of school. Still, by the 1850s the number of schools, attendance figures, and school budgets had all increased sharply. School reformers enjoyed their greatest success in the Northeast and the least in the South, where planters opposed paying taxes to educate poorer white children.

Educational opportunities for women also expanded. Teachers like Catharine Beecher and Emma Hunt Willard established a number of private girls' schools, putting to rest the objection of many male educators that fragile female minds could not absorb large doses of mathematics, physics, or geography. In 1833 Oberlin became the nation's first coeducational college. Four years later Mary Lyon founded Mount Holyoke, the first American college for women.

Female education

COUNTERPOINT   *Reform and Social Control*

What motivated advocates like Emma Willard, Charles Finney, and the Beechers? Some historians have suggested that the real purpose of the Jacksonian reform movements was not "social uplift," but to instill middle-class values in the working class in order to make them diligent (and submissive) workers. In so doing, the reformers undercut any real threat the working class might pose to society. These historians pay particular attention to the educational reform movement, which aimed in the classroom to teach good behavior to lower-class students. Textbooks like the famous McGuffey Readers stressed the middle-class virtues of self-control, punctuality, hard work, patriotism, and Protestantism. Emerson satirized the more extreme arguments of school reformers as "we must educate them or they will be at our throats."

This social control thesis has been criticized by historians who place greater emphasis on the role of religion. In their view, reformers' prefectionism sprang out of the ideals of the Second Great Awakening. Viewing social problems as manifestations of individual sin, reformers looked to create a morally perfect society. They also warned that a decline in public virtue would undermine republicanism. Education did become a way to instill proper moral values in the masses—values including self-reliance, responsible citizenship, and Christianity. But reformers saw tax-supported public schools as a means to expand rather than restrict opportunity, including opportunities for lower-class children, who otherwise would have little access to education. These historians contend that middle-class reformers were hardly indifferent to the welfare of less privileged groups in society.

The Asylum Movement

After 1820 there was also a dramatic increase in the number of asylums of every sort—orphanages, jails, and hospitals. Advocates of asylums called for isolating and separating the criminal, the insane, the ill, and the dependent from outside society. The goal of care in asylums, which earlier had focused on confinement, shifted to the reform of personal character.

Dorothea Dix, a Boston schoolteacher, took the lead in advocating state-supported asylums for the mentally ill. She attracted much attention to the movement by her report detailing the horrors to which the mentally ill were subjected, including being chained, kept in cages and closets, and beaten with rods. In response to her efforts, 28 states maintained mental institutions by 1860.

Like other reform movements, the push for new asylums and better educational facilities reflected overtones of both liberation and control. Asylums freed

Order and social control

prisoners and the mentally ill from the harsh punishments of the past, but the new techniques of "rehabilitation" forced prisoners to march in lockstep. Education brought with it the freedom to question and to acquire knowledge, but some reformers hoped that schools would become as orderly as prisons. Louis Dwight, who advocated solitary confinement for prisoners at night and total silence by day, suggested eagerly that such methods "would greatly promote order, seriousness, and purity in large families, male and female boarding schools, and colleges."

ABOLITIONISM

In the fall of 1834, Lyman Beecher, as president of Lane Seminary in Cincinnati, was continuing his efforts to "overturn and overturn" on behalf of the kingdom of God. The school had everything that an institution for training ministers to convert the West needed—everything, that is, except students. In October all but 8 of Lane's 100 scholars had departed after months of bitter controversy with Beecher and the trustees over the issue of abolition.

Beecher knew the source of his troubles: a scruffy yet magnetic student named Theodore Dwight Weld. Weld had been firing up his classmates over the need to immediately free the slaves. Beecher was not surprised, for Weld had been converted by that incendiary Finney. He knew, too, that Weld was a follower of William Lloyd Garrison, whose abolitionist writings had sent shock waves across the entire nation. Indeed, Beecher's troubles at Lane Seminary provided only one example of how the flames of reform, when fanned, could spread along paths not anticipated by those who first kindled them.

The Beginnings of the Abolitionist Movement

William Lloyd Garrison symbolized the transition from a moderate antislavery movement to the more militant abolitionism of the 1830s. A deeply religious young man, Garrison went to Baltimore in 1829 to work for Benjamin Lundy, who edited an antislavery newspaper.

But Garrison's views proved more radical than Lundy's, and within the year the young firebrand was in jail. Upon his release Garrison hurried back to

Garrison's immediatism

Boston, determined to publish a new kind of antislavery journal. On January 1, 1831, the first issue of *The Liberator* appeared, and abolitionism was born. In appearance, the bespectacled Garrison seemed frail, almost mousy, but in print he was abrasive, withering, and uncompromising. "On this subject, I do not wish to think, or speak, or write with moderation," he proclaimed. "I am in earnest—I will not equivocate—I will not excuse—I will not retreat a single inch—AND I WILL BE HEARD." Repudiating gradual emancipation and embracing "immediatism," Garrison insisted that slavery end at once. He denounced colonization as a racist movement and upheld the principle of racial equality. To those who suggested that slaveowners should be compensated for freeing their slaves, Garrison was firm. Southerners ought to be convinced by "moral suasion" to renounce slavery as a sin. Virtue was its own reward.

Prison reformers believed that rigid discipline, extensive rules, and (in some programs) solitary confinement were necessary to rehabilitate criminals. Prisoners often had to march lockstep under strict supervision and wear uniforms such as those seen in this photograph from the 1870s.

Garrison attracted the most attention, but other abolitionists spoke with equal conviction. Wendell Phillips, from a socially prominent Boston family, held listeners spellbound with his speeches. Lewis Tappan and his brother Arthur, two New York City silk merchants, boldly placed their wealth behind various humanitarian causes, including abolitionism. James G. Birney, an Alabama slaveholder, converted to abolitionism after wrestling with his conscience, and Angelina and Sarah Grimké, the daughters of a South Carolina planter, left their native state to speak against the institution. And there was Angelina's future husband, Theodore Weld, the restless student at Lane Seminary who had fallen so dramatically under Garrison's influence.

To abolitionists, slavery was a moral, not an economic, question. The institution seemed a contradiction of the principle of the American Revolution that all human beings had been created with natural rights. Abolitionists condemned slavery because of the breakup of marriages and families by sale, the harsh punishment of the lash, slaves' lack of access to education, and the sexual abuse of black women. But most of all, abolitionists denounced slavery as outrageously contrary to Christian teaching. As one Ohio antislavery paper declared, "We believe slavery to be a sin, always, everywhere, and only, sin—sin, in itself." Abolitionism forced the churches to face the question of slavery head-on, and in the 1840s the Methodist and Baptist churches each split into northern and southern organizations over the issue.

The Spread of Abolitionism

After helping organize the New England Anti-Slavery Society in 1832, Garrison joined with Lewis Tappan and Theodore Weld the following year to establish a national organization, the American Anti-Slavery Society. During the years before the Civil War, perhaps 200,000 northerners belonged to an abolitionist society.

Abolitionists were concentrated in the East, especially New England, and in areas that had been settled by New Englanders, such as western New York and northern Ohio. The movement was not strong in cities or among businesspeople and workers. Most abolitionists were young, being generally in their twenties and thirties when the movement began, and had grown up in rural areas and small towns in middle-class families. Intensely religious, many had been profoundly affected by the revivals of the Second Great Awakening.

Support for abolitionism

Certainly Theodore Weld was cut from this mold. After enrolling in Lane Seminary in 1833, he promoted immediate abolitionism among his fellow students. Unlike some abolitionists, who opposed slavery but disdained blacks as inferior, Lane students mingled freely with Cincinnati's free black population. In the sum-

An escaped slave, Harriet Tubman (far left) made several forays into the South as a "conductor" on the Underground Railroad. Shown here with one group that she led to freedom, she was noted for her stealth and firm determination, qualities that helped her repeatedly to outwit her pursuers.

mer of 1834, Beecher and Lane's trustees forbade any discussion of slavery on campus and ordered students to return to their studies. All but a handful left the school and enrolled at Oberlin College, where Charles Finney was professor of theology.

Free African Americans, who made up the majority of subscribers to Garrison's *Liberator*, provided important support and leadership for the move-

African American abolitionists

ment. Frederick Douglass assumed the greatest prominence. Having escaped from slavery in Maryland, he became an eloquent critic of its evils. Initially a follower of Garrison, Douglass eventually broke with him and started his own newspaper in Rochester. Other important black abolitionists included Martin Delany, William Wells Brown, William Still, and Sojourner Truth. Most black Americans endorsed peaceful means to end slavery, but David Walker in his *Appeal to the Colored Citizens of the World* (1829) urged slaves to use violence to end bondage.

A network of antislavery sympathizers developed in the North to convey runaway slaves to Canada and freedom. While not as extensive or as tightly organized as contemporaries claimed, the Underground Railroad hid fugitives and transported them northward from one station to the next. Free African Americans, who were more readily trusted by wary slaves, played a leading role in the Underground Railroad. One of its most famous conductors was Harriet Tubman, an escaped slave who repeatedly returned to the South and eventually escorted more than 200 slaves to freedom.

Opponents and Divisions

The drive for immediate abolition faced massive obstacles, no matter how fervent its advocates. With slavery increasingly important to the South's eco-

Hostility toward abolitionists

nomic life, the abolitionist cause encountered extreme hostility there. And in the North, where racism was equally entrenched, abolitionism provoked bitter resistance. Even abolitionists like Garrison treated blacks paternalistically, contending that they should occupy a subordinate place in the antislavery movement.

On occasion, northern resistance turned violent. An anti-abolitionist mob burned down the headquarters of the American Anti-Slavery Society in Philadelphia, and in 1837 in Alton, Illinois, Elijah Lovejoy was murdered when he tried to protect his printing press from an angry crowd. The leaders of these mobs were not from the bottom of society but, as one of their victims noted, were "gentlemen of property and standing." Prominent leaders in the community, they reacted vigorously to the threat that abolitionists posed to their power and prosperity and to the established order.

But abolitionists were also hindered by divisions among reformers. At Oberlin College Finney, too, ended up opposing Theodore Weld's fervent abo-

Divisions among reformers

litionism. More conservative than Finney, Lyman Beecher saw his son Edward stand guard over Elijah Lovejoy's printing press the evening before the editor's murder. Within another decade,

Beecher would see his daughter Harriet Beecher Stowe write the most success-ful piece of antislavery literature in the nation's history, *Uncle Tom's Cabin* (page 392). Even the abolitionists themselves splintered. More conservative reformers wanted to work within established institutions, using churches and political ac-tion to end slavery. But for Garrison and his followers, the mob violence demon-strated that slavery was only part of a deeper national disease, whose cure re-quired the overthrow of American institutions and values.

By the end of the decade, Garrison had worked out a program for the to-tal reform of society. He embraced perfectionism, denounced the clergy, and urged members to leave the churches. Condemning the Constitution as proslavery—"a covenant with death and an agreement with hell"—he argued that no person of conscience could participate in the corrupt political system. This platform was radical enough on all counts, but the final straw for Garrison's opponents was his endorsement of women's rights as an inseparable part of abolitionism.

The Women's Rights Movement

Women faced many disadvantages in American society. They were kept out of most jobs, denied political rights, and given only limited access to education be-yond the elementary grades. When a woman married, her husband became the legal representative of the marriage and gained complete control of her prop-erty. Any unmarried woman was made the ward of a male relative.

When abolitionists divided over the issue of female participation, women found it easy to identify with the situation of slaves, since both were victims of male tyranny. Sarah and Angelina Grimké took up the cause of women's rights after they were criticized for speaking to audiences that included men as well as women. Sarah responded with *Letters on the Condition of Women and the Equality of the Sexes* (1838), arguing that women deserved the same rights as men. Abby Kelly, another abolitionist, remarked that women "have good cause to be grate-ful to the slave," for in "striving to strike his irons off, we found most surely, that we were manacled *ourselves.*"

Two abolitionists, Elizabeth Cady Stanton and Lucretia Mott, launched the women's rights movement after they were forced to sit behind a curtain at a

Seneca Falls convention

world antislavery convention in London. In 1848 Stanton and Mott organized a conference in Seneca Falls, New York, that at-tracted about a hundred supporters. The meeting issued a Declaration of Sentiments, modeled after the Declaration of Independence, that began, "All men and women are created equal." The Seneca Falls convention approved resolutions calling for educational and professional opportunities for women, control by women of their property, recognition of legal equality, and repeal of laws awarding the father custody of the children in divorce. The most controversial proposal, and the only resolution that did not pass unanimously, was one demanding the right to vote. The Seneca Falls convention established

Elizabeth Cady Stanton, one of
the instigators and guiding spirits
at the Seneca Falls convention,
with two of her children at
that time.

the arguments and the program for the women's rights movement for the remainder of the century.

The women's rights movement won few victories before 1860. Several
states gave women greater control over their property, and a few made divorce
easier or granted women the right to sue in courts. But disappointments and
defeats outweighed these early victories. Still, many of the important leaders in
the crusade for women's rights that emerged after the Civil War had already
taken their places at the forefront of the movement. They included Stanton,
Susan B. Anthony, Lucy Stone, and—as Lyman Beecher by now must have
expected—one of Beecher's daughters, Isabella Beecher Hooker.

The Schism of 1840

It was Garrison's position on women's rights that finally split antislavery ranks
asunder. The showdown came in 1840 at the national meeting of the American
Anti-Slavery Society, when delegates debated whether women could hold office
in the organization. Garrison's opponents feared that this issue would drive off
potential supporters, but Garrison carried the day. His opponents, led by Lewis
Tappan, resigned to found the rival American and Foreign Anti-Slavery Society.

The schism of 1840 lessened the influence of abolitionism as a benevolent
reform movement in American society. Although abolitionism heightened moral

concern about slavery, it failed to convert the North to its program, and its supporters remained a tiny minority. For all the considerable courage they showed, their movement suffered from the lack of a realistic, long-range plan for eliminating so deeply entrenched an institution. Garrison even boasted that "the genius of the abolitionist movement is to have *no* plan." Abolitionism demonstrated the severe limits of moral suasion and individual conversions as a solution to deeply rooted social problems.

REFORM SHAKES THE PARTY SYSTEM

"What a fog-bank we are in politically! Do you see any head-land or light—or can you get an observation—or soundings?" The words came from a puzzled Whig politician writing a friend after the Massachusetts state elections of 1853. He was in such a confused state because reformers were increasingly entering the political arena to achieve their goals.

The crusading idealism of revivalists and reformers inevitably collided with the hard reality that society could not be perfected by converting individuals. In America's democratic society, politics and government coercion promised a more effective means to impose a new moral vision on the nation.

Politicians did not particularly welcome the new interest. Because the Whig and Democratic parties both drew on evangelical and nonevangelical voters, heated moral debates over the harmful effects of drink or the evils of slavery threatened to detach regular party members from their old loyalties.

Women and the Right to Vote

As the focus of change and reform shifted toward the political arena, women in particular lost influence. As major participants in the benevolent organizations of the 1820s and 1830s, they had used their efforts on behalf of "moral suasion." But since women could not vote, they felt excluded when the temperance and abolitionist movements turned to electoral action to accomplish their goals. By the 1840s female reformers increasingly demanded the right to vote as the means to reform society.

Previously, many female reformers had accepted the right of petition as their most appropriate political activity. But *The Lily*, a women's rights paper, soon changed its tack. "Why shall [women] be left only the poor resource of petition?" it asked. "For even petitions, when they are from women, without the elective franchise to give them backbone, are of but little consequence."

The Maine Law

Although drinking had significantly declined in American society by 1840, it had hardly been eliminated. After 1845 the arrival of large numbers of German and Irish immigrants, who were accustomed to consuming alcohol, made voluntary prohibition even more remote. In response, temperance advocates proposed state laws that would outlaw the manufacture and sale of alcoholic beverages. If liquor was unavailable, reformers reasoned, the attitude of drinkers was unimportant: they would be forced to reform whether they wanted to or not.

The issue of prohibition cut across party lines, with large numbers of Whigs and Democrats on both sides of the question. When party leaders tried to dodge the issue, the temperance movement adopted the strategy of endorsing the legislative candidates who pledged to support a prohibitory law. To win additional recruits, temperance leaders took up techniques used in political campaigns, including house-to-house canvasses, parades and processions, bands and singing, banners, picnics, and mass rallies.

The temperance movement's first major triumph came in 1851 in Maine. The Maine Law, as it was known, authorized search and seizure of private property and provided stiff penalties for selling liquor. In the next few years a number of states enacted similar laws, although most were struck down by the courts or later repealed.

Even though prohibition had been temporarily defeated, the issue badly disrupted the unity of the Whig and Democratic parties. It detached a number of

Effect on the party system

voters from both coalitions, greatly increased the extent of party switching, and brought to the polls a large number of new voters, including many "wets" who wanted to preserve their right to drink. By dissolving the ties between so many voters and their parties, the temperance issue played a major role in the eventual collapse of the Jacksonian party system in the 1850s.

Abolitionism and the Party System

Abolition was the most divisive issue to come out of the benevolent movement. In 1835 abolitionists distributed over a million pamphlets through the post office to southern whites. A wave of excitement swept the South when the first batches arrived. Former senator Robert Hayne led a Charleston mob that

Censorship of the mails

burned sacks of U.S. mail containing abolitionist literature, and postmasters in other southern cities refused to deliver the material. When the Jackson administration acquiesced in this censorship, abolitionists protested that their civil rights had been violated. In reaction, the number of antislavery societies in the North nearly tripled.

With access to the mails impaired, abolitionists began flooding Congress with petitions against slavery. Asserting that Congress had no power over the

The gag rule

institution, angry southern representatives persuaded the House to adopt the so-called gag rule in 1836. It tabled without consideration any petition dealing with slavery. Claiming that the right of petition was also under attack by slavery's champions, abolitionists gained new supporters. In 1844 the House finally repealed the controversial rule.

Many abolitionists outside Garrison's extreme circle were increasingly convinced that an antislavery third party offered a more effective means of attacking slavery. In 1840 these political abolitionists founded the Liberty party and nominated for president James Birney, a former slaveholder who had converted to abolitionism. Birney received only 7000 votes, but the Liberty party was the seed from which a stronger antislavery political movement would grow. In the next two decades, abolitionism's greatest importance would be in the political arena rather than as a voluntary reform organization.

After two decades of fiery revivals, benevolent crusades, utopian experiments, and Transcendental philosophizing, the ferment of reform had spread through urban streets, canal town churches, frontier clearings, and the halls of Congress. Abolition, potentially the most dangerous issue, seemed still under control in 1840. Birney's small vote, coupled with the disputes between the two national antislavery societies, encouraged political leaders to believe that the party system had turned back this latest threat of sectionalism.

But the growing northern concern about slavery highlighted differences between the two sections. Despite the strength of evangelicalism in the South, the reform impulse spawned by the revivals found little support there, since reform movements were discredited by their association with abolitionism. The party system confronted the difficult challenge of holding together sections that, although sharing much, were also diverging in important ways. To the residents of both sections, the South increasingly seemed to be a unique society with its own distinctive way of life.

SIGNIFICANT EVENTS

1787	First Shaker commune established
1794	African American Bethel Church organized
1821	New York constructs first penitentiary
1824	New Harmony established
1824–1837	Peak of revivals
1826	James Fenimore Cooper's *The Last of the Mohicans* published; American Temperance Society founded
1829	David Walker's *Appeal to the Colored Citizens of the World* published
1830–1831	Charles Finney's revival at Rochester
1831	*The Liberator* established
1833	American Anti-Slavery Society founded; Oberlin College admits women
1834	Lane Seminary rebellion
1835	Abolitionists' postal campaign
1836	Transcendental Club established; gag rule passed
1837	Massachusetts establishes state board of education; Mount Holyoke Seminary commences classes; Elijah Lovejoy killed
1838	Ralph Waldo Emerson delivers Divinity School address; Sarah Grimké's *Letters on the Condition of Women and the Equality of the Sexes* published
1840	Schism of American Anti-Slavery Society; Liberty party organized
1843	Dorothea Dix's report on treatment of the insane
1844	Gag rule repealed
1848	Oneida Community established; Seneca Falls convention
1850	Nathaniel Hawthorne's *The Scarlet Letter* published
1851	Maine adopts prohibition law; Herman Melville's *Moby-Dick* published
1854	Henry David Thoreau's *Walden* published
1855	Walt Whitman's *Leaves of Grass* published

CHAPTER THIRTEEN

The Old South

The impeccably dressed Colonel Daniel Jordan, master of 261 slaves at Laurel Hill, strolls down his oak-lined lawn to the dock along the Waccamaw River, a day's journey north of Charleston, to board the steamship *Nina*. On Fridays, it is Colonel Jordan's custom to visit the exclusive Hot and Hot Fish Club, founded by his fellow lowcountry planters, to play a game of lawn bowling or billiards and be waited on by black servants in livery as he sips an iced mint julep in the refined atmosphere that for him is the South.

Several hundred miles to the west another steamboat, the *Fashion*, makes its way along the Alabama River. One of the passengers is upset by the boat's slow pace. He has been away from his plantation in the Red River country of Texas and is eager to get back. "Time's money, time's money!" he mutters. "Time's worth more'n money to me now; a hundred percent more, 'cause I left my niggers all alone; not a damn white man within four mile on 'em." When asked what they are doing, since the cotton crop has already been picked, he says, "I set 'em to clairin', but they ain't doin' a damn thing. . . . But I'll make it up, I'll make it up when I get thar, now you'd better believe." For this Red River planter, time is money and cotton is his world—indeed, cotton is what the South is all about. "I am a cotton man, I am, and I don't car who knows it," he proclaims. "I know cotton, I do. I'm dam' if I know anythin' but cotton."

In the bayous of the Deep South, only a few miles from where the Mississippi Delta meets the Gulf, Octave Johnson hears the dogs coming. For over a year now Johnson has been a runaway slave. He fled from a Louisiana plantation in St. James Parish when the overseer threatened to whip him for staying in bed. To survive, he hides in the swamps four miles behind the plantation—stealing turkeys, chickens, and pigs and trading with other slaves. As uncertain as this life is, nearly 30 other slaves have joined him over the past year.

This time when the pack of hounds bursts upon them, the slaves do not flee but kill as many dogs as possible. Then they plunge into the bayou. For Octave

Plantation Burial, painted about 1860 by John Antrobus, portrays the black slave community from a Louisiana plantation burying a loved one. Religion played a central role in the life of slaves.

Johnson the real South is a matter of weighing one's prospects between the uncertainties of alligators and the overseer's whip—and deciding when to say no.

Ferdinand Steel and his family are not forced, by the flick of the lash, to rise at five in the morning. They rise because the land demands it. Steel, in his twenties, owns 170 acres of land in Carroll County, Mississippi. His life is one of continuous hard work, caring for the animals and tending the crops. His mother Eliza and sister Julia have plenty to keep them busy: making soap, fashioning dippers out of gourds, or sewing.

The Steel family grows cotton, too, but not with the single-minded devotion of the planter aboard the *Fashion*. Self-sufficiency and family security always come first, and Steel's total crop amounts to only five or six bales. His profit is never enough for him to consider buying even one slave. In fact, he would prefer not to raise any cotton—"We are to[o] weak handed," he says—but the cotton means cash, and cash means that he can buy things he needs in nearby Grenada. Though fiercely independent, Steel and his scattered neighbors help each other raise houses, clear fields, shuck corn, or quilt. They depend on one another and are bound together by blood, religion, obligation, and honor. For small farmers like Ferdinand Steel, these ties constitute the real South.

The portraits could go on: different people, different Souths, all of them real. Such contrasts underscore the difficulty of trying to define a regional identity. Encompassing in 1860 the 15 slave states plus the District of Columbia, the South was a land of great social and geographic diversity.

Yet despite its many differences of people and geography, the South was bonded by ties so strong, they eventually outpulled those of the nation itself. At the heart of this unity was an agricultural system that took advantage of the region's warm climate and long growing season. Most important, this rural agricultural economy was based on the institution of slavery, which had far-reaching effects on all aspects of southern society. It shaped not only the culture of the slaves themselves but the lives of their masters and mistresses, and even of farm families and herders in the hills and backwoods, who saw few slaves from day to day. To understand the Old South, then, we must understand how the southern agricultural economy and the institution of slavery affected the social class structure of both white and black southerners.

Factors unifying the South

THE SOCIAL STRUCTURE OF THE COTTON KINGDOM

We have already seen (in Chapter 10) that the spread of cotton stimulated the nation's remarkable economic growth after the War of 1812. Demand spurred by the textile industry sent the price of cotton soaring on the international market, and white southerners scrambled into the fresh lands of the Southwest to reap the profits to be made in the cotton sweepstakes.

Deep South, Upper South

As Indian lands were opened to white settlement, word spread of the "black belt" region of Alabama, where the dark soil was particularly suited to growing cotton, and of the tremendous yields from the soils along the Mississippi River's broad reaches. "The *Alabama Feaver* rages here with great violence and has *carried off* vast numbers of our Citizens," a North Carolinian wrote in 1817. "I am apprehensive if it continues to spread as it has done, it will almost depopulate the country." A generation later, in the 1830s, immigrants were still "pouring in with a ceaseless tide," an Alabama observer reported. But the booming frontier in the Deep South pushed even farther west. By the 1840s residents were leaving Alabama and Mississippi and heading for fresher cotton lands along the Red River and up into Texas. Amazingly, by the eve of the Civil War nearly a third of the total cotton crop came from *west* of the Mississippi River.

As Senator James Henry Hammond of South Carolina boasted in 1858, cotton was king in the Old South. True, the region devoted more acreage to corn, but

Cotton and southern prosperity

cotton was the primary export and the major source of southern wealth. By 1860 the United States produced three-fourths of the world's supply of cotton. Per capita income among southern whites actually exceeded that of the free states, though wealth was not so evenly distributed in the plantation South as in northern agricultural areas.

The single-crop agriculture practiced by southern farmers (especially in tobacco and corn) rapidly wore out the soil. Planters and farmers in the Upper

Environmental impact of single-crop agriculture

South increasingly shifted to wheat production to restore their soils, but because they now plowed fields rather than using the hoe, this shift accelerated soil erosion. Destruction of the forests, particularly in the Piedmont where commercial agriculture now took hold, had the same effect. In addition, reliance on a single crop increased toxins and parasites in the soil, making southern agriculture more vulnerable to destruction than diversified agriculture.

Only the South's low population density eased such environmental damage. More remote areas remained heavily forested, wetlands were still extensive, and as late as 1860 80 percent of the region was uncultivated. (Cattle and hogs, however, ranged over much of this acreage.)

Perhaps the most striking environmental consequence of the expansion of southern society was the increase in disease. The Lower South especially enjoyed a reputation for unhealthiness. Epidemic diseases such as malaria, yellow fever, and cholera were brought to the area by Europeans. The clearing of land—which increased runoff, precipitated floods, and produced pools of stagnant water—encouraged their spread.

As cotton transformed the boom country of the Deep South, agriculture in the Upper South also adjusted.* Scientific agricultural practices reversed the decline in tobacco, which had begun in the 1790s. More important,

The Upper South's new orientation

farmers in the Upper South made wheat and corn their major crops. Because the new crops required less labor, slaveholders in the Upper South sold their surplus slaves to planters in the Deep South. The demand in the Deep South for slaves drove their price steadily up, so that by the late 1850s a prime field hand commanded $1500. Even with increased labor costs, southern agriculture flourished.

The Rural South

The Old South, then, was expanding, dynamic, and booming economically. But the region remained overwhelmingly rural, with 84 percent of its labor force engaged in agriculture in 1860, compared with 40 percent in the North.

*The Upper South included the border states (Delaware, Maryland, Kentucky, and Missouri) and Virginia, North Carolina, Tennessee, and Arkansas. The states of the Deep South were South Carolina, Georgia, Florida, Alabama, Mississippi, Louisiana, and Texas.

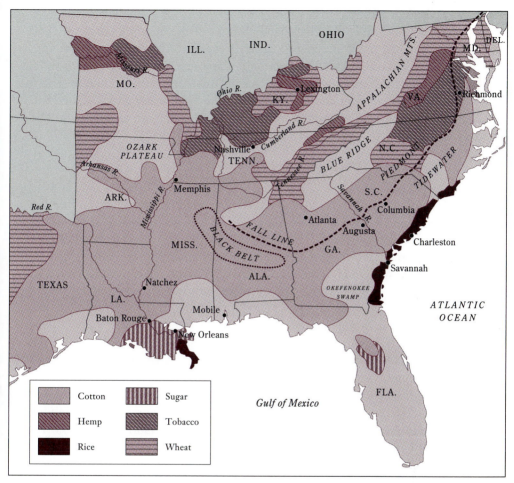

COTTON AND OTHER CROPS OF THE SOUTH   By 1860, the cotton kingdom extended across the Lower South into the Texas prairie and up the Mississippi River valley. Tobacco and hemp were the staple crops of the Upper South, where they competed with corn and wheat. Rice production was concentrated in the swampy coastal region of South Carolina and Georgia as well as the lower tip of Louisiana. The sugar district was in southern Louisiana.

Lack of manufacturing

Conversely, the South produced only 9 percent of the nation's manufactured goods. Efforts to diversify the South's economy made little headway in the face of the high profits from cotton.

With so little industry, few cities developed in the South. Only 1 in 10 southerners lived in cities and towns in 1860, compared with 1 out of 3 persons in the North. North Carolina, Alabama, Mississippi, Arkansas, and Texas did not contain a single city with a population of 10,000.

As a rural society, the South evidenced far less interest in education. Most wealthy planters opposed a state-supported school system, since they hired tutors or sent their children to private academies. Thus free public schools were rare, especially in rural areas that made up most of the South. Georgia in 1860

White illiteracy had only one county with a free school system, and Mississippi had no public schools outside its few cities. Not surprisingly, southern white children on average spent only one-fifth as much time in school as did their northern counterparts. Among native-born white citizens, the 1850 census showed that 20 percent were unable to read and write. In the middle states the figure was 3 percent; in New England, only 0.4 percent.

Distribution of Slavery

Even more than agrarian ways, slavery set the South apart. Whereas in 1776 slavery had been a national institution, by 1820 it was confined to the states south of Pennsylvania and the Ohio River. The South's "peculiar institution" bound white and black southerners together in a multitude of ways.

Slaves were not evenly distributed throughout the region. More than half lived in the Deep South, where African Americans outnumbered white southerners in both South Carolina and Mississippi by the 1850s. Elsewhere in the Deep South, the black population exceeded 40 percent in all states except Texas. In the Upper South, on the other hand, whites greatly outnumbered blacks. Only in Virginia and North Carolina did the slave population top 30 percent.

The distribution of slaves showed striking geographic variations within individual states as well. In areas of fertile soil, flat or rolling countryside, and good transportation, slavery and the plantation system dominated. In the pine barrens, areas isolated by lack of transportation, and hilly and mountainous regions, small family farms and few slaves were the rule.

Almost all enslaved African Americans, male and female, worked in agricultural pursuits, with only about 10 percent living in cities and towns. On large

Slave occupations plantations, a few slaves were domestic servants, and others were skilled artisans—blacksmiths, carpenters, or bricklayers—but most toiled in the fields.

Slavery as a Labor System

Slavery was, first and foremost, a system to manage and control labor. The plantation system, with its extensive estates and large labor forces, could never have developed without slavery. Slaves represented an enormous capital investment, worth more than all the land in the Old South.

Furthermore, slavery remained a highly profitable investment. The average slaveowner spent perhaps $30 to $35 a year to support an adult slave; some ex-

Profitability of slavery pended as little as half that. Even at the higher cost of support, a slaveowner took about 60 percent of the annual wealth produced by a slave's labor. For those who pinched pennies and drove slaves harder, the profits were even greater.

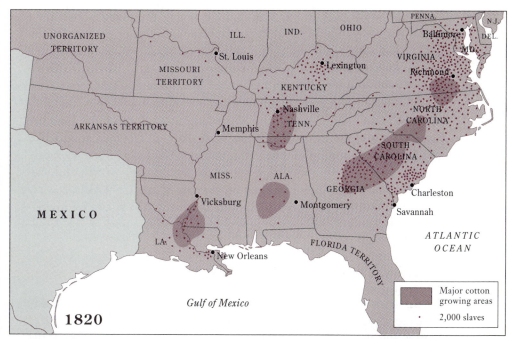

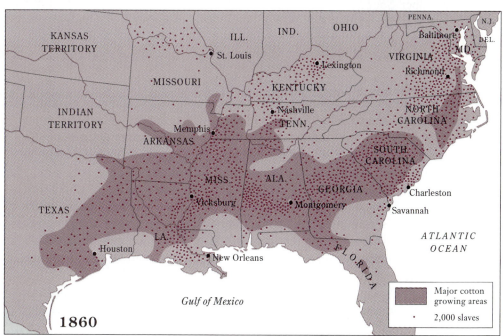

THE SPREAD OF SLAVERY, 1820–1860   Between 1820 and 1860, the slave population of
the South shifted south and westward, concentrating especially heavily in coastal
South Carolina and Georgia, in the black belt of central Alabama and Mississippi (so
named because of its rich soil), and in the Mississippi valley.

By concentrating wealth and power in the hands of the planter class, slavery shaped the tone of southern society. Planters were not aristocrats in the

Slavery and aristocratic values

European sense of having special legal privileges or formal titles of rank. Still, the system encouraged southern planters to think of themselves as a landed gentry upholding the aristocratic values of pride, honor, family, and hospitality.

Public opinion in Europe and in the North had grown more and more hostile to the peculiar institution, causing white southerners to feel increasingly like an isolated minority defending an embattled position. Yet they clung tenaciously to slavery, for it was the base on which the South's economic growth and way of life rested. As one Georgian observed on the eve of the Civil War, slavery was "so intimately mingled with our social conditions that it would be impossible to eradicate it."

CLASS STRUCTURE OF THE WHITE SOUTH

In 1860 the region's 15 states had a population of 12 million, of which roughly two-thirds were white, one-third were black slaves, and about 2 percent were free African Americans. Because of the institution of slavery, the social structure of the antebellum South differed in important ways from that of the North. Even so, southern society was remarkably fluid, and as a result, class lines were not rigid.

The Slaveowners

Of the 8 million white southerners in 1860, only about 2 million (one-quarter) either owned slaves or were members of slaveowning families. Moreover, most slaveowners owned only a few slaves. If one uses the census definition of a planter as a person who owned 20 or more slaves, only about 1 out of every 30 white southerners belonged to families of the planter class.

A planter of consequence, however, needed to own at least 50 slaves, and there were only about 10,000 such families—less than 1 percent of the white population. This privileged group made up the aristocracy at the top of the southern class structure. Although limited in size, the planter class nevertheless owned more than half of all slaves and controlled more than 90 percent of the region's total wealth.

The typical plantation had 20 to 50 slaves and 800 to 1000 acres of land. Thus larger slaveowners usually owned several plantations, with an overseer for

Plantation administration

each one. The slaves were divided into field hands, skilled workers, and house servants, with one or more slaves serving as "drivers" to assist the overseer. While planters pioneered the application of capitalistic methods, including specialization and division of labor, to agriculture, plantations remained labor-intensive operations. Of the southern staples only the production of sugar was heavily mechanized.

Tidewater and Frontier

Southern planters shared a commitment to preserve slavery as the source of their wealth and stature. Yet in other ways they were a diverse group. On the one hand, the tobacco and rice planters of the Atlantic Tidewater were part of a settled region and a culture that reached back 150 to 200 years. States such as Mississippi and Arkansas, by contrast, were at or just emerging from the frontier stage, since most residents had arrived after 1815. Consequently, the society of the Southwest was rawer and more volatile.

It was along the Tidewater, especially the bays of the Chesapeake and the South Carolina coast, that the legendary "Old South" was born. Here, masters

Tidewater society

erected substantial homes, some—especially between Charleston and Columbia—the classic white-pillared mansions in the Greek revival style. Here, more than a few planters were urbane and polished.

The ideal of the Tidewater South was the country gentleman. An Irish visitor observed that in Maryland and Virginia the great planters lived in "a style which approaches nearer to that of the English country gentleman than what is to be met with anywhere else on the continent." As in England, the local gentry often served as justices of the peace, and the Episcopal church remained the socially accepted road to heaven. Here, too, family names continued to be important in politics.

While the newer regions of the South boasted of planters with cultivated manners, as a group the cotton lords were a different breed. Whatever their

Society in the cotton kingdom

background, whether planters, farmers, overseers, or businessmen, they were basically entrepreneurs who had moved west for the same reason so many other white Americans had: to make their fortunes. By and large, the cotton gentry were self-made men who through hard work, aggressive business tactics, and good luck had risen from ordinary backgrounds. For them, the cotton boom and the exploitation of enslaved men and women offered the opportunity to move up in a new society that lacked an entrenched elite.

"Time's money, time's money." For men like the impatient Texan, time was indeed money, slaves were capital, and cotton by the bale signified cash in hand.

Slaveholders' values

This business orientation was especially apparent in the cotton kingdom, where planters sought to maximize their profits and constantly reinvested their returns in land and slaves. As one visitor said of Mississippi slaveholders: "To sell cotton in order to buy negroes— to make more cotton to buy more negroes, 'ad infinitum,' is the aim and direct tendency of all the operations of the thorough-going cotton planter: his whole soul is wrapped up in the pursuit." One shocked Virginian who visited Vicksburg claimed that its citizens ran "mad with speculation" and did business "in a kind of phrenzy." And indeed there was money to be made. The combined annual income of the richest thousand families of the cotton kingdom approached $50 million, while the wealth of the remaining 666,000 white families amounted to only about $60 million.

Stately mansions could be found in a few areas of the South. In general, though, most planters lived humbly. Although they ranked among the richest citizens in America, their homes were often simple one- or two-story unpainted wooden frame houses, and some were log cabins. "If you wish to see people worth millions living as [if] they were not worth hundreds," advised one southwestern planter in 1839, "come to the land of cotton and negroes." Practical men, few of the new cotton lords had absorbed the culture and learning of the traditional country gentleman.

The Master at Home

Whether supervising a Tidewater plantation or creating a cotton estate on the Texas frontier, the master had to coordinate a complex agricultural operation. He gave daily instructions concerning the work to be done, settled disputes between slaves and the overseer, and generally handed out rewards and penalties. In addition, the owner made the critical decisions concerning the planting, harvesting, and marketing of the crops, as well as investments and expenditures.

In performing his duties, the plantation owner was supposed to be the "master" of his crops, his family, and his slaves. Defenders of slavery often held

Paternalism

up this paternalistic ideal—the care and guidance of dependent "children"—and maintained that slavery promoted a genuine bond of affection between the caring master and his loyal slaves. In real life, however, the forces of the market made this paternalistic ideal less evident. Even in the Tidewater, planters were concerned with money and profits. Indeed, some of the most brutal forms of slavery existed on rice plantations. Except for a few domestic servants, owners of large plantations generally had little contact with their slaves. Nor could paternalism mask the reality that slavery everywhere rested on violence, racism, and exploitation.

The Plantation Mistress

Upper-class southern white women, like those in the North, grew up with the ideal of domesticity, reinforced by the notion of a paternalistic master who was lord of the plantation. But the plantation mistress soon discovered that, given the demands placed on her, the ideal was hard to fulfill.

In her youth a genteel lady enjoyed a certain amount of leisure. But once she married and became a plantation mistress, a southern woman was often shocked by the magnitude of her responsibilities. Nursing the sick, making clothing, tending the garden, caring for the poultry, and overseeing every aspect of food preparation were all her domain. She also had to supervise and plan

Mistress's duties

the work of the domestic servants and distribute clothing. After taking care of breakfast, one harried Carolina mistress recounted that she "had the [sewing] work cut out, gave orders about dinner, had the horse feed fixed in hot water, had the box filled with cork: . . . now I have to cut out

Sarah Pierce Vick, the mistress of a plantation near Vicksburg, Mississippi, pauses to speak to one of her slaves. A plantation mistress had many duties and, while enjoying the comforts brought by wealth and status, often found her life more difficult than she had anticipated before marriage.

the flannel jackets." Sarah Williams, the New York bride of a North Carolina planter, admitted that her mother-in-law "works harder than any Northern farmer's wife I know."

Unlike female reformers in the North, upper-class southern women did not openly challenge their role, but some certainly found their sphere confining.

Mistress's discontent

The greatest unhappiness stemmed from the never-ending task of managing slaves. One southern mistress confessed she was frightened at being "always among people whom I do not understand and whom I must guide, and teach and lead on like children." Yet without the labor of slaves, the lifestyle of these women was an impossibility.

Some women drew a parallel between their situation and that of the slaves. Both were subject to male dominance, and independent-minded women found the subordination of marriage difficult. Susan Dabney Smedes, in her recollection of growing up on an Alabama plantation, recalled that "it was a saying that the mistress of a plantation was the most complete slave on it."

Many women were deeply discontented, too, with the widespread double standard for sexual behavior and with the daily reminders of miscegenation

Miscegenation

some had to face. A man who fathered illegitimate children by slave women suffered no social or legal penalties, even in the case of rape (southern law did not recognize such a crime against slave women), whereas a white woman guilty of adultery lost all social respectability. One planter's wife spoke of "violations of the moral law that made mulattoes as common as blackberries," and another recalled, "I saw slavery . . . teemed with injustice and shame to all womankind and I hated it."

Still, plantation mistresses were unwilling to forgo the material comforts that slavery made possible. Moreover, racism was so pervasive within American society that the few white southern women who privately criticized the institution displayed little empathy for the plight of slaves themselves, including black women. Whatever the burdens of the plantation mistress, they were hardly akin to the bondage of slavery itself.

Yeoman Farmers

In terms of numbers, yeoman farm families were the backbone of southern society, accounting for well over half the southern white population. They owned no slaves and farmed the traditional 80 to 160 acres, like northern farmers. About 80 percent owned their own land. They settled almost everywhere in the South, except in the rice and sugar districts and valuable river bottomlands of the Deep South, which were monopolized by large slaveowners. Like Ferdinand Steel, most were semisubsistence farmers who raised primarily corn and hogs, along with perhaps a few bales of cotton or some tobacco, which they sold to obtain the cash needed to buy items like sugar, coffee, and salt. Yeoman farmers lacked the wealth of planters, but they had a pride and dignity that earned them the respect of their richer neighbors.

Lives of yeoman farmers

While southern farmers led more isolated lives than their northern counterparts, their social activities were not very different. Religion played an important role at camp meetings held in late summer, after the crops were laid by and before harvest time. As in the North, neighbors also met to exchange labor and tools. The men rolled logs to clear fields of dead trees, women met for quilting bees, and adults and children alike would gather to shuck corn. Court sessions, militia musters, political rallies—these too were occasions that brought rural folk together.

Since yeoman farmers lacked cheap slave labor, good transportation, and access to credit, they could not compete with planters in the production of staples. And when it came to selling their corn and wheat, small farmers conducted only limited business with planters, who usually grew as much of their own food as possible. In the North urban centers became a market for small farmers, but in the South the lack of towns limited this internal market. Thus while southern yeoman farmers were not poor, they suffered from a chronic lack of money and the absence of conveniences that northern farm families enjoyed. Josiah Hinds, who hacked a farm out of the isolated woods of northern Mississippi, worried that his children were growing up "wild." He complained that "education is but little prized by my neighbours," who were satisfied "if the corn and cotton grows to perfection . . . [and] brings a fare price, and hog meat is at hand to boil with the greens."

Limits on economic opportunity

A majority of white southerners were members of nonslaveholding yeoman farm families. Ruggedly independent, these families depended on their own labor and often lived under primitive conditions. (Courtesy, Museum of Fine Arts, Boston)

In some ways, then, the worlds of the yeoman farmers and the upper-class planters were not only different but also in conflict. Still, a hostility between the two classes did not emerge. Yeoman farmers admired planters and hoped that one day they would join the gentry themselves. Furthermore, they accepted slavery as a means of controlling African Americans as members of an inferior social caste based on race. "Now suppose they was free," one poor farmer told Frederick Law Olmsted, a northern visitor. "You see they'd all think themselves as good as we." Racism and fear of black people were sufficient to keep nonslaveholders loyal to southern institutions.

Absence of class conflict

Poor Whites

The poorest white southerners were confined to land that no one else wanted. They lived in rough, unchinked, windowless log cabins located in the remotest areas and were often squatters without title to the land they were on. The men spent their time hunting and fishing, while women did the domestic work, including what farming they could manage. Circumstances made their poverty difficult to escape. Largely illiterate, they suffered from malnutrition stemming from a monotonous diet of corn, pork, and whiskey, and they were afflicted with malaria and hookworm, diseases that sapped their energy. Other white southerners referred to them scornfully as crackers, white trash, sandhillers, and clay eaters.

The number of poor whites in the Old South is difficult to estimate. There may have been as few as 100,000 or as many as a million; probably they numbered about 500,000, or a little more than 5 percent of the white population.

Because poor whites traded with slaves, exchanging whiskey for stolen goods, contemptuous planters often bought them out simply to rid the neighborhood of them. For their part, poor whites keenly resented *Relations with* planters, but their hostility toward African Americans was even *planters* stronger. Poor whites refused to perform any work commonly done by slaves and vehemently opposed ending slavery. Emancipation would remove one of the few symbols of their status—that they were, at least, free.

THE PECULIAR INSTITUTION

Slaves were not free. That overwhelming fact must be understood before anything is said about the kindness or the cruelty individual slaves experienced; before any consideration of healthy or unhealthy living conditions; before any discussion of how slave families coped with hardship, rejoiced in shared pleasures, or worshiped in prayer. The lives of slaves were affected day in and day out, in big ways and small, by the basic reality that slaves were not their own masters. The master determined a slave's workload, whether a slave could visit a nearby plantation, and whether a slave family remained intact. Whatever slaves wanted to do, they had always to consider the response of their masters.

When power is distributed as unequally as it was between masters and slaves, every action on the part of the enslaved involved a certain calculation, conscious or unconscious. The consequences of every act, of every expression or gesture, had to be considered. In that sense, the line between freedom and slavery penetrated every corner of a slave's life, and it was an absolute and overwhelming distinction.

One other stark fact reinforced the sharp line between freedom and slavery: slaves were distinguished on the basis of color. While the peculiar institution *Slavery and race* was an economic system of labor, it was also a caste system based on race. The color line of slavery made it easier to defend the institution and win the support of yeoman farmers and poor white southerners, even though in many ways the system held them back. Hence slavery must be understood on many levels: not only as an economic system but also as a racial and cultural one, in terms of not only its outward conditions of life and labor but also the inner demands it made on the soul.

Work and Discipline

The conditions slaves encountered varied widely, depending on the size of the farm or plantation, the crop being grown, the personality of the master, and whether he was an absentee owner. On small farms slaves worked in the fields alongside their owners and had much closer contact with whites. On plantations, in contrast, most slaves dealt primarily with the overseer, who was paid by the size of the harvest he brought in and was therefore often harsh in his approach.

House servants and the drivers, who supervised the field hands, were accorded the highest status, and skilled artisans such as carpenters and blacksmiths were also given special recognition. The hardest work was done by the field hands, both men and women, who sometimes were divided into plowhands and hoe gangs.

Some planters organized their slaves in the gang system, in which a white overseer or a black driver supervised gangs of 20 to 25 adults. Although this approach extracted long hours of reasonably hard labor, the slaves had to be constantly supervised and shirkers were difficult to detect. Other planters preferred the task system, under which each slave was given a specific daily assignment to complete, after which he or she was finished for the day. This system allowed slaves to work at their own pace, gave them an incentive to do careful work, and freed overseers from having to closely supervise the work. On the other hand, slaves resisted vigorously if masters tried to increase the workload. The task system was most common in the rice fields, whereas the gang system predominated in the cotton districts. Many planters used a combination of the two.

Gang versus task system of labor

Toil began just before sunrise and continued until dusk. During cultivation and harvest, slaves were in the field 15 to 16 hours a day, eating a noonday meal there and resting before resuming labor. Work was uncommon on Sundays, and frequently only a half day was required on Saturdays. Even so, the routine was taxing. "We . . . have everybody at work before day dawns," an Arkansas cotton planter reported. "I am never caught in bed after day light nor is any body else on the place, and we continue in the cotton fields when we can have fair weather till it is so dark we can't see to work."

Often masters gave rewards to slaves who worked diligently, but the threat of punishment was always present. Slaves could be denied passes; their food allowance could be reduced; and if all else failed, they could be sold. The most common instrument of punishment was the whip. The frequency of its use varied from plantation to plantation, but few slaves escaped the lash entirely. "We have to rely more and more on the power of fear," planter James Henry Hammond acknowledged. "We are determined to continue masters, and to do so we have to draw the reign tighter and tighter day by day to be assured that we hold them in complete check."

Rewards and punishment

Slave Maintenance

Planters generally bought rough, cheap cloth for slave clothing and each year gave adults at most only a couple of outfits and a pair of shoes. Few had enough clothing or blankets to keep warm when the weather dipped below freezing. Some planters provided well-built housing, but more commonly slaves lived in cramped, poorly built cabins that were leaky in wet weather, drafty in cold, and furnished with only a few crude chairs or benches and a table, perhaps a mattress filled with corn husks or straw, and a few pots and dishes.

Clothing and housing

Sickness among the hands was a persistent problem. In order to keep medical expenses down, slaveowners treated sick slaves themselves and called in a doctor only for serious cases. Conditions varied widely, but on average, a slave-owner spent less than a dollar a year on medical care for each slave.

Nevertheless, the United States was the only slave society in the Americas where the slave population increased naturally—indeed, at about the same rate as the white population. Even so, infant mortality among slaves was more than double that of the white population; for every 1000 live births among southern slaves, more than 200 died before the age of 5. For those who survived infancy, enslaved African Americans had a life expectancy about 8 years less than that of white Americans. As late as 1860, fewer than two-thirds of slave children survived to the age of 10.

Lower life expectancy

Resistance

Given the wide gulf between freedom and slavery, it was only natural that slaves resisted the bondage imposed on them. Unlike Latin America, slave revolts were rare in the southern United States, where whites outnumbered blacks, the government was more powerful, a majority of slaves were native-born, and family life was stronger. Slaves recognized the odds against them, and many potential leaders became fugitives instead. What is remarkable is that American slaves revolted at all.

Infrequency of revolts

Early in the nineteenth century several well-organized uprisings were barely thwarted. In 1800 Gabriel Prosser, a slave blacksmith, recruited perhaps a couple hundred slaves in a plan to march on Richmond and capture the governor. But a few slaves betrayed the plot, and Prosser and other leaders were eventually captured and executed. Denmark Vesey's conspiracy in Charleston in 1822 met a similar fate (page 287).

The most famous slave revolt, led by a literate slave preacher named Nat Turner, was more spontaneous. Turner, who lived on a farm in southeastern Virginia, was given unusual privileges by his master, whom he described as a kind and trusting man. A religious mystic, Turner became convinced that God had selected him to punish white

Nat Turner's rebellion

people through "terror and devastation." One night in 1831 following an eclipse of the sun, he and six confederates stole out and murdered Turner's master and family. Recruiting some 70 slaves as they went, Turner's band killed 57 white men, women, and children.

The revolt lasted only 48 hours before being crushed. Turner was eventually captured, tried, and executed. While the uprising was quickly put down, it left white southerners with a haunting uneasiness. Turner seemed a model slave, yet who could read the true emotions behind the mask of obedience?

Few slaves followed Turner's violent example. But there were other, more subtle ways of resisting a master's authority. Most dramatically, they could do as

Day-to-day resistance

Octave Johnson did and run away. With the odds stacked heavily against them, few runaways escaped safely to freedom except from the border states. More frequently, slaves fled to nearby woods or swamps. Some runaways stayed out only a few days; others, like Johnson, held out for months.

Many slaves resisted by abusing their masters' property. They mishandled animals, broke tools and machinery, misplaced items, and worked carelessly in the fields. Slaves also sought to trick the master by feigning illness or injury and by hiding rocks in the cotton they picked. Slaves complained directly to the owner about an overseer's mistreatment, thereby attempting to drive a wedge between the two.

The most common form of resistance, and a persistent annoyance to slave-owners, was theft. Slaves raided the master's smokehouse, secretly slaughtered his stock, and killed his poultry. Slaves often distinguished between "stealing" from each other and merely "taking" from white masters. "Dey allus done tell us it am wrong to lie and steal," recalled Josephine Howard, a former slave in Texas, "but why did de white folks steal my mammy and her mammy? Dey lives . . . over in Africy. . . . Dat de sinfulles' stealin' dey is."

Slaves learned to outwit their masters, one former bondsman testified, by wearing an "impenetrable mask" around whites. "How much of joy, of sorrow,

Slaves' hidden feelings

of misery and anguish have they hidden from their tormentors." Frederick Douglass, the most famous fugitive slave, explained that "as the master studies to keep the slave ignorant, the slave is cunning enough to make the master think he succeeds."

SLAVE CULTURE

Trapped in bondage, slaves could at least forge a culture of their own by combining strands from their African past with customs that evolved from their life in America. This slave culture was most distinct on big plantations, where the large slave population lived farther apart from white scrutiny.

The Slave Family

Maintaining a sense of family was one of the most remarkable achievements of African Americans in bondage, given the obstacles that faced them. Southern law did not recognize slave marriages as legally binding, nor did it allow slave parents complete authority over their children. Black women faced the possibility of rape by the master or overseer without legal recourse, and husbands, wives, and children had to live with the fear of being sold and separated. From 1820 to 1860 more than 2 million slaves were sold in the interstate slave trade. Perhaps 600,000 husbands and wives were separated by such sales.

Breakup of families

Still, family ties remained strong, as slave culture demonstrated. The marriage ceremony among slaves varied from a formal religious service to jumping over the broomstick in front of the slave community to nothing more than the master's giving verbal approval. Whatever the ceremony, slaves viewed the ritual as a public affirmation of the couple's commitment to their new duties and responsibilities. Rather than adopting white norms, slaves developed their own moral code concerning sexual relations and marriage. Although young slaves often engaged in premarital sex, they were expected to choose a partner and become part of a stable family. It has been estimated that at least one in five slave women had one or more children before marriage, but most of these mothers eventually married. "The negroes had their own ideas of morality, and they held them very strictly," the

Family ties in slavery

Slaves who have been sold are being loaded into boxcars to be transported from Richmond to plantations farther south. As they say their final sad goodbyes to family and friends, a slave trader completes his business.

An Enslaved Woman Picks a Husband

My first husband . . . nice man; . . . den he sold off to Florida—neber hear from him 'gain. . . . Den I sold up here—now hab 'noder husband. . . .

Massa he want me to breed; so he say, "Violet, you must take some nigger here. . . ."

Den I say, "No, Massa, I can't take any here." Den he say, . . . "Plenty young fellers here;" but I say, "I can't hab any ob dem." Well den . . . he go down Virginia, and he bring up two niggers—and . . . Missis say, "One ob dem's for you Violet;" but I say, "No, Missis, I can't take one ob dem, 'cause I don't lub 'em. . . ." Well, den, by-and-by, Massa he buy tree more, and den Missis say, "Now, Violet, ones dem is for you." I say "I do' know—maybe I can't lub one dem neider;" but she say "You must hab one ob dese." Well, so Sam and I we lib along two year—he watchin my ways and I watchin his ways.

At last, one night, we was standin' by de wood-pile togeder, and de moon bery shine, and I do' know how 'twas, . . . he answer me, he want a wife, but he didn't know where he get one. I say, "Plenty girls in G." He say, "Yes—but maybe I shan't find any I like so well as you." Den I say maybe he wouldn't like my ways, 'cause I'se an ole woman, and I hab four children by my first husband; and anybody marry me must be jest [as] kind to dem children as dey was to me, else I couldn't lub him. . . . Well, so we went on from one ting to anoder, till at last we say we'd take one anoder, and so we've libed togeder eber since—and I's had four children by him—and he never slip away from me nor I from him. . . .

We jest takes one anoder—we asks de white folks' leave, and den takes one anoder. Some folks dey's married by de book; but den, what's de use? Dere's my fus husband, we'se married by de book, and he sold way off to Florida, and I's here. Dey . . . do what dey please wid us, . . . so [long as] we jest makes money for dem.

Harriet Beecher Stowe, *Key to Uncle Tom's Cabin* (Boston: J. P. Jewett, 1853), 299–301.

daughter of a Georgia planter recalled. "They did not consider it wrong for a girl to have a child before she married, but afterwards were very strict upon anything like infidelity on her part."

The traditional nuclear family of father, mother, and children was the rule, not the exception, among slaves. Labor in the quarters was divided according

Gender roles to sex. Women did the indoor work such as cooking, washing, and sewing, and men performed outdoor chores, such as gathering firewood, hauling water, and tending the animals and garden plots. The men also hunted and fished to supplement the spare weekly rations. "My old daddy . . . caught rabbits, coons an' possums," recalled Louisa Adams of North Carolina. "He would work all day and hunt at night."

Songs and Stories of Protest and Celebration

In the songs they sang, slaves expressed some of their deepest feelings about life. "The songs of the slave represent the sorrows of his heart," commented Frederick Douglass. Surely there was bitterness as well as sorrow when slaves sang:

> We raise the wheat
> They give us the corn
> We bake the bread
> They give us the crust
> We sift the meal
> They give us the husk
> We peel the meat
> They give us the skin
> And that's the way
> They take us in

Lewis Miller of York, Pennsylvania, painted this picture of Virginia slaves dancing in 1853. Dancing and music were important components of slave culture and provided a welcome respite from work under slavery.

Yet songs were also central to the celebrations held in the slave quarters: for marriages, Christmas revels, and after harvest time. And a slave on the way to the fields might sing:

> Saturday night and Sunday too
> Young gals on my mind.
> Monday morning 'way 'fore day,
> Old master's got me gwine.
> Peggy does you love me now?

Slaves expressed themselves through stories as well as song. Most often these folk tales used animals as symbolic models for the predicaments in which slaves

Folk tales

found themselves. In the best known of these, the cunning Brer Rabbit was a weak fellow who defeated larger animals like Brer Fox and Brer Bear by using his wits. Other stories were less symbolic and contained more overt hostility toward white people. These stories, whether direct or symbolic, taught the young how to survive in a hostile world.

The Lord Calls Us Home

At the center of slave culture was religion. Slaveowners encouraged a carefully controlled form of religion among slaves. "Church was what they called it," one former slave protested, "but all that preacher talked about was for us slaves to obey our masters and not to lie and steal. Nothing about Jesus was ever said and the overseer stood there to see that the preacher talked as he wanted him to talk." In response, some slaves rejected all religion.

Most slaves, however, sought a Christianity firmly their own, beyond the control of the master. On many plantations they met secretly at night, when

Slave religion

they broke into rhythmic singing and dancing, modeled on the ring shout of African religion. "The way in which we worshiped is almost indescribable," one slave preacher recalled. "The singing was accompanied by a certain ecstasy of motion, clapping of hands, tossing of heads, which would continue without cessation about half an hour." In an environment where slaves, for most of the day, were prevented from expressing their deepest feelings, such meetings served as a satisfying emotional release.

Religion also provided slaves with values to guide them through their daily experiences and give them a sense of self-worth. Slaves learned that God would redeem the poor and downtrodden and raise them one day to honor and glory. Just as certainly, on the final Day of Judgment, masters would be punished for their sins. "This is one reason why I believe in hell," a former slave declared. "I don't believe a just God is going to take no such man as my former master into His Kingdom."

Again, song played a central role. Slaves sang religious "spirituals" at work and at play as well as in religious services. Seemingly meek and otherworldly,

Slave spirituals the songs often contained a hidden element of protest. Frederick Douglass disclosed that when slaves sang longingly of "Canaan, sweet Canaan," they were thinking not only of the Bible's Promised Land but of the North and freedom. While a song's lyrics might speak of an otherworldly freedom from sin in heaven, their hearts were considering a this-worldly escape from physical bondage.

Religion, then, served not only to comfort slaves after days of toil and sorrow. It also strengthened the sense of togetherness and common purpose and held out the promise of eventual freedom in this world and the next. The faith that "some ob dese days my time will come" was one of the most important ways that slaves coped with bondage and resisted its pressure to rob them of their self-esteem.

COUNTERPOINT   *The Role of Regligion in the Lives of Slaves*

Modern studies of slavery recognize that religion was one of the most crucial components of slave culture. Historians have disagreed, however, over the role those religious beliefs played. Some historians have argued that slaves took the evangelical religion of whites and adapted it, creating in essence a new version of Christianity that strongly reflected their African heritage. The role of communal singing and dancing in slave services represented a continuation of African forms. The African view that gods spoke to individuals by possessing their spirits was akin to the conversion experience in evangelical churches, and the African concept of a creator god was easily adapted to the Christian concept of an all-powerful deity. This interpretation of slave religion places primary emphasis on independent black services in the quarters and secret ones held in the woods. In this view, religion helped create a distinctive African American culture, nurtured racial self-esteem, and weakened the forces of accommodation within slavery.

Other historians emphasize that the religious experience of most enslaved African Americans occurred within the regular white-controlled churches of the South. It has been estimated that one million slaves were included in the southern churches before the Civil War. Black worshipers were especially numerous in the Methodist and Baptist churches; indeed, in some areas, slaves were a majority in local congregations. As a result, most slaves worshiped together with their masters rather than in separate services. At one point during the regular service ministers delivered a special message to the slaves who were present, but they also heard the same sermon as whites, with its emphasis on faith and salvation. According to this view, secret services in the quarters and elsewhere were an extension of regular worship, not an alternative. Thus they did not provide a fundamentally different message. "The church," one historian concludes, "was the single most important institution in the 'Americanization' of the bondsman."

The Slave Community

While slaves managed to preserve a sense of self-worth in a culture of their own, they found it impossible to escape fully from white control. Even the social hierarchy within the slave quarters never was entirely free from the white world. The prestige of a slave driver rested ultimately on the authority of the white master, and skilled slaves and house servants often felt superior to other slaves,

Hierarchy of color

an attitude masters consciously promoted. Light-skinned slaves sometimes deemed their color a badge of superiority. Fanny Kemble recorded that one woman begged to be relieved of field labor, which she considered degrading, "on *'account of her color.'* "

The daughter of a driver who had been educated by her mistress, Lucy Skipwith was a member of the slave elite. At Hopewell plantation in Alabama, she was in full charge of the main residence during her master's frequent absences. Eager for her master's approval, Skipwith on several occasions reported slave disobedience, which temporarily estranged her from the slave community, yet in the end she was always welcomed back. While Skipwith never rebelled or apparently considered running away, she was far from submissive. She defined white authority, protected her family, and used her influence to get rid of an overseer the slaves disliked. Like many house servants, she lived between two worlds—her master's and the slave quarters—and was never entirely comfortable in either.

Despite these divisions, the realities of slavery and white racism inevitably drove black people closer together in a common bond and forced them to depend on one another to survive. Walled in from the individualistic white society beyond, slaves out of necessity created a community of their own.

Free Black Southerners

Of the 4 million African Americans living in the South in 1860, only 260,000—about 7 percent—were free. More than 85 percent of them lived in the Upper South, with almost 200,000 in Maryland, Virginia, and North Carolina alone. Free black southerners were also much more urban than either the southern white or slave populations. In 1860 almost a third of the free African Americans in the Upper South, and more than half in the Lower South, lived in towns and cities. As a rule, free African Americans were more literate than slaves, and they were disproportionately female and much more likely to be of mixed ancestry.

Most free black southerners lived in rural areas, although usually not near plantations. A majority eked out a living farming or in low-paying unskilled jobs, but some did well enough to own slaves themselves. In 1830 about 3600 did, although commonly their "property" was their wives or children, purchased because they could not be emancipated under state laws. A few, however, were full-blown slaveowners.

Following Nat Turner's rebellion of 1831, southern legislatures increased the restrictions on free African Americans. They were forbidden to enter a new

Tightening control

state, had to carry their free papers, could not assemble when they wished, were subject to a curfew, often had to post a bond and be licensed to work, and could not vote, hold office, or testify in court against white people.

Lighter-skinned black southerners who were free, like their counterparts in the North, tended to set themselves apart from darker-skinned African Americans, free or slave, yet they were never accepted in the white world. Free African Americans occupied an uncertain position in southern society, well above black slaves but distinctly beneath even poorer white southerners. They were victims of a society that had no place for them.

SOUTHERN SOCIETY AND THE DEFENSE OF SLAVERY

While the South was a remarkably diverse region, it was united above all by the institution of slavery. As the South's economy became more and more dependent on slave-produced staples, slavery became more central to the life of the South, to its culture and its identity.

The Virginia Debate of 1832

At the time of the Revolution, the leading critics of slavery had been southerners—Jefferson, Washington, Madison, and Patrick Henry among them. But beginning in the 1820s, in the wake of the controversy over admitting Missouri as a slave state, southern leaders became less apologetic about slavery and more aggressive in defending it. The turning point occurred in the early 1830s, when the South found itself increasingly under attack. It was in 1831 that William Lloyd Garrison began publishing his abolitionist newspaper, *The Liberator*. That was also the year Nat Turner led his revolt, which frightened so many white southerners.

In response to the Turner insurrection, a number of Virginia's western counties, where there were few slaves, petitioned the legislature to adopt a program for gradual emancipation. In the end, however, the legislature refused, by a vote of 73 to 58, to consider legislation to end slavery.

The 1832 Virginia debate represented the last significant attempt of white southerners to take action against slavery. Most felt that the subject was no

Significance of the Virginia debate

longer open to debate. Instead, during the 1830s and 1840s, southern leaders defended slavery as a positive good, not just for white but for black people as well. As John C. Calhoun proclaimed in 1837, "I hold that in the present state of civilization, where two races . . . distinguished by color and other physical differences, as well as intellectual, are brought together, the relation now existing in the slave-holding states between the two is, instead of an evil, a good—a positive good."

The Proslavery Argument

Politicians like Calhoun were not alone. White southern leaders justified slavery in a variety of ways. Ministers argued that under the law of Moses, Jews were authorized to enslave heathens, and emphasized that none of the Biblical prophets nor Christ himself had ever condemned slavery. Defenders of the institution also pointed out that classical Greece and Rome depended on slavery. They even cited John Locke, that giant of the Enlightenment, who had recognized slavery in the constitution he drafted for the colony of Carolina. African Americans belonged to an intellectually and emotionally inferior race, slavery's defenders argued, and therefore lacked the ability to care for themselves.

Religious, racial, and social arguments

Proslavery writers sometimes argued that slaves in the South lived better than factory workers in the North. Masters cared for slaves for life, whereas northern workers had no claim on their employer when they were unemployed, old, or no longer able to work. In advancing this argument, white southerners exaggerated the material comforts of slavery and minimized the average worker's standard of living—to say nothing, of course, about the incalculable psychological value of freedom. Still, to many white southerners, slavery seemed a more humane system of labor relations.

Defenders of slavery did not really expect to convert Northerners. Their target was more often slaveowners themselves. As Duff Green, a southern editor, explained, "We must satisfy the consciences, we must allay the fears of our own people. We must satisfy them that slavery is of itself right—that it is not a sin against God—that it is not an evil, moral or political. In this way only," he went on, "can we prepare our own people to defend their institutions."

Closing Ranks

Not all white southerners could quell their doubts. Still, a striking change in southern opinion seems to have occurred in the three decades before the Civil War. Outside the border states, few white southerners after 1840 would admit even in private that slavery was wrong. And those who continued to oppose slavery found themselves harassed, assaulted, and driven into exile. Southern mobs destroyed the presses of antislavery papers and threatened the editors into either keeping silent or leaving the state. Southern mails were forcibly closed to abolitionist propaganda, and defenders of the South's institutions carefully scrutinized textbooks and faculty members in southern schools. Southerners like

James Birney and Sarah and Angelina Grimké had to leave their native region to carry on the fight against slavery from the free states.

Increasingly, too, slavery entered the national political debate. Before 1836 Andrew Jackson's popularity in the South blocked the formation of a competi-

Politics of slavery

tive two-party system. The rise of the abolitionist movement in the 1830s, however, left many southerners uneasy, and when the Democrats nominated the northerner Martin Van Buren in 1836, southern Whigs charged that Van Buren could not be counted on to meet the abolitionist threat to slavery. The Whigs made impressive gains in the South in 1836, carrying several states and significantly narrowing the margin between the two parties.

In later presidential elections, each party in the South attacked the opposing party through its northern supporters as unreliable on slavery. This tactic was less successful in state elections, however, since both parties were led by slaveholders and were committed to protecting slavery. In addition, the depression that began in 1837 focused the attention of southern voters on economic

Economics and party affiliation

matters. Southern Whigs appealed to the commercially oriented members of society, whereas the Democratic party's strongholds were the more isolated regions of small independent farmers. As in the North, class and occupation were less important than one's economic and moral outlook. Southern voters most comfortable with the market and the changes it brought gravitated toward the Whig party. On the other hand, those farmers who feared the loss of personal independence that banks and commercial development brought with them tended to support the Democratic party.

During the Jacksonian era, most southern political battles did not revolve around slavery. Still, southern politicians in both parties had to be careful to avoid the stigma of antislavery, since they were under mounting pressure from John Calhoun and his followers. Frustrated in his presidential hopes by the nullification crisis, Calhoun sought to unite the South behind his leadership by agitating the slavery issue. Few southern politicians followed his lead after 1833, but they did become extremely careful about being the least bit critical of slavery or southern institutions. They knew quite well that, even if their constituents were not so fanatical as Calhoun, southern voters overwhelmingly supported slavery.

Sections and the Nation

Viewing the events of the 1830s and 1840s with the benefit of hindsight, it is natural to anticipate the Civil War looming and to focus on the major differences dividing the North and the South. Yet free white northerners and southerners had much in common as Americans.

The largest group in both sections was composed of independent farmers who cultivated their own land with their own labor and were devoted to the principles of personal independence and social egalitarianism. Although south-

Forces of national unity ern society was more aristocratic in tone, both sections were driven by the quest for material wealth. The Texas Red River planter for whom "time was money" did not take a back seat to the Yankee clockmaker Chauncey Jerome in the scramble for success and status. White Americans in both sections aspired to rise in society, and linking geographic mobility to opportunity, they pushed westward with astonishing frequency.

Many Americans, North and South, also adhered to the teachings of evangelical Protestantism. Southern churches were less open to social reform, primarily because of its association with abolitionism, and southern churches, unlike most in the North, defended slavery as a Christian institution. Eventually both the Methodist and the Baptist churches split into separate northern and southern organizations over this issue, but their attitudes on other matters often coincided.

Finally, white northerners and southerners shared a belief in democracy and white equality. Southern as well as northern states embraced the democratic reforms of the 1820s and 1830s, and the electorate in both sections favored giving all white males the vote and making public officeholders responsible to the people. Southerners insisted that the equality proclaimed in the Declaration of Independence applied only to white Americans (and really only to white males), but the vast majority of northerners in practice took no exception to this attitude. Both sections agreed on the necessity of safeguarding equality of opportunity rather than promoting equality of wealth.

With so much in common, it was not inevitable that the two sections come to blows. Certainly, before 1840 few politicians believed that the differences between the two sections were unreconcilable. It was only in the mid-1840s, when the United States embarked on a new program of westward expansion, that the slavery issue began to loom ominously in American life, and Americans began to question whether the Union could permanently endure, half slave and half free.

SIGNIFICANT EVENTS

1800	Gabriel's rebellion
1815–1860	Spread of the cotton kingdom
1822	Denmark Vesey conspiracy
1830–1840	Proslavery argument developed
1830–1860	Agricultural reform movement in Upper South
1831	Nat Turner's rebellion
1832	Virginia debate on slavery
1844	Methodist church divides into northern and southern organizations
1845	Baptist church divides

CHAPTER FOURTEEN

Western Expansion and the Rise of the Slavery Issue

At first the Crows, Arapahos, and other Indians of the Great Plains paid little attention to the new people moving out from the forests far to the east. After all, for as long as they could remember, nations like the Crow had called the plains their own. But the new arrivals were not to be taken lightly. Armed with superior weapons and bringing a great many women and children with them, their appetite for land seemed inexhaustible. They attacked the villages of the Plains Indians, massacred women and children, and forced defeated tribes to live on reservations and serve their economic interests. In little more than a century and a half—from the first days when only a handful of their hunters and trappers had come into the region—they had become the masters of the plains.

The invaders who established this political and military dominance were *not* the strange "white men," who also came from the forest. During the 1830s and early 1840s, whites were still few in number. The more dangerous people—the ones who truly worried the Plains tribes—were the Sioux.

Westward expansion is usually told as a one-dimensional tale, centering on the wagon trains pressing on toward the Pacific. But frontiers, after all, are the

Cultural interaction

boundary lines between contrasting cultures or environments; and during the nineteenth century, those in the West were constantly shifting and adapting. Frontier lines moved not only east to west, as with the white and Sioux migrations, but also south to north, as Spanish culture diffused, and west to east, as Asian immigrants came to California. Furthermore, frontiers marked not only human but also animal boundaries. Horses, cattle, and pigs, all of which had been imported from Europe, moved across the continent, usually in advance of European settlers. Often they transformed the way Indian peoples lived. Frontiers could also be technological, as in the case of trade goods and firearms. Moreover, as we have already seen, disease moved across the continent, with disastrous consequences for natives who had not acquired immunity to European microorganisms.

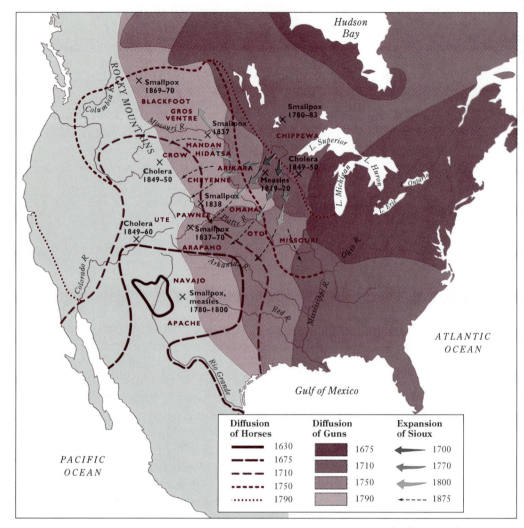

SIOUX EXPANSION AND THE HORSE AND GUN FRONTIER   In 1710 the horse and gun frontiers had not yet crossed, but by 1750 the two waves began to overlap. The Sioux pushed west during the early eighteenth century thanks to firearms; they were checked from further expansion until the 1770s, when smallpox epidemics again turned the balance in their favor.

Three frontiers altered the lives of the Sioux: those of the horse, the gun, and disease. The horse frontier spread ahead of white settlement from the southwest, where horses had first been imported by the Spanish.

Horse, gun, and disease frontiers

On the other hand, the Spanish, unlike English and French traders, refused to sell firearms to Indians, so the gun frontier moved in the opposite direction, from northeast to southwest. The two waves met and crossed along the upper Missouri during the first half of the eighteenth century. For the tribes that possessed them, horses and guns conferred advantages in hunting and fighting.

The Sioux were first lured from the forest onto the Minnesota prairie during the early 1700s to hunt beaver, whose pelts could be exchanged with white traders for manufactured goods. Having obtained guns in exchange for furs, the Sioux drove the Omahas, Otos, Cheyennes, and Missouris (who had not yet acquired guns) south and west. But by the 1770s their advantage in guns had disappeared, and any farther advance was blocked by powerful tribes like the Mandans and Arikaras. These peoples were primarily horticultural, raising corn, beans, and squash and living in well-fortified towns. They also owned more horses than the Sioux, which made it easier for them to resist attacks.

But the third frontier, disease, threw the balance of power toward the Sioux after 1779. European traders brought smallpox with them onto the prairie. The horticultural tribes were hit especially hard because they lived in densely populated villages, where epidemics spread more easily. The Sioux embarked on a second wave of westward expansion in the late eighteenth century, so that by the time Lewis and Clark came through in 1804, they firmly controlled the upper Missouri as far as the Yellowstone River.

The Sioux's nomadic life enabled them to avoid the worst ravages of disease, especially the smallpox epidemic of 1837, which reduced the plains population by as much as half. Indeed, the Sioux became the largest (and most powerful) tribe on the plains. Certainly they were the only one whose high birthrate approximated that of whites. From an estimated 5000 in 1804, they grew to 25,000 by the 1850s. Their numbers increased Sioux military power as well as the need for new hunting grounds, and during the first half of the nineteenth century, they pushed even farther up the Missouri.

These shifting frontiers of animals, disease, firearms, and trade goods disrupted the political and cultural life of the Great Plains. And as white Americans moved westward, their own frontier lines produced similar disruptions, not only between white settlers and Indians but also between Anglo-American and Hispanic cultures.

Ironically, perhaps the greatest instability created by the moving frontiers occurred in established American society. As the political system of the United States struggled to incorporate western territories, North and South engaged in a fierce debate over whether the new lands should become slave or free. Just as the Sioux's cultural identity was brought into question by the moving frontier, so too was the identity of the American Republic.

DESTINIES: MANIFEST AND OTHERWISE

"Make way . . . for the young American Buffalo—he has not yet got land enough," roared one American politician in 1844. In the space of a few years, the United States acquired Texas, California, the lower half of the Oregon Territory, and the lands between the Rockies and California: nearly 1.5 million square miles in all.

John L. O'Sullivan, a prominent Democratic editor in New York, struck a responsive chord when he declared that it had become the United States's "manifest destiny to overspread the continent allotted by Providence for the free development of our yearly multiplying millions." The cry of "Manifest Destiny" soon echoed in other editorial pages and in the halls of Congress.

The Roots of Manifest Destiny

Many Americans had long believed that their country had a special, even divine mission, which could be traced back to the Puritans' attempt to build a "city on a hill." Manifest Destiny also contained a political compo-

Religious and political components

nent, inherited from the ideology of the Revolution. In the mid-nineteenth century, Americans spoke of extending democracy, with widespread suffrage among white males, no king or aristocracy, and no established church, "over the whole North American continent."

Americans believed that their social and economic system, too, should spread around the globe. They pointed to its broad ownership of land, individualism, and free play of economic opportunity as superior features of American life. Of course, Manifest Destiny had its self-interested side. American business interests recognized the value of the fine harbors along the Pacific Coast, which promised a lucrative trade with Asia, and they hoped to make them American.

Finally, underlying the doctrine of Manifest Destiny was a persistent and deeply rooted racism. The United States had a duty to regenerate the backward

Racist aspects

peoples of America, declared politicians and propagandists. Their reference was not so much to Indians—who refused to assimilate into American society—but to Mexicans, whose Christian nation had its roots in European culture. The Mexican race "must amalgamate and be lost, in the superior vigor of the Anglo-Saxon race," proclaimed O'Sullivan's *Democratic Review*, "or they must utterly perish."

Before 1845 most Americans assumed that expansion would be achieved peacefully. When the time was right, neighboring provinces, like ripe fruit, would fall naturally into American hands. Texas, New Mexico, Oregon, and California—areas that were sparsely populated and weakly defended—dominated the American expansionist imagination. With time, Americans became less willing to wait patiently for the fruit to fall.

The Mexican Borderlands

The heart of Spain's American empire was Mexico City, where spacious boulevards spread out through the center of the city and the University of Mexico, the oldest university in North America, had been accepting students since 1553, a full 85 years longer than Harvard. From the Mexican point of view, the frontier was 1000 miles to the north, in the provinces of Texas, New Mexico, and California. These isolated provinces developed largely free from supervision.

Although most Indians worked both on Spanish missions and on *ranchos* in conditions of near slavery, Indians were encouraged to adopt Spanish religion and customs. This Indian choir at Mission San Buenaventura sang in the mass. The Indians often made their own instruments, including flutes, drums, guitars, and triangles.

When Mexico won its independence from Spain in 1821, California at first was little affected. But in 1833 the Mexican Congress stripped the Catholic church of its huge tracts of California lands. These were turned over to Mexican cattle ranchers, usually in massive grants of 50,000 acres or more. The new *rancheros* ruled their estates much like great planters of the Old South. Labor was provided by Indians, who were forced to work for little more than room and board. At this time the Mexican population of California was approximately 4000. Lured by the cattle hide trade, a few Yankees settled in California as well, but in 1845 the American population amounted to only 700.

Spanish settlement of New Mexico was more dense: the province had about 44,000 inhabitants in 1827. But like California, its society was dominated by

Society in New Mexico

ranchero families who grazed large herds of sheep along the upper Rio Grande valley between El Paso and Taos. A few individuals controlled most of the wealth, while their workers eked out a meager living. Spain had long outlawed any commerce with Americans, but after Mexico declared its independence in 1821, yearly caravans from the United States began rolling into Santa Fe. While this trade flourished over the next two decades, developments in the third Mexican borderland, neighboring Texas, worsened relations between Mexico and the United States.

The Texas Revolution

The new government in Mexico encouraged American emigration to Texas, where only about 3000 Mexicans, mostly ranchers, lived. Stephen Austin, who established a thriving colony on land granted by the goverment, was only the first of a new wave of American land agents, or *empresarios*. These *empresarios* obtained permission from Mexican authorities to settle families in Texas. Ninety percent of the new arrivals came from the South. Some, intending to grow cotton, brought slaves with them.

Tensions between Mexicans and American immigrants grew with the Texas economy. Most settlers from the States were Protestant, and although the Mexican government did not enforce its law that all citizens become Catholic, it barred Protestant churches. In 1829 Mexico abolished slavery, then looked the other way when Texas slaveholders evaded the law. But Texans were most disturbed because they had little say in their government, whose legislature lay about 700 miles to the south.

Cultural conflict in Texas

During the early 1830s the Mexican government made sporadic attempts to stop the influx of Americans. But immigration continued, until by mid-decade the American white population of 30,000 was nearly 10 times the number of Mexicans in the territory. Mexico also seemed determined to enforce the abolition of slavery. Even more disturbing to the American newcomers, in 1834 General Antonio Lopez de Santa Anna dissolved the Mexican Congress, proclaimed himself dictator, and led a military expedition north to enforce his new regime. When a ragtag Texas army clashed with the advance guard of Santa Anna's troops, a full-scale revolution was under way.

The Republic of Texas

As Santa Anna massed his forces for a decisive attack, a provisional government on March 2, 1836, proclaimed Texan independence. The constitution of the new Republic of Texas borrowed heavily from the U.S. Constitution, except that it explicitly prohibited the new Texas Congress from interfering with slavery. Meanwhile, Santa Anna's troops overran a Texan garrison at an old mission in San Antonio, known as the Alamo, and killed all of its 187 defenders. The Mexicans, however, paid dearly for the victory, losing more than 1500 men. The massacre of another force at Goliad after it surrendered further inflamed American resistance.

But anger was one thing; organized resistance was another. The commander of the Texas forces was Sam Houston, a former governor of Tennessee. Houston's intellectual ability and talent as a stump speaker thrust him to the forefront of the Texas independence movement. Houston knew his army needed seasoning, so he retreated steadily eastward, buying time in order to forge a disciplined fighting force. By late April he was ready. Reinforced by eager volunteers from the United States,

Houston defeats the Mexican army

Houston's men surprised the Mexican army camped along the San Jacinto River. Shouting "Remember the Alamo!" they took only 15 minutes to overwhelm the Mexicans (who had been enjoying an afternoon siesta) and capture Santa Anna.

Threatened with execution, the Mexican commander signed treaties recognizing Texan independence and establishing the Rio Grande as the southern boundary of the Texas republic. The Mexican Congress (which had been reestablished in 1835) repudiated this agreement and launched several unsuccessful invasions into Texas. In the meantime, Houston assumed office in October 1836 as the first president of the new republic, determined to bring Texas into the Union as quickly as possible.

But Andrew Jackson worried that such a step would revive sectional tensions and hurt Martin Van Buren in the 1836 presidential election. Only on his last day in office did he extend formal diplomatic recognition to the Texas Republic. Van Buren was soon distracted by the economic panic that began shortly after he entered office and took no action during his term.

Rebuffed, Texans decided to go their own way. In the 10 years following independence, the "Lone Star" republic attracted more than 100,000 immigrants *Texas as an independent republic* by offering free land to settlers. Mexico, however, refused to recognize Texan independence, and the vast majority of Texas citizens still wished to join the United States, where most of them, after all, had been born. There matters stood when the Whigs and William Henry Harrison won the presidency in 1840.

THE TREK WEST

As thousands of Americans were moving into Texas, a much smaller trickle headed toward the Oregon country. Since 1818 the United States and Great Britain had occupied that territory jointly, as far north as latitude 54°40'. Although white settlement remained sparse, by 1836 American settlers outnumbered the British in the Willamette valley.

Pushed by the Panic of 1837 and six years of depression and pulled by tales of Oregon's lush, fertile valleys and the frost-free climate along California's Sacramento River, many American farmers struck out for the West Coast. The wife of one Missouri farmer was adamant about heading west: "Well, Dan Waldo," she announced, "if you want to stay here another summer and shake your liver out with the fever and ague, you can do it; but in the spring I am going to take the children and go to Oregon, Indians or no Indians." The wagon trains began rolling west.

The Overland Trail

Only a few hundred emigrants reached the West in 1841 and 1842, but in 1843 more than 800 followed the Overland Trail across the mountains to Oregon. *Families migrate* From then on, they came by the thousands. The migration was primarily a family enterprise, and many couples had only re-

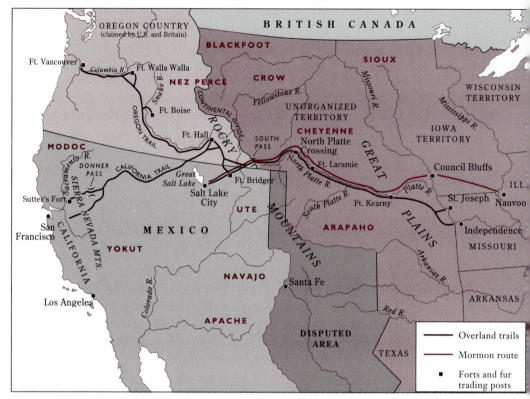

THE OVERLAND TRAIL   Beginning at several different points, the Overland Trail followed the Platte and Sweetwater rivers across the plains to South Pass, where it crossed the Continental Divide. The trail split near Fort Hall. Between 1840 and 1860 more than a quarter of a million emigrants made the trek.

cently married. Most adults were between 20 and 50, since the hard journey discouraged the elderly. Furthermore, a family of four needed about $600 to outfit their journey, an amount that excluded the poor.

Caravans of 20 to 30 wagons were not uncommon the first few years, but after 1845 parties traveled in smaller trains of 8 to 10 wagons. Large companies used up the grass quickly, disagreements were more likely, and breakdowns (and hence halts) were more frequent. The trip itself lasted about 6 months.

The journey west placed a special strain on women, for the rugged life along the trail disrupted their traditional sense of the home. At first, parties di-

Women on the Overland Trail

vided work by gender, as had been done back home. Women cooked, washed, sewed, and took care of the children, while men drove the wagons, cared for the stock, stood guard, and did the heavy labor. Within a few weeks, however, women found themselves under the force of necessity helping to repair wagons, construct bridges, stand guard, and drive the oxen. The change in work assignments proceeded only in one direction, however, for few men did "women's work."

The extra labor did not bring women new authority or power within the family. Nor, by and large, did they seek it. Women resisted efforts to blur the division between male and female work and struggled to preserve their traditional role and image. Quarrels over work assignments often brought into the open long-simmering family tensions. One woman reported that there was "not a little fighting" in their company, which was "invariably the outcome of disputes over divisions of labor." The conflicting pressures a woman might feel were well illustrated by Mary Ellen Todd, a teenaged daughter who learned the male skill of cracking the bullwhip despite her mother's disapproval. "While I felt a secret joy," she recalled, "in being able to have a power that set things going, there was also a sense of shame over this new accomplishment."

As women strove to maintain a semblance of home on the trail, they often experienced a profound sense of loss. Trains often traveled on the Sabbath,

Women's sense of loss

which had been an emblem of women's moral authority back home. Women also felt the lack of close companions to whom they could turn for comfort. One woman, whose husband separated from the train after a dispute, sadly watched the other wagons pull away: "I felt that indeed I had left all my friends to journey over the dreaded plains without one female acquaintance even for a companion—of course I wept and grieved about it but to no purpose."

Women on the trail complained, as one put it, that "we had left all civilization behind us." Civilization to women meant more than law, government, and schools; it also meant their homes and domestic mission. Once settled in the West, they strove to reestablish that order.

COUNTERPOINT   *Women in the West*

For many years historians, caught up in the trailblazing heroics of "frontiersmen," gave little attention to women in the West. But except for the mining frontier, white migration westward was largely a family process. Yet even as historians have come to recognize that women were central to western history, they continue to disagree about the effect of the western experience on white women.

Some historians have argued that women enjoyed greater freedom and status in the West. They see western women as crucial to the family economy in a way they no longer were in the industrializing market economy of the East. Thus women's wages were higher in the West, where labor was scarce and women were a minority. To a much greater extent, western schoolteachers were women; a surprising number ended up making teaching a career. Far from helpless or passive, women actually accepted frontier challenges, were economic partners with their husbands, refused to surrender their domestic mission, and took pride in their achievements. Some historians have gone on to argue that western women's greater opportunities and more equal status explain why divorce was more common in the West and why women gained political and legal rights more quickly there.

Other historians portray the impact of the western experience quite differently. Drawing on diaries women kept on the Overland Trail, they contend that the decision to migrate was almost always made by the husband and that wives often opposed the move. Moreover, many women who made the trek westward regretted going. These historians argue that the domestic work women performed was more akin to drudgery than liberating and no different from women's work in preindustrial society. They do not see western society according women greater power, and they emphasize that western women were equally subject to male dominance. "This is the Paradise of men," Martha Hitchcock wrote home in 1851. "I wonder if a paradise for poor *Women* will ever be discovered."

Indians and the Trail Experience

The nations whose lands were crossed by the wagon trains reacted in a number of ways. The Sioux were among the tribes who regularly traded with the over-

Pressures on the Plains Indians

landers. On the other hand, white migrants took a heavy toll on the Plains Indians' way of life: the emigrant parties scared off game and reduced buffalo herds, overgrazed the grass, and depleted the supply of wood. As a result, the Sioux demanded with varying success payment from the wagon trains crossing their lands. Finally in 1851 the U.S. government agreed to make an annual payment to various tribes as compensation for the damages caused by the emigrants.

Their fears aroused by sensational stories, overland parties were wary of Indians, but this menace was greatly exaggerated, especially on the plains. Few wagon trains were attacked by Indians, and more emigrants killed Indians than were killed by Indians. For overlanders the most aggravating problem posed by Indians was theft of stock. Many companies received valuable assistance from Indians, who acted as guides and directed them to grass and water.

THE POLITICAL ORIGINS OF EXPANSION

President William Henry Harrison made the gravest mistake of his brief presidential career when he ventured out one raw spring day, bareheaded and without an overcoat, to buy groceries at the Washington market. He caught pneumonia and died, only one month after his inauguration. For the first time in the nation's history, a vice president succeeded to the nation's highest office upon the death of the president.

John Tyler of Virginia had been a states' rights Democrat who left the Democratic party because of Jackson's opposition to nullification. Tyler eventually joined the Whigs, despite his strict construction principles, and in 1840 the Whig convention nominated him as Old Tip's running mate, in order to balance the ticket sectionally.

Tyler's Texas Ploy

Tyler's courteous manner and personal warmth masked a rigid, doctrinaire mind. Repeatedly, when Henry Clay and the Whigs in Congress passed a ma-

Tyler's break with the Whigs

jor bill, Tyler opposed it. After Tyler twice vetoed bills to charter a new national bank, disgusted congressional Whigs formally expelled the president from their party. Most Democrats, too, avoided him as an untrustworthy "renegade." In short, Tyler became a man without a party, his support limited to federal officeholders. Still, his intense ambition led him to believe he might win another four years in the White House if only he latched onto the right popular issue. That issue, his advisers convinced him, was the annexation of Texas.

That advice came mostly from Democrats disgruntled with Martin Van Buren, who had led the party to defeat in 1840. "They mean to throw Van overboard," reported one delighted Whig, who caught wind of the plans. Meanwhile Tyler's allies circulated rumors designed to frighten southerners into pushing for annexation. Britain was ready to offer Texas economic aid if it abolished slavery, they claimed. (The rumor was false.) In April 1844 Tyler sent to the Senate for ratification a treaty he had secretly negotiated to bring Texas into the Union.

Van Overboard

The front runners for the Whig and Democratic presidential nominations were Clay and Van Buren, moderates who feared the slavery issue. By prearrangement, both men issued letters opposing annexation on the grounds that it threatened the Union and would provoke war with Mexico.

As expected, the Whigs unanimously nominated Clay on a platform that ignored the expansion issue entirely. The Democrats, however, had a more diffi-

Polk's nomination

cult time. With Van Buren unable to get the two–thirds majority required to be nominated, the delegates finally turned to James K. Polk of Tennessee, who was pro-Texas, and approved an expansion platform calling for the annexation of Texas and the occupation of Oregon all the way to its northernmost boundary at 54°40′.

Angered by the convention's outcome, Van Buren's supporters in the Senate joined the Whigs in decisively defeating Tyler's treaty of annexation by a vote of 35 to 16. Tyler eventually withdrew from the race, but the Texas issue would not go away. Seeking to shore up his support in the South, Clay finally announced he would support Texas's annexation if it would not lead to war. And in the North, a few antislavery Whigs turned to James G. Birney, running on the Liberty party ticket.

In the end, Polk squeaked through by 38,000 votes out of nearly 3 million cast. If just half of Birney's 15,000 ballots in New York had gone to Clay, he would have carried the state and been narrowly elected president. Indignant Whigs charged that by refusing to support Clay, political abolitionists had made the annexation of Texas, and hence the addition of slave territory to the Union, inevitable. And indeed, in the atmosphere following Polk's election, Congress approved a joint resolution annexing Texas. On March 3, 1845, his last day in office, Tyler invited Texas to enter the Union.

To the Pacific

Humorless, calculating, and often deceitful, President Polk pursued his objectives with dogged determination. Embracing a continental vision of the United States, he not only endorsed Tyler's offer of annexation but looked beyond, hoping to gain the three best harbors on the Pacific: San Diego, San Francisco, and Puget Sound. That meant wresting lower Oregon from Britain and California from Mexico.

To put pressure on Great Britain, Polk induced Congress to terminate the joint occupation of Oregon. His blustering was reinforced by the knowledge

Compromise on Oregon

that American settlers in Oregon outnumbered the British 5000 to 750. On the other hand, Polk hardly wanted war with a nation as powerful as Great Britain. So when the British offered, in June 1846, to divide the Oregon Territory along the 49th parallel, he readily agreed (see map, page 375). The arrangement gave the United States Puget Sound, which had been the president's objective all along.

The Mexican War

The Oregon settlement left Polk free to deal with Mexico. In 1845 Congress admitted Texas to the Union as a slave state, but Mexico had never formally rec-

Disputed boundary of Texas

ognized Texas's independence. It insisted, moreover, that its southern boundary was the Nueces River, not the Rio Grande, 130 miles to the south, as claimed by Texas. In reality, Texas had never controlled the disputed region, but Polk, already looking toward the Pacific, supported the Rio Grande boundary.

Knowing that the Mexican government desperately needed money, the president attempted to buy New Mexico and California. But the Mexican public overwhelmingly opposed ceding any more territory to the land-hungry Yankees. Blocked on the diplomatic front, Polk ordered General Zachary Taylor to proceed south with American troops to the Rio Grande. From the Mexican standpoint, the Americans had invaded their country and occupied their territory. On April 25 Mexican forces clashed with Taylor's troops.

Polk had already resolved to send Congress a war message when word arrived of the fighting along the Rio Grande. The president quickly revised his war message, placing the entire blame for the war on Mexico. "Mexico has passed the boundary of the United States, has invaded our territory, and shed American blood upon American soil," he told Congress on May 11. "War exists, and notwithstanding all our efforts to avoid it, exists by the act of Mexico

THE MEXICAN WAR

herself." The administration sent a bill to Congress calling for volunteers and requesting money to supply American troops.

The war with Mexico posed a dilemma for Whigs. They were convinced (correctly) that Polk had provoked it in order to acquire more territory from

Opposition to the war

Mexico, and many northern Whigs accused the president of seeking to extend slavery. But they also feared that if they opposed the war, they would ruin their party. Therefore, they voted for supply bills but, at the same time, strenuously attacked the conduct of "Mr. Polk's War" and opposed the acquisition of any territory from Mexico.

The Price of Victory

Even before word of hostilities arrived in California, a group of impetuous American settlers around Sacramento launched the "Bear Flag Revolt." In June 1846 they proclaimed California an independent republic. American forces in the area soon put down any Mexican resistance, and by the following January California was safely in American hands.

Meanwhile, Taylor moved south from the Rio Grande and won several decisive battles, ending the war in the northern provinces. Polk had gained the territory he sought to reach the Pacific; now he wanted only peace. But the Mexican people refused to support any government that sued for peace, so Polk ordered an invasion into the heart of the country. Only after an American army commanded by General Winfield Scott captured Mexico City on September 14, 1847, did Mexico surrender.

Conquest of Mexico

The war had cost $97 million and 13,000 American lives, mostly as a result of disease. Yet the real cost was even higher. By bringing vast new territories into the Union, the war forced the explosive slavery issue to the center of national politics and threatened to upset the balance of power between North and South. Ralph Waldo Emerson had been prophetic when he declared that the conquest of Mexico "will poison us."

The Rise of the Slavery Issue

The annexation of so much southwestern territory left not only northern Whigs but many northern Democrats embittered. They complained that Polk, a Tennessee slaveholder, had compromised with the British on Oregon at the same time that he used military force to defend the absurd boundary claims of Texas. This discontent finally erupted in August 1846 when Polk requested $2 million from Congress. On August 8 David Wilmot, an obscure Pennsylvania congressman, startled Democratic leaders by introducing an amendment to the bill, barring slavery from any territory acquired from Mexico. The Wilmot Proviso, as the amendment became known, passed the House of Representatives several times with strong northern support, only to be rejected in the Senate, where the South had greater power.

Wilmot Proviso

Wilmot was hardly an abolitionist. Indeed, he hoped to keep not only slaves but all black people out of the territories. "I would preserve for white free labor a fair country," he explained, ". . . where the sons of toil, of my own race and color, can live without the disgrace which association with negro slavery brings upon free labor." The Wilmot Proviso aimed not to destroy slavery in the South but to confine the institution to those states where it already existed.

The status of slavery in the territories became more than an abstract question when the Senate in 1848 ratified the Treaty of Guadalupe Hidalgo.

Peace treaty with Mexico Under its terms the United States acquired Mexico's provinces of New Mexico and Upper California in return for approximately $18 million. With the United States in control of the Pacific Coast from San Diego to Puget Sound, Polk's continental vision had become a reality.

NEW SOCIETIES IN THE WEST

As Hispanic, Indian, Asian, and Anglo-American cultures mixed, the patterns of settlement along the frontier varied widely. In California the new settlements were overwhelmingly shaped by the rush for gold after 1848. And in the Great Basin around Salt Lake, the Mormons established a society whose sense of religious mission was as strong as that of the Puritans.

Farming in the West

The overlanders expected to replicate the societies they had left behind. Once a wagon train arrived at its destination, members had usually exhausted their resources and thus quickly scattered in search of employment or a good farm site.

In a process repeated over and over, settlers in a new area set up the machinery of government. Churches took longer to establish, for ministers were *Evolution of western society* hard to recruit and congregations were often not large enough to support a church. As the population grew, however, a more conventional society evolved. Towns and a middle class developed, the proportion of women increased, schools were established, and the residents became less mobile.

While opportunity was greater on the frontier and early arrivals had a special advantage, more and more the agricultural frontier of the West resembled the older society of the East. With the development of markets and transportation, wealth became concentrated, some families fell to the lower rungs of society, and those who were less successful left, seeking yet another fresh start.

The Gold Rush

In January 1848, while constructing a sawmill along the American River, James Marshall noticed gold flecks in the millrace. More discoveries followed, and when the news reached the East, it spread like wildfire. The following spring the Overland Trail was jammed with eager "forty-niners." In only two years, from 1848 to the end of 1849, California's population jumped from 14,000 to 100,000. By 1860 it stood at 380,000.

Those intent on making a fortune and returning home gave no thought to putting down roots. Mining camps literally appeared and died overnight, as

EYEWITNESS TO HISTORY

Disappointment in the Gold Diggings

My expectations are not realized. We have been unlucky—or rather, by being inexperienced, we selected a poor spot for a location and staked all on it, and it has proved worth nothing. Had it proved as it was expected when we took it up . . . I should have today been on my way to the bosom of my family in possession of sufficient means to have made them and me comfortable through life. . . . I mostly regret the necessity of staying here longer.

I was in hopes to have sent home a good pile of money before this time, but I am not able to at present. Still, my expectations are high, and in my opinion the excitement about the gold mines was not caused by exaggeration. In fact, I believe that greater amounts of gold have been and will be taken from the mines this summer than the gold news have told. . . . But I am of the opinion that the gold will soon be gathered from these washings and then will come the hardest part of this gold fever. I therefore would advise no one to come here. . . . But were I to be unfortunate in all my business here and arrive at last at home without *one cent*, I should ever be glad that I have taken the trip to California. It has learnt me to have confidence in myself, has disciplined my impetuous disposition and has learnt me to think and act for myself and to look upon men and things in a true light. Notwithstanding all these favorable circumstances, it is a fact that no energy or industry can secure certain success in the business of mining.

William Swain to Sabrina Swain, Foster's Bar, April 15, 1850, J. S. Holliday, *The World Rushed In* (New York: Simon & Schuster, 1981), 360–362. Copyright © 1981 by J. S. Holliday. Reprinted by permission of Simon & Schuster, Inc.

Life in the mining camps word of a new strike sent miners racing off to another canyon, valley, or streambed. More than 80 percent of the prospectors who poured into the gold country were Americans, including free blacks. Mexicans, Australians, Hawaiians, Chinese, French, English, and Irish also came. Whatever their nationality, the new arrivals were overwhelmingly unmarried men in their twenties and thirties.

The constant movement, the hard labor of mining, the ready cash, and the rootlessness all made camp society unstable. "There is an excitement connected with the pursuit of gold which renders one restless and uneasy—ever hoping to do something better," explained one forty-niner. Removed from the traditional forms of social control, miners engaged in gambling, swearing, drinking, and fighting. As a Denver paper complained during that territory's gold rush a few years later, as soon as "men of decent appearance" reached a mining camp, they "sang low songs, walked openly with the painted courtesans with whom the town teems, and generally gave themselves up to what they term, 'a time!'"

Only about 5 percent of gold rush emigrants were women or children; given this scarcity, men were willing to pay top dollar to women to cook, sew, and

Women in the camps

wash. Other women ran hotels and boardinghouses. "A smart woman can do very well in this country," one woman informed a friend in the East. "It is the only country I ever was in where a woman received anything like a just compensation for work." Likewise, they suffered no shortage of suitors. "I had men come forty miles over the mountains, just to look at me," Eliza Wilson recalled, "and I never was called a handsome woman, in my best days, even by my most ardent admirers." The class of women most frequently seen in the diggings were prostitutes, who numbered perhaps 20 percent of female Californians in 1850.

Violence was common in the mining districts, so when a new camp opened, miners adopted a set of rules and regulations. Justice was dispensed promptly,

Nativist and racial prejudices

either by a vote of all the miners or by an elected jury. While effective when administered fairly, the system at times degenerated into lynch law. In addition, American miners frustrated by a lack of success often directed their hostility toward foreigners. The miners ruthlessly exterminated the Indians in the area, mob violence drove Mexicans out of nearly every camp, and the Chinese were confined to claims abandoned by Americans as unprofitable. The state eventually enacted a foreign miners' tax that fell largely on the Chinese. Free African Americans felt the sting of discrimination as well. White American miners proclaimed that "colored men were not privileged to work in a country intended only for American citizens."

Before long, the most easily worked claims had been played out, and competition steadily drove down the average earnings from $20 a day in 1848 to $6 in 1852. As gold became increasingly difficult to extract, corporations using heavy equipment and employing miners working for wages came to dominate the industry. As the era of the individual miner passed, so too did mining camps and the unique society they spawned.

The damage mining did to the land endured longer. Abandoned diggings pockmarked the gold fields and created piles of debris that heavy rains washed

Environmental impact of mining

down the valley, choking streams and rivers and ruining lands below. Excavation of hillsides, construction of dams to divert rivers, and the destruction of the forest cover to meet the heavy demand for lumber and firewood caused serious erosion of the soil and spring floods. The attitude of the individual miners differed little from the capitalists who succeeded them: both sought to exploit the environment as rapidly as possible with little thought to long–term consequences. Untempered by any sense of restraint, the quest for rapid wealth left long–lasting scars on the landscape of the gold country.

Instant City: San Francisco

When the United States assumed control of California, San Francisco had a population of perhaps 200. But thousands of emigrants took the water route west, passing through San Francisco's harbor on their way to the diggings. By 1856 the city's population had jumped to an astonishing 50,000. In a mere 8 years the city had attained the size New York had taken 190 years to reach.

The product of economic self-interest, San Francisco developed in helter-skelter fashion. Since the city government took virtually no role in directing de-

San Francisco's chaotic growth

velopment, almost no land was reserved for public use. Property owners defeated a proposal to widen the streets, prompting the city's leading newspaper to complain, "To sell a few more feet of lots, the streets were compressed like a cheese, into half their width." An amazing assortment of languages could be heard on the streets; indeed, in 1860 the city was 50 percent foreign-born.

The most distinctive of the ethnic groups was the Chinese. China in the 1840s had experienced considerable economic distress, and thus between 1849

San Francisco in 1852

Chinese experience and 1854, some 45,000 Chinese went to California. Like the other gold seekers, they were overwhelmingly young and male, and they wanted only to accumulate savings and return home to their families. (Only 16 Chinese women arrived before 1854.)

When the Chinese were harassed in the mines, many opened laundries in San Francisco and elsewhere, since little capital was required. Other Chinese around San Francisco set up restaurants or worked in the fishing industry. In these early years they found Americans less hostile, so long as they stayed away from the gold fields. As immigration and the competition for jobs increased, however, anti-Chinese sentiment intensified.

Gradually, San Francisco took on the trappings of a more orderly community. The city government established a public school system, erected street lights, created a municipal water system, and halted further filling in of the bay. Fashionable neighborhoods sprouted on several hills, as high rents drove many residents from the developing commercial center. Churches and families became more common. By 1856, the city of the gold rush had been replaced by a new city whose stone and brick buildings gave it a sense of permanence.

The Mormons in Utah

The makeshift, often chaotic society spawned by the gold rush was a product of largely uncontrolled economic forces. By contrast, an entirely different society evolved in the Great Basin of Utah under the control of the Church of Jesus Christ of Latter-day Saints.

After Joseph Smith's death in 1844 (page 312), the Mormon church was led by Brigham Young, who lacked Smith's religious mysticism but was a brilliant organizer. Young decided to move his followers to the Great Basin, an isolated area a thousand miles from settled regions of the United States, where they could live and worship without interference. In 1847 the first thousand settlers arrived, the vanguard of thousands more who extended Mormon settlement throughout the valley of the Great Salt Lake and the West. The Mormons' success rested on a community-oriented effort firmly controlled by church elders. Families were given only as much farmland as they could use, and church officials, headed by Young, exercised supreme power in legislative, executive, and judicial matters as well as religious affairs.

The most controversial church teaching was the doctrine of polygamy, or plural marriage, which Young finally sanctioned publicly in 1852. Visitors reported with surprise that few Mormon wives seemed to rebel *Polygamy* against the practice. If the wives lived together, the system allowed them to share domestic work. When the husband established separate households, wives enjoyed greater freedom, since he was not constantly present. Moreover, because polygamy distinguished Mormonism from other religions, plural wives saw it as an expression of their religious faith. "I want to be assured of *my position in God's estimation,*" one such wife explained. "If polygamy is the Lord's order, we must carry it out."

The Mormons connected control of water to their sense of mission. The Salt Lake valley, where the Mormons established their holy community, lacked significant rivers or abundant sources of water. Thus their success depended on irrigating the region, something never before attempted. By constructing a coordinated series of dams, aqueducts, and ditches, they brought life–giving water to the valleys of the region. By 1850, there were more than 16,000 irrigated acres in what would become Utah.

Irrigation and community

Manipulation of water reinforced the Mormons' sense of hierarchy and group discipline. Centralization of authority in the hands of church officials made possible an overall plan of development, allowed for maximum exploitation of resources, and freed communities from the disputes over water rights that plagued many settlements in the arid West. In a radical departure from American ideals, church leaders insisted that water belonged to the community, not individuals, and vested this authority in the hands of the local bishop. Control of vital water resources reinforced the power of the church hierarchy over not just the faithful but dissidents as well. Thus irrigation did more than make the desert bloom. By checking the Jeffersonian ideal of an independent, self-sufficient farmer, it also sustained a centralized, well-regulated society under the firm control of the church.

Temple City: Salt Lake City

In laying out the Mormons' "temple city" of Salt Lake, Young was also determined to avoid the commercial worldliness and competitive individualism that had plagued Joseph Smith's settlement at Nauvoo. City lots, which were distributed by lottery, could not be subdivided for sale, and real estate speculation was forbidden.

The city itself was laid out in a checkerboard grid well suited to the level terrain. Streets were 132 feet wide (compared with 60 feet in San Francisco), and a square block contained eight home lots of 1.25 acres each. Unlike early San Francisco, in Salt Lake City the family was the basic social unit, and almost from the beginning the city had an equal balance of men and women. The planners also provided for four public squares in various parts of the city. The city was divided into 18 wards, each under the supervision of a bishop, who held civil as well as religious power.

Salt Lake City's orderly growth

As the city expanded, the original plan had to be modified to accommodate the developing commercial district by dividing lots into sizes more suitable for stores. Experience and growth also eventually dictated smaller blocks and narrower streets, but the city still retained its spacious appearance and regular design. Through religious and economic discipline church leaders succeeded in preserving a sense of common purpose.

Shadows on the Moving Frontier

Transformations like Salt Lake City and San Francisco were truly remarkable. But it is important to remember that Americans were not coming into a trackless, unsettled wilderness. As frontier lines crossed, 75,000 Mexicans had to adapt to American rule.

The Treaty of Guadalupe Hidalgo guaranteed Mexicans in the ceded territory "the free enjoyment of their liberty and property." So long as Mexicans continued to be a sizable majority in a given area, such as New Mexico, their influence was strong. But wherever Anglos became more numerous, they demanded conformity to American customs. When Mexicans remained faithful to their heritage, language, and religion, these cultural differences worked to reinforce Hispanic powerlessness, social isolation, and economic exploitation.

The rush of American emigrants quickly overwhelmed Hispanic settlers in California. Even in 1848, before the discovery of gold, Americans in California

Hispanic–Anglo conflict

outnumbered Mexicans two to one, and by 1860 Hispanics amounted to only 2 percent of the population. Changes in California land law required verification of the *rancheros'* original land grants by a federal commission. Since the average claim took 17 years to complete and imposed complex procedures and hefty legal fees, many *rancheros* lost large tracts of land to Americans. Lower-class Mexicans scratched out a bare existence on ranches and farms or in the growing cities and towns.

Mexicans in Texas were also greatly outnumbered: they totaled only 6 percent of the population in 1860. Stigmatized as inferior, they were the poorest group in free society. One response to this dislocation, an option commonly taken by persecuted minorities, was social banditry. An example was the folk hero Juan Cortina. A member of a displaced landed family in southern Texas, Cortina in the 1850s began stealing from wealthy Anglos to aid poor Mexicans, proclaiming, "To me is entrusted the breaking of the chains of your slavery." He continued to raid Texas border settlements until finally imprisoned by Mexican authorities. While failing to produce any lasting change, Cortina demonstrated the depth of frustration and resentment among Hispanics over their abuse at the hands of the new Anglo majority.

ESCAPE FROM CRISIS

With the return of peace, Congress confronted the problem of whether to allow slavery in the newly won territories. David Wilmot, in his controversial

Constitution and extension of slavery

proviso, had already proposed to outlaw slavery throughout the Mexican cession. John C. Calhoun, representing the extreme southern position, countered that slavery was legal in all territories. The federal government had acted as the agent of all the states in acquiring the land, he argued, and southerners had a right to take their property there, including slaves. Only when the residents of a territory drafted a state constitution could they decide the question of slavery.

Between these extremes were two moderate positions. One proposed extending the Missouri Compromise line of 36°30′ to the Pacific, which would have continued the earlier policy of dividing the national domain between the North and the South. The other proposal, championed by Senator Lewis Cass of Michigan and Senator Stephen A. Douglas of Illinois, was to allow the people of the territory rather than Congress to decide the status of slavery. This solution, which became known as popular sovereignty, was deliberately ambiguous, since its supporters refused to specify whether the residents could make this decision at any time or only when drafting a state constitution, as Calhoun insisted.

When Congress organized the Oregon Territory in 1848, it prohibited slavery there, since even southerners admitted that the region was too far north to grow the South's staple crops. But this seemingly straightforward decision made it impossible to apply the Missouri Compromise line to the other territories. Without Oregon as a part of the package, the bulk of the remaining land would be open to slavery, something at which the North balked. Almost inadvertently, one of the two moderate solutions had been discarded by the summer of 1848.

A Two-Faced Campaign

In the election of 1848 both major parties tried to avoid the slavery issue. The Democrats nominated Lewis Cass, a supporter of popular sovereignty, while the Whigs bypassed all their prominent leaders and selected General Zachary Taylor of Louisiana, who had taken no position on any public issue.

But the slavery issue would not go away. A new antislavery coalition, the Free Soil party, brought together northern Democrats who had rallied to the

Free Soil party Wilmot Proviso, Conscience Whigs who disavowed Taylor's nomination because he was a slaveholder, and political abolitionists in the Liberty party. To gain more votes, the Free Soil platform focused on the dangers of extending slavery rather than on the evil of slavery itself. Ironically, the party nominated Martin Van Buren—the man who for years had struggled to keep the slavery issue out of national politics.

Both the Whigs and the Democrats ran different campaigns in the North and the South. To southern audiences, each party promised it would protect slavery in the territories; to northern voters, each claimed it would keep the territories free. In this two-faced, sectional campaign, the Whigs won their second national victory. Taylor held onto the core of Whig voters in both sections (Van Buren as well as Cass, after all, had long been Democrats). But in the South, where the contest pitted a southern slaveholder against two northerners, Taylor won many more votes than Clay had in 1844. As one southern Democrat complained, "We have lost hundreds of votes, solely on the ground that General

Cass was a Northerner and General Taylor a Southern man." Furthermore, Van Buren polled five times as many votes as the Liberty party had four years earlier. Increasingly the two national political parties were being pulled apart.

The Compromise of 1850

Once he became president, Taylor could no longer remain silent. The territories gained from Mexico had to be organized; furthermore, by 1849 California had gained enough residents to be admitted as a state. In the Senate the balance of power between North and South stood at 15 states each. California's admission would break the sectional balance.

TERRITORIAL GROWTH AND THE COMPROMISE OF 1850

Called "Old Rough and Ready" by his troops, Taylor was a forthright man of action, but he was politically inexperienced and oversimplified complex prob-

Taylor's plan

lems. Since even Calhoun conceded that entering states had the right to ban slavery, Taylor proposed that the way to end the sectional crisis was to skip the territorial stage by combining all the Mexican cession into two huge states, New Mexico and California. Even more shocking to southern Whigs, he proposed to apply the Wilmot Proviso to the entire area, since he was convinced that slavery would never flourish there. When Congress convened in December 1849, Taylor recommended that California and New Mexico be admitted as free states. The president's plan touched off the most serious sectional crisis the Union had yet confronted.

Into this turmoil stepped Henry Clay, now 73 years old and nearing the end of his career. A savvy card player all his life, Clay loved the bargaining, the wheeling and dealing, the late-night trade-offs eased along by a bottle of bourbon that were part of politics. Clay decided that a grand compromise was needed to end all disputes between the North and South and save the Union. Already, Mississippi had summoned a southern convention to meet at Nashville to discuss the crisis, and extremists were pushing for secession.

Clay's compromise, submitted in January 1850, addressed all the major controversies between the two sections. California, he proposed, should be

Clay's compromise

admitted as a free state, which represented the clear wishes of most settlers there. The rest of the Mexican cession would be organized as two territories, New Mexico and Utah, under the doctrine of popular sovereignty. Thus slavery would not be prohibited from these regions. Clay also proposed that Congress abolish the slave trade but not slavery itself in the District of Columbia and that a new, more rigorous fugitive slave law be passed to enable southerners to reclaim runaway slaves. To reinforce the idea that both North and South were yielding ground, Clay combined those provisions that dealt with the Mexican cession (and several others adjusting the Texas–New Mexico border) in a larger package known as the Omnibus Bill.

With the stakes so high, the Senate debated the bill for six months. Clay, wracked by a hacking cough, spent long hours trying to line up the needed votes. But for once, the great whist enthusiast had misplayed his hand. The Omnibus Bill required that the components of the compromise be approved as a package. Extremists in Congress from both regions, however, combined against the moderates and rejected the bill.

With Clay exhausted and his strategy in shambles, Democrat Stephen A. Douglas assumed leadership of the pro-compromise forces. The sudden death

Passage of the Compromise

in July of President Taylor, who had threatened to veto Clay's plan, aided the compromise movement. One by one, Douglas submitted the individual measures for a vote. Northern representatives provided the necessary votes to admit California and abolish the slave trade in the District of Columbia, while southern representatives supplied the edge needed to organize the Utah and New Mexico territories and pass the new fugitive slave law. On the face of it, everyone had compromised. But in truth, only 61 members of Congress, or 21 percent of the membership, had not voted against some part of the Compromise.

By September 17 all the separate parts of the Compromise of 1850 had passed and been signed into law by the new president, Millard Fillmore. The Union, it seemed, was safe.

Away from the Brink

The general public, both North and South, rallied to the Compromise. At the convention of southern states in Nashville, the fire-eaters—the radical propo-

Rejection of secession

nents of states' rights and secession—found themselves voted down by more moderate voices. Even in the Deep South, coalitions of pro-Compromise Whigs and Democrats soundly defeated secessionists in state elections. Nevertheless, most southerners felt that a firm line had been drawn. With California's admission, they were now outnumbered in the Senate, so it was critical that slaveholders be granted equal legal access to the territories. They announced that any breach of the Compromise of 1850 would justify secession.

The North, for its part, found the new fugitive slave law the hardest measure of the Compromise to swallow. The controversial law denied an accused

Fugitive slave law

runaway a trial by jury, and it required that all citizens assist federal marshals in its enforcement. Harriet Beecher Stowe's popular novel *Uncle Tom's Cabin* (1852) presented a powerful moral indictment of the law—and of slavery as an institution. Despite its crude literary techniques, the book profoundly moved its readers. Emphasizing the duty of Christians toward the downtrodden, it reached a greater audience than any previous abolitionist work. Thousands more in northern cities saw theatrical productions of the story (page 394).

In reality, however, fewer than 1000 slaves a year escaped to the North, many of whom did not succeed. Despite some well-publicized cases of resis-

Both sections accept the Compromise

tance, the 1850 fugitive slave law was generally enforced in the free states. Many northerners did not like the law, but they were unwilling to tamper with the Compromise. Stephen Douglas spoke accurately enough when he boasted in 1851, "The whole country is acquiescing in the compromise measures—everywhere, North and South. Nobody proposes to repeal or disturb them."

And so calm returned. In the lackluster 1852 presidential campaign, both the Whigs and the Democrats endorsed the Compromise. Franklin Pierce, a little-known New Hampshire Democrat, soundly defeated the Whig candidate, Winfield Scott. Even more significant, the antislavery Free Soil candidate received only about half as many votes as Van Buren had four years before. With the slavery issue seemingly losing political force, it appeared that the Republic had weathered the storm unleashed by the Wilmot Proviso.

But the moving frontier still had changes to work. It had leaped from the Mississippi valley to the Pacific, but in between remained territory still unorganized. And as the North became increasingly industrialized and the South more firmly committed to an economy based on cotton and slavery, the growing conflict between the two sections would shatter the Jacksonian party system, reignite the slavery issue, and shake the Union to its foundation.

SIGNIFICANT EVENTS

1725–1850	Sioux expansion on the Great Plains
1821	Mexico wins independence; Santa Fe trade opens
1823	First American settlers in Texas
1829	Mexico tries to abolish slavery in Texas
1830	Mexico attempts to halt American migration to Texas
1835	Texas Revolution
1836	Texas republic established; Battle of the Alamo; Santa Anna defeated at San Jacinto
1841	Tyler becomes president
1843	Large-scale migration to Oregon begins
1843–1844	Tyler's secret negotiations with Texas
1844	Tyler's Texas treaty rejected by the Senate; Polk elected president
1845	United States annexes Texas; phrase "Manifest Destiny" coined
1846	War declared against Mexico; Bear Flag Revolt in California; Oregon Treaty ratified; Wilmot Proviso introduced
1847	Mormon migration to Utah; U.S. troops occupy Mexico City
1848	Gold discovered in California; Treaty of Guadalupe Hidalgo; Free Soil party founded; Taylor elected president
1849	Gold rush; California drafts free state constitution
1850	Nashville convention; Taylor dies and Fillmore becomes president; Compromise of 1850 enacted
1850–1851	South rejects secession
1852	Harriet Beecher Stowe's *Uncle Tom's Cabin* published; Pierce elected president

CHAPTER FIFTEEN

The Union Broken

Into town they rode, several hundred strong, their faces flushed with excitement. They were unshaven, rough-talking men, "armed . . . to the teeth with rifles and revolvers, cutlasses and bowie-knives." At the head of the procession flapped an American flag, and alongside it another with a crouching tiger emblazoned on black and white stripes, followed by banners proclaiming "Southern Rights" and "The Superiority of the White Race." At the rear rolled five artillery pieces, which were quickly dragged into range of the town's main street. Josiah Miller, the editor of the Lawrence *Kansas Free State*, watched intently from a window in his office. "Well, boys," he predicted, "we're in for it."

For residents of Lawrence, Kansas, the worst seemed at hand. The town had been founded by the New England Emigrant Aid Company, a Yankee association that recruited settlers in an effort to keep Kansas Territory from becoming a slave state. Accepting Stephen Douglas's idea that the people should decide the status of slavery, the town's residents intended to see to it that under popular sovereignty Kansas entered the Union as a free state. Emigrants from the neighboring slave state of Missouri were equally determined that no "abolition tyrants" control the territory. There had been conflict in Kansas almost immediately: land disputes, horse thievery, shootings on both sides.

In the ensuing turmoil, the federal government seemed to back the proslavery forces. A U.S. District Court indicted several of Lawrence's leading citizens for treason, and federal marshall Israel Donaldson called for a posse to help make the arrests. Donaldson's posse, swelled by eager volunteers from across the Missouri border, arrived outside Lawrence on the night of May 20, 1856.

Meanwhile, Lawrence's "committee of safety" had agreed on a policy of nonresistance. Most of those indicted had fled, but Donaldson arrested two men without incident and then dismissed his posse. But Sheriff Samuel Jones, who on his previous visit to Lawrence had been shot, had a score to settle. Falsely claiming that he had a court order, the irate sheriff took over the band and led the cheering throng into town at three o'clock in the afternoon.

The thoroughly liquored "army" quickly degenerated into a mob. Ignoring the pleas of some leaders, its members smashed the presses of two newspapers,

The "sack" of Lawrence

the *Herald of Freedom* and the *Kansas Free State*. Then the horde unsuccessfully tried to blow up the now-deserted Free State Hotel, which more closely resembled a fort, before finally putting it to the torch. When the mob finally rode off, it left the residents of Lawrence unharmed but thoroughly terrified.

Retaliation by free state partisans was not long in coming. Hurrying north toward Lawrence, an older man with a grim visage and steely eyes heard the news the next morning that the town had been attacked. "Old Man Brown," as everyone called him, was on his way to provide reinforcements. A severe, God-fearing Calvinist, John Brown was also a staunch abolitionist who had once remarked that he believed "God had raised him up on purpose to break the jaws of the wicked." Brooding over the failure of the free-staters to resist the "slave hounds" from Missouri, Brown decided not to push on to Lawrence; instead, he ordered his followers to sharpen their heavy cutlasses. "Caution," he announced, "is nothing but the word of Cowardice."

Three days after the Lawrence raid, Brown headed under cover of dark toward Pottawatomie Creek with a half dozen others, including four of his sons.

Pottawatomie massacre

Announcing that they were "the Northern Army" come to serve justice, they burst into the cabin of James Doyle, a proslavery man from Tennessee, with cutlasses drawn. As Brown marched Doyle and his three sons off, Doyle's terrified wife Mahala begged him to spare her youngest, and the old man relented. The others were led a hundred yards down the road and hacked to death with broadswords by Owen and Salmon Brown. Old Man Brown then walked up to James Doyle's body and put a bullet through his forehead. Before the night was done, two more cabins had been visited and two more proslavery settlers brutally executed. Not one of the five murdered men owned a single slave or had any connection with the raid on Lawrence.

Brown's action precipitated a new wave of fighting in Kansas, and the news of the tumult further angered residents in both sections of the nation. "Everybody here feels as if we are upon a volcano," remarked one congressman in Washington.

The country was indeed atop a smoldering volcano that would finally erupt in the spring of 1861, showering death and destruction across the land. Popular sovereignty, the last remaining moderate solution to the controversy over the expansion of slavery, had failed dismally in Kansas. The violence and disorder in the territory provided a stark reply to Stephen Douglas's proposition: What could be more peaceable, more fair than the notion of popular sovereignty?

SECTIONAL CHANGES IN AMERICAN SOCIETY

The road to war was not a straight or short one. Six years elapsed between the Compromise of 1850 and the crisis in "Bleeding Kansas." Another four would pass before the first shot was fired. And the process of separation involved more than popular fears, ineffective politicians, and an unwillingness to compromise. As we have seen, Americans were bound together by a growing transportation network, by national markets, and by a national political system. Increasingly, however, the changes occurring in American society heightened sectional tensions. As the North continued to industrialize, its society came into conflict with that of the South. The coming of Civil War, in other words, involved social and economic changes as well as political ones.

The Growth of a Railroad Economy

By the time the Compromise of 1850 produced a lull in the tensions between North and South, the American economy had left behind the depression of the early 1840s and was roaring again with speculative optimism. Its basic structure, however, was changing. Cotton remained the nation's major export, but it was no longer the driving force for American economic growth. After 1839 this role was taken over by the construction of a vast railroad network covering the eastern half of the continent. By 1850 the United States possessed more than 9000 miles of track; 10 years later it had over 30,000 miles, more than the rest of the world combined. Much of the new construction during the 1850s occurred west of the Appalachian Mountains—over 2000 miles in Ohio and Illinois alone.

Because western railroads ran through less settled areas, they were especially dependent on public aid. State and local governments made loans to rail companies and sometimes exempted them temporarily from taxes. About a quarter of the cost of railroad construction came from state and local governments, but federal land grants were crucial, too. By mortgaging or selling the land to farmers, the railroad raised construction capital and also stimulated settlement, which increased its business and profits. By 1860 Congress had allotted about 28 million acres of federal land to 40 different companies.

The effect of the new lines rippled through the economy. Nearby farmers began to specialize in cash crops and market them in distant locations. With the

Railroads' impact on the economy

profits they purchased manufactured goods. Before the railroad reached Athens, Tennessee, the surrounding counties produced about 25,000 bushels of wheat, selling at less than 50 cents a bushel. Once the railroad came, farmers near Athens grew 400,000 bushels and sold their crop at a dollar a bushel. Railroads also stimulated other areas of the economy, notably the mining and iron industries. By 1860 half the domestic output of bar and sheet iron was used by railroads, and pig iron production almost tripled over the previous 20 years.

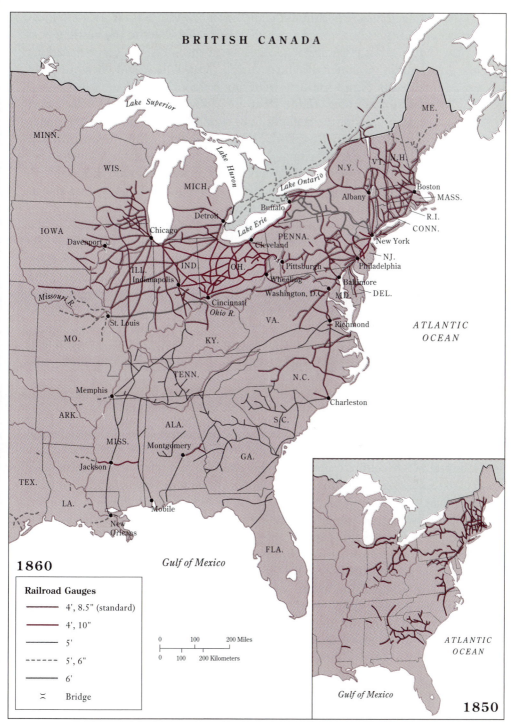

1860

Railroad Gauges

— 4', 8.5" (standard)

— 4', 10"

— 5'

- - - 5', 6"

— 6'

≍ Bridge

0   100   200 Miles

0   100   200 Kilometers

Gulf of Mexico

1850

GROWTH OF THE RAILROAD NETWORK, 1850–1860

The new rail networks shifted the direction of western trade. In 1840 most northwestern grain was shipped down the Mississippi River to the bustling port of New Orleans. But low water made steamboat travel risky in summer, and ice shut down traffic in winter. Products such as lard, tallow, and cheese quickly spoiled if stored in New Orleans's sweltering warehouses.

With the new rail lines, traffic from the Midwest increasingly flowed west to east. Chicago became the region's hub, connecting the farms of the upper

Shift in flow of western trade

Midwest to New York and other eastern cities. Thus while the value of goods shipped by river to New Orleans continued to increase, the South's overall share of western trade dropped dramatically. The old political alliance between South and West, based on shared economic interests, was weakened by the new patterns of commerce.

The growing rail network was not the only factor that led farmers in the Northeast and Midwest to become more commercially oriented. Another was the sharp rise in international demand for grain. Wheat, which in 1845 commanded $1.08 a bushel in New York City, fetched $2.46 in 1855; at the same time the price of corn nearly doubled. Farmers responded by specializing in cash crops and investing in equipment to increase productivity. "The power of cotton over the financial affairs of the Union has in the last few years rapidly diminished," the *Democratic Review* remarked in 1849, "and bread stuffs will now become the governing power."

Railroads and the Prairie Environment

As railroad lines fanned out from Chicago, farmers began to acquire open prairie land in Illinois and then Iowa, putting its deep black soil into production. Commerical agriculture transformed this remarkable treeless environment.

To settlers accustomed to woodlands, the thousands of square miles of grass taller than a person were an awesome sight. In 1838 Edmund Flagg gazed upon "the tall grasstops waving in . . . billowy beauty in the breeze; the narrow pathway winding off like a serpent over the rolling surface, disappearing and reappearing till lost in the luxuriant herbage. . . ." Long-grass prairies had their perils too: year round, storms sent travelers searching for the shelter of trees along river valleys, and stinging insects were thick in the summer.

Because normal plows could not penetrate the densely tangled roots of prairie grass, the earliest settlers erected farms along the boundary separating

Impact of technology

the forest from the prairie. In 1837, however, John Deere invented a sharp-cutting steel plow that sliced through the sod without soil sticking to the blade. Cyrus McCormick refined a mechanical reaper that harvested 14 times more wheat with the same amount of labor. By the 1850s McCormick was selling 1000 reapers a year and could not keep up with demand, while Deere turned out 10,000 plows annually.

The new commercial farming fundamentally altered the landscape and the environment. Indians had grown corn in the region for years, but never in such large

Changes in the landscape

fields as those of white farmers, whose surpluses were shipped east. Prairie farmers also introduced new crops that were not part of the earlier ecological system, notably wheat, along with fruits and vegetables. Native grasses were replaced by a small number of plants cultivated as commodities. Tame grasses replaced native grasses in pastures for making hay.

Western farmers altered the landscape by reducing the annual fires, often set by Indians, that had kept the prairie free from trees. In the absence of these fires, trees reappeared on land not in cultivation and, if undisturbed, eventually formed woodlots. The earlier unbroken landscape gave way to independent farms, each fenced off in the precise checkerboard pattern established by the Northwest Ordinance (page 176). It was an artificial ecosystem of animals, woodlots, and crops, whose large, unform layout made western farms more efficient than the more irregular farms in the East.

Railroads and the Urban Environment

Railroads transformed the urban environment as well. Communites soon recognized that their economic survival depended on creating adequate rail links to the countryside and to major urban markets and transshipment points. Large cities feared they would be left behind in the struggle to be the dominant city in the region, and smaller communities saw their very survival at stake in the battle for rail connections.

Even communities that obtained rail links found the presence of this new technology difficult to adjust to. When a railroad began serving Jacksonville,

Location of railroads

Illinois, merchants soon complained about the noise, dirt, and billowing smoke produced by locomotives passing through the business district. "The public square was filled with teams [of horses]," one resident recalled, "and whenever the engine steamed into the square making all the noise possible, there was such a stampede. . . ." After a few years, the tracks were relocated on the outskirts of town. Increasingly communities kept railroads away from fashionable neighborhoods and shopping areas. As the tracks became a physical manifestation of social and economic divisions in the town, the notion of living "on the wrong side of the tracks" became crucial to the urban landscape.

Rising Industrialization

The expansion of commercial agriculture, along with the shift from water power to steam, also spurred the growth of industry. Out of the 10 leading American industries, 8 processed raw materials produced by agriculture, including flour milling and the manufacture of textiles, shoes, and woolens. (The only exceptions were iron and machinery.)

Most important, the factory system of organizing labor and the technology of interchangeable parts spread to other areas of the economy during the 1850s.

Isaac Singer began using interchangeable parts in 1851 to mass-produce sewing machines, which made possible the ready-made clothing indus-

Expansion of industry

try, while workers who assembled farm implements performed a single step in the process over and over again. By 1860 the United States had nearly a billion dollars invested in manufacturing, almost twice as much as in 1849. And for the first time, less than half the workers in the North were working on farms.

Immigration

The surge of industry depended on a large factory labor force. Natural increase helped swell the population to more than 30 million by 1860, but only in part, since the birthrate had begun to decline. It was the beginning of mass immigration to America during the mid-1840s that kept population growth soaring.

In the 20 years from 1820 to 1840, about 700,000 newcomers had entered the United States. That figure jumped to 1.7 million in the 1840s, then to 2.6

Beginning of mass immigration

million in the 1850s. Though even greater numbers arrived after the Civil War, as a percentage of the nation's total population, the wave from 1845 to 1854 was the largest influx of immigrants in American history. Most of the newcomers were in the prime of life: in 1856 out of 224,000 arrivals, only 31,000 were under 10 and 20,000 were over 40. Certainly the booming economy and the lure of freedom drew immigrants, but they were also pushed by deteriorating conditions in Europe. In Ireland, a potato blight, which first struck in 1845, led to widespread famine. Out of a population of 9 million, as many as a million perished, while a million and a half more emigrated, two-thirds to the United States.

The Irish tended to be poorer than other immigrant groups of the day. Although the Protestant Scots-Irish continued to emigrate, as so many had dur-

New sources of immigration

ing the eighteenth century, the decided majority of the Irish who came after 1845 were Catholic. Because they were poor and unskilled, the Irish congregated in the cities, where the women performed domestic service and took factory jobs and the men did manual labor.

Germans and Scandinavians also had economic reasons for leaving Europe. They included small farmers, whose lands had become marginal or who had been displaced by landlords, and skilled workers thrown out of work by industrialization. Some, particularly among the Germans, left after the liberal revolutions of 1848 failed, in order to live under the free institutions of the United States. Since coming to America, wrote a Swede who settled in Iowa in 1850, "I have not been compelled to pay a penny for the privilege of living. Neither is my cap worn out from lifting it in the presence of gentlemen."

Although many Germans and Scandinavians arrived in modest straits, few were truly impoverished, and many could afford to buy a farm or start a business. Unlike the Irish, Germans tended to emigrate as families, and wherever they settled, they formed social, religious, and cultural organizations to maintain their language and customs. Whereas the Scandinavians, Dutch, and English immigrants were Protestant, half or more of the Germans were Catholic.

Factories came more and more to depend on immigrant labor, including children, since newcomers would work for lower wages and were less prone to

Immigrants in factories and cities

protest harsh working conditions. The shift to an immigrant workforce could be seen most clearly in the textile industry, where over half the workers in New England mills were foreign-born by 1860.

The sizable foreign-born population in many American cities severely strained urban resources. Immigrants who could barely make ends meet were forced to live in overcrowded, unheated tenement houses, damp cellars, and even shacks. Urban slums became notorious for crime and drinking, which took a heavy toll on families and the poor. In the eyes of many native-born Americans, immigrants were to blame for driving down factory wages and pushing American workers out of jobs. Overshadowing these complaints was a fear that America might not be able to assimilate the new groups, with their unfamiliar languages and customs. These fears precipitated an outburst of political nativism in the mid-1850s.

Southern Complaints

With British and northern factories buying cotton in unprecedented quantities, southern planters prospered in the 1850s. Like those of northern commercial farmers, their operations became more highly capitalized to keep up with the demand. But instead of machinery, white southerners invested in slaves. During the 1850s, the price of prime field hands reached record levels.

Nonetheless, a number of southern nationalists, who advocated that the South should be a separate nation, pressed for greater industrialization to make

Southern economic dependence

the region more independent. "At present, the North fattens and grows rich upon the South," one Alabama newspaper complained in 1851, noting that "we purchase all our luxuries and necessities from the North," including clothing, shoes, implements and ma-

chinery, saddles and carriages, and even books. But most southerners ignored such pleas. So long as investments in cotton and slaves absorbed most of the South's capital, efforts to promote southern industry made little headway.

Despite southern prosperity, the section's leaders repeatedly complained that the North had used its power over banking and commerce to convert the South into a colony. Storage and shipping charges, insurance, port fees, and commissions, which added an estimated 20 percent to the cost of cotton and other commodities, went into the pockets of northern merchants, shippers, and bankers. The idea that the South was a colony of the North was inaccurate, but southern whites found it a convincing explanation of the North's growing wealth. More important, it reinforced their resistance to federal aid for economic development, which they were convinced would inevitably enrich the

North at southern expense. This attitude further weakened the South's political alliance with the West, which needed federal aid for transportation.

White southerners also feared that the new tide of immigration would shift the sectional balance of power. Most immigrants shunned the South, not wanting to compete with cheap slave labor. The lack of industry and the limited demand for skilled labor also shunted immigrants northward. As a result, the North surged even further ahead of the South in population, thereby strengthening its control of the House of Representatives and heightening southern concern that the North would rapidly settle the western territories.

THE POLITICAL REALIGNMENT OF THE 1850s

When Franklin Pierce (he pronounced it "Purse") assumed the presidency in 1853, he was only 48 years old, the youngest man yet to be elected president. He was also a supporter of the "Young America" movement of the Democratic party, which enthusiastically anticipated extending democracy across the globe and annexing additional territory to the United States.

The believers in Young America felt it idle to argue about slavery when the nation could be developing new resources. In 1853 Pierce did manage to con-

Gadsden Purchase

clude the Gadsden Purchase, thereby gaining control of about 45,000 square miles of Mexican desert, which contained the most practical southern route for a transcontinental railroad. He had no success accomplishing his major goal, the acquisition of Cuba, a rich sugar-producing island where slavery had once been important. In any case, he soon had his hands full with the proposals of another Democrat of the Young America stamp, Senator Stephen A. Douglas of Illinois.

The Kansas–Nebraska Act

Known as the Little Giant, Douglas was ambitious, bursting with energy, and impatient to get things done. As chairman of the Senate's Committee on Territories, he was eager to organize federal lands west of Missouri as part of his program for economic development. And as a citizen of Illinois, he wanted Chicago selected as the eastern terminus of the proposed transcontinental railroad. That necessitated the organization of the remainder of the Louisiana Purchase, since any northern rail route would have to run through that region.

Under the terms of the Missouri Compromise of 1820, slavery was prohibited in this portion of the Louisiana Purchase. But Douglas had already tried once to organize the area while keeping a ban on slavery—only to have his bill voted down by southern opposition in the Senate. In January 1854 he reintroduced the measure, this time omitting the prohibition on slavery that had been in effect for 34 years.

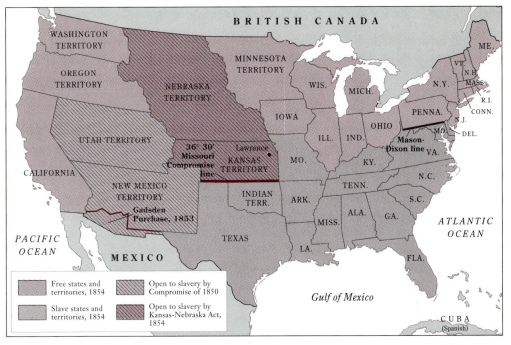

THE KANSAS–NEBRASKA ACT   When the Kansas–Nebraska Act of 1854 opened the remaining portion of the Louisiana Purchase to slavery under the doctrine of popular sovereignty, conflict between the two sections focused on control of Kansas, directly west of the slave state of Missouri.

In its final form, the bill created two territories: Kansas, directly west of Missouri, and a much larger Nebraska Territory, located west of Iowa and the Minnesota Territory. The Missouri Compromise was explicitly repealed. Instead, popular sovereignty was to determine the status of slavery in both territories, though it was left unclear whether residents of Kansas and Nebraska could prohibit slavery at any time or only at the time of statehood, as southerners insisted. It was widely assumed that Kansas would be a slave state and Nebraska a free state.

Missouri Compromise repealed

The Kansas–Nebraska Act outraged northern Democrats, Whigs, and Free Soilers alike. Critics rejected Douglas's contention that popular sovereignty would keep the territories free. The bill, they charged, was meant to give slaveholders—the "Slave Power"—new territory. Most northern opponents of the bill focused on the expansion of slavery and the Slave Power rather than the moral evil of slavery. A wave of popular indignation swept across the North.

Once President Pierce endorsed the bill, Senate passage was assured. The real fight came in the House, where the North held a large majority. The president put intense pressure on his fellow northern Democrats, and finally the bill passed by a narrow margin, 113 to 100. Pierce signed it on May 30, 1854, and the Missouri Compromise was repealed.

The Collapse of the Second American Party System

The furor over the Kansas–Nebraska Act laid bare the underlying social and economic tensions that had developed between the North and the South. These

Political realignment

tensions put mounting pressure on the political parties, and in the 1850s the Jacksonian party system collapsed. Voters who had been loyal to one party for years, even decades, began switching allegiances. By the time the process of realignment was completed, a new party system had emerged, divided this time along clearly sectional lines.

In part, the old party system decayed because new problems had replaced the traditional economic issues of both Whigs and Democrats. The Whigs alienated many of their traditional Protestant supporters by openly seeking the support of Catholics and recent immigrants. Then, too, the growing agitation for the prohibition of alcohol divided both parties, especially the Whigs. Finally, both the Whigs and the Democrats were increasingly perceived as little more than corrupt engines of plunder and became targets of popular disillusionment.

Thus the party system was already weakened when the Kansas–Nebraska Act divided the two major parties along sectional lines. In such an unstable atmosphere, with party loyalties declining, independent parties flourished. Antislavery veterans, who had earlier sparked the Liberty and Free Soil parties, united with Whigs and anti-Nebraska Democrats in the new antislavery Republican party. Their calculations were derailed, however, when another new party capitalized upon fears aroused by the recent flood of immigrants.

The Know-Nothings

In 1854 the American party, a secret nativist organization whose members were called Know-Nothings, suddenly emerged as a potent political force. (Its members, sworn to secrecy, had been instructed to answer inquiries by replying "I

Nativist fears

know nothing.") Taking as its slogan "Americans should rule America," Know-Nothings denounced illegal voting by immigrants, the rising crime and disorder in urban areas, and immigrants' heavy drinking. They were also strongly anti-Catholic and were convinced that the church's "undemocratic" hierarchy of bishops and archbishops was conspiring to undermine American democracy. Know-Nothings advocated lengthening the residency period for naturalization and ousting from office corrupt politicians who openly bid for foreign and Catholic votes.

The Know-Nothings won a series of remarkable victories in the 1854 elections. Their showing spelled doom for the Whigs, already weakened by the Kansas–Nebraska Act, as the rank and file deserted in droves to the Know-Nothings. With perhaps a million voters enrolled in its lodges in every state of the Union, Know-Nothing leaders confidently predicted in 1855 that they would elect the next president.

Yet only a year later—by the end of 1856—the party had collapsed as quickly as it had risen. The collapse came in part because inexperienced lead-

Sudden decline ers failed to enact the party's reform platform; but its real death knell was rising sectional tensions. In 1856 a majority of north-

ern delegates walked out of the American party's national convention when it adopted a proslavery platform. Significantly, they deserted to the other new party, the Republicans. This party, unlike the Know-Nothings, had no base in the South. It intended to elect a president by sweeping the free states, which controlled a majority of the electoral votes.

The Republicans and Bleeding Kansas

Initially, the Republican party made little headway in the North. Although it attracted a variety of Whigs, anti-Nebraska Democrats, and Free Soilers, many moderate Whigs and Democrats viewed the party as too radical. Observers predicted that it would soon go the way of all other failed antislavery parties.

Such predictions, however, did not take into account the emotions stirred up by developments in Kansas. Most early settlers migrated to Kansas for the same reason other white Americans headed west: the chance to prosper in a new land. But Douglas's idea of popular sovereignty transformed the new settlement into a referendum on slavery in the territories. A race soon developed between northerners and southerners to settle Kansas first. To the proslavery residents of neighboring Missouri, free state communities like Lawrence seemed ominous threats. "We are playing for a mighty stake," former Senator David Rice Atchison of Missouri insisted. "If we win, we carry slavery to the Pacific Ocean; if we fail we lose Missouri, Arkansas and Texas and all the territories; the game must be played boldly."

When the first Kansas elections were held in 1854 and 1855, Missourians poured over the border, seized the polls, and stuffed the ballot boxes. A later con-

Turmoil in Kansas gressional investigation concluded that more than 60 percent of the votes were cast illegally. This massive fraud tarnished popular sovereignty at the outset and greatly aroused public opinion in the

North. It also provided proslavery forces with a commanding majority in the Kansas legislature, where they enacted a strict legal code designed to intimidate antislavery settlers. This Kansas Code limited such time-honored rights as freedom of speech, impartial juries, and fair elections. Mobilized into action, the free-staters in the fall of 1855 organized a separate government, drafted a state constitution prohibiting slavery, and asked Congress to admit Kansas as a free state. In such a polarized situation, violence quickly broke out between the two factions.

The Caning of Charles Sumner

In May 1856, only a few days before the proslavery attack on Lawrence, Republican Senator Charles Sumner of Massachusetts delivered a scathing speech, "The Crime Against Kansas." Sumner was passionate in his condemna-

The caning of Senator Charles Sumner of Massachusetts by Representative Preston S. Brooks of South Carolina inflamed public opinion. In this northern cartoon, the fallen Sumner, a martyr to free speech, raises his pen against Brooks's club. Rushing to capitalize on the furor, printmakers did not know what the obscure Brooks looked like and thus had to devise ingenious ways of portraying the incident. In this print, Brooks's face is hidden by his raised arm.

tion of slavery, and his speech included remarks that deliberately insulted the state of South Carolina and one of its senators. Preston S. Brooks, a South Carolina congressman, was outraged that Sumner had insulted his relative and mocked his state.

Several days later, on May 22, Brooks strode into the Senate after it had adjourned, went up to Sumner, who was seated at his desk, and proceeded to beat him over the head with a cane. The cane shattered into three pieces from the violence of the attack, but Brooks, swept up in the emotion of the moment, furiously continued hitting Sumner until the senator collapsed unconscious, drenched in blood.

Northerners were electrified to learn that a senator of the United States had been beaten unconscious in the Senate chamber. But what caused them

Significance of the caning

even greater consternation was southern reaction to Sumner's caning—for in his own region, Preston Brooks was lionized as a hero. Instantly, the Sumner caning breathed life into the fledgling Republican party. Its claims about "Bleeding Kansas" and the Slave Power now seemed credible.

The Election of 1856

In the face of the storm that had arisen over Kansas, the Democrats turned to James Buchanan of Pennsylvania as their presidential nominee. Buchanan's supreme qualification was having the good fortune to have been out of the country when the Kansas–Nebraska Act was passed. The American party, split badly by the Kansas issue, nominated former president Millard Fillmore.

The Republicans chose John C. Frémont, a western explorer who had helped liberate California during the Mexican War. The party's platform denounced slavery as a "relic of barbarism" and demanded that Kansas be admitted as a free state. Throughout the summer the party hammered away on Bleeding Sumner and Bleeding Kansas. "A constantly increasing excitement is kept up by the intelligence coming every day from Kansas," wrote one observer. "I have never known political excitement—I ought rather to say exasperation—approach that which now rages."

A number of basic principles guided the Republican party, especially the ideal of free labor. Slavery degraded labor, Republicans argued, and would inevitably drive free labor out of the territories. Condemning the

Ideology of the Republican party

South as a stagnant, hierarchical, and economically backward region, Republicans praised the North as a fluid society of wide-

In this playbill advertising a dramatic production of *Uncle Tom's Cabin*, vicious bloodhounds pursue the light-skinned Eliza, who clutches her child as she frantically leaps to safety across the ice-choked Ohio River.

E Y E W I T N E S S   T O   H I S T O R Y

A Northerner Views Uncle Tom's Cabin *on the Stage*

I read Uncle Toms Cabin when first published with great interest, and since it has been dramatized, I have heard much and read much of its influence on the minds of those who make it a part of their religion to witness Theatrical performances. When I came here this time, I found the City [Chicago] was all astir, in consequence of the Marsh Troupe from New York City playing Uncle Toms Cabin every evening. . . . In as much as the play was to be in the Tremont Hall, instead of the Theater, I concluded to spend an evening for the first [time] in my life in witnessing a dramatic play. Of course I would not be competent to judge whether the play was well performed or not. But from the effect produced on my own mind, I should think the characters of St. Clair, Eva, Aunt Ophelia (from Vermont) Topsy and Uncle Tom were very correctly delineated. When Aunt Ophelia and Topsy appeared on the stage I was convulsed with laughter. . . . But my laughing was soon turned to weeping. The appeals of the dying little Eva to her father, for Uncle Toms freedom, were overwhelmingly effecting. It is not an unusual thing for me to shed tears, but it is not usual for them to roll down my cheeks in quite *so* large drops as they did on this occasion. . . . After composing myself a little, I ventured to "eyes right," and I must confess that I never saw so many white pocket handkerchiefs in use at the same time, and, for the same purpose before. I was not the only one in that large audience to shed tears I assure you. Our "name was legion."

What will be the effect, or the result, of this marvelous book of Fiction, on the destinies of the world, or upon our own Nation, time only can reveal. That it will exert a favorable influence for the rights of humanity and have a happy tendency towards the enfranchisement of the down trodden millions of our own land, I cannot for a moment doubt.

John Kirk to Mr. Elliot, Chicago, April 30, 1854.

spread opportunity, where enterprising individuals could improve their lot. Stopping the expansion of slavery, in Republican eyes, would preserve this heritage of opportunity and economic independence for white Americans. Republicans by and large remained blind to ways in which industrialization was closing off avenues of social mobility for poor workers.

Also important was the moral opposition to slavery, which works like Harriet Beecher Stowe's *Uncle Tom's Cabin* had strengthened. Republican speakers and editors stressed that slavery was a moral wrong, that it was incompatible with the ideals of the Republic and Christianity. "Never forget," Republican leader Abraham Lincoln declared on one occasion, "that we have before us this whole matter of the right and wrong of slavery in this Union, though the immediate question is as to its spreading out into new Territories and States."

More negatively, Republicans gained support by shifting their attacks from slavery itself to the Slave Power, or the political influence of the planter class.

Threat to white liberty

Pointing to the Sumner assault and the incidents in Kansas, Republicans contended that the Slave Power had set out to destroy the liberties of white northerners. Just as the nation's founders had battled against tyranny, aristocracy, and minority rule in the Revolution, so the North confronted the unrepublican Slave Power. "If our government, for the sake of Slavery, is to be perpetually the representative of a minority," argued the Cincinnati *Commercial*, "it may continue republican in form, but the substance of its republicanism has departed."

In the election, Buchanan all but swept the South (losing only Maryland to Fillmore) and won enough free states to push him over the top, with 174 electoral votes to Frémont's 114 and Fillmore's 8. Still, the violence in Kansas and Sumner's caning nearly carried Frémont into the presidency. He ran ahead of both Buchanan and Fillmore in the North and won 11 free states out of 16. Had he carried Pennsylvania plus one more, he would have been elected. For the first time in American history, an antislavery party based entirely in the North threatened to elect a president and snap the bonds of union.

THE WORSENING CRISIS

James Buchanan was one of the most experienced men ever elected president: he had served in Congress, in the cabinet, and in the foreign service. Moderates in both sections hoped that the new president would thwart Republicans in the North and secessionists of the Deep South, popularly known as "fire-eaters." Throughout his career, however, Buchanan had taken the southern position on sectional matters, and he proved remarkably insensitive to the concerns of northern Democrats. Moreover, on March 6, 1857, only two days after Buchanan's inauguration, the Supreme Court gave the new administration a jolt with one of the most controversial decisions in its history.

The Dred Scott *Decision*

The owner of a Missouri slave named Dred Scott had taken him to live for several years in Illinois, a free state, and in what is now Minnesota, where slavery had been banned by the Missouri Compromise. Eventually the owner returned with Scott to Missouri. Scott sued for his freedom on the grounds that his residence in a free state and a free territory had made him free, and his case ultimately went to the Supreme Court. Two northern justices joined all five southern members in ruling 7 to 2 that Scott remained a slave. The major opinion was written by Chief Justice Roger Taney of Maryland.

Wanting to strengthen the judicial protection of slavery, Taney ruled that African Americans could not be and never had been citizens of the United

Protection of slavery

States. Instead, he insisted that at the time the Constitution was adopted, they were "regarded as beings of an inferior order, so far inferior that they had no rights which the white man was bound to respect." In addition, the Court ruled that the Missouri Compromise was unconstitutional. Congress, it declared, had no power to ban slavery from *any* territory of the United States.

While southerners rejoiced at this result, Republicans denounced the Court for rejecting their party's main principle, that Congress should prohibit slavery in

Reaction to the decision

all territories. "We know the court . . . has often over-ruled its own decisions," Abraham Lincoln observed, "and we shall do what we can to have it over-rule this." For Republicans, the decision foreshadowed the spread of slavery throughout the West and even the nation.

But the decision also was a blow to Douglas's moderate solution of popular sovereignty. If Congress had no power to prohibit slavery in a territory, how could it authorize a territorial legislature to do so? While the Court did not rule on this point, the clear implication of the *Dred Scott* decision was that popular sovereignty was also unconstitutional. The Court, in effect, had endorsed John Calhoun's radical view that slavery was legal in all the territories. In so doing, the Court, which had intended to settle the question of slavery in the territories, instead pushed the political debate toward new extremes.

The Panic of 1857

As the nation grappled with the *Dred Scott* decision, an economic depression aggravated sectional conflict. The Panic of 1857 was nowhere near as severe as

Uneven effects of the Panic

the depression of 1839–1843. But the psychological results were far-reaching, for the South remained relatively untouched. With the price of cotton and other southern commodities still high, southern secessionists hailed the panic as proof that an independent southern nation was economically workable. Insisting that cotton sustained the international economy, James Henry Hammond, a senator from South Carolina, boasted: "No, you dare not make war on cotton. No power on earth dares to make war on it. Cotton is king."

For their part, northerners urged federal action to bolster the economy. Southerners defeated an attempt to increase the tariff duties, which were at their lowest level since 1815, and Buchanan, under southern pressure, vetoed bills to improve navigation on the Great Lakes and to give free farms to western settlers. Many northern conservatives concluded that southern obstructionism blocked national development and now endorsed the Republican party.

The Lecompton Constitution

Although the *Dred Scott* decision and economic depression weakened the bonds of the Union, Kansas remained at the center of the political stage. In June 1857, when the territory elected delegates to draft a state constitution, free-staters boycotted the election, thereby giving proslavery forces control of the convention that met in Lecompton. The delegates promptly drafted a constitution that made slavery legal. Even more boldly, they scheduled a referendum in which voters could choose only whether to admit additional slaves into the new state. They could not vote against either the constitution or slavery. Once again, free-staters boycotted the election, and the Lecompton constitution was approved.

President Buchanan had pledged earlier there would be a free and fair vote on the Lecompton constitution. But the outcome offered the unexpected opportunity to create one additional slave state and thereby satisfy his southern supporters by pushing the Lecompton constitution through Congress. This was too much for Douglas, who broke party ranks and denounced the Lecompton constitution as a fraud. Nevertheless, the administration prevailed in the Senate. But the House, where northern representation was much stronger, rejected the constitution. In a compromise, Congress, using indirect language, returned the constitution to Kansas for another vote. This time it was decisively defeated, 11,300 to 1788. No doubt remained that as soon as Kansas had sufficient population, it would come into the Union as a free state.

Defeat of Lecompton constitution

The attempt to force slavery on the people of Kansas drove many conservative northerners into the Republican party. And Douglas now found himself assailed by the southern wing of his party. On top of that, in the summer of 1858, he faced a desperate fight in his race for reelection to the Senate against Republican Abraham Lincoln.

The Lincoln–Douglas Debates

"He is the strong man of his party . . . and the best stump speaker, with his droll ways and dry jokes, in the West," Douglas commented when he learned of Lincoln's nomination to oppose him. "He is as honest as he is shrewd, and if I beat him my victory will be hardly won." Tall (6 feet, 4 inches) and gangly, Lincoln had an awkward manner as he spoke, yet his finely honed logic and sincerity carried the audience with him. His sentences had none of the oratorical flourishes common in that day. "If we could first know *where* we are, and *whither* we are tending, we could then better judge *what* to do, and *how* to do it,"

Superb debaters, Douglas and Lincoln nevertheless had very different speaking styles. The deep-voiced Douglas was constantly on the attack, drawing on his remarkable memory and showering points like buckshot in all directions. Lincoln, who had a high-pitched voice, developed his arguments more carefully and methodically, and he relied on his sense of humor and unmatched ability as a storyteller to drive his points home to the audience.

Lincoln began, in accepting his party's nomination for senator in 1858. He quoted a proverb from the Bible:

"A house divided against itself cannot stand."

I believe this government cannot endure, permanently half slave and half free.

I do not expect the Union to be *dissolved*—I do not expect the house to *fall*—but I *do* expect it will cease to be divided.

It will become *all* one thing, or *all* the other.

Either the *opponents* of slavery, will arrest the further spread of it, and place it where the public mind shall rest in the belief that it is in course of ultimate extinction; or its *advocates* will push it forward, till it shall become alike lawful in all the States, *old* as well as new—*North* as well as *South*.

The message echoed through the hall and across the pages of the national press.

Born in the slave state of Kentucky, Lincoln grown up mostly in southern Indiana and central Illinois. Yet his intense ambition lifted him above the back-

Lincoln's character woods from which he came. He compensated for a lack of schooling through disciplined self-education, and he became a shrewd courtroom lawyer of respectable social standing. Known for his sense of humor, he was nonetheless subject to fits of acute depression.

Lincoln's first love was always politics. A fervent admirer of Henry Clay and his economic program, he became a Whig and then, after the party's demise, joined the Republicans and became one of their key leaders in Illinois. In a series of seven joint debates, Lincoln challenged Douglas to discuss the issues of slavery and the sectional controversy.

In the campaign, Douglas sought to portray Lincoln as a radical who preached sectional warfare. The nation *could* endure half slave and half free, *Debate over the slavery issue* Douglas declared, so long as states and territories were left alone to regulate their own affairs. Lincoln countered by insisting that the spread of slavery was a blight on the Republic. Even though Douglas had voted against the Lecompton constitution, he could not be counted on to oppose slavery's expansion, for he admitted that he didn't care whether slavery was voted "down or up."

In the debate held at Freeport, Illinois, Lincoln asked Douglas how under the *Dred Scott* decision the people of a territory could lawfully exclude slavery *Freeport Doctrine* before statehood. Douglas answered, with what became known as the Freeport Doctrine, that slaveowners would never bring their slaves into an area where slavery was not legally protected. Therefore, Douglas explained, if the people of a territory refused to pass a slave code, slavery would never be established there.

In a close race, the legislature elected Douglas to another term in the Senate.* But on the national scene, southern Democrats angrily repudiated him and condemned the Freeport Doctrine. And although Lincoln lost, Republicans thought his impressive performance marked him as a possible presidential contender for 1860.

The Beleaguered South

While northerners increasingly feared that the Slave Power was conspiring to extend slavery into the free states, southerners worried that the "Black Republicans" would hem them in and undermine their political power.

The very factors that brought prosperity during the 1850s stimulated the South's sense of crisis. As the price of slaves rose sharply, the proportion of southerners who owned slaves had dropped almost a third since 1830. Land also was being consolidated into larger holdings, evidence of declining opportunity

---

*State legislatures elected senators until 1913, when the Seventeenth Amendment was adopted. While Lincoln and Douglas both campaigned for the office, Illinois voters actually voted for candidates for the legislature who were pledged to one of the senatorial candidates.

for ordinary white southerners. At the same time, California and Kansas had been closed to southern slaveholders—unfairly, in their eyes. Finally, Douglas's clever claim that a territory could effectively outlaw slavery using the Freeport Doctrine seemed to negate the *Dred Scott* decision that slavery was legal in all the territories.

Several possible solutions to the South's internal crisis had failed. Agricultural reform to restore worn-out lands had made significant headway in Virginia and Maryland, but elsewhere the rewards of a single-crop economy were just too great. Another alternative—industrialization—had also failed. Indeed, the gap between the North and the South steadily widened in the 1850s. Finally, private military expeditions in Latin America, which were designed to strengthen the South by adding slave territory to the United States, came to naught.

Failed solutions

The South's growing sense of isolation made this crisis more acute. By the 1850s slavery had been abolished throughout most of the Americas, and in the United States the South's political power was steadily shrinking. Only the expansion of slavery held out any promise of new slave states needed to preserve the South's political power and protect its way of life. "The truth is," fumed one Alabama politician, ". . . the South is excluded from the common territories of the Union. The right of expansion claimed to be a necessity of her continued existence, is practically and effectively denied the South."

THE ROAD TO WAR

In 1857 John Brown—the abolitionist firebrand—had returned to the East from Kansas, consumed with the idea of attacking slavery in the South itself. Financed by a number of prominent northern reformers, Brown gathered 21 followers, including 5 free blacks, in hope of fomenting a slave insurrection. On the night of October 16, 1859, his band seized the unguarded federal armory at Harpers Ferry in Virginia. But no slaves rallied to Brown's standard: few lived in the area to begin with. Before long the raiders found themselves surrounded and holed up in the town. Charging with bayonets fixed, federal troops commanded by Colonel Robert E. Lee soon captured Brown and his raiders. On December 2, 1859, Virginia hanged Brown for treason.

John Brown attacks Harpers Ferry

Brown's raid at Harpers Ferry was yet another blow weakening the forces of compromise and moderation within the nation. Although the invasion itself was a dismal failure, the old man knew well how to bear himself with a martyr's dignity. Republicans made haste to denounce Brown's raid, lest they be tarred as radicals, but other northerners were less cautious. Ralph Waldo Emerson described Brown as a "saint, whose martyrdom will make the gallows as glorious as the cross." While only a minority of northerners endorsed Brown, southerners were shocked by such displays of sympathy. And they were firmly convinced that the

Republican party was secretly connected to the raid. "I have always been a fervid Union man," one North Carolina resident wrote, "but I confess the endorsement of the Harpers Ferry outrage has shaken my fidelity and I am willing to take the chances of every probable evil that may arise from disunion, sooner than submit any longer to Northern insolence and Northern outrage."

A Sectional Election

When Congress convened in December, there were ominous signs everywhere of the growing sectional rift. Intent on destroying Douglas's Freeport Doctrine, southern radicals demanded a congressional slave code to protect slavery in the territories. To northern Democrats, such a platform spelled political death. As one Indiana Democrat put it, "We cannot carry a single congressional district on that doctrine in the state."

Disruption of the Democratic party

At the Democratic convention in April, southern radicals boldly pressed their demand for a federal slave code. But instead the convention adopted the Douglas platform upholding popular sovereignty, whereupon the delegations from eight southern states walked out. The convention finally reassembled two months later and nominated Douglas. At this point most of the remaining southern Democrats departed and, together with those delegates who had seceded earlier, nominated Vice President John C. Breckinridge of Kentucky on a platform supporting a federal slave code. The last major national party had shattered.

The Republicans turned to Abraham Lincoln, a moderate on slavery who was strong in his home state of Illinois and the other doubtful states that the party had failed to carry in 1856. Republicans also sought to broaden their appeal by adding to their platform several economic planks that endorsed a moderately protective tariff, a homestead bill, and a northern transcontinental railroad.

Lincoln's victory

The election that followed was really two contests in one. In the North, which had a majority of the electoral votes, only Lincoln and Douglas had any chance to carry a state. In the South, the race pitted Breckinridge against John Bell of Tennessee, the candidate of the new Constitutional Union party. Although Lincoln received less than 40 percent of the popular vote and had virtually no support in the South, he won 180 electoral votes, 27 more than needed for election. For the first time, the nation had elected a president who headed a completely sectional party and who was committed to stopping the expansion of slavery.

Secession

Although the Republicans had not won control of either house of Congress, Lincoln's election struck many southerners as a blow of terrible finality. Lincoln had been lifted into office on the strength of the free states alone. It was not unrealistic, many fire-eaters argued, to believe that he

Southern fears

would use federal aid to induce the border states to voluntarily free their slaves. Once slavery disappeared there, and new states were added, the necessary three-fourths majority would exist to approve a constitutional amendment abolishing slavery. Or perhaps Lincoln might send other John Browns into the South to stir up more slave insurrections. The Montgomery (Alabama) *Mail* accused Republicans of intending "to free the negroes and force amalgamation between them and the children of the poor men of the South."

Secession seemed the only alternative left to protect southern equality and liberty. South Carolina, which had challenged federal authority in the nullifica-

Confederate States of America

tion crisis, was determined to force the other southern states to act. On December 20, 1860, a popular convention unanimously passed a resolution seceding from the Union. The rest of the Deep South followed, and on February 7, 1861, the states stretching from South Carolina to Texas organized the Confederate States of America and elected Jefferson Davis president.

But the Upper South and the border states declined to secede, hoping that once again Congress could patch together a settlement. Senator John Crittenden

Failure of compromise in Congress

of Kentucky proposed extending to Calfornia the old Missouri Compromise line of 36°30′. Slavery would be prohibited north of this line and given federal protection south of it in all territories, including any acquired in the future. Furthermore, Crittenden proposed an "unamendable amendment" to the Constitution, forever preserving slavery in states where it already existed.

But the Crittenden Compromise was doomed, for the simple reason that the two groups who were required to make concessions—Republicans and secessionists—had no interest in doing so. "The argument is exhausted," representatives from the Deep South announced, even before Crittenden had introduced his package. "We have just carried an election on principles fairly stated to the people," Lincoln wrote in opposing compromise. "Now we are told in advance, the government shall be broken up, unless we surrender to those we have beaten, before we take the offices. If we surrender, it is the end of us, and of the government."

The Outbreak of War

As his inauguration approached, Lincoln pondered what to do about secession. In his inaugural address on March 4, he sought to reassure southerners that he had no intention, "directly or indirectly, to interfere with the institution of slavery in the States where it exists." But he maintained that "the Union of these states is perpetual," and he announced that he intended to "hold, occupy and possess" federal property and collect customs duties under the tariff. He closed by calling for a restoration of the "bonds of affection" that united all Americans.

The new president hoped for time to work out a solution, but on his first day in office he was given a dispatch from Major Robert Anderson, comman-

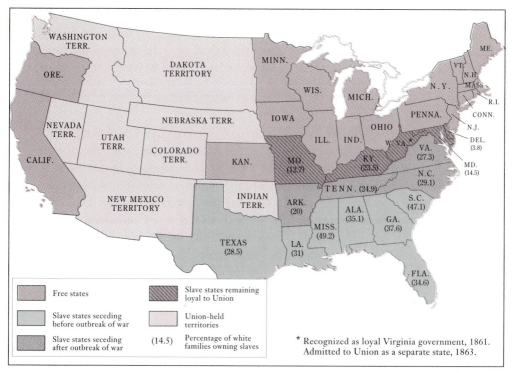

Free states

Slave states seceding before outbreak of war

Slave states seceding after outbreak of war

Slave states remaining loyal to Union

Union-held territories

(14.5) Percentage of white families owning slaves

* Recognized as loyal Virginia government, 1861. Admitted to Union as a separate state, 1863.

THE PATTERN OF SECESSION   Led by South Carolina, the Deep South seceded between Lincoln's election in November and his inauguration in March. The Upper South did not secede until after the firing on Fort Sumter. The four border slave states never seceded and remained in the Union throughout the war. As the map indicates, secession sentiment was strongest in states where the highest percentage of white families owned slaves.

Fort Sumter   der of the federal garrison at Fort Sumter in Charleston harbor. Sumter was one of the few remaining federal outposts in the South. Anderson informed the government that he was almost out of food and that, unless resupplied, he would have to surrender. For a month Lincoln looked for a way out, but he finally sent a relief expedition. As a conciliatory gesture, he notified the governor of South Carolina that supplies were being sent and that if the fleet were allowed to pass, only food, and not men, arms, or ammunition, would be landed.

The burden of decision now shifted to Jefferson Davis. From his point of view, secession was a constitutional right, and the Confederacy was not a bogus *Upper South* but a legitimate government. To allow the United States to hold *secedes* property and maintain military forces within the Confederacy would destroy its claim of independence. Davis therefore instructed the Confederate commander at Charleston to demand the immediate surrender of Fort Sumter and, if refused, to open fire. When Anderson declined the ultimatum, Confederate batteries began shelling the fort on April 12 at 4:30 A.M. Some 33 hours later Anderson surrendered. When in response Lincoln called for 75,000 volunteers to put down the rebellion, four states in the Upper South, led by Virginia, also seceded. Matters had passed beyond compromise.

COUNTERPOINT *Lincoln's Motives in the Fort Sumter Crisis*

Lincoln's decision to relieve Fort Sumter had dire consequences. Not surprisingly, historians have disagreed on the president's motives. Was the act a carefully crafted attempt to strengthen the Republican party and bolster Lincoln's own position? Certainly he faced mounting criticism in Congress and in the northern press for not dealing decisively with secession. In response, some historians argue, Lincoln maneuvered the Confederacy into firing the first shot in the war that Lincoln believed inevitable and desirable. As the commander of the unsuccessful relief expedition put it, the president's clever policy forced the Confederacy to "fire upon bread." To these historians, Lincoln was the bringer of war.

Critics of this interpretation insist that the resort to war represented a defeat of Lincoln's intentions. They emphasize that the president notified South Carolina's governor of the expedition in advance and sent only supplies, not troops or ammunition. Moreover, Lincoln's action did not force the Confederacy to attack the fort; he was merely trying to continue the stalemate that had existed for more than three months in Charleston.

Of course, the extremes of both these explanations suggest a middle ground. If Lincoln had really wanted a war, surely he would have considered it a defeat if the Confederates had allowed the resupply ships to pass unharmed. And there is no evidence to support that view. At the same time, Lincoln clearly ranked saving the Union above maintaining peace at all costs. Thus it is possible to argue that the president maneuvered the Confederate government into a position where it would have to fire first *if* any shots were fired at all. Davis did not have to give the order to attack. In the end, though, Davis preferred war to reunion, just as Lincoln preferred war to disunion.

The Roots of a Divided Nation

And so the Union was broken. After 70 years, the forces of sectionalism and separatism had finally outpulled the ties binding "these United States." Why did affairs come to such a pass?

In some ways, as we have seen, the revolution in markets, the improving technologies of transportation, the increasingly sophisticated systems of credit and finance, all served to tie the nation together. The cotton planter who rode the steamship *Fashion* along the Alabama River ("Time's money! Time's money!") was wearing ready-made clothes manufactured in New York from southern cotton. Chauncey Jerome's clocks from Connecticut were keeping time not only for commercial planters but also for Lowell mill workers like Mary Paul, who learned to measure her lunch break in minutes. Wheat farmers in Athens, Tennessee, and Ottumwa, Iowa, were interested in the price of wheat in New York, for it affected the profits that could be made shipping their grain by the new railroad lines. American society had become far more specialized, and therefore far more interdependent, since the days of Crèvecoeur's self-sufficient farmer of the 1780s.

But a specialized economy had not brought unity. For the North, specialization meant more factories, a higher percentage of urban workers, and a

Diverging economies

greater number of cities and towns. Industry affected midwestern farmers as well, for their steel plows and McCormick reapers allowed them to farm larger holdings and required greater capital investment in the new machinery. For its part, the South was transformed by the industrial revolution too, as textile factories made cotton the booming mainstay of its economy. But for all its growth, the region remained largely a rural society. Its prosperity stemmed from expansion westward into new areas of cotton production, not new forms of production or technology.

Above all, the intensive labor required to produce cotton, rice, and sugar made slavery an inseparable part of the southern way of life—"so intimately mingled with our social conditions," as one Georgian admitted, "that it would be impossible to eradicate it." An increasing number of northerners viewed slavery as evil, not so much out of high-minded sympathy toward slaves but as a labor system that threatened the republican ideals of white American society. The new territories became the battlegrounds for two contrasting ways of life, with slavery at the center of the debate.

It fell to the political system to try to adjudicate sectional conflict, through a system of national parties that represented various interest groups and pro-

Weaknesses of the political system

moted democratic debate. But the political system had critical weaknesses. The American process of electing a president gave the winning candidate a state's entire electoral vote, regardless of the margin of victory. That procedure made a northern sectional party possible, since the Republicans could never have carried an election on the basis of a popular vote alone. In addition, since 1844 the Democratic party had required a two-thirds vote to nominate its presidential candidate. Unintentionally, this requirement made it difficult to pick any truly forceful leader and gave the South a veto over the party's candidate. Yet the South, by itself, could not elect a president.

The nation's republican heritage also contributed to the political system's vulnerability. Ever since the Revolution, when Americans accused the king and

Belief in conspiracies against liberty

Parliament of deliberately plotting to deprive them of their liberties, Americans were on the watch for political conspiracies. Such an outlook often stimulated exaggerated fears, unreasonable conclusions, and excessive reactions. For their part,

Republicans emphasized the existence of the Slave Power bent on eradicating northern rights. Southerners, on the other hand, accused the Black Republicans of conspiring to destroy southern equality. Each side viewed itself as defending the country's republican tradition from an internal threat.

In 1850 southerners might have been satisfied if their section had been left alone and the agitation against slavery had ended. But a decade later, many Americans both North and South had come to accept the idea of an irrepressible conflict between two societies, one based on freedom, the other on slavery, in which only one side could ultimately prevail. At stake, it seemed, was control of the nation's future. Four years later, as a weary Abraham Lincoln looked back to the beginning of the conflict, he noted, "Both parties deprecated war, but one of them would *make* war rather than let the nation survive, and the other would *accept* war rather than let it perish, and the war came."

SIGNIFICANT EVENTS

1834	McCormick patents mechanical reaper
1837	John Deere patents steel plow
1840–1860	Expansion of railroad network
1846–1854	Mass immigration to United States
1849–1860	Cotton boom
1852	Pierce elected president
1853	Gadsden Purchase
1854	Kansas–Nebraska Act; Republican party organized; peak of immigration
1854–1855	Height of Know-Nothings' popularity
1855	Fighting begins in Kansas; Republican party organizes in key northern states
1856	Free state "government" established in Kansas; "Sack of Lawrence"; caning of Charles Sumner; Pottawatomie massacre; Buchanan elected president
1857–1861	Panic and depression
1857	*Dred Scott* decision; Lecompton constitution drafted
1858	Congress rejects Lecompton constitution; Lincoln–Douglas debates
1859	John Brown's raid on Harpers Ferry
1860	Democratic party ruptures; Lincoln elected president; South Carolina secedes
1861	Rest of Deep South secedes; Confederate States of America established; Crittenden Compromise defeated; war begins at Fort Sumter; Upper South secedes

CHAPTER SIXTEEN

Total War and the Republic

The war won't last sixty days!" Of that Jim Tinkham was confident. With dreams of a hero's return, Tinkham enlisted for three months in a Massachusetts regiment. Soon he was transferred to Washington as part of the Union army being assembled under the command of General Irvin McDowell. Tinkham was elated when in mid-July the army was finally ordered to march toward the Confederates concentrated at Manassas Junction, 25 miles away.*

The battle began at dawn on July 21, with McDowell commanding 30,000 troops against General Pierre Beauregard's 22,000. Tinkham did not arrive on the field until early afternoon. As his regiment pushed toward the front, he felt faint at his first sight of the dead and wounded, some mangled horribly. But he was soon caught up in the excitement of battle as he charged up Henry Hill. Suddenly the Confederate ranks broke and exuberant Union troops shouted, "The war is over!"

The timely arrival of fresh troops, however, enabled the Confederates to regroup and resume the fight. Among the reinforcements who rushed to Henry Hill was 19-year-old Randolph McKim of Baltimore. A student at the University of Virginia when the war began, McKim joined the First Maryland Infantry as a private when Abraham Lincoln imposed martial law in his home state. "The cause of the South had become identified with liberty itself," he explained. After only a week of drill, McKim boarded a train on July 21 bound for Manassas. The arrival of the First Maryland and other reinforcements in the late afternoon turned the tide of battle. The faltering Confederate line held, and Union troops began to withdraw.

---

*The Union and the Confederacy often gave different names to a battle. The Confederates called the first battle Manassas; the Union, Bull Run.

Once McDowell ordered a retreat, discipline dissolved, the army degenerated into a mob, and a stampede began. As they fled, terrified troops threw away their equipment, shoved aside officers who tried to stop them, and raced frantically past the wagons and artillery pieces that clogged the road. Joining the stampede was Jim Tinkham, who confessed he would have continued on to Boston if he had not been stopped by a guard in Washington.

All the next day in a drizzling rain, mud-spattered troops straggled into the capital in complete disorder. William Russell, an English reporter, asked one pale officer where they were coming from. "Well, sir, I guess we're all coming out of Virginny as far as we can, and pretty well whipped too," he replied. "I know I'm going home. I've had enough of fighting to last my lifetime."

The rout at Bull Run sobered the North. Gone were dreams of ending the war with one glorious battle. Gone was the illusion that 75,000 volunteers serving three months could crush the rebellion. As one perceptive observer noted, "We have undertaken to make war without in the least knowing how." Having cast off his earlier misconceptions, a newly determined Jim Tinkham reenlisted for a three-year hitch.

Still, it was not surprising that both sides underestimated the magnitude of the conflict. Previous warfare as it had evolved in Europe consisted largely of maneuverings that took relatively few lives, respected private property, and left civilians largely unharmed. The Civil War, on the other hand, was the first war whose major battles routinely involved more than 100,000 troops. So many combatants could be equipped only through the use of factory-produced weaponry, they could be moved and supplied only with the help of railroads, and they could be sustained only through the concerted efforts of civilian society as a whole. The morale of the population, the quality of political leadership, and the utilization of industrial and economic might were all critical to the outcome. Quite simply, the Civil War was the first total war in history.

Meaning of total war

THE DEMANDS OF TOTAL WAR

When the war began, the North had an enormous advantage in manpower and industrial capacity. The Union's population was 2.5 times larger; it contained more railroad track and rolling stock and possessed more than 10 times the industrial capacity.

From a modern perspective, the South's attempt to defend its independence against such odds seems hopeless. Yet this view indicates how much the conception of war has changed. European observers, who knew the strength and resources of the two sides, believed that the Confederacy could never be conquered. Indeed, the South enjoyed definite strategic advantages. To be victorious, it did not need to invade the North—only to defend its own land and prevent the North from destroy-

Southern advantages

RESOURCES OF THE UNION AND THE CONFEDERACY, 1861			
	UNION	CONFEDERACY	UNION ADVANTAGE
Total population	22,300,000	9,100,000*	2.5 to 1
White male population (18–45 years)	4,600,000	1,100,000	4.2 to 1
Bank deposits	$207,000,000	$47,000,000	4.4 to 1
Value of manufactured goods	$1,730,000,000	$156,000,000	11 to 1
Railroad mileage	22,000	9,000	2.4 to 1
Shipping tonnage	4,600,000	290,000	16 to 1
Value of textiles produced	$181,000,000	$10,000,000	18 to 1
Value of firearms produced	$2,290,000	$73,000	31 to 1
Pig iron production (tons)	951,000	37,000	26 to 1
Coal production (tons)	13,680,000	650,000	21 to 1
Corn and wheat production (bushels)	698,000,000	314,000,000	2.2 to 1
Draft animals	5,800,000	2,900,000	2 to 1
Cotton production (bales)	43,000	5,344,000	1 to 124

*Slaves accounted for 3,500,000, or 40 percent

Source: U.S. Census 1860 and E. B. Long, *The Civil War Day by Day* (New York: Doubleday, 1971), p. 723.

ing its armies. Southern soldiers knew the topography of their home country better, and a friendly population regularly supplied them with intelligence about Union troop movements.

The North, in contrast, had to invade and conquer the Confederacy and destroy the southern will to resist. To do so, it would have to deploy thousands of soldiers to defend long supply lines in enemy territory, a situation that significantly reduced the northern advantage in manpower. Yet by 1865 the Union forces had penetrated virtually every part of the 500,000 square miles of the Confederacy and were able to move almost at will. The Civil War demonstrated the capacity of a modern society to overcome distance and terrain with technology.

Political Leadership

To sustain a commitment to total war required effective political leadership. This task fell on Abraham Lincoln and Jefferson Davis, presidents of the rival governments.

Jefferson Davis grew up in Mississippi accustomed to life's advantages. Educated at West Point, he fought in the Mexican War, served as Franklin

Davis's character

Pierce's secretary of war, and became one of the South's leading advocates in the Senate. Although he was hard-working and committed to the cause he led, his temperament was not well suited to his new post: he was quarrelsome, resented criticism, and refused to work with those he disliked. "He cannot brook opposition or criticism," one member of the Confederate Congress testified, "and those who do not bow down before him have no chance of success with him."

Yet for all Davis's personal handicaps, he faced an institutional one even more daunting. The Confederacy had been founded on the ideology of states' rights. Yet to meet the demands of total war, Davis would need to increase the authority of the central government beyond anything the South had ever experienced.

When Lincoln took the oath of office, his national experience consisted of one term in the House of Representatives. But Lincoln was a shrewd judge of

Lincoln's leadership

character and a superb politician. To achieve a common goal, he willingly overlooked withering criticism and personal slights. He was not easily humbugged, overawed, or flattered and never allowed personal feelings to blind him to his larger objectives. "No man knew

Jefferson Davis

better how to summon and dispose of political ability to attain great political ends," commented one associate.

"This is essentially a People's contest," Lincoln asserted at the start of the war, and few presidents have been better able to communicate with the average citizen. He regularly visited Union troops in camp, in the field, and in army hospitals. "The boys liked him," wrote Joseph Twichell, from a Connecticut regiment, "in fact his popularity with the army is and has been universal." Always Lincoln reminded the public that the war was being fought for the ideals of the Revolution and the Republic. It was a test, he remarked in his famous address at Gettysburg, of whether a nation "conceived in Liberty, and dedicated to the proposition that all men are created equal" could "long endure."

He also proved the more effective military leader. Jefferson Davis took his title of commander-in-chief literally, constantly interfering with his generals, but he failed to formulate an effective overarching strategy. In contrast, Lincoln clearly grasped the challenge confronting the Union. He accepted General Winfield Scott's proposal to blockade the Confederacy, cut off its supplies, and slowly strangle it into submission. But unlike Scott, he realized that this plan was not enough. The South would also have to be invaded and defeated, not only on an eastern front in Virginia but in the West, where Union control of the Mississippi would divide the Confederacy. Lincoln understood that the Union's superior manpower and materiel would become decisive only when the Confederacy was simultaneously threatened along a broad front. It took time before the president found generals able to execute this novel strategy.

The Border States

When the war began, only Delaware of the border slave states was certain to remain in the Union. Lincoln's immediate political challenge was to retain the loyalty of Maryland, Kentucky, and Missouri. Maryland especially was crucial, for if it was lost, Washington itself would have to be abandoned.

Lincoln moved vigorously—even ruthlessly—to secure Maryland. He suppressed pro-Confederate newspapers and suspended the writ of habeas corpus,

Suppression in Maryland
the right under the Constitution of an arrested person either to be charged with a specific crime or to be released. That done, he held without trial prominent Confederate sympathizers. Intervention by the army ensured that Unionists won a complete victory in the fall state election. The election ended any possibility that Maryland would join the Confederacy.

At the beginning of the conflict, Kentucky officially declared its neutrality. Union generals requested permission to occupy the state, but the president re-

Kentucky's neutrality
fused, preferring to act cautiously and wait for Unionist sentiment to assert itself. After Unionists won control of the legislature in the summer election, a Confederate army entered the

state, giving Lincoln the opening he needed. He quickly sent in troops, and Kentucky stayed in the Union.

In Missouri, skirmishing broke out between Union and Confederate sympathizers. Only after the Battle of Pea Ridge in March 1862 was Missouri secure from any Confederate threat. Even so, guerrilla warfare continued in the state throughout the remainder of the war.

In Virginia, internal divisions led to the creation of a new border state, as the hilly western counties where slavery was not strong refused to support the Confederacy. After adopting a congressionally mandated program of gradual emancipation, West Virginia was formally admitted to the Union in June 1863.

The Union scored an important triumph in holding the border states. The population of all five equaled that of the four states of the Upper South that had joined the Confederacy, and their production of military supplies—food, animals, and minerals—was greater. Furthermore, Maryland and West Virginia contained key railroad lines and were critical to the defense of Washington, while Kentucky and Missouri gave the Union army access to the major river systems of the western theater, down which it launched the first successful invasions of the Confederacy.

Importance of the border states

OPENING MOVES

As with so many Civil War battles, the Confederate victory at Bull Run achieved no decisive military results. But Congress authorized a much larger army of long-term volunteers, and Lincoln named 34-year-old George McClellan, a West Point graduate and railroad executive, to be the new commander. Energetic and ambitious, he spent the next eight months directing the much-needed task of organizing and drilling the Army of the Potomac.

Blockade and Isolate

Although the U.S. Navy began the war with only 42 ships available to blockade 3550 miles of Confederate coastline, it had secured key supply bases by the spring of 1862. The navy also began building powerful gunboats to operate on the rivers. In April 1862 Flag Officer David G. Farragut ran a gauntlet of Confederate shore batteries to capture New Orleans, the Confederacy's largest port. Memphis, another important river city, fell to Union forces in June.

The blockade was hardly leakproof, and small, fast ships continued to slip through it. Still, southern trade suffered badly. In hopes of lifting the blockade, the Confederacy converted the wooden U.S.S. *Merrimack*, which was rechristened the *Virginia*, into an ironclad gunboat. In March 1862 a Union ironclad, the *Monitor*, battled it to a standoff, and the Confederates scuttled the *Virginia* when they evacuated Norfolk in May. After that, the Union's naval supremacy was secure.

Ironclads

The Confederacy looked to diplomacy as another means to lift the blockade. With cotton so vital to European economies, especially Great Britain's,

King cotton diplomacy

southerners believed Europe would formally recognize the Confederacy and come to its aid. The British government favored the South, but it hesitated to act until Confederate armies demonstrated that they could win the war. Meanwhile, new supplies of cotton from Egypt and India enabled the British textile industry to recover. In the end, Britain and the rest of Europe refused to recognize the Confederacy, and the South was left to stand or fall on its own resources.

Grant in the West

In the western war theater, the first decisive Union victory was won by a short, shabbily dressed, cigar-chomping general named Ulysses S. Grant. An undistinguished student at West Point, Grant eventually had resigned his commission. He had failed at everything he tried in civilian life, and when the war broke out, he was a store clerk in Galena, Illinois. Almost 39, he promptly volunteered, and two months later became a brigadier general.

Grant's quiet, self-effacing manner gave little indication of his military ability or iron determination. He had a flair for improvising, was alert to seize any

Grant's character

opening, and remained extraordinarily calm and clear-headed in battle. Most important, Grant grasped that hard fighting, not fancy maneuvering, would bring victory. "The art of war is simple," he once explained. "Find out where your enemy is, get at him as soon as you can and strike him as hard as you can, and keep moving on."

Grant realized that rivers were avenues into the interior of the Confederacy, and in February 1862, supported by Union gunboats, he captured Fort Henry

Shiloh

on the Tennessee River and Fort Donelson on the Cumberland. These victories forced the Confederates to withdraw from Kentucky and middle Tennessee. Grant continued south with 40,000 men, but he was surprised on April 6 by General Albert Johnston at Shiloh, just north of the Tennessee–Mississippi border. Johnston was killed in the day's fierce fighting, but by nightfall his army had driven the Union troops back to the Tennessee River, where they huddled numbly as a cold rain fell. William Tecumseh Sherman, one of Grant's subordinates, found the general standing under a dripping tree, his coat collar drawn up against the damp, puffing on a cigar. Sherman was about to suggest retreat, but something in Grant's eyes, lighted by the glow of his stogey, made him hesitate. So he said only, "Well, Grant, we've had the devil's own day, haven't we." "Yes," replied Grant. "Lick 'em tomorrow, though." And he did. With the aid of reinforcements, which he methodically ferried across the river all night, Grant counterattacked the next morning and drove the Confederates from the field.

But victory came at a high price, for Shiloh inflicted more than 23,000 casualties. Grant, who previously had doubted the commitment of Confederate troops,

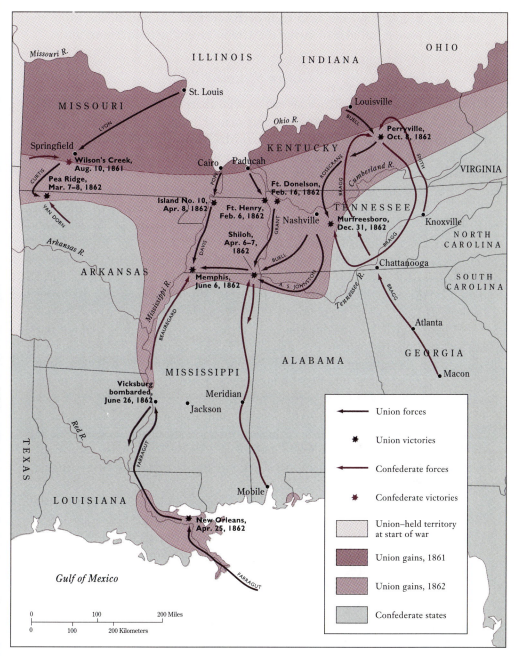

THE WAR IN THE WEST, 1861–1862   Grant's push southward stalled after his costly victory at Shiloh; nevertheless, by the end of 1862 the Union had secured Kentucky and Missouri, as well as most of Confederate Tennessee and the upper and lower stretches of the Mississippi River.

came away deeply impressed with their determination. "At Shiloh," he wrote afterward, "I gave up all idea of saving the Union except by complete conquest."

Eastern Stalemate

Grant's victories did not silence his critics, who charged he drank too much. But Lincoln was unmoved. "I can't spare this man. He fights." That was a quality in short supply in the east, where General McClellan directed operations.

McClellan looked like a general, but beneath his arrogance and bravado lay a self-doubt that rendered him excessively cautious. As the months dragged on and McClellan did nothing but train and plan, Lincoln's frustration grew. "If General McClellan does not want to use the army I would like to *borrow* it," he remarked sarcastically. In the spring of 1862 the general finally transported his 130,000 troops to the Virginia coast and began inching toward Richmond, the Confederate capital. In May General Joseph Johnston suddenly attacked him near Fair Oaks, from which he barely escaped. Worse for McClellan, when Johnston was badly wounded, the formidable Robert E. Lee took command of the Army of Northern Virginia.

"McClellan has the slows"

Where McClellan was cautious and defensive, the aristocratic Lee was daring and ever alert to assume the offensive. His first name, one of his colleagues commented, should have been Audacity: "He will take more chances, and take them quicker than any other general in this country." In the Seven Days' battles, McClellan successfully parried the attacks of Lee and Thomas "Stonewall" Jackson but stayed on the defensive. As McClellan retreated to the protection of the Union gunboats, Lincoln ordered the Peninsula campaign abandoned and formed a new army under John Pope. After Lee badly mauled Pope at the second Battle of Bull Run in August, Lincoln restored McClellan to command.

Lee's generalship

Realizing that the Confederacy needed a decisive victory, Lee invaded the North, hoping to detach Maryland and isolate Washington. Learning that he greatly outnumbered Lee, McClellan launched a series of badly coordinated assaults near Antietam Creek on September 17 that Lee barely repulsed. The bloody exchanges horrified both sides for their sheer carnage. Nearly 5000 soldiers were killed and another 18,000 wounded, making it the bloodiest single day in American history. When McClellan allowed Lee's army to escape back into Virginia, an exasperated Lincoln permanently relieved him from command in November.

Antietam

The winter of 1862 was the North's Valley Forge, as morale sank to an all-time low. It took General Ambrose Burnside, who assumed McClellan's place, little more than a month to demonstrate his utter incompetence at the Battle of Fredericksburg. The Union's disastrous defeat there prompted Lincoln to put "Fighting Joe" Hooker in charge. In the West, Grant had emerged as the dominant figure, but the Army of the Potomac still lacked a capable commander, the deaths kept mounting, and no end to the war was in sight.

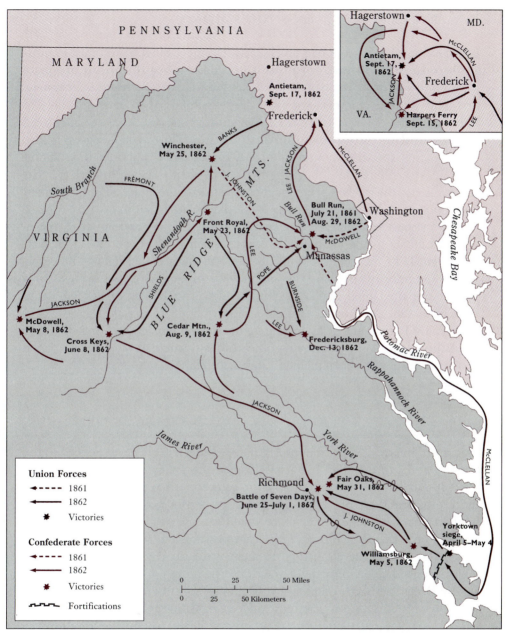

Union Forces
- ◄----- 1861
- ◄—— 1862
- ✴ Victories

Confederate Forces
- ◄----- 1861
- ◄—— 1862
- ✴ Victories
- ⌐⌐⌐⌐ Fortifications

THE WAR IN THE EAST, 1861–1862   McClellan's campaign against Richmond failed when Joseph Johnston surprised him at Fair Oaks. Taking command of the Army of Northern Virginia, Lee drove back McClellan in the Seven Days' battles, then won a resounding victory in the second Battle of Bull Run. He followed this up by invading Maryland. McClellan checked his advance at Antietam. The Army of the Potomac's devastating defeat at Fredericksburg ended a year of frustration and failure for the Union in the eastern theater.

EMANCIPATION

In 1858 Abraham Lincoln had proclaimed that the United States must eventually become either all slave or all free. When the war began, however, the president refused to make emancipation a Union war aim. He perceived, accurately, that most white northerners were not deeply committed to emancipation. He feared the social upheaval that such a revolutionary step would cause, and he did not want to alarm the wavering border slave states. Thus when Congress met in

Crittenden Resolution

special session in July 1861, Lincoln fully supported a resolution offered by John J. Crittenden of Kentucky, which declared that the war was being fought solely to save the Union. The Crittenden Resolution passed the House 117 to 2 and the Senate by 30 to 5.

Still, Republican radicals like Senator Charles Sumner and Horace Greeley pressed Lincoln to adopt a policy of emancipation. Slavery had caused the war, they argued; its destruction would hasten the war's end. Lincoln, however, placed first priority on saving the Union. "My paramount object in this struggle *is* to save the Union, and is *not* either to save or to destroy slavery," he wrote Greeley in 1862. "If I could save the Union without freeing *any* slave I would do it, and if I could save it by freeing *all* the slaves I would do it, and if I could save it by freeing some and leaving others alone, I would also do that." For the first year of the war, this remained Lincoln's policy.

The Logic of Events

As the Union army began to occupy Confederate territory, slaves flocked to the Union lines. In May 1861 the army adopted the policy of declaring runaway slaves "contraband of war" and refused to return them to their rebel owners. In the Confiscation Act of August 1861, Congress provided that slaves used for military purposes by the Confederacy would become free if they fell into Union hands. For a year Lincoln accepted that position but would go no further. When two of his generals, acting on their own authority, abolished slavery in their districts, he countermanded their orders.

By December 1861, opinion was beginning to shift. When the Crittenden

Growing congressional attack on slavery

Resolution was reintroduced in Congress, it was soundly defeated. Congress also prohibited federal troops from capturing or returning fugitive slaves and freed the 2000 slaves living in the District of Columbia with compensation to their owners. In July 1862 it passed the Second Confiscation Act, which declared that the slaves of anyone who supported the rebellion would be freed if they came into federal custody. Unlike the first act, it did not matter whether the slaves had been used for military purposes.

Lincoln signed this bill, then proceeded to ignore it. Instead, he emphasized state action, since slavery was a domestic institution. In his first annual message to Congress, he proposed that the federal government provide grants to compensate slaveowners in any state-sponsored program of gradual emancipation. Twice the president summoned white representatives from the border states and prodded them to act before the war destroyed slavery of its own momentum. Both times they rejected his plea.

Following the failure of his second meeting with the border state leaders, Lincoln on July 22, 1862, presented to his cabinet a proposed proclamation *Lincoln's decision for emancipation* freeing the slaves in the Confederacy. He was increasingly confident that the border states would remain in the Union, and he wanted to strike a blow that would weaken the Confederacy militarily. By making the struggle one of freedom versus slavery, such a proclamation would also undermine Confederate efforts to obtain diplomatic recognition. But Lincoln decided to wait for a Union military victory, so that the act would not seem like one of desperation.

The Emancipation Proclamation

On September 22, in the aftermath of the victory at Antietam, Lincoln announced that all slaves within rebel lines would be freed unless the seceded states returned to their allegiance by January 1, 1863. When that day came, the Emancipation Proclamation went into effect. Excluded from its terms were the Union slave states and areas of the Confederacy that were under Union control. In all, about 830,000 of the nation's 4 million slaves were not covered by its provisions. Since Lincoln justified his actions on strictly military grounds, he believed he had no legal right to apply it to areas not in rebellion.

After initial criticism of the Proclamation, European public opinion swung toward the Union. In the North, Republicans generally favored Lincoln's decision, *Reaction to the Proclamation* while the Democrats made it a major issue in the 1862 elections. "Every white man in the North, who does not want to be swapped off for a free Nigger, should vote the Democratic ticket," urged one party orator. The results in the elections that fall, however, offered no clear verdict on the Proclamation.

Despite the mixed popular reaction, the Emancipation Proclamation had immense symbolic importance, for it redefined the nature of the war. The North was fighting, not to save the old Union, but to create a new nation. The war had become a remorseless revolution.

COUNTERPOINT   *Who Freed the Slaves?*

For many years, the triumph of emancipation was told from the vantage point of Union politics and Abraham Lincoln's presidential leadership. Lincoln made the crucial decision, Congress enacted legislation that crippled the institution, and northern public opinion endorsed this change in policy. The result was the death of slavery.

More recently, as part of social history's emphasis on the ways in which ordinary Americans shaped their lives in meaningful ways, some historians have stressed the role slaves themselves played in ending slavery. Lincoln, after all, made it quite clear at the beginning of the war that he was willing to save the Union without ending slavery. It was thousands of slaves, voting with their feet, who flocked to the Union lines. It was thousands of African Americans who served gallantly in the Union army and navy, and thousands more who undermined the institution of slavery behind southern lines. Such behavior forced the nation to confront the issue of slavery head-on. It pushed Lincoln, finally, to conclude that freeing the slaves was the best way to save the Union. In that sense, emancipation stemmed directly from the initiative of slaves, not from congressional legislation or presidential documents.

Critics of this self-emancipation thesis readily admit that the actions of African Americans in both the Union and the Confederacy were important in destroying slavery. But were they strong enough, by themselves, to end so deeply entrenched an institution as slavery? Before the Civil War, no self-emancipation had occurred on a wide scale during slavery's 200 years of existence. And the spreading tide of freedom could be and was reversed when Union troops left an area and returning Confederates promptly restored slavery. Moreover, these historians argue that escaping to freedom was not the same thing as abolishing slavery. At bottom, slavery could never be eradicated without legal action: in this case, the passage of the Thirteenth Amendment. In that sense, Lincoln's role proved vital. It made a difference, these historians insisted, which side won the war, and how they chose to win it.

African Americans' Civil War

Under the pressure of war, slavery disintegrated. Well before federal troops entered an area, slaves took the lead in undermining the institution by openly challenging white authority and claiming greater personal freedom for themselves. One experienced overseer reported in frustration that the "slaves will do only what pleases them, go out in the morning when it suits them, come in when they please, etc."

Early in the conflict slaves concluded that emancipation would be one consequence of a Union victory. Perhaps as many as half a million—one-seventh of the total slave population of the Confederacy—fled to Union lines. The ex-slaves, called "freedmen," ended up living in refugee or contraband camps that were overcrowded and disease-ridden and provided only the most basic shelter and food.

Seeking freedom

Convinced that freed slaves would not work on their own initiative, the U.S. government put some contrabands to work assisting the army. Their wages were well below those paid white citizens for the same work. In the Mississippi valley, where two-thirds of the freed people under Union control were located, most were forced to work on plantations leased or owned by loyal planters.

Black men, including runaway slaves, joined the Union army and navy
beginning in 1863. As soldiers, former slaves developed a new sense of
pride and confidence. At his first roll call, recruit Elijah Marrs recalled that
"I felt freedom in my bones."

Most worked for little more than room and board, and the conditions often approximated slavery.

Black Soldiers

In adopting the policy of emancipation, Lincoln also announced that African
Americans would be accepted into the navy and, more controversially, the army.
Resistance to accepting black volunteers in the army remained especially strong
in the Midwest. Black northerners themselves were divided over whether to enlist, but Frederick Douglass spoke for the vast majority when he argued that
once a black man had served in the army, there was "no power on earth which
can deny that he has earned the right of citizenship in the United States."

In the end, nearly 200,000 black Americans served in the Union forces,
about 10 percent of the Union's total military manpower. Some, including two
of Douglass's sons, were free, but most were former slaves who enlisted after escaping to the Union lines. As a concession to the racism of white troops, blacks
served in segregated units under white officers. Not until June 1864 did Congress
finally grant equal pay to African American soldiers.

Relegated to the most undesirable duties, black soldiers successfully lobbied
for the chance to fight. They deeply impressed white troops with their courage

Black soldiers in combat

under fire. "I have been one of those men, who never had much confidence in colored troops fighting," one Union officer admitted, "but these doubts are now all removed, for they fought as bravely as any troops in the Fort." In the end 37,000 African American servicemen gave their lives, a rate of loss about 40 percent higher than that among white soldiers. Black recruits had good reason to fight fiercely: they knew that the freedom of their race hung in the balance, they hoped to win civil rights at home by their performance on the battlefield, they resented racist sneers about their loyalty and ability, and they knew that capture might mean death.

THE CONFEDERATE HOME FRONT

"How shall we subsist this winter?" John Jones wondered in the fall of 1862. A clerk in the War Department in Richmond, Jones found it increasingly difficult to make ends meet on his salary. Prices kept going up, essential items were in short supply, and the signs of hardship were everywhere: in the darned and patched clothing, in the absence of meat from the market, in the desperation on people's faces. Coffee was a luxury Jones could no longer afford; he sold his watch to buy fuel; and he worried incessantly about being able to feed his family. "I cannot afford to have more than an ounce of meat daily for each member of my family of six," he recorded in 1864. ". . . We see neither rats nor mice about the premises now." By the end of the year a month's supply of food and fuel was costing him $762, a sum sufficient to have supported his family for a year in peacetime. "This is war, terrible war!"

Nowhere was the effect of war more complete than within the Confederacy. These changes were especially ironic, since the southern states had seceded in order to preserve their traditional ways. The demands of war fundamentally transformed the southern economy, society, and government.

The New Economy

With the Union blockade tightening, the production of foodstuffs became crucial. More and more plantations switched from cotton to raising grain and livestock. As a result, cotton production dropped from 4.5 million bales in 1861 to 300,000 in 1864. Even so, food production declined. In the last two years of the war, the shortage was serious.

The Union blockade also made it impossible to rely on European manufactured goods. So the Confederate War Department built and ran factories,

Attempts to industrialize

took over the region's mines, and regulated private manufacturers so as to increase the production of war goods. Although the Confederacy never became industrially self-sufficient, its accomplishments were impressive. In fact, the Confederacy sustained itself far better in industrial goods than it did in agricultural produce. It was symbolic that when

Lee surrendered, his troops had sufficient guns and ammunition to continue, but they had not eaten in two days.

New Opportunities for Southern Women

Southern white women took an active role in the war. Some gained notoriety as spies; others smuggled military supplies into the South. Women also spent a good deal of time knitting and sewing clothes for soldiers. "We never went out to pay a visit without taking our knitting along," recalled a South Carolina woman. Perhaps most important, with so many men fighting, women took charge of agricultural production. On plantations the mistress often supervised the slaves, as well as the wrenching shift from cotton to foodstuffs. "All this attention to farming is uphill work with me," one South Carolina woman confessed to her army husband.

One such women was Emily Lyles Harris, the wife of a small slaveowner in upcountry South Carolina. When her husband joined the army in 1862, she was left to care for her seven childern, as well as supervise the slaves and manage the farm. She felt overwhelmed. Nevertheless, despite the disruptions of wartime, she succeeded remarkably, one year producing the largest crop of oats in the neighborhood and always making enough money for her family to live decently. She took little pride, however, in her achievements. "I shall never get used to being left as the head of affairs at home," she confessed. "The burden is very heavy, and there is no one to smile on me as I trudge wearily along in the dark with it. . . ." While she persevered in her efforts, by 1865 she openly hoped for defeat.

The war also opened up new jobs off the farm. Given the manpower shortage, "government girls" became essential to fill the growing Confederate bureaucracy. At first women were paid half the wages of male coworkers, but by the end of the war they had won equal pay. Women also staffed the new factories springing up in southern cities and towns, undertaking even dangerous work in munitions factories.

"Of all the principles developed by the late war," wrote one Alabama planter, "I think the capability of our Southern women to take care of themselves was by no means the least important."

Confederate Finance and Government

The most serious domestic problem the Confederate government faced was finance, for which officials at Richmond never developed a satisfactory program. Only in 1863 did the government begin levying a graduated income tax (from 1 to 15 percent) and a series of excise taxes. Most controversial, the government resorted to a tax-in-kind on farmers that, after exempting a certain portion, took one-tenth of their agricultural crops. Even more unpopular was the policy of impressment, which allowed the army to seize private property for its own use, often with little or no compensation.

Above all, the Confederacy financed the war effort simply by printing paper money not backed by specie, some $1.5 billion, which amounted to three

Soaring inflation

times more than the federal government issued. The result was runaway inflation, so that by 1865 a Confederate dollar was worth only 1.7 cents in gold and prices had soared to 92 times their prewar base. Prices were highest in Richmond, where flour sold for $275 a barrel by early 1864 and coats for $350.

In politics even more than finance, the Confederacy exercised far greater powers than those of the federal government before 1861. Indeed, Jefferson

Centralization of power

Davis strove to meet the demands of total war by transforming the South into a centralized, national state. He sought to limit state authority over military units, and in April 1862 the Confederacy passed the first national conscription law in American history. The same year the Congress authorized Davis to invoke martial law and suspend the writ of habeas corpus.

Critics protested that Davis was destroying states' rights, the main principle of the Confederacy. Intent on preserving states' traditional powers,

Opposition to Davis

Confederate governors obstructed the draft and retained military supplies. When President Davis suspended the writ of habeas corpus, his own vice president, Alexander H. Stephens, accused him of aiming at a dictatorship. Davis, however, used those powers for a limited time, only with the permission of Congress, and only where northern invasion threatened.

But the Confederate draft, more than any other measure, produced an outcry. As one Georgia leader complained, "It's a notorious fact if a man has influential friends—or a little money to spare he will never be enrolled." Most controversially, the draft exempted from service one white man on every plantation with 20 or more slaves (later reduced to 15). This law was designed to preserve control of the slave population, but more and more nonslaveholders complained that it was a rich man's war and a poor man's fight.

Hardship and Suffering

By the last year of the conflict, food shortages had become so severe that ingenious southerners concocted various substitutes: parched corn in place of coffee, strained blackberries in place of vinegar. Scarcity bred speculation, hoarding, and spiraling prices. The high prices and food shortages led to riots, most seriously in Richmond early in April 1863, when about 300 women and children chanting "Bread!" looted stores.

As always, war corroded the discipline and order of society. Speculation was rampant, gambling halls were crowded with revelers seeking relief, and many

Social and moral decay

southerners spent money in frenzied haste. Even in the army, theft became common, and in Richmond, the House of Representatives was robbed and Jefferson Davis's favorite horse stolen.

The frantic effort to escape the grim reality of the war led to a forced gaiety among southern civilians. "The cities are gayer than before the war," one refugee reported, "—parties every night in Richmond, suppers costing ten and twenty thousand dollars." Walking home at night after spending several hours at the bedside of a dying soldier, Judith McGuire passed a house gay with laughter, music, and dancing. "The revulsion was sickening," she wrote in her diary. "I . . . felt shocked that our own Virginians, at such a time, should remind me of scenes which we were wont to think only belonged to . . . foreign society." The war was a cancer that ate away not only at southern society but at the southern soul itself.

THE UNION HOME FRONT

Since the war was fought mostly on southern soil, northern civilians rarely felt its effects directly. Yet to be effective, the North's economic resources had to be organized and mobilized.

Government Finances and the Economy

To begin with, the North required a comprehensive system to finance its massive campaign. Taxing the populace was one obvious means, and taxes paid for

Economic legislation

21 percent of Union war expenses, compared with only 1 percent of the Confederacy's. In August 1861 Congress levied the first federal income tax of 3 percent on all incomes over $800 a year. When that, along with increased tariff duties, proved insufficient, Congress enacted a comprehensive tax law in 1862 that for the first time brought the tax collector into every northern household.

The government also borrowed heavily, through the sale of $2.2 billion in bonds. It financed the rest of the war's cost by issuing paper money. In all, the Union printed $431 million in greenbacks (so named because of their color). Congress also instituted a national banking system, allowing nationally chartered banks to issue notes backed by U.S. bonds. By taxing state bank notes out of circulation, Congress for the first time created a uniform national currency.

During the war, the Republican-controlled Congress encouraged economic development. Tariffs to protect industry from foreign competition rose to an av-

Western development

erage rate of 47 percent, compared to 19 percent in 1860. To encourage development of the West, the Homestead Act of 1862 granted 160 acres of public land—the size of the traditional American family farm—to anyone (including women) who settled and improved the land for five years. In addition, the Land Grant College Act of 1862 donated the proceeds from certain land sales to finance public colleges and universities. This aid was especially crucial in promoting higher education in the West.

A Rich Man's War

Over the course of the war the government purchased more than $1 billion worth of goods and services. In response to this heavy demand, the economy boomed and business and agriculture prospered. Since prices rose faster than wages, workers' real income dropped almost 30 percent, which meant that the working class paid a disproportionate share of financing the war.

The Republican belief that government should play a major role in the economy also fostered a cozy relationship between business and politics. In the

Corruption and fraud

rush to profit from government contracts, some suppliers succumbed to the temptation to sell inferior goods at inflated prices. Uniforms made of "shoddy"—bits of unused thread and recycled cloth—were fobbed off in such numbers that the word became an adjective describing inferior quality. A War Department investigation later revealed that at least 20 percent of government expenditures involved fraud.

Stocks and dividends rose with the economy, speculation during the last two years of the war became particularly feverish, and the fortunes made went toward the purchase of ostentatious luxuries. The Chicago *Tribune* admitted: "We are clothed in purple and fine linen, wear the richest laces and jewels and fare sumptuously every day." Like Richmond, Washington became the symbol of this moral decay. Prostitution, drinking, and corruption reached epidemic proportions in the capital, and social festivities became the means to shut out the numbing horror of the casualty lists.

Women and the Workforce

Even more than in the South, the war opened new opportunities for northern women. Countless wives ran farms while their husbands were away at war. One traveler in Iowa reported, "I met more women driving teams on the road and saw more at work in the fields than men." The war also stimulated the shift to mechanization: by 1865 three times as many reapers and harvesters were in use as in 1861. Beyond the farm, women filled approximately 100,000 new jobs in industry. As in the South, they also worked as clerks in the expanding government bureaucracy. The work was tedious and the workload heavy, but the new jobs offered good wages and satisfaction in having aided the war effort.

The war also allowed women to enter and eventually dominate the profession of nursing. "Our women appear to have become almost wild on the sub-

Women and medicine

ject of hospital nursing," protested one physician, who like many others opposed their presence. Led by Drs. Emily and Elizabeth Blackwell, Dorothea Dix, and Mary Ann Bickerdyke, women fought the bureaucratic inefficiency of the army medical corps. Their service in the hospital wards reduced the hostility to women in medicine.

One nurse was Clara Barton, who later founded the Red Cross. During the battle of Fredericksburg, she worked in a battlefield hospital. She later recalled

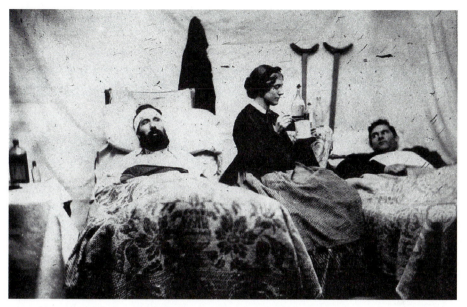

A nurse tends a wounded Union soldier in a military hospital in Nashville, Tennessee. Despite the opposition of army doctors, hundreds of female volunteers worked in army hospitals for each side.

that as she rose from the side of one soldier, "I wrung the blood from the bottom of my clothing, before I could step, for the weight about my feet." She steeled herself at the sight of amputated arms and legs casually tossed in piles outside the front door as the surgeons cut away, yet she found the extent of suffering overwhelming. Sleeping in a tent nearby, she drove herself to the brink of exhaustion until the last patients were transferred to permanent hospitals.

Before 1861 teaching too had been dominated by males, but the shortage of men forced school boards in both sections to turn to women. After the war,

Women and teaching

teaching increasingly became a female profession. Women also contributed to the war effort through volunteer work. The United States Sanitary Commission was established in 1861 to provide medical supplies and care. Women raised funds for the commission, collected supplies, and worked in hospitals alongside paid nurses.

Civil Liberties and Dissent

In mobilizing the northern war effort, Lincoln did not hesitate to curb dissenters. Shortly after the firing on Fort Sumter, he suspended the writ of habeas

Writ of habeas corpus suspended

corpus in specified areas, which allowed the indefinite detention of anyone suspected of disloyalty or activity against the war. Although the Constitution permitted such suspension in time of rebellion or invasion, Lincoln did so without consulting Congress (unlike

President Davis), and he used his power far more broadly, expanding it in 1862 to cover the entire North for cases involving antiwar activities. The president also decreed that those arrested under its provisions could be tried in a military court. Eventually more than 20,000 individuals were arrested, most of whom were never brought to trial.

Democrats attacked Lincoln as a tyrant bent on destroying the Constitution. After the war, the Supreme Court, in *Ex parte Milligan* (1866), struck down the military conviction of a civilian accused of plotting to free Confederate prisoners of war. The Court ruled that as long as the regular courts were open, civilians could not be tried by military tribunals.

Republicans labeled those who opposed the war Copperheads, conjuring up the image of a venomous snake waiting to strike the Union. Copperheads constituted the extreme peace wing of the Democratic party. They condemned the draft as an attack on individual freedom and an instrument of special privilege. According to the provisions enacted in 1863, a person would be exempt from the present draft by paying a commutation fee of $300, about a year's wages for a worker or an ordinary farmer. Or those drafted could hire a substitute, the

New York City draft riot

cost of which was beyond the reach of all but the wealthy. In July 1863, largely Irish workers in New York City rose in anger against the draft. By the time order was restored four days later, at least 105 people had been killed, the worst loss of life from any riot in American history.

GONE TO BE A SOLDIER

By war's end about 2 million men had served the Union cause and another million the Confederate. They were mostly young, with almost 40 percent of entering soldiers 21 or younger. They were not drawn disproportionately from the poor, and in both North and South, farmers and farm laborers accounted for the largest group of soldiers.

Camp Life

On average, soldiers spent 50 days in camp for every day in battle. The near-holiday atmosphere of the early months soon gave way to dull routine. Men from rural areas, accustomed to the freedom of the farm, complained about the endless recurrence of reveille, roll call, and drill. "When this war is over," one Rebel promised, "I will whip the man that says 'fall in' to me." Troops in neither army cared for the spit and polish of regular army men. "They keep us very strict here," noted one Illinois soldier. "It is the most like a prison of any place I ever saw."

Camp life was often unhealthy as well as unpleasant. Poor sanitation, miserable food, exposure, and primitive medical care contributed to widespread

*Disease and
medical care*

sickness and disease. Officers and men alike regarded army doctors as nothing more than quacks and tried to avoid them. It was a common belief that if a fellow went to the hospital, "you might as well say good bye." Conditions were even worse in the Confederate hospitals, for the Union blockade produced a shortage of medical supplies. Twice as many soldiers died from dysentery, typhoid, and other diseases as from wounds.

Morals in camp

The boredom of camp life, the horrors of battle, and the influence of an all-male society all corrupted morals. Swearing and heavy drinking were common and gambling was pervasive, especially immediately after payday. Prostitutes flooded the camps of both armies. As in the gold fields of California, the absence of women stimulated behavior that would have been checked back home by the frowns of family and society.

With death so near, some soldiers sought solace in religion, especially in Confederate camps. A wave of revivals swept their ranks during the last two winters of the war, producing between 100,000 and 200,000 conversions. Significantly, the first major revivals occurred after the South's twin defeats at Vicksburg and Gettysburg. Then, too, as battle after battle thinned Confederate ranks, the prospect of death became increasingly large.

Southern Individualism

*Southern soldiers
and discipline*

Despite obvious similarities, Confederate soldiers differed from their northern counterparts in ways that reflected fundamental qualities of southern society. While Union soldiers came grudgingly to accept discipline as a necessity in war, many southerners were "not used to control of any sort and were not disposed to obey anyone except for good and sufficient reason given," one Rebel noted. Many Confederates discarded equipment on the march and lagged behind, while others left without permission to take care of affairs back home, then returned to the ranks.

This disrespect for authority affected the ordinary soldier's relations with his officers. Like Union soldiers, Confederates complained about officers' special privileges, but they were far more likely to threaten or even physically assault their superiors when dissatisfied. Moreover, upper-class southerners often felt that social class should override military rank. Contributing to the lack of discipline, Confederates insisted on electing all officers through the rank of colonel, and those known as strict disciplinarians were eventually defeated. A Confederate general fumed that the law should have been entitled "An act to disorganize and dissolve the army," but the Confederate Congress retained it because it was popular.

*The North's
increasing
organization*

At first, the rural individualism of southerners was not a severe handicap. But as the Union army became increasingly organized, Confederate indifference to discipline took its toll. Northern soldiers were more familiar with impersonal organizations and accustomed to greater social control, and urban factory workers especially were used to a strict regimen. In a total war, which would be

won by superior organization and the mobilization of resources, this difference between the two armies became more significant with each year of the
fighting.

The Changing Face of Battle

As in all modern wars, technology revolutionized the conditions under which
Civil War soldiers fought. Smoothbore muskets, which at first served as the ba-

Impact of technology

sic infantry weapon, gave way to the rifle, so named because of
the grooves etched into the barrel to give a bullet spin. The per-
cussion cap rendered a rifle serviceable in wet weather. More important, the new weapon had an effective range of 400 yards—five times greater
than that of the old musket. As a result, soldiers fought each other from greater
distances and battles produced many more casualties.

Under such conditions, the defense became a good deal stronger than the
offense. The larger artillery pieces also adopted rifled barrels, but they were too

Strength of the defense

inaccurate to effectively support attacking troops. They were a
deadly defensive weapon, however, that decimated advancing infantry at close range. The rising casualty lists bore down heavily
on the ordinary soldier, and over 100 regiments on both sides suffered more
than 50 percent casualties in a single battle.

As the haze of gunfire covered the land and the constant spray of bullets
mimicked rain pattering through the treetops, soldiers discovered that their romantic notions about war had no place on the battlefield. Men witnessed horrors they had never envisioned as civilians and choked from the stench of decaying flesh. They realized that their efforts to convey to those back home the
gruesome truth of combat were inadequate. "No tongue can tell, no mind can
conceive, no pen portray the horrible sights I witnessed this morning," a Union
soldier wrote after Antietam. And yet they tried.

An Indiana soldier at Perryville (7600 casualties): "It was an awful sight to
see there men torn all to pieces with cannon balls and bom shells[.] the dead
and wounded lay thick in all directions." An Ohio soldier at Antietam (23,000
casualties), two days after the fighting: "The smell was offul . . . there was about
5 or 6,000 dead bodes decaying over the field . . . I could have walked on the
boddees all most from one end too the other." A Georgian, the day after
Chancellorsville (30,000 casualties): "It looked more like a slaughter pen than
anything else. . . . The shrieks and groans of the wounded . . . was heart rending beyond all description." A Maine soldier who fought at Gettysburg (50,000
casualties): "I have Seen . . . men rolling in their own blood, Some Shot in one
place, Some another. . . . our dead lay in the road and the Rebels in their hast
to leave dragged both their baggage wagons and artillery over them and they
lay mangled and torn to pieces so that Even friends could not tell them. You
can form no idea of a battle field."

In the face of what Charles Francis Adams, Jr., termed "the carnival of death," soldiers braced themselves with a grim determination to see the war through to the end. Not glorious exploits, but endurance became the true measure of heroism.

THE UNION'S TRIUMPH

In the spring of 1863 matters still looked promising for Lee. At the battle of Chancellorsville, he won another brilliant victory. But during the fighting Stonewall Jackson was accidentally shot by his own men, and he died a few days later—a grievous setback for the Confederacy. Determined to take the offensive, Lee invaded Pennsylvania in June with an army of 75,000. Lincoln's newest general, George Gordon Meade, warily shadowed the Confederates. On the first of July, advance parties from the two armies accidentally collided at the town of Gettysburg, and the war's greatest battle ensued.

For once it was Lee who had the extended supply lines and was forced to fight on ground chosen by his opponent. After two days of assaults failed to break the Union left or right, Lee made the greatest mistake of his career, sending 15,000 men under General George Pickett in a charge up the center of the Union line. "Pickett's division just seemed to melt away in the blue musketry smoke which now covered the hill," one Confederate officer wrote. "Nothing but stragglers came back." With the loss of more than a third of his troops, Lee was never again able to assume the offensive.

Gettysburg

Lincoln Finds His General

To the west, Grant had been trying for months to capture Vicksburg, a Rebel stronghold on the Mississippi. In a daring maneuver, he left behind his supply lines and marched inland, feeding his army from the produce of Confederate farms. These were the tactics of total war, and seldom had they been tried before. On July 4, the city surrendered. With the fall of Port Hudson, Louisiana, four days later, the Mississippi was completely in Union hands, thus dividing the Confederacy.

Capture of Vicksburg

Grant followed up this victory by rescuing Union forces holed up in Chattanooga. His performance confirmed Lincoln's earlier judgment that "Grant is my man, and I am his the rest of the war." In March 1864 Lincoln brought Grant east and placed him in command of all the Union armies.

Grant recognized that in the past the Union's armies had "acted independently and without concert, like a balky team, no two ever pulling together." He intended to change that. While he launched a major offensive against Lee in Virginia, William Tecumseh Sherman, who replaced Grant as commander of the western army, would drive a diagonal wedge through the Confederacy from Tennessee across Georgia.

Grant in command

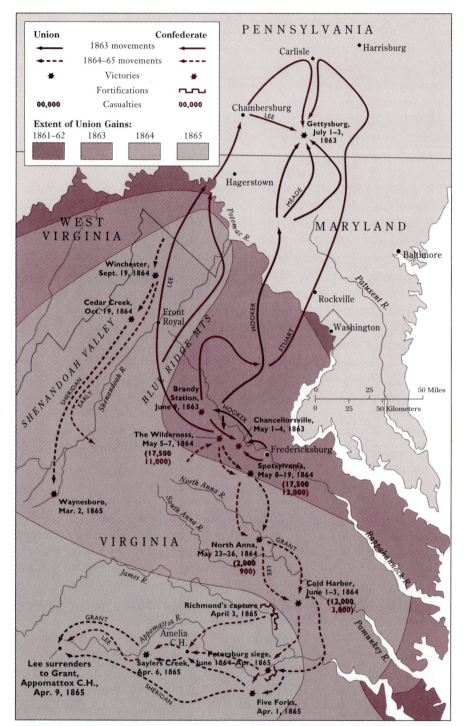

Union
- ← 1863 movements
- ←--- 1864–65 movements
- ✱ Victories
- ⊓⊔ Fortifications
- **00,000** Casualties

Confederate
- ← 1863 movements
- ←--- 1864–65 movements

00,000

Extent of Union Gains:
| 1861–62 | 1863 | 1864 | 1865 |

PENNSYLVANIA

Carlisle · Harrisburg

Chambersburg
LEE

Gettysburg, July 1–3, 1863 ✱

Hagerstown

MEADE

WEST VIRGINIA

MARYLAND

Baltimore

Potomac R.

Winchester, Sept. 19, 1864

LEE

Cedar Creek, Oct. 19, 1864 ✱

SHERIDAN EARLY

Front Royal

HOOKER

STUART

Patuxent R.

Rockville

Washington

SHENANDOAH VALLEY

Shenandoah R.

BLUE RIDGE MTS.

Brandy Station, June 9, 1863 ✱

HOOKER

Chancellorsville, May 1–4, 1863

0 — 25 — 50 Miles
0 — 25 — 50 Kilometers

The Wilderness, May 5–7, 1864 (17,500 11,000) ✱

Fredericksburg

Spotsylvania, May 8–19, 1864 (17,500 12,000) ✱

Waynesboro, Mar. 2, 1865 ✱

North Anna R.

South Anna R.

VIRGINIA

North Anna, May 23–26, 1864 (2,000 900)

GRANT

LEE

James R.

Cold Harbor, June 1–3, 1864 (12,000 3,000) ✱

Rappahannock R.

Richmond's capture April 3, 1865

GRANT

LEE

Amelia C.H.

Appomattox R.

Petersburg siege, June 1864–Apr. 1865 ✱

Pamunkey R.

Lee surrenders to Grant, Appomattox C.H., Apr. 9, 1865

Saylers Creek, Apr. 6, 1865 ✱

SHERIDAN

Five Forks, Apr. 1, 1865

THE WAR IN THE EAST, 1863–1865   Lee won his most brilliant victory at Chancellorsville, then launched a second invasion of the North, which ended in defeat at Gettysburg. In 1864 Grant delivered a series of blows against Lee's outnumbered forces in Virginia. Despite staggering losses, Grant pressed on in a ruthless demonstration of total war. (Note the casualties listed from mid-May to mid-June of 1864; Grant lost nearly 60,000 men, equal to Lee's strength.) In April 1865, too weak to defend Richmond any longer, Lee surrendered at Appomattox Courthouse.

Grant instructed Sherman to "get into the interior of the enemy's country so far as you can, inflicting all the damage you can against their war resources."

In May and June 1864 Grant tried to maneuver Lee out of the trenches and into an open battle. But Lee was too weak to win head-on, so he opted for a strategy of attrition, hoping to inflict such heavy losses that the northern will would break. It was a strategy that nearly worked, for Union casualties were staggering. In a month of fierce fighting, the Army of the Potomac lost 60,000 men. Yet at the end of the campaign Grant's reinforced army was larger than when it started, whereas Lee's was significantly weaker.

Union's summer offensive

Unable to break Lee's lines, Grant settled into a siege of Petersburg, which guarded Richmond's last remaining rail link to the south. In the west, meanwhile, the gaunt and grizzled Sherman fought his way by July to the outskirts of Atlanta, which was heavily defended and gave no sign of capitulating. "Our all depends on that army at Atlanta," wrote Mary Chesnut in August, based on her conversations with Confederate leaders. "If that fails us, the game is up."

War in the Balance

The game was nearly up for Lincoln as the 1864 election approached. As the Union war machine swept more and more northerners south to their death, and with Grant and Sherman bogged down on the Virginia and Georgia fronts, even leaders in Lincoln's own party began to mutter he was not equal to the task.

Lincoln rejected any suggestion to postpone the presidential election, which he believed would be to lose democracy itself. Exploiting his control of the party machinery, Lincoln easily won the Republican nomination, and he made certain that the Republican platform called for adoption of a constitutional amendment abolishing slavery. To balance the ticket, Lincoln selected Andrew Johnson, the military governor of Tennessee and a prowar Democrat, as his running mate. The two men ran under the label of the "Union" party.

1864 election

The Democrats nominated George McClellan, the former Union commander. Their platform pronounced the war a failure and called for an armistice and a peace conference. Warned that a cessation of fighting would lead to disunion, McClellan partially repudiated this position, insisting that "the Union is the one condition of peace—we ask no more." In private he made it clear that if elected he intended to restore slavery. Late in August, Lincoln was still gloomy about his prospects, as well as those of the Union itself. But Admiral David Farragut won a dramatic victory at Mobile Bay, and a few weeks later, in early September, Sherman finally captured Atlanta. As Secretary of State Seward gleefully noted, "Sherman and Farragut have knocked the bottom out of the Chicago [Democratic] nominations."

Polling an impressive 55 percent of the popular vote, Lincoln won 212 electoral votes to McClellan's 21. Eighteen states allowed soldiers to vote in the

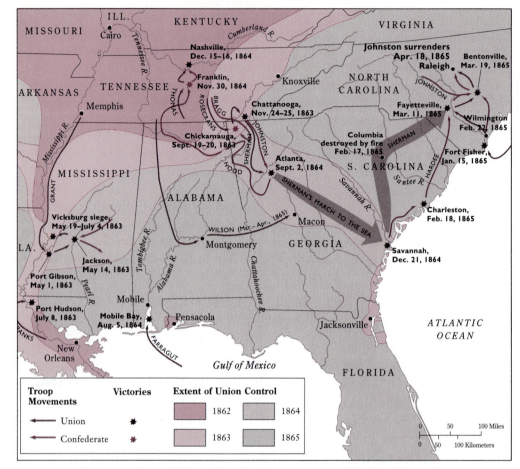

THE WAR IN THE WEST, 1863–1865 The Union continued its war of mobility in the western theater, bringing more Confederate territory under its control. After Grant captured Vicksburg, the entire Mississippi lay in Union hands. His victories at Lookout Mountain and Missionary Ridge, near Chattanooga, ended the Confederate threat to Tennessee. In 1864 Sherman divided the Confederacy by seizing Atlanta and marching across Georgia; then he turned north. When Joseph Johnston surrendered, several weeks after Lee's capitulation at Appomattox, the war was effectively over.

Significance of Lincoln's reelection

field, and Lincoln received nearly 80 percent of their ballots. One lifelong Democrat described the sentiment in the army: "We all want peace, but none any but an honorable one. I had rather stay out here a lifetime (much as I dislike it) than consent to a division of our country." Jefferson Davis remained defiant, but the last hope of a Confederate victory was gone.

Equally important, the election of 1864 ended any doubt that slavery would be abolished in the reconstructed Union. The Emancipation Proclamation had not put an end to the question, for its legal status remained unclear. Lincoln argued that as a war measure, it would have no standing once peace returned; and in any case, it had not freed slaves in the border states or those parts of the Confederacy already under Union control. Thus Lincoln and the Republicans believed that a constitutional amendment was necessary to secure emancipation.

In 1864 the Senate approved an amendment that freed all slaves without compensating their owners. The measure passed the House on January 31, 1865. By December, enough states had ratified the Thirteenth Amendment to make it part of the Constitution.

*Thirteenth
Amendment*

The Twilight of the Confederacy

For the Confederacy, the outcome of the 1864 election had a terrible finality. In March 1865 the Confederate Congress authorized recruiting 300,000 slaves for

The war's greatest generals, Ulysses S. Grant (left) and Robert E. Lee (right), confronted each other in the eastern theater during the last year of the war. A member of a distinguished Virginia family, the impeccably dressed Lee was every inch the aristocratic gentleman. Grant, a short, slouched figure with a stubby beard, dressed indifferently, but his determination is readily apparent in this picture, taken at his field headquarters in 1864.

Confederacy abandons slavery

military service. When he signed the bill, Davis announced that freedom would be given to those who volunteered and to their families. That same month he offered through a special envoy to abolish slavery in exchange for British diplomatic recognition. A Mississippi paper denounced this proposal as "a total abandonment of the chief object of this war." The British rejected the offer, and the war ended before any slaves were mustered into the Confederate army, but the demands of total war had forced Confederate leaders to forsake the Old South's most important values and institutions.

In the wake of Lincoln's reelection, the Confederate will to resist rapidly disintegrated. White southerners had never fully united behind the war effort, but the large majority had endured great suffering to uphold it. As Sherman pushed deeper into the Confederacy, however, the war came home to southern civilians as never before. "We haven't got nothing in the house to eat but a little bit o meal," wrote the wife of one Alabama soldier in December 1864. ". . . Try to get off and come home and fix us all up some and then you can go back. . . . If you put off a-coming, 'twont be no use to come, for we'll all . . . [be] in the grave yard." He deserted. In the last months of the fighting, over half the Confederacy's soldiers were absent without leave.

After the fall of Atlanta, Sherman gave a frightening demonstration of the meaning of total war. Detaching a portion of his forces to engage General John

March to the sea

Hood's army, which moved back into Tennessee, Sherman imitated Grant's strategy by abandoning his supply lines for an audacious 300-mile march to the sea. He intended to deprive Lee's army of the supplies it desperately needed to continue and to break the southern will to resist. Or as he bluntly put it, "to whip the Rebels, to humble their pride, to follow them to their recesses, and make them fear and dread us."

Moving in four columns, Sherman's army covered about 10 miles a day, cutting a path of destruction 50 miles wide. Sherman estimated that his men did $100 million in damage, of which $20 million was necessary to supply his army and the rest was wanton destruction. After he captured Savannah, he turned north and wreaked even greater havoc in South Carolina.

Meanwhile, General George H. Thomas defeated Hood's forces in December at Nashville, leaving the interior of the Confederacy essentially

Lee's surrender

conquered. Only Lee's army remained, entrenched around Petersburg. As Grant relentlessly extended his lines, Lee's troops were forced to evacuate Richmond. Westward Grant doggedly pursued the Army of Northern Virginia, until the weary gentleman from Virginia finally asked for terms. On April 9, 1865, Lee surrendered at Appomattox Courthouse. As the vanquished foe mounted his horse, Grant saluted by raising his hat; Lee raised his respectfully and rode off at a slow trot. The guns were quiet.

Remaining resistance throughout the Confederacy collapsed within a matter of weeks. Visiting the captured city of Richmond on April 4, Lincoln was enthusiastically greeted by the black population. He looked "pale, haggard, utterly worn out," noted one observer. The lines in his face showed how much

E Y E W I T N E S S   T O   H I S T O R Y

A Georgia Plantation Mistress in Sherman's Path

I saw some blue-coats coming down the hill. . . . Oh God, the time of trial has come! . . .

To my smoke-house, my dairy, pantry, kitchen, and cellar, like famished wolves they come, breaking locks and whatever is in their way. The thousand pounds of meat in my smoke-house is gone in a twinkling, my flour, my meat, my lard, butter, eggs, pickles of various kinds . . . —wine, jars, and jugs are all gone. My eighteen fat turkeys, my hens, chickens, and fowls, my young pigs, are shot down in my yard and hunted as if they were rebels themselves. . . .

As I stood there, from my lot I saw driven, first, old Dutch, my dear old buggy horse . . . then came old Mary, my brood mare, who for years had been too old and stiff for work, with her three-year-old colt, my two-year-old mule, and her last little baby colt. There they go! There go my mules, my sheep, and worse than all, my boys [slaves]! . . .

Their [slaves'] cabins are rifled of every valuable, the soldiers swearing that their Sunday clothes were the white people's, and that they never had money to get such things as they had. Poor Frank's chest was broken open, his money and tobacco taken. . . . All of his clothes and Rachel's clothes . . . were stolen from her. Ovens, skillets, coffee-mills . . . coffee-pots—not one have I left. Sifters all gone! . . .

Sherman himself and a greater portion of his army passed my house that day. All day, as the sad moments rolled on, were they passing not only in front of my house, but from behind; they tore down my garden palings, made a road through my back-yard and lot field, driving their stock and riding through, tearing down my fences and desolating my home—wantonly doing it when there was no necessity for it. . . .

As night drew its sable curtains around us, the heavens from every point were lit up with flames from burning buildings.

Dolly Lunt, November 19, 1864, *A Woman's Wartime Journal* (Macon: J. W. Burke Co., 1927), 21–31.

the war had aged him in only four years. Often his friends had counseled rest, but Lincoln had observed that "the tired part of me is *inside* and out of reach." The burden, he confessed, was almost too much to bear.

Back in Washington the president received news of Lee's surrender with relief. The evening of April 14, Lincoln, seeking a welcome escape, went to a comedy at Ford's Theater. In the midst of the performance John Wilkes Booth, a famous actor and Confederate sympathizer, slipped into the presidential box and shot him. Lincoln died the next morning. As he had called upon others to do in his Gettysburg Address, the sixteenth president had given his "last full measure of devotion" to the Republic.

Lincoln's assassination

THE IMPACT OF WAR

The assassination left a tiredness in the nation's bones—a tiredness *"inside"* and not easily within reach. In every way the conflict had produced fundamental, often devastating changes. There was, of course, the carnage. Approximately 620,000 men on both sides lost their lives, almost as many as in all the other wars the nation has fought from the Revolution through Vietnam combined. In material terms, the conflict cost an estimated $20 billion, more than 11 times the total amount spent by the federal government from 1789 to 1861. Even without adding the market value of freed slaves, southern wealth declined 43 percent, transforming what had been the richest section in the nation (on a white per capita basis) into the poorest.

Cost of war

The demands of total war also stimulated industrialization, especially in the heavy industries of iron and coal, machinery, and agricultural implements, while the probusiness finance and tax policies of the Republican party encouraged the formation of larger corporations in the years ahead. The war also forced manufacturers to supply the army on an unprecedented scale over great distances. One consequence was the creation of truly national industries in flour milling, meat packing, clothing and shoe manufacture, and machinery making.

Politically, the war dramatically changed the balance of power. The South lost its substantial influence, as did the Democratic party, while the Republicans emerged in a dominant position. The Union's military victory signaled the triumph of nationalism. The war destroyed the idea that the Union was a voluntary confederacy of sovereign states, which theorists like John C. Calhoun had argued, and that the states had the right to secede.

In the short run, the price was disillusionment and bitterness. The South had to live with the humiliation of military defeat and occupation, while former slaves anxiously waited to see what their situation would be in freedom. The war's corrosive effect on morals corrupted American life and politics, destroyed idealism, and severely crippled humanitarian reform. Millennialism and perfectionism were victims of the war's appalling slaugh-

Spiritual toll of war

ter, forsaken for a new emphasis on practicality, order, materialism, and science. As the war unfolded, the New York *Herald* recognized the deep changes: "All sorts of old fogy ideas, manners, and customs have gone under, and all sorts of new ideas, modes, and practices have risen to the surface and become popular."

George Ticknor, a prominent author and critic who was sensitive to shifting intellectual and social currents, reflected on the changes that had shaken the nation in only a few short years. The war, it seemed to him, had left "a great gulf between what happened before it in our century and what has happened since. . . . It does not seem to me as if I were living in the country in which I was born."

SIGNIFICANT EVENTS

1861 ┼ Border states remain in the Union; Union blockade proclaimed; Lincoln suspends writ of habeas corpus in selected areas; Battle of Bull Run; Crittenden Resolution; First Confiscation Act

1862 ┼ Forts Henry and Donelson captured; *Monitor* vs. *Virginia (Merrimack);* Battle of Shiloh; slavery abolished in the District of Columbia; Confederacy institutes draft; New Orleans captured; Homestead Act; Land Grant College Act; Second Confiscation Act; Union income tax enacted; McClellan's Peninsula campaign fails; Second Battle of Bull Run; Battle of Antietam; preliminary Emancipation Proclamation; Lincoln suspends writ of habeas corpus throughout the Union; Battle of Fredericksburg

1863 ┼ Emancipation Proclamation; National Banking Act; Union institutes draft; Confederacy enacts general tax laws, initiates impressment; bread riots in the Confederacy; Battle of Chancellorsville; Battle of Gettysburg; Vicksburg captured; New York City draft riots

1864 ┼ Grant becomes Union general in chief; Grant's Virginia offensive; siege of Petersburg; Battle of Mobile Bay; fall of Atlanta; Lincoln reelected; Sherman's march to the sea

1865 ┼ Congress passes Thirteenth Amendment; Sherman's march through the Carolinas; Richmond captured; Lee surrenders; Lincoln assassinated; Thirteenth Amendment ratified

1866 ┼ *Ex parte Milligan*

CHAPTER SEVENTEEN

Reconstructing the Union

Joseph Davis had had enough. Well on in years and financially ruined by the war, he decided to quit farming. So, on November 19, 1866, he sold his Mississippi plantations Hurricane and Brierfield to Benjamin Montgomery and his sons. The sale of southern plantations was common enough after the war, but this transaction was bound to attract attention, since Joseph Davis was the elder brother of Jefferson Davis. Indeed, before the war the Confederate president had operated Brierfield as his own plantation, even though his brother retained legal title to it. But the sale was unusual for another reason—so unusual that the parties involved agreed to keep it secret. The plantation's new owners were black, and Mississippi law prohibited African Americans from owning land.

Though a slave, Benjamin Montgomery had been the business manager of the two Davis plantations before the war. He had also operated a store on Hurricane Plantation with his own line of credit in New Orleans. In 1863 Montgomery fled to the North, but when the war was over, he returned to Davis Bend, where the federal government had confiscated the Davis plantations and was leasing plots of the land to black farmers. Montgomery quickly emerged as the leader of the African American community at the Bend.

Then, in 1866, President Andrew Johnson pardoned Joseph Davis and restored his lands. Davis was now over 80 years old and lacked the will and stamina to rebuild, yet unlike many ex-slave holders, he felt bound by obligations to his former slaves. Convinced that with proper encouragement African Americans could succeed economically in freedom, he sold his land secretly to Benjamin Montgomery. Only when the law prohibiting African Americans from owning land was overturned in 1867 did Davis publicly confirm the sale to his former slave.

For his part, Montgomery undertook to create a model society at Davis Bend based on mutual cooperation. He rented land to black farmers, hired others to work his own fields, sold supplies on credit, and ginned and marketed the crops. To the growing African American community, he preached the gospel of hard work, self-reliance, and education.

Various difficulties dogged these black farmers, including the destruction caused by the war, several disastrous floods, insects, droughts, and declining cotton prices. Yet before long, cotton production exceeded that of the prewar years, and in 1870 the black families at Davis Bend produced 2500 bales. The

Montgomerys eventually acquired 5500 acres, which made them reputedly the third largest planters in the state, and they won national and international awards for the quality of their cotton. Their success demonstrated what African Americans, given a fair chance, might accomplish.

The experiences of Benjamin Montgomery during the years after 1865 were not those of most black southerners, who did not own land or have a powerful white benefactor. Yet Montgomery's dream of economic independence was shared by all African Americans. As one black veteran noted, "Every colored man will be a slave, and feel himself a slave until he can raise him own *bale of cotton* and put him own mark upon it and say dis is mine!" Blacks could not gain effective freedom simply through a proclamation of emancipation. They also needed economic power, including their own land that no one could unfairly take away.

For nearly two centuries the laws had prevented slaves from possessing such economic power. If such conditions were to be overturned, black Americans needed political power too. Thus the Republic would have to be reconstructed to give African Americans political power that they had been previously denied.

War, in its blunt way, had roughed out the contours of a solution, but only in broad terms. Clearly, African Americans would no longer be enslaved. The North, with its industrial might, would be the driving force in the nation's economy and retain the dominant political voice. But beyond that, the outlines of a reconstructed Republic remained vague. Would African Americans receive effective power? How would North and South readjust their economic and political relations? These questions lay at the heart of the problem of Reconstruction.

PERSIDENTIAL RECONSTRUCTION

Throughout the war Abraham Lincoln had considered Reconstruction his responsibility. Elected with less than 40 percent of the popular vote in 1860, he was acutely aware that once the states of the Confederacy were restored to the Union, the Republicans would be weakened unless they ceased to be a sectional party. By a generous peace, Lincoln hoped to attract former Whigs in the South, who supported many of the Republicans' economic policies, and build up a southern wing of the party.

Lincoln's 10 Percent Plan

Lincoln outlined his program in a Proclamation of Amnesty and Reconstruction, issued in December 1863. When a minimum of 10 percent of the qualified voters from 1860 took a loyalty oath to the Union, they could organize a state government. The new state constitution had to abolish slavery and provide for black education, but Lincoln did not insist that high-ranking Confederate leaders be barred from public life.

Lincoln indicated that he would be generous in granting pardons to prominent Confederate leaders and did not rule out compensation for slave property.

Moreover, while he privately advocated limited black suffrage in the disloyal southern states, he did not demand social or political equality for black Americans, and he recognized pro-Union governments in Louisiana, Arkansas, and Tennessee that allowed only white men to vote.

The Radical Republicans found Lincoln's approach much too lenient. Strongly antislavery, Radical members of Congress had led the struggle to make

Radical Republicans

emancipation a war aim. Now they led the fight to guarantee the rights of the freedpeople. The Radicals believed that it was the duty of Congress, not the president, to set the terms under which states would regain their rights in the Union. Though the Radicals often disagreed on other matters, they were united in a determination to readmit southern states only after slavery had been ended, black rights protected, and the power of the planter class destroyed.

Under the direction of Senator Benjamin Wade of Ohio and Representative Henry Winter Davis of Maryland, Congress formulated a much stricter plan of

Wade–Davis bill

Reconstruction. It required half the white adult males to take an oath of allegiance before drafting a new state constitution, and restricted political power to the hard-core Unionists. When the Wade–Davis bill passed on the final day of the 1864 congressional session, Lincoln exercised his right of a pocket veto.* Still, his own program could not succeed without the assistance of Congress, which refused to recognize his governments in Louisiana and Arkansas. As the war drew to a close, Lincoln appeared ready to make concessions to the Radicals, and at his final cabinet meeting he approved placing the defeated South temporarily under military rule. But only a few days later Booth's bullet found its mark, and Lincoln's final approach to Reconstruction would never be known.

The Mood of the South

In the wake of defeat, the immediate reaction among white southerners was one of shock, despair, and hopelessness. Some former Confederates were openly antagonistic. A North Carolina innkeeper remarked bitterly that Yankees had stolen his slaves, burned his house, and killed all his sons, leaving him only one privilege: "To hate 'em. I git up at half-past four in the morning, and sit up till twelve at night, to hate 'em." Most Confederate soldiers were less defiant, having had their fill of war. Even among hostile civilians the feeling was widespread that the South must accept northern terms. A South Carolina paper admitted that "the conqueror has the right to make the terms, and we must submit."

This psychological moment was critical. To prevent a resurgence of resistance, the president needed to lay out in unmistakable terms what white southerners had to do to regain their old status in the Union. Perhaps even a clear and firm policy would not have been enough. But with Lincoln's death, the executive power came to rest in far less capable hands.

---

*If a president does not sign a bill after Congress has adjourned, it has the same effect as a veto.

Johnson's Program of Reconstruction

Andrew Johnson, the new president, had been born in North Carolina and eventually moved to Tennessee, where he worked as a tailor. Barely able to read and write when he married, he rose to political power by portraying himself as the champion of the people against the wealthy planter class. "Some day I will show the stuck-up aristocrats who is running the country," he vowed as he began his political career. He had not opposed slavery before the war, and although he accepted emancipation as one consequence of the war, Johnson remained a confirmed racist with no concern for the welfare of African Americans. "Damn the negroes," he said during the war, "I am fighting these traitorous aristocrats, their masters."

Johnson's character and values

During the war he had joined the Radicals in calling for stern treatment of southern rebels. "Treason must be made odious and traitors must be punished and impoverished," he proclaimed in 1864. After serving in Congress and as military governor of Tennessee following its occupation by Union forces, Johnson, a Democrat, was tapped by Lincoln in 1864 as his running mate on the rechristened "Union" ticket.

The Radicals expected Johnson to uphold their views on Reconstruction, and upon assuming the presidency he spoke of trying Confederate leaders and breaking up planters' estates. Unlike most Republicans, however, Johnson strongly supported states' rights and opposed government aid to business. Given such differences, conflict between the president and the majority in Congress was inevitable, but Johnson's political shortcomings made the situation worse. Scarred by his humble origins, he became tactless and inflexible when challenged or criticized, and he alienated even those who sought to work with him.

Johnson moved to quickly return the southern states to their place in the Union. He prescribed a loyalty oath white southerners would have to take to regain their civil and political rights and to have their property, except for slaves, restored. Excluded were high Confederate officials and those with property worth over $20,000, who had to apply for individual pardons. Johnson announced that once a state had drafted a new constitution and elected state officers and members of Congress, he would revoke martial law and recognize the new state government. Suffrage was limited to white citizens who had taken the loyalty oath. This plan was similar to Lincoln's, though more lenient. Only informally did Johnson stipulate that the southern states were to renounce their ordinances of secession, repudiate the Confederate debt, and ratify the proposed Thirteenth Amendment abolishing slavery.

Johnson's program

The Failure of Johnson's Program

The southern delegates who met to construct new governments soon demonstrated that they were in no frame of mind to follow Johnson's recommendations. Several states merely repealed instead of repudiating their ordinances of secession, rejected the Thirteenth Amendment, or refused to repudiate the Confederate debt.

Andrew Johnson was a staunch Unionist, but his contentious personality and inflexibility soured his relationship with Congress.

Nor did any of the new governments allow African Americans any political rights or provide in any effective way for black education. In addition, each state

Black codes

passed a series of laws, often modeled on its old slave code, that applied only to African Americans. These "black codes" did give African Americans some rights that had not been granted to slaves. They legalized marriages from slavery and allowed black southerners to hold and sell property and to sue and be sued in state courts. Yet their primary intent was to keep African Americans as propertyless agricultural laborers with inferior legal rights. The new freedpeople could not serve on juries, testify against whites, or work as they pleased. Mississippi prohibited them from buying or renting farmland, and most states ominously provided that black people who were vagrants could be arrested and hired out to landowners. Many northerners were incensed by the restrictive black codes, which violated their conception of freedom.

Southern voters under Johnson's plan also defiantly elected prominent Confederate military and political leaders to office. At this point, Johnson could have

Elections in the South

called for new elections or admitted that a different program of Reconstruction was needed. Instead he caved in. For all his harsh rhetoric, he shrank from the prospect of social upheaval, and as the lines of ex-Confederates waiting to see him lengthened, he began issuing special pardons almost as fast as they could be printed. Publicly Johnson put on a bold face, announcing that Reconstruction had been successfully completed. But many members of Congress were deeply alarmed, and the stage was set for a serious confrontation.

Johnson's Break with Congress

The new Congress was by no means of one mind. A small number of Democrats and a few conservative Republicans backed the president's program of immediate and unconditional restoration. At the other end of the spectrum, a larger group of Radical Republicans, led by Thaddeus Stevens, Charles Sumner, Benjamin Wade, and others, was bent on remaking southern society in the image of the North. Reconstruction must "revolutionize Southern institutions, habits, and manners," thundered Representative Stevens, ". . . or all our blood and treasure have been spent in vain."

As a minority, the Radicals needed the aid of the moderate Republicans, the largest bloc in Congress. Led by William Pitt Fessenden and Lyman Trumbull, the moderates hoped to avoid a clash with the president, and they had no desire to foster social revolution or promote racial equality in the South. But they wanted to keep Confederate leaders from reassuming power, and they were convinced that the former slaves needed federal protection. Otherwise, Trumbull declared, the freedpeople would "be tyrannized over, abused, and virtually reenslaved."

The central issue dividing Johnson and the Radicals was the place of African Americans in American society. Johnson accused his opponents of seeking "to

Issue of black rights

Africanize the southern half of our country," while the Radicals championed civil and political rights for African Americans. The only way to maintain loyal governments and develop a Republican party in the South, Radicals argued, was to give black men the ballot. Moderates agreed that the new southern governments were too harsh toward African Americans, but they feared that too great an emphasis on black civil rights would alienate northern voters.

In December 1865, when southern representatives to Congress appeared in Washington, a majority in Congress voted to exclude them. Congress also appointed a joint committee, chaired by Senator Fessenden, to look into Reconstruction.

The growing split with the president became clearer when Congress passed a bill extending the life of the Freedmen's Bureau. Created in March 1865, the Bureau provided emergency food, clothing, and medical care to war refugees (including white southerners) and took charge of settling freedpeople on abandoned lands. The new bill gave the Bureau the added responsibilities of supervising special courts to resolve disputes involving freedpeople and establishing schools for black southerners. Although this bill passed with virtually unanimous Republican support, Johnson vetoed it.

Johnson also vetoed a civil rights bill designed to overturn the more flagrant provisions of the black codes. The law made African Americans citizens of the

Johnson's vetoes

United States and granted them the right to own property, make contracts, and have access to courts as parties and witnesses. For most Republicans Johnson's action was the last straw, and in April 1866 Congress overrode his veto. Congress then approved a slightly revised Freedmen's Bureau bill in July and promptly overrode the president's veto. Johnson's refusal to compromise drove the moderates into the arms of the Radicals.

The Fourteenth Amendment

To prevent unrepentant Confederates from taking over the reconstructed state governments and denying African Americans basic freedoms, the Joint Committee on Reconstruction proposed an amendment to the Constitution, which passed both houses of Congress with the necessary two-thirds vote in June 1866.

The amendment guaranteed repayment of the national war debt and prohibited repayment of the Confederate debt. To counteract the president's whole-

Provisions of the amendment

sale pardons, it disqualified prominent Confederates from holding office and provided that only Congress by a two-thirds vote could remove this penalty. Because moderates balked at giving the vote to African Americans, the amendment merely gave Congress the right to reduce the representation of any state that did not have impartial male suffrage. The practical effect of this provision, which Radicals labeled a "swindle," was to allow northern states to retain white suffrage, since unlike southern states they had few African Americans in their populations and thus would not be penalized.

The amendment's most important provision, Section 1, defined an American citizen as anyone born in the United States or naturalized, thereby automatically making African Americans citizens. Section 1 also prohibited states from abridging "the privileges or immunities" of citizens, depriving "any person of life, liberty, or property, without due process of law," or denying "any person . . . equal protection of the laws." The framers of the amendment probably intended to prohibit laws that applied to one race only, such as the black codes, or that made certain acts felonies when committed by black but not white people, or that decreed different penalties for the same crime when committed by white and black lawbreakers. The framers probably did not intend to prevent segregation (the legal separation of the races) in schools and public places.

Johnson denounced the proposed amendment and urged southern states not to ratify it. Ironically, of the seceded states only the president's own state ratified the amendment, and Congress readmitted Tennessee with no further restrictions. The telegram sent to Congress by a longtime foe of Johnson officially announcing Tennessee's approval ended, "Give my respects to the dead dog in the White House."

The Elections of 1866

When Congress blocked his policies, Johnson undertook a speaking tour of the East and Midwest in the fall of 1866 to drum up popular support. But Johnson found it difficult to convince northern audiences that white southerners were fully repentant. Only months earlier white mobs in Memphis and New Orleans had attacked black residents and killed nearly 100 in two major race riots. "The negroes now know, to their sorrow, that it is best not to arouse the fury of the white man," boasted one Memphis newspaper. When the president encountered hostile audiences during his northern campaign, he only made matters worse by trading insults and proclaiming that the Radicals were traitors.

Not to be outdone, the Radicals vilified Johnson as a traitor aiming to turn the country over to former rebels. Resorting to the tactic of "waving the bloody shirt," they appealed to voters by reviving bitter memories of the war. In a classic example of such rhetoric, Governor Oliver Morton of Indiana proclaimed that "every bounty jumper, every deserter, every sneak who ran away from the draft" was a Democrat; every "New York rioter in 1863 who burned up little children in colored asylums called himself a Democrat. In short, the Democratic party may be described as a common sewer. . . ."

Voters soundly repudiated Johnson, as the Republicans won more than a two-thirds majority in both houses of Congress. The Radicals had reached the

Repudiation of Johnson

height of their power, propelled by genuine alarm among northerners that Johnson's policies would lose the fruits of the Union's victory. Johnson was a president virtually without a party.

CONGRESSIONAL RECONSTRUCTION

With a clear mandate in hand, congressional Republicans passed their own program of Reconstruction, beginning with the first Reconstruction Act in March 1867. Like all later pieces of Reconstruction legislation, it was repassed over Johnson's veto.

Placing the 10 unreconstructed states under military commanders, the act provided that in enrolling voters, officials were to include black adult males but not former Confederates who were barred from holding office under the Fourteenth Amendment. Delegates to the state conventions were to frame constitutions that provided for black suffrage and disqualified prominent ex-Confederates from office. The first state legislatures to meet under the new constitution were required to ratify the Fourteenth Amendment. Once these steps were completed and Congress approved the new state constitution, a state could send representatives to Congress.

White southerners found these requirements so obnoxious that officials took no steps to register voters. Congress then enacted a second Reconstruction

Resistance of white southerners

Act, also in March, ordering the local military commanders to put the machinery of Reconstruction into motion. Johnson's efforts to limit the power of military commanders produced a third act, passed in July, that upheld their superiority in all matters.

When elections were held to ratify the new state constitutions, white southerners boycotted them in sufficient numbers to prevent a majority of voters from participating. Undaunted, Congress passed the fourth Reconstruction Act (March 1868), which required ratification of the constitution by only a majority of those voting rather than those who were registered.

By June 1868 Congress had readmitted the representatives of seven states. Texas, Virginia, and Mississippi did not complete the process until 1869. Georgia finally followed in 1870.

The Land Issue

While the political process of Reconstruction proceeded, Congress debated whether land should be given to former slaves to foster economic independence. At a meeting with Secretary of War Edwin Stanton near the end of the war,

African American leaders declared, "The way we can best take care of ourselves is to have land, and till it by our own labor." The Second Confiscation Act of 1862 had authorized the government to seize and sell the property of supporters of the rebellion. In June 1866, however, President Johnson ruled that confiscation laws applied only to wartime.

For over a year Congress debated land confiscation off and on, but in the end it rejected all proposals to give land to former slaves. Even some Radicals were opposed. Given Americans' strong belief in self-reliance, little sympathy existed for the idea that government should support any group. In addition, land redistribution represented an attack on property rights, another cherished American value. "A division of rich men's lands amongst the landless," argued the *Nation*, a Radical journal, "would give a shock to our whole social and political system from which it would hardly recover without the loss of liberty." By 1867 land reform was dead.

Failure of land redistribution

Few freedpeople acquired land after the war, a development that severely limited African Americans' economic independence and left them vulnerable to white coercion. It is doubtful, however, that this decision was the basic cause of the failure of Reconstruction. In the face of white hostility, African Americans probably would have been no more successful in protecting their property than they were in maintaining the right to vote.

Impeachment

Throughout 1867 Congress routinely overrode Johnson's vetoes, but the president had other ways of undercutting congressional Reconstruction. He interpreted the new laws as narrowly as possible and removed military commanders who vigorously enforced them. Congress responded by restricting his power to issue orders to military commanders in the South. It also passed the Tenure of Office Act, which forbade Johnson from removing any member of the cabinet without the Senate's consent. The intention of this law was to prevent him from firing Secretary of War Edwin Stanton, the only remaining Radical in the cabinet.

Tenure of Office Act

When Johnson tried to dismiss Stanton in February 1868, the House of Representatives angrily approved articles of impeachment. The articles focused on the violation of the Tenure of Office Act, but the charge with the most substance was that Johnson had conspired to systematically obstruct Reconstruction legislation. In the trial before the Senate, his lawyers argued that a president could be impeached only for an indictable crime, which Johnson clearly had not committed. The Radicals countered that impeachment applied to political offenses and not merely criminal acts. In May 1868 the Senate voted 36 to 19 to convict, one vote short of the two-thirds majority needed. The seven Republicans who joined the Democrats in voting for acquittal were uneasy about using impeachment as a political weapon.

Johnson's acquittal

COUNTERPOINT   *Should Johnson Have Been Removed from Office?*

For the first half of the twentieth century, most historians viewed Reconstruction as an undertaking that was tragically flawed at best or vindictive and misconceived at worst. Since 1960, however, historians increasingly have found much to praise in the experiment of Reconstruction and much to condemn in Andrew Johnson's leadership. (It is no coincidence that this reevaluation gained momentum just as the civil rights movement was forcing Americans to rethink attitiudes about segregation, racism, and equality.)

Controversy persists, however, over the issue of whether congressional Republicans were wise to pursue impeachment. Some historians point out that when the Constitution was drafted, James Madison argued that impeachment should apply to political misdeeds as well as crimes. Johnson, after all, had not been elected president in his own right. Voters in the 1866 congressional elections had rejected his clumsy attempts to gain support. Furthermore, as president he had taken an oath to uphold the laws of the nation. Yet time after time Johnson interpreted those laws as narrowly as possible, refusing to enforce them in a manner that Congress clearly intended. When Congress voted to not convict the president, these historians argue, it lessened the threat that impeachment would ever be used. Yet that was one of the legislative branch's most important weapons to control presidential abuse of power.

Other historians, while not sympathetic to Johnson's policies, believe that his acquittal was fortunate. The Constitution states only that a president may be removed for "Treason, Bribery, or other high Crimes and Misdemeanors." Johnson's lawyers ably argued that whatever his "misdeeds" in the eyes of Congress, he had not comitted "high Crimes." Historians who sympathize with that view argue that a conviction would have upset the constitutional doctrine of separation of powers. Removing Johnson from office would have seriously weakened the presidency, placed too much power in the hands of Congress, and provided a dangerous precedent for the future. The best course, they conclude, was the one Congress finally followed: to let Johnson finish his term as an ineffective president.

RECONSTRUCTION IN THE SOUTH

The waning power of the Radicals in Congress, evident in the failure to remove Johnson, meant that the success or failure of Reconstruction increasingly hinged on developments in the southern states themselves. Power in these states rested with the new Republican parties, representing a coalition of black and white southerners and transplanted northerners.

Black Officeholding

Almost from the beginning of Reconstruction, African Americans had lobbied for the right to vote. After they received the franchise, black men constituted as much as 80 percent of the Republican voters in the South. They steadfastly opposed the Democratic party with its appeal to white supremacy. As one Tennessee Republican explained, "The blacks know that many conservatives [Democrats] hope to reduce them again to some form of peonage. Under the impulse of this fear they will roll up their whole strength and will go entirely for the Republican candidate whoever he may be."

Throughout Reconstruction, African Americans never held office in proportion to their voting strength. No African American was ever elected governor, and only in South Carolina, where more than 60 percent of the population was black, did they control even one house of the legislature. During Reconstruction between 15 and 20 percent of the state officers and 6 percent of members of Congress (2 senators and 15 representatives) were black. Only in South Carolina did black officeholders approach their proportion of the population.

Those who held office came from the top levels of African American society. Among state and federal officeholders, perhaps four-fifths were literate, and over

Black political leadership

a quarter had been free before the war, both marks of distinction in the black community. Their occupations also set them apart: two-fifths were professionals (mostly clergy), and of the third who were farmers, nearly all owned land. In their political and social values, African American leaders were more conservative than the rural black population, and they showed little interest in land reform.

White Republicans in the South

Black citizens were a majority of the voters only in South Carolina, Mississippi, and Louisiana. Thus in most of the South the Republican party had to secure white votes

Scalawags

to stay in power. Opponents scornfully labeled white southerners who allied with the Republican party scalawags, yet an estimated

A black politician addresses former slaves at a political meeting in the South during the 1868 presidential campaign. Although only men could vote, black women are also in the audience.

quarter of white southerners at one time voted Republican. They were primarily Unionists from the upland counties and hill areas who were largely yeoman farmers. Such voters were attracted by Republican promises to rebuild the South, restore prosperity, create public schools, and open isolated areas to the market with railroads.

The other group of white Republicans in the South were known as carpetbaggers. Originally from the North, they allegedly had arrived with all their

Carpetbaggers

worldly possessions stuffed in a carpetbag, ready to loot and plunder the defeated South. Some did, certainly, but northerners moved south for a variety of reasons. Though carpetbaggers made up only a small percentage of Republican voters, they controlled almost a third of the offices. More than half of all southern Republican governors and nearly half of Republican members of Congress were originally northerners.

The Republican party in the South had difficulty maintaining unity. Scalawags were especially susceptible to the race issue and social pressure. "Even my own kinspeople have turned the cold shoulder to me because I hold office under a Republican administration," testified a Mississippi white Republican. As black southerners pressed for greater recognition, white southerners increasingly defected to the Democrats. Carpetbaggers, by contrast, were less sensitive to race, although most felt that their black allies should be content with minor offices. The animosity between scalawags and carpetbaggers, which grew out of their rivalry for party honors, was particularly intense.

Reforms Under the New State Governments

The new southern state constitutions enacted several significant reforms. They devised fairer systems of legislative representation and made many previously ap-

Reconstruction state constitutions

pointive offices elective. The Radical state governments also assumed some responsibility for social welfare and established the first statewide systems of public schools in the South. Although the Fourteenth Amendment prevented high Confederate officials from holding office, only Alabama and Arkansas temporarily forbade some ex-Confederates from voting.

All the new constitutions proclaimed the principle of equality and granted black adult males the right to vote. On social relations they were much more

Race and social equality

cautious. No state outlawed segregation, and South Carolina and Louisiana were the only ones that required integration in public schools (a mandate that was almost universally ignored). Sensitive to status, mulattoes pushed for prohibition of social discrimination, but white Republicans refused to adopt such a radical policy.

Economic Issues and Corruption

With the southern economy in ruins at the end of the war, problems of economic reconstruction were severe. The new Republican governments sought to encourage industrial development by providing subsidies, loans, and even temporary exemptions from taxes. These governments also largely rebuilt the southern railroad system, often offering lavish aid to railroad corporations. In the two decades after 1860, the region doubled its manufacturing establishments, yet the South steadily slipped further behind the booming industrial economy of the North.

The expansion of government services offered temptations for corruption. In many southern states, officials regularly received bribes and kickbacks for

Corruption their award of railroad charters, franchises, and other contracts. By 1872 the debts of the 11 states of the Confederacy had increased $132 million, largely because of railroad grants and new social services such as schools. The tax rate grew as expenditures went up, so that by the 1870s it was four times the rate of 1860.

Corruption, however, was not only a southern problem: the decline in morality affected the entire nation. During these years, the Democratic Tweed Ring in New York City alone stole more money than all the Radical Republican governments in the South combined. Moreover, corruption in the South was hardly limited to Republicans. Many Democrats and white business leaders participated in these corrupt practices, both before and after the Radical governments were in power. Louisiana Governor Henry Warmoth, a carpetbagger, told a congressional committee, "Everybody is demoralizing down here. Corruption is the fashion."

Corruption in Radical governments undeniably existed, but southern Democrats exaggerated its extent for partisan purposes. They opposed honest Radical regimes just as bitterly as notoriously corrupt ones. In the eyes of most white southerners, the real crime of the Radical governments was that they allowed black citizens to hold some offices and tried to protect the civil rights of black Americans. Race was white conservatives' greatest weapon. And it would prove the most effective means to undermine Republican power in the South.

BLACK ASPIRATIONS

Emancipation came to slaves in different ways and at different times. Betty Jones's grandmother was told about the Emancipation Proclamation by another slave while they were hoeing corn. Mary Anderson received the news from her master near the end of the war when Sherman's army invaded North Carolina. And for Louis Napoleon, emancipation arrived after the war when Union troops occupied Tallahassee, Florida. Whatever the timing, freedom meant a host of precious blessings to people who had been in bondage all their lives.

Experiencing Freedom

The first impulse was to think of freedom as a contrast to slavery. Emancipation immediately released slaves from the most oppressive aspects of bondage—the whippings, the breakup of families, the sexual exploitation. Freedom also meant movement, the right to travel without a pass or white permission. Above all,

Meaning of freedom

freedom meant that African Americans' labor would be for their own benefit. One Arkansas freedman, who earned his first dollar working on a railroad, recalled that when he was paid, "I felt like the richest man in the world."

Freedom included finding a new place to work. Changing jobs was one concrete way to break the psychological ties of slavery. Even planters with reputations for kindness sometimes found that most of their former hands had departed. The cook who left a South Carolina family, even though they offered her higher wages than her new job did, explained, "I must go. If I stays here I'll never know I'm free."

Symbolically, freedom meant having a full name. African Americans now adopted last names, most commonly the name of the first master in the family's oral history as far back as it could be recalled. Most, on the other hand, retained their first name, especially if the name had been given to them by their parents (as most often had been the case). Whatever name they took, it was important to black Americans that they made the decision themselves.

The Black Family

African Americans also sought to strengthen the family in freedom. Since slave marriages had not been recognized as legal, thousands of former slaves insisted on being married again by proper authorities, even though this was not required

Upholding the family

by law. Those who had been forcibly separated in slavery and later remarried confronted the dilemma of which spouse to take. Laura Spicer, whose husband had been sold away in slavery, received a series of wrenching letters from him after the war. He had thought her dead, had remarried, and had a new family. "You know it never was our wishes to be separated from each other, and it never was our fault. I had rather anything to had happened to me most than ever have been parted from you and the children," he wrote. "As I am, I do not know which I love best, you or Anna." Declining to return, he closed, "Laura, truly, I have got another wife, and I am very sorry. . . ."

As in white families, black husbands deemed themselves the head of the family and acted legally for their wives. They often insisted that their wives would not work in the fields as they had in slavery. "The [black] women say they never mean to do any more outdoor work," one planter reported, "that white men support their wives and they mean that their husbands shall support them." In negotiating contracts, a father also demanded the right to control his children and their labor. All these changes were designed to insulate the black family from white control.

The Schoolhouse and the Church

In freedom, the schoolhouse and the black church became essential institutions in the black community. "My Lord, Ma'am, what a great thing learning is!" a

Black education

South Carolina freedman told a northern teacher. "White folks can do what they likes, for they know so much more than we." At first, northern churches and missionaries, working with the Freedmen's

Bureau, set up black schools in the South. Tuition at these schools represented 10 percent or more of a laborer's monthly wages, yet these schools were full. Eventually, states established public school systems, which by 1867 enrolled 40 percent of African American children.

Black adults, who often attended night classes, had good reasons for seeking literacy. They wanted to be able to read the Bible, to defend their newly gained civil and political rights, and to protect themselves from being cheated. Both races saw that education would undermine the old servility that slavery had fostered.

The teachers in the Freedmen's Bureau schools were primarily northern middle-class white women sent south by northern missionary societies. "I feel that

Teachers in black schools

it is a precious privilege," Esther Douglass wrote, "to be allowed to do something for these poor people." Many saw themselves as peacetime soldiers, struggling to make emancipation a reality. Indeed, hostile white southerners sometimes destroyed black schools and threatened and even murdered white teachers. Then there were the everyday challenges: low pay, dilapidated buildings, insufficient books, classes of 100 or more children, and irregular attendance. Meanwhile, the Freedmen's Bureau undertook to train black teachers, and by 1869 a majority of the teachers in these schools were black.

Most slaves had attended white churches or services supervised by whites. Once free, African Americans quickly established their own congregations led by

Independent black churches

black preachers. Mostly Methodist and Baptist, black churches were the only major organizations in the African American community they controlled. A white missionary reported that "the Ebony preacher who promises perfect independence from White control and direction carried the colored heart at once." Just as in slavery, religion offered African Americans a place of refuge in a hostile white world and provided them with hope, comfort, and a means of self-identification.

New Working Conditions

As a largely propertyless class, blacks in the postwar South had no choice but to work for white landowners. Except for paying wages, whites wanted to retain the old system of labor, including close supervision, gang labor, and physical punishment. Determined to remove all emblems of servitude, African Americans refused to work under these conditions, and they demanded time off to devote to their own interests. Because of shorter hours and the withdrawal of children and women from the fields, blacks' output declined by an estimated 35 percent in freedom. They also refused to live in the old slave quarters located near the master's house and instead erected cabins on distant parts of the plantation. Wages initially were $5 or $6 a month plus provisions and a cabin; by 1867, they had risen to an average of $10 a month.

These changes eventually led to the rise of sharecropping. Under this arrangement African American families farmed separate plots of land and then

Sharecropping

at the end of the year divided the crop, normally on an equal basis, with the white landowner. Sharecropping had higher status

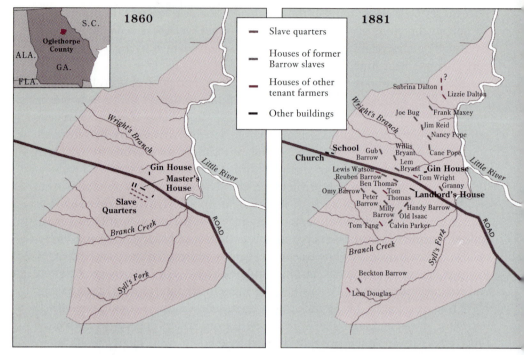

A GEORGIA PLANTATION AFTER THE WAR   After emancipation, sharecropping became the dominant form of agricultural labor in the South. Black families no longer lived in the old slave quarters but dispersed themselves to separate plots of land that they farmed themselves. At the end of the year each sharecropper turned over part of the crop to the white landowner.

and offered greater personal freedom than being a wage laborer. "I am not working for wages," one black farmer declared in defending his right to leave the plantation at will, "but am part owner of the crop and as I have all the rights that you or any other man has. . . ." Although black per capita agricultural income increased 40 percent in freedom, sharecropping was a harshly exploitative system in which black families often sank into perpetual debt.

The Freedmen's Bureau

The task of supervising the transition from slavery to freedom on southern plantations fell to the Freedmen's Bureau, a unique experiment in social policy supported by the federal government. Assigned the task of protecting freedpeople's economic rights, approximately 550 local agents regulated working conditions in southern agriculture after the war. The racial attitudes of Bureau agents varied widely, as did their commitment and competence. Then, too, they had to depend on the army to enforce their decisions.

Most agents required written contracts between white planters and black laborers, specifying not only wages but also the conditions of employment.

*Bureau's
mixed record*

Although agents sometimes intervened to protect freedpeople from unfair treatment, they also provided important help to planters. They insisted that black laborers not leave at harvest time, they arrested those who violated their contracts or refused to sign new ones at the beginning of the year, and they preached the gospel of hard work and the need to be orderly and respectful. Given such attitudes, freedpeople increasingly complained that Bureau agents were mere tools of the planter class. One observer reported, "Doing justice seems to mean seeing that the blacks don't break contracts and compelling them to submit cheerfully."

The primary means of enforcing working conditions were the Freedmen's Courts, which Congress created in 1866 in order to avoid the discrimination African Americans received in state courts. These new courts functioned as military tribunals, and often the agent was the entire court. The sympathy black laborers received varied from state to state. In 1867 one agent summarized the Bureau's experience with the labor contract system: "It has succeeded in making the freedman work and in rendering labor secure and stable—but it has failed to secure to the Freedman his just dues or compensation."

Opposed to any permanent welfare agency, Congress in 1869 decided to shut down the Bureau, and by 1872 it had gone out of business. Despite its mixed record, it was the most effective agency in protecting blacks' civil and political rights. Its disbanding signaled the beginning of the northern retreat from Reconstruction.

Planters and a New Way of Life

Planters and other white southerners faced emancipation with dread. "All the traditions and habits of both races had been suddenly overthrown," a Tennessee planter recalled, "and neither knew just what to do, or how to accommodate themselves to the new situation."

The old ideal of a paternalistic planter, which required a facade of black subservience and affection, gave way to an emphasis on strictly economic relationships. When two black laborers falsely accused her of trickery and hauled her into court, Mary Jones, a Georgia slaveholder before the war, told her assembled employees that she had previously "considered them friends and treated them as such but now they were only laborers under contract, and only the law would rule between us." Only with time did planters develop new norms to judge black behavior. What in 1865 had seemed insolence was viewed by the 1870s as the normal attitude of freedom.

Slavery had been a complex institution that welded black and white southerners together in intimate relationships. After the war, however, planters in-

*Planters'
new values*

creasingly embraced the ideology of segregation. Since emancipation significantly reduced the social distance between the races, white southerners sought psychological separation and kept dealings with African Americans to a minimum. By the time Reconstruction ended, white planters had developed a new way of life based on the institutions of sharecropping and segregation and undergirded by a militant white supremacy.

While most planters kept their land, they did not regain the economic prosperity of the prewar years. Cotton prices began a long decline, and southern per capita income suffered as a result. By 1880 the value of southern farms had slid 33 percent below the level of 1860.

THE ABANDONMENT OF RECONSTRUCTION

On Christmas Day 1875 a white acquaintance approached Charles Caldwell in Clinton, Mississippi, and invited him to have a drink. A former slave, Caldwell was a state senator and the leader of the Republican party in Hinds County. But the black leader's fearlessness made him a marked man. Only two months earlier, Caldwell had fled the county to escape an armed white mob. Despite threats against him, he had returned home to vote in the November state election. Now, as Caldwell and his "friend" raised their glasses in a holiday toast, a gunshot exploded through the window and Caldwell collapsed, mortally wounded. He was taken outside, where his assassins riddled his body with bullets. He died alone in the street.

Charles Caldwell shared the fate of a number of black Republican leaders in the South during Reconstruction. Resorting to violence and terror, southern whites challenged the commitment of the federal government to sustain Reconstruction. But following Johnson's acquittal, the Radical's influence waned, and the Republican party was increasingly drained of its crusading idealism. Ulysses S. Grant was hardly the cause of this change, but he certainly came to symbolize it.

The Election of Grant

In 1868 Republicans nominated Grant for president. Although he was elected, Republicans were shocked that his popular margin was only 300,000 votes and that, with an estimated 450,000 black Republican votes cast in the South, a majority of whites had voted Democratic. The 1868 election helped convince Republican leaders that an amendment securing black suffrage throughout the nation was necessary.

In February 1869 Congress sent the Fifteenth Amendment to the states for ratification. It forbade any state from denying the right to vote on grounds of

Fifteenth Amendment ratified

race, color, or previous condition of servitude. It did not forbid literacy and property requirements, as some Radicals wanted, because the moderates feared that only a conservative version could be ratified. As a result, the final amendment left loopholes that eventually allowed southern states to disfranchise African Americans. Furthermore, advocates of women's suffrage like Lucy Stone and Susan B. Anthony were bitterly disappointed when Congress refused to prohibit voting discrimination on the basis of sex as well as race. The amendment was ratified in March 1870, aided by the votes of the four southern states that had not completed the process of Reconstruction and thus were also required to endorse this amendment before being readmitted to Congress.

The Grant Administration

Ulysses Grant was ill at ease with the political process: his simple, quiet manner, while superb for commanding armies, did not serve him as well in public life, and his well-known resolution withered when he was uncertain of his goal.

A series of scandals wracked Grant's presidency, so much so that "Grantism" soon became a code word in American politics for corruption, cronyism, and venality. Although Grant did not profit personally, he remained loyal to his friends and displayed little zeal to root out wrongdoing. James W. Grimes, one of the party's founders, denounced the Republican party under Grant as "the most corrupt and debauched political party that has ever existed."

Corruption under Grant

Nor was Congress immune from the lowered tone of public life. In such a climate ruthless state machines, led by men who favored the status quo, came to dominate the party. Office and power became ends in themselves, and party leaders worked in close cooperation with northern industrial interests.

As corruption in both the North and the South worsened, reformers became more interested in cleaning up government than in protecting black rights. Congress in 1872 passed an amnesty act, removing the restrictions of the Fourteenth Amendment on officeholding, except for about 200 to 300 ex-Confederate leaders. That same year liberal Republicans broke with the Republican party and nominated for president Horace Greeley, the editor of the New York *Tribune*. A one-time Radical, Greeley had become disillusioned with Reconstruction and urged a restoration of

Liberal Republican movement

Grant swings from a trapeze while supporting a number of associates accused of corruption. While not personally involved in the scandals during his administration, Grant was reluctant to dismiss from office supporters accused of wrongdoing.

home rule in the South as well as adoption of civil service reform. Democrats decided to back the Liberal Republican ticket. The Republicans renominated Grant, who, despite the defection of a number of prominent Radicals, won an easy victory with 56 percent of the popular vote.

Growing Northern Disillusionment

During Grant's second term, Congress passed the Civil Rights Act of 1875, the last major piece of Reconstruction legislation. This law prohibited racial discrimination in public accommodations, transportation, places of amusement, and juries. At the same time, Congress rejected a ban on segregation in public schools, which was almost universally practiced in the North as well as the South. The federal government made little attempt to enforce the law, however, and in 1883 the Supreme Court struck down its provisions, except the one relating to juries.

Civil Rights Act of 1875

Despite passage of the Civil Rights Act, many northerners were growing disillusioned with Reconstruction. They were repelled by the corruption of the southern governments, they were tired of the violence and disorder in the South, and they had little faith in black Americans. William Dodge, a wealthy New York capitalist and an influential Republican, wrote in 1875 that the South could never develop its resources "till confidence in her state governments can be restored, and this will never be done by federal bayonets." It had been a mistake, he went on, to make black southerners feel "that the United States government was their special friend, rather than those . . . among whom they must live and for whom they must work. We have tried this long enough," he concluded. "Now let the South alone."

As the agony of the war became more distant, the Panic of 1873, which precipitated a severe depression that lasted four years, diverted public attention from Reconstruction to economic issues. Battered by the panic and the corruption issue, the Republicans lost a shocking 77 seats in Congress in the 1874 elections, and along with them control of the House of Representatives for the first time since 1861.

Depression and Democratic resurgence

"The truth is our people are tired out with the worn out cry of 'Southern outrages'!!" one Republican concluded. "Hard times and heavy taxes make them wish the 'ever lasting nigger' were in hell or Africa." Republicans spoke more and more about cutting loose the unpopular southern governments.

The Triumph of White Supremacy

As northern commitment to Reconstruction waned, southern Democrats set out to overthrow the remaining Radical governments. Already white Republicans in the South felt heavy pressure to desert their party. In Mississippi one party member justified his decision to leave on the grounds that otherwise he would have "to live a life of social isolation" and his children would have no future.

To poor white southerners who lacked social standing, the Democratic appeal to racial solidarity offered great comfort. Explained one, "I may be poor

Racism and my manners may be crude, but . . . because I am a white man, I have a right to be treated with respect by Negroes. . . . no Negro is ever going to forget that he is not a white man." The large landowners and other wealthy groups that led southern Democrats objected less to black southerners voting, since they were confident that if outside influences were removed, they could control the black vote.

Democrats also resorted to economic pressure to undermine Republican power. In heavily black counties, newspapers published the names of black res-

Terror and violence idents who cast Republican ballots and urged planters to discharge them. But terror and violence provided the most effective means to overthrow the radical regimes. A number of paramilitary organizations broke up Republican meetings, terrorized white and black Republicans, assassinated Republican leaders, and prevented black citizens from voting. The most famous of these organizations was the Ku Klux Klan, which with similar groups functioned as an unofficial arm of the Democratic party.

What became known as the Mississippi Plan was inaugurated in 1875, when Democrats decided to use as much violence as necessary to carry the state elec-

Mississippi Plan tion. Several local papers trumpeted, "Carry the election peaceably if we can, forcibly if we must." Recognizing that northern public opinion had grown sick of repeated federal intervention in southern elections, the Grant administration rejected the request of Republican Governor Adelbert Ames for troops to stop the violence. Bolstered by terrorism, the Democrats swept the election in Mississippi. Violence and intimidation prevented as many as 60,000 black and white Republicans from voting, converting the normal Republican majority into a Democratic majority of 30,000. Mississippi had been "redeemed."

Two Ku Klux Klan members pose in full regalia. Violence played a major role in overthrowing the Radical governments in the South.

The Disputed Election of 1876

With Republicans on the defensive across the nation, the 1876 presidential election was crucial to the final overthrow of Reconstruction. The Republicans nominated Ohio Governor Rutherford B. Hayes to oppose Samuel Tilden of New York. Once again, violence prevented an estimated quarter of a million Republican votes from being cast in the South. Tilden had a clear majority of 250,000 in the popular vote, but the outcome in the Electoral College was in doubt because both parties claimed South Carolina, Florida, and Louisiana, the only reconstructed states still in Republican hands.

To arbitrate the disputed returns, Congress established a 15-member electoral commission. By a straight party vote of 8 to 7, the commission awarded the disputed electoral votes—and the presidency—to Hayes.

When angry Democrats threatened a filibuster to prevent the electoral votes from being counted, key Republicans met with southern Democrats and *Compromise of 1877* reached an informal understanding, later known as the Compromise of 1877. Hayes's supporters agreed to withdraw federal troops from the South and not oppose the new Democratic state

EYEWITNESS TO HISTORY

The Mississippi Plan in Action

Seeing that nothing but intimidation would enable them [the Democrats] to carry the election they resorted to it in every possible way, and the republicans at once found themselves in the midst of a perfect organized armed opposition that embraced the entire democratic party. . . . At Sulphur Springs they came very near precipitating a bloody riot by beating colored men over the heads with pistols. . . . The republicans . . . revoked the balance of their appointments running up to the election, and did not attempt to hold any more meetings in the Co[unty]. . . . On the night before the election armed bodies of men visited almost every neighborhood in the county, threatening death to all who voted the "radical" ticket. . . .

On the morning of the election in Aberdeen . . . the White-Liners took possession of the polls. . . . The colored men who had gathered . . . to vote were told if they did not leave the town within five minutes that the last man would be shot dead in his tracks, and that not a man could vote that day unless he voted the democratic ticket. . . . The cannon was placed in position bearing on the large crowd, . . . when the whole crowd broke & run in confusion, then the infantry & cavalry had no trouble in driving everything from town; and there are over 1,300 men in this county . . . who will swear that they were driven from the polls & could not vote.

James W. Lee to Adelbert Ames, Aberdeen, Miss., February 7, 1876, 44th Cong., 1st Sess., Senate Report 527, v. 2, pp. 67–68.

governments. For their part, southern Democrats dropped their opposition to Hayes's election and pledged to respect African Americans' rights.

Without federal support, the last Republican governments collapsed, and Democrats took control of the remaining states of the Confederacy. By 1877, the entire South was in the hands of the Redeemers, as they called themselves. Reconstruction and Republican rule had come to an end.

Racism and the Failure of Reconstruction

Reconstruction failed for a multitude of reasons. The reforming impulse that had created the Republican party in the 1850s had been battered and worn down by the war. The new materialism of industrial America inspired a jaded cynicism in many Americans. In the South, African American voters and leaders inevitably lacked a certain amount of education and experience; elsewhere, Republicans were divided over policies and options.

Yet beyond these obstacles, the sad fact remains that the ideals of Reconstruction were most clearly defeated by a deep-seated racism that permeated American life. Racism stimulated white southern resistance, undercut northern support for black rights, and eventually made northerners willing to write off Reconstruction, and with it the welfare of African Americans. While Congress might pass a constitutional amendment abolishing slavery, it could not overturn at a stroke the social habits of two centuries.

Certainly the political equations of power, in the long term, had been changed. The North had secured the power to dominate the economic and political destiny of the nation. With the overthrow of Reconstruction, the white South had won back some of the power it had lost in 1865—but not all. Even with white supremacy triumphant, African Americans did not return to the social position they had occupied before the war. They were no longer slaves, and black southerners who walked dusty roads in search of family members, sent their children to school, or worshiped in churches they controlled knew what a momentous change this was. Even under the exploitative sharecropping system, black income rose significantly in freedom. Then, too, the guarantees of "equal protection" and "due process of law" had been written into the Constitution and would be available for later generations to use in championing once again the Radicals' goal of racial equality.

But this was a struggle left to future reformers. For the time being, the clear trend was away from change or hope—especially for former slaves like Benjamin

An end to the Davis Bend experiment

Montgomery and his sons, the owners of the old Davis plantations in Mississippi. In the 1870s bad crops, lower cotton prices, and falling land values undermined the Montgomerys' financial position, and in 1875 Jefferson Davis sued to have the sale of Brierfield invalidated.

A lower court ruled against Davis, since he had never received legal title to the plantation. Davis appealed to the state supreme court, which, following the overthrow of Mississippi's Radical government, had a white conservative majority. In a politically motivated decision, the court awarded Brierfield to Davis in 1878, and the Montgomerys lost Hurricane as well. The final outcome was not without bitter irony. In applying for restoration of his property after the war, Joseph Davis had convinced skeptical federal officials that he—and not his younger brother—held legal title to Brierfield. Had they decided instead that the plantation belonged to Jefferson Davis, it would have been confiscated.

But the waning days of Reconstruction were times filled with such ironies: of governments "redeemed" by violence, of Fourteenth Amendment rights designed to protect black people being used by conservative courts to protect giant corporations, of reformers taking up other causes. Disowned by its northern supporters and unmourned by public opinion, Reconstruction was over.

SIGNIFICANT EVENTS

1863 — Lincoln outlines Reconstruction program

1864 — Lincoln vetoes Wade–Davis bill; Louisiana, Arkansas, and Tennessee establish governments under Lincoln's plan

1865 — Freedmen's Bureau established; Johnson becomes president; presidential Reconstruction completed; Congress excludes representatives of Johnson's governments; Thirteenth Amendment ratified; Joint Committee on Reconstruction established

1865–1866 — Black codes enacted

1866 — Civil Rights bill passed over Johnson's veto; Memphis and New Orleans riots; Fourteenth Amendment passes Congress; Freedmen's Bureau extended; Ku Klux Klan organized; Tennessee readmitted to Congress; Republicans win decisive victory in congressional elections

1867 — Congressional Reconstruction enacted; Tenure of Office Act

1867–1868 — Constitutional conventions in the South; blacks vote in southern elections

1868 — Johnson impeached but acquitted; Fourteenth Amendment ratified; Grant elected president

1869 — Fifteenth Amendment passes Congress

1870 — Last southern states readmitted to Congress; Fifteenth Amendment ratified

1872 — General Amnesty Act; Freedmen's Bureau dismantled; Liberal Republican revolt

1873–1877 — Panic and depression

1874 — Democrats win control of the House

1875 — Civil Rights Act; Mississippi Plan

1876 — Disputed Hayes–Tilden election

1877 — Compromise of 1877; Hayes declared winner of electoral vote; last Republican governments in South fall

The United States in an Industrial Age

With some justice, the United States has been called a nation of immigrants. Looking back today, most Americans tend to view the "huddled masses" passing the Statue of Liberty as part of the stream of newcomers stretching back to the English Pilgrims, the French fur traders of Canada, and the Spanish friars of Old California. But the tide of immigration that swelled during the mid-nineteenth century was strikingly different.

Before 1820 most new arrivals in North and South America did not come voluntarily. Nearly 8 million Africans were brought to the Americas during those years, virtually all as slaves. That number was four to five times the number of Europeans who came during the same period. In contrast, between 1820 and 1920 nearly 30 million free immigrants arrived from Europe.

Nor was this new flood directed only toward America. At least as many Europeans settled in other regions of Europe or the world. From Eastern Europe millions followed the Trans-Siberian Railway (completed in 1905) into Asiatic Russia. The Canadian prairie provinces of Manitoba and Saskatchewan competed for homesteaders with Montana and the Dakotas. Before 1900 two out of three emigrating Italians booked passage not for the United States but for Brazil and Argentina.

This broad movement could not have taken place without a global network of communication, markets, and transportation. By midcentury, urbanization and industrialization were well under way in both America and Europe. The British, who led in revolutionizing industry, also discovered its harsh side effects. Urban factory workers in Britain jammed into dark, dingy row houses built with few windows along streets and alleys where open sewers flowed with garbage. Spurred by a deadly cholera epidemic in 1848, social reformer Edwin Chadwick led a campaign to install water and sewer systems throughout major cities.

Other urban planners admired the radical renovation of Paris begun in the 1850s by Baron Georges Haussmann. Haussmann's workers tore down the city's medieval fortress walls, widened major streets into boulevards, and set aside land for pleasant green parks. American innovations inspired Europeans to adopt horse-drawn streetcars and, later, electric trolleys.

As hubs of the new industrial networks, cities needed efficient links to raw materials. Much of the late nineteenth century can be seen as a scramble of Western nations for those natural resources. Miners combed the hills of California for gold in 1849, as they did two years later in Victoria, Australia. In Canada, Argentina, Australia, and New Zealand, farmers and cattle ranchers moved steadily toward larger commercial operations. All these enterprises extracted value from previously untapped natural resources.

The end result of the scramble was the age of imperialism, as the European powers sought to dominate newly acquired colonies in Africa and Asia. The United States joined the rush somewhat late, in part because it was still extracting raw materials from its own "colonial" regions, the booming West and the defeated South.

European imperialists sometimes justified their rule over nonwhite races as a noble sacrifice made on behalf of their subject peoples—"the White Man's Burden," British poet Rudyard Kipling called it. But the burdens were far greater for the coolie laborers of Kipling's India, who died by the thousands clearing jungles for tea plantations. Imperialism's costs were also harsh for black miners laboring in South Africa and for Chinese workers in Australia and the United States who found themselves excluded and segregated after both gold rushes. A similar racism thwarted Southern black sharecroppers in the United States and made it easier for successive waves of prospectors, cowhands, and sodbusters to drive American Indians off their lands.

The social strains arising out of such changes forced political systems to adjust as well. In the United States both the Populists and the Progressives called on the government to take a more active role in managing the excesses of the new industrial order. In Europe, industrializing nations went further, passing social legislation that included the first social security systems and health insurance. In the end, however, the political system was unable to manage the new global order of commerce and imperialism. With the coming of World War I, it was shaken to its roots.

CHAPTER EIGHTEEN

The New Industrial Order

It was so dark Robert Ferguson could not see his own feet. Inching along the railroad tracks, he suddenly pitched forward as the ground vanished beneath him. To his dismay, he found himself wedged between two railroad ties, his legs dangling in the air. Scrambling back to solid ground, he retreated to the railroad car, where he sat meekly until dawn.

Ferguson, a Scot visiting America in 1866, had been in Memphis only two days earlier, ready to take the "Great Southern Mail Route" east some 850 miles to Washington. Things had gone badly from the start. About 50 miles down the track, a broken river bridge had forced him to take a ferry and then spend 10 miles bumping along in a mule-drawn truck before learning that the rail line did not resume for another 40 miles. Disheartened, he had decided to return to Memphis to try again.

The train to Memphis had arrived six hours late, dawdled its way home, and then, three miles outside the city, derailed in the middle of the night. When a few passengers decided to hike the remaining distance into town, Ferguson had tagged along. It was then that he had fallen between the tracks. At dawn he discovered to his horror that the tracks led onto a flimsy, high river bridge. Ferguson had trouble managing the trestle even in daylight.

Before he finally reached Washington, Robert Ferguson faced six more days of difficult travel. One rail line would end, and passengers and freight would be forced to transfer to another because rail gauges—the width of the track—differed from line to line. Or a bridge would be out. Or there would be no bridge at all. Trains had no meals "on board"–or any sleeping cars. "It was certainly what the Americans would call 'hard travelling,'" Ferguson huffed; "—they do not make use of the word 'rough,' because roughness may be expected as a natural condition in a new country."

Less than 20 years later, rail passengers traveled in relative luxury. T. S. Hudson, another British tourist, launched a self-proclaimed "Scamper Through America" in 1882. It took him just 60 days to go from England to San Francisco and back. He crossed the continent on a ticket booked by a single agent in Boston. Such centralization would have been unthinkable in 1866 when, in any case, the transcontinental railroad was still three years from completion.

Hudson's trains had Pullman Palace cars with posh sleeping quarters, full meals, and installed air brakes. Bridges appeared where none had been before, including a "magnificent" span over the Mississippi at St. Louis. It had three arches of "five hundred feet each, approached by viaducts, and, on the western shore, also by a tunnel." Hudson also found himself in the midst of a communications revolution. Traveling across the plains, he was struck by the number of telephone poles along the route.

What made America in the 1880s so different from the 1860s was a new industrial order. The process of industrialization had begun at least three decades

An industrial transformation

before the Civil War. Small factories had produced light consumer goods like clothing, shoes, and furniture. They catered to local markets in an economy of farmers and merchants. After the 1850s the industrial economy matured, with larger factories, more machines, greater efficiency, and national markets.

The transformation, remarkable as it was, brought pain along with the progress. Virgin forests vanished from the Pacific Northwest, the hillsides of Pennsylvania and West Virginia were scarred by open-pit mines, and the rivers of the Northeast grew toxic with industrial wastes. In 1882, the year Hudson scampered by rail across America, an average of 675 people were killed on the job every week. Like most Americans, workers scrambled—sometimes literally—to adjust.

THE DEVELOPMENT
OF INDUSTRIAL SYSTEMS

The new industrial order can best be understood as a web of complex industrial systems. Look, for example, at the bridge across the Mississippi that Hudson so admired. When James B. Eads constructed his soaring arches in 1874, he needed steel, most likely made from iron ore mined in northern Michigan. Giant steam shovels scooped up the ore and loaded whole freight cars in a few strokes. A transportation system—railroads, boats, and other carriers—moved the ore to Pittsburgh, where the factory system furnished the labor and machinery to finish the steel. The capital to create such factories came itself from a system of finance, linking investment banks and stock markets to entrepreneurs in need of money. Only with a national network of industrial systems could the Eads bridge be built and a new age of industry arise.

E Y E W I T N E S S   T O   H I S T O R Y

An Englishman Visits Pittsburgh in 1898

Pittsburgh is not an Eastern City. . . . A cloud of smoke hangs over it by day. The glow of scores of furnaces light[s] the riverbanks by night. It stands at the junction of two great rivers, the Monongahela which flows down today in a turbid yellowy stream, and the Allegheny which is blackish. They join at the nose of the city where Fort Duquesne stood. A hundred and fifty years ago the whole country was desolate except for the little French blockhouse at the river junction. Today the old block-house stands in a little green patch off a filthy slum-street. . . .

I spent today seeing the [steel] works where the Bessemer rails are turned out. On the other side of the river is Homestead where the great strike was and the Duquesne works, all three of them under Carnegie and Co. . . . All nations are jumbled up here, the poor living in tenement dens or wooden shanties thrown up or dumped down (better expression) with very little reference to roads or situation, whenever a new house is wanted. It is a most chaotic city, and as yet there is no public spirit or public consciousness to make the conditions healthy or decent. Carnegie has given libraries, a Park and organs to several dozen churches. Some of the other millionaires have done the same. Otherwise the town is chaos. . . . It is industrial greatness with all the worst industrial abuses on the grandest scale.

The class of manufacturer I have met is not pleasing. There is profound contempt and dislike of Unions and all their ways, much worse than in England. A certain De Armit was recommended to me to tell me about mining, being a great controller of pits and 'having fought the unions like the devil'. He was well-nigh drunk with whiskey at 5 in the afternoon at the best town club, and as coarse a fighting-cock as I have often seen. Not much chance of conciliation with such a man. His fierce competence was evident. But he was nothing but a selfish, violent money-maker. All the men I meet here are rough; but they are a good breed and shrewd and friendly. With their immense natural resources they will do great things. I absolutely trust them to evolve order out of their social disorder in time.

Charles Philips Trevelyan, April 15, 1898. *Letters from North America and the Pacific* (London: Chatto & Windus, 1969), pp. 31–33.

Natural Resources and Industrial Technology

The earliest European settlers had marveled at the "merchantable commodities" of America, from the glittering silver mines of the Spanish empire to the continent's hardwood forests. What set the new industrial economy apart from that older America was the scale and efficiency of using resources. New technologies made it possible to employ natural riches in ways undreamed of only decades earlier.

Iron, for example, had been forged into steel swords as far back as the Middle Ages. In the 1850s, inventors in England and America discovered a
Bessemer process cheaper way—called the Bessemer process—to convert large quantities of iron into steel. By the late 1870s, the price of steel had dropped by more than half. Steel was lighter than iron, could support 20 times as much weight, and lasted 20 years instead of 3. Steel tracks soon carried most rail traffic; steel girders replaced the old cast iron frames; steel cables supported new suspension bridges.

Industrial technology made some natural resources more valuable. New distilling methods transformed a thick, smelly liquid called petroleum into kerosene for lighting lamps, oil for lubricating machinery, and paraffin for making candles. Beginning in 1859, new drilling techniques began to tap vast pools of pe-
Petroleum industry troleum below the surface. About the same time, Frenchman Etienne Lenoir constructed the first practical internal combustion engine. After 1900, new vehicles like the gasoline-powered carriage turned the oil business into a major industry.

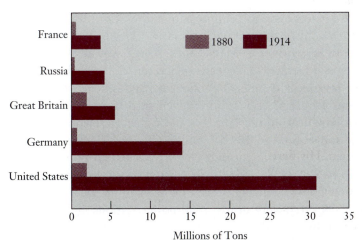

STEEL PRODUCTION, 1880 AND 1914   While steel production jumped in western industrial nations from 1880 to 1914, it skyrocketed in the United States because of rich resources, cheap labor, and aggressive management.

The environmental price of industrial technology soon became evident. Coal mining, logging, and the industrial wastes of factories produced only the most obvious environmental degradation. In California, as giant water cannons blasted away hillsides in search of gold, rock and gravel washed into rivers, raising their beds and threatening those downstream with floods. When engineers tried to cleanse the Chicago River by reversing its flow, so that it emptied into the Illinois River instead of Lake Michigan, they only succeeded in shifting pollution to rivers downstate. Some industrialists had greater success in limiting the damage. Meatpackers, for example, stretched their imaginations to use every conceivable part of the animals that came into their plants. Even blood was dried and sold as powder.

Systematic Invention

Industrial technology rested on invention. For sheer inventiveness, the 40 years following the Civil War have rarely been matched in American history. Between 1790 and 1860, 36,000 patents had been registered with the government. Over the next three decades, the U.S. Patent Office granted more than half a million. The process of invention became systematized as small-scale inventors were replaced by orderly "invention factories"—forerunners of expensive research labs.

No one did more to bring system, order, and profitability to invention than Thomas Alva Edison. In 1868, at the age of 21, Edison went to work for a New

Edison's contributions

York brokerage house and promptly improved the design of the company's stock tickers. Granted a $40,000 bonus, he set himself up as an independent inventor. For the next five years, Edison patented a new invention almost every five months.

Edison was determined to bring system and order to the process of invention. Only then could breakthroughs come in a steady and profitable stream. He moved 15 of his workers to Menlo Park, New Jersey, where in 1876 he created an "invention factory." Like a manufacturer, Edison subdivided the work among gifted inventors, engineers, toolmakers, and others.

This orderly bureaucracy soon evolved into the Edison Electric Light Company. Its ambitious owner aimed at more than perfecting his new electric lightbulb. Edison wanted to create a unified electrical power system—central stations to generate electric current, wired to users, all powering millions of small bulbs in homes and businesses. To launch his enterprise, Edison won the backing of several large banking houses by lighting up the Wall Street district in 1882. By 1898 there were nearly 3000 power stations, lighting some 2 million bulbs across America. By then, electricity was also running trolley cars, subways, and factory machinery.

George Eastman revolutionized photography by making the consumer a part of his inventive system. In 1888 Eastman marketed the "Kodak" camera. The small black box weighed two pounds and contained a strip of celluloid film that replaced hundreds of pounds of photography equipment. After 100 snaps of the shutter, the owner simply sent the camera back to the factory and waited for the developed photos, along with a reloaded camera, to return by mail. "You press the button—we do the rest" was Eastman Kodak's apt slogan.

What united these innovations was the notion of rationalizing inventions— of making a systematic business out of them. By 1913, Westinghouse Electric,

The research laboratory

General Electric, U.S. Rubber Company, and other firms had set up research laboratories. And by the middle of the century research labs had spread beyond business to the federal government, universities, trade associations, and labor unions.

Transportation and Communication

Abundant resources and new inventions remained worthless to industry until they could be moved to processing plants, factories, and offices. With more than

The problem of scale

3.5 million square miles of land in the United States, distance alone was daunting. Where 100 miles of railroad track would do for shipping goods in Germany and England, 1000 miles was necessary in America.

An efficient internal transportation network tied the country into an emerging international system. By the 1870s railroads crisscrossed the country, and steam-powered ships (introduced before the Civil War) were pushing barges down rivers and carrying passengers and freight across the oceans. Between 1870 and 1900, the value of American exports tripled. Eventually the rail and water transportation systems fused. By 1900 railroad companies owned nearly all of the country's domestic steamship lines.

A thriving industrial nation also required effective communication. Information was a precious commodity, as essential as resources or technology to industry. In the early 1840s, it took newspapers as many as 10 days to reach Indiana from New York and 3 months to arrive by ship in San Francisco. In

Telegraph

1844 Samuel Morse succeeded in sending the first message over an electrical wire between cities. By 1861 the Western Union Company had strung 76,000 miles of telegraph lines across the country. If a bank collapsed in Chicago, bankers in Dallas knew of it that day. Railroads could keep traffic unsnarled through the dots and dashes of Morse's code. So useful to railroads was the telegraph that they allowed poles and wires to be set along their rights of way in exchange for free telegraphic service. By the turn of the century a million miles of telegraph wire handled some 63 million messages a year, not to mention those flashing across underwater cables to China, Japan, Africa, and South America.

A second innovation in communication, the telephone, vastly improved on the telegraph. Alexander Graham Bell, a Scottish immigrant, was teaching the

Telephone

deaf when he began experimenting with ways to transmit speech electrically. In 1876, he transmitted his famous first words to his young assistant: "Mr. Watson, come here! I want you." No longer did messages require a telegraph office, the unwieldy Morse code, and couriers to deliver them. Communication could be instantaneous *and* direct. New York and Boston were linked in 1877 by the first intercity telephone line, and before the turn of the century, the Bell-organized American Telephone and Telegraph Company had combined more than 100 local companies to furnish business and government with long-distance service. The telephone patent proved to be the most valuable ever granted.

Along with other advances like the typewriter (1868), carbon paper (1872), and the mimeograph machine (1892), telephones modernized offices and eased business transactions. When rates dropped after the turn of the century, the telephone entered homes and helped to bring on a social revolution. Like the railroad and the telegraph, it compressed distances and reduced differences across the country.

Finance Capital

As industry grew, so did the demand for investment capital—the money spent on land, buildings, and machinery. The need for capital was great especially because so many new industrial systems were being put into place at once. In the old days, a steamboat could be set afloat for the price of the boat itself. A railroad, on the other hand, had enormous start-up costs. Track had to be laid, workers hired, engines and cars bought, depots constructed. Industrial processes involving so many expensive systems could not take shape until someone raised the money to build them.

For the first three-quarters of the nineteenth century, investment capital had come mostly from the savings of firms. In the last half of the century "cap-

Sources of capital

ital deepening"—a process essential for industrialization—took place. Simply put, as national wealth increased, people began to save and invest more of their money. This meant that more funds could be lent to companies seeking to start up or expand.

Savings and investment grew more attractive with the development of a complex network of financial institutions. Commercial and savings banks, investment houses, and insurance companies gave savers new opportunities to channel money to industry. The New York Stock Exchange, in existence since 1792, linked eager investors with money-hungry firms. By the end of the nineteenth century the stock market had established itself as the basic means of making capital available to industry.

The Corporation

For those business leaders with the skill to knit the industrial pieces together, large profits awaited. This was the era of the notorious "robber baron." And to be sure, sheer ruthlessness went a long way in the fortune-building game. "Law?

Who cares about law!" railroad magnate Cornelius Vanderbilt once boasted. "Hain't I got the power?"

But to survive in the long term, business leaders could not depend on ruthlessness alone. They needed ingenuity, an eye for detail, and the gift of foresight. The growing scale of enterprise and need for capital, for example, led them to adapt an old device, the corporation, to new needs.

The corporation had several advantages over more traditional forms of ownership, the single owner and the partnership. A corporation could raise

Advantages of the corporation

large sums quickly by selling "stock certificates" or shares in its business. It could also outlive its owners (or stockholders) because it required no legal reorganization if one died. It limited liability, since owners were no longer personally responsible for corporate debts. And it separated owners from day-to-day management of the company. Professional managers could now operate complex businesses. So clear were these advantages that before the turn of the century, corporations were making two-thirds of all manufactured products in the United States.

A Pool of Labor

Last, but hardly least important for the new industrial order, was a pool of labor. In the United States the demand for workers was so great that the native-born could not fill it. In 1860 it took about 4.3 million workers to run all the factories, mills, and shops in the United States. By 1900 there were approximately 20 million industrial workers in America.

Europe was one recruiting ground. Mechanization, poverty, and oppression pushed many laborers from farms into cities and finally off the continent en-

European sources

tirely. To lure them across the Atlantic, industrialists advertised in newspapers, distributed pamphlets, and sent agents to Europe. In the 1880s incoming iron workers from Sweden often knew only three words of English: "Charlie—Deere—Moline" (Charlie was the president of the John Deere Plow Company in Moline, Illinois).

More than 8 million immigrants arrived in the United States between 1870 and 1890, another 14 million by 1914. Most settled in industrial cities in hopes of returning home with fatter purses. Often unskilled, many of them peasants, they found jobs in factories and mines or on construction and road gangs. And they were willing to work harder for less than those they replaced. "Immigrants work for almost nothing," complained a native-born laborer, "and seem to be able to live on wind."

To get those jobs, immigrants relied on well-defined migration chains of friends and family. A brother might find work with other Slavs in the mines of

Migration chains

Pennsylvania; or the daughter of Greek parents, in a New England textile mill filled with relatives. Labor contractors also served as a funnel to industry. Tough and savvy immigrants themselves, they met newcomers at the docks and train stations with contracts.

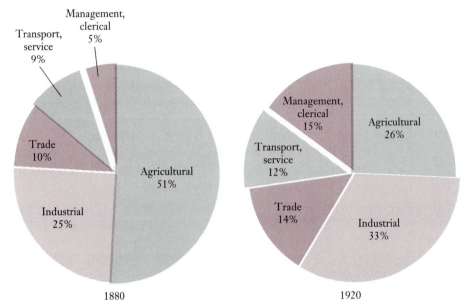

OCCUPATIONAL DISTRIBUTION, 1880 AND 1920   Between 1880 and 1920, management
and industrial work—white- and blue-collar workers—
grew at the expense of farmwork.

Among Italians they were known as *padrones;* among Mexicans, as *enganchistas.*
By 1900 they controlled two-thirds of the labor in New York.

A massive migration of rural Americans—some 11 million between 1865 and
1920—provided a home-grown source of labor. Driven from the farm by ma-

Domestic sources chines or bad times or just following dreams of a new life, they
moved first to small, then to larger cities. Most lacked the skills
for high-paying work. But they spoke English, and many could read and write.
In iron and steel cities as well as in coal-mining towns, the better industrial jobs
and supervisory positions went to them. Others found work in retail stores or offices and slowly entered the new urban middle class of white-collar workers.

Most African Americans continued to work the fields of the South. About
300,000 moved to northern cities between 1870 and 1910. Like the new immigrants, they were trying to escape discrimination and follow opportunity. One
by one, they brought their families. Discrimination still dogged them, but they
found employment. Usually they worked in low-paying jobs as day laborers or
laundresses and domestic servants. Black entrepreneurship also thrived as black-
owned businesses served growing black communities.

Mexicans, too, came in search of jobs, mainly in agriculture but also in industry. They helped to build the transcontinental railroad. After the turn of the
century, a small number turned farther north for jobs in the tanneries, meatpacking plants, foundries, and rail yards of Chicago and other midwestern industrial cities.

RAILROADS: AMERICA'S FIRST BIG BUSINESS

The system was a mess: any good railroad man knew as much. All across the country, each town—each rail station—set its clocks separately by the sun. In
Railroad time 1882, the year T. S. Hudson scampered across America, New York and Boston were 11 minutes and 45 seconds apart. Stations often had several clocks showing the time on different rail lines, along with one displaying "local mean time." So in 1883, without consulting anyone, the railroad companies divided the country into four time zones. Congress did not get around to making the division official until 1916.

At the center of the new industrial systems were the railroads, moving people and freight, spreading communications, reinventing time, ultimately tying the nation together. Railroads also stimulated economic growth, simply because they required so many resources to build—coal, wood, glass, rubber, brass, and, by the 1880s, 75 percent of all U.S. steel. By lowering transportation costs railroads allowed manufacturers to reduce prices, attract more buyers, and increase business. Perhaps most important, as America's first big business they devised new techniques of management, soon adopted by other companies.

A Managerial Revolution

To the men who ran them, railroads provided a challenge in organization and finance. In the 1850s, one of the largest industrial enterprises in America, the Pepperell textile mills of Maine, employed about 800 workers. By the early 1880s the Pennsylvania Railroad had nearly 50,000 people on its payroll. From setting schedules and rates to determining costs and profits, everything required a level of coordination unknown in earlier businesses.

The so-called trunk lines pioneered in devising new systems of management. Scores of early companies had serviced local networks of cities and com-
Pioneering trunk lines munities, often with less than 50 miles of track. During the 1850s trunk lines emerged east of the Mississippi to connect the shorter branches, or "feeder" lines. By the outbreak of the Civil War, with four great trunk lines under a single management, railroads linked the eastern seaboard with the Great Lakes and western rivers. After the war, trunk lines grew in the South and West until the continent was spanned in 1869.

The operations of large lines spawned a new managerial elite, beneath owners but with wide authority over operations. Daniel McCallum, superintendent
The new managers of the New York and Erie in the 1850s, laid the foundation for this system by drawing up the first table of organization for an American company. A tree trunk with roots represented the president and board of directors; five branches constituted the main operating divisions; leaves stood for the local agents, train crews, and others. Information moved up and down the trunk so that managers could get reports to and from the separate parts.

By the turn of the century, these managerial techniques had spread to other industries. Local superintendents were responsible for daily activities. Central offices served as corporate nerve centers, housing divisions for purchases, production, transportation, sales, and accounting. A new class of middle managers ran them and imposed new order on business operations. Executives, managers, and workers were being taught to operate in increasingly precise and coordinated ways.

Competition and Consolidation

While managers made operations more systematic, the fierce struggle among railroad companies to dominate the industry was anything but precise and rational. In the 1870s and 1880s the pain of railroad progress began to tell.

By their nature, railroads were saddled with enormous fixed costs: equipment, payrolls, debts. These remained constant regardless of the volume of traffic. To generate added revenue, railroads constructed more lines in hopes of increasing their traffic. Soon the railroads had overbuilt. With so much extra capacity, railroad owners schemed to win new accounts. They gave free passes to favored shippers, promised them free sidings at their plants, offered free land to lure businesses to their territory.

Railroad problems

The most savage and costly competition came over the rates charged for shipping goods. Managers lowered [rates] prices for freight that was shipped in bulk, on long hauls, or on return routes (since the cars were empty anyway). They used "rebates"—secret discounts to preferred customers—to drop prices below the posted rates of competitors (and then recouped the losses by overcharging small shippers like farmers). When the economy plunged or a weak line sought to improve its position, rate or price wars broke out. By 1880, 65 lines had declared bankruptcy.

Rebates

Consolidation worked better than competition. During the 1870s railroads created regional federations to pool traffic, set prices, and divide profits among members. Pooling—informal agreements among competing companies to act together—was designed to remove the incentive for cutting rates. Without the force of law, however, pools failed. Members broke ranks by cutting prices in hopes of quick gain. In the end, rate wars died down only when weaker lines failed or stronger ones bought up competitors.

Pooling

The Challenge of Finance

Earlier in the nineteenth century, many railroads relied on state governments for financial help. Backers also looked to counties, cities, and towns for bonds and other forms of aid. People living near the ends of rail lines, who stood to gain from construction, were persuaded to take stock in exchange for land or labor. In the 1850s and 1860s western promoters went to Washington for

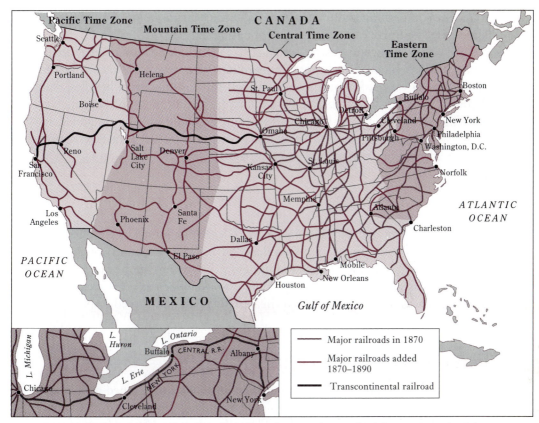

RAILROADS, 1870–1890   By 1890, the railroad network stretched from one end of the
country to the other, with more miles of track than all of Europe combined.
New York and Chicago, linked by the New York Central trunk line,
became the new commercial axis.

federal assistance. Congress loaned $65 million to six western railroads and
granted some 131 million acres of land.

Federal aid helped to build only part of the nation's railroads. Most of the
money came from private investors. The New York Stock Exchange expanded

*New ways of
raising money*

rapidly as railroad corporations began to trade their stocks there.
Large investment banks developed financial networks to track
down money at home and abroad. By 1898 a third of the assets
of American life insurance companies had gone into railroads, while Europeans
owned nearly a third of all American railroad securities.

Because investment bankers played such large roles in funding railroads,
they found themselves advising companies about their business affairs. If a company fell into bankruptcy, bankers sometimes served as the "receivers" who
oversaw the property until financial health returned. By absorbing smaller lines
into larger ones, eliminating rebates, and stabilizing rates, the bankers helped

to reduce competition and impose order and centralization. In the process, they often gained control of the companies they advised.

By 1900, the new industrial systems had transformed American railroads. Some 200,000 miles of track were in operation, 80 percent of it owned by only six groups of railroads. Time zones allowed for coordinated schedules; standardized track permitted easy cross-country freighting. Soon passengers were traveling 16 billion miles a year. To that traffic could be added farm goods, raw materials, and factory-finished products. Everything moved with new regularity that allowed businesses to plan and prosper.

THE GROWTH OF BIG BUSINESS

In 1865, near the end of the Civil War, 26-year-old John D. Rockefeller sat blank-faced in the office of his Cleveland oil refinery, about to conclude the biggest deal of his life. Rockefeller's business was thriving, but he had fallen out with his partner over how quickly to expand. Rockefeller was eager to grow fast; his partner was not. They dissolved their partnership and agreed to bid for the company. Bidding opened at $500, rocketed to $72,500, and abruptly stopped. "The business is yours," said the partner. The men shook hands, and a thin smile crept across Rockefeller's angular face.

Twenty years later, Rockefeller's Standard Oil Company controlled 90 percent of the nation's refining capacity and an empire that stretched well beyond Cleveland. Day and night, trains whisked Standard executives to New York, Philadelphia, and other eastern cities. The railroads were a fitting form of transportation for Rockefeller's company, for they were the key to his oil empire. They pioneered the business systems upon which he was building. And they carried his oil products for discounted rates, giving him the edge to squeeze out rivals. Like other American firms, Standard Oil was improving on the practices of the railroads in order to do bigger and bigger business.

Growth in Consumer Goods

But first a great riddle had to be solved: how to control the ravages of competition? In Michigan in the 1860s, salt producers found themselves fighting for their existence. The presence of too many salt makers had begun an endless round of price-cutting that was driving them all out of business. Seeing salvation in combination, they drew together in the nation's first pool. In 1869 they formed the Michigan Salt Association. They voluntarily agreed to allocate production, divide markets, and set prices—at double the previous rate.

Salt processing and other industries that specialized in consumer goods had low start-up costs, so they were often plagued by competition. Horizontal

Horizontal growth

combination—joining together loosely with rivals—had saved Michigan salt producers. By the 1880s there was a whiskey pool, a cordage pool, and countless rail and other pools. Such informal pools ultimately proved to be unenforceable and therefore unsatisfactory. (After 1890 they were also considered illegal restraints on trade.) But other forms of horizontal growth, such as formal mergers, spread in the wake of an economic panic in the 1890s.

Some makers of consumer products worried less about direct competition and concentrated on boosting efficiency and sales. They adopted a vertical-growth strategy that integrated several different activities under one company. Gustavus Swift, a New England butcher, moved to Chicago in the mid-1870s. Aware of the demand for fresh beef in the East, he acquired new refrigerated railcars to ship meat from western slaughterhouses and a network of ice-cooled warehouses in eastern cities to store it. By 1885 he had created the first national meatpacking enterprise, Swift and Company.

Vertical integration

Swift moved upward, closer to consumers, by putting together a fleet of wagons to distribute his beef to retailers. He moved down toward raw materials, extending and coordinating the purchase of cattle at the Chicago stockyards. By the 1890s Swift and Company was a fully integrated, vertically organized corporation operating on a nationwide scale. Soon Swift, Armour and Company, and three other giants—together called the "Big Five"—controlled 90 percent of the beef shipped across state lines.

Vertical growth generally moved producers of consumer goods closer to the marketplace in search of high-volume sales. The Singer Sewing Machine Company and the McCormick Harvesting Machine Company created their own retail sales arms. Manufacturers began furnishing ordinary consumers with technical information, credit, and repair services. Advertising expenditures grew, to some $90 million by 1900, in an effort to identify markets, shape buying habits, and increase sales.

Carnegie Integrates Steel

Industrialization encouraged vertical integration in heavy industry but more often in the opposite direction, toward reliable sources of raw materials. These firms made products for big users like railroads and factory builders. Their markets were easily identified and changed little. For them, success lay in securing limited raw materials and in holding down costs.

Andrew Carnegie led the way in steel. A Scottish immigrant, he worked his way up from bobbin boy to expert telegrapher to superintendent of the Pennsylvania Railroad's western division at the age of 24. A string of wise investments paid off handsomely. He owned a share of the first sleeping car and the first iron railroad bridge as well as a locomotive factory and an iron factory that became the nucleus of his steel empire.

In 1872, on a trip to England, Carnegie chanced to see the Bessemer process in action. Awestruck, he rushed home to build the biggest steel mill in the world. It opened in 1875, in the midst of a severe depression. Over the next 25 years, Carnegie added mills at Homestead and elsewhere in Pennsylvania and moved from railroad building to city building. He supplied steel for the Brooklyn Bridge, New York City's elevated railway, and the Washington Monument.

Carnegie succeeded, in part, by taking advantage of the boom-and-bust business cycle. He jumped in during hard times, building and buying when equipment

Keys to Carnegie's success

and businesses were cheap. But he also found skilled managers, who employed the administrative techniques of the railroads. And Carnegie knew how to compete. He scrapped machinery, workers, even a new mill to keep costs down and undersell competitors. The final key to Carnegie's success was expansion. His empire spread horizontally by purchasing rival steel mills and constructing new ones. It spread vertically, buying up sources of supply, transportation, and eventually sales. Controlling such an integrated system, Carnegie could ensure a steady flow of materials from mine to mill and market, as well as profits at every stage. In 1900 his company turned out more steel than Great Britain and netted $40 million.

Integration of the kind Carnegie employed expressed the logic of the new industrial age. More and more, the industrial activities of society were being linked in one giant, interconnected process.

Rockefeller and the Great Standard Oil Trust

John D. Rockefeller accomplished in oil what Carnegie achieved in steel. And he went further, developing an innovative business structure—the trust—that

Rockefeller's methods of expansion

promised greater control than even Carnegie's integrated system. At first Rockefeller grew horizontally by buying out or joining other refiners. To cut costs, he also expanded vertically, with oil pipelines, warehouses, and barrel factories. By 1870, when he and five partners formed the Standard Oil Company of Ohio, his high-quality, low-cost products could compete with any other.

Since the oil refining business was a jungle of competitive firms, Rockefeller proceeded to compete ferociously. He bribed rivals, spied on them, created phony companies, and slashed prices. His decisive edge came from the railroads. Desperate for business, they granted Standard Oil not only rebates on shipping rates but also "drawbacks," a fee for any product shipped by a rival oil company. Within a decade Standard dominated American refining with a vertically integrated empire that stretched from drilling to selling.

Throughout the 1870s Rockefeller kept his empire stitched together through informal pools and other business combinations. But they were weak and afforded him too little control. He could try to expand further, except that corporations were restricted by state law. In Rockefeller's home state of Ohio, for example, corporations could not own plants in other states or own stock in out-of-state companies.

In 1879 Samuel C. T. Dodd, chief counsel of Standard Oil, came up with a new device, the "trust." The stockholders of a corporation surrendered their

The trust   shares "in trust" to a central board of directors with the power to control all property. In exchange, stockholders received certificates of trust that paid hefty dividends. Since it did not literally own other companies, the trust violated no state law.

In 1882 the Standard Oil Company of Ohio formed the country's first great trust. It brought Rockefeller what he sought so fiercely: centralized management of the oil industry. Other businesses soon created trusts of their own—in meatpacking, wiremaking, farm machinery, and elsewhere. Just as quickly, trusts became notorious for crushing rivals and controlling prices.

The Mergers of J. Pierpont Morgan

The trust was only a stepping-stone to an even more effective means of avoiding competition, managing people, and controlling business: the corporate merger. The merging of two corporations—one buying out another—remained impossible until 1889, when New Jersey began to permit corporations to own other companies.

In 1890, the need to find a substitute for the trust grew urgent. Congress outlawed trusts under the Sherman Antitrust Act (see p. 485). The Sherman Act *The holding company* specifically banned business from "restraining trade" by setting prices, dividing markets, or engaging in other unfair practices. The ever-inventive Samuel Dodd came up with the "holding company." It had the power to own other companies. Many industries converted their trusts into holding companies, including Standard Oil, which moved to New Jersey in 1899.

Two years later came the biggest corporate merger of the era. It was the creation of a financial wizard named J. Pierpont Morgan. His orderly mind detested the chaotic competition that threatened his profits. "I like a little competition," Morgan used to say, "but I like combination more." After the Civil War he had taken over his father's powerful investment bank. For the next 50 years, the House of Morgan played a part in consolidating almost every major industry in the country.

Morgan's greatest triumph came in steel. In 1901, a colossal steel war loomed between Andrew Carnegie and other steelmakers. Morgan convinced Carnegie to put a price tag on his company. When a messenger brought the scrawled reply back—over $400 million—Morgan merely nodded and said, "I accept this price." He then bought Carnegie's eight largest competitors and announced the formation of the United States Steel Corporation.

U. S. Steel gobbled up over 200 manufacturing and transportation companies, 1000 miles of railways, and the whole Mesabi iron range. The mammoth holding company produced nearly two-thirds of all American steel. Its value of $1.4 billion exceeded the national debt and made it the country's first billion-dollar corporation.

What Morgan helped to create in steel was rapidly coming to pass in other industries. A wave of mergers swept through American business after the de-

The merger movement

pression of 1893. As the economy plunged, cutthroat competition bled businesses until they were eager to sell out. Giants sprouted almost overnight. By 1904, in each of 50 industries one firm came to account for 60 percent or more of the total output.

Corporate Defenders

As Andrew Carnegie's empire grew, his conscience turned troubled. Preaching a "gospel of wealth," he urged the rich to act as agents for the poor, "doing for them

The gospel of wealth

better than they would or could do for themselves." He devoted his time to philanthropy by creating foundations and endowing libraries and universities with some $350 million in contributions.

Defenders of the new corporate order were less troubled than Carnegie about the rough-and-tumble world of big business. They justified the system by stressing the opportunity created for individuals by economic growth. Through frugality, acquisitiveness, and discipline—the sources of cherished American individualism—anyone could rise like Andrew Carnegie.

When most ordinary workers failed to follow in Carnegie's footsteps, defenders blamed the individual. Failures were lazy, ignorant, or morally de-

Social Darwinism

praved, they said. British philosopher Herbert Spencer added the weight of science by applying Charles Darwin's theories of evolution to society. He maintained that in society, as in biology, only the "fittest" survived. The competitive social jungle doomed the unfit to poverty and rewarded the fit with property and privilege.

Spencer's American apostle, William Graham Sumner, argued that competition was natural and had to proceed without any interference, including government regulation. Millionaires were simply the "product of natural selection." Such "Social Darwinism" found strong support among turn-of-the-century business leaders. The philosophy certified their success even as they worked to destroy the very competitiveness it celebrated.

Corporate Critics

Meanwhile a group of radical critics mounted a powerful attack on corporate capitalism. Henry George, a journalist and self-taught economist, proposed a way to redistribute wealth in *Progress and Poverty* (1879). George attacked larger landowners as the source of inequality. They bought property while it was cheap and then held it until the forces of society—labor, technology, and speculation

Henry George's single tax

on nearby sites—had increased its value. George proposed to do away with all taxes except a single tax on these "unearned" profits, to end monopoly landholding. "Single-tax" clubs sprang up throughout the country, and George nearly won the race for mayor of New York in 1886.

The journalist Edward Bellamy tapped the same popular resentment against the inequalities of corporate capitalism. In his utopian novel, *Looking Backward* (1888), a fictional Boston gentleman falls asleep in 1887 and awakens Rip Van Winkle-like in the year 2000. The competitive, caste-ridden society of the nineteenth century is gone. In its place is an orderly utopia, managed by a benevolent government trust. Competition, exploitation, and class divisions have been replaced by "fraternal cooperation" and shared abundance. Like George's ideas, Bellamy's philosophy inspired a host of clubs around the nation. His followers demanded redistribution of wealth, civil service reform, and nationalization of railroads and utilities.

Less popular but equally hostile to capitalism was the Socialist Labor party, formed in 1877. Under Daniel De Leon, a West Indian immigrant, it stressed

Socialist Labor party

class conflict and called for a revolution to give workers control over production. De Leon refused to compromise his radical beliefs, and the socialists ended up attracting more intellectuals than workers. Some immigrants found its class consciousness appealing, but most rejected its radicalism and rigidity. A few party members, bent on gaining greater support, revolted and in 1901 founded the more successful Socialist Party of America. Workers were beginning to organize their own responses to industrialism.

By the mid-1880s, in response to the growing criticism of big business, several states in the South and West had enacted laws limiting the size of corporations. But state laws proved all too easy to evade when states such as New Jersey and Delaware eased their rules to cover the whole nation.

In 1890, the public clamor against trusts finally forced Congress to act. The Sherman Antitrust Act relied on the only constitutional authority Congress had

Sherman Antitrust Act

over business: its right to regulate interstate commerce. The act outlawed "every contract, combination in the form of trust or otherwise, or conspiracy, in restraint of trade or commerce." The United States stood practically alone among industrialized nations in regulating business combinations.

Its language was purposefully vague, but the Sherman Antitrust Act did give the government the power to break up trusts and other big businesses. So high was the regard for the rights of private property, however, that few in Congress expected the government to exercise that power or the courts to uphold it. They were right. Before 1901, the Justice department filed only 14 antitrust suits against big businesses, virtually none of them successful. And in 1895, the Supreme Court dealt the law a major blow by severely limiting its scope. *United States v. E. C. Knight Co* held that businesses involved in manufacturing (as opposed to "trade or commerce") lay outside the authority of the Sherman Act. Not until after the turn of the century would the law be used to bust a trust.

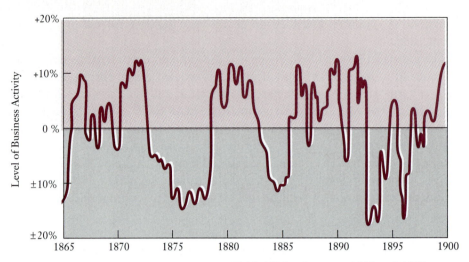

BOOM AND BUST BUSINESS CYCLE, 1865–1900   Between 1865 and 1900,
industrialization produced great economic growth but also wild swings of prosperity
and depression. During booms, productivity soared, and near-full employment
existed. But the rising number of industrial workers meant high
unemployment during deep busts.

The Costs of Doing Business

The heated debates between the critics and defenders of industrial capitalism
made clear that the changes in American society were two-edged. Big businesses
helped to rationalize the economy, increase national wealth, and tie the country together. Yet they also concentrated power, corrupted politics, and made the
gap between rich and poor more apparent than ever. In 1890, the richest 9 percent of Americans held nearly three-quarters of all wealth in the United States.
By 1900, one American in eight (nearly 10 million people) lived below the
poverty line.

More to the point, the practices of big business subjected the economy to
enormous disruptions. The banking system could not always keep pace with the

*The boom-and-
bust cycle*

demand for capital, and businesses failed to distribute enough of
their profits to sustain the purchasing power of workers. The
supply of goods periodically outstripped demand, and then the
wrenching cycle of boom and bust set in. Three severe depressions—1873–1879,
1882–1885, and 1893–1897—rocked the economy in the last third of the nineteenth century. With hard times came fierce competition as managers searched
frantically to cut costs, and the industrial barons earned their reputations for
ruthlessness.

COUNTERPOINT   *American Business Leaders: Robber Barons or Captains of Industry?*

Attacks and celebrations have continued to characterize portraits of the Carnegies, Rockefellers, and Morgans. Some historians have followed the lead of nineteenth-century critics and depicted them as hypocrites who extolled the virtues of competition while crushing it to pursue profits. Financiers and industrialists acted like medieval barons, robbing workers of the fruits of their labors, concentrating power, and threatening democracy.

Other historians see them as captains of industry: leaders and innovators who created an economy of abundance. Business historians have shown little interest in questions of morality or democracy versus economic concentration. They emphasize instead the strategies, structures, and forms of doing business.

THE WORKERS' WORLD

At seven in the morning, Sadie Frowne sat at her sewing machine in a Brooklyn garment factory. Her boss, a man she barely knew, dropped a pile of unfinished skirts next to her. She pushed one under her needle and began to rock her foot on the pedal that powered her machine. Sometimes Sadie pushed the skirts too quickly, and the needle pierced her finger. "The machines go like mad all day because the faster you work the more money you get," she explained of the world of industrial work in 1902.

The cramped sweatshops, the vast steel mills, the dank tunnels of the coal fields—all demanded workers and required them to work in new ways. Farmers or peasants who had once timed themselves by the movement of the sun now lived by the clock and labored by the twilight of gaslit factories. Instead of being self-employed, they had to deal with supervisors and were paid by the piece or hour. Not the seasons but the relentless cycle of machines set their pace. Increasingly, workers bore the brunt of depressions, faced periodic unemployment, and toiled under dangerous conditions as they struggled to bring the new industrial processes under their control.

Industrial Work

In 1881, the Pittsburgh Bessemer Steel Company opened its new mill in Homestead, Pennsylvania. Nearly 400 men and boys went to work on its 60 acres of sheds. They kept the mill going around the clock by working in two shifts: 12 hours a day the first week, 12 hours a night the next. In the furnace room, some men fainted from the heat, while the vibration and screeching of machinery deafened others. There were no breaks, even for lunch. "Home is just the place where I eat and sleep," said a steelworker. "I live in the mills."

Few industrial laborers worked under such conditions, but the Homestead mill reflected common characteristics of industrial work: the use of machines for mass production; the division of labor into intricately orga-

Pattern of industrial work

nized, menial tasks; and the dictatorship of the clock. At the turn of the century, two-thirds of all industrial work came from large-scale mills.

Under such conditions labor paid dearly for industrial progress. By 1900, most of those earning wages in industry worked 6 days a week, 10 hours a day. They held jobs that required more machines and fewer skills. Repetition of small chores replaced fine craftwork. In the 1880s, for example, almost all the 40 different steps that had gone into making a pair of shoes by hand could be performed by a novice or "green hand" with a few days of instruction at a simple machine.

With machines also came danger. Tending furnaces in a steel mill or plucking tobacco from cigarette-rolling machines was tedious. If a worker became bored or tired, disaster could strike. Each year from 1880 to 1900 industrial mishaps killed an average of 35,000 wage earners and injured over 500,000. Workers and their families could expect no payment from employers or government for death or injury.

Carnegie Furnaces, Braddock, Pennsylvania

Industrial workers rarely saw an owner. The foreman or supervisor exercised complete authority over the unskilled in his section, hiring and firing them, even setting their wages. Skilled workers had greater freedom; yet they too felt the pinch of technology and organization. Carpenters found that machine-made doors were replacing the ones they used to construct at the site. Painters no longer mixed their own paints.

Higher productivity and profits were the aims, and for Frederick W. Taylor, efficiency was the way to achieve them. During the 1870s and 1880s, Taylor un-

Taylorism

dertook careful time-and-motion studies of workers' movements in the steel industry. He set up standard procedures and offered pay incentives for beating his production quotas. On one occasion, he designed 15 ore shovels, each for a separate task. One hundred forty men were soon doing the work of 600. By the early twentieth century "Taylorism" was a full-blown philosophy, complete with its own professional society. "Management engineers" prescribed routines from which workers could not vary.

For all the high ideals of Taylorism, ordinary laborers refused to perform as cogs in a vast industrial machine. In a variety of ways, they worked to maintain control. Many European immigrants continued to observe the numerous saint's days and other religious holidays of their homelands, regardless of factory rules. When the pressure of six-day weeks became too stifling, workers took an unauthorized "blue Monday" off. Or they slowed down to reduce the

grueling pace. Or they simply walked off the job. Come spring and warm weather, factories reported turnover rates of 100 percent or more.

For some, seizing control of work was more than a matter of survival or self-respect. Many workers regarded themselves as citizens of a democratic re-

Worker citizens public. They expected to earn a "competence"—enough money to support and educate their families and enough time to stay up with current affairs. Few but highly skilled workers could realize such democratic dreams. More and more, labor was being managed as another part of an integrated system of industry.

Children, Women, and African Americans

In the mines of Pennsylvania, nimble-fingered eight-year-olds snatched bits of slate from amid the chunks of coal. In Illinois glass factories, "dog boys" dashed with trays of red-hot bottles to the cooling ovens. By 1900, the industrial labor force included some 1.7 million children, more than double the number 30 years earlier. Parents often had no choice. As one union leader observed, "Absolute necessity compels the father . . . to take the child into the mine to assist him in winning bread for the family." On average, children worked 60 hours a week and carried home paychecks a third the size of those of adult males.

Women had always labored on family farms, but by 1870 one out of every four nonagricultural workers was female. In general they earned one-half of what men did. Nearly all were single and young, anywhere from their mid-teens to their mid-twenties. Most lived in boardinghouses or at home with their parents. Usually they contributed their wages to the family kitty. Once married, they took on a life of full-time housework and child rearing.

Only 5 percent of married women held jobs outside the home in 1900. Married black women—in need of income because of the low wages paid their husbands—were four times more likely than married whites to work away from home. Industrialization inevitably pushed women into new jobs. Mainly they worked in industries considered extensions of housework: food processing, textiles and clothing, cigar making, and domestic service.

New methods of management and marketing opened positions for white-collar women as "typewriters," "telephone girls," bookkeepers, and secretaries.

Feminization of work On rare occasions women entered the professions, though law and medical schools were reluctant to admit them. Such discrimination drove ambitious, educated women into nursing, teaching, and library work. Their growing presence soon "feminized" these professions, pushing men upward into managerial slots or out entirely.

Even more than white women, all African Americans faced discrimination in the workplace. They were paid less than whites and given menial jobs. Their greatest opportunities in industry often came as strikebreakers to replace white workers. Once a strike ended, however, black workers were replaced themselves—

Clerks' jobs, traditionally held by men, came to be filled by women as growing industrial networks created more managerial jobs for men. In this typical office, male managers literally oversee female clerks.

and hated by the white regulars all the more. The service trades furnished the largest single source of jobs. Craftworkers and a sprinkling of black professionals could usually be found in cities. After the turn of the century, black-owned businesses thrived in the growing black neighborhoods of the North and South.

The American Dream of Success

Whatever their separate experiences, working-class Americans did improve their overall lot. Though the gap between the very rich and the very poor

Rising real wages

widened, most wage earners made some gains. Between 1860 and 1890 real daily wages—pay in terms of buying power—climbed some 50 percent as prices gradually fell. And after 1890, the number of hours on the job began a slow decline.

Yet most unskilled and semiskilled workers in factories continued to receive low pay. In 1890, an unskilled laborer could expect about $1.50 for a 10-hour day; a skilled one, perhaps twice that amount. It took about $600 to make ends meet, but most manufacturing workers made under $500 a year. Native-born white Americans tended to earn more than immigrants, those who spoke English more than those who did not, men more than women, and all others more than African Americans and Asians.

Few workers repeated the rags-to-riches rise of Andrew Carnegie. But some did rise, despite periodic unemployment and ruthless wage cuts. About one-quarter of the manual laborers in one study entered the lower middle class in their own lifetimes. More often such unskilled workers climbed in financial status within their own class. And most workers, seeing some improvement, believed in the American dream of success, even if they did not fully share in it.

THE SYSTEMS OF LABOR

Putting in more hours to save a few pennies, walking out in exhaustion or disgust, slowing down on the job—these were the ways individual workers coped with industrial America. Sporadic and unorganized, such actions had little chance of bringing the new industrial order under the control of labor. For ordinary workers to begin to control industrialization they had to combine, just as businesses did. They needed to join together horizontally—organizing not just locally but on a national scale. They needed to integrate vertically by coordinating action across a wide range of jobs and skills, as Andrew Carnegie coordinated the production of steel. For workers, unions were their systematic response to industrialization.

Early Unions

In the United States unions began forming before the Civil War. Skilled craft-workers—carpenters, iron molders, cigar makers—united to counter the growing power of management. Railroad "brotherhoods" also furnished insurance for those hurt or killed on the accident-plagued lines. Largely local and exclusively male, these early craft unions remained weak and unconnected to each other, as well as to the growing mass of unskilled workers.

After the war, a group of craft unions, brotherhoods, and reformers united skilled and unskilled workers in a nationwide organization. The National Labor

National Labor Union

Union (NLU) hailed the virtues of a simpler America, when workers controlled their workday, earned a decent living, and had time to be good informed citizens. NLU leaders attacked the wage system as unfair and enslaving and urged workers to manage their own factories. By the early 1870s, NLU ranks swelled to more than 600,000.

Among other things, the NLU pressed for the eight-hour workday, the most popular labor demand of the era. Workers saw it as a way not merely of limiting their time on the job but of limiting the power of employers over their lives. "Eight hours for work; eight hours for rest; eight hours for what we will!" proclaimed a banner at one labor rally. Despite the popularity of the issue, the NLU wilted during the depression of 1873.

The Knights of Labor

More successful was a national union born in secrecy. In 1869 Uriah Stephens and nine Philadelphia garment cutters founded the Noble and Holy Order of the Knights of Labor. They draped themselves in ritual and regalia to deepen their sense of solidarity and met in secret to evade hostile owners. The Knights remained small and fraternal for a decade. Their strongly Protestant tone repelled Catholics, who made up almost half the workforce in many industries.

In 1879 the Knights elected Terence V. Powderly as their Grand Master Workman. Handsome, dynamic, Irish, and Catholic, Powderly threw off the

Terence Powderly

Knights' secrecy, dropped their rituals, and opened their ranks. He called for "one big union" to embrace the "toiling millions"— skilled and unskilled, men and women, natives and immigrants, all religions, all races. By 1886, membership had leaped to over 700,000, including nearly 30,000 African Americans and 3000 women.

Like the NLU, the Knights of Labor looked to abolish the wage system and in its place create a cooperative economy of worker-owned mines, factories, and railroads. The Knights set up more than 140 cooperative workshops, where workers shared decisions and profits, and sponsored some 200 political candidates. To tame the new industrial order, they supported the eight-hour workday and the regulation of trusts. Underlying this program was a moral vision of society. If only people renounced greed, laziness, and dishonesty, Powderly argued, corruption and class division would disappear. Democracy would flourish. To reform citizens, the Knights promoted the prohibition of child and convict labor and the abolition of liquor.

It was one thing to proclaim a moral vision for his union, quite another to coordinate the activities of so many members. Locals resorted to strikes and violence, actions Powderly condemned. In the mid-1880s, such stoppages wrung concessions from the western railroads, but the organization soon became associated with unsuccessful strikes and violent extremists. Even the gains against the railroads were wiped out when the Texas and Pacific Railroad broke a strike by local Knights. By 1890, the Knights of Labor teetered near extinction.

The American Federation of Labor

The Knights' position as the premier union in the nation was taken by the rival American Federation of Labor (AFL). The AFL reflected the practicality of

Samuel Gompers

its leader, Samuel Gompers. Born in a London tenement, the son of a Jewish cigar maker, he had immigrated in 1863 with his family to New York's Lower East Side. Unlike the visionary Powderly, Gompers accepted capitalism and the wage system. What he wanted was "pure and simple unionism"—higher wages, fewer hours, improved safety, more benefits.

Gompers chose to organize highly skilled craftworkers because they were difficult to replace. He then bargained with employers, using strikes and boycotts only as last resorts. With the Cigar Makers' Union as his base, Gompers helped create the first national federation of craft unions in 1881. In 1886, it was reorganized as the American Federation of Labor. Twenty-five labor groups joined, representing some 150,000 workers.

Gompers fought off radicals and allied himself with whatever candidate supported labor. Stressing gradual, concrete gains, he made the AFL the most powerful union in the country. By 1901 it had more than a million members, almost a third of all skilled workers in America.

Gompers was less interested in vertical integration: combining skilled and unskilled workers. For most of his career, he preserved the privileges of craftsmen and accepted their prejudices against women, blacks, and immigrants. Only two locals—the Cigar Makers' Union and the Typographers' Union—enrolled women. Most affiliates restricted black membership through high entrance fees and other discriminatory practices.

Despite the success of the AFL, the laboring classes did not organize themselves as systematically as the barons of industrial America. At the turn of the century, union membership included less than 10 percent of industrial workers. Separated by different languages and nationalities, divided by issues of race and gender, workers resisted unionization during the nineteenth century. In fact, a strong strain of individualism often made them regard all collective action as un-American.

Failure of organized labor

The Limits of Industrial Systems

As managers sought to increase their control over the workplace, workers often found themselves at the mercy of the new industrial order. Even in boom times, one in three workers was out of a job at least three or four months a year. But it was in hard times that the industrial system was driven to its limits.

When a worker's pay dropped and frustration mounted, when a mother worked all night and fell asleep during the day while caring for her children, when food prices suddenly jumped—violence might erupt. "A mob of 1,000 people, with women in the lead, marched through the Jewish quarter of Williamsburg last evening and wrecked half a dozen butcher shops," reported the New York *Times* in 1902. In the late nineteenth century a wave of labor activism swept the nation. More often than mob violence, it was strikes and boycotts that challenged the authority of employers and gave evidence of working-class identity and discontent.

Spontaneous protests

Most strikes broke out spontaneously, organized by informal leaders in a factory. "Malvina Fourtune and her brother Henry Fourtune it was them who started the strike," declared a company informer in Chicopee, Massachusetts. "They go from house to house and tells the people to keep up the strike." Thousands of rallies and organized strikes were staged as well, often on behalf of the eight-hour workday, in good times and bad, by union and nonunion workers alike.

In 1877 the country's first nationwide strike opened an era of confrontation between labor and management. When the Baltimore and Ohio Railroad cut

Great Railroad Strike

wages by 20 percent, a crew in Martinsburg, West Virginia, seized the local depot and blocked the line. Two-thirds of the nation's track shut down in sympathy. When strikebreakers were brought in, striking workers torched rail yards, smashed engines and cars, and tore up track. Local police, state militia, and federal troops finally crushed the strike after 12 bloody days. In its wake, the Great Railroad Strike of 1877 left 100 people dead and $10 million worth of railroad property in rubble.

In 1886, tension between labor and capital exploded in the "Great Upheaval"—a series of strikes, boycotts, and rallies. One of the most violent

Haymarket Square riot

episodes occurred at Haymarket Square in Chicago. A group of anarchists was protesting the recent killing of workers by police at the McCormick Harvesting Company. As rain drenched the small crowd, police moved in and ordered everyone out of the square. Suddenly a bomb exploded. One officer was killed, and 6 others mortally wounded. When police opened fire, the crowd fired back. Nearly 70 more policemen were injured, and at least 4 civilians died.

Conservatives charged that radicals were responsible for the "Haymarket Massacre." Ordinary citizens who had supported labor grew fearful of its power

In this painting by Robert Koehler, entitled *The Strike* (1886), labor confronts management in a strike that may soon turn bloody. One worker reaches for a stone as an anxious mother and her children look on. Barely visible on the desolate horizon is a smoke-enshrouded factory.

to spark violence and disorder. Though the bomb thrower was never identified, a trial of questionable legality found eight anarchists guilty of conspiracy to murder. Seven were sentenced to death. Cities enlarged their police forces, and states built more National Guard armories on the borders of working-class neighborhoods.

Management Strikes Again

The strikes, rallies, and boycotts of 1886 were followed by a second surge of labor activism in 1892. In the silver mines of Coeur d'Alene, Idaho, at the Carnegie steel mill in Homestead, Pennsylvania, in the coal mines near Tracy City, Tennessee, strikes flared. Often state and federal troops joined company guards and Pinkerton detectives to crush these actions.

The broadest confrontation between labor and management took place two years later. A terrible depression had shaken the economy for almost a year

Pullman strike when George Pullman, owner of the Palace Car factory and inventor of the plush railroad car, laid off workers, cut wages (but kept rents high on company-owned housing), and refused to discuss grievances. In 1894 workers struck and managed to convince the new American Railway Union (ARU) to support them by boycotting all trains that used Pullman cars. Quickly the strike spread to 27 states and territories. Anxious railroad owners appealed to President Grover Cleveland for federal help. On the slim pretext that the strike obstructed mail delivery (strikers had actually been willing to handle mail trains without Pullman cars), Cleveland secured a court order halting the strike. He then called several thousand special deputies into Chicago to enforce it. In the rioting that followed, 12 people died and scores were arrested. But the strike was quashed.

In all labor disputes the central issue was the power to shape the new industrial systems. Employers always enjoyed the advantage. They hired and fired

Management weapons workers, set the terms of employment, and ruled the workplace. They fought unions with "yellow dog" contracts that forced workers to refuse to join. Blacklists circulated the names of labor agitators. Lockouts kept protesting workers from plants, and labor spies infiltrated their organizations. With a growing pool of labor, employers could replace strikers and break strikes.

Management could also count on local, state, and federal authorities to send troops to break strikes. In addition, businesses used a powerful new legal weapon, the injunction. These court orders prohibited certain actions, including strikes, by barring workers from interfering with their employer's business. It was just such an order that had brought federal deputies into the Pullman strike and put Eugene Debs, head of the railway union, behind bars.

In a matter of only 30 or 40 years, the new industrial order had transformed the landscape of America. Whether rich or poor, workers, entrepreneurs, or industrial barons, Americans were drawn closer by the new industrial systems. Ore scooped from Mesabi might end up in a steel girder on James Eads's Mississippi bridge, in a steel needle for Sadie Frowne's sewing machine in Brooklyn, or in a McCormick reaper slicing across the Nebraska plains. When a textile worker in Massachusetts struck, a family in Alabama might well pay more for clothes. A man in Cleveland now set his watch to agree with the time of a man in New York, regardless of the position of the sun.

Such changes might seem effortless to someone like T. S. Hudson, scampering across the rails of America in 1882. But as the nineteenth century drew to a close, material progress went hand in hand with social pain and upheaval.

SIGNIFICANT EVENTS

1859	First oil well drilled near Titusville, Pennsylvania
1866	National Labor Union founded
1869	Knights of Labor created
1870	John D. Rockefeller incorporates Standard Oil Company of Ohio
1873	Carnegie Steel Company founded; Panic of 1873
1874	Massachusetts enacts first 10-hour workday law for women
1876	Alexander Graham Bell invents telephone
1877	Railroad wage cuts lead to violent strikes; Thomas Edison invents phonograph
1879	Edison develops incandescent lightbulb; Henry George's *Progress and Poverty* published
1882	Rockefeller's Standard Oil Company becomes nation's first trust; Thomas Edison's electric company begins lighting New York City
1883	Railroads establish standard time zones
1886	American Federation of Labor organized; Haymarket Square bombing
1892	Homestead Steel strike
1893	Panic of 1893
1894	Pullman strike
1901	U.S. Steel Corporation becomes nation's first billion-dollar company

CHAPTER NINETEEN

The Rise of an Urban Order

Graziano's bootblack stand was jammed with people, mulling about, looking for help. Above the crowd, enthroned like an Irish king, sat George Washington Plunkitt, ward boss of Manhattan's Fifteenth Assembly District. There to help, Plunkitt asked little in return, only votes on election day. Plunkitt understood the close relationship between help and votes. "There's got to be in every ward," another boss explained, "somebody that any bloke can come to—no matter what he's done—and get help. *Help, you understand; none of your law and justice, but help.*" The reverse was also true: to maintain power, bosses like Plunkitt had to be able to count on the political support of those they helped.

For years Plunkitt had been a leader of Tammany Hall, the Democratic party organization that ruled New York City politics from 1850 to 1930. Much of his daily routine was taken up with helping. One typical day

A boss at work

began when a bartender roused him at two in the morning to get a friend out of jail. Plunkitt succeeded but didn't get back to bed until after three. Howling fire sirens woke him at six. Before dawn he was assisting burned-out tenants with food, clothing, and shelter. Home by eleven, he found four unemployed men waiting for him. Within hours each had a job. A quick bite of lunch and it was off again, this time to a pair of funerals. Plunkitt brought flowers for the bereaved and offered consolation, all in full view of the assembled. From there he rushed to attend a "Hebrew confirmation." Early evening found him at district headquarters, helping his election captains plot ways of "turning out the vote."

After a quick stop at a church fair, it was back to the party clubhouse where he helped some local teams by buying tickets for their next game. Before leaving, he pledged to stop the police from harassing two dozen pushcart peddlers.

He arrived at a wedding reception at half past ten (having already bestowed on the bride and groom "a handsome wedding present"). Finally, at midnight, he crawled into bed, after a day of helping all he could.

Such relentless effort helped Plunkitt as well. Born to Irish immigrants, he died a millionaire in 1924. His pluck and practicality would have made him the envy of any industrialist. Like the Carnegies and Rockefellers, fierce ambition fueled his rise from butcher boy to political boss. City politics was his way out of the slums in a world that favored the rich, the educated, and the well-established.

In the late nineteenth century the needs of rapidly growing cities gave political bosses like George Washington Plunkitt their chance. "I seen my opportunities and I took 'em," Plunkitt used to say. Every city contract and bond issue, every tax assessment, every charter for a new business offered Plunkitt and his cronies an opportunity to line their pockets. Money made from inside *Boodle* knowledge of city projects was known as "boodle." How much boodle bosses collected depended on how well their organization managed to elect sympathetic officials. And that explained why Plunkitt spent so much time helping his constituents in order to get out the vote.

Plunkitt's New York was the first great city in history to be ruled by men of the people in an organized and continuing way. Bosses and their henchmen came from the streets and saloons, the slums and tenements, the firehouses and funeral homes. Many of their families had only recently arrived in America. While the Irish of Tammany Hall ran New York, Germans governed St. Louis, Scandinavians Minneapolis, and Jews San Francisco.

In an earlier age political leadership had been drawn from the ranks of the wealthy and native-born. America had been an agrarian republic, in which most personal relationships were grounded in small communities. By the late nineteenth century, the country was in the midst of an urban explosion. Industrial cities of unparalleled size and diversity were transforming American life. They lured people from all over the globe, created tensions between natives and newcomers, reshaped the social order. For Plunkitt, as for so many Americans, the golden door of opportunity opened onto the city.

A NEW URBAN AGE

The modern city was the product of industrialization. Cities contained the great investment banks, the smoky mills and dingy sweatshops, the spreading railroad yards, the grimy tenements and sparkling mansions, the new department stores and skyscrapers. People came from places as near as the countryside and as far away as Italy, Russia, Armenia, and China. By the end of the nineteenth century America had entered a new urban age, with tens of millions of "urbanites," an urban landscape, and a growing urban culture.

The Urban Explosion

During the 50 years after the Civil War, the population of the United States quadrupled—from 31 million to 92 million. Yet the number of Americans living in cities increased nearly sevenfold. In 1860, only one American in six lived in a city with a population of 8000 or more; in 1900, one in three did. By 1910 nearly half the nation lived in cities large and small.

Cities grew in every region of the country. In the Northeast and upper Midwest early industrialization created more cities than in the West and the South, although a few big cities sprouted there as well. Atlanta, Nashville, and later Dallas and Houston boomed under the influence of railroads. Los Angeles had barely 6000 people in 1870. By 1900 it was the second-largest city on the Pacific coast, with 100,000 residents.

Large urban centers dominated whole regions, tying the country together in a vast urban network. New York, the nation's banker, printer, and chief

Realist painters like George Bellows, who were scorned by critics as the "Ashcan School," captured the grittiness and vibrancy of teeming cities, here in Bellows's *Cliff Dwellers*.

Cities' relations to regions around them — marketplace, ruled the East. Smaller cities operated within narrower spheres of influence and often specialized. Milwaukee was famous for beer, Tulsa for oil, and Hershey, Pennsylvania, for chocolate. Cities even shaped the natural environment hundreds of miles beyond their limits. Chicago became not only the gateway to the West but also a powerful agent of ecological change. As its lines of commerce and industry radiated outward, the city transformed the rich ecosystems of the West. Wheat to feed Chicago's millions replaced sheltering prairie grasses. Great stands of white pine in Wisconsin vanished, only to reappear in the furniture and frames of Chicago houses, or as fence rails shipped to prairie farms.

The Great Global Migration

Between 1820 and 1920, some 60 million people across the globe left farms and villages for cities. Mushrooming population gave them a powerful push. In Europe the end of the Napoleonic Wars in 1815 launched a cycle of baby booms that continued at 20-year intervals for the rest of the century. Improved diet and sanitation, aided by Louis Pasteur's discovery that bacteria cause infection and disease, reduced deaths. Meanwhile machinery cut the need for farmworkers. In 1896 one man in a wheat field could do what had taken 18 men just 60 years earlier.

Surplus farmworkers became a part of a vast international labor force, pulled by industry to cities in Europe and America. The prospect of factory work for better pay and fewer hours especially lured the young. In America, young farm women spearheaded the urban migration. Mechanization and the rise of commercial agriculture made them less valuable in the fields, while mass-produced goods from mail-order houses made them less useful at home.

Earlier in the century, European immigrants had come from northern and western Europe. In the 1880s, however, "new" immigrants from southern and *The "new" immigration* — eastern Europe began to arrive. Some, like Russian and Polish Jews, were fleeing religious and political persecution. Others left to evade famine or diseases such as cholera, which swept across southern Italy in 1887. But most came for the same reasons that motivated migrants from the countryside: a job, more money, a fresh start.

Ambitious, hardy, and resourceful, immigrants found themselves tested every step of the way to America. They left behind the comforting familiarity of families, friends, and old ways. The price of one-way passage by steamship— about $50 in 1904—was far too high for most to bring relatives, at least at first. And the trip was dangerous. Wayfarers often stole across heavily guarded borders. They traveled for weeks just to reach a port like Le Havre in France. At dockside, shipping lines vaccinated, disinfected, and examined them to ensure against their being returned at company expense.

It took from one to two weeks to cross the Atlantic. Immigrants spent most of the time below decks in cramped, filthy compartments called "steerage."

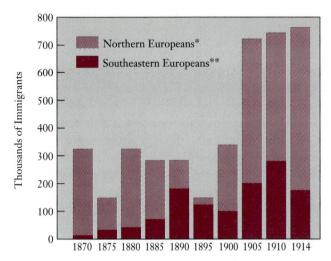

*Includes immigrants from Great Britain, Ireland, Germany, and the Scandinavian countries.

**Includes immigrants from Poland, Russia, Italy, and other Baltic and east European countries.

IMMIGRATION, 1860–1920   Between 1860 and 1920 immigration increased dramatically as the sources of immigrants shifted from northern Europe to southeastern Europe. Despite fears to the contrary, the proportion of newcomers as a percentage of population increases did not show nearly the same jump.

Most landed at New York's Castle Garden or the newer facility on nearby Ellis Island, opened in 1892. If arriving from Asia, they landed at Angel Island in San Francisco Bay. They had to pass another medical examination, have their names recorded by customs officials, and pay an entry tax. At any point, they could be detained or shipped home.

Immigrants arrived in staggering numbers—by 1900 they made up nearly 15 percent of the population. Most newcomers were young, between the ages of 15 and 40. Few spoke English or had skills or much educa-

Immigrant profile

tion. Unlike earlier arrivals, who were mostly Protestant, these new immigrants worshiped in Catholic, Greek, or Russian Orthodox churches and Jewish synagogues. Almost two-thirds were men. A large number came to make money to buy land or start businesses back home. Some changed their minds and sent for relatives, but those returning home were common enough to be labeled "birds of passage."

Jews were an exception. Between 1880 and 1914, a third of eastern Europe's Jewry left in the face of growing anti-Semitism. They made up 10 percent of all immigration to the United States. Almost all stayed and brought their families, often one by one. They had few choices. As one Jewish immigrant wrote of his Russian homeland, "Am I not despised? Am I not urged to leave? . . . Do I not rise daily with the fear lest the hungry mob attack me?"

The Shape of the City

In colonial days, Benjamin Franklin could walk from one end of Boston to the other in an hour. Only Franklin's adopted home, Philadelphia, spilled into suburbs. Over the years these colonial "walking cities" developed ringed patterns of settlement. Merchants, professionals, and the upper classes lived near their shops and offices in the city center. As one walked outward, the income and status of the residents gradually declined.

Cities of the late nineteenth century still exhibited this ringed pattern, except that industrialization had reversed the order and increased urban sprawl.

Patterns of settlement As the middle and upper classes moved out of a growing industrial core, the poor, some immigrants, African Americans, and laborers filled the inner void. They took over old factories and brownstones, shanties and cellars. By sheer weight of numbers they transformed these areas into the slums of the central city.

Curled around the slums was the "zone of emergence," an income-graded band of those on their way up. It contained second-generation city dwellers, factory workers, skilled laborers, and professional mechanics. They lived in progressively better tenements and neater row houses. Poverty no longer imprisoned them, but they could still slip back in hard times.

Farther out was the suburban fringe, home to the new class of white-collar managers and executives. They lived in larger houses with individual lots on neat, tree-lined streets. The very wealthy still maintained mansions on fashionable city avenues, but by the 1870s and 1880s, they too began to keep suburban homes.

Urban Transport

For all their differences, the circles of settlement held together as a part of an interdependent whole. One reason was an evolving system of urban transportation. By the mid-nineteenth century horse-drawn railways were conveying some 35 million people a year in New York. Their problems were legendary: so slow, a person could walk faster; so crowded (according to Mark Twain), you "had to hang on by your eyelashes and your toenails"; so dirty, tons of horse manure were left daily in the streets.

Civic leaders came to understand that the modern city could not survive, much less grow, without improved transportation. San Francisco installed trolley cars pulled by steam-driven cables. The innovation worked so well in hilly San Francisco that Chicago, Seattle, and other cities installed cable systems in the 1880s. Still other cities experimented with elevated trestles, to carry steam locomotives or cable lines high above crowded streets. But none of the breakthroughs quite did the trick. Cables remained slow and unreliable; the elevated railways, or "els," were dirty, ugly, and noisy.

Electricity rescued city travelers. In 1888 Frank Julian Sprague, a naval engineer who had once worked for Thomas Edison, installed the first electric

Role of electricity
trolley line in Richmond, Virginia. Electrified streetcars were soon speeding along at 12 miles an hour, twice as fast as horses. By 1902 electricity drove nearly all city railways. Sprague's breakthroughs also meant that "subways" could be built without having to worry about tunnels filled with a steam engine's smoke and soot. Between 1895 and 1897 Boston built the first underground electric line. New York followed in 1904 with a subway that ran from City Hall on the southern tip of Manhattan north to 145th Street.

The rich had long been able to keep homes outside city limits, traveling to and fro in private carriages. New systems of mass transit freed the middle class and even the poor to live miles from work. For a nickel or two, anyone could ride from central shopping and business districts to the suburban fringes and back. A network of moving vehicles held the segmented and sprawling city together and widened its reach out to "streetcar suburbs."

Bridges and Skyscrapers

Since cities often grew along rivers and harbors, their separate parts sometimes had to be joined over water. The principles of building large river bridges had already been worked out by the railroads. It remained for a German immigrant and his son, John and Washington Roebling, to make the bridge a symbol of

Brooklyn Bridge
urban growth. The Brooklyn Bridge, linking Manhattan with Brooklyn, took 13 years to complete. It cost $15 million and 20 lives, including that of designer John. When it opened in 1883, it stretched more than a mile across the East River, with passage broad enough for a footpath, two double carriage lanes, and two railroad lines. Its arches were cut like giant cathedral windows, and its supporting cables hung, said an awestruck observer, "like divine messages from above." Soon other suspension bridges were spanning the railroad yards in St. Louis and the bay at Galveston, Texas.

Even as late as 1880 church steeples dominated the urban landscape. They towered over squat factories and office buildings. But growing congestion and the increasing value of land pushed architects to search for ways to make buildings taller. In place of thick, heavy walls of brick that restricted factory floor space, builders used cast iron columns. The new "cloudscrapers" were strong, durable, and fire-resistant, ideal for warehouses and also for office buildings and department stores.

Steel, tougher in tension and compression, turned cloudscrapers into skyscrapers. William LeBaron Jenney first used steel in his 10-story Home Insurance Building (1885) in Chicago. By the end of the century steel frames and girders raised buildings to 30 stories or more. New York City's triangular Flatiron building (on page 505) used the new technology to project an angular, yet remarkably delicate elegance. In Chicago, Daniel Burnham's Reliance Building (1890) made such heavy use of new plate glass windows that contemporaries called it "a glass tower fifteen stories high."

The Flatiron building

It was no accident that many of the new skyscrapers arose in Chicago. The city had burned nearly to the ground in 1871. The "Chicago school" of architects helped to rebuild it. The young maverick Louis H. Sullivan promised a new urban profile in which the skyscraper would be "every inch a proud and soaring thing." In the Wainwright Building (1890) in St. Louis and the Carson, Pirie, and Scott department store (1889–1904) in Chicago, Sullivan produced towering structures that symbolized the modern industrial city.

Louis Sullivan and the "Chicago school"

Slum and Tenement

Far below the skyscrapers lay the slums and tenements of the inner city. In cramped rooms and sunless hallways, along narrow alleys and in flooded basements, lived the city poor. They often worked there, too. In "sweaters' shops" as many as 18 people labored and slept in foul two-room flats.

In New York, whose slums were among the nation's worst, crime thrived in places called "Bandit's Roost" and "Hell's Kitchen." Bands of young toughs with names like the "Sewer Rats" and the "Rock Gang" stalked the streets in search of thrills and easy money. Gambling, prostitution, and alcoholism all claimed their victims most readily in the slums. The poor usually turned to crime in despair. A 20-year-old prostitute supporting a sickly mother and four brothers and sisters made no

Perils of the slum neighborhood

apologies: "Let God Almighty judge who's to blame most, I that was driven, or them that drove me to the pass I'm in."

Slum dwellers often lived on poor diets that left them vulnerable to epidemics. Cholera, typhoid, and an outbreak of yellow fever in Memphis in the 1870s killed tens of thousands. Tuberculosis was deadlier still. Slum children—all city children—were most vulnerable to such diseases. Almost a quarter of the children born in American cities in 1890 never lived to see their first birthday.

The installation of new sewage and water purification systems helped. The modern flush toilet came into use only after the turn of the century. Until then people relied on water closets and communal privies. Some catered to as many as 800. All too often cities dumped waste into old private vaults or rivers used for drinking water. In 1881 the exasperated mayor of Cleveland called the Cuyahoga River "an open sewer through the center of the city."

Slum housing was often more dangerous than the water. The tubercle bacillus flourished in musty, windowless tenements. In 1879 New York enacted a

The dumbbell tenement

new housing law requiring a window in all bedrooms of new tenements. Architect James E. Ware won a competition with a creative design that contained an indentation on both sides of the building. When two tenements abutted each other, the indentations formed a narrow shaft for air and light. From above, the buildings looked like giant dumbbells. Up to 16 families lived on a floor, with two toilets in the hall.

Originally hailed as an innovation, Ware's dumbbell tenement spread over such cities as Cleveland, Cincinnati, and Boston "like a scab," said an unhappy reformer. Ordinary blocks contained 10 tenements and housed as many as 4000 people. The airshafts became giant silos for trash, which blocked what little light had entered and, worse still, carried fires from one story to the next. When the New York housing commission met in 1900, it concluded that conditions were worse than when reformers had started 33 years earlier.

RUNNING AND REFORMING THE CITY

Every new arrival to the city brought dreams and altogether too many needs. Schools and houses had to be built, streets paved, garbage collected, sewers dug, fires fought, utility lines laid. Running the city became a full-time job, and a new breed of full-time politician rose to the task. So, too, did a new breed of reformer, determined to help the needy cope with the ravages of urban life.

The need for reform change was clear. Many city charters dating from the eighteenth century included a paralyzing system of checks and balances. Mayors

The weaknesses of city government

vetoed city councils; councils ignored mayors. Jealous state legislatures allowed cities only the most limited and unpopular taxes, such as those on property. At the same time, city governments were often decentralized: fragmented, scattered, at odds with one another. By 1890, Chicago had 11 branches of government. Each was a tiny kingdom with its own regulations and taxing authority. As immigrants and rural newcomers flocked to factories and tenements, the structures of urban government strained to adapt.

Boss Rule

"Why must there be a boss," journalist Lincoln Steffens asked Boss Richard Croker of New York, "when we've got a mayor—and a city council?" "That's why," Croker broke in. "It's because we've got a mayor and a council and judges—*and*—a hundred other men to deal with." The boss was right. He and his system furnished cities with the centralization, authority, and services they sorely needed.

Bosses ruled through the political machine. Often, as with New York's Tammany Hall, machines dated back to the late eighteenth and early nineteenth centuries. They began as fraternal and charitable organizations. Over the years they became centers of political power. In New York the machine was Democratic; in Philadelphia, Republican. Some were less centralized, as in Chicago; some less ethnically mixed, as in Detroit. Machines could even be found in rural areas such as Duval County, Texas, where the Spanish-speaking Anglo boss Archie Parr molded a powerful alliance with Mexican American landowners.

In an age of enterprise, the boss operated his political machine like a corporation. His office might be a saloon, a funeral home, or, like George Washington Plunkitt's, a shoeshine stand. His managers were party activists, connected in a corporate-like chain of command. Local committeemen reported to district captains, captains to district leaders, district leaders to the boss or bosses who directed the machine.

The boss as entrepreneur

The goods and services of the machine were basics: a Christmas turkey, a load of coal for the winter, jobs for the unemployed, English-language classes for recent immigrants. Bosses sponsored fun too: sports teams, glee clubs, balls and barbecues.

This system, rough and uneven as it was, served as a form of public welfare at a time when private charity could not cope with the crush of demands. To the unskilled, the boss doled out jobs in public construction. For bright, ambitious young men, he had places in city offices or in the party. These represented the first steps into the middle class.

Crude welfare system

In return, citizens expressed their gratitude at the ballot box. Sometimes the votes of the grateful were not enough. "Little Bob" Davies of Jersey City was adept at mobilizing the "graveyard vote." He drew names from tombstones to pad lists of registered voters and hired "repeaters" to vote under the phony names. When reformers introduced the Australian (secret) ballot in the 1880s to prevent fraud, bosses pulled the "Tasmanian dodge" by premarking election tickets. Failing that, they dumped whole ballot boxes into the river or used hired thugs to scare unpersuaded voters away from the polls.

Rewards, Accomplishments, and Costs

Why did bosses go to such lengths? Some simply loved the game of politics. More often bosses loved money. Their ability to get it was limited only by their *Boss William Tweed* ingenuity or the occasional success of an outraged reformer. The record for brassiness must go to Boss William Tweed. During his reign in the 1860s and 1870s, Tweed swindled New York City out of a fortune. His masterpiece of graft was a chunky three-story courthouse in lower Manhattan originally budgeted at $250,000. When Tweed was through, the city had spent more than $13 million—and the building was still not finished! Tweed died in prison, but with such profits to be made, it was small wonder that bosses rivaled the pharaohs of Egypt as builders.

In their fashion bosses played a vital role in the industrial city. Rising from the bottom ranks, they guided immigrants into American life and helped some of the underprivileged up from poverty. They changed the urban landscape with a massive construction program. They modernized city government by uniting it and making it perform. Choosing the aldermen, municipal judges, mayors, and administrative officials, bosses exerted new control to provide the contracts and franchises to run cities. Such accomplishments fostered the notion that government could be called on to help the needy. The welfare state, still decades away, had some roots here.

The toll was often outrageous. Inflated taxes, extorted revenue, unpunished vice and crime were only the obvious costs. A woman whose family enjoyed Plunkitt's Christmas turkey might be widowed by an accident to her husband in a sweatshop kept open by timely bribes. Filthy buildings might claim her children, as corrupt inspectors ignored serious violations. Buying votes and selling favors, bosses turned democracy into a petty business—as much a "business," said Plunkitt, "as the grocery or dry-goods or the drug business." Yet they were the forerunners of the new breed of professional politicians who would soon govern the cities and the nation as well.

Nativism, Revivals, and the Social Gospel

Urban blight and the condition of the poor inspired social as well as political activism, especially within churches. Not all of it was constructive. The popular Congregationalist minister Josiah Strong concluded that the city was "a menace to society." Along with anxious economists and social workers, he blamed everything from corruption to unemployment on immigrant city dwellers and urged restrictions on their entry.

In the 1880s and 1890s, two depressions sharpened such anxieties. Nativism, a defensive and fearful nationalism, peaked as organizations like the new *Nativist restrictions* Immigration Restriction League attacked Catholics and foreigners. Already the victims of racial prejudice, the Chinese were an easy target. In 1882 Congress enacted the Chinese Exclusion

Act. It banned the entry of Chinese laborers and represented an important step in the drive to restrict immigration. In 1897 the first bill requiring literacy tests for immigrants passed Congress, but President Grover Cleveland vetoed it.

Some clergy took their missions to the slums to bridge the gap between the middle class and the poor. Beginning in 1870 Dwight Lyman Moody, a 300-pound former shoe salesman, won armies of lowly converts with revivals in Boston, Chicago, and other cities. Evangelists helped to found American branches of the British Young Men's Christian Association and the Salvation Army. By the end of the century the Salvation Army had grown to 700 corps staffed by some 3000 officers. They ministered to the needy with food, music, shelter, and simple good fellowship.

A small group of ministers rejected the traditional notion that weak character explained sin and that society would be perfected only as individual sin-

The Social Gospel

ners were converted. They spread a new "Social Gospel" that focused on improving the conditions of society in order to save individuals. In *Applied Christianity* (1886), the influential Washington Gladden preached that the church must be responsible for correcting social injustices in the political and economic order, including dangerous working conditions and unfair labor practices. Houses of worship, such as William Rainford's St. George's Episcopal Church in New York, became centers of social activity, with boys' clubs, gymnasiums, libraries, glee clubs, and industrial training programs.

Billy Sunday (1923), by George Bellows, depicts a revival meeting of William Ashley "Billy" Sunday. Sunday, a hard-drinking professional baseball player turned evangelist, began his religious revivals in the 1890s and drew thousands.

The Social Settlement Movement

Church-sponsored programs often repelled the immigrant poor, who saw them as thinly disguised missionary efforts. Immigrants and other slum dwellers were more

The settlement house

receptive to a bold experiment called the settlement house. Situated in the worst slums, often in renovated old houses, these early community centers were run by middle-class women and men to help the poor and foreign-born. At the turn of the century there were more than 100 of them, the most famous being Jane Addams's Hull House in Chicago. In 1898 the Catholic church sponsored its first settlement house in New York, and in 1900 Bronson House opened its doors to the Latino community in Los Angeles.

High purposes inspired settlement workers, who actually lived in the settlement houses. They left comfortable middle-class homes and dedicated themselves (like the "early Christians," said one) to service and sacrifice. They aimed to teach immigrants American ways and to create a community spirit that would foster "right living through social relations." But immigrants were also encouraged to preserve their heritages through festivals, parades, and museums. Like political bosses, settlement reformers furnished help, from day nurseries to English-language and cooking classes to playgrounds and libraries. Armed with statistics and personal experiences, they also lobbied for social legislation to improve housing, women's working conditions, and public schools.

CITY LIFE

City life reflected the stratified nature of American society in the late nineteenth century. Every city had its slums and tenements but also its fashionable avenues, where many-roomed mansions housed the rich. The rich constituted barely 1 percent of the population but owned a fourth of all wealth. In between tenement and mansion lived the broad middle of urban society, which made up nearly a third of the population and owned about half of the nation's wealth. With more money and leisure time, the middle class was increasing its power and influence.

In the impersonal city of the late nineteenth century, class distinctions, as ever, continued to be based on wealth and income. But no longer were dress and man-

Urban social stratification

ners enough to distinguish one class from another. Such differences were reflected in where people lived, what they bought, which organizations they joined, and how they spent their leisure time.

The Immigrant in the City

When they put into port, the first thing immigrants were likely to see was a city. Perhaps it was Boston or New York or Galveston, Texas, where an overflow of Jewish immigrants was directed after the turn of the century. Most immigrants, exhausted physically and financially, settled in cities.

Cities developed a well-defined mosaic of ethnic communities, since immigrants usually clustered together on the basis of their villages or provinces. But

Ethnic neighborhoods

these neighborhoods were in constant flux. As many as half the residents moved every 10 years, often because they got better-paying jobs or had more of their family working. Though one nationality usually dominated a neighborhood, there was always a sprinkling of others. Despite popular misconceptions, no other immigrants lived like the Chinese in urban ghettos of just one ethnic group. Racial prejudice forced the Chinese together, and local ordinances kept them from buying their way out like other immigrants.

Ethnic communities served as havens from the strangeness of American society and springboards to a new life. From the moment they stepped off the boat, newcomers felt pressed to learn English, don American clothes, and drop their "greenhorn" ways. Yet in their neighborhoods they also found comrades who spoke their language, theaters that performed their plays and music, restaurants that served their food.

The *Jewish Daily Forward* and scores of other foreign-language newspapers reported events from the homeland but also gave eager readers profiles of local

Entertainment in immigrant neighborhoods often resulted in a cross-fertilization of cultures. The Cathay Boys Club Band (pictured above), a marching band of Chinese Americans, was formed in San Francisco's Chinatown in 1911. It was inspired by the Columbia Park Boys Band of Italians from nearby North Beach and played American music only.

Adapting to America leaders, advice on voting, and tips on adjusting to America. Immigrant aid societies like the Polish National Alliance and the Society for the Protection of Italian Immigrants furnished fellowship and assistance in the newcomers' own languages. They fostered assimilation by sponsoring baseball teams, insurance programs, libraries, and English classes.

Sometimes immigrants combined the old and the new in creative ways. Italians developed a pidgin dialect called Italglish. It permitted them to communicate quickly with Americans and to absorb American customs. So the Fourth of July became "*Il Forte Gelato*" (literally "The Great Freeze"), a play on the sound of the words. Other immigrant groups invented similar idioms, like *Chuco*, a dialect that developed among border Mexicans in El Paso.

Houses of worship were always at the center of immigrant life. They often catered to the practices of individual towns or provinces. Occasionally they changed their ways under the cultural pressures of American life. Where the Irish dominated the American Catholic church other immigrants formed new churches with priests from their homelands. Eastern European Jews began to break the old law against sitting next to their wives and daughters in synagogues. The Orthodox churches of Armenians, Syrians, Romanians, and Serbians gradually lost their national identifications.

The backgrounds and cultural values of immigrants influenced their choice of jobs. Because Chinese men did not scorn washing or ironing, more than 7500 of them could be found in San Francisco laundries by 1880. Sewing ladies' garments seemed unmanly to many native-born Americans but not to Russian and Italian tailors. Slavs tended to be physically robust and valued steady income over education. They pulled their children out of school, sent them to work, and worked themselves in the mines for better pay than in factories.

On the whole, immigrants married later and had more children than the native-born. Greeks and eastern European Jews prearranged marriages according to tradition. They imported "picture brides," betrothed by mail with a photograph. *Family life* After marriage men ruled the household, but women managed it. Although child-rearing practices varied, immigrants resisted the relative permissiveness of American parents. Youngsters were expected to contribute like little adults to the welfare of the family.

In these "family economies" of working-class immigrants, key decisions— over whether and whom to marry, over work and education, over when to leave home—were made on the basis of collective rather than individual needs. Though immigrant boys were more likely to work outside the home than girls, daughters often went to work at an early age so sons could continue their education. It was customary for one daughter to remain unmarried so she could care for younger siblings or aged parents.

The Chinese were an exception to the pattern. The ban on the immigration of Chinese laborers in the 1880s (pages 508–509) had frozen the gender ratio of Chinese communities into a curious imbalance. Like other immigrants,

EYEWITNESS TO HISTORY

A Chinese Immigrant Names
His Children

As we children arrived, Father was confronted with a vexatious problem. It perplexed not only him, but every other Chinatown father. What names should he give us children born in this country? . . . He winced at the prospect of saddling his children with names which could be ridiculously distorted into pidgin English. He had had enough, he said, of Sing High, Sing Low, Wun Long Hop, Ching Chong, Long Song.

. . . For him the problem, when I arrived, was immensely simplified. According to the Barbarian calender, I was born on "The Double Ninth," or the ninth day of the ninth month . . . a holiday commemorating California's admission into the Union. "Why not," suggested Dr. [Mabel] LaPlace [who delivered his daughter and for whom she was named] . . . , "name your son after the Governor?" . . . At that time the Governor of California bore the name of Dr. George C. Pardee. . . . I was named for a fellow Republican.

I doubt whether Father ever quite realized the tremendous burden he placed upon our shoulders. Sister Mabel . . . never had to live up to her name in school, although she did have to live down among her playmates the discreditable fact that her brothers and sisters bore the socially forbidding names of George C. Pardee, Alice Roosevelt, Helen Taft, Woodrow Wilson, and Thomas Riley Marshall.

. . . As we grew up, our Chinese names were used less and less. When we visited Chinatown and were addressed, as always happened, by these Chinese names, it gave us a weird, uncomfortable feeling as though someone other than ourselves were being addressed . . . Our lives never seemed to be ours to do with as we saw fit. . . . In our Chinese world we had to order our lives for the happiness of our parents and the dignity of our clan; while in the American one it was no different. It was obvious that we not only had to "make a name" for ourselves, but acquit with distinction our namesakes as well.

Pardee Lowe, *Father and Glorious Descendant* (Boston: Little, Brown, and Company, 1943), pp. 12–25. Copyright renewed in 1971 by Pardee Lowe. All rights reserved.

most Chinese newcomers had been single men. In the wake of the ban, those in the United States could not bring over their wives and families. Nor by law in 13 states could they marry white Americans. With few women, Chinese communities suffered from high rates of prostitution, large numbers of gangs and secret societies, and low birth totals. When the San Francisco earthquake and fire destroyed birth records in 1906, resourceful Chinese immigrants created "paper sons" (and less often "paper daughters") by forging birth certificates and claiming their China-born children as American citizens.

Caught between past and present, immigrants clung to tradition and assimilated slowly. Their children adjusted more quickly. They soon spoke English like natives, married whomever they pleased, and worked their way out of old neighborhoods. Yet the process was not easy. Children faced heartrending clashes with parents and rejection from peers.

Assimilation

COUNTERPOINT   *The "New" Immigrants: Who Came and Why?*

With so many immigrants coming to America, it is no wonder historians have disagreed over who came and why. Early historians of immigration focused specifically on the United States and the European arrivals. The newcomers were depicted as an undifferentiated mass of peasants in search of economic opportunity and freedom from persecution. These immigrants, according to early interpretations, helped to make the American experience unique.

More recently, historians have placed immigration to the United States in global perspective by examining both receiving and sending countries. In an international framework, the United States moves from the center of immigration action to the fringes of the narrative as one of many components in an expanding world economy. Immigration to America thus becomes part of international labor exchange and the American experience less exceptional and more comparable to that of other receiving nations such as Argentina and Australia. As for the immigrants themselves, the international perspective makes the pool from which they were drawn more diverse economically and ethnically and less poverty-stricken than originally thought.

Urban Middle-Class Life

Life for the urban middle class revolved around home and family. By the turn of the century just over a third of middle-class urbanites owned their homes. Often two or three stories, made of brick or brownstone, these houses were a measure of their owners' social standing. The plush furniture, heavy drapes, antiques, and curios all signaled status and refinement.

Such homes, usually on their own lots, also served as havens to protect and nourish the family. Seventeenth-century notions of children as inherently sinful had given way to more modern theories about the shaping influence of environment. Calm and orderly households with nurturing mothers would launch children on the right course. "A clean, fresh, and well-ordered house," stipulated a domestic adviser in 1883, "exercises over its inmates a moral, no less than physical

The home as haven and status symbol

influence, and has a direct tendency to make members of the family sober, peaceable, and considerate of the feelings and happiness of each other."

A woman was judged by the state of her home. The typical homemaker prepared elaborate meals, cleaned, laundered, and sewed. Each task took time.

The middle-class homemaker

Baking a loaf of bread required nearly 24 hours, and in 1890, four of five loaves were still made at home. Perhaps 25 percent of urban households had live-in servants to help with the work. They were on call about 100 hours a week, were off but one evening and part of Sunday, and averaged $2 to $5 a week in salary.

By the 1890s a wealth of new consumer products eased the burdens of housework. Brand names trumpeted a new age of commercially prepared food—Campbell's soup, Quaker oats, Pillsbury flour, Jell-O, and Cracker Jacks, to name a few. New appliances such as "self-working" washers offered mechanical assistance but often shredded shirts. Aching arms testified to how far short mechanization still fell.

Toward the end of the century, Saturday became less of a workday and more of a family day. Sunday mornings remained a time for church, still an important center of family life. Afternoons had a more secular flavor. There were shopping trips (city stores often stayed open) and visits to lakes, zoos, and amusement parks (usually built at the end of trolley lines to attract more riders). Outside institutions—fraternal organizations, uplift groups, athletic teams, and church groups—were becoming part of middle-class urban family life.

Victorianism and the Pursuit of Virtue

Middle-class life reflected a rigid social code called Victorianism, named for Britain's long-reigning Queen Victoria. It emerged in the 1830s and 1840s as part of an effort to tame the turbulent urban-industrial society developing in Europe.

Victorianism dictated that personal conduct be based on orderly behavior and disciplined moralism. It stressed sobriety, industriousness, self-control, and sexual modesty and taught that demeanor, particularly proper manners, was the backbone of society. According to its sexual precepts, women were "pure vessels," devoid of carnal desire. Their job was to control the "lower natures" of their husbands by withholding sex except for procreation.

Women's fashion mirrored Victorian values. Strenuously laced corsets ("an instrument of torture," according to one woman) pushed breasts up, stomachs in, and rear-ends out. The resulting wasplike figure accentuated the breasts and hips, promoting the image of women as child bearers. Ankle-length skirts were draped over bustles, hoops, and petticoats to make hips look even larger and suggest fertility. Such elegant dress set off middle- and upper-class women from those below, whose plain clothes signaled lives of drudgery and want.

When working-class Americans failed to follow Victorian cues, reformers helped them to pursue virtue. In 1874 Frances Willard, fearing the ill effects of

WCTU — alcohol on the family, helped to organize the Woman's Christian Temperance Union. Under her leadership the WCTU worked relentlessly to stamp out alcohol and promote sexual purity and other middle-class virtues. By the turn of the century it was the largest women's organization in the country, with 500,000 members.

Anthony Comstock crusaded with equal vigor against what he saw as moral pollution, ranging from pornography and gambling to the use of nude art *Comstock Law* — models. In 1873 President Ulysses S. Grant signed the so-called Comstock Law, a statute banning from the mails all materials "designed to incite lust." Two days later Comstock went to work as a special agent for the Post Office. In his 41-year career, he claimed to have made more than 3000 arrests and destroyed 160 tons of vice-ridden books and photographs.

Victorian crusaders like Comstock were not simply missionaries of a stuffy morality. They were apostles of a middle-class creed of social control, responding to an increasing incidence of alcoholism, venereal disease, gambling debts, prostitution, and unwanted pregnancies. No doubt they overreacted in warning that the road to ruin lay behind the door of every saloon, gambling parlor, or bedroom. Yet the new urban environment did indeed reflect the disorder of a rapidly industrializing society.

The insistence with which moralists warned against "impropriety" suggests that many people did not heed their advice. Three-quarters of the women surveyed toward the turn of the century reported that they enjoyed sex. The growing variety of contraceptives—including spermicidal douches, sheaths made of animal intestines, rubber condoms, and forerunners of the diaphragm—testified to the desire for pregnancy-free intercourse. Abortion, too, was available. According to one estimate, a third of all pregnancies were aborted, usually with the aid of a midwife. (By the 1880s abortion had been made illegal in most states following the first antiabortion statute in England in 1803.) Despite Victorian marriage manuals, middle-class Americans became more conscious of sexuality as an emotional dimension of a satisfying union.

Challenges to Convention

A few bold men and women challenged convention more openly. Victoria Woodhull, publisher of *Woodhull & Claflin's Weekly*, divorced her husband, ran *Victoria Woodhull* — for president in 1872 on the Equal Rights Party ticket, and pressed the case for sexual freedom. "I am a free lover!" she shouted to a riotous audience in New York. "I have the inalienable, constitutional, and natural right to love whom I may, to love as long or as short a period as I can, to change that love every day if I please!" Woodhull made a strong public case for sexual freedom. In private, however, she believed in strict monogamy and romantic love for herself.

The same cosmopolitan conditions that provided protection for Woodhull's unorthodox beliefs also made possible the growth of self-conscious communi-

Urban homosexual communities

ties of homosexual men and women. Earlier in the century, Americans had idealized romantic friendships among members of the same sex, without necessarily attributing to them sexual overtones. But for friendships with an explicitly sexual dimension, the anonymity of large cities provided new meeting grounds. Single factory workers and clerks, living in furnished rooms rather than with their families in small towns and on farms, were freer to seek others who shared their sexual orientation. Homosexual men and women began forming social networks: on the streets where they regularly met, at specific restaurants and clubs, which, to avoid controversy, sometimes passed themselves off as athletic associations or chess clubs. Such places could be found in New York City's Bowery, around the Presidio military base in San Francisco, and at Lafayette Square in Washington, D.C.

Only toward the end of the century did physicians begin to notice homosexual behavior, usually to condemn it as a disease or an inherited infirmity. Indeed, not until the turn of the century did the term *homosexual* come into existence. Certainly homosexual love itself was not new. But for the first time in the United States, the conditions of urban life allowed gays and lesbians to define themselves in terms of a larger, self-conscious community, even if they were stoutly condemned by the prevailing Victorian morality.

CITY CULTURE

"We cannot all live in cities," the reformer Horace Greeley lamented just after the Civil War, "yet nearly all seemed determined to do so. . . ." Economic opportunity drew people to the teeming industrial city. But so, too, did a vibrant urban culture.

By the 1890s, cities had begun to clean up downtown business districts, pave streets, widen thoroughfares, erect fountains and buildings of marble. This "city beautiful" movement aimed also to elevate public tastes and, like Victorian culture itself, refine the behavior of urbanites. Civic leaders built museums, libraries, and parks to uplift unruly city masses. Public parks followed the model of New York's Central Park. When it opened in 1858, Central Park was meant to serve as pastoral retreat from the turbulent industrial city. Its rustic paths, woodsy views, and tranquil lakes, said designer Frederick Law Olmsted, would have "a distinctly harmonizing and refining influence" on even the rudest fellow.

For those in search of lower-brow entertainment, cities offered dance halls and sporting events, amusement parks and vaudeville shows, saloons and arcades. In the beckoning cities of the late nineteenth century, Americans sought to realize their dreams of fun and success.

Public Education in an Urban Industrial World

Those at the bottom and in the middle of city life found in public education one key to success. Although the campaign for public education began in the Jacksonian era, it did not make much headway until after the Civil War, when industrial cities began to mushroom. As late as 1870 half the children in the country received no formal education at all, and one American in five could not read.

Between 1870 and 1900, an educational awakening occurred. As more and more businesses required better-educated workers, attendance in public schools more than doubled. The length of the school term rose from 132 to 144 days. Illiteracy fell by half. By the turn of the century, nearly all the states outside the South had enacted mandatory education laws. Almost three of every four school-age children were enrolled. Even so, the average American adult still attended school for only about five years, and less than 10 percent of those eligible continued beyond the eighth grade.

The average school day started early, but by noon most girls were released under the assumption that they needed less formal education. Curricula stressed the fundamentals of reading, writing, and arithmetic. Courses in manual training, science, and physical education were added as the demand for technical knowledge grew and opportunities to exercise shrank. Students learned by memorization, sitting in silent study with hands clasped or standing erect while they repeated phrases and sums. Few schools encouraged creative thinking. "Don't stop to think," barked a Chicago teacher to a class of terrified youngsters in the 1890s, "tell me what you know!"

A strict social philosophy underlay the harsh routine. In an age of industrialization, massive immigration, and rapid change, schools taught conformity and values as much as facts and figures. Teachers acted as drillmasters, shaping their charges for the sake of society. "Teachers and books are better security than handcuffs and policemen," wrote a New Jersey college professor in 1879.

As Reconstruction faded, so did the impressive start made in black education. Most of the first generation of former slaves had been illiterate. So eager

African Americans

were they to learn that by the end of the century nearly half of all African Americans could read. But discrimination soon took its toll. For nearly 100 years after the Civil War, the doctrine of "separate but equal," upheld by the Supreme Court in *Plessy v. Ferguson* (1896), kept black and white students apart but scarcely equal (page 534). By 1882 public schools in a half dozen southern states were segregated by law, the rest by practice. Underfunded and ill-equipped, black schools served dirt-poor families whose every member had to work.

Like African Americans, immigrants saw education as a way of getting ahead. Some educators saw it as a means of Americanizing newcomers. They

Immigrant education

assumed that immigrant and native-born children would learn the same lessons in the same language and turn out the same way. Only toward the end of the century, as immigration mounted, did eastern cities begin to offer night classes that taught English, along with civics lessons, for foreigners. When public education proved inadequate, immigrants established their own schools. Catholics, for example, started an elaborate expansion of their parochial schools in 1884.

By the 1880s educational reforms were helping schools respond to the needs of an urban society. Opened first in St. Louis in 1873, American versions of innovative German "kindergartens" put four- to six-year-olds in orderly classrooms while parents went off to work. "Normal schools" multiplied to provide teachers with more professional training. And in the new industrial age, science and manual training supplemented more conventional subjects in order to supply industry with educated workers.

Higher Learning and the Rise of the Professional

Colleges served the urban industrial society, too, not by controlling mass habits but by providing leaders and managers. Early in the nineteenth century, most Americans had regarded higher learning as unmanly and irrelevant. The few who sought it often preferred the superior universities of Europe to those in the United States.

As American society grew more organized, mechanized, and complex, the need for professional, technical, and literary skills brought greater respect for college education. The Morrill Act of 1862 generated a dozen new state colleges and universities, eight mechanical and agricultural colleges, and six black colleges. Private charity added more.

Postgraduate education

Railroad barons like Johns Hopkins and Leland Stanford used parts of their fortunes to found colleges named after them (Hopkins in 1873, Stanford in 1890). The number of colleges and universities nearly doubled between 1870 and 1910, though less than 5 percent of college-age Americans enrolled in them.

A practical impulse inspired the founding of several black colleges. In the late nineteenth century, few institutions mixed races. Church groups and private foundations, such as the Peabody and Slater funds (supported by white donors from the North), underwrote black colleges after Reconstruction. By 1900, a total of 700 black students were enrolled. About 2000 had graduated. Through hard work and persistence, some even received degrees from institutions reserved for whites.

In keeping with the new emphasis on practical learning, professional schools multiplied to provide training beyond a college degree. American universities adopted the German model requiring young scholars to perform research as part of their education. The number of law and medical schools more than doubled between 1870 and 1900; medical students almost tripled. Ten percent of them were women, though their numbers shrank as physicians became more organized and exclusive.

Professionals of all kinds—in law, medicine, engineering, business, academics—swelled the ranks of the middle class. Slowly they were becoming a new force in urban America, replacing the ministers and gentlemen freeholders of an earlier day as community leaders.

Higher Education for Women

Before the Civil War women could attend only three private colleges. After the war they had new ones all their own, including Smith (1871), Wellesley (1875), and Bryn Mawr (1885). Such all-women schools, with their mostly female faculties and administrators, deepened an emerging sense of membership in a special community of women. Many land-grant colleges, chartered to serve all people, also admitted women. By 1910 some 40 percent of college students were women, almost double the 1870 figure. Only one college in five refused to accept them.

Potent myths of gender continued to plague women in college. As Dr. Edward Clarke of the Harvard Medical School told thousands of students in *Sex in Education* (1873), the rigors of a college education could lead the "weaker sex" to physical or mental collapse, infertility, and early death. Women's colleges therefore included a program of physical activity to keep students healthy. Many offered an array of courses in "domestic science"—cooking, sewing, and other such skills—to counter the claim that higher education would be of no value to women.

College students, together with office workers and female athletes, became role models for ambitious young women. These "new women," impatient with custom, cast off Victorian restrictions. Fewer of them married, and more—perhaps 25 percent—were self-supporting. They shed their corsets and bustles and donned lighter, more comfortable clothing, such as "shirtwaist" blouses (styled after men's shirts) and lower-heeled shoes. And they showed that women could move beyond the domestic sphere of home and family.

A Culture of Consumption

The city spawned a new material culture built around consumption. As standards of living rose, American industries began providing "ready-made" clothing to replace garments that had once been made at home. Similarly, food and furniture were mass-produced in greater quantities. The city became a giant market for these goods, the place where new patterns of mass consumption took hold. Radiating outward to more rural areas, this urban consumer culture helped to level American society. Increasingly city businesses sold the same goods to farmer and clerk, rich and poor, native-born and immigrant.

Well-made, inexpensive merchandise in standard sizes and shapes found outlets in new palaces of consumption known as "department stores," so called

Department
stores
because they displayed their goods in separate sections or departments. Unlike the small exclusive shops of Europe, department stores were palatial, public, and filled with inviting displays of furniture, housewares, and clothing.

The French writer Emile Zola claimed that department stores "democratized luxury." Anyone could enter free of charge, handle the most elegant and expensive goods, and buy whatever was affordable. When consumers found goods too pricey, department stores pioneered lay-away plans with deferred payments. The department store also educated people by showing them what "proper" families owned and the correct names for things like women's wear and parlor furniture. This process of socialization was occurring not only in cities but in towns and villages across America. Mass consumption was giving rise to a mass culture.

"Chain stores" (a term coined in America) spread the culture of consumption without frills. They catered to the working class, who could not afford department stores, and operated on a cash-and-carry basis. Owners
Chain stores
and mail-order
houses
kept their costs down by buying in volume to fill the small stores in growing neighborhood chains. Founded in 1859, the Great Atlantic and Pacific Tea Company (later to become A&P supermarkets) was the first of the chain stores. By 1876 its 76 branch stores had added groceries to the original line of teas.

Far from department and chain stores, rural Americans joined the community of consumers by mail. In 1872, Aaron Montgomery Ward sent his first price sheet to farmers from a livery stable loft in Chicago. Ward avoided the middleman and promised savings of 40 percent on fans, needles, trunks, harnesses, and scores of other goods. By 1884, his catalog boasted 10,000 items, each illustrated by a lavish woodcut. Similarly, Richard W. Sears and Alvah C. Roebuck built a $500 million mail-order business by 1907. Schoolrooms that had no encyclopedia used a Ward's or Sears' catalog instead. When asked the source of the Ten Commandments, one farm boy replied that they came from Sears, Roebuck.

Leisure

As mechanization gradually reduced the number of hours on the job, factory workers found themselves with more free time. So did the middle class, with free weekends, evenings, and vacations. A new, stricter division between work and play developed in the more disciplined society of industrial America. City dwellers turned leisure into a consumer item that often reflected differences in class, gender, and ethnicity.

Sports, for example, had been a traditional form of recreation for the rich. They continued to play polo, golf, and the newly imported English game of ten-
Sports and class
distinctions
nis. Croquet had more middle-class appeal. It required less skill and special equipment. Perhaps as important, it could be enjoyed in mixed company, like the new craze of bicycling. Bicycles

evolved from unstable contraptions with large front wheels into "safety" bikes with equal-sized wheels, a dropped middle bar, pneumatic tires, and coaster brakes. A good one cost about $100, far beyond the reach of a factory worker. On Sunday afternoons city parks became crowded with cyclists. Women rode the new safety bikes too, although social convention prohibited them from riding alone. But cycling broke down conventions too. It required looser garments, freeing women from corsets. And lady cyclists demonstrated that they were hardly too fragile for physical exertion.

Organized spectator sports attracted crowds from every walk of life. Baseball overshadowed all others. For city dwellers with dull work, cramped quarters,

Spectator sports for the urban masses

and isolated lives, baseball offered the chance to join thousands of others for an exciting outdoor spectacle. The first professional teams appeared in 1869, and slowly the game evolved. Umpires began to call balls and strikes, the overhand replaced the underhand pitch, and fielders put on gloves. Teams from eight cities formed the National League of Professional Baseball Clubs in 1876, followed by the American League in 1901. League players were distinctly working class. At first, teams featured some black players. When African Americans were barred in the 1880s, black professionals formed their own team, the Cuban Giants of Long Island, New York, looking to play anyone they could.

Horse racing, bicycle tournaments, and other sports of speed and violence helped to break the monotony, frustration, and routine of the industrial city. In 1869, without pads or helmets, Rutgers beat Princeton in the first intercollegiate football match. By the 1890s the service academies and state universities fielded teams. Football soon attracted crowds of 50,000 or more. Beginning in 1891 when Dr. James Naismith nailed a peach basket to the gymnasium wall at the YMCA Training School in Springfield, Massachusetts, "basketball" became the indoor interlude between the outdoor sports of spring and fall.

Arts and Entertainment

Variety also marked social life in the city. The saloon served as a workingman's club, while young working women escaped the drudgery of factory, office, or sweatshop at vaudeville shows and the new amusement parks. Coney Island's Luna Park, opened in 1903, drew 5 million customers in a single season. Jostling with crowds, eating ice cream and hot dogs, riding "Shoot-the-Chutes," young women and men, even the newest immigrants, could feel gloriously American. Instead of the Victorian values of orderly conduct and sober industry, amusement parks encouraged abandon, fantasy, and gaiety.

Workingmen took their dates to dance halls and boxing exhibitions, staged in small rings used for variety acts between fights. Wealthier couples went to concerts given by local symphony orchestras, which played a mixture of popular tunes, John Philip Sousa marches, and the music of classical European composers. At the theater, popular melodramas gave patrons a chance to avoid the

From balconies at theaters (like the one depicted in Charles Dana Gibson's pen-and-ink drawing *The Villain Dies*) rowdy patrons cheered, whistled, and booed at performers. Around the turn of the century, theater owners imposed strict rules of behavior on audiences in an effort to attract middle-class families.

ambiguities of modern life. Theatergoers booed villains and cheered heroes, as seen in the illustration above; they shuddered for heroines and marveled at tricky stage mechanics that made ice floes move and players float upward to heaven.

In villages and cities music of every tempo and style filled the air. Organ grinders churned out Italian airs on street corners. Steam-powered calliopes tooted spirited waltzes from amusement parks and riverboat decks. In bandstands brass ensembles played German-style concerts. By 1900 the sale of phonograph records had reached 3 million. Popular music became a big business, as companies hawked sentimental ballads like "My Mother Was a Lady" or topical tunes celebrating the discovery of oil or the changing styles of women's clothing. In Scott Joplin's "Maple Leaf Rag" (1899) the lively syncopation of ragtime heralded the coming of jazz.

As the nineteenth century drew to a close, the city was reshaping the country, just as the industrial system was creating a more specialized, diversified, and interlocking economy. Cities beckoned migrants from the countryside and immigrants from abroad with unparalleled opportunities for work and pleasure. The playwright Israel Zangwill celebrated the city's transforming power in his 1908 Broadway hit *The Melting Pot*. "The real American," one of his characters explained, "is only in the Crucible, I tell you—he will be the fusion of all the races, the coming superman."

Where Zangwill saw a melting pot with all its promise for a new super race, champions of traditional American values like the widely read Protestant minister Josiah Strong saw "a commingled mass of venomous filth and seething sin, of lust, of drunkenness, of pauperism, and crime of every sort." Both the champions and the critics of the late nineteenth century had a point. Corruption, crudeness, and disorder were no more or less a part of the cities than the vibrancy, energy, and opportunities that drew people to them. The gap between rich and poor yawned most widely in cities. As social critic Henry George observed, progress and poverty seemed to go hand in hand.

In the end moral judgments, whether pro or con, missed the point. Cities stood at the nexus of the new industrial order. All Americans, whatever they thought about the new urban world, had to search for ways to make that world work.

SIGNIFICANT EVENTS

1869	Cincinnati Red Stockings become first professional baseball team; Rutgers beats Princeton in first intercollegiate football game
1870	Elevated railroad begins operation in New York City
1872	William "Boss" Tweed convicted of defrauding city of New York
1873	Comstock Law enacted
1874	Woman's Christian Temperance Union founded
1875	Dwight Moody begins urban evangelical revivals
1876	Central Park completed in New York City; Johns Hopkins University opens nation's first graduate school
1882	Chinese Exclusion Act
1883	Brooklyn Bridge opens
1885	Home Life Insurance Building, world's first skyscraper, built in Chicago; first all-black professional baseball team, the Cuban Giants, organized
1888	Nation's first electric trolley line begins operation in Richmond, Virginia
1889	Hull House opens in Chicago
1891	Basketball invented
1892	Ellis Island opens as receiving station for immigrants
1894	Immigration Restriction League organized
1897	Boston opens nation's first subway station

CHAPTER TWENTY

Agrarian Domains:
The South and the West

T he news spread across the South during the late 1870s. Perhaps a man came around with a handbill, telling of cheap land; or a letter might arrive from friends or relatives and be read aloud at church. The news spread in different ways, but in the end, the talk always spelled *Kansas*.

Few black farmers had been to Kansas themselves. But more than a few knew that the abolitionist Old John Brown had lived there before coming east to raid Harpers Ferry. Black folks, it seemed, might be able to live more freely in Kansas. "You can buy land at from a dollar and a half to two dollars an acre," wrote one settler to his friend in Louisiana. There was another distinct advantage: "They do not kill Negroes here for voting."

In 1878 such prospects excited hundreds of black families already stretched to their limits by hardship and violence. With Rutherford Hayes president, Reconstruction was at an end. Southern state governments had been "redeemed" by conservative whites, and the future seemed uncertain. "COME WEST," concluded *The Colored Citizen*, a newspaper in Topeka. "COME TO KANSAS."

St. Louis learned of these rumblings in the first raw days of March 1879, as steamers from downriver began unloading freedmen in large numbers. While the weather was still cold, they sought shelter beneath tarpaulins along the river levee, built fires by the shore, and got out frying pans to cook meals while their children jumped rope nearby. By the end of 1879, more than 20,000 had arrived.

When the crowds overwhelmed the wharves and temporary shelters, the city's black churches banded together to house the "refugees," feed them, and

The Exodusters

help them continue toward Kansas. Repeated rumors that rail passage would not be free failed to shake their hopes. "We's like de chilun ob Israel when dey was led from out o' bondage by Moses," one explained, referring to the Bible's tale of exodus from Egypt. "If we sticks togeter an' keeps up our faith we'll git to Kansas and be out o' bondage for shuah." So the "Exodusters," as they became known, pressed onward.

525

In the end, most of the black emigrants settled in growing towns like Topeka, Lincoln, and Kansas City. Men worked as hired hands; women did laundry. With luck, couples made $350 a year, saved a bit for a home, and put down roots.

The host of Exodusters who poured into Kansas were part of a human flood westward. It had many sources: played-out farms of New England and the South, crowded cities, all of Europe. Special trains brought the settlers to the plains, all eager to start anew. During the 1880s the number of Kansans jumped from a million to a million and a half. Other western states experienced similar booms.

Yet the boomers' optimistic spirits could not mask serious strains in the rapidly expanding nation, especially in the South and West. The boom economies of cotton, cattle, and grain all depended on city markets. Especially during hard times, westerners and southerners saw themselves as the victims of a colonial economic system, in which their fortunes were controlled by the industries of northeastern cities and their hardships ignored by Washington.

Relations between the South, West, and Northeast

But these self-styled victims themselves exploited both people and land. Whether locking former slaves into new forms of economic bondage or conquering land from Indians and Hispanics, both Southerners and Westerners built societies of racial caste. Violence became a common means of carving out and sustaining these societies. Imbalances emerged as drought, exhausted mines, overcut timberlands, and overproduction strained these regional economies to their limits.

THE SOUTHERN BURDEN

Henry Grady, the editor of the Atlanta *Constitution*, often liked to tell the story of the poor cotton farmer buried in a pine coffin in the pine woods of Georgia. Only the coffin hadn't been made in Georgia but in Cincinnati. The nails in the coffin had been forged in Pittsburgh, though an iron mine lay near the cemetery. Even the farmer's cotton coat was made in New York and his trousers in Chicago. The "South didn't furnish a thing on earth for that funeral but the corpse and the hole in the ground!" fumed Grady. The irony of the story was the tragedy of the South. The region had human and natural resources aplenty but, alas, few factories to manufacture the goods it needed.

In the 1880s Grady campaigned to bring about a "New South" based on bustling industry, cities, and commerce. The business class and its values would displace the old planter class as southerners raced "to out-Yankee the Yankee." Grady and other publicists recognized the South's potential. Extending from Delaware south to Florida and west to Texas, the region took in a third of the nation's total area. It held a third of its arable farmlands, vast tracts of lumber, and rich deposits of coal, iron, oil, and fertilizers. To overcome the destruction of the Civil War and the loss of slave-

The gospel of a "New South"

holding wealth, apostles of the New South campaigned to catch up with the industrial North. But well into the twentieth century, Grady's New South remained the poorest section of the country. And it suffered as well the burden of an unwieldy labor system that was largely unskilled and racially divided.

Agriculture in the New South

For all the hopeful talk of industry, the economy of the postwar South remained agricultural, tied to crops like tobacco, rice, sugar, and especially cotton. By us-

A cotton-dominated economy

ing fertilizers, planters were able to introduce cotton into areas once considered marginal. The number of acres planted in cotton more than doubled between 1870 and 1900. Some southern farmers sought prosperity in crops other than cotton. George Washington Carver, of Alabama's Tuskegee Institute (page 574), persuaded many poor black farmers to plant peanuts. But most southern soils were too acidic and the spring rains too heavy for other legumes and grains to flourish. Parasites and diseases plagued cattle herds. Try as southerners might to diversify, cotton still dominated their economy.

Yet from 1880 to 1900 world demand for cotton grew slowly, and prices fell. As farms in other parts of the country were becoming larger, more efficient, and tended by fewer workers per acre, southern farms decreased in size. This reflected the breakup of large plantations, but it also resulted from a high birthrate. Across the country, the number of children born per mother was dropping, but in the South, large families remained common because more children meant more farmhands. Each year, fewer acres of land were available for each person to cultivate. Even though the southern economy kept pace with national growth, per capita income fell behind.

Tenancy and Sharecropping

To freedpeople across the South, the end of slavery brought hopes of economic independence. John Solomon Lewis was one farmer with such hopes. After the war Lewis rented land to grow cotton in Tensas Parish, Louisiana. A depression in the 1870s dashed his dreams. "I was in debt," Lewis explained, "and the man I rented land from said every year I must rent again to pay the other year, and so I rents and rents and each year I gets deeper and deeper in debt."

Lewis was impoverished like most small farmers in the cotton South. The South's best lands remained in the hands of large plantation owners. Few freed-

Tenancy

men or poor white southerners had money to acquire property. Like Lewis, most rented land—perhaps a plot of 15 to 20 acres—as tenants. Since cotton was king and money scarce, rents were generally set in pounds of cotton rather than dollars. Usually the amount added up to between one-quarter and one-half the value of the crop.

Among the most common and explotative forms of farm tenancy in the South was sharecropping. Unlike renters, who leased land and controlled what they raised, sharecroppers simply worked a parcel of land in exchange for a share of the crop, usually a third after debt was deducted. It was rarely enough to make ends meet and, like other forms of tenancy, left the farmer in perpetual debt. But this system would not have proved so ruinous if the South had possessed a fairer system of credit. Before selling crops in the fall, farmers without cash had to borrow money in the spring to buy seeds, tools, and other necessities. Most often, the only source of supplies was the local store. When John Solomon Lewis and other tenants entered the store, they saw two prices, one for cash and one for credit. The credit price might be as much as 60 percent higher. (By contrast, merchants in New York City seldom charged over 6 percent to buy on credit.) As security for the merchant's credit, the only asset most renters and sharecroppers could offer was a mortgage or "lien" on their crops. The lien gave the shopkeeper first claim on the crop until the debt was paid off.

Sharecropping and crop liens

Across the South, sharecropping and crop liens reduced many farmers to virtual slavery by shackling them to debt. Year after year, they rented land and borrowed against their harvests. This economic dependence, known as debt peonage, robbed small farmers of their freedom. The landlord or shopkeeper (often the same person) could insist that sharecroppers grow profitable crops like cotton rather than things they could eat. Most landlords also required that raw cotton be ginned, baled, and marketed

Debt peonage

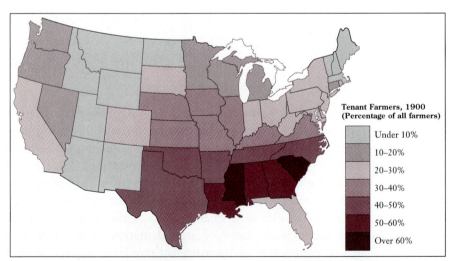

Tenant Farmers, 1900
(Percentage of all farmers)

Under 10%
10–20%
20–30%
30–40%
40–50%
50–60%
Over 60%

TENANT FARMERS, 1900   Tenant farming dominated southern agriculture after the Civil War. But notice that by 1900 it accounted for much of the farm labor in the trans-Mississippi West, where low crop prices, high costs, and severe environmental conditions forced independent farmers into tenancy.

through their mills—at a rate they controlled. "The white people do not allow us to sell our own crops," one black sharecropper remarked. "When we do, we do it at risk of our lives, getting whipped, shot at, and often some get killed." Sharecropping, crop liens, and monopolies on ginning and marketing added up to inequality and crushing poverty for the South's small farmers, black or white.

Southern Industry

The crusade for a New South did bring change. From 1869 to 1909, industrial production grew faster than the national rate. A boom in railroad building af-

Boom in textiles

ter 1879 furnished the region with good transportation. In two areas, cotton textiles and tobacco, southern advances were striking. With cotton fiber and cheap labor close at hand, 400 cotton mills were humming by 1900, when they employed almost 100,000 workers.

Most new textile workers were white southerners escaping competition from black farm laborers or fleeing the hardscrabble life of the mountains. Entire families worked in the mills. Older men had the most trouble adjusting. They lacked the experience, temperament, and dexterity to tend spindles and looms in cramped mills. Only over time, as farm folk adapted to the tedious rhythm of factories, did southerners become competitive with workers from other regions of the United States and western Europe.

The tobacco industry also thrived in the New South. Before the Civil War, American tastes had run to cigars, snuff, and chewing tobacco. In 1876, James

Tobacco and cigarettes

Bonsack invented a machine to roll cigarettes. That was just the device Washington Duke and his son James needed to boost the fortunes of their growing tobacco business. Cigarettes suited the new urban market in the North. Unlike chewing tobacco and snuff, they were, in the words of one observer, "clean, quick, and potent."

Between 1860 and 1900, Americans spent more money on tobacco than on clothes or shoes. The sudden interest in smoking offered southerners a rare opportunity to control a national market. But the factories were so hot, the stench of tobacco so strong, and the work so unskilled that native-born white southerners generally refused the jobs. Duke solved the labor problem by hiring Jewish immigrants, expert cigar makers, to train black southerners in the techniques of tobacco work. Then he promoted cigarettes in a national advertising campaign, using gimmicks like collectible picture cards. By the 1890s his American Tobacco Company led the industry.

Timber and Steel

In the postwar era, the South possessed over 60 percent of the nation's timber resources. With soaring demand from towns and cities, lumber and turpentine became the South's chief industries and employers. Aggressive lumbering, however, added little to local economies. Logging camps were isolated and temporary. Visitors described the lumberjacks as "single, homeless, and possession-less." Once loggers leveled the forests around their camps, they moved on to another site. Sawmills followed a similar pattern. Thus loggers and millers had little time to put down roots and invest their cash in the community.

The environmental costs were equally high. In the South as elsewhere, overcutting and other logging practices stripped hillsides bare. As spring rains

Environmental costs

eroded soil and unleashed floods, forests lost their capacity for self-renewal. With them went the golden eagles, peregrine falcons, and other native species.

Turpentine mills, logging, and lumbering provided young black southerners with their greatest source of employment. Occasionally an African American rose to be a supervisor, though most were white. Because the work was dirty and dangerous and required few skills, turnover was high and morale low. Workers usually left the mills for better wages or for sharecropping in order to marry and support families.

The iron and steel industry most disappointed promoters of the New South. The availability of coke as a fuel made Chattanooga, Tennessee, and Birming-

Birmingham steel

ham, Alabama, major centers for foundries. By the 1890s the Tennessee Coal, Iron, and Railway Company (TCI) of Birmingham was turning out iron pipe for gas, water, and sewer lines vital to cities. Unfortunately Birmingham's iron deposits were ill suited to produce the kinds of steel in demand. In 1907 TCI was sold to the giant U.S. Steel Corporation, controlled by northern interests.

The pattern of lost opportunity was repeated in other southern industries. Under the campaign for a New South, all grew dramatically in employment and value, but not enough to end poverty. The South remained largely rural, agricultural, and poor.

The Sources of Southern Poverty

Why did poverty persist in the New South? Many southerners claimed that the region was exploited by outside interests. In effect, they argued, the South became a colonial economy, controlled by business interests in New York or Pittsburgh, rather than Atlanta or New Orleans. Raw materials such as minerals, timber, and cotton were shipped to other regions, which earned larger profits by turning them into finished goods.

Three factors peculiar to the South offer a better explanation for the region's poverty. First, the South began to industrialize later than the Northeast,

Late start in industrializing

so northerners had a head start on learning new manufacturing techniques. Once southern workers overcame their inexperience, they competed well. Second, the South commanded only a small technological community to guide its industrial development. Northern engineers and mechanics seldom followed northern capital into the region. Few experts were available to adapt modern technology to southern conditions or to teach southerners how to do it themselves.

Education might have overcome the problem by upgrading the region's workforce. But no region in the nation spent less on schooling than the South.

Undereducated labor

Southern leaders, drawn from the ranks of the upper class, cared little about educating ordinary white residents and openly resisted educating black southerners. Education, they contended, "spoiled" otherwise contented workers by leading them to demand higher wages and better conditions. In fact, the region's low wages encouraged educated workers to leave the South in search of higher pay.

Lack of education aggravated the third and central source of southern poverty: the isolation of its labor force. In 1900 agriculture still dominated the

The isolated southern labor market

southern economy. It required unskilled, low-paid sharecroppers and wage laborers. Southerners feared outsiders, whether capitalists, industrialists, or experts in technology, who might spread discontent among workers. So southern states discouraged social services and opportunities that might have attracted human and financial resources, keeping their workforce secluded and uneducated. The South remained poor because it received too little, not too much, outside investment.

LIFE IN THE NEW SOUTH

Many a southern man, noted a son of the region, loved "to toss down a pint of raw whiskey in a gulp, to fiddle and dance all night, to bite off the nose or gouge out the eye of a favorite enemy, to fight harder and love harder than the next man, to be known far and wide as a hell of a fellow. . . ." Life in the New South was a constant struggle to balance this love of sport and leisure with the powerful pull of Christian piety.

Divided in its soul, the South was also divided by race. After the Civil War, some 90 percent of African Americans continued to live in the rural South. Without slavery, however, white southerners lost the system of social control that had defined race relations. Over time they substituted a new system of racial separation that eased, but never eliminated, white fear of black Americans.

Rural Life

Pleasure, piety, race—all divided southern life, in town and country alike. And in the country especially, where most southerners lived, life separated along lines of gender as well.

Southern males loved hunting. For rural people a successful hunt could add meat and fish to a scanty diet. Hunting also offered welcome relief from heavy

Hunting

farmwork. One South Carolinian recalled that possum hunting "gave you a wild feeling of being free." Through hunting many boys found a path to manhood. Seeing his father and brothers return with wild turkeys, young Edward McIlhenny longed "for the time when I would be old enough to hunt this bird."

The thrill of illicit pleasure drew many southern men to events of violence and chance, including cockfighting. They were convinced that their champions fought more boldly than northern bantams. Gambling between bird owners and among spectators only heightened the thrills. Such sport offended churchgoing southerners. They condemned as sinful "the beer garden, the baseball, the low theater, the dog fight and cock fight and the ring for the pugilist and brute."

On the other hand, many southern customs involved no such disorderly behavior. Work-sharing festivals celebrated the harvest and offered relief from the *Farm entertainments* daily burdens of farm life. A Mississippian spoke of "neighborhood gatherings such as house raisings, log rollings, quiltings, and road workings." These events, too, were generally segregated along gender lines. Men did the heavy chores and competed in contests of physical prowess. Women shared more domestic tasks. Quilting was a favorite, for it brought women an opportunity to work together and enjoy one another's company. Community gatherings also offered young southerners an opportunity for courtship. In one courting game, the young man who found a rare red ear of corn "could kiss the lady of his choice"—although in the school, church, or home under adult supervision, such behavior was discouraged.

For rural folk, a trip to town brought special excitement and a bit of danger. Saturdays, court days, and holidays provided an occasion to mingle. For *Town* men the saloon, the blacksmith shop, or the storefront was a place to do business and to let off steam. Few men went to town without participating in social drinking. When they turned to roam the streets, the threat of brawling and violence drove most women away. One Tennessee woman claimed that "it was never considered safe for a lady to go down on the streets on Saturdays."

Court week drew the biggest crowds as a district judge arrived to mete out rough justice. Some people came to settle disputes; most came to enjoy the spectacle or do some business like horse trading. Peddlers and entertainers worked the crowds with magic tricks, patent medicines, and other wares. Town also offered a chance to attend the theater or a traveling circus.

The Church

At the center of southern life stood the church as a great stabilizer and custodian of social order. "When one joined the Methodist church," a southern woman recalled, "he was expected to give up all such things as cards, dancing, theatres, in fact all so called worldly amusements." Many devout southerners pursued these ideals, although such restraint asked more of people, especially men, than most were willing to show, except perhaps on Sunday.

For Baptists in the South, the ceremony of adult baptism included immersion, often in a nearby river. The ritual symbolized the waters of newfound faith washing away sins. Here, a black congregation looks on, some holding umbrellas to protect against the sun.

Congregations were often so small and isolated they could attract a preacher only once or twice a month. Evangelicals counted on the Sunday sermon to *Rural religion* steer them from sin. In town, a sermon might last 30 to 45 minutes, but in the country, a preacher could go on for two hours or more, whipping up his congregation until "even the little children wept."

By 1870 southern churches were segregated by race (see page 455). Congregations, particularly in rural areas, were separated by gender, too. Upon seeing a man and woman seated together, a Virginia Baptist claimed "they were from Richmond or Lynchburg, or some other city where folks did not know any better." Churches were female domains. Considered guardians of virtue, women made up a majority of members, attended church more often, and ran many church activities.

Church was a place to socialize as well as worship. Church picnics and all-day sings brought people together for hours of eating, talk, services, and hymn singing. Still, these occasions could not match the fervor of a week-long camp meeting. In the late summer or early fall, town and countryside alike emptied as folks set up tents in shady groves and listened to two or three ministers preach day and night, in the largest event of the year. The camp meeting re-fired evangelical faith while celebrating traditional values of home and family.

Segregation

After Reconstruction, white northerners and southerners achieved sectional harmony by sacrificing the rights of black citizens. White southerners were assured that in matters of race they would be "left alone" by the federal government. The hands-off, or laissez-faire, approach also suited even white northerners who had once championed black rights. The editor of one magazine published in New York told northern readers that he doubted whether former slaves were capable of participating in "a system of government for which you and I have much respect." In the New South, African Americans would remain free but scarcely equal.

Laissez-faire race relations

During the 1880s, Redeemer governments (pages 461–462) moved to formalize a new system of segregation or racial separation. The pressure to do so increased as more African Americans moved into southern towns and cities, competing for jobs with poor whites. One way to preserve the social and economic superiority of white southerners, poor as well as rich, was to separate blacks as an inferior caste. But federal laws designed to enforce the Civil Rights Act of 1866 and the Fourteenth Amendment stood in the way. In effect, they established social equality for all races in public places such as hotels, theaters, and railroads.

In 1883, however, the Supreme Court ruled in the *Civil Rights Cases* that hotels and railroads were not "public" institutions because private individuals owned them. The Fourteenth Amendment was thus limited to protecting citizens from violations of their civil rights only by states, not by private individuals. The national policy of laissez faire in race relations could not have been made any clearer.

Within 20 years every southern state had enacted segregation as law. The earliest laws legalized segregation in trains and other public conveyances. Soon a web of "Jim Crow" statutes separated the races in almost all public places except streets and stores. (The term "Jim Crow," to denote a policy of segregation, originated in a song of the same name sung in minstrel shows of the day.) In 1896, the Supreme Court again upheld the policy of segregation. *Plessy v. Ferguson* upheld a Louisiana law requiring segregated railroad facilities. Racial separation did not constitute discrimination, the Court argued, so long as accommodations for both races were equal. In reality, of course, such separate facilities were seldom equal and always stigmatized African Americans.

Jim Crow laws

Plessy v. Ferguson

By the turn of the century segregation was firmly in place, stifling economic competition between the races and reducing African Americans to second-class citizenship. Many kinds of employment, such as work in the textile mills, went largely to whites. Skilled and professional black workers generally served black clients only. Blacks could enter some white residences only as servants and hired help, and then only by the back door. They were barred from juries and usually received far stiffer penalties than whites for the same crimes. Any African

American who crossed the color line risked violence. Some were tarred and feathered, others whipped and beaten, and many lynched. Of the 187 lynchings averaged each year of the 1890s, some 80 percent occurred in the South, where the victims were usually black.

WESTERN FRONTIERS

The black Exodusters flooding into the treeless plains of Kansas in the 1870s and 1880s were only part of the vast migration west. Looking beyond the Mississippi in the 1840s and 1850s, "overlanders" had set their sights on California and Oregon and the promise of land. So they headed into the trans-Mississippi West, pushing the frontier of Anglo settlement to the edge of the continent. They rolled over the Great Plains, through the snow-capped Rockies, and across the Great Basin, with deserts so dry rain sometimes evaporated before hitting the ground. When they reached the fertile valleys of the coast, they were ready, as one Oregonian immigrant proclaimed, "to seek their fortunes and settle an empire."

The overlanders went west in search of opportunity and "free" land. In the trans-Mississippi West, however, opportunity proved elusive to those without

Moving frontiers

money or power. They also found Indians and "Hispanos" (settlers of Spanish descent), who hardly considered the land free for use by Anglos. They discovered that the West was not one region but many, each governed by a different ecology. And its frontiers moved in many directions, not just from east to west. Before the Civil War, the frontier for easterners had moved beyond the Mississippi to the timberlands of Missouri, but skipped over the Great Plains, as the overlanders settled in California and Oregon. Another frontier then pushed east from the Pacific coast, following miners into the Sierra Nevadas. For Texans, the frontier moved from south to north as cattle ranchers sought new grazing land, as had the ancestors of the Hispanic *rancheros* of the Southwest. And for American Indians, the frontier was constantly shifting and disrupting their ways of life.

COUNTERPOINT   *How to Define the Frontier*

For historian Frederick Jackson Turner, writing in the 1890s, the West was not many frontiers but one. He defined it as a westward-moving line, "the meeting point of savagery and civilization." For Turner, the frontier represented the march of progress into isolated areas of "free land." Its significance in American history—as social safety valve, as cradle of democracy, as fountain of American self-reliance and sense of community— could no longer be ignored.

Modern historians have rejected this "Turner thesis," though not the importance of the West in American history. In the ethnocentric fashion of his day, Turner ignored the presence of rich Hispanic and Indian cultures beyond the bounds of Anglo settlement, just as he ignored the important role of women in the West. Where Turner saw a westward-moving frontier along which savagery met civilization, modern historians see a "new West" of conflict and conquest, of opportunity and cultural interplay along a series of shifting borders.

The Western Landscape

Early travellers from the United States labelled the vast lands beyond the Mississippi the "Great American Desert"—with good reason. Most of the region between the 98th meridian and the West Coast receives fewer than 20 inches of rain a year, making the Great Plains a treeless expanse of prairie grass and dunes. But the plains are only part of the trans-Mississippi West. And even they can be divided. The Great Plains west of the 98th meridian are semi-arid, but the eastern Prairie Plains are favored with good soil and abundant rain. Beyond the plains the jagged peaks of the Rocky Mountains stretch from Alaska to New Mexico. And beyond the mountains lies the Great Basin of Utah, Nevada, and eastern California, where temperatures climb above 100 degrees and the ground cracks. Near the coast rise the Sierra Nevadas and Cascades, rich in minerals and lumber and sloping to the temperate shores of the Pacific.

Already by the 1840s, the Great Plains and mountain frontier comprised a complex web of cultures and environments. The horse, for example, had been introduced into North America by the colonial Spanish. By the eighteenth century horses were grazing on prairie grass across the Great Plains. By the nineteenth century the Comanche, Cheyenne, Apache, and other tribes had become master riders and hunters, who could shoot their arrows with deadly accuracy at a full gallop. The new mobility of the Plains Indians far extended the area in which they could hunt buffalo. Their lives shifted from settled, village-centered agriculture to a more nomadic existence.

Indian Peoples and the Western Environment

Some whites embraced the myth of the Indian as "noble savage" who lived in perfect harmony with the natural world. To be sure, Plains Indians were inventive in using scarce resources. Cottonwood bark fed horses in winter, while the buffalo supplied not only meat but also bones for tools, fat for cosmetics, and sinews for thread. Yet Indians could not help but alter their environment. Plains Indians hunted buffalo by stampeding herds over cliffs, which often led to waste. They irrigated crops and set fires to improve vegetation. By the mid-nineteenth century some tribes had become so enmeshed in the white fur trade that they overtrapped their own hunting grounds. In these and other ways, Indians altered the ecological systems around them.

Ecosystems, in turn, helped shape Indian cultures. Although big-game hunting was common among many western tribes, the nomadic buffalo culture of the Plains Indians was hardly representative. In the lush forests and mountain ranges of the Pacific Northwest, Yuroks, Chinook, and other tribes hunted bear, moose, elk, and deer. Along the rocky coast they took whales, seals, and a variety of fish from the ocean. The Yakimas and Walla Wallas moved into the river valleys for the great salmon runs. Elsewhere, with land less bountiful, Indian tribes lived close to starvation. Utes, Shoshones, Paiutes, and Pavistos scoured the deserts of the Great Basin to eke out a diet of rabbits, snakes, insects, roots, and berries.

Variety of Indian cultures

Despite their diversity, Indian peoples shared certain values. Most tribes were small kinship groups of 300 to 500 people in which the well-being of all outweighed the needs of each member. Although some tribes were materially better off than others, the gap between rich and poor within tribes was seldom large. Such small material differences often promoted communal decision making. The Cheyenne, for example, employed a council of 44 to advise the chief.

Shared values

Most of all, Indians shared a reverence for nature, whatever their actual impact on the natural world. They believed human beings were part of an interconnected world of animals, plants, and other natural elements. All had souls of their own but were bound together, as if by contract, to live in balance through the ceremonial life of the tribe and the customs related to specific plants and animals. The Taos of New Mexico believed that each spring the pregnant earth issued new life. To avoid disturbing "mother" earth, they removed the hard shoes from their horses and walked themselves in bare feet or soft moccasins.

Such regard for the land endowed special places with religious meaning utterly foreign to most whites. Where the Sioux saw in the Black Hills the sacred home of Wakan Tanka, the burial place of the dead, and the site of their "vision quests," whites saw grass for grazing and gold for the taking. From such contrasting views came conflict.

Whites and the Western Environment: Competing Visions

As discoveries of gold and silver lured white settlers into Indian territory, many adopted the confident outlook of Missouri politician William Gilpin. Only a lack of vision prevented the opening of the West for exploitation, Gilpin told an Independence, Missouri, audience in 1849. What was most needed were cheap lands and a railroad linking the two coasts "like ears on a human head." In his expansive view, Indians were just another impediment to overcome.

William Gilpin, a western booster

By 1868 a generous Congress had granted western settlers their two greatest wishes: free land under the Homestead Act of 1862, and a transcontinental railroad. As the new governor of Colorado, Gilpin crowed about the region's limitless resources. One day, he believed, the West would support more than a billion peo-

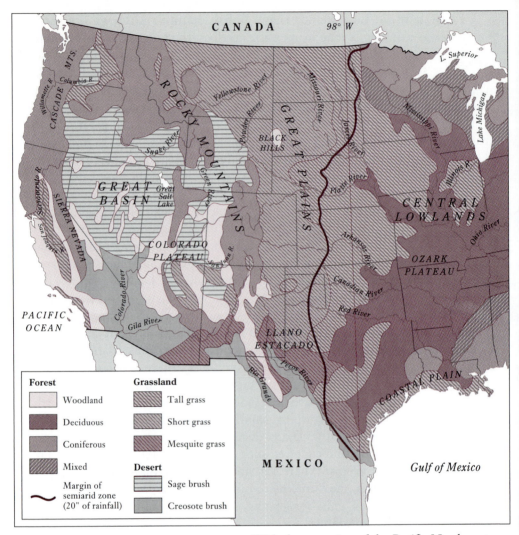

NATURAL ENVIRONMENT OF THE WEST   With the exception of the Pacific Northwest, few areas west of the 20-inch rainfall line receive enough annual precipitation to support agriculture without irrigation. Consequently water has been the key to development west of the 98th meridian, encompassing more than half the country.

ple. Scarce rainfall and water did not daunt him, for in his eyes the West was an Eden-like garden, not a desert. Once the land had been planted, Gilpin assured listeners, the rains would develop naturally. He subscribed to the popular notion that "rain follows the plow."

Unlike the visionary Gilpin, John Wesley Powell knew something about water and farming. After losing an arm in the Civil War, geologist Powell came

John Wesley Powell

west. In 1869 and 1871 he led scientific expeditions down the Green and Colorado rivers through the Grand Canyon. Navigating the swirling rapids that blocked his way, he returned to warn Congress that developing the West required more scientific planning. Much of the region had not yet been mapped nor its resources identified.

In 1880 Powell became director of the recently formed U.S. Geological Survey. He, too, had a vision of the West, but one based on the limits of its en-

Water as a key resource

vironment. The key was water, not land. In the water-rich East, the English legal tradition of river rights prevailed. Whoever owned the banks of a river or stream controlled as much water as they might take, regardless of the consequence for those downstream. Such a practice in the West, Powell recognized, would enrich the small number with access to water while spelling ruin for the rest.

The alternative was to treat water as community property. The practice would benefit many rather than a privileged few. To that end Powell suggested that the federal government establish political boundaries defined by watersheds and regulate the distribution of the scarce resource. But his scientific realism could not overcome the popular vision of the West as the American Eden. Powerful interests ensured that development occurred with the same laissez-faire credo that ruled the East.

THE WAR FOR THE WEST

Beginning in 1848, a series of gold and silver discoveries signaled the first serious interest by white settlers in the arid and semiarid lands beyond

Policy of concentration

the Mississippi. To open more land, federal officials introduced in 1851 a policy of "concentration." Tribes were pressured into signing treaties limiting the boundaries of their hunting grounds—the Sioux to the Dakotas, the Crow to Montana, the Cheyenne to the foothills of Colorado. Such treaties often claimed that their provisions would last "as long as waters run," but time after time, land-hungry pioneers broke the promises of their government by squatting on Indian lands and demanding federal protection. The government, in turn, forced more restrictive agreements on the western tribes. This cycle of promises made and broken was repeated, until a full-scale war for the West raged between whites and Indians.

Contact and Conflict

By 1862 the lands of the Santee Sioux had been whittled down to a strip 10 miles wide and 150 miles long along the Minnesota River. Lashing out in frustration, the tribe attacked several undefended white settlements along the Minnesota frontier. In response, General John Pope arrived in St. Paul declaring his intention to wipe out the Sioux. "They are to be treated as maniacs or

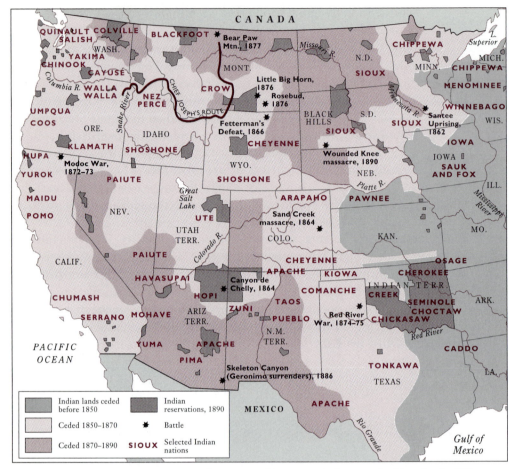

THE INDIAN FRONTIER As conflict erupted between Indians and whites in the West, the government pursued a policy of concentrating tribes on reservations. Indian resistance helped unite the Sioux and Cheyenne, traditionally enemies, in the Dakotas in the 1870s.

wild beasts and by no means as people," he instructed his officers. When Pope's forces captured 1800 Sioux, white Minnesotans were outraged that President Lincoln ordered only 38 hanged.

The campaign under General Pope was the opening of a guerrilla war that continued off and on for some 30 years. The conflict gained momentum in

Chivington massacre

November 1864, when a force of Colorado volunteers under Colonel John Chivington fell upon a band of friendly Cheyenne gathered at Sand Creek under army protection. Chief Black Kettle raised an American flag to signal friendship, but Chivington would have none of it. "Kill and scalp all, big and little," he told his men. The troops massacred well over 100, including children holding white flags of truce and mothers with babies in their arms. In 1865 virtually all Plains Indians joined in the First Sioux War to drive whites from their lands.

War was only one of several ways in which contact with whites undermined tribal cultures. Liquor and disease, including smallpox, measles, and cholera, killed more Indians than combat. On the Great Plains the railroad disrupted the migratory patterns of the buffalo and thus the patterns of the hunt. Tourist parties came west to bag the buffalo from railside. When hides became popular back East, commercial companies hired hunters who killed more than 100 bison an hour. Military commanders promoted the butchery as a way of weakening Indian resistance. In three short years, from 1872 to 1874, approximately 9 million members of the herd were slaughtered. By 1883 bison had nearly disappeared from the plains. In other areas mines, crops, grazing herds, and fences disturbed traditional hunting and farming lands of many tribes.

Custer's Last Stand—And the Indians

The Sioux War ended in 1868 with the signing of the Treaty of Fort Laramie. It established two large Indian reservations, one in Oklahoma and the other in the Dakota Badlands. Only six years later, however, Colonel George Armstrong Custer led an expedition into *Paha Sapa*, the sacred Black Hills of the Sioux. In doing so, he flagrantly disregarded the treaty of 1868. Custer, a Civil War veteran, already had a reputation as a "squaw killer" for his cruel warfare against Indians in western Kansas. To open the Black Hills to whites, his expedition spread rumors of gold "from the grass roots down." Prospectors poured into Indian country. Federal authorities tried to force yet another treaty to gain control of the Black Hills. When negotiations failed, President Grant ordered all "hostiles" in the area driven onto the reservations.

In reaction the Cheyenne for the first time allied with the Sioux, who were led by the young war chief Crazy Horse and medicine man Sitting Bull. Against

Battle of Little Big Horn

them in the summer of 1876 marched several army columns, including Custer's Seventh Cavalry of about 600 troops. Custer, eager for glory, arrived at the Little Big Horn River a day earlier than the other columns. Hearing of a native village nearby, he attacked, only to discover that he had stumbled onto an encampment of more than 12,000 Sioux and Cheyenne, extending for almost three miles. From a deep ravine Crazy Horse charged Custer, killing him and some 250 soldiers.

As he led the attack, Crazy Horse yelled "It is a good day to die!"—the traditional war cry. Even in the midst of victory he spoke truly. Although Custer had been conquered, railroads stood ready to extend their lines, prospectors to make fortunes, and soldiers to protect them. By late summer the Sioux were forced to split into small bands in order to evade the army. While Sitting Bull barely escaped to Canada, Crazy Horse and 800 with him surrendered in 1876 after a winter of suffering and starvation.

The battles along the Platte and upper Missouri rivers did not end the war between whites and Indians, but never again would it reach such proportions. Even peaceful tribes like the Nez Percé of Idaho found no security once whites began to hunger for their land. The Nez Percé had become breeders of livestock, rich in horses and cattle that they grazed in the meadows west of the Snake River canyon. That did not prevent the government from trying to force them onto a small reservation in 1877.

Rather than see his people humiliated, Chief Joseph led almost 600 Nez Percé toward Canada, pursued by the U.S. Army. In 75 days they traveled more

Chief Joseph

than 1300 miles. Every time the army closed to attack, Chief Joseph's warriors drove them off. But before they could reach the border, they were trapped and forced to surrender. The government then shipped the defeated tribe to the bleak Indian Country of Oklahoma. There disease and starvation finished the destruction the army had begun.

Killing with Kindness

By 1887 reformers recognized that the policy of concentrating Indians on reservations had failed. With a mix of good intentions and unbridled greed, Congress

The Dawes Act

adopted the Dawes Severalty Act in 1887. It ended reservation policy with the goals of drawing Indians into white society as farmers and small property owners and (less high-mindedly) their lands into the marketplace. Lands held by tribes would now be parceled out to individuals: 160 acres to the head of a family and 80 acres to single adults or orphans.

In practice, the Dawes Act was more destructive than any blow struck by the army. It undermined the communal structure upon which Indian tribal life was based. And as John Wesley Powell had warned, small homestead farms in the West could not support a family—white or Indian—unless they were irrigated. Most Indians, moreover, had no experience with farming, managing money, or other white ways. The sponsors of the Dawes Act, knowing that whites might swindle Indians out of their private holdings, arranged for the government to hold title to the land for 25 years, but that did not stop unscrupulous speculators from "leasing" lands. Furthermore, all reservation lands not allocated to Indians were opened to non-Indian homesteaders.

Against such a dismal future, some Indians sought solace in the past. In 1890 a religious revival spread when word came from the Nevada desert that a

Wounded Knee

humble Paiute named Wovoka had received revelations from the Great Spirit. Wovoka preached that if his followers adopted his mystical rituals and lived together in love and harmony, the Indian dead would come back, whites would be driven from the land, and game would be thick again. As the rituals spread, alarmed settlers called the strange shuffling and chanting the "Ghost Dance." The army moved to stop the proceedings among the Sioux for fear of another uprising. At Wounded Knee in South Dakota the

E Y E W I T N E S S   T O   H I S T O R Y

An Indian Girl Is Shorn at Boarding School

Late in the morning, my friend Judewin gave me a terrible warning. . . . She heard the paleface woman talk about cutting our long, heavy hair. Our mothers had taught us that only unskilled warriors who were captured had their hair shingled by the enemy. Among our people, short hair was worn by mourners, and shingled hair by cowards!

We discussed our fate some moments, and when Judewin said, "We have to submit, because they are strong," I rebelled.

"No, I will not submit! I will struggle first!" I answered.

I watched my chance, and when no one noticed I disappeared, I crept up the stairs as quietly as I could in my squeaking shoes—my moccasins had been exchanged for shoes. . . . Turning aside to an open door, I found a large room with three white beds in it. . . . On my hands and knees I crawled under [a] bed, and cuddled myself in the dark corner.

From my hiding place I peered out. . . . Loud voices were calling my name, and I knew that even Judewin was searching for me. . . . Then the steps were quickened and the voices became excited. . . . Women and girls entered the room. I held my breath and watched them open closet doors and peep behind large trunks. . . . What caused them to stoop and look under the bed I do not know. I remember being dragged out, though I resisted by kicking and scratching wildly. In spite of myself, I was carried downstairs and tied fast in a chair.

I cried aloud, shaking my head all the while until I felt the cold blades on the scissors against my neck, and heard them gnaw off one of my thick braids. Then I lost my spirit. Since the day I was taken from my mother I had suffered extreme indignities. People had stared at me. I had been tossed about in the air like a wooden puppet. And now my long hair was shingled like a coward's! In my anguish I moaned for my mother, but no one came to comfort me. Not a soul reasoned quietly with me, as my own mother used to do; for now I was only one of many little animals driven by a herder.

Zitkala-Sa (Gertrude Simmons Bonnin), "The School Days of an Indian Girl," *Atlantic Monthly*, Vol. 89 (1900) January–March, pp. 45–47, 190, 192–194.

cavalry fell upon one band and with devastating artillery fire killed at least 146 men, women, and children.

Wounded Knee was a final act of violence against an independent Indian way of life. After 1890 the battle was over assimilation, not extinction. The system of markets, rail networks, and extractive industries was linking the Far West with the rest of the nation. Free-roaming bison were replaced by herded cattle and sheep, nomadic tribes by prairie sodbusters, and sacred hunting grounds by gold fields. Reformers relied on education, citizenship, and allotments to move Indians from their communal lives into white society. Most Indians were equally determined to preserve their tribal ways and separateness as a people.

Borderlands

The coming of the railroad in the 1880s and 1890s brought wrenching changes to the Southwest as well, with a twist. As new markets and industries sprang up, new settlers poured in from the east but also from the south, across the Mexican border. Indians like the Navajo and the Apache thus faced the hostility of Anglos *and* Hispanos, those settlers of Spanish descent already in the region.

Like Indians, Hispanos discovered that they had either to embrace or to resist the flood of new Anglos. The elite, or *Ricos*, often aligned themselves with

Juan José Herrera and the White Caps

Anglos against their countryfolk to protect their status and property. Others, including Juan José Herrera, resisted the newcomers. When Anglo cattle ranchers began forcing Hispanos off their lands near Las Vegas, Herrera assembled a band of masked night riders known as *Las Gorras Blancas* (the White Caps). In 1889 and 1890 as many as 700 White Caps burned Anglo fences, haystacks, and occasionally barns and houses, and attacked railroads that refused to raise the low wages of Hispano workers.

New Anglos frequently fought Hispanos. But it was western lawyers and politicians, using legal tactics, who deprived Hispanos of most of their property. Thomas Catron, an ambitious New Mexico lawyer, squeezed out many Hispanos by contesting land titles so aggressively that his holdings grew to 3 million acres. In those areas of New Mexico and California where they remained a majority, Hispanos continued to play a role in public life. During the early 1890s Herrera and his allies formed a "People's Party," swept local elections, and managed to defeat a bid by Catron to represent the territory in Congress.

With the railroads came more white settlers, as well as Mexican laborers from south of the border. Just as the southern economy depended on African

Mexican immigrants

American labor, the Southwest grew on the labor of Mexicans. Mexican immigrants worked mostly as contract and seasonal laborers for railroads and large farms. Many of them settled in the growing cities along the rail lines: El Paso, Albuquerque, Tucson, Phoenix, and Los Angeles. They lived in segregated *barrios*, Spanish towns, where their cultural traditions persisted. But by the late nineteenth century, most

Hispanics, whether in barrios or on farms and ranches, had been excluded from power.

Yet to focus on cities alone would distort the experience of most southwesterners of Spanish descent, who lived in small villages like those in northern New Mexico and southern Colorado. There a pattern of adaptation and resistance to Anglo penetration developed. As the market economy advanced, Hispanic villagers turned to migratory labor to adapt. While women continued to work in the old villages, men traveled from job to job in mining, in farming, and on the railroads. The resulting "regional communities" of village and migrant workers allowed Hispanic residents to preserve the communal culture of the village, incorporating those aspects of Anglo culture—like the sewing machine—that suited their needs. At the same time, the regional community also sustained migrant workers with a base of operations and a haven to which they could return in protest against harsh working conditions.

BOOM AND BUST IN THE WEST

Opportunity in the West lay in land and resources, but wealth also accumulated in the towns. Each time a speculative fever hit a region, new communities sprouted to serve those who rushed in. The western boom began in mining—with the California Gold Rush of 1849 and the rise of San Francisco (see page 367). In the decades that followed, new hordes threw up towns in Park City, Utah; Tombstone, Arizona; Deadwood in the Dakota Territories; and other promising sites. All too often, busts followed booms, transforming boom towns into ghost towns.

Mining Sets a Pattern

The gold and silver strikes of the 1840s and 1850s set a pattern followed by other booms. Stories of easy riches attracted single prospectors with their shovels and wash pans. Almost all were male and nearly half foreign-born. Muddy mining camps sprang up, where a prospector could register a claim, get provisions, bathe, and buy a drink or a companion. Outfitting these boom societies siphoned riches into the pockets of storeowners and other suppliers. Once the quick profits were gone, a period of consolidation brought more order to towns and larger scale to regional businesses.

In the mine fields, that meant corporations with the capital for hydraulic water jets to blast ore loose and other heavy equipment to crush rock and ex-

Environmental costs   tract silver and gold from deeper veins. In their quest for quick profits, such operations often led to environmental disaster. Floods, mud slides, and dirty streams threatened the livelihood of farmers in the valleys below.

In corporate mining operations, paid laborers replaced the independent prospectors of earlier days. As miners sought better wages and working conditions, along with shorter hours, management fought back. In Coeur d'Alene, Idaho, troops crushed a strike in 1892, killing seven miners. The miners, in turn, created the Western Federation of Miners. In the decade after 1893 the union attracted some 50,000 members and gained a reputation for militancy. In a cycle repeated elsewhere, the rowdy mining frontier of small-scale prospectors was integrated into the industrial system of wage labor, large-scale resource extraction, and high finance capital.

The Transcontinental Railroad

As William Gilpin predicted in 1849, the development of the West awaited the railroads. Before the Central and Union Pacific railroads were joined in 1869, travel across the West was slow and dusty. Vast distances and sparse population gave entrepreneurs little chance to follow the eastern practice of building local railroads from city to city.

In 1862 Congress granted the Central Pacific Railroad the right to build the western link of the transcontinental railroad eastward from Sacramento. To the Union Pacific Corporation fell responsibility for the section from Omaha westward. Generous loans and gifts of federal and state lands made the venture wildly profitable. For every mile of track completed, the rail companies received between 200 and 400 square miles of land—some 45 million acres by the time the route was completed. Fraudulent stock practices, corrupt accounting, and wholesale bribery (involving a vice president of the United States and at least two members of Congress) swelled profits even more. More than 75 western railroads eventually benefited from such government generosity before the lines were linked at Promontory Point, Utah, on May 10, 1869.

Railroad land grants

General Grenville Dodge, an army engineer on leave to the Union Pacific, recruited his immense labor force from Irish and other European immigrants. Charles Crocker of the Central Pacific relied on some 10,000 Chinese laborers. With wheelbarrows, picks, shovels, and baskets they inched eastward, building trestles like the one at Secrettown (see page 547) and chipping away at the Sierras' looming granite walls.

As the railroads pushed west in the 1860s, they helped to spawn cities like Denver and later awakened sleepy communities such as Los Angeles. Railroads opened the Great Plains to cattle drives that in the 1870s brought great herds to "cow towns" like Sedalia, Missouri, and Cheyenne, Wyoming, where cattle could be shipped to market. The rail companies recognized the strategic position they held. Just by threatening to bypass a town, a railroad could extract concessions on rights of way, taxes, and loans. If a key to profiting from the gold rush was supplying miners, one way to prosper from the West was to control transportation. That was why westerners developed such mixed feelings toward the railroads.

The power of the railroads

Trestles for the transcontinental railroad at Secrettown. Nearly 10,000 Chinese laborers, some pictured above, chipped away with picks and shovels at the granite walls of the Sierra Nevadas.

Cattle Kingdom

Westerners recognized that railroads were crucial components of the cattle industry. Cow towns like Abilene, Denver, and Cheyenne flourished from the business of the growing cattle kingdom. By 1860, some 5 million head of longhorn cattle were wandering the grassy plains of Texas. Ranchers allowed their herds to roam the unbroken or "open" range freely, identified only by a distinctive brand. Each spring cowboys rounded up the herds, branded the calves, and selected the steers to send to market.

Anglo-Americans who came to Texas readily adopted the Mexican equipment: the tough mustangs and broncos (horses suited to managing mean-spirited longhorns), the branding iron for marking the herds, the corral for holding cattle, and the *riata*, or lariat, for roping. The cowboys also wore Mexican chaps, spurs, and broad-brimmed *sombrero*, or "hat that provides shade." After the Civil War, veterans of the Confederate army made up the majority of the cowhands in Texas. But at least a third of all cowboys were Mexicans and black freedmen.

Mexican ranching techniques

In 1866, as rail lines swept west, Texas ranchers began driving their herds north to railheads for shipment to market. These "long drives" lasted two to three months and might cover more than 1000 miles. When early routes to Sedalia, Missouri, proved unfriendly, ranchers scouted alternatives. The

Chisholm Trail led from San Antonio to Abilene and Ellsworth in Kansas. More westerly routes ran to Dodge City and even Denver and Cheyenne.

Since cattle grazed on the open range, early ranches were primitive. Most had a house for the rancher and his family, a bunkhouse for the hired hands,

Home on the range

and about 30 to 40 acres per animal. Women were scarce in the cattle kingdom. Most were ranchers' wives, who cooked, nursed the sick, and helped run things. Some women ranched themselves. When Helen Wiser Stewart of Nevada learned that her husband had

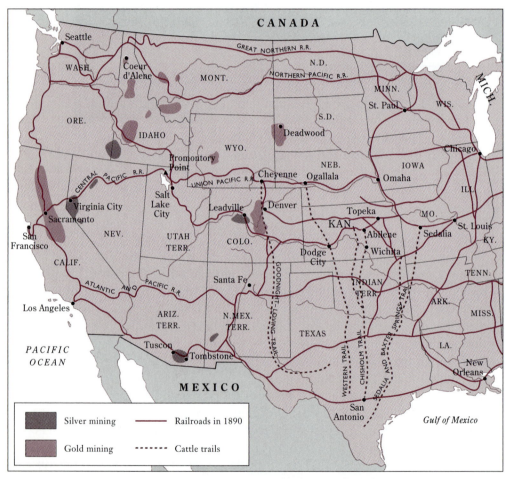

THE MINING AND CATTLE FRONTIERS   Railroads, cattle trails, and gold mines usually preceded the arrival of enough settlers to establish a town. Cattle trails ended at rail lines, where cattle could be shipped to city markets. By transecting the plains, railroads disrupted the migratory patterns of the buffalo, undermining Indian cultures and opening the land to grazing and farming.

been murdered, she took over the ranch. Her life was an endless round of buying and selling cattle, managing the hands, and tending to family and crops.

Farmers looking for their own homesteads soon became rivals to the cattle ranchers. The "nesters," as ranchers disdainfully called them, fenced off their lands, thus shrinking the open range. Vast grants to the railroads also limited the area of free land, while ranchers intent on breeding heavier cattle with more tender beef began to fence in their stock to prevent them from mixing with inferior strays. Conflicts also arose between cattle ranchers and herders of another animal introduced by the Mexicans: sheep. Sheep cropped grasses so short that they ruined land for cattle grazing. On one occasion enraged cattlemen clubbed 8000 sheep to death along the Green River in Wyoming. The feuds often burst into range wars, some more violent than those between farmers and ranchers.

Ranchers came to expect profits of 25 to 40 percent a year. As in all booms, however, forces were at work bringing the inevitable bust. High profits soon swelled the size of the herds and led to overproduction. Increased competition from cattle producers in Canada and Argentina caused beef prices to fall. And in the end, nature imposed its own limits on the boom. There was simply not enough grass along the trails to support the millions of head on their way to market. Then in 1886 and 1887 came two of the coldest winters in recorded history. The winds brought blizzards that drove wandering herds up against fences, where they either froze or starved to death. Summer brought no relief. Heat and drought scorched the grasslands and dried up waterholes. In the Dakotas, Montana, Colorado, and Wyoming, losses ran as high as 90 percent.

Western boom and bust

By the 1890s the open range and the long drives had largely vanished. What prevailed were the larger cattle corporations like the King Ranch of Texas. Only they had enough capital to acquire and fence vast grazing lands, hire ranchers to manage herds, and pay for feed during winter months. As for the cowboys, most became wage laborers employed by the ranching corporations. As with mining, the eastern pattern of economic concentration and labor specialization was being applied in the West.

THE FINAL FRONTIER

In the 1860s they had come in a trickle; in the 1870s they became a torrent. They were farmers from the East and Midwest, black freedmen from the rural South, and peasant-born immigrants from Europe. What bound them together was a craving for land. They had read railroad and steamship advertisements and heard stories from friends about millions of free acres in the plains west of the 98th meridian. Hardier strands of wheat like the "Turkey Red" (imported from Russia) improved machinery, and new farming methods made it possible to raise crops in what once had been called the "Great American Desert." The number of farms in the United States jumped from around 2 million on the eve of the Civil War to almost 6 million in 1900.

Farming on the Plains

Farmers looking to plow the plains faced a daunting task. Under the Homestead Act, government land could be bought for $1.25 an acre, or claimed free if a homesteader worked it for five years. But the best parcels—near a railroad line, with access to eastern markets—were owned by the railroads themselves or by speculators, and sold for around $25 an acre. Furthermore, successful farming on the plains demanded expensive machinery. Steel-tipped plows and harrows (which left a blanket of dust to keep moisture from evaporating too quickly) permitted "dry farming" in arid climates. Threshers, combines, and harvesters brought in the crop, while steam tractors pulled the heavy equipment.

With little rain, many farmers had to install windmills and pumping equipment to draw water from deep underground. The threat of cattle trampling the fields forced farmers to erect fences. Lacking wood, they found the answer in barbed wire, first marketed in 1874. When all was said and done, the average farmer spent what was for the poor a small fortune, about $785 on machinery and another $500 for land. Bigger operators invested 10 or 20 times as much.

Tracts of 160 acres granted under the Homestead Act might be enough for eastern farms, but in the drier West more land was needed to produce the same
Bonanza farms   harvest. Farms of more than 1000 acres, known as "bonanza farms," were most common in the wheatlands of the northern plains. A steam tractor working a bonanza farm could plow, harrow, and seed up to 50 acres a day—20 times more than a single person could do without machinery. Against such competition, small-scale farmers could scarcely survive. As in the South, many westerners became tenants on land owned by others. Bonanza farmers hired as many as 250 laborers to work each 10,000 acres in return for room, board, and 50 cents a day in wages.

A Plains Existence

For poor farm families, life on the plains meant sod houses or dugouts carved from hillsides for protection against the wind. Tough, root-bound sod was cut into bricks a foot wide and three feet long and laid edgewise to create walls; sod bricks covered rafters for a roof. The average house was seldom more than 18 by 24 feet and in severe weather had to accommodate animals as well as people. One door and a single window provided light and air. The thick walls kept the house warm in winter and cool in summer, but a heavy, soaking rain or snow could bring the roof down, or drip mud and water into the living area.

The heaviest burdens fell to women. With stores and supplies scarce, they spent long days over hot tubs preparing tallow wax for candles or soaking ashes

Plains women and boiling lye with grease and pork rinds to make soap. In the early years of settlement wool was in such short supply that resourceful women used hair from wolves and other wild animals to make cloth. Buttons had to be fashioned from old wooden spoons. Without doctors, women learned how to care for the hurt and sick, treating anything from frostbite to snakebite to burns and rheumatism.

Nature imposed added hardships. Blizzards swept the plains, piling snow to the rooftops and halting all travel. Weeks would pass before farm families saw an outsider. In the summers, searing winds blasted the plains for weeks. Grasses grew so dry that a single spark could ignite thousands of acres. Farmers in the Southwest lived in dread of stinging centipedes and scorpions that inhabited wall cracks. From Missouri to Oregon, nothing spelled disaster like locusts. They descended without warning in swarms 100 miles long. Beating against houses like hailstones, they stripped all vegetation, including the bark of trees. An entire year's labor might be destroyed in a day.

In the face of such hardships many westerners found comfort in religion. Indians turned to traditional spiritualism, Hispanics to the Catholic Church, as *Religion* a means of coping with nature and change. Though Catholics and Jews came West, evangelical Protestants dominated the Anglo frontier in the mining towns and in other western communities. Worship offered an emotional outlet, intellectual stimulation, a means of preserving old values and sustaining hope. As in the rural South, circuit riders compensated for the shortage of preachers, while camp meetings offered the chance to socialize. Both brought contact with a world beyond the prairie. In many communities it was the churches that first instilled order on public life. Through church committees westerners could deal with local problems like the need for schools or charity for the poor.

The Urban Frontier

Not all westerners lived in such isolation. By 1890, the percentage of those living in cities of 10,000 or more was greater than in any other section of the country except the Northeast.

Some western cities—San Antonio, El Paso, Los Angeles—were old Spanish towns whose growth had been reignited by the westward march of Anglo migrants, the northward push of Mexican immigrants, and the spread of railroads. Other cities, like Portland near the Columbia River in Oregon, blossomed because they stood astride commercial routes. Still others, such as Witchita, Kansas, arose to serve the cattle and mining booms. As technology freed people from the need to produce their own food and clothing, westerners turned to the business of supplying goods and services, enterprises that required the labor of densely populated cities.

Denver was typical. Founded in 1859, the city profited from the discovery of gold in nearby Cherry Creek. The completion of the Denver Pacific and Kansas Pacific railroads sparked a second growth spurt in the 1870s. By the 1890s, with a population of over 100,000, it ranked behind only Los Angeles and Omaha among western cities. Like much of the urban West, Denver grew outward rather than upward, breaking the pattern set by the cramped cities of the East. In the West, such urban sprawl produced cities with sharply divided districts for business, government, and industry. Workers lived in one section of town; managers, owners, and wealthier citizens in another.

Examining the returns from 1890, the superintendent of the census noted that landed settlements stretched so far that "there can hardly be said to be a frontier line." One after another, territories became states: Nebraska in 1867; Colorado in 1876; North Dakota, South Dakota, Montana, and Washington in 1889; Wyoming in 1890; Utah in 1896; Oklahoma in 1907; and New Mexico and Arizona in 1912. A new West was emerging as a mosaic of ethnicities, races, cultures, and climates, but with the shared identity of a single region.

That sense of a regional identity was heightened for both westerners and southerners, because so many of them felt isolated from the mainstream of industrial America. Ironically, it was not their isolation from northern industry but their links to it that marginalized them. The campaign for a New South to out-Yankee the industrial Yankee could not overcome the low wages and high fertility rates of an older South. The promoters of the West had greater success in adapting large-scale industry and investment to mining, cattle ranching, and farming. But they too confronted the limits of their region, whose resources were not endless and whose rainfall did not follow the plow. Like easterners, citizens of the West found that large corporations with near-monopoly control over markets and transportation bred inequality, corrupt politics, and resentment.

These sectional upheavals inevitably affected the political system, as conflicts of class, race, and region spilled into the national arena. By the 1890s, an agrarian revolt was sweeping the South and West. In both sections disillusionment and despair turned to bitterness as more small farmers, black and white, found themselves enslaved to debt and driven toward bankruptcy, tenancy, and wage labor. It was small wonder, then, that the South and the West gave rise to a "People's party," determined to end the "business as usual" approach of the Democratic and Republican parties.

SIGNIFICANT EVENTS

1849–1859 — Gold and silver strikes open western mining frontier

1862 — Homestead Act; Minnesota Sioux uprising begins Plains Indian wars

1864 — Chivington massacre

1866 — Drive to Sedalia, Missouri, launches cattle boom

1869 — Completion of first transcontinental railroad; Powell explores the Grand Canyon

1872–1874 — The great buffalo slaughter

1874 — Black Hills gold rush; barbed wire patented

1876 — Battle of Little Big Horn; Nez Percé resist relocation

1877 — Compromise of 1877 ends Reconstruction; Crazy Horse surrenders

1879 — Height of Exoduster migration to Kansas

1880 — Bonsack cigarette-rolling machine invented

1883 — *Civil Rights Cases*

1886–1887 — Severe winter and drought cycle in the West

1887 — Dawes Severalty Act

1889 — Oklahoma opened to settlement

1890 — Ghost Dance Indian religious revival; Wounded Knee

1892 — Union violence at Coeur d'Alene, Idaho; Wyoming range wars

1896 — *Plessy v. Ferguson* upholds separate but equal doctrine

CHAPTER TWENTY-ONE

The Political System Under Strain

O n May 1, 1893, an eager crowd of nearly half a million people jostled into a dramatic plaza fronted on either side by gleaming white buildings. Named the Court of Honor, the plaza was the center of a strange, ornamental city that was at once both awesome and entirely imaginary.

At one end stood a building whose magnificent white dome exceeded even the height of the Capitol in Washington. Unlike the marble-built Capitol, however, this building was all surface: a stucco shell plastered onto a steel frame and then sprayed with white oil paint to make it glisten. Beyond the Court of Honor stretched thoroughfares encompassing over 200 colonaded buildings, piers, islands, and watercourses. Located five miles south of Chicago's center, this city of the imagination proclaimed itself the "World's Columbian Exposition" to honor the 400th anniversary of Columbus's voyage to America.

President Grover Cleveland opened the world's fair in a way that symbolized the nation's industrial transformation. He pressed a telegrapher's key. Instantly electric current set 7000 feet of shafting into motion—motion that in turn unfurled flags, set fountains pumping, and lit 10,000 electric bulbs. The lights played over an array of exhibition buildings soon known as the "White City."

In Cleveland's judgment the neoclassical architecture was both "magnificent" and "stupendous." Surely the sheer size was astonishing, for the buildings had been laid out not by the square foot but by the acre. The Hall of Manufactures and Liberal Arts alone spread its roof over 30 acres, twice the area of Egypt's Great Pyramid.

One English visitor dismissed the displays within as "the contents of a great dry goods store mixed up with the contents of museums." In a sense he was right. Visitors paraded by an unending stream of typewriters, pins, watches, agricultural machinery, cedar canoes, and refrigerators, to say nothing of a map of the United States fashioned entirely out of pickles. But this riot of mechanical marvels, gewgaws, and bric-a-brac was symbolic, too, of the nation's industrial transformation. The fair resembled nothing so much as a living, breathing version of the new department store mail-order catalogues whose pages were now introducing the goods of the city to the hinterlands.

The connections made by the fair were international as well. This was the *World's* Columbian Exposition, with exhibits from 36 nations. Germany's famous manufacturer of armaments, Krupp, had its own separate building. It housed a 120-ton rifled gun 46 feet long, "said to be able to throw a projectile weighing one ton a distance of twenty miles." Easily within the range of its gunsights was a replica of the U.S. battleship *Illinois*, whose own bristling turrets stood just offshore of the exposition, on Lake Michigan. At the fair's amusement park, visitors encountered exotic cultures—and not just temples, huts, and totems, but exhibits in the living flesh. The Arabian village featured Saharan camels, veiled ladies, elders in turbans, and beggar children. Nearby, Irish peasants boiled potatoes over turf fires and Samoan men threw axes.

Like all such fairs, the Columbian Exposition created a fantasy. Beyond its boundaries, the real world was showing serious signs of strain. Early in 1893 the Philadelphia and Reading Railroad had gone bankrupt, setting off a financial panic. By the end of the year, nearly 500 banks and 15,000 businesses had failed. Although tourists continued to marvel at the fair's wonders, crowds of worried and unemployed workers also gathered in Chicago. On Labor Day, Governor John Altgeld of Illinois told one such assemblage that the government was powerless to avoid or even soften "suffering and distress" that this latest economic downturn would bring.

In truth, the political system was ill equipped to cope with the economic and social revolutions reshaping America. The executive branch remained weak, while Congress and the courts found themselves easily swayed by the financial interests of the industrial class. The crises of the 1890s forced the political order to try to address such inequities.

The political system also had to take into account developments abroad. Industrialization had sent American businesses around the world searching for raw materials and new markets. As that search intensified, many influential Americans argued that the United States needed, like European nations, to acquire territory overseas. By the end of the century, the nation's political system had taken its first steps toward modernization. That included a major political realignment at home and a growing empire abroad. Both changes launched the United States into the twentieth century and an era of prosperity and power.

THE POLITICS OF PARALYSIS

During the 1880s and 1890s, as the American political system came under strain, Moisei Ostrogorski was traveling across the United States. Like other foreign visitors, the Russian political scientist had come to see the new democratic experiment in action. His verdict was as blunt as it was widely shared: "the constituted authorities are unequal to their duty." It seemed that the experiment had fallen victim to private greed, middle-class indifference, and political mediocrity.

In fact, there were deeper problems: a great gulf between rich and poor; the growing power of corporate industry; the wretched poverty of city and farm; an endless cycle of boom and bust; the unmet needs of African Americans, women, Indians, and other Americans. These problems had scarcely been addressed, let alone resolved. Politics was the traditional medium of resolution, but it was grinding into a dangerous stalemate.

Political Stalemate

From 1877 to 1897 American politics rested on a delicate balance of power that left neither Republicans nor Democrats in control. Republicans inhabited the White House for 12 years; Democrats, for 8. Margins of victory in presidential elections were paper thin. And no president could count on having a majority of his party in both houses of Congress for his entire term. Usually Republicans controlled the Senate, while Democrats controlled the House of Representatives.

With elections so tight, both parties worked hard to bring out the vote. Brass bands, parades, cheering crowds of flag-wavers "are the order of the day and night from end to end of the country," reported a British visitor. In cities

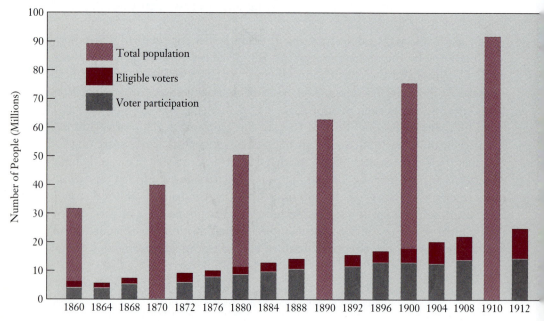

THE VOTING PUBLIC, 1860–1912   Between 1860 and 1910 the population and the number of eligible voters increased nearly threefold. As reforms of the early twentieth century increased the number of eligible voters but reduced the power of political machines to mass voters, the percentage of participation actually declined.

party workers handed out leaflets and pinned campaign buttons on anyone who passed. When Election Day arrived, stores closed and businesses shut down. At political clubs and corner saloons men lined up to get voting orders (along with free drinks) from ward bosses. In the countryside, fields went untended as farmers took their families to town, cast their ballots, and bet on the outcome.

An average of nearly 80 percent of eligible voters turned out for presidential elections between 1860 and 1900, a figure higher than at any time since. In

Voter turnout

that era, however, the electorate made up a smaller percentage of the population. About one American in five actually voted in presidential elections from 1876 to 1892. Virtually all were white males. Women could vote in national elections only in a few western states, and beginning in the 1880s, the South erected barriers that eventually disfranchised many African American voters.

Party loyalty rarely wavered. In every election, 16 states could be counted on to vote Republican and 14 Democratic. In only six states—the most important being New York and Ohio—were the results in doubt.

The Parties

What inspired such loyalty? Republicans and Democrats did have similarities but also had differences. Both parties supported business and condemned radicalism; neither offered embattled workers and farmers much help. But Democrats believed in states' rights and limited government, while Republicans

Democrats and Republicans compared

favored federal activism to foster economic growth. The stronghold of Democrats lay in the South, where they continually reminded voters that they had led the states of the Old Confederacy, "redeemed" them from Republican Reconstruction, and championed white supremacy. Republicans dominated the North with strong support from industry and business. They, too, invoked memories of the Civil War to secure voters, black as well as white. "Not every Democrat was a rebel," they chanted, "but every rebel was a Democrat."

Ethnicity and religion also cemented voter loyalty. Republicans drew on old-stock Protestants, who feared new immigrants and put their faith in promoting pious behavior. In the Republican party, they found support for immigration restriction, prohibition, and English-only schools. The Democratic party attracted urban political machines, their immigrant voters, and the working poor. Often Catholic, they saw salvation in following religious rituals, not in dictating the conduct of all society. For them, the Democratic party defended liberty because it opposed the very restrictions sought by native-born Protestants.

Region, religion, and ethnicity thus bound voters to each party. Some citizens weighed their purses at election time, but many more thought of their pastors or their parents or their communities when they went to the polls. Year after year, these cultural loyalties shaped political allegiances.

Outside the two-party system, impassioned reformers often fashioned political instruments of their own. Some formed groups that aligned themselves behind issues rather than parties. Opponents of alcohol created the Woman's Christian Temperance Union (1874) and the Anti-Saloon League (1893). Champions of women's rights joined the National American Woman Suffrage Association (1890), a reunion of two branches of the women's suffrage movement that had split in 1869.

Third political parties might also crystallize around a single concern or a particular group. Those who sought inflation of the currency formed the

Third parties

Greenback party (1874). Angry farmers in the West and South created the Populist, or People's, party (1892). All drew supporters from both conventional parties, but as single-interest groups they mobilized minorities, not majorities.

The Issues

In the halls of Congress, attention focused on well-worn issues: veterans' benefits, appointments, tariffs, and money. The presidency had been weakened by the impeachment of Andrew Johnson, the scandals of Ulysses S. Grant, and the contested victory of Rutherford B. Hayes in 1876 (see pages 462–463). So Congress enjoyed the initiative in making policy.

Some divisive issues were the bitter legacy of the Civil War. Republicans and Democrats waved symbolic "bloody shirts," each tarring the other with re-

Legacies of the Civil War

sponsibility for the war. The politics of the Civil War also surfaced in the lobbying efforts of veterans. The Grand Army of the Republic, an organization of more than 400,000 Union soldiers, petitioned Congress for pensions to make up for poor wartime pay and to support the widows and orphans of fallen comrades. By the turn of the century Union army veterans and their families were receiving $157 million annually. It was one of the largest public assistance programs in American history and laid the foundation for the modern welfare state.

COUNTERPOINT   *Origins of the Welfare State*

Historians disagree over the origins of the American welfare state. Some maintain that the United States followed the lead of industrial nations in Europe, where the first social insurance laws were passed in the 1880s and 1890s. Similar laws were not enacted in the United States until the Great Depression of the 1930s. Marxist historians see their emergence as a way for capitalism to control the working class and head off more radical change.

Other historians and social scientists place the origins of the welfare state in late nineteenth-century America. These scholars focus on the activities of interest groups, especially veterans', women's, and other voluntary organizations. Their lobbying resulted in an extensive aid program for Civil War veterans and, by the first two decades of the twentieth century, benefits for mothers and pensions for widows in over 40 states, many of them more elaborate than those in Europe.

More important than public welfare was the campaign for a new method of staffing federal offices. Since the early nineteenth century, political victors had practiced patronage by rewarding loyal followers with government or party jobs, regardless of their qualifications. After elections, winners faced an army of office seekers, "lying in wait . . . like vultures for a wounded bison."

A growing federal bureaucracy aggravated the problem. From barely 53,000 employees at the end of the Civil War, the federal government had grown to 166,000 by the early 1890s, with far more jobs requiring special skills. But dismantling this "spoils system" proved difficult. American politics rested on patronage. Without it, politicians—from presidents to lowly ward captains—feared that they could attract neither workers nor money. Reacting to the scandals of the Grant administration, a group of independents formed the National Civil Service Reform League in 1881. The league promoted the British model of civil service based on examination and merit. But in Congress neither party was willing to take action when it held power (and thus controlled patronage).

One July morning in 1881, a frustrated office seeker named Charles Guiteau unwittingly broke the log jam. As President James Garfield hurried to catch a train, Guiteau jumped from the shadows and shot him twice. Garfield's death

Pendleton Act — finally produced reform. In 1883 the Civil Service Act, or Pendleton Act, created a bipartisan civil service commission to administer competitive examinations for some federal jobs. Later presidents expanded the jobs covered. By 1896 almost half of all federal workers came under civil service jurisdiction.

As much as any issue, the protective tariff stirred Congress. As promoters of economic growth, Republicans usually championed this tax on manufactured imports. Democrats, with their strength in the agrarian South, generally sought tariff reduction to encourage foreign trade, reduce prices on manufactured goods,

McKinley Tariff — and cut the federal surplus. In 1890, when Republicans controlled the House, Congress enacted the McKinley Tariff. It raised schedules to an all-time high. The McKinley Tariff also contained a novel twist known as reciprocity: the president could lower rates if other countries did the same. In 1894 House Democrats succeeded in reducing rates, only to be thwarted by some 600 Senate amendments restoring most cuts. In 1897 the Dingley Tariff raised rates still higher but soothed reductionists by broadening reciprocity.

Just as divisive was the issue of currency. Until the mid-1800s money was coined from both gold and silver. The need for more money during the Civil

Currency debates — War had led Congress to issue "greenbacks"—currency printed on paper with a green back. For the next decade and a half Americans argued over whether to print more paper money (not backed by gold or silver) or take it out of circulation. Farmers and other debtors favored greenbacks as a way of inflating prices and reducing their debts. For the opposite reasons, bankers and creditors stood for "sound money" backed by gold. Fear of inflation led Congress first to reduce the number of greenbacks and then in 1879 to make all remaining paper money convertible into gold.

A more heated battle was developing over silver-backed money. By the early 1870s so little silver was being used that Congress stopped coining it. A silver

Bland–Allison Act

mining boom in Nevada soon revived demands for more silver money. In 1878 the Bland–Allison Act inaugurated a limited form of silver coinage. But pressure for unlimited coinage of silver— coining all silver presented at U.S. mints—mounted as silver production quadrupled between 1870 and 1890. In 1890 pressure for silver peaked in the Sherman Silver Purchase Act. It obligated the government to buy 4.5 million ounces of silver every month. Paper tender called "treasury notes," redeemable in either gold or silver, would pay for it. The compromise satisfied both sides only temporarily.

The White House from Hayes to Harrison

From the 1870s through the 1890s a string of nearly anonymous presidents presided over the country. Not all were mere caretakers. Some tried to revive the office, but Congress continued to rein in the executive.

Republican Rutherford B. Hayes was the first of the "Ohio dynasty," which included three presidents from 1876 to 1900. As president, Hayes moved quickly to end Reconstruction and tried unsuccessfully to woo southern Democrats with promises of economic support. His pursuit of civil service reform ended only in splitting his party between "Stalwarts" (who favored the spoils systems) and "Half-Breeds" (who opposed it). Hayes left office after a single term, happy to be "out of a scrape."

In 1880, Republican James Garfield, another Ohioan, succeeded Hayes by a handful of votes. He spent his first hundred days in the White House besieged by office hunters and failing to placate the rival sections of his party. After Garfield's assassination only six months into his term, Chester A. Arthur, the "spoilsman's spoilsman," became president.

To everyone's surprise, the dapper Arthur turned out to be an honest president. He broke with machine politicians, including his mentor and Stalwart leader Roscoe Conkling. He worked to lower the tariff, warmly endorsed the new Civil Service, or Pendleton, Act, and reduced the federal surplus by beginning construction of a modern navy. Such even-handed administration left him little chance for renomination divided by party leaders.

The election of 1884 was one of the dirtiest ever waged. Senator James Blaine, the beloved "Plumed Knight" from Maine and leader of the Half-

The dirty election of 1884

Breeds, ran against Democrat Grover Cleveland, the former governor of New York. Despite superb talents as a leader and vote-getter, Blaine was haunted by old charges of illegal favoritism for the Little Rock and Fort Smith Railroad. For his part, "Grover the Good" had built a reputation for honesty by fighting corruption and the spoils system in New York. So hard a worker was the portly Cleveland, sighed a reporter, that he "remains within doors constantly, eats and works, eats and works, and works and eats." The bachelor Cleveland spent enough time away from his desk to father an illegitimate child. The country rang with Republican taunts of "Ma, ma, where's my pa?"

In the last week of the tight race, Cleveland supporters in New York circulated the statement of a local Protestant minister that labeled Democrats the party of "Rum, Romanism, and Rebellion" (alcohol, Catholicism, and the Civil War). The Irish-Catholic vote swung to the Democrats. New York went to Cleveland, and with it, the election. Democrats crowed with delight over where to find the bachelor "pa": "Gone to the White House, ha, ha, ha!"

Cleveland was the first Democrat elected to the White House since James Buchanan in 1856, and he was more active than many of his predecessors. He pleased reformers by expanding the civil service, and his devotion to gold, economy, and efficiency earned him praise from business. He supported the growth of federal power by endorsing the Interstate Commerce Act (1887), new agricultural research, and federal arbitration of labor disputes.

Still, Cleveland's presidential activism remained limited. He vetoed two of every three bills brought to him, more than twice the number vetoed by all his predecessors. Toward the end of his term, embarrassed by the large federal surplus, Cleveland finally reasserted himself by attacking the tariff, but to no avail. The Republican-controlled Senate blocked his attempt to lower it.

In 1888 Republicans nominated a sturdy defender of tariffs, Benjamin Harrison, the grandson of President William Henry Harrison. President Cleveland won a plurality of the popular vote but lost in the Electoral College. The "human iceberg" (as Harrison's colleagues called him) worked hard, rarely delegated management, and turned the White House into a well-regulated office. He helped to shape the Sherman Silver Purchase Act (1890), kept up with the McKinley Tariff (1890), and accepted the Sherman Antitrust Act (1890) to limit the power and size of big businesses.

By the end of Harrison's term in 1892, Congress had completed its most productive session of the era, including the first billion-dollar peacetime budget. To Democratic jeers of a "Billion Dollar Congress," Republican House Speaker Thomas Reed shot back, "This is a billion-dollar country!"

Ferment in the States and Cities

Despite growing expenditures and more legislation, most people expected little from the federal government. Few newspapers even bothered to send correspondents to Washington. Public pressure to curb the excesses of the new industrial order mounted closer to home, in state and city governments. Experimental and often effective, state programs began to grapple with the problems of corporate power, discriminatory shipping rates, political corruption, and urban disorder.

Starting in 1869 with Massachusetts, states established commissions to investigate and regulate industry, especially railroads, America's first big business.

State commissions

By the turn of the century, almost two-thirds of the states had them. The first commissions gathered and publicized information on shipping rates and business practices and furnished advice about public policy.

In the Midwest, on the Great Plains, and in the Far West, merchants and farmers pressed state governments to reduce railroad rates and stop the rebates given to large shippers. In California, one newspaper published a schedule of freight rates to Nevada, showing that lower rates had been charged by wagon teams before the railroads were built. On the West Coast and in the Midwest, state legislatures empowered commissions to end rebates and monitor rates. In 1870 Illinois became the first of several states to define railroads as public highways subject to regulation, including setting maximum rates.

Concern over cities led to state municipal conventions, the first in Iowa in 1877. Philadelphia sponsored a national conference on good city government

National Municipal League

in 1894. A year later reformers founded the National Municipal League. It soon had more than 200 branches. Its model city charter advanced such farsighted reforms as separate city and state elections, limited contracts for utilities, and more authority for mayors. Meanwhile cities and states in the Midwest enacted laws closing stores on Sundays, prohibiting the sale of alcohol, and making English the language of public schools—all in an effort to standardize social behavior and control the habits of new immigrants.

THE REVOLT OF THE FARMERS

In 1890, the politics of stalemate cracked, as did the patience of farmers across the South and the western plains. Beginning in the 1880s, a sharp depression drove down agricultural prices, pushed up surpluses, and forced thousands from their land. Farmers also suffered from a great deal more, including heavy mortgages, widespread poverty, and railroad rates that discriminated against them. In 1890 their resentment boiled over. An agrarian revolt—called Populism—swept across the political landscape and broke the stalemate of the previous 20 years.

The Harvest of Discontent

The revolt of the farmers stirred first on the southern frontier, spreading eastward from Texas through the rest of the Old Confederacy, then west across the

Targets of farm anger

plains. Farmers blamed their troubles on obvious inequalities: manufacturers protected by the tariff, high railroad rates, bankers who held their mounting debts, and expensive middlemen who

Mary Shelley's novel of a man-made creature who turns against its creator strikes the theme for this antirailroad cartoon entitled "The American Frankenstein" (1874). "Agriculture, commerce, and manufacture are all in my power," bellows the mechanical monster with the head of a locomotive.

stored and processed their commodities. All seemed to profit at the expense of farmers.

The true picture was fuzzier. The tariff protected industrial goods but also supported some farm commodities. Railroad rates, however high, actually fell from 1865 to 1890. And while mortgages were heavy, most were short, no more than four years. Farmers often refinanced them, using the money to buy more land and machinery, which only increased their debt. Millers and operators of grain elevators earned handsome profits; yet every year more of them came under state regulation.

In hard times, of course, none of this mattered. And in the South many poor farmers seemed condemned to hard times forever. Credit lay at the root of the

Credit crunch problem, since most southern farmers had to borrow money in order to plant and harvest their crops. The inequities of sharecropping and the crop–lien system (page 528) forced them deeper into debt. When crop prices fell, they borrowed still more, stretching the financial resources of the South beyond their meager limits. Within a few years after the

E Y E W I T N E S S   T O   H I S T O R Y

A Nebraska Farmer Laments His Plight

This season is without a parallel in this part of the country. The hot winds burned up the entire crop, leaving thousands of families wholly destitute, many of whom might have been able to run through this crisis had it not been for the galling yoke put on them by the money loaners and sharks—not by charging 7 per cent per annum, which is the lawful rate of interest, or even 10 per cent, but the unlawful and inhuman country destroying rate of 3 per cent a month, some going still farther and charging 50 per cent per annum. We are cursed, many of us financially, beyond redemption, not by the hot winds so much as by the swindling games of the bankers and money loaners, who have taken the money and now are after the property, leaving the farmer moneyless and homeless. . . . I have borrowed for example $1,000. I pay $25 besides to the commission man. I give my note and second mortgage of 3 per cent of the $1,000, which is $30 more. Then I pay 7 per cent on the $1,000 to the actual loaner. Then besides all this I pay for appraising the land, abstract, recording, etc., so when I have secured my loan I am out the first year $150. Yet I am told by the agent who loans me the money, he can't stand to loan at such low rates. This is on the farm, but now comes the chattel loan. I must have $50 to save myself. I get the money; my note is made payable in thirty or sixty days for $35, secured by chattel of two horses, harness and wagon, about five times the value of the note. The time comes to pay, I ask for a few days. No I can't wait; must have the money. If I can't get the money, I have the extreme pleasure of seeing my property taken and sold by this iron handed money loaner while my family and I suffer.

W. M. Taylor to editor, *Farmer's Alliance* (Lincoln), January 10, 1891, Nebraska Historical Society, reprinted in Robert D. Marcus and David Burner, eds., *America Firsthand*, Vol. II (New York: St. Martin's Press, 1992), p. 90.

Civil War, Massachusetts' banks had five times as much money as all the banks of the Old Confederacy.

Beginning in the 1870s, nearly 100,000 debt-ridden farmers a year picked up stakes across the Deep South and fled to Texas to escape the system, only to find it waiting for them. Others stood and fought, as one pamphlet exhorted in 1889, "not with glittering musket, flaming sword and deadly cannon, but with the silent, potent and all-powerful ballot."

The Origins of the Farmers' Alliance

Before farmers could vote together, they had to get together. Life on the farm was harsh, drab, and isolated. Such conditions shocked Oliver Hudson Kelley as he traveled across the South after the Civil War. In 1867 the young govern-

Patrons of Husbandry

ment clerk founded the Patrons of Husbandry to brighten the lives of farmers and broaden their horizons. Local chapters, called granges, brought farmers and their families together to pray, sing, and learn new farming techniques. The Grangers sponsored fairs, picnics, dances, lectures—anything to break the bleakness of farm life. After a slow start the Grange grew quickly. By 1875 there were 800,000 members in 20,000 locals, most in the Midwest, South, and Southwest.

At first the Grangers swore off politics. But in a pattern often repeated, socializing led to economic and then political action. By pooling their money for supplies and equipment to store and market their crops, Grangers could avoid the high charges of middlemen. By the early 1870s they also were lobbying midwestern legislatures to adopt "Granger laws" regulating rates charged by railroads, grain elevator operators, and other middlemen.

Eight "Granger cases" came before the Supreme Court in the 1870s to test the new regulatory measures. *Munn v. Illinois* (1877) upheld the right of Illinois to

Granger cases

regulate private property (in this case, giant elevators used for storing grain) "devoted to a public use." Later decisions allowed state regulation of railroads but only within state lines. Congress responded in 1887 by creating the Interstate Commerce Commission, a federal agency that could regulate commerce across state boundaries. In practice, it had little power, but it was a key step toward establishing the public right to regulate private corporations.

Slumping prices in the 1870s and 1880s bred new farm organizations. Slowly they blended into what the press called the "Alliance Movement." The Southern

Southern Alliance

Alliance, formed in Texas in 1875, spread rapidly after Dr. Charles W. Macune took command in 1886. A doctor and lawyer as well as a farmer, Macune planned to expand Texas's network of local chapters, or suballiances, into a national network of state Alliance Exchanges. Like the Grangers, the exchanges pooled their resources in cooperatively owned enterprises for buying and selling, milling and storing, banking and manufacturing.

Soon the Southern Alliance was publicizing its activities in local newspapers, publishing a journal, and sending lecturers across the country. For a brief period, between 1886 and 1892, the Alliance cooperatives multiplied throughout the South, grew to more than a million members, and challenged accepted ways of doing business. Macune claimed that his new Texas Exchange saved members 40 percent on plows and 30 percent on wagons. But most Alliance cooperatives were managed by farmers without the time or experience to succeed. Usually opposed by irate local merchants, the ventures eventually failed.

Although the Southern Alliance admitted no African Americans, it encouraged them to organize. A small group of black and white Texans founded the

Colored Farmers' Alliance Colored Farmers' National Alliance and Cooperative Union in 1886. By 1891 a quarter of a million farmers had joined. Its operations were largely secret, since public action often brought swift retaliation from white supremacists. When the Colored Farmers' Alliance organized a strike of black cotton pickers near Memphis in 1891, white mobs hunted down and lynched 15 strikers. The murders went unpunished, and the Colored Alliance began to founder.

The Alliance Peaks

Farmer cooperation reached northward to the states of the Midwest and Great Plains in the National Farmers' Alliance, created in 1880. In June 1890 Kansas organizers formed the first People's party to compete with Democrats and Republicans. Meanwhile the Southern Alliance changed its name to the National Farmers' Alliance and Industrial Union, incorporated the strong Northern Alliances in the Dakotas and Kansas, and made the movement truly national.

The key to Alliance success was not organization but leadership, both at the top and in the middle. Alliance lecturers fanned out across the South and the Great Plains, organizing suballiances and teaching new members about finance and cooperative businesses. Women were often as active as men. "Wimmin is everywhere," noted one observer of the Alliance. The comment seemed to apply literally to Mary Elizabeth Lease, who in the summer of 1890 alone gave 160 speeches.

In 1890 members of the Alliance met in Ocala, Florida, and issued the "Ocala Demands." The manifesto reflected the populists' deep distrust of "the *Ocala Demands* money power"—large corporations and banks, whose financial power gave them the ability to manipulate the "free" market. The Ocala Demands called on government to correct such abuses by reducing tariffs, abolishing national banks, regulating railroads, and coining silver money freely. The platform also demanded a federal income tax and the popular election of senators, to make government more responsive to the public. The most innovative feature came from Charles Macune. His "subtreasury system" would require the federal government to furnish warehouses for harvested crops and low-interest loans to tide farmers over until prices rose. Under such a system farmers would no longer have to sell in a glutted market, as they did under the crop–lien system. And they could expand the money supply simply by borrowing at harvest time.

In the elections of 1890 the old parties faced hostile farmers across the nation. In the South, the Alliance worked within the Democratic party and elected four governors, won eight legislatures, and sent 44 members of Congress and three senators to Washington. In the Great Plains, Alliance candidates drew farmers from the Republican party. Newly created farmer parties elected five representatives and two senators in Kansas and South Dakota and took over both houses of the Nebraska legislature.

In the West especially, Alliance organizers began to dream of a national third party that would be free from the corporate influence, sectionalism, and

The People's Party

racial tensions that split Republicans and Democrats. It would be a party not just of farmers but of the downtrodden, including industrial workers.

In February 1892, as the presidential election year opened, a convention of 900 labor, feminist, farm, and other reform delegates (100 of them black) met in St. Louis. They founded the People's, or Populist, party and called for another convention to nominate a presidential ticket. Initially southern Populists held back, clinging to their strategy of working within the Democratic party. But when newly elected Democrats failed to support Alliance programs, southern leaders like Tom Watson of Georgia abandoned the party and began recruiting black and white farmers for the Populists.

The national convention of Populists met in Omaha, Nebraska, on Independence Day, July 4, 1892. Their impassioned platform promised to return government "to the hands of 'the plain people.'" Planks advocated the subtreasury plan, unlimited coinage of silver and an increase in the money supply, direct election of senators, an income tax, and government ownership of railroads, telegraph, and telephone. To attract wage earners the party endorsed the eight-hour workday, restriction of immigration, and a ban on the use of Pinkerton detectives in labor disputes—for the Pinkertons had engaged in a savage gun battle with strikers that year at Andrew Carnegie's Homestead steel plant. Delegates rallied behind the old greenbacker and Union general James B. Weaver, carefully balancing their presidential nomination with a one-legged Confederate veteran as his running mate.

The Election of 1892

The Populists enlivened the otherwise dull campaign, as Democrat Grover Cleveland and Republican incumbent Benjamin Harrison refought the election of 1888. This time, however, Cleveland won, and for the first time since the Civil War, Democrats gained control of both houses of Congress. The Populists too enjoyed success. Weaver polled over a million votes, the first third-party candidate to do so. Populists elected 3 governors, 5 senators, 10 representatives, and nearly 1500 members of state legislatures.

Despite these victories, the election revealed dangerous weaknesses in the People's party. Across the nation thousands of voters changed political affilia-

Populist weaknesses

tions, but most often from the Republicans to the Democrats, not to the Populists. No doubt the campaign of intimidation and repression hurt the People's party in the South, where white conservatives had been appalled by Tom Watson's open courtship of black southerners. In the North, Populists failed to win over labor and most city dwellers. Both were more concerned with family budgets than with the problems of farmers and the downtrodden.

The darker side of Populism also put off many Americans. Its rhetoric was often violent and laced with naturist slurs; it spoke ominously of conspiracies and stridently in favor of immigration restriction. In fact, the Alliance lost members, an omen of defeats to come. But for the present, the People's party had demonstrated two conflicting truths. It showed how far from the needs of many ordinary Americans the two parties had drifted, and how difficult it would be to break their power.

THE NEW REALIGNMENT

On May 1, 1893, President Cleveland was in Chicago to throw the switch that set ablaze 10,000 electric bulbs and opened the World's Columbian Exposition (pages 554–555). The gleaming "White City" with its grand displays stood as a monument to the nation's glorious progress. Four days later a wave of bankruptcies destroyed major firms across the country, and stock prices sank to all-time lows, setting off the depression of 1893.

At first Chicago staved off the worst, thanks to the business generated by the exposition. But when that closed in October, thousands of laborers found themselves out of a job. Chicago's mayor estimated the number of unemployed in the city to be near 200,000. He had some firsthand experience on which to base his calculations, for every night desperate men slept on the floors and stairways of City Hall and every police station in the city put up 60 to 100 additional homeless. Children as well as their parents rifled the city's garbage dumps for food.

The Depression of 1893

The sharp contrast between the exposition's White City and the nation's economic misery demonstrated the inability of the political system to smooth out the economy's cycle of boom and bust. The new industrial order had brought prosperity by increasing production, opening markets, and tying Americans closer together. But in 1893, the price of interdependence became obvious. A major downturn in one area affected the other sectors of the economy. And with no way to control swings in the business cycle, depression came on a scale as large as that of the booming prosperity.

The depression of 1893, the deepest the nation had yet experienced, lasted until 1897. Railroad baron and descendant of two presidents Charles Francis Adams, Jr., called it a "convulsion," but the country experienced it as crushing idleness. In August 1893, unemployment stood at 1 million; by the middle of 1894, it was 3 million. At the end of the year nearly one worker in five was out of a job.

The federal government had no program at all. "While the people should patriotically and cheerfully support their Government," President Cleveland

Charles Dana Gibson, famous for his portraits of well-bred young women in the 1890s, tackles a different subject in this drawing, a breadline of mixed classes during the depression of 1893.

declared, "its functions do not include the support of the people." The states offered little more. Relief, like poverty, was considered a private matter. The burden fell on local charities, benevolent societies, churches, labor unions, and ward bosses. In city after city, citizens organized relief committees to distribute bread and clothing until their meager resources gave out.

Others were less charitable. As the popular preacher Henry Ward Beecher told his congregation, "No man in this land suffers from poverty unless it be more than his fault—unless it be his sin." But the scale of hardship was so great, its targets so random, that anyone could be thrown out of work—an industrious neighbor, a factory foreman with 20 years on the job, a bank president. Older attitudes about personal responsibility for poverty began to give way to new ideas about its social origins and the obligation of public agencies to help.

The Rumblings of Unrest

Even before the depression, rumblings of unrest had begun to roll across the country. The Great Railroad Strike of 1877 had ignited nearly two decades of labor strife (page 495). After 1893 discontent mounted as wages were cut, employees laid off, and factories closed. During the first year of the depression, 1400 strikes sent more than half a million workers from their jobs.

Uneasy business executives and politicians saw radicalism and the possibility of revolution in every strike. But the depression of 1893 had unleashed another force: simple discontent. And in the spring of 1894, it focused on government inaction. On Easter Sunday, "General"

Coxey's Army

Jacob Coxey, a 39-year-old Populist and factory owner, launched the "Tramps' March on Washington" from Massillon, Ohio. His "Commonweal Army of Christ"—some 500 men, women, and children—descended on Washington at the end of April to offer "a petition with boots on" for a federal program of public works. Cleveland's staff tightened security around the White House, as other "armies" of unemployed mobilized: an 800-person contingent left from Los Angeles; a San Francisco battalion of 600 swelled to 1500 by the time it reached Iowa.

On May 1, Coxey's troops, armed with "clubs of peace," massed at the foot of the capitol. When Coxey entered the capitol grounds, 100 mounted police routed the demonstrators and arrested the general for trespassing on the grass. Nothing came of the protest, other than to signal a growing demand for federal action.

Federal help was not to be found. Grover Cleveland had barely moved into the White House when the depression struck. The country blamed him; he blamed silver. In his view the Sherman Silver Purchase Act of 1890 had shaken business confidence by forcing the government to use its shrinking reserves of gold to purchase (though not coin) silver. Repeal of the act, Cleveland believed, was the way to build gold reserves and restore confidence. After bitter debate, Congress complied. But this economic tinkering only strengthened the resolve of "silverites" in the Democratic party to overwhelm Cleveland's conservative "gold" wing.

Democrats under fire

Worse for the president, repeal of silver purchases brought no economic revival. In the short run abandoning silver hurt the economy by contracting the money supply just when expansion might have stimulated it by providing needed credit. As panic and unemployment spread across the country, Cleveland's popularity wilted. Democrats were buried in the congressional elections of 1894. Dropping moralistic reforms and stressing national activism, Republicans won control of both the House and the Senate.

With the Democrats confined to the South, the politics of stalemate was over. All that remained for the Republican party was to capture the White House in 1896.

The Battle of the Standards

The campaign of 1896 quickly became a "battle of the standards." Both major parties obsessed over whether gold alone or gold and silver should become the nation's monetary standard. Most Republicans saw gold as the stable base for building business confidence and economic prosperity. They adopted a platform calling for "sound money" supported by gold. Their candidate, Governor William McKinley of Ohio, cautiously supported the gold plank and firmly believed in high tariffs to protect American industry.

Silverites, on the other hand, campaigned for "free and independent" coinage of silver, in which the Treasury freely minted all the silver presented to

Free silver
it, independent of other nations. The supply of money would increase, prices would rise, and the economy would revive—or so their theory said.

But the free silver movement was more than a monetary theory. It was a symbolic protest of region and class—of the agricultural South and West against the commercial Northeast, of debt-ridden farm folk against industrialists and financiers. Silverites pressed their case like preachers exhorting their flocks, nowhere more effectively than in William Harvey's best-selling pamphlet, *Coin's Financial School* (1894). It reached tens of thousands of readers with the common sense of Coin, its young hero, fighting for silver.

At the Democratic convention in Chicago, William Jennings Bryan of Nebraska was ready to fight, as well. Just 36 years old, Bryan looked "like a young divine"—"tall, slender, handsome," with a rich melodic voice that reached the back rows of the largest halls (no small asset in the days before electric amplification). He had served two terms in Congress and worked as a journalist. He favored low tariffs, opposed Cleveland, and came out belatedly for free silver. Systematically, he coordinated a quiet fight for his nomination.

Silverites controlled the convention from the start. They paraded with silver banners, wore silver buttons, and wrote a plank into the anti-Cleveland platform calling for free and unlimited coinage of the metal. The high point came when Bryan stepped to the lectern, threw back his head, and offered himself to "a cause as holy as the cause of liberty—the cause of humanity." The crowd was in a near-frenzy as he reached the dramatic climax and spread his arms in mock crucifixion: "You shall not crucify mankind upon a cross of gold." The next day the convention nominated him for the presidency.

Populists were in a quandary. They had expected the Democrats to stick with Cleveland and gold, sending unhappy silverites headlong into their camp. Instead, the Democrats had stolen their thunder by endorsing silver and nominating Bryan. "If we fuse [with the Democrats] we are sunk," complained one Populist. "If we don't fuse, all the silver men we have will leave us for the more powerful Democrats." At a bitter convention, fusionists nominated Bryan for president. The best antifusionists could do was drop the Democrats' vice presidential candidate in favor of a fiery agrarian rebel from Georgia, Tom Watson.

Campaign and Election

Bryan knew he faced an uphill battle. Adopting a more active style that would be imitated in future campaigns, he traveled 18,000 miles by train, gave as many as 30 speeches a day, and reached perhaps 3 million people in 27 states. The nomination of the People's party actually did more harm than good by labeling Bryan a Populist (which he was not) and a radical (which he definitely was not). Devoted to the "plain people," the Great Commoner spoke for rural America and Jeffersonian values: small farmers, small towns, small government.

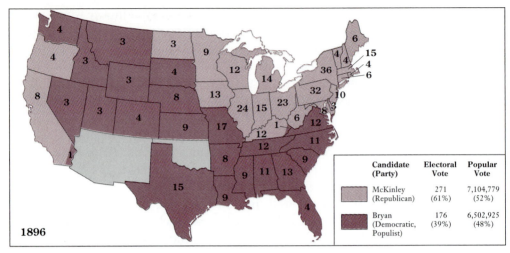

Candidate (Party)	Electoral Vote	Popular Vote
McKinley (Republican)	271 (61%)	7,104,779 (52%)
Bryan (Democratic, Populist)	176 (39%)	6,502,925 (48%)

1896

THE ELECTION OF 1896 The critical election of 1896 established the Republicans as the majority party, ending two decades of political gridlock with a new political realignment. Republican victor William McKinley dominated the large industrial cities and states, as the returns of the electoral college show.

McKinley knew he could not compete with Bryan's barnstorming, so he contented himself with sedate speeches from his front porch in Canton, Ohio. The folksy appearance of the campaign belied its reality. From the beginning, it had been engineered by Marcus Alonzo Hanna, a talented Ohio industrialist. Hanna relied on modern techniques of organization and marketing. He advertised McKinley, said Theodore Roosevelt, "as if he were patent medicine." His well-financed campaign brought to Canton tens of thousands, who cheered the candidate's promises of a "full dinner pail." Hanna also saturated the country with millions of leaflets, along with 1400 speakers attacking free trade and free silver.

On election night, Bryan sat at home in Lincoln, Nebraska, as three telegraph operators brought him bulletin after bulletin spelling defeat. Both candidates tallied more votes than any of their predecessors: Bryan, 6.5 million; McKinley, 7.1 million (making him the first president since Grant to receive a popular majority).

The election proved to be one of the most critical in the republic's history.* Over the previous three decades, political life had been characterized by vibrant

---

* Five elections, in addition to the contest of 1896, are often cited as critical shifts in voter allegiance and party alignments: the Federalist defeat of 1800, Andrew Jackson's rise in 1828, Lincoln's Republican triumph of 1860, Al Smith's Democratic loss in 1928, and—perhaps—Ronald Reagan's conservative tide of 1980.

campaigns, slim party margins, high voter turnout, and low-profile presidents. The election of 1896 signaled a new era of dwindling party loyalties and voter turnout, stronger presidents, and Republican rule. McKinley's victory broke the political stalemate and forged a powerful coalition that dominated politics for the next 30 years. It rested on the industrial cities of the Northeast and Midwest and combined old support from businesses, farmers, and Union Army veterans with broader backing from industrial wage earners. The Democrats controlled little but the South, and the Populists virtually vanished from the political scene.

The Rise of Jim Crow Politics

In 1892, despite the stumping of Populists like Tom Watson, African Americans cast their ballots for Republicans, when they were permitted to vote freely. But increasingly, their voting rights were being curtailed across the South.

As the century drew to a close, long-standing racism deepened. The arrival of "new" immigrants from eastern and southern Europe and the acquisition of new overseas colonies encouraged prejudices that stridently rationalized segregation and other forms of racial control (pages 534–535). In the South racism was enlisted in a political purpose: preventing an alliance of poor blacks and whites that might topple white conservative Democrats. So the white supremacy campaign, ostensibly directed at African Americans, also had a broader target in the world of politics: rebellion from below, whether black or white.

Mississippi, whose Democrats had led the move to "redeem" their state from Republican Reconstruction, in 1890 took the lead in disfranchising African Americans. A new state constitution required voters to pay a poll tax and pass a literacy test, requirements that eliminated the great majority of black voters. Conservative Democrats favored the plan because it also reduced the voting of poor whites, who were most likely to join opposition parties. Before the new constitution went into effect, Mississippi contained more than 250,000 eligible voters. By 1892, after its adoption, there were fewer than 77,000. Soon an all-white combination of conservatives and "reformers"—those disgusted by frequent election stealing with blocks of black votes—passed disfranchisement laws across the South. Between 1895 and 1908, disfranchisement campaigns won out in every southern state.

Sometimes disfranchisement laws relied on the complicated procedure of charging poll taxes and demanding receipts at the polls, as in Mississippi. (To *Disfranchisement* trick voters who had paid, local politicians arranged for circuses to tour black districts before elections and collect poll tax receipts as the price of admission. Without them, black voters could not cast their ballots.) Sometimes literacy tests were used as a barrier. Where African American voters were concentrated in large numbers, some states gerrymandered, or remapped the boundaries of election districts, to split up black votes. "Grandfather clauses" allowed citizens to vote only if their grandfathers had voted in elections held before 1860 (or 1866 in some cases). The provision excluded most African Americans.

The disfranchisement campaign also succeeded in barring many poor whites from the polls. In Louisiana, for example, under the new provisions the number of citizens voting was cut by more than two-thirds, excluding almost all the black voters and almost half the whites. The disfranchisement campaign had one final consequence: splitting rebellious whites from blacks, as the fate of Tom Watson demonstrated.

Only a dozen years after his biracial campaign of 1892, Watson was promoting black disfranchisement in Georgia. Like other southern Populists, Watson returned to the Democratic party still hoping to help poor whites. But he turned against black southerners. Only by playing a powerful race card could he hope to win election. "What does civilization owe the negro?" he asked bitterly. "Nothing! Nothing!! NOTHING!!!" In 1920, after a decade of baiting blacks (as well as Catholics and Jews), the Georgia firebrand was elected to the Senate. Watson, who began with such high racial ideals, gained power only by abandoning them.

The African American Response

To mount a successful campaign for disfranchisement, white conservatives inflamed racial passions. They staged "White Supremacy Jubilees" and peppered newspaper editorials with complaints of "bumptious" and "impudent" African Americans. The number of lynchings peaked during the 1890s, averaging over a hundred a year for the decade. Most took place in the South. In Atlanta and New Orleans, white mobs terrorized blacks for days in the new, heightened atmosphere of tension.

Under such circumstances, African Americans worked out responses to the climate of intolerance. One came from Booker T. Washington, a former slave and founder of an industrial and agricultural school for blacks in Tuskegee, Alabama. "I love the South," he reassured an audience of white and black southerners in Atlanta in 1895. He conceded that white prejudice existed throughout the region but nonetheless counseled African Americans to work for their economic betterment through manual labor. Every laborer who learned a trade, every farmer who tilled the land could increase his savings. And those earnings would amount to "a little green ballot" that "no one will throw out or refuse to count." Thus Tuskegee's curriculum stressed vocational skills for farming, manual trades, and industrial work.

Booker T. Washington

Many white Americans hailed Washington's "Atlanta Compromise," for it struck the note of patient humility they were so eager to hear. For African Americans, it made the best of a bad situation. Washington, an astute politician, discovered that philanthropists across the nation hoped to make Tuskegee an example of their generosity. He was the honored guest of Andrew Carnegie at his imposing Skibo Castle. California railroad magnate Collis Huntington became his friend, as did other business executives eager to discuss "public and social questions."

Throughout, Washington preached accommodation to the racial caste system. He accepted segregation (so long as separate facilities were equal) and qualifications on voting (if they applied to white citizens as well). Above all Washington sought economic self-improvement for common black folk in fields and factories. In 1900 he organized the National Negro Business League to help establish black businessmen as the leaders of their people. The rapid growth of local chapters (320 by 1907) extended his influence across the country.

Not all black leaders accepted Washington's call for accommodation. W. E. B. Du Bois, a professor at Atlanta University, leveled the most stinging attack in

W. E. B. Du Bois

The Souls of Black Folk (1903). Du Bois saw no benefit for African Americans in sacrificing intellectual growth for narrow vocational training. Nor was he willing to abide the humiliating stigma that came from the South's discriminatory caste system. A better future would come only if black citizens struggled politically to achieve suffrage and equal rights.

Instead of exhorting African Americans to pull themselves up slowly from the bottom, Du Bois called on the "talented tenth," a cultured black vanguard,

NAACP

to blaze a trail of protest. In 1905 he founded what became known as the Niagara movement for political and economic equality. In 1909 a coalition of blacks and sympathetic whites transformed the Niagara movement into the National Association for the Advancement of Colored People (NAACP). Middle class and elitist, it mounted legal challenges to the Jim Crow system of segregation. But for sharecroppers in southern cotton fields and laborers in northern factories—the mass of African Americans—the strategy offered little relief.

Neither accommodation nor legal agitation would suffice. But in the "Solid South" (as well as an openly racialized North) it was Washington's restrained approach that articulated an agenda for most African Americans. The ferment of the early 1890s, among black Populists and white, was replaced by an all-white Democratic party that dominated the region but remained in the minority on the national level.

McKinley in the White House

In William McKinley, Republicans found a skillful chief with a national agenda and personal charm. He cultivated news reporters, openly walked the streets of Washington, and courted the public with handshakes and flowers from his own lapel. Firmly but delicately, he curbed the power of old-time state bosses. When necessary, he prodded Congress to action. In all these ways, he foreshadowed "modern" presidents, who would act as party leaders rather than as executive caretakers.

Fortune at first smiled on McKinley. When he entered the White House, the economy had already begun its recovery, as the cycle of economic retrenchment hit bottom. Factory orders were slowly increasing, and unemployment dropped. Farm prices climbed. New discoveries of gold in Alaska and South Africa expanded the supply of money without causing "gold bugs" to panic that it was being destabilized by silver.

Freed from the burdens of the economic crisis, McKinley called a special session of Congress to revise the tariff. In 1897 the Dingley Tariff raised protective rates still higher but allowed the tariffs to come down if other nations lowered theirs. McKinley also sought a solution for resolving railroad strikes, like the Pullman conflict, before they turned violent. The Erdman Act of 1898 set up machinery for government mediation. McKinley even began laying plans for stronger regulation of trusts.

But the same expansiveness that had pushed an industrial nation across the continent and shipped grain and cotton abroad was also drawing the country into a race for empire and a war with Spain. Regulation—and an age of reform—would have to await the next century.

VISIONS OF EMPIRE

The crisis with Spain was only the affair of the moment that turned American attention abroad. Underlying the conflict were larger forces linking the United States with international events. By the 1890s, southern farmers were exporting half their cotton crop to factories worldwide, while western wheat farmers earned some 30 to 40 percent of their income from markets abroad. John D. Rockefeller's Standard Oil Company shipped about two-thirds of its refined products overseas, and Cyrus McCormick supplied Russian farmers with the reaper.

More than commerce turned American eyes overseas. Since the 1840s expansionists had spoken of a divine destiny to overspread the North American continent from the Atlantic to the Pacific. Some Americans still cast covetous glances at Canada to the north and Mexico and Cuba to the south. More often, however, they dreamed of empire in more distant lands.

Imperialism, European-Style and American

The scramble for empire was well under way by the time the Americans, Japanese, and Germans entered in the late nineteenth century. Spain and Portugal still clung to the remnants of colonial empires dating from the fifteenth and sixteenth centuries. Meanwhile, England, France, and Russia accelerated their drive to control foreign peoples and lands. But the late nineteenth century became the new age of imperialism because the technology of arms and the networks of communication, transportation, and commerce brought the prospect of effective, truly global empires within much closer reach.

The naked force with which Europeans took possessions in Africa in the 1880s prompted many Americans to argue for this European-style imperialism

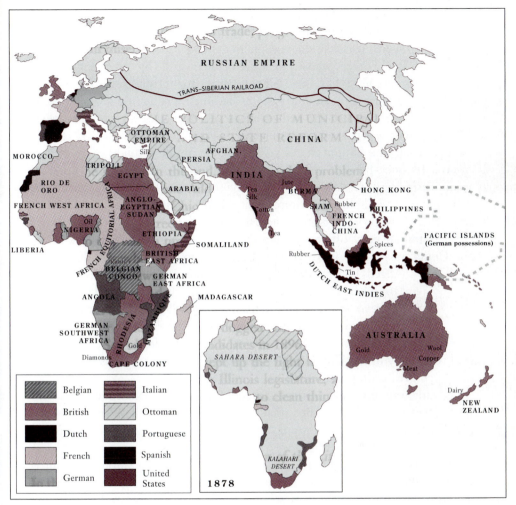

IMPERIALIST EXPANSION, 1900 Often resource-poor countries like Great Britain sought colonies for their raw materials, such as South African diamonds and tin from Southeast Asia. While China appears to be undivided, the major powers were busy establishing spheres of influence there.

American values of conquest and possession. But others preferred the more indirect imperialism that exported products, ideas, and influence. To them, this American imperialism seemed somehow purer, for they could portray themselves as bearers of their long-cherished values: democracy, free-enterprise capitalism, and Protestant Christianity. No doubt most Americans felt the world's far reaches would benefit as a result.

While Americans tried to justify imperial control in the name of democracy, social, economic, and political forces were drawing them rapidly into the impe-

Forces of imperialism

rial race. The growth of industrial networks linked them to international markets as never before. This was true whether they were Arkansas sharecroppers dependent on world cotton prices or Pittsburgh steelworkers whose jobs were made possible by orders for railroad steel from entrepreneurs like Isaac Singer, whose agents sold sewing machines from Europe to Asia. As economic systems became more tightly knit and political systems more responsive to industrialists and financiers, a rush for markets and distant lands was perhaps unavoidable.

But in 1880, the United States still lacked the military might of an imperial power. Its once-proud Civil War fleet of more than 600 warships was rotting and rusted with neglect. The U.S. Navy ranked twelfth in the world, behind Denmark and Chile. The United States had a coastal fleet but in effect no functional navy to protect its interests overseas.

Discontented navy officers joined with trade-hungry business leaders to lobby Congress for a modern navy with steam-powered, steel-hulled ships.

Alfred Thayer Mahan and the new navy

Alfred Thayer Mahan, a Navy captain and later admiral, formulated their ideas into a widely accepted theory of navalism. In *The Influence of Sea Power Upon History* (1890), Mahan argued that great nations were seafaring powers that relied on foreign trade for wealth and might. In times of overproduction and depression, as had occurred repeatedly in the United States after the Civil War, overseas markets assumed even greater importance.

The only way to gain and protect foreign markets, Mahan argued, was with large cruisers and battleships, not small coastal defenders. These ships, operating far from American shores, would need coaling stations and other resupply facilities throughout the world.

Mahan's logic was persuasive. So too were the profits a shipbuilding program would bring to American factories. In the 1880s, Congress launched a program to rebuild the navy with steam vessels made of steel rather than the wooden sailing ships of old. By 1900, the U.S. Navy ranked third in the world. With a modern navy, the country had the means to become an imperial power.

The Shaping of Foreign Policy

Although the climate for expansion and imperialism was present at the end of the nineteenth century, the small farmer or steelworker was little concerned with how the United States advanced its goals abroad. An elite group—Christian missionaries, intellectuals, business leaders, and commercial farmers—joined with navy careerists to push for a more active American imperialism.

Protestant missionaries provided a spiritual rationale that complemented Mahan's navalism. As American Protestant missionaries sought to convert "heathen" unbelievers in faraway lands, they encountered people whose cultural differences often made them unreceptive to the Christian message. Many came to believe that the natives first had to become Western in culture before becoming Christian in belief. They introduced Western goods, education, and systems of government administration—any "civilizing medium," as one minister remarked when he encouraged Singer to bring his sewing machines to China. Yet most American missionaries were not territorial imperialists. They eagerly took up what they called "the white man's burden" of introducing civilization to the "colored" races of the world. But they opposed direct military or political intervention.

From scholars, academics, and scientists came racial theories to justify European and American expansion. Charles Darwin's *On the Origin of Species*

Social Darwinism

(1859) had popularized the notion that among animal species, the fittest survived through a process of natural selection. Social Darwinists (page 484) argued that the same laws of survival governed the social order. When applied aggressively, Social Darwinism was used to justify theories of white supremacy as well as the slaughter and enslavement of nonwhite native populations that resisted conquest. When combined with the somewhat more humane "white man's burden" of Christian missionaries, conquest included uplifting natives by spreading Western ideas, religion, and government.

Perhaps more compelling than either racial or religious motives for American expansion was the need for trade. The business cycle of boom and

Commercial factors

bust reminded Americans of the unpredictability of their economy. In hard times, people sought salvation wherever they could, and one obvious road to recovery lay in markets abroad. With American companies outgrowing the home market, explained the National Association of Manufacturers, "expansion of our foreign trade is [the] only promise of relief."

In and out of government, leading public figures called for a campaign to "find markets in every part of the habitable globe." Imperialist policies, whether defined as an expansion of U.S. boundaries, the acquisition of colonies, or merely the achievement of a controlling influence, offered the chance to spread American values, increase foreign trade, enhance American prestige, and guarantee future security.

William Henry Seward

No one did more to initiate the idea of a "New Empire" for the United States than William Henry Seward. Secretary of state under Lincoln and Andrew Johnson, he had employed skillful diplomacy to avert European intervention in the Civil War. Following the war, the breadth of his vision led him to dream dreams beyond those of most politicians.

Seward rested his expansionism on his two central political laws. The first was that "empire has . . . made its way constantly westward . . . until the tides

Seward's laws of empire

of the renewed and decaying civilizations of the world meet on the shores of the Pacific Ocean." The United States must thus be prepared to win supremacy in the Far East. Seward's second maxim underscored how the battle could be won: the great empires of the future would be commercial, not military. The American empire required not colonies but markets. Equal access to foreign markets, often called the "open door," guided both British and American policy in Asia.

While he pursued ties to Japan, Korea, and China, Seward promoted a transcontinental railroad at home and a canal across the Central American isthmus. Link by link, he was trying to connect eastern factories to western ports and, from there, to markets in the Far East. But his dreams of opening Asia to American commerce bore little result in his lifetime. The transcontinental railroad, Atlantic cable, and high tariffs that he supported did come to pass. But his attempts to buy Iceland, Greenland, and a few Caribbean islands (and to annex Cuba) ran into opposition both at home and abroad.

Seward made two notable territorial acquisitions. An American naval officer raised the Stars and Stripes over the Pacific island of Midway in 1867 as a result of Seward's efforts. Unimportant by itself, the value of Midway lay as a way station to Asia and a Pacific toehold near Hawaii, where missionary planters were already establishing an American presence. Seward also engineered the purchase of Alaska in 1867. Critics called it "Seward's Folly" and the "Polar Bear Garden." But the Alaskan purchase turned out to be a bargain. The United States paid Russia $7.2 million, or about 2 cents an acre, for a mineral-rich territory twice the size of Texas.

Midway and Alaska purchases

The United States and Latin America

Many Americans did not accept Seward's conviction that their future lay in Asia. After the Civil War, some expansionists renewed talk of annexing Canada or provoking a border war with Mexico to gain territory. By the early 1870s, however, most Americans had decided that it was more profitable to trade with their northern neighbor than to possess it. Similarly, commercial and business interests pushed for friendly economic ties with Mexico. In 1881 Secretary of State James G. Blaine made it clear that the United States was not looking for the chance to acquire new territory there, only the opportunity to invest its "large accumulation of capital."

Elsewhere in Latin America, Blaine looked for ways to expand American trade and influence. One obstacle was the British presence in Central America. Blaine launched a campaign to cancel the Clayton–Bulwer Treaty (1850) sharing rights with Great Britain to any canal built in the region. At the same time, he tried to shift Central American imports from British to American goods by promoting hemispheric cooperation and stability. For years Latin America had endured political rivalries, governments rising and falling, and British and American meddling. International conflicts pitted Mexico

James G. Blaine

against Guatemala, Chile against Argentina, Nicaragua against Honduras, Chile against Peru and Bolivia, and even resulted in near-war between Chile and the United States in 1891.

To promote regional trade and ease tensions Blaine helped organize the Pan-American Congress. He presided over the opening session as representa-

Blaine's Pan-American Congress

tives from 18 nations gathered in October 1889. Blaine immediately proposed a "customs union" to reduce trade barriers in the Americas and a set of arbitration procedures to prevent disputes from erupting into war. Deep suspicions over American motives hamstrung delegates, who in the end established only the weak Pan-American Union to foster peaceful understanding.

Blaine thus found himself forced to pursue separate talks and sometimes to strong-arm his way to the tariff reductions he wanted. If Latin American nations refused to lower their tariffs, he threatened to ban the products of their often single-crop economies under provisions of the 1890 McKinley Tariff. Only three nations—Colombia, Haiti, and Venezuela—had the will to resist.

Prelude in the Pacific

In the Pacific, the United States faced Great Britain and Germany as they vied for control of the strategically located islands of Samoa. In 1878 a treaty gave America the rights to the fine harbor at Pago Pago. When the Germans sent marines to secure their interests in 1889, the British and Americans sent gunboats. As tensions peaked, a typhoon struck, sinking the rival fleets and staving off conflict. Ten years later the three powers finally carved up the islands, with the United States retaining Pago Pago.

If American expansionists wanted to extend trade across the Pacific to China, Hawaii was the crucial link. The islands had been settled some 2000

Ambitions in Hawaii

years earlier by visitors from the Polynesian Islands. In the 1780s an American merchant ship had stopped there, and by the 1840s American merchants and missionaries dominated the port at Honolulu.

Whereas the missionaries had been God-fearing idealists, their descendants were a practical lot: they saw the possibilities for a harvest in sugarcane, not Polynesian souls. Thus they acquired thousands of acres on which they produced sugar for export to the United States. In 1879 the total value of sugar estates in Hawaii was less than $10 million, but by 1898 that figure had jumped to over $40 million. Planters imported cheap laborers from China, Japan, the Philippines, Korea, and Puerto Rico to work the sugarcane fields. Soon Japanese immigrants alone made up a fourth of the population. Native Hawaiians were rapidly becoming a minority on their own islands.

By the 1880s the United States had asserted virtual control over the islands, including naval rights to a base at Pearl Harbor. European imperialists found

Polynesians were culturally ill-suited to the backbreaking labor of sugarcane cultivation in Hawaii. English and American planters, who dominated the sugar plantations, instead recruited Japanese workers like this one.

themselves hopelessly outmaneuvered. The Hawaiian sugar planters had forged particularly close ties with the U.S. because a treaty in 1875 allowed Hawaiian sugar to enter the states duty-free.

In 1890, the planters received a jolt when the McKinley Tariff added a bounty of 2 cents a pound to home-grown sugarcane. Of course, if the Hawaiian Islands

McKinley Tariff were annexed by the United States, their growers would gain this advantage—a thought that set more than a few planters to scheming. Unfortunately for them, Queen Liliuokalani ascended to the Hawaiian throne the very next year. A strong nationalist, she tried to limit foreign influence and restore the power of the monarchy.

As a nationalist, Queen Liliuokalani believed that Hawaii should remain in the hands of its native peoples. And as a monarchist, she believed those hands should be hers, not those of sugar planters who might dominate a constitutional legislature. In 1893, the planters overthrew her. Their success was ensured when a contingent of marines arrived ashore on the pretense of protecting American lives. In the face of heavily armed opposition, the queen capitulated. A commission of planters—four American and one British—took over.

Eager to dampen any British designs on the islands, President Benjamin Harrison signed an annexation treaty with the American-dominated commis-

Hawaii revolts sion early in 1893. But before the Senate could ratify it, Grover Cleveland took office and put the treaty on hold. Cleveland was no foe of expansion but was, as his secretary of state noted, "unalterably opposed to stealing territory, or of annexing people against their consent, and the people of Hawaii do not favor annexation." The idea of incorporating the non-white population also troubled Cleveland. For a time, matters stood at a stalemate.

Crisis in Venezuela

Gold, with its capacity to muddy the waters from which it is panned, stirred trouble in the jungles of Venezuela. In the 1880s prospectors unearthed a 32-pound nugget along the border between Venezuela and the colony of British Guiana. Venezuela and Britain both laid claim to the territory, which also included the mouth of the Orinoco River. The river was a gateway to trade in the interior of South America's northern coast.

For years the United States pressed Britain to submit the dispute to arbitration. In 1895 an exasperated President Cleveland warned the British that their expansive claims against Venezuela impinged on the "safety," "honor," and "welfare" of the United States. Facing an economic depression, neither the president nor Congress wanted to chance having Great Britain close off a promising market. Arbitration, Cleveland insisted, was the only way to avoid armed American intervention.

When the British rejected arbitration, Cleveland fired off what amounted to an ultimatum. The United States would send a commission to set the boundary, and if the British still refused to arbitrate, more forceful action—perhaps even war—would follow. In the end, cool heads prevailed. After all, Cleveland did not want war with Britain, only British consent to terms acceptable to the United States. In that he succeeded. Eager to avoid conflict, the British agreed to arbitration, which in the end left Venezuela with what it wanted most, control of access to the Orinoco, and the United States what it wanted, an opportunity to assert its supremacy in the hemisphere.

Tensions between the United States and Great Britain eased in the wake of the crisis. The British had no choice but to make up. In Europe, they faced a formidable rival: newly unified Germany, rapidly industrializing, seeking colonies, and building a navy. In Asia, Japan and Russia threatened to exclude Britain from important markets. In South Africa, the Boer War—with the descendants of old Dutch settlers—was draining British blood and resources. Granting the United States a free hand in the Western Hemisphere was a small price to pay for cementing Anglo-American relations.

The treaty concluded by Secretary of State John Hay and British Ambassador Sir Julian Pauncefote in 1901 symbolized the new era of Anglo-American friendship. It also ended a campaign begun by James Blaine years earlier. Under the Hay–Pauncefote Treaty, Britain ceded its interest in building a canal across the Central American isthmus, while the United States pledged to leave such a canal open to ships of all nations.

Hay–Pauncefote Treaty

THE IMPERIAL MOMENT

In 1895, after almost 15 years of planning from exile in the United States, José Martí returned to Cuba to renew the struggle for independence from Spain.

Cuba in revolt

With cries of *Cuba libre*, Martí and his rebels cut railroad lines, destroyed sugar mills, and set fire to the cane fields. Within a year, rebel forces controlled more than half the island. But even as they fought the Spanish, the rebels worried about the United States. Their island, just 90 miles off the coast of Florida, had long been a target of American expansionists and business interests. "I have lived in the bowels of the monster," Martí said in reference to the United States, "and I know it."

The Spanish overlords struck back at Martí and his followers with brutal violence. Governor-General Valeriano Weyler herded a half million Cubans from their homes into fortified camps where filth, disease, and starvation killed perhaps 200,000. Outside these "reconcentration" camps, Weyler chased the rebels across the countryside, polluting drinking water, killing farm animals, burning crops.

Mounting Tensions

Cleveland had little sympathy for the Cuban revolt. He doubted that the mostly black population was capable of self-government and feared that independence from Spain might lead to chaos on the island. Already the revolution had caused widespread destruction of American-owned property. The president settled on a policy that would throw American support neither to Spain nor to the rebels: opposing the rebellion, but pressing Spain to grant Cuba some freedoms.

In the Republican party, expansionists like Theodore Roosevelt and Massachusetts senator Henry Cabot Lodge urged a more forceful policy. In 1896 they

Republican imperialism

succeeded in writing an imperial wish list into the Republican national platform: annexation of Hawaii, the construction of a Nicaraguan canal, purchase of the Virgin Islands, and more naval expansion. They also called for recognition of Cuban independence, a step that, if taken, would likely provoke war with Spain. When the victorious William McKinley entered the White House, however, his Republican supporters found only a moderate expansionist. Cautiously, privately, he lobbied Spain to stop cracking down on the rebels and destroying American property.

In 1897 Spain promised to remove the much-despised Weyler, end the reconcentration policy, and offer Cuba greater autonomy. The shift encouraged McKinley to resist pressure at home for more hostile action. But leaders of the Spanish army in Cuba had no desire to compromise. Although Weyler was removed, the military renewed efforts to crush the rebels and stirred pro-army riots in the streets of Havana. Early in 1898, McKinley dispatched the battleship *Maine* to show that the United States meant to protect its interests and its citizens.

A grisly depiction of the explosion that sank the battleship *Maine* in Havana harbor in 1898, complete with a panel entitled "Recovering the Dead Bodies" (upper right). The causes of the explosion remain a mystery, but illustrations like this one helped jingoists turn the event into a battle cry.

Then in February 1898 the State Department received a stolen copy of a letter to Cuba sent by the Spanish minister in Washington, Enrique Dupuy de Lôme. So did William Randolph Hearst, a pioneer of sensationalist, or "yellow," journalism who was eager for war with Spain. "WORST INSULT TO THE UNITED STATES IN ITS HISTORY," screamed the headline of Hearst's New York *Journal*. What had de Lôme actually written? After referring to McKinley as a mere "would-be politician," the letter admitted that Spain had no intention of changing its policy of crushing the rebels. Red-faced Spanish officials immediately recalled de Lôme, but most Americans now believed that Spain had deceived the United States.

De Lôme letter

On February 15, 1898, as the *Maine* lay peacefully at anchor in the Havana harbor, explosions ripped through the hull. Within minutes the ship sank to the bottom, killing some 260 American sailors. The cause of the blasts remains unclear, but most Americans, inflamed by hysterical news accounts, concluded that Spanish agents had sabotaged the ship. McKinley sought a diplomatic solution but also a $50 million appropriation "to get ready for war."

Sinking of the Maine

Pressures for war proved too great, and on April 11, McKinley asked Congress to authorize "forceful intervention" in Cuba. Nine days later Congress recognized Cuban independence, insisted on the withdrawal of Spanish forces, and gave the president authority to use military force. In a flush of idealism, Congress also adopted the Teller Amendment, renouncing any aim to annex Cuba.

Teller Amendment

Certainly both idealism and moral outrage led many Americans down the path to war. But in the end, the "splendid little war" (as Secretary of State John Hay called it) came as a result of less lofty ambitions: empire, trade, glory.

The Imperial War

For the 5462 men who died, there was little splendid about the Spanish–American War. Only 379 gave their lives in battle. The rest succumbed to accidents, disease, and the mismanagement of an unprepared army. As war began, the American force totaled only 30,000, none trained for fighting in tropical climates. The sudden expansion to 60,000 troops and 200,000 volunteers overtaxed the graft-ridden system of supply. Rather than tropical uniforms troops were issued winter woolens and sometimes fed on rations that were diseased, rotten, or poisoned. Some soldiers found themselves fighting with weapons from the Civil War.

Military disorganization

The Navy fared better. Decisions in the 1880s to modernize the fleet paid handsome dividends. Naval battles largely determined the outcome of the war. As soon as war was declared, Admiral George Dewey ordered his Asiatic battle squadron from China to the Philippines. Just before dawn on May 1, he opened fire on the Spanish ships in Manila Bay. Five hours later the entire Spanish squadron lay at the bottom of the bay. Three hundred eighty-one Spaniards were killed but only one American, a ship's engineer who died of a heart attack. Dewey had no plans to follow up his stunning victory with an invasion. His fleet carried no marines with which to take Manila. So ill-prepared was President McKinley for war, let alone victory, that only after learning of Dewey's success did he order 11,000 American troops to the Philippines.

Dewey at Manila

Halfway around the globe, another Spanish fleet had slipped into Santiago harbor in Cuba just before the arrival of the U.S. Navy. The Navy, under Admiral William Sampson, blockaded the island, expecting the Spanish to flee under the cover of darkness. Instead, on July 3, the Spanish fleet made a desperate dash for the open seas in broad daylight. So startled were the Americans that several of their ships nearly collided as they rushed to attack their exposed foes. All seven Spanish ships were sunk, with 474 casualties. Only one American was killed and one wounded. With Cuba cut off from Spain, the war was virtually won.

War in Cuba

Few Americans had heard of the Philippine Islands; fewer still could locate them on a globe. McKinley himself followed news from the Pacific front on an old textbook map. But most Americans knew the location of Cuba and how close it lay to the Florida coast.

Before the outbreak of hostilities, Tampa, Florida, was a sleepy coastal town with a single railroad line. As the port of embarkation for the Cuban expeditionary force, it became a hive of activity. In the spring of 1898 alone, some 17,000 troops arrived. Tampa's overtaxed facilities soon broke down, spawning disease, tension, and racial violence as well.

President McKinley had authorized the army to raise five volunteer regiments of black soldiers. By the time war was declared, over 8000 African *Racial tensions* Americans had signed up. Like most southern towns, Tampa and nearby Lakeland were largely segregated. The 4000 black soldiers stationed there could sail off to die freeing the peasants of Cuba, but they could not buy a soda at the local drugstore. "Is America any better than Spain?" one dismayed black chaplain wondered. As the expeditionary force prepared to

Black veterans of the western Indian wars along with volunteers, segregated and commanded by white officers, made up almost a quarter of the American force that invaded Cuba. Members of the Tenth Calvary, shown here, were clearly in no mood to be subjected to the harrassment they and other black troops encountered around Tampa. Later the Tenth Calvary supported a charge by Colonel Teddy Roosevelt's Rough Riders at the battle of San Juan Hill.

leave in early June, anger turned to violence. After drunken white troops shot at a black child, black troops in Tampa rioted. Three white and 27 black Americans were wounded in the melee.

Matters were scarcely less chaotic as 17,000 disorganized troops and hundreds of reporters finally scrambled aboard ships. There they sat for a week, until finally sailing for Santiago and battle. By June 30, the Americans had landed to challenge some 24,000 Spanish, many equipped with modern rifles. The following day 7000 Americans—including the black soldiers of the Ninth and Tenth Cavalry regiments—stormed up heavily fortified San Juan Hill and nearby Kettle Hill. Their objective was the high ground north and east of Santiago.

Among them Lieutenant Colonel Theodore Roosevelt thrilled at the experience of battle. He had raised a cavalry troop of cowboys and college polo play-

The Rough Riders

ers, originally called "Teddy's Texas Tarantulas." By the time they arrived in Cuba, the volunteers were answering to the nickname "Rough Riders." As they charged toward the high ground, Roosevelt yelled: "Gentlemen, the Almighty God and the just cause are with you. Gentlemen, *charge!*" The withering fire drowned out his shrill, squeaky voice, so he repeated the call. Charge they did and conquer the enemy, though the battle cost more than 1500 American casualties.

Without a fleet for cover or any way to escape, the Spanish garrison surrendered on July 17. In the Philippines, a similar brief battle preceded the American taking of Manila on August 13. The "splendid little war" had ended in less than four months.

Peace and the Debate over Empire

Conquering Cuba and the Philippines proved easier than deciding what to do with them. The Teller Amendment had renounced any American claim to Cuba. But clearly the United States had not freed the island to see chaos reign or American business and military interests excluded. And what of the Philippines—and Spanish Puerto Rico, which American forces had taken without a struggle? Powerful public and congressional sentiment pushed McKinley to claim empire as the fruits of victory.

The president himself favored such a course. The battle in the Pacific highlighted the need for naval bases and coaling stations. "To maintain our flag in

Annexing Hawaii

the Philippines, we must raise our flag in Hawaii," the New York *Sun* insisted. On July 7 McKinley signed a joint congressional resolution annexing Hawaii, as planters had wanted for nearly a decade.

The Philippines presented a more difficult problem. Filipinos had greeted the American forces as liberators, not new colonizers. The popular leader of the

Aguinaldo

rebel forces fighting Spain, Emilio Aguinaldo, had returned to the islands on an American ship. To the rebels' dismay, McKinley

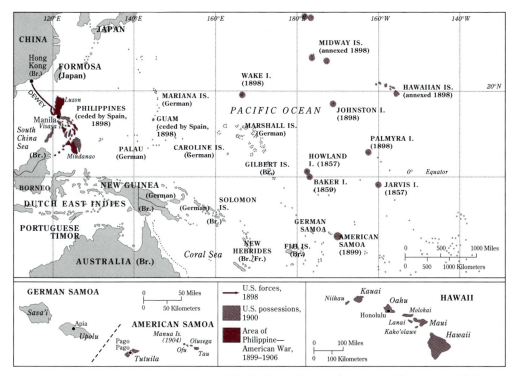

THE UNITED STATES IN THE PACIFIC In the late nineteenth century, Germany and the United States emerged as Pacific naval powers and contestants for influence and trade in China. The island groups of the Central and Southwest Pacific were of little economic value but had great strategic worth as bases and coaling stations along the route to Asia.

insisted that the islands were under American authority until the peace treaty settled matters.

Many influential Americans—former president Grover Cleveland, steel baron Andrew Carnegie, novelist Mark Twain—opposed annexation of the Philippines. Yet even these anti-imperialists favored expansion, if only in the form of trade. Business leaders especially believed that the country could enjoy the economic benefits of the Philippines without the costs of maintaining it as a colony. Annexation would mire the United States too deeply in the quicksands of Asian politics, they argued. More important, a large, costly fleet would be necessary to defend the islands. To the imperialists that was precisely the point: a large fleet was crucial to the interests of a powerful commercial nation.

Anti-imperialists

Racist ideas shaped both sides of the argument. Imperialists believed that the racial inferiority of nonwhites made occupation of the Philippines necessary,

The role of racism and they were ready to assume the "white man's burden" and govern. Gradually, they argued, Filipinos would be taught the virtues of Western civilization, Christianity,* democracy, and self-rule. Anti-imperialists, on the other hand, feared racial intermixing and the possibility of Asian workers' flooding of the American labor market. They also maintained that dark-skinned people would never develop the capacity for self-government. An American government in the Philippines could be sustained only at the point of bayonets—yet the U.S. Constitution made no provision for governing people without representation or equal rights. Such a precedent, the anti-imperialists warned, might one day threaten American liberties at home.

Still, when the Senate debated the Treaty of Paris ending the Spanish–American War in 1898, the imperialists had the support of the president, most of Congress, and the majority of public opinion. Even an anti-imperialist like William Jennings Bryan, defeated by McKinley in 1896, supported the treaty. In it Spain surrendered title to Cuba, ceded Puerto Rico and Guam to the United States, and in return for $20 million turned over the Philippines as well.

Eager to see war ended, Bryan and other anti-imperialists believed that once the United States possessed the Philippines, it could free them. The imperialists had other notions. Having acquired an empire and a modern navy to protect it, the United States could now assert its new status as one of the world's great powers.

America's First Asian War

Managing an empire turned out to be even more devilish than acquiring one. As the Senate debated annexation of the Philippines in Washington, rebels clashed *The Philippine insurrection* with an American patrol outside of Manila, igniting a guerrilla war. The few Americans who paid attention called it the "Filipino insurrection," but to those who fought, it was a brutal war. When it ended more than three years later, nearly 5000 Americans, 25,000 rebels, and perhaps as many as 200,000 civilians lay dead.

Racial antagonism spurred the savage fighting. American soldiers tended to dismiss Filipinos as nearly subhuman. Their armed resistance to American occupation often transformed the frustrations of ordinary troops into brutality and torture. To avenge a rebel attack, one American officer swore he would turn the surrounding countryside into a "howling wilderness." Before long the American force was resorting to a garrison strategy of herding Filipinos into concentration camps, while destroying their villages and crops. The policy was embarrassingly reminiscent of "Butcher" Weyler (page 584) in Cuba. In 1902, only after the Americans captured Aguinaldo himself, did the war end.

In contrast to the bitter guerrilla war, the United States ruled its new island territory with relative benevolence. Under William Howard Taft, the first civil-

*In point of fact, most Filipinos were already Catholic after many years under Spanish rule.

U.S. rule in the Philippines ian governor, the Americans built schools, roads, sewers, and factories and inaugurated new farming techniques. The aim, said Taft, was to prepare the Philippines for independence, and in keeping with it, he granted great authority to local officials. These advances—social, economic, and political—benefited the Filipino elite and thus earned their support. Finally, on July 4, 1946, the Philippines were granted independence.

The United States played a similar role in Puerto Rico. As in the Philippines, executive authority resided in a governor appointed by the U.S. president. *Puerto Rico* Under the Foraker Act of 1900 Puerto Ricans received a voice in their government, as well as a nonvoting representative in the U.S. House of Representatives, and certain tariff advantages. All the same, many Puerto Ricans chafed at the idea of such second-class citizenship. Some favored eventual admission to the United States as a state while others advocated independence, a division of opinion that persists even today.

An Open Door in China

Interest in Asia drove the United States to annex the Philippines; and annexation of the Philippines only whetted American interest in Asia. As ever, the possibility of markets in China—whether for Christian souls or consumer goods—proved an irresistible lure.

Both the British, who dominated China's export trade, and the Americans, who wanted to, worried that China might soon be carved up by other powers. Japan had defeated China in 1895, encouraging Russia, Germany, and France to join in demanding trade concessions. Each nation sought to establish an Asian "sphere of influence" in which its commercial and military interests reigned. Often this ended in commercial and other restrictions against rival powers. Since Britain and the United States wanted the benefits of trade rather than actual colonies, they tried to limit foreign demands while leaving China open to all commerce.

In 1899, at the urging of the British, Secretary of State John Hay circulated the first of two "open door" notes among the imperial powers. He did not ask *The "open door" notes* them to relinquish their spheres of influence in China, only to keep them open to free trade with other nations. The United States could hardly have enforced even so modest a proposal, for it lacked the military might to prevent the partitioning of China. Still, Japan and most of the European powers agreed in broad outline with Hay's policy, out of fear that the Americans might tip the delicate balance by siding with a rival. Hay seized on the tepid response and brashly announced that the open door in China was international policy.

Unrest soon threatened to close the door. Chinese nationalists, known to Westerners as Boxers for their clenched fist symbol, formed secret societies to

Boxer Rebellion drive out the *fon kwei*, or foreign devils. Encouraged by the Chinese empress, Boxers murdered hundreds of Christian missionaries and their followers and besieged foreign diplomats and citizens at the British Embassy in Beijing. European nations quickly dispatched troops to quell the uprising and free the diplomats, while President McKinley sent 2500 Americans to join the march to the capital city. Along the way, the angry foreign armies plundered the countryside and killed civilians before reaching Beijing and breaking the siege.

Hay feared that once in control of Beijing the conquerors might never leave. So he sent a second open-door note in 1900, this time asking foreign powers to respect China's territorial and administrative integrity. They endorsed the proposal in principle only. In fact, the open-door notes together amounted to little more than an announcement of American desires to maintain stability and trade in Asia. Yet they reflected a fundamental purpose to which the United States dedicated itself across the globe: to open closed markets and to keep open those markets that other empires had yet to close. The new American empire would have its share of colonies, but in Asia as elsewhere it would be built primarily on trade.

To expansionists like Alfred Thayer Mahan, Theodore Roosevelt, and John Hay, American interests would be secure only when they had been established worldwide, a course of action they believed to be blessed by divine providence. "We will not renounce our part in the mission of the race, trustee under God of the civilization of the world," declared Senator Albert Beveridge. But to one French diplomat, more accustomed to wheeling and dealing in the corridors of international power, it seemed that the Americans had tempted fate rather than destiny. With a whiff of Old World cynicism or perhaps a prophet's eye, he remarked, "The United States is seated at the table where the great game is played, and it cannot leave it."

On New Year's Eve at the State House in Boston a midnight ceremony ushered in the twentieth century. The crowd celebrated with psalms and hymns. There was a flourish of trumpets, and in the absence of a national anthem everyone sang "America."

Solemn and patriotic, the dawn of the new century brought an end to an era of political uncertainty and a decade of social upheaval. Prosperity returned at home; empire beckoned abroad. But deep divisions—between rich and poor, farmers and factory workers, men and women, native-born and immigrant, black and white—split America. A younger generation of leaders stood in the wings, fearful of the schisms but confident it could bridge them. As Theodore Roosevelt looked eagerly toward war with Spain and the chance to expand American horizons, he did not mince words with an older opponent. "You and your generation have had your chance. . . . Now let us of this generation have ours!"

SIGNIFICANT EVENTS

1850	Clayton–Bulwer Treaty
1867	Patrons of Husbandry ("Grange") founded; Alaska acquired
1869	Prohibition party founded; Massachusetts establishes first state regulatory commission
1874	Greenback party organized; Woman's Christian Temperance Union formed
1875	First Farmers' Alliance organized
1877	*Munn v. Illinois* establishes the right of states to regulate private property in the public interest
1881	President James Garfield assassinated; Chester Arthur sworn in; Booker T. Washington founds Tuskegee Normal and Industrial Institute in Alabama
1887	Interstate Commerce Commission created
1889	First Pan-American Congress
1890	National American Woman Suffrage Association created; Sherman Antitrust Act; Wyoming enters the Union as first state to give women the vote; Sherman Silver Purchase Act; McKinley Tariff; Southern and Northwestern Alliances adopt Ocala Demands; Mahan's *The Influence of Sea Power Upon History, 1660–1783* published
1892	Populist party formed; Grover Cleveland elected president
1893	Panic of 1893; Sherman Silver Purchase Act repealed; Anti-Saloon League created; controversy over annexation of Hawaii
1894	Coxey's Army marches on Washington to demand public works for the unemployed
1895	National Municipal League founded; Venezuelan boundary dispute; Martí revives Cuban revolution
1896	League for the Protection of the Family organized; William McKinley elected president
1898	Sinking of the USS *Maine;* war with Spain; Teller Amendment; Dewey captures the Phillipines; Tampa riots; Treaty of Paris; Hawaii formally annexed; Anti-Imperialist League established
1898–1902	Philippine insurrection
1899	First open-door notes
1900	Boxer Rebellion; second open-door notes; Foraker Act establishes civil government in Puerto Rico
1903	W. E. B. Du Bois's *The Souls of Black Folk* published
1909	National Association for the Advancement of Colored People founded

CHAPTER TWENTY-TWO

The Progressive Era

Quitting time, March 25, 1911. The long day had almost come to an end at the Triangle Shirtwaist Company in New York City. The deafening whir of some 1500 sewing machines would soon be silenced as hundreds of workers—mostly young immigrant women and their daughters—were set free. To some quitting time seemed like an emancipation. Twelve-hour days in stifling, unsafe workrooms, weekly paychecks of but $3 to $15, fines for the tiniest mistakes, deductions for needle and thread—even for electricity—made seamstresses angry. Two years earlier, their frustrations had boiled over into an industrywide strike for better wages and working conditions. Despite a union victory, the only change visible at Triangle was that every morning the doors were locked to keep workers in and labor organizers out.

The fire started in the lofts as the workers were leaving their machines. In minutes the top stories were ablaze. Terrified seamstresses groped through the black smoke, only to find exits locked or clogged with bodies. All but one of the few working fire escapes collapsed. When the fire trucks arrived, horrified firefighters discovered that their ladders could not reach the top stories. "Spectators saw again and again pitiable companionships formed in the instant of death—girls who placed their arms around each other as they leaped," read one news story. Their bodies hit the sidewalk with a sickening thud or were spiked on the iron guard rails. One hundred forty-six people died, most of them young working-class women.

A few days later 80,000 New Yorkers joined the silent funeral procession snaking slowly up Fifth Avenue in the rain. A quarter of a million watched. At the Metropolitan Opera House, union leader Rose Schneiderman told a rally, "This is not the first time that girls have been burned alive in the city. Every year thousands of us are maimed." A special state commission investigated the tragedy. Over the next four years its recommendations produced 56 state laws regulating fire safety, hours, machinery, and homework. They amounted to the most far-reaching labor code in the country.

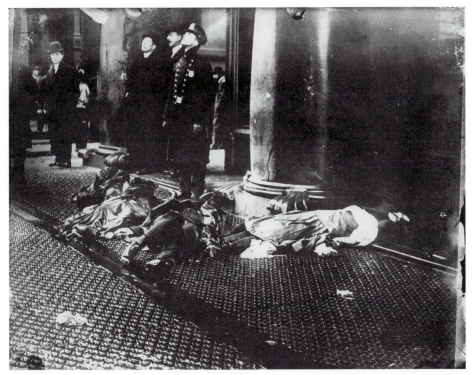

On a street littered with the bodies of dead workers, a policeman looks up at the blazing Triangle Shirtwaist factory, unable to stop more people from jumping. Firefighters arrived within minutes, but their ladders could not reach the top stories.

The Triangle fire shocked the nation and underscored a growing fear: modern industrial society had created profound strains, widespread misery, and deep class divisions. Corporations grew to unimagined size, bought and sold legislators, dictated the terms of their own profit. Men, women, and children worked around the clock in unsafe factories for wages that barely supported them. In cities across America, tenement-bred disease took innocent lives, criminals threatened people and property, saloons tied the working poor to dishonest political bosses. Even among the middle class, inflation was shrinking their wallets at the rate of 3 percent a year. "It was a world of greed," concluded one garment worker; "the human being didn't mean anything."

But human beings did mean something to followers of an influential reform movement sweeping the country. Progressivism had emerged in the mid-1890s

The rise of progressivism

and would last through World War I. The movement sprang from many impulses, mixing a liberal concern for the poor and working class with conservative efforts to stabilize business and avoid social chaos. Liberal or conservative, most progressives shared a desire to soften the harsh impact of industrialization, urbanization, and immigration.

Progressivism thus began in the cities, where those forces converged. It was organized by an angry, idealistic middle class and percolated up from neighborhoods to city halls, state capitals, and, finally, Washington. Though usually pursued through politics, the goals of progressives were broadly social—to create a "good society," where people could live decently, harmoniously, and prosperously, along middle-class guidelines.

Unlike earlier reformers, progressives saw government as a protector, not an oppressor. Only government possessed the resources for the broad-based reforms they sought. Progressivism spawned the modern activist state, with its capacity to regulate the economy and manage society. And because American society had become so interdependent, progressivism became the first nationwide reform movement. No political party monopolized it; no single group controlled it. It flowered in the presidencies of Republican Theodore Roosevelt and Democrat Woodrow Wilson. In 1912 it even spawned its own party, the Progressive, or "Bull Moose," party. By then progressivism had filtered well beyond politics into every realm of American life.

THE ROOTS OF PROGRESSIVE REFORM

Families turned from their homes; an army of unemployed on the roads; hunger, strikes, and bloody violence across the country—the wrenching depression of 1893 forced Americans to take a hard look at their new industrial order. They found common complaints that cut across lines of class, religion, and ethnicity. If streetcar companies raised fares while service deteriorated, if food processors doctored their canned goods with harmful additives, if politicians skimmed money from the public till, everyone suffered. And no one alone could stop it.

The result was not a coherent progressive movement but a set of loosely connected goals. Some progressives fought for efficient government and hon-

Aims of progressives

est politics. Others called for greater regulation of business and a more orderly economy. Some sought social justice for the urban poor; others, social welfare to protect children, women, workers, and consumers. Still other progressives looked to purify society by outlawing alcohol and drugs, stamping out prostitution and slums, and restricting the flood of new immigrants.

Paternalistic by nature, progressives often imposed their solutions no matter what the less "enlightened" poor or oppressed saw as their own best interests. And they acted partly out of nostalgia. Progressives wanted to redeem such traditional American values as democracy, opportunity for the individual, and the spirit of public service. Yet if their ends were traditional, their means were distinctly modern. They used the systems and methods of the new industrial order—the latest techniques of organization, management, and science—to fight its excesses.

COUNTERPOINT   *What Was Progressivism?*

Embracing such diversity, progressivism has generated a host of interpretations. Historians writing during the movement depicted it as progressives did: a democratic crusade by the "good people" to curb big business, fight political corruption, and promote social justice. A later generation of historians, examining individual progressives, concluded that they were a small group of once-powerful, upper-middle-class families anxious to reassert the status they had lost to rising industrialists and corporate executives.

To explain the often strong support of corporations, historians of the "New Left" have portrayed progressivism as the "triumph of conservatism," whose aim was to protect corporations from strict regulation and competition. Still others have looked at progressivism as a widespread effort by the "new middle class" of professionals, business leaders, and others to secure their power by bringing order and efficiency to the new industrial economy.

Historians with interests in women, consumers, and African Americans have all found in progressivism an opportunity for these groups to advance their separate, sometimes conflicting goals. Perhaps the most useful interpretation comes from those who see progressivism as part of the broad process of adjustment to the new industrial order. They emphasize the weakening of political parties and the growing influence of "interest groups" of workers, industrialists, consumers, and others who campaigned for the reforms they wanted.

Progressive Beliefs

Progressives were moderate modernizers. They accepted the American system as sound, only in need of adjustment. Many drew on the increasingly popular Darwinian theories of evolution to buttress this gradual approach to change. With its notion of slowly changing species, evolution undermined the acceptance of fixed principles that had guided social thought in the Victorian era. Progressives saw an evolving landscape of shifting values. They denied the old Calvinist doctrine of inborn sinfulness and instead saw people as having a greater potential for good than for evil.

Yet progressives somehow had to explain the existence of evil and wrongdoing. Most agreed that they were "largely, if not wholly, products of society or environment." People went wrong, wrote one progressive, because of "what happens to them." By changing what happened, the human potential for good could be released.

With an eye to results, progressives asked not "Is it true?" but "Does it work?" Philosopher Charles Peirce called this new way of thinking "pragma-

Pragmatism

tism." William James, the Harvard psychologist, became its most famous popularizer. For James, pragmatism meant "looking towards last things, fruits, consequences, facts."

The Pragmatic Approach

Pragmatism led educators, social scientists, and lawyers to adopt new approaches to reform. John Dewey, the master educator of the progressive era, believed that environment shaped the patterns of human thought. Instead of demanding mindless memorization of abstract and unconnected facts, Dewey tried to "make each one of our schools an embryonic community life." At his School of Pedagogy, founded in 1896, he let students unbolt their desks from the floor, move about, and learn by doing so that they could train for real life.

Psychologist John B. Watson believed that human behavior could be shaped at will. Give him control of an infant's world from birth, Watson boasted, "and

Behaviorism

I'll guarantee to take any one at random and train him to become any specialist I might select, doctor, lawyer, artist, merchant, chief, and yes, even beggarman and thief." "Behaviorism" swept the social sciences and later advertising, where Watson himself eventually landed.

Lawyers and legal theorists applied their own blend of pragmatism and behaviorism. Justice Oliver Wendell Holmes, Jr., appointed to the Supreme Court in 1902, rejected the idea that the traditions of law were constant and universal. Law was a living organism to be interpreted according to experience and the needs of a changing society.

This environmental view of the law, known as "sociological jurisprudence," found a skilled practitioner in Louis Brandeis. Shaken by the brutal suppression of the Homestead steel strike of 1892, Brandeis quit his corporate practice and proclaimed himself the "people's lawyer." The law must "guide by the light of reason," he wrote, which meant bringing everyday life to bear in any court case. When laundry owner Curt Muller challenged an Oregon law limiting his laun-

Brandeis Brief

dresses to a 10-hour workday, Brandeis defended the statute before the Supreme Court in 1908. His famous brief contained 102 pages describing the damaging effects of long hours on working women and only 2 pages of legal precedents. *In Muller v. Oregon,* the Supreme Court upheld Oregon's right to limit the working hours of laborers and thus legitimized the "Brandeis Brief."

The Progressive Method

Seeing the nation torn by conflict, progressives tried to restore a sense of community through the ideal of a single public interest. Christian ethics were the guide, to be applied after using the latest scientific methods to gather and analyze data about a social problem. The modern corporation furnished an appealing model for organization. Like corporate executives, progressives relied on careful management, coordinated systems, and specialized bureaucracies to carry out reforms.

Between 1902 and 1912 a new breed of journalists provided the necessary evidence and fired public indignation. They investigated wrongdoers, named them in print, and described their misdeeds in vivid detail. Most exposés began as articles in mass-circulation magazines such as *McClure's*. It stirred controversy (and boosted circulation) when publisher Samuel McClure sent reporter Lincoln Steffens to uncover the crooked ties between business and politics. "Tweed Days in St. Louis," which *McClure's* published in October 1902, was followed in the November issue by the first of Ida M. Tarbell's stinging, well-researched indictments of John D. Rockefeller's oil empire, collected later as the *History of the Standard Oil Company* (1904). Soon a full-blown literature of exposure was covering every ill from unsafe food to child labor.

A disgusted Theodore Roosevelt thought the new reporters had gone too far and called them "muckrakers," after the man who raked up filth in the

Muckrakers

seventeenth-century classic *Pilgrim's Progress*. But by documenting dishonesty and blight, muckrakers not only aroused people but educated them. No broad reform movement of American institutions would have taken place without them.

To move beyond exposure to solutions, progressives stressed volunteerism and collective action. They drew on the organizational impulse that seemed

Voluntary organizations

everywhere to be bringing people together in new interest groups. Between 1890 and 1920 nearly 400 organizations were founded, many to combat the ills of industrial society. Some, like the National Consumers' League, grew out of efforts to promote general causes—in this case protecting consumers and workers from exploitation. Others, such as the National Tuberculosis Association, aimed at a specific problem.

When voluntary action failed, progressives looked to government to protect the public welfare. They mistrusted legislators, who might be controlled by corporate interests or political machines. So they strengthened the executive branch by increasing the power of individual mayors, governors, and presidents. Then they watched those executives carefully.

Progressives also drew on the expertise of the newly professionalized middle class. Confident, cosmopolitan professionals—doctors, engineers, psychia-

Professionals

trists, city planners—mounted campaigns to stamp out venereal disease and dysentery, to reform prisons and asylums, and to beautify cities. At local, state, and federal levels, new agencies and commissions staffed by experts began to investigate and regulate lobbyists, insurance and railroad companies, public health, even government itself.

THE SEARCH FOR THE GOOD SOCIETY

If progressivism ended in politics, it began with social reform: the need to reach out, to do something to bring the "good society" a step closer. Ellen Richards had just such ends in mind in 1890 when she opened the New England Kitchen in downtown Boston. Richards, a chemist and home economist, designed the Kitchen to sell cheap, wholesome food to the working poor. For a few pennies, customers could choose from a nutritious menu, every dish of which had been tested in Richards's laboratory at the Massachusetts Institute of Technology.

The New England Kitchen promoted social as well as nutritional reform. Women freed from the drudgery of cooking could seek gainful employment. And as a "household experiment station" and center for dietary information, the Kitchen tried to educate the poor and Americanize immigrants by showing them how the middle class prepared meals. According to philanthropist Pauline Shaw, it was also a "rival to the saloon." A common belief was that poor diets fostered drinking, especially among the lower classes.

In the end, the New England Kitchen served more as an inexpensive eatery for middle-class working women and students than as a resource for the poor

Pattern of reform

or an agency of Americanization. Still, Ellen Richards's experiment reflected a pattern typical of progressive social reform: the mix of professionalism with uplift, socially conscious women entering the public arena, the hope of creating a better world along middle-class lines.

Poverty in a New Light

During the 1890s crime reporter and photographer Jacob Riis introduced middle-class audiences to urban poverty. Writing in vivid detail in *How the Other Half Lives* (1890), he brought readers into the teeming tenement. Accompanying the text were shocking photos of poverty-stricken Americans—Riis's "other half." He also used lantern slide shows to publicize their plight. His pictures of slum life appeared artless, merely recording the desperate poverty before the camera. But Riis used them to tell a moralistic story, as the earlier English novelist Charles Dickens had used his melodramatic tales to attack the abuses of industrialism in England. People began to see poverty in a new, more sympathetic light—the fault less of the individual than of social conditions.

A haunting naturalism in fiction and painting followed Riis's gritty photographic essays. In *McTeague* (1899) and *Sister Carrie* (1900), novelists like Frank

Naturalism

Norris and Theodore Dreiser spun dark tales of city dwellers struggling to keep body and soul intact. The "Ashcan school" painted urban life in all its grimy realism. Photographer Alfred Stieglitz and painters John Sloan and George Bellows chose slums, tenements, and dirty streets as subjects. Poverty began to look less ominous and more heartrending.

Between 1908 and 1914 the Russell Sage Foundation produced six large volumes of facts and figures documenting a vicious cycle of urban poverty that trapped its victims for generations. The children of paupers were likely to be paupers themselves, not because of heredity or sin but because of deprivation.

A new profession—social work—proceeded from this new view of poverty. Social work developed out of the old settlement house movement (page 510).

Social work Like the physicians from whom they drew inspiration, social workers studied hard data to diagnose the problems of their "clients" and worked with them to solve their problems. A social worker's "differential casework" attempted to treat individuals case by case, each according to the way the client had been shaped by environment.

In reality poverty was but a single symptom of deep-rooted personal and social ills. Most progressives, however, continued to see it as a by-product of political and corporate greed.

Expanding the "Woman's Sphere"

Progressive social reform attracted a great many women seeking what Jane Addams called "the larger life" of public affairs. In the late nineteenth century, women found that protecting their traditional sphere of home and family forced them to move beyond it. Bringing up children, making meals, keeping house, and caring for the sick now involved community decisions about schools, public health, and countless other matters.

Many middle- and upper-middle-class women received their first taste of public life from women's organizations, including mothers' clubs, temperance

Women's organizations societies, and church groups. By the turn of the century, some 500 women's clubs boasted over 160,000 members. Through the General Federation of Women's Clubs, they funded libraries and hospitals, and supported schools, settlement houses, compulsory education, and child labor laws. Eventually they moved beyond the concerns of home and family to endorse such controversial causes as woman suffrage and unionization. To that list the National Association of Colored Women added the special concerns of race, none more urgent than the fight against lynching.

The dawn of the century saw the rise of a new generation of women. Longer lived, better educated, and less often married than their mothers, they

New woman were also willing to pursue careers for fulfillment. Usually they turned to professions that involved the traditional role of nurturer—nursing, library work, teaching, and settlement housework. Custom and prejudice still restricted these new women. The faculty at the Massachusetts Institute of Technology, for example, refused to allow Ellen Richards to pursue a doctorate. Instead they hired her to run the gender-segregated "Woman's Laboratory" for training public school teachers. At the turn of the century, only about 1500 female lawyers practiced in the United States, and in 1910 women made up barely 6 percent of licensed physicians. That figure rapidly declined as

By 1900 one-fourth of the nonfarm labor force was female. On average, women earned $3 less a week than unskilled men. Here at a Labor Day parade in San Diego in 1910 women demand equal pay for equal work.

male-dominated medical associations grew in power and discouraged the entry of women.

Despite the often bitter opposition of families, some feminists tried to destroy the boundaries of the woman's sphere. In *Women and Economics* (1898) Charlotte Perkins Gilman condemned the conventions of womanhood—femininity, marriage, maternity, domesticity—as enslaving and obsolete. She argued for a radically restructured society with large apartment houses, communal arrangements for child rearing and housekeeping, and cooperative kitchens to free women from economic dependence on men.

Margaret Sanger sought to free women from chronic pregnancy. Sanger, a visiting nurse on the Lower East Side of New York, had seen too many poor women overburdened with children, pregnant year after year, with no hope of escaping the cycle. The consequences were crippling. "Women cannot be on equal footing with men until they have complete control over their reproductive functions," she argued.

Margaret Sanger

The insight came as a revelation one summer evening in 1912 when Sanger was called to the home of a distraught immigrant family on Grand Street. Sadie Sachs, mother of three, had nearly died a year earlier from a self-induced abortion. In an effort to terminate another pregnancy, she had killed herself. Sanger

E Y E W I T N E S S   T O   H I S T O R Y

Jane Addams Fights Child Labor

Our very first Christmas at Hull-House, when we as yet knew nothing of child labor, a number of little girls refused the candy which was offered them as part of the Christmas good cheer, saying simply that they "worked in a candy factory and could not bear the sight of it." We discovered that for six weeks they had worked from seven in the morning until nine at night, and they were exhausted as well as satiated. The sharp consciousness of stern economic conditions was thus thrust upon us in the midst of the season of good will. . . .

The visits we made in the neighborhood constantly discovered women sewing upon sweatshop work, and often they were assisted by incredibly small children. I remember a little girl of four who pulled out basting threads hour after hour, sitting on a stool at the feet of her Bohemian mother, a little bunch of human misery. But even for that there was no legal redress, for the only child-labor law in Illinois with any provision for enforcement had been secured by the coal miners' unions, and was confined to children employed in mines. . . .

While we found many pathetic cases of child labor and hard-driven victims of the sweating system who could not possibly earn enough in the short busy season to support themselves during the rest of the year, it became evident that we must add carefully collected information to our general impression of neighborhood conditions if we would make it of genuine value.

There was at the time no statistical information on Chicago industrial conditions, and Mrs. Florence Kelley, an early resident of Hull-House, suggested to the Illinois State Bureau of Labor that they investigate the sweating system in Chicago with its attendant child labor. The head of the Bureau adopted this suggestion and engaged Mrs. Kelley to make the investigation. When the report was presented to the Illinois Legislature, a special committee was appointed to look into the Chicago conditions. . . .

As a result of its investigations, this committee recommended to the Legislature the provisions which afterward became those of the first factory law of Illinois, regulating the sanitary conditions of the sweatshop and fixing fourteen as the age at which a child might be employed. . . .

Although this first labor legislation was but bringing Illinois into line with the nations in the modern industrial world, which "have long been obliged for their own sakes to come to the aid of the workers by which they live—that the child, the young person and the woman may be protected from their own weakness and necessity—" nevertheless from the first it ran counter to the instinct and tradition, almost to the very religion of the manufacturers, who were for the most part self-made men.

Jane Addams, *Twenty Years at Hull-House* (New York: The Macmillan Company, 1910), pp. 148–153.

vowed that night "to do something to change the destiny of mothers whose miseries were as vast as the sky." She became a crusader for what she called "birth control." By distributing information on contraception, she hoped to free women from unwanted pregnancies and the fate of Sadie Sachs.

Single or married, militant or moderate, professional or lay, white or black, more and more middle-class urban women thus became "social housekeepers." From their own homes they turned to the homes of their neighbors and from there to all of society.

Social Welfare

In the "bigger family of the city," as one woman reformer called it, settlement house workers found that they alone could not care for the welfare of the poor. If industrial America, with its sooty factories and overcrowded slums, was to be transformed into the good society, individual acts of charity would have to be supplemented by government. Laws had to be passed and agencies created to promote social welfare, including improved housing, workplaces, parks, and playgrounds, the abolition of child labor, and the enactment of eight-hour day laws for working women.

By 1910 the more than 400 settlement houses across the nation had organized into a loose affiliation, with settlement workers ready to help fashion government policy. With greater experience than men in the field, women led the way. Julia Lathrop, a Vassar College graduate, spent 20 years at Jane Addams's Hull House before becoming the first head of the new federal Children's Bureau in 1912. By then two-thirds of the states had adopted some child

Keating–Owen Act

labor legislation, although loopholes exempted countless youngsters from coverage. Under Lathrop's leadership, Congress was persuaded to pass the Keating–Owen Act (1916), forbidding goods manufactured by children to cross state lines.[*]

---

[*]The Supreme Court struck down the law in 1918 as an improper regulation of local labor; nonetheless, it focused greater attention on the abuses of child labor.

Florence Kelley, who had also worked at Hull House (page 510), spearheaded a similar campaign in Illinois to protect women workers by limiting their workday to eight hours. As general secretary of the National Consumers' League, she also organized boycotts of companies that treated employees inhumanely. Eventually most states enacted laws restricting the number of hours women could work.

Woman Suffrage

Ever since the conference for women's rights held at Seneca Falls in 1848, women reformers had pressed for the right to vote on the grounds of simple justice and equal opportunity. They adopted the slogan *"woman* suffrage" to emphasize the solidarity of women, regardless of class, ethnicity, or race. Progressives embraced woman suffrage by stressing what they saw as the practical results: protecting the home and increasing the voting power of native-born whites. The "purer sensibilities" of women—an ideal held by Victorians and progressives alike—would help cleanse the political process of selfishness and corruption.

The suffrage movement benefited, too, from new leadership. In 1900 Carrie Chapman Catt became president of the National American Woman Suffrage

Catt's "winning plan"

Association, founded by Susan B. Anthony in 1890. Politically astute and a skilled organizer, Catt mapped a grass-roots strategy of education and persuasion from state to state. She called it "the winning plan." As the map shows, victories came first in the West, where women and men had already forged a more equal partnership to overcome the hardships of frontier life. By 1914, 10 western states (and Kansas) had granted women the vote in state elections, as Illinois had in presidential elections.

The slow pace of progress drove some women to militancy. In England, turn-of-the-century suffragists had chained themselves to lampposts, refused to

Militant suffragists

eat when imprisoned, and assaulted politicians. A young American Quaker named Alice Paul had been with them and brought the aggressive tactics to America. In 1913 she organized 5000 women to parade in protest at President Woodrow Wilson's inauguration. Half a million people watched as a near-riot ensued. The suffragists were hauled to jail, stripped naked, and thrown into cells with prostitutes.

A year later Paul formed the Congressional Union, dedicated to enacting a suffrage amendment at any cost. She soon allied her organization with western women voters in the militant National Woman's party. In 1917, they picketed the White House. When Paul was thrown into jail, she refused to eat in protest. "This is a spirit like Joan of Arc," concluded the doctor who examined her.

Nineteenth Amendment

Prison officials declared her insane. But public anger over such treatment, along with the need for broad-based support for World War I, led the House of Representatives to pass a woman suffrage amendment in 1918. In 1920 it became the Nineteenth Amendment.

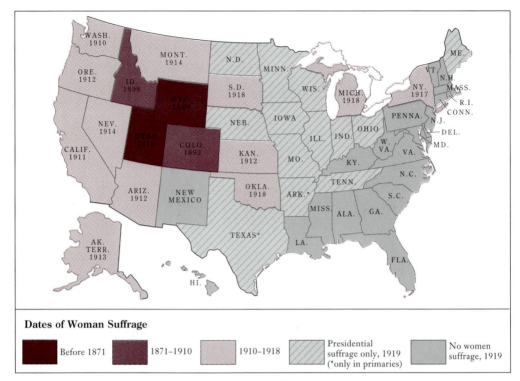

Dates of Woman Suffrage

Before 1871	1871–1910
1910–1918	Presidential suffrage only, 1919 (*only in primaries)
No women suffrage, 1919	

WOMAN SUFFRAGE   Western states were the first to grant women the right to vote. Sparsely populated and more egalitarian than the rest of the nation, the West was used to women participating more fully in settlement and work.

CONTROLLING THE MASSES

"Observe immigrants," wrote one American in 1912; "you are struck by the fact that from ten to twenty percent are hirsute, low-browed, big-faced persons of obviously low mentality. . . . They clearly belong in skins, in wattled huts at the close of the Ice Age." The writer was neither an uneducated fanatic nor a stern opponent of change. He was Professor Edward A. Ross, a progressive from Madison, Wisconsin, who prided himself on his scientific study of sociology.

Faced with the chaos of urban life, more than a few progressives feared they were losing control of their country. Saloons and dance halls lured youngsters and impoverished laborers; prostitutes walked the streets; vulgar amusements pandered to the uneducated. And worse—strange Old World cultures clashed with "all-American" customs, and races jostled uneasily. The city challenged middle-class reformers to convert this riot of diverse customs into a more uniform society. To maintain control they sometimes moved beyond education and regulation and sought restrictive laws to control the new masses.

Stemming the Immigrant Tide

A rising tide of nonwhite and ethnic Americans, often settling in cities, aggravated the fears of many progressives and native-born whites. During the 1890s, segregation laws had already begun to restrict the opportunities of African Americans in the South (page 534); after 1900, the rhetoric of reform was used to support white supremacy. Southern progressives won office by promising to disfranchise black southerners, in order to break the power of corrupt political machines that rested on the black vote, much as northern machines marshaled the immigrant vote.

The South was hardly the only region in which discrimination flourished. Asians, Latinos, and Indians faced similar curbs in the West, as did the new arrivals from southern and eastern Europe in the North. The sharp increase in immigration especially chilled native-born Americans, including reformers anxious over the changing ethnic complexion of the country. In northern cities progressives often succeeded in reducing immigrant voting power by increasing residency requirements.

The infant science of "eugenics" lent respectability to the idea that newcomers were biologically inferior. Eugenicists believed that heredity determined everything and advocated selective breeding for human improvement. By 1914 magazine articles discussed eugenics more than slums, tenements, and living standards combined. In *The Passing of the Great Race* (1916), upper-crust New Yorker and amateur zoologist Madison Grant helped to popularize the notion that the "lesser breeds" threatened to "mongrelize" America. So powerful was the pull of eugenics that it captured the support of many reformers, including birth control advocate Margaret Sanger.

Eugenics

More enlightened reformers such as Jane Addams stressed the "gifts" immigrants brought: folk rituals, dances, music, and handicrafts. With characteristic paternalism, these reformers hoped to "Americanize" the foreign-born (the term was newly coined) by teaching them middle-class ways. Education was one key. Progressive educator Peter Roberts, for example, developed a lesson plan for the Young Men's Christian Association that taught immigrants to dress, tip, buy groceries, and vote.

Americanization

Less tolerant citizens (usually native-born and white) sought to restrict immigration as a way of reasserting control and achieving social harmony. Usually not progressives themselves, they employed progressive methods of organization, investigation, education, and legislation. Active since the 1890s, the Immigration Restriction League pressed Congress in 1907 to require a literacy test for admission into the United States. Presidents Taft and Wilson vetoed it in 1913 and 1915, but Congress overrode Wilson's second veto in 1917 as war fever raised fears of foreigners to a new peak.

Literacy test

The Curse of Demon Rum

Tied closely to concern over immigrants was an attack on saloons. Part of a broader crusade to clean up cities, the antisaloon campaign drew strength from the century-old drive to lessen the consumption of alcohol. Women made up a disproportionate number of alcohol reformers. In some ways, the temperance movement reflected their growing campaign to storm male domains, in this case the saloon, and to contain male violence, particularly the wife and child abuse associated with drinking.

Reformers considered a national ban on drinking unrealistic and intrusive. Instead they concentrated on prohibiting the sale of alcohol at local and state

Anti-Saloon League

levels. Led by the Anti-Saloon League (1893), a massive publicity campaign bombarded citizens with pamphlets and advertisements. Doctors cited scientific evidence linking alcohol to cirrhosis, heart disease, and insanity. Social workers connected drink to the deterioration of the family; employers, to accidents on the job and lost efficiency.

By 1917 three out of four Americans lived in dry counties. Nearly two-thirds of the states had adopted laws outlawing the manufacture and sale of alcohol. Not all progressives were prohibitionists, but by curtailing the liquor business those who were breathed a sigh of relief at having taken some of the profit out of human pain and corruption.

Prostitution

No urban vice worried reformers more than prostitution. In their eyes it was a "social evil" that threatened young city women. The Chicago Vice Commission of 1910 estimated that 5000 full-time and 10,000 occasional prostitutes plied their trade in the city. Other cities, small and large, reported similar results.

An unlikely group of reformers united to fight the vice: feminists who wanted husbands to be as chaste as their wives, social hygienists worried about the spread of venereal disease, immigration restrictionists who regarded the growth of prostitution as yet another sign of corrupt newcomers. Progressives condemned prostitution but saw the problem in economic and environmental terms. "Poverty causes prostitution," concluded the Illinois Vice Commission in 1916.

Some reformers saw more active agents at work. Rumors spread of a vast and profitable "white slave trade." Men armed with hypodermic needles were

White slave trade

said to be lurking about streetcars, amusement parks, and dance halls in search of young women. Although the average female rider of the streetcar was hardly in danger of villainous abduction, every city had locked pens where women were held captive and forced into prostitution. By conservative estimates they constituted some 10 percent of all prostitutes.

As real abuses blended with sensationalism, Congress passed the Mann Act (1910), prohibiting the interstate transport of women for immoral purposes. By

1918 reformers succeeded in banning previously tolerated "red light" districts in most cities. As with the liquor trade, progressives went after those who made money from misery.

THE POLITICS OF MUNICIPAL AND STATE REFORM

Reform the system. In the end, so many urban problems came back to overhauling government. Jane Addams learned as much outside the doors of her beloved Hull House in Chicago. For months during the early 1890s, garbage had piled up in the streets. The filth and stench drove Addams and her fellow workers to city hall in protest—700 times in one summer—but to no avail. In Chicago, as elsewhere, a corrupt band of city bosses had made garbage collection a plum to be awarded to the company that paid the most for it.

In desperation, Addams submitted a bid for garbage removal in the ward. When it was thrown out on a technicality, she won an appointment as garbage inspector. For almost a year she dogged collection carts, but boss politics kept things dirty. So Addams ran candidates in 1896 and 1898 against the local ward boss. They lost, but Addams kept up the fight for honest government and social reform—at city hall, in the Illinois legislature, and finally in Washington. Politics turned out to be the only way to clean things up.

The Reformation of the Cities

In the smokestack cities of the Midwest, where the frustrations of industrial and agricultural America fed each other, the urban battleground furnished the first test of political reform. A series of colorful and independent mayors demonstrated that cities could be run humanely without changing the structure of government.

In Detroit, shoe magnate Hazen Pingree turned the mayor's office into an agency of reform when elected in 1889. By the end of his fourth term, Detroit had new parks and public baths, fairer taxes, ownership of the local light plant, and a work-relief program for victims of the depression of 1893. In 1901, Cleveland mayor Tom Johnson launched a similar reform campaign. Before he was through, municipal franchises had been limited to a fraction of their previous 99-year terms, and the city ran the utility company. By 1915 nearly two out of three cities in the nation had copied some form of this "gas and water socialism" to control the runaway prices of utility companies.

Gas and water socialism

Tragedy sometimes dramatized the need to alter the very structure of government. On a hot summer night in 1900 a tidal wave from the Gulf of Mexico

Commission plan

smashed the port city of Galveston, Texas. Floods killed one of every six residents. The municipal government sank into confusion. Business leaders stepped in with a new charter that replaced the mayor and city council with a powerful commission. Each of five commissioners controlled a municipal department, and together they ran the city. Nearly 400 cities had adopted the plan by 1920. Expert commissioners enhanced efficiency and helped to check party rule in municipal government.

In other cities, elected officials appointed an outside expert or "city manager" to run things, the first in Staunton, Virginia, in 1908. Within a decade,

City manager plan

45 cities had them. At lower levels experts took charge of services: engineers oversaw utilities; accountants, finances; doctors and nurses, public health; specially trained firefighters and police, the safety of citizens. Broad civic reforms attempted to break the corrupt alliance between companies doing business with the city and the bosses who controlled the wards. Citywide elections replaced the old ward system, and civil service laws helped to create a nonpartisan bureaucracy. Political machines and ethnic voters lost power, while city government gained efficiency.

Progressivism in the States

"Whenever we try to do anything, we run up against the charter," complained the reform-minded mayor of Schenectady, New York. Charters granted by state governments defined the powers of cities. The rural interests that generally dominated state legislatures rarely gave cities adequate authority to levy taxes, set voting requirements, draw up budgets, or legislate reforms. State legislatures, too, found themselves under the influence of business interests, party machines, and county courthouse rings. Reformers therefore tried to place their candidates where they could do some good: in the governors' mansions.

As with urban reform, state progressivism enjoyed its earliest success in the Midwest, under the leadership of Robert La Follette of Wisconsin. La Follette first won election to Congress in 1885 by toeing the Republican line of high tariffs and the gold standard. When a Republican boss offered him a bribe in a railroad case, La Follette pledged to break "the power of this corrupt influence." In 1900 he won the governorship of Wisconsin as an uncommonly independent Republican.

Over the next six years "Battle Bob" La Follette made Wisconsin, in the words of Theodore Roosevelt, "the laboratory of democracy." La Follette's

La Follette's Wisconsin idea

"Wisconsin idea" produced the most comprehensive set of state reforms in American history. There were new laws regulating railroads, controlling corruption, and expanding the civil service. His direct primary weakened the hold of party bosses by transferring nominations from the party to the voters. Among La Follette's notable "firsts" were a state income tax, a state commission to oversee factory safety and sanitation, and a Legislative Reference Bureau at the University of Wisconsin. University-trained experts poured into state government.

Other states copied the Wisconsin idea or hatched their own. All but three had direct primary laws by 1916. To cut the power of party organizations and

Reforming politics

make officeholders directly responsible to the public, progressives worked for three additional reforms: initiative (voter introduction of legislation), referendum (voter enactment or repeal of laws), and recall (voter-initiated removal of elected officials). By 1912 a dozen states had adopted initiative and referendum; seven, recall. A year later the Seventeenth Amendment to the Constitution permitted the direct election of senators. Previously they had been chosen by state legislatures, where political machines and corporate lobbyists controlled the selections.

Almost every state established regulatory commissions with the power to hold public hearings, examine company books, and question officials. Some

Regulating business

could set maximum prices and rates. Yet it was not always easy to define, let alone serve, the "public good." All too often commissioners found themselves refereeing battles within industries—between carriers and shippers, for example—rather than between what progressives called "the interests" and "the people." Regulators had to rely on the advice of experts drawn from the business community itself. Many commissions thus became captured by the industries they regulated.

Social welfare received special attention from the states. The lack of workers' compensation for injury, illness, or death on the job had long drawn fire

Seeds of the welfare state

from reformers and labor leaders. American courts still operated on the common-law assumption that employees accepted the risks of work. Workers or their families could collect damages only if they proved employer negligence. Most accident victims received nothing. In 1902 Maryland finally adopted the first workers' compensation act. By 1916 most states required insurance for factory accidents, and over half had employer liability laws. Thirteen states also provided pensions for widows with dependent children.

More and more it was machine politicians and women's organizations that pressed for working-class reforms. Despite the progressive attack on machine politics, political bosses survived, in part by adapting the climate of reform to the needs of their working-class constituents. After the Triangle fire of 1911, for example, it was Tammany Democrats Robert F. Wagner and Alfred E. Smith who led the fight for a new labor code.

This working-class "urban liberalism" also found advocates among women's associations, especially those concerned with mothers, children, and working women. The Federation of Women's Clubs opened a crusade for mothers' pensions (a forerunner of aid to dependent children). When in 1912 the National Consumers' League and other women's groups succeeded in establishing the Children's Bureau, it was the first federal welfare agency and the only female-run national bureau in the world. At a time when women lacked the vote, they nonetheless sowed the seeds of the welfare state and helped to make urban liberalism a powerful instrument of social reform.

PROGRESSIVISM GOES TO WASHINGTON

On September 6, 1901, at the Pan-American Exposition in Buffalo, New York, Leon Czolgosz stood nervously in line. He was waiting among well-wishers to meet President William McKinley. Unemployed and bent on murder, Czolgosz shuffled toward McKinley. As the president reached out, Czolgosz fired two bullets into his chest. McKinley slumped into a chair. Eight days later the president was dead. The mantle of power passed to Theodore Roosevelt. At 42 he was the youngest president ever to hold the office.

Roosevelt's succession was a political accident. Party leaders had seen the weak office of vice president as a way of removing him from power, but the tragedy in Buffalo foiled their plans. "It is a dreadful thing to come into the presidency this way," Roosevelt remarked, "but it would be a far worse thing to be morbid about it." Surely progressivism would have come to Washington without him, and while there, he was never its most daring advocate. In many ways he was quite conservative. He saw reform as a way to avoid more radical change. Yet without Theodore Roosevelt, progressivism would have had neither the broad popular appeal nor the buoyancy he gave it.

TR

TR, as so many Americans called him, was the scion of seven generations of wealthy, aristocratic New Yorkers. A sickly boy, he built his body through rigorous exercise, sharpened his mind through constant study, and pursued a life so strenuous that few could keep up. He learned to ride and shoot, roped cattle in the Dakota Badlands, mastered judo, and later in life climbed the Matterhorn, hunted African game, and explored the Amazon.

In 1880, driven by an urge to lead and serve, Roosevelt won election to the New York State Assembly. In rapid succession he became a civil service commissioner in Washington, New York City police commissioner, assistant secretary of the navy, and the Rough Rider hero of the Spanish–American War. At the age of 40 he won election as reform governor of New York and two years later as vice president. Through it all, TR remained a loyal Republican, personally flamboyant but committed to mild change only.

To the Executive Mansion (he renamed it the "White House"), Roosevelt brought a passion for order, a commitment to the public, and a sense of presidential possibilities. Most presidents believed that the Constitution set specific limits on their power. Roosevelt thought that the president could do anything not expressly forbidden in the document. Recognizing the value of publicity, he

Bull-necked and barrel-chested, Theodore Roosevelt was "pure act," said one admirer. Critics, less enthused with his perpetual motion, charged him with having the attention span of a golden retriever.

gave reporters the first press room in the White House and favored them with all the stories they wanted. He was the first president to ride in an automobile, fly in an airplane, and dive in a submarine—and everyone knew it.

To dramatize racial injustice, Roosevelt invited black educator Booker T. Washington to lunch at the White House in 1901. White southern journalists called such mingling with blacks treason, but for Roosevelt the gesture served both principle and politics. His lunch with Washington was part of a "black and tan" strategy to build a biracial coalition among southern Republicans. He denounced lynching and appointed black southerners to important federal offices in Mississippi and South Carolina.

Sensing the limits of political possibility, Roosevelt went no further. Perhaps his own racial narrowness stopped him too. In 1906, when Atlanta exploded in a race riot that left 12 people dead, he said nothing. Later that *Brownsville incident* year he discharged "without honor" three entire companies of African American troops because some of the soldiers were unjustly charged with having "shot up" Brownsville, Texas. All lost their pensions, including six winners of the Medal of Honor. The act stained Roosevelt's record.

(Congress acknowledged the wrong in 1972 by granting the soldiers honorable discharges.)

A Square Deal

Roosevelt could not long follow the cautious course McKinley had charted. He had more energetic plans in mind for the country. He accepted growth—

Philosophy of the Square Deal

whether of business, labor, or agriculture—as natural. In his pluralistic system, big labor would counterbalance big capital, big farm organizations would offset big food processors, and so on. Standing astride them all, mediating when needed, was a big government that could ensure fairness for all. Later, as he campaigned for a second term in 1904, Roosevelt named his program the "Square Deal."

In a startling display of presidential initiative, Roosevelt in 1902 intervened in a strike that idled 140,000 miners and paralyzed the anthracite (hard) coal in-

Anthracite coal strike

dustry. As winter approached, public resentment with the operators mounted when they refused even to recognize the miners' union, let alone negotiate. Roosevelt summoned both sides to the White House. John A. Mitchell, the young president of the United Mine Workers, agreed to arbitration, but mine owners balked. Roosevelt leaked word to Wall Street that the army would take over the mines if management did not yield.

Seldom had a recent president acted so decisively, and never had one acted on behalf of strikers. In late October 1902 the owners settled by granting miners a 10 percent wage hike and a nine-hour day in return for increases in coal prices and no recognition of the union. Roosevelt was equally prepared to intervene on the side of management, as he did when he sent federal troops to end strikes in Arizona in 1903 and Colorado in 1904. His aim was to establish a vigorous presidency ready to deal squarely with both sides.

Roosevelt especially needed to face the issue of economic concentration. Financial power had become consolidated in giant trusts following a wave of mergers at the end of the century. As large firms swallowed smaller ones, Americans feared that such consolidation would destroy individual enterprise and free competition. A series of government investigations revealed rampant corporate abuses: rebates, collusion, "watered" stock, payoffs to government officials. The conservative courts showed little willingness to break up the giants

United States v. E. C. Knight

or blunt their power. In *United States v. E. C. Knight* (1895), the Supreme Court crippled the Sherman Antitrust Act by ruling that the law applied only to commerce and not to manufacturing. The decision left the American Sugar Refining Company in control of 98 percent of the nation's sugar factories.

In his first State of the Union message, Roosevelt told Congress that he did not oppose business concentration. As he saw it, large corporations were not only inevitable but more productive than smaller operations. He wanted to regulate them to make them fairer and more efficient. Only then would the economic order be humanized, its victims protected, and class violence avoided. Like individuals, trusts had to be held to strict standards of morality. Conduct, not size, was the yardstick TR used to measure "good" and "bad" trusts.

With a progressive's faith in the power of publicity and a regulator's need for the facts, Roosevelt moved immediately to strengthen the federal power of investigation. He called for the creation of a Department of Labor and Commerce with a Bureau of Corporations that could force companies to hand over their records. Congressional conservatives shuddered at the prospect of putting corporate books on display. Finally, after Roosevelt charged that John D. Rockefeller was orchestrating the opposition, Congress enacted the legislation and provided the Justice Department with additional staff to prosecute antitrust cases.

In 1902, to demonstrate the power of government, Roosevelt had his attorney general file an antitrust suit against the Northern Securities Company.

Northern Securities The mammoth holding company virtually monopolized railroads in the Northwest. Worse still, it had bloated its stock with worthless certificates. Here, clearly, was a symbol of the "bad" trust. A trust-conscious nation cheered as the Supreme Court ordered the company to dissolve in 1904. Ultimately, the Roosevelt administration brought suit against 44 giants, including Standard Oil Company, American Tobacco Company, and Du Pont Corporation.

Despite his reputation for trustbusting, Roosevelt always preferred regulation. The problems of the railroads, for example, were newly underscored by a

Railroad regulation recent round of consolidation that had contributed to higher freight rates. Roosevelt pressed Congress to revive the ineffective Interstate Commerce Commission (ICC). In 1903 Congress passed the Elkins Act, which gave the ICC power to end rebates. Even the railroads supported the act because it saved them from the costly practice of granting special reductions to large shippers.

By the election of 1904 the president's iniatives had won him broad popular support. He trounced his two rivals, Democrat Alton B. Parker, a jurist from New York, and Eugene V. Debs of the Socialist party. No longer was he a "political accident," Roosevelt boasted.

Conservatives in his own party opposed Roosevelt's meddling in the private sector. But progressives demanded still more regulation of the railroads, in particular a controversial proposal for making public the value of all rail property. In 1906, the president finally reached a compromise typical of his restrained approach to reform. The Hepburn Railway Act allowed the ICC to set maximum rates and to regulate sleeping car companies, ferries, bridges, and terminals. Progressives did not gain the provision of disclosure of company value, but the Hepburn Act drew Roosevelt nearer to his goal of continuous regulation of business.

Bad Food and Pristine Wilds

Extending the umbrella of federal protection to consumers, Roosevelt belatedly threw his weight behind two campaigns for healthy foods and drugs. In 1905 Samuel Hopkins Adams of *Collier's Weekly* wrote that in its patent medicines "Gullible America" would get "huge quantities of alcohol, an appalling amount of opiates and narcotics," and worse—axle grease, acid, and glue. Adams sent the samples he had collected to Harvey Wiley, chief chemist at the Agriculture Department. Wiley's "Poison Squad" produced scientific evidence of Adams's charges.

Several pure food and drug bills had already died at the hands of lobbyists, despite a presidential endorsement. The appearance of Upton Sinclair's *The Jungle* in 1906 spurred Congress to act. Sinclair intended to recruit people to socialism by exposing the plight of workers in the meatpacking industry. The novel contained a brief but dramatic description of the slaughter of cattle infected with tuberculosis, of meat covered with rat dung, and of men falling into cooking vats. Readers paid scant attention to the workers, but their stomachs turned at what they might be eating for breakfast. The Pure Food and Drug Act of 1906 sailed through Congress, and the Meat Inspection Act soon followed.

Roosevelt came late to the consumer cause, but on conservation he led the nation. An outdoors enthusiast, he galvanized public concern over the reckless

Conservation through planned management

use of natural resources. His chief forester, Gifford Pinchot, persuaded him that planned management under federal guidance was needed to protect the natural domain. Cutting trees must be synchronized with tree plantings, oil pumped from the ground must be under controlled conditions, and so on.

In the western states water was the problem. Economic growth, even survival, depended on it. As uneven local and state water policies sparked controversy, violence, and waste, many progressives campaigned for a federal program to replace the chaotic web of rules. Democratic senator Frederick Newlands of Nevada introduced the Reclamation Act of 1902 to set aside proceeds from the sale of public lands for irrigation projects. The Reclamation Act signaled a progressive step toward the conservationist goal of rational resource development.

Conservation often conflicted with the more radical vision of preservationists, led by naturalist and wilderness philosopher John Muir. Muir founded the

John Muir and preservation

Sierra Club (1892) in hopes of maintaining such natural wonders as Yosemite and its neighboring Hetch-Hetchy valley in a state "forever wild" to benefit future generations. Many conservationists saw such valleys as sites for dams and reservoirs. Controversy flared after 1900 when San Francisco announced plans to create a city reservoir flooding the Hetch-Hetchy valley. For 13 years Muir waged a publicity campaign against the "devotees of ravaging commercialism." Pinchot enthusiastically backed San Francisco's claim. Roosevelt, torn by his friendship with Muir, did so less loudly.

The Sierra Club, founded by naturalist John Muir, believed in the importance of
preserving wilderness in its natural state. Muir helped to persuade President
Theodore Roosevelt to double the number of national parks. Here a group of Sierra
clubbers lounges at the base of a giant redwood in Big Basin in 1905.

Not until 1913 did President Woodrow Wilson finally decide the issue in favor
of San Francisco. Conservation had won over preservation.

Roosevelt nonetheless advanced many of Muir's goals. Over the protests of
cattle and timber interests, he added nearly 200 million acres to government
forest reserves; placed coal and mineral lands, oil reserves, and water-power
sites in the public domain; and enlarged the national park system. When
Congress balked, he appropriated another 17 million acres of forest before the
legislators could pass a bill limiting him. Roosevelt also set in motion national
congresses and commissions on conservation and mobilized governors across
the country. Like a good progressive, he sent hundreds of experts to work applying science, education, and technology to environmental problems.

As Roosevelt acted more forcefully, conservatives lashed back. So far his
record had been modest, but his chief accomplishment—invigorating the
presidency—could lead to deeper reform. When another spike in the business
cycle produced financial panic on Wall Street in 1907, business leaders and conservative politicians blamed the president. An angry Roosevelt blamed the
"speculative folly and the flagrant dishonesty of a few men of great wealth."

Clearly shaken, however, Roosevelt assured business leaders that he would do nothing to interfere with their efforts at recovery. That included a pledge not to file an antitrust suit if the giant U.S. Steel bought the Tennessee Coal and Iron Company. The economy recovered, and having declared he would not run in 1908, the 50-year-old Roosevelt prepared to give over his office to William Howard Taft, his handpicked successor.

The Troubled Taft

On March 4, 1909, as snow swirled outside the White House, William Howard Taft readied himself for his inauguration. Over breakfast with Roosevelt, he warmed in the glow of recent Republican victories. He had beaten Democrat William Jennings Bryan in the "Great Commoner's" third and last bid for the presidency. Republicans had retained control of Congress as well as a host of northern legislatures. Reform was at high tide, and Taft was eager to continue the Roosevelt program.

"Will," as Roosevelt liked to call him, was a distinguished jurist and public servant, the first American governor-general of the Philippines, and Roosevelt's secretary of war. Taft had great administrative skill and personal charm. But he disliked the political maneuvering of Washington and preferred conciliation to confrontation. Even Roosevelt had doubts. "He's all right," TR had told a reporter on inauguration day. "But he's weak. They'll get around him. They'll"—and here Roosevelt pushed the reporter with his shoulder—"lean against him."

Trouble began early when progressives in the House moved to curb the near-dictatorial power of the conservative Speaker, Joseph Cannon. Taft waffled, first supporting them, then abandoning them to preserve the tariff reductions he was seeking. When progressives later broke Cannon's power without Taft's help, they scorned him. And Taft's compromise was wasted. Senate protectionists peppered the tariff bill with so many amendments that rates jumped nearly to their old levels.

Late in 1909, the rift between Taft and the progressives reached the breaking point in a dispute over conservation. Taft had appointed Richard Ballinger

Ballinger–Pinchot affair secretary of the interior over the objections of Roosevelt's old friend and mentor, Chief Forester Pinchot. When Ballinger opened a million acres of public lands for sale, Pinchot charged that shady dealings led Ballinger to transfer Alaskan public coal lands to a syndicate that included J. P. Morgan. Early in 1910, Taft fired Pinchot for insubordination. Angry progressives saw the Ballinger–Pinchot controversy as another betrayal by Taft. They began to look longingly across the Atlantic, where TR was stalking big game in Africa.

Despite his failures, Taft was no conservative pawn. For the next two years he pushed Congress to enact a progressive program regulating safety standards

Taft's accomplishments for mines and railroads, creating a federal children's bureau, and setting an eight-hour workday for federal employees. Taft's support of a graduated income tax—sometimes heated, sometimes tepid—was finally decisive. Early in 1913 it became the Sixteenth Amendment. Historians view it as one of the most important reforms of the century, for it eventually generated the revenue for many new social programs.

Yet no matter what Taft did, he managed to alienate conservatives and progressives alike. That spelled trouble for the Republicans as the presidential election of 1912 approached.

Roosevelt Returns

In June 1910 Roosevelt came home, laden with hunting trophies and exuberant as ever. He found Taft unhappy and progressive Republicans threatening to defect. Party loyalty kept Roosevelt quiet through most of 1911, but in October, Taft pricked him personally on the sensitive matter of busting trusts. Like TR, Taft accepted trusts as natural, but he failed to make Roosevelt's distinction between "good" and "bad" ones. He demanded, more impartially, that all trusts be prevented from restraining trade. In four years as president, Taft had brought nearly twice the antitrust suits Roosevelt had in seven years.

In October 1911 the Justice Department charged U. S. Steel with having violated the Sherman Act by acquiring the Tennessee Coal and Iron Company. Roosevelt regarded the action as a personal rebuke, since he himself had allowed U. S. Steel to proceed with the acquisition. Taft, complained TR, "was playing small, mean, and foolish politics."

Roosevelt decided to play big, high-minded, and presidential. Already, in a speech at Osawatomie, Kansas, in 1910, he had outlined a program of sweeping national reform. His "New Nationalism" recognized the value of consolidation in the economy—whether big business or big labor—but insisted on protecting the interests of individuals through big government. The New Nationalism went further, stressing planning and efficiency under a powerful executive, "a steward of the public welfare." It promised taxes on incomes and inheritances and greater regulation of industry. And it embraced social justice, specifically workers' compensation for accidents, minimum wages and maximum hours, child labor laws, and "equal suffrage"—a nod to women and loyal black Republicans. Roosevelt, a cautious reformer as president, now grew daring as he campaigned for the White House.

New Nationalism

The Election of 1912

"My hat is in the ring!" Roosevelt announced in February 1912, to no one's surprise. Taft responded by claiming that the New Nationalism had won support only from "radicals," "emotionalists," and "neurotics." In fact, the enormously popular Roosevelt won most of the primaries; but by the time Republicans met in Chicago in June 1912, Taft had used presidential patronage and promises to secure the nomination.

A frustrated Roosevelt bolted and took progressive Republicans with him. Two months later, amid choruses of "Onward Christian Soldiers," delegates to

Progressive party

the newly formed Progressive party nominated Roosevelt for the presidency. "I'm feeling like a bull moose!" he bellowed. Progressives suddenly had a symbol for their new party.

The Democrats met in Baltimore, jubilant over the prospect of a divided Republican party. Delegates chose as their candidate Woodrow Wilson, the progressive governor of New Jersey. Wilson wisely concentrated his fire on

New Freedom

Roosevelt. He countered the New Nationalism with his "New Freedom." It rejected the economic consolidation that Roosevelt embraced. Bigness was a sin, crowding out competition, promoting inefficiency, and reducing opportunity. Only by strictly limiting the size of businesses could the free market be preserved. And only by keeping government small could individual freedom be preserved. "Liberty," Wilson cautioned, "has never come from government," only from the "limitation of governmental power."

Increasingly voters found Taft beside the point. And in an age of reform, even the Socialists looked good. Better led, financed, and organized than ever, the Socialist party had increased its membership to nearly 135,000 by 1912. Socialist mayors ran 32 cities. The party also had an appealing candidate in Eugene V. Debs, a homegrown Indiana radical. He had won 400,000 votes for president in 1904. Now, in 1912, he summoned voters to make "the working class the ruling class."

On election day voters gave progressivism a resounding endorsement. Wilson won 6.3 million votes; Roosevelt, 4.1 million; Taft, just 3.6 million. Debs received almost a million votes. Together the two progressive candidates amassed a three to one margin. But the Republican split had broken the party's

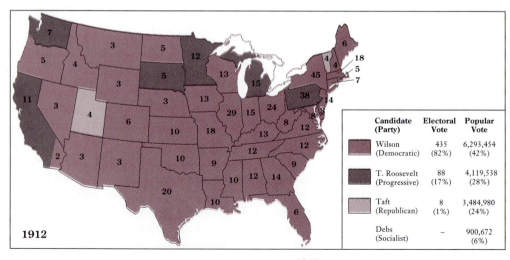

Candidate (Party)	Electoral Vote	Popular Vote
Wilson (Democratic)	435 (82%)	6,293,454 (42%)
T. Roosevelt (Progressive)	88 (17%)	4,119,538 (28%)
Taft (Republican)	8 (1%)	3,484,980 (24%)
Debs (Socialist)	–	900,672 (6%)

1912

THE ELECTION OF 1912

hold on national politics. For the first time since 1896, a Democrat would sit in the White House—and with his party in control of Congress.

WOODROW WILSON AND THE POLITICS OF MORALITY

Soon after the election Woodrow Wilson made a proud if startling confession to the chairman of the Democratic National Committee: "God ordained that I should be the next President of the United States." To the White House, Wilson brought a sense of destiny and a passion for reform. All his life, he believed he was meant to accomplish great things, and he did. Under him, progressivism peaked.

Early Career

From the moment of his birth in 1856, Woodrow Wilson felt he could not escape destiny. It was all around him. In his family's Presbyterian faith, in the sermons of his minister father, in dinnertime talk ran the unbending belief in a world predetermined by God and ruled by saved souls, an "elect." Wilson ached to be one of them and behaved as though he were.

To prepare to lead, Wilson studied the fiery debates of the British Parliament and wandered the woods reciting them from memory. Like most southerners, he loved the Democratic party, hated the tariff, and accepted racial separation. (Under his presidency, segregation returned to Washington for the first time since Reconstruction.)

An early career in law bored him, so he turned to history and political science and became a professor. His studies persuaded him that a modern president must act as a "prime minister," directing and uniting his party, molding legislation and public opinion, exerting continuous leadership. In 1910, after a stormy tenure as head of Princeton University, Wilson was helped by Democratic party bosses to win the governorship of New Jersey. In 1912 they helped him again, this time to the presidency of the country.

The Reforms of the New Freedom

As governor, Wilson had led New Jersey on the path of progressive reform. As president, he was a model of progressive leadership. More than Theodore Roosevelt, he shaped policy and legislation. He went to Congress to let members know he intended to work personally with them. He kept party discipline tight and mobilized public opinion when Congress refused to act.

Lowering the high tariff was Wilson's first order of business. Progressives had long attacked the tariff as another example of the power of trusts. By protecting American manufacturers, Wilson argued, such barriers weakened the competition he cherished. When the Senate threatened to raise rates, the new president appealed directly to the public. "Industrious" and "insidious" lobbyists were blocking reform, he cried to reporters. A "brick couldn't be thrown without hitting one of them."

Underwood–Simmons Tariff

The Underwood–Simmons Tariff of 1913 marked the first downward revision in 19 years and the biggest since before the Civil War. To compensate for lost revenue, Congress enacted a graduated income tax under the newly adopted Sixteenth Amendment. It applied solely to corporations and the tiny fraction of Americans who earned more than $4000 a year. It nonetheless began a momentous shift in government revenue from its nineteenth-century base—public lands, alcohol taxes, and customs duties—to its twentieth-century base: personal and corporate incomes.

Wilson turned next to the perennial problems of money and banking. Early in 1913 a congressional committee under Arsène Pujo revealed that a few powerful banks controlled the nation's credit system. They could choke Wilson's free market by raising interest rates or tightening the supply of money. As a banking reform bill moved through Congress in 1913, opinion divided among conservatives, who wanted centralized and private control, rural Democrats, who wanted regional banks under local bankers, and Populists and progressives—including Bryan and La Follette—who wanted government control.

Wilson split their differences in the Federal Reserve Act of 1913. The new Federal Reserve System contained 12 regional banks scattered across the country. But it also created a central Federal Reserve Board in Washington, appointed by the president, to supervise the system. The board could regulate credit and the money supply by setting the interest rate it charged member banks, by buying or selling government bonds, and by issuing paper currency called Federal Reserve notes. Thus the Federal Reserve System sought to stabilize the existing order by increasing federal control over credit and the money supply.

Federal Reserve Act

When Wilson finally took on the trusts, he inched toward the New Nationalism of Theodore Roosevelt. The Federal Trade Commission Act of 1914 created a bipartisan executive agency to oversee business activity. The end—to enforce orderly competition—was distinctly Wilsonian, but the means—an executive commission to regulate commerce—were pure Roosevelt.

Federal Trade Commission

Roosevelt would have stopped there, but Wilson made good on his campaign pledge to attack trusts. The Clayton Antitrust Act (1914) barred some of the worst corporate practices: price discrimination, holding companies, and interlocking directorates (directors of one corporate board sitting on others). Yet despite Wilson's bias against size, the advantages of large-scale production and distribution were inescapable. In practice his administration chose to regulate rather than break up bigness. The

Clayton Antitrust Act

Justice Department filed fewer antitrust suits than it had under the Taft administration.

Labor and Social Reform

For all of Wilson's impressive accomplishments, voters seemed lukewarm toward the New Freedom. In the elections of 1914 Republicans cut Democratic majorities in the House and won important industrial and farm states. To strengthen his hand in the presidential election of 1916, Wilson began edging toward the social reforms of the New Nationalism he had once criticized as paternalistic and unconstitutional. He signaled the change early in 1916 when he nominated his close adviser Louis D. Brandeis to the Supreme Court. The progressive Brandeis had fought for the social reforms lacking from Wilson's agenda. His appointment also broke the tradition of anti-Semitism that had previously kept Jews off the Court.

In other ways, Wilson showed a new willingness to intervene more actively in the economy. He helped pass laws improving the working conditions of merchant seamen and setting an eight-hour day for workers on interstate railroads. He supported the Keating–Owen Child Labor Act (page 604). Farmers benefited from legislation providing them with low-interest loans. And just before the election Wilson intervened to avert a nationwide strike of rail workers.

The Limits of Progressive Reform

Woodrow Wilson's administration capped a decade and a half of heady reform. Seeing chaos in the modern industrial city, progressive reformers had worked to reduce the damage of poverty and the hazards of industrial work, control rising immigration, and spread a middle-class ideal of morality. In city halls and state legislatures, they tried to break the power of corporate interests and entrenched political machines. In Washington, they enlarged government and broadened its mission from caretaker to promoter of public welfare.

Progressivism did not always succeed. Reformers sometimes betrayed their high ideals by denying equality to African Americans, Asians, and other minorities and by attempting to Americanize foreigners rather than accepting the contributions of their cultures. Too often government commissions meant to be "watchdog" agencies were captured by the interests they were supposed to oversee. Heavy regulation of industries like the railroads crippled them for decades. Although the direct primary, the popular election of senators, and other reforms weakened the power of political machines, boss rule survived.

For all its claims of sweeping change, progressivism left the system of market capitalism intact. Neither the New Nationalism of Theodore Roosevelt, with its emphasis on planning and regulation, nor Woodrow Wilson's New

Freedom, which promoted competition through limits on corporate size, aimed to do more than improve the system. But the Gilded Age philosophy of laissez faire—of giving private enterprise a free hand—had clearly been rejected. Both state and federal governments established their right to regulate the actions of private corporations for the public good.

The reforms thus achieved, including the eight-hour day, woman suffrage, direct election of senators, graduated income taxes, and public ownership of utilities, began to address the problems of an urban industrial society. Under progressive leadership, the modern state—active and interventionist—was born.

SIGNIFICANT EVENTS

1890 — New England Kitchen opens; General Federation of Women's Clubs organized

1892 — Sierra Club founded

1893 — Illinois legislature enacts eight-hour workday law for women; Anti-Saloon League created

1895 — *United States v. E. C. Knight*

1899 — National Consumers' League founded

1900 — Robert La Follette elected governor of Wisconsin; Galveston, Texas, creates first commission form of government

1901 — Leon Czolgosz assassinates President McKinley; Theodore Roosevelt becomes president; Socialist Party of America founded

1902 — Northern Securities Company dissolved under Sherman Antitrust Act; anthracite coal miners strike in Pennsylvania; Maryland adopts first workers' compensation law

1903 — Department of Labor and Commerce created; Elkins Act passed; Wisconsin first state to enact direct primary

1904 — Lincoln Steffens's *The Shame of the Cities* published; Theodore Roosevelt elected president

1906 — Hepburn Act strengthens Interstate Commerce Commission; Upton Sinclair's *The Jungle* published; Meat Inspection and Pure Food and Drug acts passed

1907 — William James's *Pragmatism* published

1908 — *Muller v. Oregon*; William Howard Taft elected president

1909 — Ballinger–Pinchot controversy

1910 — Mann Act passed

1911 — Triangle Shirtwaist fire

1912 — Progressive ("Bull Moose") party nominates Theodore Roosevelt for presidency; Woodrow Wilson elected president

1913 — Sixteenth and Seventeenth amendments passed; Underwood–Simmons Tariff enacted; Federal Reserve Act passed

1914 — Clayton Antitrust Act passed; Federal Trade Commission created

1916 — Margaret Sanger organizes New York Birth Control League; Keating–Owen Child Labor Act passed; Woodrow Wilson reelected president

1917 — Congress enacts literacy test for new immigrants

1920 — Nineteenth Amendment ratified

CHAPTER TWENTY-THREE

The United States and the Old World Order

I n 1898, as tens of thousands of eager young men signed up to kill Spaniards in Cuba, the USS *Oregon* left San Francisco Bay on a roundabout route toward its battle station in the Caribbean. It first headed south through the Pacific, passing Central America and leaving it thousands of miles behind. Then in the narrow Strait of Magellan at South America's tip, the ship encountered a gale so ferocious the shore could not be seen. All communication ceased, and Americans at home feared the worst. But the *Oregon* passed into the Atlantic and steamed north until finally, after 68 days and 13,000 miles at sea, it helped win the Battle of Santiago Bay.

The daring voyage electrified the nation but worried its leaders. Since the defeat of Mexico in 1848, the United States had stretched from the Atlantic to the Pacific without enough navy to go around. As an emerging power, the country needed a path between the seas, a canal across the narrow isthmus of Colombia's Panamanian province in Central America, to defend itself and to promote its growing trade.

"I took the isthmus," President Theodore Roosevelt later told a cheering crowd. In a way he did. In 1903 he reached an agreement with Colombia to lease the needed strip of land. Hoping for more money and greater control over the canal, the Colombians refused to ratify the agreement.

Privately, TR talked of seizing Panama. But when he learned of a budding independence movement there, he let it be known that he would welcome a revolt. On schedule and without bloodshed, the Panamanians rebelled late in 1903. The next day a U.S. cruiser dropped anchor offshore to prevent Colombia from landing troops. The United States quickly recognized the new Republic of Panama and signed a treaty for a renewable lease on a canal zone 10 miles wide. Panama received $10 million plus an annual rent of $250,000, the same terms offered to Colombia. Critics called it "a rough-riding assault upon another republic." (In 1921, after oil had been discovered in Colombia, Congress voted $25 million to the country.)

In November 1906 Roosevelt pulled into port at Panama City aboard the *Louisiana*, newly launched and the biggest battleship in the fleet. He spent the next three days traveling the length of the canal in the pouring rain. Soaked from head to toe, his huge Panama hat and white suit sagging about his body, he splashed through labor camps, asking workers for their complaints. He toured the hospital at Ancon and met Dr. William Gorgas, conqueror of the yellow-fever–bearing mosquito. He walked railroad ties at the cuts and made speeches in the mud. "This is one of the great works of the world," he told an assembly of black diggers.

The Panama Canal embodied Roosevelt's muscular policy of respect through strength. TR modernized the army and tripled its size, created a general staff for planning and mobilization, and established the Army War College. As a pivot point between the two hemispheres, his canal allowed the United States to flex its strength across the globe.

These expanding horizons came about largely as an outgrowth of American commercial and industrial expansion, just as the imperialist empires of Great Britain, France, Germany, Russia, and Japan reflected the spread of their own industrial and commercial might. The Americans, steeped in democratic ideals, frequently seemed uncomfortable with the naked ambitions of European empire builders. Roosevelt's embrace of the canal, however, showed how far some Americans had come in being willing to shape the world.

Expansionist diplomats at home and abroad assured each other that global order could be maintained by balancing power through a set of carefully crafted alliances. But that system of alliances did not hold. In 1914, the year the Panama Canal opened, the old world order shattered in a terrible war.

PROGRESSIVE DIPLOMACY

As the Panama Canal was being built, progressive diplomacy was taking shape. Like progressive politics, it stressed moralism and order as it stretched executive power to new limits, molding and remaking now the international environment. "Of all our race, [God] has marked the American people as His chosen nation to finally lead in the redemption of the world," said one senator in 1900. At the core of this missionary faith lay a belief in the superiority of Anglo-American institutions. Every western leader assumed that northern Europeans were racially superior, too. The darker peoples of the tropical zones, observed a progressive educator, dwelled in "nature's asylum for degenerates." In this global vision of Manifest Destiny, few progressives questioned the need to uplift them.

Foundations of progressive diplomacy

Economic expansion underlay the commitment to a "civilizing" mission. The depression of 1893 had encouraged American manufacturers and farmers to look overseas for markets, and that expansion continued after 1900. By 1918, at the end of World War I, the United States had become the largest creditor in the world. Every administration committed itself to opening doors of trade and keeping them open.

Big Stick in the Caribbean

Theodore Roosevelt liked to invoke the old African proverb, "Walk softly and carry a big stick." But in the Caribbean he moved both loudly and mightily. The Panama Canal gave the United States a commanding position in the Western Hemisphere. Its importance required the country to "police the surrounding premises," explained Secretary of State Elihu Root. Before granting Cuba independence in 1902, the United States reorganized its finances and included in the Cuban constitution the Platt Amendment. It gave American authorities the right to intervene if Cuban independence or internal order were threatened. Claiming that power, U.S. troops occupied the island twice between 1906 and 1923.

Platt Amendment

In looking to enforce a favorable environment for trade in the Caribbean, Roosevelt also worried about European intentions. The Monroe Doctrine of 1823 declared against further European colonization of the Western Hemisphere, but in the early twentieth century the rising debts of Latin Americans to Europeans invited intrusion. "If we intend to say hands off to the power of Europe, then sooner or later we must keep order ourselves," Roosevelt warned.

Going well beyond Monroe's concept of resisting foreign penetration, Roosevelt asserted American command of the Caribbean. He convinced Britain and Germany to arbitrate a debt dispute with Venezuela in 1902. Two years later, when the Dominican Republic defaulted on its debts, he added the "Roosevelt Corollary" to the Monroe Doctrine by claiming the right to police the Americas. Under it, the United States assumed responsibility for several Caribbean states, including the Dominican Republic, Cuba, and Panama.

Roosevelt Corollary to the Monroe Doctrine

A "Diplomatist of the Highest Rank"

In the Far East Roosevelt exercised ingenuity rather than force, since he considered Asia beyond the American sphere of influence. Like McKinley, TR committed himself only to maintaining an "open door" of equal access to trade in China and to protecting the Philippines, "our heel of Achilles."

The key lay in offsetting Russian and Japanese ambitions in the region. When Japan attacked Russian holdings in the Chinese province of Manchuria in 1904, Roosevelt offered to mediate. He worried that if unchecked, Japan might threaten American interests in China and the Philippines. Both sides met at the U.S. Naval Base near

Treaty of Portsmouth

Portsmouth, Maine, and, under Roosevelt's guidance, produced the Treaty of Portsmouth in 1905. It recognized the Japanese victory (the first by an Asian power over a European country) and ceded to Japan Port Arthur, the southern half of Sakhalin Island, and, in effect, control of Korea. Japan promised to leave Manchuria as part of China and keep trade open to all foreign nations. Both the balance of power in Asia and the open door in China had been preserved. Roosevelt's diplomacy earned him the Nobel Peace Prize in 1906.

Some Japanese nationalists resented the peace treaty for curbing Japan's ambitions in Asia. Their anger surfaced in a protest lodged, of all places, against the San Francisco school board. In 1906, rising Japanese immigration led San Francisco school authorities to place the city's 93 Asian students in a separate school. In Japan citizens talked of war over the insult. Roosevelt, fuming at the "infernal fools in California," summoned the mayor of San Francisco and seven school board members to the White House. In exchange for an end to the segregation order, Roosevelt offered to arrange a mutual restriction of immigration between Japan and the United States. In 1907 all sides accepted his "gentlemen's agreement."

Gentlemen's agreement

The San Francisco school crisis sparked wild rumors that Japan was bent on taking Hawaii, or the Philippines, or the Panama Canal. In case Japan or any other nation thought of upsetting the Pacific balance, Roosevelt sent 16 gleaming white battleships on a world tour. "By George, isn't it magnificent!" he crowed, as the "Great White Fleet" steamed out of Hampton Roads, Virginia, in 1907. The fleet made its most conspicuous stop in Japan. Some Europeans predicted disaster. Instead, cheering crowds turned out in Tokyo and Yokohama, where a group of Japanese children sang "The Star Spangled Banner" in English. The show of force heralded a new age of American naval might but had an unintended consequence that haunted Americans for decades: it spurred Japanese admirals to expand their own navy.

Great White Fleet

Watching Roosevelt in his second term, an amazed London *Morning Post* dubbed him a "diplomatist of the highest rank." Abroad as at home, his brand of progressivism was grounded in an enthusiastic nationalism that mixed force with finesse to achieve balance and order. Yet despite TR's efforts, imperial rivalries, an unchecked naval arms race, and unrest in Europe threatened to plunge the world into chaos.

Dollar Diplomacy

Instead of force or finesse, William Howard Taft relied on private investment to promote economic stability, keep peace, and tie debt-ridden nations to the United States. "Dollar diplomacy" simply amounted to "substituting dollars for bullets," Taft explained. He and Philander Knox, his prickly secretary of state, treated the restless nations of Latin America like ailing corporations, injecting capital and reorganizing management. By the time Taft left office in 1913, half of all American investments abroad were in Latin America.

In Nicaragua dollar diplomacy was not enough. In 1909, when the Nicaraguan legislature balked at American demands to take over its customshouse and national bank, a U.S. warship dropped anchor off the coast. The lawmakers changed their minds, but in 1912 a revolution led Taft to dispatch 2000 marines to protect American lives and property. Sporadic American intrusions lasted more than a dozen years.

Failure dogged Taft overseas as it did at home. In the Caribbean his dollar diplomacy was linked so closely with unpopular regimes, corporations, and banks that Woodrow Wilson scrapped it as soon as he entered the White House. Taft's efforts to strengthen China with investments and trade only intensified rivalry with Japan and made China more suspicious of all foreigners, including Americans. In 1911 the southern Chinese provinces rebelled against foreign intrusion and overthrew the monarchy. Only persistent pressure from the White House kept dollar diplomacy in Asia alive at all.

WOODROW WILSON AND MORAL DIPLOMACY

The Lightfoot Club had been meeting in the Reverend Wilson's hayloft for months when the question of whether the pen was mightier than the sword came up. Young Tommy Wilson, who had organized the debating society, jumped at the chance to argue that written words were more powerful than armies. But when the boys drew lots, Tommy ended up on the other side. "I can't argue for something I don't believe in," he protested. Thomas Woodrow Wilson eventually dropped his first name, but he never gave up his boyhood conviction that morality, at least as he defined it, should guide conduct.

Missionary Diplomacy

As president, Woodrow Wilson revived and enlarged Jefferson's notion of the United States as a beacon of freedom. The country had a mission: "We are chosen, and prominently chosen, to show the way to the nations of the world how they shall walk in the paths of liberty." Such paternalism only thinly masked Wilson's assumption of Anglo-American superiority and his willingness to spread western-style democracy and Christian morality through force.

Wilson's missionary diplomacy had a practical side. In the twentieth century foreign markets would serve as America's new frontier. American industries "will burst their jackets if they cannot find free outlets in the markets of the world," he cautioned in 1912. Wilson's genius lay in reconciling this commercial self-interest with a global idealism. In his eyes, exporting American democracy and capitalism would promote stability and progress throughout the world.

In Asia and the Pacific, Wilson moved to put "moral and public considerations" ahead of the "material interests of individuals." He pulled American bankers out of a six-nation railroad project in China backed by President Taft.

AMERICAN INTERVENTIONS IN THE CARIBBEAN, 1898–1930   In the first three decades of the twentieth century, armed and unarmed interventions by the United States virtually transformed the Caribbean into an American lake.

The scheme encouraged foreign intervention and undermined Chinese sovereignty, Wilson said. The United States became the first major power to recognize the new democratic Republic of China in 1911 and in 1915 strongly opposed Japan's "Twenty-One Demands" for control of the country.

In the Caribbean and Latin America, Wilson discovered that interests closer to home could not be pursued through principles alone. In August 1914 he convinced Nicaragua, already occupied by American troops, to yield control of a naval base and grant the United States an alternative canal route. Upheavals in Haiti and the Dominican Republic brought in the U.S. Marines. By the end of his administration American troops were still stationed there and also in Cuba. All four nations were economically dependent on the United States and virtual protectorates. Missionary diplomacy, it turned out, could spread its gospel with steel as well as cash.

Intervention in Mexico

A lingering crisis turned Wilson's "moral diplomacy" into a mockery in Mexico. A common border, 400 years of shared history, and millions of dollars in investments made what happened in Mexico of urgent importance to the United

Mexican Revolution

States. In 1910 a revolution plunged Mexico into turmoil. Just as Wilson was entering the White House in 1913, the ruthless general Victoriano Huerta emerged as head of the government. Wealthy landowners and foreign investors endorsed Huerta, who was likely to protect their holdings. Soon a bloody civil war was raging.

Most European nations recognized the Huerta regime, but Wilson refused to accept the "government of butchers." (Huerta had murdered the popular leader Francisco Madero with the approval of the Taft administration.) When Huerta proclaimed himself dictator, Wilson banned arms shipments to Mexico. He threw his support to rebel leader Venustiano Carranza, on the condition that Carranza participate in American-sponsored elections. No Mexican was ready to tolerate such interference. Carranza and his "constitutionalists" rejected the offer. With few options, Wilson armed the rebels anyway.

Wilson's distaste for Huerta was so great that he used a minor incident as a pretext for an invasion. In April 1914 the crew of the USS *Dolphin* landed without permission in the Mexican port city of Tampico. Local police arrested the sailors, only to release them with an apology. Unappeased, their squadron commander demanded a 21-gun salute to the American flag. Agreed, replied the Mexicans, but only if American guns returned the salute to Mexico. Learning of a German shipload of weapons about to land at Veracruz, Wilson broke the impasse by ordering American troops to take the city. Instead of the bloodless occupation they expected, U.S. marines encountered stiff resistance as they stormed ashore; 126 Mexicans and 19 Americans were killed before the city fell.

Only the combined diplomacy of Argentina, Brazil, and Chile staved off war between Mexico and the United States. When a bankrupt Huerta resigned in

Pancho Villa

1914, Carranza formed a new constitutionalist government but refused to follow Wilson's guidelines. Wilson threw his support to Francisco "Pancho" Villa, a wily, peasant-born general who had broken from Carranza. Together with Emiliano Zapata, another peasant leader, Villa kept rebellion flickering.

A year later, when Wilson finally recognized the Carranza regime, Villa turned against the United States. In January 1916 he abducted 18 Americans from a train in Mexico and slaughtered them. In March, he galloped into Columbus, New Mexico, killed 19 people, and left the town in flames. Wilson ordered 6000 troops into Mexico to capture Villa. A reluctant Carranza agreed to yet another American invasion.

For nearly two years, General John "Black Jack" Pershing (nicknamed for the all-black unit he commanded in the Spanish–American War) chased Villa on horseback, in automobiles, and with airplanes. There were bloody skirmishes with government troops, but not a single one with Villa and his rebels. As the chase turned wilder and wilder, Carranza withdrew his consent for U.S. troops on Mexican soil. Early in 1917 Wilson pulled Pershing home. The "punitive expedition," as the president called it, poisoned Mexican–American relations for the next 30 years.

THE ROAD TO WAR

In early 1917, around the time that Wilson recalled Pershing, the British liner *Laconia* was making its way home across the Atlantic. As it steamed through the black night, passengers below decks talked almost casually of the war raging in Europe since 1914. "What do you think are our chances of being torpedoed?" asked Floyd Gibbons, an American reporter. Since Germany had stepped up its submarine attacks, the question was unavoidable. "I should put our chances at 250 to 1 that we don't meet a sub," replied a British diplomat.

"At that minute," recalled Gibbons, "the torpedo hit us." As warning whistles blasted the passengers abandoned ship, watching in horror from lifeboats as a second torpedo struck. The *Laconia*'s bow rose straight in the air as its stern sank; then the entire ship slid beneath icy waters. After a miserable night spent bobbing in the waves, Gibbons was rescued. But by 1917 other neutral Americans had already lost their lives at sea. Despite its best efforts, the United States found itself dragged into war.

The Guns of August

For a century, profound strains had been pushing Europe toward war. Its population tripled, its middle and working classes swelled, and discontent with in-

Causes of World War I

dustrial society grew. Nationalism surged and with it, militarism and an aggressive imperialism. Led by Kaiser Wilhelm II and eager for empire, Germany aligned itself with Turkey and Austria–Hungary. The established imperial powers of England and France looked to contain Germany by supporting its foe, Russia. By the summer of 1914 Europe bristled with weapons, troops, and armor-plated navies. And these war machines were linked to one another through a web of diplomatic alliances—all of them committed to war, should someone or some nation set chaos in motion.

That moment came on June 28, 1914, in the streets of Sarajevo, the provincial capital of Bosnia in southwest Austria–Hungary. There, the heir to the

Assassination of Archduke Ferdinand

Austro-Hungarian throne, Archduke Franz Ferdinand, was gunned down with his wife. The young assassin who carried out the deed belonged to the Black Hand, a terrorist group that had vowed to reunite Bosnia with Serbia in yet another Slavic nation on Austria–Hungary's border.

Austria–Hungary mobilized to punish all of Serbia. In response, rival Russia called up its 6 million-man army to help the Serbs. Germany joined with Austria–Hungary; France, with Russia. On July 28, after a month of insincere demands for apologies, Austria–Hungary attacked Serbia. On August 1, Germany declared war on Russia and, two days later, on France.

The guns of August heralded the first global war. Like so many dominoes, nations fell into line: Britain, Japan, Romania, and later Italy to the side of

"Allies" France and Russia; Bulgaria and Turkey to the "Central Powers" of Germany and Austria–Hungary. Armies fought from the deserts of North Africa to the plains of Flanders. Fleets battled off the coasts of Chile and Sumatra. Soldiers came from as far away as Australia and India. Nearly 8 million never returned.

Neutral but Not Impartial

The outbreak of war in Europe shocked most Americans. Few knew Serbia as anything but a tiny splotch on a world map. Fewer still were prepared to go to war in its defense. President Wilson issued an immediate declaration of neutrality and approved a plan for evacuating Americans stranded in Belgium. "The more I read about the conflict," Wilson wrote a friend, "the more open it seems to me to utter condemnation."

Wilson came to see the calamity as an opportunity. Neutral America would lead warring nations to "a peace without victory" and a new world order. Selfish

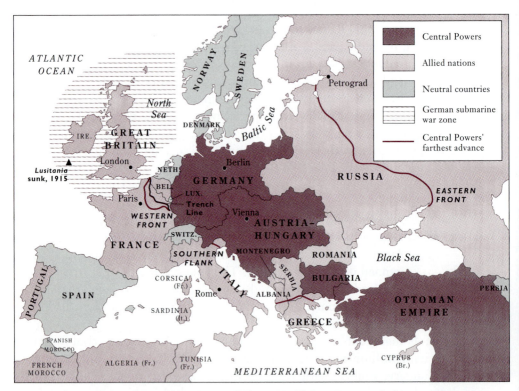

THE WAR IN EUROPE, 1914–1917   When World War I erupted, few countries in Europe remained neutral. The armies of the Central Powers penetrated as far west as France and as far east as Russia. By 1917, the war in Europe had settled into a hideous standoff along a deadly line of trenches on the western front.

nationalism would give way to cooperative internationalism; power politics, to collective security and Christian charity. Progressive faith in reason would triumph over violence. Everything hinged on maintaining neutrality. Only if America stood above the fray could it lead the way to a higher peace. Americans must remain "impartial in thought as well as action," Wilson insisted in 1914.

But true impartiality was impossible. Americans of German and Austrian descent naturally sympathized with the Central Powers, as did Irish-Americans, on the grounds of England's centuries-old domination of Ireland. But the bonds of language, culture, and history tied most Americans to Great Britain. Even Wilson, who had long admired British institutions, could not escape the tug of loyalty. And gratitude for French aid during the American Revolution still lived. When the first American division marched through Paris years later, its commander stopped to salute Lafayette's tomb with the cry, "Nous voilà, Lafayette!"—Lafayette, we are here!

Germany aroused different sentiments. Although some progressives admired German social reforms, Americans generally saw Germany as an iron military power bent on conquest. Americans read British propaganda of spike-helmeted "Huns" raping Belgian women, bayoneting their children, pillaging their towns. Some of the stories were true, some embellished, some manufactured, but all worked against Germany.

Then, too, American economic ties to Britain and France created an investment in Allied victory. After faltering briefly in 1914, the American economy boomed with the flood of war orders. Between 1914 and 1916 trade with the Allies rocketed from $800 million to $3 billion. The Allies eventually borrowed more than $2 billion from American banks to finance their purchases. By contrast, a British blockade reduced American "contraband" commerce with the Central Powers to a trickle.

The Diplomacy of Neutrality

Wilson had admired Great Britain all his life. Try as he might, he could not contain his sympathies. Although he insisted that all warring powers respect the right of neutrals to trade with any nation, he hesitated to retaliate against Great Britain's blockade. Britain's powerful navy was its key to victory over Germany, a land power. By the end of 1915 the United States had all but accepted the British blockade of Germany, while American supplies continued to flow to England. True neutrality was dead. America became the quartermaster of the Allies.

Early in 1915, Germany turned to a dreadful new weapon to even the odds at sea. It mounted a counterblockade of Great Britain with two dozen sub-

Submarine warfare

marines, or *Unterseeboote*, called U-boats. Before submarines, sea raiders usually gave crews and passengers the chance to escape. But if thin-skinned U-boats surfaced to obey these conventions, they risked being rammed or blown from the water. So submarines attacked without warning and spared no lives. Invoking international law and national honor, President Wilson threatened to hold Germany to "strict accountability" for any American losses. Germany promised not to sink any American ships, but soon a new issue grabbed the headlines: the safety of American passengers on belligerent vessels.

On the morning of May 7, 1915, the British passenger liner *Lusitania* appeared out of a fog bank off the coast of Ireland on its way from New York to Southampton. The commander of the German U-20 could hardly believe his eyes: the giant ship filled the viewfinder of his periscope. He fired a single torpedo. A tremendous roar followed as one of the *Lusitania*'s main boilers exploded. The ship listed so badly that lifeboats could barely be launched before the vessel sank. Nearly 1200 men, women, and children perished, including 128 Americans.

Former President Theodore Roosevelt charged that such an "act of piracy" demanded war against Germany. Wilson, though horrified at this "murder on the high seas," urged restraint. "There is such a thing as a nation being so right that it does not need to convince others by force," he said a few days later. He sent notes of protest but did little more.

Secretary of State Bryan, an advocate of what he called "real neutrality," wanted equal protests lodged against both German submarines and British blockaders. He suspected that the *Lusitania* carried munitions and was thus a legitimate target. (Much later, evidence proved him right.) Relying on passengers for protection against attack, Bryan argued, was "like putting women and children in front of an army." Rather than endorse Wilson's policy, Bryan resigned.

Battling on two fronts in Europe, Germany wanted to keep the United States out of the war. But in February 1916 a desperate Germany declared submarine warfare on all *armed* vessels, belligerent or neutral. A month later a U-boat commander mistook the French steamer *Sussex* for a mine layer and torpedoed the unarmed vessel as it ferried passengers and freight across the English Channel. Several Americans were injured.

In mid-April, Wilson issued an ultimatum. If Germany refused to stop sinking nonmilitary vessels, the United States would break off diplomatic relations.

Sussex pledge — War would surely follow. Without enough U-boats to control the seas, Germany agreed to Wilson's terms, all but abandoning its counterblockade. This *Sussex* pledge gave Wilson a major victory but carried a grave risk. If German submarines resumed unrestricted attacks, the United States would have to go to war. "Any little German [U-boat] commander can put us into the war at any time," Wilson admitted to his cabinet.

Peace, Preparedness, and the Election of 1916

While hundreds of young Yanks slipped across the border to enlist in the Canadian army, most Americans agreed that neutrality was the wisest course. Before the war a peace movement had taken seed in the United States, nourished in 1910 by a gift of $10 million from Andrew Carnegie. In 1914 social re-formers Jane Addams, Charlotte Perkins Gilman, and Lillian Wald founded the Women's International League for Peace and Freedom and the American Union Against Militarism. Calling on Wilson to convene a peace conference, they lob-bied for open diplomacy, disarmament, an end to colonial empires, and an in-ternational organization to settle disputes. These would become the core of Wilson's peace plan.

Pacifists might condemn the war, but Republicans and corporate leaders ar-gued that the nation was woefully unprepared to keep peace. The army num-bered only 80,000 men in 1914; the navy, just 37 battleships and a handful of new "dreadnoughts," or supercruisers. Advocates of "preparedness" called for a navy larger than Great Britain's, an army of millions of reservists, and univer-sal military training.

By the end of 1915, frustration with German submarines led Wilson to join the cause. He toured the country promoting preparedness and promising a "navy second to none." In Washington, he pressed Congress to double the army, in-crease the National Guard, and begin construction of the largest navy in the world. To foot the bill progressives pushed through new graduated taxes on higher incomes and on estates as well as additional levies on corporate profits.

Whoever paid for it, most Americans were thinking of preparedness for peace, not war. The Democrats discovered the political power of peace early in the presidential campaign of 1916. As their convention opened in St. Louis in June, the keynote speaker began what he expected to be a dull description of Wilson's recent diplomatic maneuvers—only to have the crowd roar back in each case, "What did we do? What did we do?" The speaker knew the answer

"He kept us out of war" and shouted it back: "We didn't go to war! We didn't go to war!" The next day Wilson was renominated by acclamation. "He Kept Us Out of War" became his campaign slogan.

The Republicans had already nominated Charles Evans Hughes, the former governor of New York. He endorsed "straight and honest" neutrality and peace. But despite his moderate stand, Democrats succeeded in painting him as a war-monger, partly because Theodore Roosevelt had rattled his own sabers so loudly. As the election approached, Democrats took full-page advertisements in newspapers across the country: "If You Want WAR, Vote for HUGHES! If You Want Peace with Honor, VOTE FOR WILSON!"

By the time the polls closed, Wilson had squeaked out a victory. He carried the South and key states in the Midwest and West on a tide of prosperity, pro-gressive reform, and, most of all, promises of peace.

Wilson's Final Peace Offensive

Twice since 1915 Wilson had sent his trusted advisor Colonel Edward House to Europe to negotiate a peace between the warring powers, and twice House had failed. With the election over, Wilson opened his final peace offensive. But when he asked the belligerents to state their terms for a cease-fire, neither side responded. Frustrated, fearful, and genuinely agonized, Wilson called for "peace without victory." There could only be "a peace among equals," he told the Senate in January 1917.

As Wilson spoke, a fleet of U-boats was cruising toward the British Isles. Weeks earlier German military leaders had persuaded the Kaiser to take one last gamble to starve the Allies into submission. On January 31, 1917, the German ambassador in Washington announced that unrestricted submarine warfare would resume the next day.

Wilson's dream of keeping the country from war collapsed. He asked Congress for authority to arm merchant ships and early in February severed re-

Zimmermann telegram

lations with Germany. Then British authorities handed him a bombshell—an intercepted telegram from the German foreign secretary, Arthur Zimmermann, to the Kaiser's ambassador in Mexico. In the event of war, the ambassador was instructed to offer Mexico guns, money, and its "lost territory in Texas, New Mexico, and Arizona" to attack the United States. Hot with rage, Wilson released the Zimmermann telegram to the press. Soon after, he ordered gun crews aboard merchant ships and directed them to shoot U-boats on sight.

The momentum of events now propelled a reluctant Wilson toward war. On March 12, U-boats torpedoed the American merchant vessel *Algonquin*. On March 15, a revolution in Russia toppled Czar Nicholas II. A key ally was crumbling from within. By the end of the month U-boats had sunk nearly 600,000 tons of Allied and neutral shipping. For the first time reports came to Washington of cracking morale in the Allied ranks.

On April 2, accompanied by armed cavalry, Wilson rode down Pennsylvania Avenue. He trudged up the steps of the capitol and delivered to Congress a stirring war message, full of idealistic purpose. "We shall fight for the things we have always carried nearest our hearts—for democracy, for the right of those who submit to authority to have a voice in their own governments, for the rights and liberties of small nations."

Pacifists held up the war resolution until it finally passed on April 6. Six senators and 50 House members opposed it, including the first woman in Congress, Jeannette Rankin. Cultural, economic, and historical ties to the Allies, along with the German campaign of submarine warfare, had tipped the country toward war. Wilson had not wanted it, but now the battlefield seemed the only path to a higher peace.

COUNTERPOINT   *Why Did the United States Go to War?*

Because the country was never attacked, the question of why the United States went to war has sparked heated debate. Within a decade of the First World War, an early generation of "revisionists" rejected the official explanation that for moral and practical reasons Germany's campaign of submarine warfare compelled American entry. They pointed to a conspiracy of greedy munitions makers, financiers, and others who stood to profit from Allied victory. A school of "realists" emphasized the importance of strategic, diplomatic, and other pragmatic considerations by arguing that Wilson had rightly gone to war in 1917 but for the wrong reasons: abstract moral principals such as "making the world safe for democracy."

Other historians have painted a more complex portrait that underscores the pressures from all sides limiting Wilson's choices, including the German submarine campaign and Allied blockade but also interventionists, preparedness groups, and advocates of continued trade. Finally, "New Left" historians of the 1960s and 1970s placed blame for American entry on capitalism, which required a stable, peaceful world for the United States to exert its commercial supremacy.

WAR AND SOCIETY

In 1915 the German zeppelin LZ-38, hovering at 8000 feet, dropped a load of bombs that killed 7 Londoners. For the first time in history, civilians died in an air attack. Few aerial bombardments occurred during the First World War, but they signaled the growing importance of the home front in modern combat. Governments not only fielded armies but also mobilized industry, controlled labor, even rationed food. In the United States, traditions of cooperation and volunteerism helped to organize the home front and the battlefront, often in ways that were peculiarly progressive.

The Slaughter of Stalemate

While the United States debated entry into the Great War, the Allies were coming perilously close to losing it. Following the initial German assault in 1914, the war had settled into a grisly stalemate. A continuous, immovable front stretched south from Flanders to the border of Switzerland. Troops dug ditches, _Trench warfare_ six to eight feet deep and four to five feet wide, to escape bullets, grenades, and artillery. Twenty-five thousand miles of these "trenches" slashed a muddy scar across Europe. Men lived in them for years, prey to disease, lice, and a plague of rats.

War in the machine age gave the advantage to the defense. When soldiers bravely charged "over the top" of the trenches, they were shredded by machine guns that fired 600 rounds a minute. Poison gas choked them in their tracks. Giant howitzers lobbed shells on them from positions too distant to see. Even in quiet times 7000 British soldiers died or were wounded every day. In the Battle of the Somme River in 1916 a million men were killed in just four months of fighting. Only late in the war did new armored "landships"—

Trench warfare, wrote one general, is "marked by uniform formations, the regulation of space and time by higher commands . . . fixed distances between units and individuals." The reality of life in the trenches (as pictured here) was something else again.

code-named "tanks"—return the advantage to the offense by surmounting the trench barriers with their caterpillar treads.

By then Vladimir Lenin was speeding home to Russia where food riots, coal shortages, and protests against the government had led to revolution. Lenin had been exiled to Switzerland during the early stages of the Russian Revolution but returned to lead the Bolshevik party to power in November 1917. Soon the Russians negotiated a separate peace with Germany, which then transferred a million soldiers to the western front for the coming spring offensive.

"You're in the Army Now"

The Allies' plight forced the army into a crash program to send a million men to Europe by the spring of 1918. The United States had barely 180,000 men in uniform. To raise the force, Congress passed the Selective Service

Selective Service Act

Act in May 1917. Feelings about the draft ran high. "There is precious little difference between a conscript [draftee] and a convict," protested the House Speaker in 1917. Progressives were more inclined to see military service as an opportunity to unite America and promote democracy:

"Universal [military] training will jumble the boys of America all together, . . . smashing all the petty class distinctions that now divide, and prompting a brand of real democracy."

At ten in the morning on July 20, 1917, Secretary of War Newton Baker tied a blindfold over his eyes, reached into a huge glass bowl, and drew the first number in the new draft lottery. Some 24 million men were registered. Almost 3 million were drafted; another 2 million volunteered. Most were white, and all were young, between the ages of 21 and 31. Several thousand women served as clerks, telephone operators, and nurses. In a nation of immigrants, nearly one draftee in five had been born in another country. Training often aimed at educating and Americanizing these ethnic recruits. In special "development battalions" drill sergeants barked out orders while volunteers from the YMCA taught American history and English.

African Americans volunteered in disproportionately high numbers and quickly filled the four all-black army and eight National Guard units already in existence. Abroad, where 200,000 black troops served in France, only 42,000

Members of the 369th Regiment, one of the few all-black units permitted to fight, are pictured in front of their barracks. Still in World War I commanded by whites (at center), these black troops were among the first Americans to see action and initially were attached to the French army. The unit displays the Croix de Guerre, the French medal of honor.

were permitted in combat. Southern Democrats in Congress had opposed training African Americans to arms, fearful of putting "arrogant, strutting representatives of black soldiery in every community." But four regiments of the all-black Ninety-Third Division, brigaded with the French army, were among the first Americans in the trenches and among the most decorated units in the U.S. Army.

Racial violence sometimes flared among the troops. The worst episode occurred in Houston in the summer of 1917. Harassed by white soldiers and by the city's Jim Crow laws, seasoned black regulars rioted and killed 17 white civilians. Their whole battalion was disarmed and sent under arrest to New Mexico. Thirteen troopers were condemned to death and hanged within days, too quickly for appeals even to be filed.

Houston riot

Black or white, recruits learned the ways of the army—rising before dawn, drilling in close order, marching for miles. But many of them also learned to wash regularly, use indoor toilets, and read. To fight sexually transmitted disease, the army produced thousands of pamphlets, films, and lectures. The drive constituted the first serious sex education young Americans ever received.

Progressive reformers did not miss the chance to put the social sciences to work in the army. Most recruits had fewer than seven years of education; yet they had to be classified and assigned quickly to units. Psychologists saw the chance to use new intelligence tests to help the army and prove their own theories about the value of "IQ" (intelligence quotient) in measuring the mind. In fact, these new "scientific" IQ tests often measured little more than class origins. Questions such as "Who wrote 'The Raven'?" exposed background rather than intelligence. More than half the Russian, Italian, and Polish draftees and almost 80 percent of the black draftees showed up as "inferior." The army stopped the testing program in January 1919, but schools across the country adopted it after the war, reinforcing many ethnic and racial prejudices.

Mobilizing the Economy

Armed against the enemy, clothed and drilled, the doughboys marched up the gangplanks of the "Atlantic Ferry"—the ships that conveyed them to Europe. (Infantrymen were called "doughboys," most likely because of the clay dough used by soldiers in the 1850s to clean their belts.) To equip, feed, and transport an army of nearly 5 million required a national effort.

At the Treasury Department, Secretary William Gibbs McAdoo fretted over how to finance the war, which cost, finally, $32 billion. At the time the entire national debt ran to only $2 billion. New taxes paid about a third of the war costs. The rest came from loans financed through "Liberty" and "Victory" bonds and war savings certificates. By 1920 the national debt had climbed to $20 billion.

With sweeping grants of authority provided by Congress, President Wilson constructed a massive bureaucracy to mobilize the home front. What emerged

War Industries Board was a managed economy, similar to the New Nationalism envisioned by Theodore Roosevelt. A War Industries Board (WIB) coordinated production through networks of industrial and trade associations. Although it had the authority to order firms to comply, the WIB relied instead on persuasion through publicity and "cost-plus" contracts that covered all production costs, plus a guaranteed profit. Corporate profits tripled, and production soared.

The Food Administration encouraged farmers to grow more and citizens to eat less wastefully. Publicity campaigns promoted "wheatless" and "meatless" days and exhorted families to plant "victory" gardens. Spurred by rising prices, farmers brought more marginal lands into cultivation, as their real income jumped 25 percent.

A Fuel Administration met the army's energy needs by increasing production and limiting domestic consumption. Transportation snarls required more drastic action. In December 1917 the U.S. Railroad Administration simply took over rail lines for the duration of the war. Government coordination, together with a new system of permits, got freight moving and kept workers happy. Rail workers saw their wages grow by $300 million. Railroad unions won recognition, an eight-hour day, and a grievance procedure. For the first time in decades labor unrest subsided, and the trains ran on schedule.

The modern bureaucratic state received a powerful boost during the 18 months of American participation in the war. Speeding trends already under *Bureaucratic state* way, some 5000 new federal agencies centralized authority and cooperated with business and labor. The number of federal employees more than doubled between 1916 and 1918, to over 850,000. The wartime bureaucracy was quickly dismantled at the end of the war, but it set an important precedent for the future.

War Work

The war benefited working men and women, though not as much as their employers. Government contracts guaranteed high wages, an eight-hour day, and equal pay for comparable work. To encourage people to stay on the job, federal contracting agencies set up special classes to teach employers the new science of personnel management in order to supervise workers more efficiently and humanely. American industry moved one step closer to the "welfare capitalism" of the 1920s, with its profit sharing, company unions, and personnel departments to forestall worker discontent.

Personnel management was not always enough to guarantee industrial peace. In 1917 American workers called over 4000 strikes, the most in American *National War Labor Board* history. To keep factories running smoothly, President Wilson created the National War Labor Board (NWLB) early in 1918. The NWLB arbitrated more than 1000 labor disputes, helped to increase wages, and established overtime pay. In return for pledges not to strike,

Wartime needs brought more women into the labor force, often on jobs that challenged assumptions about gender roles. These women work on a production line manufacturing bullets. The novelty of the situation seems evident from the fashionable high-button, high-heeled shoes that they wear.

the board guaranteed the rights of unions to organize and bargain collectively. Membership in the American Federation of Labor jumped from 2.7 million in 1916 to nearly 4 million by 1919.

As doughboys went abroad, the war brought about a million new women into the labor force. Most were young and single. Sometimes they took over jobs once held by men as railroad engineers, drill press operators, and electric lift truck drivers. The prewar trend toward higher-paying jobs intensified, though most women still earned less than the men they replaced. And some of the most spectacular gains in defense and government work evaporated after the war as male veterans returned and the country demobilized. Tens of thousands of army nurses, defense workers, and war administrators lost their jobs. Agencies such as the Women's Service Section of the Railroad Administration, which fought sexual harassment and discrimination, simply went out of business.

Great Migrations

War work sparked massive migrations of laborers. As the fighting abroad choked off immigration and the draft depleted the workforce, factory owners scoured the country for workers. Industrial cities, no matter how small, soon swelled with newcomers. Between 1917 and 1920, some 150,000 Mexicans crossed the

Mexican migrations

border into Texas, California, New Mexico, and Arizona. Some Mexican Americans left segregated *barrios* of western cities for war plants in Chicago, Omaha, and other northern cities, pushed out by the cheaper labor from Mexico and seeking higher paying jobs. But most worked on farms and ranches, freed from military service by the deferment granted to agricultural labor.

Northern labor agents fanned out across the rural South to recruit young African Americans, while black newspapers like the Chicago *Defender* sum-

African Americans

moned them up to the "Land of Hope." During the war more than 400,000 moved to the booming industries of the North. Largely unskilled and semiskilled, they worked in the steel mills of Pennsylvania, the war plants of Massachusetts, the brickyards of New Jersey. Southern towns were decimated by the drain. Finally, under pressure from southern politicians, the U.S. Employment Service suspended its program to assist blacks moving north.

These migrations of African Americans—into the army as well as into the city—aggravated racial tensions. Lynching parties murdered 38 black southerners in 1917 and 58 in 1918. In 1919, after the war ended, more than 70 were hanged, some still in uniform. Housing shortages and job competition helped to ignite race riots across the North. In almost every city black citizens, stirred by war rhetoric of freedom and democracy, showed new militancy. During the bloody "red summer" of 1919 race wars broke out in Washington, D.C., Omaha, Nebraska, New York City, and Chicago, where thousands of African Americans were burned out of their homes and hundreds injured as they fought white mobs.

Propaganda and Civil Liberties

"Once lead this people into war," President Wilson warned before American entry into the conflict, "and they'll forget there ever was such a thing as tolerance." Americans succumbed to a ruthless hysteria during World War I, but they had help. Wilson knew how reluctant Americans had been to enter the war, and in 1917 he created the Committee on Public Information (CPI) to cement American commitment to the war.

Under George Creel, a California journalist, the CPI launched a zealous publicity campaign that produced colorful war posters, 75 million pamphlets,

Committee on Public Information

and patriotic "war expositions" in two dozen cities across the country. An army of 75,000 fast-talking "Four-Minute Men" invaded theaters, schools, and churches to keep patriotism at "white heat" with four minutes of war tirades. The CPI organized "Loyalty Leagues" in ethnic communities and sponsored rallies, including a much-publicized immigrant "pilgrimage" to the birthplace of George Washington.

As war fever mounted, voluntary patriotism blossomed into an orgy of "100 percent Americanism" that distrusted all aliens, radicals, pacifists, and dissenters. German Americans became special targets. In Iowa the governor made it a crime to speak German in public. Hamburgers were renamed "Salisbury steak"; German measles, "liberty measles." When a mob outside of St. Louis lynched a naturalized German American who had tried to enlist in the navy, a jury found the leaders not guilty.

EYEWITNESS TO HISTORY

An African American Woman's View of the 1919 Race Riots

The Washington riot gave me the *thrill that comes once in a life time*. I . . . read between the lines of our morning paper that at last our men had stood like men, struck back, were no longer dumb driven cattle. When I could no longer read for my streaming tears, I stood up, alone in my room, held both hands high over my head and exclaimed aloud: "Oh I thank God, thank God." . . . Only colored women of the South know the extreme in suffering and humiliation.

We know how many insults we have borne silently, for we have hidden many of them from our men because we did not want them to die needlessly in our defense . . ., the deep humiliation of sitting in the Jim Crow part of a street car and hear the white men laugh and discuss us, point out the good and bad points of our bodies. . . .

And, too, a woman loves a strong man, she delights to feel that her man can protect her, fight for her if necessary, save her.

No woman loves a weakling, a coward be she white or black, and some of us have been near thinking our men cowards, but thank God for Washington colored men! All honor to them, for they first blazed the way and right swiftly did Chicago men follow [during the 1919 race riot]. They put new hope, a new vision into their almost despairing women.

God Grant that our men everywhere refrain from strife, provoke no quarrel, but they protect their women and homes at any cost.

A Southern Colored Woman

The Crisis, Vol. 19 (November 1919), p. 339. Reprinted in William Loren Katy, ed., *Eyewitness: The Negro in American History* (New York: Pittman Publishing, 1976), p. 403.

Congress gave hysteria more legal bite by passing the Espionage and the Sedition acts of 1917 and 1918. Both set harsh penalties for any actions that hindered the war effort or that could be viewed as even remotely unpatriotic. Following passage, 1500 citizens were arrested for offenses that included denouncing the draft, criticizing the Red Cross, and complaining about wartime taxes.

Espionage and Sedition acts

Radical groups received especially severe treatment. The Industrial Workers of the World (IWW), a militant union centered in western states, saw the war as a battle among capitalists and threatened to strike mining and lumber companies in protest. Federal agents raided IWW headquarters in Chicago and arrested 113 members. The crusade destroyed the union. Similarly, the Socialist party opposed the "capitalist" war. In response, the postmaster general banned a dozen Socialist publications from the mail, though the party was a legal organization that had elected mayors, municipal officials, and members of Congress. In June 1918 government agents arrested Eugene V. Debs, the Socialist candidate for president in 1912, for an anti-war speech. A jury found him guilty of sedition and sentenced him to 10 years in jail.

The Supreme Court endorsed such actions. In *Schenck v. United States* (1919), the Court unanimously affirmed the conviction of a Socialist party of-

Schenck v.
United States

ficer who had mailed pamphlets urging resistance to the draft. The pamphlets, wrote Justice Oliver Wendell Holmes, created "a clear and present danger" to a nation at war.

Over There

The first American doughboys landed in France in June 1917, but few saw battle. General John Pershing held back his raw troops until they could receive more training. He also separated them in a distinct American Expeditionary Force to preserve their identity and avoid Allied disagreements over strategy.

In the spring of 1918, as the Germans pushed toward Paris, Pershing rushed 70,000 American troops to the front. American units helped block the Germans both at the town of Château-Thierry and, a month later in June, at Belleau Wood. Two more German attacks, one at Amiens and the other just east of the Marne River, ended in costly German retreats. On September 12, 1918, half a million American soldiers and a smaller number of French troops overran the German stronghold at Saint-Mihiel in four days.

With their army in retreat and civilian morale low, Germany's leaders sought an armistice. They hoped to negotiate terms along the lines laid out by

Fourteen Points

Woodrow Wilson in a speech to Congress in January 1918. Wilson's bright vision of peace had encompassed "Fourteen Points." The key provisions called for open diplomacy, free seas and free trade, disarmament, democratic self-rule, and an "association of nations" to guarantee collective security. It was nothing less than a new world order to end selfish nationalism, imperialism, and war.

Allied leaders were not impressed. "President Wilson and his Fourteen Points bore me," French Premier Georges Clemenceau said. "Even God Almighty has only ten!" But Wilson's idealistic platform was also designed to save the Allies deeper embarrassment. Almost as soon as it came to power in 1917, the new Bolshevik government in Moscow had begun publishing secret treaties from the czar's archives. They revealed that the Allies had gone to war

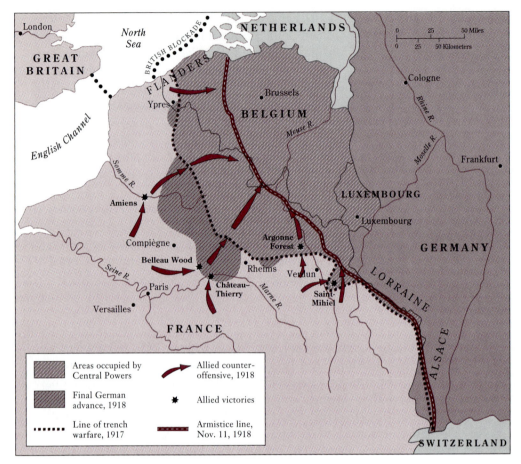

THE FINAL GERMAN OFFENSIVE AND ALLIED COUNTERATTACK, 1918   On the morning of March 21, 1918, over 60 German divisions sliced through Allied lines and plunged within 50 miles of Paris before being stopped at the Marne River in July. The Allied counterattack was marked by notable American victories at Château-Thierry, Belleau Wood, Saint-Mihiel, and Meuse-Argonne.

for territory and colonies, not for high principles. Wilson's Fourteen Points had given their cause a nobler purpose.

Wilson's ideals also stirred German liberals. On October 6 he received a telegram from Berlin requesting an immediate truce. Within a month Turkey and Austria–Hungary surrendered. Early in November the Kaiser was overthrown and fled to neutral Holland. On November 11, 1918, German officers filed into Allied headquarters in a converted railroad car near Compiègne, France, and signed the armistice.

Of the 2 million Americans who served in France, over 50,000 were killed in combat, fewer than had died in the influenza pandemic of 1918. By comparison, the war claimed 2.2 million Germans, 1.7 million Russians, 1.4 million

French, 1.2 million Austro-Hungarians, and nearly a million Britons. The American contribution had nonetheless been crucial, providing vital convoys at sea and fresh, confident troops on land. The United States emerged from the war stronger than ever. Europe, on the other hand, looked forward—as one newspaper put it—to "Disaster . . . Exhaustion . . . Revolution."

THE LOST PEACE

As the USS *George Washington* approached the coast of France in mid-December 1918, the mist suddenly lifted in an omen of good hope. Woodrow Wilson had come to represent the United States at the Paris peace conference at Versailles, once the glittering palace of Louis XIV. A world of problems awaited him and the other Allied leaders. Europe had been shelled into ruin and scarred with the debris of war. Fifty million people lay dead or maimed from the fighting. Throughout the Balkans and the old Turkish empire, ethnic rivalries, social chaos, and revolution loomed.

With the old world order so evidently in shambles, Wilson felt the need to take vigorous action. Thus the president handpicked the Peace Commission of experts that accompanied him. It included economists, historians, geographers, and political scientists—but not a single member of the Republican-controlled Senate. What promised to make peace negotiations easier created a crippling liability in Washington, where Republicans were already casting hostile eyes on the mirrored halls of Versailles.

The Treaty of Versailles

Everywhere Wilson went, cheers greeted him. In Paris 2 million people showered him with flowers. In Italy they hailed him as the "peacemaker from America." And everywhere he went, Woodrow Wilson believed what he heard, unaware of how determined the victors were to punish the vanquished. David Lloyd George of England, Georges Clemenceau of France, Vittorio Orlando of Italy, and Wilson constituted the Big Four at the conference that included some 27 nations. War had united them; now peacemaking threatened to divide them.

Wilson's sweeping reforms had taken Allied leaders by surprise. Hungry for new colonies, eager to see Germany crushed and disarmed, their secret treaties had already divided up the territories of the Central Powers. Germany had offered to surrender on the basis of Wilson's Fourteen Points, but the Allies refused to accept them. When Wilson threatened to negotiate peace on his own, Allied leaders finally agreed—but only for the moment.

Noticeably absent when the peace conference convened in January 1919 were the Russians. None of the Western democracies had recognized the Bolshevik regime in Moscow, out of fear that the communist revolution might spread. Instead, France and Britain were helping to finance a civil war to overthrow the Bolsheviks. Even Wilson had been persuaded to send several thousand American troops to join the Allied occupation of some northern Russian ports and to Siberia. The Soviets would neither forgive nor forget this intrusion.

Grueling negotiations forced Wilson to yield several of his Fourteen Points. Britain, with its powerful navy, refused even to discuss the issues of free trade and freedom of the seas. Wilson's "open diplomacy" was conducted behind closed doors by the Big Four. The only mention of disarmament involved Germany, which was permanently barred from rearming. Wilson's call for "peace without victory" gave way to a "guilt clause" that saddled Germany with responsibility for the war. Worse still, the victors imposed on the vanquished a burdensome debt of $33 billion in reparations.

Wilson did achieve some successes. His pleas for national self-determination led to the creation of a dozen new states in Europe, including Yugoslavia, Hungary, and Austria. (Poland and newly created Czechoslovakia, however, contained millions of ethnic Germans.) Former colonies gained new status as "mandates" of the victors, who were obligated to prepare them for independence. The old German and Turkish empires in the Middle East and Africa became the responsibility of France and England, while Japan took over German possessions in the Far East.

Wilson never lost sight of his main goal: a League of Nations. He had given so much ground precisely because he believed this new world organization would

League of Nations

correct any mistakes in the peace settlement. As constituted, the League was composed of a general Body of Delegates, a select Executive Council, and a Court of International Justice. Members promised to submit all war-provoking disagreements to arbitration and to isolate aggressors by cutting off commercial and military trade. Article X (Wilson called it "the heart of the covenant") bound members to respect one another's independence and territory and to join together against attack. "It is definitely a guarantee of peace," the president told the delegates in February 1919.

The Battle for the Treaty

Wilson left immediately for home to address growing opposition in Congress. In the off-year elections of 1918, voters unhappy with wartime controls, new taxes, and attacks on civil liberties gave both houses to the opposition Republicans. A slim Republican majority in the Senate put Wilson's archrival, Henry Cabot Lodge of Massachusetts, in the chairman's seat of the all-important Foreign Relations Committee.

While most of the country favored the League, Lodge was against it. For decades he had fought to preserve American freedom of action in foreign af-

Lodge opposes the League

fairs. Now he worried that the League would force Americans to subject themselves to "the will of other nations." And he certainly did not want Democrats to win votes by taking credit for the treaty. Securing the signatures of enough senators to block any treaty, Lodge rose in the Senate just before midnight on March 3 to read a "round robin" resolution against the League. "Woodrow Wilson's League of Nations died in the Senate tonight," concluded the New York *Sun*.

Wilson formally presented the treaty in July. "Dare we reject it and break the heart of the world?" he asked the senators. Fourteen Republicans and two Democrats were ready to do just that. "Irreconcilable" opponents of internationalism, they vowed to kill "the unholy thing with the holy name." Over 20 "strong reservationists," led by Lodge, sought to amend the treaty with major changes requiring yet another round of Allied negotiations. Twelve "mild reservationists" wanted minimal alterations, mainly interpretive in nature.

Wilson's only hope of winning the necessary two-thirds majority lay in compromise. Worn out by the concessions already wrung from him in Paris, afflicted by numbing headaches and a twitch in his left eye, he resisted all changes. Despite his doctor's warnings, Wilson took his case to the people in a month-long stump across the nation in 1919.

In Pueblo, Colorado, a crowd of 10,000 heard perhaps the greatest oration of his career. Wilson spoke of American soldiers killed in France and American

Wilson's stroke   boys whom the League one day would spare from death. Listeners wept openly. That evening, utterly exhausted, he collapsed in a spasm of pain. On October 2, four days after being rushed to the White House, he fell to the bathroom floor, knocked unconscious by a stroke.

For six weeks Wilson could do no work at all and for months after worked little more than an hour a day. His second wife, Edith Bolling Wilson, handled the routine business of government along with the president's secretary and his doctor. The country knew nothing of the seriousness of his condition. Wilson recovered slowly but never fully. More and more the battle for the treaty consumed his fading energies.

Late in 1919 Lodge finally reported the treaty out of committee with 14 amendments to match Wilson's Fourteen Points. The most important asserted that the United States assumed no obligation under Article X to aid League members unless Congress consented. Wilson believed Lodge had delivered a "knife thrust at the heart of the treaty" and refused to accept any change. Whatever ill will Lodge bore Wilson, his objections did not destroy the treaty, but only weakened it by protecting the congressional power to declare war.

Wilson and Lodge refused to compromise. When the amended treaty finally came before the Senate in March 1920, enough Democrats broke from the president to produce a majority—but not the required two-thirds. The Treaty of Versailles was dead in America. Not until July 1921 did Congress enact a joint resolution ending the war. The United States, which had fought separately from the Allies, made a separate peace as well.

Red Scare

Peace abroad did not bring peace at home. On May Day 1919, six months after the war ended, mobs in a dozen cities broke up Socialist parades, injured hundreds, and killed three people. Later that month, when a spectator at a Victory Loan rally in Washington refused to stand for the national anthem, a sailor shot him in the back. The stadium crowd applauded.

The spontaneous violence and extremism occurred because Americans believed they were under attack. Millions of soldiers had returned home, now un-

Radicals and labor unrest

employed and looking for jobs. With prices rising and war regulations lifted, laborers were demanding higher wages and striking when they failed to get them. In Boston even the police walked off their jobs. When a strike by conservative trade unionists paralyzed Seattle for five days in January, Mayor Ole Hanson draped his car in an American flag and led troops through the streets in a show of force. Hanson blamed radicals, while Congress ascribed the national ills to Bolshevik agents, inspired by the revolution in Russia.

The menace of radicalism was entirely overblown. With Socialist Eugene Debs in prison, his dwindling party numbered only about 30,000. Radicals at first hoped that the success of the Russian Revolution would help reverse their fortunes in the United States. But most Americans found the prospect of "Bolshevik" agitators threatening, especially after March 1919, when the new Russian government formed the Comintern to spread revolution abroad. Furthermore, the Left itself splintered. In 1919 dissidents deserted the Socialists to form the more radical Communist Labor party. About the same time, a group of mostly Slavic radicals created a separate Communist party. Both organizations together counted no more than 40,000 members.

On April 28 Mayor Hanson received a small brown parcel at his office, evidently another present from an admirer of his tough patriotism. It was a homemade bomb. Within days, 20 such packages were discovered, including ones sent to John D. Rockefeller, Supreme Court Justice Oliver Wendell Holmes, and the Postmaster General. On June 2 bombs exploded simultaneously in eight different cities. One of them demolished the front porch of A. Mitchell Palmer, attorney general of the United States. The bomb thrower was blown to bits, but enough remained to identify him as an Italian anarchist from Philadelphia. Already edgy over Bolshevism and labor militancy, many Americans assumed that an organized conspiracy was being mounted to overthrow the government.

Palmer, a Quaker and a progressive, hardened in the wake of the bombings. In November 1919 and again in January 1920, he launched raids in over 30

Palmer raids

cities across the United States. Government agents invaded private homes, meeting halls, and pool parlors, taking several thousand alleged communists into custody without warrants and beating those who resisted. Prisoners were marched through streets in chains, crammed into di-

On September 16, 1920, a wagonload of bombs exploded at the corner of Broad and Wall streets, killing 33 people and injuring more than 200. The nation was horrified but saw no communist plot behind the mysterious blast, as Attorney General A. Mitchell Palmer charged.

lapidated jails, held without hearings. Over two hundred aliens, most of whom had no criminal records, were deported to the Soviet Union.

Arrests continued at the rate of 200 a week through March. State after state passed new statutes outlawing radical unions. In Centralia, Washington, vigilantes spirited radical labor organizer Wesley Everest from jail, castrated him, and hanged him from the Chehalis River bridge as they riddled his body with bullets. The county coroner ruled it a suicide.

Such abuses of civil liberties provoked a backlash. After the New York legislature expelled five duly-elected Socialists in 1919, responsible politicians—from former presidential candidate Charles Evans Hughes to Ohio Senator Warren Harding—denounced the action. The "deportation delirium" ended early in 1920. Palmer finally overreached himself by predicting a revolutionary uprising for May 1, 1920. Buildings were put under guard and state militia called to readiness. Nothing happened. Four months later, when a wagonload of bombs exploded on Wall Street, Palmer blamed a Bolshevik conspiracy. Despite 33 deaths and more than 200 injuries, Americans saw it as the work of a few demented radicals (which it probably was) and went about business as usual.

Not for another 20 years would the United States assume a responsible position in international affairs. And the spirit of reform at home dimmed as well. When war came, progressivism had furnished the bureaucratic weapons to organize the fight, but its push for social justice and toleration had been overshadowed by a patriotic frenzy.

War changed Americans. They experienced a planned economy for the first time. Propaganda shaped diverse ethnic, racial, class, and gender differences into the uniform purpose of victory. War work drew millions from country to city, from farm to factory. The army mixed millions more, who returned from Europe with tales of its wonders. Provincial America thus became more cosmopolitan and urban. But the corrosive effects of war and the cynicism of the European victors led to disillusionment. Americans turned from idealistic crusades to the practical business of getting and spending.

SIGNIFICANT EVENTS

1901 — Canal authorized across the Central American isthmus

1902 — Platt Amendment ratified

1904 — Roosevelt Corollary to Monroe Doctrine

1905 — Treaty of Portsmouth ends Russo-Japanese War

1907 — "Gentlemen's agreement" with Japan; "Great White Fleet" embarks on world tour

1910 — Mexican Revolution erupts

1914 — U.S. Navy invades Veracruz; Archduke Franz Ferdinand assassinated; World War I begins; Panama Canal opens

1915 — Japan issues Twenty-One Demands; Germany proclaims war zone around British Isles; *Lusitania* torpedoed; Secretary of State Bryan resigns; Wilson endorses preparedness

1916 — *Sussex* pledge; General John Pershing invades Mexico in pursuit of Pancho Villa; Wilson reelected president

1917 — Wilson calls for "peace without victory"; Germany resumes unrestricted submarine warfare; Zimmermann telegram released; Russian Revolution breaks out; U.S. enters World War I; Selective Service Act passed; War Industries Board created

1918 — Wilson's Fourteen Points for peace; Eugene Debs jailed under Sedition Act; influenza epidemic; Germany sues for peace; armistice declared

1919 — Paris Peace Conference; *Schenck v. United States* affirms Espionage Act; red summer; Chicago race riot; Senate rejects Treaty of Versailles

1920 — Palmer raids; red scare

The Perils of Democracy

In the wake of World War I, the editors of *The New Republic* despaired that "the war did no good to anybody. Those of its generation whom it did not kill, it crippled, wasted, or used up." But by the mid-1920s, with a post-war recession lifting, despair gave way to hope. Woodrow Wilson's vision of a world made safe for democracy no longer seemed so naive.

In both political and material terms democracy seemed to be advancing. Great Britain eliminated restrictions on suffrage for men and by 1928 gave the vote to women as well. Hapsburg Germany transformed itself into the Weimar Republic, whose constitution provided universal suffrage and a bill of rights. Across central and eastern Europe, the new nations carved out of the old Russian and Austro-Hungarian empires, along with the previously independent Romania, Bulgaria, Greece, and Albania, attempted to create governments along similarly democratic lines.

The winds of reform also blew through Asia. Some Asians, like Mao Zedong in China and Ho Chi Minh in Indochina, saw communism as the means to liberate their peoples from imperialist rule. But even Asian Marxists aligned themselves with the powerful force of nationalism. In India, the Congress party formed by Mohandas K. Gandhi united socialists and powerful industrial capitalists in a campaign of nonviolence and boycotts of British goods that ultimately brought self-government to India. In Turkey, Kemal Atatürk in 1923 abolished the sultanate and established the Turkish Republic with all the trappings of a Western democratic state.

The spread of democracy had a material side as well. Indeed, the respect given parliamentary governments depended heavily on their ability to restore prosperity. As the world economy expanded, some optimists suggested that innovations in manufacturing, like Henry Ford's moving assembly line, would usher in an era in which plenty would replace want. Increased earnings encouraged a democratic culture of consumption, whether it was buying radios in France or Western-style fashions in Tokyo. Culture too was being spread globally, with the coming of mass media. Movies, radio, and mass-circulation magazines made once-remote people and places accessible and familiar.

But democracy's foundations were fragile. In the new Soviet Union, communists led by Lenin and the ruthless Joseph Stalin demonstrated that talk of "the masses" and "democratic socialism" could mask an iron totalitarianism. In Japan, democracy was hampered by feudal traditions. By the late 1920s nationalists from the old samurai class had joined with the nation's economically powerful families in a militarist quest for a Japanese East Asian empire.

Fear of communist revolution led some nationalists in Europe to reject democracy. With Italy's parliamentary government seemingly paralyzed by postwar unrest, Benito Mussolini and his *Fasci di Combattimento*, or fascists, used terrorism and murder to create an "all-embracing" single-party state. During the 1920s Italian fascists rejected the liberal belief in political parties in favor of a glorified nation-state dominated by the middle class, small businesspeople, and small farmers. In Germany Adolf Hitler trumpeted similar ideals and relied on equally brutal tactics to gain power in 1933. His Nazi party used its Gestapo, or secret police, to ensure that Germans expressed only ideas that conformed to the views of their national leader, the *Führer*.

Hitler succeeded partly because the prosperity of the 1920s was shattered worldwide by the Great Depression. Farmers ruined by overproduction, urban workers out of a job, shopkeepers facing bankruptcy—such people found it easy to believe that only the forceful leadership of one could unite the many. Even in the United States, the business newspaper *Barron's* mused that "a mild species of dictatorship" might "help us over the roughest spots in the road ahead."

Thus the Depression shook both the political and the material pillars of democratic culture. On the eve of World War II the number of European democracies had been reduced from 27 to 10. Latin America was ruled by a variety of dictators and military juntas, China by the corrupt one-party dictatorship of Chiang Kai-shek. Almost alone, the New Deal attempted to combat the Depression through the methods of parliamentary democracy. The totalitarian states had promised stability, national glory, and an end to the communist menace. Instead they led the world to chaos and war from which both communism and democracy emerged triumphant.

CHAPTER TWENTY-FOUR

The New Era

Just before Christmas 1918 the "Gospel Car" pulled into Los Angeles. Bold letters on the side announced: "JESUS IS COMING—GET READY." Aimee Semple McPherson, the ravishing redheaded driver, had completed a cross-country trip to seek her destiny in the West. With only "ten dollars and a tambourine" to her name, destiny at first proved hard to find. But after three years of wandering the state, she landed in San Diego, a city with the highest rates of illness and suicide in California. It was the perfect place to preach the healing message of Sister Aimee's "Foursquare Gospel." Her revival attracted 30,000 people, who witnessed her first miracle: a paralytic walked.

Sister Aimee had a Pentecostal message for her flock: "Jesus is the healer. I am only the little office girl who opens the door and says, 'Come in.'" After the miracle in San Diego, her fame spread. She returned triumphantly to Los Angeles, where nearly three-quarters of a million people, many from the nation's heartland, had migrated in search of opportunity, sun, and perhaps salvation. In heading west, more than a few had lost touch with the traditional Protestant denominations at home. Sister Aimee put her traveling gospel tent away. She would minister to the lost flock at her doorstep.

To the blare of trumpets on New Year's Day, 1923, she unveiled the $1.5 million Angelus Temple, graced by a 75-foot rotating electronic cross. It was visible at night from 50 miles away. Inside was a 5000-seat auditorium, radio station KFSG (Kall Four Square Gospel), a "Cradle Roll Chapel" for babies, and a "Miracle Room" filled with the many aids discarded by the cured faithful. Services were not simply a matter of hymn, prayer, and sermon. Sister added pageants, Holy Land slide shows, circuses, and healing sessions.

Aimee Semple McPherson succeeded because she was able to blend old and new. Her lively sermons carried the spirit of what people were calling the "New Era" of productivity and consumerism. Country preachers menaced their congregations with visions of eternal damnation, but Sister Aimee, wrote a reporter,

Sister Aimee Semple McPherson, billed as the "world's most pulchritudinous evangelist," in her robes

offered "flowers, music, golden trumpets, red robes, angels, incense, nonsense, and sex appeal." Her approach revealed a nose for publicity and a sophisticated understanding of the booming media industries of the 1920s. Here was one brand of evangelism suited to a new consumer age.

Modernizing the gospel was just one symptom of the New Era. Writing in 1931, journalist Frederick Lewis Allen found the changes of the preceding decade so overwhelming that it hardly seemed possible 1919 was *Only Yesterday*, as he titled his book. To give some sense of the transformation, Allen followed an average American couple, the fictitious "Mr. and Mrs. Smith," through the decade. Among the most striking changes was the revolution in women's fashions and behavior. Mrs. Smith's corset vanished, her hemline jumped from her ankle to her knee, and she "bobbed," or cut, her long hair to the popular near-boyish length and flattened her breasts for greater freedom of movement.

With Prohibition in full force, Mrs. Smith and other women of her day walked into illegal "speakeasy" saloons as readily as men. In the trendy hotels she and her husband danced to jazz and sprinkled their conversations with references to "repressed sexual drives" and the best methods of contraception.

Urban role in the New Era

But perhaps the most striking change about these "average" Americans was that they lived in the city. The census of 1920 showed that for the first time just over half the population were urbanites. Here, in urban America, the New Era worked its changes and sent them rippling outward.

Yet the Smiths of Frederick Allen's imagination were hardly average. Nearly as many Americans still lived on isolated farms, in villages, and in small towns as in the cities. In fact, many "city" dwellers lived there too. By defining cities

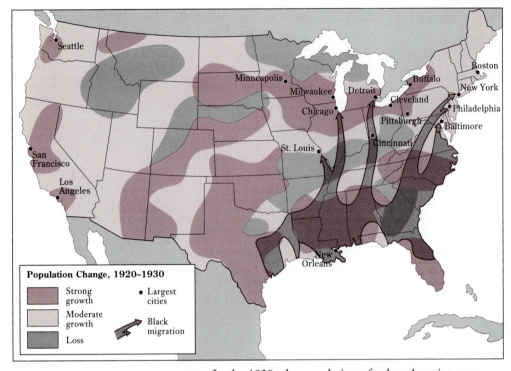

AREAS OF POPULATION GROWTH   In the 1920s the population of urban America grew by some 15 million people—at the time, the greatest 10-year jump in American history. Cities grew largely by depopulating rural areas. In the most dramatic manifestation of the overall trend, more than a million African Americans migrated from the rural South to the urban North.

as incorporated municipalities with 2500 people or more, the Census Bureau had created hundreds of statistical illusions. New York with its millions of inhabitants ranked in the census tables alongside Sac Prairie, Wisconsin, whose population hovered barely above the mystical mark of 2500, and tiny Hyden, a town along the Cumberland plateau of eastern Kentucky.

Most citizens, the Smiths aside, dwelled in an earlier America and clung to many of its values. The poet August Derleth grew up in Sac Prairie. As a 10-year-old in 1919 he could hear the "howl of wolves" at night. The town observed changing seasons not with new fashions but by the appearance and disappearance of plants and animals. In Hyden, Kentucky, Main Street was still unpaved. By 1930 there were still only 10 automobiles in the county. God-fearing Baptists worshiped together as their parents had before them and still repaired to the Middle Fork of the Kentucky River for an open-air baptism when they declared their new birth in Christ. They would have nothing to do with flapper girls or the showy miracles of Aimee McPherson.

As much as some Americans resisted the transforming forces of modern life, the New Era could not be walled out. New industrial technologies stimulated a host of consumer goods, while large corporations developed more "modern" bureaucracies to make workers and production lines more efficient. Whether Americans embraced the New Era or condemned it, change came nonetheless, in the form of a mass-produced consumer economy, a culture shaped by mass media, and a more materialistic society.

THE ROARING ECONOMY

In the 1920s, the United States was in the midst of a revolution in production. Manufacturing rose 64 percent; output per workhour, 40 percent. The sale of electricity doubled; the consumption of fuel oil more than doubled. Between 1922 and 1927 the economy grew by 7 percent a year—the largest peacetime rate ever. If anything roared in the "Roaring Twenties," it was industry and commerce.

Technology and Consumer Spending

Technology was partly responsible. Steam turbines and shovels, electric motors, belt and bucket conveyors, and countless other new machines became commonplace at work sites. Machines replaced 200,000 workers each year, and a new phrase—"technological unemployment"—entered the vocabulary. Even so, demand, especially for new consumer goods, kept the labor force growing at a rate faster than that of the population. And pay improved. Between 1919 and 1927, average income climbed nearly $150 for each American.

As the industrial economy matured, more consumer goods appeared on store shelves: cigarette lighters, wristwatches, radios, panchromatic film. The improvement in productivity helped to keep prices down. The cost of a tire and an inner tube, for example, dropped by half between 1914 and 1929. Meanwhile, the purchasing power of wage earners jumped by 20 percent. Americans enjoyed the highest standard of living any people had ever known.

Yet for all the prosperity, a dangerous imbalance in the economy developed. Most Americans were putting very little of their savings into the bank. Personal debt was rising two and a half times faster than personal income, an unhealthy sign of consumers scrambling to spend.

The Booming Construction Industry

Along with technology and consumer spending, new "boom industries" promoted economic growth. Construction was one. In a rebound after the war years, even cities the size of Beaumont, Texas, Memphis, Tennessee, and Syracuse, New York, were constructing buildings of 20 stories or more. Residential construction doubled as people moved from cities to suburbs. Suburban Grosse Point, near Detroit, grew by 700 percent; and Beverly Hills, on the outskirts of Los Angeles, by 2500 percent. Road construction made suburban life possible and pumped millions of dollars into the economy. In 1919 Oregon, New Mexico, and Colorado hit on a novel idea for financing roads: a tax on gasoline. Within a decade every state had one.

Construction stimulated other businesses too: steel, concrete, lumber, home mortgages, and insurance. It even helped change the nation's eating habits. The limited storage space of small "kitchenettes" in new apartments boosted supermarket chains and the canning industry. And as shipments of fresh fruits and vegetables sped across new roads, interest in nutrition grew. Vitamins, publicized with new zeal, appeared on breakfast tables.

The Automobile

No industry boomed more than auto manufacturing. Although cars had first appeared on streets at the turn of the century, for many years they remained little more than expensive toys. By 1920 there were 10 million in America, a sizable number. But by 1929 the total had jumped to 26 million, one for every 5 people (compared with one for every 43 in Britain). Automakers bought one-seventh of the nation's steel and more rubber, plate glass, nickel, and lead than any other industry. By the end of the decade, one American in four somehow earned a living from automobiles.

Henry Ford made it possible by pushing standardization and mass production to such ruthless extremes that the automobile became affordable. Trading

Henry Ford

on his fame as a race-car manufacturer, he founded the Ford Motor Company in 1903 with the dream of building a "motor car for the multitude." "Everybody wants to be somewhere he ain't," Ford said. The way to succeed was to reduce manufacturing costs by making all the cars alike, "just like one pin is like another pin." In 1908 Ford perfected the Model T. It had a 20-horsepower engine and a body of steel. It was high enough to ride the worst roads, and it came in only one color: black.

Priced at $845, the Model T was cheap by industry standards but still too costly and too time-consuming to build. Two Ford engineers suggested copying a practice of Chicago meatpacking houses, where beef carcasses were carried on moving chains past meat dressers. In 1914 Ford introduced the moving assembly line. A conveyor belt, positioned waist high to eliminate bending or walking, propelled the chassis at six feet per minute as stationary workers put the cars together. The process cut assembly time in half. In 1925 new Model Ts were rolling off the line every 10 seconds. At $290, almost anybody could buy one. By 1927 Ford had sold 15 million of his "tin lizzies."

Ford was also a social prophet. Breaking with other manufacturers, he preached a "doctrine of high wages." According to it, workers with extra money

Doctrine of high wages

in their pockets would buy enough to sustain a booming prosperity. In 1915 Ford's plants in Dearborn established the "Five-Dollar Day," twice the wage rate in Detroit. He reduced working hours from 48 to 40 a week and cut the workweek to five days.

Yet Ford workers were not happy. Ford admitted that the repetitive operations on his assembly line made it scarcely possible "that any man would care to continue long at the same job." The Five-Dollar Day was designed, in part, to reduce the turnover rate of 300 percent a year at Ford plants. Ford recouped his profits by speeding up the assembly line and enforcing ruthless efficiencies. Ford workers could not talk, whistle, smoke, or sit on the job. They wore frozen expressions called "Fordization of the Face" and communicated in the "Ford Whisper" without moving their lips. A "Sociological Department" spied on workers in their homes, and the "Education Department" taught plant procedures and also "Americanization" classes where immigrant workers learned English, proper dress, even etiquette.

By making automobiles available to nearly everyone, the industry changed the face of America. The spreading web of paved roads fueled urban sprawl, real

A car culture estate booms in California and Florida, and a new roadside economy of restaurants, service stations, and motels. Thousands of "auto camps" opened to provide tourists with tents and crude toilets. Automobile travel broke down rural isolation and advanced common dialects and manners. By 1930 almost two farm families in three had cars.

Across the country the automobile gave the young unprecedented freedom from parental authority. After hearing 30 cases of "sex crimes" (19 had occurred in cars), an exasperated juvenile court judge declared that the automobile was "a house of prostitution on wheels." It was, of course, much more. The automobile was to the 1920s what the railroad had been to the nineteenth century: the catalyst for economic growth, a transportation revolution, and a cultural symbol.

The Business of America

In business, said Henry Ford, the "fundamentals are all summed up in the single word, 'service.'" President Calvin Coolidge echoed the theme of service to society in 1925: "The business of America is business. The man who builds a factory builds a temple. The man who works there worships there." A generation earlier, progressives had criticized business for its social irresponsibility. But the wartime contributions of business managers and the return of prosperity in 1922 gained them a renewed respect.

Encouraged by federal permissiveness, a wave of mergers swept the economy. Between 1919 and 1930, some 8000 firms disappeared as large gobbled

Corporate consolidation small. Oligopolies (where a few firms dominated whole industries) grew in steel, meatpacking, cigarettes, and other businesses. National chains began to replace local "mom and pop" stores. By 1929, one bag of groceries in ten came from the 15,000 red-and-gold markets of the Great Atlantic and Pacific Tea Company, commonly known as A & P.

This expansion and consolidation meant that national wealth was being controlled not by affluent individuals, but by corporations. The model of modern business was the large, bureaucratic corporation, in which those who actually managed the company had little to do with those who owned it, the shareholders. Stocks and bonds were becoming so widely dispersed that few individuals held more than 1 or 2 percent of any company.

A salaried bureaucracy of executives and plant managers formed a new elite, which no longer set their sights on becoming swashbuckling entrepreneurs like

Managerial elite the Carnegies and Rockefellers of old. The new managers looked to work their way up a corporate ladder. They were less interested in risk than in productivity and stability. Managers subdivided operations and put experts in charge. Corporate leaders learned the techniques of "scientific management" taught at Harvard and other new schools of business, through journals, professional societies, and consulting firms. And they channeled earnings back into their companies to expand factories and carry on research. By the end of the decade more than a thousand firms had research laboratories.

Welfare Capitalism

The new scientific management also stressed good relations between managers and employees. There was reason to, for the rash of postwar strikes had left business leaders suspicious as ever of labor unions and determined to find ways to limit their influence.

Some tactics were more strong-armed than scientific. In 1921 the National Association of Manufacturers, the Chamber of Commerce, and other em-

The American Plan ployer groups launched the "American Plan," aimed at ending "closed shops," factories where only union members could work. Employers made workers sign agreements disavowing union membership. Labor organizers called them "yellow dog contracts." Companies infiltrated unions with spies, locked union members out of factories if they protested, and boycotted firms that hired union labor.

The benevolent side of the American Plan involved a social innovation called "welfare capitalism." Companies like General Electric and Bethlehem Steel pledged to care for their employees and give them incentives for working hard. They built clean, safe factories, installed cafeterias, hired trained dietitians, formed baseball teams and glee clubs. Several hundred firms encouraged perhaps a million workers to buy company stock. And they had more enroll in company unions. Called "Kiss-Me Clubs" for their lack of power, they nonetheless offered what few independent unions could match: health and safety insurance; a grievance procedure; and representation for African Americans, women, and immigrants.

But welfare capitalism embraced barely 5 percent of the workforce and often gave benefits only to skilled laborers, the hardest to replace. Most companies cared more for production than for contented employees. In the 1920s a family of four could live in "minimum health and decency" on $2000 a year. The average industrial wage was $1304. Thus working-class families often needed more than one wage earner just to get by. Over a million children, ages 10 to 15, still worked full-time in 1920. Some received as little as 20 cents an hour.

In 1927, in the most famous strike of the decade, 2500 mill hands in the textile town of Gastonia, North Carolina, left their jobs. Even strikebreakers walked out. Eventually, authorities broke the strike, presaging a national trend. A year later there were only 629 strikes, a record low for the nation. Union membership sank from almost 5 million in 1921 to less than 3.5 million in 1929. "The AF of L [American Federation of Labor] machinery has practically collapsed," reported one union official.

The Consumer Culture

During the late nineteenth century the economy had boomed too, but much of its growth went into nonconsumer goods: huge steel factories and rail, telephone, and electric networks. By World War I, these industrial networks had penetrated enough of the country to create mass markets. As a greater percentage of the nation's industries turned out consumer goods, prosperity hinged increasingly on consumption. If consumers purchased more goods, production would increase, at the same time bringing down costs. The lower production costs would allow for lower prices, which would lift sales still higher, increase employment, and repeat the cycle again.

Everything in this cycle of prosperity depended on consumer purchases. In the consumer economy, wives ceased to be homemakers who canned fruit and baked their own bread to become buyers of processed food and manufactured goods. Husbands were not merely workers but, equally important, consumers of mortgages and other forms of credit. Even vacationers became consumers— in this case, consumers of leisure time, as more employees got two-week (unpaid) vacations. Consumption was the key to prosperity, and increased consumption rested on two innovations: advertising to encourage people to buy and credit to help them pay.

Before World War I advertising had been a grubby business, hawking the often exaggerated virtues of products. Around the turn of the century, advertis-

Role of advertising

ers began a critical shift from emphasizing *products* to stressing a consumer's *desires:* health, popularity, social prestige. During the war, the Committee on Public Information demonstrated the power of emotional appeals as an instrument of mass persuasion. Behavioral psychologists like John B. Watson, who left Johns Hopkins University for an advertising agency in the 1920s, helped to develop more sophisticated techniques for attracting customers.

Albert Lasker, the owner of Chicago's largest advertising firm, Lord and Thomas, created modern advertising in America. His eye-catching ads were hard-hitting, positive, and often preposterous. To expand the sales of Lucky Strike cigarettes Lord and Thomas advertisements claimed that smoking made

A Mexican Laborer Sings of the Sorrows of the New Era

Desde Morelia vine enganchado	I came under contract from Morelia
ganar los dólars fué mi ilusión	To earn dollars was my dream,
compré zapatos, compré sombrero,	I bought shoes and I bought a hat
y hasta me puse de pantalón.	And even put on trousers.
Pues me decían que aquí los dólars	For they told me that here the dollars
se pepenaban y de a montón	Were scattered about in heaps;
que las muchachas y que los teatros	That there were girls and theaters
y que aquí todo era vacilón.	And that here everything was good fun.
Y ahora me encuentro ya sin resuello	And now I'm overwhelmed—
soy zapatero de profesión	I am a shoemaker by trade
pero aquí dicen que soy camello	But here they say I'm a camel
y a pura pala y puro azadón.	And good only for pick and shovel.
De qué me sirve saber mi oficio	What good is it to know my trade
si fabricantes hay de a montón	If there are manufacturers by the score,
y en tanto que hago yo dos botines	And while I make two little shoes
ellos avientan más de un millón	They turn out more than a million.
Hablar no quieren muchos paisanos	Many Mexicans don't care to speak
lo que su mamá les enseñó	The language their mothers taught them
y andan diciendo que son hispanos	And go about saying they are Spanish
y renegando del pabellón	And denying their country's flag.

people slimmer and more courageous. "Lucky's" became one of the most popular brands in America. Bogus doctors and dentists endorsed all kinds of products, including toothpaste containing potassium chloride—eight grams of which was lethal. "Halitosis" was plucked from the pages of an obscure medical dictionary and used to sell Listerine mouthwash.

Advertisers encouraged Americans to borrow against tomorrow to purchase what advertising convinced them they wanted today. Installment buying had once been confined to sewing machines and pianos. In the 1920s

Installment buying as credit

it grew into the tenth-biggest business in the United States. In 1919 automaker Alfred Sloan created millions of new customers by establishing the General Motors Acceptance Corporation, the nation's first consumer credit organization. By 1929 Americans were buying most of their

Los hay mas prietos que el chapote	Some are darker than *chapote*
pero presumen de ser sajón	But they pretend to be Saxon;
andan polveados hasta el cogote	They go about powdered to the back of
y usan enaguas por pantalón	the neck
	And wear skirts for trousers.
Van las muchachas casi encueradas	The girls go about almost naked
y a la tienda llaman estor	And call *la tienda* "estor" ["store"]
llevan las piernas rete chorreadas	They go around with dirt-streaked legs
pero con medias de esas chifón.	But with those stockings of chiffon.
Hasta me vieja me la han cambiado	Even my old woman has changed on
viste de seda rete rabón	me—
anda pintada como piñata	She wears a bob-tailed dress of silk,
y va en las noches al dancing jol.	Goes about painted like a *piñata*
	And goes at night to the dancing hall.
Mis chilpallates hablan puro "inglis"	My kids speak perfect English
ya no les cuadra nuestro español	And have no use for our Spanish
me llaman fader y no trabajan	They call me "fader" and don't work
y son regüenos pa'l chárleston.	And are crazy about the Charleston.
Ya estoy cansado de esta tonteada	I am tired of all this nonsense
yo me devuëlvo para Michoacán	I'm going back to Michoacán;
hay de recuerdo dejo a la vieja	As a parting memory I leave the old
a ver si alguno se la quiere armar.	woman
	To see if someone else wants to burden
	himself.

Paul S. Taylor, *Mexican Labor in the United States*, Vol. II (Berkeley: University of California Press, 1932), pp. vi–vii.

cars, radios, and furniture on the installment plan. Consumer debt had jumped 250 percent to $7 billion, almost twice the federal budget.

A MASS SOCIETY

In the evening after a day's work in the fields—perhaps in front of an adobe house built by one of the western sugar-beet companies—Mexican American workers might gather to chat or sing a *corrido* or two. The *corrido*, or ballad, was an old Mexican folk tradition. But the subjects changed over time, to match the concerns of those who sang them. One *corrido* during the 1920s told of a field laborer distressed that his family had rejected Mexican customs in favor of new

American fashions (see "Eyewitness to History"). His wife, he sang, now dressed in "a bob-tailed dress of silk" and, wearing makeup, went about "painted like a *piñata*." As for his children, they spoke English, not Spanish, and loved all the new dances. It was enough to make him long for Mexico.

For Americans from all backgrounds, the New Era was witness to "a vast dissolution of ancient habits," commented columnist Walter Lippmann. Mass marketing and mass distribution led not simply to a higher standard of living but to a life less regional and diverse. In place of moral standards set by local communities and churches came "modern" fashions and attitudes, spread by the new mass media of movies, radio, and magazines. In the place of "ancient habits" came the forces of mass society: independent women, freer love, standardized culture, urban energy and impersonality, and growing alienation.

The New Woman

The "New Woman," charged critics, was at the bottom of what Frederick Lewis Allen called the "revolution in manners and morals" of the twenties. The most flamboyant of them wore makeup, close-fitting felt hats, long-waisted dresses, strings of beads, and unbuckled galoshes. They called themselves "flappers." Cocktail in hand, cigarette in mouth, footloose and economically free, the New Woman became a symbol of liberation to some. To others she represented the decline of civilization.

World War I had served as a powerful social catalyst. Before the war women could be arrested for smoking cigarettes openly, using profanity, appearing on public beaches without stockings, and driving automobiles without men beside them. Wartime America ended many of these restrictions. With women bagging explosives, running locomotives, and drilling with rifles, the old taboos often seemed silly.

Disseminating birth control information by mail had also been a crime before the war. By the armistice there was a birth control clinic in Brooklyn, a
Margaret Sanger
National Birth Control League, and later an American Birth Control League led by Margaret Sanger. Sanger's crusade had begun as an attempt to save poor women from the burdens of unwanted pregnancies (page 602). By the 1920s her message had found a receptive middle-class audience. Surveys showed that by the 1930s nearly 90 percent of college-educated couples practiced contraception.

Being able to a degree to control the matter of pregnancy, women felt less guilt about enjoying sex. In 1909 Sigmund Freud had come to America to lec-
Freudian psychology
ture on his theories of coping with the unconscious and overcoming harmful repressions. Some of Freud's ideas, specifically his emphasis on childhood sexuality, shocked Americans, while most of his complex theories sailed over their heads. As popularized in the 1920s, Freudian psychology stamped sexuality as a key to health.

"Street selling was torture for me," Margaret Sanger recalled of her efforts to promote the *Birth Control Review*. A heckler once shouted: "Have you ever heard God's word to be fruitful and multiply?" The reply came back, "They've done that already."

Such changes in the social climate were real enough, but the life of a flapper girl hardly mirrored the lives and work routines of most American women.

Women and labor

Over the decade, the female labor force grew by only 1 percent. As late as 1930 nearly 60 percent of all working women were African American or foreign-born and generally held low-paying jobs in domestic service or the garment industry. At home, women found that even new, "labor-saving" appliances could increase their burdens by raising standards of household cleanliness.

The New Era did spawn new careers for women. The consumer culture capitalized on a preoccupation with appearance and led to the opening of some 40,000 beauty parlors staffed by hairdressers, manicurists, and cosmeticians. "Women's fields" carved out by progressive reformers expanded opportunities in education, libraries, and social welfare. Women earned a higher percentage of doctoral degrees (from 10 percent in 1910 to 15.4 percent in 1930) and held more college teaching posts than ever (32 percent). But in most areas, professional men resisted the "feminization" of the workforce. The number of female doctors dropped by half. Medical schools imposed restrictive quotas, and 90 percent of all hospitals rejected female interns.

In 1924 two women—Nellie Ross in Wyoming and Miriam ("Ma") Ferguson in Texas—were elected governors, the first female chief executives. For the most part, though, women continued to be marginalized in party politics while remaining widely involved in educational and welfare programs. Operating outside male-dominated political parties, women activists succeeded in winning passage of the Sheppard–Towner Federal Maternity and Infancy Act in 1921 to fight high rates of infant mortality with rural prenatal and baby care centers. It was the first federal welfare statute. Yet by the end of the decade the Sheppard–Towner Act had lapsed.

In the wake of their greatest success, the hard-won vote for women, feminists splintered. The National Woman Suffrage Association disbanded in 1920.

Equal Rights Amendment In its place the League of Women Voters was begun to encourage informed voting. For the more militant Alice Paul and her allies, that was not enough. Their National Woman's party pressed for a constitutional Equal Rights Amendment (ERA). Social workers and others familiar with the conditions under which women labored opposed it. Death and injury rates for women were nearly double those for men. To them the ERA meant losing the protection as well as the benefits women derived from mothers' pensions and maternity insurance. Joined by most men and a majority of Congress they fought the amendment to a standstill.

Mass Media

In balmy California, where movies could be made year-round, Hollywood helped give the New Woman notoriety as a temptress and trendsetter. When sexy Theda Bara (the "vamp") appeared in *The Blue Flame* in 1920, crowds mobbed theaters. And just as Hollywood dictated standards of physical attractiveness, it became the judge of taste and fashion in countless other ways because motion pictures were a virtually universal medium. There was no need for literacy or fluency, no need even for sound, given the power of the pictures parading across the screen.

Motion pictures, invented in 1889, had first been shown in tiny neighborhood theaters called "nickelodeons." For only a nickel, patrons watched a silent

Motion pictures screen flicker with moving images as an accompanist played music on a tinny piano. The audience was anything but silent. The theater reverberated with the cracking of Indian nuts, the day's equivalent of popcorn, while young cowboys shot off their Kilgore repeating cap pistols during dramatic scenes. Often children read the subtitles aloud to their immigrant parents, translating into Italian, Yiddish, or German.

After the first feature-length film, *The Great Train Robbery* (1903), productions became rich in spectacle, attracted middle-class audiences, and turned into America's favorite form of entertainment. By 1926 more than 20,000 movie houses offered customers lavish theaters with overstuffed seats, live music, and a celluloid dream world—all for 50 cents or less. At the end of the decade, they were drawing over 100 million people a week, roughly the equivalent of the national population.

In the spring of 1920 Frank Conrad of the Westinghouse Company in East Pittsburgh rigged up a research station in his barn and started transmitting phonograph music and baseball scores to local wireless opera-

Radio

tors. An ingenious Pittsburgh newspaper began advertising radio equipment to "be used by those who listen to Dr. Conrad's programs." Six months later Westinghouse officials opened the first licensed broadcasting station in history, KDKA, to stimulate sales of their supplies. By 1923 the number of licensed radio stations had jumped to 556. Nearly one home in three had a radio ("furniture that talks," comedian Fred Allen called it) by 1930.

At first radio was seen as a civilizing force. "The air is your theater, your college, your newspaper, your library," exalted one ad in 1924. But with the growing number of sets came commercial broadcasting, catering to more common tastes. Almost the entire nation listened to "Amos 'n' Andy," a comedy about African Americans created by two white vaudevillians in 1929. At night families gathered around the radio instead of the hearth, listening to a concert, perhaps, rather than going out to hear music. Ticket sales at vaudeville theaters collapsed. The aged, the sick, and the isolated, moreover, could be "at home but never alone," as one radio ad declared. Linked by nothing but airwaves, Americans were finding themselves part of a vast new community of listeners.

Print journalism also broadened its audience during the 1920s. In 1923 Yale classmates Henry R. Luce and Briton Hadden rewrote news stories in a snappy style, mixed them with photographs, and created the country's

Mass circulation weeklies

first national weekly, *Time* magazine. Fifty-five giant newspaper chains distributed 230 newspapers with a combined circulation of 13 million by 1927. Though they controlled less than 10 percent of all papers, the chains pioneered modern mass news techniques. Editors relied on central offices and syndicates to prepare editorials, sports, gossip, and Sunday features for a national readership.

A Youth Culture

By the 1920s, the drive for public education had placed a majority of teenagers in high school for the first time in American history. College enrollment reached 10 percent of the eligible population by 1928; in 1890 it had been less than 3 percent. A "peer culture" of adolescents emerged as children and teens spent more time outside the family among people their own age. Revolving around school and friends, its components were remarkably modern—athletics, clubs, sororities and fraternities, dating, proms, "bull sessions," and moviegoing.

Tolerance for premarital sex seems to have grown in the 1920s ("necking" and "petting" parties replaced sedate tea parties), but the new subculture of youth still tied sexual relations to love. Casual sex remained rare; what changed was the point at which sexual intimacy occurred. A growing minority of young women reported having premarital intercourse, for example, but only with their future husbands. Unsupervised dating and "going together" replaced chaperoned courting.

For all the frivolity and rebelliousness it promoted, the new youth culture tended to fuse the young to the larger social culture by promoting widely held values: competitiveness, merit through association, service, prestige. Even notorious young flappers, if they wed, found themselves defined by home and family.

"Ain't We Got Fun?"

"Ev'ry morning, ev'ry evening, ain't we got fun?" ran the 1921 hit song. As the average hours on the job each week decreased from 47.2 in 1920 to 42 by 1930,

Spectator sports spending on amusement and recreation shot up 300 percent. Spectator sports came of age. In 1921, some 60,000 fans paid $1.8 million to see Jack Dempsey, the "Manassas Mauler," knock out French champion Georges Carpentier. Millions more listened as radio took them ringside for the first time in sports history. Universities constructed huge stadiums for football, such as Ohio State's 64,000 seater. By the end of the decade college football games were outdrawing major league baseball.

Baseball still remained the national pastime but became a bigger business. An ugly World Series scandal in 1919 led owners to appoint Judge Kenesaw Mountain Landis "czar" of the sport early in the decade. His strict rule reformed the game. In 1920 the son of immigrants revolutionized it. George Herman "Babe" Ruth hit 54 home runs and made the New York Yankees the first club to attract a million fans in one season. A heroic producer in an era of consumption, Ruth was also baseball's bad boy. He smoked, drank, cursed, and chased every skirt in sight. Under the guidance of the first modern sports agent, Christy Walsh, Ruth became the highest-paid player in the game and made a fortune endorsing everything from automobiles to clothing.

At parties old diversions—charades, card tricks, recitations—faded in popularity as dancing took over. The ungainly camel walk, the sultry tango, and in 1924 the frantic Charleston were the urban standards. Country barns featured a revival of square dancing with music provided by Detroit's WBZ, courtesy of Henry Ford. And from the turn-of-the-century brothels and gaming houses of New Orleans, Memphis, and St. Louis came a rhythmic, compelling music that swept into nightclubs and over the airwaves: jazz.

Jazz was a remarkably complex blend of several older African American musical traditions, combining the soulfulness of the blues with the brighter synco-

Jazz pated rhythms of ragtime music. The distinctive style of jazz bands came from a marvelous improvising as the musicians embellished melodies and played off one another. The style spread when the "Original Dixieland Jazz Band" (hardly original but possessed of the commercial advantage of being white) recorded a few numbers for the phonograph. The music became a sensation in New York in 1917 and spread across the country. Black New Orleans stalwarts like Joe "King" Oliver's Creole Jazz Band began touring, and in 1924 Paul Whiteman inaugurated respectable "white" jazz in a concert at Carnegie Hall. When self-appointed guardians of good taste denounced such music as "intellectual and spiritual debauchery," Whiteman disagreed: "Jazz is the folk music of the machine age."

The Art of Alienation

Before World War I a generation of young writers had begun rebelling against Victorian purity. The savagery of the war drove many of them even further from any faith in reason or progress. Instead they embraced a "nihilism" that denied all meaning in life. When the war ended, they turned their resentment against American life, especially its small towns, big businesses, conformity, technology, and materialism. Some led unconventional lives in New York City's Greenwich

Expatriates Village. Others, called expatriates, left the country altogether for the artistic freedom of London and Paris. Their alienation helped produce a literary outpouring unmatched in American history.

On the eve of World War I the poet Ezra Pound had predicted an "American Risorgimento" that would "make the Italian Renaissance look like a tempest in a teapot." From Europe the expatriate Pound began to make it happen. Abandoning rhyme and meter in his poetry, he decried the "botched civilization" that had produced the war. Another voluntary exile, T. S. Eliot, bemoaned the emptiness of modern life in his epic poem *The Waste Land* (1922). Ernest Hemingway captured the disillusionment of the age in *The Sun Also Rises* (1926) and *A Farewell to Arms* (1929), novels in which resolution came as it had in war—by death.

At home Minnesota-born Sinclair Lewis, the first American to win a Nobel prize in literature, sketched a scathing vision of midwestern small-town life in *Main Street* (1920). The book described "savorless people . . . saying mechanical things about the excellence of Ford automobiles, and viewing themselves as the greatest race in the world." His next novel, *Babbitt* (1922), dissected small-town businessman George Follansbee Babbitt, a peppy realtor from the fictional city of Zenith. Faintly absurd and supremely dull, Babbitt was the epitome of the average.

The novels of another Minnesotan, F. Scott Fitzgerald, glorified youth and romantic individualism but found redemption nowhere. Fitzgerald's heroes, like Amory Blaine in *This Side of Paradise* (1920), spoke for a generation "grown up to find all Gods dead, all wars fought, all faiths in man shaken." Like most writers of the decade, Fitzgerald saw life largely as a personal affair—opulent, self-absorbing, and ultimately tragic.

A "New Negro"

As World War I seared white intellectuals, so too did it galvanize black Americans. Wartime labor shortages had spurred a migration of half a million African Americans out of the rural South into northern industrial cities. But postwar unemployment and racial violence quickly dashed black hopes for equality. Common folk in these urban enclaves found an outlet for their alienation in a charismatic nationalist from Jamaica named Marcus Garvey.

Garvey brought his organization, the Universal Negro Improvement Association (UNIA), to America in 1916 in hopes of restoring black pride by

Marcus Garvey returning Africans to Africa and Africa to Africans. "Up you mighty race," he told his followers, "you can accomplish what you will." When Garvey spoke at the first national UNIA convention in 1920, over 25,000 supporters jammed Madison Square Garden in New York to listen. Even his harshest critics admitted there were at least half a million members in more than 30 branches of his organization. It was the first mass movement of African Americans in history. But in 1925 Garvey was convicted of mail fraud for having oversold stock in his Black Star Line, the steamship company founded to return African Americans to Africa. His dream shattered.

As Garvey rose to prominence, a renaissance of black literature, painting, and sculpture was brewing in Harlem. The first inklings came in 1922 when

Harlem Renaissance Claude McKay, another Jamaican immigrant, published a book of poems entitled *White Shadows*. In his most famous poem, "If We Must Die," McKay mixed defiance and dignity: "Like men we'll face the murderous, cowardly pack/Pressed to the wall, dying but fighting back!"

Often supported by white patrons, or "angels," young black writers and artists found their subjects in the street life of cities, the folkways of the rural South, and the primitivism of preindustrial cultures. Poet Langston Hughes reminded his readers of the ancient heritage of African Americans in "The Negro Speaks of Rivers," while Zora Neale Hurston collected folktales, songs,

Born in Jamaica in 1887, Marcus Garvey founded his "Back to Africa" movement in 1914 and brought it to the United States in 1916. In 1925 he went to prison for mail fraud, before being deported two years later.

and prayers of black southerners. Though generally not a racial protest, the Harlem Renaissance drew on the growing assertiveness of African Americans as well as on the alienation of white intellectuals. In 1925 Alain Locke, a black professor from Howard University, collected a sampling of their works in *The New Negro*. The title reflected not only an artistic movement but also a new racial consciousness.

DEFENDERS OF THE FAITH

As mass society pushed the country into a future of machines, organization, middle-class living, and cosmopolitan diversity, not everyone approved. Dr. and Mrs. Wilbur Crafts, the authors of *Intoxicating Drinks and Drugs in All Lands and Times*, set forth a litany of modern sins that tempted young people in this "age of cities." "Foul pictures, corrupt literature, leprous shows, gambling slot machines, saloons, and Sabbath breaking. . . . *We are trying to raise saints in hell.*"

The changing values of the New Era seemed especially threatening to traditionalists like the Crafts. Their deeply held beliefs reflected the rural roots of so many Americans: an ethic that valued neighborliness, small communities, and a homogeneity of race, religion, and ethnicity. Opponents of the new ways could be found among not only country folk but also rural migrants to cities as well as an embattled Protestant elite. All were determined to defend the older faiths against the modern age.

Nativism and Immigration Restriction

In 1921, two Italian aliens and admitted anarchists presented a dramatic challenge to those older faiths. Nicola Sacco and Bartolomeo Vanzetti were sentenced to death for a shoe company robbery and murder in South

Sacco and Vanzetti

Braintree, Massachusetts. Critics charged that they were innocent and convicted only of being foreign-born radicals. During the trial, the presiding judge had scorned them in private as "anarchist bastards," and in 1927, they were executed. For protesters around the world, the execution was a symbol of American bigotry and prejudice.

By then, nativism—a rabid hostility to foreigners—had produced the most restrictive immigration laws in American history. In the aftermath of World War I immigration was running close to 1 million a year, almost as high as prewar levels. Most immigrants came from eastern and southern Europe and from Mexico; most were Catholics and Jews. Alarmed white native-born Protestants warned that if the flood continued, Americans might become "a hybrid race of people as worthless and futile as the good-for-nothing mongrels of Central America and Southeastern Europe." Appreciating the benefits of a shrunken labor pool, the American Federation of Labor supported restriction too.

In the Southwest, Mexicans and Mexican Americans became a target of concern. The Spanish had inhabited the region for nearly 400 years, producing

Mexican Americans

a rich blend of European and Indian cultures. By 1900 about 300,000 Mexican Americans lived in the United States. In the following decade Mexicans fleeing poverty and a revolution in 1910 almost doubled the Latino population of Texas and New Mexico. In California it quadrupled. During World War I, labor shortages led authorities to relax immigration laws, and in the 1920s American farmers opened a campaign to attract Mexican farmworkers.

Thousands of single young men, known as *solos*, also crossed the border to catch trains for Detroit, Kansas City, and other industrial cities. By the end of the 1920s, northern industrial cities had thriving communities of Mexicans. In these *barrios* Spanish-speaking newcomers settled into an immigrant life of family and festivals, churchgoing, hard work, and slow adaptation. Like other immigrants, many returned home, but others brought their families. The census of 1930 listed nearly 1.5 million Mexicans living in the United States, not including an untold number who had entered the country illegally.

In 1921 Senators Henry Cabot Lodge of Massachusetts and Hiram Johnson of California sponsored legislation that cut off the flood of immigrants at

National Origins acts

350,000 a year. A quota parceled out available spaces by admitting up to 3 percent of each nationality living in the United States as of 1910. Asian immigration was virtually banned. In 1924 a new National Origins Act reduced the quota to 150,000 and pushed the base year back to 1890, before the bulk of southern and eastern Europeans arrived.

The National Origins Act fixed the pattern of immigration for the next four decades. Immigration from southern and eastern Europe was reduced to a trickle. The free flow of Europeans to America, a migration of classes and nationalities that had been unimpeded for 300 years, came to an end.

The "Noble Experiment"

Nativists who distrusted immigrants usually viewed alcohol as a particular problem of the immigrant lower classes. Progressive prohibitionists stressed the need for efficiency and public health, which they contrasted with the corrupting influence of the immigrant saloon culture. German brewers and their beer gardens came under special suspicion during World War I.

For nearly a hundred years reformers had tried—with sporadic success—to reduce the consumption of alcohol. Their most ambitious campaign climaxed

Eighteenth Amendment

in January 1920, when the Eighteenth Amendment to the Constitution went into effect. It outlawed the sale of liquor. Prohibition was not total: private citizens could still drink. They simply could not make, sell, transport, or import any "intoxicating beverage" containing 0.5 percent alcohol or more. By some estimates, consumption was reduced by as much as half.

From the start, however, enforcement was underfunded and understaffed. In large cities "speakeasies"—taverns operating undercover—were plentiful. Rural stills continued to turn out "moonshine." Even so, the consequences of so vast a social experiment were significant and often unexpected. Prohibition reversed the prewar trend toward beer and wine, since hard liquor brought greater profits to bootleggers. It also advanced women's rights. While saloons had discriminated against "ladies," having them enter by a separate door, speakeasies welcomed them. Prohibition helped to line the pockets—and boost the fame—of gangsters, including "Scarface" Al Capone. Like Capone, thousands of poor immigrants looked to illegal bootlegging to move them out of the slums. As rival gangs fought over territory, cities erupted in a mayhem of violence.

Consequences of Prohibition

Prohibition can be best understood as cultural and class legislation. Support had run deepest in Protestant churches, especially the evangelical Baptists and Methodists. And there had always been a strong antiurban and anti-immigrant bias among reformers. As it turned out, the steepest decline in drinking occurred among working-class ethnics. Only the well-to-do had enough money to drink regularly without risking death or blindness, the common effects of cheap, tainted liquor. Traditionalists might celebrate the triumph of the "noble experiment," but modern urbanites either ignored or resented it.

KKK

On Thanksgiving Day 1915, just outside Atlanta, 16 men trudged up a rocky trail to the crest of Stone Mountain. There, as night fell, they set ablaze a huge wooden cross and swore allegiance to the Invisible Empire, Knights of the Ku Klux Klan. The KKK was reborn.

The modern Klan, a throwback to the hooded order of Reconstruction days (page 461), reflected the insecurities of the New Era. Klansmen worried about the changes and conflicts in American society, which they attributed to the rising tide of immigrants, "uppity women," and African Americans who refused to "recognize their place." Whereas any white man could join the old Klan, the new one admitted only "native born, white, gentile [Protestant] Americans." And the reborn Klan was not confined to the South, like the hooded night riders of old. By the 1920s its capital had become Indianapolis, Indiana. More than half of its leadership and over a third of its members came from cities of more than 100,000 people.

The new Klan drew on the culture of small-town America. It was patriotic, gave to local charities, and boasted the kind of outfits and rituals adopted by many fraternal lodges. Klansmen wore white hooded sheets and satin robes, sang songs called "klodes," and even used a secret hand-"klasp." A typical gathering brought the whole family to a barbecue with fireworks and hymn singing, the evening capped by the burning of a giant cross.

Members came mostly from the middle and working classes: small businesspeople, clerical workers, independent professionals, farmers, and laborers

Social composition of the Klan

with few skills. Sometimes they lived on the edge of unemployment and poverty. The Klan offered them status, security, and the promise of restoring an older America. It touted white supremacy, chastity, fidelity, and parental authority and fought for laissez-faire capitalism and fundamental Protestantism. When boycotts and whispering campaigns failed to cleanse communities of Jews, Mexicans, Japanese,

A brutal form of racial violence, lynching continued to be a national scourge well into the 1920s and 1930s, when Paul Cadmus drew this searing study entitled *To the Lynching!* In 1921, after a long campaign by the National Association for the Advancement of Colored People, an antilynching bill was introduced in Congress but fell victim to a Senate filibuster.

or others who offended their social code, the Klan resorted to floggings, kidnappings, acid mutilations, and murder.

Using modern methods of promotion, two professional fund-raisers, and an army of 1000 salesmen (called "kleagles"), the Klan enrolled perhaps 3 million dues-paying members by the early 1920s. Moving into politics, its candidates captured legislatures in Indiana, Texas, Oklahoma, and Oregon. The organization was instrumental in electing six governors, three senators, and thousands of local officials. In the end, however, the Klan was undone by sex scandals and financial corruption. In November 1925 David Stephenson, grand dragon of the Indiana Klan and the most powerful leader in the Midwest, was sentenced to life imprisonment for rape and second-degree murder. Across the country in elections for mayor, governor, or senator, Klan-backed candidates lost as conventional politicians fought back with hard-hitting campaigns for office.

Fundamentalism versus Darwinism

Although Aimee Semple McPherson embraced the fashions of the New Era, many Protestants, especially in rural areas, felt threatened by the secular aspects of modern life. Scientists and intellectuals spoke openly about the relativity of moral values and questioned the possibility of biblical miracles. Darwinism, pragmatism, and other scientific and philosophical theories left traditional religious teachings open to skepticism and scorn.

As early as the 1870s anxious conservatives had combined to combat modernist influences. Between 1909 and 1912 two wealthy Los Angeles churchgoers, Lyman and Milton Stewart, subsidized a series of booklets

The
Fundamentals

known as *The Fundamentals*. The 3 million copies sent across the country stressed the "verbal inerrancy" of scripture: every word of the Bible was literally true. Advocates of this view, who after 1920 were increasingly known as "fundamentalists," saw themselves as defenders of traditional religion. Yet their literal reading of scripture was hardly traditional, for over the centuries many Christian theologians had interpreted various passages of scripture symbolically.

Fundamentalists maintained effective ministries nationwide, but especially among Southern Baptists. Nothing disturbed them more than Darwinian theories of evolution. By definition Darwinism denied the divine origin of humankind and made the creation story of Adam and Eve at best a parable. In 1925 a part-time schoolteacher and clerk of the Round Lick Association of Primitive Baptists convinced his fellow Tennessee legislators to make it illegal to teach that "man has descended from a lower order of animals." Oklahoma, Florida, Mississippi, and Arkansas soon passed similar statutes.

Encouraged by the newly formed American Civil Liberties Union, a number of skeptics in the town of Dayton, Tennessee, decided to test the law. In the

Scopes trial

spring of 1925 a bespectacled biology teacher named John T. Scopes was arrested for teaching evolution. Behind the scenes,

Scopes's sponsors were preoccupied as much with the commercial boost a sensational trial could give their town as with the defense of academic freedom.

When the Scopes trial opened in July, millions listened over the radio to the first trial ever broadcast. Inside the courtroom Clarence Darrow, the renowned defense lawyer from Chicago and a professed agnostic, acted as co-counsel for Scopes. Opposing him was William Jennings Bryan, the three-time presidential candidate who had recently joined the antievolution crusade. It was urban Darrow against rural Bryan in what Bryan described as a "duel to the death" between Christianity and evolution.

The presiding judge ruled that scientists could not be used to defend evolution. He considered their testimony "hearsay" because they had not been present at the Creation. The defense virtually collapsed, until Darrow called Bryan to the stand as an "expert on the Bible." Under withering examination Bryan admitted, to the horror of his followers, that the Earth might not have been made "in six days of 24-hours." Even so, the Dayton jury took only eight minutes to find Scopes guilty and fine him $100.

By then the excesses of the Scopes trial had transformed it into more of a national joke than a confrontation between darkness and light. But the debate over evolution raised a larger question that continued to reverberate throughout the twentieth century. As scientific, religious, and cultural standards clashed, how much should religious beliefs influence public education in a nation where church and state were constitutionally separated?

REPUBLICANS ASCENDANT

"The change is amazing," wrote a Washington reporter after the inauguration of Warren G. Harding in March 1921. Woodrow Wilson had been ill, reclusive, and austere. Harding was handsome, warm, lovable. Wilson had kept his own counsel; Harding promised to bring the "best minds" into the cabinet to run things. Sentries disappeared from the gates of the White House, tourists again walked the halls, and reporters freely questioned the president. The reign of "normalcy," as Harding called it, had begun. "By 'normalcy,'" he explained, ". . . I mean normal procedure, the natural way, without excess."

The Politics of Normalcy

"Normalcy" turned out to be anything but normal. After eight years of Democratic rule, Republicans controlled the White House from 1921 to 1933 and both houses of Congress from 1918 to 1930. Fifteen years

Warren G. Harding

of reform gave way to eight years of cautious governing. The presidency, strengthened by Wilson, now fell into weak hands. The cabinet and the Congress set the course of the nation.

Harding and his successor, Calvin Coolidge, were content with delegating power. Harding appointed to the cabinet some men of quality: Charles Evans Hughes as secretary of state, Henry C. Wallace as secretary of agriculture, and Herbert Hoover as secretary of commerce. He also made, as one critic put it, some "unspeakably bad appointments": his old crony Harry Daugherty as attorney general and New Mexico Senator Albert Fall as interior secretary. Daugherty sold influence for cash and resigned in 1923. Only a divided jury saved him from jail. In 1929 Albert Fall became the first cabinet member to be convicted of a felony. In 1922 he had accepted bribes of more than $400,000 for secretly leasing naval oil reserves at Elk Hill, California, and Teapot Dome, Wyoming, to private oil companies.

Harding died suddenly in August 1923, before most of the scandals came to light. Though he would be remembered as lackluster, his tolerance and moderation had a calming influence on the strife-ridden nation. Slowly he had even begun to lead. In 1921 he created a Bureau of the Budget that brought modern accounting techniques to the management of federal revenues. Toward the end of his administration he cleared an early scandal from the Veterans' Bureau and set an agenda for Congress that included expanding the merchant marine.

To his credit Calvin Coolidge handled Harding's sordid legacy with skill and dispatch. He created a special investigatory commission, prosecuted wrong-

Calvin Coolidge doers, and restored the confidence of the nation. Decisiveness, when he chose to exercise it, was one of Coolidge's hallmarks. As governor of Massachusetts, he had ended the Boston police strike in 1919 with a firm declaration: "There can be no right to strike against the public safety by anybody, anywhere, anytime." He believed in small-town democracy and minimalist government. "One of the most important accomplishments of my administration has been minding my own business," he boasted. Above all Coolidge worshiped wealth. "Civilization and profits," he once said, "go hand in hand."

Coolidge had been in office barely a year when voters returned him to the White House by a margin of nearly two to one in the election in 1924. It was yet another sign that Americans had wearied of reform and delighted in surging prosperity. Whether the business-dominated policies served the economy or the nation well in the long term was open to question.

The Policies of Mellon and Hoover

Coolidge retained most of Harding's cabinet, including his powerful treasury secretary, Andrew Mellon. The former head of aluminum giant Alcoa, Mellon believed that prosperity "trickled down" from rich to poor through investment, which raised production, employment, and wages. In 1921 Mellon persuaded Congress to repeal the excess-profits tax on corporations; under Coolidge he convinced legislators to end all gift taxes, to halve estate and income taxes, and to reduce corporation and consumption taxes even further.

Business leaders applauded the Mellon tax program for reversing the progressive tax policies of the Wilson era. They, after all, paid the most in taxes and profited most from the tax cuts as well as from the protectionism of a new tariff. In 1922 the Fordney–McCumber Tariff increased rates on manufactured and farm goods.

Unlike Mellon, Commerce Secretary Herbert Hoover (also a Harding holdover) was not a traditional Republican. Dedicated to efficiency, distribution,

Associationalism cooperation, and service, Hoover advocated a progressive capitalism called "associationalism." It sought to bring order to the economy through the industrywide trade associations that had proved so helpful in organizing war production. Government provided advice, statistics, and forums. Business leaders exchanged ideas, set industry standards, and developed markets. Hoover also promoted the ideals of welfare capitalism by encouraging firms to sponsor company unions, pay employees decent wages, and protect workers from factory hazards and unemployment. Meanwhile the Commerce Department worked to expand foreign markets and fight international cartels.

Both Hoover and Mellon, each in his own way, placed government in the service of business. As a result, the role of government in the economy grew. So did its size, by more than 40,000 employees between 1921 and 1930. Building on their wartime partnership, government and business dropped all pretense of a laissez-faire economy. Efficiency increased, production soared, and prosperity reigned.

COUNTERPOINT   *Were the 1920s a Sharp Break with the Past?*

Historians have long argued over the meaning of the 1920s. Initially most took their cues from Frederick Lewis Allen's *Only Yesterday* and concluded that the decade represented a sharp, if frivolous, break from the serious past of reform and war. Later historians have seen the 1920s as more continuous with the past, more complex, and more important. Business historians have pointed to the trade association movement as an innovative attempt to achieve the old progressive goals of efficiency and equity in a modern industrial economy. Political historians have emphasized the remnant progressives who continued the fight for social justice and social welfare. Social historians have stressed the search for continuity amid dramatic change by fastening on the theme of shared anxiety over the future and nostalgia for a mythic past. In their eyes, the rise of nativism and religious fundamentalism, along with the drive toward Prohibition and creationism, represented reactions to the intrusion of secularism, science, and social pluralism on an older, more homogeneous America. Cultural historians have seen both change and continuity in the decade. Some see the intellectual revolt of the 1920s as having originated a decade earlier, while others have highlighted the emergence of a new American culture radiating outward from "mongrel Manhattan," with its hybrid mix of ethnicities, races, and sexes.

Distress Signals

Some economic groups remained outside the magic circle of Republican prosperity. Ironically, they included those people who made up the biggest business in America: farmers. In 1920 agriculture still had an investment value greater than manufacturing, all utilities, and all railroads combined. A third of the population made a living from farming.

Yet the farmers' portion of the national income shrank by almost half during the 1920s. The government withdrew wartime price supports for wheat and ended its practice of feeding refugees with American surpluses. *Decline of farm prosperity* As European farms began producing again, the demand for American exports dropped. New dietary habits meant that average Americans of 1920 ate 75 fewer pounds of food annually than they had 10 years earlier. New synthetic fibers drove down demand for natural wool and cotton.

In 1921 a group of southern and western senators organized the "farm bloc" in Congress, to coordinate relief for farmers. Over the next two years they succeeded in bringing stockyards, packers, and grain exchanges under federal supervision. Other legislation exempted farm cooperatives from antitrust actions and created a dozen banks for low-interest farm loans. But regulation and credit were not enough. Over the decade, farmers' purchasing power continued to slide.

For the four years that Coolidge ran a "businessman's government," workers reaped few gains in wages, purchasing power, and bargaining rights. Although welfare capitalism promised benefits, only a handful of companies put it into practice. And those that did often used it to weaken independent unions. As dangerous imbalances in the economy developed, Coolidge ignored them.

If most Americans disregarded the distress signals at home, they paid almost no heed to economic unrest abroad. At the end of World War I, Europe's victors had forced Germany to take on $33 billion in war costs or *Economic unrest abroad* reparations, partly to repay their own war debts to the United States. When Germany defaulted in 1923, French forces occupied the Ruhr valley in Germany's industrial heartland. Germany struck back by printing more money, a move that dramatized the crushing burden of its debt. Runaway inflation wiped out the savings of the German middle class, shook confidence in the new Weimar Republic, and soon threatened the economic structure of all Europe.

In 1924 American business leader Charles G. Dawes persuaded the victorious Europeans to scale down reparations. In return the United States promised to help stabilize the German economy. Encouraged by the State *The Dawes plan* Department, American bankers made large loans to Germany, with which the Germans paid their reparations. The European victors then used those funds to repay *their* war debts to the United States. It amounted to taking money out of one American vault and depositing it in another. In 1926 the United States also reduced European war debts. Canceling them altogether would have made more sense, but few Americans were that forgiving.

Despite Europe's debt problems, an arms race continued among the great powers. The United States vied with Britain, France with Italy, and Japan with nearly everyone for naval supremacy. Within the United States two factions sought to end military escalation, but for different reasons. Pacifists and peace activists blamed the arms race between Germany and England for having brought the world to war in 1914. They believed disarmament would secure a permanent peace. Saber-rattling Republicans had few qualms about military rivalry but worried about the high cost of maintaining navies in the Pacific as well as the Atlantic Ocean.

Two grand diplomatic gestures reflected the twin desires for peace and economy. In 1921, following the lead of the United States, the world's sea powers agreed to freeze battleship construction for 10 years and set ratios on the tonnage of each navy. The Five-Power Agreement was the first disarmament treaty in modern history. A more extravagant gesture came seven years later, in

Kellogg–Briand Pact

1928, when the major nations of the world (except the Soviet Union) signed an agreement outlawing war, the Kellogg–Briand Pact. "Peace is proclaimed," announced Secretary of State Frank Kellogg as he signed the document with a foot-long pen of gold.

But what seemed so bold on paper proved to be ineffective in practice. The French resented the lower limits set on their battleships under the Five-Power Agreement and began building smaller warships such as submarines, cruisers, and destroyers. The arms race now concentrated on these vessels. And the Kellogg–Briand Pact remained a hollow proclamation, with no means of enforcement.

The Election of 1928

On August 2, 1927, in a small classroom in Rapid City, South Dakota, Calvin Coolidge handed a terse typewritten message to reporters: "I do not choose to run for President in nineteen twenty-eight." Republicans honored the request and nominated Herbert Hoover. Hoover was not a politician but an administrator and had never once campaigned for public office. It didn't matter. Republican prosperity made it difficult for any Democrat to win. Hoover, perhaps the most admired public official in America, made it impossible.

The Democratic party continued to be polarized between its rural supporters in the South and West and urban laborers in the Northeast. The two factions had clashed during the 1924 convention, scuttling the presidential candidacy of New York governor Al Smith. By 1928 the shift in population toward cities had given an edge to the party's urban wing. Al Smith won the nomination on the first ballot, even though his handicaps were evident. For one, he sounded like a city slicker. When the New York City–bred Smith spoke "poisonally" on the "rha-dio," voters across America winced. Though he pledged to enforce Prohibition, he campaigned against it and even took an occasional drink

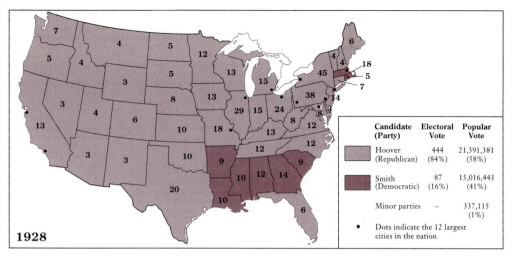

Candidate (Party)	Electoral Vote	Popular Vote
Hoover (Republican)	444 (84%)	21,391,381 (58%)
Smith (Democratic)	87 (16%)	15,016,443 (41%)
Minor parties	–	337,115 (1%)
•	Dots indicate the 12 largest cities in the nation	

1928

THE ELECTION OF 1928   In the pivotal election of 1928, Republican Herbert Hoover cracked the solidly Democratic South, which would return to the Democrats in 1932. Democrat Al Smith won the 12 largest cities in the country, all of which had voted Republican in 1924 but would stay with the Democrats in 1932.

(which produced the false rumor that Smith was a hopeless alcoholic). Most damaging of all, he was Catholic, at a time when anti-Catholicism remained strong in many areas of the country.

In the election of 1928, nearly 60 percent of the eligible voters turned out to give all but eight states to Hoover. The solidly Democratic South cracked for the first time. Still, the stirrings of a major political realignment were buried in the returns. The 12 largest cities in the country had gone to the Republicans in 1924; in 1928 the Democrats won them. The Democrats were becoming the party of the cities and of immigrants, a core around which they would build the most powerful vote-getting coalition of the twentieth century.

Early on a May morning in 1927, a silver monoplane streaked into the skies above Long Island and headed east. At the controls sat the young pilot Charles Lindbergh. Thirty-three hours and thirty minutes later, he landed just outside of Paris. An ecstatic mob swamped him and nearly tore his plane to pieces in search of souvenirs. Eight other flyers had died trying to cross the ocean. Lindbergh alone succeeded.

Lindbergh, dubbed the "Lone Eagle," and his plane, the *Spirit of St. Louis*, returned home aboard the warship *Memphis*. As he sailed up the Potomac, he received an honor previously reserved only for heads of state, a 21-gun salute. Lindbergh, wrote one reporter, "fired the imagination of mankind." Never had one person mastered a machine so completely or conquered nature so heroically. To Americans ambivalent about mass production, mass consumption, and mass society, here was a sign. Perhaps they could control the New Era without losing their cherished individualism. For a brief moment it seemed possible.

SIGNIFICANT EVENTS

1903	First feature-length film, *The Great Train Robbery*, released
1909	Sigmund Freud comes to America
1914	Henry Ford introduces moving assembly line
1915	Modern Ku Klux Klan founded
1916	Marcus Garvey brings Universal Negro Improvement Association to America
1920	First commercial radio broadcast; Eighteenth Amendment outlaws alcohol use; Nineteenth Amendment grants women right to vote; Warren Harding elected president
1921	Congress enacts quotas on immigration; Sheppard–Towner Federal Maternity and Infancy Act; American Birth Control League organized
1921–1922	Washington Naval Disarmament Conference
1922	Fordney–McCumber Tariff raises rates; Sinclair Lewis's *Babbitt* published; T. S. Eliot's *The Waste Land* published
1923	*Time* magazine founded; Harding dies; Calvin Coolidge becomes president; Harding scandals break
1924	Dawes plan to stabilize German inflation; Coolidge elected president
1925	John T. Scopes convicted of teaching evolution in Tennessee; Alain Locke's *The New Negro* published
1927	Charles Lindbergh's solo flight across the Atlantic; Sacco and Vanzetti executed
1928	Herbert Hoover elected president; Kellogg–Briand Pact signed

CHAPTER TWENTY-FIVE

Crash and Depression

igh above Columbus Circle in New York City a gigantic electric sign blinked out the happy decree: "You should have $10,000 at the age of 30; $25,000 at the age of 40; $50,000 at the age of 50." In the pages of the *Ladies Home Journal* John J. Raskob, who had run the Finance Committee at General Motors and listed his profession as "capitalist," told people how. "Everyone ought to be rich," he declared: $15 a month, "wisely invested," would be worth $80,000 in 20 years. In the 1920s, when 40 percent of American families earned less than $1500 a year, that was rich.

Possibilities for profit seemed to be everywhere, including far-off Florida. Land fever hit southern Florida in the mid-1920s. Before World War I Miami

Florida land boom

sat on mangrove jungle and bug-infested swamp. Attracted by 80-degree temperatures in winter, developers cleared the jungle, drained the swamp, put up a sea wall, and built a three-mile causeway from the beach to the mainland. Miami became the fastest-growing city in America as land speculators poured in. So many people arrived in the summer that famine threatened the state, and ice could be obtained only by doctor's prescription.

One mid-September night in 1926, Miami barometers dropped to 27.75— the lowest reading North America had ever recorded. Wind howled through the city at 130 miles per hour. Twenty-foot waves pounded sea walls and washed away beaches. Flooded swamps reclaimed landfills. Speculators discovered an awful truth: south Florida lay in the middle of the hurricane belt. In one night 100 Miamians drowned; 40,000 lost their homes. Reality punctured the vast speculative bubble. The value of oceanfront lots dropped by two-thirds. Hundreds went bankrupt; thousands lost their land to foreclosures.

The Florida land boom of the 1920s laid the foundation for later development, but stock market scams and speculation did nothing except turn the financial center of the nation into a gambling den. Phony stock deals (oil wells and mines were the most popular) netted swindlers more than $600 million a year. Some stock maneuvering was legal but deceptive. Favored "insiders"

In the 1930s Dorothea Lange pioneered a new realism in photography—grim, unvarnished, and poignant. Nowhere did she better capture the shattering effects of the Great Depression than in this picture of a heavily mortgaged Georgia cotton farmer overcome by despair.

(including President Calvin Coolidge) were placed on "preferred lists" at brokerage houses and tipped off about impending issues.

The desire for quick riches obsessed the nation. The volume of sales on the New York Stock Exchange jumped 400 percent from 1923 to 1928. Other exchanges in Chicago, St. Louis, San Francisco, and Los Angeles registered similar gains. Buyers were less concerned about wise investments—about profit and loss statements or market shares of a company—than about rising stock prices. A simple dictum governed all strategy: buy low, sell high; buy high, sell higher. "Everybody ought to be rich"—and anyone could be.

So it seemed in the late 1920s, as the New Era careened toward disaster. Behind electric signs directing the pursuit of wealth and slogans exhorting it, beneath land booms and stock deals, the economy was honeycombed with weaknesses, and in 1929 it shattered.

THE GREAT BULL MARKET

Strolling across the felt-padded floor of the New York Stock Exchange, Superintendent William Crawford greeted the New Year with swaggering confidence. Nineteen twenty-eight had been a record setter, with more than

90,500,000 shares traded. The "bulls"—buyers of stock—had routed the "bears"—those who sell. It was the greatest bull market in history as eager purchasers drove prices to new highs. At the end of the last business day of the year, Crawford surveyed the floor and declared flatly, "The millennium's arrived."

Veteran financial analyst Alexander Noyes knew better. Speculation—buying and selling on the expectation that rising prices will yield quick gains—had taken over. "Something has to give," said Noyes in September 1929. Less than a month later, the Great Bull Market collapsed in a heap.

The Rampaging Bull

No one knows exactly what caused the wave of speculation that boosted the stock market to dizzying heights. Driven alternately by greed and fear, the market succumbed to greed in a decade that considered it a virtue. A new breed of aggressive outsiders helped to spread the speculative fever. William Durant of General Motors, the Fisher brothers from Detroit, and others like them bought millions of shares, crowded out more conservative investors from the East, and helped to send prices soaring.

Money to fuel the market became plentiful. From 1922 to 1929, some $900 million worth of gold flowed into the country. The money supply expanded by

New money

$6 billion. Over the decade corporate profits grew by 80 percent. At interest rates as high as 25 percent, more could be made from lending money to brokers (who made "brokers' loans" to clients for stock purchases) than from constructing new factories. Borrowed over the phone, lent with the purchased stock as collateral, this "call money" could be collected, or called in, at any time and was usually renewable. By 1929 Bethlehem Steel had more than $157 million invested in the "call money market," and brokers' loans had almost tripled from two years earlier.

"Margin requirements," the cash actually put down to purchase stock, hovered around 50 percent for most of the decade. Thus buyers had to come up

ON THE FLOOR — N.Y. STOCK EXCHANGE   REGINALD MARSH

with only half the price of a share. The rest came from brokers' loans. As trading reached record heights in August 1929, the Federal Reserve Board tried to dampen speculation by raising the interest, or "rediscount," rate charged for loans to member banks. Higher interest rates made borrowing more expensive and, authorities hoped, would rein in the galloping bull market. But it was already too late.

The Great Crash

On Thursday morning, October 24, 1929, the gallery of the New York Stock Exchange was packed with visitors. Trouble was in the air. The day before, a sharp break downward had capped a week of falling prices. Speculators had begun to sell their stocks and take their profits.

At the opening bell, a torrent of sell orders flooded the Exchange. Prices plunged as panic set in. By the end of "Black Thursday" nearly 13 million shares had been traded—a record. Losses stood at $3 billion, another record. Thirty-five of the largest brokerage houses on Wall Street issued a joint statement of reassurance: "The worst has passed."

The worst had only begun. Prices rallied for the rest of the week, buoyed by a bankers' buying pool organized at the House of Morgan. The following Tuesday, October 29, 1929, the bubble burst. Stockholders lost $10 billion in a single day. Within a month industrial stocks lost half of what they had been worth in September. And the downward spiral continued for almost four years. At their peak in 1929 stocks had been worth $87 billion. In 1933 they bottomed out at $18 billion.

The Great Crash did not cause the Great Depression, but it did damage the economy. Although only about 500,000 people were actually trading stocks by

Role of the crash

the end of the decade, their investments had helped to sustain prosperity. Thousands of middle-class investors lost their savings and their futures. Commercial banks—some loaded with corporate stocks, others deeply in the call money market—reeled in the wake of the crash. As historian Robert McElvaine has suggested, the shock of the stock market's fall "lowered the economy's resistance to the point where already existing defects could multiply rapidly and bring down the whole organism."

The Causes of the Great Depression

What, then, were the defects in the American economy? With national attention riveted on the stock market, hardly anyone had paid them heed. But by 1928 the booming construction and automobile industries began to lose vitality as consumer demand for housing and cars sagged. In fact, increases in consumer spending for all goods and services slowed to a lethargic 1.5 percent for 1928–1929. Warehouses began to fill as business inventories climbed, from $500 million in 1928 to $1.8 billion in 1929.

In one sense, businesses had done all too well. They had increased profits during the 1920s by keeping the cost of labor and raw materials low, as well as by increasing productivity (producing more goods using fewer workers). But most of the profits reaped by business were used to expand factories rather than to pay workers higher wages. Without strong labor unions or government support to help buoy them, real wages never kept pace with productivity. And this led to a paradox. As consumers, workers did not have enough money to buy the new products so many factories were turning out. The American economy was overexpanding at the same time that purchasing power was declining.

Overexpansion and decline in mass purchasing power

People made up the difference between earnings and purchases by borrowing. Consumers bought "on time," paying for merchandise a little each month. During the decade consumer debt rose by 250 percent. Few could afford to keep spending at that rate. Nor could the distribution of wealth sustain prosperity. By 1929, 1 percent of the population owned 36 percent of all personal wealth. The wealthy had more money than they could possibly spend and saved too much. The working and middle classes had not nearly enough to keep the economy growing, spend though they might.

Consumer debt and uneven distribution of wealth

Another problem lay with the banking system. Mismanagement, greed, and the emergence of a new type of executive—half banker, half stockbroker—led banks to divert more funds into more speculative investments. The uniquely decentralized American banking system left no way to set things right if a bank failed. At the end of the decade half of the 25,000 banks in America lay outside of the Federal Reserve System. Its controls even over member banks were weak. During the decade, 6000 banks failed.

Banking system

Added to the weak banking structure was a shaky corporate structure. No government agency monitored the stock exchanges at all, while big business operated largely unchecked. Insider trading, shady deals, and outright fraud ran rampant. Meanwhile public policy encouraged corporate consolidation and control by discouraging antitrust suits. High profits and the Mellon program of tax reduction (see page 681) helped make many corporations wealthy enough to avoid borrowing. Thus changes in interest rates had little influence on them. Free from government regulation, fluctuating prices, and the need for loans, huge corporations ruled the economy. And they ruled badly.

Corporate structure and public policy

Unemployment began to increase as early as 1927, revealing a growing softness in the economy. By the fall of 1929 nearly 2 million people were out of work. Many of them were in textiles, coal mining, lumbering, and railroads. All were "sick" industries that had suffered from overexpansion, reduced demand, and weak management. Farmers were in trouble too. As European agriculture revived after World War I, farm prices tumbled. American farmers earned 16 percent of the national income in 1919 but only 9 percent in 1929. As more of them went bust, so did the rural banks that had lent them money.

"Sick" industries

Finally, plain economic ignorance contributed to the calamity. High tariffs protected American industries but discouraged foreign trade, making it harder

Economic ignorance

for European businesses to sell to the world's most profitable market. Since Europeans weren't profiting, they lacked the money to spend on American goods being shipped to Europe. Only American loans and investments supported demand for American goods abroad; when the economy began to collapse, those were withdrawn.

Furthermore, the Federal Reserve had been stimulating the economy both by expanding the money supply and by lowering interest rates. That only fed the speculative fever. A decision to raise interest rates in 1929 to stem speculation ended up speeding the slide.

COUNTERPOINT   *What Caused the Great Depression?*

Not all scholars see the causes of the Depression just so. Most historians follow the thinking of British economist John Maynard Keynes. His revolutionary ideas challenged traditional notions that the economy was a self-adjusting mechanism that would eventually recover on its own. "Keynesians" argue that the capitalist economy must expand to survive. Economic expansion requires spending by both consumers and investors. Without such spending, the economy could stagnate at low levels of productivity and employment, as was the case in the 1930s. What caused the Great Depression, according to this school, was a decline in both investments and consumption as markets for producer and consumer goods reached saturation. Simply put, not enough income was being distributed to sustain consumer purchasing power and to encourage expansion and investment.

Followers of American economist Milton Friedman disagree. Called "monetarists," they point to the money supply as the root of the problem. In the crucial years between 1930 and 1932 the money supply shrank at an annual rate of 10 percent, reversing the pre-1929 period of expansion. The failure of the Federal Reserve System to increase the supply of money, argue monetarists, fatally weakened banks and set off a "great contraction" in the economy. More money in circulation and lower interest rates on loans would have promoted a quick recovery in the wake of the stock market crash of 1929.

The Sickening Slide

The Great Crash signaled the start of a 10-year depression, the worst in the history of the nation. The gains of the twenties were wiped out in a few years. In the first three years after the crash total productivity dropped from $103 billion to $56 billion. National income fell by half; factory wages, by almost half; foreign trade, by more than two-thirds. Some 85,000 businesses failed.

The shock waves helped to topple already fragile economies in Europe. American loans, investments, and purchases had propped up Europe since the end of World War I. When they stopped, European governments defaulted on war debts. More European banks failed; more businesses collapsed; unemployment surged. Europeans scrambled to protect themselves. Led by Great Britain in 1931, 41 nations abandoned the gold standard. Foreign governments hoped to devalue their currencies by expanding their supplies of money. Exports would be cheaper, and foreign trade would increase. But at the same time, each country raised tariffs to protect itself from foreign competition, and devaluation failed. The resulting trade barriers only deepened the crisis.

Declining sales abroad sent crop prices in the United States to new lows. Farm income dropped by more than half—to a paltry $5 billion. The epidemic of rural bank failures spread to the cities as nervous depositors rushed to withdraw their cash. Even healthy banks could not bear the strain. Between 1929 and 1933 collapsing banks took more than $20 billion in assets with them. The economy was spiraling downward, and no one could stop it.

THE AMERICAN PEOPLE IN THE GREAT DEPRESSION

Long bread lines snaked around corners. Vacant-eyed apple sellers stood shivering in the wind. A man with his hat in his hand came to the back door asking for food in exchange for work. Fewer automobiles rode the streets; more hobos rode the rails. Trains were shorter and the air was cleaner as factories cut back or shut down. Between 1929 and 1932 an average of 100,000 people lost their jobs every week until some 13 million Americans were jobless. At least one worker in four could find no work at all.

The Great Depression was a great leveler that reduced differences in the face of common want. The New York seamstress without enough piecework to pay her rent felt the same frustration and anger as the Berkeley student whose college education was cut short when the bank let her father go. Not everyone was devastated. Most husbands had some job. Most wives continued as homemakers. Most Americans got by, often cooperating with one another, practicing a ruthless underconsumption to make ends meet. "We lived lean," recalled one Depression victim. So did most of the American people—northern and southern; urban and rural; black, white, yellow, and brown.

Hard Times

Even before the Great Crash many Americans were having trouble making a living. In the golden year of 1929, economists calculated that for necessities

Subsistence incomes

alone a family of four required $2000 a year—more money than 60 percent of American families earned. By 1932 the average family had an annual income of $1348, barely enough to survive.

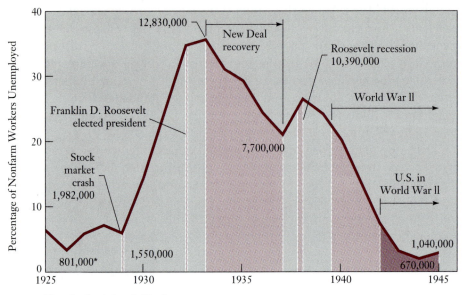

UNEMPLOYMENT, 1925–1945   Unemployment mushroomed in the wake of the stock market crash of 1929. The success of the New Deal in increasing employment did not nearly match World War II, which turned out to be the unintended agent of recovery.

As soup kitchens opened and bread lines formed in cities across the nation, survival often became the primary goal. Millions stayed alive by foraging like animals, and city hospitals began receiving new patients ill from starvation. In the coal-mining regions of West Virginia and Illinois almost every child fed by the American Friends Service Committee was underweight. Pellagra and other diseases associated with malnutrition increased. Despite official claims that "no one has starved," the New York City Welfare Council reported 29 victims of starvation and 110 dead of malnutrition in 1932. Most were children.

Unable to pay mortgages or rent, many families lived off the generosity of forgiving landlords. Some traded down to smaller quarters or simply lost their homes. By 1932 between 1 million and 2 million Americans were homeless wanderers, among them an estimated 25,000 nomadic families. For the first time, emigration out of the United States exceeded immigration into it because Americans could find so little work in their own country.

Victims of the Depression overthrew the governments of seven Latin American countries, but in the United States most citizens turned their anger

Psychological impact

inward. "People blamed themselves, not the system," explained one woman. "They felt they had been at fault: . . . 'if we hadn't bought that old radio' . . . 'if we hadn't bought that second-hand car.'" Shame, self-doubt, and pessimism became epidemic. "I'm just no good, I

Shantytowns (called "Hoovervilles" after the president) sprang up around most cities as the Depression deepened.

guess," a Houston woman lamented in 1934. Most tried to keep up appearances. Men resharpened old razor blades, rolled their own cigarettes, used 25-watt bulbs to save electricity. Women retailored their dresses for their daughters and sewed together lengths of sheets to equalize wear. Under the strain, rates of mental illness and suicide rose.

Some never forgot the humiliation of life in the Depression. "Shame? You tellin' me?" recalled a businessman. "I would go stand on that relief line [and] bend my head low so nobody would recognize me. The only scar that is left on me is my pride, my pride." The lasting legacy of humiliation and fear—that the bottom would fall out again, that life would be leveled once more, that the next depression might not end—this was what one writer called an "invisible scar."

The Depression Family

Jane Addams, 81 years old in 1931 and a tireless fighter for social justice, saw the anxiety in the faces of those living around her beloved Hull House in Chicago—"men and women who have seen their margin of savings disappear; heads of families who see and anticipate hunger for their children before it occurs. That clutch of cold fear is one of the most hideous aspects."

The "clutch of cold fear" led many young couples to put off having children: births per 1000 women of childbearing age dropped from 97.4 in 1929 to

Baby shortage

75.7 in 1933. For the first time in three centuries the curve of population growth was leveling off. The marriage rate slumped as well and did not begin to recover until 1934. Although divorce declined throughout the 1930s, desertion—the "poor man's divorce"—increased.

Studies found that the Depression did not split families so much as it magnified tendencies already present. Weak families languished or fell apart. Strong

Impact on families

ones hung together and grew closer. But in all families the Depression took a toll, especially on men. Work had defined them as productive members of society. Suddenly they had nothing to do. Husbands without jobs grew listless and discouraged after a few weeks at home. Some put on ties and jackets each morning, but instead of going to the office they sold Two-in-One shoe polish or cheap neckties door to door. In a culture that stressed self-reliance and male breadwinning, such men felt like failures.

During the Depression the routines of most of the country's 28 million homemakers were less disrupted than their husbands', but demands on them

Importance of homemaking

grew as homemaking took on added importance. Between 1929 and 1933 living costs dropped almost 25 percent, but family incomes tumbled by 40 percent. Homemakers watched family budgets with a close eye. They substituted less expensive fish for red meat or dropped meat from their menus altogether. Jell-O, the cheapest all-purpose dessert, enjoyed new popularity. Corn, tomatoes, and pole beans sprang up in backyards and vacant city lots. Families took in relatives and boarders. Some homemakers sold baked goods, made dresses, or opened kitchen beauty parlors.

After a decade of being drawn from home by automobiles and mass entertainment, the middle-class family turned inward. Church attendance declined, and a third of the Grange and rural women's clubs vanished. Home and family emerged as the center of recreation and companionship. People dreamed of the outdoors—playing tennis, swimming, or boating—but surveys showed that they spent their free time indoors, reading, listening to the radio, and going to the movies, in that order.

The Great Depression marked a generation. Countless women came to associate working outside the home with financial distress. The middle-class dream of a wife freed from working for wages, which had weakened in the 1920s, reasserted itself. Whether in the renewed importance of homemaking and family life or in the reemergence of home industries, Americans retreated into traditionalism.

Working Women, Anxious Children

As the Depression deepened, more women worked outside their homes to supplement meager family incomes. Some critics claimed they took jobs from men, and one offered a simple solution: "Fire the women, who shouldn't be working

EYEWITNESS TO HISTORY

A Salesman Loses Everything

I was in business for myself, selling clothing on credit, house to house. And collecting by the week. Up to that time, people were buying very good and paying very good. But they started to speculate, and I felt it. My business was dropping from the beginning of 1928. They were mostly middle-class people. They weren't too rich, and they weren't too poor.

All of a sudden, in the afternoon, October 1929 . . . I was going on my business and I heard the newspaper boys calling, running all around the streets and giving news and news: stock market crashed, stock market crashed. It came out just like lightning.

I remember vividly. I was on my route, going to see my customer. It didn't affect me much at the time. I wasn't speculating in the market. Of course, I had invested some money in some property and some gold bonds, they used to call it. Because I have more confidence in the gold bonds than the stock market. Because I know the stock market goes up and down. But the gold bond, I was told from the banks, is just like gold. Never lose its value. Later we found to our sorrow that it was fake. . . .

We lost everything. It was the time I would collect four, five hundred dollars a week. After that, I couldn't collect fifteen, ten dollars a week. I was going around trying to collect enough money to keep my family going. It was impossible. Very few people could pay you. Maybe a dollar if they would feel sorry for you or what.

Finally people started to talk me into going into the relief. They had open soup kitchens. Al Capone, he had open soup kitchens somewhere downtown, where people were standing in line. And you had to go two blocks, stand there, around the corner, to get a bowl of soup.

Ben Issacs in Studs Terkel, *Hard Times: An Oral History of the Great Depression* (New York: Pantheon, 1986), pp. 423–427. Copyright © 1970 by Studs Terkel. Reprinted by permission of Pantheon Books, a division of Random House, Inc.

anyway, and hire the men. Presto! No unemployment. No relief rolls. No depression."

Such thinking reflected the prejudice still dogging female wage earners. Past discrimination had relegated many women to jobs as secretaries,

Working outside
the home
schoolteachers, and social workers. Over half the female labor force worked in domestic service or the garment trades. Live-in maids, the elite of domestic servants, got $8 a week; pieceworkers in the textile mills of Lawrence, Massachusetts, $4. Most unemployed men would have been reluctant to take such "women's work," even if it were available.

Married women who sought employment faced special obstacles. Opinion polls showed that more than three in four Americans believed wives belonged at home. Few school districts would hire them, and half had a policy of firing them first. Between 1932 and 1937 federal regulations prohibited more than one family member from holding a civil service job. Three-quarters of those forced to resign were women. The proportion of women in the workforce rose anyway because they were willing to take almost any job. By 1940 it approached 25 percent. Wages for women rose too, until they were 63 percent of men's.

The nation's 21 million children could not escape anxiety. Teachers reported even kindergartners being "excitable and high-strung." Many of them were as uncertain of their future as they were of their next meal. Initially some 250,000 children took to the road, often to relieve families of their support or just to escape. But school enrollments grew as prospects for employment shrank. By 1940 three-quarters of high school-aged children were attending, compared with less than half in 1930. Extended schooling kept children out of the labor force, and the Depression fed the long-term trend toward a highly educated public.

*Childhood
anxiety*

Play

Somber faces fill the photographs of the Depression decade, but in fact Americans still had fun, although play was often conditioned by the crisis. In the midst of fear and uncertainty, games built on rationality captured middle-class imaginations: contract bridge with its systematic bidding and play; Parker Brothers' board game Monopoly, which rewarded orderly investing in real estate; pinball, the ultimate machine-age game that carried the injunction "Do Not Tilt." All relied on rules and skill as well as luck. In more physical games, endurance became a virtue. Six-day bicycle races staged a comeback. Dance marathons, another contest for survival, kept partners on the floor 45 minutes out of every hour, 24 hours a day, sometimes for weeks on end.

The Depression produced more traditional fashions for women: longer skirts and hair and more curves. A desire to escape the here-and-now helped to make bestsellers of *The Good Earth* (1931), Pearl Buck's saga of China, and Margaret Mitchell's Civil War epic, *Gone with the Wind* (1936). New skepticism about business led Fred Schlink to write *100,000,000 Guinea Pigs*, a sequel to *Your Money's Worth* (1927), his earlier exposé of false advertising. By 1935 the two books had sold half a million copies.

Hungry for diversions, people still flocked to spectacles, as they had in the 1920s. A world's fair in Chicago in 1933 and another in New York in 1939 drew millions. Families living on a limited budget took up cheaper pursuits, such as stamp collecting, knitting, and jigsaw puzzles. Boxtop contests and other games of chance held out hope of turning bad financial luck good. Inaugurated in 1930, the Irish Sweepstakes became the most successful lottery in the world within five years.

With a wider audience than ever, record sales jumped a hundredfold between 1934 and 1937. Classical music enjoyed new popularity as tastes turned to a more controlled, full-bodied sound. By 1939 there were more than 270 symphony orchestras in the country; only 17 had existed in 1915. More than 10 million families listened to symphonic music and opera each weekend on radio. Popular music became more melodic and cheerful. "Swing," a commercialized jazz, dominated the charts, and big-band orchestras played popular favorites at nightclubs and theaters.

The Golden Age of Radio and Film

By the end of the decade almost 9 out of 10 families owned radios. (The cost of one had dropped from $100 in 1929 to about $50 by the mid-1930s.) People depended on them for nearly everything—news, sports, and weather; music and entertainment; advice on how to bake a cake or find God. Radio entered a

Commercial programming

golden age of commercialism, as sponsors hawked their products on variety programs like "Major Bowes' Amateur Hour" and comedy shows with George Burns and Gracie Allen. Daytime melodramas, called "soap operas" because they were sponsored by soap companies, aimed at women with stories of the personal struggles of ordinary folk. The hair-raising adventures of "The Lone Ranger" drew young listeners. By 1939 it was being heard three times a week on 140 stations.

Radio continued to bind the country together. A teenager in Splendora, Texas, could listen to the same wisecracks from Jack Benny, the same music from Guy Lombardo, as kids in New York and Los Angeles. In 1938 Orson Welles broadcast H. G. Wells's classic science fiction tale, *The War of the Worlds*. Americans everywhere listened to breathless reports of an "Invasion from Mars," and some believed them. In Newark, New Jersey, cars jammed roads as families rushed to evacuate the city. The nation, bombarded with reports of impending war in Europe, was prepared to believe anything, even invaders from Mars.

In Hollywood an efficient but dictatorial "studio system" churned out a record number of feature films. Eight motion picture companies produced

Studio system

more than two-thirds of them. Color, first introduced in features in *Becky Sharp* (1935), soon complemented sound, which had debuted in the 1927 version of *The Jazz Singer*. Neither alone could keep movie theaters full. As attendance waned early in the Depression, big studios like Metro-Goldwyn-Mayer and Universal sought to lure audiences back with films that shocked, titillated, and just plain entertained.

Popular movies often played upon deep national emotions. Early Depression gangster movies like *Little Caesar* (1931) and *Scarface* (1932) allowed Americans ambivalent about the ethic of success to root for misfits who challenged it and still applaud their just demise. The Marx Brothers made fun of social disorder in *Monkey Business* (1931) and *Duck Soup* (1933), while teamwork and cooperation were stressed in the elaborately choreographed musicals of Busby Berkeley and in the dancing routines of Fred Astaire and Ginger Rogers. Only toward the end of the decade did Hollywood develop a social conscience in such films as *Dead End* (1937) and *The Grapes of Wrath* (1941).

By the mid-1930s more than 60 percent of Americans were going to the movies at least once a week. They saw tamer films as the industry regulated movie content in the face of growing criticism. To avoid censorship and boycotts, studios stiffened their own regulations.

Production code

According to the Motion Picture Production Code of 1934, producers could not depict homosexuality, abortion, drug use, or sex. (Even the word *sex* was banned.) If couples were shown in bed, they had to be clothed and one foot of each partner had to touch the floor. Middle-class morality reigned on the screen, and most Depression movies, like most of popular culture, preserved traditional social and economic values.

"Dirty Thirties": An Ecological Disaster

On Armistice Day 1933, the wind began to blow through Beadle County, South Dakota, not just briskly but at 60 miles an hour. "By noon," reported R. D. Lusk from a local farmhouse, "it was darker than night." When the wind finally died down, the farm, like the rest of Beadle County, was transformed. Lusk saw no fields, "only sand drifting into mounds. . . . Fences, machinery, and trees were gone, buried. The roofs of sheds stuck out through drifts deeper than a man is tall."

Between 1932 and 1939 an average of nearly 50 "black blizzards" a year turned 1500 square miles between the Oklahoma panhandle and western Kansas into a gigantic "Dust Bowl." It was one of the worst ecological disasters in modern history, and its baleful effects were felt as far

Dust Bowl

north as the Dakotas and as far south as Texas. Nature played its part, scorching the earth and whipping the winds. But the "dirty thirties" were mostly man-made. The semiarid lands west of the 98th meridian were not suitable for agriculture or livestock. Sixty years of intensive farming and grazing had stripped the prairie of its natural vegetation and rendered it defenseless against the elements. When the dry winds came, one-third of the Great Plains just blew away.

The dust storms lasted anywhere from hours to days. Walking into one, as R. D. Lusk discovered when he stepped outside, was like walking into "a wall of dirt." For protection people wore gauze masks, swabbed their nostrils with Vaseline, covered their windows with paraffin-soaked rags. Nothing worked. Tiny particles of dust covered everything, and food crunched to the bite.

"Black blizzards" dwarfed all man-made structures. The drought that helped to bring them about lasted from 1932 to 1936. In a single day in 1934, dust storms dumped 12 million tons of western dirt on Chicago.

Some 3.5 million plains people abandoned their farms. Landowners or corporations forced off about half of them, as large-scale commercial farming slowly spread east from California into the heartland of America. The Great Plains contained the only states that suffered a net loss of residents during the decade. No one knows how many of these rural refugees became migrants, but relief offices around the country reported a change in migrant families. No longer black or brown, more and more were white and native-born, typically a young married couple with one child.

Most did not travel far, perhaps to the next county. Long-distance migrants—the "Exodusters" from Oklahoma, Arizona, and Texas—usually set their sights on California. Handbills and advertisements promised jobs picking fruit and harvesting vegetables. If they were like the Joad family in John Steinbeck's classic novel *The Grapes of Wrath* (1939), they drove west along Route 66 through Arizona and New Mexico, their belongings piled high atop rickety jalopies, heading for the West Coast.

Exodusters

More than 350,000 Oklahomans migrated to California, so many that "Okie" came to mean any Dust Bowler, even though most of Oklahoma lay outside the Dust Bowl. The poor were only a small minority of new arrivals, but Californians grew edgy. By the middle of the decade Los Angeles police had formed "bum blockades" to keep out migrants. "Negroes and Okies upstairs," read one sign in a San Joaquin Valley theater. Native-born whites had never encountered such discrimination before.

Only one in two or three migrants actually found work. The labor surplus allowed growers to set their own terms. A migrant family earned about $450 a year, less than a third of the subsistence level. Those who did not work formed wretched enclaves called "little Oklahomas." The worst were located in the fertile Imperial Valley. There at the end of the decade relief officials discovered a family of 10 living in a 1921 Ford.

Mexican Americans and African Americans

The Chavez family lost their farm in the North Gila River valley of Arizona in 1934. They had owned a small homestead near Yuma for two generations, but the
Cesar Chavez   Depression pushed them out. Cesar, barely six years old at the time, remembered only images of the departure: a "giant tractor" leveling the corral, the loss of his room and bed, a beat-up Chevy hauling the family west, his father vowing to buy another plot in Arizona someday.

The elder Chavez could never keep his promise. Instead he and his family lived on the road, "following the crops" in California. In eight years Cesar went to 37 schools. The family was forced to sell their labor to unscrupulous *enganchistas*, or contractors, for less than $10 a week. The father joined strikers in the Imperial Valley in the mid-1930s, but they were crushed. "Some people put this out of their minds and forget it," said Cesar Chavez years later. "I don't." Thirty years later he founded the United Farm Workers of America, the first union of migratory workers in the country.

The Chavezes resembled the Joads in every way but one: they were Mexican Americans. The Joads had encountered at least a few sympathetic store clerks on their way west. When the Chavezes found a roadside restaurant, the sign outside read: "White trade only." In an America still strictly segregated, the owner never thought twice about refusing service to Americans who were brown or black. "Every time we thought of it, it hurt us," remembered Cesar.

A deep ambivalence had always characterized American attitudes toward Mexicans, but the Great Depression turned most Anglo communities against
Repatriation   them. Cities like Los Angeles, fearing the burden of relief, found it cheaper to ship them home. Some migrants left voluntarily. Others were driven out by frustrated officials or angry neighbors. Beginning in 1931 the federal government launched a series of deportations, or "repatriations," of Mexicans back to Mexico. These included their American-born children, who by law were citizens of the United States.

During the decade the Spanish-speaking population of the Southwest declined by 500,000. In a city like Chicago, the Mexican community shrank almost by half. Staying often turned out to be as difficult as leaving. The average income of Mexican American families in the Rio Grande valley of Texas was $506 a year. The sum represented the combined income of parents and children. Following the harvest made schooling particularly difficult: fewer than 2 Mexican American children in 10 completed five years of school.

Hard times were nothing new to African Americans. "The Negro was born in depression," opined one man. "It only became official when it hit the white man." Still, when the Depression struck, black unemployment surged. By 1932 it reached 50 percent, twice the national level. By 1933 several cities reported between 25 and 40 percent of their black residents with no support but relief payments. Even skilled black workers who retained their jobs saw their wages cut in half, according to one study of Harlem in 1935.

Migration from the rural South, up 800,000 over the 1920s, dropped by 50 percent during the 1930s. As late as 1940 three of four African Americans still lived in rural areas; yet conditions there were as bad as in cities. Forty percent of all black workers in the United States were farm laborers or tenants. In 1934 one study estimated the average income for black cotton farmers at under $200 a year.

Millions of African Americans made do by stretching meager incomes as they had for years. "Our wives could go to the store and get a bag of beans or a sack of flour and a piece of fat meat, and they could cook this. And we could eat it," explained another man. "Now you take the white fella, he couldn't do this."

Like many African Americans, George Baker refused to be victimized by the Depression. Baker had moved from Georgia to Harlem in 1915. He changed
Father Divine and Elijah Muhammad his name to M. J. Divine and founded a religious cult that promised followers an afterlife of full equality. In the 1930s "Father Divine" preached economic cooperation and opened shelters, or "heavens," for regenerate "angels," black and white. In Detroit, Elijah Poole changed his name to Elijah Muhammad and in 1931 established the Black Muslims, a blend of Islamic faith and black nationalism. He exhorted African Americans to celebrate their African heritage, to live a life of self-discipline and self-help, and to strive for a separate all-black nation.

The Depression inflamed racial prejudice. "Dust has been blown from the shotgun, the whip, and the noose," reported *The New Republic* in 1931, "and Ku
Scottsboro boys Klux Klan practices were being resumed in the certainty that dead men not only tell no tales but create vacancies." Lynchings tripled between 1932 and 1933. In 1932 the Supreme Court ordered a retrial in the most celebrated racial case of the decade. A year earlier nine black teenagers had been accused of raping two white women on a train bound for Scottsboro, Alabama. Within weeks all-white juries had sentenced eight of them to death. The convictions rested on the testimony of the women, one of whom later admitted the boys had been framed. Appeals kept the case alive for almost a decade. In the end charges against four of the "Scottsboro boys" were dropped. The other five received substantial prison sentences.

Elsewhere the Depression divided black and white Americans, but in the Arkansas delta hard times drew them together. In Arkansas poor black and white farmers joined forces to organize the Southern Tenant Farmers Union in 1934. The union published its own newspaper, the *Sharecropper's Voice*, and attracted national support from Socialists and other radicals. Landlords became uneasy with union demands for federal subsidies and an end to arbitrary evictions. Planters and riding bosses broke up union meetings and horsewhipped organizers. Although they won few concessions, union members hung together.

THE TRAGEDY OF HERBERT HOOVER

A cold, gray morning sent shivers through the crowd huddled in front of the capitol on March 4, 1929. Herbert Hoover had just been sworn in as the thirty-first president of the United States. His monotone came booming over the loudspeakers: "I have no fears for the future of our country. It is bright with hope." Within seven months a "depression" had struck. (Hoover coined the term himself to minimize the crisis.) Try as he might, he could not beat it, and the nation turned against him. "People were starving because of Herbert Hoover," cried an angry mother in 1932. "Men were killing themselves because of Herbert Hoover, and their fatherless children were being packed away to orphanages . . . because of Herbert Hoover."

The charge was unfair, but it stuck. Hoover's presidency, begun with such bright hope, became the worst ordeal of his life. Near the end of his term in 1932 he lamented that "all the money in the world could not induce me to live over the last nine months." He nonetheless felt duty-bound to accept his party's renomination for the presidency. His ordeal soon turned into a tragic and humiliating rejection.

The Failure of Relief

By the winter of 1931–1932 the story was the same everywhere: relief organizations with too little money and too few resources to combat the Depression.

Private charity

Once-mighty private charity had dwindled to 6 percent of all relief funds. Hull House in Chicago, the model of progressive benevolence, was overwhelmed by the needs of the neighborhood it served. New York City employees had been donating 1 percent of their salaries to feed the needy since 1930, yet many New Yorkers were starving to death.

Ethnic charities made similar efforts to stave off disaster. Mexican Americans and Puerto Ricans turned to *mutualistas*, traditional societies that provided members with social support, life insurance, and sickness benefits. The stress of the Depression quickly bankrupted most *mutualistas*. In San Francisco, the Chinese Six Companies offered food and clothing to needy Chinese Americans. But as one charity head warned, private efforts were failing. The government would be "compelled, by the cruel events ahead of us, to step into the situation and bring relief on a large scale."

An estimated 30 million needy people nationwide quickly depleted city treasuries, already pressed by delinquent tax rates of nearly 30 percent. In

City services

Philadelphia relief payments to a family of four totaled $5.50 a week. It was the highest rate in the country. Some cities gave nothing to unmarried people or childless couples, no matter how impoverished they were. Oklahoma City began arresting unemployed men, charging them with vagrancy and ordering them out of town. Roads went unpaved in summer; snow, unplowed in winter. By the end of 1931, Detroit, Boston, Buffalo, and scores of other cities were bankrupt.

Cities clamored for help from state capitals, but after a decade of extravagant spending and sloppy bookkeeping, many states were already running in the red. As businesses and property values collapsed, tax bases shrank and with them state revenues. Michigan, one of the few states to provide any relief, reduced funds by more than half between 1931 and 1932. Until New York established its Temporary Emergency Relief Administration (TERA) in 1931, no state had any agency at all to handle the problem.

TERA

Some people refused to accept help even when they qualified. To go on relief, said one man, was to endure a "crucifixion." Before applications could even be considered, all property had to be sold, all credit exhausted, all relatives declared flat broke. After a half-hour grilling about his family, home, and friends, one applicant left, "feeling I didn't have any business living any more." Hostile officials attached every possible stigma to aid. In 1932 residents of Lewiston, Maine, voted to bar all welfare recipients from the polls. Ten states wrote property requirements for voting into their constitutions. The destitute were being disfranchised.

Herbert Hoover

Trumpets blared, servants bowed, and the president of the United States sat down to dinner. One after another, seven full courses were set before him. When he finished, the uniformed buglers sounded his departure. Every night he stayed at the White House during the Great Depression, Herbert Hoover dined in such splendor. He thought about economizing but decided against it. If he changed his habits one bit, it might be taken as a sign of lost confidence.

It was not that Herbert Hoover was insensitive—far from it. He never visited a bread line or a relief shelter because he could not bear the sight of suffering. Yet he was doing all he could to promote recovery, more than any of his predecessors, and still he was scorned. His natural sullenness turned to self-pity. Calvin Coolidge advised patience: "You can't expect to see calves running in the field the day after you put the bull to the cows." "No," said an exasperated Hoover, "but I would expect to see contented cows."

Hoover's frustration was understandable. He had never failed before. Orphaned at nine, he graduated from the newly opened Stanford University in 1895, an engineer and soon the owner of one of the most successful mining firms in the world. Before he turned 40, he was a millionaire. As a good Quaker he balanced private gain with public service. He saved starving refugees in war-torn Europe and flood victims at home and became known as the greatest humanitarian of his generation. The people of Finland added a new word to their vocabulary: to *hoover* meant to help.

The Hoover Depression Program

From the fall of 1930 onward, Hoover took responsibility for ending the crisis—and as humanely as possible. He understood the vicious cycle of rising unemployment and falling demand and knew the necessity for investment. His unprecedented Depression program rested on his associational philosophy (see page 682), with its commitment to voluntary efforts, faith in the power of capitalism, and conviction that too much government action would undermine freedoms and initiative.

Despite Hoover's best efforts, the program failed. He secured pledges from business leaders to maintain employment, wages, and prices, only to have them back down as the economy sputtered. To bolster public confidence, he reassured Americans that "conditions are fundamentally sound," but the sagging economy quickly proved him wrong. When Hoover tax cuts to increase the purchasing power of consumers led to an unbalanced federal budget, Hoover tax increases followed in 1932, further undermining investment and consumption. Presidential commissions to discover the number of unemployed and spark local relief did neither, and Hoover's Federal Farm Board, created to stimulate the sale of farm commodities, lacked the funds to make it effective. The president endorsed the Smoot–Hawley Tariff (1930) to protect the United States from cheap foreign goods, but the new tariff ended up bringing a wave of retaliation that choked world trade. Even Hoover's spending on public works—at $1 billion, more than all the presidents before him—did not approach the $10 billion needed to put only half the unemployed to work.

Under pressure from Congress, Hoover took his boldest action to save the banks. Without the credit they supplied, there could be no recovery. Between 1930 and 1932 some 5100 banks failed as panicky depositors withdrew their funds. Losses in deposits alone amounted to more than $3.2 billion. In 1932 Hoover endorsed the Reconstruction Finance Corporation (RFC), an agency that could lend money to banks and their chief corporate debtors—insurance companies and railroads. Modeled on a similar organization that had been created during World War I, the RFC had a capital stock of $500 million and the power to borrow four times that amount. Within three months bank failures dropped from 70 a week to 1 every two weeks. The Glass–Steagall Banking Act (1932) made it easier for banks to lend money by adding $2 billion of new currency to the money supply, backed by Federal Reserve government bonds.

Reconstruction Finance Corporation

Yet in spite of this success, Hoover drew criticism for rescuing banks and not people. From the start he rejected the idea of direct federal relief for the unemployed. He feared that a dole or giveaway program (of the kind being used in Britain) would damage the character of recipients. Federal experiments with relief could have unhealthy results for the whole nation, he argued, perhaps creating a permanent underclass. The program, moreover, would be expensive, and a bureaucracy would be needed to police recipients. Inevitably it would meddle

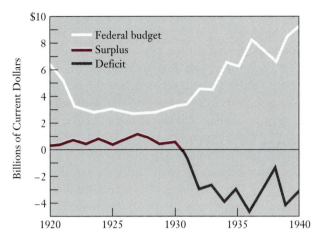

FEDERAL BUDGET AND SURPLUS/DEFICIT, 1920–1940   During the 1920s, the federal government ran a modest surplus. Beginning in 1930, federal deficits mounted as spending for Depression programs climbed and revenues from taxes and tariffs sank.

in the lives of citizens and bring a "train of corruption and waste." Hoover assumed that neighborliness and cooperation would be enough.

In 1930, as unemployment topped 4 million, Americans sent a new Congress to Washington. The off-year elections reduced the Republican majority to one in

Unemployment relief

the Senate and gave Democrats a slim lead in the House. After rejecting Democratic proposals for more public works and a federal employment service, Hoover slowly retreated on federal relief. In 1932 he finally dictated the terms of his surrender in the Emergency Relief and Construction Act. It authorized the RFC to lend up to $1.5 billion for "reproductive" public works like toll bridges and slum clearance. Another $300 million went to states as loans for the direct relief of the unemployed. They were hardly adequate: when the governor of Pennsylvania requested funds to furnish the destitute with 13 cents a day for a year, the RFC sent only enough for 3 cents a day.

Stirrings of Discontent

Hoover had given ground on relief, but like the rest of his Depression program it was too little and came too late. "The word revolution is heard at every hand," one writer warned in 1932. Some wondered if capitalism itself had gone bankrupt.

Here and there the desperate took matters into their own hands in 1932. In Wisconsin the Farm Holiday Association, under the leadership of Milo Reno,

Farm Holiday Association

dumped thousands of gallons of milk on highways in a vain attempt to raise prices. Ten thousand striking miners formed a 48-mile motor car "Coal Caravan" that worked its way in protest across southern Illinois. In March a demonstration turned ugly when communist sympathizers led a hunger march on Henry Ford's Rouge Assembly Plant in Dearborn, Michigan. As 3000 protesters surged toward the gates, Ford police drenched them with hoses, then opened fire at point-blank range. Four marchers were killed and more than 20 wounded.

For all the stirrings of discontent, revolution was never a danger. By 1932 the Communist party of the United States had only 20,000 members, up from 6500 in 1929 but hardly a political force. Under the slogan "Starve or Fight!" the Communists staged dozens of food, unemployment, and eviction protests. They led unionizing drives and courted intellectuals and the oppressed with their commitment to labor and civil rights.

Communist party

Deeply suspicious of Marxism, most Americans were unsympathetic. Fewer than 1000 African Americans joined the party in the early 1930s, despite a vigorous campaign to recruit them. In the election of 1932 Communist presidential candidate William Z. Foster polled just over 100,000 votes. At first hostile to established politics, the Communists adopted a more cooperative strategy to

Labor pickets, such as the one in Joe Jones'
We Demand, highlighted the failures of
capitalism. Here workers and their children, white
and black, display solidarity and new
"militancy" as they march in protest.

contain Adolf Hitler when his Nazi party won control of Germany in 1933. The Soviet Union ordered Communist parties in Europe and the United States to join with liberal politicians in a "popular front" against Nazism. Thereafter party membership peaked in the mid-1930s at about 80,000.

Hoover sympathized with the discontented but only to a point. When 1600 Communist-led hunger marchers came to Washington in December 1931, he was determined to protect their right to protest. The president ordered blankets, tents, a field kitchen, and medical aid for them. Washington police stood guard over their parade. Hoover himself received their petitions at the White House. But the following summer, the "Bonus Army" received a far different reception.

The Bonus Army

The "army," a ragtag collection of World War I veterans, was looking to cash in certificates they had received from Congress in 1924, as a reward for wartime service. Called "bonuses," the certificates were due to mature at an average of $1000 each in 1945. Penniless and hungry, the veterans wanted their bonuses now, whatever they were worth.

In May 1932 Congressman Wright Patman of Texas introduced a bill for immediate payment of bonuses. Three hundred veterans set out from Portland, Oregon, on a march for the bonus bill. By the time they reached Washington in June, the "Bonus Expeditionary Force" had swelled to 15,000, the biggest protest in the city's history. Bonus Army leaders met with congressional representatives, but the president refused to see them. For the first time since the end of World War I the gates of the Executive Mansion were chained shut.

Hoover dismissed the veterans as a special-interest lobby eager to feather an already soft nest. Veterans' benefits accounted for a quarter of the federal budget, the largest single item. At a cost of $2.3 billion, their bonuses would have nearly doubled the deficit. The Senate spared Hoover the trouble of vetoing the bonus bill by blocking it.

Some veterans went home, but about 10,000 stayed to dramatize their plight. When Washington police tried to evict the veterans from buildings in the Federal Triangle, Hoover called in the army to help. He wanted nothing more than unarmed military support; instead Army Chief of Staff General Douglas MacArthur arrived with four troops of cavalry brandishing sabers, followed by six tanks and a column of infantry.

On July 28, 1932, soldiers cleared the Federal Triangle with bayonets and tear gas. Major George S. Patton, Jr., rode down a crowd of marchers in the last mounted charge of the U.S. Cavalry. MacArthur then turned to the Bonus encampment on the Anacostia Flats across the Potomac River. Despite Hoover's orders to halt, the general burned the camp to the ground. As the smoke drifted over the capitol the next morning, the Bonus marchers had vanished, except for some 300 wounded veterans. Among them was Joseph T. Angelino. In 1918 he had received the Distinguished Service Cross for saving the life of a young officer—none other than George Patton.

Hoover took full responsibility. He offered the lame excuse that Bonus marchers were "not veterans" but "Communists and persons with criminal records" bent on insurrection. (A survey conducted by the Veterans Administration later belied the claim.) In Albany, New York, Governor Franklin Roosevelt exploded at the president's performance: "There is nothing inside the man but jelly." Hoover's fear of big government and commitment to private initiative and voluntarism overcame his humanitarian impulses. Like the hero of a classical tragedy, Herbert Hoover came tumbling down.

The Election of 1932

The Republicans refused to abandon Hoover. In June 1932 their national convention opened in Chicago and supported his Depression program to the last detail. Hoover was renominated, and rather thoughtlessly, the band struck up "California, here I come/Right back where I started from."

With an opportunity to recapture the White House for the first time since 1920, buoyant Democrats also gathered in Chicago. Their platform blamed the Depression on the Republicans, called for a 25 percent cut in federal spending, and promised a balanced budget. It also vowed somehow to provide federal public works and unemployment relief.

Franklin D. Roosevelt swept all challengers aside on the fourth ballot. Effervescent and inspiriting, Roosevelt broke tradition by accepting the nomination in person: "I pledge you, I pledge myself, to a new deal for the American people." In that instant, Roosevelt found his slogan—"the New Deal."

The campaign was over before it began, but Hoover fought on. He viewed the contest as a fight between two philosophies of government: the dangerous federal activism of Democrats against the voluntarism and prudent leadership of Republicans. Roosevelt, Hoover warned, would increase federal spending, inflate the currency, reduce the tariff, and "build a bureaucracy such as we have never seen in our history."

Without a national following, Roosevelt tailored his appeal to as broad a constituency as possible. In Iowa he said he was a "farmer"; in San Francisco, an economic planner. He called for a balanced budget one minute, more unemployment relief the next. He attacked Hoover as a "profligate spender," then went on to describe his own costly program for expanding public works.

Despite such fuzzy promises, election day brought a thundering rejection of Hoover and the Republicans. Roosevelt received nearly 58 percent of the popular vote. Norman Thomas won for the Socialists proportionately fewer votes than in 1912 or 1920. Democrats held majorities in both houses of Congress.

As telling as the magnitude of the victory were the returns themselves. Roosevelt carried the South and West and almost all the industrial states.

Roosevelt coalition   Dissatisfaction with Republican rule was galvanizing immigrants, Catholics and Jews, farmers and industrial laborers, city dwellers, and the rural poor into a broad coalition. With them the Democratic party would dominate politics for decades to come.

Early the next morning, Franklin Roosevelt returned to his townhouse from victory celebrations at the Biltmore Hotel in New York, only to experience a rare moment of doubt. As his son James helped him to bed, he confessed, "I am afraid I may not have the strength to do this job. After you leave me tonight, Jimmy, I am going to pray. . . . I hope you will pray for me, too."

The challenge was daunting: more than 12 million unemployed, 30 banks a week failing, factories idle, farms on the auction block, prices plummeting. People who had scorned government, including businessmen, were baffled and now looked to Washington. The nation awaited Roosevelt, but not even Roosevelt knew whether he would be equal to the job. All he knew was that he would try anything to help. In the progressive tradition, he would rely on the power of government. In one of his first acts, Roosevelt ordered that no one telephoning the White House for aid should be shut off. Someone in the administration would be found to answer every call.

SIGNIFICANT EVENTS

1926 — Miami real estate bust

1927 — First "talking" film, *The Jazz Singer*, released

1928 — Great Bull Market begins to peak

1929 — Herbert Hoover inaugurated; stock market crash; Federal Farm Board created

1930 — Smoot–Hawley Tariff raises rates

1931 — Repatriation of Mexicans; Scottsboro boys arrested; New York establishes Temporary Emergency Relief Administration

1932 — Glass–Steagall Banking Act; Reconstruction Finance Corporation established; Emergency Relief and Construction Act; Farm Holiday Association formed; Bonus Army marches on Washington, D.C.; Franklin Roosevelt elected president

1933 — Legion of Decency formed; "black blizzards" begin to create Dust Bowl

1934 — Southern Tenant Farmers Union organized

1935 — *Becky Sharp*, first color film; Communist party announces popular front

1936 — Margaret Mitchell's *Gone with the Wind* published

1938 — Orson Welles's radio broadcast of "Invasion from Mars"

1939 — John Steinbeck's *The Grapes of Wrath* published

CHAPTER TWENTY-SIX

The New Deal

Winner, South Dakota, November 10, 1933. "Dammit, I don't WANT to write to you again tonight. It's been a long, long day, and I'm tired." All the days had been long since Lorena Hickok began her cross-country trek. Four months earlier Harry Hopkins, the new federal relief administrator, had hired the newspaper journalist to report on the relief efforts of the New Deal. Forget about statistics or the "social worker angle," he told her. "Talk with the unemployed, those who are on relief and those who aren't, and when you talk to them," he added, "don't ever forget that but for the grace of God you, I, any of our friends might be in their shoes."

In 1933 and 1934, Hickok found that Roosevelt's relief program was falling short. Its half-billion-dollar subsidy to states, localities, and charities was still leaving out too many Americans, like the sharecropper Hickok discovered near Raleigh, North Carolina. He and his daughters had been living in a tobacco barn for two weeks on little more than weeds and table scraps. "Seems like we just keep goin' lower and lower," said the blue-eyed 16-year-old. To Hickok's surprise, hope still flickered in those determined eyes. Hick couldn't explain it until she noticed a pin on the girl's chest. It was a campaign button from the 1932 election—"a profile of the President." Hope sprang from the man in the White House.

Before Franklin D. Roosevelt and the New Deal, the White House was far removed from ordinary citizens. The only federal agency with which they had any contact was the post office. And these days it usually delivered bad news. But as Hickok traveled across the country in 1933, she detected a change. People were talking about government programs. Perhaps it was long-awaited contributions to relief or maybe reforms in securities and banking or the new recovery programs for industry and agriculture. Just as likely it was Franklin Roosevelt. Hickok seldom heard voters call themselves "Republicans" or "Democrats" any more. Instead, she wrote, they were "for the president."

Lorena Hickok (left) met Eleanor Roosevelt (right) in 1928.
Thereafter she served as Mrs. Roosevelt's unofficial press adviser
and became her closest friend. (In the center of this photograph
is Paul Person, governor of the Virgin Islands.)

The mail to Washington carried other signs that plain people were looking to the president. During the first weekend after the inauguration nearly half a million letters and telegrams poured into the White House. For years the average remained a record 5000 to 8000 a day. Over half the letters came from those at the bottom of the economic heap. Most sought help, offered praise, or just expressed their gratitude.

Whatever the individual messages, their collective meaning was clear: Franklin D. Roosevelt and the New Deal had begun to restore national confidence. Though it never brought full recovery, the New Deal did improve economic conditions and provided relief to millions of Americans. Equally significant, it made lasting reforms in the nation's economic system and committed the federal government to a more active role in managing the ups and downs of the business cycle. In doing so it extended the progressive drive to soften industrialization and translated decades of growing concern for the disadvantaged into a federal aid program. For the first time, Americans believed Washington would help them through a terrible crisis. In short, during the Roosevelt years the liberal state came of age: active, interventionist, and committed to social welfare.

THE EARLY NEW DEAL (1933–1935)

On March 4, 1933, as the clocks struck noon, Eleanor Roosevelt wondered if it were possible to "do anything to save America now." She looked at her husband, who had just been sworn in as thirty-second president of the United States. Franklin faced the crowd of over 100,000. Heeding the nation's call for "action, and action now," he promised to exercise "broad Executive power to wage a war against the emergency." The crowd cheered. Eleanor was terrified: "One has the feeling of going it blindly because we're in a tremendous stream, and none of us know where we're going to land."

The early New Deal unfolded in the spring of 1933 with a chaotic 100-day burst of legislation. It stressed recovery through planning and cooperation with business but also tried to aid the unemployed and reform the economic system. Above all, the early New Deal broke the cycle of despair. With Roosevelt in the White House, most Americans believed that they were in good hands, wherever they landed.

The Democratic Roosevelts

From the moment they entered it in 1933, Franklin and Eleanor—the Democratic Roosevelts—transformed the White House. No more footmen; no more buglers; above all, no more seven-course meals like those Hoover had served. Instead visitors got fare fit for a boardinghouse. Roosevelt's lunches of hash and a poached egg cost 19 cents. The gesture was symbolic, but it made the president's point of ending business as usual.

Such belt-tightening was new to Franklin Roosevelt. Born of an old Dutch family in New York, he grew up rich and pampered. He idolized his Republican

Franklin Roosevelt

cousin Theodore Roosevelt and mimicked his career, except as a Democrat. Like Theodore, Franklin was graduated from Harvard University (in 1904), won a seat in the New York State legislature (in 1910), secured an appointment as assistant secretary of the navy (in 1913), and ran for the vice presidency (in 1920). Then disaster struck. On vacation in the summer of 1921, Roosevelt fell ill with poliomyelitis. The disease paralyzed him from the waist down. For the rest of his life, he walked only with the aid of crutches and heavy steel braces.

Roosevelt emerged from the ordeal to win the governorship of New York in 1928. When the Depression struck, he created the first state relief agency in 1931, the Temporary Emergency Relief Administration. Aid to the jobless "must be extended by Government, not as a matter of charity, but as a matter

Most photographers acceded to White House wishes that President Roosevelt, a victim of polio, never be shot from the waist down. The president sits poolside at Warm Springs, Georgia, a polio treatment center that he helped to fund. Notice the newspaper held over his stricken legs.

of social duty," he explained. He considered himself a progressive but moved well beyond the cautious federal activism of most progressives. He adopted no single ideology. He cared little about economic principles. What he wanted were results. Experimentation became a hallmark of the New Deal.

Eleanor Roosevelt redefined what it meant to be First Lady. Never had a president's wife been so visible, so much of a crusader, so cool under fire. She

Eleanor Roosevelt

was the first First Lady to hold weekly press conferences. Her column, "My Day," appeared in 135 newspapers, and her twice-weekly broadcasts made her a radio personality rivaling her husband. She became his eyes, ears, and legs, traveling 40,000 miles a year. Secret Service men code-named her "Rover."

Eleanor believed she was only a spur to presidential action. But she was active in her own right, as a teacher and social reformer before Franklin became president and afterwards as a tireless advocate of the underdog. In the White House, she pressed him to hire more women and minorities but also supported antilynching and anti–poll tax measures, when he would not, and experimental towns for the homeless. By 1939 more Americans approved of her than of her husband.

Saving the Banks

Before the election Roosevelt had gathered a group of economic advisers called the "Brains Trust." Out of their recommendations came the early or "first" New

The Brains Trust

Deal of government planning, intervention, and experimentation. Brains Trusters disagreed over the means of achieving their goals, but those goals they broadly shared: economic recovery,

E Y E W I T N E S S   T O   H I S T O R Y

"My Day":
The First Lady Tours Tennessee

Johnson City, Tenn., May 31 [1939]—I looked out of the window of the train this morning while I was waiting for my breakfast, and it suddenly occurred to me that scenes from a train window might give a rather good picture of the variety in the conditions and occupations of our people in different parts of the country. I saw a little girl, slim and bent over, carrying two heavy pails of water across a field to an unpainted house. How far that water had to be carried, I do not know, but it is one thing to carry water on a camping trip for fun during a summer's holiday, and it is another thing to carry it day in and day out as part of the routine of living. On the outskirts of the town, I saw a wash line. On it hung two brown work shirts, a pair of rather frayed and faded blue dungarees, two child's sun suits and a woman's calico dress. Not much sign of wasteful living here.

Through its open door, I had a glimpse of the inside of a cabin in the hollow below us. It was divided into two rooms, one of them the bedroom with two beds in it. These two beds took up about all the available space in the room and it must have been necessary to leave the door open for air. There was a pad which looked rather like the cotton mattresses that have been made on WPA [Works Progress Administration], and a quilt neatly over each bed. I didn't notice any sheets or pillows.

There has been rain down here and the fields look in good condition. We passed a man plowing in a field with two women not far away hoeing. Beyond, in a grove of trees, there stood a stately house and under the trees was a baby carriage. I caught sight of someone in a flowered dress sitting on the porch. Then I again saw a yard of an unpainted house in the outskirts of a small town and a happy looking woman rocking a baby on the porch while a group of youngsters played in the yard. Happiness may exist under all conditions, given the right kind of people and sufficient economic security for adequate food and shelter.

Rochelle Chadakoff, ed., *Eleanor Roosevelt's My Day: Her Acclaimed Columns, 1936–1945* (New York: Pharos Books, 1989), pp. 119–120. Reprinted by permission of UFS, Inc.

relief for the unemployed, and sweeping reform to ward off future depressions. All concurred that the first step was to save the banks. By the eve of the inauguration governors in 38 states had temporarily closed their banks to stem the withdrawal of deposits. Without a sound credit structure, there could be no recovery.

On March 5, the day after his inauguration, Roosevelt ordered every bank in the country closed for four days. He shrewdly called it a "bank holiday." On March 9, the president introduced emergency banking legislation. The House passed the measure, sight unseen, and the Senate endorsed it later in the day. Roosevelt signed it that night.

Rather than nationalizing the banks as radicals wanted, the Emergency Banking Act followed the modest course of extending federal assistance to them.

Emergency Banking Act — Sound banks would reopen immediately with government support. Troubled banks would be handed over to federal "conservators," who would guide them to solvency. On Sunday, March 12, Roosevelt explained what was happening in the first of his many informal "fireside-chat" radio broadcasts. When banks reopened the next day, deposits exceeded withdrawals.

To guard against another stock crash, financial reforms gave government greater authority to manage the currency and regulate stock transactions. In April 1933, Roosevelt dropped the gold standard and began experimenting with the value of the dollar to boost prices. Later that spring the Glass–Steagall Banking Act restricted speculation by banks and, more important, created federal insurance for bank deposits of up to $2500. Under the

Federal Deposit Insurance — Federal Deposit Insurance Corporation, fewer banks failed for the rest of the decade than in the best year of the 1920s. The Securities Exchange Act (1934) established a new federal agency, the Securities and Exchange Commission, to oversee the stock market.

Relief for the Unemployed

Saving the banks and financial markets meant little if human suffering could not be relieved. Mortgage relief for the millions who had lost their homes came eventually in 1934 in the Home Owners' Loan Act. But the urgent need to alleviate starvation led Roosevelt to propose a bold new giveaway program. The Federal Emergency Relief Administration (FERA) opened its door in May 1933. Sitting amid unpacked boxes, gulping coffee and chain-smoking, former social worker Harry Hopkins spent $5 million of a $500 million appropriation in his first two hours as head of the new agency. In its two-year existence, FERA furnished more than $1 billion in grants to states, local areas, and private charities.

As the winter of 1933–1934 approached, Hopkins persuaded Roosevelt to expand relief with an innovative shift from government giveaways to a

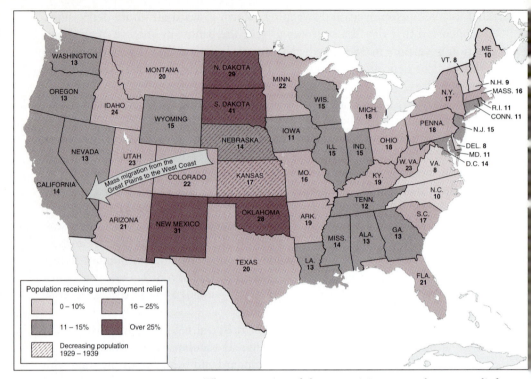

UNEMPLOYMENT RELIEF, 1934   The percentage of those receiving unemployment relief differed markedly throughout the nation. The farm belt of the plains was especially hard-hit, with 41 percent of South Dakota's citizens receiving federal benefits. In the East, the percentage dropped as low as 8 percent in some states.

Work relief work program. Paying someone "to do something socially useful," Hopkins explained, "preserves a man's morale." The Civil Works Administration (CWA) employed 4 million Americans. Alarmed at the high cost of the program, Roosevelt disbanded the CWA in the spring of 1934. It nonetheless furnished a new weapon against unemployment and an important precedent for future relief programs.

Another work relief program established in 1933 proved even more creative. The Civilian Conservation Corps (CCC) was Roosevelt's pet project. It combined his concern for conservation with compassion for youth. The CCC took unmarried 18- to 25-year-olds from relief rolls and sent them into the woods and fields to plant trees, build parks, and fight soil erosion. During its 10 years, the CCC provided 2.5 million young men with jobs (which prompted some critics to chant, "Where's the she, she, she?").

New Dealers intended relief programs to last only through the crisis. But the Tennessee Valley Authority (TVA)—a massive public works project created

Tennessee Valley Authority in 1933—made a continuing contribution to regional planning. For a decade, planners had dreamed of transforming the flood-ridden basin of the Tennessee River, one of the poorest areas of the country, with a program of regional development and social engineering. The TVA constructed a series of dams along the seven-state basin to control flooding, improve navigation, and generate cheap electric power. In cooperation with state and local officials, it also launched social programs to stamp out malaria, provide library bookmobiles, and create recreational lakes.

Like many New Deal programs, the TVA produced a mixed legacy. It saved 3 million acres from erosion, multiplied the average income in the valley ten-fold, and repaid its original investment in federal taxes. Its cheap electricity helped to bring down the rates of private utility companies. But the experiment in regional planning also pushed thousands of families from their land, failed to end poverty, and created an agency that became one of the worst polluters in the country.

The Riddle of Recovery

Planning, not just for regions but for the whole economy, seemed to many New Dealers the key to recovery. Some held that if businesses were allowed to plan and cooperate with one another, the ruthless competition that was driving down prices, wages, and employment could be controlled and the riddle of recovery solved. Business leaders had been urging such a course since 1931. In June 1933, under the National Industrial Recovery Act (NIRA), Roosevelt put planning to work for industry.

The legislation created two new agencies. The Public Works Administration (PWA) was designed to boost industrial activity and consumer spending with a *Public Works Administration* $3.3 billion public works program. The companies put under contract and unemployed workers hired would help stimulate the economy and leave a legacy of capital improvement. Harold Ickes, the prickly interior secretary who headed PWA, built the Triborough Bridge and Lincoln Tunnel in New York, the port city of Brownsville, Texas, and two aircraft carriers. But he was so fearful of waste and corruption that he never spent funds quickly enough to jumpstart the economy.

A second federal agency, the National Recovery Administration (NRA), aimed directly at controlling competition. Under NRA chief Hugh Johnson, *National Recovery Administration* representatives from government and business (and also from labor and consumer groups) drew up "codes of fair practices." Industry by industry, the codes established minimum prices, minimum wages, and maximum hours. No company could seek a competitive edge by cutting prices or wages below certain levels or by working a few employees mercilessly and firing the rest. It also required business to accept key demands of labor, including union rights to organize and bargain with management (thus ensuring that if prices jumped, so too might wages). And each code promised improved working conditions and outlawed such practices as child labor and sweatshops.

No business was forced to comply, for New Dealers feared that such government coercion might be ruled unconstitutional. The NRA relied on voluntary participation. A publicity campaign of parades, posters, and public pledges exhorted businesses to join the NRA and consumers to buy only NRA-sanctioned products. More than 2 million employers eventually signed up. In store windows and on merchandise, shiny decals with blue-eagle crests alerted customers that "We Do Our Part."

The NRA in Trouble

For all the hoopla, the NRA failed to bring recovery. Big businesses shaped the codes to their advantage. Often they limited production and raised prices, sometimes beyond what they normally had been. Not all businesses joined, and those that did often found the codes too complicated or costly to follow. The NRA tried to cover too many businesses, and its relatively few inspectors had trouble keeping up with all the complaints. Even NRA support for labor tottered, for it had no means of enforcing its guarantee of union rights. Business survived under the NRA, but without increasing production there was no incentive for expansion and new investment. Under such conditions hard times could last indefinitely. And in the short run, despite an enthusiastic start, the NRA was soon spawning little but evasion and criticism.

On May 27, 1935, the Supreme Court struck down the floundering NRA in *Schecter Poultry Corp. v. United States*. The justices unanimously ruled that the NRA had exceeded federal power over commerce among the states by regulating the Schecter brothers' poultry business in New York. Privately Roosevelt was relieved to be rid of the NRA. But he and other New Dealers were plainly shaken by the grounds of the decision. They were relying on a broad view of the commerce clause to fight the Depression. Their distress only grew when Justice Benjamin Cardozo added a chilling afterthought: the NRA's code making represented "an unconstitutional delegation of legislative power" to the executive branch. Without the ability to make rules and regulations, all the executive agencies of the New Deal might flounder.

Planning for Agriculture

As with planning for industry, New Deal planning for agriculture relied on private interests—the farmers—to act as the principal planners. Under the Agricultural Adjustment Act of 1933, farmers limited their own production. The government, in turn, paid them for not producing, while a tax on millers, cotton ginners, and other processors financed the payments. In theory, production quotas would reduce surpluses, demand for farm commodities would rise (as would prices), and agriculture would recover.

In practice the Agricultural Adjustment Administration (AAA) did help to increase prices. Unlike the code-ridden NRA, the AAA wisely confined cover-age to seven basic commodities. As a way to push prices even higher, the new Commodity Credit Corporation gave loans to farmers who stored their crops rather than sold them—a revival of the Populists' old subtreasury plan (see page 566). Farm income rose from $5.5 billion in 1932 to $8.7 billion in 1935.

Agricultural Adjustment Administration

Not all the gains in farm income were the result of government actions or free from problems. In the mid-1930s dust storms, droughts, and floods helped to reduce harvests and push up prices. The AAA, moreover, failed to distribute its benefits equally. Large landowners controlled decisions over which plots would be left fallow. In the South this frequently meant cutting the acreage of tenants and sharecroppers or forcing them out. Even when they reduced the acreage that they themselves plowed, big farmers could increase yields, since they had the money and equipment to cultivate more intensively.

In 1936 the Supreme Court voided the Agricultural Adjustment Act. In *Butler v. U.S.*, the six-justice majority concluded that the government had no right to regulate agriculture, either by limiting production or by taxing proces-sors. A hastily drawn replacement, the Soil Conservation and Domestic Allotment Act (1936), addressed the complaints. Farmers were now subsidized for practicing "conservation"—taking soil-depleting crops off the land—and paid from general revenues instead of a special tax. A second Agricultural Adjustment Act in 1938 returned production quotas.

Other agencies tried to help impoverished farmers. The Farm Credit Administration refinanced about a fifth of all farm mortgages. In 1935 the Resettlement Administration gave marginal farmers a fresh start by moving them to better land. Beginning in 1937 the Farm Security Administration fur-nished low-interest loans to help tenants buy family farms. In neither case did the rural poor have enough political clout to obtain sufficient funds from Congress. Fewer than 5000 families of a projected 500,000 were resettled, and less than 2 percent of tenant farmers received loans.

A SECOND NEW DEAL (1935–1936)

"Boys—this is our hour," crowed the president's closest advisor, Harry Hopkins, in the spring of 1935. A year earlier voters had broken precedent by returning the party in power to office, giving the Democrats their largest majorities in decades. With the presidential election of 1936 only a year away, Hopkins fig-ured that time was short: "We've got to get everything we want—a works pro-gram, social security, wages and hours, everything—now or never."

Hopkins calculated correctly. In 1935 politics, swept along by a torrent of protest, led to a "second hundred days" of lawmaking and a "Second New Deal." The emphasis shifted from planning and cooperation with business to greater regulation of business, broader relief, and bolder reform.

Voices of Protest

In 1934 a mob of 6000 stormed the Minneapolis city hall, demanding more relief and higher pay for government jobs. In San Francisco longshoremen walked off the job, setting off a citywide strike. By year's end, 1.5 million workers had joined in 1800 strikes. Conditions were improving but not quickly enough, and across the country voices of protest gathered strength.

From the right came the charges of a few wealthy business executives and conservatives that Roosevelt was an enemy of private property and a dictator in

Liberty League

the making. In August 1934 they founded the American Liberty League. Despite spending $1 million in anti-New Deal advertising, the League won little support and only helped to convince the president that cooperation with business was failing.

In California discontented voters took over the Democratic party and turned sharply to the left by nominating novelist Upton Sinclair, a Socialist, for

End Poverty in California

governor. Running under the slogan "End Poverty in California" (EPIC), Sinclair proposed to confiscate idle factories and land and permit the unemployed to produce for their own use. Republicans mounted a no-holds-barred counterattack, including fake newsreels depicting Sinclair as a Bolshevik, atheist, and free-lover. Sinclair lost the election but won nearly 1 million votes.

Huey P. Long, the flamboyant senator from Louisiana, had ridden to power on a wave of rural discontent against banks, corporations, and political ma-

Huey Long

chines. As governor of Louisiana, he pushed through reforms regulating utilities, building roads and schools, even distributing free school books. Opponents called him a "dictator"; most Louisianans simply called him the "Kingfish." Breaking with Roosevelt in 1933, Long pledged to bring about recovery by making "every man a king." "Share Our Wealth" was a drastic but simple plan: the government would limit the size of all fortunes and confiscate the rest. Every family would then be guaranteed an annual income of $2500 and an estate of $5000, enough to buy a house, an automobile, and a radio (over which Long had already built a national following).

By 1935, one year after its founding, Long's Share Our Wealth organization boasted 27,000 clubs with files containing nearly 8 million names. Democratic National Committee members shuddered at polls showing that Long might capture up to 4 million votes in 1936, enough to put a Republican in the White House. But late in 1935, in the corridors of the Louisiana capitol, Long was shot to death by a disgruntled constituent whose family had been wronged by the Long political machine.

Louisiana Governor and Senator Huey
Long promised to "make every man a
king," but critics predicted that only
Long would wear a crown. The "Kingfish"
(a nickname taken from the "Amos 'n'
Andy" radio show) made no secret
of his presidential ambitions.

Father Charles Coughlin was Long's urban counterpart. Where Long explained the Depression as the result of bloated fortunes, Coughlin blamed the banks. In weekly broadcasts from the Shrine of the Little Flower in suburban Detroit, the "Radio Priest" told his working-class, largely Catholic audience of the international bankers who had toppled the world economy by manipulating gold-backed currencies.

Charles Coughlin

Coughlin promised to end the Depression with simple strokes: nationalizing banks, inflating the currency with silver, spreading work. (None would have worked because each would have dampened investment, the key to recovery.) Across the urban North, 30 to 40 million Americans—the largest audience in the world—huddled around their radios to listen. In 1934 Coughlin organized the National Union for Social Justice to pressure both parties. As the election of 1936 approached, the Union loomed on the political horizon.

A less ominous challenge came from Dr. Francis Townsend. The 67-year-old physician had recently retired in California from the public health service. Moved by the plight of elderly Americans without pension plans or medical insurance, Townsend set up Old Age Revolving Pensions, Limited, in 1934. He proposed to have the government pay $200 a month to those 60 years or older who quit their jobs and spent

Francis Townsend

the money within 30 days. By 1936 Townsend clubs counted 3.5 million members, most of them small businessmen and farmers at or beyond retirement age.

For all their differences, Sinclair, Long, Coughlin, Townsend, and other critics struck similar chords. Although the solutions they proposed were simplistic, the problems they addressed were serious: a maldistribution of goods and wealth, inadequacies in the money supply, the plight of the elderly. They attacked the growing control of corporations, banks, and government over individuals and communities. And they created mass political movements based on social as well as economic dissatisfaction. When Sinclair supporters pledged to produce for their own use and Long's followers swore to "share our wealth," when Coughlinites damned the "monied interests" and Townsendites thumped their Bibles at foul-ups in Washington, they were also trying to protect their freedom and their communities from the intrusion of big business and big government.

The Second Hundred Days

By the spring of 1935, the forces of discontent were pushing Roosevelt to more action. And so was Congress. With Democrats accounting for more than two-thirds of both houses, they were prepared to outspend the president in extending the New Deal. The 100 days from April through mid-July, the "second hundred days," produced a legislative barrage that moved the New Deal toward Roosevelt's ultimate destination—"a little to the left of center."

To help the many Americans who were still jobless Roosevelt proposed the Emergency Relief Appropriation Act of 1935, with a record $4.8 billion for relief and employment. Some of the money went to the new National Youth

Works Progress Administration Administration (NYA) for more than 4.5 million jobs for young people. But the lion's share went to the new Works Progress Administration (WPA), where Harry Hopkins mounted the largest work relief program in history. Before its end in 1943, the WPA employed at least 8.5 million people and built or improved over 100,000 schools, post offices, and other public buildings. Constrained from competing with private industry and committed to spending 80 percent of his budget on wages, Hopkins showed remarkable ingenuity. WPA workers taught art classes in a Cincinnati mental hospital, drafted a Braille map for the blind in Massachusetts, and pulled a library by packhorse through the hills of Kentucky.

The ambitious Social Security Act, passed in 1935, sought to help those who could not help themselves: the aged poor, the infirm, dependent children.

Social security In this commitment to the destitute—which the Roosevelt administration believed were actually few in number—it laid the groundwork for the modern welfare state. But social security also acted as an economic stabilizer by furnishing pensions for retirees and insurance for those suddenly laid off from their jobs. A payroll tax on both employer and employee underwrote pensions after age 65, while an employer-financed system of insurance made possible government payments to unemployed workers.

Social security marked a historic reversal in American political values. A new social contract between the government and the people replaced the gospel of self-help and the older policies of laissez faire. At last government acknowledged a broad responsibility to protect the social rights of citizens. The welfare state, foreshadowed in the aid given veterans and their families after the Civil War, was institutionalized, though its coverage was limited. To win the votes of southern Congressmen hostile to African Americans, the legislation excluded farmworkers and domestic servants, doubtless among the neediest Americans but often black and disproportionately southern.

Roosevelt had hoped for social insurance that would cover Americans "from cradle to grave." Congress whittled down his plan, but its labor legislation pushed the president well beyond his goal of providing paternalistic aid for workers, like establishing pension plans and unemployment insurance. New York senator Robert Wagner, the son of a janitor, wanted workers to fight their own battles. In 1933 he had included union recognition in the NRA. When the Supreme Court killed the NRA in 1935, Wagner introduced what became the

National Labor Relations Act National Labor Relations Act. (So important had labor support become to Roosevelt that he gave the bill his belated blessing.) The "Wagner Act" created a National Labor Relations Board (NLRB) to supervise the election of unions and ensure union rights to bargain. Most vital, the NLRB had the power to enforce these policies. By 1941, the number of unionized workers had doubled.

Roosevelt responded to the growing hostility of business by turning against the wealthy and powerful in 1935. The popularity of Long's tirades against the rich and Coughlin's against banks sharpened his points of attack. The Revenue Act of 1935 (called the "Wealth Tax Act") threatened to "soak the rich." By the time it worked its way through Congress, however, it levied only moderate taxes on high incomes and inheritances. The Banking Act of 1935 centralized authority over the money market in the Federal Reserve Board. By controlling interest rates and the money supply, government increased its ability to compensate for swings in the economy. The Public Utilities Holding Company Act (1935) limited the size of utility empires. Long the target of progressive reformers, the giant holding companies produced nothing but higher profits for speculators and higher prices for consumers. Diluted like the wealth tax, the utility law was still a political victory for New Dealers. "I am now on your bandwagon again," a Philadelphia voter told the president as the election of 1936 approached.

The Election of 1936

In June of 1936 Roosevelt traveled to Philadelphia, not to thank the loyal voter who had hopped aboard his bandwagon but to accept the Democratic nomination for a second term as president. "This generation of Americans has a rendezvous with destiny," he told a crowd of 100,000 packed into Franklin Field.

Whatever destiny had in store for his generation, Roosevelt knew that the coming election would turn on a single issue: "It's myself, and people must be either for me or against me."

Roosevelt ignored his Republican opponent, Governor Alfred Landon of Kansas. Despite a bulging campaign chest of $14 million, Landon lacked luster as well as issues. He favored the regulation of business, a balanced budget, and much of the New Deal. For his part Roosevelt turned the election into a contest between haves and have-nots. The forces of "organized money are unanimous in their hate for me," he told a roaring crowd at New York's Madison Square Garden, "and I welcome their hatred."

The strategy deflated Republicans, discredited conservatives, and stole the thunder of the newly formed Union Party of Townsendites, Coughlinites, and old Long supporters. The election returns shocked even experienced observers. Roosevelt won the largest electoral victory ever—523 to 8—and a whopping 60.8 percent of the popular vote. The margin of victory came from those at the bottom of the economic ladder, grateful for help furnished by the New Deal.

A dramatic political realignment was now clearly in place, as important as the Republican rise to power in 1896. The Democrats reigned as the new majority party for the next 30 years. The "Roosevelt coalition"
Roosevelt coalition
rested on three pillars: traditional Democratic support in the South; the big cities, particularly ethnics and African Americans; and labor, both organized and unorganized. The minority Republicans became the party of big business and small towns.

THE NEW DEAL AND THE AMERICAN PEOPLE

Before 1939, farmers in the Hill Country of Texas spent their evenings in the light of 25-watt kerosene lamps. Their wives washed eight loads of laundry a week, all by hand. Every day they hauled home 200 gallons—about 1500 pounds—of water from nearby wells. Farms had no milking machines, no washers, no automatic pumps or water heaters, no refrigerators, and no radios. "Living—just living—was a problem," recalled one woman.

The reason for this limited life was simple: the Hill Country had no electricity. Thus no agency of the Roosevelt administration changed the way people lived more dramatically than the Rural Electrification
Rural Electrification Administration
Administration (REA), created in 1935. At the time less than 10 percent of American farms had electricity. Six years later 40 percent did, and by 1950, 90 percent. The New Deal did not always have such a marked impact. And its overall record was mixed. But time and again it changed the lives of ordinary people as government never had before.

The New Deal and Western Water

In September 1936, President Roosevelt pushed a button in Washington, D.C., and sent electricity pulsing westward from the towering Boulder Dam in Colorado to cities as far away as Los Angeles. The waters thus diverted irrigated 2.5 million acres, while the dam's floodgates protected millions of people in southern California, Nevada, and Arizona. In its water management programs, the New Deal further extended federal power, literally across the country.

Boulder Dam was one of several multipurpose dams completed under the New Deal in the arid West. The aim was simple: to control whole river systems for regional use. Buchanan Dam on the lower Colorado River, the Bonneville and Grand Coulee dams on the Columbia, and many smaller versions curbed floods, generated cheap electricity, and developed river basins from Texas to Washington state. Beginning in 1938, the All-American Canal diverted the Colorado River to irrigate the Imperial Valley in California.

The environmental price of such rewards soon became evident, as it did with the New Deal's experiment in eastern water use, the Tennessee Valley Authority. The once mighty Columbia River, its surging waters checked by dams, flowed sedately from man-made lake to lake, but without the salmon whose spawning runs were also checked. Blocked by the All-American Canal from its path to the sea, the Colorado River slowly turned salty, until by 1950 its waters were unfit for drinking or irrigation.

The Limited Reach of the New Deal

In the spring of 1939, the Daughters of the American Revolution refused to permit the black contralto Marian Anderson to sing at Constitution Hall in Washington, D.C. Eleanor Roosevelt quit the DAR in protest, and Secretary of the Interior Harold Ickes began looking for another site. On a nippy Easter Sunday, in the shadow of the Lincoln Memorial, Anderson finally stepped to the microphone and sang to a crowd of 7500. Lincoln himself would not have missed the irony.

In 1932 most African Americans cast their ballots as they had since Reconstruction—for Republicans, the party of Abraham Lincoln and emanci-

African Americans

pation. But disenchantment with decades of broken promises was spreading, and by 1934 African Americans were voting for Democrats. "Let Jesus lead you and Roosevelt feed you," a black preacher told his congregation on the eve of the 1936 election. When the returns were counted, three of four black voters had cast their ballots for Roosevelt.

The New Deal accounted for this voting revolution. Sympathetic but never a champion, Roosevelt regarded African Americans as one of many groups whose interests he brokered. Even that was an improvement. Federal offices had been segregated since Woodrow Wilson's day, and in the 1920s black leaders

California's multiethnic workforce is depicted in this detail from Paul Langley Howard's *California Industrial Scenes*. It was one of several murals painted on the walls of San Francisco's Coit Tower. The murals were begun in 1934 as a New Deal relief program for artists.

called Hoover "the man in the lily-White House." Under Roosevelt racial integration slowly returned to government. Supporters of civil rights like Eleanor Roosevelt and Secretary of the Interior Ickes brought political scientist Clark Foreman, economist Robert C. Weaver, and other black advisers into the administration. Mary McLeod Bethune, a sharecropper's daughter and founder of Bethune–Cookman College, ran a division of the National Youth Administration. Important as both symbols and activists, African American administrators created a "Black Cabinet" to help design federal policy.

Outside of government the Urban League continued to lobby for economic advancement, and the NAACP pressed to make lynching a federal crime. (Though publicly against lynching and privately in favor of an antilynching bill, Roosevelt refused to make it "must" legislation to avoid losing the white southern members of Congress he needed "to save America.") In New York's Harlem, Reverend John H. Johnson organized the Citizens' League for Fair Play in 1933 to persuade white merchants to hire black clerks. After picketers blocked storefronts, hundreds of African Americans got jobs with Harlem retailers and utility companies. Racial tension over employment and housing continued to run high, and in 1935 Harlem exploded in the only race riot of the decade.

Discrimination persisted under the New Deal. Black newspapers reported hundreds of cases of NRA codes resulting in jobs lost to white workers or wages lower than white rates of pay. Disgusted editors renamed the agency "Negroes Ruined Again." Federal efforts to promote "grass-roots democracy" often gave control of New Deal programs to local governments, where discrimination went unchallenged. New Deal showplaces like the TVA's model town of Norris, Tennessee, and the homestead village of Arthurdale, West Virginia, were closed to African Americans.

African Americans reaped a few benefits from the New Deal. The WPA hired black workers for almost 20 percent of its jobs, even though African Americans made up less than 10 percent of the population. When it was discovered that the WPA was paying black workers less than whites, Roosevelt issued an executive order to halt the practice. Public Works Administrator Ickes established the first quota system for hiring black Americans. By 1941 the percentage of African Americans working for the government exceeded their proportion of the population.

Civil rights never became a serious aspect of the New Deal, but for the nearly 1 million Mexican Americans in the United States, Latino culture some-

Mexican Americans

times frustrated meager federal efforts to help. Mexican folk traditions of self-help inhibited some from seeking aid; others remained unfamiliar with claim procedures. Still others failed to meet residency requirements. Meanwhile, low voter turnout hampered their political influence, and discrimination limited economic advancement.

In the Southwest and California, the Civilian Conservation Corps and the Works Progress Administration furnished some jobs, though fewer and for less pay than average. On Capitol Hill, Dennis Chavez of New Mexico, the only Mexican American in the Senate, channeled what funds he could into Spanish-speaking communities. But like African Americans, most Latinos remained mired in poverty. The many Mexican Americans who worked the fields as migratory laborers lay outside the reach of most New Deal programs.

Tribal Rights

The New Deal renewed federal interest in Indians. Among the most disadvantaged Americans, Indian families on reservations rarely earned more than $100 a year. Their infant mortality rate was the highest in the country; their life expectancy, the shortest; their education level—usually no more than five years—the lowest. Their rate of unemployment was three times the national average.

In the 1930s, Indians had no stronger friend in Washington than John Collier. For years he had fought as a social worker among the Pueblos to

John Collier and Indians

restore tribal culture. As the new commissioner of Indian affairs, he reversed the decades-old policy of assimilation and promoted tribal life. Under the Indian Reorganization Act of 1934, elders were urged to celebrate festivals, artists to work in native styles, children to learn the old languages. A special Court of Indian Affairs removed Indians from state jurisdiction, and tribal governments ruled reservations. Perhaps most important, tribes regained control over Indian land. Since the Dawes Act of 1887, the land had been allotted to individual Indians, who were often forced by poverty to sell to whites. By the end of the 1930s, Indian landholding had increased.

Indians split over Collier's policies. The Pueblos, with a strong communal spirit and already functioning communal societies, favored them. The tribes of Oklahoma and the Great Plains tended to oppose them. Individualism, the profit motive, and an unwillingness to share property with other tribe members fed resistance. So did age-old suspicion of all government programs. And some Indians genuinely desired assimilation. The Navajos, under the leadership of J. C. Morgan, rejected the Indian Reorganization Act in 1935. Morgan saw tribal government as a step backward.

A New Deal for Women

As the tides of change rippled across the country, a new deal for women was unfolding in Washington. The New Deal's welfare agencies offered unprecedented opportunity for social workers, teachers, and other women who had spent their lives helping the downtrodden. They were already experts on social welfare. Several were friends with professional ties, and together they formed a network of activists in the New Deal promoting women's interests and social reform. Led by Eleanor Roosevelt and Labor Secretary Frances Perkins, women served on the consumers' advisory board of the NRA, helped to administer the relief program, and won appointments to the Social Security Board.

In growing numbers women became part of the Democratic party machinery. Under the leadership of social worker Mary W. "Molly" Dewson, the Women's Division of the Democratic National Committee played a critical role in the election. Thousands of women mounted a "mouth-to-mouth" campaign, traveling from door to door to drum up support for Roosevelt and other Democrats. When the ballots were tallied, women formed an important part of the new Roosevelt coalition.

Federal appointments and party politics broke new ground for women, but in general the New Deal abided by existing social standards. Gender equality,

Progress limited

like racial equality, was never high on its agenda. One-quarter of all NRA codes permitted women to be paid less than men, while WPA wages averaged $2 a day more for men. The New Deal gave relatively few jobs to women, and when it did, they were often in gender-segregated trades such as sewing. Government employment patterns for women fell below even those in the private sector. The WPA hired nearly half a million women in 1936, roughly 15 percent of all WPA workers, at a time when women constituted almost a quarter of the workforce.

Reflecting old conceptions of reform, New Dealers placed greater emphasis on aiding and protecting women than on employing them. The Federal Emergency Relief Administration built 17 camps for homeless women in 11 states. Social security furnished subsidies to mothers with dependent children, and the WPA established emergency nursery schools (which also became the government's first foray into early childhood education). But even federal protection fell short. Social security, for example, did not cover domestic servants, most of whom were women.

The Rise of Organized Labor

Although women and minorities discovered that the New Deal had limits to the changes it promoted, a powerful union movement arose in the 1930s by taking full advantage of the new climate. It ended up pushing Roosevelt well beyond

In San Antonio, Texas, Mexican American pecan shellers worked a 54-hour week for only $3. In 1938 they struck for better wages and working conditions. Here Emma Tenayuca, one of their leaders, addresses a group of striking workers.

his limits. At the outset of the Depression barely 6 percent of the labor force belonged to unions. The nation's premier union, the American Federation of Labor (AFL), was historically bound to skilled labor and organized on the basis of craft or skill. It virtually ignored the unskilled workers who made up most of the industrial labor force by the 1930s. Thus the AFL avoided major industries like rubber, automobiles, and steel.

John L. Lewis fought to unionize unskilled laborers. Tough, charismatic, and practical, Lewis headed the United Mine Workers (UMW), an affiliate of the AFL. When he met with Roosevelt in 1933, he received little more than consolation for his shrinking union. Yet the shrewd Lewis returned to the coal fields with a message the president had never given him: "The president wants you to join a union." Within a year the UMW had 400,000 members. Raising his sights, Lewis called for the creation of a Steel Workers' Organizing Committee (SWOC) and for the admission of the United Auto Workers into the AFL.

At the annual AFL convention in Atlantic City in 1935, Lewis demanded a commitment to the "industrial organization of mass production workers." The delegates, mostly from craft unions, voted down the proposal. Near the end of the convention, as he passed "Big Bill" Hutcheson of the carpenters union, angry words passed between the two. Lewis spun and with a single punch sent Hutcheson sprawling in a bloody heap.

The blow signaled the determination of industrial unions to break the AFL's domination of organized labor. A few weeks later, Lewis and the heads of seven

Congress of Industrial Organizations

other AFL unions announced the formation of the Committee for Industrial Organization (CIO). The AFL suspended the rogue unions in 1936. The CIO, later rechristened the Congress of Industrial Organizations, turned to the unskilled.

Campaigns of the CIO

CIO representatives concentrated on the mighty steel industry, which had clung to the "open," or nonunion, shop since 1919. In other industries, the rank and file did not wait. Emboldened by the recent passage of the Wagner Act, a group

Sit-down strikes

of rubber workers in Akron, Ohio, simply sat down on the job in early 1936. Since the strikers occupied the plants, managers could not replace them with strikebreakers. Nor could the rubber companies call in the military or police without risk to their property. The leaders of the United Rubber Workers Union opposed the "sit-downs," but when the Goodyear Tire & Rubber Company laid off 70 workers, 1400 rubber workers struck on their own. An 11-mile picket line sprang up outside. Eventually Goodyear settled by recognizing the union and accepting its demands on wages and hours.

The biggest strikes erupted in the automobile industry. A series of spontaneous strikes at General Motors plants in Atlanta, Kansas City, and Cleveland spread to Fisher Body No. 2 in Flint, Michigan, late in December 1936. Singing the unionists' anthem, "Solidarity Forever," workers took over the plant while wives, friends, and fellow union members handed food and clothing through the windows. Local police tried to break up supply lines, only to be driven off by a hail of nuts, bolts, coffee mugs, and bottles.

In the wake of this "Battle of Running Bulls" (a reference to the retreating police), Governor Frank Murphy finally called out the National Guard, not to arrest but to protect strikers. General Motors surrendered in February 1937. Less than a month later U.S. Steel capitulated without a strike. By the end of the year every automobile manufacturer except Henry Ford had negotiated with the UAW.

Bloody violence accompanied some drives. On Memorial Day 1937, 10 strikers lost their lives when Chicago police fired on them as they marched peacefully toward the Republic Steel plant. And sit-down strikes often alienated an otherwise sympathetic middle class. (In 1939 the Supreme Court outlawed

Union gains

the tactic.) Yet a momentous transfer of power had taken place. By 1940 nearly one worker in three belonged to a union. The unskilled had a powerful voice in the CIO. And the craft unions of the AFL outnumbered them by more than a million. Women's membership in unions tripled between 1930 and 1940, and African Americans also made gains. Independent unions had become a significant part of industrial America.

Government played an important but secondary role in the industrial union movement by creating a hospitable environment for labor. Roosevelt courted workers, both organized and unorganized, but stood aside in the toughest labor battles. Yet doing nothing in favor of strikers was a vast improvement over the active hostility shown by earlier presidents. The Wagner Act afforded laborers an opportunity to organize and protection if they chose to request it, but nothing more. Leaders such as John L. Lewis, Walter Reuther of the United Auto Workers, and Philip Murray of the Steel Workers' Organizing Committee galvanized workers, who won their own victories.

"Art for the Millions"

No agency of the New Deal touched more Americans than Federal One, the bureaucratic umbrella of the WPA's arts program. For the first time, thousands of unemployed writers, musicians, painters, actors, and photographers went on the federal payroll. Public projects—from massive murals to tiny guidebooks—would make "art for the millions."

A Federal Writers Project (FWP) produced about a thousand publications. Its 81 state, territorial, and city guides were so popular that commercial pub-

Federal arts programs

lishers happily printed them. A Depression-bred interest in American history prompted the FWP to collect folklore, study ethnic groups, and record the reminiscences of 200 former slaves. Meanwhile, the Federal Music Project (FMP) employed some 15,000 out-of-work musicians. For a token charge, Americans could hear the music of Bach and Beethoven.

In the Federal Art Project (FAP), watercolorists and draftsmen painstakingly prepared the Index of American Design, which offered elaborate illustrations of American material culture, from skillets to cigar-store Indians. At night artists taught sculpture, painting, clay modeling, and carving in country churches, settlement houses, and schools. Jackson Pollock, Willem de Kooning, and others destined to become important painters survived the Depression by painting for the government.

The most notable contribution of the FAP came in the form of murals. Under the influence of Mexican muralists Diego Rivera and José Clemente

Muralists

Orozco, American artists covered the walls of thousands of airports, post offices, and other government buildings with wall paintings glorifying local life and work. The rare treatment of class conflict later opened the FAP to charges of communist infiltration, but most of the murals stressed the enduring qualities of American life: family, work, community.

The Federal Theater Project (FTP) reached the greatest number of people—some 30 million—and aroused the most controversy. As its head, Hallie Flanagan made government-supported theater vital, daring, and relevant. Living Newspapers dramatized headlines of the day. Under the direction of Orson Welles and John Houseman an all-black company (one of 16 "Negro Units") set Shakespeare's *Macbeth* in Haiti, with voodoo priestesses and African drummers. Occasionally frank depictions of class conflict riled congressional conservatives, and beginning in 1938, the House Un-American Activities Committee investigated the FTP as "a branch of the Communistic organization." A year later Congress slashed its budget and brought government-sponsored theater to an end.

The documentary impulse to record life permeated the arts in the 1930s. Novels such as Erskine Caldwell's *Tobacco Road*, feature films like John Ford's

Documentary realism

The Grapes of Wrath, and such federally funded documentaries as Pare Lorentz's *The River* stirred the social conscience of the country. New Dealers had practical motives for promoting documentary realism. They wanted to blunt criticism of New Deal relief measures by documenting the distress. In 1937 Rexford Tugwell established an Information Division in his Resettlement Administration. He put Roy Stryker, his former Columbia University teaching assistant, in charge of its Historical Section. Stryker hired talented photographers to produce an unvarnished record of the Great Depression. Their raw and haunting photographs turned history into both propaganda and art.

THE END OF THE NEW DEAL (1937–1940)

"I see one-third of a nation ill-housed, ill-clad, ill-nourished," the president lamented in his second inaugural address on January 20, 1937 (the first January inauguration under a new constitutional amendment). Industrial output had doubled since 1932; farm income had almost quadrupled. But full recovery remained elusive. Over 7 million Americans were still out of work, and national income was only half again as large as it had been in 1933, when Roosevelt took office. At the height of his popularity, with bulging majorities in Congress, Roosevelt planned to expand the New Deal. Within a year, however, the New Deal was largely over, drowned in a sea of economic and political troubles—many of them Roosevelt's own doing.

"Packing" the Courts

As Roosevelt's second term began, only the Supreme Court clouded the political horizon. In its first 76 years the Court had invalidated only two acts of Congress. Between 1920 and 1933 it struck down portions of 22 laws. This new judicial activism, spearheaded by a conservative majority, rested on a narrow view of the constitutional powers of Congress and the president. As the New Deal broadened those powers, the Supreme Court let loose a flood of nullifications.

In 1935 the Court wiped out the NRA on the grounds that manufacturing was not involved in interstate commerce and thus lay beyond federal regulation. In 1936 it canceled the AAA, reducing federal authority under the taxing power and the general welfare clause of the Constitution. In *Moorehead v. Tipaldo* (1936) the Court ruled that a New York minimum-wage law was invalid because it interfered with the right of workers to negotiate a contract. A frustrated Roosevelt complained that the Court had thereby created a " 'no-man's land,' where no government—State or Federal" could act.

Roosevelt was the first president since James Monroe to serve four years without making a Supreme Court appointment. Among federal judges Re-

Roosevelt's plan

publicans outnumbered Democrats by more than two to one in 1933. Roosevelt intended to redress the balance with legislation that added new judges to the federal bench, including the Supreme Court. The federal courts were overburdened and too many judges "aged or infirm," he declared in February 1937. In the interests of efficiency, said Roosevelt, he proposed to "vitalize" the judiciary with new members. When a 70-year-old judge who had served at least 10 years failed to retire, the president could add another, up to six to the Supreme Court and 44 to the lower federal courts.

Roosevelt badly miscalculated. He unveiled his plan without warning, expecting widespread support. He regarded courts as political, not sacred, institutions and had ample precedent for altering even the Supreme Court. (As recently as 1869 Congress had increased its size to nine.) But most Americans clung to the courts as symbols of stability. Few accepted Roosevelt's efficiency argument, and no one on Capitol Hill (with its share of 70-year-olds) believed that seven decades of life necessarily made one incompetent. Worse still, the proposal ignited conservative–liberal antagonisms within the Democratic party.

"Here's where I cash in my chips," declared the Democratic chairman of the House Judiciary Committee as he abandoned the President.

Suddenly the Court reversed itself. In April, *N.L.R.B. v. Jones and Laughlin Steel Corporation* upheld the Wagner Act by one vote. A month later the justices sustained the Social Security Act as a legitimate exercise of the commerce power. And when Justice Willis Van Devanter, the oldest and most conservative justice, retired later that year, Roosevelt at last made an appointment to the Supreme Court.

With Democrats deserting him, the president accepted a substitute measure that utterly ignored his proposal to appoint new judges. Roosevelt nonetheless claimed victory. After all, the Court shifted course (and eventually he appointed nine Supreme Court justices). But victory came at a high price. The momentum of the 1936 election was squandered, the unity of the Democratic party was destroyed, and opponents learned that Roosevelt could be beaten. A conservative coalition of Republicans and rural Democrats had come together around the first of several anti-New Deal causes.

The New Deal at Bay

As early as 1936 Secretary of the Treasury Henry Morgenthau began to plead for fiscal restraint. With productivity rising and unemployment falling, it was time to reduce spending, balance the budget, and let business lead the recovery. "Strip off the bandages, throw away the crutches," and let the economy "stand on its own feet," he said.

Morgenthau was preaching to the converted. Although the president had been willing to run budget deficits in a time of crisis, he had never been com-

John Maynard Keynes

fortable with them. To be sure, the British economist John Maynard Keynes had actually recommended the kind of deficit spending that Roosevelt had used. Keynes's startling theory called on government not to balance the budget but to spend its way out of depression. When prosperity returned, Keynes argued, government could pay off its debts through taxes. This deliberate policy of "countercyclical" action (spending in bad times, taxing in good) would compensate for swings in the economy.

For the present, however, Roosevelt ignored Keynes and ordered cuts in federal spending early in 1937. He slashed relief rolls by half and virtually halted spending on public works. Within six months, the economy collapsed. Industrial activity plummeted to 1935 levels. At the end of the year unemployment stood

Roosevelt recession

at 10.5 million as the "Roosevelt recession" deepened. Finally spenders convinced him to propose a $3.75 billion omnibus measure in April 1938. Facing an election, Congress happily reversed relief cuts, quadrupled farm subsidies, and embarked on a new shipbuilding program. The economy revived but never recovered. Keynesian economics was vindicated, though it would take decades before becoming widely accepted.

With Roosevelt vulnerable, conservatives in Congress struck. They cut back on public housing programs and minimum wage guarantees in the South. The president's successes came where he could act alone, principally in a renewed attack on big business. At his urging, the Justice Department opened investigations of corporate concentration. Even Congress responded by creating the Temporary National Economic Committee to examine corporate abuses and recommend revisions in the antitrust laws. These were small consolations. The president, wrote Interior Secretary Harold Ickes in August 1938, "is punch drunk from the punishment."

Vainly Roosevelt fought back. In the off-year elections of 1938, he tried to purge Democrats who had deserted him. The five senators he targeted for defeat all won. Republicans posted gains in the House and Senate and won 13 governorships. Democrats still held majorities in both houses, but conservatives had the votes to block new programs. With the economy limping toward recovery, the New Deal passed into history, and the nation turned to a new crisis: a looming war abroad.

The Legacy of the New Deal

The New Deal lasted only five years, from 1933 to 1938, and it never spent enough to end the Depression. Though it pledged itself to the "forgotten" Americans, it failed the neediest among them: sharecroppers, tenant farmers, migrant workers. In many ways, it was quite conservative. It left capitalism intact, even strengthened, and it overturned few cultural conventions. Even its reforms followed the old progressive formula of softening industrialism by strengthening the state.

Yet for all its conservatism and continuities, the New Deal left a legacy of change. Under it, government assumed a broader role in the economy than progressives had ever undertaken. To regulation was now added the complicated task of maintaining economic stability—compensating for swings in the business cycle. In its securities and banking regulations, unemployment insurance, and requirements for wages and hours, the New Deal created stabilizers to avoid future breakdowns. Bolstering the Federal Reserve system and enhancing control over credit strengthened government influence over the economy.

Franklin Roosevelt modernized the presidency. He turned the White House into the heart of government, the place where decisions were made. Americans looked to the president to set the public agenda, spread new ideas, initiate legislation, and assume responsibility for the nation. The power of Congress diminished, but the scope of government grew. In 1932 there were 605,000 federal employees; by 1939 there were nearly a million (and by 1945, after World War II, some 3.5 million). The many programs of the New Deal—home loans, farm subsidies, bank deposit insurance, relief payments and jobs, pension programs, unemployment insurance, aid to mothers with dependent children—

WHAT THE NEW DEAL DID. . .

	RELIEF	RECOVERY	REFORM
FOR THE FARMER:	Rural Electrification Administration (1936) Farm Security Administration (1937)	Agriculture Adjustment Act (1933)	
FOR THE WORKER:		National Industrial Recovery Act (1933)	National Labor Relations Act (1935) Fair Labor Standards Act (1938)
FOR THE MIDDLE CLASS:	Home Owner's Loan Act (1934)		Revenue ("Wealth Tax") Act (1935) Public Utilities Holding Company Act (1935)
FOR THE NEEDY:	Federal Emergency Relief Act (1933) Civilian Conservation Corp (1933) Civil Works Administration (1933) Emergency Relief Appropriation Act (1935) National Public Housing Act (1937)		
FOR PROTECTION AGAINST FUTURE DEPRESSIONS:			Federal Deposit Insurance Corporation (1933) Securities Exchange Act (1934) Social Security Act (1935)

touched the lives of ordinary Americans, made them more secure, bolstered the middle class, and formed the outlines of the new welfare state.

The welfare state had limits. Most of its relief measures were designed to last no longer than the crisis. Millions fell through even its more nearly permanent safety nets. Yet the commitment to furnishing minimum standards of life, not the failure to do so, marked a change so dramatic that the poor and working class threw their support to Roosevelt. He was, after all, the first president to try.

At a time when dictators and militarists took hold in Germany, Italy, Japan, and Russia, the New Deal strengthened democracy in America. Roosevelt acted as a democratic broker, responding first to one group, then another. And his "broker state" embraced groups previously spurned: unions, farm organizations, ethnic minorities, women. In short, during the 1930s the United States found a middle way avoiding the extremes of communism and fascism. Still, the broker state also had limits. The unorganized, whether in city slums or in share-croppers' shacks, too often found themselves ignored.

Under the New Deal, the Democratic party became a mighty force in politics. In a quiet revolution, African Americans came into the party's fold, as did workers and farmers. Political attention shifted to bread-and-butter issues. In 1932 people had argued about Prohibition and European war debts. By 1935 they were debating social security, labor relations, tax reform, public housing, and the TVA. With remarkable speed, the New Deal had become a vital part of American life.

COUNTERPOINT   *Assessing the New Deal*

Historians disagree sharply in assessing the New Deal. We have taken the view, shared by many liberal historians, that the New Deal was not radical or socialistic but fell within the American political tradition of pragmatic reform. Historians of the New Left, a group of radical scholars writing in the 1960s, attacked the New Deal for being too conservative and thus failing to aid those most in need—sharecroppers, for example. Instead, they say, New Dealers ended up preserving the inequities of corporate capitalism.

Other scholars have defended the New Deal, noting the obstacles faced by reformers. Some stress the absence of "state capacity," a bureaucracy of necessary size and expertise to carry out the New Deal's massive programs. Others emphasize political constraints: Congress, the Supreme Court, and the public, all of which manifested concern at one time or another over the growth of government. Still others point out that New Dealers themselves were often skeptical about growing deficits, expanding government, and mounting welfare initiatives.

SIGNIFICANT EVENTS

1933 — Franklin Roosevelt inaugurated as president; first "100 days" launched; "bank holiday"; repeal of Eighteenth Amendment (Prohibition); Townsend movement begins

1934 — Securities and Exchange Commission; American Liberty League; Indian Reorganization Act; Father Charles Coughlin creates National Union for Social Justice; Huey Long organizes Share Our Wealth Society

1935 — Emergency Relief Appropriation Act; Rural Electrification Administration authorized; *Schecter Poultry Corp. v. United States* invalidates National Recovery Administration; "second hundred days" legislation passed; Huey Long assassinated

1936 — *Butler v. U.S.* ends Agricultural Adjustment Administration; Soil Conservation and Domestic Allotment Act; Congress of Industrial Organizations formed; Roosevelt reelected; United Auto Workers union begins sit-down strikes; John Maynard Keynes's major work, *The General Theory of Employment, Interest, and Money,* published

1937 — Roosevelt announces court "packing" plan; Roosevelt recession

1938 — Fair Labor Standards Act sets minimum wages and maximum hours; Congress establishes Temporary National Economic Committee

CHAPTER TWENTY-SEVEN

America's Rise to Globalism

John Garcia, a native Hawaiian, worked at the Pearl Harbor Navy Yard in Honolulu. On Sunday, December 7, 1941, Garcia planned to enjoy a lazy day off. By the time his grandmother rushed in to wake him that morning at eight, he had already missed the worst of it. "The Japanese were bombing Pearl Harbor," he recalled her yelling at him. John listened in disbelief. "I said, 'They're just practicing.'" "No," his grandmother replied. It was real. He catapulted his huge frame from the bed, ran to the front porch, hopped on his motorcycle, and sped to the harbor.

"It was a mess," he remembered. The USS *Shaw* was in flames. The battleship *Pennsylvania*, a bomb nesting one deck above the powder and ammunition, was about to blow. When ordered to put out its fires, he told the navy officer, "There ain't no way I'm gonna go down there." Instead, he spent the rest of the day pulling bodies from the water. There were so many he lost count. Surveying the wreckage the next morning, he noted that the battleship *Arizona* "was a total washout." So was the *West Virginia*. The *Oklahoma* had "turned turtle, totally upside down." It took two weeks to get all the fires out.

The war that had been spreading around the world had, until December 7, spared the United States. The surprise attack on Pearl Harbor suddenly transformed the Pacific into an avenue for potential invasion. Panic spread up and down the West Coast. Crowds in Los Angeles turned trigger-happy. A young police officer named Tom Bradley (who later served as mayor of the city) heard "sirens going off, aircraft guns firing." "Here we are in the middle of the night," he said, "there was no enemy in sight, but somebody thought they saw the enemy." In January 1942 worried officials moved the Rose Bowl from Pasadena, California, to Durham, North Carolina. Though overheated, their fears were not entirely imaginary. Japanese submarines shelled Santa Barbara, while other enemy ships launched balloons carrying incendiary devices. One floated all the way to Iowa without doing any damage.

Although the Japanese never mounted a serious threat to the mainland, in a world with long-range bombers and submarines, no place seemed safe. This was global war, the first of its kind. Arrayed against the Axis powers of Germany, Italy, and Japan were the Allies: Great Britain, the Soviet Union, the United States, China, and the Free French. Their armies fought from the Arctic to the southwestern Pacific, in the great cities of Europe and Asia and the small villages of North Africa and Indochina, in malarial jungles and scorching deserts, on six continents and across four oceans. Perhaps as many as 100 million people took up arms; some 40 to 50 million lost their lives.

Tragedy on such a scale taught the generation of Americans who fought the war that they could no longer isolate themselves from any part of the world, no matter how remote. Manchuria, Ethiopia, and Poland had once seemed far away, yet the road to war had led from those distant places to the United States. Retreat into isolation had not cured the worldwide Depression or preserved the peace. As it waged a global war, the United States began to assume far wider responsibility for managing the world's geopolitical and economic systems.

THE UNITED STATES IN A TROUBLED WORLD

The outbreak of World War II had its roots in World War I. Many of the victorious as well as the defeated nations resented the peace terms adopted at Versailles. Over the next two decades Germany, the Soviet Union, Italy, Poland, and Japan all sought to achieve on their own what Allied leaders had denied them during the negotiations. War debts imposed at Versailles shackled Germany's economy. As Germany struggled to recover during the Great Depression, so did all of Europe. In central and eastern Europe rivalry among fascists, communists, and other political factions led to frequent violence and instability.

Faced with an unstable world, the United States turned away from collective action. Although their nation possessed the resources at least to ease international tensions, Americans declined to lead in world affairs, remaining outside of the League of Nations.

Pacific Interests

That did not mean the United States could simply ignore events abroad. In assuming colonial control over the Philippines, Americans had created a potentially dangerous rivalry with Japan over the western Pacific. So also had the American commitment to uphold China's territorial integrity, set out in the "open door" policy of 1900 (page 591). With rival Chinese warlords still fighting among themselves, Japan took the opportunity to capture much-needed overseas raw materials and markets.

The Japanese had long dominated Korea, and during the 1920s they expanded their influence on the Chinese mainland. In 1931 Japanese agents staged an explosion on a rail line in Manchuria (meant to appear as though carried out by Chinese nationalists), which provided Japan with an excuse to occupy the whole province. A year later Japan converted Manchuria into a puppet state called Manchukuo.

Here was a direct threat to the Versailles system. But neither the major powers in Europe nor the United States was willing to risk a war with Japan over China. President Hoover instructed Secretary of State Henry Stimson only to protest that the United States would refuse to recognize Japan's takeover of

Stimson Doctrine

Manchuria as legal. The policy of "nonrecognition" became known as the Stimson Doctrine, even though Stimson himself doubted its worth. He was right to doubt. Three weeks later Japan's imperial navy shelled the Chinese port city of Shanghai. When the League of Nations condemned Japan in 1933, the Japanese simply withdrew from the League. The seeds of war in Asia had been sown.

Becoming a Good Neighbor

Growing tensions in Asia and Europe gave the United States an incentive to improve relations with nations closer to home. By the late 1920s the United States had intervened in Latin America so often that the Roosevelt Corollary (page 628) had become an embarrassment. Slowly, however, American administrations began to moderate those highhanded policies. In 1927, when Mexico confiscated American-owned properties, President Coolidge decided to send an ambassador to settle the dispute rather than the marines. In 1933, when critics compared the American position in Nicaragua to Japan's in Manchuria, Secretary Stimson ordered U.S. troops to withdraw. In such gestures lay the roots of a "Good Neighbor" policy.

Franklin Roosevelt pushed the good neighbor idea. At the seventh Pan-American Conference in 1933, his administration accepted a resolution deny-

Good Neighbor policy

ing any country "the right to intervene in the internal or external affairs of another." The following year he negotiated a treaty with Cuba that renounced the American right to intervene under the Platt Amendment (page 628). Henceforth the United States would replace direct military presence with indirect (but still substantial) economic influence.

As the threat of war increased during the 1930s, the United States found a new Latin willingness to cooperate in matters of common defense. By the end of 1940 the administration had worked out defense agreements with every Latin American country but one. The United States faced the threat of war with the American hemisphere largely secured.

The Diplomacy of Isolationism

During the 1920s Benito Mussolini had appealed to Italian nationalism and fears of communism to gain power in Italy. Spinning his dreams of a new

The rise of fascism

Roman empire, Mussolini embodied the rising force of fascism. Then on March 5, 1933, one day after the inauguration of Franklin Roosevelt, the German legislature gave Adolf Hitler control of Germany. Riding a wave of anticommunism and anti-Semitism, Hitler's Nazi party promised to unite all Germans in a Greater Third Reich that would last a thousand years. A week earlier, Japan had withdrawn from the League of Nations. Its militarist leaders were intent on carving out Japan's own empire, which they called the Greater East Asia Co-Prosperity Sphere. The rise of fascism and militarism in Europe and Asia brought the world to war.

As much as Roosevelt wanted the United States to play a leading role in world affairs, he found the nation reluctant to follow. "It's a terrible thing to look over your shoulder when you are trying to lead—and to find no one there," he commented during the mid-1930s. Only when a potential economic interest

Recognition of the Soviet Union

was involved could the president command wide support for foreign initiatives. For example, in 1933 Roosevelt recognized the Communist government of the Soviet Union, hoping it would help contain Japanese expansion in Asia and fascism in Europe. But the move was accepted largely because business leaders welcomed the opportunity to increase Russian–American trade.

For every step Roosevelt took toward internationalism, the Great Depression forced him home again. Programs to revive the economy gained broad support; efforts to resolve crises abroad provoked opposition. The move to noninvolvement in world affairs gained in 1935 after Senator Gerald P. Nye of North Dakota held hearings on the role of bankers and munitions makers in World

The Nye Committee

War I. These "merchants of death," Nye's Committee revealed, had made enormous profits during World War I. The committee report implied, but could not prove, that business interests had even steered the United States into war. "When Americans went into the fray," declared Senator Nye, "they little thought that they were there and fighting to save the skins of American bankers who had bet too boldly on the outcome of the war and had two billions of dollars of loans to the Allies in jeopardy."

Nye's charges fed a fierce debate over how the United States should face the growing threat of war. Internationalists like the League of Women Voters

Internationalists versus isolationists

and former Secretary of State Henry Stimson favored a policy of collective security: working actively with other nations. Isolationists opposed the collective security formula. Two beliefs united them: a firm opposition to war and the conviction that the United States should avoid alliances with other nations. Yet the isolationist camp was a mixed one, with many strange bedfellows. It included liberal reformers and arch-conservatives, a concentration of midwesterners as well as major leaders from both coasts, and a number of Democrats as well as leading Republicans. Pacifists added yet another element to the debate. Powerful groups like the Women's International League for Peace and Freedom insisted that disarmament was the only road to peace.

Neutrality Legislation

Roused by the Nye Committee hearings, Congress debated a proposal to prohibit the sale of arms to all belligerents in time of war. Internationalists argued that an embargo should apply only to aggressor nations. Otherwise, aggressors could strike when they were better armed than their victims. The president, internationalists suggested, should use the embargo selectively. Isolationists, however, had the votes they needed. The Neutrality Act of 1935 required an impartial embargo of arms to all belligerents. The president had authority only to determine when a state of war existed.

The limitations of formal neutrality became immediately apparent. In October 1935 Mussolini ordered Italian forces into the North African country of Ethiopia. Against tanks and planes, Ethiopian troops fought back with spears and flintlock rifles. Roosevelt immediately invoked neutrality in hopes of depriving Italy of war goods. Unfortunately for Roosevelt, Italy needed not arms but oil, steel, and copper—materials not included under the Neutrality Act. When Secretary of State Cordell Hull called for a "moral embargo" on such goods, Depression-starved American businesses shipped them anyway. With no effective opposition from the League of Nations or the United States, Mussolini quickly completed his conquest. In a second Neutrality Act, Congress added a ban on providing any loans or credits to belligerents.

American isolation also benefited Nazi dictator Adolf Hitler. In March 1936, two weeks after Congress passed the second Neutrality Act, German troops thrust into the demilitarized area west of the Rhine River. This flagrant act violated the Treaty of Versailles. As Hitler shrewdly calculated, Britain and France did nothing, while the League of Nations sputtered out a worthless condemnation. Roosevelt remained aloof. The Soviet Union's lonely call for collective action fell on deaf ears.

Then came an attack on Spain's fledgling democracy. In July 1936 Generalissimo Francisco Franco, made bold by Hitler's success, led a rebellion against the newly elected Popular Front government. Hitler and *Spanish Civil War* Mussolini sent supplies, weapons, and troops to Franco's Fascists, while the Soviet Union and Mexico aided the left-leaning government. With Americans sharply divided over whom to support, Roosevelt refused to become involved. Lacking vital support, the Spanish republic fell to Franco in 1939.

For its part, Congress searched for a way to allow American trade to continue (and thus to promote economic recovery at home) without drawing the

A company of Nazi youths parades past the *Führer,* Adolf Hitler
(centered in the balcony doorway). Hitler's shrewd use of
patriotic symbols, mass rallies, and marches exploited the
new possibilities of mass politics.

Cash-and-carry — nation into war itself. Under new "cash-and-carry" provisions in the Neutrality Act of 1937, belligerents could buy supplies other than munitions. But they would have to pay beforehand and carry the supplies on their own ships. If war spread, these terms favored the British, whose navy would ensure that supplies reached England.

But the policy of cash-and-carry did not help China in 1937 when Japanese forces pushed into its southern regions. In order to give China continued ac-

Aggression in China — cess to American goods, Roosevelt refused to invoke the Neutrality Act, which would have cut off trade with both nations. But Japan had far the greater volume of trade with the United States. Since the president lacked the freedom to impose a selective embargo, he could only condemn Japan's invasion.

Inching toward War

In 1937 the three aggressor nations, Germany, Japan, and Italy, signed the Anti-Comintern Pact. On the face of it, the pact pledged them only to ally against the Soviet Union. But the agreement created a Rome–Berlin–Tokyo axis that provoked growing fear of an even wider war. Roosevelt groped for some way to

contain the Axis powers, delivering in October his first foreign policy speech in
Quarantine speech   14 months. Seeming to favor firm collective action, he called for an international "quarantine" of aggressor nations. Although most newspapers applauded his remarks, Roosevelt remained cautious about matching words with deeds. When Japanese planes sank the American gunboat *Panay* on China's Yangtze River only two months later, he meekly accepted an apology for the unprovoked attack.

In Europe, the Nazi menace continued to grow as German troops marched into Austria in 1938—yet another violation of the Versailles Treaty. Hitler then insisted that the 3.5 million ethnic Germans in the Sudetenland of Czechoslovakia be brought into the Reich. With Germany threatening to invade Czechoslovakia, the leaders of France and Britain flew to Munich in September 1938, where they struck a deal to appease Hitler. Czechoslovakia would give up
Appeasement at Munich   the Sudetenland in return for German pledges to seek no more territory in Europe. When British Prime Minister Neville Chamberlain returned to England, he told cheering crowds that the Munich Pact would bring "peace in our time." Six months later, in open contempt for the European democracies, Hitler took over the remainder of Czechoslovakia. "Appeasement" became synonymous with betrayal, weakness, and surrender.

Hitler's Invasion

By 1939 Hitler made little secret that he intended to recapture territory Germany lost to Poland after World War I. What then would the Soviet Union do? If Soviet leader Joseph Stalin joined the Western powers, Hitler might be blocked. But Stalin, who coveted eastern Poland, suspected that the West hoped to turn Hitler against him. On August 24, 1939, Russia and Germany shocked the world when they announced a nonaggression pact. Its secret protocols freed Hitler to invade Poland without fear of Soviet opposition. In turn, Stalin could extend his western borders by bringing eastern Poland, the Baltic states (Latvia, Estonia, and Lithuania), and parts of Romania and Finland into the Soviet sphere.

On the hot Saturday of September 1, 1939, German tanks and troops surged into Poland. "It's come at last," Roosevelt sighed. "God help us all." Within
Hitler invades Poland   days France and England declared war on Germany. Stalin quickly moved into eastern Poland, where German and Russian armor took just three weeks to crush the Polish cavalry. As Hitler consolidated his hold on eastern Europe, Stalin invaded Finland.

Once spring arrived in 1940, Hitler moved to protect his sea lanes by capturing Denmark and Norway. Soon after, German panzer divisions supported
German blitzkrieg   by airpower knifed through Belgium and Holland in a *blitzkrieg*— a "lightning war." The Low Countries fell in 23 days, giving the Germans a route into France. By May a third of a million British

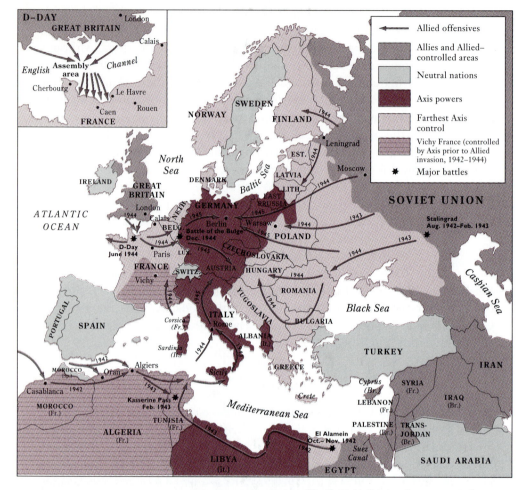

WORLD WAR II IN EUROPE AND NORTH AFRICA   Until 1944 Soviet forces carried
the brunt of the war in Europe, engaging the Axis armies across a huge front.
After winning North Africa, the Allies turned north to knock Italy out of the
war. The final key to defeating Germany was the Anglo-American invasion
of western Europe at Normandy.

and French troops had been driven back onto the Atlantic beaches of Dunkirk.
Only a strenuous rescue effort, staged by the Royal Navy and a flotilla of
English pleasure craft, managed to ferry them to safety, across the Channel to
England. With the British and French routed, German forces marched to Paris.

On June 22, less than six weeks after the German invasion, France capitulated. Hitler insisted that the surrender come in the very railway car in which
Germany had submitted in 1918. William Shirer, an American war correspondent standing 50 yards away, watched the dictator through binoculars: "He
swiftly snaps his hands on his hips, arches his shoulders, plants his feet wide
apart. It is a magnificent gesture of defiance, of burning contempt for this place

and all that it has stood for in the twenty-two years since it witnessed the humbling of the German Empire."

Retreat from Isolationism

Now, only Great Britain stood between Hitler and the United States. If the Nazis defeated the British fleet, the Atlantic Ocean could easily become a gateway to America. Isolationism suddenly seemed dangerous. By the spring of 1940 Roosevelt had abandoned impartiality in favor of outright aid to the Allies. In May he requested funds to motorize the U.S. army (it had only 350 tanks) and build 50,000 airplanes a year (fewer than 3000 existed, most outmoded). Over isolationist protests he soon persuaded Congress to adopt a bill for the first peacetime draft in history.

In the 1940 presidential election campaign both Roosevelt and his Republican opponent, Wendell Willkie, favored an internationalist course short of war. In defeating Willkie, Roosevelt promised voters that rather than fight, the United States would become "the great arsenal of democracy." The British, however, could no longer pay for arms under the provisions of cash-and-carry. So Roosevelt proposed a scheme to "lease, lend, or otherwise dispose of" arms

Lend-lease   and supplies to countries whose defense was vital to the United States. That meant sending supplies to England on the dubious premise that they would be returned when the war ended. Roosevelt likened "lend-lease" to lending a garden hose to a neighbor whose house was on fire. Isolationist Senator Robert Taft thought a comparison to "chewing gum" more apt. After a neighbor used it, "you don't want it back." In March 1941 a large majority in Congress passed the Lend-Lease Act.

Step by step Roosevelt had led the United States to the verge of war with the Nazis. Over the summer of 1941 American destroyers escorted British ships as far as Iceland (though Roosevelt insisted it was a "patrol," not a convoy). The United States extended its defensive sphere to include Greenland and Iceland. Then Hitler, as audacious as ever, broke his alliance with the Soviet Union by launching a surprise invasion of Russia in June 1941. The Allies expected a swift collapse, but when Russian troops mounted a heroic resistance, Roosevelt extended lend-lease to the Soviet Union.

That August Roosevelt secretly met with the new British prime minister, Winston Churchill, on warships off the coast of Newfoundland, in Argentia Bay. Almost every day since England and Germany had gone to war, the two men had exchanged phone calls, letters, or cables. The Argentia meetings cemented this friendship—one key to Allied victory. Roosevelt and Churchill also

Atlantic Charter   drew up the Atlantic Charter, a statement of principles that the two nations held in common. The Charter condemned "Nazi tyranny" and embraced the "Four Freedoms": freedom of speech and expression, freedom of worship, freedom from want, and freedom from fear. In effect, the Atlantic Charter was an unofficial statement of war aims.

By mid-1941, American destroyers in the North Atlantic were already stalking German U-boats (submarines) and reporting their whereabouts to British commanders. Given the harsh weather and aggressive American policy, incidents were inevitable. In October a U-boat sank the destroyer *Reuben James*, killing more than 100 American sailors. That act increased public support for the Allied cause. Yet as late as September 1941 eight of ten Americans opposed entering the hostilities. Few in the United States suspected that an attack by Japan, not Germany, would unify America and bring it into the war.

Disaster in the Pacific

Preoccupied by the fear of German victory in Europe, Roosevelt sought to avoid a showdown with Japan. The navy, the president told his cabinet, had "not got enough ships to go round, and every little episode in the Pacific means fewer ships in the Atlantic." But precisely because American and European attention lay elsewhere, Japan was emboldened to expand militarily into Southeast Asia.

Japanese leaders viewed their Greater East Asia Co-Prosperity Sphere as an Asian version of the Monroe Doctrine. Japan, the preeminent power in the region, would replace the Europeans as a promoter of economic development. To American leaders, however, Japan's actions threatened the policy of keeping an open door to China and preserving that country's independence. By the summer of 1941 Japanese forces controlled the Chinese coast and all major cities. When its army marched into French Indochina (present-day Vietnam) in July, Japan stood ready to conquer all of the Southeast Asian peninsula and the oil-rich Dutch East Indies.

Roosevelt was forced to act. He embargoed trade, froze Japanese assets in American banks, and barred shipments of vital scrap iron and petroleum. Japanese leaders indicated a willingness to negotiate with the

Embargo

United States, but diplomats from both sides were only going through the motions. The two nations' goals were totally at odds. Japan demanded that its conquests be recognized; the United States insisted that Japan withdraw from China and renounce the Tripartite Pact with Germany and Italy. As negotiations sputtered on, the Japanese secretly prepared for an attack on American positions in Guam, the Philippines, and Hawaii.

In late November American intelligence located, and then lost, a Japanese armada as it left Japan. Observing strict radio silence, the six carriers and their escorts steamed across the North Pacific. On Sunday morning, December 7, 1941, the first wave of Japanese planes roared down on the Pacific Fleet lying

Pearl Harbor

at anchor in Pearl Harbor. For more than an hour the Japanese pounded the ships and nearby airfields. Altogether 19 ships were sunk or battered. Practically all of the 200 American aircraft were damaged or destroyed. Only the aircraft carriers, by chance on maneuvers, escaped the worst naval defeat in American history.

In Washington, Secretary of War Henry Stimson could not believe the news relayed to his office. "My God! This can't be true, this must mean the Philippines." Later that day the Japanese did attack the Philippines, along with Guam, Midway, and British forces in Hong Kong and the Malay peninsula. On December 8, Franklin Roosevelt told a stunned nation that "yesterday, December 7, 1941" was "a date which will live in infamy." America, the "reluctant belligerent," was in the war at last. Three days later Hitler declared war on the "half Judaized and the other half Negrified" people of the United States; Italy quickly followed suit.

COUNTERPOINT   *Did Roosevelt deliberately invite war?*

Had Roosevelt known the attack on Pearl Harbor was coming? Some critics have charged that the president deliberately contrived to bring war about. For months, American intelligence had been cracking some of Japan's secret codes. Much information indicated that Pearl Harbor was at risk. Yet Roosevelt left the fleet exposed, seeming almost to provoke an attack to bring the United States into the war. Was it mere coincidence that the vital aircraft carriers were at sea? That only the obsolete battleships were left at Pearl Harbor?

This argument, however, is based on circumstantial, not documentary, evidence. Roosevelt's defenders (and they include most historians) have countered that he wanted to fight Germany more than Japan. If he really had wished to provoke an incident leading to war, one in Atlantic waters would have served him far better. More important, the intelligence signals intercepted by American code-breakers were confusing. Analysts lost track of the Japanese fleet as it moved toward Hawaii. Secretary of War Stimson had good reason to be astonished when the fleet attacked Pearl Harbor.

In the end, cultural misperceptions may have explained the coming of war better than any conspiracy theory. American leaders were surprised by the attack on Pearl Harbor because they could not quite believe that the Japanese were daring or resourceful enough to attack an American stronghold some 4000 miles from Japan. Japanese militarists counted on a surprise attack to give them time to build a line of defense strong enough to discourage weak-willed Westerners from continuing the war. As it turned out, both calculations were wrong.

A GLOBAL WAR

British Prime Minister Winston Churchill greeted the news of Pearl Harbor with shock but, even more, elation. Great Britain would no longer stand alone in the North Atlantic and the Pacific wars. "We have won the war," he thought, and that night he slept "the sleep of the saved and thankful."

As Churchill recognized, only with the Americans fully committed to war could the Allies make full use of the enormous material and human resources of the United States. Beyond that, the Allies needed to secure an alliance between the Anglo-American democracies and the Soviet Communist dictatorship that could win both the war and the peace to follow.

Strategies for War

Within two weeks, Churchill was in Washington, meeting with Roosevelt to coordinate production schedules for ships, planes, and armaments. The numbers they announced were so high some critics openly laughed—at first. A year later combined British, Canadian, and American production boards not only met but exceeded the schedules.

Roosevelt and Churchill also planned grand strategy. Outraged by the attack on Pearl Harbor, many Americans thought Japan should be the war's primary target. But the two leaders agreed that Germany posed the greater threat. The Pacific war, they decided, would be fought as a holding action, while the Allies concentrated on Europe. In a global war, arms and resources had to be allocated carefully, for the Allies faced daunting threats on every front.

Germany first

Gloomy Prospects

By summer's end in 1942 the Allies faced defeat. The Nazis stood outside the Soviet Union's three major cities: Leningrad, Moscow, and Stalingrad. In North Africa, General Erwin Rommel, Germany's famed "Desert Fox," swept into Egypt with his Afrika Korps to stand within striking distance of the Suez Canal—a lifeline to the resources of the British empire. German U-boats in the North Atlantic threatened to sever the ocean link between the United States and Britain. U-boat sailors called the first six months of 1942 "the American hunting season," as they sank 400 Allied ships in U.S. territorial waters. So deadly were these "Wolfpacks" that merchant sailors developed a grim humor about sleeping. Those on freighters carrying iron ore slept above decks, since the heavily laden ships could sink in less than a minute. On oil tankers, however, sailors closed their doors, undressed, and slept soundly. If a torpedo hit, no one would survive anyway.

U-boat war

In the Far East the supposedly impregnable British base at Singapore fell to Japan in just one week. Furthermore, the Japanese navy destroyed most of the Allied fleet in the western Pacific during the Battle of Java Sea. General Douglas MacArthur, commander of American forces in the Philippines, was forced to flee to Australia in April 1942. In what appeared to be an empty pledge, he vowed, "I shall return." The ill-equipped American and Philippine troops left on Bataan and Corregidor put up

Fall of the Philippines

In the face of Japanese occupation, many Filipinos actively supported the American war effort. Valentine Untalan survived capture by the Japanese and went on to serve in the American army's elite Philippine Scouts. Like a growing number of Filipinos, he moved to the United States once the war was over.

a heroic but doomed struggle. By summer no significant Allied forces stood between the Japanese and India or Australia.

The chain of spectacular victories disguised fatal weaknesses within the Axis alliance. Japan and Germany fought separate wars, each on two fronts. They never coordinated strategies. Vast armies in China and Russia drained them of both manpower and supplies. Brutal occupation policies made enemies of conquered populations, which forced Axis armies to use valuable forces to maintain control and move supplies. The Nazis were especially harsh. They launched a major campaign to exterminate Europe's Jews, Slavs, and Gypsies. Resistance movements grew as the victims of Axis aggression fought back. At the war's height 50 countries were among the Allies, who referred to themselves as the United Nations.

A Grand Alliance

The early defeats also obscured the Allies' strengths. Chief among these were the manpower of the Soviet Union and the productive capacity of the United States. Safe from the fighting, American farms and factories could produce enough food and war materials to supply two separate wars at once. By the end of the war American factories had turned out vast quantities of airplanes, ships, artillery pieces, tanks, and self-propelled guns, as well as 47 million tons of ammunition.

The Allies benefited too from exceptional leadership. The "Big Three"—Joseph Stalin, Winston Churchill, and Franklin Roosevelt—were able to main-

The Big Three   tain a unity of purpose that eluded Axis leaders. All three understood the global nature of the war. To a remarkable degree they managed to set aside their many differences in pursuit of a common goal: the defeat of Nazi Germany.

To be sure, each nation had its own needs. Russian forces faced 3.5 million Axis troops along a 1600-mile front in eastern Europe. To ease the pressure on those troops, Stalin repeatedly called upon the Allies to open a second front in western Europe. So urgent were his demands that one Allied diplomat remarked that Stalin's foreign minister knew only four words in English: *yes, no,* and *second front.* But Churchill and Roosevelt felt compelled to turn Stalin down. In August 1942 the western Allies lacked the massive, well-trained force needed for a successful invasion of Europe. Churchill himself flew to Moscow to give Stalin the bad news: no second front in Europe until 1943. Postponed again until mid-1944, the second front became a source of festering Russian discontent.

Yet after an initial surge of anger, Stalin accepted Churchill's rationale for a substitute action. That was to be a British-American invasion of North Africa

Operation Torch   at the end of 1942. Code-named Operation Torch, the North African campaign would bring British and American troops into direct combat with the Germans and stood an excellent chance of succeeding. Here was an example of how personal contact among the Big Three ensured Allied cooperation. The alliance sometimes bent but never broke.

The Naval War in the Pacific

Despite the Allied decision to defeat Germany first, the earliest successes came in the Pacific. At the Battle of Coral Sea in May 1942 planes from American aircraft carriers stopped a large Japanese invading force headed for Port Moresby in New Guinea. For the first time in history two fleets fought without seeing each other. The age of naval aviation had arrived. The Japanese fleet actually inflicted greater damage but decided to turn back to nurse its wounds. Had they captured Port Moresby, the Japanese could have severed Allied shipping routes to Australia.

To extend Japan's defenses, the Japanese military ordered the capture of Midway, a small island west of Hawaii. The Americans, in possession of decoded

Midway   Japanese transmissions, were ready. On June 3, as the Japanese main fleet bore down on Midway, American planes sank four enemy carriers, a cruiser, and three destroyers. The Battle of Midway broke Japanese naval supremacy in the Pacific and stalled Japan's offensive. In August 1942 American forces launched their first offensive, on the Solomon Islands, east of New Guinea. With the landing of American marines on the island of Guadalcanal, the Allies started on the bloody road to Japan and victory.

Turning Points in Europe

By the fall of 1942 the Allies had their first successes in the European war. In Africa, British forces under General Bernard Montgomery broke through Rommel's lines at El Alamein. Weeks later, the Allies launched Operation Torch, the invasion of North Africa. Under the command of General Dwight D. Eisenhower, Allied forces swept eastward through Morocco and Algeria. They were halted in February 1943 at the Kasserine Pass in Tunisia, but General George S. Patton regrouped them and masterminded an impressive string of victories. By May 1943 Rommel had fled from North Africa, leaving behind 300,000 German troops.

Success in North Africa provided a stirring complement to the dogged Russian stand at Stalingrad. From August 1942 until February 1943 Axis and

Stalingrad

Soviet armies, each with more than a million troops, fought one of the bloodiest engagements in history. Each side suffered more casualties than the Americans did during the entire war. When it was over, the Germans had lost an army and their momentum; Stalin's forces went on the offensive, moving south and west through the Ukraine toward Poland and Romania.

Those Who Fought

"The first time I ever heard a New England accent," recalled a midwesterner, "was at Fort Benning. The southerner was an exotic creature to me. The people from the farms. The New York street smarts." Mobilizing for war brought together Americans from all regions, classes, and ethnic backgrounds. More than any other social institution the army acted as a melting pot. It also offered educational opportunities and job skills. "I could be a technical sergeant only I haven't had enough school," reported one Navajo soldier in a letter home to New Mexico. "Make my little brother go to school even if you have to lasso him."

In waging the world's first global war, the U.S. armed forces swept millions of Americans into new worlds and experiences. In 1941, the army had 1.6 million men in uniform. By 1945 it had more than 7 million; the navy, 3.9 million; the army air corps, 2.3 million; and the marines, 600,000. Nineteen-year-olds who had never left home found themselves swept off to Europe or to the South Pacific. At basic training recruits were subjected to forms of regimentation—the army hair cut, foul-mouthed drill sergeants, and barracks life—they had seldom experienced in other areas of America's democratic culture.

As with most wars, the infantry bore the brunt of the fighting and dying. They suffered 90 percent of the battlefield casualties. In all, almost 400,000

A G.I.'s life

Americans died and more than 600,000 were wounded. But service in the military did not mean constant combat. Most battles were reasonably short, followed by long periods of waiting and preparation. The army used almost 2 million soldiers just to move supplies. Yet even during the lull in battle, the soldier's biggest enemy, disease, stalked them: malaria, dysentery, typhus, and even plague. In the Pacific theater, the thermometer sometimes rose to over 110 degrees Fahrenheit.

Wherever they fought, American soldiers usually lived in foxholes dug by hand with small shovels. Whenever possible they turned a hole in the ground into a home. "The American soldier is a born housewife," observed war correspondent Ernie Pyle. Between battles, movies were about the only entertainment many troops had. Each film was a tenuous link to a more comfortable world at home, a place American soldiers yearned for with special intensity. It was not a country or an idea for which they fought so much as a set of memories—a house, a car, Mom and Pop.

Uneasy Recruits

Minorities enlisted in unusually large numbers because the services offered training and opportunities unavailable in civilian life. Still, prejudice against

African Americans at war

African Americans and other minorities remained high. The army was strictly segregated and generally assigned black soldiers to noncombatant roles. The navy accepted them only as cooks and servants. At first the air corps and marines would not take them at all. The American Red Cross even kept "black" and "white" blood plasma separated, as if there were a difference. (Ironically, a black physician, Charles Drew, had invented the process allowing plasma to be stored.)

Despite such prejudice, more than a million black men and women served. As the war progressed, leaders of the black community pressured the military to ease segregation and allow black soldiers a more active role. The army did form some black combat units, usually led by white officers, as well as a black air corps unit. By mid-1942 black officers were being trained and graduated from integrated officer candidate schools at the rate of 200 a month. More than 80 black pilots won the Distinguished Flying Cross.

Homosexuals who wished to join the military faced a dilemma. Would their sexual orientation be discovered during the screening process? And if they were

Choices for homosexuals

rejected and word got back to their parents or communities, would they be stigmatized? Many took that chance. Charles Rowland, from Arizona, recalled that he and other gay friends "were not about to be deprived the privilege of serving our country in a time of great national emergency by virtue of some stupid regulation about being gay." Those who did pass the screening test found themselves in gender-segregated bases, where life in an overwhelmingly male or female environment allowed many, for the first time in their lives, to meet like-minded gay men and women. They served in all the ways other soldiers did, facing both the dangers of combat and the tedium of military life.

Women at War

World War II brought an end to the military as a male enclave that women entered only as nurses. During the prewar mobilization, Eleanor Roosevelt and other women had campaigned for a regular military organization for women. The War Department came up with a compromise that allowed women to join

WACs

the Women's Army Auxiliary Corps (WAAC), but only with inferior status and lower pay. By 1943 the "Auxiliary" had dropped out of the title: WAACs became WACs, with full status, equal ranks, and equal pay. (The navy had a similar force called the WAVEs.)

Women could look with a mixture of pride and resentment on their wartime military service. Thousands served close to the battlefields, working as technicians, mechanics, radio operators, postal clerks, and secretaries. Although filling a vital need, these were largely traditional female jobs that implied a separate and inferior status. Until 1944 women were prevented by law from serving in war zones, even as noncombatants. There were women pilots, but they were restricted to shuttling planes behind the lines. At many posts WAVEs and WACs lived behind barbed wire and could move about only in groups under armed escort.

WAR PRODUCTION

When Pearl Harbor brought the United States into the war, Thomas Chinn sold his publishing business and devoted full time to war work. Like many Chinese Americans, it was the first time he had worked outside of Chinatown. He served as a supervisor in the Army Quartermaster Market Center, which was responsible for supplying the armed forces with fresh food as it was harvested across California. Chinn found himself coordinating a host of cold storage warehouses all the way from the Oregon border as far south as Fresno. "At times," he recalled, "in order to catch seasonal goods such as fresh vegetables, as many as 200 or 300 railroad cars would be shuttling in and out" of the warehouses.

Food distribution was only one of many areas that demanded attention from the government. After Pearl Harbor, steel, aluminum, and electric power were all in short supply, creating bottlenecks in production lines. Roosevelt recognized the need for more direct government control of the economy.

Although the conversion from peace to war began slowly, the president used a mix of compulsory and voluntary programs to guarantee an ever-increasing supply of food, munitions, and equipment. In the end the United States worked a miracle of production that proved every bit as important to victory as any battle fought overseas. From 1939 to 1945 the gross national product grew from $91 billion to $166 billion. So successful was war production that civilians suffered little deprivation.

Mobilizing for War

Roosevelt first tried to coordinate the war economy by setting up a War Production Board (WPB) under the direction of former Sears, Roebuck president Donald M. Nelson. On paper, Nelson's powers were impressive. The WPB had authority to allocate resources and organize factories in whatever way promoted national defense. In one of its first acts, the WPB ordered an end to all civilian car and truck production. The American people would have no new cars until the war ended.

In practice, Nelson was scarcely the dictator the economy needed. Other federal agencies with their own czars controlled petroleum, rubber, and labor resources, while military agencies continued their own procurement. To end the bottlenecks, the president in 1943 made Supreme Court Justice James F. Byrnes the dictator the economy needed. His authority as director of the new Office of War Mobilization (OWM) was so great and his access to Roosevelt so direct that he became known as the "assistant president." By assuming control over vital materials such as steel, aluminum, and copper, OWM was able to allocate them more systematically. The bottlenecks disappeared.

Office of War Mobilization

Equally crucial, industries both large and small converted their factories to turning out war matériel. The "Big Three" automakers—Ford, General Motors, and Chrysler—generated some 20 percent of all war goods, as auto factories were retooled to make tanks and planes. But small business also played a vital role. A manufacturer of model trains, for example, made bomb fuses.

Henry J. Kaiser, a California industrialist, exemplified the war's creative entrepreneurship. Kaiser rustled up generous government loans for building factories. With generous wages and benefits, including day care for the children of working mothers, he lured workers to his new shipyards on the West Coast. His assembly line techniques reduced the time required to build cargo vessels, known as Liberty ships, from almost a year to only 56 days.

War production also created new industrial centers, especially in the West. When production of aircraft factories peaked in 1944, the industry had 2.1 million workers producing almost 100,000 planes. Most of the new factories were located around Los Angeles, San Diego, and Seattle. The demand for workers opened opportunities for many Asian workers who had been limited to jobs within their own ethnic communities. In Los Angeles about 300 laundry workers closed their shops so that they could work on the construction of the ship *China Victory*. By 1943, 15 percent of all shipyard workers around San Francisco Bay were Chinese.

West Coast industry

The government relied on large firms such as Ford and General Motors because they had experience with large-scale production. Thus, war contracts helped large corporations increase their dominance over the economy. Workers in companies with more than 10,000 employees amounted to just 13 percent of the workforce in 1939; by 1944 they constituted more than 30 percent. In agriculture a similar move toward bigness occurred. The number of people working on farms dropped by a fifth, yet productivity increased 30 percent, as small farms were consolidated into larger ones that relied on more machinery and artificial fertilizers to increase yields.

Productivity increased for a less tangible reason: pride in work done for a common cause. Civilians volunteered for civil defense, hospitals, and countless scrap drives. Children became "Uncle Sam's Scrappers" and "Tin-Can Colonels" as they scoured vacant lots for valuable trash. Backyard "victory" gardens added 8 million tons of food to the harvest in 1943; car pooling conserved millions of tires. As citizens put off buying new consumer goods, they helped limit inflation. Morale ran high because people believed that every contribution, no matter how small, helped defeat the Axis.

Science Goes to War

The striking success of aircraft against battleships at Pearl Harbor and Midway was just one way in which technology and science created new strategies of warfare. The Battle of Britain and the European air war spurred the development of a new generation of fighter planes and long-range bombers. To combat enemy bombers and submarines, English and American scientists rushed to perfect electronic detection devices such as radar and sonar, making it possible to hit targets obscured by darkness, fog, or smoke.

Scientific advances saved lives as well as destroying them. Insecticides, pesticides, and drugs limited the spread of infectious diseases like malaria and syphilis. Penicillin saw its first widespread use. Indeed, the health of the nation actually improved during the war. Life expectancy rose by three years overall and by five years for African Americans. Infant mortality was cut by more than a third, and in 1942 the nation recorded its lowest death rate in history. Still, scientific discoveries sometimes had unforeseen consequences. While the pesticide DDT helped control malaria and other insect-borne diseases, its harmful effects on the environment would become clear only years later.

Science made its most dramatic and frightening advances in atomic research. Before the war German scientists had discovered the process of fission: splitting the atom. Leading European physicists who had come to America to escape the Nazis understood all too well the military potential of the German discovery. In 1939 they alerted President Roosevelt to the possibility that fission research would enable the Nazis to develop atomic weapons. Their warning led Roosevelt to commit the United States to the largest research and de-

Manhattan Project

velopment effort in history, code-named the Manhattan Project. More than 100,000 scientists, engineers, technicians, and support workers from the United States, Canada, and England worked to build an atomic bomb. Yet even with increased resources, scientists feared they would not win the race to produce a weapon.

War Work and Prosperity

War production not only ended the Depression, it revived prosperity—but not without stress. Unemployment, which stood at almost 7 million in 1940, virtually disappeared by 1944. Jeff Davies, president of Hoboes of America, reported in 1942 that 2 million of his members were "off the road." Employers, eager to overcome the labor shortage, welcomed handicapped workers. Hearing-impaired people found jobs in deafening factories; dwarfs became aircraft inspectors because they could crawl inside wings and other cramped spaces. By the summer of 1943 nearly 3 million children aged 12 to 17 were working. When the war ended, average income had jumped to nearly $3000, twice what it had been in 1939.

Roosevelt had to find some means to pay the war's enormous cost without triggering severe inflation. His approach mixed conservative and liberal elements: it was voluntary and compulsory, regressive and progressive. The Treasury Department sold war bonds through advertising campaigns rather than enforced savings. Still, Secretary of the Treasury Henry Morgenthau also

Tax reform looked to raise money with a new highly progressive tax structure that taxed higher income at a higher rate. Conservatives, however, balked at such sweeping reforms. After six months of wrangling, Congress passed a compromise, the Revenue Act of 1942, which levied a flat 5 percent tax on all annual incomes over $624. That provision struck hardest at low-income workers: in 1942 almost 50 million citizens paid taxes, compared with 13 million the year before.

Organized Labor

Wartime prosperity brought substantial gains for unions. Still, the tensions between business and labor that characterized the New Deal era continued. In

War Labor Board 1941 alone more than 2 million workers walked off their jobs in protest. To end labor strife Roosevelt established the War Labor Board in 1942. Like the similar agency Woodrow Wilson had created during World War I, the new WLB had authority to impose arbitration in any labor dispute.

Despite Roosevelt's attempt to smooth labor relations, dissatisfied railroad workers tied up rail lines in a wildcat strike in 1943. To break the impasse, the

Coal strike government seized the railroads and then granted wage increases. That same year the pugnacious John L. Lewis allowed his United Mine Workers to go on strike. "The coal miners of America are hungry," he charged. "They are ill-fed and undernourished." Roosevelt seized the mines and ran them for a time; he even considered arresting union leaders and drafting striking miners. But as Secretary of the Interior Harold Ickes noted, a "jailed miner produces no more coal than a striking miner." In the end the government negotiated a settlement that gave miners substantial new benefits.

Most Americans were less willing to forgive Lewis and his miners. A huge coal shortage along the East Coast had left homes dark and cold. "John L. Lewis—Damn your coal black soul," wrote the military newspaper *Stars and Stripes*. In reaction, Congress easily passed the Smith–Connolly Act of 1943. It gave the president more authority to seize vital war plants shut by strikes and required union leaders to observe a 30-day "cooling-off" period before striking.

Despite these incidents, most workers remained dedicated to the war effort. Stoppages actually accounted for only about one-tenth of one percent of total work time during the war. When workers did strike, it was usually in defiance of their union leadership, and they left their jobs for just a few days.

Women Workers

With as many as 12 million men in uniform, women (especially married women) became the nation's largest untapped source of labor. During the high unem-

Womanpower

ployment years of the Depression, both government and business had discouraged women from competing with men for jobs. Now, magazines and government bulletins began trumpeting "the vast resource of womanpower." Having accounted for a quarter of all workers in 1940, women

During the war, many women proved that they could do work once considered exclusively for males. Lionized with nicknames such as "Rosie the Riveter," women like this aircraft worker dispelled old stereotypes.

amounted to more than a third by 1945. These women were not mostly young and single, as female workers of the past had been. A majority were either married or between 55 and 64 years old.

Many women preferred the relative freedom of work and wages to the confines of home. With husbands off at war, millions of women needed additional income and had more free time. Black women in particular realized dramatic gains in the quality of jobs available to them. Once concentrated in low-paying domestic and farm jobs with erratic hours and tedious labor, some 300,000 rushed into factories that offered higher pay and more regular hours. Whether

Social stresses

black or white, working women faced new stresses. The demands of a job were added to domestic responsibilities. The pressures of moving and crowded housing tore at families and communities already fearful for their men at war.

Although the war inspired a change in economic roles for women, it did not create a revolution in attitudes about gender. Most Americans assumed that when the war ended, veterans would pick up their old jobs and women would return home. Surveys showed that the vast majority of Americans, whether male or female, continued to believe that child rearing was a woman's primary responsibility. The birthrate, which had fallen during the Depression, began to rise in 1943 as prosperity returned.

A QUESTION OF RIGHTS

Roosevelt, who had been a government official during World War I, was determined to avoid the patriotic excesses he had witnessed then: mobs menacing immigrants, patriotic appeals to spy on neighbors, raids on pacifist radicals. Even so, the tensions over race, ethnic background, and class differences could not simply be ignored. In a society in which immigration laws discriminated against Asians by race, the war with Japan made life difficult for loyal Asian Americans of all backgrounds. Black and Hispanic workers still faced discrimination in shipyards and airplane factories as much as they had in peacetime industries.

Italians and Asian Americans

When World War II began, about 600,000 Italian aliens and 5 million Italian Americans lived in the United States. Most still lived in Italian neighborhoods centered around churches, fraternal organizations, and clubs. Some had been proud of Mussolini and supported *Fascismo*. "Mussolini was a hero," recalled one Italian American, "a superhero. He made us feel special." Those attitudes changed abruptly after Pearl Harbor. During the war, Italian Americans unquestioningly pledged their loyalties to the United States.

At first the government treated Italians without citizenship (along with Japanese and Germans) as "aliens of enemy nationality." They could not travel

E Y E W I T N E S S   T O   H I S T O R Y

A Woman Learns Shipyard Welding

I, who hate heights, climbed stair after stair after stair till I thought I must be close to the sun. I stopped on the top deck. I, who hate confined spaces, went through narrow corridors, stumbling my way over rubber-coated leads—dozens of them, scores of them, even hundreds of them. I went into a room about four feet by ten where two shipfitters, a shipfitter's helper, a chipper, and I all worked. I welded in the poop deck lying on the floor while another welder spattered sparks from the ceiling and chippers like giant woodpeckers shattered our eardrums. I, who've taken welding, and have sat at a bench welding flat and vertical plates, was told to weld braces along a baseboard below a door opening. On these a heavy steel door was braced while it was hung to a fine degree of accuracy. I welded more braces along the side, and along the top. I did overhead welding, horizontal, flat, vertical. . . . I made some good welds and some frightful ones. But now a door in the poop deck of an oil tanker is hanging, four feet by six of solid steel, by my welds. Pretty exciting. . . .

I am convinced that it is going to take backbone for welders to stick to their jobs through the summer months. It is harder on them than on any of the other workers—their leathers are so hot and heavy, they get more of the fumes, and their hoods become instruments of torture. . . . It grows unbearably hot under the hood, my glasses fog and blur my vision, and the only thing to do is to stop. . . . Yet the job confirmed my strong conviction—I have stated it before—what exhausts the woman welder is not the work, nor the heat, nor the demands upon physical strength. It is the apprehension that arises from inadequate skill and consequent lack of confidence; and this can be overcome by the right kind of training.

Augusta Clawson, "Shipyard Diary of a Woman Welder," in Rosalyn Baxandall, Linda Gordon, and Susan Reverby, eds., *America's Working Women* (New York, Vintage, 1976), pp. 289–290. Copyright 1994 by Penguin Books, Inc. Used by permission of Viking Penguin, a division of Penguin Books, USA, Inc.

Enemy aliens without permission, enter strategic areas, or possess shortwave radios, guns, or maps. By 1942 few Americans believed that German or Italian Americans posed any kind of danger. Eager to keep the support of Italian voters in the 1942 congressional elections, Roosevelt chose Columbus Day, 1942, to lift restrictions on Italian aliens.

The 127,000 Japanese living in the United States, whether aliens or citizens, did not experience similar tolerance. Ironically, prejudices against them were least high in Hawaii, where the war with Japan had begun. Newspapers there expressed confidence in the loyalty of Japanese Americans, who in any case were crucial to the success of Hawaii's economy.

The situation was far more volatile on the mainland. There, Japanese Americans remained largely separated from the mainstream of American life, often because state laws and local custom threw up complex barriers. In the western states where they were concentrated around urban areas, most Japanese Americans could not vote, own land, or live in decent neighborhoods. Approx-

Issei

imately 47,000 Japanese aliens, known as *Issei*, were ineligible for citizenship under American law. Only their children could become citizens. Despite such restrictions, some Japanese achieved success in small businesses like landscaping, while many others worked on or owned farms that supplied fruits and vegetables to growing cities.

West Coast politicians pressed the Roosevelt administration to evacuate the Japanese from their communities. It did not seem to matter that about 80,000

Nisei

were American citizens, called *Nisei*, and that no evidence indicated that they posed any threat. "A Jap's a Jap . . ." commented General John De Witt, commander of West Coast defenses. "It makes no difference whether he is an American citizen or not." In response, the War Department in February 1942 drew up Executive Order 9066, which allowed the exclusion of any person from designated military areas. Under De Witt's authority, the order was applied only on the West Coast against Japanese Americans. By late February Roosevelt had agreed that both Issei and Nisei would be evacuated. But where would they go?

The army began to ship the entire Japanese community to temporary "assembly centers." Most Nisei were forced to sell their property at far below mar-

Concentration
Camps

ket value. Furthermore, many army sites did not offer basic sanitation, comfort, or privacy. "We lived in a horse stable," remembered one young girl. Eventually, most Japanese were interned in 10 camps in remote areas of seven western states. No claim of humane intent could change the reality: these were concentration camps. Internees were held in wire-enclosed compounds by armed guards. Tar-papered barracks housed families or small groups in single rooms. Each room had a few cots, some blankets, and a single light bulb. That was home.

Some Japanese Americans protested, especially when government officials circulated a loyalty questionnaire that asked Nisei citizens if they would be willing to serve in the armed forces. "What do they take us for? Saps?" asked Dunks Oshima, a camp prisoner. "First, they change my army status to 4-C [enemy alien] because of my ancestry, run me out of town, and now they want me to volunteer for a suicide squad so I could get killed for this damn democracy." Yet thousands of Nisei did enlist, and many distinguished themselves in combat.

The bleak landscape of this camp at Manzanar, California, was typical of the internment camps to which the government sent Japanese Americans.

Other Japanese Americans challenged the government through the legal system. Fred Korematsu in California and Gordon Hirabayashi in Washington State were arrested when they refused to report for relocation. "As an American citizen, I wanted to uphold the principles of the Constitution," recalled Hirabayashi. But in *Korematsu v. United States* (1944), the Supreme Court upheld the government's relocation program as a wartime necessity. Three justices dissented, criticizing relocation as the "legalization of racism."

Hirabayashi and Korematsu

Concentration camps in America did not mirror the horror of Nazi death camps, but they were built on racism and fear. Worse, they violated the traditions of civil rights and liberties for which Americans believed they were fighting.

Minorities on the Job

Minority leaders saw the irony of fighting a war for freedom in a country in which civil rights were still limited. "A jim crow army cannot fight for a free world," the NAACP declared. Such ideas of racial justice had been the driving force in the life of A. Philip Randolph, long an advocate of greater black militancy. Randolph had already demonstrated his gifts as an organizer and leader of the Brotherhood of Sleeping Car Porters, a strong African American union. During the war he

A. Philip Randolph

launched a campaign to gain entrance to defense industries and government agencies, unions, and the armed forces, all of them segregated. "The Administration leaders in Washington will never give the Negro justice," Randolph argued, "until they see masses—ten, twenty, fifty thousand Negroes on the White House lawn." In 1941 he began to organize a march on Washington.

President Roosevelt could have issued executive orders to integrate the government, defense industries, unions, and the armed forces, as Randolph demanded. But it took the threat of the march to make him act. He issued Executive Order 8802 in June, which forbid discrimination by race in hiring either government or defense industry workers. To carry out the policy, Order

FEPC

8022 established the Fair Employment Practices Commission (FEPC). Despite its promise the new agency had only limited success in breaking down barriers against African Americans and Hispanics. It was one thing to ban discrimination and quite another to enforce that ban in a society still deeply divided by racial prejudice.

Still, the FEPC did open industrial jobs in California's shipyards and aircraft factories, which had previously refused to hire Hispanics. Thousands

Hispanic war workers

migrated from Texas, where job discrimination was most severe, to California, where war work created new opportunities. Labor shortages led the southwestern states to join with the Mexican government under the bracero program to recruit Mexican labor under specially arranged contracts. In Texas, by contrast, antagonism to braceros ran so deep that the Mexican government tried to prevent workers from going there. With support from labor unions, officials in the oil and mining industries routinely blocked Hispanics from training programs and job advancement. Not until late 1943 did the FEPC investigate the situation.

Black Americans experienced similar frustrations. More than half of all defense jobs were closed to minorities. For example, with 100,000 skilled and high-paying jobs in the aircraft industry, blacks held about 200 janitorial positions. The federal agency charged with placing workers honored local "whites only" employment practices. Unions segregated black workers or excluded them entirely. One person wrote to the president with a telling complaint: "Hitler has not done anything to the colored people—it's people right here in the United States who are keeping us out of work and keeping us down."

Eventually the combination of labor shortages, pressures from black leaders, and initiative from government agencies opened the door to more skilled

Jobs for African Americans

jobs and higher pay. Beginning in 1943 the United States Employment Service rejected requests with racial stipulations. Faced with a dwindling labor pool, many employers finally opened their doors. By 1944 blacks, who accounted for almost 10 percent of the population, held 8 percent of the jobs.

Urban Unrest

At the beginning of the war three-quarters of the 12 million black Americans lived in the South. Hispanic Americans, whose population exceeded a million, were concentrated in a belt along the United States–Mexican border. When jobs for minorities opened in war centers, African and Hispanic Americans became increasingly urban. In cities, too, they confronted entrenched systems of segregation that denied them basic rights to decent housing, jobs, and political participation. Competition with white residents for housing and the use of public parks, beaches, and transportation produced explosive racial tensions.

To ease crowding the government funded new housing. In Detroit, federal authorities had picked a site for minority housing along the edge of a Polish *Detroit riots* neighborhood. One such project, named in honor of the black abolitionist Sojourner Truth, included 200 units for black families. When the first of them tried to move in, local officials had to send several hundred National Guardsmen to protect the newcomers from menacing Ku Klux Klan members. With a hot summer approaching, riots broke out in June 1943, as white mobs beat up African Americans riding public trolleys or patronizing movie theaters, and black protesters looted white stores. Six thousand soldiers from nearby bases finally imposed a troubled calm, but not before the riot had claimed the lives of 24 black and 9 white residents.

In southern California Anglo hostility toward Latinos focused on pachucos, or "zoot suiters." These young Hispanic men and boys had adopted the stylish fashions of Harlem hipsters: greased hair swept back into a ducktail; broad-shouldered, long-waisted suit coats; baggy pants pegged at the ankles. The Los Angeles city council passed an ordinance making it a crime even to wear a zoot suit. For most "zooters" this style was a modest form of rebellion; for a few it was a badge of criminal behavior; for white servicemen it was a target for racism.

In June 1943 sailors from the local navy base invaded Hispanic neighborhoods in search of zooters who had allegedly attacked servicemen. The self-*Zoot suit riots* appointed vigilantes grabbed innocent victims, tore their clothes, cut their hair, and beat them. When Hispanics retaliated, the police arrested them, ignoring the actions of the sailors. Irresponsible newspaper coverage made matters worse. "ZOOTERS THREATEN L.A. POLICE," charged one Hearst paper. A citizens committee created at the urging of California Governor Earl Warren rejected Hearst's inflammatory accusations. Underlying Hispanic anger were the grim realities of poor housing, unemployment, and white racism. All that added up to a level of poverty that wartime prosperity eased but in no way resolved.

Minority leaders acted on the legal as well as the economic front. The Congress of Racial Equality (CORE), a nonviolent civil rights group inspired *CORE and nonviolence* by the Indian leader Mohandas K. Gandhi, used sit-ins and other peaceful tactics to desegregate some restaurants and movie theaters. In 1944 the Supreme Court outlawed the "all-white primary," an infamous device used by southerners to exclude blacks from voting in primary elections within the Democratic party. Because Democratic candidates in the South often ran unopposed in the general elections, the primary elections were usually the only true political contests. In *Smith v. Allwright* the Court ruled that since political parties were integral parts of public elections, they could not deny minorities the right to vote in primaries. Such new attitudes opened the door to future gains.

The New Deal in Retreat

After Pearl Harbor, Roosevelt told reporters that "Dr. New Deal" had retired in favor of "Dr. Win-the-War." Political debates, however, could not be eliminated, even during a global conflict. The increasingly powerful anti–New Deal coalition of Republicans and rural Democrats saw in the war an opportunity to attack programs they had long resented. They quickly ended the Civilian Conservation Corps and the National Youth Administration, reduced the powers of the Farm Security Administration, and blocked moves to extend social security and unemployment benefits. Seeming to approve such measures, voters in the 1942 elections sent an additional 44 Republicans to the House and another 9 to the Senate. The GOP began eyeing the White House.

By the spring of 1944 no one knew whether Franklin Roosevelt would seek an unprecedented fourth term. His health had declined noticeably. Pallid skin,

Election of 1944   sagging shoulders, and shaking hands seemed open signs that he had aged too much to run. In July, one week before the Democratic convention, Roosevelt announced his decision: "All that is within me cries out to go back to my home on the Hudson River. . . . But as a good soldier . . . I will accept and serve." Conservative Democrats, however, made sure that FDR's liberal vice president, Henry Wallace, would not remain on the ticket. In his place they settled on Harry S Truman of Missouri, a loyal Democrat. The Republicans chose the moderate governor of New York, Thomas E. Dewey, to run against Roosevelt, but Dewey never had much of a chance. At the polls, voters gave Roosevelt 25.6 million popular votes to Dewey's 22 million, a clear victory, although the election was tighter than any since 1916. Like its aging leader, the New Deal coalition was showing signs of strain.

WINNING THE WAR AND THE PEACE

To impress upon newly arrived officers the vastness of the war theater in the Pacific, General Douglas MacArthur laid out a map of the region with the outline of the United States laid over it. Running the war from headquarters in Australia, the distances were about the same as if, in the Western Hemisphere, the center were located in South America. On the same scale, Tokyo would lie far up in northern Canada, Iwo Jima somewhere in Hudson Bay, Singapore in Utah, Manila in North Dakota, and Hawaii off the coast of Scotland.

In a war that stretched from one end of the globe to the other, the Allies had to coordinate their strategies on a grand scale. Which war theaters would receive equipment in short supply? Who would administer conquered territories? Inevitably, the questions of fighting a war slid into discussions of the peace that would follow. What would happen to occupied territories? How would the Axis powers be punished? If a more stable world order could not be created, the cycle of violence might never end. So as Allied armies struggled mile by mile to defeat the Axis, Allied diplomacy concentrated just as much on winning the peace.

The Fall of the Third Reich

After pushing the Germans out of North Africa in May 1943, Allied strategists agreed to Churchill's plan to drive Italy from the war. Late in July, two weeks after a quarter of a million British and American troops had landed on Sicily, Mussolini fled to German-held northern Italy. Although Italy surrendered early in September, Germany continued to pour in reinforcements. It took the Allies almost a year of bloody fighting to reach Rome, and at the end of the campaign they had yet to break German lines. Along the eastern front, Soviet armies steadily pushed the Germans out of Russia and back toward Berlin.

General Dwight D. Eisenhower, fresh from battle in North Africa and the Mediterranean, took command of Allied preparations for Operation Overlord,

D-Day

the long-awaited opening of a second front in western Europe. By June 1944 all eyes focused on the coast of France, for Hitler, of course, knew the Allies would attack across the English Channel. Allied planners did their best to focus his attention on Calais, the French port city closest to the British Isles. On the morning of June 6, 1944, the invasion began—not at Calais but on the less fortified beaches of Normandy (see the map, page 748). Almost 3 million men, 11,000 aircraft, and more than 2000 vessels took part in D-Day.

As Allied forces hit the beaches, luck and Eisenhower's meticulous planning favored their cause. Still convinced that Calais was the Allied target, Hitler delayed sending in two reserve divisions. His indecision allowed the Allied forces to secure a foothold. Still, the Allied advance from Normandy took almost two months, not several weeks as expected. Once Allied tanks broke through German lines, their progress was spectacular. In August, Paris was liberated, and by mid-September, the Allies had driven the Germans from France and Belgium.

Battle of the Bulge

Hitler's desperate counterthrust in the Ardennes Forest in December 1944 succeeded momentarily, pushing back the Allies along a 50-mile bulge. But the "Battle of the Bulge" cost the Germans their last reserves. After George Patton's forces rescued trapped American units, little stood between the Allies and Berlin.

Two Roads to Tokyo

In the bleak days of 1942 General Douglas MacArthur—flamboyant and jaunty with his dark sunglasses and corncob pipe—had emerged as America's great military hero. MacArthur believed that the future of America lay in the Far East. The Pacific theater, he argued, not the European, should have top priority. In March 1943 the Combined Chiefs of Staff agreed to his plan for a westward advance along the northern coast of New Guinea toward the Philippines and Tokyo. Naval forces directed by Admiral Chester Nimitz used amphibious warfare to pursue a second line of attack, along the island chains of the central Pacific. American submarines cut Japan's supply lines.

By July 1944 the navy's leapfrogging campaign had reached the Mariana Islands, east of the Philippines. From there B-29 bombers could reach the Japanese home islands. As a result, Admiral Nimitz proposed bypassing the

WORLD WAR II IN THE PACIFIC AND ASIA Extraordinary distances complicated the war in the Pacific. As the map shows, American forces moved on two fronts: the naval war in the central Pacific and General MacArthur's campaign in the southwest Pacific.

MacArthur returns

Philippines in favor of a direct attack on Formosa (present-day Taiwan). MacArthur insisted on fulfilling a promise he had made "to eighteen million Christian Filipinos that the Americans would return." President Roosevelt himself came to Hawaii to resolve the impasse, giving MacArthur the green light. Backed by more than 100 ships of the Pacific Fleet, the general splashed ashore on the island of Leyte in October 1944.

The decision to invade the Philippines led to savage fighting until the war ended. As retreating Japanese armies left Manila, they tortured and slaughtered

Battle of Leyte Gulf

tens of thousands of Filipino civilians. The United States suffered 62,000 casualties redeeming MacArthur's pledge, but a spectacular U.S. Navy victory at the Battle of Leyte Gulf spelled the end of the Japanese Imperial Navy as a fighting force. MacArthur and Nimitz prepared to tighten the noose around Japan's home islands.

Big Three Diplomacy

While Allied cooperation gained military victories in both Europe and the Pacific, negotiations over the postwar peace proved knottier. Churchill believed that only a stable European balance of power, not an international agency, could preserve peace. In his view the Soviet Union was the greatest threat to upset that balance of power. Premier Joseph Stalin left no doubt that an expansive notion of Russian security defined his war aims. For future protection Stalin expected to annex the Baltic states, once Russian provinces, along with bits of Finland and Romania and about half of prewar Poland. In eastern Europe and other border areas such as Iran, Korea, and Turkey, he wanted "friendly" neighbors. It soon became apparent that "friendly" meant regimes dependent on Moscow.

Early on, Roosevelt had promoted his own version of an international balance of power, which he called the "Four Policemen." Under its framework, the Soviet Union, Great Britain, the United States, and China would guarantee peace through military cooperation. But by 1944 Roosevelt had rejected both this scheme and Churchill's wish to return to a balance of power that hemmed in the Russians. Instead, he looked to bring the Soviet Union into a peacekeeping system based on an international organization similar to the League of Nations. But this time, all the great powers would participate, including the United States. Whether Churchill and Stalin—or the American people as a whole—would accept the idea was not yet clear.

The Road to Yalta

The outlines and the problems of a postwar settlement emerged during several summit conferences among the Allied leaders. In November 1943, with Italy's

Teheran Conference

surrender in hand and the war against Germany going well, Churchill and Roosevelt agreed to make a hazardous trip to Teheran, Iran. There, the Big Three leaders met together for the first time. ("Seems very confident," Roosevelt said of Stalin, "very sure of himself, moves slowly—altogether quite impressive.") The president tried to charm the Soviet premier, teasing Churchill for Stalin's benefit, keeping it up "until Stalin was laughing with me, and it was then that I called him 'Uncle Joe.'"

Teheran proved to be the high point of cooperation among the Big Three. It was there that FDR and Churchill finally committed to the D-Day invasion Stalin had so long sought. In return he promised to launch a spring offensive to pin down German troops on the eastern front. He also reaffirmed his earlier pledge to declare war against Japan once Germany was beaten.

But thorny disagreements over the postwar peace remained. That was clear in February 1945, when the Big Three met at the Russian resort city of Yalta,

Yalta Conference on the Black Sea. By then, Russian, British, and American troops were closing in on Germany. Roosevelt arrived tired, ashen. At 62, limited by his paralysis, he had visibly aged. He came to Yalta mindful that although Germany was all but beaten, Japan still held out in the Pacific. Under no circumstances did he want Stalin to withdraw his promise to enter the fight against Japan or to join a postwar international organization. Churchill remained ever mistrustful of Soviet intentions. The Russians appeared only too eager to fill the power vacuum that a defeated Japan and Germany would leave.

Allied differences were most clearly reflected in their discussions over Poland. Having gone to war to protect Poland, the British wanted to ensure

Poland that it survived as an independent nation. But the presence of Soviet troops there gave Stalin the determining voice. For him, Poland was the historic corridor of invasion used by Russia's enemies. After Soviet troops reentered Poland, he insisted that he would recognize only the Communist-controlled government at Lublin. Stalin also demanded that Russia receive territory in eastern Poland, for which the Poles would be compensated with German lands. That was hardly the "self-determination" the Atlantic Charter called for. Roosevelt proposed a compromise. For the time being, Poland would have a coalition government; after the war, free elections would settle the question of who should rule. The Soviets would also receive the territory they demanded in eastern Poland, and the western boundary would be established later.

Similarly, the Allies remained at odds about Germany's postwar future. Stalin was determined that the Germans would never invade Russia again. Many

Dividing Germany Americans shared his desire to have Germany punished and its war-making capacity eliminated. At the Teheran Conference, Roosevelt and Stalin had proposed that the Third Reich be split into five powerless parts. Churchill, on the other hand, was much less eager to bring low the nation that was the most natural barrier to Russian expansion. The era after World War I, he believed, demonstrated that a healthy European economy required an industrialized Germany.

As with Poland, the Big Three put off making a firm decision. For the time being, they agreed to divide Germany into separate occupation zones (France would receive a zone carved from British and American territory). These four powers would jointly occupy Berlin, while an Allied Control Council supervised the national government.

When the Big Three turned their attention to the Far East, Stalin held a trump card. Fierce Japanese resistance on the islands of Okinawa and Iwo Jima had convinced Roosevelt that only a bloody invasion would force Japan's surrender. He thus secured a pledge from Stalin to declare war within three months of Germany's defeat. The price was high. Stalin wanted to reclaim territories that Russia had lost in the Russo-Japanese War of 1904–1906, as well as control over the Chinese Eastern and South Manchurian railroads.

The agreements reached at Yalta depended on Stalin's willingness to cooperate. In public Roosevelt put the best face on matters. He argued that the new world organization (which Stalin had agreed to support) would "provide the greatest opportunity in all history" to secure a lasting peace. "We shall take responsibility for world collaboration," he told Congress, "or we shall have to bear the responsibility for another world conflict." Privately the president was less optimistic. "When the chips were down," he confessed, he doubted "Stalin would be able to carry out and deliver what he had agreed to."

The Fallen Leader

The Yalta Conference marked one of the last and most controversial chapters of Franklin Roosevelt's presidency. Critics charged that the concessions to Stalin were far too great: Poland had been betrayed; China sold out; the United Nations crippled at birth. Yet Roosevelt gave to Stalin little that Stalin had not liberated with Russian blood and could have taken anyway. Even Churchill, an outspoken critic of Soviet ambitions, concluded that although "our hopeful assumptions were soon to be falsified . . . they were the only ones possible at the time."

What peace Roosevelt might have achieved can never be known. He returned from Yalta visibly ill. On April 12, 1945, while sitting for his portrait at

The legacy of FDR

his vacation home in Warm Springs, Georgia, he complained of a "terrific headache," then suddenly fell unconscious. Two hours later Roosevelt was dead. Not since the assassination of Lincoln had the nation so grieved. Under Roosevelt's leadership government had become a protector, the president a father and friend, and the United States the leader in the struggle against Axis tyranny. Eleanor recalled how many Americans later told her that "they missed the way the President used to talk to them. . . . There was a real dialogue between Franklin and the people."

Truman

Harry S Truman faced the awesome task of replacing Roosevelt.* "Who the hell is Harry Truman?" the chief of staff had asked when Truman was nominated for the vice presidency in 1944. As vice president, Truman had learned almost nothing about the president's postwar plans.

---

*Truman had no middle name, only a middle initial. Thus the S appears without a period.

Sensing his own inadequacies, he adopted a tough pose and made his mind up quickly. People welcomed the new president's decisiveness as a relief from Roosevelt's evasive style. Too often, though, Truman acted before the issues were clear. But he at least knew victory in Europe was at hand as Allied troops swept into Germany from the east and west.

The Holocaust

The horror of war in no way prepared the invading armies for their liberation of the Nazi concentration camps. Hitler, they discovered, had authorized the systematic extermination of all European Jews as well as Gypsies, homosexuals, and others considered deviant. The SS, Hitler's security force, had constructed six extermination centers in Poland. By rail from all over Europe the SS shipped Jews to die in the gas chambers.

No issue of World War II more starkly raised questions of human good and evil than what came to be known as the Holocaust. Tragically, the United States could have done more to save at least some of the 6 million Jews killed. Until the fall of 1941 the Nazis permitted Jews to leave Europe, but few countries would accept them—including the United States. Americans haunted by un-

At Buchenwald in April 1945, Senator Alben Barkley of Kentucky, who became vice president under Harry Truman, viewed firsthand the horror of the Nazis' death camps.

employment feared that a tide of new immigrants would make competition for jobs even worse. Tales of persecution from war refugees had little effect on most citizens: opinion polls showed that more than 70 percent of Americans opposed easing quotas. After 1938 the restrictive provisions of the 1924 Immigration Act were made even tighter.

American Jews wanted to help, especially after 1942 when they learned of the death camps. But they worried that highly visible protests might only ag-

Anti-Semitism

gravate American anti-Semitism. They were also split over support for Zionists working to establish a Jewish homeland in Palestine. Roosevelt and his advisers ultimately decided that the best way to save Jews was to win the war quickly. That still does not explain why the Allies did not do more: they could have bombed the rail lines to the camps, sent commando forces, or tried to destroy the death factories.

A Lasting Peace

After 15 years of depression and then war, the Allies sought a new framework to promote international stability. That system, many believed, needed to be

Postwar organizations

economic as well as political. At a 1944 meeting at Bretton Woods, a resort in New Hampshire, Americans led the way in creating two new economic organizations: the International Monetary Fund (IMF) and the International Bank for Reconstruction and Development, later known as the World Bank. The IMF hoped to promote trade by stabilizing national currencies, while the World Bank was designed to stimulate economic growth by investing in projects worldwide. Later that summer the Allies met at Dumbarton Oaks, a Washington estate, to lay out the structure for the proposed United Nations Organization (UNO, later known simply as the UN). An 11-member Security Council would oversee a General Assembly composed of delegates from all member nations. By the end of the first organizational meeting, held in San Francisco in April 1945, it had become clear that the United Nations would favor the Western powers in most postwar disputes.

While the United Nations was organizing itself in San Francisco, the Axis powers were collapsing in Europe. As Mussolini attempted to escape to Germany, anti-Fascist mobs in Italy captured and slaughtered him like a pig. Adolf Hitler committed suicide in his Berlin bunker on April 30. Two weeks later General Eisenhower accepted the German surrender.

In one final summit meeting, held in July 1945 at Potsdam (just outside of Berlin), President Truman met Churchill and Stalin for the first time. Two is-

Potsdam Conference

sues dominated the meeting: Germany's political fate and how much the defeated nation would pay in reparations. The three leaders agreed that Germany should be occupied and demilitarized. Stalin insisted that Russia receive a minimum of $10 billion in reparations, regardless of how much it might hurt postwar Germany or the European economy. A complicated compromise allowed Britain and the United States to restrict reparations from their zones. But in large part Stalin had his way. For the foreseeable future, Germany would remain divided into occupation zones, and without a central government of its own.

Atom Diplomacy

The issue most likely to shape postwar relations never even reached the bargaining table in Potsdam. On July 16, 1945, Manhattan Project scientists detonated their first atomic device. Upon receiving the news in Germany, Truman seemed a changed man—firmer, more confident. He "told the Russians just where they got on and off and generally bossed the whole meeting," observed Churchill. Several questions loomed. Should the United States now use the bomb? Should it warn Japan before dropping it? And perhaps equally vital, should Truman inform Stalin of the new weapon?

Over the spring and early summer of 1945 administration officials discussed the use of atomic weapons. A few scientists had recommended not using the

Stalin and the bomb

bomb, or at least attempting to convince Japan to surrender by offering a demonstration of the new weapon's power. A high-level committee of administrators, scientists, and political and military leaders dismissed that idea. Rather than tell Stalin directly about the bomb, Truman mentioned obliquely that the United States possessed a weapon of "awesome destructiveness." Stalin showed no surprise, most likely because spies had already informed him about the bomb. Privately, Truman and Churchill decided to drop the first bomb with only a veiled threat of "inevitable and complete" destruction if Japan did not surrender unconditionally. Unaware of the warning's full meaning, officials in Tokyo made no formal reply.

Some historians have charged that Secretary of State James Byrnes, a staunch anti-Communist, believed that a combat demonstration of the bomb would shock Stalin into behaving less aggressively in postwar negotiations. Most evidence, however, indicates that Truman decided to drop the bomb in order to end the war quickly. The victory in the Pacific promised to be bloody. Military leaders estimated that an invasion of Japan would produce heavy Allied casualties.

Before leaving Potsdam, Truman gave the final order for B-29s to drop two atomic bombs on Japan. On August 6 the first leveled four square miles of the

Hiroshima and Nagasaki

city of Hiroshima. Three days later a second exploded over the port of Nagasaki. About 140,000 people died instantly in the fiery blasts. A German priest came upon soldiers who had looked up as the bomb exploded. Their eyeballs had melted from their sockets. Tens of thousands more who lived through the horror began to sicken and die from radiation poisoning.

The two explosions left the Japanese stunned. Breaking all precedents, the emperor intervened and declared openly for peace. On September 3 a somber Japanese delegation boarded the battleship *Missouri* in Tokyo Bay to sign the document of surrender. World War II had ended.

"World War II changed everything," observed one admiral long after the war. The defeatism of the Depression gave way to the exhilaration of victory. Before the war Americans seldom exerted leadership in international affairs. After it, the world looked to the United States to rebuild the economies of Europe and Asia and to maintain peace. Not only had World War II shown the global interdependence of economic and political systems, but it had also increased that interdependence. Out of the war developed a truly international economy. At home the economy became more centralized and the role of the government larger.

Still, a number of fears loomed, even as victory parades snaked down the nation's main streets. Would the inevitable cutbacks in military spending bring on another Depression? Would Soviet ambitions undo the new global peace, much as fascism and economic instability had undone the peace of Versailles? And then there was the shadow of the atom bomb, looming over the victorious as well as the defeated. The United States might control atomic technology for the present, but what if the weapon fell into unfriendly hands? After World War II launched the atomic age, no nation, not even the United States, was safe anymore.

SIGNIFICANT EVENTS

1931–1932 — Japan invades Manchuria; Stimson Doctrine

1933 — Roosevelt recognizes the Soviet Union

1935 — Nye Committee hearings; first Neutrality Act

1936 — Second Neutrality Act; Pan-American Conference

1937 — Third Neutrality Act (cash-and-carry); Roosevelt's quarantine speech; *Panay* incident

1938 — Munich meetings

1939 — Fall of Czechoslovakia; Germany signs nonaggression pact with the Soviet Union; World War II begins in Europe

1940 — Germany launches blitzkrieg against Low Countries and France; Roosevelt supports peacetime draft; Roosevelt wins third term

1941 — Congress adopts Lend-Lease Act; A. Philip Randolph plans march on Washington; Roosevelt creates Fair Employment Practices Commission; Germany invades Soviet Union; Roosevelt and Churchill sign Atlantic Charter; Japan occupies Indochina; Roosevelt imposes embargo against Japan; Pearl Harbor attacked; Hitler and Mussolini declare war on the United States

1942 — War Production Board and War Labor Board created; submarine war in the Atlantic; internment of Japanese Americans; Bataan and Corregidor fall; battles of Guadalcanal, Coral Sea, and Midway fought; American and British troops invade North Africa; Manhattan Project begins

1943 — British-American forces invade Italy; Smith–Connolly Act; Office of War Mobilization replaces WPB; race riot in Detroit; zoot suit riots; Big Three meet at Teheran

1944 — War Refugee Board created; D-Day invasion of France; U.S. forces return to Philippines; Dumbarton Oaks and Bretton Woods meetings; *Smith v. Allwright*; Roosevelt wins fourth term; Allies invade Germany

1945 — Yalta Conference; Roosevelt dies; Truman becomes president; Allied troops liberate extermination camps; first United Nations Organization meeting; Germany surrenders; Potsdam Conference; atom bombs dropped on Japan; World War II ends

The United States in a Nuclear Age

D uring the victory celebrations of 1945, the threat of nuclear annihilation seemed improbably distant to most Americans. Although
President Truman had become increasingly distrustful of Joseph Stalin, the
United States preserved a clear atomic monopoly. The dangers from radioactive fallout impressed only a handful of officials and even fewer members of the
public, who were treated to cheery fantasies of the peacetime use of atomics. (A
1947 issue of *Collier's* magazine showed a smiling paraplegic emerging from the
mushroom cloud of a nuclear treatment, his wheelchair left behind.)

By 1949, when fallout from Russian atomic tests indicated that the U.S. nuclear monopoly had been broken, a grim global realignment was already well
established. Two rival superpowers, the Soviet Union and the United States,
had come to dominate world affairs, replacing the players in the old "balance
of power" politics that had defined European relations for two centuries.

In area and vastness of resources, the Soviet Union surpassed even the
United States, its boundaries encompassing 12 time zones. Given the centuries-
long tradition of authoritarian rule (*czar* is the Russian derivative of caesar), the
Russian Revolution of 1917 took a firmly centralized approach to modernization. At sometimes frightful cost Stalin brought the Soviet Union to its position as superpower by the end of World War II. By the 1960s both the Russians
and the Americans were relying on stockpiles of nuclear weapons to guarantee
their security and power.

Nuclear strategists viewed these stockpiles as essential to a policy of deterrence. Neither side, they hoped, would dare launch a missile attack, knowing
that any nuclear exchange would end in "mutual assured destruction." Yet that
strategy was frightening precisely because the globe could not be neatly divided
into communist and noncommunist halves. The world was riven by ethnic, religious, and economic rivalries, and when the prestige of either superpower became critically involved, such regional conflicts threatened to escalate into a
full-scale nuclear war.

Over time, both the Soviets and the Americans discovered the limits of pro-
jecting their power. For more than a decade, the United States fought an
unsuccessful war against North Vietnam before withdrawing in defeat. For

another decade, the Soviet Union waged a similarly unsuccessful war in Afghanistan. In both cases, regional rivalries remained strong. In the Middle East, both the Soviets and the Americans found that Arab nationalism and Islamic fundamentalism proved more influential than communist or free-market ideologies.

As the Western world recovered from the devastation of World War II, the peacetime economic expansion that benefited Americans also allowed both West Germany and Japan, their former enemies, to grow into modern industrial states. But the global economy did not expand indefinitely. In America, the boom and development mentality of the 1950s and 1960s was tempered in the 1970s as the environmental costs of air and water pollutants, strip mining, and pesticides became clearer. Similarly, by the mid-1970s major Soviet rivers like the Ural, Volga, and Dnieper were badly polluted by industrial wastes. Smog from coal-fired electrical plants plagued China's northern cities, while damage from acid rain could be charted in neighboring regions.

By the end of the 1980s the natural limits of global growth and the strains of a nuclear standoff were becoming clear. The Soviet empire saw its Eastern European satellite nations break away. The Union of Soviet Socialist Republics itself split into a host of nations divided by ethnic and religious rivalries. Although some Americans cheered at having "won" the cold war, the U.S. economy suffered from an immense federal debt run up in large part by military budgets aimed at checking Soviet power.

The multipolar world emerging in the 1990s reflected a truly global theater of markets, cultures, and politics. Growing industrialization had also created such threats as a hole in the ozone layer and the possibility of a global warming trend. The United States, no longer such a dominant economic power, gratefully left behind 50 years of a long and costly cold war. Its challenge, instead, was to rebuild its decayed public infrastructure, retrain displaced workers, and restore growth without further degrading the global environment. Half a millennium after the civilizations of two hemispheres achieved sustained contact, their ultimate fates have been indivisibly intertwined.

CHAPTER TWENTY-EIGHT

Cold War America

The war had been over for almost five months and still troop ships steamed into New York. Timuel Black was packing his duffel below decks when he heard some of the white soldiers shout, "There she is! The Statue of Liberty!"

Black felt a little bitter about the war. He'd been drafted in Chicago in 1943, just after race riots ripped the city. His father, a strong supporter of civil rights, was angry. "What the hell are you goin' to fight in Europe for? The fight is here." He wanted his son to go with him to demonstrate in Detroit, except the roads were blocked and the buses and trains screened to prevent African Americans from coming in to "make trouble."

Instead, Black went off to fight the Nazis, serving in a segregated army. He'd gone ashore during the D-Day invasion and marched through one of the German concentration camps. "The first thing you get is the stench," he recalled. "Everybody knows that's human stench. You begin to see what's happened to these creatures. And you get—I got more passionately angry than I guess I'd ever been." He thought: if it could happen to Jews in Germany, it could happen to black folk in America. So when the white soldiers called to come up and see the Statue of Liberty, Black's reaction was, "Hell, I'm not goin' up there. Damn that." But he went up after all. "All of a sudden, I found myself with tears, cryin' and saying the same thing [the white soldiers] were saying. Glad to be home, proud of my country, as irregular as it is. Determined that it could be better."

At the same time Betty Basye was working as a nurse in California. Her hospital treated soldiers shipped back from the Pacific: "Blind young men. Eyes gone, legs gone. Parts of the face. Burns—you'd land with a fire bomb and be up in flames." She'd joke with the men, trying to keep their spirits up, talking about times to come. She liked to take Bill, one of her favorites, for walks downtown. Half of Bill's face was gone, and civilians would stare. It happened to other patients, too. "Nicely dressed women, absolutely staring, just standing there staring." Some people wrote the local paper, wondering why disfigured vets couldn't be kept on their own grounds and off the streets. Such callousness made Basye indignant. But once the war ended, Basye had to think about her own future. "I got busy after the war," she recalled, "getting married and having my four children. That's what you were supposed to do. And getting your house in suburbia."

Yet as Betty Basye and Timuel Black soon discovered, the return to "normal" life was filled with uncertainties. The first truly global war had left a large part of Europe in ruins and the old balance of power shattered. So great was the rebuilding task that it soon became clear the United States would have a central role in shaping whatever new world order emerged. Isolation seemed neither practical nor desirable in an era where the power of the Soviet Union and communism seemed on the rise.

To blunt the threat of a world shaped by communism, the United States converted not so much to peace as to a "cold war" against its former Soviet ally.

Effects of the cold war   This undeclared war came to affect almost every aspect of American life. Abroad, it justified a far wider military and economic role for the United States—not just in Europe but in the Middle East and along the Asian Pacific rim, from Korea to Indochina. At home it sent politicians searching the land for communist spies and "subversives," from the State Department to the movie studios of Hollywood.

Trying to deter war in times of peace dramatically increased the role of the military-industrial-university complex formed during World War II. A people who had once resisted government intrusion into individual lives now accepted a large defense establishment. They voted, too, to maintain programs that ensured an active federal role in managing the economy.

THE RISE OF THE COLD WAR

World War II devastated lands and people almost everywhere outside the Western Hemisphere. As the world struggled to rebuild, power that had once been centered in Europe shifted to nations on its periphery. In place of Germany, France, and England the United States and the Soviet Union emerged as the world's two reigning superpowers—and as mortal enemies. This rivalry was not altogether an equal one. At war's end, the United States had a booming economy, a massive military establishment, and the atomic bomb. By contrast, much of the Soviet Union lay in ruins.

But the defeat of Germany and Japan left no power in Europe or Asia to block the still formidable Soviet army. Many Americans feared that desperate,

American worries about Soviet intentions   war-weary peoples would find the appeal of communism irresistible. If Stalin intended to extend the Soviet Union's dominion, only the United States had the economic and military might to block him. Events in the critical years of 1945 and 1946 persuaded most Americans that Stalin did have such a plan. The Truman administration concluded that "the USSR has engaged the United States in a struggle for power, or 'cold war', in which our national security is at stake and from which we cannot withdraw short of national suicide." What had happened that led Western leaders to such a dire view of their former Soviet allies? How did such a wide breach open between the two nations?

American Suspicions

Even before postwar events deepened American suspicions of the Soviets, an ideological gulf had separated the two nations. The October Revolution of

Roots of the cold war

1917 shocked most Americans. They had come to view Lenin's Bolshevik revolutionaries with a mixture of fear, suspicion, and loathing. As the communists grasped power, they had often used violence and terror to achieve their ends. As Marxists they rejected both religion and the notion of private property, two institutions central to the American dream. Furthermore, Soviet propagandists had made no secret that they intended to export revolution throughout the world, including the United States.

One event leading to World War II taught Western leaders to resist "appeasement." In 1938 British Prime Minister Neville Chamberlain's attempt to

Munich analogy

satisfy Hitler's demands on Czechoslovakia only emboldened the Nazis to expand further (page 747). After the war, Secretary of the Navy James Forrestal applied the Munich analogy to the new Europe. Appeasing Russian demands, he believed, would only seem like an attempt "to buy their understanding and sympathy. We tried that once with Hitler. . . . There are no returns on appeasement." To many of Truman's advisers, the Soviet dictator seemed as much bent on conquest as Hitler.

In April 1946 *Time* magazine portrayed communism as a disease, liable to "infect" unsuspecting populations the world over.

Communist Expansion

During the war, Stalin did make numerous demands to control territory along the Soviet borders. And with the coming of peace, he continued to push for greater influence. He asked for a role in controlling the Dardanelles, the narrow straits linking Soviet ports on the Black Sea with the Mediterranean Sea (see the map, page 788). In Iran, Soviet forces occupying northern Iran lent support to rebels seeking to break away from the Iranian government. In Greece, local Communists led the fighting to overturn the traditional monarchy.

Asia, too, seemed a target for Communist ambitions. Russian occupation forces in Manchuria were turning over captured Japanese arms to Chinese Communists under Mao Zedong. Russian troops controlled the northern half of Korea. In Vietnam leftist nationalists were fighting against the return of colonial rule.

COUNTERPOINT   *What Were Stalin's Intentions?*

Despite Russian actions, many historians have argued that American policymakers consistently exaggerated Stalin's ambitions. At war's end, much of the farmland and industry in the Soviet Union lay in ruins. Over the previous two centuries, Russians had seen their lands invaded once by Napoleon (in 1812) and twice by Germany, during the two world wars. In 1945, as the Soviets struggled to rebuild their war-ravaged economy, the United States continued to gain influence and power. When Stalin looked outward, he saw American occupation forces in Europe and Asia ringing the Soviet Union, their military might backed by a newly developed atomic arsenal. American corporations owned or controlled vast oil fields in the Middle East. Along with the French and the British, the United States was a strong presence in Southeast Asia. Given that situation, one could argue that Stalin's actions after the war were primarily defensive, designed to counter what appeared to him a threatening American–European alliance.

In the 1990s, after the breakup of the Soviet Union, historians were able to consult previously closed Russian archives. New evidence suggests that Stalin's position had not been so defensive. Despite the ravages of war, Stalin recognized that in 1945 the Soviet Union was emerging as a more powerful state. With Germany and Japan defeated, Soviet borders to the east and west were secure from invasion. Only to the south did Stalin see a problem, along the border with Iran. Further, he recognized that the people of Britain and the United States had tired of fighting. Their leaders were not about to threaten the Soviet Union with war, at least not in the near term. Equally significant, Soviet spies had informed Stalin that in 1946 the United States possessed only a few atom bombs. For the time being, the nuclear threat was more symbolic than real. These historians thus conclude that Stalin was neither a global expansionist nor a leader fearful that his nation would soon be encircled and broken apart by American imperialists. Rather, he was a political realist eager to advance the interests of the Soviet state and his own regime—so long as his actions did not risk war.

The tensions arising from the conflicting Soviet and American points of view came to a head in the first months of 1946. Stalin announced in February that the Soviet Union would act vigorously to preserve its national security. In a world dominated by capitalism, he warned, future wars were inevitable. The Russian people had to ensure against "any eventuality" by undertaking a new five-year plan for economic development.

Although some Americans thought Stalin was merely rallying Russian support for his domestic programs, others saw their worst fears confirmed. *Time*

The move to "get tough"

magazine, an early voice for a "get tough" policy, called Stalin's speech "the most warlike pronouncement uttered by any top-rank statesman since V-J day." "I'm tired of babying the Soviets," remarked President Truman, who in any case seldom wore kid gloves. Even his mother passed along a message: "Tell Harry to be good, be honest, and behave himself, but I think it is now time for him to get tough with someone." In March Winston Churchill warned that the Soviets had dropped an "Iron Curtain" between their satellite nations and the free world. Poland, East Germany, Romania, and Bulgaria lay behind it. Iran, Greece, Turkey, and much of Europe seemed at risk.

A Policy of Containment

As policymakers groped for a way to deal with these developments, the State Department received a diplomatic cable. It was extraordinary both for its length

George Kennan's "long telegram"

(8000 words) and for its impact in Washington. The author was George Kennan, chargé d'affaires in Moscow and long a student of Soviet conduct. In his "long telegram," Kennan argued that Russian leaders, including Stalin, were so paranoid that it was impossible to reach any useful agreements with them. This temperament could best be explained by "the traditional and instinctive Russian sense of insecurity." When combined with Marxist ideology that viewed capitalism as evil, that insecurity created a potent force for expansion, Kennan argued. Soviet power "moves inexorably along a prescribed path, like a toy automobile wound up and headed in a given direction, stopping only when it meets some unanswerable force."

The response Kennan recommended was "containment." The United States must apply "unalterable counterforce at every point where [the Soviets] show signs of encroaching upon the interests of a peaceful and stable world." The idea of containment was not particularly novel, but Kennan's analysis provided leaders in Washington with a clear strategic plan for responding to Soviet behavior. By applying firm diplomatic, economic, and military counterpressure, the United States could block Russian aggression. Truman wholeheartedly adopted the doctrine of containment.

The Truman Doctrine

The first major test of Soviet and American wills came in early 1947. As Europe reeled under severe winter storms and a depressed postwar economy, Great

Aid to Greece and Turkey

Britain announced that it could no longer support the governments of Greece and Turkey. Without British aid, the Communist movements within these countries seemed destined to win critical victories. Truman decided that the United States should shore up Greek and Turkish resistance. He asked Congress to provide $400 million in military and economic aid. To gain support he went before Congress in March, determined to "scare hell out of the country." The world was now divided into two hostile camps, the president warned. To preserve the American way of life, the United States must step forward and help "free people" threatened by "totalitarian regimes." This rationale for aid to Greece and Turkey soon became known as the Truman Doctrine.

The Truman Doctrine marked a new level of American commitment to a cold war. Just what responsibility the Soviets had for unrest in Greece and Turkey remained unclear. But Truman had linked communism with rebel movements all across the globe. That committed Americans to a relatively open-ended struggle, in which the president gained expanded powers to act when unrest threatened. Occasionally Congress would regret giving the executive branch so much power, but by 1947 anticommunism had become the dominant theme in American policy, both foreign and domestic.

The Marshall Plan

For all its importance, the Truman Doctrine did not aid Western Europe. There, national treasuries were empty, city streets stood dark, people starved, and factories were closed. American diplomats warned that without aid to revive the European economy, Communists would seize power in Germany, Italy, and France. If Western Europe fell, the cold war could be lost.

In June 1947 Secretary of State George C. Marshall told a Harvard commencement audience about a plan to ensure the recovery of Europe. He invited all European nations, East or West, to request assistance to rebuild their economies. Unlike Truman, Marshall did not emphasize the communist menace. All the same, his massive aid plan was designed to eliminate conditions that produced the discontent that Communists often exploited. Then, too, humanitarian aid had practical benefits. As Europe recovered, so would its interest in buying American goods. Marshall did not rule out Soviet participation in the massive aid program. Still, he gambled—correctly—that fears of American economic domination would lead the Soviets and their allies to reject his offer.

At first neo-isolationists in Congress argued that the United States could not afford such generosity. But when Communists expelled the non-Communists from Czechoslovakia's government, the cold war seemed to spread. Congress then approved the Marshall Plan, as it became known. The blame for dividing Europe fell on the Soviet Union, not the United States. And the Marshall Plan proved crucial to Western Europe's economic recovery.

NATO

American efforts to stabilize Europe placed Stalin on the defensive. In 1947 he moved against the moderate government in Hungary, which since 1945 had been chosen through relatively free elections. Soviet forces replaced the gov-

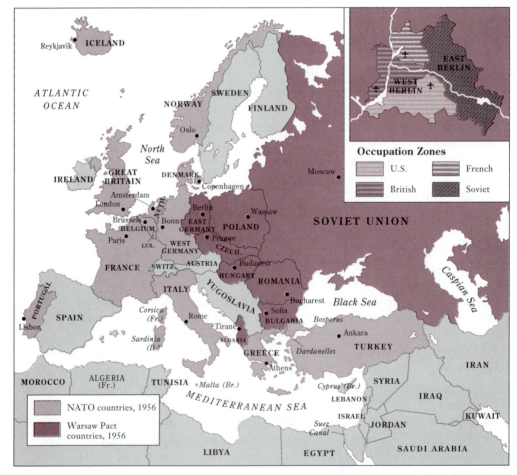

COLD WAR EUROPE By 1956 the postwar occupation of Europe had hardened into hostile spheres. As a western outpost within the Soviet bloc, West Berlin remained a source of cold war tensions.

ernment with a Communist regime dependent on Moscow. Then in February 1948 Communists toppled the elected government of Czechoslovakia. Shortly after, news came that the popular Czech foreign minister, Jan Masaryk, had fallen to his death from a small bathroom window. Suicide was the official explanation, but many suspected murder.

The spring of 1948 brought another clash between the Soviets and their former allies, this time over Germany. There, the United States, Great Britain,

Berlin airlift and France decided to transform their occupation zones into an independent West German state. The Western-controlled sectors of Berlin, however, lay over 100 miles to the east, well within the Soviet zone. On June 24 the Soviets reacted by blockading land access to Berlin. Truman did not hesitate to respond. "We are going to stay, period." But he did say no when General Lucius Clay proposed to shoot his way through the blockade. Instead, the United States began a massive airlift of supplies that lasted almost a year. In May 1949 Stalin lifted the blockade, conceding that he could not prevent the creation of West Germany.

Stalin's aggressive actions accelerated the American effort to use military means to contain Soviet ambitions. By 1949 the United States and Canada had

NATO formed joined with Britain, France, Belgium, the Netherlands, and Luxembourg to establish the North Atlantic Treaty Organization (NATO) as a mutual defense pact. For the first time since George Washington had warned against the practice in his Farewell Address of 1793, the United States during peacetime entered into entangling alliances with European nations.

Truman's firm handling of the Berlin crisis won him applause from both Democrats and Republicans. They were equally enthusiastic about another

Israel recognized presidential action. Minutes after Jewish residents of Palestine announced their independence in May 1948, Truman recognized the new state of Israel. He had previously supported the immigration of Jews into Palestine, despite the opposition of oil-rich Arab states and diplomats in the State Department. The president sympathized with Jewish aspirations for a homeland. He also faced a tough campaign in 1948 in which Jewish votes would be critical. As British Prime Minister Clement Attlee observed, "There's no Arab vote in America, but there's a heavy Jewish vote and the Americans are always having elections."

The Atomic Shield versus the Iron Curtain

The Berlin crisis forced Truman to consider the possibility of war. If it came, would atomic weapons again be used? That dilemma raised two other difficult questions. Should the decision to use atomic weapons rest in civilian or military hands? And was it possible to find a way to ease the atomic threat by creating an international system to control nuclear power?

On the question of civilian or military control of the bomb, Truman's response was firm. He was not going to have "some dashing lieutenant colonel

Atomic Energy Commission

decide when would be the proper time to drop one." In 1946 Congress seemed to have decided the issue in Truman's favor when it passed the McMahon Act. This bill established the Atomic Energy Commission (AEC) with control of all fissionable materials for both peacetime and military applications. The AEC was a civilian, not a military, agency.

But civilian control was not so complete as Truman had demanded. The wartime head of the Manhattan Project, General Leslie Groves, had been working behind the scenes to give the military a decisive voice in atomic policy. During debate over the bill, Groves had leaked information about a Canadian atomic spy ring delivering secrets to the Soviet Union. That news spread doubts that scientists and civilians could be trusted with key secrets. Thus Groves persuaded Congress to allow the military to review many civilian decisions and even severely limit their actions.

The idea of international control of atomic energy also fell victim to cold war fears. Originally a high-level government committee proposed to Truman that the mining and use of the world's atomic raw materials be supervised by the United Nations. The committee argued that in the long run the United States would be more secure under a system of international control than by relying on its temporary nuclear monopoly. But Truman chose Bernard Baruch, a staunch cold warrior, to draw up the recommendations to the United Nations

Baruch plan

in June 1946. Baruch's proposals ensured that the United States would dominate any international atomic agency. The Soviets countered with a plan calling for destruction of all nuclear bombs and a ban on their use. But Baruch had no intention of bargaining. It was either his plan or nothing, he announced. And so it was nothing. The Truman administration never seriously considered the possibility of giving up the American nuclear monopoly.

Atomic Deterrence

Ironically, because so much secrecy surrounded the bomb, many military planners knew little about it. Even Truman had no idea in 1946 how many bombs the United States possessed. (For the two years after Hiroshima, it was never more than a dozen.) Military planners, however, soon found themselves relying more and more on atomic weapons. The Soviet army had at its command over 260 divisions. The United States, in contrast, had reduced its forces by 1947 to little more than a single division. As the cold war heated up, American military planners were forced to adopt a nuclear strategy in face of the overwhelming superiority of Soviet forces. They would deter any Soviet attack by setting in place a devastating atomic counterattack.

At first, this strategy of nuclear deterrence was little more than a doomsday scenario to incinerate vast areas of the Soviet Union. A 1946 war plan, "Pincher," proposed obliterating 20 Soviet cities if the Soviets attacked Western Europe. By 1948 the war plan "Fleetwood" had raised the tally of cities to 77, with eight bombs aimed for Moscow, seven for Leningrad. Not until "Dropshot," the following year, did planners correct a major flaw in their strategy. If Moscow and Leningrad disappeared, who would be left to surrender? Dropshot recommended sparing those two cities until the second week.

By 1949, then, the cold war framed all aspects of American foreign policy. The Joint Chiefs of Staff had committed themselves to a policy of nuclear deterrence. Western Europe was on its way to economic recovery, thanks to the Marshall Plan. Soviet pressures on Greece and Turkey had abated. Many Americans had hopes that the United States might soon defeat communism.

Yet success brought little comfort. The Soviet Union was not simply a major power seeking to protect its interests and expand where opportunity permitted. In the eyes of many Americans, the Soviets were determined, if they could, to overthrow the United States from either without or within. This was a war being fought not only across the globe but right in America, by unseen agents using subversive means. In this way, the cold war mentality soon came to shape the lives of Americans at home much as it did American policy abroad.

POSTWAR PROSPERITY

At war's end, many business leaders feared that a sudden drop in government purchases would bring back the depressed conditions of the 1930s. Instead, Americans entered into the longest period of prosperity in the nation's history, lasting until the 1970s. Even the fear of communism could not dampen the simple joys of getting and spending.

Two forces drove the postwar economic boom. One was unbridled consumer and business spending that followed 16 years of depression and war. High

Sources of prosperity

war wages had piled up in savings accounts and war bonds. Eager consumers set off to find the new cars, appliances, and foods unavailable during the war. Despite a sharp drop in government spending (from $83 billion in 1945 to only $31 billion in 1946), the gross national product fell less than 1 percent, and employment actually increased. Consumers had taken up the slack.

Government spending at the local, state, and federal levels provided another boost to prosperity. The three major growth industries in the decades after World War II were health care, education, and government programs. Each of these was spurred by public spending. Equally important, the federal government poured millions of dollars into the military-industrial sector. The defense budget, which fell to $9 billion in 1947, reached $50 billion by the time Truman left office. Over the longer term, these factors promoting economic growth became clearer. In 1946, though, the road from war to peace seemed rocky, especially for those at the margins of the economy.

Postwar Adjustments

With millions of veterans looking for peacetime jobs, workers on the home front, especially women and minorities, found themselves out of work. Cultural

Women workers attitudes added to the pressure on these groups to resume more traditional roles. War employment had given many women their first taste of economic independence. As peace came, almost 75 percent of the working women in one survey indicated that they hoped to continue their jobs. But as the troops came home, male social scientists stressed how important it was for women to accept "more than the wife's usual responsibility for her marriage" and offer "lavish—and undemanding—affection" to returning GIs. One marriage counselor urged women to let their husbands know "you are tired of living alone, that you want him now to take charge."

For minorities, the end of the war brought a return of an old labor practice, "last hired, first fired." At the height of the war over 200,000 African

Minority workers Americans and Hispanics had found jobs in shipbuilding. By 1946 that number had dwindled to less than 10,000. The influx of Mexican laborers under the bracero program temporarily halted. In the South, where the large majority of black Americans lived, wartime labor shortages had become surpluses, leaving few jobs available.

At the same time, many black and Hispanic veterans who fought during the war had been treated with greater equality and freedom than they had known

Push for civil rights before enlisting. Thus they often resented returning to a deeply segregated society with limited opportunities. One observer noted that Hispanic veterans in Texas were no longer willing to tolerate discrimination. They "have acquired a new courage, have become more vocal in protesting the restrictions and inequalities with which they are confronted." Benefits received under the GI Bill allowed many Mexican Americans to enter the middle class. When confronted by "haughty, lordly, or unfriendly" businesses, they sometimes organized informal boycotts. Much of the Anglo business community learned to respect this new activism.

Black veterans exerted a similar impact on the civil rights movement. Angered by violence, frustrated by the slow pace of desegregation, they breathed new energy into civil rights organizations like the NAACP and the Congress of Racial Equality. Voting rights was one of the issues they pushed. Registration drives in the South had the greatest success in urban centers like Atlanta. Other black leaders pressed for improved education. In rural Virginia, for example, a young Howard University lawyer, Spottswood Robinson, litigated cases for the NAACP to force improvement in segregated all-black schools. In one county Robinson and the NAACP even won equal pay for black and white teachers.

Out in the countryside, however, segregationists used economic intimidation, violence, and even murder to preserve the "Jim Crow" system. White citizens in rural Georgia lynched several black veterans who had shown the determination to vote. Such instances disturbed President Truman, who saw civil rights as a key ingredient in his reform agenda. The President was especially disturbed when he learned that police in South Carolina had gouged out the eyes of a recently discharged black veteran. Truman responded in December 1946 by appointing a Committee on Civil Rights. A year later it published its report, *To Secure These Rights.*

To Secure These Rights

Discovering inequities for minorities, the committee exposed a racial caste system that denied African Americans employment opportunities, equal education, voting rights, and decent housing. But every time Truman appealed to Congress to implement the committee's recommendations southern senators threatened to filibuster. That opposition forced the President to resort to executive authority to achieve even modest results. In his most direct attack on segregation, he issued an executive order in July 1948 banning discrimination in the armed forces. Segregationists predicted disaster, but experience soon demonstrated that integrated units fought well and exhibited minimal racial tension.

The New Deal at Bay

In September 1945 Harry Truman boldly claimed his intention to extend the New Deal into the postwar era. He called for legislation to guarantee full employment, subsidized public housing, national health insurance, and a peacetime version of the Fair Employment Practices Commission to fight job discrimination. But Truman found that inflation, shortages, and labor unrest undermined his ability to pass such liberal legislation. The combination of increased demand and shortages of consumer goods temporarily in short supply triggered a sharp inflation. For two years prices rose as much as 15 percent annually. Consumers blamed the White House for not doing more to ease their burden.

As inflation ate into paychecks, strikes spread across the nation. Autoworkers walked off the job in the fall of 1945; steelworkers, in January 1946; miners, in April. In 1946 some 5 million workers struck, a rate triple that of any previous year. Antiunion sentiment soared. The crisis peaked in May 1946 with a national rail strike, which temporarily paralyzed the nation's transportation network. An angry President Truman asked, "What decent American would pull a rail strike at a time like this?"

Organized labor

At first, Truman threatened to seize the railroads and then requested from Congress the power to draft striking workers into the military. The strike was settled before the threat was carried out, but few people, whether conservative or liberal, approved the idea of using the draft to punish political foes. Labor leaders, for their part, became convinced they no longer had a friend at the White House.

With Truman's political stock falling, conservative Republicans and southern Democrats joined to block the president's attempts to revive and extend the

New Deal. All he achieved was a watered-down full-employment bill, which created the Council of Economic Advisors. The bill did establish one key principle: the government rather than the private sector was responsible for maintaining full employment. As the congressional elections of 1946 neared, Republicans pointed to production shortages, the procession of strikes, the mismanagement of the economy. "To err is Truman," proclaimed the campaign buttons—or, more simply, "Had enough?" Many voters had. The Republicans gained control of both houses of Congress. Not since 1928 had the Democrats fared so poorly.

Leading the rightward swing was Senator Robert A. Taft of Ohio, son of former President William Howard Taft. Bob Taft not only wanted to halt the spread of the New Deal—he wanted to dismantle it. "We have to get over the corrupting idea we can legislate prosperity, legislate equality, legislate opportunity," he said in dismissing the liberal

Taft–Hartley Act

agenda. Taft especially wished to limit the power of the unions. In 1947 he pushed the Taft–Hartley Act through Congress, over Truman's veto. In the event of a strike, the bill allowed the president to order workers back on the job during a 90-day "cooling-off" period while collective bargaining continued. It also permitted states to adopt "right-to-work" laws, which banned the closed shop by eliminating union membership as a prerequisite for many jobs. Union leaders criticized the new law as a "slave-labor" act. Later, they discovered they could live with it, though it did hurt union efforts to organize, especially in the South.

Despite the conservative backlash, most Americans continued to support the New Deal's major accomplishments: social security, minimum wages, a more active role for government in reducing unemployment. The administration maintained its commitment to setting a minimum wage, raising it again in 1950 from 45 to 75 cents. Social security coverage was broadened to include an additional 10 million workers. Furthermore, a growing list of welfare programs benefited not only the poor but also veterans, middle-income families, the elderly, and students.

The most striking of these was the GI Bill of 1944, which created unparalleled opportunity for returning veterans under the "GI Bill of Rights." Those with more than two years of service received all tuition and fees plus living expenses for three years of college education. By 1948 the govern-

The GI Bill

ment was paying the college costs of almost half of all male students as over 2 million veterans went to college on the GI Bill. The increase in college graduates encouraged a shift from blue- to white-collar work and self-employment. Veterans also received low-interest loans to start businesses or farms of their own and to buy homes. The GI Bill accelerated trends that would transform American society into a prosperous, better-educated, heavily middle-class suburban nation.

The Election of 1948

With his domestic program blocked, Harry Truman faced almost certain defeat in the election of 1948. The New Deal coalition that Franklin Roosevelt had held together for so long seemed to be coming apart. On the left Truman was

Henry Wallace challenged by Henry Wallace, who had been a capable secretary of agriculture and vice president under Roosevelt, then secretary of commerce under Truman. Wallace wanted to pursue New Deal reforms even more vigorously than Truman did, and he continually voiced his sympathy for the Soviet Union. Disaffected liberals bolted the Democratic party to support Wallace on a third-party Progressive ticket.

Within the southern conservative wing of the party, arch-segregationists resented Truman's moderate civil rights proposals for a voting rights bill and an *Dixiecrats* antilynching law. When the liberal wing of the party passed a civil rights plank as part of the Democratic platform, delegates from several Deep South states stalked out of the convention. They banded together to create the States' Rights or "Dixiecrat" party, with J. Strom Thurmond, the segregationist governor of South Carolina, as their candidate.

With the Democrats divided, the Republicans smelled victory. They sought to control the political center by rejecting the conservative Taft in favor of the more moderate former New York governor, Thomas Dewey. Dewey proved so aloof that he inspired scant enthusiasm. "You have to know Dewey well to really dislike him," quipped one critic. Despite such shortcomings, most observers believed that Dewey would walk away with the race. Pollster Elmo Roper stopped canvassing the voters two months before the election.

Truman, however, would not roll over and play dead. He launched a stinging attack against the "reactionaries" in Congress: that "bunch of old mossbacks . . . gluttons of privilege . . . all set to do a hatchet job on the New Deal." From the rear platform of his campaign train, he made almost 400 speeches in eight weeks. Over and over he hammered away at the "do-nothing" 80th Congress, which, he told farmers, "had stuck a pitchfork" in their backs. Still, on election day odds makers favored Dewey by as much as 20 to 1. Hours before the polls closed the archconservative Chicago *Tribune* happily headlined "Dewey Defeats Truman." But the experts were wrong. Not only did the voters return Truman by over 2 million popular votes, they gave the Democrats commanding majorities in the House and Senate.

The defection of the liberal and conservative extremes had allowed Truman to hold the New Deal coalition together, after all. Jews grateful for his stand on Israel, Catholics loyal to the Democratic party, and ethnics all supported him. He had been the first major presidential candidate to campaign in Harlem. Farmers hurt by falling prices deserted the Republicans. An easing of inflation had reminded middle-income Americans that they had benefited significantly under Democratic leadership. "I have a new car and am much better off than my parents were. Why change?" one suburban voter remarked.

The Fair Deal

As he began his new term, Harry Truman declared that all Americans were entitled to a "Fair Deal" from their government. He called for a vigorous revival of New Deal programs like national health insurance and regional TVA-style projects. Echoing an old Populist idea, Truman hoped to keep his working coalition together by forging stronger links between farmers and labor. But the conservative coalition of southern Democrats and Republicans in Congress still blocked any significant new initiatives. On the domestic front Truman remained largely the conservator of Franklin Roosevelt's legacy.

THE COLD WAR AT HOME

Bob Raymondi, a mobster serving a prison term in the late 1940s, was no stranger to racketeering or gangland killings. In fact, he was so feared, he dominated the inmate population at Dannemora Prison. Raymondi made the acquaintance of a group of Communists who had been jailed for advocating the overthrow of the government. He enjoyed talking with people who had some education. When Raymondi's sister learned about his new friends, she was frantic. "My God, Bob," she told him, "You'll get into trouble."

Was something amiss? Many Americans seemed to believe it riskier to associate with Communists than to do so with hardened criminals. Out of a population of 150 million, the Communist party in 1950 could claim a membership of only 43,000. (More than a few of those were FBI undercover agents.) But worry about Communists Americans did. Conservatives still thought of the New Deal as "creeping socialism," only an arm's length short of communism. Leftists, they believed, controlled labor unions, Hollywood, and other interest groups sympathetic to the New Deal. As Stalin extended Soviet control in Eastern Europe and Asia, American fears grew.

The Shocks of 1949

Nineteen forty-nine proved a pivotal year. American scientists reported in August that rains monitored in the Pacific contained traces of hot nuclear waste.

The Soviet A-bomb

Only one conclusion seemed possible: the Soviet Union possessed its own atom bomb. Senator Arthur Vandenberg, a Republican with wide experience in international affairs, summed up the reaction of many to the end of the American nuclear monopoly: "This is now a different world." Truman directed that research into a newer, more powerful hydrogen bomb continue.

Then in December came more bad news. The Nationalist government of Chiang Kai-shek fled mainland China to the offshore island of Formosa

China falls to the Communists

(present-day Taiwan). By January 1950 Communist troops under Mao Zedong swarmed into Beijing, China's capital city. Chiang's defeat came as no surprise to the State Department. Officials there had long regarded Chiang and his Nationalists as hopelessly corrupt and inefficient. Despite major American efforts to save his regime and stabilize China, poverty and civil unrest spread. In 1947 full-scale civil war had broken

The fall of China to the forces of Mao Zedong was one of the
chilling cold war shocks of 1949.

out. By February 1949 almost half of Chiang's demoralized troops had defected
to the Communists. So the December defeat was hardly unexpected.

But Republicans, who had formerly supported the president's foreign pol-
icy, now broke ranks. For some time, a group of wealthy conservatives and
Republican senators had resented the administration's preoccupation with
Europe. Time-Life publisher Henry Luce used his magazines to campaign for
a greater concern for Asian affairs, and especially more aid to defeat Mao
Zedong. When Chiang at last collapsed, his American backers charged the
Democrats with letting the Communists win.

Worries that subversives had sold out the country were heightened when
former State Department official Alger Hiss was brought to trial in 1949 for

*The Alger
Hiss case*

perjury. Hiss, an adviser to Roosevelt at the Yalta Conference,
had been accused by former Communist Whittaker Chambers of
passing secrets to the Soviet Union during the 1930s. Though
the evidence in the case was far from conclusive, the jury convicted Hiss for lying about his association with Chambers. And in February 1950 the nation was

further shocked by news from Britain that a high-ranking physicist, Klaus Fuchs, had spied for the Russians while working on the Manhattan Project. Here was clear evidence of conspiracy at work.

The Loyalty Crusade

As fears of subversion and espionage mounted in the postwar years, President Truman sought ways to protect himself from Republican accusations that he was "soft" on communism. Only days after proposing the Truman Doctrine in March 1947, the president signed an executive order establishing a Federal Employee Loyalty Program designed to guard against any disloyalty by "Reds, phonies, and 'parlor pinks.'" The order required government supervisors to certify the loyalties of those who worked below them, reporting to a system of federal loyalty review boards. The FBI was to follow up any "derogatory information" that came to light.

The system quickly got out of hand. The conservative head of the Loyalty Review Board, Seth Richardson, contended that the government could "discharge any employee for reasons which seem sufficient to the Government, and without extending to such employee any hearing whatsoever." Those accused would have no right to confront their accusers. But a few years' experience showed that it was difficult actually to prove disloyalty on the part of employees. Truman then allowed the boards to fire those who were "potentially" disloyal or "bad security risks," such as alcoholics, homosexuals, and debtors. Suspected employees, in other words, were assumed guilty until proven innocent. After some 5 million investigations, the program identified a few hundred employees who, though not Communists, had at one time been associated with suspect groups. Rather than calm public fears, the loyalty program gave credibility to the growing red scare.

HUAC and Hollywood

Hollywood, with its wealth, glamour, and highly visible Jewish and foreign celebrities, had long aroused a mixture of attraction and suspicion among traditional Americans. In 1947 the House Committee on Un-American Activities (HUAC) began to investigate communist influences in the film industry. "Large numbers of moving pictures that come out of Hollywood carry the communist line," charged committee member John Rankin of Mississippi.

HUAC called a parade of movie stars, screenwriters, and producers to sit in the glare of its public hearings. Some witnesses were considered "friendly" because, like Gary Cooper and Ronald Reagan, they answered committee questions or supplied names of suspected leftists. Others refused to inform on their colleagues or to answer questions about earlier ties to the Communist party. Eventually 10 uncooperative witnesses, known as the "Hollywood Ten," refused on First Amendment grounds to say whether they were or ever had been Communists. They served prison terms for contempt of Congress.

For all its probing, HUAC never offered convincing evidence that film-makers were in any way subversive. Yet the investigation did have a chilling ef-

Blacklisting fect on the entertainment industry. Nervous Hollywood produc-ers turned out patriotic films like *I Was a Communist for the FBI* (1950) in order to demonstrate their loyalty. The studios also fired any actors suspected of leftist leanings, adopting a blacklist that prevented admitted or ac-cused Communists from finding work. Since no judicial proceedings were in-volved, victims of false charges, rumors, or spiteful accusations found it nearly impossible to clear their names.

Suspicion of aliens and immigrants as subversives led finally to the passage, over Truman's veto, of the McCarran Act (1950). It required all Communists to

McCarran Act register with the attorney general, forbade the entry of anyone who had belonged to a totalitarian organization, and allowed the Justice Department to detain suspect aliens indefinitely during deportation hearings. That same year a Senate committee began an inquiry designed to root out homosexuals holding government jobs. Even one "sex pervert in a Government agency tends to have a corrosive influence upon his fellow em-ployees," warned the committee.

The Ambitions of Senator McCarthy

By 1950 anticommunism had created a climate of fear, where legitimate con-cerns mixed with irrational hysteria. Senator Joseph R. McCarthy, a mediocre Republican senator from Wisconsin, saw in that fear an opportunity to improve his political fortunes. Before an audience in Wheeling, West Virginia, in February 1950 he waved a sheaf of papers in the air and announced that he had a list of 205—or perhaps 81, 57, or "a lot" of—Communists in the State Department. (No one, including the senator, could remember the number, which he continually changed.) In the following months McCarthy leveled charge after charge. He had penetrated the "iron curtain" of the State De-partment to discover "card-carrying Communists," the "top Russian espionage agent" in the United States, "egg-sucking phony liberals," and "Communists and queers" who wrote "perfumed notes."

It seemed not to matter that McCarthy never substantiated his charges. When examined, his lists contained names of people who had left the State Department long before or who had been cleared by the FBI. Indeed, the FBI provided McCarthy with the little real evidence he did have. In the summer of 1950 a Senate committee headed by Millard F. Tydings of Maryland concluded that McCarthy's charges were "a fraud and a hoax." Such candor among those in government did not last long as "Jolting Joe" (one of McCarthy's favorite

The energetic Roy Cohn (left) served as the key strategist in the crusades of Senator Joseph McCarthy (center). David Schine (right) joined the committee at Cohn's urging.

nicknames) during the 1950 elections helped defeat Tydings and several other of his Senate critics.

In a sense, McCarthyism was the bitter fruit Truman and the Democrats reaped from their own attempts to exploit the anticommunist mood. McCarthy, more than Truman, tapped the fears and hatreds of traditional conservatives, Catholic leaders, and neo-isolationists who distrusted things foreign, liberal, or intellectual. They saw McCarthy and his fellow witch hunters as the protectors of a vaguely defined but deeply felt spirit of Americanism.

The Democrats and McCarthyism

By the time Truman stepped down as president, 32 states had laws requiring teachers to take loyalty oaths. Government loyalty boards were asking employees what newspapers they subscribed to or phonograph records they collected. A library in Indiana had banned *Robin Hood* because the idea of stealing from the rich to give to the poor seemed too leftish. As one historian commented, "Opening the valve of anticommunist hysteria was a good deal simpler than closing it."

FROM COLD WAR TO HOT WAR AND BACK

As the cold war heated up during 1949, the Truman administration searched for a more assertive foreign policy. The new approach was developed by the National Security Council (NSC), an agency created by Congress in 1947 as part of a plan to help the executive branch respond more effectively to cold war crises. Rather than merely "contain" the Soviets, as George Kennan had suggested, the National Security Council wanted the United States to "strive for victory." In April 1950 the council sent Truman a document, NSC-68, which came to serve as the framework for American policy over the next 20 years.

NSC-68 called for a dramatic increase in defense spending, from $13 billion to $50 billion a year, to be paid for with a large tax increase. Most of the *NSC-68* funds would go to rebuild conventional forces, but the NSC urged that the hydrogen bomb be developed to offset the new Soviet nuclear capacity. Efforts to carry out NSC-68 at first aroused widespread opposition. George Kennan argued that the Soviets had no immediate plans for domination outside the Communist bloc. Fiscal conservatives, both Democrat and Republican, resisted any proposal for higher taxes. All such reservations were swept away on June 25, 1950. "Korea came along and saved us," Secretary of State Dean Acheson later remarked.

Police Action

In 1950 Korea was about the last place Americans might have imagined themselves fighting a war. Since World War II the country had been divided along the 38th parallel: the north was controlled by the Communist government of Kim Il Sung, the south by the dictatorship of Syngman Rhee. Preoccupied with China and the rebuilding of Japan, the Truman administration's interest had dwindled steadily after the war. When Secretary of State Acheson discussed American policy in Asia for the National Press Club in January 1950, he did not even mention Korea.

On June 24 Harry Truman was enjoying a leisurely break from politics at the family home in Independence, Missouri. In Korea it was already Sunday morning when Acheson called the president. North Korean troops had crossed the 38th parallel, Acheson reported, possibly to fulfill Kim Il Sung's proclaimed intention to "liberate" South Korea. Soon Acheson confirmed that a full-scale invasion was in progress. The threat of a third world war, this one atomic, seemed agonizingly real. The United States had to respond with enough force to deter aggression, but without provoking a larger war with the Soviet Union or China.

Truman did not hesitate. American troops would fight the North Koreans, though the United States would not declare war. The fighting in Korea would be a "police action" supervised by the United Nations and commanded by General Douglas MacArthur. That move succeeded only because the Soviet delegate, who had veto power, was absent. Stalin had agreed to the attack, but promised only supplies. Neither Russian troops nor prestige would be involved, he had warned Kim.

Truman's forceful response won immediate approval across America. Congress voted to carry out the recommendations of NSC-68. But by the time

Inchon landing

the UN authorized the police action, on June 27, North Korean forces had pinned the South Koreans within an area around Pusan (see the map on the facing page). In a daring counterstroke, General MacArthur launched an amphibious attack behind North Korean lines at Inchon, near the western end of the 38th parallel. Fighting eastward, MacArthur's troops threatened to trap the invaders, who fled back to the North.

The Chinese Intervene

MacArthur's success led Truman to a fateful decision. With the South liberated, he permitted MacArthur to cross the 38th parallel, drive the Communists from the North, and reunite Korea under Syngman Rhee. Such a victory was just what Truman needed with Senator Joe McCarthy on the attack at home and the 1950 congressional elections nearing. By Thanksgiving American troops had roundly defeated northern forces and were advancing toward the frozen Yalu River, the boundary between Korea and China. MacArthur, made bold by success, promised that the boys would be home by Christmas.

Throughout the fall offensive, however, China's Premier Zhou Enlai cautioned that his country would not tolerate an American presence on its border. Washington officials did not take the warning seriously. Mao Zedong, they assumed, was a Soviet puppet, and Stalin had declared the Korean conflict to be merely a "civil war" and off limits. But on November 26, 400,000 Chinese troops poured across the Yalu, smashing through lightly defended UN lines. At Chosan they trapped 20,000 American and South Korean troops, inflicting one of the worst military defeats in American history. Within three weeks they had driven UN forces back behind the 38th parallel.

So total was the rout that Truman wondered publicly about using the atom bomb. That remark sent a frightened British Prime Minister Clement Attlee flying to Washington to dissuade Truman. The president readily agreed that the war must remain limited and withdrew his nuclear threat.

Truman versus MacArthur

Military stalemate in Korea brought into the open a simmering feud between General MacArthur and Truman. The general had publicized his differences with Truman, arguing UN forces should bomb Chinese and Russian supply bases across the Korean border, blockade China's coast, and unleash Chiang Kai-shek on mainland China. On March 23 he issued a personal ultimatum to Chinese military commanders demanding total surrender. To his Republican

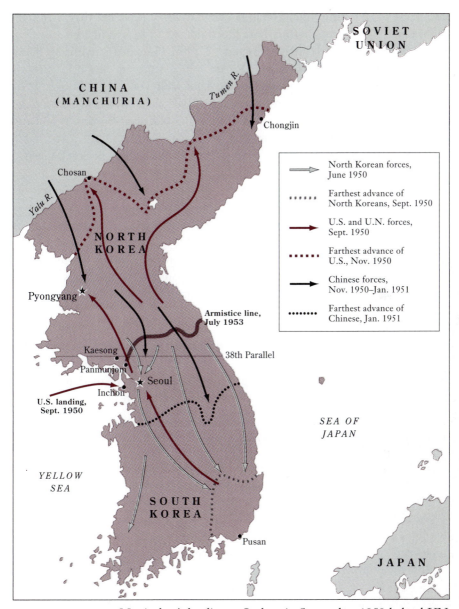

SOVIET
UNION

CHINA
(MANCHURIA)

Tumen R.

Chongjin

Chosan

Yalu R.

NORTH
KOREA

Pyongyang

Kaesong

Panmunjom

Inchon

Seoul

U.S. landing,
Sept. 1950

Armistice line,
July 1953

38th Parallel

SEA OF
JAPAN

YELLOW
SEA

SOUTH
KOREA

Pusan

JAPAN

North Korean forces,
June 1950

Farthest advance of
North Koreans, Sept. 1950

U.S. and U.N. forces,
Sept. 1950

Farthest advance of
U.S., Nov. 1950

Chinese forces,
Nov. 1950–Jan. 1951

Farthest advance of
Chinese, Jan. 1951

THE KOREAN WAR   MacArthur's landing at Inchon in September 1950 helped UN
forces take the offensive. The drive to the Yalu River provoked
the Chinese to intervene.

congressional supporters he sent a letter declaring, "We must win. There is no substitute for victory."

To Truman, MacArthur's strategy appeared to be an open invitation to another world war. Equally alarming, the general's insubordination threatened the tradition that the military remain under clear civilian control. When Truman made plans to discipline him, General Omar Bradley reported that MacArthur was threatening to resign before Truman could act. "The son of a bitch isn't going to resign on me," Truman retorted. "I want him fired!" Military leaders agreed that MacArthur had to go. On April 11 a stunned nation learned that the celebrated military commander had been relieved of his duties. When MacArthur returned to the states, cheering crowds welcomed him with a ticker-tape parade. Congress gave him the unprecedented opportunity to address a joint session before a national television audience.

Behind the scenes, however, Truman was winning this personal clash. At stake was not simply Truman or MacArthur but the future direction of American foreign policy. MacArthur insisted on an all-out effort in Asia. To Secretary of State Dean Acheson, Europe came first. He asked Congress to see Korea as only one link in a worldwide "collective security system." A wider war in Asia would threaten American interests in Europe. Or as General Omar Bradley argued, a showdown in Asia would lead to "the wrong war, at the wrong place, at the wrong time, and with the wrong enemy." Congressional leaders were persuaded of the need to accompany limited war in Korea with a military buildup in Europe.

Still, the continuing war in Korea took its toll on Truman's political fortunes. After July 1951, the war dragged on and so did the aimless peace talks.

Korean stalemate — By March 1952 Truman's popularity had sunk so low that he lost the New Hampshire presidential primary. With that defeat, he announced he would not run for reelection in 1952.

K1C2: The Election of 1952

The Republican formula for victory in 1952 played on the Truman administration's weaknesses. Those did not include the economy, which remained remarkably healthy. Wage and price controls put in place by the administration prevented the sharp inflation that was expected to follow increased wartime spending. But the Republicans could capitalize on the stalemate over Korea. And several of Truman's advisers had been forced to resign for accepting gifts in return for political favors. The campaign strategy was summed up in the formula K1C2: Korea, corruption, and communism.

Republican party regulars and the conservative wing were committed to Robert Taft, who ran surprisingly well in the party primaries. But former military hero Dwight "Ike" Eisenhower was more popular with voters. His backers maneuvered their candidate to a first-ballot nomination. To heal the breach with the Taft delegates, the convention chose the staunch anticommunist Senator Richard Nixon as Eisenhower's running mate.

The Democrats had no candidate as popular as Eisenhower. They drafted Illinois Governor Adlai E. Stevenson, an unusually eloquent speaker. But, like Dewey before him, Stevenson lacked the common touch. The GOP's campaign against communism and corruption, led by Nixon, forced the Democrats on the defensive. Eisenhower, meanwhile, remained high above the mudslinging and promised voters that if elected, he would go to Korea to seek an end to the war.

The election outcome was never much in doubt. Ike's broad smile and confident manner won him over 55 percent of the vote. "The great problem of America today," he had said during the campaign, "is to take that straight road down the middle." Most Americans who voted for him were comforted to think that was just where they were headed.

And Eisenhower kept his pledge "to go to Korea" and review the situation firsthand. Once in office, he renewed negotiations with North Korea but warned

Eisenhower and Korea

that unless the talks made speedy progress, the United States might retaliate "under circumstances of our choosing." The carrot-and-stick approach worked. On July 27, 1953, the Communists and the United Nations forces signed an armistice ending a "police action" in which 54,000 Americans had died. Korea remained divided, almost as it had been in 1950. Communism had been "contained," but at a high price in human lives.

The Fall of McCarthy

It was less clear whether anticommunism could be contained. When Eisenhower called himself a "modern" Republican, he distinguished himself from what he called the more "hidebound" members of the GOP. Their anticommunist campaigns caused him increasing embarrassment. Senator McCarthy's reckless antics, at first directed at Democrats, began to hit Republican targets as well.

By the summer of 1953 the senator was on a rampage. He dispatched two young staff members, Roy Cohn and David Schine, to investigate the State Department's overseas information agency and the Voice of America radio stations. While there, they insisted on purging government libraries of "subversive" volumes. Some librarians, fearing for their careers, burned a number of books. That drove President Eisenhower to denounce "book burners," though soon after he reassured McCarthy's supporters that he did not advocate free speech for Communists.

The administration's own behavior contributed to the hysteria on which McCarthy thrived. The president launched a loyalty campaign, which he claimed resulted in 3000 firings and 5000 resignations of government employees. It was a godsend to McCarthyites: what further proof was needed that subversives were lurking in the federal bureaucracy? Furthermore, a well-publicized spy

Rosenberg case

trial had led to the conviction of Ethel and Julius Rosenberg, a couple accused of passing atomic secrets to the Soviets. Although the evidence was not conclusive, the judge sentenced both Rosenbergs to the electric chair, an unusually harsh punishment even in cases of espionage. When asked to commute the death sentence to life imprisonment, Eisenhower refused and the Rosenbergs were executed in June 1953.

In such a climate—where Democrats remained silent for fear of being called leftists and Eisenhower cautiously refused to "get in the gutter with *that* guy"—

E Y E W I T N E S S   T O   H I S T O R Y

Harry Truman Disciplines
His "Big General"

April 6, 1951

MacArthur shoots another political bomb through Joe Martin, leader of the Republican minority in the House.

This looks like the last straw.

Rank insubordination. Last summer he sent a long statement to the Vets of Foreign Wars—not through the high command back home, but directly! He sent copies to newspapers and magazines particularly hostile to me.

I was furnished a copy from the press room of the White House which had been *accidentally* sent there.

I ordered the release suppressed and then sent him a very carefully prepared directive dated Dec. 5, 1950, setting out Far Eastern policy after I'd flown 14,404 [miles] to Wake Island to see him and reach an understanding face to face.

He told me the war in Korea was over, that we could transfer a regular division to Germany Jan 1st. He was positive Red China would not come in. He expected to support our Far Eastern policy.

---

*The army vs.
McCarthy* — McCarthy lost all sense of proportion. When the army denied his staff aide David Schine a commission, McCarthy decided to investigate communism in the army. The new American Broadcasting Company network, eager to fill its afternoon program slots, televised the hearings. The public had an opportunity to see McCarthy badger witnesses and make a mockery of Senate procedures. Soon after, his popularity began to slide and the anticommunist hysteria ebbed as well. The Senate finally moved to censure him. He died three years later, destroyed by alcohol and the habit of throwing so many reckless punches.

With the Democrats out of the White House for the first time since the Depression and with right-wing McCarthyites in retreat, Eisenhower did indeed seem to be leading the nation on a course "right down the middle." Still, it is worth noting how much that sense of "middle" had changed.

I call in Gen. Marshall, Dean Acheson, Mr. Harriman and Gen. Bradley before Cabinet to discuss situation. I've come to the conclusion that our Big General in the Far East must be recalled. I don't express any opinion or make known my decision.

Direct the four to meet again Friday afternoon and go over all phases of the situation.

April 9, 1951

. . . Meet with Acheson, Marshall, Bradley and Harriman. Go over recall orders to MacArthur and suggested public statement. Approve both and decide to send the orders to Frank Pace, Sec. of the Army, for delivery to MacArthur. . . . Gen. Bradley called about 9 P.M. Said there had been a leak. . . . I ordered messages sent at once and directly to MacArthur.

April 10, 1951

Quite an explosion. Was expected but I had to act.
Telegrams and letters of abuse by the dozens.

Harry S Truman, Diary. Reprinted in Robert H. Farrell, ed., *The Private Papers of Harry Truman* (Harper & Row: New York, 1980), pp. 210–211.

Both the Great Depression and World War II made most Americans realize that the nation's economy was closely linked to the international order. The crash in 1929, with its worldwide effects, certainly made that clear. The New Deal demonstrated that Americans were willing to give the federal government power to influence American society in major new ways. And the war led the government to intervene in the economy even more directly.

Thus when peace came in 1945, it became clear that the "middle road" did not mean a return to the laissez-faire economics of the 1920s. Nor would most Americans support the isolationist policies of the 1930s. "Modern" Republicans accepted social welfare programs like social security and recognized that the federal government had the ability to lower unemployment, control inflation, and manage the economy in a variety of ways. Furthermore, the shift from war to peace demonstrated that it was no longer possible to make global war without making a global peace. Under the new balance of power in the postwar world, the United States and the Soviet Union stood alone as "superpowers," with the potential capability to annihilate each other and the rest of the world.

SIGNIFICANT EVENTS

1945 ┼ Civil war in Greece

1946 ┼ Labor unrest; Kennan's "long telegram"; Stalin and Churchill "cold war" speeches; Republican congressional victories; Atomic Energy Commission created; Baruch plan fails at United Nations

1947 ┼ Truman Doctrine; Taft–Hartley Act; Marshall announces European recovery plan; federal loyalty oath; HUAC investigates Hollywood; National Security Council created; Truman's Committee on Civil Rights issues *To Secure These Rights*

1948 ┼ Marshall Plan adopted; Berlin airlift; Truman upsets Dewey; Truman recognizes Israel

1949 ┼ Soviet A-bomb test; China falls to the Communists; NATO established; Truman orders work on H-bomb

1950 ┼ McCarthy's Wheeling, West Virginia, speech; Korean War begins; McCarran Act; NSC-68 adopted; Alger Hiss convicted

1951 ┼ Truman fires MacArthur; peace talks in Korea

1952 ┼ Eisenhower defeats Stevenson

1953 ┼ UN armistice ends police action in Korea; Rosenbergs executed

1954 ┼ Army–McCarthy hearings; McCarthy censured

CHAPTER TWENTY-NINE

The Suburban Era

The company that epitomized the corporate culture of the 1950s was General Motors. GM executives sought to blend in rather than to stand out. They chose their suits in drab colors—dark blue, dark gray, or light gray— to increase their anonymity. Not head car designer Harley Earl. Earl brought a touch of Hollywood into the world of corporate bureaucrats. He had a closet filled with colorful suits. His staff would marvel as he headed off to a board meeting dressed in white linen with a dark blue shirt and *blue suede shoes*, the same shoes that Elvis Presley sang so protectively about.

Mr. Earl—no one who worked for him ever called him Harley—could afford to be a maverick. He created the cars that brought customers into GM showrooms across the country. Before he came to Detroit, engineering sold cars. Advertising stressed mechanical virtues—the steady ride, reliable brakes, or, perhaps, power steering. Earl made style the distinctive feature. Unlike the boxy look other designs favored, an Earl car was low and sleek, suggesting motion even when the car stood still. No feature stood out more distinctively than the fins he first put on the 1948 Cadillac. By the mid-1950s jet planes inspired Earl to design ever more outrageous fins, complemented by huge, shiny chrome grills and ornaments. These features served no mechanical purpose. Some critics dismissed Earl's designs as jukeboxes on wheels.

To Earl and GM that did not matter. Design sold cars. "It gave [customers] an extra receipt for their money in the form of visible prestige marking for an expensive car," Earl said. The "Big Three" auto manufacturers—General Motors, Ford, and Chrysler—raced one another to redesign their annual models, the more outrageous the better. Earl once joked, "I'd put smokestacks right in the middle of the sons of bitches if I thought I could sell more cars." In the lingo of the Detroit stylists, these designs were "gasaroony," an adjective *Popular Mechanics* magazine translated as "terrific, overpowering, weird." The goal was not a better car but what Earl called "dynamic obsolescence," or simply change for change's sake. "The 1957 Ford was great," its designer remarked, "but right away we had to bury it and start another." Even a successful style had to go within a year. "We would design a car to make a man unhappy with his 1957 Ford 'long about the end of 1958." Even though the mechanics of cars changed little from year to year, dynamic obsolescence persuaded Americans in the 1950s to buy new cars in record numbers.

Fins, roadside motels, "gaseterias," drive-in burger huts, interstate highways, shopping centers, and, of course, suburbs—all these were part of a culture of mobility in the 1950s. Americans continued their exodus from rural areas to cities and from the cities to the suburbs. African Americans left the South, heading for industrial centers in the Northeast, in the Midwest, and on the West Coast. Mexican Americans concentrated in southwestern cities, while Puerto Ricans came largely to New York. And for Americans in the Snowbelt, the climate of the West and South (at least when civilized by air conditioning) made the Sunbelt irresistible to ever larger numbers.

The mobility was social, too. As the economy continued to expand, the size of the American middle class grew. In an era of prosperity and peace, some com-

The 1950s as an era of consensus

mentators began to speak of a "consensus"—a general agreement in American culture, based on values of the broad middle class. In a positive light consensus reflected the agreement among most Americans about fundamental democratic values. Most citizens embraced the material benefits of prosperity as evidence of the virtue of "the American way." And they opposed the spread of communism abroad.

But consensus had its dark side. Critics worried that too strong a consensus bred a mindless conformity. Were Americans becoming too homogenized? Was there a depressing sameness in the material goods they owned, in the places they lived in, and in the values they held? In addition, wasn't any notion of consensus hollow as long as racism and segregation prevented African Americans and other minorities from fully sharing in American life?

The baby boomers born into this era seldom agonized over such issues. In the White House President Eisenhower radiated a comforting sense that the affairs of the nation and the world were in capable hands. That left teenagers free to worry about what really mattered: a first date, a first kiss, a first job, a first choice for college, and whether or not to "go all the way" in the back seat of one of Harley Earl's fin-swept Buicks.

THE RISE OF THE SUBURBS

Suburban growth accelerated sharply at the end of World War II. During the 1950s suburbs grew 40 times faster than cities, so that by 1960 half of the American people lived in them. The return of prosperity brought a baby boom and a need for new housing. Automobiles made the suburbs accessible. But the spurt in suburban growth took its toll on the cities, which suffered as the middle class fled urban areas.

A Boom in Babies and in Housing

The Great Depression caused many couples to delay beginning a family. In the 1930s birthrates had reached their low point in American history, about 18 to 19 per thousand. As prosperity returned during the war, birthrates began to rise. By 1952 they had passed 25 per thousand to reach one of the highest fertility rates in the world. New brides were also younger, which translated into unusual fertility. Americans chose to have larger families, as the number with three children tripled and those with four or more quadrupled. "Just imagine how much these extra people, these new markets, will absorb—in food, in clothing, in gadgets, in housing, in services," one journalist predicted.

The boom in marriage and families created a need for housing. At war's end, 5 million families were eager to find anything, tired of living doubled up with other families or in basements or even coal cellars. With the help of the GI Bill and rising incomes, the chance to own a house rather than rent became a reality for over half of American families. And it was the suburbs that offered the kind of residence most Americans idealized: a detached single-family house with a lawn and garden.

In the 1940s inexpensive suburban housing became synonymous with the name of real estate developer William Levitt. From building houses for war

Levittown, U.S.A.

workers, Levitt learned how to use mass production techniques. In 1947 he began construction of a 17,000-house community in the New York City suburb of Hempstead. All the materials for a

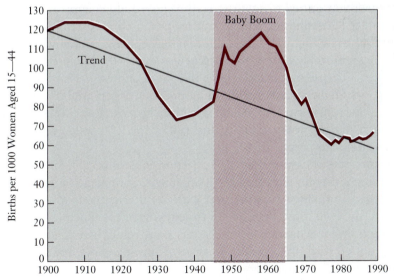

THE UNITED STATES BIRTHRATE, 1900–1989   Over the long term, the nation's birthrate has shown a steady downward trend, which became even sharper during the Depression years. But after World War II, younger marriages and prosperity triggered a baby boom.

Levittown house were precut and assembled at a factory, then moved to the site for assembly. If all went according to schedule, a new house was erected on a cement slab every 16 minutes. Buoyed by his success, Levitt later built developments in Bucks County, Pennsylvania, and Willingboro, New Jersey.

The typical early Levitt house was a "Cape Codder." It boasted a living room, a kitchen, a bath, and two bedrooms on the ground floor and an expansion attic, all for $7990. None of the houses had custom details, insulation, or any features that complicated construction. "The reason we have it so good in this country," Levitt said, "is that we can produce lots of things at low prices through mass production."

Uniformity in house style extended to behavior as well. Levitt discouraged owners from changing colors or adding distinctive features to the house or yard. Buyers promised to cut the grass each week of the summer and not to hang out wash on weekends. African Americans were expressly excluded. Other suburban communities excluded Jews and ethnic Americans through restrictive covenants that dictated who could take up residence.

Suburbs and Cities Transformed

Single-family houses with spacious lawns required plenty of open land, unlike the row houses built side by side in earlier suburban developments. That meant Levitt and other builders chose vacant areas outside of major urban centers. With the new houses farther from factories, offices, and jobs, the automobile became more indispensable than ever.

As population shifted to suburbs, traffic choked old country roads. To ease congestion, the Eisenhower administration proposed a 20-year plan to build a massive interstate highway system. In rallying support, Eisenhower addressed cold war fears as well, arguing that the new system would help cities evacuate

The Interstate Highway Act

in case of nuclear attack. In 1956 Congress passed the Interstate Highway Act, setting in motion the largest public works project in history. The federal government picked up 90 percent of the cost through a Highway Trust Fund, financed by special taxes on cars, gas, tires, lubricants, and auto parts.

The Interstate Highway Act had an enormous impact on American life. Average annual driving increased by 400 percent. Shopping centers, linked by the new roads, provided suburbanites with an alternative to the longer trip downtown. By 1960 more than 3840 of them covered as much land as the nation's central business districts. Almost every community had at least one highway strip dotted with drive-in movies, stores, bowling alleys, gas stations, and fast-food joints.

The interstates affected cities in less fortunate ways. The new highway system featured beltways, ring roads around major urban areas. Instead of leading

Declining cities

traffic downtown, the beltways allowed motorists to avoid the center city altogether. As people took to their cars, intercity rail

Like a freak of evolution run riot, automotive tailfins during the 1950s were elongated until they reached the monstrous proportions of the 1959 Cadillac, which also sported bomblike taillights.

service and mass transit declined. Seventy-five percent of all government transportation dollars went to subsidize travel by car and truck; only one percent was earmarked for urban mass transit. At the same time that middle-class home owners were moving to the suburbs, many low-paying, unskilled jobs disappeared from the cities. That forced the urban poor into reverse commuting from city to suburb. All of these trends made cities less attractive places to live or do business in. With fewer well-to-do taxpayers to draw upon, city governments lacked the tax base to finance public services. A vicious cycle ensued that proved most damaging to the urban poor, who had few means of escape.

Much of the white population that moved to the suburbs was replaced by African Americans and Hispanics. They were part of larger migrations, espe-

Black and Hispanic Americans migrate to cities

cially of millions of black families leaving the South to search for work in urban centers. Most headed for the Northeast and Upper Midwest. While central cities lost 3.6 million white residents, they gained 4.5 million African Americans. Indeed, by 1960 half of all black Americans were living in central cities.

Earlier waves of European immigrants had been absorbed by the expanding urban economy. During the 1950s, however, the flight of jobs and middle-class taxpayers to the suburbs made it difficult for African Americans and

The suburbs and race

Hispanics to follow the same path. In the cities fewer jobs awaited them, while declining school systems made it harder for newcomers to acculturate. In the hardest-hit urban areas, unemployment rose to over 40 percent.

By contrast, the suburbs remained beyond reach of most minorities. Since few black or Hispanic families could afford the cost of suburban living, they accounted for less than 5 percent of the population there. The few black suburbs that existed dated from before the war and had little in common with the newer white "bedroom communities." Black suburbanites were poorer, held lower-status jobs, lived in more ramshackle housing, and had less education than urban African Americans.

Those who could afford the suburbs discovered that most real estate agents refused to show them houses; bankers would not provide mortgages. And many communities adopted either restrictive covenants or zoning regulations that kept out "undesirable" home buyers. One African American, William Myers, finally managed in 1957 to buy a house from a white family in Levittown, Pennsylvania, but the developers did not sell directly to African Americans until 1960.

THE CULTURE OF SUBURBIA

In suburban tracts across America, a new appetizer began appearing at trendy dinner parties. Named the California Dip, it was the brainchild of the Lipton Company, which was searching for new ways to market its dehydrated onion soup. Homemakers simply mixed Lipton's soup powder with sour cream and served it up with chips. As one commentator noted,

> Using potato chips as little shovels, you gathered up the deliciously salty but drip-prone liquid and popped it, potato chip and all, into your mouth as quickly and gracefully as possible. There was anxiety in all this—particularly the fear that a great glop of the stuff would land on your tie or the rug—but also immense satisfaction.

As much genius, perhaps, went into the naming of the dip as into the recipe. Sour cream had been a mainstay in ethnic dishes like blintzes (thin Jewish pancakes) and borscht (an Eastern European beet soup). With an all-American name like "California Dip," sour cream's ethnic associations were left behind. The ingredient went mainstream—into the consensus.

The evolving culture of the suburbs reflected a similar process, a shucking off of ethnic associations. In many city neighborhoods, immigrant parents or grandparents lived on the same block or even in the same apartment with their children. In the suburbs, single-family dwellers often left their relatives and in-laws behind, which meant that ethnic lifestyles were less pronounced. The restrictive immigration policies of the 1920s had also reduced the number of newly arrived foreign-born Americans. Thus suburban culture reflected the tastes of the broad, mostly assimilated middle classes.

Class distinctions were more pronounced between suburban communities than within them. The upper middle class clustered in older developments,

Suburbs and social class

often centered around country clubs. Working-class suburbs sprouted on the outskirts of large manufacturing centers, where blue-collar families eagerly escaped the city. Within suburbs a more homogeneous suburban culture evolved. "We see eye to eye on most things," commented one Levittown resident, "about raising kids, doing things together with your husband . . . we have practically the same identical background."

American Civil Religion

If the move out of cities often reduced the ethnic flavor of suburban neighborhoods, most residents held onto their religious beliefs. Religion continued to be a distinctive and segregating factor during the 1950s. Catholics, Protestants, and Jews generally married within their own faiths, and in the suburbs they kept their social distance as well.

Communities that showed no obvious class distinctions were sometimes deeply divided along religious lines. Catholics attended parochial rather than public schools, formed their own clubs, and socialized less with their Protestant neighbors. Protestant and Catholic members of the same country club usually did not play golf or tennis in the same foursomes. As for Jews, one historian remarked that whereas a gulf divided many Catholics and Protestants, Jews and Gentiles "seem to have lived on the opposite sides of a religious Grand Canyon." Even an outward friendliness masked underlying mistrust and the persistence of old stereotypes.

Religious divisions

Although such religious boundaries remained strong, the consensus increased that religion was central to American life. Church membership rose to over 50 percent for the first time in the twentieth century, and by 1957 the census bureau reported that 96 percent of the American people cited a specific affiliation when asked the question "What is your religion?" The religious upswing was supported in part by the prevailing cold war mood, since Communists were avowedly atheists. Cold war fervor led Congress in 1954 to add the phrase "under God" to the Pledge of Allegiance.

Patriotic and anticommunist themes were strong in the preaching of clergy who pioneered the use of television. Billy Graham, a Baptist revival preacher, first attracted national attention at a tent meeting in Los Angeles in 1949. Following in the tradition of nineteenth-century revivalists like Dwight Moody, Graham soon achieved even wider impact by televising his meetings. Though no revivalist, the Roman Catholic Bishop Fulton J. Sheen made the transition from a radio to a television ministry. In his weekly program he extolled traditional values and attacked communism.

Television ministries

Indeed, throughout American culture, the benefits of religion—of *any* religion—were lauded. Historians have referred to this acceptance of generalized religious values as American civil religion. President Eisenhower made the point quite clear. "Our government makes no sense unless it is founded on a deeply religious faith," he proclaimed, "—and I don't care what it is." And every Friday afternoon children watching "The Howdy Doody Show" were exhorted by the show's host, Buffalo Bob, to worship "at the church or synagogue of your choice."

"Homemaking" Women in the Workaday World

The growth of a suburban culture revealed a contradiction in the lives of middle-class women. Never before were their traditional roles as housewives and mothers so central to American society. Yet never before did more women join the workforce outside the home.

For housewives, the single-family suburban home required more labor to keep clean. At the same time, the baby boom left suburban mothers with more children to tend and less help from relatives and grandparents, who less often lived nearby. Increased dependence on automobiles made many a suburban housewife the chauffeur for her family. In the 1920s grocers or milkmen commonly delivered their goods from door to door. By the 1950s delivery services were being replaced by housewives doing "errands."

Yet between 1940 and 1960 the percentage of wives working outside the home doubled from 15 to 30 percent. While some women took jobs simply to

Working women

help make ends meet, more than financial necessity was involved. Middle-class married women went to work as often as lower-class wives, and women with college degrees were the most likely to get a job. Two-income families were able to spend far more on extras: gifts, education, recreation, and household appliances. In addition, women found status and self-fulfillment in their jobs, as well as a chance for increased social contacts.

In the automobile-centered suburbs, many women became chauffeurs as well as housewives. The average suburban woman spent one full working day each week driving and doing errands.

More women were going to college, too, but that increased education did not translate into economic equality. The median wage for women was less than half that for men—a greater gap than in any other industrial nation. The percentage of women holding professional jobs actually dropped between 1950 and 1960.

Despite women's wider roles in society, the media most often portrayed them either as sex objects or as domesticated housewives and mothers. A typi-

Media images of women

cal article appearing in *Redbook* in 1957 made a heroine of Junior, a "little freckle-faced brunette" who had given up work. As the story closed, Junior nursed her baby at two in the morning, crooning "I'm glad, glad, glad I'm just a housewife." In 1950 Lynn White, the president of Mills College for women, advocated a curriculum that displaced traditional academic subjects with those that were "distinctly feminine," like home economics and crafts.

The Flickering Gray Screen

In the glow of postwar prosperity, most Americans found themselves with more leisure time and more income. A suburban yard to tend and a young family to raise determined that parents and children would spend much of their free time around the house. The new medium of television fit perfectly into suburban lifestyles. It provided an ideal way to entertain families at home as well as sell them consumer goods.

The entrance of television into the American mainstream came only after World War II. In 1949 Americans owned only a million televisions; by 1960 the figure had jumped to 46 million. Indeed, by then more Americans had televisions than had bathrooms. Soon attendance began dropping for pastimes like moviegoing and professional sports. Over 4000 urban movie theaters closed. Some were replaced in the suburbs by popular drive-ins, which allowed whole families to enjoy movies in the comfort of their cars. But even that novelty failed to attract as many viewers. Restaurant owners also felt the squeeze. When Sid Caesar and Imogene Coca appeared on Saturday nights in "Your Show of Shows," diners rushed home to their television sets.

In 1948 television began its involvement in politics, covering both the Democratic and Republican conventions. Two years later, it televised hearings

Television and politics

on organized crime chaired by Senator Estes Kefauver. Some 30 million viewers watched senators grill mobster Frank Costello about his criminal organization and its ties to city governments. Millions more watched Senator Joseph McCarthy's ill-fated attack on the army in 1954. With such a large audience, television clearly had the potential to shape the nation's politics. But by the mid-1950s controversy over news coverage of issues like McCarthyism led the networks to downgrade public affairs programs. As an alternative they turned to Hollywood, which developed telefilm dramas and situation comedies. By 1959 live television was virtually a thing of the past. Westerns, detective shows, and old movies led the ratings.

THE POLITICS OF CALM

In presiding over these changes in American society, President Dwight David Eisenhower projected an aura of paternal calm. Pursuing "modern Republicanism," the new president sought consensus, not confrontation. No longer would conservatives like Robert Taft call for a repeal of the New Deal and a return to laissez-faire capitalism. Eisenhower declared that he was "conservative when it comes to money and liberal when it comes to human beings."

The Eisenhower Presidency

Eisenhower had been raised in a large Kansas farm family. His parents, though poor, offered him a warm, caring home steeped in religious faith. In an era of organizational men, Eisenhower succeeded by mastering the military's bureaucratic politics. A graduate of West Point, he was neither a scholar nor an aggressive general like George Patton. In the placid years between the two world wars, the skills "Ike" demonstrated at golf, poker, and bridge often proved as valuable as his military expertise. Yet these genial ways could not hide his ambition or his ability to judge character shrewdly. It took a gifted organizer to coordinate the D-Day invasion and to hold together the egocentric generals who pushed east to Berlin.

As president, Eisenhower resisted conservative demands to dismantle New Deal programs. He even agreed to increases in social security, unemployment insurance, and the minimum wage. He accepted a small public housing program and a modest federally supported medical insurance plan for the needy. But as a conservative, Eisenhower remained uncomfortable with big government. Thus he rejected more far-reaching liberal proposals on housing and universal health care through the social security system.

Modern Republicanism in practice

To make modern Republicanism successful, Eisenhower had to woo the newly prosperous Democratic voters joining the middle class. Success in that

President Dwight D. Eisenhower

effort hinged on how well the administration managed the economy. New Deal Democrats had established a tradition of activism: when the economy faltered, they used deficit spending and tax cuts to stimulate it. Eisenhower preferred to reduce federal spending and the government's role in the economy. When a recession struck in 1953–1954, the administration was concerned more with balancing the budget and holding inflation in line than with reducing unemployment through government spending.

Eisenhower was similarly pragmatic in other areas. When major projects called for federal leadership, as with the Highway Act, he supported them. In 1954 he signed the St. Lawrence Seaway Act, which joined the United States and Canada in an ambitious engineering project to open the Great Lakes to ocean shipping. Like the highway program, the Seaway was fiscally acceptable because the funding came from user tolls and taxes rather than from general revenues.

Farm policy was one area where Eisenhower's pragmatic approach faltered. Farmers made up a major Republican voting bloc. For the president to abolish

Farm policy

the price supports established under the New Deal was to commit political suicide. On the other hand, crop surpluses continued to fill government silos with unwanted grain. Eisenhower's secretary of agriculture, Ezra Taft Benson, proposed lowering support payments so that farmers would not overproduce basic commodities like corn, cotton, and wheat. Benson also established a soil bank program to pay farmers for reducing acreage.

In the end, however, the effects of modern technology made it difficult to regulate agricultural production. Even when farmers cut back acreage, they discovered that automated harvesters, fertilizers, and new varieties of plants actually increased farm outputs. In an age of continuing centralization, more and more small farms were being replaced by agribusinesses. As power became more concentrated in these large commercial farming businesses, so did their political power to protect farm subsidies.

Despite occasional setbacks Eisenhower remained popular. Although he suffered a major heart attack in 1955, voters gladly reelected him in 1956. But

The limits of modern Republicanism

poor economic performance took its toll on the Republican party. In the wake of the 1954 recession the Democrats gained a 29-member majority in the House and a 1-vote edge in the Senate. Never again would Eisenhower work with a Republican majority in Congress. In 1958, when recession again dragged down the economy, the Democrats took a 68-seat majority in the House and a 12-vote advantage in the Senate. Modern Republicanism did not put down deep roots beyond Eisenhower's White House.

COUNTERPOINT   *Assessing Eisenhower*

In 1962, when historians rated presidential performance, Eisenhower scored near the bottom, barely ahead of Ulysses S Grant. As president, he had kept a low political profile. Critics complained that he conceived of himself as a mere figurehead, like a constitiutional monarch. Certainly, Eisenhower was reluctant to challenge the aggressive anticommunism of Senator Joseph McCarthy, and as we shall see, he only reluctantly moved to defend the civil rights of African Americans. Critics also attacked Ike's firm belief in letting the business community chart its own course without closer government regulation. Secretary of Defense Charles Wilson, former president of General Motors, expressed the administration's probusiness creed, proclaiming that "What was good for our country was good for General Motors and vice versa."

More recently, historians have been inclined to place Eisenhower among the most capable of American presidents. His aloof manner, some argue, disguised a president whose "hidden hand" acted vigorously behind the scenes. While in public Eisenhower let others speak for him (and take the heat), in private he made decisions and set directions. Ike was not activist in the energetic tradition of either Roosevelt. Then again, the three presidents who followed him took "bold" actions that were quite controversial: John Kennedy's invasion of Cuba, Lyndon Johnson's war in Vietnam, and Richard Nixon's political overreaching. In this light Eisenhower's modern Republicanism seems no longer like inactive government, but like a mature appreciation of the limits of the presidency.

The Conglomerate World

Large businesses welcomed the administration's probusiness attitudes as well as the era's general prosperity. Wages for the average worker rose over 35 percent between 1950 and 1960. At the same time, the economic distress of the 1930s had led corporate executives to devise new ways to minimize the danger of economic downturns. In various ways, each of the approaches sought to minimize shocks in specific markets by expanding the size of corporations in different ways.

One expansion strategy took the form of diversification. In the 1930s, a giant like General Electric had concentrated largely in one industrial area: equip-

Diversification and conglomeration

ment for generating electric power and light. When the Depression struck, GE found its markets evaporating. The company responded by entering markets for appliances, X-ray machines, and elevators—all products developed or enhanced by the company's research labs. In the postwar era General Electric diversified even further, into nuclear power, jet engines, and television. Diversification was most practical for large industrial firms, whose size allowed them to support extensive research and development.

Conglomeration often turned small companies into giants. Unlike earlier horizontal and vertical combinations, conglomerate mergers could join companies with seemingly unrelated products. Over a 20-year period International Telephone and Telegraph branched out from its basic communications business into baking, hotels and motels, car rental, home building, and insurance. Corporations also became multinational by expanding their overseas operations or buying out potential foreign competitors. Large integrated oil companies like Mobil and Standard Oil of New Jersey (Exxon) developed huge oil fields in the Middle East and markets around the free world.

One aid to managing these modern corporate giants was the advent of electronic data processing. In the early 1950s computers were virtually unknown in *Early computers* private industry. But banks and insurance companies saw calculating machines as an answer to their need to manipulate huge quantities of records and statistical data. Manufacturers, especially in the petroleum, chemical, automotive, and electronics industries, began to use computers to monitor their production lines, quality control, and inventory.

NATIONALISM IN AN AGE OF SUPERPOWERS

Along the Iron Curtain of Eastern Europe and across the battle lines of northern Asia, the Soviet-American cold war settled into an uneasy stalemate. But World War II had also disrupted Europe's colonial relationships. As nationalists in the Middle East, Africa, and Southeast Asia fought to gain independence, the two superpowers competed for their allegiance. Across the globe the Eisenhower administration sought ways to prevent the Soviet Union from capturing national independence movements. To do so, it sometimes used the threat of nuclear war to block communist expansion in Europe or Asia.

To the Brink?

Eisenhower, no stranger to world politics, shared the conduct of foreign policy with his secretary of state, John Foster Dulles. Coming from a family of missionaries and diplomats, Dulles had within him a touch of both. *John Foster Dulles* He viewed the Soviet–American struggle in almost religious terms, as a fight between good and evil. Eisenhower was less hostile toward the Soviets. In the end, the two men's differing temperaments led to a policy that seesawed from confrontation to conciliation.

The administration was determined to turn Truman's containment strategy into a more dynamic offensive. Dulles wanted the United States to aid in liberating the "captive peoples" of Eastern Europe and other communist nations. On the other hand, Eisenhower was equally determined to cut back military spending and troop levels in order to keep the budget balanced. The president was sometimes irked at the "fantastic programs" the Pentagon kept proposing. "If we demand too much in taxes in order to build planes and ships," he argued, "we will tend to dry up the accumulations of capital that are necessary to provide jobs for the million or more new workers that we must absorb each year."

Rather than rely on costly conventional forces, Eisenhower and Dulles used the threat of massive nuclear retaliation to intimidate the Soviets into behaving less aggressively. Dulles insisted that Americans should not shrink from the

The policy of massive retaliation

threat of nuclear war: "If you are scared to go to the brink, you are lost." And as Secretary of Treasury George Humphrey put it, a nuclear strategy was much cheaper—"a bigger bang for the buck." Henceforth American foreign policy would have a "new look," though behind the more militant rhetoric lay an ongoing commitment to containment.

Brinksmanship in Asia

Moving beyond talk of "brinksmanship" to concrete action did not prove easy. When Dulles announced American intentions to "unleash" Chiang Kai-shek to

Taiwan and mainland China

attack mainland China from his outpost on Taiwan (formerly Formosa), China threatened to invade Taiwan. At that, Eisenhower ordered the Seventh Fleet into the area to protect rather than unleash Chiang. If the Communists attacked, Dulles warned bluntly, "we'll have to use atomic weapons."

Nuclear weapons also figured in the American response to a crisis in Indochina. There, Vietnamese forces led by Ho Chi Minh were fighting the French, who had returned at the end of World War II to reestablish their colonial rule. Between 1950 and 1954, the United States provided France with over $1 billion in military aid in Vietnam. Eisenhower worried that if Vietnam fell to a Communist revolutionary like Ho, other nations of Southeast Asia would follow. "You have a row of dominoes set up," the president warned, "you knock over the first one [y]ou could have the beginning of a disintegration that would have the most profound influences."

Worn down by a war they seemed unable to win, the French in 1954 tried to force a final showdown with Ho Chi Minh's army at Dien Bien Phu. With

Vietnamese victory at Dien Bien Phu

Vietnamese and Chinese communist troops holding the surrounding hilltops, the French garrison there could not have chosen a worse place to do battle. Desperate, the French pleaded for more American aid. Admiral Arthur Radford, head of the Joint Chiefs of Staff, proposed a massive American air raid, perhaps even using tactical nuclear weapons. But again Eisenhower pulled back. The idea of American involvement in another Asian war aroused opposition from both allies and domestic political leaders.

Finally the garrison at Dien Bien Phu collapsed under the seige. In May, at an international peace conference in Geneva, Switzerland, the French negotiated the terms of their withdrawal. Ho Chi Minh agreed to pull his forces north of the 17th parallel, temporarily dividing the nation into North and South Vietnam. Because of Ho's broad popularity, he seemed assured an easy victory in elections scheduled for within the next two years. Dulles, however, viewed any communist victory as unacceptable, even if the election was democratic. He convinced Eisenhower to support a South Vietnamese government under Ngo Dinh Diem. Dulles insisted that Diem was not bound by the Geneva Accords to hold any election—a position the autocratic Diem eagerly supported. To help keep him in power, the United States sent a military mission to train South Vietnam's army. The commitment was small, but a decade later it would return to haunt Americans.

The Superpowers

Korea, Taiwan, Indochina—to Dulles and Eisenhower, the crises in Asia and elsewhere could all be traced back to the Soviet dictatorship. Although nationalist movements around the globe were leading nations like India to declare themselves neutral or nonaligned, Dulles continually warned them that they could not sit on the fence. They must choose either the "free world" or the communist bloc. Throughout the 1950s the secretary of state crisscrossed the globe, setting up mutual defense pacts patterned on NATO, to solidify American security. Yet in all this, it was becoming harder to decide what the motives of the Soviets themselves might be.

Joseph Stalin had died in March 1953, after becoming increasingly isolated, arbitrary, vengeful, and perhaps simply mad. Power soon fell to Nikita

Nikita Khrushchev

Khrushchev, a party stalwart with a formidable intellect and peasant origins in the farm country of the Ukraine. In some ways Khrushchev resembled another farm-belt politician, Harry Truman. Both were unsophisticated yet shrewd, earthy in their sense of humor, energetic, short-tempered, and largely inexperienced in international affairs. Khrushchev kept American diplomats off balance. At times genial and conciliatory, he would suddenly become demanding and boastful.

Khrushchev moderated some of the excesses of the Stalin years. At home, he gradually shifted the Soviet economy toward production of consumer goods. Internationally, he called for an easing of tensions and reduced forces in Europe, hoping to make Western Europeans less dependent on the United States. In Washington the administration was unsure of how to receive the new overtures. The spirit of McCarthyism still reigned, so that compromise with the Soviets involved great political risk. It was actually Winston Churchill who suggested that the Russians might be serious about negotiating. In 1955 the Americans, British, French, and Soviets met in a summit conference at Geneva, Switzerland. While little came of the summit other than a cordial "spirit of Geneva," the meeting hinted that a cooling in the arms race was possible.

Nationalism Unleashed

The spirit of Geneva did not long survive new nationalist upheavals. Khrushchev's moderation encouraged nationalists in Soviet-controlled Eastern Europe to

Revolt in Hungary

push for greater independence. Riots erupted in Poland, while in Hungary students took to the streets demanding that a coalition government replace the puppet regime established by Stalin. At first, Moscow accepted the new Hungarian government and began to remove Soviet tanks. But when Hungary announced it was withdrawing from the Warsaw Pact, the tanks rolled back into Budapest to crush the uprising in October 1956. The United States protested but did nothing to help liberate the "captive nations." For all its tough talk, the "new look" foreign policy recognized that the Soviets possessed a sphere of influence where the United States would not intervene.

At the same time that nationalism erupted in Eastern Europe Dulles faced a series of crises in the Middle East. When a nationalist government in Iran

Nationalism in Iran and Egypt seemed to lean toward the Soviets, he obtained Eisenhower's approval to launch a covert CIA operation in 1953 to oust its leader, Mohammad Mossadeq, and restore a firm ally, the Shah Mohammad Reza Pahlavi. Meanwhile, for several years Egyptian leader Gamal Abdel Nasser, a nationalist, had been attempting to modernize his country and rebuild his army. Dulles tried to befriend Nasser by offering American aid to build the Aswan Dam, a massive power project on the Nile River. But when Nasser formed an Arab alliance against the young state of Israel and continued to pursue economic ties with the Warsaw bloc, Dulles withdrew the American pledge on Aswan. In 1956 Nasser angrily countered by seizing the British-owned Universal Suez Canal Company. The company ran the waterway through which tankers carried most of Europe's oil.

Events then moved quickly. Israel, alarmed at Nasser's Arab alliance, invaded the Sinai peninsula of Egypt on October 29—the same day Hungary announced it was leaving the Warsaw Pact. Three days later French and British forces seized the canal in an attempt to restore their own interests and prestige. Angered that his allies had not consulted him, Eisenhower joined the Soviet Union in supporting a United Nations resolution condemning Britain, France, and Israel and demanding an immediate cease-fire. By December American pressures forced Britain and France to remove their forces. Few events placed so much strain on the Western alliance as the Suez crisis. At the same time, Nasser had demonstrated to the industrial powers the potential force of Third World nationalism.

Given the unstable situation in the Middle East, Eisenhower convinced Congress to give him the authority to use force against any communist attack

Eisenhower Doctrine in that region. What became known as the Eisenhower Doctrine in effect allowed the president in times of crisis to preempt Congress's power to declare war. In 1958 he used that power to send U.S. marines into Lebanon, a small nation that claimed to have been infiltrated by Nasser's supporters. Since no fighting had yet occurred, sunbathers on the beaches of Beirut, Lebanon's capital, were startled as 5000 combat-clad marines stormed ashore. In the end, the crisis blew over, and the American forces withdrew. Dulles claimed that the United States had once again turned back the communist drive into the emerging nations. In reality, nationalism more than communism had been at the root of Middle Eastern turmoil.

Nationalist forces were also in ferment in Latin America, where only 2 percent of the people controlled 75 percent of the land. Given this unequal distribution of wealth and a rapidly growing population, social tensions were rising. Yet any move toward more democratic government seemed unlikely. Repressive dictatorships exercised power, and foreign interests—especially American ones—dominated Latin American economies. In 1954, Eisenhower authorized the CIA to send a band of Latin American mercenaries into Guatemala to overthrow a nationalist government there. Although the government was democratically elected, it had seized 400,000 acres from United Fruit, a U.S. corporation. The new military dictatorship promptly returned the confiscated lands to United Fruit.

Similar economic tensions were reflected in Cuba, where the United States owned 80 percent of the country's utilities and operated a major naval base at

Castro's revolution in Cuba

Guantánamo Bay. Cuban dictator Fulgencio Batista had close ties both to the U.S. government and to major crime figures who operated gambling, prostitution, and drug rings in Havana. A disgruntled middle-class lawyer, Fidel Castro, gained the support of impoverished peasants in Cuba's mountains and, in January 1959, drove Batista from power.

At first many Americans applauded the revolution, welcoming Castro when he visited the United States. But Eisenhower was distinctly cool to the cigar-smoking Cuban, who dressed in green military fatigues and sported a full beard. By summer Castro had filled key government positions with Communists, launched a sweeping agricultural reform, and confiscated American properties. Retaliating, Eisenhower embargoed Cuban sugar and mobilized opposition to Castro in other Latin American countries. Cut off from American markets and aid, Castro turned to the Soviet Union.

The Response to Sputnik

Castro's turn to the Soviets seemed all the more dangerous because of Soviet achievements in their missile program. In 1957 they stunned America by launching into outer space the first satellite, dubbed *Sputnik*. By 1959, the Soviets had crash-landed a much larger payload on the moon. If the Russians could target the moon, surely they could launch nuclear missiles against America. In contrast, the American space program suffered so many delays and mishaps that rockets exploding on launch were nicknamed "flopniks" and "kaputniks."

How had the Soviets managed to catch up with American technology so quickly? Some Americans blamed the schools, especially weak programs in science and math. In 1958 Eisenhower joined with Congress to enact a National Defense Education Act, designed to strengthen graduate education and the teaching of science, math, and foreign languages. At the same time, crash programs were undertaken to build basement fallout shelters to protect Americans in case of a nuclear attack. Democrats charged that the administration had allowed the United States to face an unacceptable "missile gap."

Thaws and Freezes

Throughout this series of crises, each superpower found it difficult to interpret the other's motives. The Russians exploited nationalist revolutions where they could—less successfully in Egypt, more so in Cuba. "We will bury you," Khrushchev admonished Americans, though it was unclear whether he meant

Controversy over Berlin

through peaceful competition or military confrontation. More menacingly, in November 1958 he demanded that the Western powers withdraw all troops from West Berlin within six months. Berlin would then become a "free city," and the Western powers could negotiate further access to it only with East Germany, a government the West had refused to recognize. When Eisenhower flatly rejected the ultimatum, Khrushchev backed away from his hard-line stance.

Rather than adopt a more belligerent course, Eisenhower determined to use the last 18 months of his presidency to improve Soviet–American relations. The shift in policy was made easier because Eisenhower knew from American intelligence (but could not admit publicly) that the "missile gap" was not real. While willing to spend more on missile development, he refused to heed the calls for a crash defense program at any cost. Instead, he took a more conciliatory approach by inviting Khrushchev to visit the United States in September 1959. Though the meetings produced no significant results, they eased tensions. And

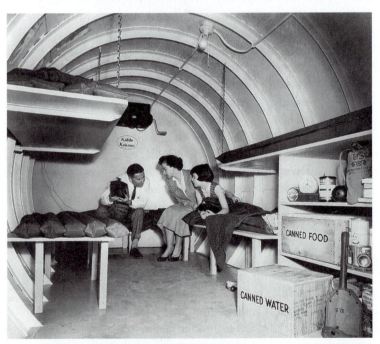

The nuclear arms race inspired many Americans to build basement fallout shelters in case of an attack.

E Y E W I T N E S S   T O   H I S T O R Y

Growing Up with
the Threat of Atomic War

And so whenever the civil defense sirens interrupted my school days with their apocalyptic howls, I folded my papers neatly and filed into the hallway and squatted in front of the lockers with my head between my knees and my hands on the back of my neck, like everyone else. . . .

In those days we did not know if we would survive from month to month. . . . Everyone was thinking about large questions and What Is to Be Done? . . . Should you shoot a person who seeks safety in your shelter? That was a question we debated in church, without satisfaction. Our pastor recalled the parable of the Good Samaritan, but it didn't seem appropriate to the occasion. "I can see letting one or two guys in," said a member of the congregation, "but what about ten? fifty? You've got to draw a line somewhere." Another woman, slightly ecstatic, said we were all going to die in the blast and meet Jesus, so what's the problem? . . .

Properly prepared, we were told, the rest of us could expect a 97 percent chance of survival—a figure universally recognized as a lie. Nonetheless, we kept a small store of canned goods in our house, and Mother stored bottled water in the closet. We had a small store of candles, flashlight batteries, and a transistor radio with the Conelrad stations marked with the nuclear triangles. Parents were told not to rescue their children from school; presumably we were safe in the hallways. The mother of a friend of mine told him if she *ever* came to school to get him, he was to go with her and never mind what the teachers or the principal might say. One day he was gazing out the window of his classroom and saw his mother drive up, and he jumped out the window and ran to her car. She was bringing his lunch money.

Lawrence Wright, *In the New World: Growing Up with America, 1960-1984* (New York, Knopf, 1987), pp. 53–55. Copyright © 1983, 1986, 1987 by Lawrence Wright. Reprinted by permission of Alfred A. Knopf, Inc.

Khrushchev undertook a picturesque tour across America, swapping comments about manure with Iowa farmers, reacting puritanically to movie cancan dancers, and grousing when his visit to the new capitalist marvel, Disneyland, was canceled for security reasons.

In May, Eisenhower's plans for a return visit to the Soviet Union were abruptly canceled. Only weeks earlier the Russians had shot down a high-altitude U-2 American spy plane over Soviet territory. At first

The U-2 incident

Eisenhower claimed the plane had strayed off course during weather research, but Khrushchev sprang his trap: the CIA pilot, Gary Powers, had been captured alive. The president then admitted that he had personally authorized the U-2 overflights for reasons of national security.

That episode ended Eisenhower's hopes that his personal diplomacy might create a true thaw in the cold war. Yet a less mature president might have led the United States into more severe conflict or even war. Eisenhower was not readily impressed by the promises of new weapon systems. He left office with a warning that too much military spending would lead to "an unwarranted influence, whether sought or unsought" by the "military–industrial complex" at the expense of democratic institutions.

CIVIL RIGHTS AND THE NEW SOUTH

The struggle of African Americans for equality during the postwar era is filled with ironies. By the time barriers to legal segregation in the South began to fall, millions of black families were leaving for regions where discrimination was less easily challenged in court. The South they left behind was in the early stages of an economic boom. The cities where many migrated had entered a period of decline. Yet, as if to close a circle, the rise of large black voting blocs in major cities created political pressures that forced the nation to dismantle the worst legal and institutional barriers to racial equality. For black Americans, it might be said that these were the best and the worst of times.

The Changing South and African Americans

Before World War II, 80 percent of African Americans lived in the South. Most raised cotton as sharecroppers and tenant farmers. But the war created a labor

Mechanizing cotton farms

shortage at home, as millions went off to fight and others to armament factories. This shortage gave cotton growers an incentive to mechanize cotton picking. In 1950 only 5 percent of the crop was picked mechanically; by 1960 it was at least half. Farmers began to consolidate land into larger holdings. Tenant farmers, sharecroppers, and hired labor of both races left the countryside for the city.

The national level of wages also profoundly affected southern labor. When federal minimum wage laws forced lumber or textile mills to raise their pay scales, the mills no longer expanded. In addition, steel and other industries with strong national unions and manufacturers with plants around the country set wages by national standards. That brought southern wages close to the national average by the 1960s. As the southern economy grew, what had for many years been a distinct regional economy became more diversified and more integrated into the national economy.

As wages rose and unskilled work disappeared, job opportunities for black southerners declined. Outside of cotton farming, the lumber industry provided the largest number of jobs for young black men. There, the number of black teenagers hired by lumber mills dropped 74 percent between 1950 and 1960. New high-wage jobs were reserved for white southerners, since outside industries arriving in the South made no effort to change local patterns of discrimination. So the ultimate irony arose. As per capita income rose and industrialization brought in new jobs, black laborers poured out of the region in search of work. They arrived in cities that showed scant tolerance for racial differences and little willingness or ability to hire unskilled black labor.

The NAACP and Civil Rights

In the postwar era the National Association for the Advancement of Colored People led the legal fight against racial segregation. Their hard-hitting campaign reflected the increased national political influence African Americans achieved as they migrated out of the South. No longer could northern politicians readily ignore the demands black leaders made for greater equality. At first, however, the NAACP focused its campaign on the courts.

Thurgood Marshall was the association's leading attorney. Marshall had attended law school in the 1930s at Howard University in Washington. There, *Thurgood Marshall* the law school's dean, Charles Houston, was in the midst of revamping the school and turning out sharp, dedicated lawyers. Not only was Marshall sharp, but he had the common touch as well. "Before he came along," one observer noted,

> the principal black leaders—men like Du Bois and James Weldon Johnson and Charles Houston—didn't talk the language of the people. They were upper-class and upper-middle-class Negroes. Thurgood Marshall was of the people. . . . Out in Texas or Oklahoma or down the street here in Washington at the Baptist church, he would make these rousing speeches that would have 'em all jumping out of their seats. . . . "We ain't gettin' what we should," was what it came down to, and he made them see that.

During the late 1930s and early 1940s Marshall toured the South (in "a little old beat-up '29 Ford"), typing out legal briefs in the back seat, trying to get teachers to sue for equal pay, and defending blacks accused of murder in a Klan-infested county in Florida. He was friendly with whites and not shy, and black citizens who had never even considered the possibility that a member of their race might win a legal battle "would come for miles, some of them on muleback or horseback, to see 'the nigger lawyer' who stood up in white men's courtrooms."

For years NAACP lawyers worked hard to organize local chapters, to support members of the community willing to risk their jobs, property, and lives in order to challenge segregation. But they waged a moderate, pragmatic campaign. They chose not to attack head-on the Supreme Court decision (*Plessy v. Ferguson*, 1896) that permitted "separate but equal" segregated facilities. They simply demonstrated that a black college or school might be separate, but it was hardly equal if it lacked a law school or even indoor plumbing.

The Brown *Decision*

In 1950 the NAACP changed tactics: it would now try to convince the Supreme Court to overturn the separate but equal doctrine itself. Oliver Brown of Topeka, Kansas, was one of the people who provided a way. Brown was dissatisfied that his daughter Linda had to walk past an all-white school on her way to catch the bus to her segregated black school. A three-judge federal panel rejected Brown's suit because the schools in Topeka, while segregated, did meet the legal standards for equality. The NAACP appealed the case to the Supreme Court and, in 1954, won a striking decision. *Brown v. Board of Education of Topeka* overturned the lower court ruling and overthrew the doctrine of "separate but equal."

Marshall and his colleagues succeeded in part because of a change in the Court itself. The year before, President Eisenhower had appointed Earl Warren, a liberal Republican from California, as chief justice. Warren, a forceful advocate, managed to persuade the last of his reluctant judicial colleagues that segregation as defined in *Plessy* rested on an insupportable theory of racial supremacy. The Court ruled unanimously that separate facilities were inherently unequal. To keep black children segregated solely on the basis of race, it ruled, "generates a feeling of inferiority as to their status in the community that may affect their hearts and minds in a way unlikely ever to be undone."

Overruling Plessy

At the time of the *Brown* decision, 21 states and the District of Columbia operated segregated school systems. All had to decide, in some way, how to comply with the new ruling. The Court allowed some leeway, handing down a second ruling in 1955 that required states to carry out desegregation "with all deliberate speed." Some border states reluctantly decided to comply, but in the Deep South, many pledged diehard defiance. In 1956, a "Southern Manifesto" was issued by 19 United States senators and 81 representatives: they intended to use "all lawful means" to reestablish legalized segregation.

A New Civil Rights Strategy

The *Brown* decision did not end segregation, but it combined with political and economic forces to usher in a new era of southern race relations. In December

Rosa Parks arrested 1955 Rosa Parks, a 43-year-old black civil rights activist, was riding the bus home in Montgomery, Alabama. When the driver ordered her to give up her seat for a white man, as Alabama Jim Crow laws required, she refused. Police took her to jail and eventually fined her $14.

Determined to overturn the law, black leaders organized a boycott of Montgomery buses, whose riders were largely black. Many in the white community responded angrily to this challenge. No local insurance agent would insure cars used to carpool black workers. A bomb exploded in the house of the Reverend Martin Luther King, Jr., the key boycott leader. Ninety black leaders were arrested for organizing the boycott. Still they held out until November 23, 1956, when the Supreme Court ruled that bus segregation was illegal.

The triumph was especially sweet for Martin Luther King, Jr., whose leadership in Montgomery brought him national fame. Before becoming a minister *Martin Luther King, Jr.* at the Dexter Street Baptist Church, King had had little personal contact with the worst forms of white racism. He had grown up in the relatively affluent middle-class black community of Atlanta, Georgia, the son of one of the city's most prominent black ministers. He attended Morehouse College, an academically respected black school in Atlanta, and Crozer Theological Seminary in Philadelphia, before entering the doctoral program in theology at Boston University. As a graduate student, King embraced the pacifism and nonviolence of the Indian leader Mohandas Gandhi and the activism of Christian reformers of the progressive era. King accepted the call to Dexter Street in 1954 with the idea of becoming a theologian after he served his active ministry and finished his dissertation.

As boycott leader, it was King's responsibility to rally black support without triggering violence. Since local officials were all too eager for any excuse to use force, King's nonviolent approach proved an effective strategy. King offered his audience two visions. First, he reminded them of the many injustices they had been forced to endure. The boycott, he asserted, was a good way to seek redress. Then he counseled his followers to avoid the actions of their oppressors: "In our protest there will be no cross burnings. No white person will be taken from his home by a hooded Negro mob and brutally murdered." And he evoked the Christian and republican ideals that would become the themes of his civil rights crusade. "If we protest courageously, and yet with dignity and Christian love," he said, "when the future history books are written, somebody will have to say, 'There lived a race of people, of black people, of people who had the moral courage to stand up for their rights. And thereby they injected a new meaning into the history of civilization.'"

Indeed, the African Americans of Montgomery did set an example of moral courage that rewrote the pages of American race relations. The firm stand of Montgomery's black community caught the attention of the national news media. King and his colleagues were developing the tactics needed to launch a more aggressive phase of the civil rights movement.

Little Rock and the White Backlash

The civil rights spotlight moved the following year to Little Rock, Arkansas. There, white officials had reluctantly adopted a plan to integrate the schools with a most deliberate lack of speed. Nine black students were scheduled to enroll in September 1957 at the all-white Central High School. Instead, the school board urged them to stay home. Governor Orval Faubus, generally a moderate on race relations, called out the Arkansas National Guard on the excuse of maintaining order. President Eisenhower tacitly supported Faubus in his defiance of court-ordered integration by remarking that "you cannot change people's hearts merely by laws."

Still, the Justice Department could not simply let Faubus defy the federal courts. It won an injunction against the governor, but when the nine blacks returned on September 23, a mob of 1000 abusive white protesters greeted them. So great was national attention to the crisis that President Eisenhower felt compelled to send in 1000 federal troops and take control of the National Guard. For one year the Guard preserved order until Faubus, in a last-ditch maneuver, closed all the schools. Only in 1959, under the pressure of another federal court

Angry white students menace black students during the integration crisis at Little Rock's Central High School.

ruling, did the Little Rock schools reopen and resume the plan for gradual integration.

In the face of such attitudes, King and other civil rights leaders recognized that the skirmishes of Montgomery and Little Rock were a beginning, not the end. Cultural attitudes and customs were not about to give way overnight.

CRACKS IN THE CONSENSUS

The fifties, then, were not a time of consensus on civil rights. In other ways, too, the era could hardly be painted as a decade of undisturbed calm. Intellectuals and social critics spoke out against the stifling features of a conformist corporate culture. Even a moderate like Eisenhower had warned of giving too much power to military, governmental, and industrial bureaucracies. At the fringes of American society, the "beatniks" rejected conformity, while the more mainstream rock 'n' roll movement broadcast its own brand of youthful rebellion. Such cultural ferment undercut the notion that the fifties were merely a decade of consensus.

Critics of Mass Culture

In Levittown, New Jersey, a woman who had invited her neighbors to a cocktail party eagerly awaited them dressed in newly fashionable Capri pants—a tight-fitting calf-length style. Alas, one early-arriving couple glimpsed the woman through a window. What on earth was the hostess wearing? *Pajamas?* Who in their right mind would entertain in pajamas? The couple sneaked home, afraid they had made a mistake about the day of the party. They telephoned another neighbor, who anxiously called yet others on the guest list. The neighbors finally mustered enough courage to attend the party. But when the hostess later learned of their misunderstanding, she put her Capri pants in the closet for good. Levittown was not ready for such a change in fashion.

Was America turning into a vast suburban wasteland, where the neighbors' worries over Capri pants would stifle all individuality? Many "highbrow" intellectuals worried openly about the effects of mass culture: the homogenized lifestyle created by mass consumption, conformity, and mass media. Critics like Dwight Macdonald sarcastically attacked the culture of the suburban middle classes: Reader's Digest Condensed Books or uplifting film spectacles like *The Ten Commandments*. "Midcult," Macdonald called it, which was his shorthand for uninspired middlebrow culture.

Other critics charged that the skyscrapers and factories of giant conglomerates housed an impersonal world. In large, increasingly automated workplaces, skilled laborers seemed little more than caretakers of machines. Large corporations required middle-level executives to submerge their personal goals

David Riesman's The Lonely Crowd

in the processes and work routines of a large bureaucracy. David Riesman, a sociologist, condemned stifling conformity in *The Lonely Crowd* (1950). In nineteenth-century America, Riesman argued, Americans had been "inner directed." It was their own consciences that formed their values and drove them to seek success. In contrast, modern workers had developed a personality shaped not so much by inner convictions as by the opinions of their peers. The new "other-directed" society of suburbia preferred security to success. "Go along to get along" was its motto. In a bureaucratized economy, it was important to please others, to conform to the group, and to cooperate.

William Whyte carried Riesman's critique from the workplace to the suburb in *The Organization Man* (1956). Here he found rootless families, shifted

William Whyte's Organization Man

from town to town by the demands of corporations. (IBM, went one standard joke, stood for "I've Been Moved.") The typical "organization man" was sociable but not terribly ambitious. He sought primarily to "keep up with the Joneses" and the number of consumer goods they owned. He lived in a suburban "split-level trap," as one critic put it, one among millions of "haggard" men, "tense and anxious" women, and "the gimme kids."

No doubt such portraits were overdrawn and overly alarmist. (Where, after all, did Riesman's nineteenth-century inner-directed Americans get their values, if not from the society around them?) But such critiques indicated the problems of adjustment faced by those working within large bureaucratic organizations and living in suburbs that were decentralized and self-contained.

Juvenile Delinquency, Rock and Roll, and Rebellion

Young Americans were among suburbia's sharpest critics. Dance crazes, outlandish clothing, slang, rebelliousness, and sexual precociousness—all these behaviors challenged middle-class respectability. More than a few educators warned that America had spawned a generation of rebellious "juvenile delinquents." Psychologist Frederic Wertheim told a group of doctors, "You cannot understand present-day juvenile delinquency if you do not take into account the pathogenic and pathoplastic [infectious] influence of comic books." Others laid the blame on films and the lyrics of popular music.

The center of the new teen culture was the high school. Whether in consolidated rural school districts, new suburban schools, or city systems, the large,

Teenage culture

comprehensive high schools of the 1950s were often miniature melting pots where middle-class students were exposed to, and often adopted, the style of the lower classes. They wore jeans and T-shirts, challenged authority, and defiantly smoked cigarettes, much like the motorcycle gang leader portrayed by Marlon Brando in the film *The Wild One* (1954).

In many ways the debate over juvenile delinquency was an argument about social class and, to a lesser degree, race. When adults complained that "delinquent" teenagers dressed poorly, lacked ambition, were irresponsible and sexually promiscuous, these were the same arguments traditionally used to denigrate other outsiders—immigrants, the poor, and African Americans. Nowhere were these racial and class undertones more evident than in the hue and cry that greeted the arrival of rock and roll.

Before 1954 popular music had been divided into three major categories: pop, country and western, and rhythm and blues. A handful of major record companies with almost exclusively white singers dominated the pop charts. On one fringe of the popular field was country and western, often split into cowboy musicians like Roy Rogers and Gene Autry and the hillbilly style associated with Nashville. The music industry generally treated rhythm and blues as "race music," whose performers and audience were largely black. Each of these musical traditions, it is worth noting, grew out of regional cultures. As the West and the South merged into the national culture, so these musical subcultures were gradually integrated into the national mainstream.

By the mid-1950s the distinctiveness of the three styles began to blur. Singers on the white pop charts recorded a few songs from country and from

The rock revolution

rhythm and blues. The popularity of crossovers such as "Sh-boom," "Tutti-Frutti," and "Earth Angel" indicated that a major shift in taste and market was under way. Lyrics still reflected the pop field's preoccupation with young love, marriage, and happiness, but the music reflected the rawer, earthier style of rhythm and blues. Country and western singer Bill Haley brought the new blend to the fore in 1954 with "Shake, Rattle, and Roll," the first rock song to reach the top ten on the pop charts.

And then—calamity! Millions of middle-class roofs nearly blew off with the appearance in 1955 of the rhythmic and raucous Elvis Presley. By background, Elvis was a country boy whose musical style combined elements of gospel, country, and blues. But it was his hip-swinging, pelvis-plunging performances that electrified teenage audiences. To more conservative adults, Presley's long hair, sideburns, and tight jeans seemed menacingly delinquent, an expression of hostile rebellion. What they often resented but rarely admitted was that Elvis looked lower class, sounded black, and really could sing.

Beyond the frenetic rhythms of rock and roll, and even further beyond the pale of suburban culture, a subculture flourished known as the beat generation.

The "beats"

In run-down urban neighborhoods and college towns this motley collection of artists, intellectuals, musicians, and middle-class students dropped out of mainstream society. In dress and behavior the "beatniks" self-consciously rejected what they viewed as the excessive spiritual bankruptcy of America's middle-class culture. Cool urban "hipsters"—especially black jazz musicians like John Coltrane or Sonny Rollins—were their models. They read poetry, listened to jazz, explored Oriental philosophy, and experimented openly with drugs, mystical religions, and sex.

The "beats" viewed themselves as driven to the margins of society by the culture of abundance, materialism, and conformity. "I saw the best minds of my generation destroyed by madness, starving hysterical naked," wrote Allen Ginsberg in his 1955 poem *Howl.* They had become "angelheaded hipsters . . . who in poverty and tatters and hollow-eyed and high sat up smoking in the supernatural darkness of cold-water flats floating across the tops of cities contemplating jazz." Jack Kerouac tapped the frenzied energy beneath the beatniks' cool facade in *On the Road* (1957), a novel based on his travels across the country with his friend Neal Cassady. Kerouac finished the novel in one three-week binge, feeding a 120-foot roll of paper through his typewriter and spilling out tales of pot, jazz, crazy sex, and all-night raps undertaken in a search for "IT"— the ultimate transcendental moment when mind and experience mesh.

The dreams of Kerouac and Ginsberg came from a world starkly different from that of the manicured lawns of suburbia. The world of the suburbs seemed content, middle-of-the-road, prosperous. The beats seemed restless, nonconformist, beyond the fringe. Yet the 1960s would demonstrate that the suburban era contained enough cracks in the consensus to launch an era of rebellion and reform. Those upheavals would test the limits of a liberal, even radical vision of American society. The fringes and the middle-of-the-roaders were perhaps not so far apart as they seemed.

SIGNIFICANT EVENTS

1947	Levittown construction begins
1950	David Riesman's *The Lonely Crowd* published; Kefauver crime hearings
1952	Fertility rate in the United States reaches new high
1954	*Brown v. Board of Education;* St. Lawrence Seaway Act; CIA overthrows government in Guatemala; Geneva summit
1955	Montgomery bus boycott; Elvis Presley ignites rock and roll
1956	Interstate Highway Act; Eisenhower reelected; Suez crisis; "Southern Manifesto"
1957	*Sputnik* launched; Little Rock crisis; Eisenhower Doctrine
1958	Marines sent into Lebanon; Berlin crisis; National Defense Education Act
1959	Castro seizes power in Cuba; Khrushchev visits United States
1960	Soviet Union captures CIA pilot; Paris summit canceled
1961	Eisenhower's farewell address warns of military–industrial complex

CHAPTER THIRTY

Liberalism and Beyond

Six-year-old Ruby knew the lessons. She was to look straight ahead—not to one side or the other—and especially not at *them*. She was to keep walking. Above all, she was not to look back once she'd passed, because that would encourage them. Ruby knew these things, but it was hard to keep her eyes straight. The first day of school, her parents came, along with federal marshals to keep order. And all around hundreds of angry white people were yelling things like, "You little nigger, we'll get you and kill you." Then she was within the building's quiet halls and alone with her teacher. She was the only person in class: none of the white students had come. As the days went by during that autumn of 1960, the marshals stopped walking with her but the hecklers still waited. And once in a while Ruby couldn't help looking back, trying to see if she recognized the face of one woman in particular.

Ruby's parents were not social activists. They signed their daughter up for the white school in this New Orleans neighborhood because "we thought it was for all the colored to do, and we never thought Ruby would be alone." Her father's white employer fired him; letters and phone calls threatened the family. Through it all Ruby seemed to take things in stride, though her parents worried that she was not eating well. Often she left her school lunch untouched or refused anything other than packaged food such as potato chips. It was only after a time that the problem was traced to the hecklers. "They tells me I'm going to die, and that it'll be soon. And that one lady tells me every morning I'm getting poisoned soon, when she can fix it." Ruby was convinced that the woman owned the variety store nearby and would carry out her threat by poisoning the family's food.

Desegregation in New Orleans, 1960

Over the course of a year, white students gradually returned to class and life settled into a new routine. By the time Ruby was 10, she had developed a remarkably clear perception of herself. "Maybe because of all the trouble going to school in the beginning I learned more about my people. Maybe I would have anyway; because when you get older you see yourself and the white kids; and you find out the difference. You try to forget it, and say there is none; and if there is you won't say what it be. Then you say it's my own people, and so I can be proud of them instead of ashamed."

The new ways were not easy for white southerners either—even those who saw the need for change. One woman, a teacher from Atlanta, recalled the summer 10 years earlier, when she went to New York City to take courses in education. There were black students in her dormitory, an integrated situation she was not used to. One day as she stepped from her shower, so did a black student from the nearby stall. "When I saw her I didn't know what to do," the woman recalled. "I felt sick all over, and frightened. What I remember—I'll never forget it—is that horrible feeling of being caught in a terrible trap, and not knowing what to do about it. . . . My sense of propriety was with me, though—miraculously—and I didn't want to hurt the woman. It wasn't *her* that was upsetting me. I knew that, even in that moment of sickness and panic." So she ducked back into the shower until the other woman left.

It took most of the summer before she felt comfortable eating with black students. Back in Atlanta, she told no one about her experiences. "At that time people would have thought one of two things: I was crazy (for being so upset and ashamed) or a fool who in a summer had become a dangerous 'race mixer.'" She continued to love the South and to defend its traditions of dignity, neighborliness, and honor, but she saw the need for change. And so in 1961 she volunteered to teach one of the first integrated high school classes in Atlanta. "I've never felt so useful," she concluded after two years; ". . .not just to the children but to our whole society. American as well as Southern. Those children, all of them, have given me more than I've given them."

A LIBERAL AGENDA FOR REFORM

For Americans in all walks of life, the changes that swept the United States in the 1960s were wrenching. From the schoolrooms and lunch counters of the South to the college campuses of the North, from eastern slums to western migrant labor camps, American society was in ferment.

On the face of it, such agitation seemed to be a dramatic reversal of the placid fifties. Turbulence and change had overturned stability and consensus. Yet the events of the 1960s grew naturally out of the social conditions that preceded them.

The Social Structures of Change

The prosperity of the 1950s encouraged a confidence that problems like poverty and discrimination might finally be solved. At the same time, that prosperity did not reach all areas of the nation equally. While suburbs flourished, urban areas decayed. While more white Americans went to college, more African Americans found themselves out of work on southern farms or desperate for jobs in northern ghettos. As Mexican American migrant workers picked grapes in California or followed the harvest north from Texas, they saw their employers resist every attempt to unionize and improve their wages. Yet the general prosperity remained for all to see. And the success of the NAACP in wringing a policy of integration from the Supreme Court gave minorities new hopes that they too could win the rights due them.

The expansive years of the 1950s, in other words, proved to be a seedbed for reform movements of the 1960s. Time and again, the dissenters challenged the political system to deal with what the 1950s had done—and what had been left undone. As one friend of Martin Luther King predicted in 1958, "If the young people are aroused from their lethargy through this fight, it will affect broad circles throughout the country. . . ."

Inevitably, these forces for change brought hope and energy to the liberal tradition. Like the New Dealers and the Progressives before them, liberals of

The liberal tradition

the 1960s did not wish to overturn capitalism. They looked primarily to tame its excesses, taking a pragmatic approach to reforming American society. Like Franklin Roosevelt, they believed that the government should play an active role in managing the economy in order to soften the boom-and-bust swings of capitalism. Like Progressives from the turn of the century, liberals looked to improve society by applying the intelligence of "experts."

The confidence of liberals that poverty could be eliminated and the good society achieved sometimes verged on arrogance—as the end of the decade would prove. Yet during the early sixties, the optimism of liberal politicians and thinkers was both heady and energizing.

The Election of 1960

The first president to ride these currents of reform was John Fitzgerald Kennedy, at 43 the youngest ever elected to the office. On the face of it, Kennedy's 1960 campaign promised to bring change to Washington. The nation needed to find "new frontiers," he proclaimed. Kennedy's rhetoric was noble, but the direction in which he would take the nation was far from clear.

Aside from political issues, there was a social one to be met. Jack Kennedy was a Roman Catholic out of Irish Boston, and no Catholic had ever been

Kennedy's Catholicism

elected president. Conservative Protestants, many concentrated in the heavily Democratic South, were convinced that a Catholic president would never be "free to exercise his own judgment" if the pope ordered otherwise. Kennedy confronted the issue head-on, addressing an association of hostile ministers in Houston. "I believe in an America where the separation of church and state is absolute," he said, "—where no Catholic prelate would tell the President (should he be Catholic) how to act, and no Protestant minister would tell his parishioners how to vote." House Speaker

Sam Rayburn, an old Texas pol, was astonished by Kennedy's bravura performance. "My God! . . . He's eating them blood raw."

Kennedy's opponent, Vice President Richard Nixon, ran on his political experience and staunch anti-Communism. His campaign faltered in October as unemployment rose. Nixon was also hurt by a series of televised debates with Kennedy—the first broadcast nationally. Despite his debating skill, Nixon was overtired, and his "Lazy Shave" makeup failed to hide his five-o'clock shadow. Election Day saw the largest turnout in 50 years: 64 percent of all voters. Out of 68.3 million ballots cast, Kennedy won by a margin of just 118,000. The whisker-thin victory was made possible by strong Catholic support in key states. "Hyphenated" Americans—Hispanic, Jewish, Irish, Italian, Polish, and German—voted Democratic in record numbers, while much of the black vote that had gone to Eisenhower in 1956 returned to the Democratic fold.

The Hard-Nosed Idealists of Camelot

Many observers compared the Kennedy White House to Camelot, King Arthur's magical court. A popular musical of 1960 pictured Camelot as a land where skies were fair, men brave, women pretty, and the days full of challenge. With similar vigor, Kennedy surrounded himself with bright, energetic liberal advisers. Touch football games on the White House lawn displayed a rough-and-tumble playfulness, akin to Arthur's jousting tournaments of old.

In truth, Kennedy was not a liberal by temperament. Handsome and intelligent, he possessed an ironic, self-deprecating humor. Yet in Congress, he had led an undistinguished career, supported Senator Joe McCarthy, and earned a reputation as a playboy. Once Kennedy set his sights on the White House, however, he revealed an astonishing capacity for political maneuver and organization. To woo the liberals, he surrounded himself with a distinguished group of intellectuals and academics.

Robert Strange McNamara typified the pragmatic, liberal bent of the new Kennedy team. Steely and brilliant, McNamara was one of the postwar breed of young executives known as the "whiz kids." As a Harvard Business School professor and later as president of Ford Motors, he specialized in using new quantitative tools to streamline business. As the new secretary of defense, McNamara intended to find more flexible and efficient ways of conducting the cold war.

McNamara and the whiz kids

Kennedy liked men like this—witty, bright, intellectual—because they seemed comfortable with power and were not afraid to use it. If Khrushchev spoke of waging guerrilla "wars of liberation," Americans could play that game too. The president's leisure reading reflected a similar adventurous taste: the popular James Bond spy novels. Agent 007, with his license to kill, was sophisticated, a cool womanizer (as Kennedy himself continued to be), and ready to use the latest technology to deal with Communist villains. Ironically, Bond demon-

The urbane John F. Kennedy was associated with both King Arthur and the spy James Bond (played by Sean Connery, right). Kennedy and his advisers prided themselves on their pragmatic, hard-nosed idealism. But while Bond used advanced technology and covert operations to save the world, in real life such approaches had their downside, as the growing civil war in Vietnam would demonstrate.

strated that there could be plenty of glamour in being "hard-nosed" and pragmatic. That illicit pleasure was the underside, perhaps, of Camelot's high ideals.

NEW FRONTIERS

Abroad, Kennedy was convinced that the cold war had shifted from the traditional battlefronts of Europe to the developing nations in Asia, Africa, and Latin America. That meant the United States needed a more flexible range of military and economic options.

The Alliance for Progress, announced in the spring of 1961, indicated the Kennedy approach. He promised to provide $20 billion in foreign aid over 10 years—about four times the aid given to Latin America under Eisenhower. In return, Latin American nations would agree to reform unfair tax policies and begin agricultural land reforms. If successful, the Alliance would discourage future Castro-style revolutions. With similar fanfare, the administration set up the Peace Corps. This program sent idealistic young men and women to Third World nations to provide technical, educational, and public health services. Under the Alliance, most Peace Corps volunteers were assigned to Latin America.

Alliance for Progress and the Peace Corps

To back the new economic policies with military muscle, the Pentagon directed jungle warfare schools, both in North Carolina and in the Canal Zone. The programs were designed to train Latin American police and paramilitary groups, as well as American special forces like the Green Berets. If the Soviets or their allies entered wars of liberation, United States commandos would be ready to fight back.

Kennedy believed, too, that the Soviets had made space the final frontier of the cold war. Only a few months after the president's inauguration, a Russian

The cold war's race to the moon

cosmonaut orbited the world for the first time. In response, Kennedy challenged Congress to authorize a manned space mission to the moon that would land by the end of the decade. In February 1962 John Glenn circled the earth three times in a "fireball of a ride." Gradually, the American space program gained on the Russians.

Cold War Frustrations

In more down-to-earth ways, high ideals did not translate easily into practical results. Latin American governments eagerly accepted aid, but they were less willing to carry out reforms. During the first five years of the Alliance for Progress, nine Latin American governments were overthrown by military coups. The Peace Corps, for its part, helped thousands of Third World farmers on a people-to-people basis. But individual Peace Corps workers could do little to change corrupt policies on a national level.

Nor did Kennedy succeed in countering "wars of liberation." The Eisenhower administration had authorized the CIA to overthrow Fidel Castro's

Bay of Pigs invasion

Communist regime in Cuba, 90 miles south of Florida. Eager to establish his own cold war credentials, Kennedy approved an attack by a 1400-member army of Cuban exiles in April 1961. The invasion turned into a mismanaged disaster. The poorly equipped rebel forces landed at the swampy Bay of Pigs, and no discontented rebels flocked to their support. Within two days Castro's army had rounded them up. Taking responsibility for the fiasco, Kennedy suffered a bitter humiliation.

Kennedy's advisers took a similar covert approach in South Vietnam. There, the American-backed Prime Minister, Ngo Dinh Diem (see page 822), grew

Vietnam

more unpopular by the month. South Vietnamese Communists, known as the Vietcong, waged a guerrilla war against Diem with support from North Vietnam. Buddhists and other groups backed the rebellion, since Diem, a Catholic, ruthlessly persecuted them. In May 1961, a month after the Bay of Pigs invasion, Kennedy secretly ordered 500 Green Berets and military advisers to Vietnam to prop up Diem. By 1963 the number of "military advisers" had risen to more than 16,000.

As the situation degenerated, Diem's corruption and police-state tactics made it unlikely he could defeat the Vietcong. Thus the Kennedy administration tacitly encouraged the military to stage a coup. The plotters captured Diem and, to Washington's surprise, shot him in November 1963. Despite Kennedy's policy of pragmatic idealism, the United States found itself mired in a Vietnamese civil war, which it had no clear strategy for winning.

Confronting Khrushchev

Vietnam and Cuba were just two areas in the Third World where the Kennedy administration sought to battle Communist forces. But the conflict between the United States and the Soviet Union soon overshadowed developments in Asia, Africa, and Latin America.

In June 1961, a summit held in Vienna gave the president his first chance to take the measure of Nikita Khrushchev. For two long days, Khrushchev was *The Berlin Wall* brash and belligerent. East and West Germany must be reunited, he demanded. The problem of Berlin, where dissatisfied East Germans were fleeing to the city's free western zone, must be settled within six months. Kennedy left Vienna worried that the Soviet leader perceived him as weak and inexperienced. By August events in Berlin confirmed his fears. The Soviets threw up a heavily guarded wall sealing off the enclave of West Berlin from the rest of the eastern zone. Despite American protests, the wall stayed up.

Tensions with the Soviet Union also led the administration to rethink the American approach to nuclear warfare. Under the Dulles doctrine of massive retaliation, almost any incident threatened to trigger a full launch *Flexible response doctrine* of nuclear missiles. Kennedy and McNamara sought to establish a "flexible response doctrine" that would limit the level of a first nuclear strike and thus leave room for negotiation.

But what if the Soviets were tempted to launch a first-strike attack to knock out American missiles? McNamara's flexible response policy required that enough American missiles survive in order to retaliate. So McNamara began a program to bury missile sites underground and develop submarine-launched missiles. The new flexible response policies resulted in a 15 percent increase in the 1961 military budget, compared with only 2 percent increases during the last two years of Eisenhower's term.

The Missiles of October

The peril of nuclear confrontation became dramatically clear in the Cuban missile crisis of October 1962. President Kennedy had warned repeatedly that the United States would treat any attempt to place offensive weapons in Cuba as an unacceptable threat. For his part, Khrushchev promised that the Soviets had no such intention. Thus Kennedy was outraged when a CIA flight over Cuba confirmed that offensive missile sites were being constructed. "He can't do that to me," the president snapped.

For a week, top security advisers met secretly to plan a response. Military advisers urged air strikes against the missile sites, but Kennedy worried that the strikes might trigger nuclear war. Indeed, recent evidence from Soviet archives indicates that, unknown to American officials, Soviet commanders in Cuba

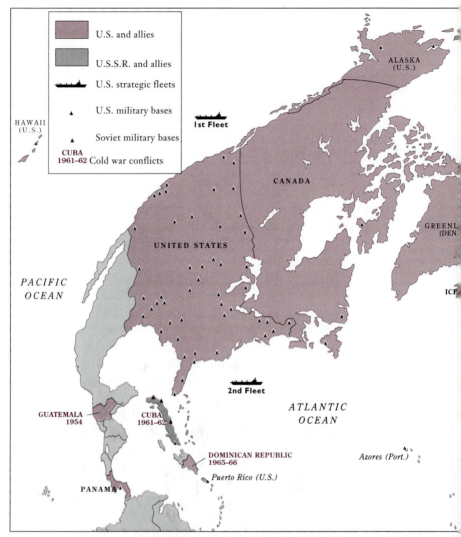

THE WORLD OF THE SUPERPOWERS Across the globe, the United States and the
Soviet Union stood astride a network of military bases and regional alliances that
marked the extent of their powers. Around these strategic perimeters, centers of
conflict continued to emerge.

possessed the authority to launch short-range nuclear missiles if American
forces attacked. In the end Kennedy chose the more restrained option of imposing a naval quarantine to intercept "all offensive military equipment under
shipment to Cuba." On October 22, Americans were stunned when the president announced news of the crisis and his response. Tensions mounted as Soviet
vessels approached the line of American ships, then stopped or reversed course.

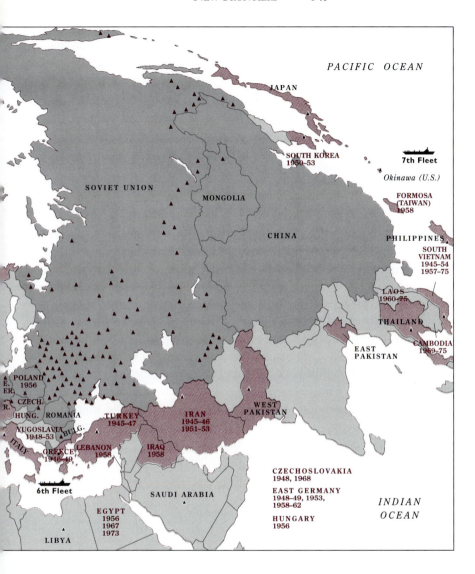

Meanwhile, Kennedy scrambled to resolve the crisis through diplomatic channels. On October 26 he received a rambling message from Khrushchev agreeing to remove the missiles in return for an American promise not to invade Cuba. The next day came a more troubling message, insisting the United States must also dismantle its missile bases in Turkey, which bordered on the Soviet Union. Unwilling to strike that deal publicly, Kennedy decided to ignore the second letter and accept the offer in the first. When the Soviets agreed, the face-off ended on terms that saved either side from overt humiliation.

The nuclear showdown prompted Kennedy and his advisers to seek ways to control the nuclear arms race. "We all inhabit this small planet," he warned in

Nuclear test ban treaty June 1963. "We all breathe the same air. We all cherish our children's future. And we are all mortal." The administration negotiated a nuclear test ban with the Soviets, outlawing all aboveground nuclear tests. At the same time Kennedy's prestige soared for "standing up" to the Soviets.

The (Somewhat) New Frontier at Home

It proved more difficult to take bold initiatives at home than abroad. Kennedy and his advisors had no broad vision for reform. They preferred to tackle problems one by one. In making domestic policy Kennedy found himself hemmed in by a Democratic Congress dominated by conservatives. As a result, the president's legislative achievements were modest. He passed a bill providing some financial aid to depressed industrial and rural areas. But on key issues, including aid to education and medical health insurance, Kennedy made no headway.

He wavered, too, on how to manage the economy. The president's liberal advisers favored increased government spending to reduce unemployment, even *Relations with business and big steel* if that meant a budget deficit. Even so, Kennedy believed that prosperity for big business spelled growth for the whole nation. Thus the president asked Congress to ease antitrust restrictions and grant investment credits and tax breaks—actions that pleased corporate interests. But he was convinced that the government needed to limit the power of both large corporations and unions to set prices and wages. The alternative was an inflationary spiral, in which wage increases would spark price increases, followed by even higher wage demands.

To prevent that, the Council of Economic Advisors proposed that wage increases be given to workers only if their increased productivity kept prices stable. In April 1962 the United Steel Workers, like most other major unions, agreed to a contract that held down wage increases. The large steel corporations, however, broke their part of the informal bargain by sharply raising steel prices. Angered, Kennedy called for investigations into price fixing and shifted Pentagon purchases to smaller steel companies that had not raised prices. The intense pressure caused the big companies to drop the price increases but soured relations between the president and the business community.

The Reforms of the Warren Court

With Kennedy's promise of new frontiers blocked by a conservative Congress, the Supreme Court broke the logjam. Chief Justice Earl Warren turned what was traditionally the least activist branch of government into a center of liberal reform. Until Warren's retirement in 1969, the Court continued to hand down landmark decisions in broad areas of civil liberties and civil rights.

In 1960 the rights of citizens accused of a crime but not yet convicted were often unclear. Those too poor to afford lawyers could be forced to go to trial

I was sentenced to the state Penitentiary
by the Circuit Court of Bay County, State of
Florida. The present proceeding was commenced
on a ~~r~~ petition for a writ of Habeus Corpus
to the Supreme Court of the State of
Florida to vacate the sentence, on the
grounds that I was made to stand
Trial with out the aid of counsel, and, at all
times of my incarseretion. The said Court
refused to appoint counsel and therefore
deprived me of Due process of law, and violeta
my rights in the Bill of Rights and the
constitution of the United States.

Clarence Earl Gideon

5th day of Jan 1962 Petitioner.

Laurence C. Duyya

NoTary PubliC

Notary Public
My Com... ...11, 1962
Bonded by American Surety Co. of N. Y.

Gideon's Letter to the Supreme Court
John F. Davis, Clerk, Supreme Court of the United States

Clarence Earl Gideon, a prisoner in a Florida jail, used this handwritten letter to bring his successful appeal to the Supreme Court. In the *Gideon* case the court ruled that even poor defendants have the right to legal counsel.

Protection of due process

without representation. Often they were not informed of their constitutional rights when arrested. In a series of decisions, the Court ruled that the Fourteenth Amendment provided broad guarantees of due process under the law. *Gideon v. Wainwright* (1963), an appeal launched by a Florida prisoner, made it clear that all citizens were entitled to legal counsel in any case involving a possible jail sentence. In *Escobedo v. Illinois* (1964) and *Miranda v. Arizona* (1966), the Court declared that individuals detained for a crime must be informed of the charges against them, of their right to remain silent, and of their right to have an attorney present during questioning. Though these decisions applied to all citizens, they were primarily intended to benefit the poor, who were most likely to be in trouble with the law and least likely to understand their rights.

Other decisions promoted a more liberal social climate. In *Griswold v. Connecticut* (1964) the Warren Court overturned a nineteenth-century law banning the sale of contraceptives or medical advice about their use.

Liberal social decisions

The Court also demonstrated its distaste for censorship by greatly narrowing the legal definition of obscenity. A book had to be "utterly without redeeming social value" to permit censorship. And the Court strengthened the constitutional separation of church and state by ruling in *Engle v. Vitale* that prayers could not be read in public schools.

Banning official school prayer may have been one of the Court's most controversial decisions; *Baker v. Carr* was one of its most far-reaching. Most states had not redrawn their legislative districts to reflect the growth of urban and suburban population since the nineteenth century. The less populated (and most often conservative) rural areas elected the most legislators. In *Baker v. Carr* the Court ruled that the states must redraw legislative lines to follow as closely as possible the principle of "one person, one vote."

THE CIVIL RIGHTS CRUSADE

In Greensboro, North Carolina, in 1960, four black students attending a local college read a pamphlet describing the 1955 bus boycott in Montgomery, Alabama. They decided it was time to make their own protest against segregation. Proceeding to the "whites only" lunch counter at a local store, they sat politely waiting for service. "The waitress looked at me as if I were from outer space," recalled one of the protesters. Rather than serve them, the manager closed the counter. Word of the action spread, and within two weeks, the courage of the Greensboro students had inspired 15 sit-ins across the South. By year's end, 50,000 people had demonstrated; 3000 had gone to jail.

Nothing did more to propel the liberalism of the 1960s—and, in the end, to push beyond it—than the campaign for civil rights. By the late 1950s a new generation of southern African Americans, many having moved from farms to cities, increasingly rejected their second-class citizenship. But how could they overturn the legal framework of segregation in the South? How could they overturn the racism evident in everyday life across the nation?

Riding to Freedom

During the 1950s the push for desegregation had centered on court actions launched by the NAACP and the Urban League. Martin Luther King's Southern Christian Leadership Conference (SCLC) hinted at newer, more direct challenges to the social order. Since organizing the Montgomery boycott, King had continued to advocate nonviolent protest: "To resist without bitterness; to be cursed and not reply; to be beaten and not hit back." A second key organization, the Congress of Racial Equality (CORE), was even more willing to force confrontations with the segregationist system. Another group, the Student Non-Violent Coordinating Committee (SNCC, pronounced "Snick"), grew out of the Greensboro sit-in. SNCC represented the militant, younger generation of black activists, impatient with the slow pace of reform.

The SCLC, CORE, and SNCC

In May 1961 CORE director James Farmer led a group of black and white "freedom riders" on a bus trip from Washington to New Orleans. They intended to focus national attention on the inequality of segregated facilities. Violent southern mobs gave the freedom riders the kind of attention they feared. In South Carolina, thugs beat divinity student John Lewis as he tried to enter an all-white waiting room. Mobs in Anniston and Birmingham, Alabama, assaulted the freedom riders as police ignored the violence. One of the buses was burned.

Sensitive to the power of conservative southern Democrats, President Kennedy tried to avoid sending federal forces to protect the demonstrators. But his hopes were dashed. From a phone booth outside the bus terminal, John Doar, a Justice Department official in Montgomery, relayed the horror to Attorney General Robert Kennedy:

> Now the passengers are coming off. They're standing on a corner of the platform. Oh, there are fists, punching! A bunch of men led by a guy with a bleeding face are beating them. There are no cops. It's terrible! It's terrible! There's not a cop in sight. People are yelling, "There those niggers are! Get 'em, get 'em!" It's awful.

Appalled, Robert Kennedy ordered in 400 federal marshals, who barely managed to hold off the crowd. Martin Luther King, addressing a meeting in town, phoned the attorney general to say that their church had been surrounded by a mob of several thousand—jeering, throwing rocks, and carrying firebombs. Kennedy later recalled, "I said that we were doing the best that we could and that he'd be as dead as Kelsey's nuts if it hadn't been for the marshals and the efforts that we made."

Both Kennedys understood that civil rights was the most divisive issue the administration faced. The president needed the votes of African Americans and liberals to win reelection. Yet an active federal role threatened to drive white southerners from the Democratic party. Thus Kennedy hedged on his promise to introduce civil rights legislation. He assured black leaders that executive orders would eliminate discrimination in the government and in businesses filling government contracts. He appointed several blacks to high positions and five, including Thurgood Marshall, to the federal courts. But the freedom riders, by their bold actions, forced the Kennedys to do more.

Civil Rights at High Tide

By the fall of 1961 Robert Kennedy had persuaded SNCC to shift its energies to voter registration, which he assumed would stir less violence. Voting booths, Kennedy noted, were not like schools, where people would protest, "We don't want our little blond daughter going to school with a Negro."

As SNCC and CORE workers arrived in southern towns in the spring of 1962, they discovered that voting rights was not a peaceful issue. Over two years in Mississippi they registered only 4000 out of 394,000 black adults. Angry

E Y E W I T N E S S   T O   H I S T O R Y

A Mississippi College Student Attends the NAACP Convention

In mid September [1962] I was back on campus. But didn't very much happen until February when the NAACP held its annual convention in Jackson [Mississippi]. They were having a whole lot of interesting speakers: Jackie Robinson, Floyd Patterson, Curt Flood, Margaretta Belafonte, and many others. I wouldn't have missed it for anything. I was so excited that I sent one of the leaflets home to Mama and asked her to come.

Three days later I got a letter from Mama with dried-up tears on it, forbidding me to go to the convention. It went on for more than six pages. She said if I didn't stop that shit she would come to Tougaloo and kill me herself. She told me about the time I last visited her, on Thanksgiving, and she had picked me up at the bus station. She said she picked me up because she was scared some white in my hometown would try to do something to me. She said the sheriff had been by, telling her I was messing around with that NAACP group. She said he told her if I didn't stop it, I could not come back there any more. He said that they didn't need any of those NAACP people messing around in Centreville. She ended the letter by saying that she had burned the leaflet I sent her. "Please don't send any more of that stuff here. I don't want nothing to happen to us here," she said. "If you keep that up, you will never be able to come home again."

I was so damn mad after her letter, I felt like taking the NAACP convention to Centreville. I think I would have, if it had been in my power to do so. The remainder of the week I thought of nothing except going to the convention. I didn't know exactly what to do about it. I didn't want Mama or any one at home to get hurt because of me.

I had felt something was wrong when I was home. During the four days I was there, Mama tried to do everything she could to keep me in the house.

racists countered with legal harassment, jailings, beatings, bombings, and murders. Terrorized workers who called for protection found it woefully lacking. FBI agents often stood by taking notes while SNCC volunteers were assaulted. Undaunted, the workers fanned out across the countryside to speak with farmers and sharecroppers who had never dared ask for the vote.

When I said I was going to see some of my old classmates, she pretended she was sick and said I would have to cook. I knew she was acting strangely, but I hadn't known why. I thought Mama just wanted me to spend most of my time with her, since this was only the second time I had been home since I entered college as a freshman.

Things kept running through my mind after that letter from Mama. My mind was so active, I couldn't sleep at night. I remembered the one time I did leave the house to go to the post office. I had walked past a bunch of white men on the street on my way through town and one said "Is that the gal goin' to Tougaloo?" He acted kind of mad or something, and I didn't know what was going on. I got a creepy feeling, so I hurried home. When I told Mama about it, she just said, "A lotta people don't like that school." I knew what she meant. Just before I went to Tougaloo, they had housed the Freedom Riders there. The school was being criticized by whites throughout the state.

The night before the convention started, I made up my mind to go, no matter what Mama said. I just wouldn't tell Mama or anyone from home. Then it occurred to me—how did the sheriff or anyone at home know I was working with the NAACP chapter on campus? Somehow they had found out. Now I knew I could never go to Centreville safely again. I kept telling myself that I didn't really care too much about going home, that it was more important to me to go to the convention.

I was there from the very beginning. Jackie Robinson was asked to serve as moderator. This was the first time I had seen him in person. I remembered how when Jackie became the first Negro to play Major League baseball, my uncles and most of the Negro boys in my hometown started organizing baseball leagues. It did something for them to see a Negro out there playing with all those white players. Jackie was a good moderator, I thought. He kept smiling and joking. People felt relaxed and proud. They appreciated knowing and meeting people of their own race who had done something worth talking about.

Meredith enters University of Mississippi
Confrontation increased when a federal court ordered the segregated University of Mississippi to admit James Meredith, a black applicant. When Governor Ross Barnett personally blocked Meredith's registration in September 1962, Kennedy ordered several hundred federal marshals to escort Meredith into a university dormitory.

The marshals were met by a mob on campus, which shot out street lights and threw rocks and bottles. The president finally sent in federal troops, but not before 2 people were killed and 375 wounded.

In Mississippi, President Kennedy had begun to lose control of the civil rights issue. The House of Representatives, influenced by television coverage of the violence, introduced a number of civil rights measures. And in 1963 Martin Luther King led a group to Birmingham, Alabama, to force a showdown against segregation. From a prison cell there, he produced one of the most eloquent documents of the civil rights movement, his "Letter from Birmingham Jail." Addressed to local ministers who had called for an end to confrontation, King defended the use of civil disobedience. The choice, he warned, was not between obeying the law and nonviolently breaking it to bring about change. It was between his way and streets "flowing with blood," as frustrated black citizens turned toward more militant ideologies.

"Letter from Birmingham Jail"

On August 28, 1963, more than 250,000 demonstrators joined the great civil rights march on Washington. The day belonged to the Reverend Martin Luther King Jr., who movingly called on black and white Americans to join together in a color-blind society.

Once freed, King led new demonstrations. Television cameras were on hand that May as Birmingham police chief "Bull" Connor, a man with a short fuse, unleashed attack dogs, club-wielding police, and fire hoses powerful enough to peel the bark off trees. When segregationist bombs went off in African American neighborhoods, black mobs retaliated with their own riot, burning a number of shops and businesses owned by white citizens. In the following 10 weeks, more than 750 riots erupted in 186 cities and towns, both North and South. King's warning of streets "flowing with blood" no longer seemed far-fetched.

Kennedy sensed that he could no longer compromise on civil rights. "If [an American with dark skin] cannot enjoy the full and free life all of us want," he asked Americans, "then who among us would be content to have the color of his skin changed and stand in his place? Who among us would then be content with counsels of patience and delay?" The president followed his words with support for a strong civil rights bill to end segregation and protect black voters. When King announced a massive march on Washington for August 1963, Kennedy objected that it would undermine support for his bill. "I have never engaged in any direct action movement which did not seem ill-timed," King replied. Faced with the inevitable, Kennedy convinced the organizers to use the event to promote the administration's bill, much to the disgust of militant CORE and SNCC factions.

On August 28 some 250,000 people gathered at the Lincoln Memorial to march and sing in support of civil rights and racial harmony. Appropriately, *The march on Washington* the day belonged to King. In the powerful tones of a southern preacher, he reminded the crowd that the Declaration of Independence was a promise that applied to all people, black and white. "I have a dream," he told them, that one day "all of God's children, black men and white men, Jews and Gentiles, Protestants and Catholics, will be able to join hands and sing in the words of the old Negro spiritual, 'Free at last! Free at last! Thank God Almighty, we are free at last!'"

The Fire Next Time

While liberals applauded Kennedy's civil rights stand and appreciative African Americans rejoined the Democratic party, many southern whites and northern ethnics deserted. The president scheduled a trip to Texas to recoup some southern support. On November 22, 1963, the people of Dallas lined *Assassination* the streets for his motorcade. Suddenly, a sniper's rifle fired several times. Kennedy slumped into his wife's arms, fatally wounded. His assassin, Lee Harvey Oswald, was caught several hours later. Oswald seemed a mysterious figure. Emotionally unstable, he had spent several years in the Soviet Union. But his actions were never fully explained, because only two days after his arrest—in full view of television cameras—he was gunned down by a disgruntled nightclub operator named Jack Ruby.

In the face of such violence, many Americans came to doubt that gradual reform or nonviolence could hold the nation together. Many younger black leaders observed that civil rights received the greatest national coverage when white, not black, demonstrators were killed. They wondered too how Lyndon Johnson, a consummate southern politician, would approach the civil rights programs.

The new president, however, saw the need for action. Just as the Catholic issue had tested Kennedy's ability to lead, Johnson knew that without strong leadership on civil rights, "I'd be dead before I could ever begin." *Civil Rights Act of 1964* On his first day in office, he promised one civil rights leader after another that he would pass Kennedy's bill. Despite a southern filibuster in the Senate, the Civil Rights Act of 1964 became law. Embodying the provisions of the Kennedy bill, it barred discrimination in public accommodations like lunch counters, bus stations, and hotels. It also prohibited employers from discriminating by race, color, religion, sex, or national origin.

The Civil Rights Act, however, did not strike down literacy tests and other laws used to prevent black citizens from voting. With King and other black leaders keeping up the pressure, President Johnson persuaded *Voting Rights Act of 1965* Congress to pass a strong Voting Rights Act in August 1965. The act outlawed literacy tests and permitted federal officials to monitor elections in many southern districts. With some justice Johnson called the act "one of the most monumental laws in the entire history of American freedom." Within a five-year period black registration in the South jumped from 35 to 65 percent.

Black Power

But even the new civil rights laws did not strike at the de facto segregation found outside the South. This was segregation not spelled out in laws but practiced through unwritten custom. In large areas of America, African Americans were locked out of suburbs, kept out of decent schools, barred from clubs, and denied all but the most menial jobs. Nor did the Voting Rights Act deal with the sources of urban black poverty. The median income for urban black residents was about half of what white residents earned.

In such an atmosphere, militants sharply questioned the liberal goal of integration. Since the 1940s the Black Muslim religious sect, dedicated to complete separation from white society, had attracted as many as 100,000 members, mostly young men. During the early 1960s the sect drew wider attention through the efforts of Malcolm X. Provocative, shrewd, and charismatic, *Malcolm X* Malcolm had learned the language of the downtrodden from his own experience as a former hustler, gambler, and prison inmate. His militancy alarmed whites, though by 1965 he was in fact becoming more moderate. He accepted integration, but emphasized black community action. After breaking with the Black Muslims, Malcolm was gunned down by rivals.

But by 1965, even CORE and SNCC had begun to give up working with white liberals for nonviolent change. If black Americans were to liberate themselves fully, militants argued, they could not merely accept rights "given" to them by whites: they had to claim them. Some members began carrying guns to defend themselves. In 1966 Stokely Carmichael of SNCC gave the militants a slogan—"Black Power"—and the defiant symbol of a gloved fist raised in the air.

In its moderate form, the black power movement encouraged African Americans to recover their cultural roots, their African heritage, and a new sense of identity. African clothes and natural hairstyles became popular. On college campuses black students pressed universities to hire black faculty, create black studies programs, and provide segregated social and residential space.

For black militants, on the other hand, violence became a revolutionary tool. The Black Panther party of Oakland, California, called on the black community to arm. Panther leader Huey Newton and his followers openly brandished shotguns and rifles as they patrolled the streets protecting blacks from police harassment. After a gun battle with police left a wounded Newton in jail, Eldridge Cleaver assumed leadership of the party. Cleaver later attracted the attention of whites with his searing autobiography, *Soul on Ice.* But even at the height of their power, the Panthers never counted more than 2000 members nationwide.

Black Panthers

Violence in the Streets

No ideology shaped the reservoir of frustration and despair that existed in the ghettos. Often, a seemingly minor incident like an arrest or an argument on the streets would trigger an eruption of violence. A mob would gather, and police cars and white-owned stores would be firebombed or looted. Riots broke out in Harlem and Rochester, New York, in 1964; the Watts area of Los Angeles in 1965; Chicago in 1966; and Newark and Detroit in 1967. It took nearly 5000 troops to end the bloodiest rioting in Detroit, where 40 died, 2000 were injured, and 5000 were left homeless.

To most white Americans the violence was unfathomable and inexcusable. Martin Luther King, still pursuing the tactics of nonviolence, was saddened by the destruction but came to understand the anger behind it. Touring Watts only days after the riots, he was approached by a band of young blacks. "We won," they told him proudly. "How can you say you won," King countered, "when thirty-four Negroes are dead, your community is destroyed, and whites are using the riot as an excuse for inaction?" The youngsters were unmoved. "We won because we made them pay attention to us."

For Lyndon Johnson, ghetto violence and black militance mocked his efforts to achieve racial progress. The Civil Rights and Voting Rights acts were essential parts of the "Great Society" he hoped to build. In that effort he had achieved a legislative record virtually unequaled by any other president in the nation's history. What Kennedy had promised, Johnson delivered. But the anger exploding in the nation's cities exposed serious flaws in the theory and practice of liberal reform.

LYNDON JOHNSON AND THE GREAT SOCIETY

Like the state he hailed from, Lyndon Baines Johnson was in all things bigger than life. His gifts were greater, his flaws more glaring. Insecurity was his Achilles heel and the engine that drove him. If Kennedy had been good as president, Johnson would be "the greatest of them all, the whole bunch of them." His folksy style often verged on the offensive: after a 1965 operation, he shocked a national audience by lifting his shirt to expose a jagged scar and corpulent belly. The president was sometimes driven to ask why so few people genuinely liked him; once a courageous diplomat actually answered: "Because, Mr. President, you are not a very likable man."

Johnson was born in the hill country outside Austin, Texas, where the dry, rough terrain only grudgingly yielded up a living. He arrived in Washington in 1932 as an ardent New Dealer who loved the political game. As majority leader of the Senate after 1954, Johnson was regarded as a moderate conservative who knew what strings to pull to get the job done. On an important bill, he latched onto the undecided votes until they succumbed to the famous "Johnson treat-

The Johnson treatment

ment," a combination of arguments, threats, rewards, and patriotic appeals. (Once, before meeting with Johnson, President Eisenhower pleaded with his attorney general, William Rogers, to run interference: "Bill, if Lyndon tries to get around my desk, block him off. I can't stand it when he grabs me by the lapel.")

Despite his compulsion to control every person and situation, Johnson was best at hammering out compromises among competing interest groups. To those who served him well he could be loyal and generous. And as president, he cared sincerely about society's underdogs. His support for civil rights, aid to the poor, education, and the welfare of the elderly came from genuine conviction. He made the betterment of such people the goal of his administration.

The Origins of the Great Society

In the first months after the assassination, Johnson acted as the conservator of the Kennedy legacy. "Let us continue," he told a grief-stricken nation. Liberals who had dismissed Johnson as an unprincipled power broker came to respect the energy he showed in quickly steering Kennedy's Civil Rights Act and tax cut legislation through Congress.

Kennedy had come to believe that prosperity alone would not ease the plight of America's poor. In 1962 Michael Harrington's book *The Other America*

Michael Harrington's The Other America

brought attention to the persistence of poverty despite the nation's affluence. Harrington focused attention on the hills of Appalachia that stretched from western Pennsylvania south to Alabama. In some counties a quarter of the population survived on a diet of flour and dried-milk paste supplied by federal surplus food programs. Under Kennedy, Congress had passed a new food stamp program as well as laws designed to revive the economies of poor areas. Robert Kennedy also headed a presidential committee to fight juvenile delinquency in urban slums by involving the poor in "community action" programs.

It fell to Lyndon Johnson to fight Kennedy's "war on poverty." By August 1964 this master politician had driven through Congress the most sweeping social welfare bill since the New Deal. The Economic Opportunity Act addressed almost every major cause of poverty. It included training programs such as the Job Corps, which brought poor and unemployed recruits to rural or urban camps to learn new job skills. It granted loans to rural families and urban small businesses as well as aid to migrant workers. The price tag for these programs was high—almost $1 billion to fund the new Office of Economic Opportunity (OEO).

Economic Opportunity Act

The speed Johnson demanded led inevitably to confusion, conflict, and waste. Officials at OEO often found themselves in conflict with other cabinet departments, as well as state and local officials. For example, OEO workers organized voter registration drives in order to oust corrupt city officials. Others led rent strikes to force improvements in public housing. The director of city housing in Syracuse, New York, reacted typically: "We are experiencing a class struggle in the traditional Karl Marx style in Syracuse, and I do not like it." Such battles for bureaucratic turf undermined federal poverty programs.

Lyndon Johnson had difficulty playing second fiddle to anyone, even as vice president under John F. Kennedy (right).

The Election of 1964

In 1964, however, these long-term flaws were not yet evident. Johnson's political stock remained high as he announced his ambition to forge a "Great Society," in which poverty and racial injustice no longer existed. The chance to fulfill his dreams seemed open to him, for the Republicans nominated Senator Barry Goldwater of Arizona as their presidential candidate. Though ruggedly handsome and refreshingly candid, Goldwater believed that government should not dispense welfare, subsidize farmers, or aid public education. Few Americans subscribed to such conservative views. Many worried, too, at Goldwater's willingness to give military commanders the power to launch tactical nuclear weapons without presidential authority.

Thus the election produced the landslide Johnson craved. Carrying every state except Arizona and four in the Deep South, he received 61 percent of the vote. Democrats gained better than two-to-one majorities in the Senate and House. The president moved rapidly to exploit the momentum of his 1964 majority.

The Great Society

In January 1965 Johnson announced a legislative vision that would extend welfare programs on a scale beyond even Franklin Roosevelt's New Deal. By the end of 1965, some 50 bills had been passed, many of them major pieces of legislation.

As a former teacher, Johnson made education the cornerstone of his program. Stronger schools would compensate the poor for their disadvantaged homes, he believed. Under the Elementary and Secondary School Act, students in low-income school districts were to receive educational equipment, money for books, and enrichment programs like Project Headstart for nursery-age children. As schools scrambled to create programs that would tap federal money, they sometimes spent more to pay middle-class educational professionals than to teach lower-income students.

Programs in education

Johnson also pushed through the Medicare Act, to provide the elderly with health insurance to cover their hospital costs. Studies had shown that older people used hospitals three times more than other Americans and generally had incomes only half as large. Since Medicare made no provision for the poor who were not elderly, Congress also passed a program called Medicaid. Participating states would receive matching grants from the federal government to pay the medical expenses of those on welfare or those too poor to afford medical care.

Medicare and Medicaid

In many ways, Medicare and Medicaid worked. Over the next two decades, their benefits helped to lower significantly the number of elderly poor. But as more patients used hospital services, Medicare budgets rose. In addition, nothing in the act restricted hospitals or doctors from raising their fees or charging for care they had once given for free. The cost of the programs soared by more than 500 percent in the first 10 years.

The Great Society also reformed immigration policy, striking down a discriminatory quota system based on national origins that had been in effect since

Immigration

1924 (page 675). Only about 150,000 immigrants a year had been allowed to enter the United States, almost all from northern Europe. The Immigration Act of 1965 abolished the national origins system. Now, 170,000 people a year would be admitted on a first-come, first-served basis. Racial provisions restricting Asian immigration were eliminated, although new limits were placed on immigration from the Western Hemisphere.

Nor did Johnson, in his efforts to outdo the New Deal, slight the environment. By the mid-1960s many Americans had become increasingly concerned

The environment

about smog from factories and automobiles; lakes and rivers polluted by detergents, pesticides, and industrial wastes; and the disappearance of wildlife. In 1964 Congress had already passed the National Wilderness Preservation System Act to set aside 9.1 million acres of wilderness as "forever wild." Congress first established pollution standards for interstate waterways and a year later provided funds for sewage treatment and water purification. Legislation also tightened standards on air pollution. Despite opposition from entrenched interests, the new standards did result in a gradual improvement in water and air quality in many areas.

For all he had done, Johnson wanted more. In 1966 he pushed through bills to raise the minimum wage, improve auto safety, aid mass transit, and develop "model cities." But in time opposition mounted. "Doesn't matter what kind of majority you come in with," Johnson had predicted early on. "You've got just one year when they treat you right, and before they start worrying about themselves." Even so, Johnson pushed major legislation through Congress as late as 1968.

Historians have difficulty measuring the Great Society's impact. It produced more legislation and more reforms than the New Deal. It also carried a higher

Evaluating the Great Society

price tag than anyone predicted. Economic statistics suggested that general prosperity, boosted by the tax cut bill, did more to fight poverty than all the OEO programs. Conservatives and radicals alike objected that the liberal welfare state was intruding into too many areas of people's lives.

For all that, the Great Society proved to be the high-water mark of a trend toward activist government that had grown steadily since the progressive era and the Great Depression. While Americans continued to pay lip service to the notion that government should remain small and interfere little in citizens' lives, no strong movement emerged to eliminate Medicare or Medicaid. Few Americans disputed the right of the government to regulate industrial pollution or to control the excesses of large corporations or powerful labor unions. In this sense, the tradition of liberalism prevailed, whatever Johnson's failings.

THE COUNTERCULTURE

In 1964 some 800 students from Berkeley, Oberlin, and other colleges met in western Ohio to be trained for the voter registration campaign in the South. Middle-class students who had grown up in peaceful white suburbs found themselves being instructed by protest-hardened SNCC coordinators. The lessons were sobering. When beaten by police, the SNCC staff advised, assume the fetal position—hands protecting the neck, elbows covering the temples. That minimized injuries from nightsticks. A few days later, grimmer news arrived. Three volunteers who had left for Mississippi two days earlier had already been arrested by local police. Now they were reported "missing." Six weeks later, their mangled bodies were found, bulldozed into the earthworks of a freshly finished dam.

By the mid-1960s conservatives, civil rights organizations, and the poor were not the only groups rejecting liberal solutions. Dissatisfied members of the middle class—and especially the young—had joined them. The students who returned to campus from the voter registration campaign that summer of 1964 were the shock troops of a much larger movement.

Activists on the New Left

More than a few students had become disillusioned with the slow pace of reform. Tom Hayden, from a working-class family in a suburb of Detroit, went
to college at the University of Michigan, then traveled to
Berkeley, and soon joined civil rights workers in Mississippi.
Along with other radical students, Hayden helped form Students
for a Democratic Society (SDS). Members of SDS gave up on
change through the electoral system. Direct action was needed if the faceless, bureaucratic society of the "organization man" were to be made truly democratic. SDS advocated sit-ins, protest marches, and confrontation.

Students for a Democratic Society

COUNTERPOINT   *What Triggered the Upheavals of the 1960s?*

Historians have debated the causes of the turbulent 1960s. Some scholars have favored a generational explanation. The United States has undergone periodic cycles of reform as each new generation has come of age—about once every 30 years. Thus the twentieth century began with progressive reformers pushing for change, only to give way to the "normalcy" of the 1920s, which in turn was succeeded by the activist New Deal. Similarly, the "consensus" decade of the 1950s preceded liberalism's high tide in the 1960s. In that light, the Port Huron Statement can be read as a call for new cycle of reform led by the nation's baby boomers, who grew up during the 1950s. "There had to be a critical mass of students, and enough economic fat to cushion them," suggested one historian.

Other historians are more leery of the "generational" approach. Consider some of the figures who played pivotal roles in the decade's social reforms: civil rights advocates like Martin Luther King and Cesar Chavez, feminist Betty Friedan, environmentalist Rachel Carson, consumer advocate Ralph Nader, drug promoter Timothy Leary, and rock stars like Bob Dylan and the Beatles. All were born before or during World War II and were not a part of the baby boom generation. In fact, it is possible to argue that by and large baby boomers served mainly as foot soldiers in a crusade led by a generation that came of age during the consensus years of the 1950s.

In the end, it may be more useful to focus on specific catalytic events that bonded different generations. Mississippi Freedom Summer was such an event. Young student volunteers gave up their surburban dress for overalls and work shirts of the sort worn by poor African American laborers in the Mississippi Delta. Volunteers and local folks shared in the terror of frequent harassment and even possible death. Once SNCC volunteers returned to their college campuses, they themselves became catalysts for much of the turmoil that followed. That is not to say necessarily that they "caused" the rebellion of the 1960s. But they did help shape much of the discontent stirring beneath the veneer of campus conformity.

These discontents surfaced most dramatically in the Free Speech Movement at the University of California's Berkeley campus. To most liberals, Berkeley was

Free Speech Movement

the gem of the California state system. Like so many other universities, it had educated a generation of GIs following World War II. But to people like Tom Hayden and the SDS, Berkeley was a bureaucratic monster, enrolling more than 30,000 students who filed into large impersonal halls to endure lectures from remote professors. In the fall of 1964, Berkeley officials declared off limits the one small area in which political organizations had been allowed to advertise their causes. When university police tried to remove a recruiter for CORE, thousands of angry students surrounded the police car for 32 hours.

To Mario Savio, a graduate student in philosophy and veteran of the Mississippi Freedom summer, the issue was clear: "In our free-speech fight, we have come up against what may emerge as the greatest problem of our nation— depersonalized, unresponsive bureaucracy." When the university's president, Clark Kerr, threatened to expel Savio, 6000 students took control of the administration building, stopped classes with a strike, and convinced many faculty members to join them. Kerr backed down, placing no limits to free speech on campus except those that applied to society at large. But the lines between students and administrators had been drawn. The rebellious spirit spread to other major universities like Michigan, Yale, and Columbia, and then to campuses across the nation.

The Rise of the Counterculture

Other youthful rebels were less interested in political dissent. Instead, they condemned American society as materialistic and shallow. These alienated students began to grope toward spiritual, nonmaterial goals. "Turn on to the scene, tune in to what is happening, and drop out of high school, college, grad school, junior executive," advised Timothy Leary, a Harvard psychology professor who dropped out himself. Those who heeded Leary's call to spiritual renewal rejected politics for a lifestyle of experimentation with music, sex, and drugs. Observers labeled their movement a "counterculture."

The counterculture of the 1960s had much in common with earlier religious revival and utopian movements. It admired the quirky individualism of Henry David Thoreau. Like Thoreau, it turned to Asian philosophies such as Zen Buddhism. Like Brook Farm and other nineteenth-century utopian communities, the new "hippie" communes sought perfection along the fringes of society. Communards "learned how to scrounge materials, tear down abandoned buildings, use the unusable," as one member of the "Drop City" commune put it. Sexual freedom became a means to liberate members of the counterculture from the repressive inhibitions that distorted the lives of their "uptight" parents. Drugs appeared to offer access to a higher state of consciousness or pleasure.

Communal living

The early threads of the sixties counterculture led back to the fifties and the subculture of the beat generation (page 835). For the beats, unconventional

This couple at their wedding reflect many of the motifs of the counterculture—long hair, casual dress, informal setting, and racial equality.

The drug scene   drugs had long been a part of the scene, but now their use expanded dramatically. Timothy Leary began experimenting with hallucinogenic mushrooms in Mexico and soon moved on to LSD. The drug "blew his mind," he announced, and he became so enthusiastic in making converts that Harvard blew him straight out of its hallowed doors. By 1966 Leary was lecturing across the land on the joys of drug use.

Where Leary's approach to LSD was cool and contemplative, novelist Ken Kesey (*One Flew Over the Cuckoo's Nest*) embraced it with antic frenzy. His ragtag company of druggies and freaks formed the "Merry Pranksters" at Kesey's home outside San Francisco. Writer Tom Wolfe chronicled their travels in *The Electric Kool-Aid Acid Test*, as the Pranksters headed east on a psychedelic school bus in search of Leary. Their example inspired others to drop out.

The Rock Revolution

In the 1950s rock and roll defined a teen culture preoccupied with young love, cars, and adult pressures. One exception was the Kingston Trio, which in 1958 popularized folk music and historical ballads, especially among college audiences. As the interest in folk music grew, the lyrics increasingly focused on social or political issues. Joan Baez, with a voice one critic found as pure and clear "as air in autumn," dressed simply, wore no makeup, and rejected the commercialism of popular music. She joined folk singer Bob Dylan in the civil rights march on Washington in 1963, singing "We Shall Overcome" and "Blowin' in the Wind." Such folk singers reflected the activist side of the counterculture as they sought to provoke their audiences to political commitment. Dylan, who

Bob Dylan   had played his songs of social protest on an unamplified guitar, shocked fans in 1965 by donning a black leather jacket and shifting to a "folk rock" style featuring an electric guitar. His new songs seemed to suggest that the old America was almost beyond redemption.

In 1964 a new sound, imported from England, exploded on the American scene. The Beatles, four musicians from Liverpool, attracted frenzied teen audiences who screamed and swooned as the "mod" crooners sang "I Want to Hold Your Hand." Along with other English groups, like the Rolling Stones, the Beatles reconnected American audiences with the rhythm-and-blues roots of rock and roll. And, like Dylan, their style influenced pop culture almost as much as their music. After a pilgrimage to India to study transcendental meditation, they returned to produce *Sergeant Pepper's Lonely Hearts Club Band*, possibly the most influential album of the decade. It blended sound effects with music, alluded to trips taken with "Lucy in the Sky with Diamonds" (LSD), and concluded, "I'd love to turn you on." Out in San Francisco, bands like the Grateful Dead pioneered "acid rock" with long pieces aimed to echo drug-induced states of mind.

The debt of white rock musicians to rhythm and blues led to increased integration in the music world. Before the 1960s black rhythm-and-blues bands played primarily to black audiences, in segregated clubs or over black radio stations. Black artists like Little Richard, Chuck Berry, and Ray Charles wrote many hit songs made popular by white performers. The civil rights movement and a rising black social and political consciousness gave rise to "soul" music. Blacks became "soul brothers" and "soul sisters," and for the first time their music was played on major radio stations. One black disc jockey described soul as "the last to be hired, first to be fired, brown all year round, sit-in-the-back-of-the-bus feeling." Soul was the quality that expressed black pride and separatism. Out of Detroit came the Motown sound, which combined elements of gospel, blues, and big band jazz.

Soul

The West Coast Scene

The heady visibility of the counterculture also signaled an increasing importance of the West Coast in American popular culture. In the 1950s the shift of television production from the stages of New York to the film lots of Hollywood helped establish Los Angeles as a communications center. San Francisco became notorious as a center of the beat movement. By 1963 the "surfing sound" of West Coast rock groups like the Beach Boys and Jan and Dean had made southern California's preoccupation with surfing and cars into a national fad. And Mario Savio and his Free Speech Movement attracted the attention of the nation.

Before 1967 Americans were only vaguely aware of another West Coast phenomenon, the "hippies." But in January a loose coalition of drug freaks, Zen cultists, and political activists banded together to hold the first well-publicized "Be-In." The beat poet Allen Ginsberg was on hand to offer spiritual guidance. The Grateful Dead and Jefferson Airplane, acid rock groups based in San Francisco, provided entertainment. An unknown organization called the Diggers somehow managed to supply free food and drink, while the notorious Hell's Angels motorcycle gang policed the occasion. In that way the Bay Area emerged as a spiritual center of the counterculture. Politically conscious dropouts gravitated toward Berkeley. Flower children who cared less about politics moved into Haight-Ashbury, a run-down San Francisco neighborhood of apartments and Victorian houses, where head shops sold drug paraphernalia, wall posters, and Indian bedspreads. Haight-Ashbury became a model replicated across the nation.

Hippies and Haight-Ashbury

In the summer of 1969 all the positive forces of the counterculture converged on Bethel, New York, in the Catskill Mountains resort area, to celebrate the promise of peace, love, and freedom. The Woodstock Music Festival attracted 400,000 people to the largest rock concert ever organized. For one long weekend the audience and performers joined to form an ephemeral community based on sex, drugs, and rock and roll. Even then, the counterculture was dying. Violence intruded on the laid-back urban communities hippies had formed. Organized crime and drug pushers muscled in on the

Woodstock

lucrative trade in LSD, amphetamines, and marijuana. Bad drugs and addiction took their toll. Free sex often became an excuse for rape, exploitation, and loveless gratification.

Much that had once seemed outrageous in the hippie world was readily absorbed into the marketplace. Rock groups became big business enterprises commanding huge fees. Yogurt, granola, and herbal teas appeared on supermarket shelves. Ironically, much of the world that hippies forged was embraced and tamed by the society they had rejected.

By the late 1960s most dreams of human betterment seemed shattered—whether John Kennedy's New Frontier, Lyndon Johnson's Great Society, or the communal society of the hippie counterculture. Recession and inflation brought an end to the easy affluence that made liberal reform programs and alternative lifestyles seem so easily affordable. Poverty and unemployment menaced even middle-class youth who had found havens in communes, colleges, and graduate schools. Racial tensions divided black militants and the white liberals of the civil rights movement into sometimes hostile camps.

But the Vietnam War more than any other single factor destroyed the promise of Camelot and the Great Society. After 1965 the nation divided sharply as the American military role in Southeast Asia grew. Radicals like the SDS condemned a capitalist system that promoted race and class conflict at home and imperialism abroad. Conservatives who supported the war called for a return to traditional values and law and order. Both the left and the right attacked the liberal center. Their combined opposition helped to undermine the consensus Lyndon Johnson had worked so hard to build.

SIGNIFICANT EVENTS

1958 — Kingston Trio popularizes folk music

1960 — Kennedy–Nixon debates; Greensboro sit-ins; Kennedy elected president

1961 — Alliance for Progress; Peace Corps begun; Bay of Pigs invasion; Kennedy steps up U.S. role in Vietnam; Vienna summit; Berlin Wall built; CORE freedom rides begin

1962 — John Glenn orbits earth; Michael Harrington's *The Other America* published; Cuban missile crisis; James Meredith desegregates University of Mississippi; *Engel v. Vitale; Baker v. Carr*

1963 — Diem assassinated in Vietnam; nuclear test ban treaty; University of Alabama desegregation crisis; Kennedy introduces Civil Rights Bill; March on Washington; *Gideon v. Wainwright;* Kennedy assassinated

1964 — *Escobedo v. Illinois; Griswold v. Connecticut;* Civil Rights Act passed; Harlem and Rochester race riots; Johnson enacts Kennedy tax cuts; Economic Opportunity Act; VISTA established; Wilderness Preservation System Act; Johnson defeats Goldwater; Berkeley "Free Speech" Movement; Beatles introduce British rock

1965 — Johnson launches the Great Society; Voting Rights Act; Watts riots; Malcolm X assassinated; Medicare and Medicaid acts; Elementary and Secondary School Act; Immigration Act; escalation in Vietnam

1966 — *Miranda v. Arizona;* Stokely Carmichael of SNCC coins "Black Power" slogan; Model Cities Act

1967 — Black Panthers battle Oakland, California, police; first "Be-In"

1968 — Fair Housing Act

1969 — Woodstock Music Festival; American astronauts land on moon

CHAPTER THIRTY-ONE

The Vietnam Era

Vietnam from afar: it looked like an emerald paradise. Thomas Bird, an army rifleman sent there in 1965, recalled his first impression: "A beautiful white beach with thick jungle background. The only thing missing was naked women running down the beach, waving and shouting 'Hello, hello, hello.'" Upon landing, Bird and his buddies were each issued a "Nine-Rule" card outlining proper behavior toward the Vietnamese. "Treat the women with respect, we are guests in this country and here to help these people."

But who were they helping and who were they fighting? When American troops searched out Vietcong forces, the VC generally disappeared into the jungle beyond the villages and rice fields. John Muir, a Marine rifleman, walked into a typical hamlet with a Korean lieutenant. To Muir the place looked ordinary, but the Korean had been in Vietnam a while. "We have a little old lady and a little old man and two very small children," he pointed out. "According to them, the rest of the family has been spirited away . . . either been drafted into one army or the other. So there's only four of them and they have a pot of rice that's big enough to feed fifty people. And rice, once it's cooked, will not keep. They gotta be feeding the VC." Muir watched in disbelief as the lieutenant set the house on fire. The roof "started cooking off ammunition because all through the thatch they had ammunition stored."

GIs soon learned to walk down jungle trails with a cautious shuffle, looking for a wire or a piece of vine that seemed too straight. "We took more casualties from booby traps than we did from actual combat," recalled David Ross, a medic. "It was very frustrating because how do you fight back against a booby trap? You're just walking along and all of a sudden your buddy doesn't have a leg. Or you don't have a leg." Yet somehow the villagers would walk the same paths and never get hurt. Who was the enemy and who the friend?

The same question was being asked half a globe away, on the campus of Kent State University in May 4, 1970. By then the Vietnam War had dragged

Kent State on for more than five years, driving President Lyndon Johnson from office and embroiling his successor, Richard Nixon, in controversy. When Nixon expanded the war beyond Vietnam into Cambodia, protest erupted even at Kent State, just east of Akron, Ohio. Opposition to the war had become so intense in this normally apolitical community that 300 students had torn the Constitution from a history text and, in a formal ceremony, buried it. "President Nixon has murdered it," they charged. That evening demonstrators spilled into the nearby town, smashed shop windows, and returned to campus to burn down an old army ROTC building. Governor James Rhodes ordered in 750 of the National Guard. Student dissidents were the "worst type of people we harbor in America," he announced. "We are going to eradicate the problem."

By background and education, the National Guard troops were little different from the students they had come to police. Almost all were white, between 18 and 30, and from Ohio. But Guard veterans who had fought in World War II or Korea particularly disapproved of students who avoided their military obligation. As his troops arrived at Kent, Guard Commander General Robert

A student lies dead at Kent State, May 1970. Who was the enemy, who was the friend?

Canterbury remarked that "these students are going to have to find out what law and order is all about."

When demonstrators assembled for a rally on the college commons, the Guard ordered them to disperse. Whether they had the authority to do so was debatable. The protesters stood their ground. Then the guardsmen advanced, wearing full battle gear and armed with M-1 rifles, whose high-velocity bullets had a horizontal range of almost two miles. Some students scattered; a few picked up rocks and threw them. The guardsmen suddenly fired into the crowd, many of whom were students passing back and forth from classes. Incredulous, a young woman knelt over Jeffrey Miller; he was dead. By the time calm was restored, three other students had been killed and nine more wounded, some caught innocently in the Guard's indiscriminate fire.

News of the killings swept the nation. At Jackson State, a black college in Mississippi, antiwar protesters seized a women's dormitory. On May 14 state po-

Jackson State lice surrounding the building opened fire without provocation, killing two more students and wounding a dozen. In both incidents the demonstrators had been unarmed. The events at Kent State and Jackson State turned sporadic protests against the American invasion of Cambodia into a nationwide student strike. Many students believed the ideals of the United States had been betrayed by those forces of law and order sworn to protect them.

Who was the friend and who the enemy? Time and again the war in Vietnam led Americans to ask that question. Not since the Civil War had the nation been so deeply divided. As the war dragged on, debate moved off college campuses and into the homes of middle Americans, where sons went off to fight and the war came home each night on the evening news. As no other war had, Vietnam seemed to stand the nation on its head. When American soldiers shot at Vietnamese "hostiles," who could not always be separated from "friendlies," or when National Guardsmen fired on their neighbors across a college green, who were the enemies and who were the friends?

THE ROAD TO VIETNAM

"The enemy must fight his battles far from his home base for a long time," one Vietnamese strategist wrote. "We must further weaken him by drawing him into protracted campaigns. Once his initial dash is broken, it will be easier to destroy him." The enemy in question was not American soldiers nor the French, but the Mongol invaders of A.D. 1284. For several thousand years Vietnam had struggled periodically to fight off foreign invasions. Buddhist culture had penetrated eastward from India. More often Indochina faced invasion and rule by the Chinese from the north. After 1856 the French entered as a colonial power, bringing with them a strong Catholic tradition.

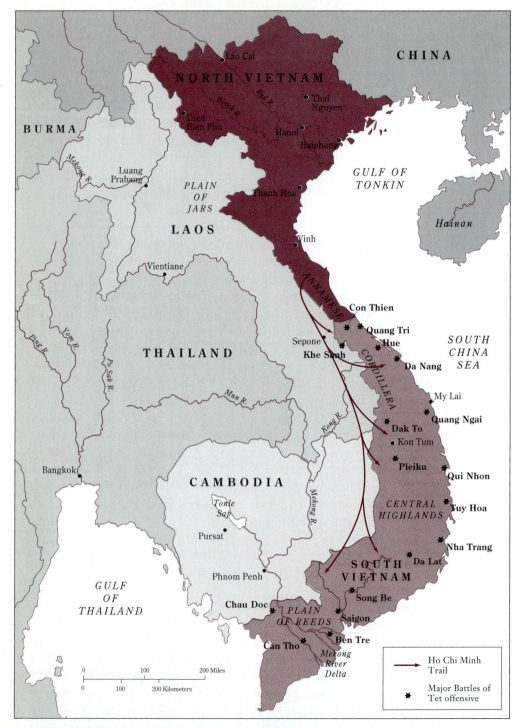

THE WAR IN VIETNAM For the United States, one strategic problem was to locate and destroy the supply routes known as the Ho Chi Minh Trail. Rugged mountains and triple canopy jungles hid much of the trail from aerial observation and attack.

Ho Chi Minh was one Vietnamese who hoped to throw off French influence as well as the Chinese. Since the end of World War I, he had worked to create an independent Vietnam. After World War II, he organized a guerrilla war against the French, which finally led to their defeat at Dien Bien Phu in 1954 (page 822). He agreed at the Geneva peace conference to withdraw his forces north of the 17th parallel, in return for a promise to hold free elections in both the North and the South. Having supported what they saw as a French struggle against communism, the Americans wanted to block Ho. They helped install Ngo Dinh Diem in South Vietnam and supported his decision not to hold elections, which Ho's forces seemed sure to win. Frustrated South Vietnamese Communists—the Vietcong—renewed their guerrilla war. "I think the Americans greatly underestimate the determination of the Vietnamese people," Ho remarked in 1962, as President Kennedy was committing more American advisers to South Vietnam.

Ho Chi Minh

Lyndon Johnson's War

For Kennedy, Vietnam had been just one of many anti-Communist skirmishes his activist advisers wanted to fight. As attention focused increasingly on Vietnam, Kennedy accepted President Eisenhower's "domino theory": if the pro-Western Catholic government fell to the Communists, the other nations of Southeast Asia would collapse one after the other. But even 16,000 American "advisers" had been unable to help the unpopular Diem, who was overthrown by the military in November 1963. When Kennedy was assassinated in the same month as Diem, the problem of Vietnam was left to Lyndon Johnson.

Domino theory

Johnson's political instincts told him to keep the Vietnam War at arm's length. He felt like a catfish, he remarked, who had "just grabbed a big juicy worm with a right sharp hook in the middle of it." Johnson's heart was in his Great Society programs. Yet fear of the political costs of defeat in Vietnam led him steadily toward deeper American involvement. He shared the assumption of Kennedy holdovers like National Security Advisor McGeorge Bundy and Defense Secretary Robert McNamara that Vietnam was a key cold war test.

Until August 1964 American advisers had focused on training and supporting the South Vietnamese army, which fought the Vietcong reluctantly. North Vietnam, for its part, had been infiltrating men and supplies along the Ho Chi Minh Trail, a network of jungle routes threading through Laos and Cambodia into the highlands of South Vietnam. But American support seemed to be having little impact. The Vietcong controlled some 40 percent of South Vietnam. Johnson strategists decided to relieve the South by increasing pressure on North Vietnam itself.

American ships patrolling the Gulf of Tonkin began to provide cover for secret South Vietnamese raids against the North. On August 2, three North

Tonkin Gulf incident

Vietnamese patrol boats exchanged fire with the American destroyer *Maddox*, neither side hurting the other. Two nights later, in inky blackness and a heavy thunderstorm, a second incident occurred. But a follow-up investigation could not be sure whether enemy ships had even been near the scene. President Johnson was not pleased. "For all I know our navy might have been shooting at whales out there," he remarked privately.

Whatever his doubts, the president publicized the incidents as "open aggression on the high sea" and ordered retaliatory air raids on North Vietnam. He did not disclose that the navy and South Vietnamese forces had been conducting secret military operations at the time. When Johnson then asked for the authority to take "all necessary measures" to "repel any armed attack" on American forces and to "prevent future aggression," Congress overwhelmingly passed what became known as the Tonkin Gulf Resolution.

Senator Ernest Gruening of Alaska, one of only two lawmakers to vote no, objected that the resolution gave the president "a blank check" to declare war, a power the Constitution specifically reserved to Congress. Johnson insisted— no doubt sincerely at the time—that he had limited aims. But as pressure for an American victory increased, the president exploited the powers the resolution gave him.

Rolling Thunder

In January 1965 Johnson received a disturbing memorandum from McGeorge Bundy and Robert McNamara, two of his most trusted advisers on foreign policy. "Both of us are now pretty well convinced that our present policy can lead

Escalation

only to disastrous defeat," they said. The United States should either increase its attack—*escalate* was the term coined in 1965— or simply withdraw. In theory escalation would increase military pressure to the point at which further resistance would cost more than the enemy was willing to pay. By taking gradual steps, the United States would demonstrate its resolve to win while leaving the door open to negotiations.

But the theory that made so much sense in the White House did not work well in practice. Each stage of American escalation only hardened the resolve of the Vietcong and North Vietnamese. When a Vietcong mortar attack in February killed seven Marines stationed at Pleiku airbase, Johnson ordered U.S. planes to begin bombing North Vietnam. Privately, McGeorge Bundy admitted that Pleiku was only an excuse. "Pleikus are like streetcars," he remarked; "there's one every ten minutes."

Restricted air strikes did not satisfy more hawkish leaders. Retired Air Force Chief of Staff Curtis LeMay complained, "We are swatting flies when we should

Air strikes

be going after the whole manure pile." In March Johnson ordered Operation Rolling Thunder, a systematic bombing campaign aimed at bolstering confidence in South Vietnam and cutting the flow of supplies from the North. At the same time, he declared his willingness to negotiate an end to the war once North Vietnamese troops had left the South.

Rolling Thunder achieved none of its goals. American pilots could seldom spot the Ho Chi Minh Trail under its dense jungle canopy. Even when bombs hit, North Vietnamese crews kept the supplies moving by filling bomb craters or improvising pontoon bridges from bamboo stalks. Equally discouraging, South Vietnamese leaders spent their energy on political intrigue. One military government after another proved equally inept.

Once the Americans established bases from which to launch the new air strikes, these too became targets for guerrilla attacks. General William Westmoreland, the chief of American military operations in Vietnam, requested combat troops to defend the bases. Johnson sent in 3500 Marines, almost without considering the implication of his decision. With the crucial decision to commit combat troops, the urge to shore up and protect those already there became stronger. Another 40,000 soldiers arrived in May and 50,000 more by July.

Combat troops

Johnson, as before, downplayed the escalation, because he feared a political backlash. McNamara ordered the decision carried out in a "low-keyed manner," both to prevent Soviet or Chinese intervention and "to avoid undue concern and excitement in the Congress and in domestic public opinion." By the end of 1965 almost 185,000 American troops had landed—and still the call for more continued. In 1968, at the height of the war, 536,000 American troops were being supported with helicopters, jet aircraft, and other advanced military technologies. This was "escalation" with a vengeance.

SOCIAL CONSEQUENCES OF THE WAR

The impact of the war fell hardest on the baby-boom generation of the 1950s. As these young people came of age, draft calls for the armed services were rising. At the same time, the civil rights movement and the growing counterculture were encouraging students to question the goals of establishment America. Whether they fought in Vietnam or protested at home, supported the government or demonstrated against it, eventually these baby boomers—as well as Americans of all ages—were forced to take a stand on Vietnam.

The Soldiers' War

Most Americans sent to Vietnam were chosen by the draft. The Selective Service System, as it was called, favored the middle and upper classes. College students could avoid service, as well as those in "critical" occupations like teachers and engineers. As the war escalated, the draft was changed, so that some students were called up through

Composition of U.S. forces

a lottery system. Still, those who knew the medical requirements might be able to produce a doctor's affidavit certifying a weak knee, flat feet, or bad eyes—all grounds for flunking the physical. Of the 1200 men in Harvard's class of 1970, only 56 served in the military, and only 2 of them in Vietnam.

The poorest and least educated were also likely to escape service, because the Armed Forces Qualification Test and the physical often screened them out. Thus the sons of blue-collar America were most likely to accept Uncle Sam's letter of induction. Once in uniform, the sons of Hispanic and black Americans who had fewer skills were more often assigned to combat duty. The draft also made it a relatively young man's war. The average age of soldiers serving in Vietnam was 19, compared with the average of 26 for World War II.

Most American infantry came to Vietnam ready and willing to fight. But physical and psychological hardships took their toll. An American search-and-destroy mission would fight its way into a Communist-controlled hamlet, clear and burn it, and move on—only to be ordered back days or weeks later because the enemy had moved in again. Since success could not be measured in terri-

Body counts

tory gained, the measure became the "body count": the number of Vietcong killed. Unable to tell who was friendly and who was hostile, GIs regularly took out their frustrations on innocent civilians. Officers counted those victims to inflate the numbers that suggested the Americans were winning.

Most Americans assumed that superior military technology could guarantee success. But technology alone could not tell friend from foe. Since

Technology and its limits

the Vietcong routinely mixed with the civilian population, the chances for deadly error increased. Bombs of napalm (jellied gasoline) and white phosphorus rained liquid fire from the skies, coating everything from village huts to the flesh of fleeing humans. To clear jungle canopies and expose Vietcong camps and roads, American planes spread more than 100 million pounds of defoliants. The forests destroyed totaled more than one-third of South Vietnam's timberlands—an area approximately the size of the state of Rhode Island. The long-term health and ecological effects were severe.

The miracles of modern technology also made the war more demanding. Helicopters could whisk GIs from one firefight to another or from the front lines of a steaming jungle back to Saigon. There they could catch overnight flights to Hawaii or the mainland. The sudden shift from the hell of war to civilian peace could be wrenching. "I fell asleep [on the plane to New York] and woke up yelling, probably a nightmare," recalled John Kerry, later a senator from Massachusetts. "The other passengers moved away from me—a reaction I noticed more and more in the months ahead. . . . The feeling toward [Vietnam vets] was, 'Stay away—don't contaminate us with whatever you've brought back from Vietnam.'"

By 1967 the war was costing more than $2 billion a month. The United States dropped more bombs on Vietnam than it had during all of World

Vietnam's difficult terrain of mountains, jungles, and rice paddies made helicopters especially useful to move troops quickly.

War II. After one air attack on a Communist-held provincial capital, American troops walked into the smoldering ruins. "We had to destroy the town in order to save it," an officer explained. As the human and material costs of the war increased, that statement stuck in the minds of many observers. What sense was there in a war that saved people by burning their homes?

The War at Home

As the war dragged on, such questions provoked anguished debate among Americans, especially on college campuses. Faculty members held "teach-ins"

Teach-ins

to explain the issues to concerned students. Scholars familiar with Southeast Asia questioned every major assumption the president used to justify escalation. The United States and South Vietnam had brought on the war, they charged, by violating the Geneva accords of 1954. Moreover, the Vietcong were an indigenous rebel force with legitimate grievances against Saigon's corrupt government. The war was a civil war among the Vietnamese, not an effort by Soviet or Chinese Communists to conquer Southeast Asia, as Eisenhower, Kennedy, and Johnson had claimed.

By 1966 national leaders had similarly divided into opposing camps of "hawks" and "doves." The hawks argued that America must win in Vietnam to

Hawks and doves

save Southeast Asia from communism, to preserve the nation's prestige, and to protect the lives of American soldiers fighting the war. Most Americans supported those views. The doves were nonetheless a prominent minority. African Americans as a group were far less likely than white Americans to support the war. Some resented the diversion of resources from the cities to the war effort. Many black Americans' heightened sense of racial consciousness led them to identify with the Vietnamese people. Martin Luther King, SNCC, and CORE all opposed the war. Heavyweight boxing champion Muhammad Ali, a black Muslim, refused on religious grounds to serve in the army, even though the decision cost him his title.

By 1967 college students and faculty turned out in crowds to express their outrage: "Hey, hey, LBJ, how many kids have you killed today?" More than 300,000 people attended the demonstration organized in April 1967 in New York City. Some college protesters even burned their draft cards in defiance of federal law. In the fall more violent protests erupted as antiwar radicals stormed a draft induction center in Oakland, California. The next day 55,000 protesters ringed the Pentagon in Washington. Again, mass arrests followed.

Antiwar demonstrations

Student protests forced policymakers and citizens to take a sobering look at the war. Key moderates became increasingly convinced the United States could not win the war. Senator William Fulbright of Arkansas was among them. Having helped President Johnson push the Tonkin Gulf Resolution through the Senate, Fulbright now held hearings sharply critical of American policy. The hawkish publisher of *Time* and *Life* magazines, Henry Luce, turned his editorials against the war in 1967.

Defense Secretary Robert McNamara became the most dramatic defector. For years the statistically minded secretary had struggled to quantify the suc-

Lyndon Johnson once shocked reporters by lifting his shirt to show them a surgical scar. In the whimsical hands of cartoonist David Levine, the scar took the shape of Vietnam.

McNamara loses faith

cess of the war effort. But by 1967 McNamara had become skeptical. If Americans were killing 300,000 Vietnamese, enemy forces should be shrinking. Instead, intelligence estimates indicated that North Vietnamese infiltration had risen from 35,000 a year in 1965 to 150,000 by the end of 1967. McNamara came to have deep moral qualms. "The picture of the world's greatest superpower killing or seriously injuring 1,000 noncombatants a week, while trying to pound a tiny, backward nation into submission on an issue whose merits are hotly disputed, is not a pretty one," he advised.

Johnson thought of himself as a moderate on the war. He weighed doves like McNamara against hawks who pressed to escalate further. But since the president did not want to be remembered as the first American leader who lost a war, he sided more with the hawks. And so McNamara resigned.

COUNTERPOINT   *Whose War?*

In 1995 Robert McNamara published a memoir that stunned long-time defenders of the war and confirmed the beliefs of those who had opposed it. The war had been a great mistake, he concluded. The Johnson administration could—and should—have avoided sending hundreds of thousands of Americans into the conflict. Moreover, McNamara implied that if Kennedy had lived, he would not have escalated the war as Lyndon Johnson had. In other words, even though presidents from Truman through Kennedy had involved the United States in Southeast Asia, Vietnam was truly Lyndon Johnson's war. Some historians have argued that by the summer of 1963, Kennedy had become convinced that American forces had to be withdrawn gradually but that politically he dared not do so until after the election of 1964. "If I tried to pull out now from Vietnam," one aide recalls him saying, "we would have another Joe McCarthy red scare on our hands."

Other historians have been skeptical. They argue that even in 1965, no official of importance suggested that the United States should allow Vietnam to fall to the Communists. Senators Fulbright and Mike Mansfield, who criticized Johnson by 1968, all backed the Tonkin Gulf resolution in 1965. Further, historians have evidence that President Kennedy would have escalated the war, though perhaps not as quickly. "We want the war to be won, the Communists to be contained, and the Americans to go home," Kennedy asserted only two months before his death; ". . . But we are not there to see a war lost." As one historian concluded, "The widespread and prevailing opinion in the administration, Congress, and the press and among the mass of Americans was that the United States simply could not walk away from Vietnam and sacrifice a pro-Western country to Communist aggression." In his view Vietnam was America's war: a product of the cold war mentality that had arisen over the previous two decades, not the act of a single, stubborn president.

As the war's annual cost soared to more than $50 billion a year, it fueled a rising inflation. Medicare, education, housing, and other Great Society pro-

Inflation

grams raised the domestic budget sharply too. Through it all Johnson refused to raise taxes, even though wages and prices rose rapidly. From 1965 to 1970 inflation jumped from about 2 percent to around 4 percent. The economy was headed for trouble.

THE UNRAVELING

Almost all the forces dividing America seemed to converge in 1968. Until January of that year, most Americans had reason to believe General West-moreland's estimate of the war. There was, he suggested, "light at the end of the tunnel." Johnson and his advisers, whatever their private doubts, in public painted an optimistic picture. With such optimism radiating from Washington, few Americans were prepared for the events on the night of January 30, 1968.

Tet Offensive

As the South Vietnamese began their celebration of Tet, the Vietnamese lunar New Year, Vietcong guerrillas launched a series of concerted attacks. Assault targets included Saigon's major airport, the South Vietnamese presidential palace, and Hue, the ancient Vietnamese imperial capital. Perhaps most unnerving to Americans, 19 crack Vietcong commandos blasted a hole in the wall of the American embassy compound in Saigon and stormed in. They fought in the courtyard until all 19 lay dead. One reporter, stunned by the carnage, compared the courtyard to a butcher shop.

Tet must rank as one of the great American intelligence failures, on a par with the failure to anticipate Japan's attack on Pearl Harbor or China's intervention in the Korean War. For nearly half a year the North Vietnamese had lured American troops away from Vietnam's cities into pitched battles at remote outposts like Khe Sanh and Con Thien. As American forces dispersed, the Vietcong infiltrated major population areas of Saigon and the Mekong Delta region. A few audacious VC, disguised as South Vietnamese soldiers, even hitched rides on American jeeps and trucks. Though surprised by the Tet offensive, American and South Vietnamese troops repulsed most of the assaults. General Westmoreland announced that the Vietcong had "very deceitfully" taken advantage of the Vietnamese holiday "to create maximum consternation" and that their "well-laid plans went afoul."

In a narrow military sense, Westmoreland was right. The enemy had been driven back, sustaining perhaps 40,000 deaths. Only 1100 American and 2300

Stalemate

South Vietnamese soldiers had been killed—a ratio of more than 10 to 1 (though 12,500 civilians died). But Americans at home received quite another message. Tet created a "credibility gap" between the administration's optimistic reports and the war's harsh reality. Westmoreland, Johnson, and other officials had repeatedly claimed that the Vietcong were on their last legs. Yet as Ho Chi Minh had coolly informed the French after World War II, "You can kill ten of my men for every one I kill of yours . . . even at those odds, you will lose and I will win." Highly respected CBS news anchor Walter Cronkite drew a gloomy lesson of Tet for his national audience: "To say that we are mired in stalemate seems the only realistic, yet unsatisfactory, conclusion."

The Tet offensive sobered Lyndon Johnson as well as his new secretary of defense, Clark Clifford. Clifford was a Johnson loyalist and a stalwart believer

Clark Clifford

in the war. But as he reviewed the American position in Vietnam, he could get no satisfactory answers from the Joint Chiefs of Staff, who had requested an additional 206,000 troops. "How long would it take to succeed in Vietnam?" Clifford recalled asking them.

> They didn't know. How many more troops would it take? They couldn't say. Were two hundred thousand the answer? They weren't sure. Might they need more? Yes, they might need more. Could the enemy build up [their own troop strength] in exchange? Probably. So what was the plan to win the war? Well, the only plan was that attrition would wear out the Communists, and they would have had enough. Was there any indication that we've reached that point? No, there wasn't.

Clifford decided to build a case for deescalation. To review policy, he formed a panel of "wise men," respected pillars of the cold war establishment that included Dean Acheson, Harry Truman's secretary of state; Henry Cabot Lodge, a Republican and former ambassador to South Vietnam; and several retired generals. The war could not be won, they concluded, and Johnson should seek a negotiated settlement.

Meanwhile, the antiwar forces had found a political champion in Senator Eugene McCarthy from Wisconsin. McCarthy was something of a senatorial maverick who wrote poetry in his spare time. He announced that no matter how long the odds, he intended to challenge Lyndon Johnson in the 1968 Democratic

"Clean for Gene"

primaries. Idealistic college students got haircuts and shaves in order to look "clean for Gene." Thus transformed, they canvassed New Hampshire voters. Johnson won the primary vote, but his margin was so slim (300 votes) that it amounted to a stunning defeat. To the anger of McCarthy supporters, Robert Kennedy, John Kennedy's younger brother, quickly announced his own antiwar candidacy.

"I've got to get me a peace proposal," the president told Clifford. White House speechwriters finally put together an announcement that bombing raids against North Vietnam would be halted, at least partially, in hopes that peace talks could begin. They were still trying to write an ending when Johnson told

LBJ withdraws

them, "Don't worry; I may have a little ending of my own." On March 31 he supplied it, announcing: "I have concluded that I should not permit the presidency to become involved in the partisan divisions that are developing in this political year. . . . Accordingly I shall not seek, and I will not accept, the nomination of my party for another term as your president."

The announcement shocked nearly everyone. The Vietnam War had pulled down one of the savviest, most effective politicians of the era. North Vietnam responded to the speech by sending delegates to a peace conference in Paris, where negotiations quickly bogged down. And American attention soon focused on the chaotic situation at home, where all the turbulence, discontent, and violence of the 1960s seemed to be coming together.

The Shocks of 1968

On April 4 Martin Luther King, Jr., traveled to Memphis to support striking sanitation workers. He was relaxing on the balcony of his motel when James

King and Kennedy killed

Earl Ray, an escaped convict, fatally shot him with a sniper's rifle. King's campaign of nonviolence was overshadowed by the violent reaction to his murder. Riots broke out in ghetto areas of the nation's capital; by the end of the week, disturbances rocked 125 more neighborhoods across the country. Almost before Americans could recover, a disgruntled Arab nationalist, Sirhan Sirhan, assassinated Robert Kennedy on the evening of June 5. Running in opposition to the war, Kennedy had just won a crucial primary victory in California.

The deaths of King and Kennedy pained Americans deeply. In their own ways, both men exemplified the liberal tradition, which reached its high-water mark in the 1960s. King had retained his faith in a Christian theology of nonviolence. He sought reform for the poor of all races without resorting to the language of the fist and the gun. Robert Kennedy had come to reject the war his brother had supported, and he seemed genuinely to sympathize with the poor and minorities. At the same time, he was popular among traditional white ethnics and blue-collar workers. Would the liberal political tradition have flourished longer if these two charismatic figures had survived the turbulence of the sixties?

Once violence silenced the clearest liberal voices, it became clear that Democrats would choose Hubert Humphrey to replace Lyndon Johnson.

A tumultuous Democratic convention

Humphrey had begun his career as a progressive and a strong supporter of civil rights. But as Johnson's loyal vice president, he was intimately associated with the war and the old-style liberal reforms that could never satisfy radicals. The Republicans had chosen Richard Nixon, a traditional anti-Communist (now reborn as the "new," more moderate Nixon). As much as radicals disliked Johnson, they truly abhorred Nixon, "new" or old.

Chicago, where the Democrats met for their convention, was the fiefdom of Mayor Richard Daley, long a symbol of machine politics and backroom deals. Daley was determined that the dissatisfied radicals who poured into Chicago would not disrupt "his" Democratic convention. The radicals were equally determined that they would. For a week the police skirmished with demonstrators: police clubs, riot gear, and tear gas versus the demonstrators' eggs, rocks, and balloons filled with paint and urine. When Daley refused to allow a peaceful march past the convention site, the radicals marched anyway, and then the police, with the mayor's blessing, turned on the crowd in what a federal commission later labeled a police riot. In one pitched battle, many officers took off their badges and waded into the crowd, nightsticks swinging, chanting "Kill, kill, kill." Reporters, medics, and other innocent bystanders were injured; at 3 A.M. police invaded candidate Eugene McCarthy's hotel headquarters and pulled some of his assistants from their beds.

With feelings running so high, President Johnson did not dare appear at his own party's convention. Theodore White, a veteran journalist covering the assemblage, scribbled his verdict in a notebook as police chased hippies down Michigan Avenue. "The Democrats are finished," he wrote.

Whose Silent Majority?

Radicals were not the only Americans alienated from the political system in 1968. Governor George Wallace of Alabama sensed the frustration among the "average man on the street, this man in the textile mill, this man in the steel mill, this barber, this beautician, the policeman on the beat." In running for president, Wallace sought the support of blue-collar workers and the lower middle classes.

Wallace had first come to national attention in 1963, when he barred integration of the University of Alabama. Briefly, he pursued the Democratic presidential nomination in 1964. For the race in 1968 he formed his
George Wallace own American Independent party with the hawkish General Curtis LeMay as his running mate. (LeMay spoke belligerently of bombing North Vietnam "back to the stone age.") Wallace's enemies were the "liberals, intellectuals, and long hairs [who] have run this country for too long."

Wallace did not simply appeal to law and order, militarism, and white backlash; he was too sharp for that. With roots in southern Populism, he called for federal job-training programs, stronger unemployment benefits, national health insurance, a higher minimum wage, and a further extension of union rights. Polls in September revealed that many Robert Kennedy voters had shifted to Wallace. A quarter of all union members backed him.

In fact, Wallace had tapped true discontent among the working class. Many blue-collar workers despised hippies and peace marchers, yet wanted the United States out of Vietnam. And they were suspicious, as Wallace was, of the upperclass "establishment" that held power. "We can't understand how all those rich kids—the kids with beards from the suburbs—how they got off when my son

EYEWITNESS   TO   HISTORY

A Disabled Vietnam Veteran Joins a
Los Angeles Antiwar Demonstration

The noon traffic is moving along Wilshire Boulevard just as if the line of veterans and ordinary citizens picketing Nixon's campaign headquarters were not there. "Join us!" we cry. "Stop the war!" Heavy curtains are drawn over the windows of the campaign headquarters where volunteers are working for the reelection of the president. We have been there for two days and not one of the volunteers has ever looked out, the people in their cars pass us quickly, intent on their steering wheels. Who are these people going to work, going to lunch as if nothing is more important than that? "Here!" I scream. "Look at the war!" They never so much as turn their heads. I wheel out into traffic, pushing myself in front of cars. "Take a good look at the war!" I cry, racing my wheel chair in front of a truck. I do not think—or even care—about getting killed. I am screaming at them to look at me. Up on the rooftop of the headquarters the hidden police cameras are taking pictures, and I know that all by myself I have at least succeeded in stopping traffic.

One by one the other demonstrators are breaking from the line. They sit down among the cars, banging their picket sticks and yelling, their voices hoarse. . . . We have taken the streets. People are honking their horns now, workers and secretaries hanging out their windows, bus drivers shouting their approval. Some of the demonstrators are dancing and I grab both wheels of my chair, then let go with one hand and raise my middle finger in the air as a salute to the cops and the FBI. I spin on my two wheels in front of everyone, as the shouting goes on for the war to end, for the killing to be stopped forever. I keep doing my wheelies as the police look on with envy and utter contempt, frozen on their side of the street. They seem torn between wanting to kill us and wanting to tear off their uniforms and throw away their guns. "Come join us!" we shout to them, but they do not take us up on our invitation.

Ron Kovic, *Born on the Fourth of July* (Camp Hill, PA.: Quality Paperback Books, 1976), pp. 138–139. Copyright © 1976 McGraw-Hill, Inc. Reprinted by permission of McGraw-Hill, Inc.

had to go over there and maybe get his head shot off," one blue-collar parent complained.

Richard Nixon too sought the votes of these traditionally Democratic voters, especially disaffected southern Democrats. The Republicans, of course, had

Nixon and the
"silent majority"

been reviled by the Populists of old as representatives of the money power, monopoly, and the old-line establishment. But Nixon himself had modest roots. His parents owned a general store in Whittier, California, where he had worked to help the family out. At Duke Law School he was so pinched for funds he lived in an abandoned tool-shed. His dogged hard work earned him the somewhat dubious nickname of "iron pants." If ever there had been a candidate who could claim to be self-made, it was Nixon. And he well understood the disdain ordinary laborers felt for "kids with beards from the suburbs" who seemed always to be insisting, protesting, *demanding*. Nixon believed himself a representative of the "silent majority," as he later described it, not a vocal minority.

He thus set two fundamental requirements for his campaign: to distance himself from President Johnson on Vietnam and to turn Wallace's "average Americans" into a Republican majority. The Vietnam issue was delicate, because Nixon had generally supported the president's efforts to end the war. He told his aide Richard Whalen, "I've come to the conclusion that there's no way to win the war. But we can't say that, of course. In fact, we have to seem to say the opposite." For most of his campaign he hinted that he had a secret plan to end the war but steadfastly refused to disclose it. He pledged only to find an honorable solution. As for Wallace's followers, Nixon promised to promote "law and order" while cracking down on "pot," pornography, protest, and permissiveness.

Hubert Humphrey had the more daunting task of surmounting the ruins of the Chicago convention. All through September antiwar protesters dogged his

The 1968
election

campaign with "Dump the Hump" posters. Although Humphrey picked up steam late in the campaign (partly by cautiously criticizing Johnson's war policies), the last-minute surge was not enough. Nixon captured 43.4 percent of the popular vote to 42.7 percent for Humphrey and 13.5 percent for Wallace. Some voters had punished the Democrats not just for the war but also for supporting civil rights. The majority of the American electorate had turned its back on liberal reform.

THE NIXON ERA

In Richard Nixon, Americans had elected two men to the presidency. On the public side, he appeared as the traditional small-town conservative who cherished individual initiative, chamber-of-commerce capitalism, Fourth-of-July patriotism, and middle-class Victorian values. The private Nixon was a troubled man. His language among intimates was caustic and profane. He waxed bitter toward those he saw as enemies. Never a natural public speaker, he was physically rather awkward—a White House aide once found toothmarks on a "childproof" aspirin cap the president had been unable to pry open. But Nixon seemed to search out challenges—"crises" to face and conquer.

Vietnamization—and Cambodia

A settlement of the Vietnam "crisis" thus became one of Nixon's first priorities. He found a congenial ally in National Security Advisor Henry Kissinger.

Henry Kissinger Kissinger, an intensely ambitious Harvard academic, shared with the new president a global vision of foreign affairs. Like Nixon, Kissinger had a tendency to pursue his ends secretly, circumventing the traditional channels of government such as the Department of State.

Nixon and Kissinger wanted to bring the war to an end, but insisted on "peace with honor." That meant leaving a pro-American South Vietnamese government behind. The strategy Nixon adopted was "Vietnamization," which involved a carrot and a stick. On its own initiative, the United States began gradually withdrawing troops as a way to advance the peace talks in Paris. The burden of fighting would shift to the South Vietnamese army. Critics likened this strategy to little more than "changing the color of the corpses." All the same, it helped reduce antiwar protests at home. As the media shifted their focus to the peace talks, the public had the impression the war was winding down.

Using the stick, President Nixon hoped to drive the North Vietnamese into negotiating peace on American terms. Quite consciously, he traded on his reputation as a cold warrior who would stop at nothing. As he explained to his chief of staff, Robert Haldeman,

> I call it the Madman Theory, Bob. I want the North Vietnamese to believe that I've reached the point where I might do anything to stop the war. We'll just slip the word to them that, "for God's sake, you know Nixon is obsessed about Communists. We can't restrain him when he's angry—and he has his hand on the nuclear button"—and Ho Chi Minh himself will be in Paris in two days begging for peace.

To underline his point, in the spring of 1969 Nixon launched a series of bombing attacks against North Vietnamese supply depots inside neighboring Cambodia. Johnson had refused to widen the war in this manner, fearing domestic reaction. Nixon simply kept the raids secret.

The North Vietnamese refused to cave in to the bombing. Ho Chi Minh's death in 1969 changed nothing. His successors continued to reject any offer that did not end with complete American withdrawal and an abandonment of the South Vietnamese military government. Once again Nixon turned up the heat.

Cambodian invasion Over the opposition of his secretaries of defense and state, he ordered American troops into Cambodia to wipe out North Vietnamese bases there. On April 30, 1970, he announced the "incursion" of American troops, proclaiming that he would not allow "the world's most powerful nation" to act "like a pitiful helpless giant."

The wave of protests that followed included the fatal clashes between authorities and students at Kent State and Jackson State as well as another march on Washington by 100,000 protesters. Even Congress was upset enough to repeal the Tonkin Gulf Resolution, a symbolic rejection of Nixon's invasion. After two months American troops left Cambodia, having achieved little.

Fighting a No-Win War

For a time, Vietnamization seemed to be working. As more American troops went home, the South Vietnamese forces improved modestly. But for American GIs still in the country, morale became a serious problem. Obviously the United States was gradually pulling out its forces. After Tet, it was clear there would be no victory. So why were the "grunts" in the field still being asked to put their lives on the line? The anger surfaced increasingly in incidents known as "fragging," in which GIs threw fragmentation grenades at officers who pursued the war too aggressively.

Nor could the army isolate itself from the trends dividing American society. Just as young Americans "turned on" to marijuana and hallucinogens, so soldiers in Vietnam used drugs. The Pentagon estimated that by 1971 nearly a third of American troops there had experimented with either opium or heroin, easily obtained in Southeast Asia.

Black GIs brought with them the black power issues from home. One white medic noticed that Muhammad Ali's refusal to be drafted caused the blacks in
_____

GIs and black power

his unit "to question why they were fighting the Honky's war against other Third World people. I saw very interesting rela-
_____
tionships happening between your quick-talking, sharp-witted Northern blacks and your kind of easygoing, laid-back Southern blacks. . . . Many Southern blacks changed their entire point of view by the end of their tour and went home extremely angry."

The problem with morale only underlined the dilemma facing President Nixon. As the troops became restive, domestic opposition to the war grew and the North Vietnamese refused to yield.

The Move toward Détente

Despite Nixon's insistence on "peace with honor," Vietnam was not a war he had chosen to fight. And both Kissinger and Nixon recognized that by 1968 the United States no longer had the resources to exercise unchallenged dominance across the globe. The Soviet Union remained their prime concern. Ever since Khrushchev had backed down at the Cuban missile crisis in 1962, the Soviets had steadily expanded their nuclear arsenal. Furthermore, the growing economies of Japan and Western Europe challenged American leadership in world trade. Continued instability in Southeast Asia, the Middle East, and other Third World areas threatened the strength of the non-Communist bloc. Thus Vietnam diverted valuable military and economic resources from more critical areas.

In what the White House labeled the "Nixon Doctrine," the United States would shift some of the military burden for containment to other allies: Japan in the Pacific, the shah of Iran in the Middle East, Zaire in central Africa, and the apartheid government in South Africa. Over the next six years American foreign military sales jumped from $1.8 billion to $15.2 billion. At the same time, Nixon and Kissinger looked for new ways to contain Soviet power not simply by the traditional threat of arms but through negotiations to ease tensions. This policy was named, from the French, détente.

Kissinger and Nixon looked to create "linkages" among many cold war issues. For example, the arms race burdened the Soviet economy. To ease that pressure, they would make concessions to the Soviets on nuclear arms. The Soviets in return would have to limit their arms buildup and, in a linked concession, pressure North Vietnam to negotiate an end to the war. To add lever-
The China card age, Nixon and Kissinger developed a "China card." The United States would stop treating Communist Mao Zedong as an arch-enemy and, instead, open diplomatic relations with the Chinese. Fearful of a more powerful China, the Soviets would be more conciliatory toward the United States.

It took a shrewd diplomatist to sense an opportunity to shift traditional cold war policy. Conservative Republicans denounced the idea of recognizing Mao's government, even after 20 years. They believed that the Soviets responded only to force and that they were united with China in a monolithic Communist conspiracy. Now Richard Nixon, the man who had built a career fighting commu-

Richard Nixon's trip to China included this visit to the Great Wall. Perhaps precisely because he had been so staunch an anticommunist, Nixon appreciated the enormous departure his trip marked in Sino-American relations.

nism, made overtures to the Communist powers. Kissinger slipped off to China on a secret mission (he was nursing a stomachache, his aides assured the press) and then reappeared having arranged a trip to China for the president. During that visit in early 1972, Nixon pledged to normalize relations, a move the public enthusiastically welcomed.

A new overture to the Soviet Union followed the China trip. Eager to acquire American grain and technology, Soviet Premier Leonid Brezhnev invited Nixon to Moscow in May 1972. Nixon saw in the Soviet market a chance to ease American trade deficits by selling surplus wheat to the Russians. But the meeting's most important result was the signing of the first Strategic Arms

SALT I

Limitation Treaty (SALT I). In the agreement, both sides pledged not to develop a new system of antiballistic missiles (ABMs), which would have accelerated the costly arms race. And they agreed to limit the number of intercontinental ballistic missiles (ICBMs) each side would deploy.

Both the China and the Moscow visits strengthened Nixon's reputation as a global strategist. Americans were pleased at the prospect of lower cold war tensions. But it was not clear that the linkages achieved in Moscow and Beijing would help extricate the United States from Vietnam.

Nixon's New Federalism

As a Republican, Nixon wanted to scale back many New Deal and Great Society programs. "After a third of a century of power flowing from the people and the states to Washington," he proclaimed, "it is time for a New Federalism in which power, funds, and responsibility will flow from Washington to the states and to the people."

The New Federalism involved a system of revenue sharing, where Washington gave money in block grants to state and local governments. Instead of

Revenue sharing

the funds being earmarked for specific purposes, localities could decide which problems needed attention and how best to attack them. Congress passed a revenue sharing act in 1972, which distributed $30 billion over the following five years. A similar approach influenced aid to individuals. In contrast, liberal programs from the New Deal to the Great Society often provided specific services to individuals: job retraining programs, Head Start programs for preschoolers, food supplement programs for nursing mothers. Republicans argued that such a "service strategy" too often assumed that federal bureaucrats best understood what the poor needed. Nixon favored an "income strategy" instead, which simply gave recipients money and allowed them to spend it as they saw fit. Such grants were meant to encourage individual initiative, increase personal freedom, and reduce government bureaucracy.

Even if Nixon was determined to reverse the liberalism of the 1960s, critics were wrong to dismiss him as a knee-jerk conservative. His appeal to local

Nixon reforms

authority and individual initiative in some ways echoed the New Left's rhetoric of "power to the people." In 1970 he signed a bill establishing an Occupational Safety and Health Agency (OSHA) to enforce health and safety standards in the workplace. And although the president was no crusader for the environment, he did support a Clean Air Act to reduce car exhaust emissions, as well as a Clean Water Act to make polluters liable for their negligence and to deal with disastrous oil spills.

Stagflation

Ironically, a worsening economy forced Nixon to adopt liberal remedies. By 1970 the nation had entered its first recession in a decade. Traditionally a recession brought a decrease in demand for goods and a rise in unemployment as workers were laid off. Manufacturers then cut prices in order to encourage demand for their goods and cut wages in order to preserve profit margins. But in the recession of 1970, while unemployment rose as economists would have expected, wages and prices were also rising in an inflationary spiral—a condition described as "stagflation."

Unfriendly Democrats labeled the phenomenon "Nixonomics," although in truth Lyndon Johnson had brought on inflation by refusing to raise taxes to pay for the war and for Great Society social programs. In addition, wages continued their inflationary rise partly because powerful unions had negotiated automatic cost-of-living increases into their contracts. Similarly, in industries dominated by a few large corporations, like steel and oil, prices did not follow the market forces of a recession. So prices and wages continued to rise as demand and employment fell.

Mindful that his own "silent majority" were the people most pinched by the slower economy, Nixon decided that unemployment posed a greater threat than inflation. Announcing "I am now a Keynesian," he adopted a deficit budget designed to stimulate the growth of jobs. More surprising, in August 1971 he announced that to provide short-term relief, wages and prices would be frozen for 90 days. For a Republican to advocate wage and price controls was near heresy, almost as heretical as Nixon's overtures to China. For a year federal wage and price boards enforced the ground rules for any increases until the economy grew again. Controls were lifted in January 1973. As in foreign policy, Nixon had reversed long-cherished economic policies to achieve practical results.

Wage and price controls

"SILENT" MAJORITIES AND VOCAL MINORITIES

During the 1968 campaign Richard Nixon had noticed a placard carried by a hopeful voter: "Bring Us Together." That became his campaign theme. Yet of necessity political coalitions cannot bring everyone together. Their goal is simply to assemble a majority on Election Day. Nixon recognized quite well that in the three-way race of 1968, his 43 percent did not add up to a majority. But when Wallace's vote was added, the total came to an impressive 60 percent. If Nixon could add discontented southerners and blue-collar workers to the traditional GOP base, he could win again in 1972.

These groups resented much that the civil rights movement had done to overcome racial inequalities. To add to that resentment, the civil rights movement inspired other minorities to demand greater equality for themselves. Just as the civil rights campaign gave way to black power militancy, so too other minority activists adopted increasingly disruptive tactics to press their causes. Their new, more assertive visibility was crucial to Nixon's attempt to form his own countermajority.

Hispanic Activism

Part of that increased visibility resulted from a new wave of immigration from Mexico and Puerto Rico after World War II and, in the case of Cubans, after the 1959 revolution that brought Castro to power. Historical, cultural, ethnic, and geographic differences among the three major Hispanic groups made it difficult to develop a common political agenda. Still, some activists did seek greater Hispanic unity.

Cesar Chavez (center left) mobilized the largely Hispanic migrant workers into the United Farm Workers Union. In 1969 a call for boycotts against grapes and lettuce gained Chavez and the union national attention.

After World War II a weak island economy and the lure of prosperity on the mainland brought more than a million Puerto Ricans into New York City.

Puerto Rican migration As citizens of the United States, they could move freely to the mainland and back home again. That dual consciousness discouraged many from establishing deep roots stateside. Equally important, the newcomers were startled to discover that, whatever their status at home, on the mainland they were subject to racial discrimination and most often segregated into urban slums. In 1964 approximately half of all recent immigrants lived below the poverty level, according to the Puerto Rican Forum. Light-skinned migrants escaped those conditions by blending into the middle class as "Latin Americans." The Puerto Rican community thereby lost some of the leadership it needed to assert its political rights.

Still, during the 1960s, the urban barrios gained greater political consciousness as groups like *Aspira* adopted the strategies of civil rights activists and organizations like the Black and Puerto Rican Caucus created links with other minority groups. The Cubans who arrived in the United States after 1959—some 350,000 over the course of the decade—forged fewer ties with other Hispanics. Most settled around Miami. An unusually large number came from Cuba's professional, business, and government class and were racially white and politically conservative.

Mexican Americans, on the other hand, constituted the largest segment of the Hispanic population. Until the 1940s most were farmers and farm laborers in Texas, New Mexico, and California. But during the 1950s, the process of mechanization had affected them, just as it had black southerners. By 1969 about 85 percent of Mexican Americans had settled in cities. With urbanization came a slow improvement of the range and quality of jobs they held. A body of skilled workers, middle-class professionals, and entrepreneurs emerged.

In 1960, frustrated by years of neglect by major parties, Hispanic political leaders from the region formed the Mexican American Political Association. MAPA declared its intent to be "proudly Mexican American, openly political, and necessarily bipartisan." By 1964 four Mexican Americans had been elected to Congress, but the growing activism across the nation altered traditional Hispanic approaches to politics. Younger Mexican Americans began to call

Cesar Chavez themselves Chicanos. In 1965 Cesar Chavez gained national attention by his efforts to organize migrant laborers into the United Farm Workers. He led them in *La Huelga*—The Strike—which they supported with a national boycott of California lettuce and grapes.

By the late 1960s Mexican Americans had clearly established greater ethnic consciousness. Like African Americans, Chicanos saw themselves as a people whose culture had been taken from them. Their heritage had been rejected, their labor exploited, and their opportunity for advancement denied. The new ethnic militancy led to the formation of *La Raza Unida* (The Race United). This third-party movement sought to gain power in communities in which Mexican

Americans were a majority and to extract concessions from the Democrats and Republicans. The more militant "Brown Berets" adopted the paramilitary tactics and radical rhetoric of the Black Panthers.

The Choices of American Indians

Like African Americans and Hispanics, Indians began to protest; yet the unique situation of Native Americans (as many had begun to call themselves) set them apart from other minorities. A largely hostile white culture had in past centuries sought to either exterminate or assimilate American Indians. Ironically, the growing strength of the civil rights movement created another threat to Indian tribal identities. Liberals came to see the reservations not as oases of Indian culture but as rural ghettos. During the 1950s they joined conservatives eager to repeal the New Deal and western state politicians eyeing tribal resources to

Termination adopt a policy of "termination." The Bureau of Indian Affairs would reduce federal services, gradually sell off tribal lands, and push Indians into the "mainstream" of American life. Although most full-blooded Indians objected to the policy, some people of mixed blood and Indians already assimilated into white society supported the move. The resulting relocation of approximately 35,000 Indians accelerated a shift from rural areas to cities. The urban Indian population, which had been barely 30,000 in 1940, reached more than 300,000 by the 1970s.

The social activism of the 1960s inspired Indian leaders to shape a new political agenda. In 1968 urban activists in Minneapolis created AIM, the American

American Indian Movement Indian Movement. A year later similarly minded Indians living around San Francisco Bay formed Indians of All Tribes. Because the Bureau of Indian Affairs refused to address the problems of urban Indians, more militant members of the organization dramatized their dissatisfaction by seizing the abandoned federal prison on Alcatraz Island in San Francisco Bay.

The Alcatraz action inspired a national Pan-Indian rights movement. Richard Oakes, a Mohawk Indian from New York, declared that the Alcatraz protest was not "a movement to liberate the island, but to liberate ourselves."

Occupation of Wounded Knee Then in 1973, AIM organizers Russell Means and Dennis Banks led a dramatic takeover of a trading post at Wounded Knee, on a Sioux reservation in South Dakota. Ever since white cavalry had gunned down over a hundred Sioux in 1890 (page 542), Wounded Knee had symbolized for Indians the betrayal of white promises and the bankruptcy of reservation policy. Even more, Wounded Knee now demonstrated the problems that Indian activists faced. When federal officers surrounded the trading post, militants discovered that other Indians did not support their tactics and were forced to leave. A Pan-Indian movement was difficult to achieve when so many tribes were determined to go their own ways, as distinct, self-regulating communities. Thus even activists who supported the Pan-Indian movement found themselves splintering. During the 1970s more than 100 different organizations were formed to unite various tribes pursuing political and legal agendas at the local, state, and federal levels.

Gay Rights

In 1972, Black Panther leader Huey Newton observed that homosexuals "might be the most oppressed people" in American society. Certainly Newton was qualified to recognize oppression when he saw it. But by then a growing number of homosexuals had embraced liberation movements that placed them among minorities demanding equal rights.

Even during the "conformist" 1950s, gay men founded the Mattachine Society (1951) to fight antihomosexual attacks and to press for a wider public acceptance of their lifestyle. Lesbians formed a similar organization, the Daughters of Bilitis, in 1955. Beginning in the mid-1960s, more radical gay and lesbian groups began organizing to raise individual consciousness and to establish a gay culture in which they felt free. One group called for "acceptance as full equals . . . basic rights and equality as citizens; our human dignity; . . . [our] right to love whom we wish."

The movement's defining moment came on Friday, June 27, 1969, when New York police raided the Stonewall Inn, a Greenwich Village bar. Such raids

Stonewall incident

were common enough: gay bars were regularly harassed by the police in an attempt to control urban "vice." This time the patrons fought back, first with taunts and jeers, then with paving stones and parking meters. Increasingly, gay activists called on homosexuals to "come out of the closet" and publicly affirm their sexuality. In 1974 gays achieved a major symbolic victory when the American Psychiatric Association removed homosexuality from its list of mental disorders.

Social Policies and the Court

Many of the blue-collar and southern Democratic voters Nixon sought to attract especially resented the use of school busing to achieve court-ordered de-

School busing

segregation. Fifteen years after *Brown v. Board of Education* had ruled that racially separate school systems must be desegregated, many localities still had not complied. In white neighborhoods, parents opposed having their children bused to more distant, formerly all-black schools, as part of a plan to achieve racial balance. Although black parents for their part worried about the reception their children might receive in hostile white neighborhoods, by and large they supported busing as a means to better education.

Under Nixon, federal policy on desegregation took a 180-degree turn. In 1969 when lawyers for Mississippi asked the Supreme Court to delay an integration plan, the Nixon Justice Department supported the state. The Court rejected that proposal, holding in *United States v. Jefferson County Board of Education* that all state systems, including Mississippi's, had an obligation "to terminate dual systems at once and to operate now and hereafter only unitary schools." Two years later, in *Swann v. Charlotte–Mecklenburg Board of Education* (1971), the Court further ruled that busing, balancing ratios, and redrawing school district lines were all acceptable ways to achieve integration.

To end the Court's liberal activism, Nixon looked to fill vacancies with more conservative justices. He replaced Chief Justice Earl Warren in 1969 with Warren Burger, a jurist who had no wish to break new ground.

Nixon and the Court

When another vacancy occurred in 1969, Nixon tried twice to appoint conservative southern judges with reputations for opposing civil rights and labor unions. Congress rejected both. In the end, Nixon chose Minnesotan Harry Blackmun, a moderate judge of unimpeachable integrity. Two additional conservative appointments guaranteed that the Court would no longer lead the fight for minority rights. But neither would it reverse the achievements of the Warren Court.

Us versus Them

In so many of his battles, as in the struggle to shape the Supreme Court, Nixon portrayed those who opposed him as foes of traditional American values. Just as Nixon had tended to equate liberal reformers with Communist "pinkos" during the 1950s, now his administration blurred the lines between honest dissent and radical criminals. In doing so, it reflected a side of the president that tended to see issues in terms of "us against them."

With Nixon's consent (and Lyndon Johnson's before him), the FBI and intelligence agencies conducted a covert and often illegal war against dissent. Attorney General John Mitchell and his Justice Department aggressively prosecuted civil rights activists, antiwar groups like Vietnam Veterans Against the War, socially liberal members of the Catholic clergy, the Black Panthers, SDS activists, and leaders of the peace movement. In its war on the drug culture of hippies and radicals, the administration proposed a bill that would allow police to stage "no-knock" raids and use "preventive detention" to keep suspected criminals in jail without bail.

In the political arena, Nixon gave Vice President Spiro Agnew the task of mudslinging that Nixon had once performed for Eisenhower. Agnew launched an alliterative assault on the administration's adversaries. He referred to the press and television news commentators as "nattering nabobs of negativism" and "troubadours of trouble" who contributed to the "creeping permissiveness that afflicted America." In the campaign between "us" and "them," the national press corps was clearly "them," a hostile establishment slanting the news.

Triumph

As the election of 1972 approached, Nixon's majority seemed to be falling into place, especially after the Democrats nominated Senator George McGovern of
_____ South Dakota. Under new party rules, which McGovern had
George
McGovern helped write, the delegate selection process was opened to all
_____ party members. No longer would party bosses handpick the delegates. Minorities, women, and young people all received proportional representation. McGovern's nomination gave Nixon the split between "us" and "them" he sought. The Democratic platform embraced all the activist causes that the silent majority resented. It called for immediate withdrawal from Vietnam, abolition of the draft, amnesty for war resisters, and a minimum guaranteed income for the poor.

By November the only question that remained to be settled was the size of Nixon's majority. An unsolved burglary at the Watergate complex in Washington, D.C., while vaguely linked to the White House, had not touched the president. Nixon even captured some antiwar votes by announcing on election eve that peace in Vietnam was at hand. When the smoke cleared, only liberal Massachusetts and the heavily black District of Columbia gave McGovern a majority. Nixon received almost 61 percent of the popular vote.

An overwhelming victory did not bring peace to Richard Nixon. He still felt that he had scores to settle with his political opponents. "We have not used the power in the first four years, as you know," he remarked to Haldeman during the campaign. "We haven't used the Bureau [FBI] and we haven't used the Justice Department, but things are going to change now. And they are going to change and they're going to get it, right?" Haldeman could only agree.

THE END OF AN ERA

Nixon was particularly frustrated because peace in Vietnam still eluded him. The North Vietnamese refused any settlement that left the South Vietnamese government. Nixon wanted to subdue the enemy through force, but he recognized that it would have been political suicide to send back American troops. Instead, he ordered North Vietnam's major port, Haiphong, mined and blockaded in May 1972, along with a sustained bombing campaign. Then on December 18 the president launched an even greater wave of attacks, as American planes dropped more bombs on the North in 12 days than they had during the entire campaign from 1969 to 1971.

Once again, Kissinger returned to Paris, hoping that the combination of threats and conciliation would bring a settlement. Ironically South Vietnamese officials had thrown up the greatest stumbling blocks, for they were rightly convinced that General Thieu's regime would not last once the United States

Peace treaty departed. But in January 1973 a treaty was finally arranged, smoothed by Kissinger's promise of aid to the North Vietnamese to help in postwar reconstruction. By March the last American units were home.

"The enemy must fight his battles . . . [in] protracted campaigns," wrote the Vietnamese strategist in 1284. For all concerned the American phase of the Vietnam Wars had been bloody and wearying. Between 1961 and 1973 the war claimed 57,000 American lives and left more than 300,000 wounded. The cost to Southeast Asia in lives and destruction was almost impossible to calculate. More than a million Vietnamese soldiers and perhaps half a million civilians died. Some 6.5 million South Vietnamese became refugees, along with 3 million Cambodians and Laotians.

At a frightful price in human lives and material destruction, Nixon could claim the "peace with honor" he had insisted on. But experienced observers predicted that South Vietnam's days were numbered. (Indeed they were: the Communist armies united the two Vietnams in 1975.) By any real measure of military success the Vietcong peasant guerrillas and their lightly armed North Vietnamese allies had held off—and in that sense defeated—the world's greatest military power.

Truman may have started the United States down the road to Vietnam by promoting the doctrine of containment all across the globe. Certainly Eisenhower and Kennedy increased American involvement. But *Vietnam in the perspective of the cold war* fairly or not, Vietnam is remembered as Lyndon Johnson's war. He committed both the material and the human resources of the United States to defeat communism in Southeast Asia. That decision to escalate eventually destroyed the political consensus that had unified Americans since the late 1940s. And ironically, it was Richard Nixon, the ardent cold warrior, who recognized that the United States did not have the inexhaustible resources to contain communism everywhere. To end the war in Vietnam, he had to open new relations with the People's Republic of China and the Soviet Union. Where containment assumed a bipolar world, Nixon's policy of détente saw the world as multipolar.

Liberal dreams died with Vietnam, too. The war in Southeast Asia shattered the optimism of the early sixties: the belief that the world could be remade with the help of brilliant intellectuals and federal programs. The war also eroded the prosperity upon which the optimism of the postwar era had rested. After 1973 the economy slid into a long recession that forced Americans to recognize they had entered an era of limits both at home and abroad. Lyndon Johnson, who sought to preserve both liberal dreams and the cold war consensus, died on January 22, 1973, one day before the American war in Vietnam ended.

SIGNIFICANT EVENTS

1945 ┼ Ho Chi Minh unifies Vietnam

1954 ┼ French defeat at Dien Bien Phu; Geneva accords

1963 ┼ Diem assassinated; United States has 16,000 "advisers" in Vietnam

1964 ┼ Tonkin Gulf incident; Tonkin Gulf Resolution

1965 ┼ Rolling Thunder begins bombing of North Vietnam; antiwar "teach-ins" on college campuses; Cesar Chavez leads national campaign on behalf of farmworkers

1967 ┼ March on the Pentagon; Johnson's advisers oppose war

1968 ┼ U.S. troop levels in Vietnam peak at 536,000; Tet offensive; peace talks begin in Paris; Eugene McCarthy challenges Johnson in New Hampshire primary; Johnson withdraws from race; Martin Luther King, Jr., assassinated; Robert Kennedy enters race and is assassinated; riots at Democratic Convention in Chicago; George Wallace candidacy; Nixon wins election

1969 ┼ Secret bombing of Cambodia; Vietnamization leads to reduction of American forces; Nixon Doctrine

1970 ┼ U.S. troops invade Cambodia; killings at Kent State and Jackson State; antiwar march on Washington; Clean Air and Water acts; creation of OSHA; recession creates stagflation; repeal of Tonkin Gulf Resolution

1971 ┼ Nixon adopts wage and price controls; *Swann v. Charlotte–Mecklenburg Board of Education*

1972 ┼ Nixon trip to China; détente with Soviet Union; SALT I; Revenue Sharing Act; Watergate break-in; Nixon reelected; mining of Haiphong Harbor; Christmas bombings of North Vietnam

1973 ┼ Vietnam peace treaty; AIM supporters occupy Wounded Knee

CHAPTER THIRTY-TWO

The Age of Limits

In July 1969, tens of thousands of spectators gathered at Cape Kennedy to witness the launching of *Apollo 11*, the first manned space flight to the moon. Among the crowd was a mule-cart procession led by civil rights leader Ralph Abernathy. The Reverend Abernathy had brought his Poor People's March to dramatize the problem of poverty. The *Saturn 5*'s thunderous ignition proved so awesome that it caught Abernathy up just as it did the millions of Americans who watched on television. He found himself praying for the safety of the crew. Days later, he too celebrated when astronauts Neil Armstrong and Buzz Aldrin walked across a lunar landscape.

The triumph had been epochal. And yet some uncertainty lingered over what it all meant. One scientist took comfort that after Apollo the human race could always go elsewhere, no matter how much a mess was made of the planet earth. That was no small consideration given the increasing problems of smog, water pollution, and toxic wastes. There had been some dramatic warnings. In 1967 an oil tanker spilled 100,000 tons of oil into the English Channel. Detergents used to clean up the spill left the area clean but without plant and animal life for years after.

Such dangers worried city officials in Santa Barbara, California, an outpost of paradise along the Pacific Coast. In the channel stretching between there and Los Angeles, 90 miles to the south, oil companies had drilled some 925 wells in the coastal tidelands. State efforts to impose stringent regulations on federal oil leases offshore had failed. The Department of the Interior repeatedly assured local officials they had "nothing to fear." That changed on January 28, 1969, when Union Oil Company's well A-21 blew a billow of thick crude oil into the channel. Crews quickly capped the hole, only to discover that pressure from the well had opened a fissure in the ocean floor, through which natural gas and oil were seeping to the surface. "It looked like a massive, inflamed abscess bursting with reddish-brown pus," one observer commented.

In the 11 days it took to seal the leak, more than 200,000 barrels of oil had left a slick extending some 800 miles. Tarry goo coated beaches, boats, and wildlife as far south as San Diego. "Cormorants and grebes dived into the oily swells for fish, most never to surface alive. All along the mucky shoreline, birds lay dead or dying, unable to raise their oil-soaked feathers," one reporter wrote. Detergents used to clean up the spill claimed the coast's population of limpets, abalones, lobsters, sea urchins, mussels, and clams, as well as some fish.

Santa Barbara, not *Apollo 11*, served as a portent of the coming decade. Having reached the moon, Americans discovered more pressing concerns closer to home. A political scandal spread so far that, for the first time in American history, a president was forced to resign from office. Renewed war in the Middle East sent the price of oil and gasoline skyrocketing. Pollution from factory smokestacks, poisonous pesticides, and oil spills like the one at Santa Barbara led some scientists to warn of a "drastic ecological imbalance" that threatened the health of the earth itself. Americans began to doubt that technological know-how could solve any problem or that economic growth was both inevitable and beneficial. Elliot Richardson, the Nixon administration's secretary of health, education and welfare (HEW), remarked, "We must recognize, as we have with both foreign affairs and natural resources, that resources we thought were boundless . . . are indeed severely limited."

THE LIMITS OF REFORM

Like the space program, the reform movements of the early 1960s sprang from an optimistic faith in the perfectibility of society. But as the war in Vietnam dragged on, American society seemed to become more fragmented. And as inflation dogged the economy and unemployment grew, Americans set their sights lower. According to social observer Tom Wolfe, in the 1970s the self-obsessed "Me Generation" displaced the crusading New Left.

Some elements of the reform movement kept alive the idea of restructuring society. Environmentalists, feminists, and consumer advocates used many of the same strategies of nonviolent protest and legal maneuver that worked so effectively in the civil rights crusade. But unlike much of the radicalism of the 1960s, these movements each had long been associated with the American reform tradition. Though they often pursued radical goals, their leadership was likely to come from the political mainstream. Consumer advocates, environmentalists, and feminists all won major victories, even if they failed to achieve the transformation of society they sought.

Consumerism

In 1965 a thin, intense young man shocked the automotive world by publishing *Unsafe at Any Speed*. The author, Ralph Nader, argued that too many automobiles were unsafe even in minor accidents. Nader's particular target was the

Chevrolet Corvair, a rear-engined small car built by General
Motors. Crash reports indicated that the Corvair sometimes
rolled over in routine turns and quickly lost control when it skid-
ded. Even more damning, Nader accused General Motors of being aware of the flaw, from its own internal engineering studies.

Ralph Nader's Unsafe at Any Speed

GM, the corporate Goliath, at first decided that rather than defend the
Corvair, it would attack Nader, this countercultural David. It sent out private
investigators to dig up dirt from his personal life. They discovered no hippie
disguised in a suit, but the hard-working son of Lebanese immigrants, who had
fulfilled the American dream. Nader had graduated from Princeton and Harvard
Law School, wore his hair short, and never used drugs. And when he discovered GM's conspiracy against him, he sued.

GM's embarrassed president publicly apologized, but by then Nader was
a hero and *Unsafe at Any Speed* a bestseller. In 1966 Congress passed legislation (the National Traffic and Motor Vehicle Safety Act), which
for the first time required safety standards for cars, tires, and
roads. Nader used $425,000 from his successful lawsuit to

Highway Safety Act

launch his Washington-based Center for the Study of Responsive Law (1969)
with a staff of five lawyers and a hundred college volunteers. "Nader's Raiders,"
as the group became known, investigated a range of issues, including water
pollution, congressional reform, fraud in old-age homes, and auto safety.

Nader's Raiders were part of a diverse consumer movement that ranged
from modest reformers to radicals. The radicals viewed the free market system
as deeply flawed. Only with a thorough overhaul carried out by an active, interventionist government could citizen-consumers be empowered. Nader suggested both the radicals' tone and their agenda when he called on corporations
"to stop stealing, stop deceiving, stop corrupting politicians with money, stop
monopolizing, stop poisoning the earth, air and water, stop selling dangerous
products, stop exposing workers to cruel hazards. . . ."

More moderate reformers viewed the problem in terms of making the existing market economy more open and efficient. To be better consumers, people needed better information about unsafe toys, dangerous food additives, and
defective products. These reformers also exposed unethical marketing strategies
like hidden credit costs that plagued the poor. Many consumer organizations
concentrated on a single issue, such as auto safety, smoking, insurance costs, or
health care.

Diversity of goals broadened the movement's appeal but also fragmented
support. Nader was never able to establish consumerism as a mass political
movement. Its strongest supporters remained within the ranks of the upper
middle classes. Then, too, a weak economy created fears that more government
regulations would add to inflation. Still, the consumer movement had placed its
agenda in the mainstream of political debate, and powerful consumer groups
continued to represent the public interest.

Environmentalism

The Santa Barbara oil spill was hardly the first warning that Americans were abusing the environment. As early as 1962 marine biologist Rachel Carson had warned in *Silent Spring* of the environmental damage done by the pesticide DDT. Though chemical companies tried to discredit her as a woman and an eccentric scientist, 40 state legislatures passed laws restricting DDT. Certainly, no one with a sense of irony could help but marvel that the oil-polluted Cuyahoga River running through Cleveland, Ohio, had burst into flames. Smog from auto emissions, nuclear fallout, dangerous pesticides, hazardous consumer goods, and polluted rivers were the not-so-hidden costs of a society wedded to technology and unbridled economic growth.

Barry Commoner and ecology

The environmental movement of the 1960s drew heavily on the field of ecology. Since the early twentieth century this biological science had demonstrated how closely life processes throughout nature depend on one another. Barry Commoner in his book *The Closing Circle* (1971) argued that modern society courted disaster by recklessly trying to "improve on nature." American farmers, for example, had shifted from animal manures to artificial fertilizers to increase farm productivity. But the change also raised costs, left soil sterile, and poisoned nearby water sources. After laundry detergents artificially "whitened" clothes, they created foamy scum in lakes and rivers while nourishing deadly algae blooms. Industry profited in the short run, Commoner argued, but in the long run the environment was going bankrupt.

By the 1970s, environmentalists were organizing to implement what microbiologist René Dubos called a "new social ethic." They brought a lawsuit in an effort to block the building of an 800-mile oil pipeline across Alaska's fragile wilderness. In addition, they successfully lobbied in Congress to defeat a bill authorizing support for the supersonic plane, the SST, whose high-altitude flights appeared to be depleting the earth's ozone layer. Similarly, environmental groups fought a proposed jet airport that threatened south Florida's water supply and the ecology of Everglades National Park.

EPA established

Even President Nixon, normally a friend of business and real estate interests, responded to the call for tougher environmental regulations. His administration banned all domestic use of DDT and supported the National Environmental Policy Act of 1969. The act required environmental impact statements for most public projects and made the government responsible for representing the public interest. Nixon also established the Environmental Protection Agency to enforce the law. Echoing Barry Commoner, he announced, "We must learn not how to master nature but how to master ourselves, our institutions, and our technology."

Earth Day

By the spring of 1970 a healthy environment had become a popular cause. Senator Gaylord Nelson of Wisconsin suggested a national "Earth Day" to celebrate the new consciousness. On April 22, 1970, for at least a few hours pedestrians replaced exhaust-belching cars on downtown city streets, millions of schoolchildren planted trees and picked up trash, college students demonstrated, and Congress adjourned. But at least one member of Congress recognized the movement's more radical implications: "The Establishment sees this as a great big anti-litter campaign. Wait until they find out what it really means . . . to clean up our earth."

Earth Day did not signal a consensus on an environmental ethic. President Nixon, for one, was unwilling to restrict economic development, including the oil industry's Alaskan pipeline. Despite a long series of court challenges, construction began in 1973. "We are not going to allow the environmental issue . . . to destroy the system," he announced in 1972.

Nixon's political instincts were shrewd. Conflict between social classes underlay the environmental debate. To those he courted for his silent majority, the issue came down to jobs versus the environment. "Out of work? Hungry? Eat an environmentalist," declared one bumper sticker. During the 1960s many middle Americans came to resent the veterans of the counterculture, civil rights, and antiwar movements who now found an outlet in environmental activism. But so long as pollution threatened, the environmental movement would not go away. From conservative hunters in Ducks Unlimited to mainstream nature lovers in the Wilderness Society to radical "enviro-freaks" in Earth First, numerous groups fought to save the environment.

COUNTERPOINT *Interpreting the Environmental Movement*

Because historians have often been sympathetic to the goals of environmentalists, they have tended to interpret the movement somewhat uncritically. Mainstream accounts often point out flattering continuities with the progressive movement, such as a reliance on the authority of science. Biology, for example, caused progressives to discard once-popular theories of human exceptionalism and to see nature not as a simple warehouse of useful resources but as a series of interlinking systems. In similar ways, environmentalists have relied on ecological studies to provide a more sophisticated understanding of how those systems were interacting.

Recently some historians have become more critical of environmentalism. One confessed, "Where once I saw a movement founded in science, now I see a utopian political program." He compared modern environmentalism to the temperance crusade at the turn of the century. Although temperance advocates were divided over how to attack alcohol abuse, the more extreme factions successfully promoted prohibition and the Eighteenth Amendment. It was a utopian experiment that, in the end, was doomed to fail. Similarly, some environmental reformers have called for "global schemes of economic and political control," according to this point of view. Environmentalist Paul Ehrlich's popular book *The Population Bomb* (1968), for example, warned of the dire consequences of overpopulation. Ehrlich suggested that voluntary efforts at family planning were likely to fail and that the state might have to step in to control birthrates, especially in developing nations.

The parallel between the environmentalists and the temperance reformers is instructive. Progressivism, we have seen, displayed a mix of reform and control. Its middle- and upper-middle-class advocates worried about what the unruly masses might do without the guidance of "experts." A similar tension can be seen in the environmental movement, whose professional, white-collar advocates during the 1960s and 1970s paid scant attention to the environmental problems specific to poor urban residents. Only in the 1980s did a number of new organizations focus greater attention on the effects of hazardous industrial sites on lower-class neighborhoods or the danger of pesticides to migrant workers.

Feminism

Organized struggle for women's rights and equality in the United States began before the Civil War. Sustained political efforts had won women the vote in 1920. But the women's movement of the 1960s and 1970s began to push for equality in broader, deeper ways.

Writer Betty Friedan was one of the earliest to voice dissatisfaction with the cultural attitudes that flourished after World War II. Even though more women

The Feminine Mystique

were entering the job market, the media routinely glorified housewives and homemakers, while discouraging those who aspired to independent careers. In *The Feminine Mystique* (1963) Friedan identified the "problem that has no name," a dispiriting boredom or emptiness in the midst of affluent lives. "Our culture does not permit women to accept or gratify their basic need to grow and fulfill their potentialities as human beings."

The Feminine Mystique gave new life to the women's rights movement. The Commission on the Status of Women appointed by President Kennedy proposed the 1963 Equal Pay Act and helped add gender to the forms of discrimination outlawed by the 1964 Civil Rights Act. Women also assumed an important role in both the civil rights and antiwar movements. They accounted for half the students who went south for the "Freedom Summers" in 1964 and 1965.

Even women who joined the protests of the 1960s found themselves belittled and limited to providing menial services such as cooking and laundry. Casey Hayden, a veteran of Students for a Democratic Society and the civil rights organization SNCC, told her male comrades that the "assumptions of male superiority are as widespread . . . and every much as crippling to the woman as the assumptions of white superiority are to the Negro."

By 1966 activist women were less willing to remain silent. Friedan joined a group of 24 women and 2 men who formed the National Organization

E Y E W I T N E S S   T O   H I S T O R Y

Recounting the Early Days of the Feminist Movement

I remember meeting with a group of women in Missouri who, because they had come in equal numbers from the small town and from its nearby campus, seemed to be split between wives with white gloves welded to their wrists and students with boots who talked about "imperialism" and "oppression." Planning for a child care center had brought them together, but the meeting seemed hopeless until three of the booted young women began to argue among themselves about a young male professor, the leader of the radicals on campus, who accused all women unwilling to run mimeograph machines of not being sufficiently devoted to the cause. As for child care centers, he felt their effect of allowing women to compete with men for jobs was part of the "feminization" of the American male and American culture. "He sounds just like my husband," said one of the white-gloved women, "only he wants me to have bake-sales and collect door-to-door for his Republican Party."

The young women had sense enough to take it from there. What did boots or white gloves matter if they were all getting treated like servants and children? Before they broke up, they were discussing the myth of the vaginal orgasm and planning to meet every week. "Men think we're whatever it is we do for men," complained one of the housewives. "It's only by getting together with other women that we'll ever find out who we are."

Gloria Steinem, "Sisterhood," *Ms.* magazine (Spring 1972), p. 49. Reprinted by permission.

National Organization for Women for Women (NOW). In arguing that "sexism" was much like racism, they persuaded President Johnson in 1967 to include women along with African Americans, Hispanics, and other minorities as a group covered by federal affirmative action programs.

Many social trends in American society gave women more freedom in their lives, both to work outside the home and to control their individual destinies. After 1957 the birthrate began a rapid decline; improved methods of contraception, such as the birth control pill, permitted smaller families. By 1970 more than 40 percent of all women, an unprecedented number, were employed outside the home.

The creation of *Ms.* magazine in 1972 gave feminists a means to reach a broader audience. The cover of its first issue used the image of a many-armed Hindu goddess to satirize the many roles of the modern housewife.

Education also spurred the shift from home to the job market, since higher educational levels allowed women to enter an economy oriented increasingly to white-collar service industries rather than blue-collar manufacturing.

Equal Rights and Abortion

As its influence grew, the feminist movement translated women's grievances into a political agenda. In 1967 NOW proclaimed a "Bill of Rights" that called for maternity leave for working mothers, federally supported day-care facilities, child-care tax deductions, and equal education and job training. But feminists divided on two other issues: the passage of an Equal Rights Amendment to the Constitution and a repeal of state antiabortion laws.

At first, support seemed strong for an Equal Rights Amendment that forbade all discrimination on the basis of gender. In 1972 both the House and

ERA and Roe v. Wade

the Senate passed the Equal Rights Amendment (ERA) virtually without opposition. Within a year 28 of the necessary 38 states had approved the ERA. It seemed only a matter of time before 10 more state legislatures would complete its ratification. Many in the women's movement also applauded the Supreme Court's decision, in *Roe v. Wade* (1973), to strike down 46 state laws restricting a woman's access to abortion. In his opinion for the majority, Justice Harry Blackmun observed that a woman in the nineteenth century had "enjoyed a substantially broader right to terminate a pregnancy than she does in most states today." As legal abortion in the first three months of pregnancy became more readily available, the rate of maternal deaths from illegal operations, especially among minorities, declined.

But the early success of the Equal Rights Amendment and the feminist triumph in *Roe v. Wade* masked underlying divisions among women's groups. *Roe*

Women divided *v. Wade* triggered a sharp backlash from many Catholics, Protestant fundamentalists, and socially conservative women. Their opposition inspired a crusade for a "right to life" amendment to the Constitution. A similar conservative reaction breathed new life into the "STOP ERA" crusade of Phyllis Schlafly, an Illinois political organizer. Although Schlafly was a professional working woman herself, she believed that women should embrace their traditional role as homemakers subordinate to their husbands. "Every change [that the ERA] requires will deprive women of a right, benefit, or exemption that they now enjoy," she argued.

In the middle ground stood women (and a considerable number of men) who wanted to use the political system, rather than a constitutional amendment, to correct the most glaring inequalities between the sexes. Within a year after Congress passed the ERA, the National Women's Political Caucus conceded that the momentum to ratify was waning. Although Congress in 1979 extended the deadline for state legislatures to act for another three years, it became clear that the amendment would fail. Determined feminists vowed to continue the fight, but they too had discovered the limits of the 1970s.

The environmental, consumer, and feminist movements may have lost ground after the early 1970s, but that is not to say they failed. Rather, each cru-

The activist legacy sade fell short in its effort to forge a consensus. There would be no sweeping new ecological consciousness, no consumer-directed economy, and no absolute gender equality. Indeed, none of the movements could ever agree on just what those ideas should mean in practice. But the advocates of reform had created new organizations, like NOW and Friends of the Earth, that became regular and active players in the political process. Within government the Environmental Protection Agency, the Federal Trade Commission, and other agencies had been given a mandate to enforce the court decisions and reform legislation. In that way these social movements had renewed the activist tradition of progressivism and the New Deal.

POLITICAL LIMITS: WATERGATE

To Richard Nixon, his 1972 reelection offered sweet revenge. In 49 of the 50 states he had defeated George McGovern, the candidate of liberal environmentalists, consumer advocates, feminists, and the youthful counterculture. Yet while Nixon sought to stem the liberal tide, he continued to concentrate federal power away from Congress and the Court and more in an "imperial presidency." That trend had been under way since the early twentieth century, but the cold war with its sense of ongoing crisis had accelerated the shift.

The President's Enemies

Encouraged by his victory, Nixon determined to use the power of his office even more broadly. The president wanted to destroy the radical counterculture that he saw as a menace to American society. Members of his staff began compiling an "enemies list"—including everyone from CBS correspondent Daniel Schorr to actress and antiwar activist Jane Fonda. Some on the list were targeted for audits by the Internal Revenue Service or similar harassment.

Then in June 1971 the *New York Times* published a secret, often highly critical military study of the Vietnam War, soon dubbed the Pentagon Papers.

The plumbers   Nixon was so irate he authorized his aide John Ehrlichman to organize a team known as "the plumbers" to find and plug security leaks. The government prosecuted Daniel Ellsberg, the disillusioned official who had leaked the Pentagon Papers. The plumbers also went outside the law: they illegally burglarized the office of Ellsberg's psychiatrist in hopes of finding personally damaging material.

When Congress passed a number of programs Nixon opposed, he simply refused to spend the appropriated money. Some members of Congress claimed

Impoundment   that the practice, called impoundment, violated the president's constitutional duty to execute the laws of the land. By 1973 Nixon had used impoundment to cut some $15 billion out of more than 100 federal programs. The courts eventually ruled that impoundment was illegal. But the president continued his campaign to consolidate power and reshape the more liberal social policies of Congress to his own liking.

Conviction of the need for firm action in a crisis, suspicion of his "enemies" —such traits made it easier for Richard Nixon to break or bend the rules in the service of what he believed was a good cause. In the end, his refusal to acknowledge the limits of power brought him down.

Break-In

Nixon's fall began with what seemed a minor event. In June 1972 burglars entered the Democratic National Committee headquarters, located in Washington's plush Watergate apartment complex. The *Washington Post* assigned this routine story to a couple of cub reporters, Bob Woodward and Carl Bernstein. But the five burglars proved an unusual lot. They wore business suits, carried walkie-talkies as well as bugging devices and tear-gas guns, and had more than $2000 in crisp new hundred-dollar bills. One of the burglars had worked for the CIA. Another was carrying an address book whose phone numbers included that of a Howard Hunt at the "W. House."

Woodward and Bernstein sensed that this was no simple break-in. When Woodward called the mysterious "W. House" number, he discovered that Hunt

A "third rate burglary"

was indeed a White House consultant. Nixon's press secretary dismissed the break-in as "a third rate burglary attempt" and warned that "certain elements may try to stretch this beyond what it is." In August, Nixon himself announced that after a thorough investigation, White House counsel John Dean had concluded that "no one on the White House staff . . . was involved in this very bizarre incident. What really hurts in matters of this sort is not the fact that they occur," the president continued. "What really hurts is if you try to cover up."

Matters were not so easily settled, however. Woodward and Bernstein traced some of the burglars' money back to the Nixon reelection campaign, which had a secret "slush fund" to pay for projects to harass the Democrats. The dirty tricks included forged letters, false news leaks, and spying on Democratic campaign workers. But by election time, Woodward and Bernstein had run out of fresh leads.

To the Oval Office

In January 1973 the five burglars plus former White House aides E. Howard Hunt, Jr., and G. Gordon Liddy went on trial before Judge John Sirica. Sirica, a no-nonsense judge tagged with the nickname "Maximum John," was not satisfied with the defendants' guilty plea. He wanted to know whether anyone else had directed the burglars and why "these hundred dollar bills were floating around like coupons."

Facing a stiff jail sentence, one of the Watergate burglars cracked. He admitted that other government officials had been involved, that the defendants had been bribed to plead guilty, and that they had perjured themselves. The White House then announced on April 17 that all previous administration statements on the Watergate scandal had become "inoperative." Soon after, the president accepted the resignations of his two closest aides, H. R. Haldeman and John Ehrlichman. He also fired John Dean, his White House counsel, after Dean agreed to cooperate with prosecutors.

Over the summer of 1973 a string of administration officials testified at televised Senate hearings. Each witness took the trail of the burglary and its

Senate hearings

cover-up higher into White House circles. Then White House counsel John Dean gave his testimony. Young, with a Boy Scout's face, Dean declared in a quiet monotone that the president had personally been involved in the cover-up as recently as April. The testimony stunned the nation. Still, it remained Dean's word against the president's— until Senate committee staff discovered, almost by chance, that since 1970 Nixon had been secretly recording all conversations and phone calls in the Oval Office. The reliability of Dean's testimony was no longer central, for the tapes could tell all.

Obtaining that evidence proved no easy task. In an effort to restore confidence in the White House, Nixon agreed to the appointment of a special

Special prosecutor

prosecutor, Harvard law professor Archibald Cox, to investigate the new Watergate disclosures. When Cox subpoenaed the tapes, the president refused to turn them over, citing executive privilege and matters of national security. The courts, however, overruled this position.

As that battle raged and the astonished public wondered if matters could possibly get worse, they did. Evidence unrelated to Watergate revealed that Vice President Spiro Agnew had systematically solicited bribes, not just as governor of Maryland but while serving in Washington. To avoid jail, he agreed to resign the vice presidency in October and to plead no contest to a single charge of federal income tax evasion. Under provisions of the Twenty-Fifth Amendment, Nixon appointed Representative Gerald R. Ford of Michigan to replace Agnew.

Meanwhile, when Special Prosecutor Cox demanded the tapes, the president offered to submit written summaries instead. Cox no longer had any reason to trust the president and rejected the offer. On Saturday night, October 20, Nixon ordered Attorney General Elliot Richardson to fire Cox. Rather than comply, Richardson and his deputy secretary both resigned, leaving the third in command to do the dirty work. Reaction to the "Saturday Night Massacre" was overwhelming: 150,000 telegrams poured into Washington, and by the following Tuesday, 84 House members had sponsored 16 different bills of impeachment. The beleaguered president agreed to hand over the tapes. And he appointed Texas lawyer Leon Jaworski as a new special prosecutor. By April 1974, Jaworski's investigations led him to request additional tapes. Again the president refused, although he grudgingly supplied some 1200 pages of typed transcripts of the tapes.

"Saturday Night Massacre"

Even the transcripts damaged the president's case. Littered with cynicism and profanity, they revealed Nixon talking with his counsel John Dean about how to "take care of the jackasses who are in jail." When Dean estimated it might take a million dollars to shut them up, Nixon replied, "We could get that. . . . You could get a million dollars. And you could get it in cash. I know where it could be gotten." When the matter of perjury came up, Nixon suggested a way out: "You can say, 'I don't remember.' You can say, 'I can't recall.'"

Even those devastating revelations did not produce the "smoking gun" demanded by the president's defenders. When Special Prosecutor Jaworski petitioned the Supreme Court to order release of additional tapes, the Court in *United States v. Nixon* ruled unanimously in Jaworski's favor.

United States v. Nixon

Resignation

The end came quickly. The House Judiciary Committee adopted three articles of impeachment, charging that Nixon had obstructed justice, had abused his constitutional authority in improperly using federal agencies to harass citizens, and had hindered the committee's investigation.

The tapes produced the smoking gun. Conversations with Haldeman on June 23, 1972, only a few days after the break-in, showed that Nixon knew the

The smoking gun

burglars were tied to the White House staff and knew that his attorney general had acted to limit an FBI investigation. Not willing to be the first president convicted in a Senate impeachment trial, Nixon resigned on August 8, 1974. The following day Gerald Ford became president. "The Constitution works," Ford told a relieved nation. "Our long national nightmare is over."

Had the system worked? In one sense, yes. The wheels of justice had turned, even if slowly. For the first time a president had been forced to leave office. Four cabinet officers, including Attorney General John Mitchell, the highest law officer in the nation, were convicted of crimes. Twenty-five Nixon aides eventually served prison terms ranging from 25 days to more than 4 years. Yet the corrupt compaign practices that financed Watergate continue to plague the political system. The system works, as the Founding Fathers understood, only when citizens and public servants respect the limits of government power.

A FORD, NOT A LINCOLN

Gerald Ford inherited a presidential office badly diminished by the Watergate scandals. As the first unelected president, he had no popular mandate. He was little known outside Washington and his home district around Grand Rapids, Michigan. Ford's success as the House minority leader came from personal popularity, political reliability, and party loyalty, qualities that suited a member of Congress better than an unelected president.

Yet Ford's easy manner and modest approach to government came as a relief after the mercurial styles of Johnson and Nixon. By all instincts a conservative, Ford was determined to continue Nixon's foreign policy of cautious détente and a domestic program of social and fiscal conservatism.

Kissinger and Foreign Policy

As Nixon's star fell, that of Secretary of State and National Security Advisor Henry Kissinger rose. Kissinger viewed himself as a realist, a man for whom order and stability were more important than principle. Quoting the German writer Goethe, he acknowledged, "If I had to choose between justice and disorder, on the one hand, and injustice and order on the other, I would always choose the latter."

Kissinger had struggled to prevent Vietnam and Watergate from eroding the president's power to conduct foreign policy. He believed Congress was too

War Powers Act

sensitive to public opinion and special-interest groups to pursue consistent long-term policies. But after Vietnam congressional leaders were eager to curtail presidential powers. The War Powers Act of 1973 required the president to consult Congress whenever possible before committing troops, to send an explanation for his actions within 2 days, and to withdraw any troops after 60 days unless Congress voted to retain them. Such limits often led Kissinger to take a covert approach to foreign policy, as he did in an attempt to quell political ferment in Chile.

In 1970 Chile ranked as one of South America's few viable democracies. When a coalition of Socialists, Communists, and radicals elected Salvador

Overthrow of Allende

Allende Gossens as president that year, the Central Intelligence Agency viewed his victory as dangerous to the United States. To drive Allende from power, Kissinger resorted to economic pressure, bribery of the Chilean congress, and the encouragement of a military coup. By 1973 a conservative Chilean coalition with CIA backing had driven the Socialists from power, attacked the presidential palace, and murdered Allende. Kissinger argued that the United States had the right to destroy this democracy because Communists themselves threatened an even longer-term dictatorship.

Economic Limits and American Diplomacy

Kissinger recognized that a weakening economy limited American ability to dominate the affairs of the non-Communist world. That weakness came not merely from the soaring inflation generated by the Vietnam War and Johnson's Great Society programs. Key American industries were crippled by inefficient production, products of poor quality, and high wages. They faced mounting competition from more efficient manufacturers in Europe and in nations along the Pacific rim, such as Japan, South Korea, and Taiwan. Reacting to these changes, American-based multinational corporations moved high-wage jobs overseas to take advantage of lower costs and cheap labor. The AFL–CIO complained that the United States would soon become "a country stripped of industrial capacity . . . , a nation of citizens busily buying and selling cheeseburgers and root beer floats."

War in the Middle East soon made inflation at home even worse. On October 6, 1973, Syria and Egypt launched a devastating surprise attack against

Yom Kippur War and the energy crisis

Israel, on the Jewish holy day of Yom Kippur. The Soviet Union airlifted supplies to the Arabs; the United States countered by re-supplying its Israeli allies while pressing the two sides to accept a cease-fire. The seven Arab members of the Organization of Petroleum Exporting Countries (OPEC) imposed a boycott of oil sales to countries seen as friendly to Israel. Lasting from October 1973 until March 1974, the boycott staggered the economies of Western Europe and Japan, which imported 80 to 90 percent of their oil from the Middle East.

The United States, too, was far more dependent on foreign oil than most Americans had appreciated. With just 7 percent of the world's population, the United States consumed about 30 percent of its energy. In November 1973

President Nixon warned the nation, "We are heading toward the most acute shortage of energy since World War II." Americans felt the crunch in every aspect of their lives. In some places motorists hoping to buy a few gallons of gas waited for hours in lines miles long.

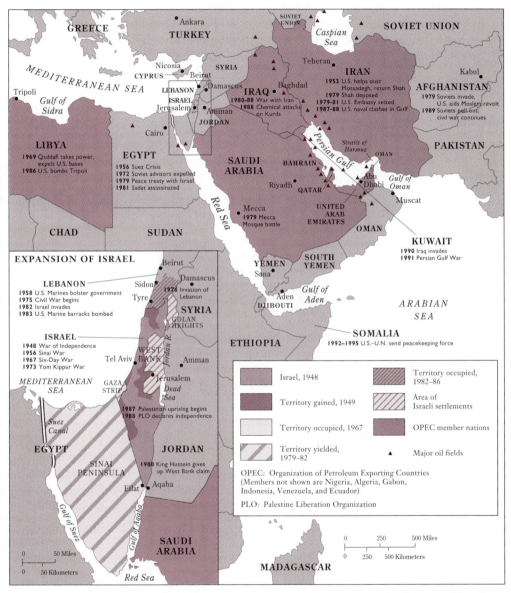

OIL AND CONFLICT IN THE MIDDLE EAST, 1948–1995 With so much of the world's oil supply coming from the Middle East, political stability in the region is vital to the health of the global economy. Yet the conflict between Israel and the Arab states, the regional political unrest, and the cold war rivalry after World War II have all contributed to the area's chronic instability.

Kissinger sought economic relief at home by promoting stability in the Middle East. If the Arab states saw the United States as neutral in their conflict with Israel, they would be less likely to resort to future oil blackmail. And as American prestige rose, Kissinger could move to reduce Soviet influence in the region. Egypt's President Anwar Sadat had recently expelled 10,000 Russian advisers from his country. From January to April 1974 Kissinger intermittently flew back and forth in "shuttle diplomacy" between Sadat's government in Cairo and the Israeli government in Jerusalem. He persuaded Israel to withdraw its troops from the west bank of the Suez Canal and arranged a disengagement between Israel and Syria in the Golan Heights.

Still, Kissinger's whirlwind efforts could not stem the erosion of American power. By the spring of 1975, the American-backed government in South Vietnam faced certain defeat at the hands of North Vietnam. President Ford asked Congress for $1 billion in aid to South Vietnam, Cambodia, and Laos, but Congress refused to spend money on a lost cause. As North Vietnamese forces marched into Saigon in April, desperate South Vietnamese civilian and military leaders rushed to escape Communist retribution.

South Vietnam falls

Détente

Vietnam, Chile, the Yom Kippur War, and other crises demonstrated that the spirit of détente had not ended the rivalry between the Soviets and the Americans to win influence in the Third World. Seeking to ease tensions, Ford met with Soviet leader Leonid Brezhnev in November 1974. Since economic stagnation also dogged the Soviet Union, Brezhnev came to this summit, in Vladivostok, eager for more American trade. Ford and Kissinger wanted a limit on nuclear weapons that preserved the current American advantage. Though many issues could not be resolved, the two sides agreed in principle to a framework for a second Strategic Arms Limitation Treaty.

A similar hope to extend détente brought Ford and Brezhnev together with European leaders at Helsinki, Finland, in August 1975. There they agreed to recognize the political boundaries that had divided Eastern and Western Europe since 1945. For the first time the United States sent an ambassador to East Germany. In return Brezhnev eased restrictions on the rights of Soviet Jews to emigrate.

Helsinki summit

The Limits of a Post-Watergate President

After only a month in office Gerald Ford granted Richard Nixon a pardon for any crimes he had committed during Watergate. That attempt to put the scandals in the past only managed to reopen the wounds. Pardon meant no prosecution of the former president, leaving charges unanswered and crimes unpun-

After having won a Nobel Peace Prize in 1973 for his role in ending the Vietnam War, Henry Kissinger (left) entered the Ford administration as something of a hero. But his efforts to improve relations with the Soviet Union by strengthening détente aroused the ire of the Republican right wing, while liberals accused Kissinger of being too secretive and friendly to dictators. Here, he briefs President Ford on a train, on the way to a 1974 summit meeting in Vladivostok in the Soviet Union.

ished. The move was especially controversial because at the same time, Ford refused to provide any similar full pardon to draft resisters from the Vietnam War. (He did offer a conditional amnesty, but only after review by a government panel. Most resisters rejected the offer.)

If Ford was willing to forgive and forget presidential sins, Congress was not, especially after reports surfaced of misconduct by the nation's intelligence agen-

Intelligence abuses

cies. Investigations revealed that the CIA had routinely violated its charter by spying on American citizens at home. It had opened private mail, infiltrated domestic protest organizations—even conducted experiments on unwitting subjects using the hallucinogenic drug LSD. Abroad, the CIA had been involved in the assassination or attempted murder of foreign leaders in Cuba, Chile, South Vietnam, the Dominican Republic, and the Congo. The FBI had also used illegal means to infiltrate and disrupt domestic dissidents, including an attempt by J. Edgar Hoover to drive Martin Luther King to suicide. In an effort to bring the executive branch under control, the Senate created an oversight committee to monitor the intelligence agencies.

Fighting Inflation

By the time Ford gave Congress his first State of the Union message in January 1975, he faced twin scourges: inflation and recession. Inflation had climbed to almost 14 percent, and unemployment exceeded 7 percent. At the heart of the economic crisis lay rising energy costs. Imports of Middle Eastern oil were needed to supply the nation's increasing thirst for energy. The price of that oil had jumped from $2 to almost $14 a barrel.

Recession

The 1975 Energy Policy and Conservation Act authorized the Federal Energy Administration to order utilities to burn abundant (though more polluting) coal rather than expensive oil. In addition, the act ordered the auto industry to improve the energy efficiency of the engines it produced. And as a final—but environmentally dangerous—stopgap measure, the government encouraged the rapid development of nuclear power plants.

Energy policy

The energy-driven recession struck hardest at the older industrial centers of the Northeast and Upper Midwest, which imported most of their energy. Housing and plants built in the days of cheap energy proved wasteful and inefficient. Nixon's and Ford's cutbacks in federal spending fell hardest on major cities with shrinking tax bases, outmoded industries, and heavy social service costs. The crisis for "rust belt" cities came to a head in October 1975, when New York City announced that it faced bankruptcy. New York's plight reflected the wrenching adjustments Americans faced in an era of economic limits.

The Election of 1976

In the 1976 presidential campaign the greatest debates occurred within rather than between the major parties. Ford's challenge came from former California governor, movie actor, and television pitchman Ronald Reagan. The polished Reagan won crowds with an uncompromising but amiable conservatism, and Ford barely squeaked by Reagan to win the nomination.

Before 1976 few Democrats had ever heard of presidential hopeful James Earl (Jimmy) Carter. That allowed Carter, a peanut farmer and former governor of Georgia, to run as a Washington outsider, an advantage after the Watergate scandals. As a southerner and a born-again Christian he appealed to many voters who had recently left the Democratic party.

Since both candidates rejected Great Society activism, party loyalty determined the outcome. Most voters backed their party's candidate, giving Carter 50.1 percent of the vote. Carter's overwhelming margin among African Americans (90 percent) carried the South and offset Ford's margin among white voters, especially in the western states. Resounding Democratic majorities in Congress indicated more accurately than the presidential race how much the weak economy had hurt Ford's campaign.

Jimmy Carter

JIMMY CARTER: RESTORING THE FAITH

Jimmy Carter looked to invest the White House with a new simplicity and directness. Rather than the usual Inauguration Day ride down Pennsylvania Avenue in the presidential limousine, the new president and his wife Rosalynn walked. He shunned the formal morning coat and tails for a business suit. But Congress too was determined to see that the executive branch would no longer be so imperial. Because the president and many of his staff were relative newcomers, Carter found his program stymied by Washington's special-interest politics.

The Search for Direction

Carter struggled, often unsuccessfully, to give his presidency a clear sense of direction. Although the president was able to absorb tremendous amounts of information, too often he focused on details. That left his larger goals obscure. Carter's key appointments reflected this confusion. In foreign policy, for

The support of African Americans proved critical to Carter's victory in 1976.
Here he and his wife Rosalynn worship with Coretta Scott King,
Andrew Young, and other black leaders.

example, a rivalry arose between National Security Advisor Zbigniew Brzezinski and Secretary of State Cyrus Vance. Brzezinski harbored the staunch cold warrior's preoccupation with containing the Communist menace. Vance believed negotiations with the Communist bloc were both possible and potentially profitable. Stronger economic ties would reduce the risk of superpower conflict. Carter gravitated in both directions.

The President found that it was no easy task to make government more efficient, responsive to the people, and ethical. His first push for efficiency—a call for the elimination of 19 expensive pork-barrel water projects—angered many in Congress, including the leaders of his own party. They promptly threatened to bury his legislative program. Even the weather seemed to conspire against Carter, when the winter of 1976–1977 proved to be one of the most severe in modern history. Supplies of heating fuels dwindled, and prices shot up. Like Ford, Carter preferred voluntary restraint to mandatory rules for conserving energy and controlling fuel costs. The nation had to adopt energy conservation measures as the "moral equivalent of war," he announced in April 1977.

The President correctly sensed that conservation was the cheapest, most practical way to reduce dependence on foreign oil. But homilies about "helping our neighbors" did not persuade Congress. Most controversial were new taxes to discourage wasteful consumption. The American way, as domestic oil producers were quick to argue, was to produce more, not to live *Department of Energy* with less. Most Americans were too wedded to gas-guzzling cars, air conditioners, and warm houses to accept limits as long as fuel was available. Although Congress did agree to establish a cabinet-level Department of Energy, it rejected most of Carter's energy program.

By 1978 the "moral equivalent of war" was sounding more like its acronym: MEOW. Renewed administration efforts resulted in a weak National Energy Act of modest tax incentives and deregulation of natural gas prices. As a result, the nation was ill-prepared for the dislocation in international oil markets that followed the 1978 revolution against the shah of Iran. Oil shortages allowed OPEC to raise prices nearly 15 percent. Carter could only complain that such hikes were unfair while asking Americans to lower thermostats to 65 degrees, take only essential car trips, and "drive 55."

Many Americans saw nuclear energy as the best alternative. But on March 28, 1979, a valve stuck in the cooling system of the Three Mile Island nuclear *Three Mile Island* power plant near Harrisburg, Pennsylvania. A cloud of radioactive gas floated into the atmosphere, and for a time, officials worried that the plant's nuclear fuels might overheat, causing a meltdown of the reactor core. About 100,000 nearby residents fled their homes. The debate that followed revealed that public utilities had often constructed nuclear power plants before installing adequate safeguards or solving the problem of where to dispose of the nuclear radioactive wastes produced by the plants. By the time of the accident at Three Mile Island, many energy experts believed that nuclear plants were at best a temporary response to the nation's long-term needs.

A Sick Economy

Long lines at the gas pumps were a symbol of a sick economy built on cheap energy. As OPEC hiked prices inflation shot from just below 6 percent in 1976 to almost 14 percent by 1979. Other factors also helped drive up the price of goods and services, including higher minimum wages, import protection for key industries like steel, and new social security taxes. So too did declines in the productivity of American labor, where output for each workhour kept dropping. And as productivity dropped, so did the competitiveness of American industry in world markets.

"Hard choices" were needed to restore the economy to health, the *Wall Street Journal* argued. That might mean higher taxes and cuts in popular programs like social security or subsidy payments to farmers. Yet Carter called only for voluntary restraints on prices and wages, while seeking to restore the strength of the dollar in international trade. But even before the president's economic remedies could be tried, OPEC raised the price of oil again. Energy costs rose almost 60 percent. Interest rates shot up to almost 20 percent. Such high rates struck hard at American consumers addicted to buying on credit. Mortgage money disappeared. With the Federal Reserve raising interest rates to dampen inflation, the recession grew worse. As the economy slumped, so did Carter's political future. At the same time he found himself bedeviled by crises abroad.

Leadership, Not Hegemony

Carter approached foreign policy with a set of ambitious, yet reasonable, goals. Like Nixon and Kissinger, he accepted the fact that in a postcolonial world, American influence could not be heavy-handed. The United *Human rights* States had to exert "leadership without hegemony." Unlike Nixon and Kissinger, Carter believed that a knee-jerk fear of Soviet ambition had led Americans to support too many right-wing dictators, simply because they claimed to be anti-Communist. Carter reasserted the nation's moral purpose by giving a higher priority to preserving human rights.

Though this policy was often jeered at by foreign policy "realists," it did make a difference. At least one Argentinian Nobel Peace Prize winner, Adolfo Pérez Esquivel, claimed he owed his life to it. So did hundreds of others in countries like the Philippines, South Korea, Argentina, and Chile, where dissidents were routinely tortured and murdered. The Carter administration exerted economic pressures to promote more humane policies.

Debate over American influence in the Third World soon focused on the Panama Canal, long a symbol of American intervention in Latin America. Most *Panama Canal* Americans were under the impression that the United States owned the canal—or if it didn't, at least deserved to. Senator S. I. Hayakawa of California spoke for defenders of the American imperial tradition when he argued, "It's ours. We stole it fair and square." In reality the

United States held sovereignty over a 10-mile-wide strip called the Canal Zone and administered the canal under a perpetual lease. Since the 1960s Panamanians had resented, and sometimes rioted against, the American presence. Secretary of State Vance believed conciliation would reduce anti-American sentiment in the region. He convinced Carter in 1977 to sign treaties that would return the canal to Panama by 1999. The United States did reserve the right to defend and use the waterway.

From 1979 on, however, it was not Vance but National Security Advisor Zbigniew Brzezinski who dominated the administration's foreign policy.

Brzezinski in charge Brzezinski preferred a hard-line anti-Communist approach, even in Latin America. Unrest troubled all the region's struggling nations, especially Nicaragua. Its dictator, Anastasio Somoza, proved so corrupt and greedy that he alienated the normally conservative propertied classes. The United States, at Brzezinski's urging, continued to support Somoza, but with cooperation from Nicaragua's business leaders, the Sandinistas toppled him. They then rejected American aid in favor of a nonaligned status and closer ties to Cuba. Hard-line American anti-Communists grew especially alarmed when the Sandinistas began supplying leftist rebels in neighboring El Salvador. To contain the threat, Carter agreed to assist the brutal right-wing dictatorship in El Salvador while encouraging the overthrow of the leftist government in Nicaragua.

Saving Détente

The United States was not the only superpower with a flagging economy and problems in the Third World. The Soviet Union struggled with an aging leadership and an economy that produced guns but little butter. Even though the Russians led the world in oil production, income from rising oil prices was drained off by an inefficient economy. Support for impoverished allies in Eastern Europe, Cuba, and Vietnam and attempts to extend Soviet influence in the Middle East and Africa proved costly.

Economic weakness made the Soviets receptive to greater cooperation with the United States. In that spirit President Carter and Soviet premier Leonid Brezhnev in 1977 issued a joint statement on a Middle East peace. But domestic opposition to any Soviet role as a peacemaker in the Middle East was immediate and powerful. Carter quickly rendered his understanding with Brezhnev inoperative.

A revived China card The Soviets then renewed arms shipments to Israel's archenemy, Syria. And in that troubled environment, Zbigniew Brzezinski flew off to Beijing to revive the "China card": Kissinger's old hope of playing the two Communist superpowers against each other. The United States extended formal recognition to China in 1979, and trade doubled within a year.

For the Russians the China card was a blow to détente. A potential Japanese–Chinese–American alliance threatened their Asian border. In an attempt to save détente Brezhnev met Carter at Vienna in 1979. Following through on the summit with President Ford, their talks produced an arms con-

SALT II

trol treaty—SALT II—to limit nuclear launchers and missiles with multiple warheads (MIRVs). But neither the Americans nor the Soviets would agree to scrap key weapons systems. Conservative critics saw the SALT agreements as another example of the bankruptcy of détente. Nuclear "parity" (an equal balance of weapons on the American and the Soviet sides) was to them yet another insulting symbol of declining American power. They successfully blocked ratification of the treaty in the Senate.

Such hostility to détente caused Carter to adopt Brzezinski's harder line. Confrontation and a military buildup replaced the Vance policy of negotiation and accommodation. The president expanded the defense budget, built American bases in the Persian Gulf region, and sent aid to anti-Communist dictators whatever their record on human rights. The Soviet Union responded with similar hostility.

The Middle East: Hope and Hostages

What the unstable Balkans were to Europe before World War I, the Middle East promised to be for the superpowers in the 1970s and 1980s. Oil and the Soviets' nearby southern border gave the area its geopolitical importance. The United States had strong ties to oil-rich Saudi Arabia, a commitment to the survival of Israel, and a determination to prevent the Soviet Union from extending its influence into the area. That commitment was tested each time war broke out between Israel and its Arab neighbors in 1948, 1956, 1967, and 1973.

Preservation of the peace was one key to American policy. As a result, Americans were greatly encouraged when President Anwar Sadat of Egypt

Camp David accords

made an unprecedented trip to Israel to meet with Prime Minister Menachem Begin. To encourage the peace process, Carter invited Begin and Sadat to Camp David in September 1978. After 13 difficult days of heated debate, Carter brought the two archrivals to an agreement. Israel agreed to withdraw from the Sinai peninsula, which it had occupied since defeating Egypt in 1967; Carter compensated Israel by offering $3 billion in military aid. Begin and Sadat shared a Nobel Peace Prize that might just as fairly have gone to Carter.

The shah of Iran, with his American-equipped military forces, was another key to American hopes for stability in the Middle East. A strong Iran, after all,

The Iranian Revolution

blocked Soviet access to the Persian Gulf and its oil. But in the autumn of 1978, the shah's regime was challenged by Iranian Islamic fundamentalists. They objected to the Western influences flooding their country, especially the tens of thousands of American advisers. Brzezinski urged Carter to support the shah with troops if necessary; Vance recommended meetings with the revolutionary leaders, distance from the shah, and military restraint.

Carter waffled between the two approaches. He encouraged the shah to use force but refused any American participation. When the shah's regime collapsed

Jimmy Carter brought together Israeli Prime Minister Menachem Begin (right) and Egypt's Anwar Sadat (left). Together at Camp David they hammered out a "Framework for Peace in the Middle East."

in February 1979, fundamentalists established an Islamic republic, led by a religious leader, the Ayatollah Ruhollah Khomeini. The new government was particularly outraged when Carter admitted the ailing shah to the United States for cancer treatment. In November student revolutionaries stormed the American embassy in Teheran, occupying it and taking 53 hostages. In the face of this insult the United States seemed helpless to act. Would Muslim Shiite fundamentalists spread their revolution to neighboring Arab states? Worse yet, would the Soviets prey upon a weakened Iran?

In fact, the Soviets were equally worried that religious zeal might spread to their own restless minorities, especially to Muslims within their borders. In December 1979 Leonid Brezhnev ordered Soviet troops to subdue anti-Communist Muslim guerrillas in neighboring Afghanistan. President Carter condemned the invasion, but the actions he took to protest were largely symbolic, especially the decision to withdraw the American team from the 1980 Olympic games in Moscow. And he announced a Carter Doctrine: the United States would intervene unilaterally if the Soviet Union threatened American interests in the Persian Gulf.

U.S.S.R. invasion of Afghanistan

A President Held Hostage

Even more than the 53 Americans in Teheran, the president himself seemed to have been taken hostage by events. His ratings in national polls sank to record lows (77 percent negative). Carter responded by reviving the cold war rhetoric of the 1950s and accelerating the development of nuclear weapons. But where the CIA in 1953 had successfully overthrown an Iranian government, an airborne rescue mission launched in 1980 ended in disaster. Eight Marines died when two helicopters and a plane collided in Iran's central desert. Cyrus Vance, a lonely voice of moderation, finally resigned.

By 1980 the United States was mired in what Carter himself described as "a crisis of confidence." Turmoil in Vietnam, Central America, and the Middle

Crisis of confidence

East produced a nightmare of waning American power. Economic dislocations at home revived fears of a depression. None of these problems had begun with Jimmy Carter. The inflationary cycle and declining American productivity had their roots in the Vietnam era. And ironically, America's declining influence abroad reflected long-term success in bringing economic growth to Europe and the Pacific rim.

In that sense, Carter's failure was largely symbolic. But the uneasiness of the late 1970s reflected a widespread disillusionment with liberal social programs, and even with pragmatic "engineers" like Carter. Had the government become a drag on the American dream? Tom Wolfe's "Me Generation" seemed to be rejecting Carter's appeals to sacrifice. It turned instead to promoters of self-help therapy, fundamentalist defenders of the faith, and staunch conservatives who promised both spiritual and material renewal for the 1980s.

SIGNIFICANT EVENTS

1962 ── Rachel Carson's *Silent Spring* published

1965 ── Ralph Nader's *Unsafe at Any Speed* published

1966 ── National Traffic and Motor Vehicle Safety Act; NOW established

1969 ── *Apollo 11* moon mission; Santa Barbara oil spill; National Environmental Policy Act

1970 ── First Earth Day; Environmental Protection Agency created

1971 ── Barry Commoner's *The Closing Circle* published; *Pentagon Papers* published

1972 ── Congress passes Equal Rights Amendment; Woodward and Bernstein investigate Watergate burglary

1973 ── *Roe v. Wade;* Senate hearings on Watergate; Spiro Agnew resigns; Saturday Night Massacre; OPEC oil boycott triggers U.S. recession

1974 ── *United States v. Nixon;* House adopts articles of impeachment; Nixon resigns; Ford becomes president; Kissinger Arab–Israeli "shuttle diplomacy"; Ford pardons Nixon; CIA and FBI abuses exposed

1975 ── Thieu government falls in South Vietnam; Helsinki summit; Energy Policy and Conservation Act; New York City faces bankruptcy

1976 ── Carter elected president

1977 ── Department of Energy established; Panama Canal treaties signed

1978 ── Revolution in Iran; Camp David meetings on the Middle East

1979 ── Three Mile Island crisis; United States recognizes People's Republic of China; SALT II agreement; Iran hostage crisis; Soviet Union invades Afghanistan

1980 ── Inflation and recession hurt economy; Carter adopts sanctions against the Soviet Union; U.S. hostage mission fails

1982 ── Ratification of ERA fails

CHAPTER THIRTY-THREE

A Nation Still Divisible

I n the early 1970s San Diego city officials looked out at a downtown that was growing seedier each year, as stores and shoppers fled to more than a dozen suburban malls that ringed the city. Nor was San Diego's experience unusual. Across the nation many downtown retail centers were disintegrating, becoming virtual ghost towns at the close of the business day. But San Diego found a way to bounce back. The city launched a $3 billion redevelopment plan, calling for a convention center, a marina, hotels, and apartment complexes.

At the core of the plan was Horton Plaza, an ambitious mall designed to look like a quaint Italian hill town. When it opened in 1985, its stucco facades and Renaissance arches lured customers to upscale stores like Banana Republic, prosperous jewelers, and leisure sporting goods shops. Jugglers and clowns wandered the mall's twisting thoroughfares, while guitarists serenaded passersby. Horton Plaza soon ranked just behind the zoo and Sea World as San Diego's prime tourist attractions.

For all its extravagance, Horton Plaza was hardly an innovation. The first enclosed mall, Southdale Center, had been completed nearly 20 years earlier in Edina, Minnesota, near Minneapolis. With chilling winters and 100 days a year of rain, shopping conditions in Edina were hardly ideal. Southdale provided an alternative: a climate-controlled marketplace where shoppers could browse or get a bite to eat without dodging cars or inhaling exhaust fumes. At first, retailers had worried that customers who couldn't drive by or park in front of their stores wouldn't stop and shop. But the success of the new malls quickly dispelled such fears. By 1985, when Horton Plaza opened, Minnesota's Southdale had expanded to a three-level complex with 144 stores. Nationwide, there were more shopping centers (25,000) than either school districts or hospitals.

With their soaring atriums and splashing fountains, malls became for consumers the cathedrals of American material culture. Shopping on Sunday rivaled churchgoing as the weekly family ritual. Where American youth culture centered on high schools in the 1950s and on college campuses in the 1960s, in the 1970s and 1980s it had gravitated toward mall fast-food stores and video amusement arcades. Older people in search of moderate exercise discovered that the controlled climate was ideal for "mall walking." Malls even had their counterculture: "mall rats" who "hung out" and survived by shoplifting.

Malls as the symbol of an age

The new cathedrals of consumption served as an appropriate symbol of a society that in the 1980s and 1990s turned from protests and crusades to more private paths of spiritual fulfillment. Confronted by an age of limits, some turned to evangelical religion, with its emphasis on the conversion of "born-again" individuals. Others extolled the virtues of the traditional family and lauded private charity and volunteerism as an alternative to activist social policies of a modern welfare state. Along less orthodox paths, the "human potential movement" focused on techniques like yoga, transcendental meditation, and "bioenergetics" to bring spiritual fulfillment.

So it was not surprising, perhaps, that in 1980 Ronald Reagan chose to evoke Puritan John Winthrop's seventeenth-century vision of an American "city on a hill"—that city Winthrop hoped would inspire the rest of the world. For conservatives, the image carried strong religious overtones. The Puritans, after all, sought to create a Christian commonwealth that was both well-ordered and moral. Reagan's vision, of course, had been updated. It embraced nineteenth-century ideals of "manifest destiny." (America should "stand tall," he insisted, as the world's number one military power.) And Reagan affirmed the laissez-faire ideals of the late nineteenth century, encouraging citizens to promote the public good through the pursuit of private wealth. "Government is not the solution to our problem," he asserted. "Government is the problem."

Critics contended that Reagan was no more likely than the Puritans to succeed with his revolution. History, they argued, had shown that private enterprise was unable to prevent or regulate the environmental damage caused by acid rain, oil spills, or toxic waste dumps. Furthermore, a severely limited federal government would prove unable to cope with declining schools, urban violence, or the AIDS epidemic. To many liberals the Reagan agenda amounted to a flight from public responsibility into a fantasy world no more authentic than the Italian hill town nestled in downtown San Diego. John Winthrop's austere vision risked being transformed into a city on a hill with climate control, where the proprietors of Muzak-filled walkways banished all problems beyond the gates of the parking lots.

Yet conservatives in the 1980s and 1990s demonstrated the abiding attraction of their ideals. Although an economic downturn brought the Democrats into the White House in 1992, Republican control of Congress after the elections of 1994 and 1996 kept alive the campaign for a born-again America.

THE CONSERVATIVE REBELLION

In 1964 billboards for conservative candidate Barry Goldwater had proclaimed across America: "In Your Heart You Know He's Right." Beneath one of the billboards an unknown Democratic wag unfurled his own banner: "Yes—Extreme Right." Most citizens voted with the wag, perceiving Goldwater's platform as too conservative, too extreme, too dangerous for the times.

By 1980 rising prices, energy shortages, and similar economic uncertainties fed a growing resistance to a liberal agenda. Hard-pressed workers resented increased competition from minorities, especially those supported

Issues of the 1970s and 1980s

by affirmative action quotas and government programs. Citizens resisted the demands for higher taxes to support social welfare spending. The traditional family, too, seemed under siege, as divorce rates and births to single mothers soared. Sexually explicit media, an outspoken gay rights movement, and the availability of legal abortions struck many religious conservatives as part of a wholesale assault on decency. Increasingly the political agenda was determined by those who wanted to restore a strong family, traditional religious values, patriotism, and limited government.

Born Again

At one center of the conservative rebellion was the call for a revival of religion. It came most insistently from white Protestant evangelicals. Fundamentalist Protestants had since the 1920s increasingly separated themselves from the older, more liberal denominations. In the decades after World War II their membership grew dramatically—anywhere from 400 to 700 percent, compared with less than 90 percent for main-line denominations. By the 1980s they had become a significant third force in Christian America, after Roman Catholics and traditional Protestants. The election of Jimmy Carter, himself a born-again Christian, reflected their newfound visibility.

Like fundamentalists of the 1920s, the evangelicals of the 1980s resisted the trend toward more secular ideas, especially in education. They pressed states

Evangelicals

and the federal government to adopt a "school prayer" amendment allowing officially sanctioned prayer in classrooms. They urged the teaching of "creationism" as an alternative to Darwinian evolution. Frustrated with public schools, they created private Christian academies to insulate their children from the influence of "secular humanism." Fundamentalists applied this term to the modernist notions of a materially determined world in which all truths were relative and in which circumstances rather than moral precepts determined ethical behavior.

Although evangelicals condemned the secularism of the modern media, they used broadcast technology to sell their message. Cable and satellite broadcasting brought "televangelists" to national audiences. The Reverend Pat Robertson introduced his "700 Club" over the Christian Broadcast Network from Virginia Beach, Virginia. Another "700 Club" regular, Jim Bakker, launched a spinoff program called the "Praise the Lord Club"—PTL for short. Within a few years PTL had the largest audience of any daily show in the world.

But it was the Reverend Jerry Falwell, spiritual leader of the Thomas Road Baptist Church in Lynchburg, Virginia, who first made the step from religious to political activism. In 1979 Falwell formed the Moral Majority, Inc., an organization to attract campaign contributions and examine candidates around the country on issues important to Christians. In the 1980 election the Moral Majority sent out more than a billion pieces of mail in an attempt to unseat liberals in Congress.

The Moral Majority

The Catholic Conscience

American Catholics faced their own decisions about the lines between religion and politics. In the 1960s Catholic social activism reflected a movement that had arisen out of the church council known as Vatican II (1962–1965). The council sought to revitalize the church and to reappraise its role in the modern world. The reforms of Vatican II invited greater participation by ordinary church members and encouraged closer ties to other Christians and to Jews.

Disturbed by these currents, Catholic conservatives found support for their views when the magnetic John Paul II became pope in 1979. Pope John Paul reined in the modern trends inspired by Vatican II. The pope resisted a wider role for women and stiffened Church policy against birth control. That put him at odds on such issues with a majority of American Catholics.

Catholic conservatism

Though conservative Catholics and Protestant evangelicals were sometimes wary of one another, they shared certain views. Both groups lobbied the government to provide federal aid to parochial schools and fundamentalist academies. And on the issue of abortion, Pope John Paul reaffirmed the church's teaching that all life began at conception, so that any abortion amounted to the murder of the unborn. Evangelicals, long suspicious of the power of secular technology and science, attacked abortion as another instance in which science had upset the natural moral order of life.

COUNTERPOINT   *Defining the New Conservatism*

It is not an easy task to pinpoint the wellsprings of the conservative rebellion. Some analysts, focusing on the movement's political leadership, have viewed matters cynically. They argue that Ronald Reagan, George Bush, and other Republican leaders are simply members of the established business elite, who have tapped the resentments of ordinary people in order to provide others of their class with tax and regulatory relief. "Hot button" issues like school prayer, abortion, and gun control can be used "as a means to ignite people who do not normally support Republicans," in the words of one conservative political

Many conservative Christians adopted the militant style of 1960s radicals to protest issues like abortion. Here they clash with pro-choice demonstrators outside Faneuil Hall in Boston.

adviser. Such an analysis emphasizes the differences within the conservative movement. On the one side, libertarians and free-enterprising businessmen would keep the government out of regulating public morals as well as out of regulating the economy. On the other side, cultural conservatives urge the government to take an active role in restoring morality.

Other historians stress the cultural roots that unite conservatives: the rejection of a liberalism that brought activism to government and a secular perspective to society at large. Conservatives of all stripes, one can argue, uphold the values of a purer, idealized past, one free from government interference and invigorated by a clear moral order. In 1955, when William F. Buckley, Jr., began his conservative magazine, *National Review*, he proclaimed it his job to "stand athwart History and shout Stop!" In the eyes of some historians, it is this fixation on a past—an idealized one, at that—that unites the new right. "People became conservatives," suggested one analyst, "when they experienced 'the horrible feeling' that a society they took for granted might suddenly cease to exist."

The Media as Battleground

Both evangelists and political conservatives viewed the mass media as an establishment that was politically liberal and morally permissive. Certainly by the 1980s American popular culture had come to portray sex and violence more explicitly than ever, as well as to treat openly such sensitive social issues as racial and ethnic prejudice. Because the media—and especially television—played such a prominent role in American life, it became a battleground where conservatives and liberals clashed.

The conflict could be seen in producer Norman Lear's situation comedy *All in the Family*, introduced in 1971. Its main character, Archie Bunker, was a blue-collar father seething with fears and prejudices. Americans were supposed to laugh at Archie's outrageous references to "Hebes," "Spics," and "Commie crapola," but many in the audience were not laughing. Some minority leaders charged that by making Archie lovable, the show legitimized the very prejudices it seemed to attack.

Topical sitcoms

M*A*S*H, a popular sitcom launched in 1972, was more clearly liberal in tone. Although set in a medical unit during the Korean War, its real inspiration was the growing disillusionment with the Vietnam war. M*A*S*H twitted bureaucracy, authority, pretense, bigotry, and snobbery. For conservatives, the antiauthoritarian bent of such shows seemed to spill over into newspaper and television reporting. On the other hand, feminists and minority groups complained that television portrayed them through stereotypes, when it bothered to portray them at all.

Perhaps inevitably, the wars for the soul of prime time spilled into the political arena. Norman Lear, Archie Bunker's creator, went on to form People for the American Way, a lobbying group that campaigned for more diversity in American life and attempted to counteract pressure groups like the Moral Majority. Conservatives, looking to make a stronger political impact, in 1980 embraced an amiable former movie actor who had long preached their gospel.

The Election of 1980

Jimmy Carter might be born again, but Ronald Reagan spoke the language of true conservatism. "I think there is a hunger in this land for a spiritual revival, a return to a belief in moral absolutes," he told his followers. Such a commitment to fundamentalist articles of faith was more important than the fact that Reagan actually had no church affiliation and seldom attended services.

The defection of many evangelical Protestants meant that the Democrats had lost the majority of white Southern voters. The Republican Party became

Reagan supporters

the home of most conservatives. When undecided voters saw Reagan as the candidate with the power to lead, the race turned into a landslide. Equally impressive, Republicans won their first majority in the Senate since 1954. They cited the margin of victory as a popular mandate for a conservative agenda.

On that count, the verdict was not clear. Only 52 percent of the eligible electorate went to the polls, the lowest total in 32 years. "It's a fed-up vote," argued Carter's political analyst Patrick Caddell. Still, the New Deal Democratic coalition had been splintered. Although Reagan's majority was greatest among white voters over 45 who earned more than $50,000 a year, he made striking gains among union workers, southern white Protestants, Catholics, and Jews.

PRIME TIME WITH RONALD REAGAN

Ronald Reagan brought the bright lights of Hollywood to Washington. His managers staged one of the most extravagant inaugurations in the nation's history. Nancy Reagan became the most fashion-conscious first lady since Jackie Kennedy, while the new administration made the conspicuous display of wealth once again a sign of success and power. During Reagan's first term sales of stretch limousines doubled every year. Poverty rates rose, too, as the gulf between rich and poor widened.

The Great Communicator

Ronald Reagan brought a simple message to Washington. "It is time to reawaken the industrial giant, to get government back within its means, and to lighten our punitive tax burden," he announced on inauguration day. Commentators began referring to the president as "the great communicator," because of his mastery of television and radio.

Reagan used his skill as an actor to obscure contradictions between his rhetoric and reality. With his jaunty wave and jutting jaw, he projected phys-

The Reagan style

ical vitality and the charismatic good looks of John Kennedy. Yet at age 69, he was the oldest president to take office, and none since Calvin Coolidge had slept so soundly or so much. Reagan had begun his political life as a New Deal Democrat, but by the 1950s he had become an ardent anti-Communist, Republican. In 1966 he began two terms as governor of California with a promise to pare down government programs and balance budgets. In fact, spending jumped sharply during his term in office.

Similar inconsistencies marked Reagan's leadership as president. Outsiders applauded his "hands-off" management: Reagan set the tone and direction, let-

As president, Ronald Reagan often evoked the image of a cowboy hero. Yet the Reagan revolution in practice led to sharply increased federal spending and federal deficits.

ting his advisers take care of the details. On the other hand, many within the administration, like Secretary of the Treasury Donald Regan, were shocked to find the new president remarkably ignorant about and uninterested in important matters of policy. "The Presidential mind was not cluttered with facts," Regan lamented. Yet Reagan's cheerful ability to deflect responsibility for mistakes earned him a reputation as the "Teflon president," since no criticism seemed to stick.

In addition, Reagan was blessed by remarkably good luck. The deaths of three aging Soviet leaders, from 1982 through 1985, compounded that country's economic weakness and reduced Russian influence abroad. Members of the OPEC oil cartel quarreled among themselves, exceeded production quotas, and thus forced oil prices lower. That removed a major inflationary pressure on the American economy. And when a would-be assassin shot the president in the chest on March 30, 1981, the wound was not life threatening. His courage in the face of danger impressed even his critics.

Reagan's fortune

The Reagan Agenda

As president, Reagan's primary goal was to weaken big government. His budget would become an instrument to reduce bureaucracy and to undermine activist federal agencies in the areas of civil rights, environmental and consumer protection, poverty programs, the arts, and education. In essence, the new president wanted to return government to the size and responsibility it possessed in the 1950s before the reforms of Kennedy and Johnson.

At the heart of the Reagan revolution was a commitment to "supply-side" economics, a program that in many ways resembled the trickle-down economic theories of the Harding-Coolidge era. Supply-side theorists argued that high taxes and government regulation stifled enterprising businesses and economic expansion. The key to revival lay in a large tax cut, a politically popular though economically controversial proposal. Such a cut threatened to reduce revenues and increase an already large deficit. Not so, argued economist Arthur Laffer. The economy would be so stimulated that tax revenues would actually rise, even though the tax rate was cut.

Supply-side economics

The president's second target for action was inflation, the "silent thief" that had burdened the economy during the Ford-Carter years. Reagan resisted certain traditional cures for inflation: tight money, high interest rates, and wage and price controls. He preferred two approaches unpopular with Democrats: higher unemployment and weakened unions to reduce labor costs.

Lower public spending, a favorite Republican remedy, might have seemed one likely method of reducing inflation. But the third element of Reagan's agenda was a sharp rise in military outlays: a total of $1.5 trillion to be spent over five years. The president wanted to create an American military presence with the strength to act unilaterally anywhere in the world to beat back Communist threats. This was a remarkably expansive goal: Presidents Nixon, Ford, and Carter had all looked to scale back American commitments, either through détente or by shifting burdens to allies in Western Europe. Reagan recognized no such limits. And rather than emphasize either nuclear defense or conventional weapons, Defense Secretary Caspar Weinberger successfully lobbied Congress for both.

Military buildup

The Reagan Revolution in Practice

The administration soon found an opportunity to "hang tough" when air traffic controllers went on strike, claiming that understaffing and long working hours threatened air safety. Because the controllers were civil service employees, the strike was technically illegal. Without addressing the merits of the controllers' complaints, Reagan simply fired them for violating their contract. The defeat of the air controllers signaled a broader attack on unions. When a recession enveloped the nation, major corporations wrung substantial concessions on wages and work rules. Organized labor witnessed a steady decline in membership and political power.

The president's war against government regulation took special aim at environmental rules. Conservatives, especially in the West, dismissed the environmental lobby as "nature lovers." Preservation of wild lands restricted mining, cattle grazing, farming, and real estate development—all powerful western industries. Reagan appointed westerner James Watt, an outspoken champion of this "sagebrush rebellion," to head the Interior Department. Watt, in turn, devoted himself to opening federal

Environmental controversy

The President's Budget Director
Discusses the "Reagan Revolution"

L ike all revolutionaries, we wanted to get our program out of the fringe cell group where it had been hatched and into the mainstream. . . . So we pitched it in tones that were music to every politician's ears. We highlighted the easy part—the giant tax cut. The side of the doctrine that had to do with giving to the electorate, not taking from it.

My blueprint for sweeping, wrenching change in national economic governance would have hurt millions of people in the short run. . . . It meant complete elimination of subsidies to farmers and businesses. It required an immediate end to welfare for the able-bodied poor. It meant no right to draw more from the Social Security fund than retirees had actually contributed, which was a lot less than most were currently getting.

These principles everywhere clashed with the political reality. Over the decades, the politicians had lured tens of millions of citizens into milking . . . cows, food stamps, Social Security, the Veterans Hospitals, and much more. . . . For the Reagan Revolution to add up, they had to be cut off. The blueprint was thus riddled with the hardship and unfairness of unexpected change. Only an iron chancellor would have tried to make it stick. Ronald Reagan wasn't that by a long shot.

Even [after I criticized the administration publicly] my private exoneration at lunch in the Oval Office by a fatherly Ronald Reagan showed why a Reagan Revolution couldn't happen. He should have been roaring mad like the others—about either the bad publicity or my admission of a flawed economic plan.

But Ronald Reagan proved to be too gentle and sentimental for that. He always went for the hard luck stories. He sees the plight of real people before anything else. Despite his right-wing image, his ideology and philosophy always takes a back seat when he learns that some individual human being might be hurt.

That's also why he couldn't lead a real revolution in American economic policy.

Selected excerpts from David Stockman, *The Triumph of Politics: Why the Reagan Revolution Failed* (New York, HarperCollins, 1986), pp. 9–12. Copyright © 1986 by David A. Stockman. Reprinted by permission of HarperCollins Publishers, Inc.

lands for private development, including lumbering and offshore oil drilling. After offending Indians, African Americans, Jews, the handicapped, as well as many Republicans, Watt was forced to resign in 1983, but the administration continued to oppose environmental initiatives.

Most important to conservatives, Reagan had by the summer of 1981 pushed his supply-side legislation through Congress. The Economic Recovery Tax Act provided a 25 percent across-the-board reduction for all taxpayers. The president hailed it, along with recently passed budget cuts, as an antidote to "big government's" addiction to spending and a stimulus to the economy.

Tax cuts

The Impact of Reaganomics

The impact of Reagan's supply-side economics (nicknamed "Reaganomics" by the press) was mixed. By 1982 a recession had pushed unemployment above 10 percent. But the following year marked the beginning of an economic expansion that lasted through Reagan's presidency, thanks in part to increased federal spending and lowered interest rates. Then, too, falling energy costs and improved industrial productivity contributed to renewed prosperity.

Even so, the Reagan tax cut was one of a series of policy changes that brought about a substantial transfer of wealth from poor and lower-middle-class workers to the upper middle classes and the rich. For the wealthiest Americans, the 1980s were the best of times. The top 1 percent commanded a greater share of the nation's wealth (37 percent) than at any time since 1929. Their earnings averaged about $560,000 per year, as opposed to $20,000 or less for the bottom 40 percent. What counterculture hippies were to the 1960s, high-salaried "yuppies" (young, upwardly mobile professionals) were to the 1980s.

On the surface, the buoyant job market seemed to signal a more general prosperity as well. By the end of Reagan's second term, more than 14.5 million jobs had been created for Americans. Yet these jobs were spread unevenly by region, class, and gender. More than 2 million were in finance, insurance, real estate, and law, all services used more by the wealthy than the poor. In highly paid "Wall Street" jobs—those involving financial services—more than 70 percent went to white males, only 2 percent to African Americans. New employment for women was concentrated in the areas of health, education, social services, and government, where approximately 3 million jobs opened, most dependent on government support. New jobs for the poor (more than 3 million) were largely restricted to minimum-wage, part-time, dead-end jobs in hotels, fast-food restaurants, and retail stores.

Factors encouraging the transfer of wealth

Because Reaganomics preached the virtues of free markets and free trade, the administration did little to discourage high-wage blue-collar jobs from flowing to cheap labor markets in Mexico and Asia. Furthermore, Reagan aimed the sharpest edge of his budget axe at programs for the poor: food stamps, Aid to Families with Dependent Children, Medicaid, school lunches, and housing

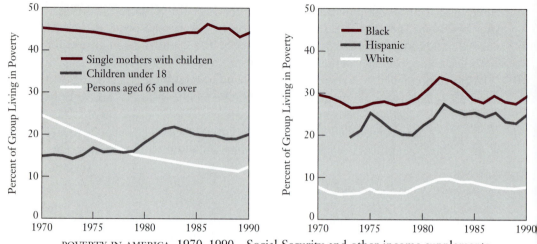

POVERTY IN AMERICA, 1970–1990   Social Security and other income supplements account for the reduced level of poverty among those over 65. For all other traditionally impoverished groups the Reagan–Bush years left them slightly worse off.

assistance. The programs trimmed back least were middle-class entitlements like Social Security and Medicare. Those programs affected Americans over 65 who, as social activist Michael Harrington observed, as a general class "are not now, and for a long time have not been, poor."

As more income flowed toward the wealthy and as jobs were lost to overseas competitors, the percentage of Americans below the poverty level rose from 11.7 percent in 1980 to 15 percent by 1982. There the level remained through the Bush administration. Reagan's successful war on inflation, which dropped to less than 2 percent by 1986, contributed to a rise in unemployment. Even during the recovery, the figure dropped below 6 percent of the workforce only in the months before the 1988 election. (By contrast, the highest rate under Jimmy Carter was 5.9 percent.) Thus the Reagan boom was an uneven one, despite continued economic expansion.

The Military Buildup

The heart of the Reagan revolution was a sharp rise in military spending. Outlays rose from less than $200 billion under Presidents Ford and Carter to almost $300 billion in 1985. The largest increases were for expensive strategic nuclear weapons systems.

Huge costs were not the only source of criticism. When Reagan's tough-talking defense planners spoke about "winning" a nuclear exchange, they revived the antinuclear peace movement across Europe and America. The bishops of the

Star Wars American Catholic church announced their opposition to nuclear war. Scientists warned that the debris in the atmosphere from an atomic exchange might create a "nuclear winter" fatal to all life on earth. Other critics singled out runaway Pentagon costs. Stories of $600 toilet seats and $7000 coffee pots made headlines, but more serious were the failures of entire multi-billion-dollar weapons systems. One of the president's favorite programs was the Strategic Defense Initiative, or SDI. Nicknamed "Star Wars," after a popular science fiction film, it spent billions of dollars trying to establish a space-based missile defense system. Most scientists contended that the project was as fantastic as the movie.

The combination of massive defense spending and substantial tax cuts left the federal government awash in red ink. Annual deficits climbed to more than $200 billion. Furthermore, with interest rates so high, the value of the dollar soared on world markets, pushing up the cost of American exports. As American exports declined, imports from abroad (such as Japanese autos) competed more successfully in America. The United States, a creditor nation since World War I, had by 1986 become the world's largest debtor.

Growing deficits

The spending excesses of the Reagan agenda would come to haunt his conservative successors. For the time being, however, Ronald Reagan's popularity seemed unassailable. In 1984 he easily won a second term, gaining 59 percent of the vote in his run against Democrat Walter Mondale of Minnesota. (Mondale's running mate, Geraldine Ferraro of New York, was the first female candidate for the vice presidency.) Reagan remained his sunny, unflappable self, seeming to enjoy the presidency immensely. "The 75-year-old man is hitting home runs," rhapsodized *Time* magazine at the beginning of his second term. In reality, Reagan would soon be tested by a series of crises arising out of his aggressive foreign policy.

STANDING TALL IN A CHAOTIC WORLD

Reagan brought to the conduct of foreign policy the same moral stance that shaped his approach to domestic affairs. Reagan wanted the United States to stand tall: to adopt a policy that drew bold, clear lines as a means of restoring American prestige. But turmoil abroad demonstrated that bold policies were not always easy to carry out. And because the president remained indifferent to most day-to-day details, he was at the mercy of those officials who put into effect his aggressive anti-Communist foreign policy.

Terrorism in the Middle East

In the Middle East, the passions of religious factions suggested how difficult it was to impose order, even for a superpower like the United States. In 1982 President Reagan sent American marines into Lebanon as part of a European-American peacekeeping force. His hope was to bring a measure of stability to a region torn by civil war. But in trying to mediate between Lebanon's religious and political sects, the American "peacekeepers" found themselves dragged into the fighting. Terrorists retaliated by blowing up a U.S. Marine barracks in October 1983, killing 239. The president then ordered American troops withdrawn.

Just as hostage-taking in Iran had frustrated the Carter administration, terrorist attacks by Islamic fundamentalists bedeviled Reagan. In 1985 terrorists took new hostages in Lebanon; others hijacked American airline flights, killed an American hostage on a Mediterranean cruise ship, and bombed a nightclub where American soldiers met in West Germany. Reagan's public response was always uncompromising: "Let terrorists beware: . . . our policy will be one of swift and effective retribution."

But against whom should the United States seek revenge? American intelligence agencies found it extremely difficult to collect reliable information on the many political and terrorist factions. In 1986 the president sent bombers to attack targets in Libya, whose anti-American leader Colonel Muammar Qadhafi had links to terrorists. But so did the more powerful states of Syria and Iran.

Mounting Frustrations in Central America

At first, a policy of standing tall seemed easier closer to home. In 1983, the administration launched an invasion of Grenada, a small Caribbean island whose

Grenada invasion

government was challenged by pro-Castro revolutionaries. U.S. forces crushed the rebels, but the invasion was largely a symbolic gesture.

More frustrating to the president, Nicaragua's left-wing Sandinista government had established increasingly close ties with Cuba. In 1981 Reagan extended aid to the antigovernment "Contra" forces. When critics warned that Nicaragua could become another Vietnam, the president countered that the Contras were "freedom fighters," battling in the spirit of America's Founding Fathers. Although the Contras did include some moderate democrats and disillusioned Sandinistas, most of their leaders had served the brutal Somoza dictatorship that the Sandinistas had toppled in 1979.

Reagan might have sought a negotiated settlement between the Contras and the Sandinistas; instead he allowed CIA to help the Contras mine Nicaraguan har-

Boland Amendment

bors, in hopes of overthrowing the Sandinistas outright. When some of the mines exploded, damaging foreign ships in violation of international law, even some conservative senators were dismayed.

Congress adopted an amendment sponsored by Representative Edward Boland of Massachusetts, explicitly forbidding the CIA or "any other agency or entity involved in intelligence activities" from spending money to support the Contras "directly or indirectly." The president signed the Boland Amendment, though only grudgingly.

The Iran-Contra Connection

Thus by mid-1985 Reagan policymakers felt two major frustrations. First, Congress had forbidden support of the Contras in Nicaragua. And second,

Iranian-backed terrorists continued to hold American hostages in Lebanon. In the summer of 1985 a course of events was set in motion that eventually linked these two issues.

The president let his advisers know that he wanted to find a way to free the remaining hostages. National Security Advisor Robert McFarlane suggested opening a channel to "moderate factions" in the Iranian government. If the United States sold Iran a few weapons, the grateful moderates might use their influence in Lebanon to free the hostages. But an agreement to exchange arms for hostages would violate the president's often-repeated vow never to pay ransom to terrorists. Still, Reagan apparently approved the initiative. Over the following year, four secret arms shipments were made to Iran. One hostage was set free.

Reagan's secretaries of state and defense both had strongly opposed the trading of arms for hostages. "This is almost too absurd to comment on,"

Arms for hostage deals

Defense Secretary Weinberger protested. Thus, both men were kept largely uninformed of the arms shipments, precisely because their opposition was well known. McFarlane's successor, Admiral John Poindexter, had the president sign a secret intelligence "finding" that allowed him and his associates to pursue their mission without informing anyone in Congress or even the secretaries of defense and state. Since the president ignored the details of foreign policy, McFarlane, Poindexter, and their aides had assumed the power to act on their own.

The man most often pulling the strings seemed to be Lieutenant Colonel Oliver "Ollie" North, a junior officer under McFarlane and later Poindexter. A Vietnam veteran with a flair for the dramatic, North was impatient with bureaucratic rules and procedures. He and McFarlane had already discovered a way to evade the Boland Amendment, in order to secretly aid the Nicaraguan Contras. McFarlane told Saudi Arabia and several other American allies that the Contras desperately needed funds. As a favor, the Saudis deposited at least $30 million in Swiss bank accounts he used to launder the money. North then arranged to spend the money to buy the weapons that were delivered to Central America.

The two secret strands came together in January 1986. North hit upon the idea that the profits made selling arms to Iran could be siphoned off to buy weapons for the Contras. The Iranian arms dealer who brokered the deal thought it a great idea. "I think this is now, Ollie, the best chance, because . . . we never get such good money out of this," he laughed, as he was recorded on a tape North himsef made. "We do everything. We do hostages free of charge; we do all terrorists free of charge; Central America free of charge."

Cover Blown

The secrecy that surrounded both operations through much of 1986 abruptly lifted when reports of the Iranian arms deal were leaked to a Lebanese

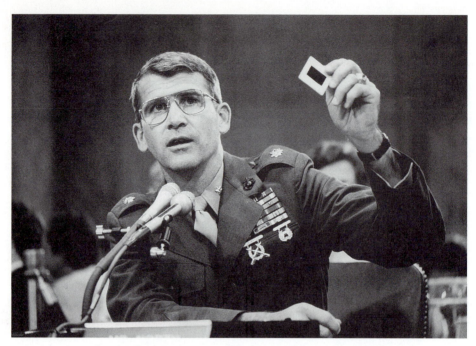

As Colonel Oliver North himself admitted during the Iran–Contra
hearings, he purposefully misled Congress about the Reagan
administration's secret aid to the Contras.

newspaper. Astonished reporters besieged the administration. How did secret
arms sales to a terrorist regime benefit the president's antiterrorist campaign,
they asked. Further inquiry revealed the link between the arms sales and the
Contras. Attorney General Edwin Meese moved so slowly to investigate that
North and his secretary had time to shred crucial documents. Still, enough evidence remained to make the dimensions of the illegal operations clear.

The press immediately began referring to the scandal as "Irangate," com-
paring it to Richard Nixon's Watergate scandal. But Irangate raised more trou-

Irangate

bling issues. Watergate sprang from political tricks that ran amok.
The president had led the cover-up to save his own political skin.
The Irangate hearings, held during the summer of 1987, left the role of the
president unexplained. Admiral Poindexter testified that he had kept Reagan in
ignorance, "so that I could insulate him from the decision and provide some future deniability for the president if it ever leaked out. . . ." In that way, Iran-
Contra revealed a presidency out of control. An unelected segment within the
government had taken upon itself the power to pursue its own poilicies beyond
legal channels. In doing so, Reagan, North, Poindexter, and McFarlane sub-
verted the constitutional system of checks and balances.

From Cold War to Glasnost

Since few in Congress wanted to impeach a popular president, the Iran-Contra hearings came to a sputtering end. Reagan's popularity returned, in part because of substantial improvement in Soviet-American relations.

In 1985 a fresh spirit entered the Kremlin. Unlike the aged leaders who preceded him, Mikhail Gorbachev was young, saw the need for reform within the Soviet Union, and rivaled Reagan as a shaper of world opinion. Gorbachev's fundamental restructuring, or *perestroika*, set about improving relations with the United States, reducing military commitments, and adopting a policy of openness (*glasnost*) about problems in the Soviet Union. In October, the two leaders held a summit meeting in Reykjavík, Iceland. Gorbachev dangled the possibility of abolishing all nuclear weapons. Reagan seemed receptive to the idea, apparently unaware that if both sides eliminated all nuclear weapons, Soviet conventional forces would far outnumber NATO troops in Europe. In the end, the president refused to sacrifice his Star Wars system for so radical a proposal.

Mikhail Gorbachev

Despite the immediate impasse, negotiations continued. In December 1987 Reagan traveled to Moscow to sign the Intermediate Nuclear Force treaty, which eliminated an entire class of intermediate-range nuclear missiles with ranges of 600 to 3400 miles. Both sides agreed to allow on-site inspections of missile bases and the facilities where missiles would be destroyed. That agreement greatly eased cold war tensions.

The Election of 1988

As the election of 1988 approached, the president could claim credit for improved relations with the Soviet Union. Loyalty to Reagan made Vice President George Bush the Republican heir. Bush appealed most to party professionals, white Protestants, and the affluent middle class that had benefited from Reaganomics.

The Democratic challenger, Governor Michael Dukakis of Massachusetts, tried to call attention to weaknesses in the American economy. An alarming number of savings and loan institutions had failed, and Dukakis recognized that poor and even many middle-class Americans had lost ground during the 1980s. But under attack from Bush the lackluster Dukakis appeared weak. With the economy reasonably robust, Bush won by a comfortable margin, taking 54 percent of the popular vote. The Reagan agenda remained on track.

AN END TO THE COLD WAR

President George Herbert Walker Bush was born to both privilege and politics. The son of a powerful Connecticut senator, he attended an exclusive boarding school and the ivy-league Yale University. That background made him part of the Eastern establishment often condemned by more populist Republicans. Yet once the oil business lured Bush to Texas, he moved to the right, becoming a Goldwater Republican when he ran for the Senate in 1964. Although he once supported Planned Parenthood and a woman's right to abortion, Bush eventually adopted the conservative right-to-life position. In truth, however, foreign policy interested him far more than domestic politics.

A Post–Cold War Foreign Policy

To the astonishment of most western observers, Mikhail Gorbachev's reform policies led not only to the collapse of the Soviet empire but to the breakup of the Soviet Union itself. In December 1988, Gorbachev spoke in the United Nations of a "new world order." To that end he began liquidating the Soviet cold war legacy, as the last Russian troops began leaving Afghanistan and then Eastern Europe.

Throughout 1989 Eastern Europeans began to test their newfound freedom. In Poland, Hungary, Bulgaria, Czechoslovakia, and most violently in

The fall of Communism

Romania, Communist dictators fell from power. Nothing inspired the world more than the stream of celebrating East Germans pouring through the Berlin Wall in November 1989. Within a year the Wall, a symbol of Communist oppression, had been torn down and Germany reunified. Although Gorbachev struggled to keep together the 15 republics that made up the U.S.S.R., the forces of nationalism and reform pulled the Soviet Union apart. The Baltic republics—Lithuania, Latvia, and Estonia—declared their independence in 1991. Then in December, the Slavic republics of Ukraine, Belarus, and Russia formed a new Commonwealth of Independent States. By the end of December eight more of the former Soviet republics had joined the loose federation. Boris Yeltsin, the charismatic president of Russia, became the Commonwealth's dominant figure. With no Soviet Union left to preside over, Gorbachev resigned as president.

President Bush responded cautiously to these momentous changes. Although the president increasingly supported Gorbachev's reforms, he distrusted the more popular yet unpredictable maverick, Yeltsin. Even if Bush had wished to launch a campaign to aid Eastern Europe and the new Commonwealth states, soaring deficits and a stagnant American economy limited his options. The administration seemed to support the status quo in Communist China, too. When in June 1989 China's aging leadership crushed students rallying for democratic reform in Beijing's Tiananmen Square, Bush muted American protests.

The fall of the Soviet Union signaled the end of a cold war that, more than once, had threatened a nuclear end to human history. At a series of summits with

START Treaty

Russian leaders, the United States and its former rivals agreed to sharp reductions in their stockpiles of nuclear weapons. The Strategic Arms Reduction Treaty (or START), concluded in July 1991, far sur-

President George Bush met with Soviet President Mikhail Gorbachev at a Moscow summit meeting in 1991. Clearly the policy of *glasnost* extended to American beverages: the Kremlin's conference table is stocked with Coke.

passed the limits negotiated in earlier SALT talks. By June 1992 Bush and Yeltsin had agreed to even sharper cuts.

The Persian Gulf War

With two superpowers no longer facing off against each other, what would the "new world order" look like? If anything, regional crises loomed larger. President Bush moved to project American power more forcefully in the Middle East. But civil wars in Eastern Europe and Africa demonstrated that a world order beyond the shadow of the cold war might be more chaotic and unpredictable than ever.

Instability in the Middle East brought Bush's greatest foreign policy challenge. From 1980 to 1988 Iran and Iraq had battered each other in a debilitating war. During those years the Reagan administration assisted *Saddam Hussein* Iraq with weapons and intelligence, until at last it won a narrow victory over Iran's fundamentalists. But Iraq's ruthless dictator, Saddam Hussein, had run up enormous debts. To ease his financial crisis, Saddam cast a covetous eye on his neighbor, the small oil-rich sheikdom of Kuwait. In August 1990, 120,000 Iraqi troops invaded and occupied Kuwait, catching the Bush administration off guard. Would Saddam stop there?

"We committed a boner with regard to Iraq and our close friendship with Iraq," admitted Ronald Reagan. Embarrassed by having supported the pro-Iraqi policy, Bush was determined to thwart Saddam's invasion of Kuwait. The president successfully coordinated a United Nations–backed economic boycott. Increasing the pressure further, he deployed half a million American troops in Saudi Arabia and the Persian Gulf. By November Bush had won a resolution from the Security Council permitting the use of military force if Saddam did not withdraw.

On January 17, 1991, planes from France, Italy, Britain, Saudi Arabia, and the United States began bombing Baghdad and Iraqi bases. Operation Desert Storm had begun. After weeks of merciless pounding from the air, ground operations shattered Saddam's vaunted Royal Guards in less than 100 hours. By the end of February Kuwait was liberated and nothing stood between Allied forces and Baghdad. Bush was unwilling to go that far—and most other nations in the coalition agreed. If Hussein were toppled, it was not clear who in Iraq would fill the vacuum of power. But long after the war ended, the United States still worried about Saddam and his potential possession of biological and atomic weapons.

Operation Desert Storm

Domestic Doldrums

Victory in the Gulf War so boosted the president's popularity that aides brushed aside the need for any bold domestic program. "Frankly, this president doesn't need another single piece of legislation, unless it's absolutely right," asserted John Sununu, his cocky chief of staff. That attitude suggested a lack of direction that proved fatal to Bush's reelection hopes.

At first, Bush envisioned a domestic program that would soften the harsher edges of the Reagan revolution. He promised to create a "kinder, gentler" nation. Yet pressures from conservative Republicans kept the new president from straying too far in the direction of reform. Although Bush appointed a well-respected conservationist, William Reilly, to head the Environmental Protection Agency, Reilly often found his programs opposed by others in the administration. When delegates from 178 nations met at an "Earth Summit" in Rio de Janiero in 1992, the president opposed efforts to draft stricter rules to lessen the threat of global warming. Bush did sign into law the sweeping Clean Air Act passed by Congress in 1990. But soon after, Vice President Dan Quayle established a "Council on Competitiveness" to rewrite environmental regulations that corporations found burdensome.

Environmental issues

The Conservative Court

Although Presidents Reagan and Bush both spoke out against abortion, affirmative action, the banning of prayer in public schools, and other liberal social positions, neither made action a legislative priority. Even so, both presidents shaped social policy through their appointments to the Supreme Court. Reagan placed three members on the bench, including in 1981 Sandra Day O'Connor, the first woman to sit on the high court. Bush nominated two justices. As more liberal members of the Court retired (including William Brennan and Thurgood Marshall), the decisions handed down became distinctly more conservative.

On two occasions, the Senate challenged this trend. In 1987, it rejected Robert Bork, a nominee whose opposition to long-established Court policies on privacy and civil rights led even some Republicans to oppose him. But this fight proved so exhausting that the Senate quickly approved President Reagan's alternate choice, Antonin Scalia. Scalia proved to be the Court's most conservative member.

In 1991 the Senate also hotly debated President Bush's nomination of Clarence Thomas, an outspoken black conservative and former member of the

The Clarence Thomas hearings

Reagan administration. The confirmation hearings became even more heated when Anita Hill, a woman who had worked for Thomas, testified that he had sexually harassed her. Because Hill was a professor of law and herself a Reagan conservative, her often graphic testimony riveted millions of television viewers. Suddenly the hearings raised new issues. Women's groups blasted the all-male Judiciary Committee for keeping Hill's allegations private until reporters uncovered the story. Thomas and his defenders accused his opponents of using a disgruntled woman to help conduct a latter-day lynching. In the end the Senate narrowly voted to confirm, and Thomas joined Scalia as one of the Court's most conservative members.

Evidence of the Court's changing stance came most clearly in its attitude toward affirmative action, those laws that gave preferred treatment to minority groups in order to remedy past racial discrimination. State and federal courts and legislatures had used techniques like busing and the setting of quotas as ways to overturn past injustices. In 1978, however, even before Reagan's appointments, the Court began to set limits on affirmative action. In *Bakke v. Regents of the University of California* (1978), the majority ruled that college admissions staffs could not set fixed quotas, although they could still use race as a guiding factor in trying to create a more diverse student body. Increasingly, the Court made it easier for white citizens to challenge affirmative action programs. At the same time it set higher standards for those who wished to put forward a claim of discrimination. "An amorphous claim that there has been past discrimination in a particular industry cannot justify the use of an unyielding racial quota," wrote Justice O'Connor in 1989. By 1996 a federal circuit court had gone so far as to state (in *Hopwood v. State of Texas et al.*) that race could not be a factor in college admissions.

Court decisions on abortion and religion in public schools demonstrated a similar desire to set limits on the established precedents. *Planned Parenthood v. Casey* (1992) upheld a woman's constitutional right to an abortion, but it also allowed states to place new restrictions on the procedure. Other Court decisions let stand laws restricting abortions and even abortion counseling by clinics or hospitals receiving federal funds. And while the Court affirmed that religious teachings or prayer could have no official status in public schools, it allowed students to engage in voluntary prayer as well as to form religious clubs meeting after school.

Disillusionment and Anger

Ronald Reagan had given a sunny face to conservatism. He assured voters that if taxes were cut, the economy would revive and deficits fall. Yet after a decade of conservative leadership, the deficit had ballooned and state and local governments were larger than ever. A growing number of Americans felt that the institutions of government had come seriously off track.

A series of longer-term crises contributed to this disillusionment. One of the most threatening centered on the nation's savings and loan institutions. By the end of the 1980s these "thrifts" were failing at the highest rate since the Great Depression. To help banks, the Reagan administration and Congress had cut back federal regulations, allowing savings banks to invest their funds more speculatively. Reagan's advisers ignored the warnings that fraud and mismanagement were increasing sharply. Only during the Bush administration did it become clearer that the cost of restoring solvency would run into hundreds of billions of taxpayers' dollars.

S&L crisis

The late 1980s also brought a public health crisis. Americans were spending a higher percentage of their resources on medical care than citizens in other nations, yet they were no healthier. As medical costs soared, more than 30 million Americans had no health insurance. The crisis was worsened by a fatal disorder that physicians began diagnosing in the early 1980s: Acquired Immune Deficiency Syndrome, or AIDS. With no cure available, the disease threatened to take on epidemic proportions, not only in the United States but across the globe. Yet because the illness at first struck hardest at the male homosexual community and intravenous drug abusers, many groups in American society resisted addressing the problem.

Health crises

The anger felt in the country had a social edge as well. In 1991 Los Angeles police were videotaped while arresting a black motorist for speeding and drunken driving. The tape showed Rodney King being struck more than 50 times by officers wielding nightsticks. When a suburban white jury acquitted the officers, the black community of central Los Angeles exploded. Stores were looted, some 600 buildings were set ablaze, and more than 50 people were killed. Clearly, the anger in central Los Angeles over racism was also fueled by the stresses of high unemployment, urban poverty, and economic decline.

Los Angeles riots

Bank failures, skyrocketing health costs, an increase in unemployment and poverty—by themselves none of these problems could derail the conservative rebellion that had swept Ronald Reagan into office. Still, the crises demonstrated how pivotal government had become in providing social services and limiting the abuses of powerful private interests in a highly industrialized society. Neither the Reagan nor the Bush administrations had developed a clear way to address such problems without the intervention of government—the sort of intervention envisioned by a more activist Republican, Teddy Roosevelt, at the turn of the century.

The Election of 1992

In the end, George Bush's inability to rein in soaring government deficits proved most damaging to his reelection prospects. "Read my lips! No new taxes," he had pledged to campaign audiences in 1988. But the president and Congress were at loggerheads over how to reach the holy grail of so many conservatives: a balanced budget. In 1985 Congress had passed the Gramm–Rudman Act, establishing a set of steadily increasing limits on federal spending. These limits were meant to force Congress and the president to make hard choices needed to reach a balanced budget. If they did not, automatic across-the-board cuts would go into effect. By 1990 the law's automatic procedures were threatening programs like Medicare, which Republicans and Democrats alike supported. Facing such unpopular cuts, Bush agreed to a package of new taxes along with budget cuts. Conservatives felt betrayed, and in the end, the deficit grew larger all the same.

Gramm-Rudman Act

As the election of 1992 approached, unemployment stood at more than 8 percent, penetrating to areas of the economy not affected by most recessions. Statistics showed that real wages for middle-class families had not increased since the early 1970s and had actually declined during Bush's presidency. Many Reagan Democrats seemed ready to return to the party of Franklin Roosevelt, who had mobilized an activist government in a time of economic depression. Other disillusioned voters were drawn to the maverick candidacy of Texas computer billionaire H. Ross Perot. The blunt-talking Perot demanded a government run like a business, but free of big-business lobbyists.

White-collar unemployment

Meanwhile, the Democrats gave their nomination to Governor Bill Clinton of Arkansas, who hammered away at Bush for failing to revive the economy. "It's the economy, stupid!" read the sign tacked up at headquarters, to remind Clinton workers of the campaign's central theme. Clinton painted himself as a new kind of Democrat: moderate, willing to work with business, and not a creature of liberal interest groups.

"It's the economy . . ."

The Bush campaign badly miscalculated by allowing the most conservative members of the party to dominate the Republican convention. On election day, Clinton captured 43 percent of the popular vote (to Bush's 38 and Perot's 19) in the largest turnout—55 percent—in 20 years. The election of four women to the Senate, including the first African American woman, Carol Moseley Braun, indicated that gender had become an electoral factor.

THE CLINTON PRESIDENCY

Did Clinton's victory in 1992 signal a reversal of fortune for the conservatives? Sixty-two percent of the electorate had voted against the Republicans, but only 43 percent had voted for the man who now looked to lead the nation.

Still, William Jefferson Clinton intended to bring change. He shared with his wife, Hillary Rodham Clinton, a love for politics and government as well as a determination to address problems neglected by the "hands-off" policies of Reagan and Bush. An activist executive could accomplish much, he insisted, "even a president without a majority mandate coming in, if the president has a disciplined, aggressive agenda. . . ." Certainly Clinton's agenda was ambitious. Beyond seeking to revive the economy and rein in the deficit, he called for systematic reform of the welfare and health care systems, as well as measures to lessen the increasing violence in American life.

The New World Disorder

Determined to focus on domestic issues, Clinton hoped to pay less attention to foreign affairs. Yet the "new world order" hailed by both Mikhail Gorbachev and George Bush seemed more than ever to be disrupted by regional conflicts.

In sub-Saharan Africa, corruption and one-party rule had severely weakened most economies, tribal violence mounted, and AIDS became epidemic. Brutal civil wars broke out in both Somalia and Rwanda. Clinton did support President Bush's decision in December 1992 to send troops to aid famine-relief efforts in Somalia. But when U.S. troops withdrew in 1994, a stable government had not been established. Similarly, the United States as well as European nations remained reluctant to intervene in Rwanda, where over a million people were massacred in 1994.

Civil wars in Somalia and Rwanda

In Yugoslavia, Serbs fought Croats and Muslims who had broken off to form the independent state of Bosnia-Herzegovina. Western Europeans and Americans were dismayed by the systematic slaughter and rape of Muslims that Serbs justified in the name of "ethnic cleansing." In November 1995 the United States hosted peace talks between the warring factions in Dayton, Ohio. The resulting Dayton Accord called for Bosnia to remain a single nation, but governed as two separate republics. To help guarantee the peace, Clinton sent 20,000 American ground troops to Bosnia as part of an international peacekeeping mission.

Instability closer to home posed greater political problems for the president. With the economies of both Cuba and Haiti in shambles, desperate refugees built boats and homemade rafts in their attempts to reach the United States. Thousands who arrived on American shores severely taxed the ability of local governments, especially in Florida. Instability in Haiti pushed the president to take a bold approach. In 1991 Haitian military leaders had forced their country's elected president, Jean-Bertrand Aristide, to leave the country. When a U.N.–sponsored economic embargo failed to oust the military regime, the Security Council in 1994 approved an invasion of Haiti by a multinational force. American troops proved crucial in convincing the military to leave and in reinstalling Aristide. The following year a smaller U.N. force replaced the Americans.

Intervention in Haiti

Whether in Africa, Eastern Europe, or the Caribbean, such regional crises demonstrated that a new global "world order" would be difficult to maintain. Despite the president's willingness to intervene in Haiti, his foreign policy marked a pulling back from the high-spending, high-profile style of the Reagan era. Clearly, Clinton believed his most important work remained at home.

Recovery—but Reform?

The president emphasized his domestic priorities in his first appearance before a joint session of Congress in February 1993. In a graceful performance, Clinton improvised nearly half of his speech when his teleprompter broke down, a feat that would have eluded either Ronald Reagan or George Bush. The new president proposed a program of economic recovery that combined deficit reduction with a package of investments to stimulate the economy and repair the nation's decaying infrastructure.

But the president's facility for public speaking by no means ensured his command of Congress. Republicans filibustered to death the stimulus portion of Clinton's program. In August 1993 a compromise budget bill passed by only a single vote in the Senate. Still, it was a remarkable achievement. During the Reagan-Bush years deficits had

Clinton's successes

President Bill Clinton's most ambitious attempt at reform was to overhaul the nation's health care system to provide all Americans with basic health care (along with a card to guarantee it). But powerful interest groups opposed the legislation, which went down to defeat.

risen sharply, despite conservative rhetoric about balancing the budget. As prosperity returned to the economy, annual budget deficits steadily dwindled.

The budget bill victory provided Clinton with some momentum in other battles. In the fall he hammered together a bipartisan coalition to pass NAFTA, the North American Free Trade Agreement. With the promise of greater trade and jobs, the pact linked the United States more closely with Canada and Mexico. The president even helped supporters of gun control overcome the powerful opposition of the National Rifle Association to pass the Brady Bill, requiring a five-day waiting period on gun purchases.

Clinton's most ambitious reform was health care—and in that area he stumbled. A task force led by Hillary Rodham Clinton developed a plan designed to

Health care reform

provide health coverage for all Americans, including the 37 million who in 1994 remained uninsured. The plan proposed more far-reaching changes than a Republican proposal merely to reform insurance laws in order to make private medical coverage more readily available. If the bill had passed, the president and the Democratic majority in Congress might have staked their claim to a government that actively responded to some of the long-term problems facing American society. But the failure of health care reform heightened the perception of an ill-organized adminstration and a well-entrenched Democratic-controlled Congress content with the status quo.

Revolution Reborn

The 1994 midterm elections confirmed the public's anger over political gridlock. For the first time since the Eisenhower years, Republicans captured majorities in both the House and the Senate. The combative new speaker of the house, Newt Gingrich of Georgia, proclaimed himself a "genuine revolutionary," and vowed to complete what Ronald Reagan had begun. Gingrich used the first hundred days of the new Congress to bring to a vote ten popular proposals from his campaign document, "The Contract with America." The proposals included a balanced budget amendment, tax cuts, and term limits for all members of Congress. Term limits was the only one of the ten proposals not passed by the House.

"When you look back five years from now," enthused Republican Governor Tommy Thompson of Wisconsin, "you're going to say they came, they saw,

The revolution stumbles

they conquered." But as Republicans assembled their budget, the public became increasingly worried. To pay for a $245 billion tax cut (and still balance the federal budget by the year 2002), Gingrich and his followers proposed scaling back Medicare expenditures and allowing Medicare premiums to double. Republicans also sought to roll back environmental legislation that had been passed over the previous quarter century. Their proposals reduced protection for endangered species, relaxed pollution controls set up by the Clean Water Act, and gave mining, ranching, and logging interests greater freedom to develop public lands.

When President Clinton threatened to veto the congressional budget, Republicans pushed for confrontation. Twice they forced the federal government to shut down. The result was a public relations disaster for the self-proclaimed revolutionaries, who were forced to back down.

At the same time, President Clinton began moving steadily toward the political center. In 1995, he proposed his own route toward a balanced budget by 2002. Similarly, in August 1996 the president signed into law a sweeping reform of welfare. The law owed as much to Republican ideas as it did to his. For the first time in sixty years, the social welfare policies of the liberal democratic state were being substantially reversed. The bill ended guarantees of federal aid to poor children, turning over such programs to the states. Food stamp spending was cut, and the law placed a five-year limit on payments to any family. Most adults receiving payments had to find work within two years.

Clinton moves to the center

As the election of 1996 approached, the Republican revolution had been chastened. At the same time, Clinton had adroitly adopted many issues that Republicans once called their own. Following a lackluster primary campaign, the Republicans nominated former Senator Bob Dole, an aging political technician, to run for president. In vain Dole and his running mate Jack Kemp sought to stir voters with promises of a 15 percent tax cut. With the economy robust, voters reelected Clinton by a comfortable margin (49 percent to Dole's 40 percent, with Ross Perot taking under 10 percent). Bill Clinton became the first Democrat since Franklin Roosevelt to win a second term in the White House.

Morality and Politics

Clinton seemed to draw several lessons from his first four years in office. Republican victories in 1994 led him to accept much of the conservative rhetoric. "The era of 'big government' is over," he proclaimed. The defeat of his health care proposal led him to avoid large and complicated reforms.

Instead, Clinton looked to achieve more progressive reform through a succession of smaller, incremental changes. Some changes were largely symbolic, such as his promotion of school uniforms to promote discipline and civility. Other reforms were substantive. He championed a bill designed to make health insurance more readily available to citizens who had changed or lost their jobs. Even more ambitious, in 1997 a proposal to provide health insurance for children passed with his support. The president's cautious approach, combined with a prosperous economy, led Clinton's popularity in polls to rise above 60 percent.

Incremental reforms

But the president confronted a potential political disaster in January 1998: allegations that he had carried on an extramarital affair with a 21-year-old White House intern, and then pressed her to deny the affair under oath. Reporters raised the possibility that associates of the president had solicited jobs for the intern in return for her silence.

Accusations of personal misconduct by the president were not new. A long-running controversy, known as the Whitewater affair, centered on special treat-

Presidential scandals

ment that the Clintons might have received in a failed real estate venture during the early 1980s. In 1994 a panel of federal judges appointed Special Prosecutor Kenneth Starr to investigate. Starr prosecuted and convicted several friends of the president for fraud. Even so, four years of investigation produced little evidence implicating the president in any illegal activities.

Feverish press coverage of the alleged White House infidelity reignited controversy over the president's conduct. Clinton already faced a lawsuit accusing him of sexual harrassment while he served as governor of Arkansas. In response to the intern scandal, Special Prosecutor Starr enlarged his investigation. News reports suggested Starr was seeking to prove that the White House had participated in a cover-up, both of this scandal and of Whitewater. Television commentators spoke ominously of the president's resignation or, failing that, his impeachment.

To the amazement of Clinton's foes, the president's popularity ratings rose. A federal judge dismissed the sexual harrassment suit in March 1998. Unemployment reached new lows, while the stock market hit record highs. Preferring prosperity to political turmoil, the public refused to link the president's personal conduct with his job performance. In addition, Starr found himself embroiled in controversy. His aggressive pursuit of witnesses dismayed even some of his staunch supporters. Unless the investigation produced convincing evidence of legal wrongdoing, President Clinton appeared likely to serve out his second term, regardless of what Americans believed about his private life.

A NATION OF NATIONS IN THE TWENTY-FIRST CENTURY

When George Washington took the oath of office in 1789, he understood all too well the odds against the survival of the United States. History offered no example of such a large and diverse republic ever enduring for long. As the United States approaches the twenty-first century, its population and territory have grown even larger and ever more diverse. More than 250 million inhabit a nation exceeding 3.6 million square miles. Such size and diversity would have astonished Washington. Given the present state of the world, in which ethnic, religious, and nationalist rivalries threaten so many nations, the survival of the American republic should perhaps astonish us as well.

How well the republic has dealt with the conflicts among its diverse citizenry has depended on the ability of different groups to participate equally and openly in the political system. The republic's most dramatic failure came with the Civil War. That breakdown occurred, it might be argued, because enslaved African Americans were forbidden any participation in the system—indeed, were treated as the property of other Americans who could and did exercise political power. Many pivotal moments in American history have turned on the attempts of groups to exercise effective political power—whether western Populists or eastern immigrants, militant suffragettes or concerned evangelicals. In a nation where half the people have moved over the past decade and immigration has reached new highs, diversity and mobility define the social fabric. As a consequence, the debate over equal participation will continue.

The New Immigration

During the 1980s, more than 7 million immigrants entered the country legally—more than in any decade in American history except 1901–1910. Adding another 300,000 to 500,000 illegal immigrants each year, the total was even greater than the 8.8 million arriving in the first decade of the century.

Latin American immigrants accounted for as much as 40 percent of the yearly influx, as they had since the 1960s. But in addition to Mexicans, Cubans, and Puerto Ricans, the Latino population in the 1980s included communities of Dominicans and Central Americans. Like immigrants at the turn of the century, established Hispanic families provided housing for newer immigrants, who were often single. The newcomers hoped to save money from their weekly paychecks to send to relatives in Mexico or Central America. However, in an economy increasingly divided between skilled jobs in the service sectors and low-paying unskilled jobs, Latinos lagged behind Anglos and black Americans in education. Often, the lack of adequate English-language skill discouraged success.

Latin immigrants

The political climate of the 1990s alarmed many Latinos. The welfare reform bill passed in 1996 prohibited legal immigrants who had not become citizens from receiving most federal welfare benefits. Furthermore, pressures to restrict immigration were rising, especially in California. In response, applications by legal immigrants to become U.S. citizens rose sharply: from almost 446,000 in 1995 to 1.2 million in 1996.

Once the Immigration Act of 1965 eliminated the national origins quota system, immigration from Asia increased heavily. By 1990 about 7.3 million Asian Americans lived in the United States. Like earlier immigrants from Europe, those from the Pacific rim came in waves. Some, like the Vietnamese "boat people" of the late 1970s, were driven from their homes by economic or political turmoil. Others were drawn to reunite families or realize greater opportunities in the Western Hemisphere. "My brother-in-law left his wife in Taiwan and came here as a student to get a Ph.D. in engineering," explained Subi Lin Felipe. "After he received his degree, he got a job in San Jose. Then he brought in a sister and his wife, who brought over one of her brothers and me. And my brother's wife then came."

Asian Americans

Professional Asian-Indians emigrated in search of better jobs. Doctors and nurses constituted a large percentage of the early Korean immigrants. But

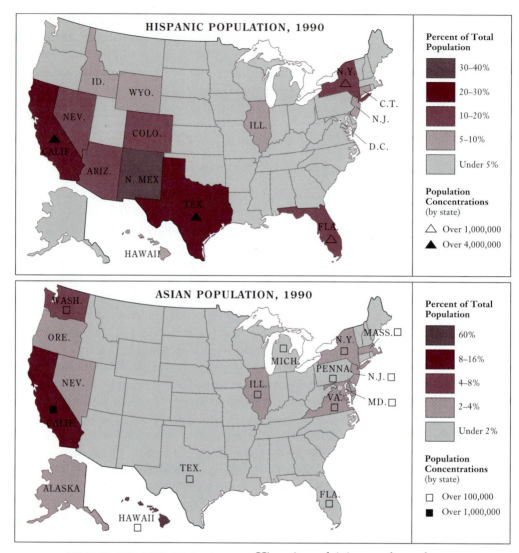

HISPANIC AND ASIAN POPULATIONS   Hispanics and Asians made up the two fastest-growing population groups in the United States over the past several decades. Demographers predict that Hispanics will soon displace African Americans as the nation's single largest minority group.

letters home soon attracted a more diverse population, which concentrated in small businesses. The presence of other Asian Americans and an international atmosphere drew many Asians to New York City, but climate made Hawaii and California particulary popular destinations. Of more than 800,000 Korean-Americans, about a quarter lived around Los Angeles in 1990. So, too, the 1.4 million Japanese-Americans settled primarily in California and Hawaii. By contrast, the federal government attempted to disperse around the country nearly half a million Vietnamese (as well as Cambodians and Laotians) who fled after the American withdrawal from Southeast Asia.

The relative success of many Asian Americans has led the media often to stereotype them as a "model minority"; yet the experience of Asian immigrants remains widely diverse, encompassing high-income Filipino-American doctors and low-income agricultural laborers, Japanese-Americans who are poor and elderly as well as those who are younger, upwardly mobile technicians. Ethnic tensions, made worse by job losses and an American trade deficit with Asian countries, gave rise periodically to acts of violence. During the 1992 Los Angeles riots, for example, Korean shops were often the targets of looters and arsonists.

A "model minority"

Equality Still Denied

By the 1980s the African American community had seemingly split in two. A significant minority was successfully living the American dream. Almost three times more black Americans held public office in the 1970s and 1980s than had in the 1960s. They made substantial strides in the professions, management, sports, and entertainment. The earnings of black households rose faster than those for whites in the 1970s and 1980s, although they remained 20 percent lower.

But the surge of African Americans into middle-class occupations tended to disguise the persistence of poverty tied to race. In the 1970s and 1980s, more young families were counted among the nation's poor. Those families were increasingly headed by single women. More than 40 percent of all black families (versus 12 percent for whites) were headed by women, and the number was growing. To make matters worse, the largest numbers of black families were concentrated in urban areas hard hit by the recessionary economy. Black unemployment, particularly severe among teenagers and young adults, was twice the national average. More shocking still, the infant mortality rate for African Americans was double the white average and worse than that for some Third World nations. Homicide was the leading cause of death for black males between 15 and 34, and in that group about 20 percent had prison records. These were the cruelest realities of poverty.

The persistence of poverty

One event starkly dramatized the ongoing currents of racial tension in America: the murder trial of O. J. Simpson. Born into a ghetto family, Simpson had become first a football legend, then a movie star and television personality. He seemed to defy all notions that race prejudice restricted African Americans. But in June 1994 police charged Simpson with the murders of his white wife, Nicole, and a friend. During televised proceedings Simpson's attorneys transformed what seemed to be a strong prosecution case into a debate over whether Simpson had been the victim of systematic police racism. The defense revealed that the lead police officer in the case lied on the stand about his own prejudices and his use of racial slurs. After a trial

The OJ case

lasting almost a year, a jury took just four hours to acquit. Regardless of Simpson's guilt or innocence, the trial demonstrated the lines of race dividing American society. The vast majority of whites believed Simpson guilty; most African Americans thought he was innocent. White and black Americans disagreed because they held differing opinions of whether the American system of justice permitted a fair trial for all its citizens.

In the United States, where diversity—and therefore conflict—remains central to its history, the debate continues over how strongly government should intervene to manage the conflicts of a modern industrial state. For better or worse, the long-term trend has been clear. As economic power became more concentrated in the late nineteenth century and as cycles of boom and bust periodically wracked the nation, government has increased its powers to curb the excesses of the market and to provide both economic protection and social guarantees for its citizens. Undoubtedly the debate will continue, as it has for the past 200 years, over how to make diversity the strength, not the weakness, of a nation of nations.

SIGNIFICANT EVENTS

1978 — *Bakke v. Regents of the University of California*
1979 — Moral Majority established
1980 — Ronald Reagan elected president
1981 — Reagan breaks air controllers' strike; Economic Recovery Tax Act; United States begins aiding Nicaraguan Contras
1982 — Attack on U.S. Marine barracks in Lebanon
1983 — Invasion of Grenada
1984 — Boland Amendment passed; Reagan reelected
1985 — Gramm–Rudman Act; United States begins secret arms-for-hostages negotiations with Iran
1986 — Reykjavík summit
1987 — Iran-Contra hearings
1988 — George Bush elected president
1989 — Fall of the Berlin Wall
1990 — Iraq invades Kuwait; Clean Air Act
1991 — Operation Desert Storm launched; Strategic Arms Reduction Treaty (START) concluded; Clarence Thomas hearings; 11 former republics of the Soviet Union become the Commonwealth of Independent States
1992 — Los Angeles riots; *Planned Parenthood v. Casey;* Bill Clinton elected president
1993 — Deficit-reduction budget passed; North American Free Trade Agreement approved
1994 — Health care reform fails; Republicans win control of Congress
1995 — O. J. Simpson acquitted in murder trial; Dayton accords signed
1996 — Welfare reform legislation signed; Clinton defeats Dole
1998 — Scandal over President Clinton's personal conduct

APPENDIX

THE DECLARATION OF INDEPENDENCE

In Congress, July 4, 1776,

THE UNANIMOUS DECLARATION OF THE
THIRTEEN UNITED STATES OF AMERICA

When, in the course of human events, it becomes necessary for one people to dissolve the political bands which have connected them with another, and to assume, among the powers of the earth, the separate and equal station to which the laws of nature and of nature's God entitle them, a decent respect to the opinions of mankind requires that they should declare the causes which impel them to the separation.

We hold these truths to be self-evident, that all men are created equal; that they are endowed by their Creator with certain unalienable rights; that among these, are life, liberty, and the pursuit of happiness. That, to secure these rights, governments are instituted among men, deriving their just powers from the consent of the governed; that, whenever any form of government becomes destructive of these ends, it is the right of the people to alter or to abolish it, and to institute a new government, laying its foundation on such principles, and organizing its powers in such form, as to them shall seem most likely to effect their safety and happiness. Prudence, indeed, will dictate that governments long established, should not be changed for light and transient causes; and, accordingly, all experience hath shown, that mankind are more disposed to suffer, while evils are sufferable, than to right themselves by abolishing the forms to which they are accustomed. But, when a long train of abuses and usurpations, pursuing invariably the same object, evinces a design to reduce them under absolute despotism, it is their right, it is their duty, to throw off such government and to provide new guards for their future security. Such has been the patient sufferance of these colonies, and such is now the necessity which constrains them to alter their former systems of government. The history of the present King of Great Britain is a history of repeated injuries and usurpations, all having, in direct object, the establishment of an absolute tyranny over these States. To prove this, let facts be submitted to a candid world:

He has refused his assent to laws the most wholesome and necessary for the public good.

He has forbidden his governors to pass laws of immediate and pressing importance, unless suspended in their operation till his assent should be obtained; and, when so suspended, he has utterly neglected to attend to them.

He has refused to pass other laws for the accommodation of large districts of people, unless those people would relinquish the right of representation in the legislature; a right inestimable to them, and formidable to tyrants only.

He has called together legislative bodies at places unusual, uncomfortable, and distant from the depository of their public records, for the sole purpose of fatiguing them into compliance with his measures.

He has dissolved representative houses repeatedly for opposing, with manly firmness, his invasions on the rights of the people.

He has refused, for a long time after such dissolutions, to cause others to be elected; whereby the legislative powers, incapable of annihilation, have returned to the people at large for their exercise; the state remaining, in the meantime, exposed to all the danger of invasion from without, and convulsions within.

He has endeavored to prevent the population of these States; for that purpose, obstructing the laws for naturalization of foreigners, refusing to pass others to encourage their migration hither, and raising the conditions of new appropriations of lands.

He has obstructed the administration of justice, by refusing his assent to laws for establishing judiciary powers.

He has made judges dependent on his will alone, for the tenure of their offices, and the amount and payment of their salaries.

He has erected a multitude of new offices, and sent hither swarms of officers to harass our people, and eat out their substance.

He has kept among us, in time of peace, standing armies, without the consent of our legislatures.

He has affected to render the military independent of, and superior to, the civil power.

He has combined, with others, to subject us to a jurisdiction foreign to our Constitution, and unacknowledged by our laws; giving his assent to their acts of pretended legislation:

For quartering large bodies of armed troops among us:

For protecting them by a mock trial, from punishment, for any murders which they should commit on the inhabitants of these States:

For cutting off our trade with all parts of the world:

For imposing taxes on us without our consent:

For depriving us, in many cases, of the benefit of trial by jury:

For transporting us beyond seas to be tried for pretended offences:

For abolishing the free system of English laws in a neighboring province, establishing therein an arbitrary government, and enlarging its boundaries, so as to render it at once an example and fit instrument for introducing the same absolute rule into these colonies:

For taking away our charters, abolishing our most valuable laws, and altering, fundamentally, the powers of our governments:

For suspending our own legislatures, and declaring themselves invested with power to legislate for us in all cases whatsoever.

He has abdicated government here, by declaring us out of his protection, and waging war against us.

He has plundered our seas, ravaged our coasts, burnt our towns, and destroyed the lives of our people.

He is, at this time, transporting large armies of foreign mercenaries to complete the works of death, desolation, and tyranny, already begun, with circumstances of cruelty and perfidy scarcely paralleled in the most barbarous ages, and totally unworthy the head of a civilized nation.

He has constrained our fellow citizens, taken captive on the high seas, to bear arms against their country, to become the executioners of their friends, and brethren, or to fall themselves by their hands.

He has excited domestic insurrections amongst us, and has endeavored to bring on the inhabitants of our frontiers, the merciless Indian savages, whose known rule of warfare is an undistinguished destruction of all ages, sexes, and conditions.

In every stage of these oppressions, we have petitioned for redress, in the most humble terms; our repeated petitions have been answered only by repeated injury. A prince, whose character is thus marked by every act which may define a tyrant, is unfit to be the ruler of a free people.

Nor have we been wanting in attention to our British brethren. We have warned them from time to time, of attempts made by their legislature to extend an unwarrantable jurisdiction over us. We have reminded them of the circumstances of our emigration and settlement here. We have appealed to their native justice and magnanimity, and we have conjured them, by the ties of our common kindred, to disavow these usurpations, which would inevitably interrupt our connections and correspondence. They, too, have been deaf to the voice of justice and consanguinity. We must, therefore, acquiesce in the necessity which denounces our separation, and hold them as we hold the rest of mankind, enemies in war, in peace, friends.

We, therefore, the representatives of the United States of America, in general Congress assembled, appealing to the Supreme Judge of the world for the rectitude of our intentions, do, in the name, and by the authority of the good people of these colonies, solemnly publish and declare, that these united colonies are, and of right ought to be, free and independent states: that they are absolved from all allegiance to the British Crown, and that all political connection between them and the state of Great Britain is and ought to be, totally dissolved; and that, as free and independent states, they have full power to levy war, conclude peace, contract alliances, establish commerce, and to do all other acts and things which independent states may of right do. And, for the support of this declaration, with a firm reliance on the protection of Divine Providence, we mutually pledge to each other our lives, our fortunes, and our sacred honor.

The foregoing Declaration was, by order of Congress, engrossed, and signed by the following members:

JOHN HANCOCK

New Hampshire
Josiah Bartlett
William Whipple
Matthew Thornton

Massachusetts Bay
Samuel Adams
John Adams
Robert Treat Paine
Elbridge Gerry

Rhode Island
Stephen Hopkins
William Ellery

Connecticut
Roger Sherman
Samuel Huntington
William Williams
Oliver Wolcott

New York
William Floyd
Philip Livingston
Francis Lewis
Lewis Morris

New Jersey
Richard Stockton
John Witherspoon
Francis Hopkinson
John Hart
Abraham Clark

Pennsylvania
Robert Morris
Benjamin Rush
Benjamin Franklin
John Morton
George Clymer
James Smith
George Taylor
James Wilson
George Ross

Delaware
Caesar Rodney
George Reed
Thomas M'Kean

Maryland
Samuel Chase
William Paca
Thomas Stone
Charles Carroll,
    of Carrollton

Virginia
George Wythe
Richard Henry Lee
Thomas Jefferson
Benjamin Harrison
Thomas Nelson, Jr.
Francis Lightfoot Lee
Carter Braxton

North Carolina
William Hooper
Joseph Hewes
John Penn

South Carolina
Edward Rutledge
Thomas Heyward, Jr.
Thomas Lynch, Jr.
Arthur Middleton

Georgia
Button Gwinnett
Lyman Hall
George Walton

Resolved, That copies of the Declaration be sent to the several assemblies, conventions, and committees, or councils of safety, and to the several commanding officers of the continental troops; that it be proclaimed in each of the United States, at the head of the army.

THE CONSTITUTION OF THE UNITED STATES OF AMERICA[1]

We the People of the United States, in Order to form a more perfect Union, establish Justice, insure domestic Tranquility, provide for the common defence, promote the general Welfare, and secure the Blessings of Liberty to ourselves and our Posterity, do ordain and establish this CONSTITUTION for the United States of America.

ARTICLE 1

Section 1. All legislative Powers herein granted shall be vested in a Congress of the United States, which shall consist of a Senate and House of Representatives.

Section 2. The House of Representatives shall be composed of Members chosen every second Year by the People of the several States, and the Electors in each State shall have the Qualifications requisite for Electors of the most numerous Branch of the State Legislature.

No Person shall be a Representative who shall not have attained to the Age of twenty-five Years, and been seven Years a Citizen of the United States, and who shall not, when elected, be an Inhabitant of that State in which he shall be chosen.

[Representatives and direct Taxes[2] shall be apportioned among the several States which may be included within this Union, according to their respective Numbers, which shall be determined by adding to the whole Number of free Persons, including those bound to Service for a Term of Years, and excluding Indians not taxed, three fifths of all other Persons.][3] The actual Enumeration shall be made within three Years after the first Meeting of the Congress of the United States, and within every subsequent Term of ten Years, in such Manner as they shall by Law direct. The Number of Representatives shall not exceed one for every thirty Thousand, but each State shall have at Least one Representative; and until such enumeration shall be made, the State of New Hampshire shall be entitled to chuse three, Massachusetts eight, Rhode-Island and Providence Plantations one, Connecticut five, New York six, New Jersey four, Pennsylvania eight, Delaware one, Maryland six, Virginia ten, North Carolina five, South Carolina five, and Georgia three.

When vacancies happen in the Representation from any State, the Executive Authority thereof shall issue Writs of Election to fill such Vacancies.

The House of Representatives shall chuse their Speaker and other Officers; and shall have the sole Power of Impeachment.

Section 3. The Senate of the United States shall be composed of two Senators from each State, chosen by the Legislature thereof, for six Years; and each Senator shall have one Vote.

Immediately after they shall be assembled in Consequence of the first Election, they shall be divided as equally as may be into three Classes. The Seats of the Senators of the first Class shall be vacated at the Expiration of the second Year, of the second Class at the Expiration of the fourth Year, and of the third Class at the Expiration of the sixth Year, so that one-third may be chosen every second Year; and if Vacancies happen by Resignation, or otherwise, during the Recess of the Legislature of any State, the Executive thereof may make temporary Appointments until the next Meeting of the Legislature, which shall then fill such Vacancies.

---

[1]This version follows the original Constitution in capitalization and spelling. It is adapted from the text published by the United States Department of the Interior, Office of Education.

[2]Altered by the Sixteenth Amendment.

[3]Negated by the Fourteenth Amendment.

No Person shall be a Senator who shall not have attained to the Age of thirty Years, and been nine Years a Citizen of the United States, and who shall not, when elected, be an Inhabitant of that State for which he shall be chosen.

The Vice President of the United States shall be President of the Senate, but shall have no vote, unless they be equally divided.

The Senate shall chuse their other Officers and also a President pro tempore, in the absence of the Vice President, or when he shall exercise the Office of President of the United States.

The Senate shall have the sole Power to try all Impeachments. When sitting for that purpose they shall be on Oath or Affirmation. When the President of the United States is tried, the Chief Justice shall preside: And no person shall be convicted without the Concurrence of two thirds of the Members present.

Judgment in Cases of Impeachment shall not extend further than to removal from Office, and disqualification to hold and enjoy any Office of honor, Trust, or Profit under the United States: but the Party convicted shall nevertheless be liable and subject to Indictment, Trial, Judgment, and Punishment, according to Law.

Section 4. The Times, Places and Manner of holding Elections for Senators and Representatives, shall be prescribed in each State by the Legislature thereof; but the Congress may at any time by Law make or alter such Regulations, except as to the Places of Chusing Senators.

The Congress shall assemble at least once in every Year, and such Meeting shall be on the first Monday in December, unless they shall by Law appoint a different Day.

Section 5. Each House shall be the Judge of the Elections, Returns and Qualifications of its own Members, and a Majority of each shall constitute a Quorum to do Business; but a smaller number may adjourn from day to day, and may be authorized to compel the Attendance of absent Members, in such Manner, and under such Penalties, as each House may provide.

Each House may determine the Rules of its Proceedings, punish its Members for disorderly Behaviour, and, with the Concurrence of two thirds, expel a Member.

Each House shall keep a Journal of its Proceedings, and from time to time publish the same, excepting such Parts as may in their Judgment require Secrecy; and the Yeas and Nays of the Members of either House on any question shall, at the Desire of one fifth of those Present, be entered on the Journal.

Neither House, during the Session of Congress, shall, without the Consent of the other, adjourn for more than three days, nor to any other Place than that in which the two Houses shall be sitting.

Section 6. The Senators and Representatives shall receive a Compensation for their Services, to be ascertained by Law, and paid out of the Treasury of the United States. They shall in all Cases, except Treason, Felony, and Breach of the Peace, be privileged from Arrest during their Attendance at the Session of their respective Houses, and in going to and returning from the same; and for any Speech or Debate in either House, they shall not be questioned in any other Place.

No Senator or Representative shall, during the Time for which he was elected, be appointed to any civil Office under the Authority of the United States, which shall have been created, or the Emoluments whereof shall have been increased, during such time; and no Person holding any Office under the United States shall be a Member of either House during his continuance in Office.

Section 7. All Bills for raising Revenue shall originate in the House of Representatives; but the Senate may propose or concur with Amendments as on other bills.

Every Bill which shall have passed the House of Representatives and the Senate, shall, before it become a Law, be presented to the President of the United States; If he approve he shall sign it, but if not he shall return it, with his Objections, to that House in which it shall have originated, who shall enter the Objections at large on their Journal, and proceed to reconsider it. If after such Reconsideration two thirds of that House shall agree to pass the bill, it shall be sent, together with the objections, to the other House, by which it shall likewise be reconsidered, and if approved by two thirds of that House, it shall become a Law. But in all such Cases the Votes of both Houses shall be determined by Yeas and Nays, and the Names of the Persons voting for and against the Bill shall be entered on the Journal of each House respectively. If any Bill shall not be returned by the President within ten Days (Sundays excepted) after it shall have been presented to him, the Same shall be a Law, in like Manner as if he had signed it, unless the Congress by their Adjournment prevent its Return, in which Case it shall not be a Law.

Every Order, Resolution, or Vote to which the Concurrence of the Senate and House of Representatives may be necessary (except on a question of Adjournment) shall be presented to the President of the United States; and before the Same shall take Effect, shall be approved by him, or being disapproved by him, shall be repassed by two thirds of the Senate and House of Representatives, according to the Rules and Limitations prescribed in the Case of a Bill.

Section 8.   The Congress shall have Power To lay and collect Taxes, Duties, Imposts and Excises, to pay the Debts and provide for the common Defence and general Welfare of the United States; but all Duties, Imposts and Excises shall be uniform throughout the United States;

To borrow money on the credit of the United States;

To regulate Commerce with foreign Nations, and among the several States, and with the Indian Tribes;

To establish an uniform rule of Naturalization, and uniform Laws on the subject of Bankruptcies throughout the United States;

To coin Money, regulate the Value thereof, and of foreign Coin, and fix the Standard of Weights and Measures;

To provide for the Punishment of counterfeiting the Securities and current Coin of the United States;

To establish Post Offices and post Roads;

To promote the Progress of Science and useful Arts, by securing for limited Times to Authors and Inventors the exclusive Right to their respective Writings and Discoveries;

To constitute Tribunals inferior to the Supreme Court;

To define and punish Piracies and Felonies committed on the high Seas, and Offenses against the Law of Nations;

To declare War, grant Letters of Marque and Reprisal, and make Rules concerning Captures on Land and Water;

To raise and support Armies, but no Appropriation of Money to that Use shall be for a longer Term than two Years;

To provide and maintain a Navy;

To make Rules for the Government and Regulation of the land and naval forces;

To provide for calling forth the Militia to execute the Laws of the Union, suppress Insurrections and repel Invasions;

To provide for organizing, arming, and disciplining the Militia, and for governing such Part of them as may be employed in the Service of the United States, reserving to the States respectively, the Appointment of the Officers, and the Authority of training the Militia according to the discipline prescribed by Congress;

To exercise exclusive Legislation in all Cases whatsoever, over such District (not exceeding ten Miles square) as may, by Cession of particular States, and the acceptance of Congress, become the Seat of the Government of the United States, and to exercise like Authority over all Places purchased by the Consent of the Legislature of the State in which the Same shall be, for the Erection of Forts, Magazines, Arsenals, Dock-yards, and other needful Buildings;—And

To make all Laws which shall be necessary and proper for carrying into Execution the foregoing Powers, and all other Powers vested by this Constitution in the Government of the United States, or in any Department or Officer thereof.

Section 9.   The Migration or Importation of such Persons as any of the States now existing shall think proper to admit, shall not be prohibited by the Congress prior to the Year one thousand eight hundred and eight, but a tax or duty may be imposed on such Importation, not exceeding ten dollars for each Person.

The privilege of the Writ of Habeas Corpus shall not be suspended, unless when in Cases of Rebellion or Invasion the public Safety may require it.

No bill of Attainder or ex post facto Law shall be passed.

No capitation, or other direct, Tax shall be laid unless in Proportion to the Census or Enumeration herein before directed to be taken.

No Tax or Duty shall be laid on Articles exported from any State.

No Preference shall be given by any Regulation of Commerce or Revenue to the Ports of one State over those of another: nor shall Vessels bound to, or from, one State, be obliged to enter, clear, or pay Duties in another.

No Money shall be drawn from the Treasury, but in Consequence of Appropriations made by Law; and a regular Statement and Account of the Receipts and Expenditures of all public Money shall be published from time to time.

No Title of Nobility shall be granted by the United States: And no Person holding any Office of Profit or Trust under them, shall, without the Consent of the Congress, accept of any present, Emolument, Office, or Title, of any kind whatever, from any King, Prince, or foreign State.

Section 10.   No State shall enter into any Treaty, Alliance, or Confederation; grant Letters of Marque and Reprisal; coin Money; emit Bills of Credit; make any Thing but gold and silver Coin a Tender in Payment of Debts; pass any Bill of Attainder, ex post facto Law, or Law impairing the Obligation of Contracts, or grant any Title of Nobility.

No State shall, without the Consent of the Congress, lay any Imposts or Duties on Imports or Exports, except what may be absolutely necessary for executing its inspection Laws; and the net Produce of all Duties and Imposts, laid by any State on Imports or Exports, shall be for the use of the Treasury of the United States; and all such Laws shall be subject to the Revision and Control of the Congress.

No state shall, without the Consent of Congress, lay any duty of Tonnage, keep Troops, or Ships of War in time of Peace, enter into any Agreement or Compact with another State, or with a foreign Power, or engage in War, unless actually invaded, or in such imminent Danger as will not admit of delay.

ARTICLE II

Section 1.   The executive Power shall be vested in a President of the United States of America. He shall hold his Office during the Term of four years, and, together with the Vice President, chosen for the same Term, be elected, as follows:

Each State shall appoint, in such Manner as the Legislature thereof may direct, a Number of Electors, equal to the whole Number of Senators and Representatives to which the State may be entitled in the Congress: but no Senator or Representative, or Person holding an Office of Trust or Profit under the United States, shall be appointed an Elector.

[The Electors shall meet in their respective States, and vote by Ballot for two persons, of whom one at least shall not be an Inhabitant of the same State with themselves. And they shall make a List of all the Persons voted for, and of the Number of Votes for each; which List they shall sign and certify, and transmit sealed to the Seat of the Government of the United States, directed to the President of the Senate. The President of the Senate shall, in the Presence of the Senate and House of Representatives, open all the Certificates, and the Votes shall then be counted. The Person having the greatest Number of Votes shall be the President, if such Number be a Majority of the whole Number of Electors appointed; and if there be more than one who have such Majority, and have an equal Number of Votes, then the House of Representatives shall immediately chuse by Ballot one of them for President; and if no Person have a Majority, then from the five highest on the List the said House shall in like Manner chuse the President. But in chusing the President, the Votes shall be taken by States, the Representation from each State having one Vote; a quorum for this Purpose shall consist of a Member or Members from two-thirds of the States, and a Majority of all the States shall be necessary to a Choice. In every Case, after the Choice of the President, the Person having the greatest Number of Votes of the Electors shall be the Vice President. But if there should remain two or more who have equal votes, the Senate shall chuse from them by Ballot the Vice President.][4]

The Congress may determine the Time of chusing the Electors, and the Day on which they shall give their Votes; which Day shall be the same throughout the United States.

No person except a natural-born Citizen, or a Citizen of the United States, at the time of the Adoption of this Constitution, shall be eligible to the Office of President; neither shall any Person be eligible to that Office who shall not have attained to the Age of thirty-five years, and been fourteen Years a Resident within the United States.

In Case of the Removal of the President from Office, or of his Death, Resignation, or Inability to discharge the Powers and Duties of the said Office, the same shall devolve on the Vice President, and the Congress may by Law provide for the Case of Removal, Death, Resignation, or Inability, both of the President and Vice President, declaring what Officer shall then act as President, and such Officer shall act accordingly, until the disability be removed, or a President shall be elected.

The President shall, at stated Times, receive for his Services a Compensation, which shall neither be increased nor diminished during the Period for which he shall have been elected, and he shall not receive within that Period any other Emolument from the United States, or any of them.

Before he enter on the execution of his Office, he shall take the following Oath or Affirmation:— "I do solemnly swear (or affirm) that I will faithfully execute the Office of President of the United States, and will, to the best of my Ability, preserve, protect, and defend the Constitution of the United States."

Section 2. The President shall be Commander in Chief of the Army and Navy of the United States, and of the Militia of the several States, when called into the actual Service of the United States; he may require the Opinion, in writing, of the principal Officer in each of the executive Departments, upon any subject relating to the Duties of their respective Offices, and he shall have Power to Grant Reprieves and Pardons for Offenses against the United States, except in Cases of Impeachment.

He shall have Power, by and with the Advice and Consent of the Senate, to make Treaties, provided two-thirds of the Senators present concur; and he shall nominate, and by and with the Advice and Consent of the Senate, shall appoint Ambassadors, other public Ministers and Consuls, Judges of the Supreme Court, and all other Officers of the United States, whose Appointments are not herein otherwise provided for, and which shall be established by Law: but the Congress may by Law vest the Appointment of such inferior Officers, as they think proper, in the President alone, in the Courts of Law, or in the Heads of Departments.

The President shall have Power to fill up all Vacancies that may happen during the Recess of the Senate, by granting Commissions which shall expire at the End of their next Session.

Section 3. He shall from time to time give to the Congress Information of the State of the Union, and recommend to their Consideration such Measures as he shall judge necessary and expedient; he may, on extraordinary occasions, convene both Houses, or either of them, and in Case of Disagreement between them, with respect to the Time of Adjournment, he may adjourn them to such Time as he shall think proper; he shall receive Ambassadors and other public Ministers; he shall take care that the Laws be faithfully executed, and shall Commission all the Officers of the United States.

Section 4. The President, Vice President and all civil Officers of the United States, shall be removed from Office on Impeachment for, and Conviction of, Treason, Bribery, or other high Crimes and Misdemeanors.

---

[4]Revised by the Twelfth Amendment.

ARTICLE III

Section 1. The judicial Power of the United States, shall be vested in one supreme Court, and in such inferior Courts as the Congress may from time to time ordain and establish. The Judges, both of the supreme and inferior Courts, shall hold their Offices during good Behaviour, and shall, at stated Times, receive for their Services, a Compensation, which shall not be diminished during their Continuance in Office.

Section 2. The judicial Power shall extend to all Cases, in Law and Equity, arising under this Constitution, the Laws of the United States, and Treaties made, or which shall be made, under their Authority;—to all Cases affecting ambassadors, other public ministers and consuls;—to all cases of admiralty and maritime Jurisdiction;—to Controversies to which the United States shall be a Party;—to Controversies between two or more States;—between a State and Citizens of another State;[5]—between Citizens of different States—between Citizens of the same State claiming Lands under Grants of different States, and between a State, or the Citizens thereof, and foreign States, Citizens, or Subjects.

In all Cases affecting Ambassadors, other public Ministers and Consuls, and those in which a State shall be Party, the supreme Court shall have original Jurisdiction. In all the other Cases before mentioned, the supreme Court shall have appellate Jurisdiction, both as to Law and Fact, with such Exceptions, and under such Regulations as the Congress shall make.

The trial of all Crimes, except in Cases of Impeachment, shall be by Jury; and such Trial shall be held in the State where the said Crimes shall have been committed; but when not committed within any State, the Trial shall be at such Place or Places as the Congress may by Law have directed.

Section 3. Treason against the United States, shall consist only in levying War against them, or in adhering to their Enemies, giving them Aid and Comfort. No Person shall be convicted of Treason unless on the Testimony of two Witnesses to the same overt Act, or on Confession in open Court.

The Congress shall have power to declare the Punishment of Treason, but no Attainder of Treason shall work Corruption of Blood, or Forfeiture except during the Life of the Person attainted.

ARTICLE IV

Section 1. Full Faith and Credit shall be given in each State to the public Acts, Records, and judicial Proceedings of every other State. And the Congress may by general Laws prescribe the Manner in which such Acts, Records and Proceedings shall be proved, and the Effect thereof.

Section 2. The Citizens of each State shall be entitled to all Privileges and Immunities of Citizens in the several States.

A Person charged in any State with Treason, Felony, or other Crime, who shall flee from Justice, and be found in another State, shall on demand of the executive Authority of the State from which he fled, be delivered up, to be removed to the State having Jurisdiction of the crime.

No Person held to Service or Labour in one State, under the Laws thereof, escaping into another, shall, in Consequence of any Law or Regulation therein, be discharged from such Service or Labour, but shall be delivered up on Claim of the Party to whom such Service or Labour may be due.

---

[5]Qualified by the Eleventh Amendment.

Section 3. New States may be admitted by the Congress into this Union; but no new State shall be formed or erected within the Jurisdiction of any other State; nor any State be formed by the Junction of two or more States, or parts of States, without the Consent of the Legislatures of the States concerned as well as of the Congress.

The Congress shall have Power to dispose of and make all needful Rules and Regulations respecting the Territory or other Property belonging to the United States; and nothing in this Constitution shall be so construed as to Prejudice any Claims of the United States, or of any particular State.

Section 4. The United States shall guarantee to every State in this Union a Republican Form of Government, and shall protect each of them against Invasion; and on Application of the Legislature, or of the Executive (when the Legislature cannot be convened) against domestic Violence.

ARTICLE V

The Congress, whenever two-thirds of both Houses shall deem it necessary, shall propose Amendments to this Constitution, or, on the Application of the Legislatures of two-thirds of the several States, shall call a Convention for proposing Amendments, which, in either Case, shall be valid to all Intents and Purposes, as part of this Constitution, when ratified by the Legislatures of three-fourths of the several States, or by Conventions in three-fourths thereof, as the one or the other Mode of Ratification may be proposed by the Congress; Provided that no Amendment which may be made prior to the Year One thousand eight hundred and eight shall in any Manner affect the first and fourth Clauses in the Ninth Section of the first Article; and that no State, without its Consent, shall be deprived of its equal Suffrage in the Senate.

ARTICLE VI

All Debts contracted and Engagements entered into, before the Adoption of this Constitution, shall be as valid against the United States under this Constitution, as under the Confederation.

This Constitution, and the Laws of the United States which shall be made in Pursuance thereof; and all Treaties made, or which shall be made, under the Authority of the United States, shall be the supreme Law of the Land; and the Judges in every State shall be bound thereby, any Thing in the Constitution or Laws of any State to the Contrary notwithstanding.

The Senators and Representatives before mentioned, and the Members of the several State Legislatures, and all executive and judicial Officers, both of the United States and of the several States, shall be bound by Oath or Affirmation to support this Constitution; but no religious Tests shall ever be required as a qualification to any Office or public Trust under the United States.

ARTICLE VII

The Ratification of the Conventions of nine States shall be sufficient for the Establishment of this Constitution between the States so ratifying the same.

Done in Convention by the Unanimous Consent of the States present the Seventeenth Day of September in the Year of our Lord one thousand seven hundred and Eighty seven, and of the Independence of the United States of America the Twelfth. In Witness whereof We have hereunto subscribed our Names.[6]

---

[6]These are the full names of the signers, which in some cases are not the signatures on the document.

GEORGE WASHINGTON

PRESIDENT AND DEPUTY FROM VIRGINIA

New Hampshire
John Langdon
Nicholas Gilman

New Jersey
William Livingston
David Brearley
William Paterson
Jonathan Dayton

Delaware
George Read
Gunning Bedford, Jr.
John Dickinson
Richard Bassett
Jacob Broom

North Carolina
William Blount
Richard Dobbs
  Spaight
Hugh Williamson

Massachusetts
Nathaniel Gorham
Rufus King

Connecticut
William Samuel
  Johnson
Roger Sherman

New York
Alexander Hamilton

Pennsylvania
Benjamin Franklin
Thomas Mifflin
Robert Morris
George Clymer
Thomas FitzSimons
Jared Ingersoll
James Wilson
Gouverneur Morris

Maryland
James McHenry
Daniel of
  St. Thomas Jenifer
Daniel Carroll

Virginia
John Blair
James Madison, Jr.

South Carolina
John Rutledge
Charles Cotesworth
  Pinckney
Charles Pinckney
Pierce Butler

Georgia
William Few
Abraham Baldwin

Articles in Addition to, and Amendment of, the Constitution of the United States of America, Proposed by Congress, and Ratified by the Legislatures of the Several States, Pursuant to the Fifth Article of the Original Constitution[7]

[AMENDMENT I]

Congress shall make no law respecting an establishment of religion, or prohibiting the free exercise thereof; or abridging the freedom of speech, or of the press; or the right of the people peaceably to assemble, and to petition the Government for a redress of grievances.

[AMENDEMENT II]

A well regulated Militia, being necessary to the security of a free State, the right of the people to keep and bear Arms shall not be infringed.

[AMENDMENT III]

No Soldier shall, in time of peace, be quartered in any house, without the consent of the Owner, nor in time of war, but in a manner to be prescribed by law.

[AMENDMENT IV]

The right of the people to be secure in their persons, houses, papers, and effects, against unreasonable searches and seizures, shall not be violated, and no Warrants shall issue, but upon proba-

---

[7]This heading appears only in the joint resolution submitting the first ten amendments, known as the Bill of Rights.

ble cause, supported by Oath or affirmation, and particularly describing the place to be searched, and the persons or things to be seized.

[AMENDMENT V]

No person shall be held to answer for a capital or otherwise infamous crime, unless on a present-ment or indictment of a Grand Jury, except in cases arising in the land or naval forces, or in the Militia, when in actual service in time of War or public danger; nor shall any person be subject for the same offence to be twice put in jeopardy of life or limb; nor shall be compelled in any crim-inal case to be a witness against himself, nor be deprived of life, liberty, or property, without due process of law; nor shall private property be taken for public use, without just compensation.

[AMENDMENT VI]

In all criminal prosecutions, the accused shall enjoy the right to a speedy and public trial, by an impartial jury of the State and district wherein the crime shall have been committed, which dis-trict shall have been previously ascertained by law, and to be informed of the nature and cause of the accusation; to be confronted with the witnesses against him; to have compulsory process for obtaining witnesses in his favour, and to have the Assistance of Counsel for his defence.

[AMENDMENT VII]

In suits at common law, where the value in controversy shall exceed twenty dollars, the right of trial by jury shall be preserved, and no fact tried by a jury, shall be otherwise reexamined in any Court of the United States, than according to the rules of the common law.

[AMENDMENT VIII]

Excessive bail shall not be required, nor excessive fines imposed, nor cruel and unusual punish-ments inflicted.

[AMENDMENT IX]

The enumeration of the Constitution, of certain rights, shall not be construed to deny or dispar-age others retained by the people.

[AMENDMENT X]

The powers not delegated to the United States by the Constitution, nor prohibited by it to the States, are reserved to the States respectively, or to the people.

[Amendments I–X, in force 1791.]

[AMENDMENT XI][8]

The Judicial power of the United States shall not be construed to extend to any suit in law or equity, commenced or prosecuted against one of the United States by Citizens of another State, or by Citizens or Subjects of any Foreign State.

[AMENDMENT XII][9]

The Electors shall meet in their respective States and vote by ballot for President and Vice-President, one of whom, at least, shall not be an inhabitant of the same State with themselves; they shall name in their ballots the person voted for as President, and in distinct ballots the person voted for as Vice-President, and they shall make distinct lists of all persons voted for as President, and of all persons voted for as Vice-President, and of the number of votes for each, which lists they shall sign and certify, and transmit sealed to the seat of the government of the United States, directed to the President of the Senate;—The President of the Senate shall, in the presence of the Senate and House of Representatives, open all the certificates and the votes shall then be counted;—The person having the greatest number of votes for President, shall be the President, if such number be a majority of the whole number of Electors appointed; and if no person have such majority, then from the persons having the highest numbers not exceeding three on the list of those voted for as President, the House of Representatives shall choose immediately, by ballot, the President. But in choosing the President, the votes shall be taken by states, the representation from each state having one vote; a quorum for this purpose shall consist of a member or members from two-thirds of the states, and a majority of all the states shall be necessary to a choice. And if the House of Representatives shall not choose a President whenever the right of choice shall devolve upon them, before the fourth day of March next following, then the Vice-President shall act as President, as in the case of the death or other constitutional disability of the President.—The person having the greatest number of votes as Vice-President, shall be the Vice-President, if such number be a majority of the whole number of Electors appointed, and if no person have a majority, then from the two highest numbers on the list, the Senate shall choose the Vice-President; a quorum for the purpose shall consist of two-thirds of the whole number of Senators, and a majority of the whole number shall be necessary to a choice. But no person constitutionally ineligible to the office of President shall be eligible to that of Vice-President of the United States.

[AMENDMENT XIII][10]

Section 1.   Neither slavery nor involuntary servitude, except as a punishment for crime whereof the party shall have been duly convicted, shall exist within the United States, or any place subject to their jurisdiction.

Section 2.   Congress shall have power to enforce this article by appropriate legislation.

[AMENDMENT XIV][11]

Section 1.   All persons born or naturalized in the United States, and subject to the jurisdiction thereof, are citizens of the United States and of the State wherein they reside. No State shall

---

[8]Adopted in 1798.
[9]Adopted in 1804.
[10]Adopted in 1865.
[11]Adopted in 1868.

abridge the privileges or immunities of citizens of the United States; nor shall any State deprive any person of life, liberty, or property, without due process of law; nor deny to any person within its jurisdiction the equal protection of the laws.

Section 2.   Representatives shall be apportioned among the several States according to their respective numbers, counting the whole number of persons in each State, excluding Indians not taxed. But when the right to vote at any election for the choice of electors for President and Vice-President of the United States, Representatives in Congress, the Executive and Judicial officers of a State, or the members of the Legislature thereof, is denied to any of the male inhabitants of such State, being twenty-one years of age, and citizens of the United States, or in any way abridged, except for participation in rebellion, or other crime, the basis of representation therein shall be reduced in the proportion which the number of such male citizens shall bear to the whole number of male citizens twenty-one years of age in such State.

Section 3.   No person shall be a Senator or Representative in Congress, or elector of President and Vice-President, or hold any office, civil or military, under the United States, or under any State, who, having previously taken an oath, as a member of Congress, or as an officer of the United States, or as a member of any State legislature, or as an executive or judicial officer of any State, to support the Constitution of the United States, shall have engaged in insurrection or rebellion against the same, or given aid or comfort to the enemies thereof. But Congress may by a vote of two-thirds of each House, remove such disability.

Section 4.   The validity of the public debt of the United States, authorized by law, including debts incurred for payment of pensions and bounties for services in suppressing insurrection or rebellion, shall not be questioned. But neither the United States nor any State shall assume or pay any debts or obligation incurred in aid of insurrection or rebellion against the United States, or any claim for the loss or emancipation of any slave; but all such debts, obligations, and claims shall be held illegal and void.

Section 5.   The Congress shall have the power to enforce, by appropriate legislation, the provisions of this article.

[AMENDMENT XV][12]

Section 1.   The right of citizens of the United States to vote shall not be denied or abridged by the United States or by any State on account of race, color, or previous condition of servitude—

Section 2.   The Congress shall have power to enforce this article by appropriate legislation.

[AMENDMENT XVI][13]

The Congress shall have power to lay and collect taxes on incomes, from whatever source derived, without apportionment among the several States, and without regard to any census or enumeration.

---

[12]Adopted in 1870.
[13]Adopted in 1913.

[AMENDMENT XVII][14]

The Senate of the United States shall be composed of two Senators from each State, elected by the people thereof, for six years; and each Senator shall have one vote. The electors in each State shall have the qualifications requisite for electors of the most numerous branch of the State legislatures.

When vacancies happen in the representation of any State in the Senate, the executive authority of such State shall issue writs of election to fill such vacancies: *Provided*, That the legislature of any State may empower the executive thereof to make temporary appointments until the people fill the vacancies by election as the legislature may direct.

This amendment shall not be so construed as to affect the election or term of any Senator chosen before it becomes valid as part of the Constitution.

[AMENDMENT XVIII][15]

Section 1. After one year from the ratification of this article the manufacture, sale, or transportation of intoxicating liquors within, the importation thereof into, or the exportation thereof from the United States and all territory subject to the jurisdiction thereof for beverage purposes is hereby prohibited.

Section 2. The Congress and the several States shall have concurrent power to enforce this article by appropriate legislation.

Section 3. This article shall be inoperative unless it shall have been ratified as an amendment to the Constitution by the legislatures of the several States, as provided in the Constitution, within seven years from the date of the submission hereof to the States by the Congress.

[AMENDMENT XIX][16]

The right of citizens of the United States to vote shall not be denied or abridged by the United States or by any State on account of sex.

Congress shall have power to enforce this article by appropriate legislation.

[AMENDMENT XX][17]

Section 1. The terms of the President and Vice-President shall end at noon on the 20th day of January, and the terms of Senators and Representatives at noon on the 3d day of January, of the years in which such terms would have ended if this article had not been ratified; and the terms of their successors shall then begin.

---

[14]Adopted in 1913.
[15]Adopted in 1918.
[16]Adopted in 1920.
[17]Adopted in 1933.

Section 2. The Congress shall assemble at least once in every year, and such meeting shall begin at noon on the 3d day of January, unless they shall by law appoint a different day.

Section 3. If, at the time fixed for the beginning of the term of the President, the President elect shall have died, the Vice-President elect shall become President. If a President shall not have been chosen before the time fixed for the beginning of his term or if the President elect shall have failed to qualify, then the Vice-President elect shall act as President until a President shall have qualified; and the Congress may by law provide for the case wherein neither a President elect nor a Vice-President elect shall have qualified, declaring who shall then act as President, or the manner in which one who is to act shall be selected, and such person shall act accordingly until a President or Vice-President shall have qualified.

Section 4. The Congress may by law provide for the case of the death of any of the persons from whom the House of Representatives may choose a President whenever the right of choice shall have devolved upon them, and for the case of the death of any of the persons from whom the Senate may choose a Vice-President whenever the right of choice shall have devolved upon them.

Section 5. Sections 1 and 2 shall take effect on the 15th day of October following the ratification of this article.

Section 6. This article shall be inoperative unless it shall have been ratified as an amendment to the Constitution by the legislatures of three-fourths of the several States within seven years from the date of its submission.

[AMENDMENT XXI][18]

Section 1. The eighteenth article of amendment to the Constitution of the United States is hereby repealed.

Section 2. The transportation or importation into any State, Territory, or possession of the United States for delivery or use therein of intoxicating liquors, in violation of the laws thereof, is hereby prohibited.

Section 3. This article shall be inoperative unless it shall have been ratified as an amendment to the Constitution by conventions in the several States, as provided in the Constitution, within seven years from the date of the submission hereof to the States by the Congress.

[AMENDMENT XXII][19]

No person shall be elected to the office of the President more than twice, and no person who has held the office of President, or acted as President, for more than two years of a term to which some other person was elected President shall be elected to the office of the President more than once.

But this Article shall not apply to any person holding the office of President when this Article was proposed by the Congress, and shall not prevent any person who may be holding the office of President, or acting as President, during the term within which this Article becomes operative from holding the office of President or acting as President during the remainder of such term.

---

[18]Adopted in 1933.
[19]Adopted in 1961.

This article shall be inoperative unless it shall have been ratified as an amendment to the Constitution by the legislatures of three-fourths of the several states within seven years from the date of its submission to the states by the Congress.

[AMENDMENT XXIII][20]

Section 1. The District constituting the seat of Government of the United States shall appoint in such manner as the Congress may direct:

A number of electors of President and Vice-President equal to the whole number of Senators and Representatives in Congress to which the District would be entitled if it were a State, but in no event more than the least populous State; they shall be in addition to those appointed by the States, but they shall be considered, for the purpose of the election of President and Vice-President, to be electors appointed by a State; and they shall meet in the District and perform such duties as provided by the twelfth article of amendment.

Section 2. The Congress shall have power to enforce this article by appropriate legislation.

[AMENDMENT XXIV][21]

Section 1. The right of citizens of the United States to vote in any primary or other election for President or Vice-President, for electors for President or Vice-President, or for Senator or Representative in Congress, shall not be denied or abridged by the United States or any state by reason of failure to pay any poll tax or other tax.

Section 2. The Congress shall have the power to enforce this article by appropriate legislation.

[AMENDMENT XXV][22]

Section 1. In case of the removal of the President from office or of his death or resignation, the Vice-President shall become President.

Section 2. Whenever there is a vacancy in the office of the Vice-President, the President shall nominate a Vice-President who shall take office upon confirmation by a majority vote of both Houses of Congress.

Section 3. Whenever the President transmits to the President Pro Tempore of the Senate and the Speaker of the House of Representatives his written declaration that he is unable to discharge the powers and duties of his office, and until he transmits to them a written declaration to the contrary, such powers and duties shall be discharged by the Vice-President as Acting President.

Section 4. Whenever the Vice-President and a majority of either the principal officers of the executive departments or of such other body as Congress may by law provide, transmit to the President Pro Tempore of the Senate and the Speaker of the House of Representatives their written declaration that the President is unable to discharge the powers and duties of his office, the Vice-President shall immediately assume the powers and duties of the office as Acting President.

---

[20]Adopted in 1961.

[21]Adopted in 1964.

[22]Adopted in 1967.

Thereafter, when the President transmits to the President Pro Tempore of the Senate and the Speaker of the House of Representatives his written declaration that no inability exists, he shall resume the powers and duties of his office unless the Vice-President and a majority of either the principal officers of the executive departments or of such other body as Congress may by law provide, transmit within four days to the President Pro Tempore of the Senate and the Speaker of the House of Representatives their written declaration that the President is unable to discharge the powers and duties of his office. Thereupon Congress shall decide the issue, assembling within forty-eight hours for that purpose if not in session. If the Congress, within twenty-one days after receipt of the latter written declaration, or, if Congress is not in session, within twenty-one days after Congress is required to assemble, determines by two-thirds vote of both Houses that the President is unable to discharge the powers and duties of his office, the Vice-President shall continue to discharge the same as Acting President; otherwise, the President shall resume the powers and duties of his office.

[AMENDMENT XXVI][23]

Section 1.   The right of citizens of the United States, who are eighteen years of age or older, to vote shall not be denied or abridged by the United States or by any State on account of age.

Section 2.   The Congress shall have power to enforce this article by appropriate legislation.

[AMENDMENT XXVII][24]

No law, varying the compensation for the services of the Senators and Representatives, shall take effect, until an election of Representatives shall have intervened.

---

[23]Adopted in 1971.
[24]Adopted in 1992.

PRESIDENTIAL ELECTIONS

Year	Candidates	Parties	Popular Vote	% of Popular Vote	Electoral Vote	% Voter Partici- pation
1789	George Washington				69	
	John Adams				34	
	Other candidates				35	
1792	George Washington				132	
	John Adams				77	
	George Clinton				50	
	Other candidates				5	
1796	John Adams	Federalist			71	
	Thomas Jefferson	Dem.-Rep.			68	
	Thomas Pinckney	Federalist			59	
	Aaron Burr	Dem.-Rep.			30	
	Other candidates				48	
1800	Thomas Jefferson	Dem.-Rep.			73	
	Aaron Burr	Dem.-Rep.			73	
	John Adams	Federalist			65	
	Charles C. Pinckney	Federalist			64	
	John Jay	Federalist			1	
1804	Thomas Jefferson	Dem.-Rep.			162	
	Charles C. Pinckney	Federalist			14	
1808	James Madison	Dem.-Rep.			122	
	Charles C. Pinckney	Federalist			47	
	George Clinton	Dem.-Rep.			6	
1812	James Madison	Dem.-Rep.			128	
	DeWitt Clinton	Federalist			89	
1816	James Monroe	Dem.-Rep.			183	
	Rufus King	Federalist			34	
1820	James Monroe	Dem.-Rep.			231	
	John Quincy Adams	Indep.-Rep.			1	
1824	John Quincy Adams	Dem.-Rep.	108,740	31.0	84	26.9
	Andrew Jackson	Dem.-Rep.	153,544	43.0	99	
	Henry Clay	Dem.-Rep.	47,136	13.0	37	
	William H. Crawford	Dem.-Rep.	46,618	13.0	41	
1828	Andrew Jackson	Democratic	647,286	56.0	178	57.6
	John Quincy Adams	National Republican	508,064	44.0	83	
1832	Andrew Jackson	Democratic	688,242	54.5	219	55.4
	Henry Clay	National Republican	473,462	37.5	49	
	William Wirt	Anti-Masonic	101,051	8.0	7	
	John Floyd	Democratic			11	

Year	Candidates	Parties	Popular Vote	% of Popular Vote	Electoral Vote	% Voter Partici-pation
1836	**Martin Van Buren**	Democratic	765,483	50.9	170	57.8
	William H. Harrison	Whig			73	
	Hugh L. White	Whig	739,795	49.1	26	
	Daniel Webster	Whig			14	
	W. P. Mangum	Whig			11	
1840	**William H. Harrison**	Whig	1,275,016	53.0	234	80.2
	Martin Van Buren	Democratic	1,129,102	47.0	60	
1844	**James K. Polk**	Democratic	1,338,464	49.6	170	78.9
	Henry Clay	Whig	1,300,097	48.1	105	
	James G. Birney	Liberty	62,300	2.3		
1848	**Zachary Taylor**	Whig	1,360,967	47.4	163	72.7
	Lewis Cass	Democratic	1,222,342	42.5	127	
	Martin Van Buren	Free Soil	291,263	10.1		
1852	**Franklin Pierce**	Democratic	1,601,117	50.9	254	69.6
	Winfield Scott	Whig	1,385,453	44.1	42	
	John P. Hale	Free Soil	155,825	5.0		
1856	**James Buchanan**	Democratic	1,832,955	45.3	174	78.9
	John C. Fremont	Republican	1,339,932	33.1	114	
	Millard Fillmore	American	871,731	21.6	8	
1860	**Abraham Lincoln**	Republican	1,866,452	39.8	180	81.2
	Stephen A. Douglas	Democratic	1,375,157	29.5	12	
	John C. Breckinridge	Democratic	847,953	18.1	72	
	John Bell	Constitutional Union	590,631	12.6	39	
1864	**Abraham Lincoln**	Republican	2,206,938	55.0	212	73.8
	George B. McClellan	Democratic	1,803,787	45.0	21	
1868	**Ulysses S. Grant**	Republican	3,013,421	52.7	214	78.1
	Horatio Seymour	Democratic	2,706,829	47.3	80	
1872	**Ulysses S. Grant**	Republican	3,596,745	55.6	286	71.3
	Horace Greeley	Democratic	2,843,446	43.9	66	
1876	**Rutherford B. Hayes**	Republican	4,036,298	48.0	185	81.8
	Samuel J. Tilden	Democratic	4,300,590	51.0	184	
1880	**James A. Garfield**	Republican	4,453,295	48.5	214	79.4
	Winfield S. Hancock	Democratic	4,414,082	48.1	155	
	James B. Weaver	Greenback-Labor	308,578	3.4		
1884	**Grover Cleveland**	Democratic	4,879,507	48.5	219	77.5
	James G. Blaine	Republican	4,850,293	48.2	182	
	Benjamin F. Butler	Greenback-Labor	175,370	1.8		
	John P. St. John	Prohibition	150,369	1.5		
1888	**Benjamin Harrison**	Republican	5,477,129	47.9	233	79.3
	Grover Cleveland	Democratic	5,537,857	48.6	168	
	Clinton B. Fisk	Prohibition	249,506	2.2		
	Anson J. Streeter	Union Labor	146,935	1.3		

Year	Candidates	Parties	Popular Vote	% of Popular Vote	Electoral Vote	% Voter Partici-pation
1892	**Grover Cleveland**	Democratic	5,555,426	46.1	277	74.7
	Benjamin Harrison	Republican	5,182,690	43.0	145	
	James B. Weaver	People's	1,029,846	8.5	22	
	John Bidwell	Prohibition	264,133	2.2		
1896	**William McKinley**	Republican	7,104,779	52.0	271	79.3
	William J. Bryan	Democratic	6,502,925	48.0	176	
1900	**William McKinley**	Republican	7,218,491	51.7	292	73.2
	William J. Bryan	Democratic; Populist	6,356,734	45.5	155	
	John C. Wooley	Prohibition	208,914	1.5		
1904	**Theodore Roosevelt**	Republican	7,628,461	57.4	336	65.2
	Alton B. Parker	Democratic	5,084,223	37.6	140	
	Eugene V. Debs	Socialist	402,283	3.0		
	Silas C. Swallow	Prohibition	258,536	1.9		
1908	**William H. Taft**	Republican	7,675,320	51.6	321	65.4
	William J. Bryan	Democratic	6,412,294	43.1	162	
	Eugene V. Debs	Socialist	420,793	2.8		
	Eugene W. Chafin	Prohibition	253,840	1.7		
1912	**Woodrow Wilson**	Democratic	6,293,454	42.0	435	58.8
	Theodore Roosevelt	Progressive	4,119,538	28.0	88	
	William H. Taft	Republican	3,484,980	24.0	8	
	Eugene V. Debs	Socialist	900,672	6.0		
	Eugene W. Chafin	Prohibition	206,275	1.4		
1916	**Woodrow Wilson**	Democratic	9,129,606	49.4	277	61.6
	Charles E. Hughes	Republican	8,538,221	46.2	254	
	A. L. Benson	Socialist	585,113	3.2		
	J. Frank Hanly	Prohibition	220,506	1.2		
1920	**Warren G. Harding**	Republican	16,143,407	60.4	404	49.2
	James M. Cox	Democratic	9,130,328	34.2	127	
	Eugene V. Debs	Socialist	919,799	3.4		
	P. P. Christensen	Farmer-Labor	265,411	1.0		
1924	**Calvin Coolidge**	Republican	15,718,211	54.0	382	48.9
	John W. Davis	Democratic	8,385,283	28.8	136	
	Robert M. La Follette	Progressive	4,831,289	16.6	13	
1928	**Herbert C. Hoover**	Republican	21,391,381	58.2	444	56.9
	Alfred E. Smith	Democratic	15,016,443	40.9	87	
1932	**Franklin D. Roosevelt**	Democratic	22,821,857	57.4	472	56.9
	Herbert C. Hoover	Republican	15,761,841	39.7	59	
	Norman Thomas	Socialist	881,951	2.2		
1936	**Franklin D. Roosevelt**	Democratic	27,751,597	60.8	523	61.0
	Alfred M. Landon	Republican	16,679,583	36.5	8	
	William Lemke	Union	882,479	1.9		

Year	Candidates	Parties	Popular Vote	% of Popular Vote	Electoral Vote	% Voter Partici-pation
1940	**Franklin D. Roosevelt**	Democratic	27,307,819	54.8	449	62.5
	Wendell L. Wilkie	Republican	22,321,018	44.8	82	
1944	**Franklin D. Roosevelt**	Democratic	25,606,585	53.5	432	55.9
	Thomas E. Dewey	Republican	22,014,745	46.0	99	
1948	**Harry S Truman**	Democratic	24,105,812	50.0	303	53.0
	Thomas E. Dewey	Republican	21,970,065	46.0	189	
	J. Strom Thurmond	States' Rights	1,169,021	2.0	39	
	Henry A. Wallace	Progressive	1,157,172	2.0		
1952	**Dwight D. Eisenhower**	Republican	33,936,234	55.1	442	63.3
	Adlai E. Stevenson	Democratic	27,314,992	44.4	89	
1956	**Dwight D. Eisenhower**	Republican	35,590,472	57.6	457	60.6
	Adlai E. Stevenson	Democratic	26,022,752	42.1	73	
1960	**John F. Kennedy**	Democratic	34,227,096	49.7	303	62.8
	Richard M. Nixon	Republican	34,107,646	49.6	219	
	Harry F. Byrd	Independent	501,643		15	
1964	**Lyndon B. Johnson**	Democratic	43,129,566	61.1	486	61.7
	Barry M. Goldwater	Republican	27,178,188	38.5	52	
1968	**Richard M. Nixon**	Republican	31,785,480	44.0	301	60.6
	Hubert H. Humphrey	Democratic	31,275,166	42.7	191	
	George C. Wallace	American Independent	9,906,473	13.5	46	
1972	**Richard M. Nixon**	Republican	47,169,911	60.7	520	55.2
	George S. McGovern	Democratic	29,170,383	37.5	17	
	John G. Schmitz	American	1,099,482	1.4		
1976	**Jimmy Carter**	Democratic	40,830,763	50.1	297	53.5
	Gerald R. Ford	Republican	39,147,793	48.0	240	
1980	**Ronald Reagan**	Republican	43,899,248	51.0	489	52.6
	Jimmy Carter	Democratic	35,481,432	41.0	49	
	John B. Anderson	Independent	5,719,437	7.0	0	
	Ed Clark	Libertarian	920,859	1.0	0	
1984	**Ronald Reagan**	Republican	54,451,521	58.8	525	53.3
	Walter Mondale	Democratic	37,565,334	40.5	13	
1988	**George H. Bush**	Republican	48,881,221	53.9	426	48.6
	Michael Dukakis	Democratic	41,805,422	46.1	111	
1992	**William J. Clinton**	Democratic	44,908,254	43.0	370	55.9
	George H. Bush	Republican	39,102,343	37.4	168	
	H. Ross Perot	Independent	19,741,065	18.9	0	
1996°	**William J. Clinton**	Democratic	47,401,054	49.3	379	49
	Robert Dole	Republican	39,197,350	40.7	159	
	H. Ross Perot	Reform	8,085,285	8.4	0	

°Preliminary figures

JUSTICES OF THE SUPREME COURT

	Term of Service	Years of Service	Life Span		Term of Service	Years of Service	Life Span
John Jay	1789–1795	5	1745–1829	Lucius Q. C. Lamar	1888–1893	5	1825–1893
John Rutledge	1789–1791	1	1739–1800	*Melville W. Fuller*	1888–1910	21	1833–1910
William Cushing	1789–1810	20	1732–1810	David J. Brewer	1890–1910	20	1837–1910
James Wilson	1789–1798	8	1742–1798	Henry B. Brown	1890–1906	16	1836–1913
John Blair	1789–1796	6	1732–1800	George Shiras, Jr.	1892–1903	10	1832–1924
Robert H. Harrison	1789–1790	—	1745–1790	Howell E. Jackson	1893–1895	2	1832–1895
James Iredell	1790–1799	9	1751–1799	Edward D. White	1894–1910	16	1845–1921
Thomas Johnson	1791–1793	1	1732–1819	Rufus W. Peckham	1895–1909	14	1838–1909
William Paterson	1793–1806	13	1745–1806	Joseph McKenna	1898–1925	26	1843–1926
John Rutledge°	1795	—	1739–1800	Oliver W. Holmes	1902–1932	30	1841–1935
Samuel Chase	1796–1811	15	1741–1811	William R. Day	1903–1922	19	1849–1923
Oliver Ellsworth	1796–1800	4	1745–1807	William H. Moody	1906–1910	3	1853–1917
Bushrod Washington	1798–1829	31	1762–1829	Horace H. Lurton	1909–1914	4	1844–1914
Alfred Moore	1799–1804	4	1755–1810	Charles E. Hughes	1910–1916	5	1862–1948
John Marshall	1801–1835	34	1755–1835	*Edward D. White*	1910–1921	11	1845–1921
William Johnson	1804–1834	30	1771–1834	Willis Van Devanter	1911–1937	26	1859–1941
H. Brockholst				Joseph R. Lamar	1911–1916	5	1857–1916
Livingston	1806–1823	16	1757–1823	Mahlon Pitney	1912–1922	10	1858–1924
Thomas Todd	1807–1826	18	1765–1826	James C. McReynolds	1914–1941	26	1862–1946
Joseph Story	1811–1845	33	1779–1845	Louis D. Brandeis	1916–1939	22	1856–1941
Gabriel Duval	1811–1835	24	1752–1844	John H. Clarke	1916–1922	6	1857–1945
Smith Thompson	1823–1843	20	1768–1843	William H. Taft	1921–1930	8	1857–1930
Robert Trimble	1826–1828	2	1777–1828	George Sutherland	1922–1938	15	1862–1942
John McLean	1829–1861	32	1785–1861	Pierce Butler	1922–1939	16	1866–1939
Henry Baldwin	1830–1844	14	1780–1844	Edward T. Sanford	1923–1930	7	1865–1930
James M. Wayne	1835–1867	32	1790–1867	Harlan F. Stone	1925–1941	16	1872–1946
Roger B. Taney	1836–1864	28	1777–1864	*Charles E. Hughes*	1930–1941	11	1862–1948
Philip P. Barbour	1836–1841	4	1783–1841	Owen J. Roberts	1930–1945	15	1875–1955
John Catron	1837–1865	28	1786–1865	Benjamin N. Cardozo	1932–1938	6	1870–1938
John McKinley	1837–1852	15	1780–1852	Hugo L. Black	1937–1971	34	1886–1971
Peter V. Daniel	1841–1860	19	1784–1860	Stanley F. Reed	1938–1957	19	1884–1980
Samuel Nelson	1845–1872	27	1792–1873	Felix Frankfurter	1939–1962	23	1882–1965
Levi Woodbury	1845–1851	5	1789–1851	William O. Douglas	1939–1975	36	1898–1980
Robert C. Grier	1846–1870	23	1794–1870	Frank Murphy	1940–1949	9	1890–1949
Benjamin R. Curtis	1851–1857	6	1809–1874	*Harlan F. Stone*	1941–1946	5	1872–1946
John A. Campbell	1853–1861	8	1811–1889	James F. Byrnes	1941–1942	1	1879–1972
Nathan Clifford	1858–1881	23	1803–1881	Robert H. Jackson	1941–1954	13	1892–1954
Noah H. Swayne	1862–1881	18	1804–1884	Wiley B. Rutledge	1943–1949	6	1894–1949
Samuel F. Miller	1862–1890	28	1816–1890	Harold H. Burton	1945–1958	13	1888–1964
David Davis	1862–1877	14	1815–1886	*Fred M. Vinson*	1946–1953	7	1890–1953
Stephen J. Field	1863–1897	34	1816–1899	Tom C. Clark	1949–1967	18	1899–1977
Salmon P. Chase	1864–1873	8	1808–1873	Sherman Minton	1949–1956	7	1890–1965
William Strong	1870–1880	10	1808–1895	*Earl Warren*	1953–1969	16	1891–1974
Joseph P. Bradley	1870–1892	22	1813–1892	John Marshall Harlan	1955–1971	16	1899–1971
Ward Hunt	1873–1882	9	1810–1886	William J. Brennan,	1956–1990	33	1906–
Morrison R. Waite	1874–1888	14	1816–1888	Jr.			
John M. Harlan	1877–1911	34	1833–1911	Charles E. Whittaker	1957–1962	5	1901–1973
William B. Woods	1880–1887	7	1824–1887	Potter Stewart	1958–1981	23	1915–
Stanley Matthews	1881–1889	7	1824–1889	Byron R. White	1962–1993	31	1917–
Horace Gray	1882–1902	20	1828–1902	Arthur J. Goldberg	1962–1965	3	1908–1990
Samuel Blatchford	1882–1893	11	1820–1893	Abe Fortas	1965–1969	4	1910–1982

	Term of Service	Years of Service	Life Span		Term of Service	Years of Service	Life Span
Thurgood Marshall	1967–1991	24	1908–1993	*William H. Rehnquist*	1986–	–	1924–
Warren C. Burger	1969–1986	17	1907–	Antonin Scalia	1986–	–	1936–
Harry A. Blackmun	1970–1994	24	1908–	Anthony M. Kennedy	1987–	–	1936–
Lewis F. Powell, Jr.	1972–1987	15	1907–	David H. Souter	1990–	–	1939–
William H. Rehnquist	1972–	–	1924–	Clarence Thomas	1991–	–	1948–
John P. Stevens III	1975–	–	1920–	Ruth Bader Ginsburg	1993–	–	1933–
Sandra Day O'Connor	1981–	–	1930–	Stephen G. Breyer	1994–	–	1938–

*Appointed and served one term, but not confirmed by the Senate.
Note: Chief justices are in italics.

A SOCIAL PROFILE OF THE AMERICAN REPUBLIC

POPULATION

Year	Population	Percent Increase	Population Per Square Mile	Percent Urban/ Rural	Percent Male/ Female	Percent White/ Nonwhite	Persons Per Household	Media Age
1790	3,929,214		4.5	5.1/94.9	NA/NA	80.7/19.3	5.79	NA
1800	5,308,483	35.1	6.1	6.1/93.9	NA/NA	81.1/18.9	NA	NA
1810	7,239,881	36.4	4.3	7.3/92.7	NA/NA	81.0/19.0	NA	NA
1820	9,638,453	33.1	5.5	7.2/92.8	50.8/49.2	81.6/18.4	NA	16.7
1830	12,866,020	33.5	7.4	8.8/91.2	50.8/49.2	81.9/18.1	NA	17.2
1840	17,069,453	32.7	9.8	10.8/89.2	50.9/49.1	83.2/16.8	NA	17.8
1850	23,191,876	35.9	7.9	15.3/84.7	51.0/49.0	84.3/15.7	5.55	18.9
1860	31,443,321	35.6	10.6	19.8/80.2	51.2/48.8	85.6/14.4	5.28	19.4
1870	39,818,449	26.6	13.4	25.7/74.3	50.6/49.4	86.2/13.8	5.09	20.2
1880	50,155,783	26.0	16.9	28.2/71.8	50.9/49.1	86.5/13.5	5.04	20.9
1890	62,947,714	25.5	21.2	35.1/64.9	51.2/48.8	87.5/12.5	4.93	22.0
1900	75,994,575	20.7	25.6	39.6/60.4	51.1/48.9	87.9/12.1	4.76	22.9
1910	91,972,266	21.0	31.0	45.6/54.4	51.5/48.5	88.9/11.1	4.54	24.1
1920	105,710,620	14.9	35.6	51.2/48.8	51.0/49.0	89.7/10.3	4.34	25.3
1930	122,775,046	16.1	41.2	56.1/43.9	50.6/49.4	89.8/10.2	4.11	26.4
1940	131,669,275	7.2	44.2	56.5/43.5	50.2/49.8	89.8/10.2	3.67	29.0
1950	150,697,361	14.5	50.7	64.0/36.0	49.7/50.3	89.5/10.5	3.37	30.2
1960	179,323,175	18.5	50.6	69.9/30.1	49.3/50.7	88.6/11.4	3.33	29.5
1970	203,302,031	13.4	57.4	73.5/26.5	48.7/51.3	87.6/12.4	3.14	28.0
1980	226,545,805	11.4	64.0	73.7/26.3	48.6/51.4	86.0/14.0	2.76	30.0
1990	248,709,873	9.8	70.3	NA	48.7/51.3	80.3/19.7	2.63	32.9
2000*	276,382,000	7.1	75.8	NA	48.9/51.1	82.6/17.4	NA	NA

NA = Not available.
*Projections.

VITAL STATISTICS (rates per thousand)

Year	Births	Year	Births	Deaths°	Marriages°	Divorces°
1800	55.0	1900	32.3	17.2	NA	NA
1810	54.3	1910	30.1	14.7	NA	NA
1820	55.2	1920	27.7	13.0	12.0	1.6
1830	51.4	1930	21.3	11.3	9.2	1.6
1840	51.8	1940	19.4	10.8	12.1	2.0
1850	43.3	1950	24.1	9.6	11.1	2.6
1860	44.3	1960	23.7	9.5	8.5	2.2
1870	38.3	1970	18.4	9.5	10.6	3.5
1880	39.8	1980	15.9	8.8	10.6	5.2
1890	31.5	1990	16.7	8.6	9.8	4.6

NA = Not available.
°Data not available before 1900.

LIFE EXPECTANCY (in years)

Year	Total Population	White Females	Nonwhite Females	White Males	Nonwhite Males
1900	47.3	48.7	33.5	46.6	32.5
1910	50.1	52.0	37.5	48.6	33.8
1920	54.1	55.6	45.2	54.4	45.5
1930	59.7	63.5	49.2	59.7	47.3
1940	62.9	66.6	54.9	62.1	51.5
1950	68.2	72.2	62.9	66.5	59.1
1960	69.7	74.1	66.3	67.4	61.1
1970	70.9	75.6	69.4	68.0	61.3
1980	73.7	78.1	73.6	70.7	65.3
1990	75.4	79.3	76.3	72.6	68.4

REGIONAL ORIGIN OF IMMIGRANTS (percent)

Years	Total Number of Immigrants	Europe — Total Europe	North and West	East and Central	South and Other	Western Hemisphere	Asia
1821–1830	143,389	69.2	67.1	–	2.1	8.4	—
1831–1840	599,125	82.8	81.8	–	1.0	5.5	—
1841–1850	1,713,251	93.8	92.9	0.1	0.3	3.6	—
1851–1860	2,598,214	94.4	93.6	0.1	0.8	2.9	1.6
1861–1870	2,314,824	89.2	87.8	0.5	0.9	7.2	2.8
1871–1880	2,812,191	80.8	73.6	4.5	2.7	14.4	4.4
1881–1890	5,246,613	90.3	72.0	11.9	6.3	8.1	1.3
1891–1900	3,687,546	96.5	44.5	32.8	19.1	1.1	1.9
1901–1910	8,795,386	92.5	21.7	44.5	6.3	4.1	2.8
1911–1920	5,735,811	76.3	17.4	33.4	25.5	19.9	3.4
1921–1930	4,107,209	60.3	31.7	14.4	14.3	36.9	2.4
1931–1940	528,431	65.9	38.8	11.0	16.1	30.3	2.8
1941–1950	1,035,039	60.1	47.5	4.6	7.9	34.3	3.1
1951–1960	2,515,479	52.8	17.7	24.3	10.8	39.6	6.0
1961–1970	3,321,677	33.8	11.7	9.4	12.9	51.7	12.9
1971–1980	4,493,300	17.8	4.3	5.6	8.4	44.3	35.2
1981–1990	7,338,000	10.4	5.9	4.8	1.1	49.3	37.3

Dash indicates less than 0.1 percent.

RECENT TRENDS IN IMMIGRATION (in thousands)

	1961–1970	1971–1980	1981–1990	1991	Percent 1961–1970	Percent 1971–1980	Percent 1981–1990
All countries	3,321.7	4,493.3	7,338.0	1,827.2	100.0	100.0	100.0
Europe	1,123.5	800.4	761.5	146.7	33.8	17.8	10.4
Austria	20.6	9.5	18.9	3.5	0.6	0.2	0.3
Hungary	5.4	6.6	5.9	0.9	0.2	0.1	0.1
Belgium	9.2	5.3	6.6	0.7	0.3	0.1	0.1
Czechoslovakia	3.3	6.0	5.4	0.6	0.1	0.1	0.1
Denmark	9.2	4.4	2.8	0.6	0.3	0.1	0.1
France	45.2	25.1	92.1	4.0	1.4	0.6	1.3
Germany	190.8	74.4	159.0	10.9	5.7	1.7	2.2
Greece	86.0	92.4	31.9	2.9	2.6	2.1	0.4
Ireland	33.0	11.5	67.2	4.6	1.0	0.3	0.9
Italy	214.1	129.4	12.3	30.3	6.4	2.9	0.2
Netherlands	30.6	10.5	4.2	1.3	0.9	0.2	0.1
Norway	15.5	3.9	83.2	0.6	0.5	0.1	1.1
Poland	53.5	37.2	40.3	17.1	1.6	0.8	0.5
Portugal	76.1	101.7	20.5	4.6	2.3	2.3	0.3
Spain	44.7	39.1	11.1	2.7	1.3	0.9	0.2
Sweden	17.1	6.5	8.0	1.2	0.5	0.1	0.1
Switzerland	18.5	8.2	57.6	1.0	0.6	0.2	0.8
USSR	2.5	39.0	18.7	31.6	0.1	0.9	0.3
United Kingdom	213.8	137.4	159.4	16.8	6.4	3.1	2.2
Yugoslavia	20.4	30.5	37.3	2.8	0.6	0.7	0.5
Other Europe	9.1	18.9	7.7	1.2	0.2	0.2	0.0
Asia	427.6	1,588.2	2,738.1	342.2	12.9	35.2	37.3
China	34.8	124.3	298.9	24.0	1.0	2.8	4.1
Hong Kong	75.0	113.5	98.2	15.9	2.3	2.5	1.3
India	27.2	164.1	250.7	42.7	0.8	3.7	3.4
Iran	10.3	45.1	116.0	9.9	0.3	1.0	1.6
Israel	29.6	37.7	44.2	5.1	0.9	0.8	0.6
Japan	40.0	49.8	47.0	5.6	1.2	1.1	0.6
Korea	34.5	267.6	333.8	25.4	1.0	6.0	4.5
Philippines	98.4	355.0	548.7	68.8	3.0	7.9	7.5
Turkey	10.1	13.4	23.4	3.5	0.3	0.3	0.3
Vietnam	4.3	172.8	281.0	14.8	1.1	3.8	3.8
Other Asia	36.5	176.1	631.4	126.4	1.1	3.8	8.6
America	1,716.4	1,982.5	3,615.6	1,297.6	51.7	44.3	49.3
Argentina	49.7	29.9	27.3	4.2	1.5	0.7	0.4
Canada	413.3	169.9	158.0	19.9	12.4	3.8	2.2
Colombia	72.0	77.3	122.9	19.3	2.2	1.7	1.7
Cuba	208.5	264.9	144.6	9.5	6.3	5.9	2.0
Dominican Rep.	93.3	148.1	252.0	42.4	2.8	3.3	3.4
Ecuador	36.8	50.1	56.2	10.0	1.1	1.1	0.8
El Salvador	15.0	34.4	213.5	46.9	0.5	0.8	2.9
Haiti	34.5	56.3	138.4	47.0	1.0	1.3	1.9
Jamaica	74.9	137.6	208.1	23.0	2.3	3.1	2.8
Mexico	453.9	640.3	1,655.7	947.9	13.7	14.3	22.6
Other America	264.4	373.8	639.3	128.4	7.9	8.3	8.7
Africa	29.0	80.8	176.8	33.5	0.9	1.8	2.4
Oceania	25.1	41.2	45.2	7.1	0.8	0.9	0.6

Figures may not add to total due to rounding.

AMERICAN WORKERS AND FARMERS

Year	Total Number of Workers (thousands)	Percent of Workers Male/Female	Percent of Female Workers Married	Percent of Workers in Female Population	Percent of Workers in Labor Unions	Farm Population (thousands)	Farm Population as Percent of Total Population
1870	12,506	85/15	NA	NA	NA	NA	NA
1880	17,392	85/15	NA	NA	NA	21,973	43.8
1890	23,318	83/17	13.9	18.9	NA	24,771	42.3
1900	29,073	82/18	15.4	20.6	3	29,875	41.9
1910	38,167	79/21	24.7	25.4	6	32,077	34.9
1920	41,614	79/21	23.0	23.7	12	31,974	30.1
1930	48,830	78/22	28.9	24.8	7	30,529	24.9
1940	53,011	76/24	36.4	27.4	27	30,547	23.2
1950	59,643	72/28	52.1	31.4	25	23,048	15.3
1960	69,877	68/32	59.9	37.7	26	15,635	8.7
1970	82,049	63/37	63.4	43.4	25	9,712	4.8
1980	108,544	58/42	59.7	51.5	23	6,051	2.7
1990	117,914	55/45	58.4	44.3	16	4,591	1.8

THE ECONOMY AND FEDERAL SPENDING

Year	Gross National Product (GNP) (in billions)	Foreign Trade (in millions) Exports	Imports	Balance of Trade	Federal Budget (in billions)	Federal Surplus/Deficit (in billions)	Federal Debt (in billions)
1790	NA	$ 20	$ 23	$ −3	$ 0.004	$ +0.00015	$ 0.076
1800	NA	71	91	−20	0.011	+0.0006	0.083
1810	NA	67	85	−18	0.008	+0.0012	0.053
1820	NA	70	74	−4	0.018	−0.0004	0.091
1830	NA	74	71	+3	0.015	+0.100	0.049
1840	NA	132	107	+25	0.024	−0.005	0.004
1850	NA	152	178	−26	0.040	+0.004	0.064
1860	NA	400	362	−38	0.063	−0.01	0.065
1870	$ 7.4	451	462	−11	0.310	+0.10	2.4
1880	11.2	853	761	+92	0.268	+0.07	2.1
1890	13.1	910	823	+87	0.318	+0.09	1.2
1900	18.7	1,499	930	+569	0.521	+0.05	1.2
1910	35.3	1,919	1,646	+273	0.694	−0.02	1.1
1920	91.5	8,664	5,784	+2,880	6.357	+0.3	24.3
1930	90.7	4,013	3,500	+513	3.320	+0.7	16.3
1940	100.0	4,030	7,433	−3,403	9.6	−2.7	43.0
1950	286.5	10,816	9,125	+1,691	43.1	−2.2	257.4
1960	506.5	19,600	15,046	+4,556	92.2	+0.3	286.3
1970	992.7	42,700	40,189	+2,511	195.6	−2.8	371.0
1980	2,631.7	220,783	244,871	+24,088	590.9	−73.8	907.7
1990	5,524.5	421,730	487,129	−65,399	1,251.8	−220.5	3,233.3

AMERICAN WARS

	U.S. Military Personnel (thousands)	Personnel as % of Population	U.S. Deaths	U.S. Wounds	Direct Cost 1990 Dollars (millions)
American Revolution					
Apr. 1775–Sept. 1783	184–250	9–12	4,004	6,004	$100–140
War of 1812					
June 1812–Feb. 1815	286	3	1,950	4,000	87
Mexican War					
May 1846–Feb. 1848	116	0.5	13,271	4,102	82
Civil War: Union	3,393	14	360,222	275,175	2,302
Civil War: Confederacy					
Apr. 1861–Apr. 1865	1,034	11	258,000	NA	1,032
Spanish-American War					
Apr. 1898–Aug. 1898	307	0.4	2,446	1,662	270
World War I					
Apr. 1917–Nov. 1918	4,714	5	116,516	204,002	32,740
World War II					
Dec. 1941–Aug. 1945	16,354	12	405,399	670,846	360,000
Korean War					
June 1950–June 1953	5,764	4	54,246	103,284	50,000
Vietnam War					
Aug. 1964–June 1973	8,400	4	47,704	219,573	140,644
Persian Gulf War					
Jan. 1991–Feb. 1991	467	0.1	293	467	NA

BIBLIOGRAPHY

CHAPTER 1: OLD WORLD, NEW WORLDS

Discovery and Exploration in the Sixteenth Century
Kenneth R. Andrews, *Trade, Plunder, and Settlement: Maritime Enterprise and the Genesis of the British Empire, 1480–1630* (1985); K. R. Andrews, N. P. Canny, and P. E. H. Hair, eds., *The Westward Enterprise: English Activities in Ireland, the Atlantic, and America, 1480–1650* (1979); Ralph Davis, *The Rise of Atlantic Economies* (1973); J. H. Elliott, *The Old World and the New, 1492–1650* (1970); Paul E. Hoffman, *A New Andalucia and a Way to the Orient: The American Southeast during the Sixteenth Century* (1990); James Lang, *Conquest and Commerce: Spain and England in the Americas* (1975); W. H. McNeil, *The Rise of the West* (1963); Samuel Eliot Morison, *The European Discovery of America: The Northern Voyages, 500–1600* (1971) and *The European Discovery of America: The Southern Voyages, 1492–1616* (1974); J. H. Parry, *The Age of Reconnaissance* (1963); David Beers Quinn, *England and the Discovery of America, 1481–1620* (1974), *North America from Earliest Discovery to First Settlements* (1977), and *Set Fair for Roanoke* (1985).

Indian Civilizations
Alfred W. Crosby, Jr., *The Columbian Exchange: Biological and Cultural Consequences of 1492* (1972); Nigel Davies, *The Aztecs* (1973); Harold Driver, *Indians of North America*, 2d ed. (1970); Peter Farb, *Man's Rise to Civilization* (1968); R. C. Padden, *The Hummingbird and the Hawk* (1962); Miguel Leon-Portilla, *The Broken Spears: The Aztec Account of the Conquest of Mexico* (1962); Wilcomb E. Washburn, *The Indian in America* (1975).

The Spanish Empire in the Sixteenth Century
Fernand Braudel, *The Mediterranean and the Mediterranean World in the Age of Philip the Second*, vols. 1 and 2 (1976); J. H. Elliott, *Imperial Spain, 1469–1716* (1963); Charles Gibson, *The Aztecs under Spanish Rule* (1964); James Lockhart, *Spanish Peru, 1532–1560* (1968); James Lockhart and Stuart B. Schwartz, *Early Latin America: A History of Colonial Spanish America and Brazil* (1983).

The Protestant Reformation
Owen Chadwick, *The Reformation* (1964); Patrick Collinson, *The Elizabethan Puritan Movement* (1967) and *The Religion of Protestants* (1982); A. G. Dickens, *The English Reformation* (1974); Richard Dunn, *The Age of Religious Wars, 1159–1689* (1979); Erik Erikson, *Young Man Luther* (1962); Charles George and Katherine George, *The Protestant Mind of the English Reformation* (1961); De Lamaar Jensen, *Reformation Europe, Age of Reform and Revolution* (1981); Steven Ozment, *The Age of Reform, 1250–1550* (1980) and *The Reformation in the Cities* (1975); Keith Thomas, *Religion and the Decline of Magic* (1971); H. R. Trevor-Roper, *Religion, Reformation, Social Change, and Other Essays* (1967).

Elizabethan and Stuart England
Trevor Ashton, ed., *Crisis in Europe, 1560–1660* (1965); Carl Bridenbaugh, *Vexed and Troubled Englishmen, 1590–1642* (1968); Peter Laslett, *The World We Have Lost* (1965); Lawrence Stone, *The Crisis of the Aristocracy, 1558–1641* (1965); Keith Wrightson, *English Society, 1580–1680* (1982).

Ireland in the Sixteenth Century
Nicholas Canny, *The Elizabethan Conquest of Ireland* (1976) and *Kingdom and Colony: Ireland in the Atlantic World, 1560–1800* (1988); David Beers Quinn, *The Elizabethans and the Irish* (1976).

CHAPTER 2: THE FIRST CENTURY OF SETTLEMENT IN THE COLONIAL SOUTH

General Histories
Charles M. Andrews, *The Colonial Period in American History (1934–1938);* Wesley Frank Craven, *The Southern Colonies in the Seventeenth Century, 1607–1689* (1949); David Galenson, *White Servitude in Colonial America* (1981); Sidney Mintz, *Sweetness and Power: The Place of Sugar in Modern History* (1985); Gary Nash, *Red, White and Black: The Peoples of Early America* (1974); John E. Pomfret, *Founding the American Colonies, 1583–1660* (1970); R. C. Simmons, *The American Colonies* (1976).

Indians in the Early South
Nancy Lurie, "Indian Cultural Adjustment to European Civilization," in James M. Smith, ed., *Seventeenth-Century America,* (1959); Gary Nash, *Red, White and Black: The Peoples of Early America* (1974).

Race and Slavery

Wesley Frank Craven, *White, Red, and Black: The Seventeenth-Century Virginian* (1971); Philip Curtin, *The Atlantic Slave Trade* (1969); Basil Davidson, *The African Genius* (1970); David B. Davis, *The Problem of Slavery in Western Culture* (1966); Carl N. Degler, *Neither White Nor Black: Slavery and Race Relations in Brazil and the United States* (1971); Winthrop Jordan, *White over Black* (1968); Herbert Klein, *The Middle Passage* (1978) and *Slavery in the Americas: A Comparative Study of Virginia and Cuba* (1967); Richard Olaniyan, *African History and Culture* (1982); Roland Oliver, ed., *The Cambridge History of Africa*, vol. 3: c. 1050–c. 1600 (1977); Orlando Patterson, *Slavery and Social Death: A Comparative Study* (1982); John Thornton, *Africa and Africans in the Making of the Atlantic World, 1400–1680* (1992); Peter Wood, "'I Did the Best I Could for My Day': The Study of Early Black History during the Second Reconstruction, 1960 to 1976," *William and Mary Quarterly* (1978).

The Early Chesapeake Colonies

Lois Green Carr, Philip D. Morgan, and Jean B. Russo, *Colonial Chesapeake Society* (1989); Lois Green Carr and Lorena Walsh, "The Planter's Wife: The Experience of White Women in Seventeenth-Century Maryland," *William and Mary Quarterly* (1977); Lois Green Carr, Russell R. Menard, and Lorena S. Walsh, *Robert Cole's World: Agriculture and Society in Early Maryland* (1991); Ivor Noel Hume, *Martin's Hundred: The Discovery of a Lost Virginia Settlement* (1979); Gloria Main, *Tobacco Colony: Life in Early Maryland, 1650–1720* (1982); James Russell Perry, *The Formation of a Society on Virginia's Eastern Shore, 1615–1655* (1990); Thad Tate and David Ammerman, eds., *The Chesapeake in the Seventeenth Century* (1979).

The English Revolution

Christopher Hill, *The Century of Revolution, 1603–1714* (1961), *Puritanism and Revolution* (1964), and *The World Turned Upside Down* (1972); R. C. Richardson, *The Debate on the English Revolution* (1977); Lawrence Stone, *The Causes of the English Revolution, 1529–1642* (1972); Michael Walzer, *The Revolution of the Saints* (1965).

The Carolinas

Verner Crane, *The Southern Frontier, 1670–1732* (1929); H. T. Merrens, *Colonial North Carolina* (1964); M. Eugene Sirmans, *Colonial South Carolina* (1966).

Georgia

Harold E. Davis, *The Fledgling Province: Social and Cultural Life in Colonial Georgia, 1733–1776* (1976); Hardy Jackson and Phinizy Spalding, eds., *Forty Years of Diversity; Essays on Colonial Georgia* (1984); Phinizy Spalding, *Oglethorpe in America* (1977).

The British Caribbean

Hilary McD. Beckles, *White Servitude and Black Slavery in Barbados, 1627–1715* (1989); Sidney Mintz, *Sweetness and Power: The Place of Sugar in Modern History* (1985); Gary Puckrein, *Little England: Plantation Society and Anglo-Barbadian Politics, 1627–1700* (1984).

The Spanish Empire in the Southwest

Sherbune F. Cook, *The Conflict between the California Indian and White Civilization* (1943); Charles Gibson, *Spain in America* (1966); Ramón A. Gutiérrez, *When Jesus Came, the Corn Mothers Went Away: Marriage, Sexuality and Power in New Mexico, 1500–1846* (1991); Edward H. Spicer, *Cycles of Conquest: The Impact of Spain, Mexico, and the United States on the Indians of the Southwest, 1533–1960* (1962).

CHAPTER 3: THE FIRST CENTURY OF SETTLEMENT IN THE COLONIAL NORTH

Indians and Northern Colonials

James Axtell, *The European and the Indian* (1981); William Cronon, *Changes in the Land: Indians, Colonists and the Ecology of New England* (1983); Francis Jennings, *The Ambiguous Iroquois Empire* (1984) and *The Invasion of America* (1975); Daniel K. Richter and James H. Merrell, *Beyond the Covenant Chain: The Iroquois and Their Neighbors in Indian North America, 1600–1800* (1987); Neal Salisbury, *Manitou and Providence: Indians, Europeans and the Making of New England* (1982); Bruce G. Trigger, *The Children of Aataentsic: A History of the Huron People to 1660* (1976); Alden Vaughan, *The New England Frontier* (1965); Anthony F. C. Wallace, *The Death and Rebirth of the Seneca* (1972).

The French in North America

W. J. Eccles, *The Canadian Frontier, 1534–1760* (1969) and *France in America* (1972); Allan Greer, *Peasant, Lord and Merchant: Rural Society in the Three Quebec Parishes, 1740–1840* (1985); Richard Colebrook Harris, *The Seigneurial System in Early Canada* (1966); C. E. O'Neill, *Church and State in French Colonial Louisiana* (1966).

New England Puritanism

Charles L. Cohen, *God's Caress: The Psychology of Puritan Religious Experience* (1986); Stephen Foster, *The Long Argument: English Puritanism and the Shaping of New England Culture, 1570–1700* (1991) and *Their Solitary Way: The Puritan Social Ethic in the First Century of Settlement in New England* (1971); Richard Godbeer, *The Devil's Dominion: Magic and Religion in Early New England* (1992); Charles Hambrick-Stowe, *The Practice of Piety: Puritan Devotional Literature in Seventeenth-Century New England* (1982); Robert Middlekauff, *The Mathers* (1971); Perry Miller, *The New*

England Mind: From Colony to Province (1953); Edmund S. Morgan, *Visible Saints* (1963); Amanda Porterfield, *Female Piety in Puritan New England: The Emergence of Religious Humanism* (1992); Harry Stout, *The New England Soul* (1986).

The New England Colonies
Virginia DeJohn Anderson, *New England's Generation: The Great Migration and the Formation of Society and Culture in the Seventeenth Century* (1991); Paul Boyer and Stephen Nissenbaum, *Salem Possessed: The Social Origins of Witchcraft* (1974); John P. Demos, *Entertaining Satan: Witchcraft and the Culture of Early New England* (1982) and *A Little Commonwealth: Family Life in Plymouth Colony* (1970); Philip Greven, *Four Generations: Land, Population, and Family in Colonial Andover, Massachusetts* (1970); Stephen Innes, *To Labor in a New Land: Economy and Society in Seventeenth-Century Springfield* (1983); Carol Karlsen, *The Devil in the Shape of a Woman: Witchcraft in Colonial New England* (1987); George Langdon, *Pilgrim Colony* (1960); John Frederick Martin, *Profits in the Wilderness: Enterpreneurship and the Founding of New England Towns in the Seventeenth Century* (1991); Edmund S. Morgan, *The Puritan Family*, rev. ed. (1966); Darrett Rutman, *Winthrop's Boston* (1965); Laurel Thatcher Ulrich, *Good Wives: Image and Reality in the Lives of Women in Northern New England* (1982).

The Middle Colonies
Randall H. Balmer, *A Perfect Babel of Confusion: Dutch Religion and English Culture in the Middle Colonies* (1989); Patricia Bonomi, *A Factious People: Politics and Society in Colonial New York* (1971); Mary Maples Dunn, *William Penn* (1967); Melvin B. Endy, *William Penn and Early Quakerism* (1973); Michael Kammen, *Colonial New York* (1975); Gary B. Nash, *Quakers and Politics: Pennsylvania, 1681–1726* (1968); J. E. Pomfret, *Colonial New Jersey* (1973); Oliver A. Rink, *Holland on the Hudson: An Economic and Social History of Dutch New York* (1986); Robert C. Ritchie, *The Duke's Province: A Study of Politics and Society in Colonial New York, 1660–1691*; Alan Tully, *William Penn's Legacy* (1977).

The Imperial Connection
Michael Hall, *Edward Randolph and the American Colonies, 1676–1703* (1960); Ian K. Steele, *Politics of Colonial Policy: The Board of Trade in Colonial Administration* (1968); Stephen Saunders Webb, *The Governors-General: The English Army and the Definition of Empire, 1569–1681* (1979).

CHAPTER 4: THE MOSAIC OF EIGHTEENTH-CENTURY AMERICA

General Histories
Jon Butler, *Awash in a Sea of Faith: Christianizing the American People* (1990); Jack P. Greene, *Pursuits of Happiness: The Social Development of Early Modern British Colonies and the Formation of American Culture* (1988); Philip Greven, *The Protestant Temperament: Patterns of Childrearing, Religious Experience, and Self in Early America* (1977); James Henretta, *The Evolution of American Society, 1700–1815* (1973); Stephen Innes, ed., *Work and Labor in Early America* (1988); Alice Hanson Jones, *Wealth of a Nation to Be: The American Colonies on the Eve of the Revolution* (1980); Jackson Turner Main, *The Social Structure of Revolutionary America* (1965); D. W. Meinig, *The Shaping of America: A Geographical Perspective on 500 Years of History*, vol. 1: *Atlantic America, 1492–1800* (1986); Mary Beth Norton, *Liberty's Daughters: The Revolutionary Experience of American Women, 1750–1800* (1980); Carole Shammas, *The Pre-Industrial Consumer in England and America* (1990); Gary M. Walton and James F. Shepherd, *The Economic Rise of Early America* (1979); Robert V. Wells, *The Population of the British Colonies in America before 1776* (1975).

Immigration
Jon Butler, *The Huguenots in America* (1983); R. J. Dickson, *Ulster Immigration to Colonial America, 1718–1775* (1966); Ned Landsman, *Scotland and Its First American Colony, 1683–1765* (1985).

Rural Society in Eighteenth-Century America
James Henretta, "Farms and Families: Mentalité in Pre-Industrial America," *William and Mary Quarterly* (1978); Christopher M. Jedrey, *The World of John Cleaveland* (1979); Sung Bok Kim, *Landlord and Tenant in Colonial New York* (1978); James T. Lemon, *The Best Poor Man's Country: A Geographical Study of Early Southeastern Pennsylvania* (1972); Gregory Stiverson, *Poverty in the Land of Plenty: Tenancy in Eighteenth-Century Maryland* (1978); Michael Zuckerman, *Peaceable Kingdoms: New England Towns in the Eighteenth Century* (1970).

The Frontier
Richard Beeman, *The Evolution of the Southern Backcountry* (1984); Michael Bellesiles, *Revolutionary Outlaws: Ethan Allen and the Struggle for Independence in the Early American Frontier* (1994); Richard M. Brown, *The South Carolina Regulators* (1963); David H. Corkran, *The Cherokee Frontier: Conflict and Survival, 1740–1762* (1962) and *The Creek Frontier, 1540–1783* (1967); John Mack Faragher, *Daniel Boone: The Life and Legend of an American Pioneer* (1992); Michael N. McConnell, *A Country Between: The Upper Ohio Valley and Its Peoples, 1724–1774* (1992); Peter Mancall, *Valley of Opportunity: Economic Culture along the Upper Susquehanna, 1700–1800* (1991); Robert D. Mitchell, *Commercialism and Frontier: Perspectives on the Early Shenandoah Valley* (1977); Gregory H. Nobles, "Breaking into the Back-country: New Approaches to the Early American Frontier," *William and Mary Quarterly* (1989); Daniel K. Richter, *The Ordeal of the*

Longhouse: The Peoples of the Iroquois League in the Era of European Colonization (1992); Malcolm J. Rohrbough, *The Trans-Appalachian Frontier* (1978); Alan Taylor, *Liberty Men and Great Proprietors: The Revolutionary Settlement on the Maine Frontier, 1760–1820* (1990); Albert H. Tillson, Jr., *Gentry and Common Folk: Political Culture on a Virginia Frontier, 1740–1789* (1991); Daniel H. Usner, Jr., *Indians, Settlers, and Slaves in a Frontier Exchange Economy: The Lower Mississippi Valley before 1783* (1992); Richard White, *The Middle Ground: Indians, Empires, and Republics in the Great Lakes Region, 1650–1815* (1991).

Provincial Seaports
Carl Bridenbaugh, *Cities in the Wilderness* (1938) and *Cities in Revolt* (1955); Elaine Forman Crane, *A Dependent People: Newport, Rhode Island in the Revolutionary Era* (1985); Thomas Doerflinger, *A Vigorous Spirit of Enterprise: Merchants and Economic Development in Revolutionary Philadelphia* (1986); Christine Leigh Heyrman, *Commerce and Culture: The Maritime Communities of Colonial Massachusetts, 1690–1750* (1984); Jacob M. Price, "Economic Function and the Growth of American Port Towns in the Eighteenth Century," *Perspectives in American History* (1974); Marcus Rediker, *Between the Devil and the Deep Blue Sea: Merchant Seamen, Pirates, and the Anglo-American Maritime Works, 1700–1750* (1987); Frederick B. Tolles, *Meetinghouse and Countinghouse: The Quaker Merchants of Colonial Philadelphia* (1948); Gerald B. Warden, *Boston, 1687–1776* (1970); Stephanie Grauman Wolf, *Urban Village: Population, Community, and Family Structure in Germantown, Pennsylvania, 1683–1800* (1976).

Blacks in Eighteenth-Century America
Thomas J. Davis, *A Rumor of Revolt: The "Great Negro Plot" in Colonial New York* (1985); Herbert Gutman, *The Black Family in Slavery and Freedom, 1750–1925* (1976); Jean Butenhoff Lee, "The Problem of the Slave Community in the Eighteenth-Century Chesapeake," *William and Mary Quarterly* (1986); Gerald W. Mullin, *Flight and Rebellion: Slave Resistance in Eighteenth-Century Virginia* (1972); Jean R. Soderlund, *Quakers and Slavery* (1985); Betty Wood, *Slavery in Colonial Georgia, 1730–1775* (1984).

The Eighteenth-Century South
Carl Bridenbaugh, *Myths and Realities: Societies of the Colonial South* (1952); A. Roger Ekirch, *"Poor Carolina": Politics and Society in Colonial North Carolina, 1729–1776* (1981); Jan Lewis, *The Pursuit of Happiness: Family and Values in Jefferson's Virginia* (1983); Daniel Blake Smith, *Inside the Great House: Planter Family Life in Eighteenth-Century Chesapeake Society* (1980); Julia Cherry Spruill, *Women's Life and Work in the Southern Colonies* (1938); Charles Sydnor, *Gentlemen Freeholders: Political Practices in Washington's Virginia* (1956).

The Enlightenment
Henry May, *The Enlightenment in America* (1976); Esmond Wright, *Franklin of Philadelphia* (1986); Louis B. Wright, *The Cultural Life of the American Colonies* (1957).

The Great Awakening
Edwin Scott Gaustad, *The Great Awakening in New England* (1957); Patricia Tracy, *Jonathan Edwards, Pastor* (1979); Marilyn Westerkamp, *The Triumph of the Laity: Scots-Irish Piety and the Great Awakening, 1625–1760* (1988).

Colonial Political Development in the Eighteenth Century
Edward M. Cook, *The Fathers of the Towns: Leadership and Community Structure in Eighteenth-Century New England* (1976); Jack P. Greene, *The Quest for Power: The Lower Houses of Assembly in the Southern Royal Colonies, 1689–1776* (1963); Robert Zemsky, *Merchants, Farmers, and River Gods: An Essay on Eighteenth Century American Politics* (1971).

CHAPTER 5: TOWARD THE WAR FOR AMERICAN INDEPENDENCE

General Histories
Charles M. Andrews, *The Colonial Background of the American Revolution*, rev. ed. (1931); Ian Christie and Benjamin Labaree, *Empire or Independence, 1760–1776* (1976); Edward Countryman, *The American Revolution* (1985); Lawrence Henry Gipson, *The Coming of the Revolution, 1763–1775* (1954); Alfred Young, ed., *The American Revolution: Explorations in the History of American Radicalism* (1976).

The Seven Years' War
Francis Jennings, *Empire of Fortune: Crown, Colonies, and Tribes in the Seven Years War in America* (1989); Howard H. Peckham, *The Colonial Wars, 1689–1762* (1963).

British Society and Politics
John Brooke, *King George III* (1972); J. C. D. Clark, *English Society, 1688–1832* (1985); M. Dorothy George, *London Life in the Eighteenth Century* (1965); Lawrence Henry Gipson, *The British Empire before the American Revolution (1936–1970)*; Lewis B. Namier, *England in the Age of the American Revolution*, 2d ed. (1961); Richard Pares, *King George III and the Politicians* (1953); W. A. Speck, *Stability and Strife: England, 1714–1760* (1979).

The Intellectual Sources of Resistance and Revolution
Nathan O. Hatch, *The Sacred Cause of Liberty: Republican Thought and the Millennium in Revolutionary New England* (1977); Isaac Kramnick, *Bolingbroke and His Circle: The Politics of Nostalgia in the Age of Walpole* (1968) and *Republicanism and Bourgeois*

Radicalism: Political Ideology in Late Eighteenth-Century England and America (1990); Edmund S. Morgan, *The Challenge of the American Revolution* (1976) and *Inventing the People: The Rise of Popular Sovereignty in England and America* (1988); J. G. A. Pocock, *The Machiavellian Moment: Florentine Political Thought and the Atlantic Republican Tradition* (1975); Caroline Robbins, *The Eighteenth-Century Commonwealthman: Studies in the Transmission, Development, and Circumstances of English Liberal Thought from the Restoration of Charles II until the War with the Thirteen Colonies* (1959).

A Decade of Resistance
David Ammerman, *In the Common Cause: The American Response to the Coercive Acts of 1774* (1974); Richard D. Brown, *Revolutionary Politics in Massachusetts: The Boston Committee of Correspondence and the Towns, 1772–1774* (1970); Joseph Ernst, *Money and Politics in America, 1755–1775* (1973); Paul A. Gilje, *The Road to Mobocracy: Popular Disorder in New York City, 1763–1834* (1987); Benjamin Labaree, *The Boston Tea Party* (1964); Gregory H. Nobles, *Divisions throughout the Whole: Politics and Society in Hampshire County, Massachusetts, 1740–1775* (1983); William Penack, *War, Politics, and Revolution in Provincial Massachusetts* (1981); Peter Shaw, *American Patriots and the Rituals of Revolution* (1981); John Shy, *Toward Lexington: The Role of the British Army in the Coming of the American Revolution* (1965); Richard Walsh, *Charleston's Sons of Liberty: A Study of the Artisans, 1763–1789* (1959); Hiller B. Zobel, *The Boston Massacre* (1970).

Leaders of the American Resistance
David Hawke, *Paine* (1974); Peter Shaw, *The Character of John Adams* (1976); John J. Waters, *The Otis Family in Provincial and Revolutionary Massachusetts* (1968).

CHAPTER 6: THE AMERICAN PEOPLE AND THE AMERICAN REVOLUTION

General Histories
John R. Alden, *The American Revolution* (1964); Ira Gruber, *The Howe Brothers and the American Revolution* (1972); Piers Makesy, *The War for America* (1964).

Thomas Jefferson and the Declaration of Independence
Carl Becker, *The Declaration of Independence* (1922); Jay Fliegelman *Declaring Independence: Jefferson, Natural Language, and the Culture of Performance* (1993); Garry Wills, *Inventing America* (1978).

The Loyalists
Wallace Brown, *The King's Friends* (1966); Robert M. Calhoon, *The Loyalists in Revolutionary America* (1973); Mary Beth Norton, *The British-Americans* (1972).

George Washington and the Continental Army
E. Wayne Carp, *To Starve the Army at Pleasure: Continental Army Administration and American Political Culture, 1775–1783* (1984); James T. Flexner, *George Washington in the American Revolution* (1968); Douglas Southall Freeman, *George Washington* (1948–1957); Ronald Hoffman and Peter J. Albert, eds., *Arms and Independence: The Military Character of the American Revolution* (1984); James Kirby Martin and Mark Lender, *A Respectable Army: The Military Origins of the Republic, 1763–1789* (1982).

Diplomacy
Samuel F. Bemis, *The Diplomacy of the American Revolution* (1935); Jonathan R. Dull, *A Diplomatic History of the American Revolution* (1985); Ronald Hoffman and Peter J. Albert, eds., *Peace and the Peacemakers: The Treaty of 1783* (1986); Richard B. Morris, *The Peacemakers: The Great Powers and American Independence* (1965); Gerald Stourzh, *Benjamin Franklin and American Foreign Policy*, rev. ed. (1969).

The North and the American Revolution
John Brooke, *The Heart of the Commonwealth: Society and Political Culture in Worcester County, Massachusetts, 1713–1861* (1991); Edward Countryman, *A People in Revolution: The American Revolution and Political Society in New York, 1760–1790* (1981); Robert J. Taylor, *Western Massachusetts in the Revolution* (1954); Donald Wallace White, *A Village at War: Chatham, New Jersey and the American Revolution* (1979); Alfred F. Young, "George Robert Twelves Hewes (1742–1840): A Boston Shoemaker and the Memory of the American Revolution," *William and Mary Quarterly* (1981).

Indians and the Revolutionary Frontier
Barbara Graymont, *The Iroquois in the American Revolution* (1972); Isabel Thomson Kelsey, *Joseph Brant, 1743–1807: Man of Two Worlds* (1984); James H. O'Donnell III, *Southern Indians in the American Revolution* (1973); J. M. Sosin, *The Revolutionary Frontier, 1763–1783* (1967).

The South and the American Revolution
John R. Alden, *The South in the Revolution, 1763–1789* (1957); Jeffrey J. Crow and Larry E. Tise, eds., *The Southern Experience in the American Revolution* (1978); Ronald Hoffman, Thad W. Tate, and Peter J. Albert, eds., *An Uncivil War: The Southern Backcountry during the American Revolution* (1985); Jerome J. Nadelhaft, *The Disorders of War: The Revolution in South Carolina* (1981).

The Black Experience and the American Revolution
Duncan MacLeod, *Slavery, Race, and the American Revolution* (1974); Benjamin Quarles, *The Negro in the American Revolution* (1961).

CHAPTER 7: CRISIS AND CONSTITUTION

General Histories
Curtis P. Nettels, *The Emergence of a National Economy, 1775–1815* (1962); Robert R. Palmer, *The Age of Democratic Revolution: A Political History of Europe and America, 1760–1800* (1959, 1964).

State Politics and State Constitutions
Willi Paul Adams, *The First American Constitutions* (1980); Ronald Hoffman and Peter Albert, eds., *Sovereign States in an Age of Uncertainty* (1981); Jackson Turner Main, *The Sovereign States, 1775–1783* (1973) and *Political Parties before the Constitution* (1973); Stephen E. Patterson, *Political Parties in Revolutionary Massachusetts* (1973); David Szatmary, *Shays' Rebellion: The Making of an Agrarian Insurrection* (1980).

The Articles of Confederation
Joseph L. Davis, *Sectionalism in American Politics, 1774–1787* (1977); E. James Ferguson, *The Power of the Purse: A History of American Public Finance, 1776–1790* (1961); H. James Henderson, *Party Politics in the Continental Congress* (1974); Merrill D. Jensen, *The Articles of Confederation*, rev. ed. (1959) and *The New Nation* (1950); Peter S. Onuf, *The Origins of the Federal Republic: Jurisdictional Controversies in the United States, 1775–1787* (1983); Jack N. Rakove, *The Beginnings of National Politics* (1979).

Society in the New Republic
Christopher Clark, *The Roots of Rural Capitalism: Western Massachusetts, 1780–1860* (1990); Nancy Cott, "Divorce and the Changing Status of Women in Massachusetts," *William and Mary Quarterly* (1976); Joseph J. Ellis, *After the Revolution: Profiles of Early American Culture* (1979); Jay Fliegelman, *Prodigals and Pilgrims: The American Revolution against Patriarchal Authority, 1750–1800* (1982); J. Franklin Jameson, *The American Revolution Considered as a Social Movement* (1962); Benjamin W. Labaree, *The Merchants of Newburyport, 1764–1815* (1962); Jan Lewis, "The Republican Wife: Virtue and Seduction in the Early Republic," *William and Mary Quarterly* (1987); Forrest McDonald and Ellen Shapiro McDonald, "The Ethnic Origins of the American People, 1790," *William and Mary Quarterly* (1980); Gary Nash, *Forging Freedom: The Formation of Philadelphia's Black Community, 1720–1840* (1988); Donald L. Robinson, *Slavery in the Structure of American Politics, 1765–1820* (1971); Howard Rock, *Artisans of the New Republic: Tradesmen of New York City in the Age of Jefferson* (1979); Charles G. Steffen, *The Mechanics of Baltimore: Workers and Politics in the Age of Revolution, 1763–1812* (1984); Lynne Withey, *Dearest Friend: A Life of Abigail Adams* (1981); Arthur Zilversmit, *The First Emancipation: The Abolition of Slavery in the North* (1967).

The Federal Constitution
Douglass Adair, *Fame and the Founding Fathers* (1974); Lance Banning, "James Madison and the Nationalists, 1780–1783," *William and Mary Quarterly* (1983); Charles Beard, *An Economic Interpretation of the Constitution of the United States* (1913); Richard Beeman, Stephen Botein, and Edward C. Carter II, eds., *Beyond Confederation: Origins of the Constitution and American National Identity* (1987); Irving Brant, *James Madison: The Nationalist, 1780–1787* (1948); Robert E. Brown, *Charles Beard and the Constitution*, (1956); Linda Grant DePauw, *The Eleventh Pillar: New York State and the Federal Constitution* (1966); John P. Diggins, *The Lost Soul of American Politics: Virtue, Self-Interest, and the Foundations of Liberalism* (1984); Max Farrand, *The Framing of the Constitution* (1913); Ralph Ketcham, *James Madison* (1971); Leonard Levy, ed., *Essays on the Making of the Constitution* (1969); Forrest McDonald, *We the People: The Economic Origins of the Constitution* (1958); Gerald Stourzh, *Alexander Hamilton and the Idea of Republican Government* (1970); Garry Wills, *Explaining America: The Federalist* (1981).

CHAPTER 8: THE REPUBLIC LAUNCHED

Society
Jeanne Boydston, *Home and Work: Housework, Wages, and the Ideology of Labor in the Early Republic* (1990); Nancy F. Cott, *The Bonds of Womanhood: "Woman's Sphere" in New England, 1780–1835* (1977); Joseph J. Ellis, *After the Revolution: Profiles of Early American Culture* (1979); Malcolm J. Rohrbough, *The Trans-Appalachian Frontier: Peoples, Societies, and Institutions, 1775–1850* (1978); Thomas P. Slaughter, *The Whiskey Rebellion: Frontier Epilogue to the American Revolution* (1986); Billy G. Smith, *The "Lower Sort": Philadelphia's Laboring People, 1759–1800* (1990); Charles G. Steffen, *The Mechanics of Baltimore: Workers and Politics in the Age of Revolution, 1763–1812* (1984).

National Government
Ralph Adams Brown, *The Presidency of John Adams* (1975); Manning J. Dauer, *The Adams Federalists* (1953); Richard H. Kohn, *Eagle and Sword: The Federalists and the Creation of a Military Establishment in America, 1783–1802* (1975); Ralph Ketcham, *Presidents over Party: The First American Presidency, 1789–1829* (1984); Forrest McDonald, *The Presidency of George Washington* (1974); John C. Miller, *The Federalist Era, 1789–1801* (1960); Wiley Sword, *President Washington's Indian War: The Struggle for the Old Northwest, 1790–1795* (1985).

Party Politics
Joseph Charles, *The Origins of the American Party System* (1956); Paul Goodman, *The Democratic*

Republicans of Massachusetts (1964); John F. Hoadley, Origins of American Political Parties, 1789–1803 (1986); Richard Hofstadter, The Idea of a Party System: The Rise of Legitimate Opposition in the United States, 1780–1840 (1969); Norman Risjord, Chesapeake Politics, 1781–1800 (1978); Alfred Young, The Democratic Republicans of New York: The Origins, 1763–1797 (1967).

Party Ideology
Joyce Appleby, Capitalism and a New Social Order: The Republican Vision of the 1970s (1984) and Liberalism and Republicanism in the Historical Imagination (1992); Richard W. Buel, Jr., Securing the Republic: Ideology in American Politics, 1789–1815 (1972); John R. Howe, Jr., The Changing Political Thought of John Adams (1966); Gerald Stourzh, Alexander Hamilton and the Idea of Republican Government (1970); John Zvesper, Political Philosophy and Rhetoric: A Study of the Origins of Party Politics (1977).

Constitutional Developments
Bernard Schwartz, The Great Rights of Mankind: A History of the American Bill of Rights (1977); James M. Smith, Freedom's Fetters: The Alien and Sedition Laws and American Civil Liberties (1956); Leonard Levy, Legacy of Suppression: Freedom of Speech and Press in Early American History (1960); Robert A. Rutland, The Birth of the Bill of Rights, 1776–1791 (1955).

Foreign Policy
Harry Ammon, The Genet Mission (1973); Jerald Combs, The Jay Treaty: Political Battleground of the Founding Fathers (1970); Alexander DeConde, Entangling Alliance: Politics and Diplomacy under George Washington (1958) and The Quasi-War: The Politics and Diplomacy of the Undeclared War with France, 1797–1801 (1966); Felix Gilbert, To the Farewell Address: Ideas of Early American Foreign Policy (1961); Bradford Perkins, The First Rapprochement: England and the United States, 1795–1805 (1955); Paul A. Varg, Foreign Policies of the Founding Fathers (1963).

Biographies
Charles W. Aikers, Abigail Adams (1980); Irving Brant, James Madison: Father of the Constitution, 1787–1800 (1950); John C. Miller, Alexander Hamilton: Portrait in Paradox (1959); Merrill Peterson, Thomas Jefferson and the New Nation (1970); Page Smith, John Adams (1962); Garry Wills, Cincinnatus: George Washington and the Enlightenment (1984).

CHAPTER 9: THE JEFFERSONIAN REPUBLIC

General Histories
Richard Hofstadter, The Idea of a Party System: The Rise of Legitimate Opposition in the United States, 1780–1840 (1969); George Dangerfield, The Era of Good Feelings (1952); James Sterling Young, The Washington Community, 1800–1828 (1966).

Jeffersonians in Power
Alexander Balinky, Albert Gallatin: Fiscal Theories and Policy (1958); James Banner, To the Hartford Convention: The Federalists and the Origins of Party Politics in the Early Republic, 1789–1815 (1970); Theodore J. Crackel, Mr. Jefferson's Army: Political and Social Reform of the Military Establishment, 1801–1809 (1987); Noble Cunningham, The Jeffersonian Republicans in Power: Party Operations, 1801–1809 (1963) and The Process of Government under Jefferson (1978); Paul Goodman, The Democratic Republicans of Massachusetts (1964); Robert M. Johnstone, Jr., Jefferson and the Presidency: Leadership in the Young Republic (1978); Linda K. Kerber, Federalists in Dissent: Imagery and Ideology in Jeffersonian America (1970); Norman K. Risjord, The Old Republicans: Southern Conservatism in the Age of Jefferson (1965); Robert A. Rutland, The Presidency of James Madison (1990); Robert W. Tucker and David C. Hendrickson, Empire of Liberty: The Statecraft of Thomas Jefferson (1990).

Indian Affairs and Western Expansion
Paul K. Conklin, Cane Ridge: America's Pentecost (1990); R. David Edmunds, Tecumseh and the Quest for Indian Leadership (1984); Reginald Horsman, Expansion and American Indian Policy, 1783–1812 (1967) and The Frontier in the Formative Years, 1783–1815 (1970); T. Scott Miyakawa, Protestants and Pioneers: Individualism and Conformity on the American Frontier (1964); Bernard W. Sheehan, Seeds of Extinction: Jeffersonian Philanthropy and the American Indians (1973); Michael Williams, Americans and Their Forests: A Historical Geography (1989).

The Judiciary
Richard E. Ellis, The Jeffersonian Crisis: Courts and Politics in the Early Republic (1971); Robert K. Faulkner, The Jurisprudence of John Marshall (1968); Morton J. Horwitz, The Transformation of American Law, 1780–1860 (1977); R. K. Newmyer, The Supreme Court under Marshall and Taney (1968).

Foreign Affairs and the War of 1812
Alexander DeConde, This Affair of Louisiana (1976); Donald C. Hickey, The War of 1812: A Forgotten Conflict (1989); Bradford Perkins, Prologue to War: England and the United States, 1805–1812 (1961); Robert A. Rutland, Madison's Alternatives: The Jeffersonian Republicans and the Coming of War, 1805–1812 (1975); Burton Spivak, Jefferson's English Crisis: Commerce, Embargo, and the Republican Revolution (1978); J. C. A. Stagg, Mr. Madison's War: Politics, Diplomacy, and Warfare in the Early American Republic, 1783–1830 (1983).

Biographies

Harry Ammon, *James Monroe: The Quest for National Identity* (1979); Leonard Baker, *John Marshall: A Life in Law* (1974); Ralph Ketcham, *James Madison: A Biography* (1971); Drew R. McCoy, *The Last of the Fathers: James Madison and the Republican Legacy* (1989); Dumas Malone, *Jefferson the President: First Term, 1801–1805* (1970) and *Jefferson the President: Second Term, 1805–1809* (1974); Merrill Peterson, *Thomas Jefferson and the New Nation: A Biography* (1970); Robert Remini, *Andrew Jackson and the Course of American Empire, 1767–1821* (1977).

CHAPTER 10: THE OPENING OF AMERICA

General Histories

W. Elliot Brownlee, *Dynamics of Ascent: A History of the American Economy* (1974); Stuart Bruchey, *The Roots of American Economic Growth, 1607–1861* (1965); Susan Previant Lee and Peter Passell, *A New Economic View of American History* (1979); Peter Temin, *Causal Factors in American Economic Growth in the Nineteenth Century* (1975).

Transportation

Carter Goodrich, *Government Promotion of American Canals and Railroads, 1800–1860* (1974); Erik F. Haites et al., *Western River Transportation: The Era of Early Internal Development, 1810–1860* (1975); Louis C. Hunter, *Steamboats on the Western Rivers: An Economic and Technological History* (1949); Ronald Shaw, *Canals for a Nation: The Canal Era in the United States, 1790–1860* (1990); Carol Sheriff, *The Artificial River: The Erie Canal and the Paradox of Progress, 1817–1862* (1996); George R. Taylor, *The Transportation Revolution, 1815–1860* (1951); Peter Way, *Common Labour: Workers and the Digging of North American Canals, 1780–1860* (1993).

Industrialization and the Economy

Thomas C. Cochran, *Frontiers of Change: Early Industrialism in America* (1981); Gary Cross and Rick Szostak, *Technology and American Society* (1995); Robert F. Dalzell, Jr., *Enterprising Elite: The Boston Associates and the World They Made* (1987); Constance M. Green, *Eli Whitney and the Birth of American Technology* (1956); David J. Jeremy, *Transatlantic Industrial Revolution: The Diffusion of Textile Technology between Britain and America, 1790–1830* (1981); Diane Lindstrom, *Economic Development in the Philadelphia Region, 1810–1850* (1978); Nathan Rosenberg, *Technology and American Economic Growth* (1972); Darwin H. Stapleton, *The Transfer of Early Industrial Technologies to America* (1987); Peter Temin, *Iron and Steel in Nineteenth Century America* (1964); Barbara M. Tucker, *Samuel Slater and the Origins of the American Textile Industry, 1790–1860* (1984).

Agriculture

Jeremy Atack and Fred Bateman, *To Their Own Soil: Agriculture in the Antebellum North* (1987); Clarence Danhof, *Changes in Agriculture: The Northern United States, 1820–1870* (1969); Paul W. Gates, *The Farmer's Age: Agriculture, 1815–1860* (1960); Lewis C. Gray, *History of Agriculture in the Southern United States*, 2 vols. (1933); Winifred Barr Rothenberg, *From Market-Places to a Market Economy: The Transformation of Rural Massachusetts, 1750–1850* (1992).

Workers and Community Studies

Mary H. Blewett, *Men, Women, and Work: Class, Gender, and Protest in the New England Shoe Industry, 1780–1910* (1988); Don H. Doyle, *The Social Order of a Frontier Community: Jacksonville, Illinois, 1825–70* (1983); Thomas Dublin, *Transforming Women's Work: New England Lives in the Industrial Revolution* (1994); Paul A. Gilje, *The Road to Mobocracy: Popular Disorder in New York City, 1763–1834* (1987); Bruce Laurie, *Working People of Philadelphia, 1800–1850* (1980) and *Artisans into Workers: Labor in Nineteenth-Century America* (1989); Brian C. Mitchell, *The Paddy Camps: The Irish of Lowell, 1821–61* (1988); Jonathan Prude, *The Coming of Industrial Order: Town and Factory Life in Rural Massachusetts, 1810–1860* (1983); W. J. Rorabaugh, *The Craft Apprentice: From Franklin to the Machine Age in America* (1986); Steven J. Ross, *Workers on the Edge: Work, Leisure, and Politics in Industrializing Cincinnati, 1788–1890* (1985); Christine Stansell, *City of Women: Sex and Class in New York, 1789–1860* (1986); Richard B. Stott, *Workers in the Metropolis: Class, Ethnicity, and Youth in Antebellum New York City* (1990); David A. Zonderman, *Aspirations and Anxieties: New England Workers and the Mechanized Factory System, 1815–1850* (1992).

Society and Values

Daniel J. Boorstin, *The Americans: The National Experience* (1965); Richard D. Brown, *Knowledge Is Power: The Diffusion of Information in Early America, 1700–1865* (1989); Richard L. Bushman, *The Refinement of America: Persons, Houses, Cities* (1992); Clyde and Sally Griffen, *Natives and Newcomers: The Ordering of Opportunity in Mid-Nineteenth Poughkeepsie* (1978); Lawrence W. Levine, *High Brow/Low Brow: The Emergence of Cultural Hierarchy in America* (1988); Russel B. Nye, *Society and Culture in America, 1830–1860* (1974); Michael O'Malley, *Keeping Watch: A History of American Time* (1990); William H. and Jane H. Pease, *The Web of Progress: Private Values and Public Styles in Boston and Charleston, 1828–1843* (1985); Edward Pessen, *Jacksonian America: Society, Personality, and Politics*, rev. ed. (1978) and *Riches, Class, and Power before the Civil War* (1973); Alexander Saxton, *The Rise and Fall of the White Republic: Class Politics and Mass Culture in Nineteenth-Century America* (1990); Stephan Thernstrom, *Poverty and Progress: Social Mobility in a Nineteenth-Century City* (1964); Robert H. Wiebe, *The Opening of American Society: From the Adoption of the Constitution to the Eve of Disunion* (1984).

Land and the West
Daniel Feller, *The Public Lands in Jacksonian Politics* (1984); Malcolm J. Rohrbough, *The Land Office Business: The Settlement and Administration of American Public Lands, 1789–1837* (1968); David J. Wishart, *The Fur Trade of the American West, 1817–1840* (1979).

Environment
Carolyn Merchant, *Ecological Revolutions: Nature, Gender, and Science in New England* (1989); Theodore Steinberg, *Nature Incorporated: Industrialization and the Waters of New England* (1991); Michael Williams, *Americans and Their Forests: A Historical Geography* (1989).

Politics and Law
George Dangerfield, *The Awakening of American Nationalism, 1815–1828* (1965); Robert K. Faulkner, *The Jurisprudence of John Marshall* (1968); Morton J. Horwitz, *The Transformation of American Law, 1780–1860* (1977); James Willard Hurst, *Law and the Conditions of Freedom in the Nineteenth-Century United States* (1956); Glover Moore, *The Missouri Controversy, 1819–1821* (1953); R. Kent Newmyer, *The Supreme Court under Marshall and Taney* (1968); M. N. Rothbard, *The Panic of 1819: Reactions and Policies* (1962); Charles Sydnor, *The Development of Southern Sectionalism, 1819–1848* (1948).

CHAPTER 11: THE RISE OF DEMOCRACY

General Histories
George Dangerfield, *The Awakening of American Nationalism, 1815–1828* (1965); Edward Pessen, *Jacksonian America: Society, Personality, and Politics*, rev. ed. (1978); Glyndon G. Van Deusen, *The Jacksonian Era, 1828–1845* (1959).

Society and Values
Michel Chevalier, *Society, Manners, and Politics in the United States* (1961); Charles Dickens, *American Notes for General Circulation* (1842, reprinted 1972); Francis J. Grund, *Aristocracy in America* (1839, reprinted 1959); Harriet Martineau, *Society in America* (1837); Douglas T. Miller, *Jacksonian Aristocracy: Class and Democracy in New York, 1830–1860* (1967); Russel B. Nye, *Society and Culture in America, 1830–1860* (1960); Edward Pessen, *Riches, Class, and Power before the Civil War* (1973); Alexis de Tocqueville, *Democracy in America* (1945); Frances Trollope, *Domestic Manners of the Americans* (1832); John William Ward, *Andrew Jackson: Symbol for an Age* (1955); Julie Winch, *Philadelphia's Black Elite: Activism, Accommodation, and the Struggle for Autonomy, 1787–1848* (1988).

The Emergence of Democracy
James S. Chase, *Emergence of the Presidential Nominating Convention, 1789–1832* (1973); Richard Hofstadter, *The Idea of a Party System: The Rise of Legitimate Opposition in the United States, 1780–1840* (1969); Richard P. McCormick, *The Presidential Game: The Origins of American Presidential Politics* (1982); Chilton Williamson, *American Suffrage from Property to Democracy, 1760–1860* (1960).

The Jacksonian Party System
Lee Benson, *The Concept of Jacksonian Democracy: New York as a Test Case* (1961); James C. Curtis, *The Fox at Bay: Martin Van Buren and the Presidency, 1837–1841* (1970); Mary W. M. Hargreaves, *The Presidency of John Quincy Adams* (1985); Richard B. Latner, *The Presidency of Andrew Jackson: White House Politics, 1829–1837* (1979); Richard P. McCormick, *The Second American Party System: Party Formation in the Jacksonian Era* (1966); Mary P. Ryan, *Women in Public: Between Banners and Ballots, 1825–1880* (1990); Joel H. Silbey, *The American Nation, 1838–1893* (1991).

Banking and the Economy
Bray Hammond, *Banks and Politics in America from the Revolution to the Civil War* (1957); John M. McFaul, *The Politics of Jacksonian Finance* (1972); James Roger Sharp, *The Jacksonians versus the Banks: Politics in the States after the Panic of 1837* (1970); Peter Temin, *The Jacksonian Economy* (1969).

Nullification
Richard Ellis, *The Union at Risk: Jacksonian Democracy, States' Rights and the Nullification Crisis* (1987); Merrill D. Peterson, *Olive Branch and Sword: The Compromise of 1833* (1982).

Indian Removal
Arthur H. DeRosier, Jr., *The Removal of the Choctaw Indians* (1970); William G. McLoughlin, *Cherokee Renascence in the New Republic* (1986); John K. Mahon, *History of the Second Seminole War, 1835–1842* (1967); Francis P. Prucha, *American Indian Policy in the Formative Years* (1962); Ronald N. Satz, *American Indian Policy in the Jacksonian Era* (1975).

Biographies
Maurice G. Baxter, *One and Inseparable: Daniel Webster and the Union* (1984); Samuel F. Bemis, *John Quincy Adams and the Union* (1956); Donald Cole, *Martin Van Buren and the American Political System* (1984); Thomas P. Govan, *Nicholas Biddle: Nationalist and Public Banker* (1959); John Niven, *John C. Calhoun and the Price of Union: A Biography* (1988) and *Martin Van Buren: The Romantic Age of American Politics* (1983); Merrill D. Peterson, *The Great Triumvirate: Webster, Clay, and Calhoun* (1987); Robert V. Remini, *The Life of Andrew Jackson* (1988) and *Henry Clay: Statesman for the*

Union (1991); Charles W. Wiltse, *John C. Calhoun, Nullifier, 1829–1839* (1949).

CHAPTER 12: THE FIRES OF PERFECTION

General Histories
John D'Emilio and Estelle B. Freedman, *Intimate Matters: A History of Sexuality in America* (1988); John F. Kasson, *Rudeness and Civility: Manners in Nineteenth Century America* (1990); Perry Miller, *The Life of the Mind in America: From the Revolution to the Civil War* (1966); Russel B. Nye, *Society and Culture in America, 1830–1860* (1974); Lewis Perry, *Boats Against the Current: American Culture between Revolution and Modernity, 1820–1860* (1993).

Religion and Revivalism
William G. McLoughlin, *Modern Revivalism: Charles Grandison Finney to Billy Graham* (1959); Paul E. Johnson and Sean Wilentz, *The Kingdom of Matthias: A Story of Sex and Salvation in 19th-Century America* (1994); T. Scott Miyakawa, *Protestants and Pioneers: Individualism and Conformity on the American Frontier* (1964); Jan Shipps, *Mormonism: The Story of a New Religious Tradition* (1985).

Women's Sphere and Feminism
Norma Balsch, *In the Eyes of the Law: Women, Marriage, and Property in Nineteenth-Century New York* (1982); Ann Douglas, *The Feminization of American Culture* (1977); Timothy J. Gilfoyle, *City of Eros: New York City, Prostitution, and the Commercialization of Sex, 1790–1920* (1992); Nancy Hewitt, *Women's Activism and Social Change: Rochester, New York, 1822–1872* (1984); Sylvia D. Hoffert, *Private Matters: American Attitudes toward Childbearing and Infant Nurture in the Urban North, 1800–1860* (1989); Mary Kelley, *Private Woman, Public Stage: Literary Domesticity in Nineteenth-Century America* (1984); Keith E. Melder, *Beginnings of Sisterhood: The American Women's Rights Movement, 1800–1850* (1977); James Reed, *From Private Vice to Public Virtue: The Birth Control Movement in America* (1978); Jean Fagan Yellin, *Women and Sisters: The Antislavery Feminists in American Culture* (1989).

Family
W. Andrew Achenbaum, *Old Age in the New Land: The American Experience since 1790* (1978); Clifford E. Clark, Jr., *The American Family Home, 1800–1860* (1986); Thomas R. Cole, *The Journey of Life: A Cultural History of Aging in America* (1992); Steven Mintz and Susan Kellogg, *Domestic Revolutions: A Social History of American Family Life* (1988); Walter T. K. Nugent, *Structures of American Social History* (1981); Maris A. Vinovskis, *Fertility in Massachusetts from the Revolution to the Civil War* (1981); Robert V. Wells, *Revolutions in*

Americans' Lives: A Demographic Perspective on the History of Americans, Their Families, and Their Society (1982); Bernard Wishy, *The Child and the Republic: The Dawn of Modern American Child Nurture* (1967); Yasukichi Yasuba, *Birth Rates of the White Population in the United States, 1800–1860* (1962).

American Romanticism
Paul F. Boller, Jr., *American Transcendentalism, 1830–1860: An Intellectual Inquiry* (1974); Mary Kupiec Cayton, *Emerson's Emergence: Self and Society in the Transformation of New England, 1800–1845* (1989); Susan P. Conrad, *Perish the Thought: Intellectual Women in Romantic America, 1830–1860* (1976); F. O. Matthiessen, *American Renaissance: Art and Expression in the Age of Emerson and Whitman* (1941); Anne C. Rose, *Transcendentalism as a Social Movement, 1830–1850* (1981); Lazar Ziff, *Literary Democracy: The Declaration of Cultural Independence in America* (1982).

Utopian Communities
Arthur Bestor, *Backwoods Utopias: The Sectarian and Owenite Phases of Communitarian Socialism in America, 1663–1829* (1950); Carl J. Guarneri, *The Utopian Alternative: Fourierism in Nineteenth-Century America* (1991); J. F. C. Harrison, *Quest for the New Moral World: Robert Owen and the Owenites in Britain and America* (1969); Lawrence Foster, *Religion and Sexuality: Three American Communal Experiments of the Nineteenth Century* (1981); Louis Kern, *An Ordered Love: Sex Roles and Sexuality in Victorian Utopias* (1981); Carol A. Kolmerten, *Women in Utopia: The Ideology of Gender in the American Owenite Communities* (1990); Stephen Stein, *The Shaker Experience in America* (1992).

Reform Movements
Robert H. Abzug, *Cosmos Crumbling: American Reform and the Religious Imagination* (1994); Charles Leslie Glenn, Jr., *The Myth of the Common School* (1988); Clifford S. Griffin, *Their Brothers' Keepers: Moral Stewardship in the United States, 1800–1865* (1960); W. J. Rorabaugh, *The Alcoholic Republic: An American Tradition* (1979); David Rothman, *The Discovery of the Asylum: Social Order and Disorder in the New Republic* (1971); Ian R. Tyrrell, *Sobering Up: From Temperance to Prohibition in Antebellum America, 1800–1860* (1979); Rush Welter, *Popular Education and Democratic Thought in America* (1962).

Abolitionism
Aileen Kraditor, *Means and Ends in American Abolitionism: Garrison and His Critics on Strategy and Tactics, 1834–1850* (1967); John R. McKivigan, *The War against Proslavery Religion: Abolitionism and the Northern Churches* (1984); William Lee Miller, *Arguing about Slavery: The Great Battle in the United States Congress* (1996); Russel B. Nye, *Fettered Freedom: Civil Liberties and the Slavery*

Controversy, 1830–1860, rev. ed. (1963); William H. and Jane H. Pease, *They Who Would be Free: Blacks' Search for Freedom, 1830–1861* (1974); Lewis Perry, *Radical Abolitionism: Anarchy and the Government of God in Antislavery Thought* (1973); Leonard Richards, *"Gentlemen of Property and Standing": Anti-Abolition Mobs in Jacksonian America* (1970).

Biographies

Robert H. Abzug, *Passionate Liberator: Theodore Dwight Weld and the Dilemma of Reform* (1980); Lois Banner, *Elizabeth Cady Stanton: A Radical for Woman's Rights* (1980); Fawn Brodie, *No Man Knows My History: The Life of Joseph Smith, the Mormon Prophet*, 2d ed. (1971); Richard L. Bushman, *Joseph Smith and the Beginnings of Mormonism* (1984); Charles Capper, *Margaret Fuller: An American Romantic Life, the Private Years* (1992); Keith J. Hardman, *Charles Grandison Finney, 1792–1875: Revivalist and Reformer* (1987); Gerda Lerner, *The Grimké Sisters of South Carolina: Rebels against Slavery* (1967); William S. McFeely, *Frederick Douglass* (1991); Nell Painter, *Sojourner Truth: A Life, a Symbol* (1996); Katherine Kish Sklar, *Catharine Beecher: A Study in American Domesticity* (1973); John L. Thomas, *The Liberator: William Lloyd Garrison* (1963); Robert D. Thomas, *The Man Who Would Be Perfect: John Humphrey Noyes and the Utopian Impulse* (1977); Bertram Wyatt-Brown, *Lewis Tappan and the Evangelical War against Slavery* (1969).

CHAPTER 13: THE OLD SOUTH

General Histories

John B. Boles, *The South through Time: A History of an American Region* (1995); William J. Cooper and Thomas Terrill, *The American South*, 2d ed. (1996); Albert Cowdrey, *This Land, This South: An Environmental History*, rev. ed. (1996); Charles S. Sydnor, *The Development of Southern Sectionalism, 1819–1848* (1948).

Southern Economy

Fred Bateman and Thomas Weiss, *A Deplorable Scarcity: The Failure of Industrialization in the Slave Economy* (1981); Lewis C. Gray, *History of Agriculture in the Southern United States to 1860*, 2 vols. (1933); Gavin Wright, *The Political Economy of the Cotton South: Households, Markets, and Wealth in the Nineteenth Century* (1978).

Southern Society

John B. Boles, ed., *Masters and Slaves in the House of the Lord: Race and Religion in the American South, 1740–1870* (1988); Orville Vernon Burton, *In My Father's House Are Many Mansions: Family and Community in Edgefield, South Carolina* (1985); Dickson D. Bruce, Jr., *Violence and Culture in the Antebellum South* (1979); Bill Cecil-Fronsman, *Common Whites: Class & Culture in Antebellum*

North Carolina (1992); Clement Eaton, *The Growth of Southern Civilization, 1790–1860* (1961); J. William Harris, *Plain Folk and Gentry in a Slave Society: White Liberty and Black Slavery in Augusta's Hinterlands* (1985); Michael P. Johnson and James L. Roark, *Black Masters: A Free Family of Color in the Old South* (1984); James Hugo Johnston, *Race Relations in Virginia and Miscegenation in the South, 1776–1860* (1970); Stephanie McCurry, *Masters of Small Worlds: Yeoman Households, Gender Relations, and the Political Culture of the Antebellum South Carolina Low Country* (1995); Donald G. Mathews, *Religion in the Old South* (1977); John Hebron Moore, *The Emergence of the Cotton Kingdom in the Old Southwest: Mississippi, 1770–1860* (1988); William H. and Jane H. Pease, *The Web of Progress: Private Values and Public Styles in Boston and Charleston, 1828–1843* (1985); Bertram Wyatt-Brown, *Honor and Violence in the Old South* (1986).

Southern Women

Victoria E. Bynum, *Unruly Women: The Politics of Social and Sexual Control in the Old South* (1992); Jane Turner Censer, *North Carolina Planters and Their Children, 1800–1860* (1984); Catherine Clinton, *The Plantation Mistress: Woman's World in the Old South* (1983); Suzanne Lebsock, *Free Women of Petersburg: Status and Culture in a Southern Town, 1784–1860* (1984); Brenda E. Stevenson, *Life in Black and White: Family and Community in the Slave South* (1996); Deborah G. White, *Arn'n't I a Woman?: Female Slaves in the Plantation South* (1985); C. Vann Woodward, ed., *Mary Chesnut's Civil War* (1981).

Slavery and Slaveowners

Shearer Davis Bowman, *Masters and Lords: Mid-Nineteenth Century U.S. Planters and Prussian Junkers* (1993); Peter A. Coclanis, *The Shadow of a Dream: Economic Life and Death in the South Carolina Low Country, 1670–1920* (1989); Paul A. David et al., *Reckoning with Slavery: A Critical Study in the Quantitative History of American Negro Slavery* (1976); Drew Gilpin Faust, *James Henry Hammond and the Old South: A Design for Mastery* (1982); Ulrich B. Phillips, *American Negro Slavery* (1918) and *Life and Labor in the Old South* (1929); Todd L. Savitt, *Medicine and Slavery: The Diseases and Health Care of Blacks in Antebellum Virginia* (1978); Robert S. Starobin, *Industrial Slavery in the Old South* (1970); Richard H. Steckel, *The Economics of U.S. Slave and Southern White Fertility* (1985); Michael Tadman, *Speculators and Slaves: Masters, Traders, and Slaves in the Old South* (1989); William L. Van Deburg, *The Slave Drivers: Black Agricultural Labor Supervisors in the Antebellum South* (1988); Richard C. Wade, *Slavery in the Cities* (1964).

Slave Culture

John W. Blassingame, *The Slave Community: Plantation Life in the Ante-Bellum South*, rev. ed.

(1979); John B. Boles, *Black Southerners, 1619–1869* (1984); Margaret Washington Creel, *"A Peculiar People": Slave Religion and Community among the Gullahs* (1988); Herbert G. Gutman, *The Black Family in Slavery and Freedom, 1750–1925* (1976); Wilma King, *Stolen Childhood: Slave Youth in Nineteenth Century America* (1995); Lawrence Levine, *Black Culture and Black Consciousness: Afro-American Folk Thought from Slavery to Freedom* (1977); Ann Patton Malone, *Sweet Chariot: Slave Family and Household Structure in Nineteenth-Century Louisiana* (1993); Albert J. Raboteau, *Slave Religion: The "Invisible Institution" in the Antebellum South* (1978); Mechal Sobel, *Trabelin' On: The Slave Journey to an Afro-Baptist Faith* (1979); Sterling Stuckey, *Slave Culture: Nationalist Theory and the Foundations of Black America* (1987).

Slave Resistance
Norrece T. Jones, *Born a Child of Freedom, Yet a Slave: Mechanisms of Control and Strategies of Resistance in Antebellum South* (1990); Winthrop Jordan, *Tumult and Silence at Second Creek* (1993); John Lofton, *Denmark Vesey's Revolt: The Slave Plot That Lit a Fuse to Fort Sumter* (1983); Stephen B. Oates, *The Fires of Jubilee: Nat Turner's Fierce Rebellion* (1975).

The Defense of Slavery
Clement Eaton, *Freedom of Thought in the Old South* (1940); George M. Fredrickson, *The Black Image in the White Mind: The Debate on Afro-American Character and Destiny, 1817–1914* (1971); Alison Goodyear Freehling, *Drift toward Dissolution: The Virginia Slavery Debate of 1831–1832* (1982); Larry E. Tise, *Proslavery: A History of the Defense of Slavery in America, 1701–1840* (1987).

CHAPTER 14: WESTERN EXPANSION AND THE RISE OF THE SLAVERY ISSUE

General Histories
Ray A. Billington, *The Far Western Frontier, 1830–1860* (1956); Ray A. Billington and Martin Ridge, *Westward Expansion*, 5th ed. (1982); William H. Goetzmann, *Exploration and Empire: The Explorer and the Scientist in the Winning of the American West* (1978); Frederick Merk, *History of the Westward Movement* (1978); Henry Nash Smith, *Virgin Land: The American West as Symbol and Myth* (1950).

American Expansionism
Norman A. Graebner, *Empire on the Pacific: A Study of American Continental Expansionism* (1955); Reginald Horsman, *Race and Manifest Destiny: The Origins of American Racial Anglo-Saxonism* (1981); Frederick Merk, *Manifest Destiny and Mission in American History* (1963), *The Monroe Doctrine and American Expansionism, 1843–1849* (1966), and *The Oregon Question: Essays in Anglo-American Diplomacy and Politics* (1967).

Societies in the West
Gunther Barth, *Instant Cities: Urbanization and the Rise of San Francisco and Denver* (1975); William C. Binkley, *The Texas Revolution* (1952); Malcolm Clark, Jr., *Eden Seekers: The Settlement of Oregon, 1812–1862* (1981); Thomas D. Hall, *Social Change in the Southwest, 1350–1880* (1989); Robert F. Heizer and Alan J. Almquist, *The Other Californians: Prejudice and Discrimination under Spain, Mexico, and the United States to 1920* (1971); Dorothy O. Johansen and Charles M. Gates, *Empire on the Columbia: A History of the Pacific Northwest*, 2d ed. (1967); Sandra L. Myres, *Westering Women and the Frontier Experience, 1800–1915* (1982); Leonard Pitt, *The Decline of the Californios: A Social History of the Spanish-Speaking Californians, 1846–1890* (1966); Elliott West, *Growing Up with the Country: Childhood on the Far Western Frontier* (1989); Donald Worster, *Rivers of Empire: Water, Aridity, and the Growth of the American West* (1985).

Expansion and the Party System
Paul B. Bergeron, *The Presidency of James K. Polk* (1987); Frederick Merk, *Slavery and the Annexation of Texas* (1972); Robert J. Morgan, *A Whig Embattled: The Presidency under John Tyler* (1954); Norma L. Peterson, *The Presidencies of William Henry Harrison and John Tyler* (1989).

The War with Mexico
K. Jack Bauer, *The Mexican War, 1846–1848* (1974); Seymour V. Connor and Odie B. Faulk, *North America Divided: The Mexican War, 1846–1848* (1971); Neal Harlow, *California Conquered: The Annexation of a Mexican Province, 1846–1850* (1982); Robert W. Johannsen, *To the Halls of the Montezumas: The Mexican War in the American Imagination* (1985); David M. Pletcher, *The Diplomacy of Annexation: Texas, Oregon, and the Mexican War* (1973); John H. Schroeder, *Mr. Polk's War: American Opposition and Dissent, 1846–1848* (1973).

The Sectional Crisis and the Expansion of Slavery
Eugene H. Berwanger, *The Frontier against Slavery: Western Anti-Negro Prejudice and the Slavery Extension Controversy* (1967); Frederick J. Blue, *The Free Soilers: Third Party Politics, 1848–1854* (1973); William J. Cooper, Jr., *The South and the Politics of Slavery, 1828–1856* (1978); Michael F. Holt, *The Political Crisis of the 1850s* (1978); Chaplain W. Morrison, *Democratic Politics and Sectionalism: The Wilmot Proviso Controversy* (1967); Allan Nevins, *Ordeal of the Union*, 2 vols. (1947); David M. Potter, *The Impending Crisis, 1848–1861* (1976); Joseph G. Rayback, *Free Soil: The Election of 1848* (1970); Richard H. Sewell, *Ballots for Freedom: Antislavery*

Politics in the United States, 1837–1860 (1976); Elbert B. Smith, *The Presidencies of Zachary Taylor and Millard Fillmore* (1988).

Biographies
Leonard J. Arrington, *Brigham Young: American Moses* (1985); K. Jack Bauer, *Zachary Taylor: Soldier, Planter, Statesman of the Old Southwest* (1985); Robert F. Dalzell, *Daniel Webster and the Trial of American Nationalism, 1843–1852* (1972); Holman Hamilton, *Zachary Taylor: Soldier in the White House* (1951); Robert W. Johannsen, *Stephen A. Douglas* (1973); Glyndon G. Van Deusen, *The Life of Henry Clay* (1937).

CHAPTER 15: THE UNION BROKEN

General Histories
Avery Craven, *The Coming of the Civil War*, 2d ed. rev. (1957) and *The Growth of Southern Nationalism, 1848–1861* (1953); James McPherson, *Ordeal by Fire: The Civil War and Reconstruction* (1982).

Economic Development and the Environment
William Cronon, *Nature's Metropolis: Chicago and the Great West* (1991); Albert Fishlow, *American Railroads and the Transformation of the Antebellum Economy* (1965); Robert William Fogel, *Without Consent or Contract: The Rise and Fall of American Slavery* (1989); Paul W. Gates, *The Farmer's Age: Agriculture, 1815–1860* (1960); James Huston, *The Panic of 1857 and the Coming of the Civil War* (1987); John F. Stover, *Iron Road to the West: American Railroads in the 1850s* (1978).

Immigration and Nativism
Tyler Anbinder, *Nativism and Slavery: The Northern Know Nothings and the Politics of the 1850s* (1992); John P. Dolan, *The Immigrant Church: New York's Irish and German Catholics, 1815–1865* (1975); Robert Ernst, *Immigrant Life in New York City, 1825–1863* (1949); Oscar Handlin, *Boston's Immigrants: A Study of Acculturation*, rev. ed. (1959); Michael F. Holt, "The Antimasonic and Know Nothing Parties," in Arthur M. Schlesinger, Jr., ed., *History of U.S. Political Parties*, vol. 1, pp. 575–737 (1973); Bruce Levine, *The Spirit of 1848: German Immigrants, Labor Conflict, and the Coming of the Civil War* (1992); Stanley Nadel, *Little Germany: Ethnicity, Religion, and Class in New York City, 1845–80* (1990).

Southern Sectionalism and Nationalism
Charles H. Brown, *Agents for Manifest Destiny: The Lives and Times of the Filibusterers* (1979); William J. Cooper, Jr., *The South and the Politics of Slavery, 1828–1856* (1978); Robert E. May, *The Southern Dream of a Caribbean Empire, 1854–1861* (1973); Eric H. Walther, *The Fire-Eaters* (1992).

Sectionalism and National Politics
Jean H. Baker, *Affairs of Party: The Political Culture of Northern Democrats in the Mid-Nineteenth Century* (1983); Eugene H. Berwanger, *The Frontier against Slavery: Western Anti-Negro Prejudice and the Slavery Extension Controversy* (1967); Don E. Fehrenbacher, *Slavery, Law, and Politics: The Dred Scott Case in Historical Perspective* (1981); Larry Gara, *The Presidency of Franklin Pierce* (1991); Roy F. Nichols, *The Disruption of American Democracy* (1948); Richard H. Sewell, *Ballots for Freedom: Antislavery Politics in the United States, 1837–1860* (1976); Mark W. Summers, *The Plundering Generation: Corruption and the Crisis of the Union, 1849–1861* (1987).

Secession and the Outbreak of War
William L. Barney, *The Secessionist Impulse: Alabama and Mississippi in 1860* (1974); Daniel W. Crofts, *Reluctant Confederates: Upper South Unionists in the Secession Crisis* (1989); Richard N. Current, *Lincoln and the First Shot* (1963); Lacy K. Ford, Jr., *Origins of Southern Radicalism: The South Carolina Upcountry, 1800–1860* (1988); George N. Knoles, ed., *The Crisis of the Union, 1860–1861* (1965); David M. Potter, *Lincoln and His Party in the Secession Crisis* (1942); J. Mills Thornton, *Politics and Power in a Slave Society: Alabama, 1800–1860* (1978).

The Causes of the Civil War
Thomas J. Pressly, *Americans Interpret Their Civil War* (1954); David M. Potter, *The South and the Sectional Conflict* (1969); Kenneth M. Stampp, ed., *The Causes of the Civil War*, rev. ed. (1991).

Biographies
Don E. Fehrenbacher, *Prelude to Greatness: Lincoln in the 1850s* (1962); Robert W. Johannsen, *Stephen A. Douglas* (1973); Philip Shriver Klein, *President James Buchanan* (1962); Roy F. Nichols, *Franklin Pierce: Young Hickory of the Granite Hills*, 2d ed. rev. (1958); Stephen B. Oates, *To Purge This Land with Blood: A Biography of John Brown* (1970).

CHAPTER 16: TOTAL WAR AND THE REPUBLIC

General Histories
Daniel Aaron, *The Unwritten War: American Writers and the Civil War* (1973); Richard F. Bensel, *Yankee Leviathan: The Origins of Central State Authority in America, 1859–1877* (1990); Richard E. Beringer et al., *The Elements of Confederate Defeat: Nationalism, War Aims, and Religion* (1989); Allan Nevins, *The War for the Union*, 4 vols. (1959–1971); Edmund Wilson, *Patriotic Gore: Studies in the Literature of the American Civil War* (1962).

Military History
Bern Anderson, *By Sea and by River: The Naval History of the Civil War* (1962); Bruce Catton, *The*

Centennial History of the Civil War, 3 vols. (1961–1965); Thomas L. Connelly, *Army of the Heartland: The Army of Tennessee, 1861–1862* (1967) and *Autumn of Glory: The Army of Tennessee, 1862–1865* (1971); Thomas L. Connelly and Archer Jones, *The Politics of Command: Factions and Ideas in Confederate Strategy* (1973); Herman Hattaway and Archer Jones, *How the North Won: A Military History of the Civil War* (1983); Archer Jones, *Civil War Command and Strategy: The Process of Victory and Defeat* (1992); Charles Royster, *The Destructive War: William Tecumseh Sherman, Stonewall Jackson, and the Americans* (1991); T. Harry Williams, *Lincoln and His Generals* (1952); Steven E. Woodworth, *Jefferson Davis and His Generals: The Failure of Confederate Command in the West* (1990).

Common Soldiers
Joseph T. Glatthaar, *Forged in Battle: The Civil War Alliance of Black Soldiers and White Officers* (1990) and *The March to the Sea and Beyond: Sherman's Troops in the Savannah and Carolinas Campaigns* (1985); James M. McPherson, *What They Fought For, 1861–1865* (1994); Reid Mitchell, *Civil War Soldiers: Their Expectations and Their Experiences* (1988), and *The Vacant Chair: The Northern Soldier Leaves Home* (1993); James I. Robertson, *Soldiers Blue and Gray* (1988); Bell I. Wiley, *The Life of Johnny Reb* (1943) and *The Life of Billy Yank* (1952).

The Confederacy
Mary A. DeCredico, *Patriotism for Profit: Georgia's Urban Entrepreneurs and the Confederate War Effort* (1990); Wayne K. Durrill, *War of Another Kind: A Southern Community in the Great Rebellion* (1990); Paul D. Escott, *After Secession: Jefferson Davis and the Failure of Confederate Nationalism* (1978); Drew Gilpin Faust, *The Creation of Confederate Nationalism: Ideology and Identity in the Civil War South* (1988); Mary Elizabeth Massey, *Refugee Life in the Confederacy* (1964); Frank L. Owsley, *State Rights in the Confederacy* (1925); Charles W. Ramsdell, *Behind the Lines in the Southern Confederacy* (1944); Richard C. Todd, *Confederate Finance* (1954); Bell I. Wiley, *The Plain People of the Confederacy* (1943) and *The Road to Appomattox* (1956); Wilfred B. Yearns, *The Confederate Congress* (1960).

Union Politics
Leonard P. Curry, *Blueprint for Modern America: Non-Military Legislation of the First Civil War Congress* (1968); William B. Hesseltine, *Lincoln and the War Governors* (1948); Harold M. Hyman, *A More Perfect Union: The Impact of the Civil War and Reconstruction on the Constitution* (1973); Philip S. Paludan, *The Presidency of Abraham Lincoln* (1994); James A. Rawley, *The Politics of Union: Northern Politics during the Civil War* (1974); Joel H. Silbey, *A Respectable Minority: The Democratic Party in the Civil War Era* (1977).

Union Home Front
Ralph Andreano, ed., *The Economic Impact of the American Civil War* (1962); Iver Bernstein, *The New York City Draft Riots: Their Significance for American Society and Politics in the Age of the Civil War* (1990); Adrian Cook, *The Armies of the Streets: The New York City Draft Riots of 1863* (1974); George Fredrickson, *The Inner Civil War: Northern Intellectuals and the Crisis of the Union* (1965); J. Matthew Gallman, *Mastering Wartime: A Social History of Philadelphia during the Civil War* (1990); Paul W. Gates, *Agriculture and the Civil War* (1965); Earl J. Hess, *Liberty, Virtue, and Progress: Northerners and Their War for the Union* (1988); James W. Geary, *We Need Men: The Union Draft in the Civil War* (1991); Frank L. Klement, *The Copperheads in the Middle West* (1960); Ernest A. McKay, *The Civil War and New York City* (1990); James H. Moorhead, *American Apocalypse: Yankee Protestants and the Civil War, 1860–1869* (1978); Philip S. Paludan, *"A People's Contest": The Union and Civil War, 1861–1865* (1988); George Winston Smith and Charles Burnet Judah, *Life in the North during the Civil War* (1966).

Women and the Civil War
Catherine Clinton and Nina Silber, eds., *Divided Houses: Gender and the Civil War* (1992); Marilyn M. Culpepper, *Trials and Triumphs: Women of the American Civil War* (1991); Ellen Leonard, *Yankee Women: Gender Battles in the Civil War* (1994); Mary Elizabeth Massey, *Bonnet Brigades: American Women and the Civil War* (1966); George C. Rable, *Civil Wars: Women and the Crisis of Southern Nationalism* (1989); C. Vann Woodward, ed., *Mary Chesnut's Civil War* (1981); Agatha Young, *Women and the Crisis: Women of the North in the Civil War* (1959).

Emancipation and the Black Experience
Dudley T. Cornish, *The Sable Arm: Negro Troops in the Union Army, 1861–1865* (1956); LaWanda Cox, *Lincoln and Black Freedom: A Study in Presidential Leadership* (1981); Barbara Jeanne Fields, *Slavery and Freedom on the Middle Ground: Maryland during the Nineteenth Century* (1985); John Hope Franklin, *The Emancipation Proclamation* (1963); Louis Gerteis, *From Contraband to Freedman: Federal Policy toward Southern Blacks, 1861–1865* (1973); James M. McPherson, *The Struggle for Equality: Abolitionists and the Negro in the Civil War and Reconstruction* (1964); Clarence L. Mohr, *On the Threshold of Freedom: Masters and Slaves in Civil War Georgia* (1986); Willie Lee Rose, *Rehearsal for Reconstruction: The Port Royal Experiment* (1964); V. Jacque Voegli, *Free but Not Equal: The Midwest and the Negro during the Civil War* (1967).

Diplomacy
David P. Crook, *Diplomacy during the American Civil War* (1975); Norman Ferris, *The Trent Affair: A Diplomatic Crisis* (1977); Brian Jenkins, *Britain*

and the War for the Union (1974); Howard Jones, *Union in Peril: The Crisis Over British Intervention in the Civil War* (1992); Frank L. Owsley, *King Cotton Diplomacy*, rev. ed. (1959).

Biographies
David W. Blight, *Frederick Douglass' Civil War: Keeping Faith in Jubilee* (1989); Bruce Catton, *Grant Moves South* (1960) and *Grant Takes Command* (1969); William C. Davis, *Jefferson Davis: The Man and His Hour* (1991); William S. McFeely, *Grant: A Biography* (1981); Mark E. Neely, Jr. *The Last Best Hope of Earth: Abraham Lincoln and the Promise of America* (1993); Alan T. Nolan, *Lee Considered: General Robert E. Lee and Civil War History* (1991); Stephen B. Oates, *A Woman of Valor: Clara Barton and the Civil War* (1994); James G. Randall and Richard N. Current, *Lincoln the President*, 4 vols. (1945–1955*)*; Emory M. Thomas, *Robert E. Lee* (1995).

CHAPTER 17: RECONSTRUCTING THE UNION

General Histories
James McPherson, *Ordeal by Fire: The Civil War and Reconstruction* (1982); Kenneth M. Stampp, *The Era of Reconstruction, 1865–1877* (1965).

National Politics
Herman Belz, *Emancipation and Equal Rights: Politics and Constitutionalism in the Civil War Era* (1978); Michael Les Benedict, *A Compromise of Principle: Congressional Republicans and Reconstruction* (1974); W. R. Brock, *An American Crisis: Congress and Reconstruction, 1865–1867* (1963); John and LaWanda Cox, *Politics, Principles, and Prejudice, 1865–1866* (1963); James M. McPherson, *The Struggle for Equality: Abolitionists and the Negro in the Civil War and Reconstruction* (1964); Hans L. Trefousse, *The Radical Republicans: Lincoln's Vanguard for Racial Justice* (1969).

Reconstruction and the Constitution
William Gillette, *The Right to Vote: Politics and the Passage of the Fifteenth Amendment* (1965); Harold M. Hyman, *A More Perfect Union: The Impact of the Civil War and Reconstruction on the Constitution* (1973); Joseph James, *The Framing of the Fourteenth Amendment* (1956); William E. Nelson, *The Fourteenth Amendment: From Political Principle to Judicial Doctrine* (1988).

The Black Experience in Reconstruction
James D. Anderson, *The Education of Blacks in the South, 1860–1935* (1988); Herbert G. Gutman, *The Black Family in Slavery and Freedom, 1750–1925* (1976); Janet Sharp Hermann, *The Pursuit of a Dream* (1981); Howard Rabinowitz, ed., *Southern Black Leaders in Reconstruction* (1982); Vernon L. Wharton, *The Negro in Mississippi, 1865–1890* (1947); Joel Williamson, *After Slavery: The Negro in South Carolina during Reconstruction* (1966).

Reconstruction in the South
Richard N. Current, *Those Terrible Carpetbaggers: A Reinterpretation* (1988); William C. Harris, *Day of the Carpetbagger: Republican Reconstruction in Mississippi* (1979); Michael Perman, *Reunion without Compromise: The South and Reconstruction, 1865–1868* (1973); George C. Rable, *But There Was No Peace: The Role of Violence in the Politics of Reconstruction* (1984); James Sefton, *The United States Army and Reconstruction, 1865–1877* (1967); Ted Tunnell, *Crucible of Reconstruction: War, Radicalism, and Race in Louisiana, 1862–1877* (1974); Allen Trelease, *White Terror: The Ku Klux Klan Conspiracy and Southern Reconstruction* (1967); Sarah Woolfolk Wiggins, *The Scalawag in Alabama Politics, 1865–1881* (1977).

Social and Economic Reconstruction
George R. Bentley, *A History of the Freedmen's Bureau* (1955); Eric Foner, *Nothing But Freedom: Emancipation and Its Legacy* (1983); Steven Hahn, *The Roots of Southern Populism: Yeoman Farmers and the Transformation of the Georgia Upcountry, 1850–1890* (1983); Jacqueline Jones, *Soldiers of Light and Love: Northern Teachers and Georgia Blacks, 1865–1873* (1980); Donald Nieman, *To Set the Law in Motion: The Freedmen's Bureau and the Legal Rights of Blacks, 1865–1868* (1979); Claude F. Oubre, *Forty Acres and a Mule: The Freedmen's Bureau and Black Landownership* (1978); Lawrence N. Powell, *New Masters: Northern Planters during the Civil War and Reconstruction* (1984); Roger L. Ransom and Richard Sutch, *One Kind of Freedom: The Economic Consequences of Emancipation* (1977); Mark W. Summers, *Railroads, Reconstruction, and the Gospel of Prosperity* (1984).

The End of Reconstruction
Paul Buck, *The Road to Reunion, 1865–1900* (1937); Keith Ian Polakoff, *The Politics of Inertia: The Election of 1876 and the End of Reconstruction* (1973); C. Vann Woodward, *Reunion and Reaction: The Compromise of 1877 and the End of Reconstruction* (1951).

Biographies
Fawn M. Brodie, *Thaddeus Stevens: Scourge of the South* (1959); David Donald, *Charles Sumner and the Rights of Man* (1970); William S. McFeely, *Yankee Stepfather: General O. Howard and the Freedmen* (1968) and *Grant: A Biography* (1981); Brooks D. Simpson, *Let Us Have Peace: Ulysses S. Grant and the Politics of War and Reconstruction, 1861–1868* (1991); Hans L. Trefousse, *Andrew Johnson: A Biography* (1989).

CHAPTER 18: THE NEW INDUSTRIAL ORDER

General Studies
Daniel Boorstin, *The Americans: The Democratic Experience* (1973); John A. Garraty, *The New*

Commonwealth (1968); Ray Ginger, *The Age of Excess* (1963); Samuel P. Hays, *The Response to Industrialism, 1885–1914* (1957); Edward C. Kirkland, *Industry Comes of Age: Business, Labor, and Public Policy, 1860–1897* (1967); Martin V. Melosi, *Coping with Abundance: Energy and Environment in Industrial America* (1985); Robert Wiebe, *The Search for Order, 1877–1920* (1968).

The Economy
Frederick Lewis Allen, *The Great Pierpont Morgan* (1949); W. Elliot Brownlee, *Dynamics of Ascent: A History of the American Economy*, rev. ed. (1979); Stuart Bruchey, *Growth of the Modern American Economy* (1975); Milton Friedman and Anna Schwartz, *Monetary History of the United States, 1867–1960* (1963); Robert L. Heilbroner, *The Economic Transformation of America* (1977); Robert Higgs, *The Transformation of the American Economy, 1865–1914* (1971); Susan Previant Lee and Peter Passell, *A New Economic View of American History* (1979); Harold G. Vatter, *The Drive to Industrial Maturity: The United States Economy, 1860–1914* (1975).

The Railroads
Alfred D. Chandler, Jr., *The Railroads: The Nation's First Big Business* (1965); Robert Fogel, *Railroads and American Economic Growth* (1964); Julius Grodinsky, *Jay Gould* (1957); Gabriel Kolko, *Railroads and Regulation, 1877–1916* (1965); Albro Martin, *James J. Hill and the Opening of the Northwest* (1976) and *Railroads Triumphant: The Growth, Rejection, and Rebirth of a Vital American Force* (1992); John F. Stover, *American Railroads* (1970).

The Rise of Big Business
Alfred Chandler, Jr., *Strategy and Structure: Chapters in the History of American Industrial Enterprise* (1962), *The Visible Hand: The Managerial Revolution in American Business* (1977) and *Scale and Scope: The Dynamics of Industrial Capitalism* (1990); Thomas Cochrane, *Business in American Life* (1972); Naomi Lamoreaux, *The Great Merger Movement in American Business, 1895–1904* (1985); Harold C. Livesay, *Andrew Carnegie and the Rise of Big Business* (1975); Alan Nevins, *Study in Power: John D. Rockefeller*, 2 vols. (1953); Glenn Porter, *The Rise of Big Business* (1973); Martin J. Sklar, *The Corporate Recon-struction of American Capitalism, 1890–1916: The Market, Law and Politics* (1988); Richard Tedlow, *The Rise of the American Business Corporation* (1991); Alan Trachtenberg, *The Incorporation of America* (1982); Joseph Wall, *Andrew Carnegie* (1970); Olivier Zunz, *Making America Corporate, 1870–1920* (1990).

Invention and Industry
Robert Bruce, *Alexander Graham Bell and the Conquest of Solitude* (1973); Robert Conot, *A Streak of Luck* (1979); Ruth Schwartz Cowan, *A Social History of American Technology* (1996); Siegfried Giedion, *Mechanization Takes Command* (1948); David Hounshell, *From the American System to Mass Production, 1800–1932* (1984); John F. Kasson, *Civilizing the Machine* (1976); Carolyn Marvin, *When Old Technologies Were New: Thinking about Electric Communication in the Late Nineteenth Century* (1988); David Nye, *Electrifying America: Social Meanings of a New Technology, 1890–1940* (1990); Harold Passer, *The Electrical Manu-facturers, 1875–1900* (1953); Leonard S. Reich, *The Making of Industrial Research: Science and Business at GE and Bell, 1876–1926* (1985); Nathan Rosenberg, *Technology and American Economic Growth* (1972); Peter Temin, *Iron and Steel in Nineteenth Century America* (1964); Frederick A. White, *American Industrial Research Laboratories* (1961).

Capitalism and Its Critics
Robert Bannister, *Social Darwinism: Science and Myth in Anglo-American Social Thought* (1979); Robert H. Bremner, *American Philanthropy* (1988); Carl N. Degler, *In Search of Human Nature: The Decline and Revival of Darwinism in America* (1991); Sidney Fine, *Laissez Faire and the General Welfare State: A Study of Conflict in American Thought, 1865–1900* (1956); Louis Galambos, *The Public Image of Big Business in America, 1880–1940: A Quantitative Study of Social Change* (1975); Richard Hofstadter, *Social Darwinism in American Thought*, rev. ed. (1955); Edward C. Kirkland, *Dream and Thought in the Business Community, 1860–1900* (1956); Ellen Condliffe Lagemann, *The Politics of Knowledge: The Carnegie Corporation, Philanthropy, and Public Policy* (1989); T. Jackson Lears, *No Place of Grace: Antimodernism and the Transformation of American Culture, 1880–1920* (1981); George E. Pozzetta, ed., *Americanization, Social Control, and Philanthropy* (1991); John Thomas, *Alternative America: Henry George, Edward Bellamy, Henry Demarest Lloyd, and the Adversary Tradition* (1983).

The Culture of Work
American Social History Project, *Who Built America? Working People and the Nation's Economy, Politics, Culture, Society*, Volume Two: *From the Gilded Age to the Present* (1992); Cindy Sondik Aron, *Ladies and Gentlemen of the Civil Service: Middle-Class Workers in Victorian America* (1987); James R. Barrett, *Work and Community in the Jungle: Chicago's Packinghouse Workers, 1894–1922* (1990); John Bodnar, *Immigration and Industrial-ization: Ethnicity in an American Mill Town* (1977); John T. Cumbler, *Working Class Community in Industrial America: Work, Leisure, and Struggle in Two Industrial Cities, 1880–1930* (1979); David Emmons, *The Butte Irish: Class and Ethnicity in an American Mining Town, 1875–1925* (1989); Michael Frisch and Daniel Walkowitz, eds., *Working-Class America: Essays on Labor, Community, and American Society* (1983); James R. Green, *World of the Worker: Labor in Twentieth Century*

America (1980); Herbert Gutman, *Work, Culture and Society in Industrializing America: Essays in American Working-Class History* (1976); Tamara Hareven, *Family, Time, and Industrial Time: The Relationship between the Family and Work in a New England Industrial Community* (1982); William H. Harris, *The Harder We Run: Black Workers since the Civil War* (1982); Jacqueline Jones, *Labor of Love, Labor of Sorrow: Black Women, Work and the Family, from Slavery to the Present* (1985); Susan Kennedy, *If All We Did Was to Weep at Home: A History of White Working Class Women in America* (1979); Walter Licht, *Working for the Railroad: The Organization of Work in the Nineteenth Century* (1983); Joanne J. Meyerowitz, *Women Adrift: Independent Wage Earners in Chicago, 1880–1930* (1988); David Montgomery, *Workers' Control in America: Studies in the History of Work, Technology, and Labor Struggles* (1979); Daniel Nelson, *Managers and Workers: Origins of the New Factory System* (1975); Richard Jules Oestreicher, *Solidarity and Fragmentation: Working People and Class Consciousness in Detroit, 1875–1900* (1986); Daniel T. Rodgers, *The Work Ethic in Industrial America, 1850–1920* (1978); Stephan Thernstrom, *The Other Bostonians: Poverty and Progress in the American Metropolis, 1880–1970* (1973).

The Labor Movement
Eric Arnesen, *Waterfront Workers of New Orleans: Race, Class, and Politics, 1863–1923* (1991); Paul Avrich, *The Haymarket Tragedy* (1984); Mary H. Blewett, *Men, Women, and Work: Class, Gender, and Protest in the New England Shoe Industry, 1880–1910* (1988); Jeremy Brecher, *Strike!* (1977); Mari Jo Buhle, *Women and American Socialism, 1870–1920* (1981); Melvyn Dubofsky, *Industrialism and the American Worker, 1865–1920* (1975) and *We Shall Be All: A History of the Industrial Workers of the World* (1969); Philip Foner, *Women and the American Labor Movement*, 2 vols. (1979); James R. Grossman, *Land of Hope: Chicago, Black Southerners, and the Great Migration* (1989); William H. Harris, *The Harder We Run: Black Workers since the Civil War* (1982); Stuart Kaufman, *Samuel Gompers and the Origins of the American Federation of Labor* (1973); Paul Krause, *The Battle for Homestead: Politics, Culture and Steel* (1992); Susan Levine, *Labor's True Women: Carpet Weavers, Industrialization, and Labor Reform in the Gilded Age* (1984); Gwendolyn Mink, *Old Labor and New Immigrants in American Political Development: Union, Party, and State, 1875–1920* (1986); David Montgomery, *The Fall of the House of Labor: The Workplace, the State, and American Labor Activism, 1865–1925* (1987); Leon Fink, *Workingmen's Democracy: The Knights of Labor and American Politics* (1983); Alice Kessler-Harris, *Out to Work: A History of Wage-Earning Women in the United States* (1982); Nick Salvatore, *Eugene V. Debs: Citizen and Socialist* (1982); David Shannon, *The Socialist Party* (1955); Sheldon Stromquist, *A Generation of Boomers: The Pattern of Railroad Labor*

Conflict in Nineteenth-Century America (1987); Lloyd Ulman, *The Rise of the National Trade Union: The Development and Significance of Its Structure, Governing Institutions, and Economic Policies* (1955).

CHAPTER 19: THE RISE OF AN URBAN ORDER

General Studies
Howard B. Chudacoff, *The Evolution of American Urban Society*, rev. ed., (1981); William Cronon, *Nature's Metropolis: Chicago and the Great West* (1991); Charles Glabb and A. Theodore Brown, *A History of Urban America*, rev. ed., (1976); Blake McKelvey, *The Urbanization of America, 1860–1915* (1963); Allan Pred, *Spatial Dynamics of U.S. Urban Growth, 1800–1914* (1971); John Stilgoe, *Borderland: The Origins of the American Suburb, 1820–1929* (1988); Stephan Thernstrom and Richard Sennett, eds., *19th Century Cities: Essays in the New Urban History* (1969); Sam Bass Warner, Jr., *Streetcar Suburbs* (1962) and *The Urban Wilderness* (1972).

Immigration and Immigrants
John Bodnar, *The Transplanted: A History of Immigrants in Urban America* (1985); Josef Barton, *Peasants and Strangers: Italians, Rumanians and Slovaks in an American City* (1975); John J. Bukowczyk, *And My Children Did Not Know Me: A History of Polish Americans* (1987); Sucheng Chan, *Asian Americans: An Interpretive History* (1991); Jack Chen, *The Chinese of America* (1970); Roger Daniels, *Coming to America: A History of Immigration and Ethnicity in American Life* (1990); Hasia A. Diner, *Erin's Daughters in America: Irish Immigrant Women in the Nineteenth Century* (1983); Leonard Dinnerstein, Roger Nichols, and David Reimers, *Natives and Strangers* (1979); John Duff, *The Irish in the United States* (1971); Mario Garcia, *Desert Immigrants: The Mexicans of El Paso, 1880–1920* (1981); Susan A. Glenn, *Daughters of the Shtetl: Life and Labor in the Immigrant Generation* (1990); Richard Griswold del Castillo, *La Familia: Chicano Families in the Urban Southwest, 1848 to the Present* (1984); Irving Howe, *World of Our Fathers: The Journey of the East European Jews to America and the Life They Found and Made* (1976); Yuji Ichioka, *The Issei: The World of the First Generation Japanese Americans, 1885–1924* (1988); Jenna Weissman Joselit, *The Wonders of America: Reinventing Jewish Culture, 1880–1950* (1994); Edward Kantowicz, *Polish-American Politics in Chicago* (1975); Thomas Kessner, *The Golden Door: Italian and Jewish Immigrant Mobility in New York City, 1880–1915* (1977); Alan M. Kraut, *The Huddled Masses: The Immigrant in American Society, 1880–1921* (1982); Michael La Sorte, *La Merica: Images of Italian Greenhorn Experience* (1985); Joseph Lopreato, *Italian Americans* (1970); Kerby A. Miller, *Emigrants and Exiles: Ireland and the Irish Exodus to North America* (1985); Ewa

Morawska, *For Bread and Butter: The Life-Worlds of East Central Europeans in Johnstown, Pennsylvania, 1890–1940* (1985); James Stuart Olsen, *The Ethnic Dimension in American History,* vol. II (1979); Moses Rischin, *The Promised City: New York's Jews* (1962); Jacob Riis, *How the Other Half Lives* (1890); Howard M. Sachar, *A History of Jews in America* (1992); Ronald Takaki, *Strangers from a Different Shore: A History of Asian Americans* (1989) and *A Different Mirror: A History of Multicultural America* (1993); Philip Taylor, *The Distant Magnet: European Emigration to the U.S.A.* (1971); Virginia Yans-McLaughlin, *Family and Commu-nity: Italian Immigrants in Buffalo, 1880–1930* (1977), and as ed., *Immigration Reconsidered: History, Sociology, Politics* (1990); Anzia Yezierska, *Bread Givers* (1925); Olivier Zunz, *The Changing Face of Inequality: Urbanization, Industrial Development, and Immigrants in Detroit, 1880–1920* (1982).

Nativism and Race
Leonard Dinnerstein, *Anti-Semitism in America* (1994); Louis Harlan, *Booker T. Washington: The Making of a Black Leader, 1856–1901* (1972) and *Booker T. Washington: The Wizard of Tuskegee, 1901–1915* (1983); John Higham, *Strangers in the Land: Patterns of American Nativism, 1880–1925* (1955) and *Send These to Me* (1975); Kenneth Kusmer, *A Ghetto Takes Shape: Black Cleveland, 1870–1930* (1976); Stanley Lieberson, *A Piece of the Pie: Blacks and White Immigrants Since 1880* (1980); Gilbert Osofsky, *Harlem: The Making of a Ghetto* (1966); Joel Perlman, *Ethnic Differences: Schooling and Social Structure among the Irish, Italians, Jews, and Blacks in an American City, 1880–1935* (1988); Elizabeth Hafkin Pleck, *Black Migration and Poverty, Boston, 1865–1900* (1979); Allan H. Spear, *Black Chicago* (1967); Donald Spivey, *Schooling for the New Slavery: Black Industrial Education, 1868–1915* (1978).

Politics and Poverty
John Allswang, *Bosses, Machines, and Urban Voters* (1977); Robert H. Bremner, *From the Depths: The Discovery of Poverty in the United States* (1956); Alexander B. Callow, ed., *The City Boss in America* (1976); Lyle Dorsett, *The Pendergast Machine* (1968); Steven P. Erie, *Rainbow's End: Irish-Americans and the Dilemmas of Urban Machine Politics, 1840–1985* (1988); Leo Hershkowitz, *Tweed's New York: Another Look* (1977); Zane Miller, *Boss Cox's Cincinnati* (1968); James T. Patterson, *America's Struggle against Poverty* (1981); Thomas Philpott, *The Slum and the Ghetto* (1978); William L. Riordon, *Plunkitt of Tammany Hall* (1963); Lloyd Wendt and Herman Kogan, *Bosses in Lusty Chicago,* 2d ed. (1971).

Reform
Jane Addams, *Twenty Years at Hull-House* (1910); Ruth Bordin, *Woman and Temperance: The Quest for Power and Liberty, 1860–1900* (1981); Paul

Boyer, *Urban Masses and Moral Order in America, 1820–1920* (1978); Allen Davis, *Spearheads for Reform: The Social Settlements and the Progressive Movement, 1890–1914* (1967) and *American Heroine: The Life and Legend of Jane Addams* (1973); Marvin Lazerson, *Origins of the Urban School* (1971); Eric Monkonnen, *Police in Urban America, 1860–1920* (1981); David Pivar, *Purity Crusade: Sexual Morality and Social Control, 1868–1900* (1973); James Reed, *The Birth Control Movement and American Society: From Private Vice to Public Virtue* (1983); Barbara Rosencrantz, *Public Health and the State* (1972); Martin Schiesl, *The Politics of Efficiency: Municipal Administration and Reform in America* (1977); David Tyack, *The One Best System: A History of American Urban Education* (1974); Morris Vogel, *The Invention of the Modern Hospital: Boston, 1870–1930* (1980); James C. Whorton, *Crusaders for Fitness: The History of American Health Reformers* (1982).

Urban Life, Work, and Culture
Cindy Aron, *Ladies and Gentlemen of the Civil Service: Middle Class Workers in Victorian America* (1987); Gunther Barth, *City People: The Rise of Modern City Culture in 19th Century America* (1980); Susan Porter Benson, *Counter Cultures: Saleswomen, Managers, and Customers in Department Stores, 1890–1940* (1986); Allan Brandt, *No Magic Bullet: A Social History of Venereal Disease in the United States Since 1880,* rev. ed. (1985); Robert Cross, *The Church and the City* (1967); Ronald Davies, *A History of Music in American Life,* Volume II: *The Gilded Years, 1865–1920* (1980); Lewis A. Erenberg, *Steppin' Out: New York Nightlife and the Transformation of American Culture, 1890–1930* (1981); Ellen Garvey, *The Adman in the Parlor: Magazines and the Gendering of Consumer Culture, 1880s to 1910s* (1996); James Gilbert, *Perfect Cities: Chicago Utopias of 1893* (1991); Thomas J. Gilfoyle, *City of Eros: New York City, Prostitution, and the Commercialization of Sex, 1790–1920* (1992); Tamara K. Hareven and Randolph Langenbach, *Amoskeag: Life and Work in an American Factory* (1978); Neil Harris, *Humbug: The Art of P. T. Barnum* (1973); Lawrence Kasson, *Amusing the Million: Coney Island at the Turn of the Century* (1978) and *Rudeness & Civility: Manners in Nineteenth-Century Urban America* (1990); William Leach, *Land of Desire: Merchants, Power, and the Rise of a New American Culture* (1993); Lawrence Levine, *Highbrow/Lowbrow: The Emergence of Cultural Hierarchy in America* (1988); Richard Lingeman, *Theodore Dreiser: At the Gates of the City, 1871–1907* (1986); John Lucas and Ronald Smith, *Saga of American Sport* (1978); Henry F. May, *Protestant Churches and Urban America* (1949); Katherine Morello, *The Invisible Bar: The Woman Lawyer in America, 1638 to the Present* (1986); Joseph Musselman, *Music in the Cultured Generation: A Social History of Music in America, 1870–1900* (1971); David Nasaw,

Schooled to Order: A Social History of Public Schooling in the United States (1979), *Children of the City: At Work and at Play* (1986), and *Going Out: The Rise and Fall of Public Amusements* (1993); Kathy Peiss, *Cheap Amusements: Working Women and Leisure in Turn-of-the-Century New York* (1986); Roy Rosenzweig, *Eight Hours for What We Will: Workers & Leisure in an Industrial City, 1870–1920* (1983); Russel Nye, *The Unembarrassed Muse: The Popular Arts in America* (1970); Thomas J. Schlereth, *Victorian American: Transformations in Everyday Life, 1876–1915* (1991); Robert H. Walker, *Life in the Age of Enterprise, 1865–1900* (1967).

Women, Family, and Social Mores
Elaine S. Abelson, *When Ladies Go A-Thieving: Middle-Class Shoplifters in the Victorian Department Store* (1990); Allan M. Brandt, *No Magic Bullet: A Social History of Venereal Disease since 1880* (1985); John D'Emilio and Estelle B. Freedman, *Intimate Matters: A History of Sexuality in America* (1988); Harvey Green, *The Light of the Home: An Intimate View of the Lives of Women in Victorian America* (1983); John S. Haller and Robin M. Haller, *The Physician and Sexuality in Victorian America* (1986); N. Ray Hiner and Joseph Hawes, eds., *Growing Up in America: Children in Historical Perspective* (1985); David Katzman, *Seven Days a Week: Women and Domestic Service in Industrializing America* (1978); Judith Leavitt, *Brought to Bed: Childbearing in America, 1750–1950* (1988); Elizabeth Lunbeck, *The Psychiatric Persuasion: Knowledge, Gender and Politics in Modern America* (1994); Elaine May, *Great Expectations: Marriage and Divorce in Post-Victorian America* (1980); Steven Mintz, *A Prison of Expectations: The Family in Victorian Culture* (1983); Steven Mintz and Susan Kellogg, *Domestic Revolutions: A Social History of American Family Life* (1988); Ellen Rothman, *Hands and Hearts: A History of Courtship in America* (1984); Gar Scharnhorst, *Charlotte Perkins Gilman* (1985); Carroll Smith-Rosenberg, *Disorderly Conduct: Visions of Gender in Victorian America* (1986); Susan Strasser, *Never Done: A History of American Housework* (1983).

CHAPTER 20: AGRARIAN DOMAINS: THE SOUTH AND THE WEST

The New South: History, Politics, and Culture
Edward L. Ayers, *The Promise of the New South: Life after Reconstruction* (1992) and *Southern Crossing: A History of the American South, 1877–1906* (1995); Orville Vernon Burton, *In My Father's House* (1985); W. J. Cash, *The Mind of the South* (1941); Thomas D. Clark and Albert Kirwan, *The South since Appomattox* (1967); David L. Carlton, *Mill and Town in South Carolina, 1880–1920* (1982); John M. Cooper, *Walter Hines Page: The South-*
erner as American, 1855–1918 (1977); Pete Daniel, *Breaking the Land: The Transformation of Cotton, Tobacco, and Rice Cultures since 1880* (1985); Carl N. Degler, *The Other South: Southern Dissenters in the Nineteenth Century* (1974); Robert Durden, *The Self-Inflicted Wound: Southern Politics in the Nineteenth Century* (1985); John S. Ezell, *The South since 1865* (1975); Paul Gaston, *The New South Creed: A Study in Southern Mythmaking* (1970); Richard Gray, *Writing the South: The Idea of an American Region* (1986); Patrick H. Hearden, *Independence and Empire: The New South's Cotton Mill Campaign, 1865–1920* (1982); J. Morgan Kousser, *The Shaping of Southern Politics: Suffrage Restriction and Establishment of the One Party South* (1974); J. Morgan Kousser and James McPherson, eds., *Region, Race, and Reconstruction* (1982); Lawrence Karsen, *The Rise of the Urban South* (1985); I. A. Newby, *Plain Folk in the New South: Social Change and Cultural Persistence, 1880–1915* (1989); Raymond B. Nixon, *Henry W. Grady: Spokesman of the New South* (1969); Ted Ownby, *Subduing Satan* (1990); David M. Potter, *The South and the Concurrent Majority* (1972); Allen Tullos, *Habits of Industry: White Culture and the Transformation of the Carolina Piedmont* (1989); Marjorie Spruill Wheeler, *New Women of the New South: The Leaders of the Woman Suffrage Movement in the Southern States* (1993); Charles R. Wilson, *Baptized in Blood: The Religion of the Lost Cause, 1865–1920* (1980); C. Vann Woodward, *Tom Watson: Agrarian Rebel* (1938), and *The Origins of the New South* (1951).

The Southern Economy and Race
David Carlton, *Mill and Town in South Carolina, 1880–1920* (1982); Pete Daniel, *Breaking the Land: The Transformation of Cotton, Tobacco, and Rice Cultures since 1880* (1985); Steven Hahn, *The Roots of Southern Populism: Yeoman Farmers and the Transformation of the Georgia Upcountry, 1850–1890* (1983); Louis T. Harlan, *Booker T. Washington: The Making of a Black Leader, 1865–1901* (1972); Robert Higgs, *Competition and Coercion: Blacks in the American Economy, 1865–1890* (1977); Gerald David Jaynes, *Branches without Roots: Genesis of the Black Working Class in the American South, 1862–1882* (1986); Neil R. McMillen, *Dark Journey: Black Mississippians in the Age of Jim Crow* (1989); J. M. McPherson, *The Abolitionist Legacy: From Reconstruction to the NAACP* (1975); August Meier, *Negro Thought in America, 1880–1915: Racial Ideologies in the Age of Booker T. Washington* (1963); Howard Rabinowitz, *Race Relations in the Urban South, 1865–1890* (1978); Roger Ransom and Richard Sutch, *One Kind of Freedom: The Economic Consequences of Emancipation* (1977); Donald Spivey, *Schooling for the New Slavery: Black Industrial Education* (1978); J. F. Stover, *The Railroads of the South* (1955); Edward Wheeler, *Uplifting the Race: The Black Minister in the New South, 1865–1902* (1986); Joel Williamson, *The Crucible of Race: Black-White Relations in the American South since Emancipation*

(1984) and *After Slavery* (1965); C. Vann Woodward, *The Strange Career of Jim Crow*, 3d rev. ed. (1974); Gavin Wright, *Old South, New South: Revolutions in the Southern Economy since the Civil War* (1986).

Opening of the West
Walton Bean, *California* (1978); Thomas Berger, *Little Big Man* (1964); Ray A. Billington, *Westward Expansion* (1967); Thomas D. Clark, *Frontier America*, rev. ed. (1969); William Cronon, *Nature's Metropolis: Chicago and the Great West* (1991); William Cronon, George Miles, and Jay Gitlin, *Under an Open Sky: Rethinking America's Western Past* (1992); Sarah Deutsch, *No Separate Refuge: Culture, Class, and Gender on an Anglo-Hispanic Frontier in the American Southwest, 1880–1940* (1987); Robert Hine, *The American West*, 2d rev. ed. (1984); Paul Hutton, ed., *Soldiers West: Biographers from the Military Frontier* (1987); Howard Lamar, *The Reader's Encyclopedia of the American West* (1977) and *The Far Southwest, 1846–1912* (1966); Patricia Nelson Limerick, *The Legacy of Conquest: The Unbroken Past of the American West* (1987); Gerald McFarland, *A Scattered People: An American Family Moves West* (1985); Leo Marx, *The Machine in the Garden* (1964); Donald W. Meinig, *The Southwest: Three People in Geographical Change, 1600–1970* (1971); Frederick Merk, *History of the Westward Movement* (1978); Clyde A. Milner II, *A New Significance: Re-Envisioning the History of the American West* (1996); Clyde A. Milner II, Carol A. O'Connor, and Martha A. Sandweiss, eds., *The Oxford History of the American West* (1994); Roderick Nash, *Wilderness and the American Mind*, 3d ed. (1982); Earl Pomery, *The Pacific Slope* (1968); Richard Slotkin, *The Fatal Environment: The Myth of the West in the Age of Industrialization* (1985) and *Gunfighter Nation: The Myth of the Frontier in Twentieth-Century America* (1992); Wallace Stegner, *Beyond the Hundredth Meridian: John Welsey Powell and the Second Opening of the West* (1954); Henry Nash Smith, *Virgin Land* (1950); Jane Tompkins, *West of Everything: The Inner Life of Westerns* (1992); Mark Twain, *Roughing It* (1872); Elliott West, *The Way to the West: Essays on the Central Plains* (1995); Richard White, *"It's Your Misfortune and None of My Own": A New History of the American West* (1992); Donald Worster, *Rivers of Empire: Water, Aridity, and the Growth of the American West* (1992) and *Under Western Skies: Nature and History in the American West* (1992).

The Peoples of the West
Rudolfo Acuna, *Occupied America: A History of Chicanos* (1981); Ralph Andrist, *The Long Death: The Last Days of the Sioux Nation* (1964); Robert Athearn, *In Search of Canaan: Black Migration in Kansas, 1879–1880* (1978); Gunther Barth, *Bitter Strength: A History of the Chinese in the United States, 1850–1870* (1964); Gretchen Bataille and Charles Silet, *The Pretend Indians: Images of Native*

Americans in the Movies (1980); Beverly Beeton, *Women Vote in the West: The Woman Suffrage Movement, 1869–1896* (1986); Robert Berkhofer, Jr., *The White Man's Indian* (1978); Dee Brown, *Bury My Heart at Wounded Knee: An Indian History of the American War* (1970); Anne M. Butler, *Daughters of Joy, Sisters of Misery: Prostitutes in the American West, 1865–1890* (1985); Colin G. Calloway, ed., *Our Hearts Fell to the Ground: Plains Indian Views of How the West Was Lost* (1996); Edward Curtis, *The North American Indian* (1972); David Dary, *Cowboy Culture* (1981); Everett Dick, *Sod House Frontier* (1954); Carol Fairbanks, *Prairie Women: Images in American and Canadian Fiction* (1986); John Mack Faragher, *Women and Men on the Overland Trail* (1979); Christine Fisher, ed., *Let Them Speak for Themselves: Women in the American West, 1849–1900* (1977); Joe B. Frantz and Julian Choate, *The American Cowboy: The Myth and Reality* (1955); Carl Guarneri and David Alvarez, *Religion and Society in the American West* (1987); Julie Roy Jeffrey, *Frontier Women: The Trans-Mississippi West, 1840–1880* (1979); Alvin Josephy, *The Indian Heritage in America* (1969); William Katz, *The Black West* (1971); Polly W. Kaufman, *Women Teachers on the Frontier* (1984); William Leckie, *The Buffalo Soldiers: A Narrative History of the Negro Cavalry* (1967); Frederick Luebke, *Ethnicity on the Great Plains* (1980); Janet A. McDonnell, *The Dispossession of the American Indian, 1887–1934* (1991); M. S. Meier and Feliciano Rivera, *The Chicanos: A History of the Mexican Americans* (1972); David Montejano, *Anglos and Mexicans in the Making of Texas, 1836–1986* (1987); Sandra Myres, *Western Women and the Frontier Experience, 1880–1915* (1982); James S. Olsen and Raymond Wilson, *Native Americans in the Twentieth Century* (1984); Nell Painter, *The Exodusters: Black Migration to Kansas after Reconstruction* (1976); Peggy Pascoe, *Relations of Rescue: The Search for Female Moral Authority in the American West, 1874–1939* (1990); Paul Prucha, *American Indian Policy in Crisis* (1976); Harriet and Fred Rochlin, *Pioneer Jews: A New Life in the Far West* (1984); Mari Sandoz, *Cheyenne Autumn* (1954); William Savage, *The Cowboy Hero: His Image in American History and Culture* (1979) and as ed., *Cowboy Life* (1975); Kent Steckmesser, *The Western Hero in History and Legend* (1965); Elinor Pruitt Stewart, *Letters of a Woman Homesteader* (1913, 1914); Joanna Stratton, *Pioneer Women: Voices of the Kansas Frontier* (1981); John Tebbel and Keith Jennison, *The American Indian Wars* (1960); Robert Utley, *High Noon in Lincoln: Violence on the Western Frontier* (1987), *The Indian Frontier of the American West, 1846–1890* (1984) and *Frontier Regulars: The United States Army and the Indian, 1866–1890* (1984); Sylvia Van Kirk, *Many Tender Ties: Women in Fur Trade Society* (1983); Wilcomb Washburn, *The Indian in America* (1975).

The Western Economy
Lewis Atherton, *Cattle Kings* (1961); Gunther Barth, *Instant Cities* (1975); Edward Dale, *The*

Range Cattle Industry, rev. ed., (1969); David Dary, *Entrepreneurs of the Old West* (1986); Alan Derickson, *Workers' Health, Workers' Democracy: The Western Miners' Struggle, 1891–1925* (1988); Robert Dykstra, *The Cattle Towns* (1968); Gilbert Fite, *The Farmer's Frontier* (1966); David Emmons, *The Butte Irish: Class and Ethnicity in an American Mining Town, 1875–1925* (1989); Paul Gates, *History of Public Land Development* (1968); William Greever, *The Bonanza West: The Story of the Western Mining Rushes* (1963); Gene M. Gressley, *Bankers and Cattlemen* (1966); Robert West Howard, *The Great Iron Trail: The Story of the First Transcontinental Railroad* (1963); Donald Jackson, *Gold Dust* (1980); Richard Lingenfelter, *The Hardrock Miners: A History of the Mining Labor Movement in the American West, 1863–1893* (1974); Rodman Paul, *The Far West and the Great Plains in Transition, 1865–1900* (1988); Mari Sandoz, *Old Jules* (1962) and *The Buffalo Hunters: The Story of the Hide Men* (1978); Fred A. Shannon, *The Farmer's Last Frontier, 1860–1897* (1945); J. M. Skaggs, *The Cattle Trailing Industry* (1973); George R. Taylor and Irene Neu, *The American Railroad Network, 1861–1890* (1956); James Ward, *Railroads and the Character of America, 1820–1887* (1986); Walter Prescott Webb, *The Great Plains* (1931); Donald Worster, *Rivers of Empire* (1985); Mark Wyman, *Hard Rock Epic: Western Miners and the Industrial Revolution, 1860–1910* (1979).

CHAPTER 21: THE POLITICAL SYSTEM UNDER STRAIN

General Studies

James Bryce, *The American Commonwealth,* 2 vols. (1888); Sean Cashman, *America and the Gilded Age: From the Death of Lincoln to the Rise of Theodore Roosevelt* (1984); John Dobson, *Politics in the Gilded Age* (1978); Harold Faulkner, *Politics, Reform, and Expansion, 1890–1900* (1959); John Garraty, *The New Commonwealth, 1877–1890* (1968); Richard Hofstadter, *The Age of Reform: From Bryan to FDR* (1955); Nancy Eleanor Flexner, *Century of Struggle: The Women's Rights Movement in the United States* (1959); Morton Keller, *Affairs of State: Public Life in the Late 19th Century America* (1977); H. Wayne Morgan, *From Hayes to McKinley: National Party Politics, 1877–1896* (1969), and as ed., *The Gilded Age* (1970); Nell Irvin Painter, *Standing at Armageddon: The United States, 1877–1919* (1987); Stephen Skowronek, *Building a New American State: The Expansion of National Administrative Capacities* (1982); Robert Wiebe, *The Search for Order, 1877–1929* (1967).

Ideology and Politics

Kenneth Davison, *The Presidency of Rutherford B. Hayes* (1972); Margaret Forster, *Significant Sisters: The Grass-roots of Active Feminism, 1839–1939* (1986); Lewis Gould, *The Presidency of William McKinley* (1981); David C. Hammack, *Power and Society: Greater New York at the Turn of the Century* (1982); S. P. Hirshon, *Farewell to the Bloody Shirt: Northern Republicans and the Southern Negro, 1877–1893* (1962); Ari Hoogenboom, *Rutherford B. Hayes: Warrior and President* (1995); Richard Jensen, *The Winning of the Midwest: Social and Political Conflict, 1888–1896* (1971); David Jordan, *Roscoe Conkling of New York* (1971); Paul Kelppner, *The Cross of Culture: A Social Analysis of Midwestern Politics, 1850–1900* (1970) and *The Third Electoral System, 1853–1892: Voters, Parties, and Political Cultures* (1979); Robert Marcus, *Grand Old Party: Political Structure in the Gilded Age* (1971); Robert McCloskey, *American Conservatism in the Age of Enterprise* (1951); Michael McGerr, *The Decline of Politics: The American North, 1865–1928* (1988); Allan Nevins, *Grover Cleveland: A Study in Courage* (New York, 1932); Arnold Paul, *Conservative Crisis and the Rule of Law: Attitudes of Bar and Bench, 1887–1895* (1969); Allan Peskin, *Garfield* (1978); Thomas Reeves, *Gentlemen Boss: The Life of Chester Alan Arthur* (1975); Martin Ridge, *Ignatius Donnelly* (1962); David Rothman, *Politics and Power: The United States Senate, 1869–1901* (1966); Martin J. Sklar, *The Corporate Reconstruction of American Capitalism, 1890–1916* (1988); Homer E. Socolofsky and Allan B. Spetter, *The Presidency of Benjamin Harrison* (1987); Richard Welch, *The Presidencies of Grover Cleveland* (1988); R. Hal Williams, *Years of Decision: American Politics in the 1890s* (1978).

Protest and Reform

Geoffrey Blodgett, *The Gentle Reformers* (1966); William Dick, *Labor and Socialism in America* (1972); John Diggins, *The American Left in the Twentieth Century* (1973); Louis Harlan, *Booker T. Washington: The Making of a Black Leader, 1856–1901* (1972) and *Booker T. Washington: The Wizard of Tuskegee* (1983); Ari Hoogenboom, *Outlawing the Spoils: A History of the Civil Service Movement, 1865–1883* (1961); John Laslett, *Labor and the Left* (1970); Charles Lofgren, *The Plessy Case: A Legal-Historical Interpretation* (1987); Walter Nugent, *Money and American Society* (1968); Theda Skocpol, *Protecting Soldiers and Mothers: The Political Origins of Social Policy in the United States* (1992); John Sproat, *The Best Men: Liberal Reformers in the Gilded Age* (1968); Irwin Unger, *The Greenback Era: A Social and Political History of American Finance, 1865–1879* (1964); C. Vann Woodward, *The Strange Career of Jim Crow,* 3d rev. ed. (1974).

Populism

Peter Argersinger, *Populism and Politics: William Alfred Peffer and the People's Party* (1974); Gene Clanton, *Populism: The Humane Preferences, 1890–1900* (1991); Gerald H. Gaither, *Blacks and the Populist Revolt* (1977); Lawrence Goodwyn, *Democratic Promise: The Populist Movement in America* (1976) and *The Populist Moment: A Brief History of the Agrarian Revolt* (1978); Steven Hahn,

The Roots of Southern Populism: Yeoman Farmers and the Transformation of the Georgia Upcountry (1983); Sheldon Hackney, *Populism to Progressivism in Alabama* (1969); John Hicks, *The Populist Revolt* (1931); Robert W. Larson, *Populism in the Mountain West* (1986); Robert C. McMath, Jr., *Populist Vanguard: A History of the Southern Farmers' Alliance* (1975) and *American Populism: A Social History, 1877–1898* (1993); Scott G. McNall, *The Road to Rebellion: Class Formation and Kansas Populism, 1865–1900* (1988); Theodore R. Mitchell, *Political Education in the Southern Farmers' Alliance, 1887–1900* (1987); Bruce Palmer, *Man over Money* (1980); Norman Pollack, *The Populist Response to Industrial America* (1962) and *The Just Polity: Populism, Law, and Human Welfare* (1987); Theodore Saloutos, *Farmer Movements in the South, 1865–1933* (1960); Barton Shaw, *The Wool-Hat Boys: Georgia's Populist Party* (1984); John L. Shover, *First Majority–Last Minority: The Transforming of Rural Life in America* (1976); Lala Carr Steelman, *The North Carolina Farmers' Alliance* (1985); C. Vann Woodward, *Tom Watson, Agrarian Rebel* (1938); Allan Weinstein, *Prelude to Populism: Origins of the Silver Issue* (1970).

The Depression of 1893 and the Election of 1896
Paolo Coletta, *William Jennings Bryan*, 3 vols. (1964–1969); Robert F. Durden, *The Climax of Populism: The Election of 1896* (1965); Ray Ginger, *Altgeld's America* (1958); Paul W. Glad, *McKinley, Bryan, and the People* (1964) and *The Trumpet Soundeth* (1960); Charles Hoffman, *The Depression of the Nineties: An Economic History* (1970); J. Rogers Hollingsworth, *The Whirligig of Politics: The Democracy of Cleveland and Bryan* (1963); Stanley Jones, *The Presidential Election of 1896* (1964); Louis Koenig, *Bryan* (1971); Samuel McSeveney, *The Politics of Depression* (1972); Carlos A. Schwantes, *Coxey's Army: An American Odyssey* (1985).

The New American Empire
Richard Bannister, *Social Darwinism* (1979); Robert Beisner, *From the Old Diplomacy to the New, 1865–1900* (1975); Charles Campbell, *The Transformation of American Foreign Relations, 1865–1900* (1976) and *From Revolution to Rapprochement: The United States and Great Britain, 1783–1903* (1974); Richard Challener, *Admirals, Generals and American Foreign Policy, 1889–1914* (1973); John Dobson, *America's Ascent: The United States Becomes a Great Power, 1880–1914* (1978); John Lewis Gaddis, *Russia, the Soviet Union, and the United States*, 2d ed. (1990); John A. S. Grenville and George Young, *Politics, Strategy, and American Diplomacy* (1967); Richard Hofstadter, *Social Darwinism in American Thought*, rev. ed. (1959); Michael Hunt, *Ideology and American Foreign Policy* (1984); Ronald Jensen, *The Alaska Purchase and Russian-American Relations* (1970); Walter

LaFeber, *The New Empire: An Interpretation of American Expansion, 1860–1898* (1963) and *The American Age* (1989); David Pletcher, *The Awkward Years* (1962); Emily Rosenberg, *Spreading the American Dream* (1982); Tom Terrill, *The Tariff, Politics, and American Foreign Policy, 1874–1901* (1973); Mira Wilkins, *The Emergence of the Multinational Enterprise* (1970); William A. Williams, *The Tragedy of American Diplomacy*, rev. ed. (1962) and *Empire as a Way of Life: An Essay on the Causes and Character of America's Present Predicament* (1982).

The Question of Imperialism
David Anderson, *Imperialism and Idealism: American Diplomats in China, 1861–1898* (1986); William Becker, *The Dynamics of Business-Government Relations* (1982); Robert L. Beisner, *Twelve against Empire* (1968); Phillip Darby, *Three Faces of Imperialism: British and American Approaches to Asia and Africa, 1870–1970* (1987); Philip S. Foner, *The Spanish-Cuban-American War and the Birth of American Imperialism*, 2 vols. (1972); Frank Friedel, *The Splendid Little War* (1958); Willard Gatewood, Jr., *Black Americans and the White Man's Burden, 1898–1903* (1975); Kenneth Hagan, *American Gunboat Diplomacy, 1877–1889* (1973); David Healy, *U.S. Expansionism* (1970); Michael Hunt, *Ideology and U.S. Foreign Policy* (1987); Frederick Merk, *Manifest Destiny and Mission in American History* (1963); Wolfgang Mommsen and Jurgen Osterhammel, eds., *Imperialism and After* (1986); H. Wayne Morgan, *America's Road to Empire: The War with Spain and Overseas Expansion* (1965); Thomas J. Osborne, *Empire Can Wait: American Opposition to Hawaiian Annexation, 1893–1898* (1981); Ernest Paolino, *The Foundations of American Empire* (1973); Thomas Paterson, ed., *Imperialism and Anti-Imperialism* (1973); Bradford Perkins, *The Great Rapprochement* (1968); Julius Pratt, *The Expansionists of 1898* (1936); Tony Smith, *The Pattern of Imperialism: The United States, Great Britain and the Late Industrializing World since 1815* (1982); Richard Turk, *The Ambiguous Relationship: Theodore Roosevelt and Alfred Thayer Mahan* (1987).

The United States and Asia
David Anderson, *Imperialism and Idealism: American Diplomacy in China, 1861–1898* (1985); Jongsuk Chay, *Diplomacy of Asymmetry: Korean-American Relations to 1910* (1990); Warren Cohen, *America's Response to China*, rev. ed. (1980); Michael Hunt, *The Making of a Special Relationship: The United States and China to 1914* (1983); Jane Hunter, *The Gospel of Gentility: American Women Missionaries in Turn-of-the-Century China* (1984); Akira Iriye, *Across the Pacific* (1967) and *Pacific Estrangement: Japanese and American Expansion, 1897–1911* (1972); Stanley Karnow, *In Our Image* (1989); Yur-Bok Lee and Wayne Patterson, eds., *One Hundred Years of Korean-American Relations,*

1882–1982 (1986); Brian M. Linn, *The U.S. Army and Counterinsurgency in the Philippine War, 1899–1902* (1989); Ernest May and John Fairbanks, eds., *America's China Trade in Historical Perspective* (1986); Glenn May, *Social Engineering in the Philippines* (1980); Thomas McCormick, *China Market: America's Quest for Informal Empire, 1893–1901* (1968); Charles Neu, *The Troubled Encounter* (1975); Gary Okihiro, *Cane Fires: The Anti-Japanese Movement in Hawaii, 1865–1945* (1991); Peter Stanley, *A Nation in the Making: The Philippines and the United States* (1974); Randall Stross, *The Hard Earth: American Agriculturalists on Chinese Soil, 1898–1937* (1986); James Thomson, Peter Stanley, and John Perry, *Sentimental Imperialists: The American Experience in East Asia* (1981); Robert Welch, Jr., *Response to Imperialism: The United States and the Philippine-American War, 1899–1902* (1979); Marilyn B. Young, *Rhetoric of Empire: American China Policy, 1895–1901* (1968).

The United States and the Americas
Robert Brown, *Canada's National Policy, 1883–1900* (1964); Kenneth Bourne, *Britain and the Balance of Power in North America, 1815–1908* (1967); Walter LaFeber, *Inevitable Revolutions: The United States in Central America*, rev. ed. (1993); Lester Langley, *The Banana Wars* (1983) and *The United States and the Caribbean, 1900–1970* (1980); Louis Perez, Jr., *Cuba under the Platt Amendment, 1902–1934* (1986) and *Cuba between Empires, 1878–1902* (1983); Dexter Perkins, *The Monroe Doctrine, 1867–1907* (1937); Ramon Ruiz, *Cuba* (1968); Karl Schmitt, *Mexico and the United States, 1821–1973* (1974); Josefina Vazquez and Lorenzo Meyer, *The United States and Mexico* (1985).

CHAPTER 22: THE PROGRESSIVE ERA

General Studies
John Chambers II, *The Tyranny of Change: America in the Progressive Era, 1900–1917* (1980); John M. Cooper, Jr., *The Pivotal Decades: The United States, 1900–1920* (1990); Alan Dawley, *Struggles for Justice: Social Responsibility and the Liberal State* (1991); Arthur Ekrich, *Progressivism in America* (1974); Peter Filene, "An Obituary for 'the Progressive Movement,'" *American Quarterly* 22 (1970); Lewis Gould, ed., *The Progressive Era* (1974); Richard Hofstadter, *The Age of Reform: From Bryan to FDR* (1955); James T. Kloppenberg, *Uncertain Victory: Social Democracy and Progressivism in European and American Thought, 1870–1920* (1986); Gabriel Kolko, *The Triumph of Conservativism* (1963); Arthur Link and Richard L. McCormick, *Progressivism* (1985); William O'Neill, *The Progressive Years* (1975); Dan Rogers, "In Search of Progressivism," *Reviews in American History* 10 (1982); James Weinstein, *The Corporate Ideal in the Liberal States, 1900–1918* (1969);

Robert Wiebe, *Busi-nessmen and Reform: A Study of the Progressive Movement* (1962).

The Progressive Impulse
Daniel Aaron, *Men of Good Hope: A Story of American Progressives* (1951); Richard Abrams, *The Burdens of Progress* (1978); Walter M. Brasch, *Forerunners of Revolution: Muckrakers and the American Social Conscience* (1990); Robert H. Bremner, *From the Depths: The Discovery of Poverty in the United States* (1956); Mina Julia Carson, *Settlement Folk: Social Thought and the American Settlement Movement, 1885–1930* (1990); David Chalmers, *The Social and Political Ideas of the Muckrakers* (1964); Clarke Chambers, *Paul U. Kellog and the Survey* (1971); Robert Crunden, *Ministers of Reform: The Progressives' Achievements in American Civilization, 1889–1920* (1982); Charles Forcey, *The Crossroads of Liberalism: Croly, Weyl, Lippmann and the Progressive Era, 1900–1925* (1961); William Hutchinson, *The Modernist Impulse in American Protestantism* (1976); Rivka Shpak Lissak, *Pluralism and Progressives: Hull House and the New Immigrants, 1890–1919* (1989); Roy Lubove, *The Professional Altruist: The Emergence of Social Work as a Career, 1880–1930* (1965); D. W. Marcell, *Progress and Pragmatism: James, Dewey, Beard and the American Idea of Progress* (1974); Daniel Nelson, *Frederick W. Taylor and the Rise of Scientific Management* (1980); David Nobel, *The Progressive Mind, 1890–1917* rev. ed. (1981); Martin Schiesl, *The Politics of Efficiency: Municipal Administration and Reform in America, 1880–1920* (1977); Robert B. Westbrook, *John Dewey and American Democracy* (1991); Morton White, *Social Thought in America: The Revolt against Formalism,* (1949); Harold Wilson, *McClure's Magazine and the Muckrakers* (1970).

Social Reform, Radical Politics, and Minority Rights
Mari Jo Buhle, *Women and American Socialism, 1870–1920* (1981); Allen F. Davis, *American Heroine: The Life and Legend of Jane Addams* (1973); James R. Green, *Grass-Roots Socialism: Radical Movements in the Southwest, 1895–1943* (1978); Louis Harlan, *Separate and Unequal: Public School Campaigns and Racism in the Southern Seaboard States, 1900–1915* (1968); Charles F. Kellogg, *NAACP: A History of the National Association for the Advancement of Colored People, 1909–1920* (1967); David L. Lewis, *W. E. B. Dubois: Biography of a Race* (1994); Roy Lubove, *The Progressives and the Slums: Tenement House Reform in New York City* (1962); James McPherson, *The Abolitionist Legacy: From Reconstruction to the NAACP* (1975); David Musto, *The American Disease: Origins of Narcotics Control* (1973); Elliot M. Rudwick, *W. E. B. DuBois* (1968); Nick Salvatore, *Eugene V. Debs: Citizen and Socialist* (1982); James Timberlake, *Prohibition and the Progressive Campaign* (1963); John D. Weaver, *The Brownsville Raid* (1970); James Weinstein, *The Decline of Socialism in America,*

1912–1925 (1967); Nancy Weiss, *The National Urban League, 1910–1940* (1974).

Women's Rights, Gender, and Sexuality
Paula Baker, *Gender and the Transformation of Politics: Public and Private Life in New York, 1870–1930* (1989); George Chester, *Gay New York: Gender, Urban Culture, and the Making of the Gay Male World, 1890–1940* (1994); Ellen Chesler, *Woman of Valor: Margaret Sanger and the Birth Control Movement in America* (1992); Nancy F. Cott, *The Grounding of Modern Feminism* (1987); Nancy Dye, *As Equals and Sisters: Feminism, the Labor Move-ment, and the Women's Trade Union League of New York* (1980); Linda Gordon, *Woman's Body, Woman's Right: A Social History of Birth Control* (1976), *Heroes of Their Own Lives: The Politics and History of Family Violence, 1880–1960* (1988), and *Pitied but Not Entitled: Single Mothers and the History of Welfare* (1994); David Kennedy, *Birth Control in America: The Career of Margaret Sanger* (1970); Aileen Kraditor, *Ideas of the Woman Suffrage Movement* (1965); Ellen Lagemann, *A Generation of Women: Education in the Lives of Progres-sive Reformers* (1979); Christine Lunardini, *From Equal Suffrage to Equal Rights: Alice Paul and the National Women's Party* (1986); David Morgan, *Suffragists and Democrats: The Politics of Woman Suffrage in America* (1972); Robyn Muncy, *Creating a Female Dominion in American Reform, 1890–1935* (1991); William O'Neil, *Divorce in the Progressive Era* (1967); Dorothy Richardson, *The Long Day: The Story of a New York Working Girl* (1905); Ruth Rosen, *The Lost Sisterhood: Prostitutes in America, 1900–1918* (1982); Rosalind Rosenberg, *Beyond Separate Spheres: Intellectual Roots of Modern Feminism* (1982); Anne Firor Scott, *Natural Allies: Women's Associations in American History* (1992); Anne Firor Scott and Andrew MacKay Scott, *One Half the People: The Fight for Woman Suffrage* (1982); Meredith Tax, *The Rising of the Women: Feminist Solidarity and Class Conflict, 1880–1917* (1980).

Education, the New Professionalism, and Entertainment
Burton Bledstein, *The Culture of Professionalism* (1976); Darlene Clark Hine, *Black Women in White: Racial Conflict and Cooperation in the Nursing Profession, 1890–1950* (1989); Lawrence Cremin, *The Transformation of the School: Progressivism in American Education* (1961); John DiMeglio, *Vaudeville U.S.A.* (1973); Lewis Erenberg, *Steppin' Out: New York Nightlife and the Transformation of American Culture, 1890–1930* (1981); James Farrell, *Inventing the American Way of Death, 1830–1920* (1980); Thomas Haskell, *The Emergence of Professional Social Science* (1977); Bruce Kuklick, *The Rise of American Philosophy* (1977); Martin Laforse and James Drake, *Popular Culture and American Life: Selected Topics in the Study of American Popular Culture* (1981); Cathy Peiss, *Cheap Amusements: Working Women and*

Leisure in Turn-of-the-Century New York (1986); Robert Sklar, *Movie-Made America: A Social History of the American Movies* (1975); Paul Starr, *The Social Transformation of American Medicine* (1982); David Tyack and Elizabeth Hansot, *Managers of Virtue: Public School Leadership in America, 1820–1980* (1982); Lawrence Vesey, *The Emergence of the American University* (1970).

Local and State Reform
Richard Abrams, *Conservatism in a Progressive Era: Massachusetts Politics, 1900–1912* (1964); John D. Buenker, *Urban Liberalism and Progressive Reform* (1973); Thomas E. Cronin, *Direct Democracy: The Politics of Initiative, Referendum and Recall* (1989); James Crooks, *Politics and Progress: The Rise of Urban Progressivism in Baltimore, 1895–1911* (1968); Dewey Grantham, *Southern Progressivism: The Reconciliation of Progress and Tradition* (1983); Melvin Holli, *Reform in Detroit: Hazen S. Pingree and Urban Politics* (1969); J. Joseph Huthmacher, "Urban Liberalism and Progressive Reform," *Mississippi Valley Historical Review* (1962); Jack Kirby, *Darkness at Dawning: Race and Reform in the Progressive South* (1972); Richard L. McCormick, *From Realignment to Reform: Political Change in New York State, 1893–1910* (1981); George Mowry, *The California Progressives* (1951); Bradley Rice, *Progressive Cities: The Commission Government Movement in America, 1901–1920* (1977); Jack Tager, *The Intellectual as Urban Reformer: Brand Whitlock and The Progressive Movement* (1968); David P. Thelen, *The New Citizenship: Origins of Progressivism in Wisconsin* (1972).

National Politics and Public Policy
Donald Anderson, *William Howard Taft* (1973); John M. Blum, *The Republican Roosevelt* (1954) and *Woodrow Wilson and the Politics of Morality* (1954); John Milton Cooper, Jr., *The Warrior and the Priest: Woodrow Wilson and Theodore Roosevelt* (1983); Stephen R. Fox, *The American Conservation Movement: John Muir and His Legacy* (1981); John Gable, *The Bull Moose Years* (1978); Alexander George and Juliette George, *Woodrow Wilson and Colonel House: A Personality Study* (1956); Lewis Gould, *Reform and Regulation: American Politics, 1900–1916* (1978) and *The Presidency of Theodore Roosevelt* (1991); Samuel P. Hays, *Conservation and the Gospel of Efficiency: The Progressive Conservation Movement, 1890–1920* (1959); James Holt, *Congressional Insurgents and the Party System* (1969); Arthur Link, *Woodrow Wilson*, 5 vols. (1947–1965); Albro Martin, *Enterprise Denied: Origins of the Decline of American Railroads, 1897–1917*; David McCullough, *Mornings on Horseback* (1981); Robert T. McCulley, *Banks and Politics during the Progressive Era: The Origins of the Federal Reserve System* (1992); Michael McGerr, *The Decline of Popular Politics: The American North, 1865–1928* (1986); Edmund Morris, *The Rise of Theodore Roosevelt* (1979); George Mowry, *The Era of Theodore Roosevelt* (1958); James Penick, *Progressive Politics and*

Conservation: The Ballinger-Pinchot Affair (1968); Harold Pinkett, *Gifford Pinchot: Private and Public Forester* (1970); Edwin Weinstein, *Woodrow Wilson and Colonel House: A Personality Study* (1956); Craig West, *Banking Reform and the Federal Reserve, 1863–1923* (1977); Clifton Yearley, *The Money Machines* (1970).

CHAPTER 23: THE UNITED STATES AND THE OLD WORLD ORDER

General Studies
Paul Abrahams, *The Foreign Expansion of American Finance and Its Relationship to Foreign Economic Policies of the United States, 1907–1921* (1976); Robert Beisner, *From the Old Diplomacy to the New, 1865–1900* (1975); John Dobson, *America's Ascent: The United States Becomes a Great Power, 1880–1914* (1978); Morrell Heald and Lawrence Kaplan, *Culture and Diplomacy* (1977); Peter Karsten, *The Naval Aristocracy* (1972); Robert Osgood, *Ideals and Self-Interest in America's Foreign Relations* (1953); Emily Rosenberg, *Spreading the American Dream: American Economic and Cultural Expansion, 1890–1945* (1982); Robert Schulzinger, *American Diplomacy in the Twentieth Century* (1984); Tom Terrill, *The Tariff, Politics, and American Foreign Policy, 1874–1901* (1973); Rubin Weston, *Racism and U.S. Imperialism, 1865–1946* (1971); Mira Wilkins, *The Emergence of the Multinational Enterprise* (1970).

Roosevelt, Taft, and Wilson
Howard K. Beale, *Theodore Roosevelt and the Rise of America to World Power* (1956); David Burton, *Theodore Roosevelt: Confident Imperialist* (1968); Robert W. Cherney, *A Righteous Cause: The Life of William Jennings Bryan* (1985); Richard H. Collin, *Theodore Roosevelt, Culture, Diplomacy, and Expansion* (1985); John Cooper, Jr., *Walter Hines Page* (1977); Lloyd Gardner, *Wilson and Revolutions, 1913–1921* (1976) and *William Jennings Bryan: Missionary Isolationist* (1983); Arthur Link, *Wilson: The Diplomatist* (1957) and *Woodrow Wilson: Revolution, War, and Peace* (1968); Frederick Marks III, *Velvet on Iron: The Diplomacy of Theodore Roosevelt* (1979); Ralph E. Minger, *William Howard Taft and United States Foreign Policy* (1975).

Asia, the Pacific, and Latin America
Warren Cohen, *America's Response to China*, rev. ed. (1980); David Healy, *Gunboat Diplomacy in the Wilson Era: The U.S. Navy in Haiti, 1915–1916* (1976) and *Drive to Hegemony: The United States in the Caribbean, 1898–1917* (1988); Akira Iriye, *Pacific Estrangement: Japanese and American Expansion, 1897–1911* (1972); Jerry Israel, *Progressivism and the Open Door: America and China, 1905–1921* (1971); Lester Langley, *Struggle for the American Mediterranean* (1980) and *The United States and the Caribbean, 1900–1970* (1980); Glenn May, *Social Engineering in the Philippines* (1980); Robert McClellan, *The Heathen Chinese: A Study of American Attitudes toward China* (1971); David McCullough, *The Path between the Seas: The Creation of the Panama Canal, 1870–1914* (1977); Dana Munro, *Intervention and Dollar Diplomacy in the Caribbean, 1900–1920* (1964); Charles Neu, *The Troubled Encounter* (1975); Robert Smith, *The United States and Revolutionary Nationalism in Mexico, 1916–1932* (1972); Peter Stanley, *A Nation in the Making: The Philippines and the United States, 1899–1921* (1974).

From Neutrality to War
Thomas Baily and Paul Ryan, *The Lusitania Disaster* (1975); John Coogan, *The End of Neutrality: The United States, Britain, and Maritime Rights, 1899–1915* (1981); John Cooper, *The Vanity of Power: American Isolationism and the First World War* (1969); Patrick Devlin, *Too Proud to Fight: Woodrow Wilson's Neutrality* (1974); Ross Gregory, *The Origins of American Intervention in the First World War* (1977); Burton Kaufman, *Efficiency and Expansion: Foreign Trade Organization in the Wilson Administration* (1974); Roland Marchand, *The American Peace Movement and Social Reform, 1898–1918* (1972); Ernest R. May, *The World War and American Isolation, 1914–1917* (1957); Jeffrey Safford, *Wilsonian Maritime Diplomacy* (1977).

The First World War Abroad
Arthur Barbeau and Henri Florette, *The Unknown Soldiers: Black American Troops in World War I* (1974); J. Gary Clifford, *The Citizen Soldiers* (1972); Edward Coffman, *The War to End All Wars: The American Military Experience in World War I* (1968); Frank Freidel, *Over There: The Story of America's First Great Overseas Crusade* (1964); Paul Fussell, *The Great War and Modern Memory* (1975); John Gifford, *The Citizen Soldiers* (1972); Otis Graham, *The Great Campaigns* (1971); Maurine Greenwald, *Women, War, and Work* (1980); James Joll, *The Origins of the First World War* (1984); N. Gordon Levin, Jr., *Woodrow Wilson and World Politics: America's Response to War and Revolution* (1968); Laurence Stallings, *The Doughboys: The Story of the AEF, 1917–1918* (1963); David F. Trask, *The AEF and Coalition Warmaking, 1917–1918* (1973); Frank Vandiver, *Black Jack: The Life and Times of John J. Pershing*, 2 vols. (1977); Russell Weigley, *The American Way of War* (1973).

The Home Front
Daniel R. Beaver, *Newton D. Baker and the American War Effort, 1917–1919* (1966); John W. Chambers, *To Raise an Army: The Draft Comes to Modern America* (1987); Valerie Jean Connor, *The National War Labor Board: Stability, Social Justice, and the Voluntary State in World War I* (1983); Robert Cuff, *The War Industries Board: Business-Government Relations during World War I* (1973);

Maurine W. Greenwald, *Women, War, and Work* (1980); Keith Grieves, *The Politics of Manpower, 1914–1918* (1988); Frank L. Grubb, *Samuel Gompers and the Great War* (1982); Carol Gruber, *Mars and Minerva: World War I and the Uses of Higher Learning in America* (1975); Ellis Hawley, *The Great War and the Search for Modern Order* (1979); Robert Haynes, *A Night of Violence: The Houston Riot of 1917* (1976); David M. Kennedy, *Over Here: The First World War and American Society* (1980); Seward Livermore, *Politics Is Adjourned: Woodrow Wilson and the War Congress, 1917–1918* (1966); Frederick Luebke, *Bonds of Loyalty: German Americans and World War I* (1974); Paul Murphy, *World War I and the Origins of Civil Liberties* (1979); Richard Polenberg, *Fighting Faiths: The Abrams Case, the Supreme Court, and Free Speech* (1987); Walton Rawls, *Wake Up America! World War I and the American Poster* (1987); Ronald Schaffer, *America in the Great War: The Rise of the War Welfare State* (1991); Jordan Schwarz, *The Speculator: Bernard M. Baruch in Washington, 1917–1965* (1981); Dale N. Shook, *William G. McAdoo and the Development of National Economic Policy, 1913–1918* (1987); Barbara Steinson, *American Women's Activism in World War I* (1982); John A. Thompson, *Reformers and War: Progressive Publicists and the First World War* (1987); Joe William Trotter, Jr., ed., *The Great Migration in Historical Perspective* (1991); Stephen Vaughn, *Holding Fast the Inner Lines: Democracy, Nationalism, and the Committee on Public Information* (1979); James Weinstein, *The Decline of Socialism in America, 1912–1923* (1967); Neil A. Wynn, *From Progressivism to Prosperity: World War I and American Society* (1986).

Versailles
Thomas Bailey, *Woodrow Wilson and the Great Betrayal* (1945) and *Woodrow Wilson and the Lost Peace* (1944); Robert Ferrell, *Woodrow Wilson and World War I* (1985); Inga Floto, *Colonel House at Paris* (1980); John Gaddis, *Russia, the Soviet Union, and the United States* (1978); Lloyd Gardner, *Safe for Democracy: The Anglo-American Response to Revolution, 1913–1923* (1984); Thomas J. Knock, *To End All Wars: Woodrow Wilson and the Quest for a New World Order* (1992); Arno Mayer, *Politics and Diplomacy of Peacemaking: Containment and Counterrevolution at Versailles* (1965); Charles Mee, Jr., *The End of Order, Versailles, 1919* (1980); Ralph Stone, *The Irreconcilables: The Fight against the League of Nations* (1970); William C. Widenor, *Henry Cabot Lodge and the Search for an American Foreign Policy* (1980).

Aftermath
David Brody, *Labor in Crisis: The Steel Strike of 1919* (1965); Stanley Coben, *A. Mitchell Palmer: Politician* (1963); Stanley Cooperman, *World War I and the American Mind* (1970); Roberta Feuerlicht, *Justice Crucified* (1977); Dana Frank, *Purchasing Power: Consumer Organizing, Gender,* *and the Seattle Labor Movement, 1919–1929* (1994); Robert Murray, *The Red Scare* (1955); Burl Noggle, *Into the Twenties* (1977); Stuart Rochester, *American Liberal Disillusionment in the Wake of World War I* (1977); Francis Russell, *A City in Terror* (1975); William Tuttle, Jr., *Race Riot: Chicago in the Red Summer of 1919* (1970); Stephen Ward, ed., *The War Generation: Veterans of the First World War* (1975).

CHAPTER 24: THE NEW ERA

General Studies
Frederick Lewis Allen, *Only Yesterday: An Informal History of the 1920s* (1931); John Braeman et al., eds., *Change and Continuity in Twentieth Century America: The 1920s* (1968); Ann Douglas, *Terrible Honesty: Mongrel Manhattan in the 1920s* (1995); Lynn Dumenil, *Modern Temper: American Culture and Society in the 1920s* (1995); Ellis Hawley, *The Great War and the Search for a Modern Order* (1979); John Hicks, *The Republican Ascendancy, 1921–1933* (1960); Isabel Leighton, ed., *The Aspirin Age* (1949); William Leuchtenburg, *The Perils of Prosperity, 1914–1932* (1958); Donald McCoy, *Coming of Age* (1973); Geoffrey Perrett, *America in the Twenties* (1982); Arthur Schlesinger, Jr., *The Crisis of the Old Order* (1957); David Shannon, *Between the Wars: America, 1919–1940* (1979).

Economics, Business, and Labor
Irving Bernstein, *The Lean Years: A History of the American Worker, 1920–1933* (1960); David Brody, *Steelworkers in America* (1960) and *Workers in Industrial America* (1980); Lizabeth Cohen, *Making a New Deal: Industrial Workers in Chicago, 1919–1939* (1990); Alfred D. Chandler, Jr., *Strategy and Structure: Chapters in the History of American Industrial Enterprise* (1962); Ed Cray, *Chrome Colossus: General Motors and Its Times* (1980); Gilbert Fite, *George Peek and the Fight for Farm Parity* (1954); James Flink, *The Car Culture* (1975); Louis Galambos, *Competition and Cooperation* (1966); James Gilbert, *Designing the Industrial State* (1972); Allan Nevins and Frank Hill, *Ford*, 3 vols. (1954–1963); Jim Potter, *The American Economy between the Wars* (1974); John Rae, *American Automobile* (1965) and *The Road and the Car in American Life* (1971); George Soule, *Prosperity Decade* (1947); Keith Sward, *The Legend of Henry Ford* (1948); Leslie Woodcock Tentler, *Wage Earning Women: Industrial Work and Family Life in the United States, 1900–1930* (1979); Bernard Weisberger, *The Dress Maker* (1979); Robert Zieger, *Republicans and Labor, 1919–1929* (1969) and *American Workers, American Unions, 1920–1980* (1986).

Mass Society and Mass Culture
Erick Barnouw, *A Tower of Babel: A History of American Broadcasting in the United States to 1933* (1966); Daniel Boorstin, *The Americans: The*

Democratic Experience (1973); Paul Carter, Another Part of the Twenties (1977); Robert Creamer, Babe (1974); Kenneth Davis, The Hero: Charles A. Lindbergh (1954); Stuart Ewen, Captains of Consciousness: Advertising and the Social Roots of the Consumer Culture (1976); Richard Wrightman Rox and T. J. Jackson Lears, eds., The Culture of Consumption: Critical Essays in American History, 1880–1980 (1983); Jackson Lears, Fables of Abundance: A Cultural History of Advertising in America (1994); Robert Lynd and Helen Lynd, Middletown: A Study in Modern Culture (1929); Roland Marchand, Advertising the American Dream: Making Way for Modernity, 1920–1940 (1985); Lary May, Screening Out the Past (1980); Leonard Mosley, Lindbergh: A Biography (1976); Otis Pease, The Responsibilities of American Advertising (1959); Daniel Pope, The Making of Modern Advertising (1983); Randy Roberts, Jack Dempsey, The Manassa Mauler (1979); Philip Rosen, The Modern Stentors: Radio Broadcasting and the Federal Government, 1920–1933 (1980); Robert Sklar, Movie-Made America: A Cultural History of American Movies (1975); Kevin Starr, Material Dreams: Southern California through the 1920s (1990); Susan Strasser, Satisfaction Guaranteed: The Making of the American Mass Market (1990).

High Culture
Carlos Baker, Hemingway (1956); Malcolm Cowley, Exile's Return (1934); Robert Crunden, From Self to Society: Transition in Modern Thought, 1919–1941 (1972); Frederick Hoffman, The Twenties (1949); Arthur Mizner, The Far Side of Paradise (1951); Roderick Nash, The Nervous Generation: American Thought, 1917–1930 (1969); Mark Shorer, Sinclair Lewis (1961); Marvin Singleton, H. L. Mencken and the "American Mercury" Adventure (1962).

Women, Youth, and Minorities
Lois Banner, American Beauty (1983); Susan D. Becker, The Origins of the Equal Rights Amendment (1981); Kathlenn M. Blee, Women of the Klan: Racism and Gender in the 1920s (1991); Dorothy M. Brown, Setting a Course: American Women in the 1920s (1987); William Chafe, The American Women: Her Changing Social, Economic, and Political Roles, 1920–1970 (1972); Nancy Cott, The Grounding of Modern Feminism (1987); David Cronon, Black Moses: The Story of Marcus Garvey (1955); Melvin Patrick Ely, The Adventures of Amos 'n' Andy: A Social History of an American Phenomenon (1991); Paula Fass, The Damned and Beautiful: American Youth in the 1920s (1977); Linda Gordon, Woman's Body, Woman's Right: A Social History of Birth Control in America (1976); Peter Gottlieb, Making Their Own Way: Southern Blacks' Migration to Pittsburgh, 1916–1930 (1987); Florette Henri, Black Migration: Movement North, 1900–1920 (1975); Nathan Huggins, Harlem Renaissance (1971); Jacqueline Jones, Labor of Love, Labor of Sorrow: Black Women,

Work, and Family, from Slavery to the Present (1985); J. Stanley Lemons, The Woman Citizen: Social Feminism in the 1920s (1973); David Levering Lewis, When Harlem Was in Vogue (1981); Glenna Matthews, "Just a Housewife!" The Rise and Fall of Domesticity in America (1987); Cary D. Mintz, Black Culture and the Harlem Renaissance (1988); Wilson Moses, The Golden Age of Black Nationalism, 1850–1925 (1988); Kathy H. Ogren, The Jazz Revolution: Twenties America and the Meaning of Jazz (1989); Arnold Rampersed, The Life of Langston Hughes, 2 vols. (1986–1988); Ricardo Romo, East Los Angeles: History of a Barrio (1983); George J. Sanchez, Becoming Mexican American: Ethnicity, Culture and Identity in Chicano Los Angeles, 1900–1945 (1993); Lois Scharf, To Work and to Wed (1980); Virginia Scharff, Taking the Wheel: Women and the Coming of the Motor Age (1991); Alan Spear, Black Chicago (1967); Judith Stein, The World of Marcus Garvey: Race and Class in Modern Society (1986); Joe William Trotter, Jr., Black Milwaukee: The Making of an Industrial Proletariat (1985); Theodore Vincent, Black Power and the Garvey Movement (1971); Winifred Wandersee, Women's Work and Family Values, 1920–1940 (1981).

Political Fundamentalism
Paul Avrich, Sacco-Vanzetti: The Anarchist Background (1991); David Burner, The Politics of Provincialism (1968); David Chalmers, Hooded Americanism: The History of the Ku Klux Klan (1965); Norman Clark, Deliver Us from Evil (1976); Robert Divine, American Immigration Policy (1957); Norman Furniss, The Fundamentalist Controversy, 1918–1933 (1954); Ray Ginger, Six Days or Forever? Tennessee v. John Scopes (1958); Joseph Gusfeld, Symbolic Crusade (1963); John Higham, Strangers in the Land: Patterns of American Nativism, 1860–1925 (1955); Kenneth Jackson, The Ku Klux Klan in the City, 1915–1930 (1967); Don Kirschner, City and Country: Rural Responses to Urbanization in the 1920s (1970); Shawn Lay, ed., The Invisible Empire in the West: Toward a New Historical Appraisal of the Ku Klux Klan of the 1920s (1992); Nancy MacLean, Behind the Mask of Chivalry: The Making of the Second Ku Klux Klan (1994); George Maraden, Fundamentalism and American Culture (1980); Leonard J. Moore, Citizen Klansmen: The Ku Klux Klan in Indiana, 1921–1928 (1991); Andrew Sinclair, Prohibition: The Era of Excess (1962); William Wilson, Coming of Age: Urban America, 1915–1945 (1974).

Politics, Public Policy, and the Election of 1928
Kristi Andersen, The Creation of a Democratic Majority (1979); Paula Edler, Governor Alfred E. Smith: The Politician as Reformer (1983); James Giglio, H. M. Daugherty and the Politics of Expediency (1978); Oscar Handlin, Al Smith and His America (1958); Ellis Hawley, Herbert Hoover as Secretary of Commerce: Studies in New Era Thought and Practice (1974); Robert Himmelberg,

The Origins of the National Recovery Administration: Business, Government, and the Trade Association Issue, 1921–1933 (1976); J. Joseph Huthmacher, *Massachusetts People and Politics, 1919–1933* (1959); Alan Lichtman, *Prejudice and the Old Politics* (1979); Richard Lowitt, *George Norris*, 2 vols. (1971); Donald McCoy, *Calvin Coolidge* (1967); Robert Murray, *The Harding Era* (1969) and *The Politics of Normalcy* (1973); Burl Noggle, *Teapot Dome* (1962); Elisabeth Perry, *Belle Moskowitz: Feminine Politics and the Exercise of Power in the Age of Alfred E. Smith* (1987); George Tindall, *The Emergence of the New South* (1967); Eugene Trani and David Wilson, *The Presidency of Warren G. Harding* (1977).

CHAPTER 25: CRASH AND DEPRESSION

General Studies
Frederick Lewis Allen, *Since Yesterday* (1939); John A. Garraty, *The Great Depression* (1987); Robert McElvaine, *The Great Depression: America, 1929–1941* (1984); Broadus Mitchell, *Depression Decade* (1947); Arthur Schlesinger, Jr., *The Crisis of the Old Order* (1957); T. H. Watkins, *The Great Depression: America in the 1930s* (1991).

The Great Crash and the Origins of the Great Depression
Michael A. Bernstein, *The Great Depression: Delayed Recovery and Economic Change in America, 1929–1939* (1987); Lester Chandler, *America's Greatest Depression, 1929–1941* (1970); Milton Friedman and Ana Schwartz, *The Great Contraction, 1929–1933* (1965); John Kenneth Galbraith, *The Great Crash*, rev. ed. (1988); Susan Kennedy, *The Banking Crisis of 1933* (1973); Charles Kindleberger, *The World in Depression* (1973); Robert Sobel, *The Great Bull Market: Wall Street in the 1920s* (1968); Peter Temin, *Did Monetary Forces Cause the Great Depression?* (1976); Gordon Thomas and Max Morgan-Witts, *The Day the Bubble Burst: The Social History of the Wall Street Crash of 1929* (1979).

Depression Life
Edward Anderson, *Hungry Men* (1935); Robert Angel, *The Family Encounters the Depression* (1936); Ann Banks, *First Person America* (1980); Caroline Bird, *The Invisible Scar* (1966); The Federal Writers' Project, *These Are Our Lives* (1939); John Garraty, *Unemployment in History: Economic Thought and Public Policy* (1978); Mirra Komarovsky, *The Unemployed Man and His Family* (1940); Robert Lynd and Helen Lynd, *Middletown in Transition* (1937); Robert McElvaine, ed. *Down & Out in the Great Depression* (1983); Harvey Levenstein, *Paradox of Plenty: A Social History of Eating in Modern America* (1993); H. Wayne Morgan, *Drugs in America: A Social History, 1800–1980* (1981); David Musto, *The American Disease,*

Origins of Narcotics Control, rev. ed. (1988); Lois Scharf, *To Work and to Wed: Female Employment, Feminism, and the Great Depression* (1980); Tom Terrill and Jerrold Hirsch, eds., *Such as Us: Southern Voices of the Thirties* (1978); Studs Terkel, *Hard Times: An Oral History of the Great Depression* (1970); Winifred Wandersee, *Women's Work and Family Values, 1920–1940* (1981); Susan Ware, *Holding Their Own: American Women in the 1930s* (1982); Jeane Westin, *Making Do: How Women Survived the '30s* (1976).'

Ethnicity and Race
Rodolfo Acuna, *Occupied America*, rev. ed. (1981); Ralph Bunche, *The Political Status of the Negro in the Age of FDR* (1973); Dan Carter, *Scottsboro: A Tragedy of the American South* (1969); Sarah Deutsch, *No Separate Refuge: Culture, Class, and Gender on an Anglo-Hispanic Frontier in the American Southwest, 1880–1940* (1987); Abraham Hoffman, *Unwanted Mexican-Americans in the Great Depression* (1974); Richard Polenberg, *One Nation Divisible: Class, Race, and Ethnicity in the United States since 1938* (1980); Bernard Sternsher, ed., *The Negro in Depression and War* (1969); Robert Weisbrot, *Father Divine and the Struggle for Racial Equality* (1983); Nancy Weiss, *The National Urban League* (1974); Raymond Wolters, *Negroes and the Great Depression* (1970).

Depression Culture
Daniel Aaron, *Writers on the Left* (1961); James Agee, *Let Us Now Praise Famous Men* (1941); Andrew Bergman, *We're in the Money: Depression America and Its Films* (1971); Eileen Eagan, *Class, Culture and the Classroom* (1981); Neal Gabler, *An Empire of Their Own: How the Jews Invented Hollywood* (1988); Lawrence Levine, *The Unpredictable Past: Explorations in American Cultural History* (1993); Jeffrey Meikle, *Twentieth Century Limited: Industrial Design in America, 1925–1939* (1979); Richard Pells, *Radical Visions and American Dreams: Culture and Social Thought in the Depression Years* (1973); Thomas Schatz, *The Genius of the System: Hollywood Filmmaking in the Studio Era* (1988); John Steinbeck, *The Grapes of Wrath* (1939); William Stott, *Documentary Expressionism and Thirties America* (1973); Warren Susman, *Culture as History: The Transformation of American Society in the Twentieth Century* (1984); Twelve Southerners, *I'll Take My Stand: The South and the Agrarian Tradition* (1937).

Radicalism and Protest
Irving Bernstein, *The Lean Years: A History of the American Worker, 1920–1933* (1960); Robert Cohen, *When the Old Left Was Young: Student Radicals and America's First Mass Student Movement, 1929–1941* (1993); Roger Daniels, *The Bonus March* (1971); John Hevener, *Which Side You On? The Harlan County Coal Miners, 1931–1939* (1978); Harvey Klehr, *The Heyday of American Communism: The Depression Decade* (1984); Donald

Lisio, *The President and Protest: Hoover, Conspiracy, and the Bonus Riot* (1974); Mark Naison, *Communists in Harlem during the Depression* (1983); Theodore Saloutos and John Hicks, *Twentieth Century Populism: Agrarian Protest in the Middle West, 1900–1939* (1951); John Shover, *Cornbelt Rebellion: The Farmers' Holiday Association* (1965).

The Hoover Years
David Burner, *Herbert Hoover: A Public Life* (1979); Roger Daniels, *The Bonus March* (1971); Martin Fausold, *The Presidency of Herbert C. Hoover* (1985); Martin Fausold and George Mazuzun, eds., *The Hoover Presidency* (1974); George Nash, *The Life of Herbert Hoover* (1983); James Olson, *Herbert Hoover and the Reconstruction Finance Corporation* (1977); Albert Romasco, *The Poverty of Abundance: Hoover, the Nation, the Depression* (1965); Elliot A. Rosen, *Hoover, Roosevelt, and the Brains Trust: From Depression to New Deal* (1977); Jordan Schwarz, *The Interregnum of Despair* (1970); Joan Hoff Wilson, *Herbert Hoover: Forgotten Progressive* (1975).

CHAPTER 26: THE NEW DEAL

General Studies
John Braeman et al., *The New Deal*, 2 vols. (1975); Paul Conkin, *The New Deal* (1967); Steve Fraser and Gary Gerstle, eds., *The Rise and Fall of the New Deal Order, 1930–1980* (1989); Otis Graham, Jr., *Encore for Reform: The Old Progressives and the New Deal* (1967); Barry Karl, *The Uneasy State* (1983); William Leuchtenburg, *Franklin D. Roosevelt and the New Deal, 1932–1940* (1963); Robert McElvaine, *The Great Depression: America, 1929–1941* (1984); Gerald Nash, *The Great Depression and World War II* (1979); Harvard Sitkoff, ed., *Fifty Years Later: The New Deal Evaluated* (1985).

Franklin and Eleanor
James Burns, *Roosevelt: The Lion and the Fox* (1956); Rochelle Chadakoff, ed., *Eleanor Roosevelt's My Day: Her Acclaimed Columns, 1936–1945* (1989); Blanche Wiesen Cook, *Eleanor Roosevelt*, Volume One, *1884–1933* (1992); Kenneth Davis, *FDR*, 4 vols. (1972–1993); Frank Freidel, *Franklin D. Roosevelt*, 4 vols. (1952–1973) and *Franklin D. Roosevelt: A Rendezvous with Destiny* (1990); Joseph Lash, *Eleanor and Franklin* (1971); Ted Morgan, *FDR: A Biography* (1985); Eleanor Roosevelt, *This Is My Story* (1937) and *This I Remember* (1949); Lois Scharf, *Eleanor Roosevelt: First Lady of American Liberalism* (1987); Arthur Schlesinger, Jr., *The Age of Roosevelt*, 3 vols. (1957–1960); Rexford Tugwell, *The Democratic Roosevelt: A Biography of Franklin D. Roosevelt* (1957); Geoffrey Ward, *Before the Trumpet: Young Franklin Roosevelt* (1985) and *A First Class Temperament: The Emergence of Franklin Roosevelt* (1989).

The New Deal and New Dealers
Anthony J. Badger, *The New Deal: The Depression Years, 1933–1940* (1989); Barton J. Bernstein, "The New Deal: The Conservative Achievements of New Deal Reform," in Barton J. Bernstein, ed., *Towards a New Past: Dissenting Essays in American History* (1968); Michael Beschloss, *Kennedy and Roosevelt: The Uneasy Alliance* (1980); John Blum, *From the Morgenthau Diaries*, 3 vols. (1959–1965); Harold Ickes, *The Secret Diaries of Harold L. Ickes*, 3 vols. (1953–1954); Peter Irons, *The New Deal Lawyers* (1982); Joseph Lash, *Dealers and Dreamers: A New Look at the New Deal* (1988); Katie Lockheim, ed., *The Making of the New Deal: The Insiders Speak* (1983); Richard Lowitt, *George W. Norris: The Triumph of a Progressive, 1933–1944* (1978); George Martin, *Madame Secretary: Frances Perkins* (1976); George McJimsey, *Harry Hopkins: Ally of the Poor and Defender of Democracy* (1987); Raymond Moley, *After Seven Years* (1939); Frances Perkins, *The Roosevelt I Knew* (1946); Samuel Rosenman, *Working for Roosevelt* (1952); Jordan Schwarz, *Liberal: Adolf A. Berle and the Vision of an American Era* (1987) and *The New Dealers: Power Politics in the Age of Roosevelt* (1993); Robert Sherwood, *Roosevelt and Hopkins: An Intimate History* (1948); Bernard Sternsher, *Rexford Tugwell and the New Deal* (1964); Susan Ware, *Beyond Suffrage: Women and the New Deal* (1981) and *Partner and I: Molly Dewson, Feminism, and New Deal Politics* (1987); T. H. Watkins, *The Righteous Pilgrim: The Life and Times of Harold L. Ickes* (1990).

Recovery and Reform
Bernard Belush, *The Failure of the NRA* (1975); Donald R. Brand, *Corporatism and the Rule of Law: A Study of the National Recovery Administration* (1988); Walter L. Creese, *TVA's Public Planning: The Vision, the Reality* (1990); Colin Gordon, *New Deals: Business, Labor, and Politics in America, 1920–1935* (1994); Ellis Hawley, *The New Deal and the Problems of Monopoly* (1966); Barry Karl, *Executive Reorganization and Reform in the New Deal* (1963); Susan E. Kennedy, *The Banking Crisis of 1933* (1973); Mark Leff, *The Limits of Symbolic Reform: The New Deal and Taxation, 1933–1939* (1984); Thomas McCraw, *TVA and the Public Power Fight* (1970); James Olson, *Saving Capitalism: The RFC and the New Deal, 1933–1940* (1988); Michael Parrish, *Securities Regulation and the New Deal* (1970); Richard Polenberg, *Reorganizing Roosevelt's Government* (1966); Albert Romasco, *The Politics of Recovery: Roosevelt's New Deal* (1983).

Agriculture and Conservation
Sidney Baldwin, *Poverty and Politics: The Rise and Decline of the Farm Security Administration* (1967); David Conrad, *The Forgotten Farmers: The Story of Sharecroppers in the New Deal* (1965); James Gregory, *American Exodus: The Dust Bowl Migration and Okie Culture in California* (1989); Richard Kirkendall, *Social Scientists and Farm*

Politics in the Age of Roosevelt (1966); Richard Lowitt, *The New Deal and the West* (1984); Percy H. Merrill, *Roosevelt's Forest Army: A History of the Civilian Conservation Corps, 1933–1942* (1981); Paul Mertz, *The New Deal and Southern Rural Poverty* (1978); Van Perkins, *Crisis in Agriculture* (1969); Donald Worster, *Dust Bowl: The Southern Plains in the 1930s* (1979) and *Rivers of Empire: Water, Aridity, and the Growth of the American West* (1986).

Relief and the Rise of the Semi-Welfare State
Searle Charles, *Minister of Relief* (1963) [about Harry Hopkins]; Paul Conkin, *FDR and the Origins of the Welfare State* (1967); Phoebe Cutler, *The Public Landscape of the New Deal* (1986); Linda Gordon, *Pitied but Not Entitled: Single Mothers and the History of Welfare* (1994); Richard Lowitt and Maurine Beasley, eds., *One Third of a Nation: Lorena Hickok Reports on the Great Depression* (1981); Roy Lubove, *The Struggle for Social Security* (1968); Jerre Mangione, *The Dream and the Deal: The Federal Writers' Project, 1935–1943* (1972); Jane deHart Matthews, *The Federal Theater, 1935–1939* (1967); Richard McKinzie, *The New Deal for Artists* (1973); Barbara Melosh, *Engendering Culture: Manhood and Womanhood in New Deal Public Art and Theater* (1991); Francis O'Connor, ed., *Art for the Millions: Essays from the 1930s by Artists and Administrators of the WPA Federal Art Project* (1973); Karen Benker Orhn, *Dorothea Lange and the Documentary Tradition* (1980); Marlene Park and Gerald Markowitz, *Democratic Vistas: Post Offices and Public Art in the New Deal* (1984); John Salmond, *The Civilian Conservation Corps* (1967); Bonnie Schwartz, *The Civil Works Administration, 1933–1934* (1984).

Dissent and Protest
Alan Brinkley, *Voices of Protest: Huey Long, Father Coughlin, and the Great Depression* (1982); Donald Grubbs, *Cry from Cotton: The Southern Tenant Farmers Union and the New Deal* (1971); Abraham Holzman, *The Townsend Movement* (1963); Glen Geansonne, *Gerald L. K. Smith: Minister of Hate* (1988); Robin D. G. Kelly, *Hammer and Hoe: Alabama Communists during the Great Depression* (1990); R. Alan Lawson, *The Failure of Independent Liberalism, 1930–1941* (1971); Greg Mitchell, *The Campaign of the Century: Upton Sinclair's Epic Race for Governor of California and the Birth of Media Politics* (1992); Mark Naison, *Communists in Harlem during the Depression* (1983); Leo Ribuffo, *The Old Christian Right: The Protestant Far Right from the Great Depression to the Cold War* (1983); Vicki Ruiz, *Cannery Women/Cannery Lives: Mexican Women, Unionization, and the California Food Processing Industry, 1930–1950* (1987); Charles Tull, *Father Coughlin and the New Deal* (1965); T. Harry Wiliams, *Huey Long* (1969); Frank Warren, *Liberals and Communism: The "Red Decade" Revisited* (1966) and *An Alternative Vision: The Socialist Party in the 1930s* (1976); George

Wolfskill, *Revolt of the Conservatives: A History of the American Liberty League, 1934–1940* (1962).

Labor
Jerold Auerback, *Labor and Liberty: The La Follette Committee and the New Deal* (1966); John Barnard, *Walter Reuther and the Rise of the Auto Workers* (1983); Irving Bernstein, *Turbulent Years: A History of the American Worker, 1933–1941* (1969); Lizabeth Cohen, *Making a New Deal: Industrial Workers in Chicago, 1919–1939* (1990); Melvyn Dubofsky and Warren Van Tine, *John L. Lewis: A Biography* (1977); Sidney Fine, *Sit-Down: The General Motors Strike of 1936–1937* (1969); Steven Fraser, *Labor Will Rule: Sidney Hillman and the Rise of American Labor* (1991); Peter Friedlander, *The Emergence of a UAW Local* (1975); Nelson Lichenstein, *"The Most Dangerous Man in Detroit": Walter Reuther and the Fate of American Labor* (1995); August Meier and Elliott Rudwick, *Black Detroit and the Rise of the UAW* (1979); David Milton, *The Politics of U.S. Labor: From the Great Depression to the New Deal* (1980); Ronald Schatz, *The Electrical Workers* (1983); Robert H. Zieger, *John L. Lewis* (1988).

New Deal Politics
John Allswang, *The New Deal in American Politics* (1978); Frank Freidel, *FDR and the South* (1965); J. Joseph Huthmacher, *Senator Robert Wagner and the Rise of Urban Liberalism* (1968); Gregg Mitchell, *The Campaign of the Century: Upton Sinclair's Race for Governor and the Birth of Media Politics* (1992); James Patterson, *Congressional Conservatism and the New Deal* (1967) and *The New Deal and the States* (1969); William Leuchtenburg, "The Origins of Franklin D. Roosevelt's 'Court Packing' Plan," in Philip Kurland, ed., *The Supreme Court Review* (1966).

Minorities
Laurence Kelly, *The Assault on Assimilation: John Collier and the Origins of Indian Policy Reform, 1920–1954* (1983); Harry A. Kersey, Jr., *The Florida Seminoles and the New Deal, 1933–1942* (1989); John Kirby, *Black Americans in the Roosevelt Era: Liberalism and Race* (1980); Carey McWilliams, *North from Mexico* (1949); Donald Parman, *The Navajoes and the New Deal* (1976); Kenneth Philp, *John Collier's Crusade for Indian Reform, 1920–1934* (1977); Francis Prucha, *The Indians in American Society: From the Revolutionary War to the Present* (1985); Mark Reisler, *By the Sweat of Their Brow: Mexican Immigrant Labor in the United States, 1900–1940* (1976); Harvard Sitkoff, *A New Deal for Blacks* (1978); Raymond Walters, *Negroes and the Great Depression: The Problem of Economic Recovery* (1970); Graham D. Taylor, *The New Deal and American Indian Tribalism: The Administration of the Indian Reorganization Act, 1934–1945* (1980); Nancy Weiss, *Farewell to the Party of Lincoln: Black Politics in the Age of FDR* (1983); Robert Zangrando, *The NAACP Crusade against Lynching* (1980).

CHAPTER 27: AMERICA'S RISE TO GLOBALISM

The Roosevelt Era and the Coming of World War II

Dorothy Borg, *The United States and the Far Eastern Crisis of 1933–1938* (1964); James MacGregor Burns, *Roosevelt: The Lion and the Fox* (1956); Wayne S. Cole, *Roosevelt and the Isolationists, 1932–1945* (1983); Robert Dallek, *Franklin D. Roosevelt and American Foreign Policy, 1932–1945* (1979); Charles DeBenedetti, *The Peace Reform Movement in American History* (1980); John Findling, *Close Neighbors, Distant Friends: United States–Central American Relations* (1987); Lloyd Gardner, *Economic Aspects of New Deal Diplomacy* (1964) and *The Great Powers Partition Europe, from Munich to Yalta* (1993); Irwin Gellman, *Good Neighbor Diplomacy* (1979); Patrick Headen, *Roosevelt Confronts Hitler: America's Entry into World War II* (1987); Edwin Herzstein, *Roosevelt and Hitler: Prelude to War* (1989); Akira Iriye and Warren Cohen, eds., *American, Chinese, and Japanese Perspectives on Asia, 1931–1949* (1990); Warren Kimball, *The Most Unsordid Act: Lend Lease, 1939–1941* (1969); Walter LaFeber, *Inevitable Revolutions: The United States in Central America* (1993); Douglas Little, *Malevolent Neutrality: The United States, Great Britain, and the Origins of the Spanish Civil War* (1985); Arthur Morse, *While Six Million Died* (1968); Arnold Offner, *The Origins of the Second World War* (1975); Gordon Prange, *At Dawn We Slept* (1981); Michael Slackman, *Target: Pearl Harbor* (1990); John Toland, *Infamy* (1982); Jonathan Utley, *Going to War with Japan, 1937–1941* (1985); Roberta Wohlstetter, *Pearl Harbor: Warning and Decision* (1962); Bryce Wood, *The Making of the Good Neighbor Policy* (1961); David Wyman, *The Abandonment of the Jews* (1984).

War and Strategy

John Dower, *War without Mercy: Race and Power in the Pacific War* (1986); David Eisenhower, *Eisenhower at War, 1943–1945* (1986); Richard B. Frank, *Guadalcanal* (1990); B. H. Liddell Hart, *History of the Second World War* (1970); Max Hastings, *OVERLORD: D-Day and the Battle of Normandy* (1984); Akira Iriye, *Power and Culture: The Japanese-American War, 1941–1945* (1981); D. Clayton James with Anne Sharp Wells, *A Time for Giants: Politics of the American High Command during World War II* (1987); John Keegan, *The Second World War* (1989); Eric Larabee, *Commander in Chief: Franklin Delano Roosevelt, His Lieutenants, and Their War* (1987); William Manchester, *American Caesar* (1979); Karal Ann Marling and John Wetenhall, *Iwo Jima* (1991); Ken McCormick and Hamilton Perry, *Images of War: The Artists' Vision of World War II* (1990); Nathan Miller, *War at Sea: A Naval History of World War II* (1995); Samuel Eliot Morison, *The Two Ocean War* (1963); Bernard C. Nalty, *Strength for the Fight: A History of Black Americans in the Military* (1986); Geoffrey Perret, *There's a War to Be Won: The United States Army and World War II* (1991) and *Winged Victory: The American Air Force in World War II* (1993); Forrest Pogue, *George C. Marshall*, 3 vols. (1963–1975); Paul P. Rogers, *The Good Years: MacArthur and Sutherland* (1990); Ronald Schaffer, *Wings of Judgment: American Bombing in World War II* (1985); Michael Sherry, *The Rise of American Air Power* (1987); Bradley Smith, *The Shadow Warriors: O.S.S. and the Origins of the C.I.A.* (1983); Ronald Spector, *The Eagle against the Sun: The American War with Japan* (1985); James Stokesbury, *A Short History of World War II* (1980).

The Home Front at War

Michael Adams, *The Best War Ever: Americans and World War II* (1994); Karen T. Anderson, *Wartime Women: Sex Roles, Family Relations, and the Status of American Women during World War II* (1981); Matthew Baigall and Julia Williams, eds., *Artists against War and Fascism* (1986); M. Joyce Baker, *Images of Women on Film: The War Years, 1941–1945* (1981); David Brinkley, *Washington Goes to War* (1988); John Costello, *Virtue under Fire: How World War II Changed Our Social and Sexual Attitudes* (1985); George Q. Flynn, *The Draft, 1940–1973* (1993); Paul Fussell, *Wartime* (1989); Sherna Berger Gluck, *Rosie the Riveter Revisited: Women, the War, and Social Change* (1987); Doris Kearns Goodwin, *No Ordinary Time, Franklin and Eleanor Roosevelt: The Homefront in World War II* (1994); Susan Hartmann, *The Home Front and Beyond: American Women in the 1940s* (1982); Maurice Isserman, *Which Side Were You On? The American Communist Party during the Second World War* (1982); Clayton Koppes and Gregory Black, *Hollywood Goes to War* (1987); Ruth Milkman, *Gender at Work: The Dynamics of Job Segregation by Sex during World War II* (1987); Gerald Nash, *The American West Transformed: The Impact of the Second World War* (1985); Richard Polenberg, *War and Society: The United States, 1941–1945* (1972); David Robertson, *Sly and Able: A Political Biography of James F. Byrnes* (1994); George H. Roeder, Jr., *The Censored War: American Visual Experience during World War II* (1993); Studs Turkel, *The Good War: An Oral History of World War II* (1984); William Tuttle, *Daddy's Gone to War: The Second World War in the Lives of America's Children* (1993); Harold Vatter, *The American Economy in World War II* (1985).

Minorities and the War

Robert Abzug, *Inside the Vicious Heart: Americans and the Liberation of the Nazi Concentration Camps* (1985); Allan Bérubé, *Coming Out under Fire: Gay Men and Women in World War Two* (1990); Richard Breitman and Alan Kraut, *American Refugee Policy and European Jewry, 1933–1945* (1987); A. Russell Buchanan, *Black Americans in World War II* (1977); Dominic Capeci, Jr., *Race Relations in Wartime*

Detroit (1984) and *The Harlem Race Riot of 1943* (1977); Richard Dalfiume, *Desegregation of the U.S. Armed Forces* (1969); Clete Daniel, *Chicano Workers and the Politics of Fairness: The Fair Employment Practices Commission and the Southwest 1941–1945* (1990); Roger Daniels, *Concentration Camps U.S.A.* (1981) and *Prisoners without Trials: The Japanese-Americans in World War II* (1993); Leonard Dinnerstein, *America and the Survivors of the Holocaust* (1982); Masayo Umezawa Duus, *Unlikely Liberators: The Men of the 100th and 442nd* (1987); Lee Finkel, *Forum for Protest: The Black Press during World War II* (1975); Peter Irons, *Justice at War: The Story of the Japanese American Internment Cases* (1983); Deborah Lipstadt, *Beyond Belief: The American Press and the Coming of the Holocaust, 1933–1945* (1986); Mauricio Mazon, *The Zoot Suit Riots* (1984); Phillip McGuire, ed., *Taps for a Jim Crow Army: Letters from Black Soldiers in World War II* (1982); Sandra Taylor, *Jewel of the West: Japanese-American Internment at Topaz* (1993); Patrick Washburn, *A Question of Sedition: The Federal Government and the Investigation of the Black Press during World War II* (1986); Neil Wynn, *The Afro-American and the Second World War* (1976); Norman Zucker and Naomi Flink Zucker, *The Guarded Gate: The Reality of American Refugee Policy* (1987).

Atoms and Diplomacy
Gar Alperovitz, *The Decision to Use the Bomb* (1995); Edward M. Bennett, *Franklin D. Roosevelt and the Search for Victory: American-Soviet Relations, 1935–1945* (1990); Henry Blumenthal, *Illusion and Reality in Franco-American Diplomacy, 1914–1945* (1982); McGeorge Bundy, *Danger and Survival: Choices about the Atom Bomb in the First Fifty Years* (1988); James MacGregor Burns, *Roosevelt: The Soldier of Freedom* (1970); Winston Churchill, *The Second World War,* 6 vols. (1948–1953); Herbert Feis, *Roosevelt, Churchill, Stalin: The War They Waged and the Peace They Sought* (1957), *Between War and Peace: The Potsdam Conference* (1960), and *The Atomic Bomb and the End of World War II* (1966); John L. Gaddis, *The United States and the Origins of the Cold War* (1972); Fraser J. Harbutt, *The Iron Curtain: Churchill, America, and the Origins of the Cold War* (1986); George Herring, *Aid to Russia, 1941–1946* (1977); John Hersey, *Hiroshima* (1946); Richard Hewlett and Oscar Anderson, *The New World* (1962); "Hiroshima in History and Memory: A Symposium," *Diplomatic History,* vol. 19, No. 2, Spring, 1995, 197–365; Godfrey Hodgson, *The Colonel: The Life and Wars of Henry Stimson* (1990); Warren Kimball, ed., *Churchill and Roosevelt: The Complete Correspondence, 1939–1945* (1984); Gabriel Kolko, *The Politics of War* (1968); William Roger Louis, *Imperialism at Bay: The United States and the Decolonization of the British Empire, 1941–1945* (1978); Mark H. Lytle, *The Origins of the Iranian-American Alliance, 1941–1953* (1987); David Painter, *Oil and the American Century: The Political Economy of U.S. Foreign Oil Policy, 1941–*

1954 (1986); Richard Rhodes, *The Making of the Atomic Bomb* (1986); Keith Sainsbury, *Roosevelt, Stalin, Churchill, and Chiang Kai-shek, 1943: The Moscow, Cairo, and Tehran Conferences* (1985); Gaddis Smith, *American Diplomacy during the Second World War, 1941–1945* (1985); Michael B. Stoff, *Oil, War, and American Security: The Search for a National Policy on Foreign Oil, 1941–1947* (1980), and as ed., *The Manhattan Project: A Documentary Introduction* (1991); Randall B. Woods, *A Changing of the Guard: Anglo-American Relations, 1941–1946* (1990).

CHAPTER 28: COLD WAR AMERICA

The Postwar Era
Paul Boyer, *By the Bomb's Early Light* (1986); H. W. Brands, *The Devil We Knew: America and the Cold War* (1993); Robert Ferrell, *Harry S Truman: A Life* (1994); Eric Goldman, *The Crucial Decade and After* (1960); Landon Jones, *Great Expectations: America and the Babyboom Generation* (1980); George Lipsitz, *Class and Culture in Postwar America* (1981); James O'Connor, ed., *American History/American Television* (1983); William O'Neill, *American High* (1986); Richard Pells, *The Liberal Mind in a Conservative Age* (1985); Dana Polan, *Power and Paranoia: History, Narrative, and the American Cinema, 1940–1950* (1986); Leila Rupp and Verta Taylor, *Survival in the Doldrums: The American Women's Rights Movement, 1945 to the 1960s* (1987); Mark Silk, *Spiritual Politics: Religion and America since World War II* (1988); Jules Tygiel, *Baseball's Great Experiment: Jackie Robinson and His Legacy* (1983); Martin Walker, *The Cold War: A History* (1994).

The Cold War in the West
Dean Acheson, *Present at the Creation* (1969); Stephen Ambrose, *The Rise to Globalism* (1983); Douglas Brinkley, ed., *Dean Acheson and the Making of American Foreign Policy* (1993); Richard Wightman Fox, *Reinhold Niebuhr: A Biography* (1985); Richard Freeland, *The Truman Doctrine and the Origins of McCarthyism* (1970); John L. Gaddis, *Strategies of Containment* (1982) and *The Long Peace: Inquiries into the History of the Cold War* (1987); Lloyd Gardner, *Architects of Illusion* (1970); David Green, *The Containment of Latin America* (1971); Gregg Herken, *The Winning Weapon* (1980); Michael Hogan, *The Marshall Plan: America, Britain, and the Reconstruction of Western Europe, 1947–1952* (1987); Walter Isaacson and Evan Thomas, *The Wise Men* (1986); Fred Kaplan, *The Wizards of Armageddon* (1983); Laurence Kaplan, *The United States and NATO* (1984); George Kennan, *Memoirs,* 2 vols. (1967, 1972); Bruce Kuniholm, *The Origins of the Cold War in the Near East* (1980); Mark H. Lytle, *The Origins of the Iranian-American Alliance, 1941–1953* (1987); James Miller, *The United States and*

Italy, 1940–1950 (1986); Ronald Pruessen, *John Foster Dulles* (1982); Cheryl Rubenberg, *Israel and the American National Interest* (1986); Gaddis Smith, *Dean Acheson* (1972) and *The Last Years of the Monroe Doctrine, 1945–1993* (1994); Adam Ulam, *The Rivals* (1971); Lawrence Wittner, *American Intervention in Greece, 1943–1949* (1982); Randall B. Woods and Howard Jones, *Dawning of the Cold War* (1991).

The Cold War in Asia
Robert Blum, *Drawing the Line: The Origin of the American Containment Policy in East Asia* (1982); Bruce Cumings, *The Origins of the Korean War* (1980) and vol. 2 (1990), and as ed., *Child of Conflict: The Korean-American Relationship, 1943–1953* (1983); William Head, *America's China Sojourn* (1983); Gary Hess, *The United States' Emergence as a Southeast Asian Power, 1940–1950* (1987); Akira Iriye, *The Cold War in Asia* (1974); Burton Kaufman, *The Korean War* (1986); Michael Schaller, *The United States and China in the Twentieth Century* (1979) and *The American Occupation of Japan: The Coming of the Cold War to Asia* (1985); John W. Spanier, *The Truman–MacArthur Controversy and the Korean War* (1959); William Stueck, Jr., *The Road to Confrontation* (1981) and *The Korean War: An International History* (1995); Nancy Tucker, *Patterns in the Dust: Chinese-American Relations and the Recognition Controversy, 1949–1950* (1983).

The Domestic Cold War
Michael Belknap, *Cold War Political Justice: The Smith Act, the Communist Party, and American Civil Liberties* (1977); David Caute, *The Great Fear* (1978); Bernard F. Dick, *Radical Innocence: A Critical Study of the Hollywood Ten* (1988); Stanley I. Kutler, *The American Inquisition: Justice and Injustice in the Cold War* (1982); Robert Lamphere and Tom Shachtman, *The FBI-KGB War* (1986); Victor Navasky, *Naming Names* (1980); Robert Newman, *Owen Lattimore and the "Loss" of China* (1992); William O'Neill, *A Better World: Stalinism and the American Intellectuals* (1983); Michael Oshinsky, *A Conspiracy So Immense: The World of Joe McCarthy* (1983); Ronald Radosh and Joyce Radosh, *The Rosenberg File* (1983); Thomas Reeves, *The Life and Times of Joe McCarthy* (1982); Richard Rovere, *Senator Joe McCarthy* (1959); Ellen Shrecker, *No Ivory Tower: McCarthyism and the Universities* (1984); Athan Theoharis, *Seeds of Repression: Harry S. Truman and the Origins of McCarthyism* (1971); Allen Weinstein, *Perjury: The Hiss-Chambers Case* (1978); Robert Williams, *Klaus Fuchs: Atom Spy* (1987).

The Truman Administration
Jack Ballard, *The Shock of Peace: Military and Economic Demobilization after World War II* (1983); Clark Clifford with Richard Holbrooke, *Counsel to the President, A Memoir* (1991); Richard Dalfiume, *Desegregation of the U.S. Armed Forces* (1969); Andrew Dunar, *The Truman Scandals and the Politics of Morality* (1984); Robert Ferrell, *Harry S. Truman and the Modern American Presidency* (1983); Donald Fixico, *Termination and Relocation: Federal Indian Policy, 1945–1960* (1986); David Goldfield, *Black, White, and Southern: Race Relations and Southern Culture* (1990); Alton Lee, *Truman and Taft–Hartley* (1966); Allen Matusow, *Farm Politics and Policies in the Truman Years* (1967); Donald McCoy, *The Presidency of Harry S. Truman* (1984); Donald McCoy and Richard Ruetten, *Quest and Response: Minority Rights and the Truman Administration* (1973); Merle Miller, *Plain Speaking* (1973); Richard Miller, *Truman: The Rise to Power* (1986); Allen Yarnell, *Democrats and Progressives: The 1948 Presidential Election as a Test of Postwar Liberalism* (1974).

CHAPTER 29: THE SUBURBAN ERA

General
Paul Carter, *Another Part of the Fifties* (1983); John Diggins, *The Proud Decades: America in War and Peace, 1941–1960* (1988); James Gilbert, *A Cycle of Outrage* (1986); Godfrey Hodgson, *America in Our Time* (1976); Martin Jezer, *The Dark Ages: Life in the United States, 1945–1960* (1982); William Leuchtenberg, *A Troubled Feast* (1979); Douglas Miller and Marion Nowak, *The Fifties: The Way We Really Were* (1977); Ronald Oakley, *God's Country: America in the 1950s* (1986); Stephen Whitfield, *The Culture of the Cold War* (1991).

American Life and Culture
Erik Barnouw, *Tube of Plenty: The Evolution of American Television* (1975); James L. Baughman, *The Republic of Mass Culture: Journalism, Filmmaking, and Broadcasting in America since 1941* (1992); Daniel Bell, *The End of Ideology* (1960); Carl Belz, *The Story of Rock* (1972); Wini Breines, *Young, White, and Miserable: Growing Up Female in the Fifties* (1992); Victoria Byerly, *Hard Times Cotton Mill Girls* (1986); Bruce Cook, *The Beat Generation* (1970); Stephanie Coontz, *The Way We Never Were: American Families and the Nostalgia Trap* (1992); John D'Emilio and Estelle Freedman, *Intimate Matters: A History of Sexuality in America* (1988); Colin Escott, *Good Rockin' Tonight: Sun Records and the Birth of Rock and Roll* (1991); Betty Friedan, *The Feminine Mystique* (1963); Neil Gabler, *Winchell: Gossip, Power and the Culture of Celebrity* (1994); John Kenneth Galbraith, *The Affluent Society* (1958); Herbert Gans, *The Levittowners* (1967); Carol George, *God's Salesman: Norman Vincent Peale and the Power of Positive Thinking* (1994); Serge Gilbaut, *How New York Stole the Idea of Modern Art* (1983); Charlie Gillett, *The Sound of the City: The Rise of Rock and Roll* (1970); William Graebner, *Coming of Age in Buffalo: Youth and Authority in the Postwar Era* (1990); Will Herberg, *Protestant-Catholic-Jew* (1956); Thomas Hine, *Populux* (1986); Kenneth Jackson, *Crabgrass Frontier: The*

Suburbanization of the United States (1985); Wendy Kozol, *Life's America: Family and Nation in Postwar Photojournalism* (1994); William Martin, *A Prophet with Honor: The Billy Graham Story* (1991); C. Wright Mills, *The Power Elite* (1956) and *White Collar* (1951); George Nash, *The Conservative Intellectual Movement in America* (1976); Richard Pells, *The Liberal Mind in a Conservative Age* (1985); David Potter, *People of Plenty* (1956); David Riesman, *The Lonely Crowd* (1950); Lynn Spiegel, *Make Room for TV: Television and the Family Ideal in Postwar America* (1992); Gaye Tuchman et al., eds., *Hearth and Home: Images of Women in the Mass Media* (1978); Ed Ward et al., *Rock of Ages: The Rolling Stone History of Rock and Roll* (1986); Carol Warren, *Madwives: Schizophrenic Women in the 1950s* (1987); William Whyte, *The Organization Man* (1956).

Foreign Policy in the Eisenhower Era
Stephen Ambrose, *Ike's Spies: Eisenhower and the Espionage Establishment* (1981); Blanche Weisen Cook, *The Declassified Eisenhower* (1981); Robert Divine, *Eisenhower and the Cold War* (1981) and *Blowin' in the Wind: The Nuclear Test Ban Debate, 1954–1960* (1978); Townsend Hoopes, *The Devil and John Foster Dulles* (1973); Richard Immerman, *The CIA in Guatemala* (1982); Madeline Kalb, *The Congo Cables: The Cold War in Africa from Eisenhower to Kennedy* (1982); Frederick Marks III, *Power and Peace: The Diplomacy of John Foster Dulles* (1993); Richard Melanson and David Mayers eds., *Reevaluating Eisenhower: American Foreign Policy in the 1950s* (1987); Thomas Paterson, *Contesting Castro: The United States and the Triumph of the Cuban Revolution* (1994); Richard Rhodes, *Dark Sun: The Making of the Hydrogen Bomb* (1995); Evan Thomas, *The Very Best Men: Four Who Dared: The Early Years of the CIA* (1995); Richard Welch, Jr., *Response to Revolution: The United States and the Cuban Revolution, 1954–1961* (1985).

Civil Rights
Numan Bartley, *The Rise of Massive Resistance: Race and Politics in the South during the 1950s* (1969); Jack Bloom, *Class, Race, and the Civil Rights Movement* (1987); Taylor Branch, *Parting the Waters: America in the King Years, 1954–1963* (1988); James Duram, *Moderate among Extremists: Dwight D. Eisenhower and the School Desegregation Crisis* (1981); David Garrow, *Bearing the Cross* (1986); Henry Louis Gates, Jr., *Colored People: A Memoir* (1994); Vincent Harding, *There Is a River: The Black Struggle for Freedom in America* (1981); Elizabeth Huckaby, *The Crisis at Central High: Little Rock, 1957–1958* (1980); Richard Kluger, *Simple Justice: The History of Brown v. Board of Education and Black America's Struggle for Equality* (1975); Anthony Lewis et al., *Portrait of a Decade* (1964); August Meier and Elliott Rudwick, *CORE: A Study in the Civil Rights Movement, 1942–1968* (1975); Stephen Oates, *Let the Trumpet Sound: The Life and Times of Martin Luther King, Jr.* (1982); Bernard Schwartz, *Inside the Warren Court* (1983);

Harvard Sitkoff, *The Struggle for Black Equality, 1954–1992* (1992); Juan Williams, *Eyes on the Prize: America's Civil Rights Years, 1954–1965* (1987); C. Vann Woodward, *The Strange Career of Jim Crow* (1974).

Domestic Politics
Stephen Ambrose, *Eisenhower the President* (1984); Piers Brendon, *Ike* (1986); Jeff Broadwater, *Eisenhower and the Anti-Communist Crusade* (1992); Larry Burt, *Tribalism in Crisis: Federal Indian Policy, 1953–1961* (1982); Barbara Clowse, *Brainpower for the Cold War: The Sputnik Crisis and the National Defense Education Act of 1958* (1981); Donald Fixico, *Termination and Relocation: Federal Indian Policy, 1945–1960* (1986); Fred Greenstein, *The Hidden Hand Presidency: Eisenhower as Leader* (1982); Chester Pach, *The Presidency of Dwight D. Eisenhower* (1991); Mark Rose, *Interstate Express Highway Politics, 1939–1989* (1991); Gary Wills, *Nixon Agonistes* (1970).

CHAPTER 30: LIBERALISM AND BEYOND

General
John M. Blum, *Years of Discord: American Politics and Society, 1961–1974* (1991); David Faber, *The Age of Great Dreams: America in the 1960s* (1994), and as ed., *The Sixties: From Memory to History* (1994); Richard Goodwin, *Remembering America: A Voice from the Sixties* (1988); Godfrey Hodgson, *America in Our Time* (1976); Edward P. Morgan, *The 60s Experience: Hard Lessons about Modern America* (1991); David Steigenwald, *The Sixties and the End of the Modern Era* (1995); Lawrence Wright, *The New World: Growing Up in America, 1960–1984* (1988).

The Counterculture and New Left
Serge Denisoff, *Great Day Coming: Folk Music and the American Left* (1971); Morris Dickstein, *The Gates of Eden* (1976); Todd Gitlin, *The Whole World Is Watching: The Mass Media in the Making and Unmaking of the New Left* (1981); Richard Goldstein, *Reporting the Counterculture* (1989); Paul Goodman, *Growing Up Absurd* (1960); Emmett Grogan, *Ringolevio* (1972); Maurice Isserman, *If I Had a Hammer . . . : The Death of the Old Left and the Birth of the New Left* (1987); Judy Kaplan and Linn Shapiro, *Red Diaper Babies: Children on the Left* (1985); Martin Lee and Bruce Shlain, *Acid Dreams: The CIA, LSD, and the Sixties Rebellion* (1985); Christine Mamiya, *Pop Art and the Consumer Culture: American Super Market* (1992); Timothy Miller, *The Hippies and American Values* (1991); W. J. Rorabaugh, *Berkeley at War: The 1960s* (1989); Theodore Roszak, *The Making of a Counter Culture* (1969); Kirkpatrick Sale, *SDS* (1973), Mark Spitz, *Dylan: A Biography* (1989); Students for a Democratic Society, *The Port Huron Statement* (1962); Hunter Thompson, *Hell's Angels* (1967) and *Fear and Loathing in Las Vegas* (1971); Ed Ward et al., *Rock of*

Ages: The Rolling Stone History of Rock and Roll (1986); Tom Wolfe, *Electric Kool-Aid Acid Test* (1968).

The Civil Rights Revolution
Michael Belknap, *Federal Law and Southern Order: Racial Violence and Constitutional Conflict in the Post-Brown South* (1987); Derrick Bell, *And We Are Not Saved: The Elusive Quest for Racial Justice* (1987); Jack Bloom, *Class, Race, and the Civil Rights Movement* (1987); Eric Burner, *And Gently He Shall Lead Them: Robert Parris Moses and Civil Rights in Mississippi* (1994); Stokely Carmichael and Charles Hamilton, *Black Power* (1967); Clayborne Carson, *In Struggle: SNCC and the Black Awakening of the 1960s* (1981); Dan T. Carter, *The Politics of Rage: George Wallace and the New Conservatism* (1995); William Chafe, *Civilities and Civil Rights* (1980); John Dittmar, *Local People: The Struggle for Civil Rights in Mississippi* (1994); Michael Eric Dyson, *Making Malcolm: The Myth and Meaning of Malcolm X* (1995); David Garrow, *The FBI and Martin Luther King* (1981); Hugh Davis Graham, *Civil Rights and the Presidency: Race and Gender in American Politics, 1960–1972* (1992); Otto Kerner et al., *The Report of the National Advisory Commission on Civil Disorders* (1968); Doug McAdam, *Freedom Summer* (1988); Malcolm X (with Alex Haley), *The Autobiography of Malcolm X* (1966); Adam Nossiter, *Of Long Memory: Mississippi and the Murder of Medgar Evers* (1994); Stephen Oates, *Let the Trumpet Sound: The Life and Times of Martin Luther King, Jr.* (1982); Hugh Pearson, *The Shadow of the Panther: Huey Newton and the Price of Black Power in America* (1994); Bruce Perry, *Malcolm* (1992); Bernard Schwartz, *Inside the Warren Court* (1983); Harvard Sitkoff, *The Struggle for Black Equality, 1954–1992* (1993); Mark Stern, *Calculating Visions: Kennedy, Johnson, and Civil Rights* (1992); Harris Wofford, *Of Kennedy and Kings* (1980); Eugene Wolfenstein, *The Victims of Democracy: Malcolm X and the Black Revolutionaries* (1981); Miles Wolff, *Lunch at the 5 & 10* (1990).

The Kennedys and Lyndon Johnson
David Burner and Thomas West, *The Torch Is Passed: The Kennedy Brothers and American Liberalism* (1984); Paul Ronnie Dugger, *The Politician* (1982); John Giglio, *The Presidency of John F. Kennedy* (1991); Lyndon Johnson, *Vantage Point* (1971); Gerald Posner, *Case Closed: Lee Harvey Oswald and the Assassination of John F. Kennedy* (1993); Thomas Reeves, *A Question of Character: A Life of John F. Kennedy* (1992); Arthur Schlesinger, Jr., *The Thousand Days* (1965) and *Robert Kennedy and His Times* (1978); Earl Warren et al., *The Report of the Warren Commission* (1964); Theodore White, *The Making of the President, 1960* (1961).

Politics and Foreign Policy in the Kennedy – Johnson Era
Graham Allison, *Essence of Decision: Explaining the Cuban Missile Crisis* (1971); James Anderson and Jared Hazelton, *Managing Macroeconomic Policy: The Johnson Presidency* (1986); Michael Beschloss, *The Crisis Years, Kennedy and Khrushchev, 1960–1963* (1991); H. W. Brands, *The Wages of Globalism: Lyndon Johnson and the Limits of American Power* (1994); Warren Cohen, *Dean Rusk* (1980); Hugh Graham Davis, *Uncertain Trumpet* (1984); Greg Duncan, *Years of Poverty, Years of Plenty* (1984); Trumbell Higgins, *Perfect Failure: Kennedy, Eisenhower and the Bay of Pigs* (1987); Diane Kunz, ed., *The Diplomacy of the Crucial Decade: American Foreign Policy in the 1960s* (1995); Richard Mahoney, *JFK: Ordeal in Africa* (1983); Walter McDougall, . . . *The Heavens and the Earth: A Political History of the Space Age* (1985); Charles Murray, *Losing Ground: American Social Policy, 1950–1980* (1984); Thomas Noer, *Cold War and Black Liberation: The United States and White Rule in Africa, 1948–1968* (1985); Gerald Rice, *The Bold Experiment: JFK's Peace Corps* (1985); R. B. Smith, *An International History of the Vietnam War: The Kennedy Strategy* (1985); Mary Ann Watson, *The Expanding Vista, American Television in the Kennedy Years* (1990); Tom Wicker, *JFK and LBJ* (1968); Bryce Wood, *The Dismantling of the Good Neighbor Policy* (1985).

CHAPTER 31: THE VIETNAM ERA

The United States and the Vietnam War
Christian Appy, *Working Class War: American Combat Soldiers and Vietnam* (1993); Loren Baritz, *Backfire: A History of How American Culture Led Us into Vietnam and Made Us Fight the Way We Did* (1985); Larry Berman, *Planning a Tragedy* (1982); Larry Cable, *Conflict of Myths: The Development of American Counterinsurgency Doctrine and the Vietnam War* (1986); Mark Clodfelter, *The Limits of Airpower* (1989); Lloyd Gardner, *Pay Any Price: Lyndon Johnson and the War for Vietnam* (1995); Francis Fitzgerald, *Fire in the Lake* (1972); Leslie Gelb and Richard Betts, *The Irony of Vietnam: The System Worked* (1979); Mike Gravel et al., *The Pentagon Papers* (1975); David Halberstam, *The Best and the Brightest* (1972) and *The Making of Quagmire* (1987); Le Ly Hayslip, *When Heaven and Earth Changed Places* (1989), and with James Hayslip, *Child of War, Woman of Peace* (1993); George Herring, *LBJ and Vietnam* (1994); George Kahin, *Intervention* (1986); Stanley Karnow, *Vietnam* (1983); Gabriel Kolko, *Anatomy of a War* (1985); Andrew Krepinevich, Jr., *The Army and Vietnam* (1986); David Levy, *The Debate Over Vietnam* (1991); Kathryn Marshall, *In the Combat Zone: An Oral History of Women in the Vietnam War, 1966–1975* (1987); Harold G. Moore and Joseph Galloway, *We Were Soldiers Once . . . and Young* (1992); Tim Page, *Nam* (1983); Bruce Palmer, Jr., *The 25-Year War* (1984); Archimedes Patti, *Why Viet Nam?* (1983); Norman Podhoretz, *Why We Were in Vietnam* (1982); Al Santoli, *Everything We Had: An Oral History of the Vietnam War by Thirty-Three American Soldiers Who Fought It* (1981); Neil Sheehan, *A Bright Shining Lie: John Paul Vann and*

America in Vietnam (1988); Ronald Spector, *The United States Army in Vietnam* (1983) and *After Tet: The Bloodiest Year in Vietnam* (1993); Harry Summers, Jr., *On Strategy: A Critical Analysis of the Vietnam War* (1981); Wallace Terry, *Bloods: An Oral History of the Vietnam War by Black Veterans* (1984); William Turley, *The Second Indochina War: A Short Political and Military History* (1986); Jim Wilson, *The Sons of Bardstown* (1994).

Dissent against the War
William Berman, *William Fulbright and the Vietnam War* (1988); David Caute, *The Year of the Barricades, 1968* (1988); Charles DeBenedetti and Charles Chatfield, *An American Ordeal: The Antiwar Movement and the Vietnam Era* (1990); Gloria Emerson, *Winners and Losers* (1976); David Farber, *Chicago '68* (1988); Myra MacPherson, *Long Time Passing: Vietnam and the Haunted Generation* (1984); Kim McQuaid, *The Anxious Years* (1989); Norman Mailer, *Armies of the Night* (1968) and *Miami and the Siege of Chicago* (1969); James Miller, *Democracy Is in the Streets* (1987); Melvin Small, *Covering Dissent: The Media and the Anti-Vietnam War Movement* (1994); William Strauss, *Chance and Circumstance* (1978); Amy Swerdlow, *The Women's Strike for Peace: Traditional Motherhood and Radical Politics in the 1960s* (1993); Lawrence Wittner, *Rebels against War: The American Peace Movement, 1933–1983* (1984) Nancy Zaroulis and Gerald Sullivan, *Who Spoke Up? American Protest against the War in Vietnam* (1984).

The Nixon Presidency before Watergate
Stephen Ambrose, *Nixon, the Triumph of a Politician, 1962–1972* (1989); John Erlichmann, *Witness to Power* (1982); Raymond Garthoff, *Détente and Confrontation: American–Soviet Relations from Nixon to Reagan* (1985); H. R. Haldeman, *The Haldeman Diaries: Inside the Nixon White House* (1994); Seymour Hersh, *The Price of Power: Kissinger in the Nixon White House* (1983); Walter Isaacson, *Kissinger* (1992); Henry Kissinger, *The White House Years* (1979) and *Years of Upheaval* (1982); Robert Litwack, *Détente and the Nixon Doctrine* (1984); Morris Morley, *The United States and Chile* (1975); Richard Nixon, *RN* (1978); William Shawcross, *Sideshow: Nixon, Kissinger, and the Destruction of Cambodia* (1978); Robert Sutter, *The China Quandary* (1983); Theodore White, *The Making of the President, 1968* (1969); Tom Wicker, *One of Us: Richard Nixon and the American Dream* (1991).

Minorities: Background and Politics
Rodolfo Acuna, *Occupied America* (1981); Mario Barerra, *Race and Class in the Southwest* (1979); John Burma, ed., *Mexican-Americans in the United States* (1970); Albert Camarillo, *Hispanics in a Changing Society* (1979); Tony Castro, *Chicano Power* (1974); Vine Deloria, *Behind the Veil of Broken Treaties* (1974); Patrick Gallagher, *The Cuban Exile* (1980); Hazel W. Hertzberg, *The Search for an American Indian Identity: Modern Pan-Indian Movements* (1971); Peter Iverson, *The Navajo Nation* (1981); Virginia Sanchez Korrol, *From Colonia to Community* (1983); Darcy McNickle, *Native American Tribalism* (1973); Joan Moore and Harry Pachon, *Hispanics in the United States* (1985); Joan Moore et al., *Homeboys* (1978); Roger Nichols, *The American Indian: Past and Present* (1986); James Olsen and Raymond Wilson, *Native Americans in the Twentieth Century* (1984); A. Petit, *Images of the Mexican-American in Fiction and Film* (1980); Ronald Taylor, *Chavez and the Farm Workers* (1975); Arnulfo Trejo, ed., *The Chicanos: As We See Ourselves* (1979); Karl Wagenheim, *Puerto Rico: A Profile* (1975).

CHAPTER 32: THE AGE OF LIMITS

American Society and the Economy in the 1970s
Barry Bluestone and Bennett Harrison, *The Deindustrialization of America* (1982); Paul Boyer, *When Time Shall Be No More: Prophecy Belief in Modern American Culture* (1992); Peter Calleo, *The Imperious Economy* (1982); Barry Commoner, *The Politics of Energy* (1979); Ronald Formisano, *Boston against Busing: Race, Class, and Ethnicity in the 1960s and 1970s* (1991); Christopher Lasch, *The Culture of Narcissism* (1978); Michael Lienesch, *Redeeming America: Piety and Politics in the New Christian Right* (1993); J. Anthony Lukas, *Common Ground: A Turbulent Decade in the Lives of Three American Families* (1986); George Marsden, *Fundamentalism and Evangelicalism* (1991); Martin Melosi, *Coping with Abundance: Energy and Environment in Industrial America* (1985); Timothy O'Neill, *Bakke and the Politics of Equality* (1985); Daniel Yergin, *The Prize* (1991).

Environmentalism
Rachel Carson, *Silent Spring* (1962); Barry Caspar and Paul Wellstone, *Powerline* (1981); Albert Cowdry, *This Land, This South: An Environmental History* (1983); Thomas Dunlap, *DDT: Scientists, Citizens, and Public Policy* (1981); Robert Booth Fowler, *The Greening of Protestant Thought* (1995); Ian McHarg, *Design with Nature* (1969); Daniel Martin, *Three Mile Island* (1980); Lester Milbrath, *Environmentalists: Vanguard for a New Society* (1984); Roderick Nash, *The Rights of Nature* (1989); Marc Reisner, *Cadillac Desert: The American West and Its Disappearing Water* (1986); Kirkpatrick Sale, *The Green Revolution, The American Environmental Movement, 1962–1993* (1993); Philip Shabecoff, *A Fierce Green Fire: The American Environmental Movement* (1993); Andrew Szasz, *EcoPopulism: Toxic Waste and the Movement for Environmental Justice* (1994); James Trefethen, *An American Crusade for Wildlife* (1975); Donald Worster, *Rivers of Empire: Water, Aridity, and the Growth of the American West* (1985).

Feminism, Sexual Politics, and the Family

Barry D. Adam, *The Rise of a Gay and Lesbian Movement* (1987); Rae Andre, *Homemakers: The Forgotten Workers* (1981); Peter Berger and Brigitte Berger, *The War over the Family: Capturing the Middle Ground* (1983); Mary Frances Berry, *Why ERA Failed: Politics, Women's Rights, and the Amending Process of the Constitution* (1986) and *The Politics of Parenthood: Childcare, Women's Rights and Feminism* (1993); Susan Brownmiller, *Against Our Will: Men, Women, and Rape* (1975); Robert Coles and Geoffrey Stokes, *Sex and the American Teenager* (1985); Angela Davis, *Women, Race, and Class* (1981); Susan Douglas, *Where the Girls Are: Growing Up Female with the Mass Media* (1994); John D'Emilio, *Sexual Politics, Sexual Communities: The Making of a Homosexual Minority in the United States, 1940–1970* (1983); Martin Duberman, *Stonewall* (1993); Andrea Dworkin, *Right-Wing Women* (1983); Barbara Ehrenreich, *The Hearts of Men: American Dreams and the Flight from Commitment* (1983); Susan Estebrook, *If All We Did Was to Weep at Home: A History of White Working-Class Women in America* (1979); Shulamith Firestone, *The Dialectic of Sex: The Case for the Feminist Revolution* (1970); Jo Freeman, *The Politics of Women's Liberation* (1975); David Garrow, *Liberty and Sexuality: The Right and Privacy in the Making of Roe v. Wade* (1994); Carol Gilligan, *In Another Voice: Psychological Theory and Women's Development* (1982); Germaine Greer, *The Female Eunuch* (1972); Alice Kessler Harris, *Out to Work* (1982); Gloria Hull et al., *But Some of Us Are Brave: Black Women's Studies* (1982); Christopher Lasch, *Haven in a Hostile World* (1979); Kristen Luker, *Abortion and the Politics of Motherhood* (1984); Norma McCorvey, *I Am Roe: My Life, Roe v. Wade and Freedom of Choice* (1994); Kate Millett, *Sexual Politics* (1970); Steven Mintz and Susan Kellogg, *Domestic Revolutions: A Social History of American Family Life* (1988); Robin Morgan, ed., *Sisterhood Is Powerful: An Anthology* (1970); Maureen Muldoon, *The Abortion Debate in the United States and Canada: A Source Book* (1991); La Frances Rodgers-Rose, ed., *The Black Woman* (1980); Gloria Steinem, *Outrageous Acts and Everyday Rebellions* (1983).

Politics and Diplomacy in the Age of Limits

Stephen Ambrose, *Nixon: Ruin and Recovery, 1973–1990* (1991); James Bill, *The Eagle and the Lion: The Tragedy of American–Iranian Relations* (1987); Zbigniew Brzezinski, *Power and Principle* (1983); James Cannon, *Time and Chance: Gerald Ford's Appointment with History, 1913–1974* (1993); Jimmy Carter, *Keeping the Faith* (1982); Rosalynn Carter, *First Lady from Plains* (1984); John Dean, *Blind Ambition* (1976); John Dumbull, *The Carter Presidency: A Re-evaluation* (1993); Gerald Ford, *A Time to Heal* (1979); Raymond Garthoff, *Détente and Confrontation: American–Soviet Relations from Nixon to Reagan* (1985); Millicent Gates and Bruce Geelhoed, *The Dragon*

and the Snake: An American Account of the Turmoil in China, 1976–1977 (1986); Michael Hogan, *The Panama Canal in American Politics* (1986); Henry Jackson, *From the Congo to Soweto: U.S. Foreign Policy toward Africa since 1960* (1982); Burton Kaufman, *The Presidency of James Earl Carter, Jr.* (1993); Walter LaFeber, *The Panama Canal*, rev. ed. (1989); J. Anthony Lukas, *Nightmare: The Underside of the Nixon Years* (1988); Richard Pipes, *U.S.–Soviet Relations in the Era of Détente* (1981); William Quandt, *Camp David* (1986); A. James Reichley, *Conservatives in an Age of Change: The Nixon and Ford Administrations* (1981); Robert Schulzinger, *Henry Kissinger: Doctor of Diplomacy* (1989); Gary Sick, *All Fall Down* (1985); John Sirica, *To Set the Record Straight* (1979); Seth Tillman, *The U.S. in the Middle East* (1982); Cyrus Vance, *Hard Choices* (1983); Theodore White, *Breach of Faith* (1975); Bob Woodward and Carl Bernstein, *All the President's Men* (1974) and *The Final Days* (1976).

CHAPTER 33: A NATION STILL DIVISIBLE

Contemporary American Society

Bruce Bawer, *A Place at the Table: The Gay Individual and American Society* (1994); Robert Bellah et al., *Habits of the Heart: Individualism and Commitment in American Life* (1985) and *The Good Society* (1991); Dallas Blanchard, *The Anti-Abortion Movement* (1994); Stephen Carter, *The Culture of Disbelief: How American Law and Politics Trivialize Religious Devotion* (1993); William Dietrich, *In the Shadow of the Rising Sun: The Political Roots of American Economic Decline* (1991); Thomas Byrne Edsall, *The New Politics of Inequality* (1984); Barbara Ehrenreich, *Fear of Falling: The Inner Life of the Middle Class* (1989) and *The Worst Years of Our Lives* (1990); Susan Faludi, *Backlash: The Undeclared War against American Women* (1991); Elizabeth Fee and Daniel Fox, eds., *AIDS: The Burdens of History* (1992); Henry Louis Gates, Jr., *Loose Canons: Notes on the Culture Wars* (1993); Michael Goldfield, *The Decline of Organized Labor in the United States* (1987); Otis Graham, Jr., *Losing Time: The Industrial Policy Debate* (1992); Michael Harrington, *The New American Poverty* (1984); Richard Herrnstein and Charles Murray, *The Bell Curve: Intelligence and Class Structure in American Life* (1994); Robert Hughes, *Culture of Complaint: The Fraying of America* (1993); Paul Krugman, *Peddling Prosperity: Economic Sense and Nonsense in the Age of Diminished Expectations* (1994); Frank Levy, *Dollars and Dreams: The Changing American Income Distribution* (1987); Steve Levy, *Insanely Great: The Life and Times of Macintosh, the Computer That Changed Everything* (1994); Jane Maysbridge, *Why We Lost the ERA* (1986); Joseph Nocera, *A Piece of the Action: How the Middle Class Joined the Money Class* (1994); Juliet Schor, *The Overworked American: The Unexpected Decline of Leisure* (1991); Studs Terkel, *The Great*

Divide (1988); Thomas Toch, *In the Name of Excellence: The Struggle to Reform the Nation's Schools* (1991); James Trabor and Eugene Gallagher, *Why Waco? Cults in the Battle for Religious Freedom* (1995).

Politics from Reagan to Clinton
Charles Allen, *The Comeback Kid: The Life and Career of Bill Clinton* (1992); Earl Black and Merle Black, *The Vital South: How Presidents Are Elected* (1992); Sidney Blumenthal, *The Rise of the Counter-Establishment from Conservative Ideology to Political Power* (1988), and with Thomas Byrne Edsall, eds., *The Reagan Legacy* (1988); Paul Boyer, ed., *Reagan as President: Contemporary Views of the Man, His Politics, and His Policies* (1990); William Brennan, *America's Right Turn from Nixon to Bush* (1994); Barbara Bush, *Barbara Bush: A Memoir* (1994); Michael Deaver, *Behind the Scenes* (1987); Theodore Draper, *A Very Thin Line: The Iran-Contra Affairs* (1991); Elizabeth Drew, *On the Edge: The Clinton Presidency* (1994); Ken Gross, *Ross Perot: The Man Behind the Myth* (1992); David Hoeveler, Jr., *Watch on the Right: Conservative Intellectuals in the Reagan Era* (1991); Peter Irons, *Brennan vs. Rehnquist: The Battle for the Constitution* (1994); Jonathan Kwitny, *The Crimes of Patriots: A True Tale of Dope, Dirty Money, and the CIA* (1987); Jonathan Lash, *A Season of Spoils: The Story of the Reagan Administration's Attack on the Environment* (1984); Theodore Lowi, *The End of the Republican Era* (1995); Mary Matlin and James Carville, *All's Fair: Love, War, and Running for President* (1994); *The New Yorker*, "Special Politics Issue," October 21 & 28, 1996; Kevin Phillips, *The Politics of Rich and Poor: Wealth and the American Electorate in the Reagan Aftermath* (1990) and *Boiling Point: Republicans: Democrats and the Decline of Middle Class Prosperity* (1993); John Podhoretz, *Hell of a Ride: Backstage at the White House Follies, 1989–1993* (1993); Dan Quayle, *Standing Firm: A Vice-Presidential Memoir* (1994); Donald Regan, *For the Record* (1988); Tom Rosenstiel, *Strange Bedfellows: How Television and the Presidential Candidates Changed American Politics, 1992* (1993); Randy Shilts, *And the Band Played On: Politics, People and the AIDS Epidemic* (1987); David Stockman, *The Triumph of Politics: The Inside Story of the Reagan Revolution* (1986); Stephen Vaugh, *Ronald Reagan in Hollywood: Movies and Politics* (1994); Gary Wills, *Reagan's America* (1987); Daniel Wirls, *The Politics of Defense in the Reagan Era* (1992); Bob Woodward, *The Agenda: Inside the Clinton White House* (1994).

Foreign Policy into the 1990s
Michael Beschloss and Strobe Talbot, *At the Highest Levels: The Inside Story of the End of the Cold War* (1993); Raymond Bonner, *Weakness and Deceit: U.S. Policy and El Salvador* (1984); William Broad, *Teller's War: The Top Secret Story behind the Star Wars Deception* (1992); Bradford Burns, *At War with Nicaragua* (1987); Leslie Cockburn, *Out of Control* (1987); Christopher Coker, *The United States and South Africa, 1968–1985* (1986); Thomas Friedman, *From Beirut to Jerusalem* (1989); John Lewis Gaddis, *The United States and the End of the Cold War* (1992); Roy Gutman, *Banana Diplomacy* (1988); Alexander Haig, Jr., *Caveat: Realism, Reagan, and Foreign Policy* (1984); Delip Hiro, *Desert Shield to Desert Storm* (1992); Bruce Jentleson, *Pipeline Politics: The Complex Political Economy of East–West Trade* (1986); Robert Kaplan, *Balkan Ghosts* (1993); Walter LaFeber, *Inevitable Revolutions* (1993); John Mueller, *Policy and Opinion in the Gulf War* (1994); Robert Pastor, *Condemned to Repetition: The United States and Nicaragua* (1987); Jonathan Schell, *The Fate of the Earth* (1982); David Schoenbaum, *The United States and the State of Israel* (1993); Strobe Talbott, *Deadly Gambits: The Reagan Administration and the Stalemate in Nuclear Arms Control* (1984); Sanford Ungar, *Africa* (1985); William Vogele, *Stepping Back: Nuclear Arms Control and the End of the Cold War* (1994). Thomas Walker, ed., *Reagan versus the Sandinistas* (1987); Bob Woodward, *Veil: The Secret Wars of the CIA* (1987).

Minorities and American Culture
Ken Auletta, *The Underclass* (1982); Richard Bernstein, *Multiculturalism and the Battle for America's Future* (1994); Ellis Cose, *The Rage of the Privileged Class: Why Are Middle Class Blacks Angry?* (1994); Roger Daniels et al., eds., *Japanese-Americans: From Relocation to Redress* (1986); Reynolds Farley and Walter Allen, *The Color Line and the Quality of Life in America* (1987); Lawrence Fuchs, *The American Kaleidoscope: Race, Ethnicity, and the Civic Culture* (1990); Douglas Glasgow, *The Black Underclass* (1980); Andrew Hacker, *Two Nations: Black and White, Separate, Hostile, Unequal* (1992); Denis Heyck, ed., *Barrios and Borderlands: Cultures of Latinos and Latinas in the United States* (1993); Bill Ong Hing, *Making and Remaking Asian America through Immigration Policy, 1850–1990* (1993); David Hollinger, *Postethnic America: Beyond Multiculturalism* (1995); Christopher Jencks, *The Homeless* (1994); Jonathan Kozol, *Savage Inequalities: Children in America's Schools* (1991); Oscar Martinez, *Border People: Life and Society in the U.S.–Mexico Border Lands* (1994); Joan Moore and Harry Pachon, *Hispanics in the United States* (1985); Adolph Reed, *The Jesse Jackson Phenomenon: The Crisis of Purpose in Afro-American Politics* (1986); Sam Roberts, *Who Are We? A Portrait of America Based on the Latest U.S. Census* (1994); Arthur Schlesinger, Jr., *The Disuniting of America* (1991); Peter Skerry, *Mexican-Americans: The Ambivalent Minority* (1993); Robert C. Smith, *Racism in the Post–Civil Rights Era: Now You See It, Now You Don't* (1995); The Staff of the Chicago Tribune, *The American Millstone: An Examination of the Nation's Permanent Underclass* (1986); Shih-Shan Henry Tsai, *The Chinese Experience in America* (1986); William Wei, *The Asian American Movement* (1993).

Credits

PHOTO CREDITS

Chapter 1 8: © The British Museum; 19: Museo de America, Madrid, Spain; 29: Bettmann.

Chapter 2 36: Courtesy of the A. H. Robins Company. Photo by Don Eiler's Custom Photography; 47: Colonial Williamsburg Foundation; 56: Arizona State Museum, University of Arizona.

Chapter 3 63 left: Centre Marguerite-Bourgeoys, Montreal; 63 right: Courtesy of the Archives Departmentales de la Gironde, Bordeaux, France; 74: Bettmann; 79: George Heriot, Calumet Dance, 1799. Art Gallery of Windsor; 81: Bettmann.

Chapter 4 99: Abby Aldrich Rockefeller Folk Art Center, Williamsburg, VA; 105: © The British Museum; 108: © The British Museum.

Chapter 5 129: Victoria and Albert Museum, London; 139: Engraving by Wm. Sharp, after Romney. Prints Division. The New York Public Library. Astor, Lenox and Tilden Foundations.

Chapter 6 144: Yale University Art Gallery, Trumbull Collection; 147: Library of Congress; 155: By permission of the Houghton Library, Harvard University.

Chapter 7 168: Print Collection Miriam & Ira D. Wallach Division of Arts, Prints and Photographs. The New York Public Library. Astor, Lenox and Tilden Foundations; 171: Bettmann; 178: The Metropolitan Museum of Art, Rogers Fun, 1942. (42.95.19); 182: Abby Aldrich Rockefeller Folk Art Center, Williamsburg, VA; 187: Gilbert Stuart, James Madison. Bowdoin College Museum of Art.

Chapter 8 194: Culver Pictures, Inc.; 200: Courtesy John and Lillian Harney; 202: John Trumbull, Alexander Hamilton. Oil on canvas. 30 1/4 x 24 inches. Yale University Art Gallery; 208: The New-York Historical Society; 213: Courtesy, Winterthur Museum, (detail).

Chapter 9 219: The New-York Historical Society; 227: Library of Congress. Illustration by A. Rider; 229; © The Field Museum, Neg# A93851c.

Chapter 10 252: Beinecke Rare Book and Manuscript Library, Yale University; 254: Missouri Historical Society (Neg. #CT SS831); 258: Bettmann; 260: Lowell Historical Society.

Chapter 11 277: The St. Louis Art Museum; 280: Collection of The New York Historical Society; 286: Collection of Jay P. Altmayer; 88: Boston Art Commission, Office of the Arts and Humanities; 293: Museum of the City of New York, The J. Clarence Davies Collection.

Chapter 12 299: The Stowe-Day Foundation, Hartford, CT; 306: Stock Montage; 310: Print Collection Miriam & Ira D. Wallach Division of Arts, Prints and Photographs. The New York Public Library. Astor, Lenox and Tilden Foundations; 316: from Adirondack Life Dec. 1997 p. 40; 317: Bettmann; 320: Courtesy of Rhoda Barney Jenkins.

Chapter 13 326 & 335: Historic New Orleans Collection; 337: Bequest of Henry Lee Shattuck, in memory of the late Ralph W. Gray. Courtesy, Museum of Fine Arts, Boston; 342: Chicago Historical Society,

ICHi-08428; 344: Print Collection Miriam & Ira D. Wallach Division of Arts, Prints and Photographs. The New York Public Library. Astor, Lenox and Tilden Foundations.

Chapter 14 356: Seaver Center for Western History Research, Los Angeles County Museum of Natural History; 369: The New-York Historical Society.

Chapter 15 390: Print Collection Miriam & Ira D. Wallach Division of Arts, Prints and Photographs. New York Public Library. Astor, Lenox and Tilden Foundations; 396 left: Bettmann; 396 right: Illinois State Historical Society.

Chapter 16 408: Chicago Historical Society, ICHi 09975; 418: Chicago Historical Society, ICHi 07774; 424: U.S. Army Military History Institute, Carlisle Barracks, PA; 432 left: Library of Congress; 432 right: The Valentine Museum of the Life and History of Richmond, Cook Collection.

Chapter 17 441: Library of Congress; 447: General Research Division. The New York Public Library. Astor, Lenox and Tilden Foundations; 456: Stock Montage; 458: Rutherford B. Hayes Presidential Center.

Chapter 18 488: Library of Congress; 491: Courtesy MetLife Archive; 495: Collection of Lee Baxandall.

Chapter 19 500: George Wesley Bellows, *Cliff Dwellers*. Los Angeles County Museum of Art, Los Angeles County Funds; 505: National Archives, photo courtesy Rudolph Vetter/Interpretive Photography; 509: Albert H. Wiggins Collection, by Courtesy of the Trustees of the Boston Public Library; 511: Photo reproduced courtesy Thomas W. Chinn. From *Bridging the Pacific: SF Chinatown and Its People* by Thomas W. Chinn. © 1989 Chinese Historical Society of America, San Francisco; 523: Drawing by Charles Dana Gibson.

Chapter 20 533: Billy Graham Center Museum.

Chapter 21 563: Courtesy of Cornell University Library, Ithaca, NY; 569:

Courtesy Dover Publications, NY; 582: Hawaii State Archives; 585: Chicago Historical Society; 587: Huntsville Public Library.

Chapter 22 595: Brown Brothers; 602: San Diego Historical Society, Ticor Collection, Photograph Collection; 613: Library of Congress; 617: The Bancroft Library, University of California, Berkeley.

Chapter 23 640: Trustees of the Imperial War Museum, London; 641: Culver; 644: National Archives, U.S. War Department.

Chapter 24 659: Bettmann; 669 & 674: Bettmann; 678: Paul Cadmus, *To the Lynching!* 1935. Pencil and watercolor on paper. 20 1/2 x 15 1/4 inches. Collection of Whitney Museum of American Art. Purchase 36.32.

Chapter 25 688: Library of Congress; 689: Library of Congress; 695: Brown Brothers; 701: Library of Congress; 708: The Butler Institute of American Art, Youngstown, OH.

Chapter 26 713: Franklin D. Roosevelt Library; 715: UPI/ Bettmann; 723: UPI/ Bettmann; 728: John Langly Howard (b. 1902), California Industrial Scenes, Coit Tower, S.F., PWAP, 1934. Don Beatty © 1983; 731: U.T. The Institute of Texan Cultures, The San Antonio Light Collection.

Chapter 27 746: UPI/ Bettmann; 753: James W. Davidson. Private collection; 761: Library of Congress; 765; Eliot Elisofon, Life Magazine © Time Warner Inc.; 774: National Archives, U.S. Army Signal Corps.

Chapter 28 784: Time map by R.M. Chapin, Jr.; 797: Bettmann; 800: Eve Arnold/ Magnum.

Chapter 29 813: Courtesy Cadillac Motor Cars; 816: © The Curtis Publishing Company; 818: AP/Wide World; 826: AP/Wide World; 832: Burt Glinn/ Magnum.

Chapter 30 841(left): UPI/ Corbis/ Bettmann; 841(right): Photofest; 852: UPI/ Corbis/ Bettmann; 857: Richard Pipes; 862: Leonard Freed/ Magnum.

Chapter 31 868: John Filo © 1970, Valley News Dispatch, Tarentum, PA ; 875: Tim Page; 876: Drawing by David Levine. Reprinted with permission from The New York Review of Books. Copyright © 1965 Nyrev, Inc.; 886: UPI/ Bettmann; 889: UPI/ Bettmann.

Chapter 32 904: MS Magazine; 913: Courtesy Gerald R. Ford Library; 915:

Courtesy Jimmy Carter Library; 920: Wally McNamee/Woodfin Camp and Associates.

Chapter 33 927: UPI/ Bettmann; 930: Bettmann; 938: Lana Harris/AP/Wide World; 941: Rick Wilking/Reuters/ Bettmann; 947: Gary Hershorn/Reuters/ Bettmann.

EYEWITNESS CREDITS

Chapter 1 A Spanish Conquistador Visits the Aztec Marketplace in Tenochtitlan. From Bermal Diaz, THE COMPANY OF NEW SPAIN, translated by J.M. Cohen (New York: Penguin Classics, 1963), pp 232–233. Copyright © J.M. Cohen 1963.

Chapter 2 A Virginia Settler Describes the Indian War of 1622 to Officials in England. Edward Waterhouse, A DECLARATION OF THE STATE OF THE COLONIE AND AFFAIRES IN VIRGINIA (1622). Susan Myra Kingsbury, ed. THE RECORDS OF THE VIRGINIA COMPANY OF LONDON, (Washington, DC 1906–1935)III, pp 459–556.

Chapter 3 A Puritan New Englander wrestles with Her Faith. John Harvard Ellis, (ed.) THE WORKS OF ANNE BRADSTREET IN PROSE AND VERSE (Charlestown, MA: A.E. Cutter, 1867) pp 3–10.

Chapter 4 Benjamin Franklin Attends the Preaching of George Whitefield. Reprinted with the permission of Pocket Books, a division of Simon & Schuster from THE AUTOBIOGRAPHY OF BENJAMIN FRANKLIN. Copyright © 1965 by Washington Square Press. Copyrights © renewed 1993 by Ralph Ketcham.

Chapter 5 Thomas Hutchinson Recounts the Destruction of His Boston Home during the Stamp Act Riots. Thomas Hutchinson to Richard Jackson, August 30, 1765, Massachusetts Archives, IIVI, pp 146–147.

Chapter 6 A North Carolina Solider Witnesses the Partisan War in the Southern Backcountry. Moses Hall in John C. Dann, ed. THE REVOLUTION REMEMBERED: EYEWITNESS ACCOUNTS OF THE WAR FOR INDEPENDENCE (Chicago: University of Chicago Press, 1980), pp 202–203.

Chapter 7 A Traveler from Virginia Considers the Ruins of an Ancient Indian Civilization in the Ohio Valley. 18 November 1795, Journal of the Reverend James Smith. Richard H. Collins Papers. Durrett Collections, University of Chicago.

Chapter 8 A Farmer Becomes Involved in the World of Commerce. A Farmer THE PITTSBURGH GAZETTE, November 18, 1786.

Chapter 9 Issac Clark is Impressed by the British Navy. Clement Cleveland Sawtell, "Impressment of American Seamen by the British," ESSEX INSTITUTE HISTORICAL COLLECTIONS v. 76 (October 1940), pp 318–318. Courtesy of the Peabody Essex Museum, Salem Massachusetts.

Chapter 10 The Mere Love of Moving. Basil Hall, TRAVELS IN THE UNITED STATES (Edinburgh: 3 vols. Cadell and Co., 1829), v. 3, pp 129–132.

Chapter 11 Andrew Jackson's Tumultuous Inauguration. Margaret Bayard Smith, THE FIRST FORTY YEARS OF WASHING-

Index

Note: Page numbers in *italics* indicate illustrations and their captions; page numbers followed by *M* indicate maps and their captions.

AAA (Agricultural Adjustment Administration), 721, 735
Abenaki tribe, 76, 77
Abernathy, Ralph, 897
ABMs (antiballistic missiles), 887
Abolitionism, 315–321
  beginnings of, 315–316, *316*
  effect on political parties, 322–323
  opponents and conflicts, 318–319
  party system and, 322–323
  schism of 1840, 320–321
  spread of, *317*, 317–318
  women's rights movement and, 319–320, *320*
Abortion, 516, 904–905, *927*
Acadians, 117
Acheson, Dean, 801, 804, 879
Acquired Immune Deficiency Syndrome (AIDS), 944, 946
Act of Supremacy (1534), 25
Adams, Charles Francis, Jr., 431, 568
Adams, John, 144, *144*, 148, 163, 166, 187
  on British abuses, 143
  death of, 240–241
  elected first vice president, 199
  election of 1796, 208, 210
  election of 1800, 212–213, *213*
  presidency of, 210–216
    Federalist legacy, 215–216
    political violence and, 213–215
    Quasi-War with France, 211
    suppression of disloyalty, 211–212
Adams, John Quincy, 246, 274
  on Great Britain, 235
  on impressment, 232
  presidency of, 278
  as secretary of state, 239
Adams, Louisa, 344
Adams, Samuel, 130, 131, 132, 135, 187
Adams, Samuel Hopkins, 615
Adams-Onís Treaty (1819), 239
Addams, Jane, 510, 603–604, 607, 609, 637, 695
Admiralty courts, 124, 130
Advertising, 665–666
Afghanistan, 781, 920, 940
AFL (American Federation of Labor), 493–494, 644, 676, 732
AFL-CIO, 910
Africa, 3, 8, *8*, 45, 98–99
African Americans
  in Alliance Movement, 565–566
  antiblack riots in free states, 285
  black writers of 1920s, 674–675
  in changing South, 828–829
  civil rights and (*See* Civil rights)
  after Civil War, 441–442, 445
  in Communist party, 708
  community response to racism, 285–286, *286*
  declining cities and, 813
  in Democratic party, 739
  education and, 518
  effects of *Plessy v. Ferguson* (1896), 534
  employment of, 476
    as cowboys, 547
    discriminatory labor practices, 792
    in industrial work, 490–491
    in labor unions, 493, 494
    in timber industry, 530

    unemployment, 838–839
    war workers, 762, 765–766
  in Federal Theater Project, 734
  free blacks, 161–162
    communities of, 179
    families, 454
    freedmen of Civil War, 420–421
    in Jacksonian Era, 276, 278
    literacy of, 347
    in North, 284–285
  Great Depression and, 703–704
  great migrations of, 645, 673–674
  Jim Crow laws and, 573–575
  for Jimmy Carter, 914
  job opportunities in South, 829
  New Deal and, 727–729, *728*
  in 1920s, 673–675, *674*
  numbers in 1790, 195
  in professional baseball, 522
  racism and
    minstrel shows, 286–287
    self-help societies, 285–286, *286*
  Reconstruction and, 453–458
    education and religion, 454–455
    effects on families, 454
    experience of freedom, 453–454
    Freedmen's Bureau, 446, 454–455, 456–457
    issue of black rights, 446
    limited economic independence, 449
    officeholding, 451, *451*
    planters and, 457–458
    working conditions, 455–456, *456*
  religious life, *178*, 227, 303–304, 455
  repression after Nat Turner's rebellion, 348
  revivalism and, 227
  segregation laws, 607
  settlement of Kansas, 525–526, 535
  slavery (*See* Slavery; Slave trade)
  as soldiers, 756
    in Civil War, *421*, 421–422
    lack of support for Vietnam War, 875–876
    in Revolutionary War, *147*
    in Spanish-American War, *587*, 587–588
    in World War I, *641*, 641–642
  in South, 347–348
  support of abolitionism, 318
  tenancy and sharecropping, 527–529, *528M*
  See also Segregation; Slavery
African Methodist Episcopal (AME) Church, 303–304
Afrika Korps, 752
Age of the Common Man, 276
Agnew, Spiro, 893, 908
Agrarianism, 219
Agrarian unrest, 186–187
Agricultural Adjustment Act (1933; 1936), 720–721
Agricultural Adjustment Administration (AAA), 721, 735
Agriculture
  agricultural economy of South, 327
  British *vs.* American, 106–107
  colonial
    in Carolinas, 51, 54
    in Chesapeake region, 41*M*
    native crops, 114
    rice, 51, 54

Agriculture *(Cont.)*:
  encomienda system, 22
  farming in West, 367
  improvements in equipment, 550
  Jefferson's views of, 209–210, 219
  market economy and, 248, 250
  in Native American societies, 13
  under New Deal, 720–721
  Populism and (*See* Populism)
  prehistoric, 11
  scientific farming methods, 248
  in South
    failure of reform, 400
    "New South," 527, 531
    sugar, 581
  in World War I, 643
  See also Cotton; Tenancy and sharecropping
Aguinaldo, Emilio, 588, 590
AIDS (Acquired Immune Deficiency Syndrome), 944, 946
AIM (American Indian Movement), 891
Air pollution, 859
Air traffic controllers' strike, 931
Air war in World War I, 639
Alamance, Battle of (1771), 94
Alamo, Battle of (1836), 358
Alaska, purchase of (1867), 580
Alaskan pipeline, 901
Albany Congress, 88–90, 106, 112, 113, 136
Albany Plan of Union (1754), 88–90, 115
Alcatraz Island, 891
Alcoa Aluminum, 681
Alcohol
  effect on Indians, 228, 540
  Prohibition, 321–322, 659, 676–677, 684–685
  in rural life, 532
  See also Temperance movement
Alcott, Bronson, 307
Aldrin, Buzz, 897
Algonquin, sinking of, 638
Algonquin tribe, 62
Ali, Muhammad, 876, 885
Alien Act (1798), 211, 212
Alienation, of 1920s, 673
All-American Canal, 727
Allen, Ethan, 94, 171
Allen, Frederick Lewis, 659, 668, 671, 682
Allen, Gracie, 699
Allende, Salvador, 910
Alliance Exchanges, 565
Alliance for Progress (1961), 841
Alliance Movement, 565–567
Allied Powers (WWII), 753–754
Allies (World War I), 633–634, 634*M*
All in the Family, 928
Altgeld, John, 555
Amadas, Philip, 30
Amendments to Constitution. *See* Constitution; *specific amendments*
American and Foreign Anti-Slavery Society, 320
American Anti-Slavery Society, 317, 318, 320
American Birth Control League, 668
American Broadcasting Company, 806
American Civil Liberties Union, 679
American Expeditionary Force, 647
American Federation of Labor (AFL), 493–494, 644, 676, 732
"American Frankenstein, The," *563*
American Friends Service Committee, 694
American Fur Company, 263–264
American Independent Party, 881
American Indian Movement (AIM), 891
American League (baseball), 522
American Liberty League (1934), 722
American party (Know-Nothings), 390–391, 393
"American Plan," 664
American Psychiatric Association, 892
American Railway Union (ARU), 496

American Red Cross, 756
American Revolution
  beginning of, 135–140
    collapse of royal authority, 137
    Common Sense and, 138–140, *139*
  causes of, 115, 116–117
  chronology of, 140, 165
  decision for independence and, 143–146
    Declaration of Independence, *144*, 144–145
    loyalists (tories), 145–146
    Second Continental Congress, 143–144
  end of, 163–165
    significance of revolution and, 164–165
    surrender at Yorktown, 163–164
  fighting in North, 146–152
    Burgoyne's surrender, 152
    capture of Philadelphia, 151–152
    in New York and New Jersey, 150–151, 150*M*
    opposing armies, *147*, 147–149
    strategies of, 149–150
  fighting in South, 157–162
    African Americans and, 161–162
    under Nathaniel Greene, 159–161, 160*M*
    partisan struggle, 158, 159
    siege of Charleston, 157
  First Continental Congress, 135–137
  imperial crisis and, 121–134
    beginning of resistance, 124–126
    Boston massacre, 131–132
    Boston tea party, 132–133
    Coercive Acts, 133–134
    frontier conflicts, 121, 122*M*
    Grenville's measures, 121–124
    organized resistance, 130–131
    repeal of Stamp Act, 128–129
    riots and resolves, 126–128
    Townshend Acts, *129*, 129–130
  postwar period (*See* Confederation)
  Seven Years' War and (*See* Seven Years' War)
  turning point in, 153–157
    alliance with France, 153
    end of war in North, 154–155
    northern homefront, 156–157
    war in West, 156
  views of radicalism during, 184–185
"American Scholar, The" (Emerson), 308
American Sugar Refining Company, 614
American Telephone and Telegraph Company, 474
American Temperance Society (1826), 313
American Tobacco Company, 529, 615
American Union Against Militarism, 637
Ames, Adelbert, 461
Amiens, Battle of (1918), 647, 648*M*
Amnesty Act (1872), 459
"Amos 'n' Andy," 671
Amusement parks, 522
Ancient civilizations, remnants of, 175
Anderson, Marian, 727
Anderson, Mary, 453
Anderson, Robert, 402–404
Andros, Sir Edmund, 84, 85
Angelino, Joseph T., 709–710
Angel Island, 502
Angelus Temple, 658
Anglican Church. *See* Church of England
Anthony, Susan B., 320, 458, 605
Anthracite coal strike (1902), 614
Antiballistic missiles (ABMs), 887
Antiblack riots, 285
Anti-Comintern Pact (1937), 746–747
Antietam, Battle of (1862), 416, 417*M*, 430
Anti-Federalists, 190–191, 192
Anti-imperialists, 589–590
Antinuclear peace movement, 934
Antisaloon campaign, 608

Anti-Saloon League (1893), 558, 608
Anti-Semitism, 502, 775
Antislavery societies, 178
Antitrust cases, 615
Antiwar movement, 879, 884
Antrobus, John, *326*
Apache tribe, 536, 544
Apollo 11, 897, 898
Appalachian frontier, 122*M*
Appeal to the Colored Citizens of the World (Walker), 318
Appeasement, 747, 784
Applied Christianity (Gladden), 509
Appomattox Courthouse, 432*M*, 434*M*, 436
Apprenticeship, 95, 96, 245, 256, 260–261
A&P supermarkets, 521
Arab alliance of 1950s, 824
Arapaho tribe, 353
Arawak tribe, 9
Architecture, urban, 504–505, *505*
Arikara tribe, 355
Aristide, Jean-Bertrand, 946
Aristocracy, 183–184, 196–197, 352
"Aristocracy of merit," 181
Arizona, statehood (1912), 552
Armed Forces Qualification Test, 874
Armour and Company, 481
Arms race, 684, 780, 845–846
Armstrong, Neil, 897
Army of the Potomac. *See* Union; *specific commanders and battles*
Army War College, 627
Arnold, Benedict, 152, 163
Art, New Deal and, 733–734
Arthur, Chester A., 560
Articles of Confederation, 169, 172–173, 187
Artisans, 95, 181, 256
Artisan system, 95, 96, 245, 256, 260–261
ARU (American Railway Union), 496
"Ashcan school" of painting, *500*, 600
Asia
    brinksmanship in, 822–823
    expansionism in, 591–592
    reform in, 656
    See also specific countries
Asian immigrants, 951–953, 952*M*
Aspira, 890
Assassinations, 559, 612, 633, 853–854, 880
Assembly line, 663
Assimilation, 224–225, 514
Associationalism, 682, 706
Astaire, Fred, 700
Astor, John Jacob, 263–264, 266
Aswan Dam, 824
Asylum movement, 314–315
Atatürk, Kemal, 656
Atlanta (Georgia), 433, 434*M*
Atlantic Charter (1941), 749
Atlanta *Constitution*, 526
Atomic bomb
    capabilities, 789–790, 796
    deterrence, 790–791
    first tests, 776
    use in World War II, 776
    See also Hydrogen bomb; Nuclear weapons
Atomic Energy Commission (AEC), 790
Atomic research in World War II, 759
Attlee, Clement, 789, 802
Attorney General, 199
Austin, Ann, 73
Austin, Stephen, 358
Australian (secret) ballot, 507
Austria-Hungary, 633
Autobiography of Benjamin Franklin, The (Franklin), 104, 108
Auto industry, 690
    conversion to tank production, 758
    in 1920s, 662–663

Automobile
    "big three" manufacturers, 809–810
    importance in suburban era, 812–814, *813*
    safety of, 898–899
    social significance of, 663
Autry, Gene, 835
Axis Powers (WWII), 753
Aztec civilization, 3, 14, 15–16, 18, 19, 21, 23

Babbit (Lewis), 673
Baby boom, 816
Baby-boom generation in Vietnam War, 873
Bacon, Nathaniel, 44, 47
Bacon's Rebellion (1676), 43–44, 45, 47
Baker, George ("Father Divine"), 703
Baker, Newton, 641
Baker v. Carr, 848
Bakker, Jim, 926
Bakke v. Regents of the University of California (1978), 943
Balanced budget amendment, 945
Balance of power, 807
Balboa, Vasco Nuñez de, 18
Ballinger, Richard, 618
Ballinger-Pinchot controversy, 618
Baltic republics, 940
Baltimore and Ohio Railroad, 495
"Bank holiday," 717
Banking Act of 1935, 725
Bank of the United States
    Bank War (*See* Bank War)
    first charter (1791), 202
    second charter (1816), 246, 250
    speculators and, 203
Banks, Dennis, 891
Banks and banking
    Bank of England, 106, 203
    Bank War, 289–292
    defects of banking system in 1920s, 691
    economic boom and, 281
    goals of New Deal, 715, 717
    national banking system, 425
    Panic of 1893, 555
    See also Bank of the United States
Bank War, 289–292, 294
    Biddle's policies, 290
    destruction of Second Bank, 291
    impact on presidency, 291–292
    Panic of 1819 and, 290
Baptism by immersion, *533*, 660
Baptist church, 105, 316, 351, 455, 677, 679
Bara, Theda, 670
Barbados, 50, 51, 52*M*
Barkley, Alben, *774*
Barlowe, Arthur, 30
Barnett, Ross, 851
Barrios, 544, 644
Barron's, 657
Barter economy, 197, 199
Barton, Clara, 426
Baruch, Bernard, 790
Baseball, 522, 672
Basketball, 522
Basye, Betty, 782–783
Bataan, fall of, 752–753
Batista, Fulgencio, 825
Battle of Britain, 759
Battle of the Bulge (1944), 769
Bayard, Margaret, 217
Bay of Pigs invasion (1961), 842
Beach Boys, 864
Bear Flag Revolt, 366
Beat generation, 835–836, 862–863
Beatles, 861, 863
Beauregard, Pierre, 408
Beautification movement (urban), 517

Becky Sharp (film), 699
Beecher, Catharine, *299*, 305, 313
Beecher, Edward, 318
Beecher, Henry Ward, 569
Beecher, Isabella, *299*, 320
Beecher, Lyman, 298–300, *299*, 301, 315, 318–319, 320
Begin, Menachem, 919, *920*
Behavioral psychology, 665
Behaviorism, 598
Belafonte, Margaretta, 850
Bell, Alexander Graham, 473–474
Bell, John, 401
Bellamy, Edward, 485
Belleau Wood, Battle of (1918), 647, 648*M*
Bellows, George, *500*, *509*, 600
Benny, Jack, 699
Benson, Ezra Taft, 819
Berkeley, Busby, 700
Berkeley, William, 43–44, 49, 80
Berkeley campus (U. of California), 861–862, 864
Berlin, controversy over, 826
Berlin airlift, 789
Berlin Wall, 843, 940
Bernstein, Carl, 906
Berry, Chuck, 864
Bessemer process, 481–482
Bethlehem Steel Corporation, 664, 689
Bethune, Mary McLeod, 728
Bethune-Cookman College, 728
Beveridge, Albert, 592
Bicameral legislatures, 71, 109, 168–169
Bickerdyke, Mary Ann, 426
Bicycling, 521–522
Biddle, Nicholas, 290, 291
Big business. *See* Business; Corporations; Industrialization
Bill of Rights, 200–201
Bird, Thomas, 867
Birmingham (Alabama), 530
Birney, James G., 316, 323, 349–350, 363
Birth control, 602, 604, 668, *669*, 847
Birth Control Review, 669
Birthrate. *See* Fertility rates
Black, Timuel, 782, 783
"Black and tan" strategy, 613
"Black blizzards," 700–701, *701*
"Black codes," 445
Black Death (A.D. 1347–1351), 16–17
Black Hawk (Sauk and Fox chief), 284
Black Hills (S. Dakota), 537, 541
Black Hoof (Shawnee chief), 224–225, 228
Black Kettle (Cheyenne chief), 539–540
Blacklists, 496, 799
Blackmun, Harry, 893, 904
Black Muslims, 703, 854
Black Panther party, 855
Black power, 854–855, 885
Black Star Line fraud, 674
Blackwell, Elizabeth, 426
Blackwell, Emily, 426
Blaine, James G., 560–561, 580–581
Bland-Allison Act (1878), 560
Bleecker, Ann Eliza, 156
"Bleeding Kansas," 391
Blitzkrieg, 747
Blue Flame, The, 670
Board of Customs Commissioners, 130
Board of Trade (England), 121
Board of Trade and Plantations (1696), 86, 110
Boer War, 583
Boland, Edward, 936
Boland Amendment, 936, 937
Boleyn, Anne, 25
Bolsheviks (Russia), 640, 647, 649–650
Bombings, 652, 653, *653*
"Bonanza farms," 550
Bonaparte, Napoleon, 222–223, 232, 236

Bonnin, Gertrude Simmons (Zitkala-Sa), 543
Bonsack, James, 529
Bonus Army, 709–710
Bonus Bill, 246
"Boodle," 499
Book of Mormon, 311
Boom and bust cycle. *See* Economy
Boone, Daniel, 122*M*
Booth, John Wilkes, 438, 443
Bootleggers, 677
Border states, 412–413
Bork, Robert, 943
Born on the Fourth of July (Kovic), 882
Bosnia-Herzegovina, 946
Boston Associates, 257, 259
Boston Massacre (1770), 131–132
Boston Port Bill (1774), 133
Boston Tea Party, 132–133
Boucher, Jonathan, 146
Boulder Dam, 727
Boundary disputes among settlers, 94
Bourgeoys, Marguerite, *63*
Boxer Rebellion, 591–592
Boxing, 672
Bracero program, 766
Braddock, Edward, 117
Bradford, William, 66
Bradley, Omar, 804
Bradley, Tom, 741
Bradstreet, Anne, 70
"Brain Trust," 715, 717
Brandeis, Louis D., 598, 623
Brando, Marlon, 834
Brant, Joseph (Thayendanegea), 156
Braun, Carol Moseley, 945
Bread lines, *569*, 693, 694
Breckinridge, John C., 401
Breed's Hill, 141–142
Brennan, William, 943
Bretton Woods Conference (1944), 775
Brezhnev, Leonid, 887, 912, 918, 920
Bridger, Jim, 263
Bridges, 504
Briefe and True Reporte of the New Found Land of Virginia, A (Hariot), 30
Brinksmanship, 821–823
Broadsides, 195
Bronson House, 510
Brooklyn Bridge, 504
Brooks, Preston S., 392, *392*, 393
Brotherhood of Sleeping Car Porters, 765–766
Brown, John, 381, 400–401, 525
Brown, Owen, 381
Brown, Salmon, 381
Brown, William Wells, 318
"Brown Berets," 891
Brownson, Orestes, 307
Brownsville incident (1906), 613–614
Brown v. Board of Education of Topeka (1950), 830, 839, 892
Bryan, William Jennings, 571–572, 590, 618, 622, 636, 680
Bryn Mawr College (1885), 520
Brzezinski, Zbigniew, 916, 918
Buchanan, James
    election of 1856, 393, 395
    presidency of, 395–400, 561
        Dred Scott decision, 395–396, 399
        Lecompton constitution (1857), 397, 399
        Panic of 1857, 396–397
Buck, Pearl, 698
Buckley, William F., 927
Buffalo, slaughter of, 540
Buffalo Bob, 815
"Bull Moose" (Progressive) party, 596, 620
Bull Run
    First Battle of (1861), 408–409, 408*n*, 413
    Second Battle of (1862), 416, 417*M*

Bundy, McGeorge, 871
Bunker Hill, Battle of (1775), 141–142
Bureaucracy, 559, 642–643, 664
Bureau of Corporations, 615
Bureau of Indian Affairs, 891
Bureau of the Budget (1921), 681
Burger, Warren, 893
Burgoyne, John, 152
Burnham, Daniel, 504
Burns, George, 699
Burnside, Ambrose, 416
Burr, Aaron, 212–213, 213
Bush, George Herbert Walker, 926, 946
    election of 1988 and, 939
    election of 1992 and, 945
    presidency of, 939–945
        crises, 944
        domestic issues, 942
        foreign policy, 940–941, 941
        Gulf War, 941–942
        Supreme Court and, 942–943
Business
    conglomerate mergers, 820–821
    Kennedy's economic policy, 846
    multinational corporations, 910
    in New Era, 663–664
    See also Corporations; Industrialization
"Businessman's government," 683
Business regulation, 614
Butler, John, 156
Butler v. United States (1936), 721
Byrnes, James F., 758, 776

Cabot, John, 5–6, 7
Caddell, Patrick, 929
Cadillac automobiles, 813
Cadmus, Paul, 678
Caesar, Sid, 817
Caldwell, Charles, 458
Caldwell, Erskine, 734
Calhoun, John C., 36, 246, 274, 373, 438
    compromise tariff (1833), 289
    defense of slavery, 348–349, 350
    theory of nullification, 288, 288–289
California
    acquisition of Upper California (1848), 366–367
    Bear Flag Revolt, 366
    building of San Francisco, 370, 370–371
    Chinese emigration to, 369–370
    Gold Rush (1849), 545, 546
    Hispanic-Anglo conflict, 373
    redevelopment of San Diego, 923–924
    Spanish settlement of, 355, 355
    statehood (1849), 375, 375M
    See also San Francisco
California Industrial Scenes (Howard), 728
Calliope, 523
"Call money," 689
Calvert family, 40–42, 44, 59
Calvin, John, 24–25, 63, 65, 72
Calvinism, 64–65, 103
Cambodia, 868, 884
Cameras, 472–473
Campbell, John, 117
Camp followers, 148–149
Camp meetings, 226–228, 227, 336, 533
Canada, 62, 235
Canals, 247, 249M, 260
Cane Ridge Revival, 226–228, 227, 309, 310
Caning of Charles Sumner, 391–392, 392, 393
Canning, George, 239
Cannon, Joseph, 618
Canterbury, Robert, 868–869
Capital. See Investment capital
Capital, location of, 202, 218
Capitalism, 623–624, 664–665

Capone, Al "Scarface," 677
Cardozo, Benjamin, 720
Caribbean islands
    American intervention in, 631M
    Anglo-French conflict over, 89
    colonization of, 18, 19, 35
    link to Carolinas, 48–55
    slave trade in, 45
    Spain's lost colonies, 49–50
Carleton, Sir Guy, 149, 152
Carmichael, Stokely, 855
Carnegie, Andrew, 483, 492, 588
    philanthropy of, 470, 484, 574, 637
    steel industry, 481–482, 567
Carnegie Furnaces (Braddock, Pa.), 488–489
Carpentier, Georges, 672
Carpetbaggers, 452
Carranza, Venustiano, 632
Carson, Pirie, and Scott department store, 505
Carson, Rachel, 861, 900
Carter, James Earl "Jimmy," 934
    election of 1976, 914
    presidency of, 915–921
        difficulties of, 920–921
        economy, 917
        foreign policy, 917–918
        Middle East and, 919–920, 920
        saving détente, 918–919
        search for direction, 915, 915–916
    religion of, 925
Carter, Rosalynn, 915, 915
Carter Doctrine, 920
Carteret, Sir George, 80
Cartier, Jacques, 61–62
Cartwright, Peter, 309
Carver, George Washington, 527
Cash-and-carry policy, 745–746
Cass, Lewis, 374, 375
Cassady, Neal, 836
Casualties
    of Civil War
        battlefield deaths, 430–431, 438
        wounds and disease, 426–427, 427, 429
    of Mexican War, 366
    of Vietnam War, 895
    of World War II, 782–783
Catawba tribe, 51
Cathay Boys Club Band, 511
Catherine of Aragon, 25
Catherine the Great, 115
Catron, Thomas, 544
Catt, Carrie Chapman, 605
Cattle industry, 547–549, 548M
Caughnawaga tribe, 63
Cayuga tribe, 80
CCC (Civilian Conservation Corps), 718, 729, 768
Celibacy, 310
Censorship, 322, 700, 847
Center for the Study of Responsive Law (1969), 899
Central Intelligence Agency (CIA), 825, 842, 913
Central Pacific Railroad, 546
Central Park (New York City), 517
Central Powers (World War I), 634, 634M
Chadwick, Edwin, 466
Chain stores, 521, 663
Chamberlain, Neville, 747, 784
Chamber of Commerce, 664
Chambers, Whittaker, 797
Champlain, Samuel de, 62
Chancellorsville, Battle of (1863), 431, 432M
Charles, Ray, 864
Charles I, king of England, 42, 50, 59, 66
Charles II, king of England, 42, 43, 69, 78, 84
Charleston, South Carolina, 50, 157, 402–404
Charter of Liberties, 78
Charter of Privileges (1701), 83

Château-Thierry, Battle of (1918), 647, 648*M*
Chavez, Cesar, 702, 861, *889*, 890
Chavez, Dennis, 729
Cherokee Phoenix, The, 282
Cherokee tribe, 13, 118, 196, 281, 282, 283*M*, 284
Chesapeake (U.S. warship), 232
Chesapeake Bay region, 31, 32, 64
  changing economic conditions, 177
  English settlement of, 35–42, 41*M*, 92*M*
    changes in English policy, 42
    founding of Maryland, 40–42
    growth of settlements, 40, 41*M*
    Indian War of 1622 and, 39
    mercantilism and, 35–36
    reforms and tobacco boom, 37–38, 40
    Virginia Company of London, 36–37
  inequality of white society in, 44–45
  society in crisis, 43–48
    changing society, 46–47
    conditions of unrest, 43
    new gentry, 47–48
    rebellions, 43–45
    role of slavery, 45–46
Chesnut, Mary, 433
Chevalier, Michel, 253
Cheyenne tribe, 355, 536, 537, 539
  battle of Little Big Horn, 541
  Sand Creek massacre, 539–540, 539*M*
Chiang Kai-shek, 657, 796–797, 823
Chicago (Illinois), 501, 504, 510
  corrupt government, 609
  Democratic convention of 1968, 880–881
  World's Columbian Exposition, 568
  World's Fair (1933), 698–699
Chicago *Defender,* 645
Chicago school, of architecture, 505
Chicago *Tribune,* 426, 795
Chicago Vice Commission (1910), 608
Chicanos, 890
Chickasaw tribe, 172, 196, 281, 282, 283*M*
Chief Joseph (Nez Percé), 542
Child labor, 603–604
Children, 490, 698
Children's Bureau, 611–612
Chile, 910
China
  Communist takeover, 796–797
  formal recognition of (1979), 918
  invasion of Korea, 802, 803*M*
  Japanese control of, 750
  Nixon's trip to, *886*, 886–887
  "open door" policy, 591
  U.S. commitment to, 742
Chinatown (San Francisco), 511, *511*
Chinese Exclusion Act (1882), 508–509
Chinese immigrants
  emigration to California, 369–370
  family life of, 513
  gender ratio among, 512–514
  racial discrimination and, 369, 371
  racial prejudice against, 511, *511*
  urban ghettoes of, 511, *511*
Chinn, Thomas, 757
Chippewa tribe, 177
Chivington, John, 539–540
Choctaw tribe, 118, 172, 196, 281, 282, 283*M*
Cholera, 259, 328, 506, 540
Christian Broadcasting Network, 925–926
Chrysler Corporation, 809
Chuco dialect, 512
Churches in immigrant life, 512
Churchill, Winston, 749, 751–752, 823
  balance of power and, 771–772
  Iron Curtain speech, 786
  leadership capabilities, 754
  Potsdam Conference (1945), 775

Church of England, 53, 71
  Act of Supremacy, 25
  conflicts with Puritans, 65, 66
  disestablishment of, 184
Church of Jesus Christ of Latter-Day Saints (Mormons),
    311–312, 371, 372
CIA (Central Intelligence Agency), 825, 842, 913
Cigar Makers' Union, 494
Cincinnati (Ohio), 254
CIO (Congress of Industrial Organizations), 732–733
Cities
  bankruptcies of, 705
  political reform in, 609–610
  progressivism and (*See* Progressive era)
  relief during Great Depression, 704–705
Cities and urbanization (late 19th century),
    498–524
  chronology of, 524
  city life, 510–517
    challenges to convention, 516–517
    immigrants and, 510–514, *511*
    middle class and, 514–515
    Victorianism, 515–516
  culture (*See* Culture)
  effect of railroads on, 546
  new urban age, 499–506
    architecture, 504–505, *505*
    global migration and, 501–502, *502*
    patterns of settlement, 503
    slums and tenements, 505–506
    transportation and, 503–504
    urban explosion, *500*, 500–501
  politics and reform, 506–510
    boss rule, 507
    "business" of democracy, 508
    settlement houses, 510
    social activism and, 508–509, *509*
  in West, 551–552
Citizenship, 447
Citizens' League for Fair Play (1933), 728–729
City charters, 610
City manager plan, 610
Civic virtue, 191
Civil defense, in cold war, 827
Civil disobedience, 136, 852
Civilian Conservation Corps (CCC), 718, 729, 768
Civil law, 71
Civil liberties, suspension of, 427–428
Civil liberties, Warren court and, 847
Civil rights
  under black codes, 445
  for blacks after Civil War, 446
  crusade for, 848–856
    assassination of King, 853–854
    black power and, 854–855
    Freedom Summer, 848–849, 861, 902
    height of crusade, 849–853, *852*
    historical analysis of, 860
    race riots and, 855–856
  denied to northern blacks, 285
  Johnson's veto of bill, 446
  for Mexican Americans, 729
  New South and, 828–833
    African Americans and, 828–829
    Brown v. Board of Education, 830, 839, 892
    integration in Little Rock, 832–833
    NAACP and, 829–830
    new strategy, 830–831
    Supreme Court rulings, 534, 767–768, 830, 831
    Warren court and, 846–847, *847*
Civil Rights Act (1866), 534
Civil Rights Act (1875), 460
Civil Rights Act (1964), 854, 902
Civil rights movement
  backlash against, 850–851
  black veterans and, 792

nonviolence in, 831
after World War II, 792–793
Civil Service Act (1883), 559
Civil War, 408–440, 950–951
aftermath of
"black codes," 445
divisive issues, 558
pardons, 441, 442
suffrage, 443, 444, 452
See also Reconstruction
chronology of, 440
conduct of, 431–438, 432M
election of 1864 and, 433–435, 434M
end of fighting, 435, 435–436, 438
Grant as commander, 431, 433
Confederacy (See Confederate States of America)
demands of total war, 409–413, 410
border states, 412–413
political leadership, 409–413, 410, 411
emancipation of slaves, 418–422
black soldiers, 421, 421–422
conditions for freedmen, 420–421
conflicting views of, 419–420
Emancipation Proclamation (1863), 419
logic of, 418–419
impact of, 438–439
naval engagements (See Naval war)
opening moves, 413–417
Confederate blockade, 412, 413–414, 422
eastern stalemate, 416, 417M
western theater, 414, 415M, 416
postwar period (See Reconstruction)
road to war, 400–406
attack on Fort Sumter, 402–403, 404
divided nation, 404–406
outbreak of war, 402–404
secession, 401–402, 403M
sectional election, 401
soldier's life in, 428–431
black soldiers, 421, 421–422
camp life, 428–429
Southern individualism and, 429–430
technology and battle, 430–431
Union (See Union)
western theater
opening moves, 414, 415M, 416
war of mobility (1863–1865), 434M
Civil Works Administration (CWA), 718
Clark, George Rogers, 156
Clark, Isaac, 233
Clark, Mollie, 305
Clark, William, 1, 2, 223–224, 224M
Clarke, Edward, 520
Clawson, Augusta, 763
Clay, Henry, 238, 246, 278, 363, 398
American System of, 292
compromise tariff (1833), 289
election of 1824 and, 274, 275
election of 1832 and, 291
Missouri Compromise, 269–270
Clay, Lucius, 789
Clayton Antitrust Act (1914), 622
Clayton-Bulwer Treaty (1850), 580
Clean Water Act, 948
Cleaver, Eldridge, 855
Clemenceau, Georges, 647, 649
Clermont (steamboat), 248
Cleveland, Grover, 588
election of 1884, 560–561
election of 1892, 567
presidency of, 496, 554, 561, 568–569, 582–583
Cliff Dwellers (Bellows), 500
Clifford, Clark, 879
Climate, 114
Clinton, Hillary Rodham, 946
Clinton, Sir Henry, 154, 155, 157, 162

Clinton, William Jefferson "Bill," 945
election of 1996, 949
presidency of, 945–950
domestic issues, 947, 947–948
foreign policy, 946–947
"Republican revolution" and, 948–949
scandals, 949–950
Clocks, 244–245
Closing Circle, The (Commoner), 900
"Coal Caravan," 707
Coca, Imogene, 817
Cockfighting, 532
Coercive Acts (1774), 133–134, 135
Cohn, Roy, 800, 805
Coin's Financial School (Harvey), 571
Cold War, 782–808
beginnings of, 783–791
American suspicions, 784, 784
atomic capabilities and, 789–790
atomic deterrence, 790–791
Communist expansion, 785, 786
containment policy, 786–787
historical analysis, 785–786
Marshall Plan, 787–788
NATO and, 788–789, 788M
Truman Doctrine, 787
chronology of, 808
economic prosperity and (See Economy)
effects of, 783
end of, 939–945
Korean War and (See Korean War)
nationalism and
in Asia, 822–823
brinksmanship, 821–822
new upheavals, 823–825
response to Sputnik, 825
Soviet-American relations and, 826, 826–828
superpowers and, 823
social effects of, 796–800
fall of McCarthy, 805–806
HUAC and Hollywood, 798–799
loyalty crusade, 798
McCarthyism, 799–800, 800
shocks of 1949, 796–798, 797
Colleton, John, 40
Collier, John, 729–730
Collier's magazine, 616, 780
Colonial assemblies
attempts to control, 129–130
conflict over equitable representation, 93–94
in Jamestown colony, 37
in Maryland, 41
in Pennsylvania, 82–83
royally appointed councils and, 86
Colonial charters, 28, 36–37, 67, 69, 172
Colonial North, settlement of, 61–63, 63, 91M
chronology of, 87
founding of New England, 64
Massachusetts Bay Colony, 66–67
Plymouth Colony, 65–66
Puritan movement and, 64–65
Middle Colonies, 77
English rule in New York, 78, 83–84
Iroquois nation and, 79, 79–80, 88
New Jersey, 80–81
New Netherlands, 77–78
Pennsylvania colony, 82–83
Quakers in, 81, 81–83
New England communities, 67–68, 68M
colonial governments, 71
conflict in, 71–72
congregational church order, 69–71
heretics and, 72–74
stability and order in, 68–69
whites and Indians in, 76–77
women's roles in, 74–75

Colonial North (*Cont.*):
  relations with England, 83–84
    Dominion of New England, 84
    Glorious Revolution and, 84–85, 86
    imperial policy in 1700, 85–86
    Leisler's rebellion, 85
  settlement of backcountry, 92–93
Colonial South, settlement of, 33–35, 91*M*
  Carolinas
    early instability, 51, 52*M*, 53
    founding of, 50–51
    founding of Georgia and, 54–55
    link to Caribbean colonies, 48–55
    race issues, 53–54
    Spain's losses in Caribbean, 49–50
    strife between North and South Carolina, 93–94
    Yamasee War (1715), 53
  Chesapeake region (*See* Chesapeake Bay region)
  chronology of, 60
  instability of colonies, 35
  revivalism, 105
  Spanish borderlands and, 55–60
Colonies and colonization, 88–113
  Albany Congress, 88–90, 106, 112, 113
  chronology of, 113
  by England (*See* England)
  English influence, 106
    on economic and social development, 106–107
    imperial system, 110–112, 111*M*
    inequality of class, 107–108
    politics, 108–110
  enlightenment and awakening, 101–102
    aftermath of Great Awakening, 103–106
    The Enlightenment, 102–103
    First Great Awakening, 103
  European background of, 16–18
    hunger and disease, 16–17
    Protestant Reformation, 23–26
    social and technological change, 17–18
  forces of division in, 90
    boundary disputes, 94
    population growth, 90, 92
    seaports, 95–97
    social conflict, 93–94, 97
    tenant wars, 94–95
  loyalty to Britain, 119–121
  Seven Years' War and, 112–113
  slave societies in South (*See* Slavery)
  by Spain (*See* Spain)
  See also specific colonies
Colorado, statehood (1876), 552
Colorado River dams, 727
Colored Citizen, The, 525
Colored Farmers' National Alliance and Cooperative Union
    (1886), 565–566
Coltrane, John, 835
Columbia Park Boys Band, *511*
Columbus, Christopher, 2, 6, 7, 9, 10*M*, 11, 17, 31, 48
Comanche tribe, 536
Commerce. *See* Trade and commerce
Commercial, 395
Commercial agriculture, 385
Commercial economy, 197–199, 209
Commercially prepared food, 515
Commission on the Status of Women, 902
Commission plan of city government, 609–610
Committee on Civil Rights, 793
Committee on Public Information (CPI), 645, 665
Committees of Correspondence, 132
Committees of inspection, 131, 137
Commodity Credit Corporation, 721
Commoner, Barry, 900
Common Sense (Paine), 138–140, *140*, 143, 146
"Commonweal Army of Christ," 570
Communications, 469, 473–474
Communications, revolution in, 257

Communism, 796
  American fears of, 784, *784*
  expansion during World War II, 785, 786
  fall of, 940–941, *941*
Communist Labor party (1919), 652
Communist party, 708–709
"Community action" programs, 857
Company of the Hundred Associates, 62
Competition, in business, 482
  in railroads, 478
"Complex marriage," 311
Compromise of 1850, 375–378, 375*M*, 382
Compromise of 1877, 463
Comptoir, 62
Comstock, Anthony, 516
Comstock Law (1873), 516
Concentration camps
  Holocaust, 774, 774–775, 782
  for Japanese Americans, 764–765, 765
Concerts, 523
Concord, Battle of (1775), 138, 139
Coney Island, 522
Confederate States of America, 402
  advantages of, 409–410, *410*
  attempts to industrialize, 422–423
  desertion as problem, 436
  end of Civil War and, *435*, 435–436, 438
  home front, 422–425
    economy and, 422–423
    finance and government, 423–424
    hardships, 424–425
    opportunities for women, 423
  ideal of states' rights and, 411
Confederation, 169–170
  Articles of Confederation, 169–170
  disputes among states, 172–173, 173*M*
  economic disruption, 179–180
  foreign intrusion, 171–172
  Northwest Territory, 174–177, *176*
  slavery and, 177–179, *178*
  state constitutions, 167–169, *168*
  in West, 170, *171*, 174
Confiscation Acts (1861; 1862), 418, 449
Conglomerate corporations, 820–821, 833
Congregational Church
  church order, 69–71
  disestablishment of, 184
  Puritans, 64, 65
  revival among, 103, 105
  settlement at Plymouth Colony, 65–66
  settlement in Massachusetts Bay Colony, 66–67
  settlement on Long Island, 78
Congress
  bank recharter bill (1832), 291
  conflict over tariffs, 559
  currency issues, 559–560
  diminished power of, 737
  education legislation, 519
  farm bloc (1921), 683
  gag rule (1836), 322
  on immigration, 508–509
  Indian legislation, 542
  Marshall Plan, 788
  nullification crisis and, 287–289
  railroad regulation, 565
  Reconstruction Acts (1867–1868), 448
  Reconstruction and, 445–446, 448–449, 450, 459
  representation in, 188, 189
  settlement of West and, 537–538
  Sherman Antitrust Act (1890), 483, 485
Congressional Union, 605
Congress of Industrial Organizations (CIO), 732–733
Congress of Racial Equality (CORE), 767, 792, 848, 853, 855,
    861, 876
Connecticut, 69, 71
Connery, Sean, *841*

Connor, "Bull," 853
Conquistadors, 20–21
Conscience Whigs, 374
Conscription, 424, 428
Consensus, era of, 810
Conservation, 616–617, *617*
Conservatism
  historical analysis of, 926–928
  issues of 1970s and 1980s, 925–929
    Catholic social activism, 926, *927*
    election of 1980 and, 928
    historical analysis of, 926–928
    media and, 928
    religious revival, 925–926
  of Reagan era, 924
Constitution, 166–192
  amendments to
    Bill of Rights, 191, 200–201
    Eighteenth Amendment, 676–677
    Fifteenth Amendment, 458
    Fourteenth Amendment, 446–447, 459, 534
    Nineteenth Amendment, 605
    process for, 190
    Seventeenth Amendment, 399*n*, 611
    Sixteenth Amendment, 618–619, 622
    Thirteenth Amendment, 420, 435, 444
    Twelfth Amendment, 274–275
  chronology of development, 192
  commercial economy and, 198–199
  compromise, 189–190
  Confederation and (*See* Articles of Confederation;
    Confederation)
  Constitutional Convention, *187*, 187–188
  ratification of, 190–191
  Virginia and New Jersey plans, 188–189
Constitutional Union party, 401
Construction industry, 661–662, 690
Consumer culture of 1920s, 665–667
Consumer debt, 691
Consumerism, 520–521, *521*, 898–899
Consumer products, 480–481, 515, 520, 661
Consumer spending, 690, 791
Containment doctrine, 786–787, 895
Contemporary issues, 950–954
  new immigration, 951–953, 952*M*
  past conflicts and, 950–951
  racial equality issue, 953–954
Continental Army, *147*, 148–149, 164
  authorization for, 143
  camp followers, 148–149
  mutinies in, 155, *155*
  Society of Cincinnati, 184
  winter at Valley Forge, 154, *155*
Continental Association, 136
Continental Congress
  First, 135–137
  Second, 143–144, 147
Contraceptives, availability of, 516
Contract law, 250–251
"Contract with America," 948
Contra forces, 936
Conversion experience, 302
Coode, John, 44
Coode's rebellion (1689), 44, 45
Coolidge, Calvin, 688, 705, 743, 929
  presidency of, 681, 683
  refusal to run in 1928, 684
Cooper, Anthony Ashley, 50, 51, 59
Cooper, Gary, 798
Cooper, James Fenimore, 308
Copperheads, 428
Coral Sea, Battle of (1942), 754
CORE (Congress of Racial Equality), 767, 848, 853, 855, 861, 876
Cornwallis, Lord Charles
  defeat and surrender, 163–165, 170
  Southern campaign, 157, 158, 160*M*, 161

Coronado, Francisco Vásquez de, 19, *56*
Corporate culture, 809
Corporate mergers, 663–664
Corporate structure, 664, 691
Corporations
  industrialization and, 474–475
  as organizational models, 599
  See also specific companies and industries
Corregidor, fall of, 752–753
Corrido, 666–668
Corruption, 453, 459, *459*, 546
Cortés, Hernando, 7, 18, 19, 20, 21, 23, 31
Cortina, Juan, 373
Costello, Frank, 817
Cotton, 329*M*
  cultivation by Cherokees, 282
  decline during Civil War, 414, 422
  demand for, 527
  economic growth and, 327–328
  from Egypt and India, 414
  export of, 382
  growing cotton trade, 246–247
  mechanized picking, 828
  Panic of 1819, 268, 270
  postwar production, 441–442, 458
  society in cotton kingdom, 333
Cotton, John, 73
Coughlin, Charles, 723, 725
Council of Economic Advisors, 794, 846
"Council on Competitiveness," 942
Counterculture, 860–865
  activists of new left, 860, 861
  rise of, *862*, 862–863
  rock revolution and, 863–864
  West Coast scene, 864–865
"Countercyclical" action, 736
County governments, 82
Coureurs du bois (French traders), 63
Court of Indian Affairs, 730
Court of International Justice, 650
Courts
  admiralty courts, 124, 130
  federal court system, 221–222
  Freedmen's Courts (1866), 457
  General Court of Massachusetts Bay Colony, 67, 71
  military, 428, 457
  Supreme Court (*See* Supreme Court)
  vice-admiralty courts, 85–86
Court week, in rural life, 532
Cowboys, 547, 549
Cowpens, Battle of (1781), 161
Cox, Archibald, 908
Coxey, Jacob, 569–570
Coxey's Army, 569–570
CPI (Committee on Public Information), 645
Crafts, Wilbur, 675
Crawford, William H., 274, 688–689
Crazy Horse (Sioux chief), 541
"Credibility gap," 878–879
Credit, 201, 290, 563–564
Creek tribe, 51, 118, 172, 196, 236, 281, 282, 283*M*
Creel, George, 645
Creole Jazz Band, 672
Crèvecoeur, Hector St. John de, 196–197
Crime, in slums, 505–506
Crittenden, John J., 402, 418
Crittenden Compromise, 402
Crocker, Charles, 546
Croker, Richard, 507
Cromwell, Oliver, 42
Cronkite, Walter, 879
Crop lien system, 528, 563, 566
Crow tribe, 353, 539
Cuba, 9
  battle of San Juan Hill, *587*, 588
  blockade of (1898), 586

Cuba *(Cont.)*:
  Castro's revolution, 825
  immigration from, 890
  rebellion in, 584–586
Cuban Giants (black baseball team), 522
Cuban missile crisis (1962), 843–846, 844–845*M*, 885
Cultural diversity, 1, 367–373
Culture, 517–524
  arts and entertainment, 522–523, *523*
  education for women, 520
  higher education, 519–520
  leisure and, 521–522
  mass consumption, 520–521
  public education, 518–519
  See also Education; Literature; Music
Currency
  Biddle's control of, 290
  Confederate, 424
  Continental currency, 179, 203
  devaluation of, 693
  as divisive issue, 559–560
  gold *vs.* silver standard, 560, 570–571
  uniform currency of Union, 425
Custer, George Armstrong, 541
CWA (Civil Works Administration), 718
Czechoslovakia, Soviet occupation of (1948), 789
Czolgosz, Leon, 612

Daley, Richard, 880–881
Dancing, *310*, 672
Dannemora Prison, 796
Darrow, Clarence, 680
Dartmouth College v. Woodward (1819), 251
Darwin, Charles, 484, 579
Darwinian theory, 597, 679
Daugherty, Harry, 681
Daughters of Bilitis (1955), 892
Daughters of Liberty, 131, 156–157
Daughters of the American Revolution, 727
Davies, Jeff, 760
Davies, "Little Bob," 507
Davis, Henry Winter, 443
Davis, Jefferson, 441, 464
  capabilities of, 410–411, *411*, 412
  conscription of slaves, 435–436
  powers during wartime, 424, 427–428
Davis, Joseph, 441, 464
Dawes, Charles G., 683
Dawes, William, 138
Dawes Plan (1924), 683
Dawes Severalty Act (1887), 542, 730
Dead End (film), 700
Dean, John, 907, 908
Dearborn, Henry, 224–225
Debs, Eugene V., 496, 615, 620, 647, 652
Debt peonage, 528–529
Declaration of Independence (1776), *144*, 144–145, 166
Declaration of Sentiments (1848), 319
Declaration of the Rights of Man, 242
Declaratory Act (1766), 128–129
Deep South, 327–328, 328*n*
Deere, John, 384
de Kooning, Willem, 734
DeLancey, James (governor), 88
Delaney, Martin, 318
Delaware (Lenni Lenape) tribe, 82, 83, 121, 231
Delaware Colony, 82
De Leon, Daniel, 485
Democracy
  equality and opportunity in, 273–274
  imperialism and, 577–578
  perils of, 656–657
  as petty business, 507, 508
  political culture of, 274–277
    election of 1824 and, 274–275
    Jacksonian democracy, 277–278

    political parties and, 276–277, *277*
    social sources, 275–276
  race and, 281–287
  rise of, 271–297, 297
  strengthened by New Deal, 738–739
Democratic National Committee, 722, 730, 906
Democratic party
  composition of, 557
  discontent with, 570
  effects of Civil War on, 438
  election of 1928, 684–685, 685*M*
  election of 1932, 710–711
  extreme peace wing, 428
  hostility to black rights, 284–285
  Jacksonian, 278, 294–295
  overthrow of Radicals, 460–462, *461*
  party affiliations in South, 350
  peace platform (1916), 637
  reform movements and, 321
  stalemate with Republicans, *556*, 556–557
  Tammany Hall, 498–499
  weaknesses of, 405
  "Young America" movement, 388
Democratic Review, 294, 356, 384
Democratic South, 685, 685*M*
Demographics, 659–660, *660*
Demonstrations, 605, 722
Dempsey, Jack, 672
Denmark, German invasion of, 747
Denver (Colorado), 551, 552
Denver Pacific railroad, 552
Department of Energy, 916
Department of Interior, 897
Department of Labor and Commerce, 615
Department stores, 520–521
Depression. *See* Economic depressions
Derleth, August, 660
Détente, 885–887, *886*, 912, 918–919
Devanter, Willis Van, 736
Dewey, George, 586
Dewey, John, 598
Dewey, Thomas E., 768, 795
De Witt, John, 764
Dewson, Mary W. "Molly," 730
Dias, Bartholomeu, 8
Dickens, Charles, 252
Dickinson, John, 110, 130, 143, 187
Dien Bien Phu, fall of (1954), 822, 871
Diggers, 864
Dingley Tariff (1897), 559, 576
Diplomacy, 414
  isolationism of 1930s and, 744–745
  moral diplomacy, 630–632
    intervention in Mexico, 631–632
    missionary diplomacy, 630–631, 631*M*
  progressive, 627–630
    in Caribbean, 628
    "Dollar Diplomacy," 629–630
    in Far East, 628–629
  Wilson's peace offensive, 637–638
Direct primary elections, 611
Discontent and unrest
  depression of 1893 and, 569–570
  Great Depression and, 707–709, *708*
Discrimination against Okies, 701
Disease
  among colonists, 37, 48, 49, 51, 59
  among poor whites, 338
  among slaves, 46, 340
  associated with malnutrition, 694
  effect on Indians, 21, 58, 540
  environmental damage and, 259, 328
  health crises, 944
  importation of, 114
  Pasteur's discoveries, 501
  as reason for colonization, 16–17

in slums, 506
war and
   casualties in Mexican War and, 366
   in Civil War military camps, 428–429
   during Revolutionary War, 156
   in World War II, 756, 759
   westward movement of, 353, 354*M*, 355
   See also specific diseases
Disenfranchisement laws, 573–574, 705
Disneyland, 827
Divorce, 183
Dix, Dorothea, 314, 426
Dixiecrat (States' Rights) party, 795
"Doctrine of high wages," 662
Dodd, Samuel C. T., 482–483
Dodge, Grenville, 546
Dodge, William, 460
Dole, Bob, 949
"Dollar Diplomacy," 629–630
Domestic animals, 49, 353
Domesticity, ideal of, 304–306, *306*, 334
Domestic markets, 250
Domestic servants, 96
  employment of blacks, 534
  excluded from Social Security, 725
  live-in, 515
Dominion of New England, 84
Donaldson, Israel, 380
"Do-nothing Congress," 795
"Doughboys," 642
Douglas, Stephen A., 374, 376–377, 380, 381, 388
  election of 1860 and, 401
  Lincoln-Douglas debates, 397–399, *398*
Douglass, Esther, 455
Douglass, Frederick, 318, 341, 346, 421–422
Doyle, James, 381
Drake, Francis, 30
Drayton, William Henry, 181
Dred Scott decision (1857), 395–396, 399
Dreiser, Theodore, 600
Drinker, Elizabeth, 152
Drugs
  AIDS and, 944
  counterculture and, 862, 864–865
  use in Vietnam, 885
Du Bois, W. E. B., 575
Dubos, René, 900
Duck Soup (film), 700
Ducks Unlimited, 901
Due process, protection of, 846–847, *847*
Dukakis, Michael, 939
Duke, James, 529
Duke, Washington, 529
Dulles, John Foster, 821–822, 823, 824, 843
Dumbarton Oaks Conference (1944), 775
Dumbbell tenements, 506
Dunkirk, 747–748
Dunmore, Lord, 143, 162
Du Pont Corporation, 615
Durand, Asher, *280*
Durant, William, 689
Dust Bowl, 700–701, *701*
Dutch Reformed Church, 78
Dutch West India Company, 77, 78
Dwight, Louis, 315
Dwight, Timothy, 222
Dyer, Mary, 73, 74
Dylan, Bob, 861, 863
Dynamic obsolescence, 809–810
Dysentery, 156, 259, 429, 756

Eads, James B., 469, 497
Earl, Harley, 809
Earth Day, 900–901
Earth First, 901
Eastern Europe, new freedom in, 940

Eastman, George, 472–473
Ecology, 900
Economic depressions
  depression of 1819, 287–288, *288*
  depression of 1893, 568–569, *569*, 596
  in late 19th century, 486, *486*
  Panic of 1837, 292–293, *293*
  Panic of 1857, 396–397
  Panic of 1873, 460
  See also Great Depression
Economic expansion, 627–628, 781
Economic Opportunity Act (1964), 857
Economic Recovery Tax Act (1981), 933
Economy
  boom and bust cycles, 267, 482, 486, *486*
    depression of 1893 and, 568–569, *569*
    imperialism and, 579, 580
    panic of 1907, 617
    in West, 545–549
  British *vs.* American, 106–107
  colonization and, 17
  commercial economy, 197–198
  of Confederacy, 422–423
  of Confederation, 179–180
  cotton-dominated Southern economy, 527
  economic inequality, 48, 59–60, 263
  economic opportunity, 336
  economic policy, 275
  fall of European economies, 692–693
  government role in, 737
  Great Society and, 859
  impact of railroads on, 382
  inflation, 914, 917
  link with international order, 807
  mercantilism, 35–36
  New Frontier, 846
  in 1920s
    damage caused by Great Crash, 690
    defects of, 690–692
    indications of distress, 683–684
  plantation economy, 177, 179–180
  prosperity, effects of, 267–270
    Missouri crisis and, 268–270, *269M*
    Panic of 1819 and, 268
  prosperity after World War II, 791–792
    adjustments, 792–793
    election of 1948 and, 794–795
    "Fair Deal," 795–796
    New Deal and, 793–794
  "Reaganomics," 933–934, *934*
  recession of 1958, 819
  under Reconstruction, 452–453
  semisubsistence, 196–197
  setbacks for Eisenhower, 819
  specialization, 264
  stagflation, 888
  supply-side economics, 931
  weakening, 910–912, *911M*
Edison, Thomas Alva, 472, 503–504
Edison Electric Light Company, 472
Education
  drawbacks of "New South," 531
  gender segregation in, 601
  higher education
    growth of, 519–520
    for women, 519, 520, 817, 904
  lacking in South, 329–330
  public education in cities, 518–519
  during Reconstruction, 452, 454–455
  of women, 183, 305
Educational reform, 313
Edwards, Jonathan, 103
Edwards, Malenda, *258*
Edward VI, king of England, 25
Ehrlich, Paul, 901–902
Ehrlichman, John, 906, 907

Eighteenth Amendment, 676–677, 901
Eight-hour workday, 492, 618
Eisenhower, Dwight D. "Ike," 755, 769, 804, 856, 895
    German surrender, 775
    presidency of, *818*, 818–819
        historical analysis of, 819–820
        nationalism (*See* Cold war)
        Soviet-American relations, 826–827
        support of Ngo Dinh Diem, 822–823
        support of Orval Faubus, 832
    on religion, 815
El Alamein, Battle of (1942), 755
Elections, *556*, 556–557
    of 1796, *208*, 208–209, 210
    of 1800, 212–213, *213*, 572*n*
    of 1812, 238
    of 1816, 238
    of 1824, 274–275, 276
    of 1828, 278, 572*n*
    of 1832, 291
    of 1836, 359
    of 1840, 293–294, 359, 362
    of 1844, 363–364
    of 1848, 374–375
    of 1856, *393*, 393–395
    of 1860, 401, 572*n*
    of 1864, 433–435, 434*M*, 444
    of 1866, 447–448
    of 1868, 458
    of 1872, 460
    of 1876, 462–463
    of 1884, 560–561
    of 1890, 566
    of 1892, 567–568
    of 1896, 570–573, 572*M*, 572*n*, 573
    of 1904, 615
    of 1912, 619–621, 620*M*
    of 1916, 637
    of 1928, 572*n*, 684–685, 685*M*
    of 1932, 710–711
    of 1936, 725–726
    of 1940, 749
    of 1944, 768
    of 1948, 794–795
    of 1952, 804–805
    of 1960, 839–840, 880
    of 1964, 858
    of 1968, 888–889
    of 1972, 894
    of 1976, 914
    of 1980, 572*n*, 928–929
    of 1988, 939
    of 1992, 945
    of 1996, 949
        African American vote, 727–728
        congressional elections of 1946, 794
        demographics of voting, *556*, 557
        direct primary elections, 611
        historically critical elections, 572–573, 572*n*
        "Negro election day," 96
        recall elections, 611
Electoral College, 189, 294, 462–463
Electric Kool-Aid Acid Test, The (Wolfe), 863
Electric trolleys, 503–504
Elementary and Secondary School Act, 858
Elevated railways ("els"), 503
Elijah Muhammad, 703
Eliot, T. S., 673
Elizabeth I, queen of England, 26, 28, 31, 64, 65
Elkins Act (1903), 615
Ellis, Powhatan, 271
Ellis Island, 502
Ellsberg, Daniel, 906
Ellsworth, Oliver, 187
Emancipation, 418–422
    black soldiers, *421*, 421–422

    differing views of, 419–420
    freed slaves and, 420–421
    logic of, 418–419
Emancipation Proclamation (1863), 419, 434–435
Embargo, 232–234
Embargo Act (1807), 233–234
Emergency Banking Act, 717
Emergency Relief and Construction Act (1932), 707
Emergency Relief Appropriation Act (1935), 724
Emerson, Ralph Waldo, 307, 308, 314, 366, 400
"Empire of liberty," 222, 240
Employment of immigrants, 512
Empresarios, 358
Encomienda system, 22
"End Poverty in California" (EPIC), 722
Energy conservation, 916
Energy Policy and Conservation Act (1975), 914
Enganchistas, 475–476, 702
England (before 1707), 2
    colonization by
        in Americas, 27–28
        Caribbean colonies, 49, 52*M*
        Chesapeake region (*See* Chesapeake
            Bay region)
        founding of New England, 64–67
        indifference to colonies, 110–112
        influence of, 83–86, 106–112
        in Ireland, 26–27
        Jamestown Colony, 32, 33–35
        Roanoke Colony, 30, 31
        role of Frobisher and Gilbert, 28–29, *29*
        See also specific colonies
    English Civil War (1642–1649), 42, 68
    exploration by, 5–6
    imperial system before 1760, 110–112, 111*M*
    North Atlantic fisheries, 6
    Protestant Reformation in, 25–26
    war with France, 2, 112
    See also Great Britain
Engle v. Vitale, 847
English Civil War (1642–1649), 42, 68
Enlightenment, 115, 218, 242, 307
Entertainment
    church-centered, 533
    in cities, 517, 522–524, *523*
    diversions of Great Depression, 698–699
    farm entertainments, 532
    in 1920s, 672–673
    politics as, 276
Entrepreneurship, 181, 476, 507
Environment
    artificial ecosystem, 385
    cost of industrialization, 472
    damage to
        disease and, 259, 328
        effects of deforestation, 226, 328
        impact of gold mining, 369–370
        by mining industry, 545
        railroads and, 384–385
        Santa Barbara oil spill, 897–898
        by textile mills, 259, *260*
        by timber industry, 530
    Dust Bowl (1930s), 700–702, *701*
    "Earth Summit," 942
    effect of Indians on, 536–537
    importance of water, 538–539, 538*M*
    industrial pollutants, 781
    influence of, 514–515
    Johnson's legislation for, 859
    under Reagan administration, 931, 933
    Republican proposals, 948
Environmentalism, 900–902
Environmental Protection Agency, 905, 942
Equality
    importance to political culture, 272, 351
    opportunity and, 273–274

of rural farmers, 196–197
social inequality and (See Social inequality)
Equal Pay Act (1963), 902
Equal Rights Amendment (ERA), 670, 904
Equal Rights Party, 516
ERA (Equal Rights Amendment), 670, 904
Era of Good Feelings, 239
Erdman Act (1898), 576
Ericsson, Leif, 2
Erie Canal, 247, 249M
Escobedo v. Illinois (1964), 847
Espionage, fears of, 798
Espionage Act (1917), 646
Esquivel, Adolfo Pérez, 917
Eternal marriage (Mormon), 312
Ethnic communities for immigrants, 511–512
Ethnicity
conflict and, 94, 97, 106
political parties and, 557
suburbia and, 814
Europe
favorable opinion of Union, 419
in 14th and 15th centuries, 16–17
hostility toward slavery, 332
reasons for 1880s immigration, 501–502, 502
Reformation in (See Protestant Reformation)
territorial expansion, 2
background of American colonization, 16–18
changes in Europe and, 6–7
Portuguese, 7–8, 8
Spain, 9, 10M, 11
See also specific European countries
Evangelical Christianity, 301, 303, 346, 925–926
Evangelists, 509, 509
Evans, Wesley, 653
Evolution, debate over, 679–680
Excise taxes, 193, 202, 205
Executive Order 8802, 766
Executive Order 9066, 764
Executive power, 167–168, 168
Exodusters, 525–526, 535, 701–702
Ex parte Milligan (1866), 428
Expatriates, 673
Exploration, in 15th century, 5–6
Exports and imports, 43, 95, 136
Exxon (Standard Oil of New Jersey), 821

Factories, 256–262
differing views of, 262–263
industrial labor force, 260–261
labor movement and, 262
Lowell textile mills, 256, 259, 260
shoe industry, 261–262
technological advances and, 256–257
textile factories, 257–259, 258
Factory system
beginnings of, 244–245
textile industry, 257–259, 258
"Fair Deal," 795–796
Fair Employment Practices Commission, 766, 793
Fair Oaks, Battle of (1862), 416, 417M
Fall, Albert, 681
Fallen Timbers, Battle of (1794), 205
Fallout shelters, 826
Falwell, Jerry, 926
Family
effects of Revolutionary War, 156
family economy, 156, 512
free black families, 454
in Great Depression, 695–696
immigrants, 512
married women in work force, 490
middle-class, 265, 306–307, 514–515
in Mormon Church, 371–372
New England settlers, 66, 69

slave families, 342, 342–344
smaller size, 306
FAP (Federal Art Project), 734
Farewell to Arms, A (Hemingway), 673
Farm bloc (1921), 683
Farm Credit Administration, 721
Farm entertainments, 532
Farmer, James, 848–849
Farmers
conflicts in West, 549
decreasing income, 683
drop in farm prices, 691, 693
in Dust Bowl of 1930s, 700–701, 701
growth of commerce and, 214–215
revolt of (See Populism)
in South, 326, 350–351
support of Whigs and Democrats, 295, 296
See also Agriculture
Farmer's Alliance, 564
Farm Holiday Association, 707
Farm policy, Eisenhower and, 819
Farm Security Administration, 721, 768
Farm workers, 501, 702, 725
Farragut, David G., 413, 433
Fascism, 657, 744
Fashion, 698
"Father Divine," 703
Faubus, Orval, 832
FBI (Federal Bureau of Investigation), 893, 894, 913
Federal aid, for railroads, 479
Federal Art Project (FAP), 734
Federal budget during Great Depression, 707
Federal Bureau of Investigation (FBI), 893, 894, 913
Federal Deposit Insurance Corporation, 717
Federal Emergency Relief Administration (FERA), 717, 731
Federal Employee Loyalty Program (1947), 798
Federal Energy Administration, 914
Federal Farm Board, 706
Federalist Papers, The, 190
Federalist party, 202, 202n
differences with Jeffersonian Republicans, 210
election of 1796 and, 208, 208–209
election of 1800 and, 212–213, 213
end of, 238
ideology of, 209–210
legacy of, 215–216
Federalists, 190–191, 192
Federal marshals, 851–852
Federal Music Project (FMP), 733
Federal One (arts program), 733–734
Federal Reserve Act (1913), 622
Federal Reserve Board, 622, 690, 725, 917
Federal Reserve System, 622, 691, 692
Federal Theater Project (FTP), 734
Federal Trade Commission, 905
Federal Trade Commission Act (1914), 622
Federal troops, 832–833, 849
Federal Writers Project (FWP), 733
Federation of Women's Clubs, 611
Felipe, Subi Lin, 951
Feminine Mystique, The (Friedan), 902
Feminism, 902–904, 904
Feminization of work force, 490, 491, 669
FERA (Federal Emergency Relief Administration), 717, 731
Ferdinand, king of Spain, 9, 17
Ferdinando, Simon, 30
Ferguson, Miriam ("Ma"), 669
Ferguson, Robert, 468
Ferraro, Geraldine, 935
Fertility rates, 68–69
baby boom, 811, 811–812
in Great Depression, 696
in World War II, 762
Fessenden, William Pitt, 446
Fifteenth Amendment, 458
Fillmore, Millard, 377, 393, 395

Financial institutions, 474
Finney, Charles Grandison, 300–301, 311, 314, 318
Fireside chats, 717
First Continental Congress
  actions of, 135–137
  British denunciation of, 137
  call for, 134
First Sioux War, 539–541, 540*M*
Fisher, Mary, 73
Fishing, in North Atlantic, 5, 6
Fitzgerald, F. Scott, 673
Five Nations (League of the Iroquois), 79, 79–80
Five-Power Agreement (1921), 684
Fixed costs of railroads, 478
Flagg, Edmund, 384
Flanagan, Hallie, 734
"Flappers," 668
Flatiron Building, 504, *505*
Fletcher v. Peck (1810), 222, 250–251
Flexible response doctrine, 843
Flood, Curt, 850
Florida, 172, 239
FMP (Federal Music Project), 733
Folk music, 863
Folk tales, in slave culture, 345
Fonda, Jane, 906
Food Administration (WWI), 643
Food shortages, in Confederacy, 424
Football, 522
Foraker Act (1900), 591
Force Bill (1832), 289
Ford, Gerald R., 908
  presidency of, 909–914
    détente, 912
    economy and diplomacy, 910–912, 911*M*
    election of 1976 and, 914
    fall of South Vietnam and, 912
    fighting inflation, 914
    Kissinger and foreign policy, 909–910
    limits of, 912–913, *913*
    pardons Nixon, 912–913
Ford, Henry, 656, 662, 672, 733
Ford, John, 734
Ford Motor Company, 662, 708, 758, 809
Fordney-McCumber Tariff (1922), 682
Foreign policy
  Bush administration, 940–941, *941*
  Carter administration, 917–918
  Clinton administration, 946–947
  Henry Kissinger and, 909–910
  imperialism and, 578–579
  post-cold war, 940–941, *941*
  Reagan administration (*See* Reagan, Ronald)
Foreman, Clark, 728
Formosa (Taiwan), 771, 796, 823
Forrestal, James, 784
Fort Donelson, capture of (1862), 414, 415*M*
Fort Duquesne, 89, 112, 117
Forten, Charlotte, 285
Fort Frontenac, fall of (1758), 119
Fort Henry, capture of (1862), 414, 415*M*
Fort McHenry, 236
Fort Necessity, 112, 117
Fort Orange (Albany) trading outpost, 77
Fort Sumter, 402–404
Fort Wayne, Treaty of (1809), 231
"Four Freedoms," 749
"Four-Minute Men," 645
"Four Policemen," 771
"Foursquare Gospel," 658
Fourteenth Amendment, 446–447, 459, 534, 847
Fragging, 885
France, 2
  Acadian colony (Nova Scotia; 1605), 62
  confiscation of cargoes, 207
  dreams of empire, 86

French and Indian War (*See* Seven Years' War)
  North Atlantic fisheries, 6
  Protestant Reformation in, 24–25
  Quasi-War with, 211, 220
  settlements in North America, 61–63
  surrender to Germany, 748–749
  West Indies colonies, 49
Francis I, king of France, 17
Franco, Francisco, 745
Franklin, Benjamin, 93, 94, 114, 118, 144, *144*, 163, 503
  Albany Congress, 88–90, 112, 113
  on commercial values, 198
  on English social classes, 108
  Enlightenment and, 102
  on George Whitefield, 104, 106
  on government, 195
  negotiations with France, 153
  opinions on slavery, 100–101
  role in Constitutional Convention, 189
Franz Ferdinand, Austrian Archduke, 633
Fredericksburg, Battle of (1862), 417*M*, 426–427
Free blacks. *See* African Americans
Freedmen's Bureau, 446, 454–455, 456–457
Freedmen's Courts (1866), 457
Freedom, experience of, 453–454
Freedom of the press, 212
Freedom riders, 848–849
Freedom Summer, 848–849, 861, 902
"Free" land, 535–536
Free love, 516
Freeport Doctrine, 399, 400, 401
Free silver movement, 570–571
Free Soil party, 374, 377–378
Free Speech Movement, 861–862, 864
Free states, 266*M*, 268–270
Free will doctrine, 301
Frémont, John C., 393, 395
French and Indian War. *See* Seven Years' War
French Revolution, 206
Freneau, Philip, 204
Freud, Sigmund, 668
Freudian psychology, 668
Friedan, Betty, 861, 902
Friedman, Milton, 692
Friends of the Earth, 905
Frobisher, Martin, 28, *29*, 30
Frontier, definition of, 535–536
Frontier settlements, 92–93
Frowne, Sadie, 487, 497
FTP (Federal Theater Project), 734
Fuchs, Klaus, 798
Fuel Administration (WWI), 643
Fugitive slave law, 377
Fulbright, William, 876, 877
Fuller, Margaret, 307
Fulton, Robert, 248
Fundamental Constitutions, 51
Fundamentalism, 679, 905
Fundamentals, The (Stewart), 679
Funding and assumption program, 201–202, 220, 221
Fur trade, 263–264
  with Iroquois tribe, 79
  in New France, 62, 63, 89, 91*M*
FWP (Federal Writers Project), 733

Gadsden Purchase (1853), 388
Gage, Thomas, 137, 138, 141, 142
Gag rule (1836), 322
Galloway, Joseph, 136, 146
Gama, Vasco da, 8
Gandhi, Mohandas K., 656, 767, 831
Gangsters, 677
Gang system (slavery), 339
Garcia, John, 741
Gardoqui, Don Diego de, 186
Garfield, James, 559, 560

Garment factories, 487
Garrison, William Lloyd, 315, 317, 318, 320–321, 348
Garvey, Marcus, 674, *674*
"Gas and water socialism," 609
Gasoline, taxed for road building, 662
Gaspee (schooner), 132
Gaspee Commission, 132, 136
Gastonia (North Carolina) strike (1927), 664
Gates, Horatio, 152, 158
Gay rights movement, 892
Gender equity, New Deal and, 730
Gender roles, 74–75, 343–344
Gender separation, 531–532, 533
General Court of Massachusetts Bay Colony, 67, 71
General Electric Corporation, 664, 820
General Federation of Women's Clubs, 601
General Motors, 732–733, 758, 809, 898–899
General Motors Acceptance Corporation, 666
Geneva summit conference (1955), 823
Gentry, of Chesapeake region, *47*, 47–48
Geographic mobility, 253–254, 255
George, Henry, 484–485, 524
George II, king of England, 54
George III, king of England, 116, 128, 136, 139, 143, 146
Georgia, 54–55, *57M*, 281
Germain, Lord George, 143, 149
German immigrants, 94
Germany, 23–24, 386–387
  divided into occupation zones, 772–773
  invasion of Poland, 747
  Nazi party, 657
  reparations, 683, 775–776
  wars (*See* World War I; World War II)
Gerry, Elbridge, 187
Gerrymandering, 573–574
Gettysburg, Battle of (1863), 429, 430, 431, *432M*
Ghent, Treaty of (1814), 238
Ghost Dance religion, 542, 544
Gibbons, Floyd, 633
Gibbons v. Ogden (1924), 250
GI Bill (1944), 792, 794
Gibson, Charles Dana, *523*, *569*
Gideon v. Wainwright (1963), 847, *847*
Gilbert, Humphrey, 7, 26, 27, 28–29, 31
Gilman, Charlotte Perkins, 602, 637
Gilpin, William, 537–538, 546
Gingrich, Newt, 948
Ginsberg, Allen, 835–836, 864
Gladden Washington, 509
Glasnost, 939
Glass-Steagall Banking Act (1932), 706
Glenn, John, 842
Glorious Revolution, 84–85, 86
Gold
  in Black Hills, 541
  California Gold Rush (1849), 545, 546
  discovery of, 539
  in Venezuela, 583
Gold Rush (1848–1849), 367–370
Gold standard, 560, 570–571, 693
Goldwater, Barry, 858, 925
Goliad, Battle of (1836), 358
Gompers, Samuel, 493–494
Gone with the Wind (Mitchell), 698
Good Earth, The (Buck), 698
Good Neighbor policy, 743
Goodyear Tire & Rubber Company, 732
Gorbachev, Mikhail, 939, 940, *941*, 946
Gorgas, William, 627
Gorras Blancas (White Caps), 544
Government
  after 1789, 199–204, *200*
    Bill of Rights, 200–201
    chronology of, 216
    fear of aristocracy, 204
    Hamilton's financial program, 201–202, *202*

opposition to Hamilton's program, 202–204, *202n*
  organization of, 199–200
colonial, 109
cuts in spending, 220
emergence of political parties (*See* Political parties; *specific parties*)
involvement in economy, 246
limited, 295
See also Politics
Government bonds, sale of, 425
"Government girls," in Civil War, 423
Government spending, 791–792
Governors, state constitutions and, 167–168
Grady, Henry, 526
Graham, Billy, 815
Grain, 384
Gramm-Rudman Act (1985), 945
Grand Army of the Republic, 558
Granges, 565
Grant, Madison, 607
Grant, Ulysses S., 558
  character of, 414, *435*
  election of 1868, 458
  election of 1872, 460
  presidency of, *459*, 459–460, 516
  role in Civil War, 414, *415M*, 416, *432M*, 433, *434M*
Grapes of Wrath, The (Steinbeck), 700, 701, 734
Grasse, Comte de, 163
Grateful Dead, 863, 864
"Graveyard vote," 507
"Great American Desert," 536, 549
Great Atlantic and Pacific Tea Company (A&P), 521, 663
Great Awakening, 103–105
Great Britain (after 1707), 656. *See also* England
  abandonment of gold standard, 693
  American aid to, 749–750
  balanced constitution, 108–109
  beginning of industrial revolution, 243
  blockade of Germany (WWI), 635
  bureaucracy in, 109
  compromise on Oregon, 364
  economic development, 106–107
  economic ties in WWI, 635
  financial problems of, 121–124
  imperial crisis (*See* American Revolution)
  impressment and confiscation, 97, 207, 208, 232, 233, 234
  Orders in Council (1807), 232, 234–235
  refusal to recognize Confederacy, 414
  Seven Years' War (*See* Seven Years' War)
  social classes in, 107–108, *108*
  social development, 107
Great Crash, 690
Great Depression, 687–711
  background of, 687–688, *688*
  chronology of, 711
  effects of, 657
  fertility rates and, 811, *811*
  Hoover's presidency and, 704–711
    Bonus Army, 709–710
    depression program, 706–707, *707*
    election of 1932 and, 710–711
    failure of relief, 704–705
    indications of discontent, 707–709, *708*
  social effects of, 693–704
    ecological disaster, 700–702, *701*
    entertainment, 698–699
    families, 695–696
    hard times, 693–695, *694*, *695*
    minorities, 702–704
    radio and film, 699–700
    unemployment, 697
    on women and children, 696–698
  stock market and (*See* Stock market)
Greater East Asia Co-Prosperity Sphere, 744, 750
Great Lakes, 235

Great migrations
  of African Americans, 645, 673–674
  global migration, 501–502, *502*
  during World War I, 644–645
Great Plains
  Dust Bowl, 700–701, *701*
  effect of railroads on, 546
  in late 19th century, 549–552
    daily life, 550–551
    farming, 550
  natural environment of, 536, 538*M*
Great Railroad Strike of 1877, 495, 569
Great Society programs, 856–859
  aspects of, 858–859
  election of 1964 and, 858
  origins of, 856–857, *857*
Great Train Robbery, The, 670
Greece, Truman Doctrine and, 787
Greeley, Horace, 418, 459–460, 517
Green, Duff, 349
Greenback party (1874), 558
"Greenbacks," 559–560
Greene, Nathanael, 158, 159–161, 160*M*
Green Mountain Boys, 94, 171
Greenough, Horatio, 252
Greenville, Treaty of (1795), 205, 225
Grenada, invasion of, 936
Grenville, George, 121–124, 126, 128
Grenville, Richard, 30
Grimes, James W., 459
Grimké, Angelina, 316, 319, 349–350
Grimké, Sarah, 316, 319, 349–350
Griswold, Roger, 213
Griswold v. Connecticut (1964), 847
Groves, Leslie, 790
Gruening, Ernest, 872
Guadalcanal, Battle of (1942), 754
Guadalupe Hidalgo, Treaty of (1848), 366–367, 373
Gulf War, 941–942
Gun frontier, 354, 354*M*
Gypsies, Holocaust and, 774

Habeas corpus, writ of, 424, 427–428
Haddon, Briton, 671
Haight-Ashbury neighborhood, 864
Haiphong, blockade and bombing (1972), 894
Haiti, intervention in, 946
Hakluyt, Richard, 30
Haldeman, H. R., 884, 894, 907, 909
Haley, Bill, 835
Hall, Moses, 159
Hamilton, Alexander, 187, 190, 199
  character of, 201, *202*
  clashes with John Adams, 211
  election of 1796, 208
  French Revolution and, 206, 207
  funding and assumption program, 201–204, 202*n*, 220, 221
  opposition to Jefferson, 204, 240
  organization of Federalist party, 207
  Whiskey Rebellion and, 205
Hammond, James Henry, 327–328, 339, 396
Hancock, John, 130
Hanna, Marcus Alonzo, 572
Harding, Warren G., 653, 680–681
Hard money advocates, 290
Hard Times: An Oral History of the Great Depression (Terkel), 697
Hariot, Thomas, 30
Harlem Renaissance, 674–675
Harper, William, 287, 289
Harper's Ferry, Virginia, 400–401
Harrington, Michael, 856–857, 934
Harris, Emily Lyles, 423
Harrison, Benjamin, 561, 567, 582
Harrison, William Henry, 236, 362, 561
  election of 1840, 293–294, 359
  on Tecumseh, 229, 231

Hartford Convention (1814), 238
Harvard Medical School, 520
Harvey, William, 571
Haussmann, Georges, 466
Hawaii, 581–583, *582*, 588
"Hawks" and "doves," 875
Hawthorne, Nathaniel, 309
Hay, John, 583, 586, 591, 592
Hayakawa, S. I., 917
Hayden, Casey, 902
Hayden, Tom, 860, 861
Hayes, Rutherford B., 462, 463, 525, 558, 560
Haymarket Square Riot (1886), 495–496
Hayne, Robert, *288*, 322
Hay-Pauncefote Treaty (1901), 583
Hazardous working conditions, 488
Headright system, 37
Health care reform, failure of, *947*, 947–948
Hearst, William Randolph, 585, 767
Helicopters, use in Vietnam, 874, *875*
Hell's Angels, 864
Helsinki summit (1975), 912
Hemingway, Ernest, 673
Henry, Patrick, 126, 166, 192
Henry VII, king of England, 5, 17
Henry VIII, king of England, 25
Henry the Navigator, Prince of Portugal, 7, 8
Hepburn Railway Act (1906), 615
Herald of Freedom, 381
Heresy, 72–74
  Antinomianism, 73
  Quakers, 73–74, 75
Heriot, George, 79
Herrera, Juan José, 544
Hessians, 151
Hickok, Lorena, 712, *713*
Highways, 812–813
Highway Trust Fund, 812
Hill, Anita, 943
Hillsborough, Lord, 130–131
Hinds, Josiah, 336
Hippie communes, 862
Hirabayashi, Gordon, 765
Hiroshima, bombing of, 776
Hispanic Americans
  activism of, *889*, 889–891
  declining cities and, 813
  Hispano settlers in Southwest, 544–545
  veterans of World War II, 792
  See also Mexican Americans
Hispanic immigrants, 951, 952*M*
Hispanic war workers, 766
Hispaniola (Haiti), 9, 17
Hispanos, 544–545
Hiss, Alger, 797–798
History of the Standard Oil Company (Tarbell), 599
Hitler, Adolf, 657, 709, 744, *746*, 769
  death of, 775
  invasion of Russia (1941), 749
  invasions, 747–749, 748*M*
  violation of Versailles Treaty, 745
  See also Germany; World War II
Hoboes of America, 760
Ho Chi Minh, 656, 822, 871, 879, 884
Ho Chi Minh Trail, 870*M*, 871
Holding companies, 483
"Hollywood Ten," 798–799
Holmes, Oliver Wendell, Jr., 598, 647, 652
Holocaust, 774, 774–775, 782
Holy Roman Empire, 2
Home Insurance Building, 504
Homemaking, 696
Home Owners' Loan Act, 717
Homestead Act (1862), 425, 537, 550
Homestead steel mill, 482, 487–488, 567
Homestead steel strike (1892), 598

Homosexuals
  AIDS and, 944
  in armed services, 756
  gay rights movement, 892
  Holocaust and, 774
  investigation of, 799
  urban life and, 517
Hone, Philip, 293
Hood, John, 436
Hooker, "Fighting Joe," 416
Hooker, Isabella Beecher, *299*, 320
Hooker, Thomas, 72
Hookworm, 338
Hoover, Herbert, 681, 743
  election of 1928, 684–685, *685M*
  election of 1932, 710
  personal habits, 705
  presidency of, 682
  See also Great Depression
Hoover, J. Edgar, 913
Hoovervilles (shantytowns), *695*
Hopi tribe, 13
Hopkins, Harry, 712, 717, 721–722, 724
Hopkins, Johns, 519
Hopwood v. State of Texas et al (1996), 943
Horizontal growth of businesses, 480–481
Horses, *56*, 353, *354M*
  in cattle industry, 547
  horse-drawn railways, 503
  use in West, 536
Horseshoe Bend, Battle of (1814), 236
Hospitals, 314
House, Edward, 637
House Committee on Un-American Activities (HUAC), 798–799
Houseman, John, 734
House of Burgesses, 37
House of Representatives, 212–213
Housing, 92, 340, 811, 812
Houston, Charles, 829
Houston, Sam, 358–359
Houston race riots (1917), 642
Howard, Josephine, 341
Howard, Paul Langley, *728*
Howard University, 792, 829
"Howdy Doody Show," 815
Howe, Lord Richard, 150
Howe, William, 141, 142, 149–150, 151–152, 154
Howl (Ginsberg), 835–836
How the Other Half Lives (Riis), 600
HUAC (House Committee on Un-American Activities), 798–799
Hudson, T. S., 469, 477, 497
Hue, David, 190
Huerta, Victoriano, 632
Hughes, Charles Evans, 637, 653, 681
Hughes, Langston, 674
Hull, Cordell, 745
Hull House, 510, 609, 695, 704
Human perfectibility doctrine, 301
"Human potential movement," 924
Human resources of "New South," 526, 527
Human rights issues, 917–918
Human sacrifice, 15–16
Humphrey, George, 822
Humphrey, Hubert, 880, 883
Hungary, Soviet occupation of (1947), 788–789
Hunt, E. Howard, 906, 907
Hunting, for sport, 531–532
Hunting and gathering, 12
Huntington, Collis, 574–575
Huron (Indian nation), 62
Huron tribe, 79
Hurston, Zora Neale, 674
Hussein, Saddam, 941–942
Hutcheson, "Big Bill," 732

Hutchinson, Anne, 73, 74
Hutchinson, Thomas, 127
Hydrogen bomb, 796, 801

ICBMs (Intercontinental ballistic missiles), 887
ICC (Interstate Commerce Commission), 615
Ickes, Harold, 727, 728, 729, 737, 760
"If We Must Die" (McKay), 674
Illinois Vice Commission (1916), 608
IMF (International Monetary Fund), 775
Immigrants
  characteristics of, 501, 502
  city life and, 510–514, *511*
  education for, 518–519
  prejudice against, 606
Immigration, 386–387, 466
  colonial population and, 90, 92
  differing reasons for, 514
  illegal, 951
  immigrant aid societies, 512
  Irish textile workers, 259
  Mexican immigrants, 544–545, 889
  population growth and, 253, 254
  from Puerto Rico, 889
  reasons for 1880s immigration, 501–502, *502*
  reform of policy, 859
  restriction of, 607, 675–676
  since 1980s, 951–953, *952M*
  Southern fear of, 388
  workers, 475–476
Immigration Act (1924), 775
Immigration Act (1965), 859, 951
Immigration Restriction League, 508, 607
Impartial Administration of Justice Act (1774), 134
Impeachment
  of Andrew Johnson, 449–450
  of Nixon, 908–909
Imperialism, 576–592
  Age of Imperialism, 467
  chronology of, 593
  foreign policy, 578–579
  in Latin America, 580–581
  in Pacific, 581–582, *582*
  scramble for empire, 576–578, *577M*
  Seward's diplomacy, 579–580
  Venezuelan crisis, 583
Implied powers, 203–204, 250
Impoundment, 906
Impressment, 97, 207, 208, 232, 233, 234, 423
Inca civilization, 21
Inchon (Korea), 802, *803M*
Income tax, 423, 618–619, 622, 760
Incorporation laws, 251
Indentured servitude, 38, 45, 50, 59, 96
Index of American Design, 734
Indianapolis (Indiana), KKK capital in 1920s, 677
Indian Reorganization Act of 1934, 730
Indians of All Tribes, 891
Indian War of 1622, 38, 39
Individualism of Confederate soldiers, 429–430
Individuality, mass culture and, 833
Indochina, 869
Industrialization, 466–497
  chronology of, 497
  cities and (*See* Cities and urbanization)
  corporate greed and, 595
  development of industrial systems, 469–476
    corporations, 474–475
    investment capital, 474
    labor resources, 475–476, *476*
    resources and technology, *471*, 471–472
    systematic invention, 472–473
    transportation and communication, 473–474
  drawbacks of "New South," 530
  failure to aid South, 400
  growth of big business, 480–486

Industrialization *(Cont.):*
  growth of big business *(Cont.):*
    consumer goods, 480–481
    corporate critics, 484–485
    costs of, 486, *486*
    mergers and holding companies, 483–484
    petroleum industry, 482–483
    social Darwinism and, 484
    steel industry, 481–482
  imperialism and, 555, 578
  labor unions *(See* Labor unions)
  railroads *(See* Railroads)
  Reconstruction and, 453
  role in Civil War, 438
  roots of progressivism and, 597
  Southern complaints about, 387–388
  spread of factory system, 385–386
  urbanization and *(See* Cities and urbanization)
  workers and, 487–492
Industrial revolution, 242, 243, 405
Industrial technology, *471*, 471–472
Industrial work, 260–261, 487–490, *488–489*
Industrial Workers of the World (IWW), 647
Industry, in "New South," 529
Infant mortality, 340
Inflation, 179–180, 424, 914, 917, 931
Influence of Sea Power Upon History, The (Mahan), 578
Information Division of Resettlement Administration, 734
Infrastructure, federal aid for, 246
Inheritance, 183, 307
Initiative legislation, 611
Installment buying, 666–667, 691
Institutes of the Christian Religion, The (Calvin), 25
Integrated systems, in business, 482
Intellectuals, 102
Intelligence tests, 642
Intercontinental ballistic missiles (ICBMs), 887
Intermediate Nuclear Force treaty (1987), 939
Internal combustion engine, 471
Internal Revenue Service, 906
International Bank for Reconstruction and Development, 775
Internationalism, 744–745
International Monetary Fund (IMF), 775
International relations, 238, 239–240
Interstate commerce, 250
Interstate Commerce Act (1887), 561
Interstate Commerce Commission (ICC), 565, 615
Interstate Highway Act (1956), 812
Interstate highway system, 812–813
Interstate slave trade, 342, *342*
"Intolerable Acts," 133–134
Intoxicating Drinks and Drugs in All Lands and Times
    (Crafts), 675
Inventions, 256, 384, 472–473
Investment bankers, 479–480, 483
Investment capital, 474, 478–480, *479M*
Invisible Empire, Knights of the Ku Klux Klan, 677–679, *678*
Iran, revolution in, 919–920
Iran-Contra affair, 936–938, *938*
"Irangate," 938
Iraq, 941–942
Ireland, 26–27, 386
Irish Sweepstakes, 699
Ironclads, battle of, 413
Iron Curtain, 786
Iroquois league
  Five Nations, 79, 79–80
  Six Nations, 88–90
Iroquois tribe, 13, 77, 88–90, 118
Irrigation, 616
Isabella, queen of Spain, 9, 17
Islam, 3
Islamic fundamentalists, 936
Isolationism, 744–745
Israel
  formal recognition of (1948), 789

wars with Arab neighbors, 919
  Yom Kippur War, 910
Issacs, Ben, 697
"Italglish" dialect, 512
Italian Americans, in World War II, 762–763
Italian immigrants, *511*, 512
Italy, fascism in, 657
I Was a Communist for the FBI, 799
Iwo Jima, Battle of, 773
IWW (Industrial Workers of the World), 647

Jackson, Andrew, 236, 237*M*, 238, 572*n*
  bank war and, 289–292
  character of, 280, *280*
  election of 1824 and, 274, 275
  election of 1828 and, 278
  on equality, 274
  Farewell Address (1837), 284
  as land speculator, 281
  mistrust of banks, 291
  new politics and, 276
  nullification crisis and, 287–289
  rise to power, 278–281, *280*
  as strong president, 295
  Texas independence and, 359
Jackson, Thomas "Stonewall," 416, 431
Jacksonian Era, 276, 350
Jackson State University, 869, 884
Jails, 314, *316*
James, William, 598
James I, king of England, 31–32, 59
  Chesapeake region settlement and, 34, 35, 36, 42
  conflict with Puritans, 64, 65
  dissolution of Virginia Company, 38, 40
James II, king of England, 43
  authority over colonies, 83–84, 86
  deposed by Parliament, 84–85
  as Duke of York, 78, 80
James Bond novels, 840–841, *841*
Jamestown Colony, 32, 33–35
  Bacon's rebellion, 43–44, 45, 47
  fort construction, *36*
  founding of, 37
Jan and Dean, 864
Japan
  attack on Manchuria, 628–629, 743
  embargo of, 750
  surrender in World War II, 776
  "Twenty-One Demands," 631
  See also World War II
Japanese Americans, in World War II, 764–765, *765*
Java Sea, Battle of, 752
Jaworski, Leon, 908
Jay, John, 163, 186, 190, 200
Jay-Gardoqui Treaty, 185–186
Jazz, 672–673
Jazz Singer, The, (film), 699
Jefferson, Thomas, *144*, 144–145, 166, 187, 217, 242
  on Andrew Jackson, 280
  appointment of Lewis and Clark, 1
  death of, 240–241
  election of 1796, *208*, 208–209
  election of 1800, 212–213, *213*
  Jeffersonian Republican party and, 207–208, 216
  opposition to Hamilton, 204, 240
  ordinances for Northwest Territory, 174–177, *176*
  presidency of, 217–218
    character and philosophy, 218–220, *219*
    economic policies, 220–221
    Indian policy, 228
    judicial review, 221–222
    republican principles, 220
    western expansion *(See* The West)
  views of French Revolution, 206
  War of 1812 and *(See* War of 1812)
Jefferson Airplane, 864

Jemmy (slave leader), 100
Jenney, William LeBaron, 504
Jeremiah, Thomas, 162
Jerome, Chauncey, 244–245, 257, 266, 405
Jesuits (Society of Jesus), 62, 63, *63*, 86
Jewish Daily Forward, 511–512
Jews, 54–55, 106
  immigration of, 502
  in tobacco industry, 529
Jim Crow laws, 573–575
  Houston riot and, 642
  after World War II, 793
Job Corps, 857
John Paul II (pope), 926
Johns Hopkins University, 519, 665
Johnson, Andrew, 433, 558, 579
  break with Congress, 445–446
  on confiscation laws, 449
  impeachment of, 449, 450
  pardon of Davis, 441
  Reconstruction program, 444–445, *445*
Johnson, Hiram, 676
Johnson, John H., 728–729
Johnson, Lyndon B., 820, 854, 876, *876*, 895
  background and character of, 856
  presidency of
    affirmative action program, 903
    race riots, 855–856
    Vietnam War, 868, 871–872
  withdrawal from 1968 race, 879–880
  See also Great Society programs
Johnson, Octave, 325–326, 341
Johnson, Tom, 609
Johnston, Albert, 414, 416, 417*M*, 434*M*
Joint Chiefs of Staff, 791, 879
Joint Committee on Reconstruction, 446–447
Jones, Betty, 453
Jones, Joe, *708*
Jones, John, 422
Jones, Mary, 457
Jones, Samuel, 380–381
Joplin, Scott, 523
Jordan, Daniel, 325
Journalism, 659
  growth in 1920s, 671
  power press and, 257
  role in progressive movement, 599
  "yellow" journalism, 585
  See also Newspapers; *specific publications*
Judicial review doctrine, 221
Judiciary Act of 1789, 200, 221
Judiciary Act of 1801, 221
Judiciary Committee, 943
Jungle, The (Sinclair), 616
Jungle warfare schools, 841–842
Justice Department, 615, 619, 737
"Justification by faith alone," 24
"Juvenile delinquency," 834–835

Kaiser, Henry J., 758
Kansas
  conflict over slavery, 380–381
  effect of conflict on political parties, 391
  settlement of, 525–526, 535
Kansas Code (1855), 391
Kansas Free State, 380, 381
Kansas-Nebraska Act (154), 388–389, *389*
Kansas Pacific railroad, 552
Kasserine Pass, Battle of (1943), 755
K1C2 (Korea, corruption, and communism), 804–805
KDKA radio (Pittsburgh), 671
Keating-Owen Act (1916), 604, 623
Kefauver, Estes, 817
Kelley, Florence, 603, 605
Kelley, Oliver Hudson, 565
Kellogg, Frank, 684

Kellogg-Briand Pact (1928), 684
Kelly, Abby, 319
Kemble, Fanny, 347
Kemp, Jack, 949
Kendall, Amos, 279–280
Kennan, George, 786, 801
Kennedy, Jacqueline, 929
Kennedy, John Fitzgerald, 820, 895, 929
  assassination of, 853
  background and character, 840–841, *841*
  election of 1960 and, 839–840
  presidency of, *857*
    Bay of Pigs invasion, 842
    Cuban missile crisis (1962), 843–846, 844–845*M*, 885
    New Frontier, 865
    Vietnam War and, 871
    women's rights and, 902
Kennedy, Robert, 849, 857, 879, 880
Kent State University, 867–868, *868*, 884
Kentucky, 412–413
Kentucky resolution (1798), 212
Kerouac, Jack, 836
Kerr, Clark, 861
Kerry, John, 874
Kesey, Ken, 863
Key, Francis Scott, 236
Keynes, John Maynard, 692, 736
Keynesian economics, 692, 736
Khomeini, Ayatollah Ruholla, 919
Khrushchev, Nikita, 823, 826, 828, 840
  confrontation with, 843
  Cuban missile crisis (1962), 843–846, 844–845*M*, 885
Kim Il Sung, 801
Kindergarten, 519
King, Coretta Scott, *915*
King, Martin Luther, Jr., 831, 833, 839, 861, 876, 913
  assassination of, 880
  "Letter from Birmingham Jail," 852
  march on Washington, *852*, 853
  race riots and, 855
  Southern Christian Leadership Conference (SCLC), 848
King, Rodney, 944
King, Rufus, 187, 238
King George's War (1744–1748), 89, 112
King Ranch (Texas), 549
Kingston Trio, 863
King William's War, 89
Kipling, Rudyard, 467
Kirk, John, 394
Kissinger, Henry, 884, 894, *913*
  economy and diplomacy, 910–912, 911*M*
  foreign policy and, 909–910
  Nixon's trip to China, 886, 887
Knights of Labor, 493
Know-Nothings (American party), 33, 390–391
Knox, Philander, 629
Kodak cameras, 472–473
Koehler, Robert, *495*
Korea, Russian occupation of, 785
Korean War, 801–806
  Chinese intervention, 802
  election of 1952 and, 804–805
  police action, 801–802, 803*M*
  Truman *vs.* MacArthur, 802–804, 806–807
Korematsu, Fred, 765
Korematsu v. United States (1944), 765
Kovic, Ron, 882
Krimmel, John Lewis, *213*
Krupp armaments company, 555
Ku Klux Klan, 461, *461*, 677–679, *678*
  Detroit housing riots (1943), 767
  during Great Depression, 703
Kuwait, Iraqi invasion of, 941–942

Labor
  in colonial seaports, 96

Labor *(Cont.):*
  limited working hours, 492, 598
  shift to immigrants, 387
  slavery as control of, 330, 332
  See also Labor unions; Workers
Labor contractors, 475–476
Labor legislation, 603–604
Labor movement, 262, 263
Labor unions, 262, 492–496
  African American, 765–766
  decline under Reagan, 931
  early unions, 492
  limits of, 494–496, *495*
  management response to, 496
  New Deal and, *731*, 731–732
  Triangle Shirtwaist fire and, 594–595, *595*
  after World War II, 793
  in World War II, 760
  See also specific unions
Laconia, sinking of (1917), 633
Ladies' Home Journal, 687
Laffler, Arthur, 931
La Follette, Robert, 610, 622
La Huelga (The Strike), 890
Laissez-faire, 534, 539, 924
Lake Champlain, Battle of (1814), 236
Lake Erie, Battle of (1813), 235, 237*M*
Lalawethika (the Prophet), Shawnee leader, 229, 230*M,* 231
Land
  cattle industry and, 547
  demand for, 281
  "free" land, 535–536
  Indian lands, 204–205, 281
  as issue in Reconstruction, 448–449, 463–464
  land speculation, 176, *176,* 253
    Andrew Jackson in, 281
    inflation and depression, 292
    Miami land boom, 687–688
  See also Plantations; Tenancy and sharecropping
Landed and landless states, 172, 173*M*
Land Grant College Act (1862), 425
Land-grant colleges, 520
Landis, Kenesaw Mountain, 672
Landon, Alfred, 726
Land speculation. *See* Land
Lane, Ralph, 30
Lane Seminary, 315
Lange, Dorothea, *688*
Language, diversity of, 1
La Raza Unida (The Race United), 890–891
Las Casas, Bartolomé de, 19, 22
Lasker, Albert, 665
Lathrop, Julia, 604
Latin America
  defense agreements in, 743
  "Dollar Diplomacy," 629–630
  effects of Great Depression, 694
  imperialism and, 580–581
  missionary diplomacy, 631
  Monroe Doctrine and, 239–240
  nationalism in, 825
  nationalist movements in, 242
  Peace Corps in, 841
  Southern expeditions to, 400
Laud, William, 66
Lawrence, Kansas, 380–381
Lawrence (Mass.) dam, 259
Law schools, 519
League of Augsburg, 89
League of Nations, 650–651, 743, 745
League of Women Voters, 670
Lear, Norman, 928
Leary, Timothy, 861, 862, 863
Lease, Mary Elizabeth, 566
Leatherstocking Tales (Cooper), 308

Leaves of Grass (Whitman), 309
Lebanon, 824, 935–936
Lee, Ann, 310
Lee, Henry "Lighthorse Harry," 159–160
Lee, James W., 462
Lee, Richard Henry, 143–144
Lee, Robert E., 400, 416, 417*M,* 422–423, *435*
  surrender at Appomattox, 432*M,* 434*M,* 436
  victory at Chancellorsville, 431, 432*M*
Legal status of women, 183
Legislation
  mandatory education laws, 518
  racist, 46
  for social welfare, 604–605
  See also specific laws
Legislative districts, Supreme Court on, 848
Legislative Reference Bureau, 610–611
Leisler, Jacob, 85
Leisler's Rebellion (1689), 85
Leisure, 265, 521–522
LeJau, Francis, 98
LeMay, Curtis, 872, 881
Lend-Lease Act (1941), 749
Lenin, Vladimir, 640, 657, 784
Lenni Lenape (Delaware) tribe, 82, 83, 121, 231
Lenoir, Etienne, 471
Leonard, Daniel, 146
"Letter from a Farmer in Pennsylvania, A," (Dickinson), 130
Letters from and American Farmer (Crèvecoeur), 196–197
Levitt, William, 811
Levittown developments, 811–812, 814
Lewis, John, 849
Lewis, John L., 732, 733, 760, 761
Lewis, John Solomon, 527, 528
Lewis, Meriwether, 1, 2, 223–224, 224*M,* 355
Lewis, Sinclair, 673
Lewis and Clark expedition, 223–224, 224*M,* 355
Lexington, Battle of (1775), 138, 139
Leyte Gulf, Battle of, 771
Liberalism, 837–866
  agenda for reform, 838–841
    election of 1960 and, 839–840
    Kennedy White House, 840–841, *841*
    social structures of change, 838–839
  chronology of, 866
  civil rights campaign and (*See* Civil rights)
  counterculture and, 860–865
  disillusionment with, 921
  Great Society programs (*See* Great Society programs)
  historical analysis, 860–861
  new frontiers, 841–848
    cold war frustrations, 842
    Cuban missile crisis, 843–846, 844–845*M,* 885
    economy and, 846
    Khrushchev and, 843
    reforms of Warren court, 846–848, *847*
  Vietnam War and, 895
Liberal Republicans, 460
Liberator, The, 315, 348
Liberty party (1840), 323
Liberty party (1874), 374
Liberty poles, 195
Liddy, G. Gordon, 907
Life expectancy
  in Chesapeake region, 38
  in New England colonies, 68–69
  of slaves, 340
Liliuokalani, queen of Hawaii, 582
Lily, The, (women's rights paper), 321
Limited government, 220, 295
Lincoln, Abraham, 395, 396, 406, 540, 572*n,* 579
  assassination of, 438
  capabilities of, 410, 411–412
  character of, 398–399
  differing views of emancipation, 419–420

election of 1860 and, 401
election of 1864, 433–435, 434*M*, 436, 444
Fort Sumter crisis and, 402–404
Lincoln-Douglas debates, 397–399, *398*
plan for Reconstruction, 442–443
views of motives, 404
visit to Richmond, 436, 438
Lincoln, Benjamin, 164
Lincoln-Douglas debates, 397–399, *398*
Lindbergh, Charles, 685–686
Lippmann, Walter, 668
Literacy
of African Americans, 451
of colonials, 102
of free blacks, 347
illiteracy of poor Southern whites, 330, 338
Literacy tests, 573, 854
Literature, 308–309
black writers of 1920s, 674–675
of Great Depression, 698
journalistic exposés, 599
of 1920s, 673
Little Big Horn, battle of (1876), 541
Little Caesar (film), 700
Little Richard, 864
Little Rock (Arkansas), 832–833
Little Rock and Fort Smith Railroad, 560–561
Livingston, Margaret, 181–182
Livingston, Robert, 144, 223
Lloyd George, David, 649
Lobbies for social legislation, 510
Locke, Alain, 675
Locke, John, 51, 124, 349
Lodge, Henry Cabot, 584, 650–651, 676, 879
Lombardo, Guy, 699
Lôme, Enrique Dupuy de, 585
London, England, 107, *108*
"Lone Ranger, The," 699
Long, Huey P., 722, *723*, 725
Long, Jacob, 193
"Long telegram," 786
Looking Backward (Bellamy), 485
Lord and Thomas advertising company, 665
Lorentz, Pare, 734
Louis XIII, king of France, 62
Louis XIV, king of France, 86
Louisbourg, fall of (1758), 118–119
Louisiana Purchase
acquisition of (1803), 222–223
exploration of, 223–224, 224*M*
financial burden of, 221
slavery in, 269
Louisiana Territory, 1
Louis-Philippe, king of France, 273
Lovejoy, Elijah, 31
Lowe, Pardee, 513
Lowell, Francis Cabot, 256
Lowell, Massachusetts, 259, *260*
Lowell Offering (magazine), 257
Lowell textile mills, 256, 259, *260*
Loyalists (tories), 145–146, 158, 159
Loyalty crusade, 798, 805
Loyalty oath, 444
Loyalty Review Board, 798
Luce, Henry R., 671, 797, 876
Luna Park (Coney Island), 522
Lundy, Benjamin, 315
Lunt, Dolly, 437
Lusitania, sinking of, 636
Lusk, R. D., 700
Luther, Martin, 23–24
Lutheranism, 26, 78
Lynchings, 535
during Great Depression, 703
in World War I, 645

Lynch law, 369
Lyon, Mary, 313
Lyon, Matthew, 213

McAdoo, William Gibbs, 642
MacArthur, Douglas, 709, 752, 768, 770, 770*M*
conflict with Truman, 802–804, 806–807
in Korean War, 701
Macbeth (Shakespeare), 734
McCarran Act (1950), 799
McCarthy, Eugene, 879, 881
McCarthy, Joseph R., 817, 840
ambitions of, 799–800, *800*
fall of, 805–806
McCarthyism, 800
McClellan, George, 413, 416, 417*M*, 433
McClure, Samuel, 599
McClure's, 599
McCormick, Cyrus, 384, 576
McCormick Harvesting Machine Company, 481, 495
McCulloch v. Maryland (1819), 250, 291
Macdonald, Dwight, 833
Macdonough, Thomas, 236
McDowell, Irvin, 408, 409
McElvaine, Robert, 690
McFarlane, Robert, 937
McGillivray, Alexander, 172
McGovern, George, 894, 905
McGuffey Readers, 314
McGuire, Judith, 425
McIlhenny, Edward, 532
McKay, Claude, 674
McKim, Randolph, 408
McKinley, William
assassination of, 612
election of 1896, 570, 572, 572*M*, 573
presidency of, 575–576
annexation of Philippines, 588–589
Boxer Rebellion, 592
intervention in Cuba, 584, 586
McKinley Tariff (1890), 559, 561, 581, 582
McMahon Act (1946), 790
McNamara, Robert Strange, 840, 871, 876–877
McPherson, Aimee Semple, 658–659, *659*, 679
McTeague (Norris), 600
Macune, Charles W., 565, 566
Madero, Francisco, 632
Madison, James, 192, 450
Bill of Rights submitted, 200–201
declaration of war (1812), 235
election of 1808, 234
election of 1812, 238
federal involvement in economy, 246
Jeffersonian Republican party and, 207–208
Marbury v. Madison (1803), 221
opposition to Hamilton, 204
role in Constitutional Convention, *187*, 188, 189, 190
Magellan, Ferdinand, 18–19
Mahan, Alfred Thayer, 578, 592
Mahican tribe, 79
Maine, 92, 321–322
Maine (battleship), 584, 585, *585*
Main Street (Lewis), 673
"Major Bowes' Amateur Hour," 699
Malaria, 37, 46, 51, 328, 338, 756, 759
Malcolm X, 854
Malnutrition, 338, 694
Management
managerial elite, 477–478, 664
response to strikes and boycotts, 496
Manassas, Battles of (1861; 1862). *See* Bull Run
Manchuria, Russian occupation of, 785
Mandan tribe, 355
Manhattan Project, 759, 776, 790, 798
Manifest Destiny, 355–359

Mann, Horace, 313
Mann Act (1910), 608–609
Mansfield, Mike, 877
Manufacturing, lacking in South, 329
Manumission, 177, 179
Mao Zedong, 656, 785, 796–797, 797, 802, 886
MAPA (Mexican American Political Association), 890
"Maple Leaf Rag" (Joplin), 523
Marblehead, Massachusetts, 71–72
Marbury, William, 221
Marco Polo, 7
Margin requirements, 689–690
Marion, Francis ("Swamp Fox"), 157, 160
Maritime trades, 95
Market economy
    effects on Jackson presidency, 281
    importance of concept, 245
    Jacksonian party system and, 294–295
    religion and, 301, 303
    after War of 1812, 243, 245
Market revolution, 245–251
    agriculture and, 248, 250
    cotton trade and, 246–247
    effect on social structure, 263–267, 273
    general incorporation laws, 251
    growth of markets and, 245–246
    new nationalism, 246
    new politics and, 275
    promotion of enterprise, 250–251
    transportation revolution and, 247–248, 249M
Marne, Battle of (1918), 647, 648M
Maroon settlements, 99
Marriage
    among slaves, 342, 343
    eternal marriage (Mormon), 312
    Great Depression and, 696
    legal reforms and, 183
    middle class and, 265
    obstacles to women's employment, 698
    polygamy (Mormon), 312
    postwar boom in, 811
    slave marriages legalized, 445
    See also Family; Women
Marrs, Elijah, 421
Marshall, George C., 787
Marshall, James, 367
Marshall, John, 221, 250–251, 282
Marshall, Thurgood, 829, 849, 943
Marshall Plan, 787–788, 791
Martí, José, 584
Marx Brothers, 700
Mary II, queen of England, 85
Maryland, 40–42, 41M, 44, 45
Mary Tudor, queen of England, 25–26
Masaryk, Jan, 789
M*A*S*H, 928
Massachusetts, 256, 259, 260
Massachusetts Bay Colony, 66–67, 69
    under direct British control, 133–134, 137
    General Court of, 67, 71
    religious beliefs, 72
    reputation of, 135
Massachusetts Bay Company (1629), 67
Massachusetts Government Act (1774), 133–134, 135
Massachusetts Institute of Technology, 600, 601
Massachusett tribe, 76
Mass consumption, 520–521
Mass culture, 833–834
Mass media, 670–671, 928
Mass transit, 503–504
Master-apprentice system, 95, 96, 245, 256, 260–261
Materialism, 264–265
Matrilineal kinship, 80
Mattachine Society (1951), 892
Mayan civilization, 13, 15
Mayflower, 65–66

Mayflower Compact, 66
Meade, George Gordon, 431
Means, Russell, 891
Measles, 540
Meatpacking industry, 472, 481
Mechanical reaper, 384
Medicaid program, 858–859
Medical schools, 519
Medicare Act, 858–859
Meese, Edwin, 938
"Me generation," 898, 921
Mellon, Andrew, 681–682, 691
Melting Pot, The, (Zangwill), 523
Melville, Herman, 309
Mental asylums, 314
Mental illness, 695
Mercantilism, 35–36
Meredith, James, 851–852
Mergers, corporate, 484
Merrimack, U.S.S., 413
"Merry Pranksters," 863
Mesabi iron range, 483
Mesoamerica, 13, 15
Metacomet (Wampanoag sachem), 77
Metacomet's War (1676), 77
Methodist church, 226, 228, 316, 351, 455
    role in Prohibition, 677
Metro-Goldwyn-Mayer movie studio, 699
Mexican American Political Association (MAPA), 890
Mexican Americans
    activism of, 889, 890
    changes of 1920s and, 666–667
    deportation of, 676, 702
    Great Depression and, 702
    great migration of, 644
    migrant workers, 839
    under New Deal, 729
    private charities, 704
Mexican immigrants, 356, 369, 373, 512
    in labor pool, 476
Mexican War (1845), 364–365, 365M
Mexico
    resistance in California, 366
    settlement of Southwest and, 356–357, 357
    Texas Revolution and, 358
    Wilson's intervention in, 631–632
Mexico City, 356, 366
Miami (Florida) land boom, 687–688
Miami Confederacy, 196, 204–205
Miami tribe, 231
Michigan, relief during Great Depression, 705
Michigan Salt Association, 480–481
Micmac tribe, 61
Middle class
    appeal of revivals, 303
    emergence of, 265
    families in transition, 306–307
    in KKK, 668
    morality and, 700
    professionalized, 599
    urban life of, 514–515
    wooing Democratic voters to, 818–819
Middle East, 919–920, 920
    terrorism in, 935–936
    Yom Kippur War, 910
Middle managers, 477–478
Middle Passage, 45–46
Midway, Battle of (1942), 754
Midway island, purchase of (1867), 580
Migrant workers
    of Great Depression, 701–702
    unionization of, 702, 889
Milburne, Jacob, 85
Militancy, 605, 855
Military
    army budget cuts, 220

buildup in Reagan presidency, 931, 934–935
life in camps, 428–429
"Military advisors" in South Vietnam, 842
Military draft, 640–641, 749
Militia, 157
Miller, Jeffrey, 869
Miller, Josiah, 380
Miller, Lewis, *344*
Miller, William, 193, 194
Mills College, 817
Minimum wage laws, 828–829
Mining, 22, 545–546
Mining camps, 367–369
Minstrel shows, 286
Miranda v. Arizona (1966), 847
Miscegenation, 335
Missionaries, 56–58, *57M*, 578–579, 581
Missionary diplomacy, 630–631, *631M*
Mississippi, 573
Mississippi Plan (1875), 461–462
Mississippi River, 171–172, 186, 431
"Miss Liberty," *182*
Missouri, 413
Missouri Compromise (1820), *266M*, 268–270, 374, 388, 389, 396
Missouri tribe, 355
Mitchell, John A., 614, 893, 909
Mitchell, Margaret, 698
Mobility, culture of, 810
Mobilization for World War II, 758–759
Mobil Oil, 821
Moby-Dick (Melville), 309
Moctezuma II, Aztec ruler, 18, 19
Model T Ford, 662
Model towns, 729
Mohawk tribe, 80
Molasses Act (1733), 123
Mondale, Walter, 935
Monetarists, 692
Money supply, 689, 692
Monitor, U.S.S., 413
Monkey Business (film), 700
Monmouth Courthouse, Battle of (1778), 155
Monopoly (board game), 698
Monroe, James
    election of 1816, 238
    election of 1824 and, 274
    Louisiana Purchase, 223
Monroe Doctrine, 239–240
Montagnai tribe, 62
Montana, statehood (1889), 552
Montcalm, Louis Joseph, marquis de, 117–118
Montgomery (Alabama) *Mail*, 402
Montgomery, Benjamin, 441–442, 463–464
Montgomery, Bernard, 755
Montgomery bus boycott, 831, 848
Montreal, surrender of (1760), 119
Moody, Anne, 850–851
Moody, Dwight, 509, 815
Moorehead v. Tipaldo (1936), 735
Moralists, 516
Morality
    abolitionism and, 316
    corruption in military camps, 429
    effects of Civil War on, 438–439
    war speculation and, 426
    women as guardians of, 305, 361
    See also Reform movements
Moral Majority, 926
More, Thomas, 29
Morehouse College, 831
Morgan, Daniel, 160, *160M*
Morgan, J. C., 730
Morgan, J. Pierpont, 483–484, 618
Morgenthau, Henry, 736, 760
Mormons (Church of Jesus Christ of Latter-Day Saints), 311–312, 371, 372

Morrill Act (1862), 519
Morris, Gouverneur, 187, 190
Morris, Robert, 187
Morse, Samuel F. B., 257, 473
Mortality rates, 40, 46
Morton, Oliver, 447
Moscow summit, 940, *941*
Mossadeq, Mohammed, 824
Motion Picture Production Code (1934), 700
Motion pictures, 670, 699–700
Mott, Lucretia, 319
Mountain men, 263
Mount Holyoke College, 313
Ms. magazine, 903, *904*
"Muckrakers," 599
Muir, John, 616, *617*
Mulattoes, 286
Muller, Curt, 598
Muller v. Oregon (1908), 598
Munich analogy, 784
Munich Conference, 747
Munn v. Illinois (1877), 565
Muralists, 734
Murphy, Frank, 733
Murray, Judith Sargent, 183
Murray, Philip, 733
Music
    classical music, 699
    folk music, 863
    integration in music world, 863–864
    record sales in Great Depression, 699
    rock and roll, 835
    in slave culture, *344*, 344–346
    soul music, 864
    in urban life, 523
Mussolini, Benito, 657, 744, 745, 762, 769, 775
Mutualistas, 704
Myers, William, 814

NAACP. *See* National Association for the Advancement of Colored People
Nader, Ralph, 861, 898–899
Nader's Raiders, 899
NAFTA (North American Free Trade Agreement), 948
Nagasaki, bombing of, 776
Naismith, James, 522
Napalm, 874
Napoleon, Louis, 453
Narragansett tribe, 76, 77
Nasser, Gamal Abdel, 824
Natchez tribe, 13
Nation (radical journal), 449
National American Woman Suffrage Association (1890), 558
National Association for the Advancement of Colored People (NAACP), 575, *678*, 728, 765
    black veterans in, 792–793
    Brown v. Board of Education of Topeka (1950), 830, 839, 892
    civil rights and, 829–830
National Association of Colored Women, 601
National Association of Manufacturers, 579, 664
National Birth Control League, 668
National character
    movement west and, 253–254
    population growth and, 252–253
    restlessness, 251–252, *252*, 255
    urbanization and, *254*, 254–255
National Civil Service Reform League (1881), 559
National Consumers' League, 599, 605, 611–612
National Defense Education Act (1958), 825
National Energy Act, 916
National Environmental Policy Act (1969), 900
National Farmers' Alliance (1880), 566
National Farmers' Alliance and Industrial Union, 566
National Guard, 733, 832, 868
National Industrial Recovery Act (NIRA), 719
National Intelligencer, 217

Nationalism
  in black communities, 285
  Civil War and, 438
  in Cold War (*See* Cold War)
National Labor Relations Act (1935), 725, 732, 733, 736
National Labor Relations Board (NLRB), 725
National Labor Union (NLU), 492
National League of Professional Baseball Clubs (1876), 522
National Municipal League (1895), 562
National Negro Business League, 575
National Organization for Women (NOW), 902–903, 904
National Origins Act (1924), 676
National park system, 617, *617*
National Recovery Administration (NRA), 719–720, 735
National Republican party (1824), 275, 278
National Review, 927
National Security Council (NSC), 801
National Trades' Union (1834), 262
National Traffic and Motor Vehicle Safety Act (1966), 899
National Tuberculosis Association, 599
National Union for Social Justice (1934), 723
National War Labor Board (NWLB), 643–644
National Wilderness Preservation System Act (1964), 859
National Woman's party, 605, 670
National Woman Suffrage Association, 670
National Women's Political Caucus, 905
National Youth Administration (NYA), 724, 728, 768
Native Americans
  alliances with Spain, 172
  assimilation of, 224–225
  battle of Little Big Horn, 541
  boarding schools, 543
  complex societies, 12–13
  conflict with other tribes, 76–77
  destruction of culture, 228
  in early New England, 76–77
  First Sioux War, 539–541, 540*M*
  French and Indian War (*See* Seven Years' War)
  Indian removal, 281–282, 283*M*, 284
  in Jacksonian Era, 276, 278
  in Mexican society, 357, *357*
  New Deal and, 729–730
  Northwest Ordinance and, 177
  numbers in 1790, 195–196
  Plains Indians, 353–355, 354*M*, 362
  political activism of, 891–892
  Pontiac's Rebellion, 121
  prehistoric, 11–12, 12*M*
  racial discrimination in mining camps, 369
  reservations, 542
  in Revolutionary War, 156
  Sand Creek massacre, 539–540, 539*M*
  semisubsistence economy of, 197
  as slaves, 51
  Spanish colonists and, 56, 57–58, 57*M*
  trade with Carolinas, 51
  Trail of Tears, 282, 283*M*, 284
  Wounded Knee massacre, 542, 544, 891
  See also specific tribes and leaders
Nativism, 508–509, 675–676
  immigration and, 387
  Know-Nothing party, 390
  prejudice in mining camps, 369
NATO (North Atlantic Treaty Organization), 788–789, 788*M*
Nat Turner's Rebellion (1831), 340–341, 348
Naturalism, in fiction and art, 600
Naturalization Act (1798), 211, 212
Natural resources, 467
  industrial technology and, *471*, 471–472
  of South, 526
Nauvoo (Illinois), 312
Navajo tribe, 544, 730
Naval aviation, 754
Naval war
  British impressment and confiscation, 97, 207, 208, 232, 233, 234

Civil War
  battle of Ironclads, 413
  Confederate blockade, 412, 413–414, 422
  victory at Mobile Bay, 413
  Quasi-War with France, 211, 220
  War of 1812, 236
Navigation Acts (1660, 1663, 1673), 42, 43, 84, 85, 123
Nazi Party, 744
Nazi party (Germany), 657
Nebraska, statehood (1867), 552
Necessary and proper clause, 203–204, 250
"Negro election day," 96
Negro Methodists Holding a Meeting in a Philadelphia Alley, 178
"Negro Speaks of Rivers, The," (Hughes), 674
Nelson, Donald M., 758
Nelson, Gaylord, 900
Neolin (Lenni Lenape prophet), 121
Netherlands, 27–28, 45, 49, 89
Neutrality, 207, 634–636
Neutrality Acts (1935; 1936; 1937), 745–746
Neville, John, 193–195, *194*, 205
New Amsterdam village, 77
New Deal, 710, 712–740
  chronology of, 740
  early stages (1933–1935), 714–721
    NRA in trouble, 720
    planning for agriculture, 720–721
    planning for recovery, 719–720
    relief for unemployed, 717–719, *718*
    role of First Lady, 716
    Roosevelts and, 714–715, *715*
    saving banks, 715, 717
  effect on unemployment, *694*
  effects on population, 726–734
    arts projects, 733–734
    CIO and, 732–733
    limitations of New Deal, 727–729, *728*
    Native Americans and, 729–730
    organized labor and, *731*, 731–732
    western water supply, 727
    women and, 730–731
  final stage (1937–1940), 734–739
    conflict over New Deal, 736–737
    effects of New Deal, 737–739, *738*
    historical assessment, 739
    "packing" courts, 735–736
  second stage (1935–1936), 721–726
    election of 1936 and, 725–726
    indications of discontent, 722–724, *723*
    second hundred days, 724–725
New England Anti-Slavery Society (1832), 317
New England colonies
  founding of, 64–67
  patterns of settlement, 69
  stability and order in, 68–69
New England Emigrant Aid Company, 380
New England Kitchen, 600
New Era (early 20th century)
  chronology of, 686
  mass society
    African Americans and, 673–675, *674*
    art and literature, 673
    cultural effects of, 666–667
    entertainments, 672–673
    mass media and, 670–671
    new woman and, 668–670, *669*
    youth culture and, 671–672
  opponents of new ways, 675–680
    fundamentalism, 679–680
    Ku Klux Klan, 677–679, *678*
    nativism and immigration restriction, 675–676
    Prohibition, 676–677
  Republican party in, 680–685
  "Roaring Twenties," 661–667
    automobile and, 662–663
    construction boom, 661–662

consumer culture of, 665–667
corporate growth, 663–664
technology and consumer spending, 661
welfare capitalism, 664–665
social changes, 659–661, 682
New Federalism, 887–888
Newfoundland, 5–6
New France, 62
"New Freedom," 620, 621–624
New Hampshire, 69, 83–84, 92
New Harmony, Indiana, 312
New Jersey, 80–81, 94, 150*M*, 151
New Jersey Plan, 188
Newlands, Frederick, 616
New Mexico
  acquisition of (1848), 366–367
  popular sovereignty proposed, 376
  Spanish settlement of, 355
  statehood (1912), 376, 552
"New Nationalism," 246, 619, 623
New Negro, The, (Locke), 675
New Netherlands, 77–78
New Orleans (Louisiana)
  Battle of (1814), 236, 238, 274
  capture of (1862), 413
  desegregation in, 837–838
New Republic, The, 656, 703
"New South." *See* The South
Newspapers
  colonial resistance and, 126
  first national newspaper, 217
  freedom of the press, 212
  power press and, 257
  in 1790, 196
  See also Journalism; *specific newspapers*
New theology of revivalism, 300–301
Newton, Huey, 855, 892
New York (colony)
  border war with Vermont, 94
  British campaign in (1776), 150–151, 150*M*
  English rule in, 78, 83–84
  Leisler's Rebellion (1689), 85
  tenant revolts in, 94–95
New York City, 500–501
  British attack on, 149–150
  Central Park, 517
  transportation revolution and, 247
  Tweed Ring in, 453
  World's Fair (1939), 698–699
New York Herald, 439
New York Stock Exchange, 474, 479, 688–689, *689,* 690
New York Times, 494, 906
New York Tribune, 459
Nez Percé tribe, 542
Ngo Dinh Diem, 842
Niagara movement, 575
Nicaragua, 918, 936
Nicholas II, Czar of Russia, 638
Nickelodeons, 670
Nicolls, Richard, 80
Nihilism, 673
Nimitz, Chester, 770–771
Nineteenth Amendment (1920), 605
NIRA (National Industrial Recovery Act), 719
Nixon, Richard, 804, 820, 840, 883–888
  background and character of, 883
  campaign of 1968, 888–889
  election of 1968, 880, 888–889
  election of 1972, 894
  pardoned by Ford, 912–913
  presidency of
    desegregation policy, 892–893
    détente, 885–886, *886*
    election of 1972 and, 894
    environmental regulation, 900
    expansion of Vietnam War, 868

gay rights, 892
Hispanic activism, *889,* 889–891
Native American activism, 891–892
New Federalism and, 887–888
no-win war, 885
social policies and, 892–893
stagflation, 887–888
trip to China, *886,* 886–887
us *versus* them mentality, 893
Vietnamization and Cambodia, 884–885
"Nixon Doctrine," 885–886
Nixonomics, 888
NLRB (National Labor Relations Board), 725
N.L.R.B. v. Jones & Laughlin Steel Corporation (1937), 736
NLU (National Labor Union), 492
Nobel Peace Prize, 629, *913,* 917, 919, *920*
Noble and Holy Order of the Knights of Labor, 493
Nonviolence, 831
Norris, Frank, 600
North, Lord, 131–132, 138
North, Oliver, 937, *938*
North, Simeon, 257
North America
  colonization of (*See* Colonies and colonization)
  early cultures, 11–16, 12*M*
  population in 15th century, 3
North American Free Trade Agreement (NAFTA), 948
North Atlantic Treaty Organization (NATO), 788–789, 788*M*
North Carolina, 50, 94, 106
North Dakota, statehood (1889), 552
Northern Securities Company, 615
North Vietnam, 780–781
Northwest Ordinance (1787), 176–177
Northwest Passage, 61–62
Northwest Territory, 174–177, *176*
Norway, German invasion of, 747
Notes on the State of Virginia (Jefferson), 219
NOW (National Organization for Women), 902–903, 904
Noyes, Alexander, 689
Noyes, John Humphrey, 311
NRA (National Recovery Administration), 719–720, 735
NSC (National Security Council), 801
NSC-68, 801, 802
Nuclear age, 780–781
Nuclear deterrence strategies, 791
Nuclear energy, development of, 916
Nuclear test ban treaty, 846
Nuclear weapons, 780
  arms race, 845–846
  civilian *vs.* military control of, 790
  deterrence and, 790–791
  dilemma of cold war and, 789–790
  parity, 919
  threat of massive retaliation, 821–822
"Nuclear winter," 934
Nullification crisis, 287–289
  Calhoun's theory, 288–289
  Jackson's solution, 289
  in South Carolina, 287–288, *288*
Nursing, 426–427, *427*
NWLB (National War Labor Board), 643–644
NYA (National Youth Administration), 724, 728, 768
Nye, Gerald P., 744
Nye Committee, 744

Oakes, Richard, 891
Oberlin College, 313
"Ocala Demands" (1890), 566
Occupational Safety and Health Agency (OSHA), 887–888
O'Connor, Sandra Day, 942, 943
October Revolution (1917), 784
Office of Economic Opportunity (OEO), 857
Office of War Mobilization (OWM), 758
Offices (office work), 265, 474, 490, *491*
Oglethorpe, James, 54
Ohio Territory, 225–226, *226*

Oil crisis, 910–912, 911M
Oil shortages, 916
Okies, 701–702
Okinawa, Battle of, 773
Oklahoma, statehood (1907), 552
Old Age Revolving Pensions, Limited (1934), 723–724
"Old South," 333
Oligopolies, 663
"Olive Branch Petition" (1775), 143
Oliver, Joe "King," 672
Olmsted, Frederick Law, 337, 517
Omaha tribe, 355
One Flew Over the Cuckoo's Nest (Kesey), 863
Oneida Community, 311
Oneida tribe, 80
100,000 Guinea Pigs (Schlink), 698
Only Yesterday (Allen), 659, 682
Onondaga tribe, 80
On the Origin of Species (Darwin), 579
On the Road (Kerouac), 836
OPEC (Organization of Petroleum Exporting Countries),
910–912, 911M, 916, 930
Opechancanough, brother of Powhatan, 34, 38, 42
Operation Desert Storm, 942
Operation Overlord, 769
Operation Rolling Thunder, 872
Operation Torch (1942), 754
Opportunity, 272, 273–274, 296
"Opposition," 124–125
Orders in Council (1807), 232, 234–235
Oregon Territory, 364, 374
Organization Man, The (Whyte), 834
Organization of Petroleum Exporting Countries (OPEC),
910–912, 911M, 916, 930
Organized labor. See Labor unions
Original Dixieland Jazz Band, 672
Orlando, Vittorio, 649
Orozco, José Clemente, 734
Orphanages, 314
Osceola (Seminole chief), 284
OSHA (Occupational Safety and Health Agency), 887–888
Oshima, Dunks, 764
Ostrogorski, Moisei, 555–556
O'Sullivan, John L., 356
Oswald, Lee Harvey, 853
Other America, The (Harrington), 856–857
Oto tribe, 355
Overexpansion of industry, 691
Overland Trail, 359–361, 360M, 362, 367
Overseers, role of, 339
Owen, Robert, 312
Owenite community, 312
OWM (Office of War Mobilization), 758

Pacific
American imperialism in, 581–582, 582
annexation of Hawaii and Philippines, 588–590, 590
Japanese aggression in, 588–590, 590, 750–751,
752–753
naval war in, 754
Pacific Northwest, 13
Pacific theater, war in, 770–771, 770M
Padrones, 475–476
Pago Pago (Samoa), 581
Pahlavi, Mohammad Reza, 824
Paine, Thomas, 138–140, 140, 242
Painting, 600
Paiute tribe, 537, 542, 544, 891
Palmer, A. Mitchell, 652, 653
Pamunkey Indians, 33–35
Panama Canal, 626–627, 917–918
Pan-American Conference (1933), 743
Pan-American Congress (1889), 581
Pan-American Union, 581
Panay incident, 747
Panic of 1819, 268, 270, 275, 290

Panic of 1837, 262, 359
Panic of 1857, 396–397
Panic of 1873, 460
Pan-Indian movement, 231, 232
Pan-Indian rights movement, 891–892
Pardons
after Civil War, 441, 442
Nixon pardoned by Ford, 912–913
Parker, Alton B., 615
Parks, Rosa, 831
Parliament (England)
Act of Supremacy (1534), 25
authority over colonies, 128, 135
bureaucracy and, 109
conflicts with James I, 64, 66
dissolved by Charles I, 42, 66
Glorious Revolution and, 84–85, 86
Grenville's measures, 123–124
indifference to colonies, 110
right to levy taxes, 86
Parochial schools, 519
Parr, Archie, 507
Passing of the Great Race, The (Grant), 607
Pasteur, Louis, 501
Paternalism, 334, 596, 630–631, 631M
Paterson, William, 188
Patman, Wright, 709
Patronage, 559
Patrons of Husbandry (1867), 565
Patterson, Floyd, 850
Patton, George S., Jr., 709, 710, 755, 769, 818
Paul, Alice, 605, 670
Paul, Mary, 256, 405
Pauncefote, Julian, 583
Pavisto tribe, 537
Pawtucket tribe, 76
Paxton Boys, 93
Pay equity, 602
Peabody fund, 519
Peace Commission (WWI), 649
Peace Corps (1961), 841
Peace movement, World War I and, 636–637
"Peace with honor," 884
Peanuts, 527
Pea Ridge, Battle of (1862), 413, 415M
Pearl Harbor (Hawaii), 581, 741–742, 750–751
Peirce, Charles, 597–598
Pellagra, 694
Pendleton Act (1883), 559
Penicillin, use in World War II, 759
Penn, William (the elder), 81
Penn, William (the younger), 81, 81–82, 83
Pennsylvania
British campaign in (1776–1777), 151–152
as colony, 81, 81–83, 92
Fort Duquesne, 89
Paxton Boys, 93
political strife in, 83
Whiskey Rebellion, 193–195, 194, 205
Pennsylvania Gazette, 89
Pennsylvania Railroad, 477, 481
Pentagon Papers, 906
People for the American Way, 928
People's (Populist) party (1892), 552, 558, 567–568, 571
People's party (1890), 566
People's Republic of China, 895
Pequot tribe, 77
Perestroika, 939
Perkins, Frances, 730
Perot, H. Ross, 945, 949
Perry, Oliver Hazard, 235
Pershing, John "Black Jack," 632, 647
Person, Paul, 713
Pesticides, use in World War II, 759
Petersburg, siege of (1864), 433
Peter the Great, 115

Petroleum industry, 471–472, 821
Philadelphia (Pennsylvania), 82, 95, 152
Philadelphia and Reading Railroad, 555
Philanthropy, 470, 484, 574, 637, 705
Philippines
  annexation of, 588–589
  attack on Manila, 586
  insurrection in, 590–591
  U.S. control of, 742
Philippine Scouts, 753
Phillips, Wendell, 316
Philosophes, 102
Photography, 600, 688, 734
Pickett, George, 431
Pickett's charge, 431
"Picture brides," 512
Pierce, Franklin, 377, 388, 411
Pike, Zebulon, 224M
Pinchot, Gifford, 616, 618
Pinckney, Charles Cotesworth, 187, 232, 234
Pinckney, Thomas, 205
Pinckney's Treaty (1796), 205, 223
Pingree, Hazen, 609
Pinkerton detectives, 567
Pitcairn, John, 138
Pitt, William, 112–113, 118–119, 129, 129
Pittsburgh (Pennsylvania), 470
Pittsburgh Bessemer Steel Company, 487–488
Pittsburgh Gazette, 214–215
Pizarro, Francisco, 7, 21
Plague, 756
Plains Indians, 353–355, 354M, 362, 536–537, 730
Planned Parenthood v. Casey (1992), 943
Planned reproduction, 311
Plantation Burial (Antrobus), 326
Plantations
  administration of, 352
  mistress of, 334–336, 335, 437
  owners, 325, 334
  plantation economy, 177
  during Reconstruction, 455–456, 456
  slave culture (See Slavery)
  social structure, 48, 55
Planter class, 332, 395, 457–458
Platt Amendment (1902), 638
Platt Amendment (1934), 743
Pledge of Allegiance, 815
Plessy v. Ferguson (1896), 518, 534, 830
Plow, improvements to, 384
Plummer, Franklin E., 271–272, 273
Plunkitt, George Washington, 498–499, 507
Plymouth Colony, 65–66, 72
Pocahontas, daughter of Powhatan, 34–35
Pocket veto, 443, 443n
Poetry, 674
Poison gas, in World War I, 639
Poland, 747, 772
Poliomyelitis, 714, 715
Polish National Alliance, 512
Political activism, 905
Political cartoons, 208, 563
Political culture of democracy, 274–277
Political machines, 498–499, 507
Political parties
  Jacksonian party system, 294–296
    collapse of, 390
    Democrats and Whigs, 294–295
    social bases of, 295–296
    triumph of market, 296
  Jefferson on, 220
  party conventions, 275
    American neutrality and, 207
    election of 1796, 208, 208–209
    Federalists and Republicans, 207–208
    French Revolution and, 206
    party ideologies, 209–210

party loyalty, 557
  political reforms and, 275–276
  sectional conflicts and, 390
  social bases of, 295–296
  social conditions and emergence of, 206
  stalemates of late 19th century, 556, 556–557
  third parties, 558, 567, 890–891
  See also specific parties
Political power
  executive power, 167–168, 168
  failure of reconstruction and, 463
  power of presidency, 291–292
  slavery and, 338
  transfer of, 217–218
  wartime powers, 424, 427–428
Politicians, full-time, 506
Politics
  Britain vs. colonies, 108–110
  Ku Klux Klan in, 679
  Manifest Destiny and, 356
  of slavery, 350
  tactics of politicians, 271–272
  Watergate crisis (See Watergate)
  weaknesses of political system, 405
  women in, 669–670
  See also Government; Politics of late 19th century
Politics of late 19th century, 554–593
  chronology of, 593
  imperialism (See Imperialism)
    Cuban revolt, 584–586, 585
    interest in China, 591–592
    Spanish-American War, 584–591
  new realignment in, 568–576
    African American response to, 574–575
    conflict over currency, 569–570
    depression of 1893, 568–569, 569
    discontent and unrest, 569–570
    election of 1896, 571–573, 572M, 572n
    Jim Crow politics, 573–574
    McKinley's presidency and, 575–576
  politics of paralysis, 555–556
    ferment in states and cities, 561–562
    ineffective presidents, 560–561
    issues and, 558–560
    origins of welfare state, 558–559
    political parties, 557–558
    stalemate, 556, 556–557
  revolt of farmers (See Populism)
Polk, James K., 363–365, 365M
Pollock, Jackson, 734
Poll tax, 573
Polygamy (Mormon), 312, 371–372
Ponce de León, Juan, 19
Pontiac (Ottawa chief), 121
Pontiac's Rebellion (1763), 121
Poole, Elijah (Elijah Muhammad), 703
Pooling, 478
Poor People's March, 897
Poor Richard's Almanack (Franklin), 198
Poor whites, 337–338
Pope, John, 416, 539–540
Popé (Indian spiritual leader), 58
Popular culture, counterculture and, 864
Popular Front (Spain), 745
Popular Mechanics magazine, 809
Popular melodramas, 522–523, 523
Popular music, 523
Popular sovereignty, 374, 376, 381, 389, 396
Population
  birthrate in 18th century, 92
  demographic pressure, 228
  distribution in 18th century, 100M
  European expansion and, 7, 17
  at first census (1790), 195–196
  growth of, 114, 252–253
Population Bomb, The (Ehrlich), 901–902

Populism, 562–568
  discontented farmers, 562–564, *563*
  election of 1892 and, 567–568
  formation of Populist party, 566–567
  origins of Alliance movement, 565–566
Populist (People's) party (1892), 558, 567–568, 571
Port Huron Statement, 860
Port Royal, Acadia (Nova Scotia), 62
Portsmouth, Treaty of (1905), 628–629
Portugal, 2, 6, 7–8, *8*
Postal system, 196
Post Office, Comstock Law and, 516
Pottawatomie massacre, 381
Pound, Ezra, 673
Poverty
  budget cuts in programs, 933–934, *934*
  in "New South," 530–531
  persistence of, 953
  social reform and, 600–601
Powderly, Terence V., 493
Powell, John Wesley, 538–539, 542
Power. *See* Political power
Power press, 257
Powers, Gary, 828
Powhatan, Pamunkey chief, 33–35, *36*, 57
Powhatan confederacy, 33–35, 38, 42, 79
Pragmatism, 597–598
Prairie, effect of railroads on, 384–385
Pratt, Micajah, 261–262
Prejudice against working women, 697–698
Premarital sex, 342
"Preparedness," for World War I, 637
Presbyterians
  Puritans, 64
  revival among, 103, 105
  settlement in Massachusetts Bay Colony, 66
Prescott, William, 141, 152
Presidency
  ineffective presidents, 560–561
  modernized under FDR, 737
Presley, Elvis, 809, 835
"Press gangs," 97
Prester John, 7, 8
Prisons, 314, *316*
Private charity, 704
Proclamation of 1763, 121
Proclamation of Amnesty and Reconstruction (1863), 442
Proclamation on Nullification (1832), 289
Product endorsements, 666
Productivity
  in factory system, 258, 261
  Taylorism and, 489–490
  World War II production, 758–759
Professional schools, 519
Professions, 601–602, 669
Profits from slavery, 330, 332
Progress and Poverty (George), 484
Progressive ("Bull Moose") party, 596, 620
Progressive era, 594–625
  chronology of, 625
  definition of progressivism, 597
  diplomacy of (*See* Diplomacy)
  municipal and state reform, 609–612
  national politics and, 612–621
    consumers and environment, 616–618, *617*
    "Square Deal," 614–615
    Theodore Roosevelt, 612–614, *613*
    William Howard Taft, 618–619
  politics of morality, 621–624
    character of Woodrow Wilson, 621
    labor and social reform, 623
    limits of reform, 623–624
    new freedom and, 621–623
  roots of reform, 596–599
    beliefs, 597–598
    pragmatic approach to, 598
    progressive method and, 598–599
    social control (*See* Social control)
    social reform (*See* Social reform)
    Triangle Shirtwaist fire, 594–595, *595*
Progressivism, 635, 640–641
Prohibition, 321–322, 659, 676–677, 684–685
Propaganda, 645, 761, 792
Property, importance of, 124, 178, 183–184
Prophecies of millennium, 298
Prophet (Shawnee leader), 229, 230*M*, 231
Prophetstown, Indiana, 229, 230*M*, 231
Proportional representation, 188
Proprietary colonies
  Maryland, 40–42, 41*M*
  South Carolina, 50–51, 53
Proslavery argument, 349
Prosperity. *See* Economy
Prosser, Gabriel, 340
Prostitution, 369, 429
  in slums, 505–506
  social control and, 608–609
Protective tariffs. *See* Tariffs
Protestant Reformation
  background of, 23
  in England, 25–26
  John Calvin, role of, 24–25
  Martin Luther, role of, 23–24
Psychological hardships, 694–695, 874
Psychology, Freudian, 668
PTL Club, 926
Public education, in cities, 518–519
Public interest, 598–599
Public lands, 175–176, *176*
Public policy, 691
Public Utilities Holding Company Act (1935), 725
Public works, 706
Public Works Administration (PWA), 719, 729
Pueblo Revolt (1680), 58
Pueblo tribe, 13, 56–57, 58, 80, 730
Puerto Rico, 889–890
Pugachev, Emelian, 115
Pujo, Arsène, 622
Pullman, George, 496
Pullman Palace Car factory, 496
Pullman Palace railroad cars, 469
Purchasing power, decline in, 691
Pure Food and Drug Act (1906), 616
Puritans, 26, 64–65
  Massachusetts Bay Colony, 66–67
  in New Jersey, 80
  Plymouth Colony, 65–66, 72
  Separatists, 65, 73
PWA (Public Works Administration), 719, 729
Pyle, Ernie, 756

Qadhafi, Muammar, 936
Quakers (Society of Friends), 78
  antislavery societies of, 178
  beliefs of, 81
  objections to slavery, 100–101
  role of women, 73, *74*, 75, 81
  sale of New Jersey to, 80
  settlement in Pennsylvania, *81*, 81–82
Quartering Act (1765), 123, 129–130
Quasi-War with France, 211, 220
Quayle, Dan, 942
Quebec, founding of (1608), 62
Quebec Act (1774), 134
Quitrents, 41, 51, 82

Race, 281–287, 338–339
"Race music," 835
Race riots. *See* Rioting
Racial discrimination

in housing, 812
suburbs and, 813
during World War II, 782
in World War II, 762
Racial prejudice
against Chinese, 511
in Great Depression, 703
intelligence testing and, 642
of Theodore Roosevelt, 613
Racial segregation. *See* Segregation
Racial violence, 642
Racism
of Andrew Johnson, 444
annexation of Philippines and, 589–590
of Benjamin Franklin, 100–101
in Chesapeake society, 46
Democratic appeal to, 461
Jim Crow laws, 573–575
Manifest Destiny and, 356
minstrel shows and, 286
in Old South, 336, 337
prejudice in mining camps, 369
Reconstruction and, 463
white fear of failure and, 286–287
Radar, 759
Radford, Arthur, 822
Radicalism, 184–185, 647, 652–654
Radical Republicans, 443, 445–446, 447–448
Radio
first commercial station, 671
golden age of, 699
Voice of America, 805
"Radio priest," 723
Ragtime, 523
Railroads, 473, 477–480
antirailroad sentiment, 562, 563, *563*
bankruptcies, 555
boom in "New South," 529
in border states, 413
competition and consolidation, 478
effects on Southwest, 544
growth of railroad economy, 382, 383*M*, 384
investment capital, 478–480, 479*M*
managerial revolution and, 477–478
national rail strike (1946), 793
prairie environment and, 384–385
pressure for regulation of, 562
railroad "brotherhoods," 492
rebuilt during Reconstruction, 453
regulation of, 615
settlement of West and, 537–538
transcontinental, 546, *547*
transportation revolution and, 248
trunk lines, 477
urban environment and, 385
urbanization and, 500
western cities and, 552
Rainford, William, 509
Raleigh, Walter, 7, 26, 27, 30, 31–32
Randolph, A. Philip, 765–766
Range wars, 549
Rankin, Jeannette, 638
Rankin, John, 798
Raskob, John J., 687
Ratification of Constitution, 190–191
Ray, James Earl, 880
Rayburn, Sam, 839–840
Raymondi, Bob, 796
REA (Rural Electrification Administration), 726
Readers Digest Condensed Books, 833
Reagan, Nancy, 929
Reagan, Ronald, 572*n*, 798, 924, 926
election of 1976, 914
election of 1980 and, 928–929
election of 1988 and, 939
foreign policy, 935–939

in Central America, 936
cover-up, 937–938, *938*
glasnost, 939
Iran-Contra, 936–937
terrorism in Middle East, 935–936
presidency of, 929–935
agenda, 930–931
foreign policy, 935–939
military buildup, 934–935
"Reagan Revolution," 931–933
Reagan style, 929–930, *930*
Supreme Court appointments, 942
"Reaganomics," 933–934, *934*
Rebates, 478
Rebels (American Revolution), 145–146, 161
Recall elections, 611
Recession of 1958, 819
Recession of 1973, 895
Recession of 1975, 914
Reciprocity, in tariffs, 559
Reclamation Act (1902), 616
Reconstruction, 441–465
abandonment of, 458–464
disputed election of 1876, 462–463
election of Grant and, 458
Grant administration, *459*, 459–460
Mississippi Plan and, 462
Northern disillusionment, 460
racism and, 463–464
white supremacy and, 457, 460–462, *461*, 463
black aspirations (*See* African Americans)
chronology of, 465
congressional, 448–450
presidential, 442–448
elections of 1866 and, 447–448
failure of Johnson's program, 444–445
Fourteenth Amendment (1866), 446–447, 459
Johnson's break with Congress and, 445–446
Johnson's program, 444, *445*
Lincoln's 10 percent plan, 442–443
mood of South and, 443
in South, 450–453
black officeholders, 451, *451*
economy and corruption, 452–453
reforms of new state governments, 452
white Republicans, 451–452
Reconstruction Acts (1867–1868), 448
Reconstruction Finance Corporation (RFC), 706
Recruitment for Continental Army, 148
Redbook magazine, 817
Red Cross, 426
Redeemer governments, 534
Redeemers, 463
Reed, Thomas, 561
Referendum, 611
Reform
in city governments, 506–507
liberal agenda for (*See* Liberalism)
limits of, 898–905
consumerism, 898–899
environmentalism, 900–901
equal rights and abortion, 904–905
feminism, 902–904, *904*
Nixon's reforms, 887–888
Reformation. *See* Protestant Reformation
Reform movements, 298–324, *299*
abolitionism (*See* Abolitionism)
Age of Reform, 309–315
asylum movement, 314–315
educational reform, 313
Mormonism, 311–312
social control and, 314
socialist communities, 312
temperance movement, 312–313
Utopian communities, 309–311, *310*
chronology of, 324

Reform movements (Cont.):
  party system and, 321–323
    temperance law, 321–322
    woman suffrage, 321
  revivalism (See Revivalism)
  Romanticism (See Romanticism)
  union reformers, 262
  women in, 304–307
Regan, Donald, 930
Regulation movements, 93–94, 106
Reilly, William, 942
Reliance Building, 504
Relief efforts
  in depression of 1893, 569
  failure in Great Depression, 704–705
Religion
  black religious life, 178, 345–346, 351, 455
  in Confederate camps, 429
  conservatism and, 925
  "conversion," 70–71
  conversion experience, 302
  differences within colonies, 72, 97
  disestablishment of state-supported churches, 184
  European exploration and, 7
  evangelical Christianity, 301, 303, 346, 924, 925
  evangelists of 20th century, 658–659, 659
  French colonies and, 62
  heresy, 72–74
  human sacrifice by Aztecs, 15–16
  of immigrants, 386–387
  importance in "New South," 532–533, 533
  liberal theology, 102
  in life on Great Plains, 551
  Manifest Destiny and, 356
  market economy and, 301, 303
  Mayan, 13, 15
  Native American, 12, 13, 229, 230M, 231
  political parties and, 557
  Protestant Reformation (See Protestant Reformation)
  Puritan faith, 70
  reform movements, 509, 509
  revivalism (See Revivalism)
  role in farm life, 336
  role in Prohibition, 677
  as segregating factor in 1950s, 815
  settlement movement and, 510
  traditional beliefs, 102–103
  See also specific faiths and denominations
Remington, Benjamin, 267
Reno, Milo, 707
Reparations, 650, 775–776
Representative assembly. See Colonial assemblies
Representative institutions, 71
Republican ideology, 183–184
Republicanism, 214, 220, 240–241
"Republican motherhood," 183
Republican party (Jeffersonian), 202, 202n
  differences with Federalists, 210
  election of 1796 and, 208, 208–209
  election of 1800 and, 212–213, 213
  ideology of, 209–210
  organization of, 207–208
Republican party (modern), 390, 391
  composition of, 557
  Cuban rebellion and, 584
  effects of Civil War on, 438
  election of 1860, 401
  election of 1928, 684–685, 685M
  election of 1932, 710–711
  election of 1952, 804–805
  ideology of, 393–395
  "modern" Republicans, 807, 818
  in New Era, 680–685
    economic policies of, 681–682
    election of 1928 and, 684–685, 685M
    indications of distress, 683–684

  politics of normalcy, 680–681
  Radical Republicans, 443, 445–446, 447–448
  scalawags and carpetbaggers, 451–452
  stalemate with Democrats, 556, 556–557
Republic of China (1911), 631
Republic of Panama, 626
Republic of Texas, 358–359
Republic Steel Company, 733
Reservations, 542
Resettlement Administration, 734
Restrictive covenants, 812, 814
Reuben James, sinking of (1941), 750
Reuther, Walter, 733
Revenue, 201
Revenue Act (1764), 123, 124, 125
Revenue Act (1935), 725
Revenue Act (1942), 760
Revenue sharing, 887
Revere, Paul, 138
Revivalism, 103–106, 226–228, 227
  in Confederate camps, 429
  conversion experience, 302
  market economy and, 301, 303
  new theology and, 300–301
  rise of African American churches, 303–304
  Second Great Awakening and, 304
Revolutionary ideals, 191–192
Reward and punishment, in slavery, 339
Reykjavík summit, 939
RFC (Reconstruction Finance Corporation), 706
Rhee, Syngman, 801, 802
Rhode Island, 69, 71, 72–74
Rhodes, James, 868
Rice, Sally, 258
Richards, Ellen, 600, 601
Richardson, Elliot, 898, 908
Richardson, Seth, 798
Richelieu, Armand du Plessis de, 62
Riesman, David, 834
Rights
  Bill of Rights, 191, 200–201
  right of petition, 321, 322
  rights of inheritance, 183
  states' rights, 411, 424
  women's rights movement, 319–320, 320
  See also Civil rights; Human rights issues
"Right to life" amendment, 905
Right-to-work laws, 794
Riis, Jacob, 600
Rioting
  antiblack riots in free states, 285
  Haymarket Square Riot (1886), 495–496
  Irish draft protesters, 428
  in Poland and Hungary, 823–824
  race riots, 447, 645, 646
    civil rights movement and, 853, 855
    Detroit housing riots (1943), 767
    Harlem riots (1935), 729
    Houston riots (1917), 642
    Los Angeles riots (1991), 944, 953
    Tampa (Florida), 587–588
  against Stamp Act, 127
  Stonewall riot (1969), 892
  against Townshend Acts, 130–131
Ripley, George, 307
Rivera, Diego, 734
River, The (Lorentz), 734
River rights, 539
River transportation, 247–248, 384, 414
Roanoke Colony, 30, 31
"Roaring Twenties." See New Era
"Robber barons," 474–475, 487
Roberts, Peter, 607
Robertson, Pat, 925
Robin Hood (banned), 800
Robinson, Jackie, 850, 851

Robinson, Spottswood, 792
Rochambeau, Comte de, 163, 164
Rochester, New York, 301, 303
Rockefeller, John D., 480, 482–483, 576, 599, 615, 652
Rock groups, 865
Rockingham, marquis of, 128
Roebling, John, 504
Roebling, Washington, 504
Roebuck, Alvah C., 521
Roe v. Wade (1973), 904–905
Rogers, Ginger, 700
Rogers, Roy, 835
Rogers, William, 856
Rolfe, John, 34–35
Rollins, Sonny, 835
Roman Catholic Church, 65, 78
  on abortion, 905
  in England, 25
  in Maryland, 41–42
  missionaries in Southwest, 56–58, 57*M*
  opposition to Luther, 24
  parochial schools, 519
  power and authority of, 23, 71
  presidency and, 839
  recognition by Quebec Act, 134
  social activism of, 926, *927*
Romantic friendships, 517
Romanticism, 307–309
  nature *vs.* civilization in, 308
  self-reliance and, 308–309
  Transcendentalism, 307–308
Rommel, Erwin, 752
Roosevelt, Eleanor, *713*, 714, 715, 716, 773
  promotion of women's interests, 730
  racial integration, 727, 728
Roosevelt, Franklin D., 710
  background and character of, 714–715, *715*
  balance of power and, 771–772
  closeness with citizens, 712–713
  death of, 773–774
  election of 1932, 710–711
  election of 1944, 768
  failing health, 768
  leadership capabilities, 754
  presidency of
    court "packing" plan, 735–736
    New Deal (*See* New Deal)
    racial integration and, 727–729, *728*
    second hundred days, 724–725
Roosevelt, Theodore, 572, 584, 592, 610, 612, 636, 714
  character and background, 612–614, *613*
  consumer causes and, 616–618, *617*
  election of 1912, 619–620, 620*M*
  election of 1916 and, 637
  on "muckrakers," 599
  presidency of
    Caribbean trade and, 638
    diplomacy in Far East, 628–629
    Panama Canal and, 626–627
    Square Deal, 614–615
  progressivism of, 596
  return to politics, 619
  in Spanish-American War, *587*, 588
Roosevelt corollary to Monroe Doctrine, 638, 743
Root, Elihu, 638
Roper, Elmo, 795
Rosenberg, Ethel, 805
Rosenberg, Julius, 805
"Rosie the Riveter," *761*
Ross, David, 867
Ross, Edward A., 606
Ross, John, 281–282, 284
Ross, Nellie, 669
Rough Riders, *587*, 588
Round Lick Association of Primitive Baptists, 679
Royal African Company, 45

Royale, Anne, 312
Ruby, Jack, 853
"Rum, Romanism, and Rebellion," 561
Runaway slaves, 341
Rural Electrification Administration (REA), 726
Rural society
  equality of rural farmers, 196–197
  in "New South," 531–532
  rate of urbanization and, *254*, 254–255
Rush, Benjamin, 183
Russell, William, 409
Russell Sage Foundation, 601
Russia, 649–650, 749
Russian Revolution (1917), 780
"Rust belt," 914
Ruth, George Herman "Babe," 672
Rutledge, John, 187
Rwanda, 946

Sacajawea, 1
Sacco, Nicola, 675
Sachs, Sadie, 602, 604
Sadat, Anwar, 912, 919, *920*
Safety standards, regulation of, 618
St. Augustine, Florida, 55, 56, 57*M*
St. George's Episcopal Church, 509
St. Lawrence River, 62
St. Lawrence Seaway Act (1954), 819
St. Louis, Missouri, growth of, 254, *254*
Saint-Mihiel, Battle of (1918), 647, 648*M*
Salem, Massachusetts, 67, 75–76
Salvation Army, 509
Samoset, 66
Sampson, William, 586
Sand Creek massacre, 540–541
San Diego (California), redevelopment of, 923–924
Sandinistas, 918, 936
San Francisco (California), *370*, 370–371
  cable cars, 503
  Chinatown, *511*
  earthquake and fire, 514
  rise of, 545
  school crisis, 629
Sanger, Margaret, 602, 604, 607, 668, *669*
San Jacinto, Battle of (1836), 358–359
San Juan Hill, battle of, *587*, 588
San Salvador, discovery of, 9
Santa Anna, Antonio Lopez de, 358
Santa Barbara oil spill, 897–898
Santa Fe, New Mexico, 55, 56
Saratoga, Battle of (1777), 152
"Saturday Night Massacre," 908
Sauk and Fox tribe, 284
Savings and loan crisis, 944
Savio, Mario, 861
Scalawags, 451–452
Scalia, Antonin, 943
Scandals, 681, 949–950
Scandinavia, immigration from, 386–387
Scarface (film), 700
Scarlet Letter, The (Hawthorne), 309
Schaw, Janet, 162
Schecter Poultry Corp. v. United States (1935), 720
Schenck v. United States (1919), 647
Schine, David, *800*, 805, 806
Schism of 1840 (abolitionism), 320–321
Schlafly, Phyllis, 905
Schlink, Fred, 698
Schneiderman, Rose, 594
School busing, 892
School of Pedagogy (1896), 598
School prayer issue, 925
Schorr, Daniel, 906
Science, 102
SCLC (Southern Christian Leadership Conference), 848
Scopes, John T., 679–680

Scopes trial, 679–680
Scott, Dred, 395–396
Scott, Winfield, 366, 377, 412
"Scottsboro boys," 703
SDI (Strategic Defense Initiative), 934–935
SDS (Students for a Democratic Society), 860, 861
Seaports, 95–97
Sears, Richard W., 521
Sears, Roebuck Co., 521
Secession, 401–402, 403M
Second Bank of the United States (1816), 246, 250.
    See Bank War
Second Confiscation Act (1862), 449
Second Continental Congress
    Articles of Confederation approved, 169
    decision for independence, 143–144
    lack of power over inflation, 180
    Washington made commander-in-chief, 147
Second Great Awakening, 226–228, 227
    conversions in, 298
    effect on abolitionism, 317
    reform movements and, 314
    techniques of, 301
Secrettown, 546, 547
Sectional conflict
    balance of power, 388
    chronology of, 407
    crisis of, 395–400
        beleaguered South, 399–400
        Dred Scott decision, 395–396, 399
        Lecompton constitution, 397, 399
        Lincoln-Douglas debates, 397–399, 398
        Panic of 1857, 396–397
    effects on political system, 552
    immigration and, 386–387
    Kansas, 380–381, 391
    political parties and, 557
    political realignment of 1850s and, 388–395
        caning of Charles Sumner and, 391–392, 392
        collapse of party system, 390
        election of 1856, 393, 393–395
        Kansas-Nebraska Act, 388–389, 389M
        Know-Nothings, 390–391
        turmoil in Kansas, 391
    rising industrialization and, 385–386
    road to war (See Civil War)
    slavery and, 177–179, 178, 350–351
    social changes and, 382–388
    Southern complaints, 387–388
    specialized economy and, 404–405
Secular humanism, 925
Securities and Exchange Commission, 717
Securities Exchange Act (1934), 717
Sedition Act (1798), 211–212
Sedition Act (1918), 646
Segregation, 792
    in churches, 533
    in free states, 285
    legalization of, 518
    of middle-class neighborhoods, 265
    in "New South," 534–535
    Plessy v. Ferguson (1896), 534
    in public schools, 460, 830
    segregation laws, 607
    values of planters and, 457–458
Selective Service Act (1917), 640–641
Selective Service System, 873
Self-emancipation thesis, 420
Self-help societies (black), 285
Self-interest, 191, 201, 370
Seminole tribe, 196, 281, 284
Semiskilled workers, low wages for, 491
Semisubsistence economy, 196–197
    agriculture in West, 225–226
    Federalist support and, 209
    Hamilton's financial program and, 203

Senate Watergate hearings, 907–908
Seneca Falls Convention (1848), 319, 320
Seneca tribe, 80
Separate but equal doctrine, 830
Separation of church and state, 71, 847–848
Separation of powers, 189, 450
Sephardim (Spanish and Portuguese Jews), 54–55, 106
Sergeant Pepper's Lonely Hearts Club Band (Beatles), 863
Serra, Junípero, 58
Servants. See Domestic servants
Service trades, 491
Settlement house movement, 510, 601
Seven Days, Battles of (1862), 416, 417M
Seventeenth Amendment, 399n, 611
Seventh Cavalry, 541
Seven Years' War, 116, 117–121, 118M, 153
    American expectations following, 119–121, 120M
    background of, 112–113
    British victory, 118–119
    early years of, 117–118
Sewage systems, 506
Seward, William Henry, 579–580
Sewing machine, 386
Sex education, in World War I, 642
Sexism, 903
Sexuality
    free love, 516
    premarital sex, 342, 671
    romantic friendships, 517
    sexual freedom, 862
    sexual standards, 335, 342–343
    Victorianism and, 515
    See also Birth control; Homosexuals
Sexually transmitted disease, in World War I, 642
Shah of Iran, 886
"Shake, Rattle, and Roll," 835
Shakers, 309, 310, 310–311
Shakespeare, William, 734
Shamans, 12
Shantytowns ("Hoovervilles"), 695
Sharecropper's Voice, 703
Sharecropping. See Tenancy and sharecropping
"Share Our Wealth" plan, 722
Shaw, Pauline, 600
Shawnee tribe, 177, 224–225
    cultural stresses, 228–229
    defeat at Battle of Tippecanoe (1811), 231, 293
Shays, Daniel, 186–187
Shays' Rebellion, 186–187
Sheen, Fulton J., 815
Sheep ranching, 549
Shelley, Mary, 563
Sheppard-Towner Federal Maternity and Infancy
    Act (1921), 670
Sherman, Roger, 144, 187
Sherman, William Tecumseh, 414
    march to the sea, 437
    seizure of Atlanta, 431, 433, 434M, 436
Sherman Antitrust Act (1890), 483, 485, 561, 614
Sherman Silver Purchase Act (1890), 560, 561, 570
Shiloh, Battle of (1862), 414, 415M, 416
Shipbuilding, in 1880s, 578
Shirer, William, 748–749
Shirley, William, 90
"Shoddy," 426
Shoe industry, 261–262
Shopping centers and malls, 813, 923–924
Shoshone tribe, 537
"Shuttle diplomacy," 912
"Sick" industries, 691
Sierra Club (1892), 616–617, 617
Silent majority, 881–883, 888
Silent Spring (Carson), 900
Silver, discovery of, 539
Silver standard, 560, 570–571
Simpson, Nicole, 953–954

Simpson, O. J., 953–954
Sinclair, Upton, 616, 722
Singapore, fall of, 752
Singer, Isaac, 386, 578, 579
Singer Sewing Machine Company, 481
"Single-tax" clubs, 484–485
Sioux tribe, 353–355, 354*M*, 362, 537, 539
  battle of Little Big Horn, 541–542
  First Sioux War, 539–541, 540*M*
Sirhan Sirhan, 880
Sirica, John, 907
Sister Carrie (Dreiser), 600
Sit-down strikes, 732–733
Sit-ins, 848
Sitting Bull (Sioux medicine man), 541
Six Companies (Chinese charity), 704
Six Nations (League of the Iroquois), 88
Sixteenth Amendment, 618–619, 622
Skilled craftworkers, in AFL, 493–494
Skipwith, Lucy, 347
Skyscrapers, 504–505, *505*
Slater, Samuel, 256
Slater fund, 519
Slaveowners, 352
Slave Power, 395, 399
Slavery
  in Aztec civilization, 14
  in Caribbean cane fields, 49
  Cherokees as slaveholders, 282
  in Chesapeake region, 45–46, 60
  conflict in Kansas Territory, 380–381
  cotton production and, 246–247
  defense of, 348–351
    commonalities of North and South, 350–351
    proslavery argument, 349
    unity of whites in, 349–350
    Virginia debate of 1832, 348–349
  distribution in South, 330, 331*M*
  in 18th century, 97–98
    African American response to, 101
    geographical differences and, 98
    resistance and escape, 99–101
    slave families and community, 98–99, *99*
  fear of slave revolts, 162
  Indians as slaves, 51
  as issue in Mexican War, 365
  as issue in West (*See* The West)
  in Jacksonian Era, 276, 278
  limited by Northwest Ordinance, 177
  Lincoln-Douglas debates, 397–399, *398*
  Maroon settlements, 99
  in Old South, 338–341
    resistance to, 340–341
    slave maintenance, 340
    work and discipline, 339
  plantation mistress and, 335
  resistance and escape, 325–326
  sectionalism and, 177–179, *178*
  slave culture and, 341–348
    common bonds, 347
    families, *342*, 342–344
    free blacks and, 347–348
    music, *344*, 344–345
    religion, 345–346
  in South Carolina, 53–54
  in territories, 388–389, *389*
  wealth of gentry and, 47
  in West Indies, 50
  Wilmot Proviso (1846), 366
Slave states, 266*M*, 268–270
Slave trade, 45, 90, 269
Slavic republics, new freedom in, 940
Sloan, Alfred, 666
Sloan, John, 600
Slums, 503, 505–506
Smallpox, 156, 354*M*, 355, 540

Smedes, Susan Dabney, 335
Smith, Adam, 35
Smith, Alfred E., 572*n*, 611, 684
Smith, James, 175
Smith, Jedediah, 263
Smith, John, 34
Smith, Margaret Bayard, 279
Smith, Samuel H., 217
Smith College (1871), 520
Smith-Connolly Act (1943), 761
Smith v. Allwright (1944), 767–768
Smoot-Hawley Tariff (1930), 706
SNCC. *See* Student Non-Violent Coordinating Committee
Social banditry, 373
Social change, automobile and, 663
Social class
  Britain *vs.* colonies, 107–108, *108*
  class resentment, 97
  distinctions in suburbia, 814–815
  inequality in colonies, 107–108
  juvenile delinquency and, 834–835
  status of industrial workers, 261
  wealth and, 265, 266
Social control, 606–609
  alcohol, 608
  Comstock Law, 516
  effect of Civil War on, 424–425
  immigration, 607
  lacking in gold camps, 369
  prostitution, 608–609
  reform movements as, 314
Social Darwinism, 484, 579
"Social Gospel," 509
Social inequality
  in colonies, 44–45, 48, 134–135
  English influence and, 107–108
  after Revolutionary War, 167
Socialist communities, 312
Socialist Labor party (1877), 485
Socialist party
  election of 1912, 620
  election of 1932, 710
  during World War I, 647
Socialist Party of America (1901), 485
Social mobility, 266, 303, 810
Social philosophy, education and, 518
Social reform, 600–605
  fight against child labor, 603
  social welfare and, 604–605
  views of poverty, 600–601
  "woman's sphere" and, 601–602, *602*, 604
  woman suffrage, 605, 606*M*
Social Security Act (1935), 724, 736
Social status. *See* Social class
Social stresses on women war workers, 762
Social structure
  changes of 1920s and 1930s (*See* New Era)
  of Confederation, 180–184
    attack on aristocracy, 183–184
    opportunities, 181
    women and, 181–182, *182*, 183
  emergence of political parties and, 206
  geographic mobility and, 253–254, 255
  of gold camps, 367–369
  inequality of wealth in commercial society, 198
  of late 18th century, 195–199
    commercial economy, 197–198
    Constitution and commerce, 198–199
    semisubsistence economy, 196–197
  liberalism and change, 838–839
  life in colonial seaports, 96–97
  of market society, 263–267
    distribution of wealth and, 266
    economic specialization, 264
    emerging middle class, 265
    materialism, 264–265

Social structure *(Cont.):*
  of market society *(Cont.):*
    sensitivity to time, 266–267
    social mobility, 266
  mass consumption and, 520–521
  revivalism and, 228
  source of new politics and, 275–276
  of South (*See* The South)
  stratification of, 272
  stratified nature of, 510
Social welfare, 604–605, 611
Social work, 601
Society for the Protection of Italian Immigrants, 512
Society of Cincinnati, 184
Society of Friends. *See* Quakers
Society of Jesus (Jesuits), 62, 63, *63*, 86
"Sociological jurisprudence," 598
Sod houses, 550
Soil Conservation and Domestic Allotment Act (1936), 721
Soldiers
  of Civil War (*See* Civil War)
  life in World War II, 755–756
  National Guard, 733, 832, 868
  of Revolutionary War, *147*, 147–149
  in Vietnam, 873–875, *875*
  See also Casualties; *specific wars*
Solomon Islands, Battle of (1942), 754
Solos, 676
Somalia, 946
Somme, Battle of (1916), 639
Somoza, Anastasio, 918
Sonar, 759
Sons of Liberty, 126–128, 130
Soto, Hernando de, 19
Soul music, 864
Soul on Ice (Cleaver), 855
Souls of Black Folk, The (Du Bois), 575
Soup kitchens, 694
Sousa, John Philip, 522
South,The, 325–352, *326*
  agriculture in, 248
  civil rights in (*See* Civil rights)
  class structure of white South, 48, 332–338
    plantation mistress, 334–336, *335*
    plantation owners, 334
    poor whites, 337–338
    slaveowners, 332
    Tidewater and frontier, 333–334
    yeoman farmers, 336–337, *337*
  colonial (*See* Colonial South, settlement of)
  complaints about Northern industrialization, 387–388
  Deep South, 327–328, 328*n*
  drop in western trade, 384
  importance of slavery to economy, 318
  internal crisis of 1850s, 399–400
  Lower South, rice culture of, 179
  "New South," 526–531
    agriculture in, 527
    industry in, 529
    religion, 532–533, *533*
    rural life in, 531–532
    segregation, 534–535
    sources of poverty, 530–531
    tenancy and sharecropping, 527–529, *528*
    timber and steel industries, 529–530
  "the peculiar institution" (*See* Slavery)
  Reconstruction and (*See* Reconstruction)
  Revolutionary War in, 157–162
  rural South, 328–330, 329*M*
  social structure of, 327–332
    Deep South and Upper South, 327–328, 328*n*
    distribution of slavery in, 330, 331*M*
    rural South, 328–330, 329*M*
    slavery as labor system, 330, 332
  strained relations with West and Northeast, 526

  Upper South, 328, 328*n*
  weakening alliance with West, 388
South Africa, 583
South America, 3
South Carolina
  depression of 1819, 287–288, *288*
  establishment of, 50
  ethnic and religious diversity, 53
  Regulators, 93, 106
  secession of, 402
  West Indian influence, 49, 52*M*
South Carolina Exposition and Protest, 288
South Dakota, statehood (1889), 552
Southern Alliance, 565, 566
Southern Christian Leadership Conference (SCLC), 848
"Southern Manifesto" (1956), 830
Southern Tenant Farmers Union (1934), 703–704
South Vietnam, "military advisors" in, 842
Southwest, Hispanic-Anglo conflict in, 544–545
Soviet Union
  atomic bomb capabilities, 796
  containment policy toward, 786–787
  economic five-year plan, 786
  occupation of Czechoslovakia, 789
  occupation of Hungary, 788–789
  recognition of (1933), 744
  Soviet-American relations, *826*, 826–828
  totalitarianism, 657
Space missions, 842, 897
Spain, 2
  alliance with colonies, 153
  colonization of New World, 18–22
  Cuban rebellion and, 584
  designs on southwest, 171–172
  exploration by, 9, 10*M*, 11
  Jay-Gardoqui Treaty, 185–186
  Louisiana ceded to France, 222
  Pinckney's Treaty (1796), 205
  rebellion of Netherlands, 27–28
  U.S. annexation of west Florida, 239
Spanish-American War (1898), 584–591, 626
  annexation of Philippines, 588–590, 589*M*
  conduct of war, 586
  conquest of Cuba, *587*, 587–588
  Cuban revolt, 584–586, *585*
  fighting in Philippines, 590–591
Spanish Civil War, 745
Speakeasies, 659, 677
Specialized economy, sectional conflict and, 404–405
Specie Circular (1836), 292
Spectator sports, 522, 672
Speculation
  Miami (Florida) land boom, 687–688
  stock market (*See* New York Stock Exchange; Stock market)
Spencer, Herbert, 484
Spicer, Laura, 454
Spirit of St. Louis, 685–686
Spiritual Autobiography, A (Bradstreet), 70
"Spoils system," 280, 559
Sports, class distinctions and, 521–522
Sprague, Frank Julian, 503–504
Sputnik, launch of (1959), 825
Squanto, 66
Square Deal, 614–615
Stagflation, 888
Stalin, Joseph, 657, 780, 823
  American concerns about, 783–784
  balance of power and, 771–772
  efforts to strengthen position, 788–789, 788*M*
  historical analysis of, 785–786
  leadership capabilities, 754
  Potsdam Conference (1945), 775
Stalingrad, Battle of (1942–1943), 755
Stamp Act (1765), 123–124
  opposition to, 146

repeal of (1766), 128–129
resistance to, 125–126
riots against, 127
Standard Oil Company, 480, 482–483, 576, 615
Standard Oil of New Jersey (Exxon), 821
Stanford, Leland, 519
Stanford University, 519, 705
Stanton, Edwin, 448–449
Stanton, Elizabeth Cady, 319, 320, *320*
Starr, Kenneth, 950
"Star Spangled Banner, The," 236
START (Strategic Arms Reduction Treaty), 940–941
Starvation, 37
"Star Wars" defense system, 934–935
State charters, 251
State colleges and universities, 519
State constitutions, 167–169, *168*, 452
State Department, 199
Statehood for Western territories, 552
States
   business regulation by, 482
   government reform, 610–612
   independence of, 166–167
   investment capital from, 478
   regulation of industry, 561–562
   regulatory commissions of, 611
States' rights, 411, 424
States' Rights (Dixiecrat) party, 795
State-supported churches, 184
Steamboats, 248, 249M, *254*
Steam engine, 243
Steel, Ferdinand, 326, 336
Steel industry, 481–482, 529, 530
   Bessemer process, 471
   production in, *471*
   steel mills, 482, 487–488, 567, 598
   See also specific companies and unions
Steel Workers' Organizing Committee (SWOC), 732, 733
Steffens, Lincoln, 507, 599
Steger, Mary, 294
Steinbeck, John, 701
Steinem, Gloria, 903
Stephens, Uriah, 493
Stephenson, David, 679
Steuben, Baron von, 154–155, 159, 164
Stevens, Thaddeus, 445–446
Stevenson, Adlai E., 804
Stewart, Helen Wiser, 548–549
Stewart, Lyman, 679
Stewart, Milton, 679
Stieglitz, Alfred, 600
Stiles, Ezra, 174
Still, William, 318
Stimson, Henry, 743, 751
Stimson Doctrine, 743
Stock certificates (shares), 475
Stockman, David, 932
Stock market, 688–693
   causes of Great Depression and, 690–692
   Great Crash, 690
   N.Y. Stock Exchange, 474, 479, 688–689, *689*, 690
   slide into Depression, 692–693
   wave of speculation, *689*, 689–690
Stone, Lucy, 320, 458
Stonewall riot (1969), 892
STOP ERA crusade, 905
Story, Joseph, 238
Stowe, Harriet Beecher, *299*, 319, 343, 377, *393*, 394, 395
Strategic Arms Limitation Treaty (SALT I & II), 887, 912, 919
Strategic Arms Reduction Treaty (START), 940–941
Strategic Defense Initiative (SDI), 934–935
Strict constructionism, 203–204, 223
Strike, The (Koehler), *495*
Strikes
   air traffic controllers' strike, 931

coal strikes, 614, 760
Coeur d'Alene miners' strike (1892), 546
   following World War I, 652
   Gastonia (North Carolina), 664
   Great Railroad Strike of 1877, 569
   Homestead steel strike (1892), 598
   pecan shellers, *731*
   sit-down strikes, 732–733
   spontaneous, 494–495, *495*
   strike breaking, 493
   in textile mills, 258
   after World War II, 793
Strong, Josiah, 508, 524
Stryker, Roy, 734
Student Non-Violent Coordinating Committee (SNCC), 848, 855, 860, 876
Students for a Democratic Society (SDS), 860, 861
Submarine warfare
   in World War I, 635–636, 638
   in World War II, 750, 752
Subsistence incomes, 693–695, *694*, *695*
Suburban era, 809–836
   chronology of, 836
   cracks in consensus, 833–836
      mass culture and, 833–834
      youth culture, 834–836
   culture of suburbia, 814–817
      religion, 815
      television, 817
      women in, *816*, 816–817
   rise of suburbs, 810–814
      boom in papies and housing, *811*, 811–812
      transformation of cities and, 812–814, *813*
Suburbs, 503
Subversion, fears of, 798
Sudbury, Massachusetts, 68M
Suez Canal, conflict over, 824
Suffrage
   after Civil War, 443, 444, 452
   impartial male suffrage, 447
   property requirements, 109
   universal manhood suffrage, 168
   white manhood suffrage, 275
   woman suffrage, 319, 321, 458
Sugar Act (1764), 123, 124, 125
Sugar cultivation, 49, 352, 581
Suicide, Great Depression and, 695
Sullivan, John, 156
Sumner, Charles, 391–392, *392*, 395, 418, 445–446
Sumner, William Graham, 484
Sumter, Thomas ("Gamecock"), 157
Sun Also Rises, The (Hemingway), 673
Sunday, William Ashley ("Billy"), *509*
Sununu, John, 942
Superpowers, 823, 844–845M
Supply-side economics, 931
Supreme Court
   abortion rulings, 943
   appointments to, 623, 942
   on birth control, 847
   business regulation, 614
   on censorship, 847
   civil rights cases, 534, 767–768, 830, 831
   conservatism of, 942–943
   court "packing," 735–736
   creation of, 200
   "granger cases," 565
   labor legislation and, 604n
   on legislative districts, 848
   New Deal cases, 720, 721
   Nixon and, 893
   pragmatism of, 598
   promotion of enterprise, 250–251
   rulings on desegregation, 892–893
   separate but equal doctrine, 518

Supreme Court *(Cont.)*:
on separation of church and state, 847–848
on Sherman Antitrust Act, 485
on strikes, 733
Warren court, 846–847, *847*
WWI radicals and, 647
See also specific cases
"Surfing sound," 864
Surplus agriculture, 226
Sussex pledge, 636
Swain, William, 368
Swann v. Charlotte-Mecklenburg Board of Education (1971), 893
Sweatshops, 487
Swift, Gustavus, 481
Swift and Company, 481
SWOC (Steel Workers' Organizing Committee), 732, 733
Syphilis, 759

Taft, Robert A., 749, 794, 804, 818
Taft, William Howard, 607, 794
governor of Philippines, 590–591
presidency of, 618, 629–630
Taft-Hartley Act (1947), 794
Taiwan (Formosa), 771, 796, 823
Tallmadge, James, 269
Tammany Hall, 498–499, 507
Tampa (Florida), riots in, 587–588
Taney, Roger, 291, 396
Tanks, use in World War I, 639–640
Taos tribe, 537
Tappan, Arthur, 316
Tappan, Lewis, 316, 317, 320
Tarbell, Ida M., 599
Tariff of Abominations (1828), 288
Tariffs, 240
blamed for depression of 1819, 287
conflict over, 559
confrontation over, 281
lowered by Wilson, 621–622
in Union, 425
See also specific tariffs
Tarleton, Banastre, 159, 160*M*, 161
Task system, in slavery, 339
Taxation
colonial resistance to, 126–128
first federal income tax, 425
graduated income tax, 618–619, 622, 760
for highway construction, 662, 812
Jefferson's tax cuts, 220
as Parliamentary right, 86
poll tax, 573
"single-tax" clubs, 484–485
"Wealth Tax Act," 725
whiskey tax (1791), 193, 202, 205
Taylor, Frederick W., 489
Taylor, W. M., 564
Taylor, Zachary, 364, 366, 376
election of 1848 and, 374, 375
presidency of, 375–376, 375*M*
Taylorism, 489–490
TCI (Tennessee Coal, Iron, and Railway Company), 530
Tea Act (1773), 132
Teaching, as female profession, 427, 455
Teach-ins, 875
Technical education, 518
Technological unemployment, 661
Technology
colonization and, 17–18, 21
drawbacks of "New South," 530–531
European exploration and, 7, 8
factory system and, 256–257
military technology, 430
in New Era, 661
scientific farming methods, 248
in Vietnam War, 874
in World War II, 759

Tecumseh, 229, *229*, 231, 236
"Teflon president," 930
Teheran Conference (1943), 771–772
Telegraph, 257, 473
Telephone, 473–474
Televangelists, 925–926
Television, 817, 840, 928
Teller Amendment (1898), 586, 588
Temperance movement, 312–313, 321–322, 608
environmental movement and, 902
formation of WCTU, 515–516, 558
Temporary Emergency Relief Administration (TERA), 705, 714
Temporary National Economic Committee, 737
Tenancy and sharecropping
in "New South," 527–529, 528*M*, 563
during Reconstruction, 455–456, *456*, 463
in West, 550
Tenant wars, among settlers, 94
Tenayca, Emma, *731*
Tenement houses, 387
Tenements, 506, 600
Tennessee Coal, Iron, and Railway Company (TCI), 530
Tennessee Coal and Iron Company, 618, 619
Tennessee Valley Authority (TVA), 718–719, 727, 729
Tenochtitlán, Aztec capital, 3, 15, 19, 21, 23
Tenskwatawa (Open Door), 229, 230*M*, 231
Tenure of Office Act (1867), 49
TERA (Temporary Emergency Relief Administration), 705, 714
Terkel, Studs, 697
"Termination" policy, 891
Terrorism, 935–936
Tet offensive, 878–880
Texas
admission as slave state, 364
annexation of, 363–364
Hispanic-Anglo conflict, 373
immigration into, 358
Republic proclaimed, 358–359
Texas and Pacific Railroad, 493
Texas Revolution, 358
Textile industry
economic specialization and, 264
employment of whites, 529, 534
factory system, 257–259, *258*
in "New South," 529
technological advances and, 256
See also Cotton
Thames, Battle of (1813), 236, 237*M*
Thayendanegea (Mohawk chief), 156
Thayer, Webster, 675
Theater, popular melodramas, 522–523, *523*
Theft, 341
Theocracy (Mormon), 311–312, 371, 372
Thieu, General, 894–895
Third parties, 558, 890–891
Third-party candidates, 567
Third Reich, fall of, 769
Third World, 917
Thirteenth Amendment, 420, 435, 444
This Side of Paradise (Fitzgerald), 673
Thomas, Clarence, 943
Thomas, George H., 436
Thomas, Norman, 710
Thompson, Tommy, 948
Thoreau, Henry David, 308, 862
Three Lower Counties, 82, 83
Three Mile Island, 916
Thurmond, J. Strom, 795
Tiananmen Square, 940
Ticknor, George, 439
Tidewater area, 333
Tilden, Samuel, 462
Timber industry, 529–530
Time, industrialization and, 266–267
Time magazine, 671, 935
Time zones, 477

Tinkham, Jim, 408, 409
Tippecanoe, Battle of (1811), 231, 293
Tobacco industry, in "New South," 529
Tobacco production, 35, 38, 42, 43, 47–48, 49
Tobacco Road (Caldwell), 734
Tocqueville, Alexis de, 251–252, 264, 274
Todd, Mary Ellen, 361
Toleration, religious, 73
Tonkin, Gulf of, 871–872
Tonkin Gulf Resolution, 872, 876, 877, 884–885
Tories. *See* Loyalists
To Secure These Rights, 793
To the Lynching! (Cadmus), *678*
Tougaloo College, 850–851
Town meetings, 71
Towns, rural life and, 532
Townsend, Francis, 723–724
Townsend clubs, 724
Townsendites, 726
Townshend, Charles, 129–130, 131
Townshend Acts, *129*, 129–130
Trade and commerce
    Aztec marketplaces, 14
    Caribbean trade, 638
    "company towns," 72
    Dutch colonization for, 77–78
    England's regulation of, 110–111
    in Europe, 2–3
    imperialism and, 579
    with Indian tribes, 51
    Jeffersonian Republican ideology and, 209–210
    merchant stock companies, 28
    overseas trade networks, 111*M*
    Portuguese merchants, 8
    seaports and, 95–96
    in Southwest, 357
    Soviet challenges, 885
Traditional values, progressivism and, 596
Trail of Tears, 282, 283*M*, 284
"Tramps' March on Washington," 570
Transcendentalism, 307–308
Transfer of power, 217–218
Transportation, 468–469
    in 1790, 196
    in Europe, 2–3
    expansion of transportation network, 473
    frontier settlement and, 92–93
    revolution in, 247–248, 249*M*
    urban transport, 503–504
    water transport, 92, 198
    See also Canals; Railroads; River transportation
Treasury Department, 199, 292–293, *293*
Treaty of Paris (1763), 116, 119
Treaty of Paris (1783), 163
Treaty of Paris (1898), 590
Trench warfare, 639–640, *640*
Trevelyan, Charles Philips, 470
Trial by jury, 124
Triangle Shirtwaist Company fire (1911), 594–595, *595*
Trolleys, electric, 503–504
Trollope, Frances, 273
Truman, Harry S, 768, *774*, 784, 895
    conflict with MacArthur, 802–804, 806–807
    election of 1948 and, 794–795
    presidency of, 773–774
        atomic bomb, 776
        concern for civil rights, 793
        extension of New Deal, 793–794
        Fair Deal, 795–796
        hydrogen bomb research, 796, 801
        Korean War (*See* Korean War)
        mistrust of Stalin, 780
        Potsdam Conference (1945), 775
        Truman Doctrine, 787
    on Soviets, 786
Truman Doctrine, 787, 798

Trumbull, John, *144*
Trumbull, Lyman, 446
Trunk lines (railroad), 477
Trusts, 482–483, 614
Truth, Sojourner, 318
Tubman, Harriet, *317*, 318
Tugwell, Rexford, 734
Turkey, Truman Doctrine and, 787
Turner, Frederick Jackson, 535
Turner, Nat, 340–341
Tuscarora tribe, 80
Tuskegee Institute, 527, 574
TVA (Tennessee Valley Authority), 718–719, 727, 729
Twain, Mark, 588
Tweed, William ("Boss Tweed"), 508
Twelfth Amendment, 274–275
"Twenty-One Demands," 631
Twichell, Joseph, 412
Tydings, Millard F., 799–800
Tyler, John, 362, 363
Typhoid, 259, 429, 506
Typhus, 756
Typographers' Union, 494

U-boats, 635–636, 750, 752
U-2 incident, 828
UMW (United Mine Workers), 624, 732, 760
Uncle Tom's Cabin (Stowe), 319, 377, *393*, 394, 395
Underconsumption, in Great Depression, 693
Underground Railroad, *317*, 318
Underwood-Simmons Tariff (1913), 622
Unemployment, 691
    federal relief, *718*
    in Great Depression, 693, *694*
    "Roosevelt recession," 736
    technological, 661
    white-collar, 945
UNIA (Universal Negro Improvement Association), 674
Unicameral legislatures, 83
Union
    advantages of, 409, *410*
    discipline of soldiers, 429–430
    Grant as commander, 431, 432*M*, 433
    home front, 425–428
        civil liberties and dissent, 427–428
        finance and economy, 425
        opportunities for women, 426–427, *427*
        prosperity, 425
Union Pacific Railroad, 546
Union Party, 726
Unitarians, 307
United Auto Workers, 732, 733
United Farm Workers Union, 702, *889*, 890
United Fruit corporation, 825
United Mine Workers (UMW), 614, 732, 760
United Nations, 775, 790, 942
United Rubber Workers Union, 732
United States Employment Service, 766
United States Sanitary Commission, 427
United States Steel Corporation, 483, 530, 618, 619
United States v. E. C. Knight Co. (1895), 485, 614
United States v. Jefferson County Board of Education, 893
United States v. Nixon, 908
United Steel Workers, 846
Universal movie studio, 699
Universal Negro Improvement Association (UNIA), 674
Universal Suez Canal Company, 824
Universities, 519
University of Mexico, 356
University of Mississippi, 851–852
Unsafe at Any Speed (Nader), 898–899
Unskilled labor, 285
Unskilled workers, low wages for, 491
Untalan, Valentine, *753*
Unterseeboote (U-boats), 635–636, 750, 752

Upper South
  agriculture in, 328, 328n
  declines to secede, 402
  distribution in South, 330, 331M
Uprisings, 340–341
Urban environment, 385
Urbanization, 466. See Cities and urbanization
Urban League, 728
U.S. Census, 195–196, 352, 552, 659
U.S. Geological Survey, 539
U.S. Navy, 578
U.S. Patent Office, 256
U.S. Railroad Administration, 643, 644
U.S. Rubber Company, 473
USS Dolphin, 632
USS Oregon, 626
Utah, 371, 372, 376, 552
Ute tribe, 537
Utopia (More), 29
Utopian communities, 309–311, 310
Utopian design of Georgia Colony, 55

Valley Forge, Pennsylvania, 154
Van Buren, Martin, 277, 292–294, 363
  depression and, 292–293, 293
  election of 1836, 359
  election of 1848 and, 374, 375
  Indian removal and, 284
  as new politician, 276
  Whig triumph and, 293–294
Vance, Cyrus, 916, 917, 921
Vandenberg, Arthur, 796
Vanderbilt, Cornelius, 266, 474–475
Vanzetti, Bartolomeo, 675
Vatican II (1962–1965), 926
Vaudeville, 522
Venezuela, crisis in, 583
Veracruz (Mexico), 632
Vergennes, Charles Gravier de, 153
Vermont, 92, 94, 171
Versailles, Treaty of, 649–650, 745, 747
Versailles peace conference, 649
Vesey, Denmark, 287, 340
Vespucci, Amerigo, 11
Veterans, 558, 709–710
Veterans Administration, 710
Vice-admiralty courts, 85–86
Vick, Sarah Pierce, 335
Vicksburg, Battle of, 429, 431
Victoria, Queen of England, 515
Victorianism, 515–516
Vietcong, 842, 872, 878–880
Vietnamization, 885
Vietnam War, 865, 867–896
  chronology of, 896
  end of, 894–895
  historical analysis of, 877
  Kent State massacre, 867–869, 868, 884
  Nixon era (See Nixon, Richard)
  road to Vietnam, 869, 870M, 871–873
    Lyndon Johnson and, 871–872
    Operation Rolling Thunder, 872–873
  social consequences, 873–878
    soldiers, 873–875, 875
    war at home, 875–878, 876
  treaty arranged (1973), 895
  unraveling of, 878–883
    antiwar demonstrations, 882
    shocks of 1968 and, 880–881
    "silent majority" and, 881–883
    Tet offensive, 878–880
Villa, Francisco "Pancho," 632
Villain Dies, The (Gibson), 523
Vinland (Ericsson's colony), 2
Violence
  among workers, 494

political, 213–215, 461, 461–462
  See also Rioting
Virginia
  English rule in, 83–84
  importance in Civil War, 413
  raid on Harper's Ferry, 400–401
  settlement of Carolinas from, 50
  women in, 40
Virginia, C.S.S., 413
Virginia Company of London, 36–37, 38, 40
Virginia debate of 1832, 348–349
Virginia Plan, 188
Virginia resolution (1798), 212
Vladivostok summit (1974), 912
Voice of America, 805
Volunteerism, 599
Voting, 109–110, 182
Voting Rights Act (1965), 854

WACs (Women's Army Corps), 756
Wade, Benjamin, 443, 445–446
Wade-Davis Bill (1864), 443
Wages
  in 1920s, 664–665
  minimum wage laws, 828–829
  rise in women's wages, 698
  rising real wages, 491
Wagner, Robert F., 611, 725
"Wagner Act," 725, 732, 733, 736
Wainwright Building, 505
Wald, Lillian, 637
Walden (Thoreau), 308
Walker, David, 318
Walker, James, 263
Walker, Thomas, 122M
"Walking cities," 503
Wallace, George, 881, 888–889
Wallace, Henry C., 681, 768, 795
Walla Walla tribe, 537
"Wall Street" jobs, 933
Wall Street Journal, 917
Walsh, Christy, 672
Wampanoag tribe, 66, 77
War bonds, 760
Ward, Aaron Montgomery, 521
Ward, Addison, 267–268
Ward bosses, 498–499, 507
War Department, 199
War Hawks, 234, 235, 238
War Industries Board (WIB), 643
War Labor Board (1942), 760
Warmoth, Henry, 453
War of 1812, 232–238
  British invasion, 236, 237M, 238
  decision for war, 234–235
  embargo, 232–234
  Hartford Convention, 238
  Indian uprising and, 236
  Madison presidency and, 234
  national unpreparedness, 235
  neutral rights and, 232
War of the Roses, 2
War of the Worlds, The (Wells), 699
"War on poverty," 857
War Powers Act (1973), 910
War production, 757–762
War Production Board (WPB), 758
Warren, Earl, 767, 830, 846, 893
Warren court, 846–847, 847
Warsaw Pact, 824
War work, 643–644, 644
Washington, Booker T., 574–575, 613
Washington, D.C., 218
Washington, George, 187, 188, 208
  as commander-in-chief, 147, 147, 148–149, 164
  at Fort Necessity, 112, 113, 117

as president
  bank bill and, 203–204
  French Revolution and, 207
  organization of Federalist party, 207, 215–216
  unanimously elected, 199, *200*
Washington, statehood (1889), 552
Washington Post, 906
Waste Land, The (Eliot), 673
Water
  effects of textile mills, 259, *260*
  in environment of West, 538–539, 538*M*
  irrigation of Salt Lake valley, 372
  New Deal water management, 727
  Reclamation Act of 1902 and, 616
  transportation by, 92, 198
Watergate, 905–909
  break-in, 894, 906–907
  cover-up, 907–908
  Nixon's enemies and, 906
  Nixon's resignation and, 908–909
Water purification systems, 506
Watson, John B., 598, 665
Watson, Tom, 567, 571, 574
Watt, James, 243, 931, 933
WAVEs, 756
Wayne, "Mad Anthony," 205
WCTU (Women's Christian Temperance Union),
    515–516, 558
Wealth
  Civil War and, 426
  goal of Southern economy, 351
  inequality of distribution, 266
  social mobility and, 266
  social status and, 265
"Wealth Tax Act," 725
Weaver, James B., 567
Weaver, Robert C., 728
Webster, Daniel, *288*, 289
Webster, Noah, 212
We Demand (Jones), *708*
Weimar Republic, 656, 683
Weinberger, Caspar, 931, 937
Weld, Theodore Dwight, 315, 316, 317, 318
Welfare capitalism, 664–665
Welfare reform, 949
Welfare state, 507, 508, 558–559
Welles, Orson, 699, 734
Wellesley College (1875), 520
Wells, H. G., 699
Wertheim, Frederic, 834
West, The
  boom and bust cycle in, 545–549
    cattle industry, 547–549, 548*M*
    mining, 545–546
    railroads, 546, *547*
  chronology of settlement, 379
  evolution of society in, 367
  expansion under Confederation, 170, *171*
  expansion under Jefferson, 222
    Lewis and Clark expedition, 223–224, 224*M*, 355
    Louisiana Purchase, 222–223
  Great Plains (*See* Great Plains)
  land claims in, 172, 173*M*
  in late 19th century, 535–539
    chronology of, 553
    competing views of, 537–539, 538*M*
    defining "frontier," 535–536
    natural environment, 535, 536, 538*M*
    treatment of Hispanics, 544–545
    urban frontier, 551–552
  Manifest Destiny, 355–359
    Mexican borderlands, 356–357, *357*
    Republic of Texas, 358–359
    roots of, 356
    Texas revolution and, 358
  Native American agriculture, 13

  Native Americans, 536–537
    conflict with Indians, 539–541, 540*M*
    Custer's last stand, 541–542
    treatment by whites, 542, 544
  patterns of settlement, 367–373
    farming, 367
    gold rush, 367–370
    Hispanic-Anglo conflict, 373
    Mormons in Utah, 371–372
    Salt Lake City, 372
    San Francisco, *370*, 370–371
  political origins of expansion, 362–367
    annexation of Texas, 363
    Bear Flag Revolt, 366
    continental vision, 364
    election of Polk and, 363–364
    Mexican War, 364–365, 365*M*
    slavery issue, 366–367
  question of slavery in, 373–378
    Compromise of 1850, 375–378, 375*M*
    legal issue, 373–374
    political parties and, 374–375
  railroads and western trade, 384
  rapid settlement of, 253–254
  resistance of Miami Confederacy, 204–205
  settlement of, 359–362
    Indians and, 362
    Overland Trail, 359–361, 360*M*
    women and, 361–362
  Sioux expansion and, 353–355, 354*M*
  Spanish colonization of, 55
  state legislators of, 174
  strained relations with South and Northeast, 526
  Whiskey Rebellion, 193–195, *194*, 205
  whites and Indians, 224–231
    changing environment and, 226
    course of white settlement, 225–226
    Indian response, 229, *229*, 230*M*, 231
    pressure on Indians, 228–229
    Second Great Awakening and, 226–228, *227*
  as World War II production center, 758
West Coast, counterculture and, 864–865
Western Federation of Miners, 546
West Indies, 48, 49, 50
  closed to U.S. by Britain, 207
  colonization of South Carolina and, 49, 52*M*
  Dutch West India Company, 77, 78
Westinghouse Electric Co., 473
Westmoreland, William, 873, 878, 879
West Virginia, 413
Weyler, Varleriono, 584, 590
Whalen, Richard, 883
Whigs, 275
  Clay's American System and, 292
  Democrats blamed for depression, *293*
  election of 1848 and, 374
  in Jacksonian party system, 294–295
  opposition to Mexican War, 365
  party affiliations in South, 350
  reform movements and, 321
  triumph in election of 1840, 293–294
Whiskey Rebellion, 193–195, *194*, 205
Whiskey tax (1791), 193, 202, 205
White, John, 30, 31
White, Lynn, 817
White, Theodore, 881
White Caps (*Gorras Blancas*), 544
Whitefield, George, 103, 104, *105*, 106
Whiteman, Paul, 672–673
Whites
  settlers
    ethnic differences among, 94
    Indians and, 76–77
    inequality in Chesapeake region, 44–45
    inequality in Plantation society, 48
    opportunities in Chesapeake region, 46–47

Whites (Cont.):
  in South
    class structure (See The South)
    defense of slavery, 349–350
    illiteracy of poor Southern whites, 330, 338
    poor whites, 337–338
    racism and fear of failure, 286–287
    Reconstruction and, 451–452, 460–462, 461
    Republicans, 451–452
    white supremacy, 457, 460–462, 461, 463
  as teachers of blacks, 455
  in West (See The West)
  white manhood suffrage, 275
White Shadows (McKay), 674
"White slave trade," 608
White supremacy, 457, 460–462, 461, 463
Whitewater affair, 950
Whitman, Walt, 2, 308–309
Whitney, Eli, 246, 256
Whyte, William, 834
WIB (War Industries Board), 643
Widows, 183
Wilderness Society, 901
Wild One, The, 834
Wiley, Harvey, 616
Wilhelm II, German Kaiser, 633, 648
Wilkinson, Eliza, 182
Willard, Abijah, 141, 142
Willard, Emma Hunt, 313, 314
Willard, Frances, 515–516
William of Orange, king of England, 85
Williams, Roger, 72–73
Williams, Sarah, 335
Willkie, Wendell, 749
Wilmot, David, 366, 373
Wilmot Proviso (1846), 366, 374, 376, 378
Wilson, Charles, 820
Wilson, Edith Bolling, 651
Wilson, Eliza, 369
Wilson, James, 187
Wilson, Woodrow, 607, 617, 656, 680
  early career of, 621
  election of 1912, 620–621, 620M
  election of 1916 and, 637
  inauguration protests, 605
  presidency of, 621–624
    declaration of neutrality, 634–635
    Fourteen Points (1918), 647, 649, 650
    labor and social reform, 623
    limits of progressive reform and, 623–624
    reforms, 621–623
    Treaty of Versailles and, 649–650
    WWI bureaucracy, 642–643
  progressivism of, 596
  suffers stroke, 651
Wingina, chief of Roanoke tribe, 30, 31
Winthrop, Hannah, 142
Winthrop, John, 67, 72, 924
Wisconsin, governmental reforms in, 610
Wisconsin, University of, 611
"Wisconsin idea," 610
Witchcraft, 75–76
Wolfe, James, 119
Wolfe, Tom, 863, 898, 921
Woman suffrage, 319, 321, 458, 605, 606M
Women
  in Alliance Movement, 566
  in armed services, 641, 756
  in cattle industry, 548–549
  Civil War and
    opportunities for Southern women, 423
    opportunities in North, 426–427, 427
  in colonial Virginia, 40
  in Confederation
    assertion of independence, 181–182
      education and legal status, 183
      exclusion from politics, 182
  duties of plantation mistress, 334–336, 335
  educational opportunities for, 313
  employment in seaports, 96
  equality in Shaker communities, 310–311
  higher education for, 519, 520
  impact of Great Depression, 696–698
  involvement in election of 1840, 294
  of Iroquois tribe, 80
  in Jacksonian Era, 276, 278
  in labor unions, 493, 494
  legal disadvantages, 75
  life on frontier, 93
  life on Great Plains, 550–551
  middle-class homemakers, 515
  in mining camps, 369
  New Deal and, 730–731
  "New Woman," 668–670, 669
  in 1950s suburbia, 816, 816–817
  political activism of, 131, 134
  in political office, 945
  poverty of single-parent families, 953
  in progressive social reform, 600, 601–602, 602, 604
  right to vote and, 319, 321
  role in Quaker church, 73, 74, 75, 81
  role in revivalism, 304–307
    ideal of domesticity, 304–306, 306
    middle class family and, 306–307
  role in semisubsistence economy, 197
  roles in colonies, 74
  Second Great Awakening and, 304
  spheres of influence and, 305
  teaching blacks, 455
  in temperance movement, 313
  in textile factories, 257–258, 258
  traditional home manufacturing, 264, 304–305
  Victorian fashion and, 515
  view of influence in West, 361–362
  witchcraft hysteria and, 75–76
  working women, 792–793
    African American war workers, 762
    in industrial work, 490
    in labor unions, 493, 494
    married women, 490, 698
    in 1950s suburbia, 816, 816–817
    postwar adjustments, 698
    in professions, 669
    rise in wages, 698
    in war work, 644, 761, 761–762, 763
    work during Great Depression, 697–698
  work on Overland Trail, 360–361, 362
Women's Army Corps (WACs), 756
Women's associations, 611–612
Women's Christian Temperance Union (WCTU),
  515–516, 558
Women's Division of Democratic National Committee, 730
Women's International League for Peace and Freedom,
  637, 745
Women's rights, Prohibition and, 677
Woodhull, Victoria, 516–517
Woodhull & Claflin's Weekly, 516
Woodmason, Charles, 94
Woodstock Music Festival, 864
Woodward, Bob, 906
Worcester v. Georgia (1832), 282
Worker-citizens, 490
Workers
  children, women, and African Americans, 490–491, 491
  improvements in lot of, 491–492
  industrial work, 487–490, 488–489
  recruitment for labor pool, 475–476, 476
  support for George Wallace, 881–882
  See also Labor unions; Women
Workers' compensation, 611

Work habits, industrialization and, 261
Working class, 259, 668
Working women. *See* Women
Works Progress Administration (WPA), 716, 724, 729
World Bank, 775
"World's Columbian Exposition" (1893), 554–555, 568
World Series scandal (1919), 672
World War I
　background of, 633–638
　　American neutrality, 634–635, 634*M*
　　assassination of Austrian archduke, 633–634
　　election of 1916 and, 636–637
　　historical analysis of, 638–639
　　support of Allies, 635–636
　　Wilson's peace negotiations, 637–638
　Bonus Army, 709–710
　casualties, 648–649
　chronology of, 655
　effect on society, 639–649
　　conduct of war, 647–649, 648*M*
　　labor migrations, 644–645
　　propaganda and civil liberties, 645–647
　　Selective Service Act (1917), 640–641
　　trench warfare, 639–640, *640*
　　war financing, 642–643
　　war work, 643–644, *644*
　peace and, 649–654
　　menace of radicalism and, 652–654
　　opposition to League of Nations, 650–651
　　Treaty of Versailles, 649–650
　postwar reparations, 683
　roots of World War II, 742
　social change caused by, 668
World War II, 741–778
　background of, 742–751
　　aid to Allies, 749–750
　　American interests in Pacific, 742–743
　　Good Neighbor policy, 743
　　historical assessment, 751
　　invasion of Poland, 747–749, 748*M*
　　isolationism, 744–745
　　neutrality legislation, 745–746, *746*
　　Pearl Harbor, 741–742, 750–751
　　prelude to war, 746–747
　chronology of, 778
　discrimination, 762–768
　　Italians and Asian Americans, 762–765, *765*
　　minority war workers, 765–766
　　urban unrest and, 767–768
　effects of, *694*, 777
　global war, 751–757
　　Allied strength, 753–754
　　initial German victories, 752–753, *753*
　　naval war in Pacific, 754
　　soldiers' life, 755–756
　　strategies, 752
　　successes in Europe, 755
　　women at war, 757
　Pearl Harbor, 741–742, 750–751
　postwar period, Marshall Plan, 787–788

　strategies for war and peace, 752, 768–777
　　attacks on Japan, 770–771, 770*M*
　　Big Three diplomacy, 771
　　death of Roosevelt and, 773–774
　　fall of Third Reich, 769
　　Hiroshima and Nagasaki, 776–777
　　Holocaust, *774*, 774–775
　　Potsdam Conference, 775–776
　　Yalta Conference, 771–773
　war production, 757–762
　　mobilization, 758–759
　　organized labor and, 760–761
　　prosperity and, 760
　　technological advances, 759
　　women workers, *761*, 761–762, 763
Wounded Knee massacre (1890), 542, 544, 781
Wovoka (Paiute prophet), 542
WPA (Works Progress Administration), 716, 724, 729
WPB (War Production Board), 758
Wright, Lawrence, 827
Wyoming, statehood (1889), 552

X, Malcolm, 854
XYZ Affair, 211

Yakima tribe, 537
Yalta Conference (1945), 772, 797
Yamasee tribe, 51, 53
Yamasee War (1715), 53
Yellow-dog contracts, 496, 664
Yellow fever, 328, 506, 627
"Yellow" journalism, 585
Yeltsin, Boris, 940
Yeoman farmers, 336–337, *337*, 452
Yom Kippur War, 910
Yorktown, 163–164, 170
Young, Andrew, *915*
Young, Brigham, 312
"Young America" movement, 388
Young Men's Christian Association, 509
Your Money's Worth (Schlink), 698
Youth
　freedom from parental authority, 663
　youth culture of 1920s, 671–672
Yugoslavia, 946
Yuppies, 933

Zangwill, Israel, 523, 524
Zapata, Emiliano, 632
Zeppelins, 639
Zhou Enlai, 802
Zimmerman, Arthur, 638
Zimmerman telegram, 638
Zionism, 775
Zitkala-Sa (Gertrude Simmons Bonnin), 543
Zola, Emile, 521
"Zone of emergence," 503
Zoning regulations, racial discrimination and, 814
"Zoot suiters," 767
Zuñi tribe, 13